Brief Contents

Contents

ETHICS IN PRACTICE CASES

CASES

Preface

Business & Society: Ethics, Sustainability, and Stakeholder Management, Tenth Edition, provides a conceptual framework, analysis, and discussion of the issues surrounding the business and society relationship. The book's structure, chapters, and cases identify and engage the major topics involved in developing a robust understanding of business *and* society, or business *in* society. The latest research, examples, and cases provide you with a broad, yet detailed, analysis of the subject matter; they also offer a solid basis for thoughtful learning, reflection, and analysis of the domestic and global issues facing businesses today.

The book employs a managerial perspective that identifies and integrates current and relevant thought and practice. The managerial perspective is embedded within the book's major themes of business ethics, sustainability, and stakeholder management. Each of these themes is essential today. Each theme builds upon its own perspective but is consistent with and overlaps with the others. Taken together, they capture the challenges of the past and provide frameworks for thinking about the current and future role of business in society.

The *business ethics* dimension is central because it has become clear that value considerations are and need to be woven into the fabric of the public issues that organizations face today. An emphasis is placed on business ethics essentials and how ethics integrates into managerial and organizational decision making. Special spheres of business ethics discussed include the realms of technology and global capitalism, where ethical questions increasingly have arisen for the past 20 years. The subject of each chapter, moreover, is infused with ethics considerations that are vital to their full treatment.

Sustainability is now one of business's most pressing mandates. This dimension has been developed further since the ninth edition of this book because it has become more evident in the business world today that a concern for the natural, social, and financial environments are interconnected and that all three must be maintained in balance for both current and future generations. Hence, topics of the new circular economy, as well as measures of sustainability, are highlighted in this edition.

The *stakeholder management* perspective is crucial and enduring and it helps managers to (1) identify the various groups or individuals who have stakes in the firm or its actions, decisions, policies, and practices and (2) incorporate the stakeholders' concerns into the firm's daily operations and strategic plans. Stakeholder management is an approach that increases the likelihood decision makers will integrate ethical wisdom with management wisdom with respect to all salient parties to the business and society relationship.

As this edition goes to press, the country and world economies are still striving to recover from one of the most perilous financial periods since the Great Depression. The world stock market collapse beginning in the fall of 2008 had devastating repercussions for economies, governments, businesses, and individuals, and still we have not resolved completely the uncertainty associated with what began as financial turmoil and bankruptcies on Wall Street. This major event and its consequences will be with us for many years, and we urge readers to keep in mind the extent to which our world has now changed as they read the book and consider its content and application. Major events have the power to change the business and society relationship in significant ways—and instantaneously—so it is essential that the book's topics be read with an ever present eye on the events breaking in the news each day.

Applicable Courses for Book

This text is appropriate for college and university courses that carry such titles as Business and Society; Business *in* Society; Business and Its Environment; Business Ethics; Business and Public Policy; Social Issues in Management; Business, Government, and Society; Social Responsibility of Business; and Stakeholder Management. The book is appropriate for either a required or an elective course seeking to meet the most recent accrediting standards of the Association to Advance Collegiate Schools of Business (AACSB International). The book has been used successfully in both undergraduate and graduate courses.

Though the AACSB does not require any specific courses in this subject matter, its recently updated (January 31, 2016) standards specify that a business school's curriculum should include the topics covered throughout this textbook in both undergraduate and graduate degree programs. For undergraduate and graduate degree programs, learning experiences should be addressed and are addressed in General Skill Areas such as *ethical understanding and reasoning (able to identify ethical issues and address the issues in a socially responsible way)* and *diverse and multicultural work environments*.

In terms of AACSB's General Business and Management Knowledge Areas, the following topics should be addressed and are addressed in this textbook: *economic, political, regulatory, legal, technological, and social contexts of organizations in a globalized society*; and *social responsibility, including sustainability, and ethical behavior and approaches to management.*

This book is ideal for coverage of perspectives that form the context for business: ethical and global issues; the influence of political, social, legal, environmental, technological, and regulatory issues; and the impact of diversity on organizations. The book provides perspectives on business, society, and ethics in the United States, along with examples from Europe, Asia, and other parts of the world. As the world has grown closer due to technology, communications, and transportation, there has been more convergence than divergence in applicability of the ideas presented herein. The book has proved suitable in a number of different countries outside of the United States. In previous editions, versions were published in Canada and China. Publication in Japan is under consideration. Though written from the perspective of American society, a special effort has been made to include some examples from different parts of the world to illustrate major points. Most of the book applies in developed economies around the world.

Objectives in Relevant Courses

Depending on the placement of a course in the curriculum or the individual instructor's philosophy or strategy, this book could be used for a variety of objectives. The courses for which it is intended typically include several essential goals, including the following:

1. Students should be made aware of the expectations and demands that emanate from the stakeholder environment and are placed on business firms.
2. As prospective managers, students need to understand appropriate business responses and management approaches for dealing with social, political, environmental, technological, and global issues and stakeholders.
3. An appreciation of ethics and sustainability issues and the influence these have on society, management decision making, behavior, policies, and practices is important.
4. The broad question of business's legitimacy as an institution in a global society is at stake and must be addressed from both business and societal perspectives. These topics are essential to business building trust with society and all stakeholders.
5. The increasing extent to which social, ethical, public, environmental, and global issues must be considered from a strategic perspective is critical in such courses.

New to the Tenth Edition

This tenth edition has been updated and revised to reflect recent research, laws, cases, and examples. Material in this new edition includes:

- New research, surveys, and examples throughout all the chapters
- Coverage throughout the text on the most recent ethics scandals and their influence on business, society, organizations, and people
- New concepts and examples on the developing theme of "behavioral ethics"
- Discussion of recent developments with the Dodd Frank Wall Street Reform and Consumer Financial Protection Act, the Net Neutrality Act, the Consumer Drone Safety Act, the Affordable Care Act, and other laws with significant importance to managers today
- Expanded coverage of social media issues, including issues of usage, privacy, and liability
- Coverage of competing corporate governance perspectives
- Incorporation of the issue of risk management and its relation to business in society
- Updated coverage of social entrepreneurship and social enterprises
- Discussion of the emerging topic of Political Corporate Social Responsibility (PCSR)
- Expanded coverage of sustainability reporting and integrated reports
- Extended coverage of Citizens United, Super PACs, and Dark Money, and the importance of Corporate Political Accountability and Transparency
- Consideration of diversity, employee rights, and recent legislation regarding discrimination, including LGBT rights and updated protections, updated affirmative action issues, and new EEOC reforms
- Updated "Spotlight on Sustainability" features in each chapter, which demonstrate how sustainability is relevant and applicable to each chapter's topics
- Fifty-five "Ethics in Practice Cases" embedded in chapters throughout the book, many of which are brand new to this edition
- Thirty-nine end-of-text "Cases" that may be assigned with any of the book's chapter topics, 11 of which are brand new to this edition
- A revised and updated Instructor's Manual
- A brand new MindTap product that includes a digital version of the book, plus practice, graded, and media quizzes

"Ethics in Practice Cases"

Integral to this tenth edition are in-chapter features titled "Ethics in Practice Cases." Interspersed throughout the chapters, these short cases and incidents present (1) actual ethical situations faced by companies, managers, consumers, or employees; (2) topics currently being discussed in the news; or (3) dilemmas faced personally in the work experiences of our former students in university or executive education classes. These latter types of cases are real-life situations actually encountered in their full- and part-time work experiences. Students and managers wrote some of these cases, and we are pleased they gave us permission to use them. They provide ready examples of the ethical issues people face today as citizens, consumers, and employees. We would like to acknowledge the authors of these for their contributions to the book. Instructors may wish to use these as mini-cases for class discussion when a lengthier case is not assigned. They can be read quickly, but they contain considerable substance for class discussion and analysis.

"Spotlight on Sustainability" Features

The "Spotlight on Sustainability" features in each chapter highlight an important and relevant linkage of sustainability concepts that augment each chapter's text material. The feature sometimes highlights a pertinent organization covered in the chapter and further discusses its activities or issues. Other features highlight a sustainability challenge that a range of organizations face or a sustainability success that organizations or individuals can emulate. These features permit readers to quickly and easily discover how the sustainability theme applies to each topic covered in the text. The concept of sustainability extends to virtually all business, society, and ethics topics and embraces people and profits, as well as the planet.

Structure of the Book

Part 1. Business, Society, and Stakeholders

Part 1 of the book provides foundational coverage of pertinent business, society, and stakeholder topics and issues. Because most courses that will use this book relate to the issue of corporate social responsibility (CSR), this concept is discussed at the outset. Part 1 explores vital issues in the business and society relationship and discusses how corporate social responsibility and its complementary concepts—corporate citizenship and sustainability—provide basic frameworks to understanding. Also given early coverage is the stakeholder management concept, because it provides a way of thinking and analyzing all topics in the book, as well as a helpful perspective for thinking about organizations.

Part 2. Corporate Governance and Strategic Management Issues

The second part of the text addresses corporate governance and strategic management for stakeholder responsiveness. The purpose of this part is to discuss management considerations and implications for dealing with the issues discussed throughout the text. Corporate governance is covered early because in the past decade this topic has been identified as central to effective strategic management. The strategic management perspective is useful because these issues have impacts on the total organization and have become intense ones for many upper-level managers. Special treatment is given to corporate public policy; issue, risk, and crisis management; and public affairs management.

Some instructors may elect to cover Part 2 later in their courses. It could easily be covered after Part 4 or 5. This option would be most appropriate for those who use the book for a business ethics course or who desire to spend less time on the governance, strategy, and management perspectives.

Part 3. Business Ethics and Leadership

Four chapters dedicated to business ethics and leadership topics are presented in Part 3. In actual practice, business ethics cannot be separated from the full range of external and internal stakeholder concerns, but the topic's importance merits the more detailed treatment presented here. Part 3 focuses on business ethics essentials, managerial and organizational ethics, business ethics and technology, and ethical issues in the global arena. Taken together, these chapters examine business and society issues that require ethical thinking.

Part 4. External Stakeholder Issues

Vital topics in Part 4 include business's relations with government, consumers, the natural environment, and the community. In each of these topic areas, we encounter social and ethical issues and challenges that are integral to business today. The business–government relationship is divided into the regulatory initiatives to monitor business practices and business's attempts to influence government. Consumers, environment, and community stakeholders are then treated in separate chapters.

Part 5. Internal Stakeholder Issues

The primary internal stakeholders addressed in this part are employees. Here, we consider workplace issues and the key themes of employee rights, diversity, employment discrimination, and affirmative action. Two chapters address the changing social contract between business and employees and the urgent subjects of employee rights. A final chapter treats the vital topic of diversity and employment discrimination. Owner stakeholders may be seen as internal stakeholders too, but we cover them in Part 2, where the subject of corporate governance has been placed.

Case Studies

Throughout each of the chapters, there are "Ethics in Practice Cases," 55 in total, that pertain to the chapter in which they are located, but also can be used with other chapters as needed. The 39 end-of-text Cases address a broad range of topics and decision situations. The cases are of varying length. They include classic cases (involving such corporate giants as Walmart, The Body Shop, Nike, McDonald's, Volkswagen, Chipotle, Coke, Pepsi, and Apple) with ongoing deliberations, as well as new cases touching upon issues that have arisen in the past several years.

All the cases are intended to provide instructors and students with real-life situations within which to further analyze course issues, concepts, and topics covered throughout the book. Both the Ethics in Practice Cases and the end-of-text Cases may be used with various chapters depending on the emphasis of the course. Many of the cases carry ramifications that spill over into several subject areas or issues. Immediately preceding the end-of-text Cases is a set of guidelines for case analysis that the instructor may wish to use in place of or in addition to the questions that appear at the end of each case. A case matrix, located inside the front cover of the instructor edition of the textbook and in the instructor's manual, provides guidance as to which of the cases in the book, both Ethics in Practice and end of text, work best with each chapter.

Support for the Student

MindTap

MindTap® Management for Carroll/Brown/Buchholtz, *Business & Society: Ethics, Sustainability, and Stakeholder Management,* 10th edition is the digital learning solution that powers students from memorization to mastery. It gives you complete control of your course—to provide engaging content, to challenge every individual, and to build their confidence. Empower students to accelerate their progress with MindTap. MindTap: Powered by You.

CourseMate Student Resources

The CourseMate site, accessible at www.cengagebrain.com, includes student support resources to enhance and assess learning, including PowerPoint slides, key terms, and learning objectives.

Support for the Instructor

Instructor's Manual

The Instructor's Manual includes learning objectives, teaching suggestions, complete chapter outlines, highlighted key terms, answers to discussion questions, case notes, and group exercises. The Instructor's Manual is available on the Instructor Companion Site.

Test Bank

Cengage Learning Testing Powered by Cognero is a flexible, online system that allows you to author, edit, and manage test-bank content from multiple Cengage Learning solutions;

create multiple test versions in an instant; and deliver tests from your LMS, your classroom, or wherever you want. The test bank for each chapter includes true/false, multiple-choice, short-answer, and essay questions, all correlated to AACSB guidelines and learning standards, and questions are identified by the level of difficulty.

PowerPoint Slides

The PowerPoint presentations are colorful and varied, designed to hold students' interest and reinforce each chapter's main points. The PowerPoint presentations are available on the Instructor Companion Site.

Online Instructor Resources

To access the online course materials, please visit www.cengage.com, and log in with your credentials.

Acknowledgments

First, we would like to remember our dear friend, co-author, and colleague, Ann Buchholtz, whose contributions to the study of business and society will remain with us forever, as will our memories of her generous spirit. When Ann won the Sumner Marcus Award for the Social Issues in Management Division at the 2015 Academy of Management Conference, the words used to describe her included "top tier scholar," "mentor," "servant leader," and "teacher." Beyond the stories of her incredible research impact in the areas of ethics, corporate governance, corporate social responsibility, and strategy, Ann was someone who stood out among her peers in every dimension of performance and service. She loved the phrase from Mahatma Gandhi, "Be truthful, gentle and fearless," and it described her nature perfectly. Ann leaves behind many friends, colleagues, and students who will miss her dearly, as well as a beloved brother, Dick Buchholtz, who has been a friend to us over the years. Ann's spirit will live on in this textbook, and we dedicate this edition to her.

Second, we would like to express gratitude to our professional colleagues in the Social Issues in Management (SIM) Division of the Academy of Management, the International Association for Business and Society (IABS), and the Society for Business Ethics (SBE). Over the years, members of these organizations have meant a great deal to us and have helped provide a stimulating environment in which we could intellectually pursue these topics in which we have a common interest. Many of these individuals are cited in this book and their work is sincerely appreciated.

Third, we would like to thank the many reviewers of the nine previous editions who took the time to provide us with helpful critiques. Many of their ideas and suggestions have been used for this edition and led to improvements in the text:

Steven C. Alber, Hawaii Pacific University

Paula Becker Alexander, Seton Hall University

Laquita C. Blockson, St. Leo University

Mark A. Buchanan, Boise State University

Peter Burkhardt, Western State College of Colorado

Preston D. Cameron, Mesa Community College

William B. Carper, University of West Florida

George S. Cole, Shippensburg University

Brenda Eichelberger, Portland State University

Jeanne Enders, Portland State University
Joshua S. Friedlander, Baruch College
John William Geranios, George Washington University
Kathleen Getz, Loyola University Maryland
Peggy A. Golden, University of Northern Iowa
Russell Gough, Pepperdine University
Michele A. Govekar, Ohio Northern University
Wade Graves, Grayson College
Frank J. Hitt, Mountain State University
Robert H. Hogner, Florida International University
Sylvester R. Houston, University of Denver
Ralph W. Jackson, University of Tulsa
David C. Jacobs, American University
Leigh Redd Johnson, Murray State University
Ed Leonard, Indiana University–Purdue University Fort Wayne
Charles Lyons, University of Georgia
Timothy A. Matherly, Florida State University
Kenneth R. Mayer, Cleveland State University
Douglas M. McCabe, Georgetown University
Douglas McCloskey, Washington University School of Law
Bill McShain, Cumberland University
Geralyn Miller, Indiana University–Purdue University Fort Wayne
Nana Lee Moore, Warner University
Harvey Nussbaum, Wayne State University
Nathan Oliver, University of Alabama Birmingham
E. Leroy Plumlee, Western Washington University
Richard Raspen, Wilkes University
Dawna Rhoades, Embry-Riddle Aeronautical University
William T. Rupp, Austin Peay State University
Robert J. Rustic, The University of Findlay
John K. Sands, Western Washington University
William Sodeman, University of Alabama in Huntsville (UAH)
Valarie Spiser-Albert, University of Texas at San Antonio
David S. Steingard, St. Joseph's University
John M. Stevens, The Pennsylvania State University
Diane L. Swanson, Kansas State University
Dave Thiessen, Lewis-Clark State College
Jeff R. Turner, Howard Payne University
Ivan R. Vernon, Cleveland State University
Marion Webb, Cleveland State University

George E. Weber, Whitworth College
Ira E. Wessler, Robert Morris University

We would also like to express gratitude to our students, who have not only provided comments on a regular basis but also made this tenth edition even more interesting with the ethical dilemmas they have personally contributed, as highlighted in the Ethics in Practice Cases features found in many of the chapters or at the end of the text. In addition to those who are named in the Ethics in Practice Cases features and end-of-text Cases and have given permission for their materials to be used, we would like to thank the following individuals for their contributions: Michelle Alen, Kristine Calo, Chad Cleveland, Ken Crowe, Lee Askew Elkins, Charles Lyons, William Megathlin, Jr., Madeline Meibauer, Laura Rosario, Paul Rouland, Sr., William Sodeman and Clayton Wilcox. We express grateful appreciation to the authors of the other cases that appear at the end of the text, and their names are mentioned there. We also would like to thank Bruce F. Freed and Karl Sandstrom of the Center for Political Accountability for their support as we incorporated the issues stemming from Citizens United into our discussion of corporate political activity.

Finally, we wish to express heartfelt appreciation to our family members and friends for their patience, understanding, and support when work on the book altered our priorities and plans.

Archie B. Carroll
Jill A. Brown

About the Authors

Archie B. Carroll

Archie B. Carroll is Robert W. Scherer Chair of Management & Corporate Public Affairs *emeritus* and professor of management *emeritus* in the Terry College of Business, University of Georgia. He also served as director of the Nonprofit Management and Community Service Program in the Terry College of Business. Dr. Carroll received his three academic degrees from The Florida State University in Tallahassee. He is the co-author of *Corporate Responsibility: The American Experience* (Cambridge University Press, 2012), which won the Academy of Management, Social Issues in Management, Book of the Year Award in 2014. He was recognized with the first Lifetime Achievement Award in Corporate Social Responsibility (2012) given by the Institute of Management, Humboldt University, Berlin, Germany.

Professor Carroll has published numerous books, chapters, articles, and encyclopedia entries. His research has appeared in the *Academy of Management Journal, Academy of Management Review, Business and Society, Journal of Management, Business Ethics Quarterly, Journal of Business Ethics*, and many others.

He is former Division Chair of the Social Issues in Management (SIM) Division of the Academy of Management, a founding board member of the International Association for Business and Society (IABS), and past president of the Society for Business Ethics (SBE). He is an elected Fellow of the Southern Management Association (1995), Fellow of the Academy of Management (2005), and Fellow of the International Association for Business and Society (2012).

Other important professional recognitions include the Sumner Marcus Award (1992) for Distinguished Service by the SIM Division of the Academy of Management; Distinguished Research Award (1993) by Terry College of Business, University of Georgia; Distinguished Service Award (2003) by the Terry College of Business; and the Hunt SMA Sustained Outstanding Service Award (2016) by the Southern Management Association. He was named professor *emeritus* (2005) at the University of Georgia, and in 2008, he was recognized with the Outstanding Ph.D. Award from the College of Business, Florida State University.

Jill A. Brown

Jill Brown is the Harold S. Geneen Research Professor of Corporate Governance at Bentley University. She received her Ph.D. at the University of Georgia; Ann Buchholtz served as her Dissertation Chair.

Dr. Brown's research and teaching interests include ethics, corporate social responsibility, corporate governance, and strategic leadership—with a focus on understanding how businesses can create both financial and social value. Brown's work has been published in the *Journal of Business Ethics, Organization Science, Business Ethics Quarterly, the Journal of Management Studies, the Oxford Handbook of Corporate Social Responsibility, Strategic Organization*, and *Corporate Governance: An International Review (CGIR)*, where she is an associate editor. She also serves as an associate editor for *Business and Society*.

She is an elected Representative-at-Large of the International Association of Business and Society (IABS), an international organization committed to understanding relationships between business, government, and society. She has also served in many capacities for the SIM (Social Issues in Management) Division at the Academy of Management, including Co-Chair of the Doctoral Consortium, elected Representative-at-Large, and most recently as Program Chair-Elect. Dr. Brown has received numerous teaching and reviewing awards, including the Robert and Christine Staub Faculty Excellence Award at Lehigh University, and Best Reviewer awards from *CGIR* and *Business & Society*.

Ann K. Buchholtz

The late Ann K. Buchholtz was professor of Leadership and Ethics at Rutgers University and served as research director of the Institute for Ethical Leadership at the Rutgers Business School. She received her Ph.D. from the Stern School of Business at New York University. She passed away in September 2015.

Professor Buchholtz's research focused on the social and ethical implications of corporate governance, in particular, and the relationship of business and society in general. Journals in which her work has appeared include *Business and Society*, *Business Ethics Quarterly*, the *Academy of Management Journal*, the *Academy of Management Review*, the *Journal of Management*, *Organization Science*, the *Journal of Management Studies*, and *Corporate Governance an International Review*, among others. Her research on board processes received an ANBAR citation of excellence award.

Her teaching and consulting activities were in the areas of business ethics, social issues, strategic leadership, and corporate governance. Her service learning activities in the classroom received a Trailblazer Advocate of the Year award from the Domestic Violence Council of Northeast Georgia. She was the recipient of numerous teaching awards, including Profound Effect on a Student Leader, and was named a Senior Teaching Fellow at the University of Georgia.

Professor Buchholtz served as past Division Chair of the Social Issues in Management Division of the Academy of Management. She served on the ethics task force that designed a Code of Ethics for the Academy of Management and then became the inaugural chairperson of the Academy's Ethics Adjudication Committee when the Academy's ethics code was put into effect. She completed a three-year term on the Academy of Management's Board of Governors. In 2015, she was honored with the Sumner Marcus Award for outstanding service given by the SIM Division of the Academy of Management. Prior to entering academe, Dr. Buchholtz's work focused on the education, vocational, and residential needs of individuals with disabilities. She worked in a variety of organizations, in both managerial and consultative capacities, and consulted with numerous public and private firms.

PART 1

Business, Society, and Stakeholders

1

The Business and Society Relationship

CHAPTER LEARNING OUTCOMES

After studying this chapter, you should be able to:

1 Define and explain business and society as foundational concepts. Describe how society is viewed as the macroenvironment.

2 Explain the characteristics of a pluralistic society. Describe pluralism and identify its attributes, strengths, and weaknesses.

3 Clarify what is a special-interest society and how it evolves.

4 Identify, discuss, and illustrate the factors leading up to business criticism and corporate response. What is the general criticism of business? How may the balance of power and responsibility be resolved? What is the changing social contract?

5 Make clear the major focuses or themes of the book: managerial approach, business ethics, sustainability, and stakeholder management.

The business and society relationship has generated many economic, social, ethical, and environmental challenges over the decades. Though the business system has served most market-based societies well, criticism of business and its practices has become commonplace. Aided by the media persistently looking for stories of conflict, this may be a reflection of the natural tendency to highlight the negative and to take for granted the beneficial aspects of the relationship. This tendency propels a focus on the stresses and strains of business operating in society. A Bloomberg BusinessWeek article in 2016 says that it is still "open season on big business."[1]

Beginning with the Enron scandal in the early 2000s, a number of major companies have been in the news because of their ethical violations. In the fall of 2008, a collapsing U.S. stock market and worldwide recession had a deeper and more far-reaching impact on the world economy and began to raise questions about the future of the business system as we have known it. In what is now believed to be the most serious financial collapse since the 1920s, this financial crisis centered on Wall Street and many of the large firms that historically had been the backbone of the U.S. financial system.

The causes of the financial collapse and the ensuing economic chaos continue to be debated. The housing bubble burst and years of lax lending standards put big investment banks and Wall Street at the center of the collapse.[2] Faced with an unprecedented financial crisis, the federal government got into the bailout business as Congress approved a $700 billion rescue plan[3] for Wall Street financial firms, such as Merrill Lynch, Bear Stearns, Citigroup, Lehman Brothers, AIG, and notable industries, like the auto industry.

There was plenty of blame to go around for the financial crisis, and the finger-pointing continues to this day. Some of those identified as guilty parties included greedy home buyers who took on more debt than they could handle; mortgage lenders who ceased using conventional lending standards; credit rating agencies that did not do their job; commission-hungry brokers; builders who conspired with crooked appraisers; and the Federal Reserve, which was accused of flooding the market with easy money.[4] Significant criticism was targeted toward Wall Street and the businesses themselves as being central to the financial collapse. Others claimed that capitalism itself was behind the mess because the Wall Street firms were just doing what the capitalist system encourages. The recent movie, *The Big Short*, provided a dramatic reminder of how this financial crisis unfolded.

By the fall of 2011, Big Business and the capitalistic system were targeted by a new protest movement, which called itself "Occupy Wall Street." The movement reflected some of the built up discontent with the business system, which had resulted in high unemployment and financial stress for millions. In spite of protestations that continued beyond 2012, the Occupy Wall Street (OWS) movement never had a clear list of criticisms or demands but it was understood that the enemy was the big business system and modern capitalism. The movement's broad list of accusations reflected a litany of complaints that included crony capitalism, inequality of wealth, poor housing, obscenely high executive compensation, business greed, the lack of good jobs, a culture that puts profits before people, and a general discontent with capitalism and the economic system.[5] Though most of OWS's complaints were targeted at business and the capitalistic system, some observers criticized the protestors because they failed to see the complicity of big government in developing and supporting housing policies that led to the financial crisis in the first place.[6] In short, though many critics were preoccupied with Wall Street and the capitalistic system, Big Government also had a hand in the crisis as well.

Business is a more inviting target than government, however, because it is seen as being motivated only by profit while government is not seeking profits but is charged with acting in the public interest. Consequently, business and the capitalistic system have become the primary targets of the critics though flaws in the business-government relationship played a huge role in the controversy. The Wall Street protestors framed the battle as if they represented the 99 percent of citizens who were angry at the 1 percent of wealthy, primarily business people. This focus on the "One Percent" who own most of the wealth had become center stage by 2015 and continues today as the One Percent movement. Global income inequality has become the rallying point for many critics of the business system.[7] Only time will tell whether the OWS and One Percent movements will continue, but in the meantime, it has raised public awareness of weaknesses in the capitalistic system. One major consequence of the OWS movement is that Wall Street, especially the big banks, have lost their "cool" factor and a lot of their prestige. Many of today's top grads are more interested in going to Silicon Valley rather than Wall Street, believing they can make good money there and also have a chance to change the world.[8] In addition, more and more commentaries questioning the capitalistic system have emerged, so it appears to be an issue the business community will need to address to repair its bruised image.[9]

The business system and society suffered another high profile blow when the Deepwater Horizon/BP oil spill occurred in the spring of 2010. Called the worst environmental disaster in history, the cleanup is still ongoing, with significant ecological and business consequences. The spill heightened the public's awareness of the impact business can have on the natural environment and doubtless heightened support for the sustainability movement that was already well underway. In the fall of 2015, the Justice Department announced a record setting $20 billion settlement with BP, the British energy giant, after five years of negotiations over the effects of the Deepwater Horizon oil spill. The oil spill damaged more than 1,300 miles of the Gulf of Mexico's coastline, and it has been called the largest environmental disaster in U.S. history.[10]

By 2016, a number of different business scandals had surfaced and damaged the business and society relationship further. These included the Volkswagen emissions scandal, admission by General Motors' that it had schemed to conceal deadly safety defects in its ignition switches, revelations that Takata Corporation had been selling defective air bags, and disclosure that Toshiba had engaged in at least $1 billion in accounting irregularities. In addition to these scandals, a national malaise seemed to have set in as many in the general public began experiencing a middle class financial squeeze due to a jobless economic recovery.[11]

According to a 2015 Gallup poll, many Americans began thinking that the country has been heading in the wrong direction. This has led to countless people questioning the major institutions of society, and according to one observer, a period of political distrust has taken over.[12] A 2016 poll by the Edelman public relations firm confirmed that America has a trust issue with business and government, especially financial companies, and that this erosion of trust is not only in the United States but also around the world.[13]

In light of the business criticisms that have arisen, it is little wonder that the "conscious capitalism" movement is gaining increased attention. This movement has been inspired by the book *Conscious Capitalism: Liberating the Heroic Spirit of Business*, co-authored by John Mackey, CEO and cofounder of Whole Foods Market and Rajendra Sisodia, professor of marketing at Bentley University. Their book has helped to spawn a whole new way of thinking about capitalism that is based on four principles—seeking a higher purpose, using a stakeholder orientation, embracing conscious leadership, and promoting a conscious culture that seeks to improve the social fabric of business. According to one writer, Mackey's latest mission is cleansing America's free-enterprise soul.[14]

Other serious questions continue to be raised about a host of other ongoing day-to-day business issues: corporate governance, ethical conduct, executive compensation, the use of illegal immigrants as employees, fluctuating energy prices, government involvement in the economy, healthiness of fast food, international corruption, and so on. The listing of such issues could go on and on, but these examples illustrate the enduring tensions between business and society, which in part can be traced to recent high-profile incidents, trends, or events.

Undergirding the recent scandals and issues, familiar worries embodying social or ethical implications have continued to be debated within the business and society interface. Some of these have included businesses moving offshore, downsizing of pension programs, high unemployment, underemployment, level of the minimum wage, reduced health insurance benefits, abuses of corporate power, toxic waste disposal, insider trading, whistle-blowing, product liability, deceptive marketing, and questionable lobbying by business to influence the outcome of legislation. These examples of both general and specific issues are typical of the kinds of stories about business and society that one finds in newspapers and magazines today and on television, social media, and the Internet.

At the broadest level, the role of business in society is the subject of this book. Many key questions will be addressed—the role of business relative to the role of government in the socioeconomic system; what a firm must do to be considered socially responsible; what managers must do to be considered ethical; and what responsibilities companies have to consumers, employees, shareholders, and communities in an age of economic uncertainty and globalization. And, throughout all this, an escalating mandate for sustainability has captured the attention of business leaders, critics, and public policymakers.

As we approach the end of the second decade of the new millennium, many economic, legal, ethical, and technological issues concerning business and society continue on. This period is turbulent and has been characterized by significant and rapid changes in the world, the economy, society, technology, and global relationships. Against this setting of ongoing instability in the business and society relationship, some basic concepts and ideas are worth considering first.

SPOTLIGHT ***on Sustainability***

Sustainability—What Does It Mean?

- Sustainability is … providing for the needs of the present generation while not compromising the ability of future generations to meet theirs (*original definition in the U.N. Brundtland Commission Report on "Our Common Future."*)
- Sustainability is … creating shareholder and social value while decreasing the environmental footprint along the value chains in which we operate (*DuPont*).
- Corporate sustainability is about being able to sustain your business responsibly, with one eye on new external risks and the other on future consequences of your decisions (*PwC*).
- Corporate sustainability can be broadly defined as the pursuit of a business growth strategy by allocating financial or in-kind resources of the corporation to a social or environmental initiative (*The Conference Board, Sustainability Matters*).
- Sustainability involves the simultaneous pursuit of economic prosperity, environmental quality, and social equity (World Business Council on Sustainable Development).

1.1 Business and Society

There are some basic concepts that are central to understanding the continuing business and society relationship. Some have chosen to frame it as business *in* society. Either way it is framed, important concepts include pluralism, our special-interest society, business criticism, corporate power, and corporate social response to stakeholders. First, it is important to define and describe two key terms that are central to the discussion: *business* and *society*.

1.1a Business Defined

Business may be defined as the collection of private, commercially oriented (profit-oriented) organizations, ranging in size from one-family proprietorships (e.g., DePalma's Italian Café, Half-Moon Outfitters, and Taqueria del Sol) to corporate giants (e.g., Coca-Cola, UPS, Microsoft, Apple, Google, and Delta Airlines). Between these two extremes are many medium-sized proprietorships, partnerships, and corporations.

When businesses are thought of in this collective sense, all sizes and types of industries are included. However, in embarking on a study of business and society, there is a tendency to focus more on *big* businesses in highly visible industries. Big businesses' products, services and advertising are widely known and they are more frequently in the critical public eye. Size is often associated with power, and the powerful are given closer scrutiny. Although it is well known that small businesses far outnumber large ones, the prevalence, power, visibility, and impact of large firms keep them in the spotlight most of the time.

In addition, some industries are simply more conducive than others in the creation of visible, social problems. For example, many manufacturing firms by their very nature cause observable air, water, and solid waste pollution and contribute to climate changes. Such firms, therefore, are more likely to be subject to criticism than a life insurance company, which emits no obvious pollutant. The auto industry with the manufacture of trucks and sport utility vehicles (SUVs) is a specific case in point. Criticism of Volkswagen, General Motors (GM), and other automakers is raised because of their high profile as manufacturers, the omnipresence of the products they make (which are the largest single source of air pollution), and the popularity of their products (many families own multiple cars), and road congestion is experienced daily.

Some industries are highly visible because of the advertising-intensive nature of their products (e.g., Procter & Gamble, FedEx, Anheuser-Busch, and Home Depot). Other industries (e.g., the cigarette, toy, and fast food industries) are scrutinized because of the possible effects of their products on health or because of their roles in providing health-related products (e.g., pharmaceutical firms, vitamin firms).

For these reasons, when discussing business in its relationship with society, the focus of attention tends to be on large businesses in well-known industries. However, we should not lose sight of the fact that small- and medium-sized companies increasingly represent settings in which our discussions also apply. In recent years, the social responsibilities of smaller enterprises and the developing movement toward social entrepreneurship has captivated increasing attention.

1.1b Society Defined

Society may be thought of as a community, a nation, or a broad grouping of people with common traditions, values, institutions, and collective activities and interests. As such, when speaking of business and society relationships, this may be referring to business and the local community (business and Nashville), business and the United States as a whole, global business, or business and a specific group of stakeholders (consumers, employees, investors, environmentalists).

When discussing business and the *total* society, society is thought of as being composed of numerous interest groups, more or less formalized organizations, and a wide variety of institutions. Each of these groups, organizations, and institutions is a purposeful aggregation of people who are grouped together because they represent a common cause or share a set of common beliefs about a particular issue. Examples of special interest groups are numerous: The Sierra Club, Center for Science in the Public Interest, chambers of commerce, National Small Business Association, People for the Ethical Treatment of Animals (PETA), and the Forest Stewardship Council.

1.2 Society as the Macroenvironment

The environment of society is a key element in analyzing business and society relationships. At its broadest level, the societal environment might be thought of as a **macroenvironment** that includes the total environment outside the firm. The macroenvironment is the comprehensive societal context in which organizations reside. The idea of the macroenvironment is just another way of thinking about society as a whole. In fact, early courses on business and society were sometimes (and some still are) titled "Business and Its Environment." The concept of the macroenvironment evokes different images or ways of thinking about business and society relationships and is therefore valuable in terms of analyzing and understanding the total business context.

A useful conceptualization of the macroenvironment is to think of it as being composed of four identifiable but interrelated segments: social, economic, political, and technological.[15]

The **social environment** focuses on demographics, lifestyles, culture, and social values of the society. Of particular interest here is the manner in which shifts in these factors affect the organization and its functioning. For example, the influx of undocumented workers and immigrants over the past decade has brought changes to the demographic profile of countries. The **economic environment** addresses the nature and direction of the economy in which business operates. Variables of interest include such indices as gross national product, inflation, interest rates, unemployment rates, foreign exchange fluctuations, national debt, global trade, balance of payments, and various other indices of economic activity. Hypercompetition in the world economy has dominated the economic segment of this environment and global competitiveness is now a huge issue for businesses.[16] Underwhelming business growth during the past several years has been a serious problem.

The economic picture has darkened since the start of the new millennium. Lackluster growth has been typical and the recovery from the recession of 2007–2008 has been even weaker and the middle class has felt it the most.[17] Businesses moving jobs offshore to lower labor costs have been a controversial trend. Enduring levels of high unemployment, underemployment and use of part-time workers have been problematic economic issues. Many people have become frustrated about finding jobs and have left the workforce completely. An important overlay to these problems has been the growing belief by some that a significant income inequality has taken hold in American society and globally.

The **political environment** focuses on the processes by which laws get passed and officials get elected and all other aspects of the interaction between firms, political practices, and government. Of particular interest to business in this segment are taxation, the regulatory process, and the changes that occur over time in business regulation of various industries, products, and different issues. Beginning in 2009, Congress ramped up its regulatory ambitions as it sought to improve the global economic system. Passage of the Affordable Care Act (ACA) in 2010 introduced considerable uncertainty in business decision making because of its dramatic impact on business costs and this concern continues. At this writing, the 2016 presidential election process is well underway and an issue that keeps coming to the surface is the inability of Congress to get anything done because of paralysis in the political process. Part of the public's reaction has been to favor "outsiders" to the Washington-centered political process when it comes to national elections.

Finally, the **technological environment** represents the total set of technology-based advancements taking place in society and the world. This rapidly changing segment includes new products, processes, materials, and means of communication (e.g., social networking), as well as the status of knowledge and scientific advancement. The process and speed of technological change is of significant importance here.[18] The rate of invention, innovation, and diffusion seems to become more dynamic with each passing year. In recent years, information technologies and biotechnology have been driving this segment of environmental turbulence.

Understanding that business and society relationships are embedded in a macroenvironment provides us with a constructive way of understanding the kinds of issues that constitute the broad milieu in which business functions. Throughout this book, evidence of these ever-changing environmental segments will become apparent and it will become easier to appreciate what challenges managers face as they strive to operate effective organizations while interfacing with society. Each of the thousands of specific groups and organizations that make up our pluralistic society can typically be traced to one of these four environmental segments.

1.3 A Pluralistic Society

Societies as macroenvironments are typically pluralistic. Pluralistic societies make for business and society relationships that are complex and dynamic. **Pluralism** refers to a diffusion of power among society's many groups and organizations. A long-standing definition of a pluralistic society is helpful: "A pluralistic society is one in which there is wide decentralization and diversity of power concentration."[19]

The key terms in this definition are *decentralization* and *diversity*. In other words, power is decentralized—dispersed among many groups and people. Power is not held

FIGURE 1-1 The Virtues of a Pluralistic Society

A pluralistic society ...

- Prevents power from being concentrated in the hands of a few
- Maximizes freedom of expression and action and strikes a balance between monism (social organization into one institution), on the one hand, and anarchy (social organization into an infinite number of persons), on the other[a]
- Is one in which the allegiance of individuals to groups is dispersed
- Creates a widely diversified set of loyalties to many organizations and minimizes the danger that a leader of any one organization will be left uncontrolled[b]
- Provides a built-in set of checks and balances, in that groups can exert power over one another with no single organization (business or government) dominating and becoming overly influential

Sources: [a]Keith Davis and Robert L. Blomstrom, *Business and Society: Environment and Responsibility*, 3d ed. (New York: McGraw-Hill, 1975), 63. [b]Joseph W. McGuire, *Business and Society* (New York: McGraw-Hill, 1963), 132. Also see "What Are Pluralistic Societies?" http://www.ask.com/world-view/pluralistic-societies-798b3a7163095a11. Accessed March 28, 2015.

in the hands of any single institution (e.g., business, government, labor, military) or a small number of groups. Pluralistic societies are found all over the world now, and some of the virtues of a pluralistic society are summarized in Figure 1-1.

1.3a Pluralism Has Strengths and Weaknesses

All social systems have strengths and weaknesses. A pluralistic society prevents power from being concentrated in the hands of a few. It also maximizes freedom of expression and action. Pluralism provides for a built-in set of checks and balances so that no single group dominates. However, a weakness of a pluralistic system is that it creates an environment in which diverse institutions pursue their own self-interests with the result that there is no unified direction to bring together individual pursuits. Another weakness is that groups and institutions proliferate to the extent that their goals start to overlap, thus causing confusion as to which organizations best serve which functions. Pluralism forces conflict, or differences in opinions, onto center stage because of its emphasis on autonomous groups, each pursuing its own objectives. In light of these concerns, a pluralistic system does not appear to be very efficient though it does provide a greater balance of power among groups in society.

1.3b Multiple Publics, Systems, and Stakeholders

Knowing that society is composed of so many different semiautonomous and autonomous groups might cause one to question whether we can realistically speak of society in a definitive sense that has any generally agreed-upon meaning. Nevertheless, we do speak in such terms, knowing that, unless we specify a particular societal subgroup or subsystem, we are referring to the total collectivity of all those persons, groups, and institutions that constitute society. Thus, references to business and society relationships may refer either to particular segments or subgroups of society (consumers, women, minorities, environmentalists, millennials, senior citizens) or to business and some *system* in our society (politics, law, custom, religion, economics). These groups of people or systems also may be referred to in an institutional form (business and the courts, business and labor unions, business and the church, business and the Federal Trade Commission, and so on).

Figure 1-2 depicts in graphic form the points of interface between business and some of the multiple publics, systems, or stakeholders with which business interacts. Stakeholders

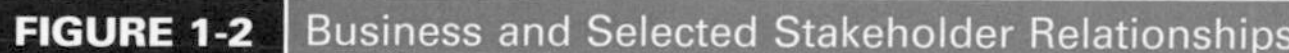

FIGURE 1-2 Business and Selected Stakeholder Relationships

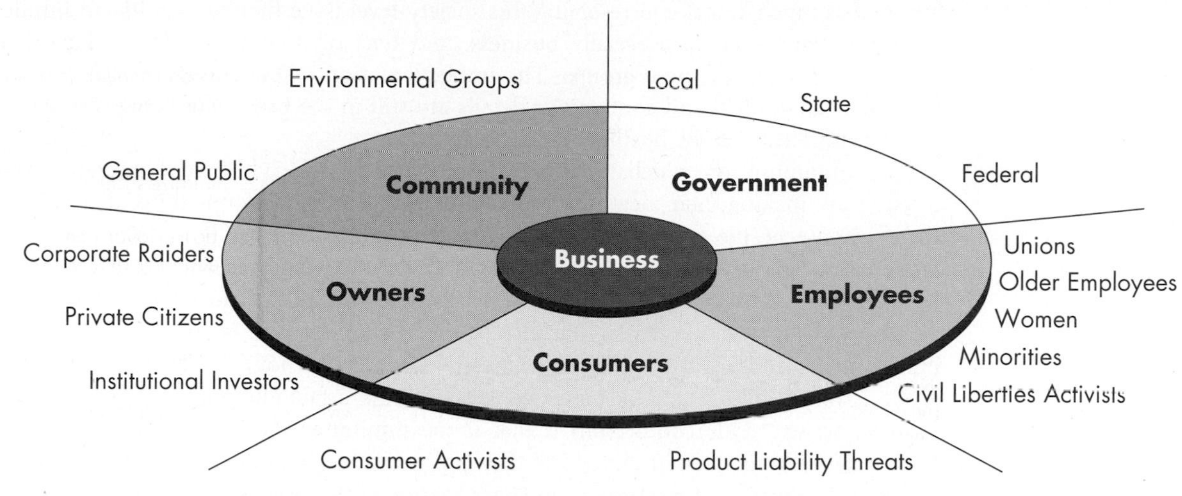

are those groups or individuals with whom an organization interacts or has interdependencies. The stakeholder concept will be developed further in Chapter 3. It also should be noted that each of the stakeholder groups may be further subdivided into more specific stakeholder subgroups, each of them posing special challenges for business.

If sheer numbers of relationships and interactions are an indicator of complexity, it is easily seen that business's current relationships with different segments of society constitute a truly complex macroenvironment. Today, managers must deal with these interfaces on a daily basis and the study of business and/in society is designed to improve that understanding.

1.4 A Special-Interest Society

A pluralistic society often becomes a **special-interest society**. As pluralism expands, a society develops that is characterized by tens of thousands of special-interest groups, each pursuing its own specific agenda. General-purpose interest organizations, often called advocacy groups, such as Common Cause and the U.S. Chamber of Commerce, still exist. However, the past several decades have been characterized by increasing specialization on the part of interest groups representing all sectors of society—consumers, employees, investors, communities, the natural environment, government, and business itself. In many parts of the world, these nonprofit organizations are frequently called **nongovernmental organizations (NGOs)**. They are citizens' groups that may be organized on a local, national, or international level. Today, many NGOs are long-lived, robust, and ever active watchdogs and actors in the business and society relationship.[20] One newspaper headline noted that "there is a group for every cause." Special-interest groups not only have grown in number at an accelerated pace but they also have become increasingly activist, intense, and focused on single issues. Such groups are strongly committed to their causes and strive to bring pressure to bear on businesses to meet their needs and on governments to accommodate their agendas.

The health-care debate in the United States that continues to rage on illustrates how a pluralistic, special-interest society works. Consider that the following special-interest groups have all been active and continue to be so in the fine-tuning of the health-care system. The major interest groups include doctors, hospitals, drug companies, insurance companies, employers, insured people, seniors, and uninsured people.[21] Each of these groups has much at stake in resolving this society-level issue that has significant implications for many sectors, especially business, and tens of millions of dollars have been spent on lobbying by these groups. The implementation of the current health-care system has been gradual and contentious details are still in the process of being worked out. The full implications for business are not yet clear.

The minimum wage debate is another context in which different interest groups recently are making their views known. A number of interest groups think that a "living wage" should be the minimum wage and have sought a $15 per hour minimum wage. Some cities have taken this action. Other interest groups disagree and think the market should determine the minimum wage. Yet another nonprofit organization, "Business for a Fair Minimum Wage," thinks that the current minimum wage is outdated and that the minimum wage should be gradually increased to $12 per hour by the year 2020. This group is made up of many business people who think a fair minimum wage makes good business sense.[22] One conundrum is that if the minimum wage is raised too quickly it hurts smaller businesses and layoffs of these minimum wage employees typically follows.

The consequence of interest group specialization is that each of these groups has been able to attract a significant following that is dedicated to the group's goals. Increased memberships have meant increased revenues and a sharper focus as each of these groups has aggressively sought its specific, narrow purposes. The likelihood of these groups working at cross-purposes and with no unified set of goals has made life immensely more complex for the major institutions, such as business and government. But this is how a pluralistic society works.

1.5 Business Criticism and Corporate Response

It is inevitable in a pluralistic, special-interest society that the major institutions that make up that society, such as business and government, will become the subjects of considerable analysis and criticism. The purpose here is not so much to focus on the negative as it is to illustrate how the process of business criticism has shaped the emergence of the business and society relationship today. Were it not for the fact that individuals and groups have been critical of business and have such high expectations and demands, there would be no articles, books or courses on this subject, and fewer improvements would occur in the business and society relationship over time.

Figure 1-3 illustrates how certain factors or social forces that have arisen in the social environment have created an atmosphere in which business criticism has taken place and flourished. Though a fair degree of resistance to change has been apparent on business's part, the more positive responses on the part of business have been (1) an increased awareness and concern for the social environment in which it operates and (2) a changed social contract (relationship) between business and society. Each of these factors merits closer attention.

1.5a Factors in the Social Environment

Over the decades, many factors in the social environment have created a climate in which criticism of business has taken place and flourished. Some of these factors arise independent of one another, but some are interrelated; that is, they occur and grow hand in hand, often feeding off of one another.

Affluence and Education. Two factors that have advanced side by side in developed economies are affluence and education. As a society becomes more prosperous and

FIGURE 1-3 Social Environment Factors, Business Criticism, and Corporate Response

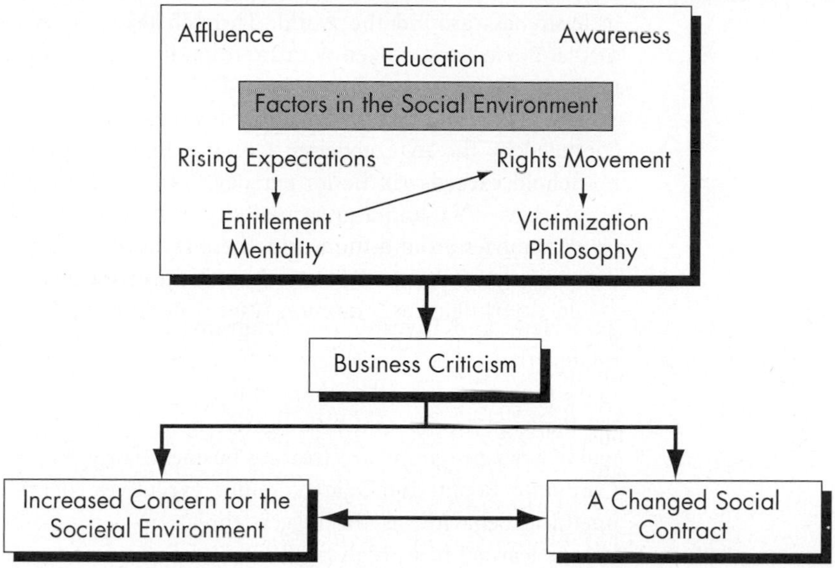

better educated, higher expectations of its major institutions, such as business, naturally follow.

Affluence refers to the level of wealth, disposable income, and standard of living of the society. Measures of the U.S. standard of living indicate that it has been rising for decades, but leveling off during the recent decade. In the past several years, questions have been raised as to whether successive generations will be better off or not. In spite of recent events, overall affluence remains high, though this could change. This movement toward affluence is found in many of the world's developed countries and also is occurring in emerging economies as global capitalism spreads. The recent, worldwide economic recession raises valid questions about continuing affluence, however.

Alongside a relatively high standard of living has been a growth in the average formal **education** of the populace. The U.S. Census Bureau's most recent data reports that the number of American adults who were high school graduates have grown to 86 percent, and the numbers who were college graduates increased to 29 percent.[23] As citizens continue to gain more formal education, these percentages will increase and their expectations of life generally rise. The combination of relative affluence and rising education has formed the underpinning for a society in which criticism of major institutions, such as business, naturally arises. Moderating factors such as unemployment, underemployment, and mounting educational costs resulting in huge student loans are also at work. It might also be added that when income and educational levels plateau or decline, business is often singled out to be a major culprit. There is significant uncertainty today as to whether past trends will continue.

Awareness through Television, Movies, Internet, and Social Media. Closely related to formal education is the widespread and growing level of public awareness in society today. Although newspapers and magazines are read by a declining fraction of the population, more powerful media—television, movies, social media, and the Internet—are accessed by virtually the entire society. Through television, the citizenry gets a profusion of information that contributes to a climate of business criticism.

In recent decades, especially, movies have bashed both the capitalist system and businesses. In addition, the Internet and smartphone explosion have brought elevated levels of awareness around the world. Through texts, tweets, e-mails, blogs, and other social media, the average citizen is extraordinarily aware of what is going on in the world on a real-time basis.

The prevalence and power of TV touches all socioeconomic classes. According to data compiled by the A. C. Nielsen Co., the average daily time spent viewing television per household exceeds six hours per day.[24] In the United States today, over 99 percent of homes have TVs, and a great majority of homes have two or more televisions. In developed countries around the world, these statistics are becoming more common. Television remains a pervasive and powerful medium in society.

24/7 News and Investigative Programs There are at least three ways in which information that leads to criticism of business appears on television. First, there are straight news shows, such as the ubiquitous 24-hour cable news channels, the evening news on the major networks, and investigative news programs. It is debatable whether or not the major news programs are treating business fairly, but in one major study conducted by Corporate Reputation Watch, senior executives identified media criticism, along with unethical behavior, as the biggest threats to a company's reputation. Reflecting on the lessons learned from high-profile cases of corporate wrongdoing, half the executives surveyed thought unethical behavior and media criticism were the biggest threats to their corporate reputations.[25] Coverage of Wall Street's complicity in the recent worldwide recession has been particularly damaging because it has called into question society's basic trust of corporate executives and the business system, especially the financial system. And, business has demonstrated a low level of preparedness for dealing with the social media criticism it has received.[26]

Business has to deal not only with the scrutiny of 24/7 news coverage but also with a myriad of different investigative news programs, such as *60 Minutes, 20/20, Dateline NBC*, and PBS's *Frontline*, that often present exposés of corporate wrongdoings or questionable practices. *American Greed* is a "true crime" documentary that focuses on the stories behind some of the biggest corporate and white collar crimes going on today, including Ponzi schemes, real estate and investment fraud, embezzlement, insurance fraud, and money laundering. Whereas the straight news programs make some effort to be objective, the investigative shows are tougher on business, tending to favor stories that expose the dark side of the enterprises or their executives. These shows are enormously popular and influential, and many companies squirm when reporters show up on their premises complete with camera crews.

Prime-Time Television Programs A second way in which criticisms of business appear on TV is through prime-time programs. Television's depiction of businesspeople in negative ways always brings to mind the scheming oilman J. R. Ewing of *Dallas*, whose backstabbing shenanigans dominated prime-time TV for years (1978–1991) before it went off the air. In 2012, *Dallas* came roaring back on TV and J. R. and his son were typically up to no good. Just as the second season of Dallas was being filmed, Larry Hagman, who played J. R., died of cancer, and TV's most delightful scoundrel would no longer be around.[27] One of J. R.'s favorite quips was "never tell the truth when a good lie will do."

More often than not, the businessperson has been portrayed across the nation's television screens as smirking, scheming, cheating, and conniving "bad guys." *The Economist* magazine summed it up nicely in its recent article in which it has declared that "businessmen are always the villains."[28] Even the enormously popular Don Draper on the successful TV series *Mad Men* didn't leave much of a positive reputation behind when he went off the air after eight seasons. Though more urbane and subtle than J. R.

Ewing, Don Draper and his Madison Avenue cronies made millions while creating artificial appetites in the unsuspecting TV viewer. One writer called the deeply cynical Draper a "moral vandal," as he let down, abandoned, or lied to every person who had ever loved him and spent his professional advertising life reducing every emotion to a slogan and every desire into slick copy.[29]

On one show, *Law & Order*, half of the felons were businesspeople.[30] A few other TV shows where this unfavorable portrayal of business people has been evident include *CSI, Mad Men, Empire, Horrible Bosses, Damages, Banshee, Criminal Minds*, and *Vinyl*. In 2016, the new Showtime drama, *Billions*, took questionable business people to new heights by featuring the unethical executive of a successful hedge fund, Bobby Axelrod, who introduced the world to a ruthlessness that was frightening.[31]

Any redeeming social values that business and businesspeople may have rarely show up on television. Rather, businesspeople are often cast as evil and greedy social parasites whose efforts to get more for themselves are justly condemned and often thwarted.[32]

One of Hollywood's latest themes is to demonize business people in children's movies. Although the "Lego Movie" did not win the Academy Award, tens of millions of children have witnessed the evil deeds of its villain, President Business. Other children's movies depicting business people as bad guys have included Big Boss in Rio 2, Clayton in the new Tarzan, and Chester V in "Cloudy with a Chance of Meatballs 2."[33] Negative portrayals of business people and the business system are probably here to stay. TV narratives demand heroes and villains and film makers typically find it easier to portray business folks in negative roles.[34]

Commercials A third way in which television contributes to business criticism is through its own commercials. To the extent that business does not accurately and fairly portray its products and services on TV, it undermines its own credibility. Commercials are a two-edged sword. On the one hand, they may sell more products and services in the short run. On the other hand, they could damage business's long-term credibility if they promote products and services deceptively and dishonestly. It is also believed by many that TV today promotes excessive commercialism as well as sedentary lifestyles.

In sum, there are three specific TV settings—news coverage, prime-time programming, and commercials—in which a tense, antibusiness environment is fostered by this "awareness" factor made available through the power and pervasiveness of television and social media.

Movies Movies also are a significant birthplace of business criticism. Hollywood seems to perceive corporations as powerful, profit-seeking enterprises that have no redeeming values. In these movies, corporate life is depicted as amoral, at best, and possibly deadly. In 2010, the sequel to *Wall Street* was released—*Wall Street: Money Never Sleeps*—with Michael Douglas again playing the malevolent Gordon Gekko. Gekko is released from 14 years in prison just in time to witness the financial system's collapse and to visit his old ways. Hollywood writers seem to love advancing the "greed is good" portrayal of business, and they go out of their way to perpetuate this image of the corporate community.[35] The release of *The Social Network* did not focus on the positive aspects of Facebook, but portrayed its cofounder Mark Zuckerberg as a conniving, antisocial individual who had to make a few enemies to succeed. The movie *Margin Call* cast its characters as flawed and cynical as they sought to save their financial institution from imminent collapse.[36] *Side Effects* portrayed a hotshot trader on Wall Street who's just done time for insider trading. The movie appears to be a modest film about the victims of a greedy pharmaceutical industry but it turns into a murder mystery set in the world of white-collar crime.[37] And, Leonardo DiCaprio's scams in *The Wolf of Wall Street* are especially memorable of the dark side of business people.

Social Media No discussion would be complete without the mention of social media that now are able to instantaneously bring information, awareness, and criticism to the public's attention. Social media have now made it possible for consumers and employees to communicate with hundreds or thousands of others about companies' products, services, or policies. Popular social media, such as Twitter, Facebook, YouTube, Google+, Snapchat, and many others, are growing by numbers and influence every day. Social media have taken on a new momentum in the digital age. And, while many businesses have been taking advantage of these for promotion purposes, they also have had a potential downside for businesses as customers now have quick and ready platforms for complaining and pointing out businesses' shortcomings. Businesses are quickly learning that social media is a double-edged sword and that they are ill prepared to deal with social media criticism. As an example of how speedy social media consequences can be, a communications director was fired immediately due to an inflammatory tweet she made before boarding her plane toward Africa. By the time her flight had landed 12 hours later, her tweet had generated so much social media opposition and uproar that her employer fired her, though she didn't know it until her plane had landed. With social media, a new world of business criticism has been opened up and large businesses as well as small ones now have to be prepared to deal with it.[38]

To be fair, the media are not to blame for all business's problems. If it were not for the fact that the behavior of some businesses and business people is deeply questionable, the media would not be able to create such an environment. The media makes the public more aware of questionable practices and should be seen as only one influential factor that contributes to the environment in which business continues to find itself criticized.

Revolution of Rising Expectations. In addition to affluence, formal education, and awareness through television, movies, social media, and the Internet, other societal trends have fostered the climate in which business criticism has flourished. When these factors work together in concert, one emerging result has been a **revolution of rising expectations** that is held by many in spite of the tougher economic times. This is a belief or an outlook that each succeeding generation ought to have a standard of living higher than that of its predecessor. A study conducted in 2014 found that most people are still living the American dream though they don't recognize it. Though only 40 percent of American adults *felt* that they were "living the American dream," this same study found sizable majorities reporting owning their own home, receiving a good education, finding a good job, and giving their children better lives than they themselves had—all characteristics of the "American dream."[39]

A mitigating factor for young people recently is that many of them have had to move back in with their parents because they couldn't find jobs, they wanted to pay off student loans, or some just want to save some money so that they can live better once they get out on their own. A 2016 study of Millennials found that they still embrace high hopes and expectations for a better life than their predecessors, but that they might define success a little differently than in the past and it may take longer to achieve it.[40] It is also worth noting that in spite of the tougher economic times, society is still very much characterized as an "impulse society" wherein we continue to live in an age of instant gratification.[41]

If rising expectations continue as they have in the past, people's hopes for major institutions, such as business, should be greater too. Building on this line of thinking, it could be argued that business criticism continues today because society's rising expectations of business's social performance have outpaced business's ability to meet these growing expectations. To the extent that this has occurred over the past and continues, business will find itself with a larger social problem.[42] To be balanced, some have observed that we may have entered an era of diminishing economic expectations[43] but whether this turns out to apply to business' social performance remains to be seen.

FIGURE 1-4 Society's Expectations versus Business's Actual Social Performance

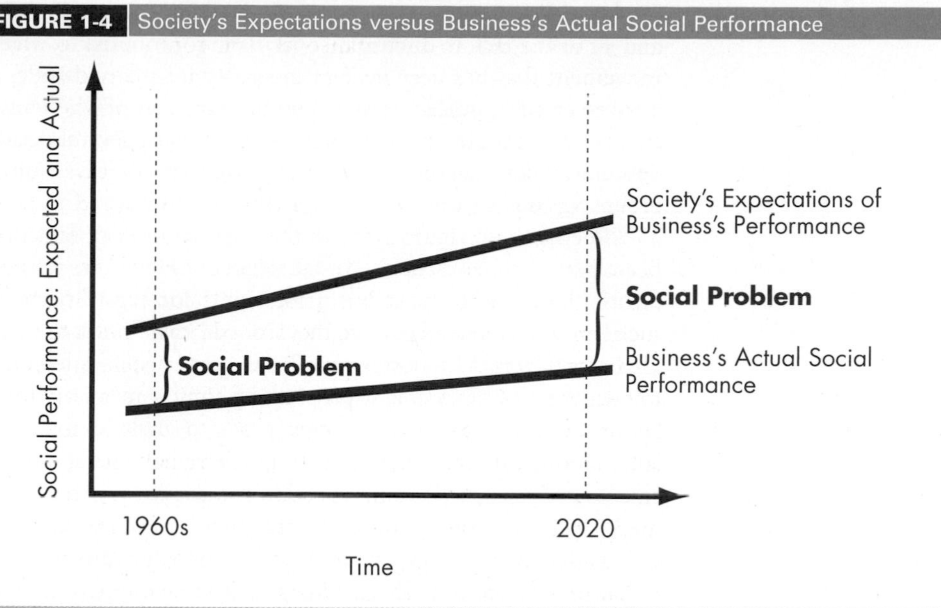

One helpful way to think about a **social problem** is that it is a gap between society's expectations of social conditions and the current social realities.[44] From the viewpoint of a business firm, the social problem it faces is experienced as the gap grows between society's *expectations* of the firm's social performance and its *actual* social performance. Rising expectations typically outpace the responsiveness of institutions such as business, thus creating a constant predicament in that it is subject to endless criticism for not meeting the public's expectations of it. Figure 1-4 illustrates the larger "social problem" that business faces today. It is depicted by the growing "gap" between society's expectations of business and business's actual social performance.

Although the general trend of rising expectations may continue, the revolution moderates at times when the economy is not as robust. Historically, job situations, health, family lives, and overall quality of life have continued to improve, though the effect of the recent economic recession makes their future hard to predict. The persistence of problems in society, such as poverty, crime, homelessness, unemployment, illegal immigration, crime, environmental pollution, and alcohol and drug abuse, along with terrorism and potential pandemics, are always present to moderate rising expectations.[45]

Entitlement Mentality. One noteworthy outgrowth of the revolution of rising expectations has been the emergence of an **entitlement mentality** on the part of some individuals and groups in society. The entitlement mentality is the general belief that someone is owed something (e.g., a job, an education, a living wage, or health care) just because she or he is a member of society. Much of this entitlement mentality impacts businesses because businesses are a central provider for many in society such as consumers, employees, and communities. Much of the entitlement mentality falls upon government but governments have a way of transferring some of these expectations to businesses.

As we approach the end of the second decade of the 2000s, jobs, expectations of "living" wages, insurance, retirement programs, "fair treatment," and health care continue to be issues on which entitlement thinking has centered though these have been moderated somewhat by the stagnant economy. Each of these has significant implications for business when they are perceived to be "entitlements" but are not received.

Rights Movement. The revolution of rising expectations, the entitlement mentality, and all of the factors discussed so far have contributed to what has been termed the **rights movement** that has been evident in society for many decades now. "Rights" thinking may have received significant impetus by the adoption of The Universal Declaration of Human Rights by the United Nations in 1948. In the past several decades, and continuing, the U.S. Supreme Court has heard increasing numbers of cases aimed at establishing for some groups various legal rights that perhaps never occurred to the founders of the nation.[46]

Some of these rights, such as the right to privacy and the right to due process, have been perceived as generic for all citizens. However, in addition to these generalized rights, there has been activism for rights for many particular groups in society. This modern movement began in the United States with the civil rights movement of the 1950s and 1960s. Many groups have been inspired by the success of the civil rights movement and have sought progress by similar means. Thus, we have seen the protected status of individuals and groups grow to include many others. At various levels—international, federal, state, and local—there have been claims for the rights of many different groups each claiming they are due special protections or privileges.

Business, as one of society's prominent institutions, has been affected with an ever-expanding array of expectations as to how people want to be treated, not only as employees but also as shareholders, consumers, environmentally conscious citizens, and members of the community. The "rights" movement is interrelated with the special-interest society discussed earlier and sometimes follows an "entitlement" mentality among some people and within some sectors of society.

Victimization Philosophy. It has become apparent during the past several decades that there are increasing numbers of individuals and groups who see themselves as having been victimized by society, thus leading to a culture of victimhood.[47] The *New York* magazine featured a cover story on "The New Culture of Victimization," with the title "Don't Blame Me!"[48] *Esquire* probed what it called "A Confederacy of Complainers."[49] Charles Sykes published *A Nation of Victims: The Decay of the American Character.*[50] Sykes's thesis, with which these other observers might agree, is that modern cultures have become a "society of victims."

What is particularly interesting about the novel **victimization philosophy** is the extent to which it is dispersing in the population. According to these writers, the victim mentality is just as likely to be seen among many groups in society—regardless of race, gender, age, or any other classification. Sykes observed that previous movements may have been seen as a "revolution of rising expectations," but the victimization movement might be called a "revolution of rising sensitivities" in which grievance begets grievance. In such a society of victims, "feelings" rather than reason or facts prevail, and people start perceiving that they are being unfairly "hurt" by society's institutions—business, government, and education. The victimization philosophy is intimately related to and sometimes inseparable from the rights movement and the entitlement mentality. Taken together, these emerging ways of viewing one's plight—as someone else's unfairness—pose special challenges for business managers now and in the future.

In summary, affluence and education; awareness through television, movies, social media, and the internet; the revolution of rising expectations; an entitlement mentality; the rights movement; and the victimization philosophy have formed a backdrop against which criticism of business has developed and flourished. This helps explain why we have a societal environment that is conducive to criticism of business. Though the U.S. and world economies have been through their worst fiscal slump since World War II, some of these same general trends are bound to continue but may be moderated if economies improve.

In the next two subsections, some of the general criticisms of business and some of the general responses to such criticisms are identified and discussed.

ETHICS IN PRACTICE CASE

Working for My Cup or the House?

For those who are not familiar with the service industry, employees are paid minimally by the company they work for and their pay rate is determined by the tips received from customers. As a bartender, a person is exposed to having to deal with all sorts of peoples' needs as well as employee competition and standard operating procedures set forth by management. Every time a drink is poured, a decision must be made whether to follow company standards or give away extra alcohol in order to receive a larger tip.

When first being promoted to bartender at an established golf resort, I witnessed firsthand the different factors that can affect one's "pour." A pour can be defined as how much liquor is added to a customer's drink. The three factors that affect one's pour are as follows: comparisons to other employees' pours, the requests of customers for extra pours with compensation of a larger tip, and what the company designates as a pour.

When working as a team or having repeat customers, bartenders are compared based on their pour. If one bartender uses two pours and another uses one pour (the latter is the standard for the company), the rule-following bartender is not viewed as favorably as the one using the larger pour. This is clearly reflected in tips from customers. Similarly, the customer might say, "Put a little extra in there and I'll take care of you." The employee is put on the spot to choose between the company and him or herself.

The bartender with the heavier pour or who gives away drinks for free may receive more money in their tip cup but the company suffers from lost revenues. If a bartender makes an average of 100 drinks a night and uses two pours instead of one for each drink, that bartender is giving away 100 drinks worth of alcohol each night which reduces nightly revenues, and has a huge effect on yearly liquor revenues.

In this highly competitive and profitable industry, over pouring is a practice that can cripple a business. As the newest bartender, one wants to fit in with the other bartenders and earn as much money as possible though it costs the company or "house" profits. Which is more important, filling your own tip cup or maximizing the house's profits that does not directly benefit the bartender?

1. Is it ethical to over pour customers' drinks in order to develop better customer relations to earn more tips at the expense of company revenues? Are the bartenders using the "entitlement mentality" here to justify their self-serving actions? Do bartenders have a "right" to take care of their own cups?
2. If the customer wants or expects over pouring, should the companies allow over pouring in order to satisfy the customers' wants and desires?
3. Is it ethical to witness and not report over pouring on the part of fellow bartenders who have been there longer? Should I inform management what is happening?

Contributed by Matthew DePasquale

1.5b A General Criticism of Business: Use and Abuse of Power

Many different criticisms have been directed toward business over the years: Business is too big, it is too powerful, it pollutes the environment and exploits people for its own gain, it takes advantage of workers and consumers, it does not tell the truth, its' executives are too highly paid, and so on. If one were to identify a common thread that seems to run through all the grievances, it would be business's use and perceived abuse of power. This is an issue that will not go away. In one cover story, *Bloomberg BusinessWeek* posed the question: "Too Much Corporate Power?" In this featured article, the magazine presented its surveys of the public regarding business power. In their survey, nearly two-thirds of Americans said they thought business had too much power over various aspects of their lives.[51] Many citizens also are deeply distrustful of employers because they believe business has derived power by virtue of being big.[52]

In the book, *Power, Inc.*, the case is made that companies, not kings, now rule the world. The author maintains that global corporations wield greater power today than most nation-states.[53] In Michael Moore's provocative movie, *Capitalism: A Love Story*, the filmmaker continued his assault on business power by laying the blame for the worldwide recession on both big business and government. Whether at the general level or the level of the firm, questions about business's use or abuse of power continue to be raised. As recently as 2016, a major Bloomberg BusinessWeek article asserted that "fairly or not, Big Business is taking heat for the stagnation of living standards and the widening gap between rich and poor."[54]

So, what exactly is **business power**? Business power refers to the capacity or ability to produce an effect, have impact, or to bring influence to bear on a situation or people. Power may be perceived or felt either positively or negatively. In the context of business criticism, however, power typically is perceived as being "abused." Business certainly does have enormous power, but whether it *abuses* power is an issue that needs to be carefully examined. The allegation that business abuses power remains the central theme behind the discussion in this section.

Levels of Power. Business power exists at and may be manifested at several different levels. Four such levels include the macrolevel, the intermediate level, the microlevel, and the individual level.[55] The *macrolevel* refers to the entire corporate system—"Corporate America," Big Business—the totality of business organizations. Power here emanates from the sheer size, resources, and dominance of the corporate system over society and our lives. As the corporate system has globalized, its impact has become more far reaching as well. At the 2012 World Economic Forum, it was noted that the worlds' major companies are now larger than many governments and are operating in a universe that is increasingly supranational, often disconnected from local issues and home markets.[56] During the election year of 2016, it was asserted that there remains "contempt for Big Business."[57] This is a refrain that just does not seem to go away.

The *intermediate level* of business power refers to groups of corporations acting in concert in an effort to produce a desired effect—to set prices, control markets, dominate purchasers, promote an issue, or pass or defeat legislation. Prime examples include OPEC (gas prices), airlines, cable TV companies, banks, pharmaceutical companies, and defense contractors pursuing the interests they have in common. The combined effect of companies acting in concert is substantial.

The *microlevel* of business power is the level of the individual firm. This might refer to the exertion of power or influence by any major corporation—Google, Wal-Mart, Apple, Microsoft, Nike, or Exxon—for example. The final level at which business power may be manifested is the *individual level.* This refers to the individual corporate leader exerting power—for example, Indra Nooyi (Pepsi), Mark Zuckerberg (Facebook), Daniel Amos (Aflac), Virginia Rometty (IBM), Tim Cook (Apple), Marissa Mayer (Yahoo), Muhtar Kent (Coca-Cola), Elon Musk (Tesla Motors), or Warren Buffett (Berkshire Hathaway).

The key point here is that as one analyzes corporate power, one should think in terms of the different levels at which that power is manifested or felt. When this is done, it is not easy to generalize whether corporate power is excessive or has been abused. The results are often mixed. Specific levels of power need to be delineated and examined before conclusions can be reached.

Spheres of Power. In addition to levels of power, there are also many different spheres or arenas in which business power may be manifested. Figure 1-5 depicts one way of looking at the four levels identified and some of the spheres of power that also exist. *Economic power* and *political power* are two spheres that are dominant, but business has other, more subtle forms of power as well. These other spheres include *social and cultural power, power over the individual, technological power,* and *environmental power.*[58]

Is the power of business excessive? Does business abuse its power? Apparently, many people think so. To provide sensible and fair answers to these questions, however, one must carefully specify which level of power is being referred to and in which sphere the power is being exercised. When this is done, it is not simple to arrive at answers that are generalizable. Furthermore, the nature of power is such that it is sometimes wielded

FIGURE 1-5 Corporate Power–Levels and Spheres

Levels / Spheres	Macrolevel (the business system)	Intermediate Level (several firms)	Microlevel (single firm)	Individual Level (single executive)
Economic				
Social/Cultural				
Individual				
Technological				
Environmental				
Political				

ETHICS IN PRACTICE CASE

Is Business Power Too Great?

The "business system," that totality of all businesses in a nation or the world, is said to be one of the most powerful institutions known to humankind. The other major candidates for this honor are typically government and the military. One of the most often repeated accusations about large businesses is that they have too much power. It is also claimed that they abuse this power.

Business power is the ability to produce an effect—to get things done and to bring about its desired state of affairs. It's about business getting its way. One way of thinking about business power is to frame it in terms that analysts have claimed are relevant in understanding power. John French and Bertram Raven have argued that business has five types of power: coercive power, legitimate power, reward power, referent power, and expert power. Each of these may be thought of from the perspective of a large business.

Coercive power occurs when a manager in authority forces someone to do something—usually with some threat of punishment. *Legitimate* power exists when a person in the chain of command has a title or position that implies he or she has the authority to take some action. *Reward* power is manifested when a boss uses rewards to get things done. The rewards may not only be monetary, such as pay increases and promotions, but may also be psychological, such as praise. The flip side of reward is punishment and it is part of reward power as well. *Referent* power is gained by leaders due to others admiring him or her as a role model. Finally, *Expert* power arises when someone becomes highly regarded due to their superior training, expertise, and/or experience.

1. Which type of power do businesses display the most? Give an example.
2. As an employee, with which type of power would you be most concerned? Why?
3. As a consumer, with which type of power would you be most troubled? Why?
4. Have you been the "victim" of business power? Explain.
5. Is business power too great? Does business abuse its' power?

Sources: John French and Bertram Raven, "Bases of Social Power." *Studies in Social Power*. Dorwin Cartwright (ed.) University of Michigan, Ann Arbor, 1959. Jeffrey Pfeffer, *Power—Why Some People Have It—and Others Don't*, Harper Business, 2010; Justin Johnson, "Five Types of Power in Business," *Chron*, http://smallbusiness.chron.com/5-types-power-businesses-18221.html. Accessed March 28, 2016.

unintentionally. Sometimes the use of power is *consequential*; that is, it is not wielded intentionally, but nevertheless exerts its influence even though no attempt is made to exercise it.[59] Whether business abuses its power is a question we will continue to examine and certainly one that the business system and companies need to keep in the forefront of their thinking.

1.5c Balancing Power with Responsibility

Whether or not business abuses its power or allows its use of power to become excessive is a central issue that cuts through all the topics examined in this book. But power should not be viewed in isolation from responsibility, and this power–responsibility relationship is the foundation for appeals for corporate social responsibility that are at the heart of business and society discussions.

Iron Law of Responsibility. The **Iron Law of Responsibility** is a concept that addresses this: "In the long run, those who do not use power in a manner which society considers responsible will tend to lose it."[60] Stated another way, whenever power and responsibility become substantially out of balance, forces will be generated to bring them into closer balance.

When power gets out of balance with responsibility, a variety of forces may come to bear on business to be more responsible and more responsive to the criticisms being made against it. Some of these more obvious forces include governmental actions such as increased regulations, or consumer actions such as boycotts or refusing to buy. The investigative news media may become interested in what is going on, and a whole host of special-interest groups may bring pressure to bear. In the *Business Week* story cited earlier, the point was made that "it's this power imbalance that's helping to breed the current resentment against corporations."[61]

The tobacco industry is an excellent example of an industry that has felt the brunt of efforts to address allegations of abuse of power. After years of perceived abuse, the Food and Drug Administration (FDA) was given additional authority to address the power imbalance between the industry and customers.

The stream of corporate scandals beginning with Enron in 2001 led to government action in this sphere. In 2002, the U.S. Congress quickly passed the Sarbanes–Oxley Act, which was designed to rein in the power and abuse that were manifested in such corporate scandals as Enron, WorldCom, Arthur Andersen, and Tyco. Beginning in 2011, a new federal regulatory body began its work—The Consumer Financial Protection Bureau (CFPB). CFPB was created to make markets fairer for consumers wanting to apply for a mortgage, choose among competing credit cards, or engage in a number of other consumer financial transactions in which business has traditionally held the upper hand.[62] A major point of view presented in this book is that many such governmental regulations may have been circumvented by business if it had done a better job of balancing its power with responsibility in these sectors. This is what corporate social responsibility (CSR) is all about, and this topic will be developed further in Chapter 2.

1.5d Business's Response: Concern and a Changing Social Contract

Growing out of criticisms of business and unease regarding the power–responsibility imbalance has been an increased concern on the part of business for the stakeholder environment and a changed social contract. Previously it was discussed how the social environment was composed of such factors as demographics, lifestyles, and social values of the society. It may also be seen as a collection of conditions, events, and trends that reflect how people think and behave and what they value. As firms have sensed that the social environment, social values, and the expectations of business have been changing, they have realized that they must adapt as well. Many positive changes have been made by businesses but as the discussion of the characteristics of a "social problem" indicated, business seldom catches up with stakeholder expectations. As we will see in Chapter 2 and later, businesses' attempts to be socially responsible or sustainable reflect how this concern is being expressed. Just to get a quick glimpse at how many major businesses have been expressing their social concern, *Fortune* magazine recently published its first ever list of companies that are "changing the world." Some of the companies recognized and what they have been doing include the following:[63]

Vodafone and Safaricom—connecting the unbanked masses to the global economy

Google (Alphabet)—knocking down barriers to knowledge

Toyota—building ways to lower automobile emissions

Walmart—pushing an army of suppliers to eliminate waste

Enel—cleaning up as it cleans up the power grid

GSK—bringing hope with an innovative malaria vaccine

Novartis—bringing essential medicines to the poor

Facebook—philanthropy? we have an app for that

Social contract. One way of thinking about the business–society relationship is through the concept of **social contract**. The social contract is a set of reciprocal understandings and expectations that characterize the relationship between major institutions—in our case, business and society. It also is seen as understood and tacit agreements that guide behavior in relationships among members of a community or group.[64] The social contract between business and society has been changing, and these changes have been a direct outgrowth of the increased importance of the social environment to many stakeholders. The social contract has been changing to reflect society's expanded expectations of business, especially in the social, ethical, and sustainability realms. Businesses have responded to these changing expectations though seldom as quickly or as much as the public would like.

The social contract between business and society, as illustrated in Figure 1-6, is articulated or expressed primarily in two main ways:

1. *Laws and regulations* that society has established as the framework within which business must operate in its relationships with stakeholders, and
2. *Shared understandings* that evolve over time as to each group's expectations of the other.

FIGURE 1-6 Elements in the Social Contract

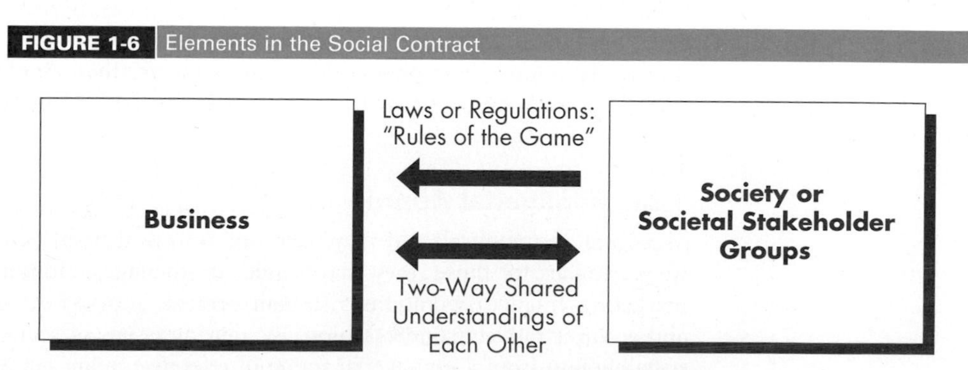

Laws and regulations spell out the "rules of the game" for business for which they are held accountable. Shared understandings, on the other hand, are more subtle and create room for misunderstandings. These shared understandings reflect mutual expectations regarding each other's roles, responsibilities, and ethics. These unspoken elements of the social contract represent what might be called the normative perspective on the relationship (i.e., what "ought" to be done by each party to the social contract).[65] The mounting importance of social responsibility, sustainability, and business ethics are reflected here.

If these shared understandings were spelled out, a company might adopt the following hypothetical principles as part of its social contract with consumers:

- We believe our company has a right to innovation, entrepreneurship, and profit-making, whereas our consumers have a right to a healthy society and planet for living.
- We believe that the interests of our company and our customers are best served through a sustainable practice of capitalism—economically, morally, environmentally, and socially.
- We believe that our customers and our company owe each other an equal duty of transparent, authentic, and accountable communication.
- We believe that our company and our customers are duty-bound to serve as custodians of global well-being for this and all future generations.[66]

Unfortunately, a shared understanding of an aspect of the social contract is seldom expressed in clear, written format such as this. Since there are so many of the shared understandings existing in the world of perceptions and expectations, the opportunities for disagreements are always with us.

A *BusinessWeek* editorial on the subject of the social contract summarizes well the current era of business and society relationships:

> *Today it is clear that the terms of the contract between society and business are, in fact, changing in substantial and important ways. Business is being asked to assume broader responsibilities to society than ever before, and to serve a wider range of human values.... Inasmuch as business exists to serve society, its future will depend on the quality of management's response to the changing expectations of the public.*[67]

Another *BusinessWeek* editorial commented on the new social contract by saying, "Listen up, Corporate America. The American people are having a most serious discussion about your role in their lives." The editorial was referring to the criticisms coming out about the abuse of corporate power.[68] Such a statement suggests that changes in the social contract between business and society will be an ongoing process.

1.6 Focus of the Book

This book takes a **managerial approach** to the business and society relationship. This managerial approach emphasizes three main themes that are of vital importance to managers, organizations, and society today: business ethics, sustainability, and stakeholder management.

1.6a Managerial Approach

Managers are practical, and they have begun to deal with social and ethical concerns in ways similar to those they have used to manage traditional business functions—marketing, finance, operations, risk management, and so forth—in a rational, systematic, and administratively sound fashion. By viewing issues of social and ethical concern and sustainability from a managerial frame of reference, managers have been able to convert seemingly unmanageable issues into ones that can be dealt with in a balanced and impartial fashion. At the same time, managers have had to integrate traditional economic and financial considerations with ethical and social considerations.

Urgent versus Enduring Issues. From the standpoint of urgency in organizational response, management is concerned with two broad types or classes of social issues. First, there are those *urgent* issues or crises that arise instantaneously and for which management must formulate relatively quick responses. A typical example might be a protest group that shows up on management's doorstep one day, arguing vehemently that the company should withdraw its sponsorship of a violent television show scheduled to air the next week or a crisis could occur with respect to a company's products, services, or operations.

Second, there are issues that management has time to deal with on more of a long-term basis. These *enduring* issues include environmental pollution, sustainability, employment discrimination, and occupational safety and health. These are continuing long-term issues that will be of concern to society on an ongoing basis and for which management must develop planned, thoughtful organizational responses. Management must be concerned with both short-term and long-term capabilities for dealing with social problems and the organization's social performance.

The measure of success of the managerial approach will be the extent to which leaders can improve an organization's social, ethical, and sustainability performance by taking a managerial approach rather than dealing with issues and crises on an ad hoc basis. This managerial approach will require balancing the needs of urgency with the requirements of enduring issues.

1.6b Business Ethics Theme

The managerial focus attempts to take a practical look at the social issues and expectations business faces, but ethical questions inevitably and continuously come into play. In the workplace, ethics essentially refers to issues of fairness, and justice, and **business ethics** focuses on ethical issues that arise in the organizational realm. Ethical factors appear throughout our discussion because questions of fairness, and justice, no matter how slippery they are to deal with, permeate business's activities as it attempts to interact successfully with major stakeholder groups. In light of the ongoing ethical scandals in recent years, the ethics theme resonates as one of the most urgent aspects of business and society relationships.

1.6c Sustainability Theme

The concept of **sustainability** has become one of businesses' most pressing mandates. Discussions of sustainability began with respect to the natural environment. As time has passed, however, it has become evident that it is a broader concept that applies not only to the natural environment but to the entirety of businesses' operations and processes as well, especially business's global role and development. At a basic level, sustainability is about business's ability to survive and thrive over the long term.[69] The concept of sustainability is derived from the notion of **sustainable development**, which is a pattern of resource use that aims to meet current human needs while preserving the environment so that these needs can be met not only in the present but also for future generations. The term *sustainability* was initiated by the Brundtland Commission, which coined what has become the most often-quoted definition of sustainable development:

> *Development that meets the needs of the present without compromising the ability of future generations to meet their own needs.*[70]

Today, sustainability is understood to embrace environmental, economic, and social criteria, and this is the general sense in which it will be used in this book.[71] Thus, discussions of sustainability and its implications will be explicit or implicit in most chapters, not just in the chapter on the natural environment.

1.6d Stakeholder Management Theme

As suggested throughout this chapter, **stakeholders** are individuals or groups with which business interacts who have a "stake," or vested interest, in the firm. Stakeholders are integral constituents in the business and society relationship.

Two broad groups of stakeholders are considered in this book—external and internal. Though all chapters touch on the **stakeholder management** theme, Chapter 3 develops the concept in detail and Chapter 4 provides early treatment of shareholding stakeholders within the topic of corporate governance.

Later, *external stakeholders*, which include government, consumers, the natural environment, and community members, are considered. Both domestic and global stakeholders are major concerns throughout. Government is treated first because ostensibly it represents the public interests. It is helpful to understand the role and workings of government to best appreciate business's relationships with other groups. Consumers may be business's most important external stakeholders. Members of the community are crucial, too, and they are concerned about a variety of issues. One of the most important is the natural environment and the topic of sustainability.

The second broad grouping of stakeholders is *internal stakeholders*. Shareholders are treated in our discussion of corporate governance (Chapter 4), and then later in the book (Chapters 17–19) employees are addressed as the principal group of internal stakeholders. We live in an organizational society, and many people think that their roles as employees are just as important as their roles as shareholders. Both of these groups have legitimate legal and ethical claims on the organization, and the management's task is to address their needs and balance these needs against those of the firm and of other stakeholder groups.

1.7 Structure of the Book

The structure and flow of the parts and chapters of this book are outlined in Figure 1-7.

In Part 1, "Business, Society, and Stakeholders," there are three chapters. Chapter 1 provides an overview of the business and society relationship. Chapter 2 introduces a number of different Corporate Social Responsibility (CSR) and Sustainability concepts. Companies being socially and sustainably responsible is a central theme of this entire book. Chapter 3 defines and elaborates on stakeholder management. These first three chapters provide a crucial foundation and context for understanding the business and society relationship.

Part 2 is titled "Corporate Governance and Strategic Management Issues." Chapter 4 covers the highly relevant and timely topic of corporate governance, which has become more prominent during the past decade. The next two chapters address management-related topics. Chapter 5 covers strategic management and corporate public affairs. Chapter 6 addresses issues, risk and crisis management.

Part 3, "Business Ethics and Leadership," focuses exclusively on business ethics topics. Business ethics essentials are established in Chapter 7, and managerial and organizational ethics are further developed in Chapter 8. Chapter 9 addresses the ever-changing topic of business ethics and technology. Chapter 10 treats business ethics in the global or international sphere. Although ethical issues cut through and permeate virtually all discussions in the book, this dedicated treatment of business ethics is warranted by a need to explore in greater detail the ethical dimension in organizations and management.

Part 4, "External Stakeholder Issues," deals with the foremost external stakeholders of business. Because government is such an active participant in all the groups to follow, in

FIGURE 1-7 Organization and Flow of the Book

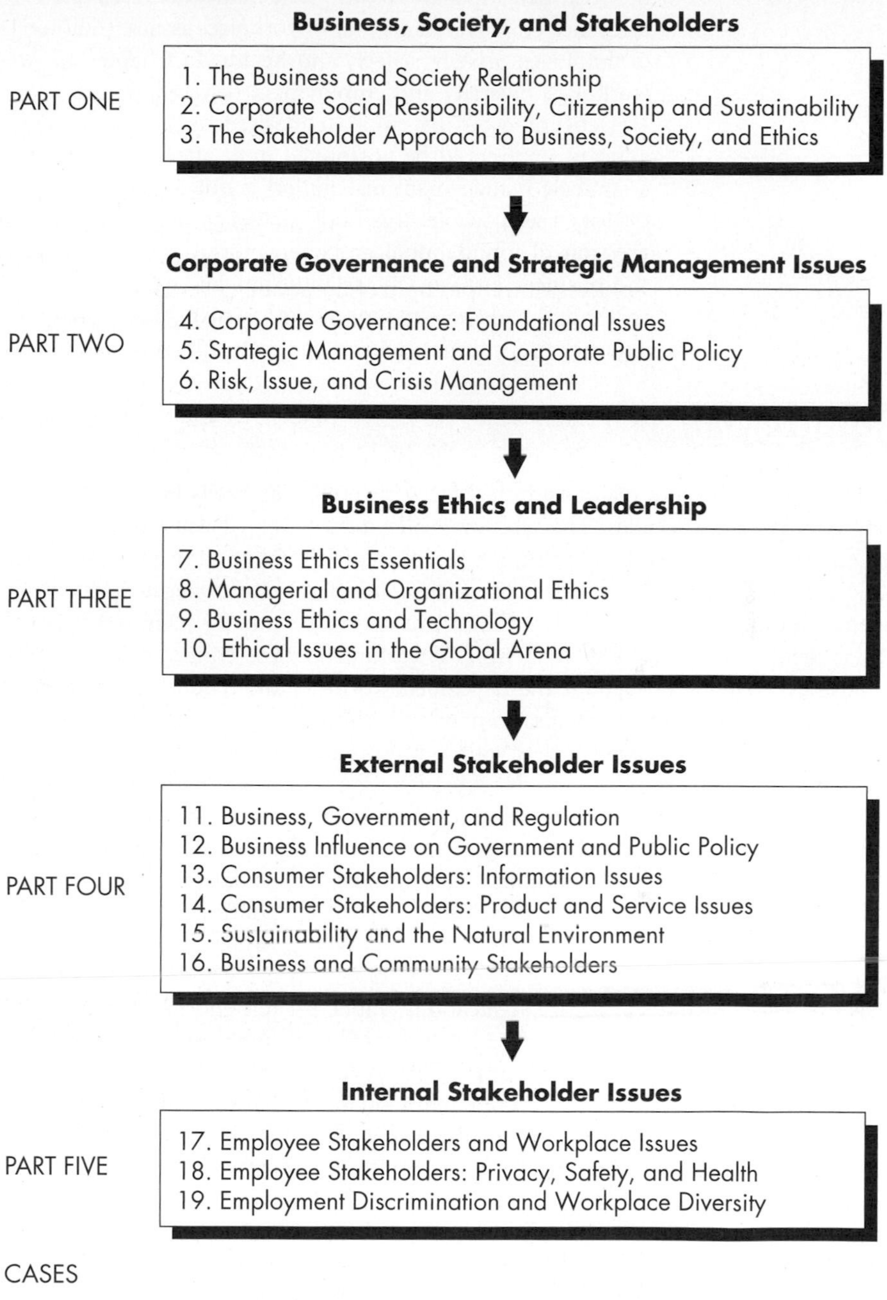

Business, Society, and Stakeholders

PART ONE

1. The Business and Society Relationship
2. Corporate Social Responsibility, Citizenship and Sustainability
3. The Stakeholder Approach to Business, Society, and Ethics

Corporate Governance and Strategic Management Issues

PART TWO

4. Corporate Governance: Foundational Issues
5. Strategic Management and Corporate Public Policy
6. Risk, Issue, and Crisis Management

Business Ethics and Leadership

PART THREE

7. Business Ethics Essentials
8. Managerial and Organizational Ethics
9. Business Ethics and Technology
10. Ethical Issues in the Global Arena

External Stakeholder Issues

PART FOUR

11. Business, Government, and Regulation
12. Business Influence on Government and Public Policy
13. Consumer Stakeholders: Information Issues
14. Consumer Stakeholders: Product and Service Issues
15. Sustainability and the Natural Environment
16. Business and Community Stakeholders

Internal Stakeholder Issues

PART FIVE

17. Employee Stakeholders and Workplace Issues
18. Employee Stakeholders: Privacy, Safety, and Health
19. Employment Discrimination and Workplace Diversity

CASES

Chapter 11 business–government relationships and government regulations are discussed. In Chapter 12, it is seen how business endeavors to shape and influence government and public policy. Chapters 13 and 14 address consumer stakeholders, arguably the most important because without them businesses fail. Chapter 15 addresses sustainability and the natural environment as stakeholder. Chapter 16 examines business and community stakeholder issues, including corporate philanthropy.

Part 5, "Internal Stakeholder Issues," centers on employees as stakeholders because the treatment of shareholding stakeholders is discussed earlier in Chapter 4. Chapter 17 examines employees and major workplace issues. Chapter 18 looks carefully at the issues of employee privacy, safety, and health. In Chapter 19, we focus on the special case of workplace diversity and employment discrimination.

Depending on the emphasis desired in the course, Part 2 could be covered where it appears, or it could be postponed until after Part 5. Alternatively, it could be omitted if a strategic management orientation is not desired.

Taken as a whole, this book strives to take the reader through a building-block progression of foundational and then more developed concepts and ideas that are vital to the business and society relationship and to explore the nature of social and ethical issues and stakeholder groups with which management must interact. It considers the external and internal stakeholder groups in considerable depth.

Summary

The business and society relationship has faced severe testing over the past decades. The Occupy Wall Street and One Percent movements have been a recent manifestation of the tensions that have arisen. In spite of this, the pluralistic system is still at work, presenting business firms with a variety of challenges. The pluralistic business system throughout the developed world has several advantages and some disadvantages. Within this context, business firms must deal with a multitude of stakeholders and an increasingly special-interest society represented by nonprofit organizations and non-governmental organizations (NGOs).

A major force that shapes the public's view of business is the criticism that business receives from a variety of sources. Factors in the social environment that have contributed to an atmosphere in which business criticism thrives include affluence, education, public awareness developed through the media (especially TV, movies, social media, and the Internet), the revolution of rising expectations, a growing entitlement mentality, the rights movement, and a philosophy of victimization. The global economic situation may result in changes in business criticism and its antecedents. In addition, actual questionable practices on the part of business have made it a natural target. The recent ethics scandals involving well-known companies such as Wells Fargo, Volkswagen, General Motors, Toshiba, and Takata have kept business ethics on the front page. Not all firms are guilty, but questionable practices attract negative attention to the entire business community. One result is that the trust and legitimacy of the entire business system is called into question and the reputational capital of businesses decline.

A common criticism of business is that it abuses its power. Power operates on four different levels: the level of the entire business system, by groups of companies acting in concert, by the individual firm, and by the individual corporate executive. Business power may be manifested in several different spheres—economic, political, technological, environmental, social, and individual. It is difficult to conclude whether business is actually abusing its power, but it is clear that business has enormous power and that it must exercise it carefully. Power evokes responsibility, and this is the central reason that appeals for corporate responsibility have continued. The Iron Law of Responsibility highlights the need for greater balance in business power and its responsible use. These concerns have led to a changing social environment for business and a changed social contract. The changing terms of the social contract will become evident throughout the book's chapters.

Key Terms

affluence, p. 11
business, p. 5
business ethics, p. 23
business power, p. 18
economic environment, p. 6
education, p. 11
entitlement mentality, p. 15
Iron Law of Responsibility, p. 20
macroenvironment, p. 6
managerial approach, p. 22
nongovernmental organizations (NGOs), p. 9

pluralism, p. 7
political environment, p. 7
revolution of rising expectations, p. 14
rights movement, p. 16
social contract, p. 21
social environment, p. 6
social problem, p. 15
society, p. 6
special-interest society, p. 9
stakeholder management, p. 24
stakeholders, p. 24
sustainability, p. 23
sustainable development, p. 23
technological environment, p. 7
victimization philosophy, p. 16

Discussion Questions

1. In discussions of business and society, why is there a tendency to focus on large-sized rather than small- or medium-sized firms? Have the corporate ethics scandals of the past decade affected small- and medium-sized firms? If so, in what ways have these firms been affected?
2. What is the one greatest strength of a pluralistic society? What is the one greatest weakness? Do these characteristics work for or against business?
3. Identify and explain the major factors in the social environment that create an atmosphere in which business criticism takes place and prospers. Provide examples. How are the factors related to one another? Has the revolution of rising expectations run its course? Or is it still a reality among young people today?
4. Give an example of each of the four levels of power discussed in this chapter. Also, give an example of each of the spheres of business power.
5. Explain in your own words the Iron Law of Responsibility and the social contract. Give an example of a shared understanding between you as a consumer or an employee and a firm with which you do business or for which you work.

Endnotes

1. Peter Coy, "Open Season on Big Business," *Bloomberg BusinessWeek*, February 25, 2016.
2. Casey B. Mulligan, "Capitol Hill Pickpockets," *The Wall Street Journal*, February 25, 2015, A11.
3. Ellen Simon, "Business Year in Review: At Least You've Got Your Health," *The Atlanta Journal-Constitution* (December 26, 2008), E4.
4. Mara Der Hovanesian, "Pointing a Finger at Wall Street," *BusinessWeek* (August 11, 2008), 80.
5. L. Gordon Crovitz, "Occupy Wall Street's Crony Capitalism," *The Wall Street Journal*, October 17, 2011, A15.
6. Mulligan, ""ibid.
7. Anna Bruce-Lockhart, "Who Are the World's One Percent? The Answer Might Surprise You." WEF Agenda Blog, October 17, 2015.
8. CNN Money, "Wall Street Has Lost Its Cool Factor," http://money.cnn.com/2015/11/17/investing/occupy-wall-street-banks-change/. Accessed February 15, 2016.
9. Lynn Forester de Rothschild and Adam S. Posen, "How Capitalism Can Repair Its Bruised Image," *The Wall Street Journal*, January 2, 2013, A17.
10. Kevin Johnson, "BP to Pay Record $20B Settlement in Gulf Spill," *USA Today*, October 6, 2015, 3A.
11. Charles Moore, "The Middle Class Squeeze," *The Wall Street Journal*, September 26–27, 2015, C1.
12. Jay Cost, "The Politics of Mistrust," *The Wall Street Journal*, October 17–18, 2015, C1.
13. Gail Marks Jarvis, "America Has an Issue with Trust and It's Getting Worse," *Atlanta Journal-Constitution*, February 14, 2016, D2.
14. Bet Kowitt, "The Conscious Capitalist," *Fortune*, September 1, 2015, 77–84.
15. Liam Fahey and V. K. Narayanan, *Macroenvironmental Analysis for Strategic Management* (St. Paul: West, 1986), 28–30.
16. Michael Porter and Jan Rivkin, "What Business Should Do to Restore U.S. Competiveness," *Fortune*, October 29, 2012, 168–171.
17. Quoted in Jay Cost, "The Politics of Mistrust," *The Wall Street Journal*, October 17–18, 2015, C2.
18. Porter and Rivkin, 2012, ibid.
19. Joseph W. McGuire, *Business and Society* (New York: McGraw-Hill, 1963), 130.
20. Bob Lurie, *BloombergBusiness*, "A New Social Contract for Green Business," http://www.businessweek.com/managing/content/may2009/ca20090512_004263.htm. Accessed March 28, 2016.
21. "Interest Groups Have a Lot at Stake in Health Care Debate," *USA Today* (November 23, 2009), 15A.
22. Business for a Fair Minimum Wage, http://www.businessforafairminimumwage.org/. Accessed March 28, 2016.

23. United States Census Bureau, USA Quickfacts, http://quickfacts.census.gov/qfd/states/00000.html. Accessed February 1, 2016.
24. "Television and Health," *The Sourcebook for Teaching Science*, http://www.csun.edu/science/health/docs/tv&health.html#tv_stats. Accessed March 28, 2016.
25. "Executives See Unethical Behavior, Media Criticisms as Threats," *Nashville Business Journal* (June 11, 2002).
26. Renilde DeWit, "Businesses Remain Unprepared for Social Media Criticism," http://www.i-scoop.eu/businesses-remain-unprepared-social-media-criticism/,i-scoop. Accessed March 28, 2016.
27. Karen Valby, "Remembering Larry Hagman," *EW.COM*, December 7, 2012, 12–13; James Poniewozik, "Milestones: Larry Hagman Texas-size Villain," *Time*, December 10, 2012, 23.
28. "Businessmen Are Always the Villains," *The Economist*, October 16, 2015.
29. Gina Berreca, "What Did Don Draper Really Leave Behind?" *Athens Banner-Herald*, May 22, 2015, A6.
30. Timothy Lamer, "Crooks in Suits," *World* (July 29, 2006), 29.
31. "Billions, Season One," *IMDb*, http://www.imdb.com/title/tt4270492/. Accessed March 28, 2016.
32. Linda S. Lichter, S. Robert Lichter, and Stanley Rothman, "How Show Business Shows Business," *Public Opinion* (November 1982), 10–12.
33. Doug Haugh, "Businessmen as Hollywood Bogeymen," *The Wall Street Journal*, February 28-March 1, 2015, A9.
34. *The Economist*, October 16, 2015, ibid.
35. Michael Medved, "Hollywood's Business-Bashing: Biting the Hand That Is You," *USA Today* (February 3, 2010), 9A.
36. Rachel Dodes, "Hollywood's Favorite Villain," *The Wall Street Journal*, October 14, 2011, D1.
37. Logan Hill, "Movie Math," *Bloomberg Businessweek*, February 11–17, 2013, 70.
38. Kami Dimitrova, "Justine Sacco, Fired after Tweet on AIDS in Africa, Issues Apology," *ABCNews*, http://abcnews.go.com/International/justine-sacco-fired-tweet-aids-africa-issues-apology/story?id=21301833. Accessed March 28, 2016.
39. Everett Rosenfeld, *USA Today*, July 5, 2014, http://www.usatoday.com/story/money/business/2014/07/05/american-dream-unrecognized/12047675/ Accessed October 26, 2015.
40. Susan Page and Jenny Ung, "American Dream Survives among Millennials, Poll Finds," *USA Today*, March 16, 2016, 2A.
41. Paul Roberts, *The Impulse Society: America in the Age of Instant Gratification*, New York: Bloomsbury USA, 2014.
42. Robert J. Samuelson, *The Good Life and Its Discontents: The American Dream in the Age of Entitlement, 1945–1995* (New York: Times Books, 1996).
43. "The Age of Diminished Expectations," *The Economist*, February 20, 2013. Accessed March 18, 2013.
44. Neil H. Jacoby, *Corporate Power and Social Responsibility* (New York: Macmillan, 1973), 186–188.
45. Linda DeStefano, "Looking Ahead to the Year 2000: No Utopia, but Most Expect a Better Life," *The Gallup Poll Monthly* (January 1990), 21.
46. Charlotte Low, "Someone's Rights, Another's Wrongs," *Insight* (January 26, 1987), 8.
47. David J. Ley, "The Culture of Victimhood," *Psychology Today*, June 28, 2014, https://www.psychologytoday.com/blog/women-who-stray/201406/the-culture-victimhood. Accessed March 28, 2016.
48. John Taylor, "Don't Blame Me!" *New York* (June 3, 1991).
49. Pete Hamill, "A Confederacy of Complainers," *Esquire* (July 1991).
50. Charles J. Sykes, *A Nation of Victims: The Decay of the American Character* (New York: St. Martin's Press, 1991).
51. Aaron Bernstein, "Too Much Corporate Power?" *Business Week*, September 11, 2000, http://www.businessweek.com/2000/00_37/b3698001.htm. Accessed March 28, 2016.
52. Jarvis, 2016, ibid.
53. David Rothkopf, *Power, Inc.: The Epic Rivalry between Big Business and Government—and the Reckoning that Lies Ahead*, (New York: Farrar, Straus & Giroux, 2012).
54. Coy, 2016, ibid., 11.
55. Edwin M. Epstein, "Dimensions of Corporate Power: Part I," *California Management Review* (Winter 1973), 11.
56. Rana Foroohar, "Companies Are the New Countries," *Time*, February 13, 2012, 21.
57. Coy, 2016, ibid., 10.
58. Epstein, ibid.
59. Ibid.
60. Keith Davis and Robert L. Blomstrom, *Business and Its Environment* (New York: McGraw-Hill, 1966), 174–175.
61. Bernstein, 2000, ibid.
62. Consumer Financial Protection Bureau, http://www.consumerfinance.gov/. Accessed March 28, 2016.
63. Erika Fry, "Fortune's Changing the World List," *Fortune*, September 1, 2015, 57–74.
64. BusinessDictionary.com, "Social Contract," http://www.businessdictionary.com/definition/social-contract.html. Accessed March 28, 2016.
65. Thomas Donaldson and Thomas W. Dunfee, "Toward a Unified Conception of Business Ethics: Integrative Social Contracts Theory," *Academy of Management Review* (April 1994), 252–253.
66. Simon Mainwaring, "The Corporate Social Contract," *CR Corporate Responsibility Magazine*, http://www.thecro.com/topics/business-ethics

/the-corporate-social-contract/. Accessed March 28, 2016.

67. "The New 'Social Contract'," *BusinessWeek* (July 3, 1971).

68. "New Economy, New Social Contract," *BusinessWeek* (September 11, 2000), 182.

69. Wayne Visser, "Sustainability," in Wayne Visser, Dirk Matten, Manfred Pohl, and Nick Tolhurst, *The A to Z of Corporate Social Responsibility*, 2007 (West Sussex, England: John Wiley & Sons), 445–446.

70. United Nations, "Sustainable Development," 1987. *Report of the World Commission on Environment and Development.* General Assembly Resolution 42/187, December 11, 1987.

71. International Institute for Sustainable Development, "What Is Sustainable Development?" https://www.iisd.org/sd/. Accessed March 28, 2016.

2

Corporate Social Responsibility, Citizenship, and Sustainability

CHAPTER LEARNING OUTCOMES

After studying this chapter, you should be able to:

1 Describe some early views of corporate social responsibility (CSR). Explain how CSR evolved and encompasses economic, legal, ethical, and philanthropic components. Explain the Pyramid of CSR.

2 Articulate the traditional arguments both against and for CSR. Explain how the business case for CSR has strengthened the concept's acceptance.

3 Describe how the concept of corporate social *responsiveness* differs from CSR.

4 Explain how corporate social *performance* (CSP) became more popular. Describe how it is different than CSR. Elaborate on how it differs from corporate social *responsiveness.*

5 Describe how corporate citizenship is a valuable way of thinking about CSR. Explain its broad and narrow views. Explain how corporate citizenship develops and proceeds in stages.

For many decades now business has been undergoing the most intense scrutiny it has ever received from the public. Business has been charged with a variety of allegations—that it has little concern for the consumer, exploits employees, cares nothing about the deteriorating social order, has no concept of principled ethical decision making, and is indifferent to the problems of minorities and the environment. Issues about what responsibilities business has to society continue to be raised. These claims have generated an unprecedented number of pleas for companies to be more socially responsible.

For some, the concept of corporate social responsibility (CSR) has been embraced in the broader term *corporate citizenship*. Other terms that have been derived from CSR include corporate social *responsiveness* and corporate social *performance*. Today, many business executives prefer the term *sustainability* as an inclusive reference to social responsibility issues. The term *conscious capitalism* is preferred by others. Some arguments have been made for the expression *creating shared value (CSV)*. These terms are often employed as synonyms for CSR. For others, they represent similar but somewhat distinct expressions. In the final analysis, these terminologies are often overlapping in their meanings. Though the terms are frequently used interchangeably, a careful inspection of each is needed to understand the user's intent. In this book, the terminology of CSR will continue to be used and other terms and frameworks will be invoked when appropriate. The CSR concept seems to be the centerpiece of the competing and complementary frameworks being used.[1] The language of sustainability appears to be rising in popular usage among business practitioners, and this also is a vital theme in this book.

CSR has been a "front-burner" issue within the business community and continues to grow in importance each year. An important landmark in its growth was the formation of an organization called **Business for Social Responsibility (BSR)** in 1992. BSR claims to have been formed to fill an urgent need for a national business alliance that fosters socially responsible corporate policies. In 2016, BSR claimed over 250 member corporations and reported among its membership such recognizable names as Apple, Inc., Abbott Laboratories, Coca-Cola Co., Google, Inc., Johnson & Johnson, Target Corp., Hitachi, Michelin, and hundreds of others. The mission statement of BSR is illuminating: "We work with business to create a just and sustainable world."[2] Today many of the world's leading corporations have a high echelon officer who is responsible for the firm's corporate social responsibility, corporate citizenship, or sustainability.[3]

In this chapter, several different aspects of the CSR topic are explored and some deeper insights into what CSR means and how businesses carry it out are explored. This entire chapter is dedicated to CSR-related issues, concepts, and

6 Summarize the three perspectives on the relationship between corporate social performance (CSP) and corporate financial performance (CFP).

7 Explain how sustainability is a broad concept that embraces profits, people, and the planet. Describe how the triple bottom line is a vehicle for implementing sustainability.

8 Elaborate on the ages and stages of CSR. Define CSR Greenwashing and how it may lead to misleading reputational profiles of companies.

9 Describe and characterize the socially responsible investing movement. Differentiate between negative and positive screens that are used in investment decisions.

practices that have emerged because it is a core idea that undergirds most of our discussions in the book.

2.1 Corporate Social Responsibility as a Concept

In Chapter 1, it was described how criticisms of business led to increased concern for the social environment and a changed social contract between business and society. Out of these developments has grown the notion of CSR. Before providing some historical perspective, it is useful to impart an initial view of what CSR means.

An early view of CSR stated: "**Corporate social responsibility (CSR)** is seriously considering the impact of the company's actions on society."[4] Another early definition was that "social responsibility … requires the individual to consider his [or her] acts in terms of a whole social system, and holds him [or her] responsible for the effects of his [or her] acts anywhere in that system."[5] Both of these early definitions provide useful insights into the idea of social responsibility. Figure 2-1 illustrates the business criticism–social response cycle, depicting how the concept of CSR grew out of the ideas introduced in Chapter 1—business criticism, the increased concern for the social environment, and the changed social contract. Figure 2-1 also clarifies that businesses' commitment to social responsibility has led to increased corporate *responsiveness* toward stakeholders and improved social (stakeholder) *performance*—ideas that are developed more fully in this chapter.

The growth of social responsibility practices has brought about a society more satisfied with business. However, this satisfaction, despite reducing the number of factors leading to business criticism, has at the same time led to increased expectations that have resulted in *more* criticism. Figure 2-1 illustrates this double effect. The net result is that overall levels of business social performance and societal satisfaction should increase with time in spite of this interplay of positive and negative influences. Should business not be responsive to societal expectations, it could conceivably enter a downward spiral, resulting in significant deterioration in the business and society relationship. The tidal wave of corporate fraud beginning in 2001 (Enron), followed by the Wall Street financial collapse beginning in 2008, has seriously called businesses' concern for society into question, and this concern continues today as ethical controversies at major companies such as Volkswagen, General Motors, Wells Fargo, Toshiba, and Takata have captured the public's attention.

Many academics and practitioners today use the terms ***corporate citizenship***, ***sustainability***, ***conscious capitalism***, or others to collectively embrace the host of concepts related to CSR. *Creating Shared Value (CSV)* is another term that has entered the discussion. It refers to companies generating economic value in a way that produces value for society. For now, a useful summary of the themes or emphases of each of these concepts helps to clarify how the flow of ideas has extended as these concepts have developed. In Figure 2-2, a summary of the various terminologies that are in use today are presented along with a brief indication of their emphases. These terms will be developed further in later discussions.

Some of the positions in industry which today manage the CSR activities carry a variety of titles as well, and these illustrate how companies use an assortment of position titles for the lead position in their companies. Following are some that were in use by companies in 2016 and more recently:[6]

Senior Director, CSR (Hershey Company)
Vice President, Corporate Social Responsibility (Marriott International)
Director, Corporate Responsibility (Adobe)
Vice President, Corporate Citizenship (State Street)
Senior Manager Global Sustainability (Gap, Inc.)
Corporate Director, Ethics & Business Conduct (Northup Grumman Corp.)

FIGURE 2-1 Business Criticism–Social Response Cycle

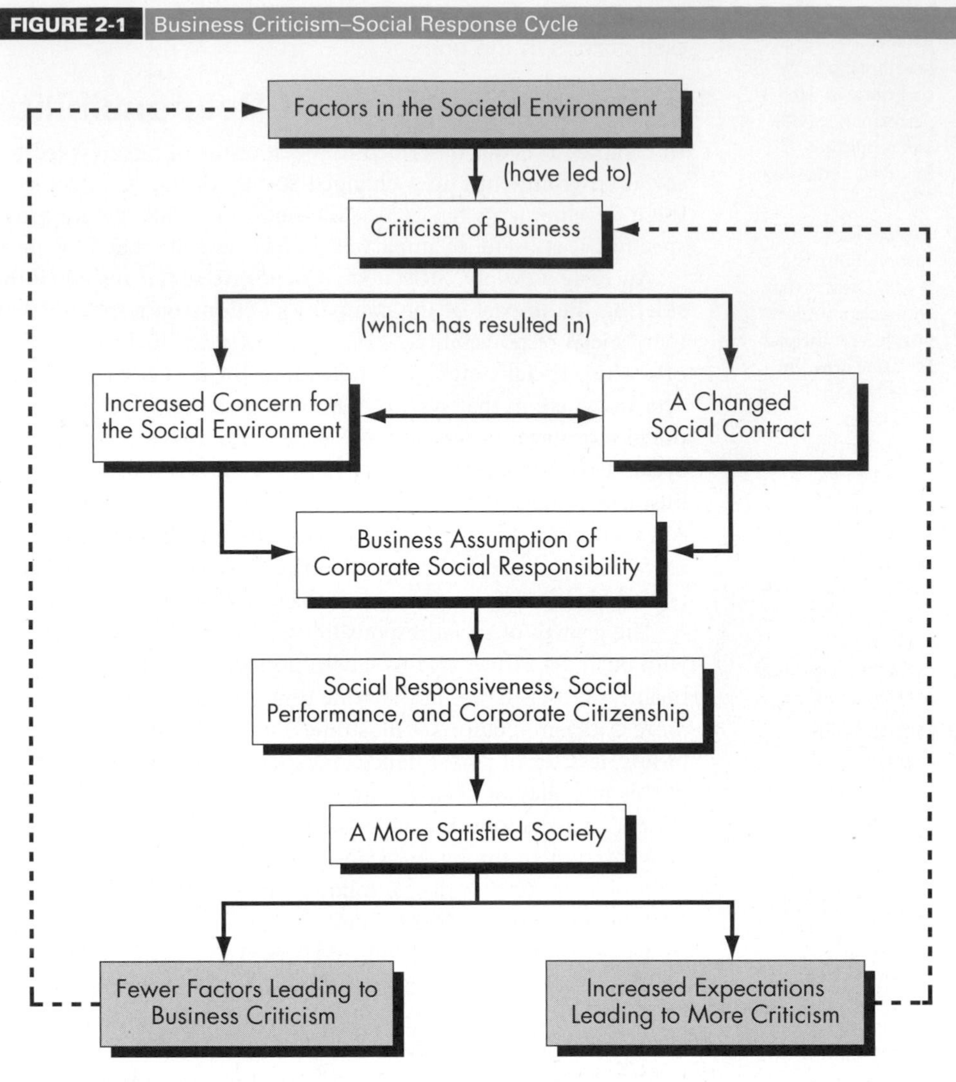

2.1a Historical Perspectives on CSR

The concept of business responsibility that prevailed in the United States and among free market societies since the Industrial Revolution of the 1800s has been fashioned after the traditional, or classical, *economic model.*[7] Adam Smith's concept of the "invisible hand" was its major starting point. The classical view holds that a society could best determine its needs and wants through the marketplace. In this view, the "invisible hand" of the market transforms self-interest into societal interest. Although the marketplace has done a fairly good job in deciding what goods and services should be produced, it had not fared quite as well in ensuring that business always acted fairly and ethically.

Over the decades, when laws constraining business behavior began to proliferate, a *legal model* emerged. Society's expectations of business changed from being strictly

FIGURE 2-2 Corporate Social Responsibility Related Concepts

Traditional CSR Concepts and Patterns	Newer Concepts with Similar Meanings
Corporate Social *Responsibility* (CSR) Emphasizes *obligation, accountability* ⇩ **Corporate Social *Responsiveness*** Emphasizes *action, activity* ⇩ **Corporate Social *Performance* (CSP)** Emphasizes *outcomes, results*	**Corporate Citizenship (CC)** Views companies as *citizens* and all this implies **Corporate Responsibility (CR)** Broadly focuses on *all categories of corporate responsibility* **Sustainability (SUS)** Emphasizes *longer-term concern for people, planet, and profits* **Creating Shared Value (CSV)** Focuses on how companies *generate economic value in a way that produces value for society* **Conscious Capitalism** Mindful business based on four key principles: higher purpose, stakeholder orientation, conscious leadership and conscious culture

economic in nature to encompassing issues that had been previously at business's discretion and eventually laws were passed to reflect these concerns. Over time, a *social model*, focusing more on society's expectations beyond what was legally required emerged, eventually transforming to a *stakeholder model*. Throughout, there has continued to be a tension between the interests of shareholders and other stakeholders. In the stakeholder model, sustainability has become a prominent focus and this idea will be developed further in Chapter 3.

2.1b Adaptations of the Economic Model

Early on, variations of the classical economic model were seen in practice in at least three areas: philanthropy, community obligations, and paternalism.[8] Historical practice documents that businesspeople did engage in **philanthropy**—contributions to charity and other worthy causes—even during periods dominated by the traditional economic view. Voluntary **community obligations** to improve, beautify, and uplift were also visible adaptations. An early example of this was the post–Civil War cooperative effort between the railroads and the YMCA to provide community services in railroad-served areas. Although these services economically benefited the railroads, they were at the same time philanthropic in nature.[9]

During the latter part of the 19th century and into the 20th century, **paternalism** appeared in many forms.[10] One of the most observable examples was the company town. Although business's motives for creating company towns (e.g., the Pullman,

Illinois, experiment) were mixed, business had to do a considerable amount of the work in governing them. Thus, some companies took on a kind of protective, paternalistic social responsibility.[11]

The emergence of large corporations during the late 1800s played a major role in hastening movement away from the classical economic view. As society developed from the economic structure of small, powerless firms governed primarily by the marketplace to large corporations in which power was more concentrated, questions of the responsibility of business to society surfaced more frequently.[12]

Although the idea of CSR had not yet fully developed in the 1920s, managers even then often had a more positive view of their role. Community service was popular during this time. The most visible example was the Community Chest movement. This was the first large-scale endeavor in which business leaders became involved with other nongovernmental community groups for a common, non-business purpose that necessitated their contribution of time and money to community welfare projects.[13] The social responsibility of business, then, had received a further broadening of its meaning.

The 1930s signaled a transition from a predominantly laissez-faire economy to a mixed economy in which business found itself one of the constituencies monitored by a more activist government. From this time well into the 1950s, business's social responsibilities grew to include employee welfare (pension and insurance plans), safety, medical care, retirement programs, and so on. These new developments were spurred by social activists, governmental compulsion, and by a broadened concept of business responsibility.[14]

In his book *The Generous Corporation*, Neil J. Mitchell presents an interesting thesis regarding how CSR evolved.[15] He argued that American business leaders developed the ideology of CSR, particularly philanthropy, as a strategic response to the antibusiness fervor that was beginning in the late 1800s and early 1900s. The antibusiness reaction was the result of questionable practices, such as railroad price gouging, and public resentment of the emerging gigantic fortunes being made by late 19th-century moguls, such as John D. Rockefeller and Andrew Carnegie.[16]

As business leaders came to realize that the government had the power to intervene in the economy and, in fact, was being encouraged to do so by public opinion, there was a need for a philosophy that promoted large corporations as a force for social good. Thus, Mitchell argued, business leaders attempted to persuade those affected by business power that such power was being used properly. An example of this early progressive business ideology was reflected in Carnegie's 1889 essay, "The Gospel of Wealth," which asserted that business must pursue profits but that business wealth should be used for the benefit of the community. Philanthropy, or corporate giving, became the most popular means of using corporate wealth for public benefit. A prime example of this was Carnegie's funding and building of more than 2,500 libraries.[17]

In a discussion of little-known history, Mitchell documents by specific examples how business developed this idea of the generous corporation and how it had distinct advantages: It helped business gain support from national and local governments, and it helped achieve in America a social stability that was unknown in Europe during that period. Berenbeim, in his review of Mitchell's book, argues that the main motive for corporate generosity in the early 1900s was essentially the same as it was in modern times—to keep the government at arm's length.[18]

Over the last half of the 20th century, the concept of CSR gained considerable acceptance and broadening of meaning. During this time, the emphasis moved from little more than a general awareness of social and moral concerns to a period in which specific issues, such as corporate governance, product safety, honesty in advertising, employee rights, affirmative action, environmental sustainability, ethical behavior, and global CSR took over center stage. The *issue* orientation eventually gave way to the more recent focus on corporate social *performance*, corporate *citizenship*, and *sustainability*. It is helpful to expand upon the modern view of CSR by examining a few definitions or understandings of this term that have developed over the years.

2.1c Evolving Meanings of CSR

Let's return to the basic question: What does CSR really mean? Up to this point, a rather simple definition of social responsibility has been used:

> *Corporate social responsibility is seriously considering the impact of the company's actions on society.*

Although this definition has inherent ambiguities, most of the evolving definitions also have limitations. A second definition is more specific:

> *Social responsibility is the obligation of decision makers to take actions which protect and improve the welfare of society as a whole along with their own interests.*[19]

This description suggests two active aspects of social responsibility—*protecting* and *improving*. To protect the welfare of society implies the *avoidance of negative impacts* on society. To improve the welfare of society implies the *creation of positive benefits* for society. Like the first definition, this second characterization also contains several words that are perhaps unavoidably vague.

A third definition that has been useful is also rather general. But, unlike the previous two, it places social responsibilities in context vis-à-vis economic and legal objectives of business:

> *The idea of social responsibility supposes that the corporation has not only economic and legal obligations, but also certain responsibilities to society which extend beyond these obligations.*[20]

This description is attractive in that it acknowledges the importance of economic objectives (e.g., profits) side by side with legal obligations while also encompassing a broader conception of the firm's responsibilities. It is limited, however, in that it does not clarify what the *certain* responsibilities that extend beyond these are. Over the years, a number of different definitions or views on CSR have evolved.[21] One study found 37 different definitions of CSR and that is why it is important that we focus on one widely used definition that will be helpful to us in moving through the book.[22]

2.1d A Four-Part Definition of CSR

Each of the definitions of CSR presented earlier is valuable. At this point, it is useful to present Carroll's four-part definition of CSR that focuses on the *types* of social responsibilities business has. This definition helps us identify, isolate, and understand the component obligations that make up CSR, and it is the definition that will be used most frequently throughout this book:

> *The social responsibility of business encompasses the economic, legal, ethical, and discretionary (philanthropic) expectations that society has of organizations at a given point in time.*[23]

This four-part definition places economic and legal expectations of business in context by linking them to more socially oriented concerns. These social concerns include ethical responsibilities and philanthropic (voluntary/discretionary) responsibilities. This set of four responsibilities creates a foundation or infrastructure that helps to delineate and frame businesses' responsibilities to the society of which it is part.

Economic Responsibilities. At a foundational level, business has **economic responsibilities**. It may seem odd to call an economic responsibility a social responsibility, but, in effect, this is what it is. First and foremost, free enterprise systems call for business to be an economic institution; that is, as an institution, it should have the objective to produce goods and services that society needs and wants and to sell them at fair prices—prices that societal members think represent the value of the goods and services delivered and that provide business with profits sufficient to ensure its survival and growth and to reward its investors.

While thinking about its economic responsibilities, business employs many management concepts that are directed toward financial effectiveness—attention to revenues, costs, investments, strategic decision making, and the host of business concepts focused on augmenting the long-term financial performance of the organization. Today, global hypercompetition in business has underscored the importance of business's economic responsibilities. Economic sustainability has become an urgent topic. Though economic responsibilities are essential, they are not enough; without them, everything else is moot because firms go out of business. With them, this is just part of what they must do to meet society's expectations of them.

Legal Responsibilities. Business also has **legal responsibilities**. Just as society has sanctioned economic systems by permitting businesses to assume the productive role, as a partial fulfillment of the social contract, it has also established the ground rules—the laws and regulations—under which businesses are expected to operate. Legal responsibilities reflect society's view of "codified ethics" in the sense that they articulate basic notions of fair practices that are established by lawmakers. It is business's responsibility toward society to comply with these laws. It is not an accident that compliance officers now have an important role on company organization charts. If business does not agree with laws that have been passed or are about to be passed, however, society has provided a mechanism by which dissenters can be heard through the political process. In the past decades, society has witnessed a proliferation of laws and regulations striving to monitor and control business behavior. A notable *Newsweek* cover story titled "Lawsuit Hell: How Fear of Litigation Is Paralyzing Our Professions" emphasized the burgeoning role that the legal responsibility of organizations has assumed.[24] And, with the proliferation of technological innovations, regulations affecting the digital economy are becoming a more urgent topic.[25] The legal aspect of the business and society relationship will be examined further in other chapters as pertinent issues arise.

As important as legal responsibilities are, they do not capture the full range of standards and practices expected of business by society. On its own, law is inadequate for at least three reasons. First, the law cannot possibly address all the topics or issues that business may face. New issues continuously emerge in such realms as technology, e-commerce, genetically modified foods, dealing with undocumented workers, and the use of cell phones while driving—just to mention a few examples. Second, the law often lags behind more recent interpretations of what is considered appropriate behavior. For example, as technology permits more precise measurements of environmental contamination, laws based on measures made by obsolete equipment become outdated but not frequently updated. Third, laws are made by elected lawmakers and often reflect the personal interests and political motivations of legislators rather than appropriate ethical justifications. A wise sage once said: "Never go to see how sausages or laws are made. It may not be a pretty picture." Although we would like to believe that lawmakers are focusing on "what is right and best for society," the history of political maneuvering, compromising, and self-interested decision making often suggests otherwise. Hence, laws and regulations, on their own, are not enough.

Ethical Responsibilities. Because laws are essential but not sufficient, **ethical responsibilities** are needed to embrace those activities, standards, and practices that are expected or prohibited by society even though they are not codified into law. Ethical responsibilities embody the full scope of norms, standards, values, and expectations that reflect what consumers, employees, shareholders, and the community regard as fair, just, and consistent with respect for or protection of stakeholders' moral rights.[26]

Historically, changes in the public's concept of ethics or values precede the establishment of new laws and they become the driving forces behind the initial creation of laws and regulations. For example, the civil rights, environmental, and consumer movements activated in the 1960s reflected basic alterations in societal values and thus were ethical bellwethers foreshadowing and leading to later legislation. Secondly, ethical responsibilities may be seen as embracing and reflecting newly emerging values and norms that society expects business to meet, and they may reflect a higher standard of performance than that previously or currently required by law. Ethical responsibilities in this sense are continually evolving—usually rising and expanding. As a result, debate about their acceptability continues. Regardless, business is expected to be responsive to newly emerging concepts of what constitutes ethical practices. One example might be Whole Foods Market and other stores selling only those foods it considers organic and free from genetically modified organisms (GMOs). These practices are not required by law, but many consumers expect companies today to engage in these practices. In recent years, ethics issues in the global arena have multiplied and extended the study of acceptable business norms and practices.

Superimposed on these ethical expectations originating from societal and stakeholder groups are the implicit levels of ethical performance suggested by a consideration of the great universal ethical principles of moral philosophy, such as justice, rights, and utilitarianism.[27] Because ethical responsibilities are so important, Part 3 of this textbook, composed of four chapters, is dedicated to the subject of business ethics. For the moment, it is useful to think of ethical responsibilities as encompassing those decision and behavior arenas in which society expects certain levels of moral or principled performance but for which it has not yet been articulated or codified into law.

Philanthropic Responsibilities. Finally, there are business's voluntary, discretionary, or **philanthropic responsibilities**. Though not responsibilities in the literal sense of the word, these are perceived as responsibilities because they reflect current expectations of business by the public. The amount and nature of these activities are voluntary or discretionary, guided only by business's desire to engage in social activities that are not mandated, not required by law, and not generally expected of business in an ethical sense. Nevertheless, the public has an expectation that business will "give back," and thus this category has become a part of the implied social contract between business and society. Such activities might include corporate giving, product and service donations, employee volunteerism, community development, and any other kind of voluntary use of the organization's resources and its employees with the community or other stakeholders.

Examples of companies expressing their philanthropic responsibilities, and "doing well by doing good," are many:

- **Chick-fil-A**, the fast-food restaurant, through the WinShape Centre® Foundation, operates foster homes, sponsors a summer camp that hosts more than 1,900 campers every year, and has provided college scholarships for more than thousands of students.[28]

- **Aflac, Inc**. For two decades, Aflac, the supplement insurance provider, has raised and contributed more than $100 million for the treatment and research of childhood cancer and has made the Aflac Cancer Center and Blood Disorders Service at Children's Healthcare of Atlanta its primary philanthropic cause.[29] It is little wonder the Aflac Duck has become an international icon.
- **General Mills**, the food company, goes the extra mile to support community causes. In its Hunger-Free Minnesota and General Mills Foundation, it recently gave a $220,000 grant award to Children's Defense Fund to support its School Breakfast Program.[30]
- **Timberland**, the products company, has a Sustainable Living Environment (SLE) program that was developed to help ensure that the workers who make Timberland products are able to meet their basic needs and have opportunities to better their lives. Timberland has been actively looking for ways to bring financial literacy and awareness to workers where the need exists[31]

Although there is sometimes an ethical motivation for companies getting involved in philanthropy,[32] it typically is considered to be a practical way for the company to demonstrate that it is a good corporate citizen. A major distinction between ethical and philanthropic responsibilities is that the latter typically are not *expected* in a moral or an ethical sense. Communities desire and expect business to contribute its money, facilities, and employee time to humanitarian programs or purposes, but they do not regard firms as unethical if they do not provide these services at the desired levels. Therefore, these responsibilities are more discretionary, or voluntary, on business's part, although the societal expectation that these be provided has been around for some time. This category of responsibilities is often referred to as good "corporate citizenship" because it entails the company giving back to the community just because it is a member of the community.

To summarize, the four-part CSR definition forms a conceptualization or framework that includes the economic, legal, ethical, and discretionary/philanthropic expectations society places on organizations at a given point in time. In turn, these expectations are seen by businesses as "responsibilities" for which they need to provide some positive response. Figure 2-3 summarizes the four components, society's expectation regarding each component, and explanations.

FIGURE 2-3 Understanding the Four Components of CSR

Type of Responsibility	Societal Expectation	Explanations
Economic responsibility	REQUIRED of business by society	Be profitable. Maximize sales, minimize costs. Make sound strategic decisions. Be attentive to dividend policy. Provide investors with adequate and attractive returns on their investments.
Legal responsibility	REQUIRED of business by society	Obey all laws, adhere to all regulations. Environmental and consumer laws. Laws protecting employees. Fulfill all contractual obligations. Honor warranties and guarantees.
Ethical responsibility	EXPECTED of business by society	Avoid questionable practices. Respond to spirit as well as to letter of law. Assume law is a floor on behavior, operate above minimum required. Do what is right, fair, and just. Assert ethical leadership.
Philanthropic responsibility	DESIRED/EXPECTED of business by society	Be a good corporate citizen. Give back. Make corporate contributions. Provide programs supporting community—education, health or human services, culture and arts, and civic. Provide for community betterment. Engage in volunteerism.

The four-part definition of CSR provides us with a structure or framework within which to identify and situate the different expectations that society has of business. With each of these four categories considered to be an indispensable facet of the total social responsibility of business, they comprise a conceptual model that more completely and specifically describes the kinds of expectations that society has of business. A major advantage of this definitional model is its ability to accommodate those who have argued against CSR by characterizing an economic emphasis as separate from a social emphasis.

This four-part definition offers these two categories (economic, legal) along with two others (ethical, philanthropic) that collectively make up CSR. Other writers sometimes limit CSR to initiatives that companies take that go beyond what is economically and legally required. Sometimes the term is used only for those activities that are discretionary, but the four-part model more comprehensively characterizes businesses total responsibilities.

2.1e The Pyramid of Corporate Social Responsibility

A useful way of graphically depicting the four-part definition of CSR is to envision it as a pyramid with four layers. This **Pyramid of Corporate Social Responsibility (CSR)** is shown in Figure 2-4.[33]

The pyramid portrays the four components of CSR, beginning with the basic building block of economic performance at the base. The infrastructure of CSR begins at the point of a successful, profit-making enterprise that has demonstrated its economic

FIGURE 2-4 The Pyramid of Corporate Social Responsibility

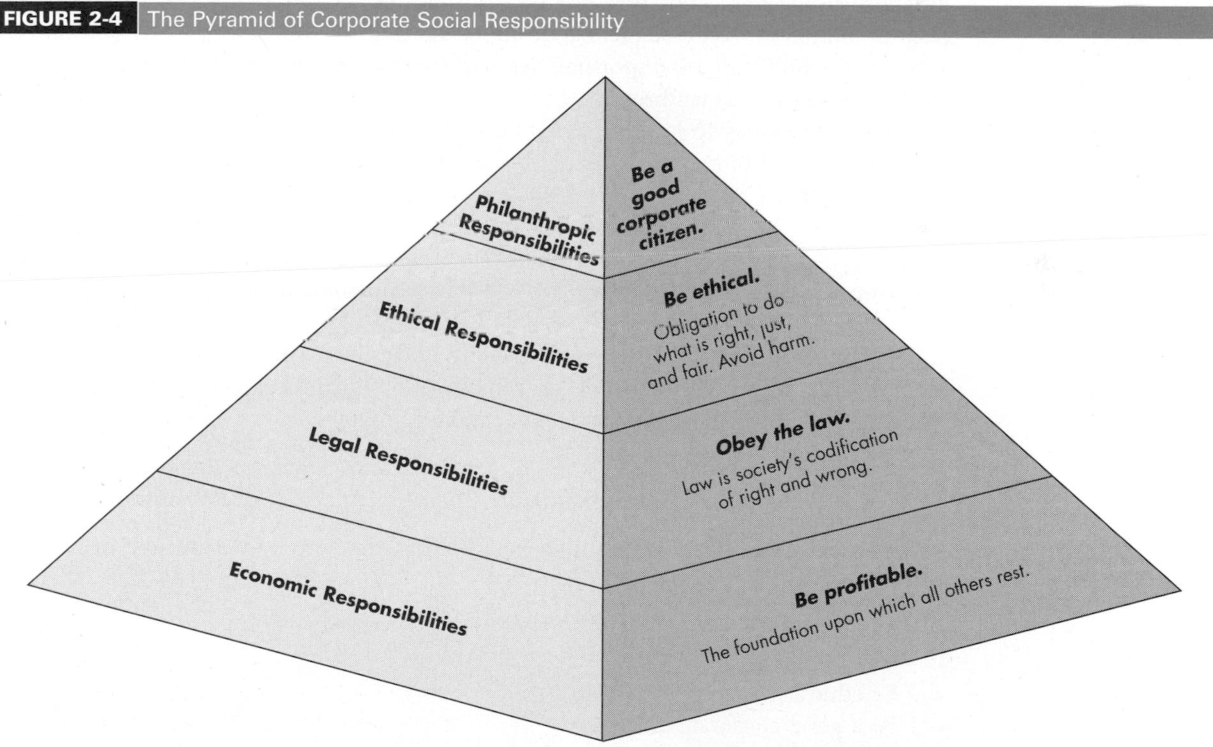

Source: Adapted from: Archie B. Carroll, "The Pyramid of Corporate Social Responsibility: Toward the Moral Management of Organizational Stakeholders," *Business Horizons* (July–August 1991), 42. Copyright © 1991 by the Foundation for the School of Business at Indiana University. Used with permission. Also see Archie B. Carroll, "Managing Ethically with Global Stakeholders: A Present and Future Challenge," *Academy of Management Executive,* Vol. 18, No. 2, May 2004, 114–120.

sustainability. At the same time, business is expected to obey the law, because the law is society's codification of acceptable and unacceptable practices. In addition, there is business's responsibility to be ethical. At its most basic level, this is the obligation to do what is right, just, and fair and to avoid or minimize harm to stakeholders (employees, consumers, the environment, and others). Finally, business is expected to be a good corporate citizen—to fulfill its philanthropic responsibility to contribute financial and human resources to the community and to improve the quality of life.

No metaphor is perfect, and the Pyramid of CSR is no exception. It intends to illustrate that the *total* social responsibility of business is composed of four distinct components which, when taken together, make up the whole. Although the components have been treated as separate concepts for discussion purposes, they are not mutually exclusive and are not intended to juxtapose a firm's economic responsibilities with its other responsibilities. At the same time, a consideration of the separate components helps the manager see more clearly that the different types or kinds of obligations are in constant and dynamic tension with one another. The most critical tensions are those between economic and legal, economic and ethical, and economic and philanthropic. Some might see this as a conflict between a firm's "concern for profits" and its "concern for society," but it is suggested here that this is an oversimplification because the two are so intertwined. Their reconciliation is what CSR is all about.

Pyramid as a Unified Whole. A CSR or stakeholder perspective would focus on the total pyramid as a unified whole and on how the firm should engage in decisions, actions, policies, and practices that *simultaneously* fulfill its four component parts. This pyramid should *not* be interpreted to mean that business is expected to fulfill its social responsibilities in some sequential fashion, starting at the base. Rather, business is expected to fulfill *all* its responsibilities simultaneously. The positioning of economic, legal, ethical, and philanthropic strives to portray the fundamental or basic nature of these four categories to business's existence in capitalistic economic systems. Economic and legal responsibilities are *required* by society; ethical and philanthropic responsibilities are *expected and desired* by society. In noncapitalistic economic systems, the sequencing of the four responsibilities might be seen differently by those societies. For example, Wayne Visser has maintained that developing countries present a distinctive set of CSR agenda challenges that are collectively different to those faced in the developed world.[34]

In summary, the total social responsibility of business entails the concurrent fulfillment of the firm's economic, legal, ethical, and philanthropic responsibilities. This might be illustrated in the form of an equation, as follows:

Economic Responsibilities + Legal Responsibilities + Ethical Responsibilities
+ Philanthropic Responsibilities = Total Corporate Social Responsibility

Stated in more practical and managerial terms, the socially responsible firm should strive to

- Make a profit
- Obey the law
- Be ethical
- Be a good corporate citizen

CSR Pyramid Is a Dynamic, Sustainable Stakeholder Model. It is especially important to note that the four-part CSR definition and the Pyramid of CSR represent dynamic, sustainable stakeholder models. Each of the four components of responsibility addresses different stakeholders in terms of the varying priorities in which the stakeholders are affected and these responsibilities may change over time. Economic responsibilities most dramatically impact owners, shareholders, and employees (because if the business is not financially sustainable, owners, shareholders, and employees will be directly affected). When the latest global economic recession hit, owners and shareholders lost money and employees were displaced and significantly affected. Legal responsibilities are certainly crucial with respect to owners and shareholders, but in today's society, the threat of litigation against businesses arises most frequently from employees and consumer stakeholders. Ethical responsibilities affect all stakeholder groups, but an examination of the ethical issues business faces today suggests that they involve consumers, employees, and the environment most frequently. Finally, philanthropic responsibilities most affect the community, but it could be reasoned that employees are next affected because some research has suggested that a company's philanthropic performance significantly affects its employees' morale and satisfaction. The definition and pyramid are sustainable in that they represent long-term responsibilities that overarch into future generations of stakeholders as well.

The role of stakeholders in discussions of CSR is inseparable. In fact, there have been recent calls for CSR to be redefined as corporate "stakeholder" responsibility, rather than corporate "social" responsibilities.[35] Others have suggested that CSR stands for corporate "sustainability" responsibilities. These views would be entirely consistent with the models presented in this chapter because a concern for stakeholders and sustainability is implicit in their understanding and application.

As business's major areas of social and stakeholder concerns are presented in various chapters in the book, it will be seen how the model's four facets (economic, legal, ethical, and philanthropic) provide a useful framework for conceptualizing the issue of CSR. The social contract between business and society is, to a large extent, formulated from mutual understandings that exist and evolve in each of these areas. But it should be noted that the ethical and philanthropic categories, taken together, more frequently capture the essence of what many people generally mean today when they speak of the social responsibility of business. Situating these two categories relative to the legal and economic obligations, however, keeps them in proper perspective and provides a more comprehensive understanding of CSR.

Ethics Permeates and Global Applications. Two additional comments of explanation regarding the Pyramid of CSR should be made. First, it should be emphasized that even though there is a separate ethics category in the model, the ethical dimension cuts through and permeates all categories in the model. Ethical considerations are involved in the economic category in that in capitalistic societies, it is believed that profit-seeking is the ethically right system for the production and distribution of goods and services. That is, in profit-oriented societies, such as capitalism, the economic responsibility is the ethically best form of economic system. Regarding the legal responsibility category, it should be emphasized that practically all laws were predicated on an ethical rationale before they became formalized into law. For example, concern for the deteriorating natural environment occurred as an ethical issue back in the 1960s before the Environmental Protection Agency laws were created in the early 1970s. The ethical category stands on its own, of course, but the philanthropic responsibility has historically, and ideally by some, been seen as an ethical concern for others and thus ethics sometimes permeates philanthropic giving; however, more recently, many companies have seen philanthropy not from an ethical point of view but from a practical, public relations or reputation-building perspective. In short, ethics permeates and cuts through all four of the levels in the pyramid.

Concerning global applications, it should be pointed out that in other countries, continents, and cultures, the CSR pyramid may not as accurately reflect the priorities present there. One may well argue that the four categories do exist in other environments but that their sequence may not adhere to the CSR pyramid that was developed primarily based on American-styled, primarily capitalistic, economies. In Europe, for example, many countries are social democracies and the government plays a much larger role in providing goods and services than in the United States and thus CSR and the levels in the pyramid might have a different significance and be interlinked in a somewhat different manner.[36] Or, as stated earlier, in developing countries or emerging economies, it may be argued that responsibilities in the pyramid may occur in a different foundational sequence.[37] To the extent that countries' socioeconomic systems become more similar to free market, capitalism, however, it would be expected that the pyramid as presented would more accurately reflect CSR in those countries.

2.1f CSR in Practice

CSR in practice is seen both in those firms that are generally perceived to be socially responsible and also in firms that are beginning to be known as CSR Exemplar firms.

Activities of Socially Responsible Firms. What do companies have to do to be seen as socially responsible? A study by Walker Information, a research organization, sought to discover what the general public perceived to be the activities or characteristics of socially responsible companies. Figure 2-5 summarizes what the sample said were the top 20 activities or characteristics of socially responsible companies.[38] The items in this listing are quite compatible with our discussion of CSR. Most of these activities would be representative of the legal, ethical, and philanthropic or discretionary components of our four-part CSR definition.

Walker Information concluded that the public thinks CSR factors impact a company's reputation just as do traditional business factors such as quality, service, and price. A related question on its survey pertained to the impact of social *irresponsibility* on

FIGURE 2-5 Top 20 Activities or Characteristics of Socially Responsible Companies

Following are activities or characteristics of socially responsible companies as identified by citizens.

- Makes products that are safe.
- Does not pollute air or water.
- Obeys the law in all aspects of business.
- Promotes honest or ethical employee behavior.
- Commits to safe workplace ethics.
- Does not use misleading or deceptive advertising.
- Upholds stated policy banning discrimination.
- Utilizes "environmentally friendly" packaging.
- Protects employees against sexual harassment.
- Recycles within company.
- Shows no past record of questionable activity.
- Responds quickly to customer problems.
- Maintains waste reduction program.
- Provides or pays portion of medical costs.
- Promotes energy conservation program.
- Helps displaced workers with placement.
- Gives money toward charitable or educational causes.
- Utilizes only biodegradable or recyclable materials.
- Employs friendly or courteous or responsive personnel.
- Tries continually to improve quality.

Source: Walker Information. Used with permission.

firm reputation. The study found that ethical and law-abiding companies can reap rewards from CSR activities and enjoy enhanced reputations. However, those companies perceived to be unethical or non–law abiding can do little in the way of other CSR activities to improve their images. Thus, the penalties for disobeying the law are greater than the rewards for helping society.

Rise of CSR Exemplar Firms. In the past several decades, a number of different socially responsible firms have become models for other firms. We call these **CSR exemplar firms** because they have tended to go well beyond the typical and established patterns for business firms in terms of their social responsibility excellence. These firms have taken the lead in advocating or integrating a social, environmental, or sustainability dimension to their missions. Though larger firms typically get most of the attention with respect to CSR, it should be emphasized that medium-sized and smaller-firms are also organizational types in which CSR is important and practiced.[39] There are at least three main categories of socially responsible firms addressed here: social entrepreneurship firms, social intrapreneurship firms, and mainstream adopters.

Social entrepreneurship firms are those that began their CSR initiatives at the very beginning of their founding and strategically carried it forward. A large part of their initial mission was to bring about social change or to reflect certain social values as a part of their organization's character. Porter and Kramer have argued that social entrepreneurship has been moving capitalism toward the creation of "shared value" in which economic value is created in a way that also creates value for society by "addressing its needs and challenges."[40] Three examples of social entrepreneurship firms would be The Body Shop International, founded by social activist Anita Roddick; Ben & Jerry's Ice Cream, also founded by two social activists, Ben Cohen and Jerry Greenfield; and more recently, Toms Shoes, founded by Blake Mycoskie. Since its beginning, Toms Shoes has sought not only to produce and sell quality products but also to bring about social change by giving away to poor children a pair of shoes for every pair it sells: "one for one."[41] Generally speaking, social entrepreneurship has led to the creation of what some have called "social enterprises." A social enterprise typically has at least two goals: to achieve social, cultural, or community outcomes; and to earn revenue.[42] A new organizational form, called the Benefit Corporation, or B-Corps, is an emerging area of social entrepreneurship and enterprise wherein states permit companies to charter themselves on both a social and economic mission. B-Corps are permitted by charter to pursue both societal welfare and shareholder welfare, so the social mission is "built into" the business from the very beginning.[43] B Corporations will be discussed further in Chapter 5.

Social *intrapreneurship* firms are companies that did not have a specific social agenda as part of their *initial* formation but later developed a highly visible social agenda or program. Social intrapreneurs are people who work inside major companies to develop and promote practical solutions to social, environmental, or sustainability challenges as a part of their financial missions. *Sustainability*, a leading nonprofit advocacy organization, says "These corporate change makers work inside big business, often against the prevailing status quo, to innovate and deliver market solutions to some of the world's most pressing social and environmental challenges."[44] Companies today that illustrate this model might include Timberland, Starbucks, Panera Bread, Microsoft, and Patagonia. As a result of innovation and risk taking, these firms have become high-profile exemplars of social responsibility and sustainability.

Mainstream adopters, a third group of CSR exemplar firms, would include all other conventional businesses that have adopted, practiced, and achieved some degree of excellence or recognition for socially responsible policies and practices. Their motives might include one or more of the following: gaining competitive advantage, reducing costs, enhancing their reputations, emulating what other firms are doing, or fulfilling their own concept of corporate citizenship. Firms that would fall into this third category include, but are not limited to, Apple, General Electric, Xerox, Aflac, Coca-Cola, Unilever, DuPont, AT&T, UPS, General Mills, and Walmart. While it is not always easy to clearly identify which category each firm is in, because some overlaps occur, the three types do offer a good way to understand the range of strategies by which different business firms have taken on a socially conscious mission and have become highly visible role models for other firms seeking to integrate social responsibility and sustainability into their everyday operations.[45]

2.2 Traditional Arguments against and for CSR

In an effort to provide a balanced, historically accurate view of CSR, it is useful to consider the arguments that traditionally have been raised against and for it.[46] It should be stated clearly at the outset, however, that those who argue *against* CSR are not using in their considerations the comprehensive four-part CSR definition and model presented in this chapter. Rather, it appears that the critics are viewing CSR more narrowly—as only the businesses' efforts to pursue social goals (primarily the philanthropic category). Some critics equate CSR with only the philanthropic category because they see this as clearly "giving away" the shareholders' money.

Very few businesspeople and academics argue against the fundamental notion of CSR today. The debate among businesspeople more often centers on the kinds and degrees of CSR and on subtle ethical questions, rather than on the basic question of whether or not business should be socially responsible, sustainable, or a good corporate citizen. Today, very few any longer resist CSR on the grounds of economic theory. The following arguments have historically been cited regarding CSR and it is helpful to appreciate them to see CSR's development over the years.

2.2a Arguments against CSR

Classical Economics. This traditional view holds that management has one responsibility—to maximize shareholder wealth. This classical economic school of thought, often attributed to the late Milton Friedman, argued that social issues are not the concern of businesspeople and that these problems should be resolved by the unfettered workings of the free market system.[47] Further, this view holds that if the free market cannot solve the social problem, then it falls upon government and legislation to do the job. This view is consistent with the prevailing Anglo-American view of corporate governance, which is based on shareholder primacy. We discuss this in more detail in Chapter 4.

A careful reading of Friedman's writings, however, reveals that he softened his argument somewhat by his assertion that management is "to make as much money as possible *while conforming to the basic rules of society, both those embodied in the law and those embodied in ethical customs*"[48] (italics added). When Friedman's entire statement is considered, it appears that he accepts three of the four categories of the four-part model—economic, legal, and ethical. The only category not specifically embraced in his quote is the voluntary or philanthropic category. It is clear that the economic argument views CSR more narrowly than depicted in the four-part model. Though not held my many today, the classical economic argument against CSR continues to be discussed, mostly by academics.[49]

Business Not Equipped. This objection to CSR holds that managers are oriented toward finance and operations and do not have the necessary expertise (social skills) to make social decisions.[50] Although this may have been true at one point in time, it is less true today as CSR has become integral to business school education and executive education and has been integrated into corporate strategic decisions.

Dilutes Business Purpose. Closely related to business not being equipped is a third issue: If managers were to pursue CSR vigorously, it would tend to dilute business's primary purpose.[51] The objection here is that CSR would put business into fields not related to its "proper aim."[52] There is little practical evidence, however, that this dilution has been realized. Moreover, the rise of social enterprises documents that some entrepreneurs see the decision to pursue social goals as a desirable choice not a dilution of business purpose.

Too Much Power Already. A fourth argument against CSR is that business already has enough power—economic, environmental, political, and technological—and so why place in its hands the opportunity to wield additional power?[53] In reality, today, business has this social power regardless of CSR. Further, this view tends to ignore the potential use of business's social power for the public good.

Global Competitiveness. Another argument that merits consideration is that by encouraging business to assume social responsibilities, businesses might be placed in a vulnerable position in terms of global competition. One consequence of being socially responsible is that business must internalize costs that it formerly passed on to society in the form of dirty air, unsafe products, consequences of discrimination, and so on. The increase in the costs of products caused by inclusion of social or environmental considerations in the price structure might necessitate raising the prices of products, thereby making them less competitive in international markets. This once prominent argument weakens considerably when we consider the reality that today social responsibility has become widespread globally, not one restricted to domestic firms and operations. Indeed, today, firms must be socially responsible to be competitive because most countries now expect it and the global community is watching carefully.

The arguments presented here constitute the principal claims that have historically been made by those who oppose the CSR concept, as it once was narrowly conceived. Many of the reasons given appear engaging. Value choices as to the type of society the citizenry would like to have, at some point, become part of the total social responsibility decision. Whereas some of these objections might have had more validity at one point in time, most of them do not carry much weight today though they continue to be raised by some critics.

2.2b Arguments in Support of CSR

In response to the traditional arguments presented against CSR, a number of arguments have been presented in support of the concept.

Enlightened Self-Interest. The long-term self-interest view, sometimes referred to as "enlightened self-interest," holds that if business is to have a healthy climate in which to operate in the future, it must take actions now to ensure its long-term sustainability. The reasoning behind this view is that society's expectations are such that if business does not respond on its own initiative, its role in society may be altered by the public—for example, through government regulations or, more dramatically, through alternative economic systems for the production and distribution of goods and services.

For managers who often have a short-term orientation, it is sometimes difficult to appreciate that their rights and roles in the economic system are determined by society. Business must be responsive to society's expectations over the long term if it is to survive in its current form or in a less restrained form. This concern for the long-term viability of business and society is the primary driver in the current emphasis on sustainability, which has become a synonym for CSR in the minds of many.

Warding Off Government Regulations. One of the most practical reasons for business to be socially responsible is to ward off government intervention and regulations. Today, there are numerous areas in which government intervenes with an expensive, elaborate regulatory apparatus to fill a void left by business's self-regulatory inaction. To the extent that business polices itself with self-disciplined standards and guidelines, future government intervention can be somewhat forestalled.

Resources Available. Two additional arguments supporting CSR deserve mention together—"Business has the resources" and "Let business try."[54] These two views maintain that because business has a reservoir of management talent, functional expertise, and capital, and because so many others have tried and failed to solve societal problems, business should be given a chance. These arguments have considerable merit, because there are some social problems that best can be handled, in the final analysis, only by business. Examples include creating a fair workplace, providing safe products, and engaging in fair advertising. Admittedly, government can and does assume a role in these areas, but business has primary responsibility for these decisions.

Proaction Better than Reaction. Another argument supporting CSR is that "proaction is better than reaction." This position holds that *proacting* (anticipating and initiating) is more practical and less costly than simply *reacting* to problems that have already occurred. Environmental pollution is a good example, particularly business's experience with attempting to clean up rivers, lakes, and other waterways that have been neglected for decades. A wiser and more cost effective approach would have been to prevent environmental deterioration in the first place. *Proaction* is a basic idea that undergirds the notion of sustainable development. Furthermore, simply reacting, rather than proacting, puts business in a crisis management mode and this is an obstacle to effective management.

Public Support. A final argument in favor of CSR is that the public strongly supports it.[55] A recent Nielsen survey has revealed what has been frequently found in recent years—consumers are increasingly more willing to pay more for products and services that are provided by companies committed to positive environmental and social impact.[56] This public support for CSR has grown over the years.[57]

2.2c The Business Case for CSR

After considering the pros and cons of CSR, most businesses and managers today embrace the idea. In recent years, the "business case" for CSR has been unfolding.[58] At the same time, the business case for sustainability has been advancing as well.[59] The "business case" refers to the reasons why businesspeople believe that CSR brings distinct benefits or advantages to their organizations and the business community. In this line of thinking, CSR directly benefits the "bottom line." The astute business guru, Michael Porter, perhaps the most respected consultant today in upper-level management circles and boardrooms, has pointed out how corporate and social initiatives are intertwined. According to Porter, "Today's companies ought to invest in corporate social responsibility as part of their business strategy to become more competitive." In a competitive context, "the company's social initiatives—or its philanthropy—can have great impact, not only for the company but also for the local society."[60]

In his perceptive book, *The Civil Corporation*, Simon Zadek has identified four ways in which firms respond to CSR pressures, and he argues that these form a composite business case for CSR. His four approaches are as follows:[61]

1. *Defensive approach.* This is an approach designed to alleviate negative consequences. Companies will do what they have to do to avoid pressure that makes them incur costs.

Companies do this through innovating products, services, and processes and by supporting progressive national and international policies.

In an ideal situation, companies would dwell at the Strategic or Systemic levels while trying to build on each previous stage of maturity. Visser argues that if companies remain stuck in any of the early stages, their ability to bring about significant change will be seriously compromised and authentic CSR will not be achieved but will fail.[65] These ages and stages may be considered not only as categories through which companies' progress but also as distinct categories or strategies that companies choose to employ as approaches to handling their CSR. In other words, some companies may not see themselves "stuck" at the charitable or promotional levels but rather have decided that is the CSR approach they wish to pursue.

2.4 CSR Greenwashing

As an addendum to the discussion of CSR and its related terms, it is important to point out that not all companies that promote their CSR images are serious about being responsible to stakeholders. Some are attempting to convey an image of responsibility when in fact they are conducting business as usual—focusing on their own profits with superficial attention to responsible business practices. Greenwashing, an offshoot of the term "white washing," is a concept that originated when it was observed that some companies sought to convey to the public that they were "green," that is, environmentally friendly, when in fact it was all a facade. According to one consulting firm that has studied the phenomenon, TerraChoice, 95 percent of the products that are marketed as eco-friendly have committed at least one of the greenwashing sins, ranging from using weak data to support marketing claims to more deliberate deceptions such as inventing bogus certifications.[66]

In a similar way, some companies may be participating in a more generalized version of the environmental subterfuge and we might call it **CSR Greenwashing**—that is, intentionally seeking to convey the image of a socially responsible firm when the evidence of their practices does not support this conclusion. Companies do this in a variety of ways including deceptive public relations, making claims without evidence to support it, misleading labeling, executive speeches that are more PR than fact, and promoting a relatively unimportant but visible CSR initiative and hoping that observers will not notice their overall record or that there may be acts of irresponsibility taking place behind the scenes.

Some critics might accuse the auto giant, Volkswagen, of a form of CSR Greenwashing. On the one hand, VW has strongly promoted its company as a progressive, inclusive, and caring corporation while at the same time it was engaging in a massive deception in that it had falsified emissions data on its vehicles by installing software in its cars' computers that hid the amount of nitrogen oxide emissions that were being produced when the cars were undergoing emissions testing.[67] As we think about Volkswagen and will see in our later discussions of business ethics, even companies that have strong CSR programs and are spending millions on CSR initiatives may still engage in questionable practices. They may not be intentionally engaging in CSR Greenwashing, but ethical mistakes can ruin years of reputational capital.

The conclusion we must reach concerning CSR and sustainability is that in order to truly understand companies' motives and strategies we have to carefully analyze the consistency of their practices and policies with their stated missions and aspirations particularly in the CSR arena. There are no 100 percent pure CSR companies but some do better than others. In any event, we need to examine carefully their practices and claims lest they fall victim to CSR Greenwashing. We need to watch carefully if companies start parading their virtues when their internal standards or other practices may not be consistent with the image they are seeking to convey.

2.5 Political CSR

In the past decade, there has been developing a concept known as political corporate social responsibility, or *Political CSR (PCSR),* that is an emerging version of CSR that has gained more attention and application especially in European or similar contexts where the government historically has assumed a larger role in providing societal benefits. Scherer, Rasche, Palazzo, and Spicer have defined PCSR as follows:

> *PCSR entails those responsible business activities that turn corporations into political actors, by engaging in public deliberations, collective decisions, and the provision of public goods or the restriction of public bads in cases where public authorities are unable or unwilling to fulfil this role.*[68]

In some countries, companies have increasingly taken on responsibilities traditionally left to governments. In addition, some businesses have engaged in political activity via philanthropy, often seen as lobbying, to help bring about a more beneficial business or social environment. Political CSR is a concept that emphasizes activities that have an intended or unintended political impact. Among the CSR activities of companies that might have a political dimension include companies as providers of community services (e.g., health and education) that previously have been seen as the purview of the state. Another aspect of PCSR occurs when companies try to usurp government regulations or be responsive to government policies.[69]

Some see Political CSR more as a governance mechanism wherein corporations contribute to global regulation and in providing public goods.[70] One goal of those advocating political CSR has been to integrate corporate political activity with traditional CSR theory and practice.[71] The field of Political CSR is defined differently by experts and is still in its infancy; we will consider many of these same topics in Chapter 11 where business, government, and regulation is addressed and in Chapter 12 where businesses' influence on government and public policy is discussed. Clearly, the government is an important stakeholder and business-government relations are a vital topic of importance.

2.6 Corporate Social *Responsiveness*

It is now worthwhile to consider a related idea that arose over the distinction between the terms *responsibility* and *responsiveness* in the evolution of the CSR field. **Corporate social *responsiveness*** represents an *action-oriented* variant of CSR.

An early argument that generated considerable discussion in CSR's development holds that the term *responsibility* is too suggestive of efforts to pinpoint accountability or obligation. Therefore, it is not dynamic enough to fully describe business's willingness and activity—apart from obligation—to respond to social demands. Ackerman and Bauer criticized CSR by stating, "The connotation of 'responsibility' is that of the process of assuming an obligation. It places an emphasis on motivation rather than on performance." They go on to say, "Responding to social demands is much more than deciding what to do. There remains the management task of *doing* what one has decided to do, and this task is far from trivial."[72] They maintain that "social responsiveness" is a more appropriate description of what is essential in the social arena.

This point has some merit. *Responsibility,* taken quite literally, does imply more of a state or condition of having assumed an obligation, whereas *responsiveness* connotes a dynamic, action-oriented condition. It should not be overlooked, however, that much of what business has done and is doing has resulted from a particular motivation—an assumption of an obligation—whether assigned by government, forced by special-interest groups, or voluntarily assumed. Perhaps business, in some instances, has failed to accept and internalize the obligation, and thus it may seem odd to refer to it as a responsibility. Nevertheless, some motivation that led to social responsiveness had to be present, even though in some cases it was not articulated as a responsibility or an obligation. Accordingly, the corporate social responsiveness dimension that has been discussed by some as an alternative focus to that of social responsibility is, practically speaking, an *action phase* of management's response in the social sphere.

2.7 Corporate Social *Performance*

For many years now, there has been a trend toward making the concern for social, environmental and ethical issues more and more *practical and results-oriented*. The responsiveness thrust was a step in this direction. Another step has been to integrate these concerns into a **corporate social performance (CSP) model**. The *performance* focus suggests that what really matters is what companies are able to achieve—the results or outcomes of their acceptance of social responsibility and the adoption of a responsiveness viewpoint. Performance is a bottom-line concept.

In developing a conceptual framework for CSP, it is important to specify the nature (economic, legal, ethical, or philanthropic) of the responsibility and also to identify a particular philosophy, pattern, mode, or strategy of responsiveness. Finally, it is important to identify the stakeholder issues to which these responsibilities are manifested and applied. The issues, and especially the degree of organizational interest in the issues, are always in a state of flux. As times change, so does the emphasis on the range of social or ethical issues that business feels compelled to address.

Also of interest is that businesses' concerns toward particular issues may vary depending on the industry in which they are a part as well as other factors. A bank, for example, may not be as pressed about environmental issues as a manufacturer. Likewise, a manufacturer is considerably more concerned with the issue of environmental protection than is an insurance company.

2.7a Carroll's CSP Model

Figure 2-7 presents Carroll's corporate social performance (CSP) model, which brings together the three major dimensions in a graphical depiction:

1. *Social responsibility categories*—economic, legal, ethical, and discretionary (philanthropic).
2. *Philosophy (or mode) of social responsiveness*—strategies ranging from reaction, defense, accommodation, and proaction.
3. *Social (or stakeholder) issues involved*—consumers, environment, employees, and others.[73]

The first dimension of this CSP model pertains to all that is included in the *definition of social responsibility* presented earlier—the economic, legal, ethical, and discretionary (philanthropic) components. The second is a *social responsiveness continuum* or dimension. The third dimension concerns the *scope or range of social or stakeholder issues* (e.g., consumerism, environment, product safety, and discrimination) that management must address in the first two dimensions.

The CSP model is intended to be useful to both academics and managers. For academics, the model is primarily a conceptual aid to understanding the distinctions among the concepts of CSR that have appeared in the literature (responsibility, responsiveness, performance). What were previously regarded as separate explanations of CSR are treated here as three separate aspects or dimensions of CSP. The model's major educational use, therefore, is in helping to organize the important concepts that must be understood in an effort to clarify the CSP concept.

FIGURE 2-7 Carroll's Corporate Social Performance Model

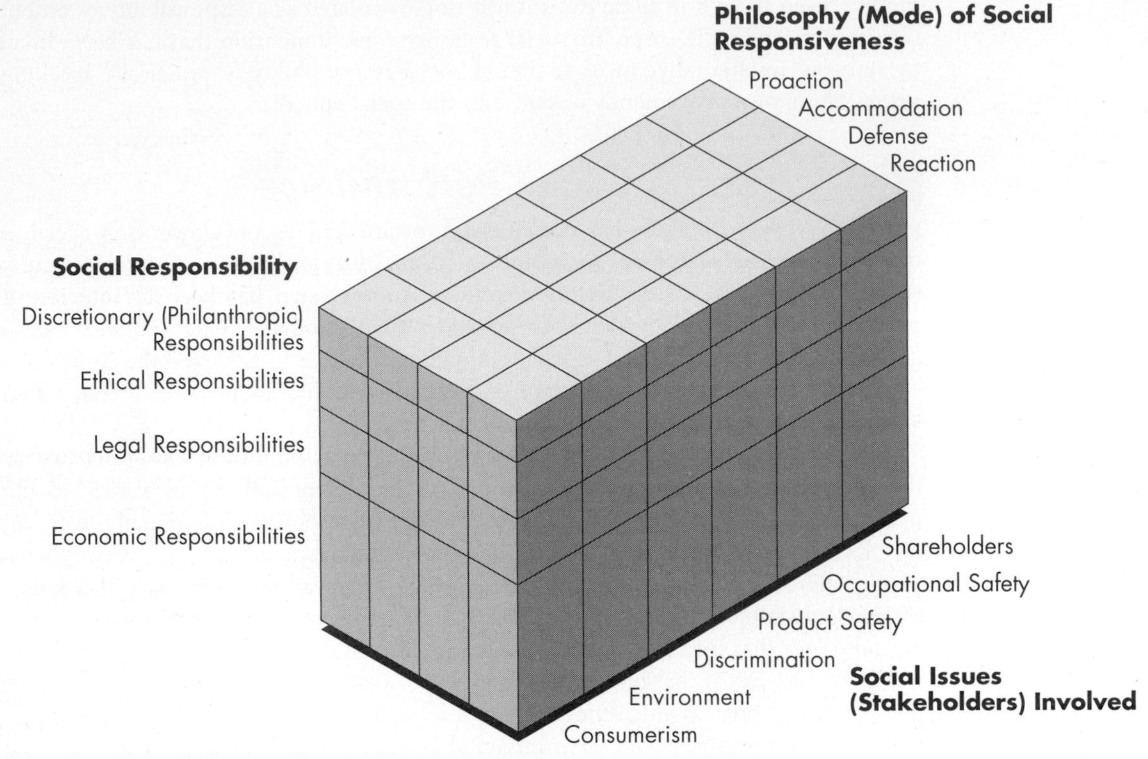

Source: Archie B. Carroll, "A Three-Dimensional Conceptual Model of Corporate Social Performance," *Academy of Management Review* (Vol. 4, No. 4, 1979), 503. Reproduced with permission.

The conceptual model can assist managers in understanding that social responsibility is not separate and distinct from economic performance. The model integrates economic concerns into a social performance framework. Also, it places ethical and philanthropic expectations into a rational economic and legal framework.

The model provides a template for the manager to systematically think through major stakeholder issues. Although it does not provide guidance as to how far the organization should go, it does provide a framework that may lead to more effective social performance. Companies may vary in which issues are most critical to them and what strategies of responsiveness they decide to pursue. An excellent example of this is the recent decision of CVS pharmacy to discontinue selling tobacco products. CVS decided that selling tobacco was no longer ethically consistent with selling pharmaceuticals and that proactive action (discontinuance of tobacco) was needed.

In addition, the CSP model could be used as a planning and diagnostic problem-solving tool. It can assist the manager by identifying categories within which the organization and its decisions can be situated. There have been several extensions, reformulations, or reorientations of the CSP model. Figure 2-8 summarizes the most important of these.

Though corporate social *responsibility, responsiveness*, and *performance* each represented periods in the development of CSR, today most believe that when CSR is referenced it would implicitly embrace the responsibility, responsiveness and performance dimensions of the concept. That will be our assumption as we move forward with CSR

FIGURE 2-8 Corporate Social Performance: Extensions, Reformulations, Reorientations

Wartick and Cochran's CSP Extensions

Wartick and Cochran proposed several changes/extensions to the CSP model. They proposed that the "social issues" dimension had matured into a new management field known as "social issues management." They extended the CSP model further by proposing that the three dimensions be viewed as depicting *principles* (corporate social responsibilities, reflecting a philosophical orientation), *processes* (corporate social responsiveness, reflecting an institutional orientation), and *policies* (social issues management, reflecting an organizational orientation).

Wood's Reformulated CSP Model

Wood elaborated and reformulated Carroll's model and Wartick and Cochran's extensions and set forth a reformulated model. Her definition of corporate social performance was "A business organization's configuration of principles of social responsibility, processes of social responsiveness, and policies, programs, and other observable outcomes as they relate to the firm's societal relationships." Wood took this definition further by proposing that each of the three components—principles, processes, and outcomes—is composed of specific elements.

Swanson's Reorientation of CSP

Swanson elaborated on the dynamic nature of the principles, processes, and outcomes reformulated by Wood. Relying on research from corporate culture, Swanson's reoriented model links CSP to the personally held values and ethics of executive managers and other employees. She proposed that the executive's sense of morality highly influences the policies and programs of environmental assessment, stakeholder management, and issues management, carried out by employees. These internal processes are means by which organizations can impact society through *economizing* (efficiently converting inputs into outputs) and *ecologizing* (forging community minded collaborations).

Sources: Steven L. Wartick and Philip L. Cochran, "The Evolution of the Corporate Social Performance Model," *Academy of Management Review* (Vol. 10, 1985), 765–766; Donna J. Wood, "Corporate Social Performance Revisited," *Academy of Management Review* (October 1991), 691–718; D. L. Swanson, "Addressing a Theoretical Problem by Reorienting the Corporate Social Performance Model," *Academy of Management Review* (Vol. 20, No. 1, 1995), 43–64; D. L. Swanson, "Toward an Integrative Theory of Business and Society: A Research Strategy for Corporate Social Performance," *Academy of Management Review* (Vol. 24, No. 3, 1999), 596–521.

discussions in this book. At the same time, moreover, many use the concepts of corporate citizenship and sustainability interchangeably.

2.8 Corporate Citizenship

Business practitioners and academics alike have grown fond of the term **corporate citizenship** in reference to businesses' CSR and CSP. Earlier in the chapter, corporate citizenship was presented as another term used synonymously with *corporate social responsibility/responsiveness* and *sustainability*, which have also been described earlier in the text. Despite its widespread popularity, it is appropriate to ask whether it has a meaning distinct from these concepts. A careful look at the concept and its literature shows that although it is a useful and attractive term, it is not dissimilar than the other terminologies, except in the eyes of some writers who have attempted to give it a specific, narrow meaning. Nevertheless, it is a popular term and one worth briefly exploring.

If one thinks about companies as "citizens" of the countries in which they reside, corporate citizenship means that these companies have certain duties or responsibilities they must fulfill in order to be perceived as good corporate citizens. In today's global business environment, some have argued that multinational enterprises are citizens of the world. Windsor has argued that corporate citizenship has become an important practitioner-based movement and that it conveys a sense of responsibility for social impacts or a sense of neighborliness in local communities.[74]

2.8a Broad and Narrow Views

Corporate citizenship has been described by some as a broad, inclusive term that essentially embraces all that is implied in the concepts of social responsibility, responsiveness, and performance. Corporate citizenship has been defined as "serving a variety of stakeholders well."[75] Fombrun also proposed a broad conception. He holds that corporate citizenship is composed of a three-part view that encompasses (1) a reflection of shared moral and ethical principles, (2) a vehicle for integrating individuals into the communities in which they work, and (3) a form of enlightened self-interest that balances all stakeholders' claims and enhances a company's long-term value.[76]

Also in the broad view, Carroll framed his four categories of CSR as embracing the "four faces of corporate citizenship"—economic, legal, ethical, and philanthropic. Each face, aspect, or responsibility category reveals an important facet of corporate citizenship that contributes to the whole. He suggests that "just as private citizens are expected to fulfill these responsibilities, companies are as well."[77]

At the narrow end of the spectrum, corporate citizenship is often viewed as "corporate community relations." In this view, it embraces the functions through which business intentionally interacts with nonprofit organizations, citizen groups, and other stakeholders at the community level.[78] The focus in the narrow view is on one stakeholder group—the community. Other definitions of corporate citizenship fall between these broad and narrow perspectives, and some refer to global corporate citizenship as well, because increasingly companies are expected to conduct themselves appropriately wherever they do business around the world.[79]

2.8b Stages of Corporate Citizenship

Like individual development, companies develop and grow in their maturity for dealing with corporate citizenship issues. A major contribution to how this growth occurs has been presented by Philip Mirvis and Bradley Googins at the Center for Corporate Citizenship at Boston College. The center holds that the essence of corporate citizenship is how companies deliver on their core values in a way that minimizes harm, maximizes benefits, is accountable and responsive to key stakeholders, and supports strong financial results.[80] This definition is quite compatible with the four-part definition of CSR presented earlier. The **stages of corporate citizenship** model helps to explain their points.

The development of the corporate citizenship model reflects a stage-by-stage process in which seven dimensions (*citizenship concept, strategic intent, leadership, structure, issues management, stakeholder relationships, and transparency*) evolve as companies move through five stages and become more sophisticated in their approaches to corporate citizenship. The five stages include *elementary, engaged, innovative, integrated, and transforming.*

As seen in Figure 2-9, the citizenship concept starts with an emphasis on "jobs, profits, and taxes" in Stage 1 and progresses through several emphases such as "philanthropy, environmental protection," "stakeholder management," "sustainability or triple bottom line," and, finally, "change the game." Similarly, the other vital dimensions change orientations as they evolve through the five stages. Company examples help to illustrate the various stages. GE is pictured as a company coming to the realization in Stage 1 that it must extend its emphases beyond financial success. Chiquita, Nestlé, and Shell Oil are depicted as companies becoming engaged in Stage 2. In Stage 3, Baxter International and ABB are identified as innovative companies striving to create coherence. BP's commitment to sustainability is provided as an example of Stage 4, where the theme is integration. Finally, the experiences of Unilever, widely noted for its socioeconomic investments in emerging markets, is presented as a company at Stage 5, with an emphasis on transformation in its corporate citizenship.

FIGURE 2-9 Stages of Corporate Citizenship

Stages of Corporate Citizenship

CENTER FOR CORPORATE CITIZENSHIP — BOSTON COLLEGE CARROLL SCHOOL OF MANAGEMENT

Dimensions	Stage 1: Elementary	Stage 2: Engaged	Stage 3: Innovative	Stage 4: Integrated	Stage 5: Transforming
Citizenship Concept	Jobs, Profits & Taxes	Philanthropy, Environmental Protection	Stakeholder Management	Sustainability or Triple Bottom Line	Change the Game
Strategic Intent	Legal Compliance	License to Operate	Business Case	Value Proposition	Market Creation or Social Change
Leadership	Lip Service, Out of Touch	Supporter, In the Loop	Steward, On Top of It	Champion, In Front of It	Visionary, Ahead of the Pack
Structural	Marginal: Staff Driven	Functional Ownership	Cross-Functional Coordination	Organizational Alignment	Mainstream: Business Driven
Issues Management	Defensive	Reactive, Policies	Responsive, Programs	Pro-Active, Systems	Defining
Stakeholder Relationships	Unilateral	Interactive	Mutual Influence	Partnership Alliance	Multi-Organization
Transparency	Flank Protection	Public Relations	Public Reporting	Assurance	Full Disclosure

Source: Philip Mirvis and Bradley K. Googins, *Stages of Corporate Citizenship:* A Boston: Carroll School of Management's Center for Corporate Citizenship at Boston College Monograph, 2006, p. 3. Used with permission.

The stages of corporate citizenship framework effectively presents the challenges of credibility, capacity, coherence, and commitment that firms move through as they come to grips with developing more comprehensive and integrated citizenship agendas. From the researchers' work, it is apparent that corporate citizenship is not a static position but is one that progresses through different themes and challenges as firms get better and better over time.[81]

The terminology and concepts of corporate citizenship are especially attractive because they resonate so well with the business community's attempts to describe its own socially responsive activities and practices. Therefore, it is expected that this concept will be around for some years to come. When reference is made to CSR, social responsiveness, social performance, and sustainability, these also embrace activities, programs, and practices that would typically fall under the purview of a firm's corporate citizenship.[82]

As indicated earlier, in addition to CSR and corporate citizenship, related concepts that have competed to become central terms in the field include *business ethics, stakeholder management*, and *sustainability.* These concepts are overlapping and complementary and they each have attributes that help reveal vital dimensions of interest in the pursuit of a common core in the business and society field.[83] All of these topics are dealt with fully throughout the book.

2.8c Global Corporate Citizenship

Global CSR and **global corporate citizenship** are topics that are becoming more relevant with each passing year. As global capitalism has become the marketplace stage for large- and medium-sized enterprises, the expectations that they address citizenship issues at a world level also multiply. Chapter 10 examines global business ethics in detail. Here, it is noted that there are also challenges for global CSR and global citizenship. To some extent, these are international extensions of the concepts treated throughout this book. Because cultures have features that are both divergent and common, however, adaptations of traditional CSR and corporate citizenship concepts often are necessary. Over time, countries are adapting CSR understandings to best fit their cultures and economies.

There are two aspects of the global dimension worthy of mention. First, U.S.-based and other multinational enterprises from countries around the world are expected to be good corporate citizens in the countries in which they are doing business. Further, they are expected to tailor as carefully as possible their citizenship initiatives to conform to the cultural environment in which they find themselves. Second, it is important to note that educators and businesspeople around the world are now doing research on and advocating CSR and corporate citizenship concepts. In fact, there has been a virtual explosion of interest in these topics, especially in the United Kingdom, Europe, and Australia/New Zealand, as well as in Asia and South America.[84] Of course, these two points are related to one another because academic interest is sparked by business interest and helps to explain the growing appeal of the topic.

Two items illustrate the kind of thinking behind the idea of global corporate citizenship. First is a definition of a global business citizen presented in an important book on the topic:

> *A global business citizen is a business enterprise (including its managers) that responsibly exercises its rights and implements its duties to individuals, stakeholders, and societies within and across national and cultural borders.*[85]

This view of a global business citizen is consistent with the discussions of this topic from a domestic perspective, but points to its expanded application across national and cultural borders. With this working definition, it can be understood how the citizenship concepts presented in this chapter can be naturally expanded and adapted to embrace multinational enterprises.

A second illustration of the global reach is provided by a distinction between frameworks for understanding CSR in America versus Europe. Earlier we discussed these differences with respect to the Pyramid of CSR. This distinction illustrates how CSR around the world has much in common, but specific, national contexts must be considered to fully grasp the topic. Dirk Matten and Jeremy Moon maintain that CSR (and corporate citizenship) is more "explicit" in America, whereas it is more "implicit" in Europe. In their distinctions, they argue that *explicit CSR* would normally consist of voluntary, self-interest driven policies, programs, and strategies as is typical in U.S.-based understandings of CSR.

By contrast, *implicit CSR* would embrace the entirety of a country's formal and informal institutions that assign corporations an agreed upon share of responsibility for society's concerns. Implicit CSR, such as that seen in the United Kingdom and Europe, would embrace the values, norms, and rules evident in the local culture.[86] The authors contend that CSR is more implicit, or understood, in Europe because it is more a part of the culture than in the United States. In Europe, some aspects of CSR are more or less decreed or imposed by institutions, such as government, whereas in the United States,

CSR is more voluntary, often pressured, and driven by companies' specific, explicit actions. And, when thinking about CSR and corporate citizenship in the global context, a special case has to be made for their applications in developing countries.[87]

In short, although CSR and corporate citizenship have much in common in terms of their applicability around the world and in diverse countries, national differences may also exist, which might suggest divergent or dissimilar strategies depending on where business is being conducted. One study of firms from 42 countries found that the *political* system followed by the *labor* and *education* systems and the *cultural* system were the most important variables that affected corporate social performance and citizenship in different countries.[88] Following this, Political CSR, discussed earlier, would be more applicable in Europe and other social democracies. As the world economic stage becomes more of a common environment within which businesses function, convergence in CSR approaches seems predictable.

2.8d CSR and Corporate Citizenship Awards by Business Media

Although there has been considerable academic research on the subjects of CSR, CSP corporate citizenship, and sustainability over the past decades, we should stress that the business media and organizations are also quite interested in this topic. Prominent business organizations and periodicals that report on corporate citizenship and social performance and provide awards for company social performance include *Fortune* magazine, the Conference Board, *CR* magazine, and the U.S. Chamber of Commerce. In addition, there are many other business groups with a keen interest in the topic.

For many years now, *Fortune* magazine has conducted rankings of the "World's Most Admired Companies" and has included "social responsibility" as one of its nine key attributes of reputation. The rankings are the result of a poll of thousands of senior executives, outside directors, and financial analysts. *Fortune's* 2016 rankings of most admired corporations were as follows:[89] Apple, Alphabet (Google), Amazon.com, Berkshire Hathaway, Starbucks, Walt Disney, Southwest Airlines, and FedEx. In a related vein, *Fortune* also publishes "The 100 Best Companies to Work For" on an annual basis. The 2016 top employers included Google (Alphabet), Acuity Insurance, Boston Consulting Group, Wegmans Food Market, Quicken Loans, Robert W. Baird (financial services), Kimley-Horn (design consulting), and SAS (business software).[90] It is not clear what specific impact the *Fortune* rankings have on these businesses, but surely they are an integral part of the firms' reputational capital. The important point to note here is that the social responsibility category is one major indicator of corporate citizenship and that it continues to be included as a criterion of admired companies by one of the country's leading business magazines.

Annual Business Corporate Citizenship Awards are also given each year by *CR: Corporate Responsibility* magazine. The magazine calls its program "The 100 Best Corporate Citizens List." Its most recent top five firms were Microsoft Corporation, Hasbro, Johnson & Johnson, Xerox Corporation, and Sigma-Aldrich Corporation.[91]

2.9 The Social Performance and Financial Performance Relationship

An issue that surfaces frequently in considerations of CSR-related concepts is whether or not there is a demonstrable relationship between a firm's social responsibility performance and its financial performance. Attempts to measure this relationship have typically been hampered by definitional and measurement problems. The appropriate performance criteria for measuring financial performance and social responsibility are subject to debate. Furthermore, the accurate measurement of social responsibility is difficult at best.

Over the years, many studies on the social responsibility–financial performance relationship have produced mixed results.[92] In a comprehensive meta-analysis, one review of research on the relationship supports the conclusion that social and financial performance are positively related. The researchers conclude by saying, "…portraying managers' choices with respect to CSP and CFP as an either/or trade-off is not justified in light of 30 years of empirical data."[93] In another study, the conclusion was reached that "there is a small, but positive relationship between corporate social performance and company financial performance."[94] Finally, another major study concluded that research supports a positive association between corporate social and financial performance.[95]

2.9a Three Perspectives on the Social–Financial–Reputation Relationship

To understand the relationship between social performance, financial performance, and reputation, it is important to note that there have been at least three different perspectives that have dominated these discussions and research.

ETHICS IN PRACTICE CASE

Burgers with a Soul—Fresh, Local, Sustainable

Burgerville sells not only burgers but also good work. But if you don't live in Oregon or the State of Washington, you may have never heard about Burgerville, a company founded in 1961 in Vancouver, Washington. Today, there are 40 Burgerville restaurants spanning those two states with more scheduled to come.

In the 1990s, when Burgerville began losing sales of its burgers to the national chains, Chief Executive Tom Mears decided to differentiate his product and sell "burgers with a soul." Mears, the son-in-law of the founder, decided to combine good food with good works. The company began to build its strategy around three key words—"fresh, local, and sustainable." It pursued this strategy through partnerships with local businesses, farms, and producers. In 2003, *Gourmet* magazine recognized Burgerville the home of the nation's freshest fast food.

According to the company Web site, "At Burgerville, doing business responsibly means doing business sustainably. One example of this is our commitment to purchasing 100 percent local wind power equal to the energy use of all our restaurants and corporate office." The company purchases its electricity from local windmills. Burgerville uses "sustainable agriculture," which means that its meat and produce are free from genetically modified seeds or livestock. In its cooking, the company avoids trans-fats, and once the cooking oils are used up, they are converted into biodiesel. The company buys its antibiotic- and hormone-free beef locally.

In addition to burgers, Burgerville offers a wild Coho salmon and Oregon Hazelnut Salad. Meals for children often come with seeds and gardening tools rather than the usual cheap toy offered at the national chains.

Burgerville extends its good works to its employees. The company pays 95 percent of the health insurance for its hundreds of workers. This adds $1.5 million to its annual compensation expense. To get its affordable health care, employees have to work a minimum of 20 hours a week for at least six months, a more generous arrangement than most provided by stores.

Being a good corporate citizen is expensive when done the Burgerville way. Though the company won't reveal its financial bottom line, one industry consultant estimated that its margin is closer to 10 percent compared with McDonald's 15 percent.

1. Is the world ready for a socially responsible, sustainable, hamburger? How much extra would you be willing to pay, assuming the burgers really taste good?
2. What tensions among its economic, legal, ethical, and philanthropic responsibilities do you think are most pressing to Burgerville?
3. Does Burgerville sound like a business that might work in Oregon and Washington, but maybe not elsewhere? What is the future of Burgerville?

Sources: "Fast Food: Want a Cause with That?" *Forbes* (January 8, 2007), 83. Washington Business Journal, http://www.bizjournals.com/washington/how-to/human-resources/2015/10/4-secrets-from-hr-experts-on-workplace-wellness.html. Accessed March 30, 2016; "About Burgerville," http://www.burgerville.com/about/. Accessed March 30, 2016.

SPOTLIGHT ***on Sustainability***

Sustainability's Stock Is Rising

A comprehensive study conducted by Deloitte Touche Tohmastsu Ltd., a private financial services provider, interviewed 250 CFOs representing 14 countries and 15 different industries with annual revenues averaging US$12 billion, and found the following:

- Sustainability is seen as a key driver of financial performance.
- Organizations are transforming to meet the sustainability imperative.
- Sustainability is becoming operationalized.
- CFO involvement with sustainability is deepening.
- Sustainability aspects of tax and financial reporting have gained significant mindshare among CFOs.
- Energy management still tops the list of issues.
- CFOs strongly believed employees are becoming increasingly concerned with sustainability.

Sources: Summarized from "Sustainability: CFOs Are Coming to the Table," Deloitte Touche Tohmatsu, Ltd., 2012, unpublished report. Also see "Nearly 50% of CFOs Say Sustainability is Key Driver of Financial Performance," September 9, 2012, *Environmental Leader*, http://www.environmentalleader.com/2012/09/19/nearly-50-of-cfos-say-sustainability-is-key-driver-of-financial-performance/. Accessed March 30, 2016; "How to Align Profit and Sustainability," *Environmental Leader*, March 8, 2013, http://www.environmentalleader.com/2013/03/08/how-to-align-profit-and-sustainability/. Accessed March 30, 2016.

Perspective 1. Perhaps the most popular view is the belief that *socially responsible firms are more financially profitable*. To those who advocate the concept of social performance, it is apparent why they would like to think that social performance is a driver of financial performance and, in addition, a corporation's reputation. If it could be demonstrated that socially responsible firms, in general, are more financially successful and have better reputations, this would significantly bolster the CSP view, even in the eyes of its critics.

Perspective 1 has been studied extensively. The findings of many of the studies that have sought to demonstrate this relationship have been inconclusive. In spite of this, some studies have claimed to have successfully established this linkage. The most positive conclusion linking CSP with CFP were the two studies reported earlier in the text.[96] Despite the lack of conclusive evidence, a Deloitte study found that chief financial officers (CFOs) of major firms are not only engaging with sustainability practices but that 49 percent of all CFOs see a strong link between sustainability performance and financial performance. These CFOs perceive sustainability to be a key driver of financial performance.[97]

Perspective 2. This view, which has not been studied as extensively, argues that a firm's financial performance is a driver of its social performance. This perspective is built somewhat on the notion that social responsibility is a "fair weather" concept. That is, when times are good and companies are enjoying financial success, higher levels of social performance are observed. In one major study, it was found that financial performance either precedes or is contemporaneous with social performance. This evidence supports the view that social–financial performance correlations are best explained by positive synergies or by "available funding."[98]

Perspective 3. A third perspective argues that there is an *interactive* relationship between and among social performance, financial performance, and corporate reputation. In this symbiotic view, the three major factors influence each other, and, because they are so interrelated, it is not easy to identify which factor is driving the process. In a recent, major study, researchers concluded that the relationships flow in each direction; that is, what is profitable performance is social performance and what is social is

FIGURE 2-10 Relationships among Corporate Social Performance (CSP), Corporate Financial Performance (CFP), and Corporate Reputation (CR)

Perspective 1: CSP Drives the Relationship

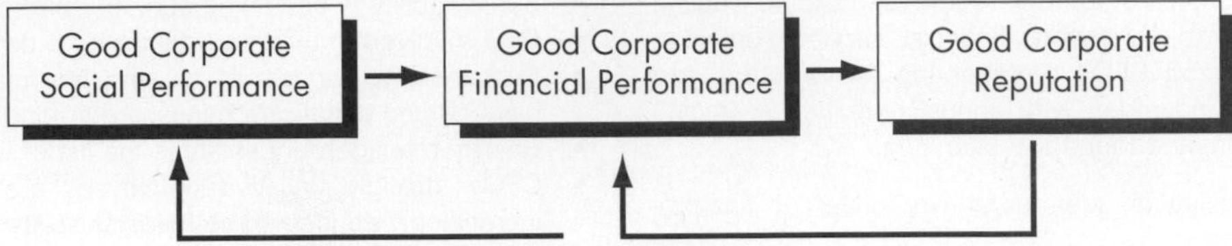

Perspective 2: CFP Drives the Relationship

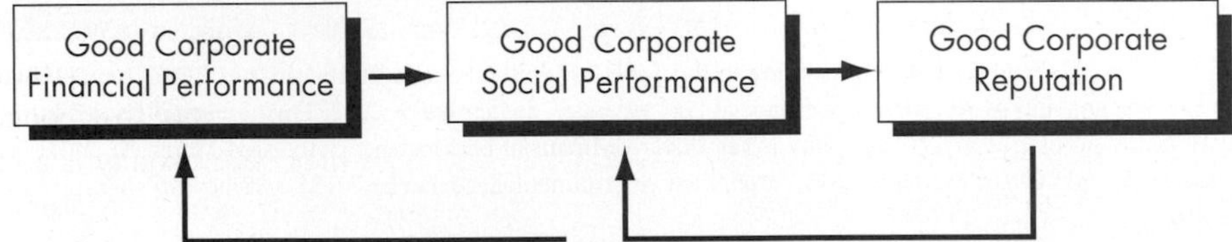

Perspective 3: Interactive Relationships Among CSP, CFP, and CR

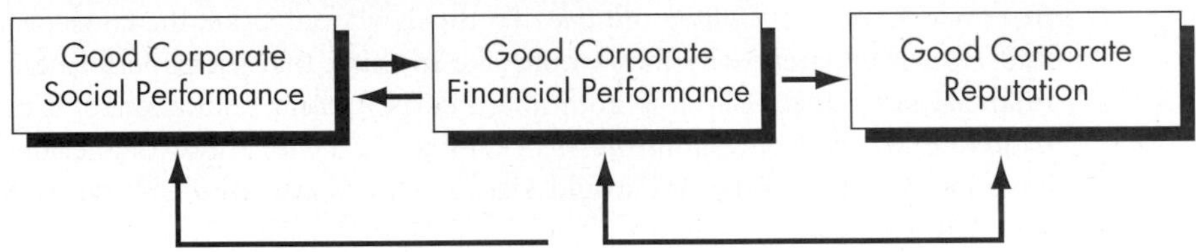

profitable thereby resulting in a positive feedback circle.[99] Regardless of the perspective taken, each view advocates a significant role for CSP, and it is expected that researchers will continue to explore these perspectives for years to come. Figure 2-10 depicts the essentials of each of these views.

Finally, it should be mentioned that a "contingency" view suggests that CSP should be seen as a function of the "fit" between specific strategies and structures and the nature of the social issue. According to Husted's research, the social issue is determined by the expectation gaps between the firm and its stakeholders that occur within or between views of what is and/or ought to be, and high CSP is achieved by closing these expectation gaps with the appropriate strategy and structure.[100]

A basic premise of all these perspectives is that there is only one "bottom line"—a corporate *financial* bottom line—that addresses primarily the shareholders' investments in the firm. An alternative view is that the firm has "multiple bottom lines" that benefit from CSP. This **stakeholder–bottom line** perspective argues that the impacts or benefits of social performance cannot be fully measured or appreciated by considering only the impact on the firm's financial bottom line.

To truly employ a stakeholder perspective, companies need to accept the stakeholder–bottom line view as reflective of reality. Thus, CSP cannot be fully comprehended unless its impacts on stakeholders, such as consumers, employees, the community, and other stakeholder groups, are recognized and measured. Research may never conclusively demonstrate a simple relationship between CSP and financial performance. If a stakeholder perspective is taken, however, it may be more straightforward to assess the impact of CSP on multiple stakeholders.

2.10 Sustainability—Profits, People, Planet

As introduced in Chapter 1, sustainability is one of the major themes of this book. It is also one of the key concepts or terms that often has been used interchangeably in recent years with CSR, CSP, and corporate citizenship. Because of this rising status, it is important to highlight it in this chapter as well. As first used by the Bruntland Commission, the term *sustainability* was derived from the idea of **sustainable development**, which is a pattern of resource use that aims to meet human needs while preserving the environment so that these needs can be met not only in the present but also for future generations.

Taking a future-oriented, longer-term perspective is a key aspect of sustainability thinking. Earlier versions of sustainability focused primarily on the natural environment and that use continues as it will be apparent throughout the book, especially in Chapter 15. More recently, it has become evident that sustainability is a broader concept that applies not only to the natural environment but to other environments of business as well. In recent years, the idea of sustainability has been expressed in the well-known and popular concept of the triple bottom line. A brief examination of this notion conveys how sustainability is now a broader concept.

The Triple Bottom Line. A variant of the multiple-stakeholder–bottom line perspective discussed earlier is popularly known as the **triple bottom-line** concept. The phrase *triple bottom line* has been attributed to John Elkington, a British consultant who founded a company called SustainAbility in 1994.[101] The concept seeks to encapsulate for business the three key spheres of **sustainability** that it must attend to—*economic, social,* and *environmental.* The "economic" bottom line refers to the firm's creation of material wealth, including financial income and assets. The emphasis is on *profits.* The "social" bottom line is about the quality of people's lives and about equity between people, communities, and nations. The emphasis is on *people.* The "environmental" bottom line is about protection and conservation of the natural environment.[102] The emphasis is on the *planet.*

In spite of the fact that sustainability refers broadly to each of these three areas, many practitioners and academics continue to speak as though sustainability is only about business and its natural environment. Each of these three—profits, people, and planet—is implicit in the Pyramid of CSR and represents a version of the stakeholder–bottom line concept. At its narrowest, the term "triple bottom line" is used as a framework for measuring and reporting corporate performance in terms of economic, social, and environmental indicators. At its broadest, the concept is used to capture the whole set of values, issues, and processes that companies must address to minimize harm resulting from their activities and to create economic, social, and environmental value.[103]

Corporate sustainability is the goal of the triple bottom-line approach. The goal of sustainability is to create long-term shareholder value by taking advantage of opportunities and managing risks related to economic, environmental, and social developments. Leaders in this area try to take advantage of the market's demand for sustainable products and services while successfully reducing and avoiding sustainability costs and risks. To help achieve these goals, the Dow Jones Sustainability Indexes were created to monitor and assess the sustainability of corporations.[104] As it will become apparent throughout the book, the concept of sustainability is intertwined with other social responsibility concepts and terminology, and it has become so important in business and academic usage that it needs to be emphasized in various contexts.

SPOTLIGHT *on Sustainability*

Myths about Sustainability

There are many myths and misconceptions about sustainability. Often these misconceptions, or myths, serve as barriers to companies pursuing sustainable development. Myths about sustainability are eliminated when the experiences of leading companies are considered. Following are some insights running counter to some of these misconceptions.

1. *Sustainability is a cost we can't afford right now.* Xerox CEO Anne Mulcahy said that being "a good corporate citizen" saved the company from bankruptcy.
2. *There's no money to be made from sustainability.* Johnson & Johnson has undertaken 80 sustainability projects since 2005 and achieved $187 million in savings with an ROI of nearly 19 percent, and rising.
3. *It's just for big companies.* Actually, smaller companies have an advantage because their competitiveness often depends on being lean, resourceful, and nimble, which sustainability makes possible.
4. *We'll be accused of greenwashing if we pursue sustainability.* Companies that set and achieve meaningful goals have the right to publicize their successes.
5. *Since we don't make things, we don't have to worry about the supply chain.* Walmart doesn't make things, but it has developed a supplier index for its thousands of suppliers to gauge the carbon impact from supplies they sell to the business.

Sources: Vijay Kanal, "The Eight Biggest Myths about Sustainability in Business," http://www.greenbiz.com/blog/2009/11/23/8-myths-about-sustainability-business. Accessed March 30, 2016; Michael D. Lemonick, "Top 10 Myths about Sustainability," http://web.chem.ucsb.edu/~feldwinn/greenworks/Top%2010%20Myths%20about%20Sustainability.pdf. Accessed March 30, 2016; "Twelve Myths about Sustainability," *Everblue*, http://www.everblue.edu/blog/12-myths-about-sustainability-12122012. Accessed March 30, 2016.

2.10a Creating Shared Value and Conscious Capitalism

In addition to CSR, corporate citizenship, and sustainability, two other concepts have become popular in recent years—creating shared value and conscious capitalism. Since they overlap significantly with the earlier presented CSR-related frameworks, their treatment here will be brief.

The **creating shared value (CSV)** concept was introduced by Porter and Kramer as a response to what they saw as too narrow a view of value creation on the part of businesses. They argued that business and society could be brought back together again if businesses redefined their basic purpose as creating shared value; that is, generating economic value in a way that also produces value for society by addressing its challenges. They argued that companies could do this in three ways: by reconceiving products and markets, by redefining productivity in the value chain, or by building supportive industry clusters at the company's locations. They believed that CSV has the potential to reshape capitalism and improve the business and society relationship.[105] Their concept has gained a lot of attention and its merits continue to be discussed.

The concept of **conscious capitalism** was developed by John Mackey, cofounder of Whole Foods. According to Mackey, "conscious capitalism is a more complex form of capitalism that reflects and leverages the interdependent nature of life and all of the stakeholders in business."[106] Companies that practice conscious capitalism are said to be ones that follow the four pillars guiding their practice. These four basic pillars include a *higher purpose, stakeholder orientation, conscious leadership*, and a *conscious culture.*[107] It is significant to observe that the companies that are embracing either CSV or conscious capitalism are typically the same companies that we identify as high on their CSR, corporate citizenship, and sustainability characteristics. Examples would include Whole Foods, Starbuck's, Chipotle, Costco, Panera, and The Container Store.[108] The overlapping characteristics of these two ideas with concepts already presented are numerous and, therefore, they will not be treated in more detail. A careful examination of the features of all these frameworks, however, is worthwhile as each has something important to contribute to the improvement of business and society relationships.

2.11 Socially Responsible, Sustainable, Ethical Investing

Special-interest groups, business, the media, and academics are not alone in their interest in business's social performance. Investors are also interested. The **socially responsible, sustainable, or ethical investing** movement arrived on the scene in the 1970s and has continued to grow and prosper. Today it is sometimes called ***impact investing***, or ***environmental, social, and governance (ESG) investing***. Socially responsible investing (SRI), or sustainable investing, has matured into a comprehensive investing approach complete with social and environmental screens, shareholder activism, and community investment, accounting for nearly $7 trillion of investments in the United States, according to the Forum for Sustainable and Responsible Investing.[109] The SRI Forum refers to it as sustainable, responsible, impact investing that considers environmental, social, and corporate governance (ESG) criteria aimed at generating long-term competitive financial returns and positive societal impact. A 2015 report by the Morgan Stanley Institute for Sustainable Investing found that "investing in sustainability has usually met, and often exceeded, the performance of comparable traditional investments."[110] Today, the socially responsible investing movement embraces social screening, shareholder advocacy, and community investing.

Historically, socially responsibility investing can be traced back to the early 1900s, when church endowments refused to buy the so-called sin stocks—then defined as shares in tobacco, alcohol, and gambling companies. During the Vietnam War era of the 1960s and early 1970s, antiwar investors refused to invest in defense contracting firms. In the early 1980s, universities, municipalities, and foundations sold off their shares of companies that had operations in South Africa to protest apartheid. By the 1990s, self-styled socially responsible investing came into its own.[111] In the 2000s, social investing began celebrating the fact that it is now part of the mainstream.

Socially conscious investments have been continuing to grow.[112] However, managers of socially conscious mutual funds do not use only ethical or social responsibility criteria to decide which companies to invest in. They consider a company's financial health before all else. Moreover, a growing corps of brokers, financial planners, and portfolio managers are available to help people evaluate investments for their social impacts.[113]

The concept of *social screening* is the backbone of the socially conscious investing movement. Investors seeking to put their money into socially responsible firms want to *screen out* those firms they consider to be socially irresponsible or to actively *screen in* those firms they think of as socially responsible or sustainable. Thus, there are negative social screens and positive social screens. Some of the *negative social screens* that have been used include the avoidance of investing in tobacco manufacturers, gambling casino operators, defense or weapons contractors, and firms doing business in South Africa.[114] In 1994, however, with the elimination of the official system of apartheid in South Africa, this was eliminated as a negative screen by many.

It is more difficult, and thus more challenging, to implement *positive social screens*, because these require the potential investor to make judgment calls as to what constitutes an acceptable or a strong level of social performance on social investment criteria. Criteria that may be used as either positive or negative screens, depending on the firm's performance, might include the firm's demonstrated record on issues such as equal employment opportunity and affirmative action, environmental sustainability, treatment of employees, corporate citizenship (broadly defined), and treatment of animals.[115]

One experience of Pax World Funds, a socially responsible mutual fund investor, illustrates how tricky social screening can be. When Starbucks first introduced a coffee liqueur containing Jim Beam bourbon, Pax World Fund thought it had no choice but to sell its $23 million stake in Starbucks, even though it had long believed Starbucks to have a strong record of social responsibility. Pax World did divest of its Starbucks stock. By 2006, however, Pax World shareholders concluded that the company needed to eliminate its zero-tolerance policy on alcohol and gambling and they approved more flexible guidelines for the future. Under the new guidelines, the company would focus more on positive social screens, like a company's record on corporate governance, climate change, and other social issues.[116]

The financial performance of socially conscious mutual funds shows that investors do not have to sacrifice profitability for principles. An increasing number of studies have demonstrated that socially responsible funds perform competitively with non-CSR funds over time. A study from Morningstar showed that in a comparison of five year returns, non-socially responsible returns for large-cap stock funds was 2.9%, whereas the returns from socially responsible firms during the same period was 3.0%.[117] In addition to stock mutual funds, bond funds that are screened for the socially conscious investors are also on the rise.[118] The fast growth of socially conscious investing is the most convincing evidence that competitive returns are being achieved. As *Kiplinger's Personal Finance* magazine concluded, investors can "make money and do good, too."[119]

Over the past 20 years, the total dollars invested in SRI has grown exponentially, as has the number of institutional, professional, and individual investors involved in the field. One out of every six dollars managed professionally in the U. S. today is investing using some mix of socially responsible criteria.[120] The Council on Economic Priorities has suggested that there are at least three reasons why there has been an upsurge in social or ethical investing: more reliable research on CSP than in the past, firms using social criteria have established a solid track record demonstrating that investors do not have to sacrifice gains for principles, and the socially conscious 1960s generation is now making investment decisions through their own IRAs and 401(k) plans.[121] Further, more citizens are seeing social investments as a way in which they can exert their priorities concerning the balance of financial and social concerns.[122]

Whether it be called social investing, ethical investing, socially responsible investing, impact investing, or sustainable investing, it is clear that social investing has "arrived" on the scene and has become a major part of the mainstream. Socially responsible investing is growing globally as well.[123] Socially conscious mutual funds will continue to be debated in the investment community. The fact that they exist, have grown, and have prospered, however, provides evidence that the practice is a serious one and that there truly are investors in the real world who take the social responsibility and sustainability issue quite seriously.

Summary

Corporate social responsibility–responsiveness–performance, corporate citizenship, and sustainability are important and related concepts. The CSR concept has a rich history. It has grown out of many diverse views. A four-part conceptualization was presented that broadly conceives CSR as encompassing economic, legal, ethical, and philanthropic obligations. The four responsibilities were also depicted as part of the Pyramid of CSR—building upon the basic economic foundations of business.

The concern for CSR has been expanded to include a concern for social responsiveness and social performance. The responsiveness theme suggests more of an action-oriented focus by which firms not only must address their basic obligations but also must decide on basic strategies of responding to these obligations. A CSP model was presented that brought the responsibility and responsiveness dimensions together into a framework that also identified categories of social or stakeholder issues that must be considered.

Ages and stages of CSR were presented along with an introduction to the concept of CSR Greenwashing. Political CSR (PCSR) was identified as a topic that is growing in importance, especially in Europe.

The term *corporate citizenship* arrived on the scene to embrace a whole host of socially conscious activities and practices on the part of businesses. This term has become quite popular in the business community. It is not clear that the concept is different than the emphases on corporate social responsibility, responsiveness, and performance, but it is a terminology being frequently used. A "stages of corporate citizenship" model was presented that depicted how companies progress and grow in their increasing sophistication and maturity in dealing with corporate citizenship issues.

Three possible perspectives on the relationship between and among corporate social performance, financial performance and corporate reputation were explored. The positive relationships among these concepts have been found to be modest and research continues on them to flesh out more definitive conclusions.

Today, a concern for sustainability has taken its place at the table. Sustainability is frequently expressed through the triple bottom line and may be viewed as a narrow concept focusing on the natural environment or more broadly as including economic (profits), social (people), and environmental (planet) arenas. The language of sustainability has become quite popular among businesses, academics, and the media.

Relatively new concepts in the CSR field were explored to include the notions of creating shared value (CSV) and conscious capitalism. Both of these concepts align nicely with other CSR-related ideas discussed.

The interest in CSR extends beyond the academic community. The business media is interested as well. Such publications from *Fortune, Forbes, CR: Corporate Responsibility* as well as the U.S. Chamber of Commerce recognize outstanding "corporate citizens" in a variety of ways each year. Achieving such status has become a symbol of pride for the companies receiving these recognitions.

Finally, the socially responsible, sustainable, or ethical investing movement is flourishing. This success documents that there is a growing body of investors who are sensitive to business's social and ethical (as well as financial) performance. Studies of social investing have demonstrated that investors do not have to give up financial performance to achieve social performance. The industry has been growing consistently and is now considered to be a part of the mainstream of investing.

Key Terms

Business for Social Responsibility (BSR), p. 30
conscious capitalism, p. 62
community obligations, p. 33
corporate citizenship, p. 53
corporate social performance (CSP) model, p. 51
corporate social responsibility (CSR), p. 31
corporate social responsiveness, p. 50
corporate sustainability, p. 61
CSR exemplar firms, p. 43
CSR Greenwashing, p. 49
creating shared value (CSV), p. 62
economic responsibilities, p. 36
environmental, social, and governance (ESG) investing, p. 63
ethical responsibilities, p. 37
global corporate citizenship, p. 56
impact investing, p. 63
legal responsibilities, p. 36
mainstream adopters (of CSR), p. 43
paternalism, p. 33
philanthropic responsibilities, p. 37
philanthropy, p. 33
Pyramid of Corporate Social Responsibility (CSR), p. 39
Social entrepreneurship, p. 43
Social intrapreneurship, p. 43
socially responsible, sustainable, or ethical investing, p. 63
stages of corporate citizenship, p. 54
stakeholder–bottom line, p. 60
sustainability, p. 61
sustainable development, p. 61
triple bottom line, p. 61

Discussion Questions

1. Explain the Pyramid of Corporate Social Responsibility. Provide several examples of each "layer" of the pyramid. Identify and discuss some of the tensions among and between the layers or components. In what sense do the different layers of the pyramid "overlap" with each other?
2. In your view, what is the single strongest argument *against* the idea of corporate social responsibility? What is the single strongest argument *for* corporate social responsibility? Briefly explain.
3. Differentiate between corporate social *responsibility* and corporate social *responsiveness*. Give an example of each. How does corporate social *performance* relate to these terms? Where do corporate citizenship and sustainability fit in?
4. Analyze how the triple bottom line and the Pyramid of CSR are similar and different. Draw a schematic that shows how the two concepts relate to one another.
5. Compare and contrast the socially oriented concepts: CSR, corporate citizenship, sustainability, creating shared value, and conscious capitalism. Do these represent different forms of the business and society relationship or do they represent how and why companies respond in a socially conscious manner?
6. Does socially responsible, sustainable, or ethical investing seem to you to be a legitimate way in which the average citizen might demonstrate her or his concern for CSR? Why is it also called impact investing? Discuss.

Endnotes

1. Archie B. Carroll, "Corporate Social Responsibility: The Centerpiece of Competing and Complimentary Frameworks," *Organizational Dynamics* (2015), 44: 87–96.
2. Business for Social Responsibility, http://www.bsr.org/en/. Accessed March 30, 2016.
3. Robert Strand, "The Chief Officer of Corporate Social Responsibility: A Study of Its Presence in Top Management Teams," *Journal of Business Ethics* (2013), 112: 721–734.
4. Quoted in John L. Paluszek, *Business and Society: 1976–2000* (New York: AMACOM, 1976), 1.
5. Keith Davis, "Understanding the Social Responsibility Puzzle," *Business Horizons* (Winter 1967), 45–50.
6. CR 2015 Superstar Winners, Leading the Way, CR Corporate Responsibility Magazine, January/February 2016, 34–39.
7. For a more complete history of corporate responsibility in the U.S., see Archie B. Carroll, Kenneth J. Lipartito, James E. Post, Patricia H. Werhane, and Kenneth E. Goodpaster, executive editor, 2012, *Corporate Responsibility: The American Experience*. Cambridge: Cambridge University Press.
8. Davis, 45–50.
9. See Morrell Heald, *The Social Responsibilities of Business: Company and Community, 1900–1960* (Cleveland: Case Western Reserve University Press, 1970), 12–14.
10. Carroll, et al. 2012.
11. James W. McKie, "Changing Views," in *Social Responsibility and the Business Predicament* (Washington, DC: The Brookings Institute, 1974), 22–23.
12. Ibid., 25. Also see Carroll, et al. 2012.
13. Heald, 119.
14. McKie, 27–28.
15. Neil J. Mitchell, *The Generous Corporation: A Political Analysis of Economic Power* (New Haven, CT: Yale University Press, 1989).
16. Ronald E. Berenbeim, "When the Corporate Conscience Was Born" (A review of Mitchell's book), *Across the Board* (October 1989), 60–62.
17. For more on Andrew Carnegie, see his biography, *Andrew Carnegie*, by David Nasaw, The Penguin Press, 2006. For a book review, see Bob Dowling, "The Robin Hood Robber Baron," *BusinessWeek* (November 27, 2006), 116.
18. Berenbeim, 62.
19. Keith Davis and Robert L. Blomstrom, *Business and Society: Environment and Responsibility*, 3d ed. (New York: McGraw-Hill, 1975), 39.
20. Joseph W. McGuire, *Business and Society* (New York: McGraw-Hill, 1963), 144.
21. For a more complete history of the CSR concept, see Archie B. Carroll, "Corporate Social Responsibility: Evolution of a Definitional Construct," *Business and Society* (Vol. 38, No. 3, September 1999), 268–295.
22. Alexander Dahlsrud, "How Corporate Social Responsibility Is Defined: an Analysis of 37 Definitions,"

Corporate Social Responsibility and Environmental Management, 15, 2008, 1–13.

23. Archie B. Carroll, "A Three-Dimensional Conceptual Model of Corporate Social Performance," *Academy of Management Review* (Vol. 4, No. 4, 1979), 497–505. Also see Archie B. Carroll, "The Pyramid of Corporate Social Responsibility: Toward the Moral Management of Organizational Stakeholders," *Business Horizons* (July–August 1991), 39–48.

24. Stuart Taylor, Jr., and Evan Thomas, "Civil Wars," *Newsweek* (December 15, 2003), 43–53.

25. Symposium: Regulating the Digital Economy, *Democracy: A Journal of Ideas*, Fall 2014.

26. Archie B. Carroll, "The Pyramid of Corporate Social Responsibility: Toward the Moral Management of Organizational Stakeholders," *Business Horizons* (July–August 1991), 39–48. Also see Archie B. Carroll, "The Four Faces of Corporate Citizenship," *Business and Society Review* (Vol. 100–101, 1998), 1–7.

27. Ibid. Also see Mark S. Schwartz, *Corporate Social Responsibility: An Ethical Approach*, 2011, Peterborough, Ontario: Broadview Press.

28. Winshape Foundation, http://www.chick-fil-a.com/Company/Winshape. Accessed March 30, 2016.

29. Aflac, http://www.aflac.com/aboutaflac/pressroom/pressreleasestory.aspx?rid=1535927. Accessed March 30, 2016.

30. General Mills, http://www.generalmills.com/en/Responsibility/Overview. Accessed March 30, 2016.

31. Timberland, http://responsibility.timberland.com/factories/?story=1. Accessed March 30, 2016.

32. Mark Schwartz and Archie Carroll, "Corporate Social Responsibility: A Three Domain Approach," *Business Ethics Quarterly*, 13:4, 2003, 503–530.

33. Carroll, ibid., 1–7.

34. Wayne Visser, "Corporate Social Responsibility in Developing Countries," in Andrew Crane, Abagail McWilliams, Dirk Matten, Jeremy Moon, and Donald S. Siegel (eds.), *The Oxford Handbook of Corporate Social Responsibility*, Oxford: Oxford University Press, 2008, 473–499.

35. R. Edward Freeman, S. Ramakrishna Velamuri, and Brian Moriarty, "Company Stakeholder Responsibility: A New Approach to CSR," *Business Roundtable Institute for Corporate Ethics Bridge Paper* (2006), 10.

36. Dirk Matten and Jeremy Moon, "Implicit and Explicit CSR: A Conceptual Framework for Understanding CSR in Europe," *Research Paper Series, International Centre for CSR*, Nottingham University Business School, U. K. 2004, 9. Also see N. A. Dentchey, M. Balen and E. Haezendonck, "On Voluntarism and the Role of Governments in CSR: Towards a Contingency Approach," *Business Ethics: A European Review*, 2015.

37. Wayne Visser, "Corporate Social Responsibility in Developing Countries," in Andrew Crane, Abagail McWilliams, Dirk Matten, Jeremy Moon, and Donald Siegel (eds.), *The Oxford Handbook of Corporate Social Responsibility*, Oxford: Oxford University Press, 2008, 473–502). Also see D. Jamali, "CSR in developing countries through an institutional lens." *Corporate Social Responsibility and Sustainability: Emerging Trends in Developing Economies (Critical Studies on Corporate Responsibility, Governance and Sustainability, Volume 8) Emerald Group Publishing Limited*, 2014, 8, 21–44.

38. Walker Group, "Corporate Character: It's Driving Competitive Companies: Where's It Driving Yours?" Unpublished document, 1994.

39. Laura J. Spence, "Small Business Social Responsibility: Expanding Core CSR Theory," *Business and Society*, 2016, Vol. 55(1), 23–55.

40. M. E. Porter and M. R. Kramer, "Creating Shared Value," *Harvard Business Review*, January-February 2011, 64.

41. Toms, http://www.toms.com/. Accessed March 30, 2016.

42. "What Is Social Enterprise?" BC Centre for Social Enterprise, http://www.centreforsocialenterprise.com/what-is-social-enterprise/. Accessed March 30, 2016.

43. "What are B Corps?" https://www.bcorporation.net/what-are-b-corps. Accessed December 7, 2015.

44. "The Social Intraprenuer," Sustainability, http://www.sustainability.com/library/the-social-intrapreneur?path=library/the-social-intrapreneurs#.ULfAZaxZUn0. Accessed December 7, 2015.

45. Carroll, et al. 2012, 373–374.

46. For further discussion, see Duane Windsor, "Corporate Social Responsibility: Cases for and against It," in Marc J. Epstein and Kirk O. Hanson, eds., *The Accountable Corporation: Corporate Social Responsibility*, Vol. 3 (Westport, CN and London: Praeger, 2006), 31–50.

47. Milton Friedman, "The Social Responsibility of Business Is to Increase Its Profits," *The New York Times* (September 1962), 126. Also see "Special Report: Milton Friedman," *The Economist* (November 25, 2006), 79.

48. Ibid., 33 (emphasis added).

49. Aneel Karnani, "The Case against Corporate Social Responsibility," *The Wall Street Journal*, August 23, 2010, R1; R4.

50. Christopher D. Stone, *Where the Law Ends* (New York: Harper Colophon Books, 1975), 77.

51. Keith Davis, "The Case for and against Business Assumption of Social Responsibilities," *Academy of Management Journal* (June 1973), 312–322.

52. F. A. Hayek, "The Corporation in a Democratic Society: In Whose Interest Ought It and Will It Be Run?" in H. Ansoff (ed.), *Business Strategy* (Middlesex: Penguin, 1969), 225.

53. Davis, 320.

54. Davis, 316.

55. For further discussion, see Duane Windsor, "Corporate Social Responsibility: Cases for and against," in Marc J. Epstein and Kirk O. Hanson (eds.), *ibid.*

56. Nielsen, "Global consumers Are Willing to Put Their Money Where Their Heart Is When It Comes to Goods and Services from Companies Committed to Social Responsibility," http://www.nielsen.com/us/en/press-room/2014/global-consumers-are-willing-to-put-their-money-where-their-heart-is.html. Accessed March 30, 2016.

57. James Epstein-Reeves, "Consumers Overwhelmingly Want CSR," *Forbes*, December 15, 2010, http://www.forbes.com/sites/csr/2010/12/15/new-study-consumers-demand-companies-implement-csr-programs/#52255c345e1d. Accessed March 30, 2016.

58. Archie B. Carroll and Kareem M. Shabana, "The Business Case for Corporate Social Responsibility: A Review of Concepts, Research and Practice," *International Journal of Management Reviews*, Vol. 12, Issue 1, March 2010, 85–105

59. Archie B. Carroll and K. M. Shabana, "The Business Case for Sustainability," in *Sustainability Matters: Why and How Corporate Boards Should Become Involved,*" Matteo Tonello (ed.), Research Report R-1481-11-RR, New York: The Conference Board, 2011, pp. 21–26

60. Reported in "CSR—A Religion with Too Many Priests," *European Business Forum* (Issue 15, Autumn 2003).

61. Simon Zadek, *The Civil Corporation: The New Economy of Corporate Citizenship* (London: Earthscan, 2001). See also Lance Moir, "Social Responsibility: The Changing Role of Business," Cranfield School of Management, U.K.

62. Kasturi Rangan, Lisa Chase, and Sohel Karim, "The Truth about CSR," *Harvard Business Review*, January-February 2015, 41–49.

63. Project ROI, http://projectroi.com/. Accessed March 11, 2016; Also see Susan Nickbarg, "Tying Corporate Responsibility to Return on Investment (ROI)," *CR Magazine*, January/February 2016, 25–28.

64. Wayne Visser, "The Age of Responsibility: CSR 2.0 and the New DNA of Business," *Journal of Business Systems, Governance and Ethics*, 2010, Vol. 5, No. 3, 7–22.

65. Visser, ibid., 9.

66. David Gelles, "Social Responsibility That Rubs Right Off," *The New York Times*, October 18, 2015, BU 3.

67. Matthew Lynn, "Corporate Social Responsibility Has Become a Racket—and a Dangerous One," *The Telegraph,* September 29, 2015.

68. A. G. Scherer, A. Rasche, G. Palazzo, and A. Spicer, "Managing for Political Corporate Social Responsibility—New Challenges and Directions for PCSR 2.0," *Journal of Management Studies*, Vol. 53, 2016. Also see BOS Business and Society, "What Do We Mean by Political CSR—Towards a Definition," http://blog.cbs.dk/BOS/2016/03/19/what-do-we-mean-by-political-csr-towards-a-definition/. Accessed March 30, 2016.

69. Jedrzej George Frynas and Sian Stephens, "Political Corporate Social Responsibility: Reviewing Theories and Setting New Agendas," *International Journal of Management Reviews*, 2015, Vol. 17, 483–509.

70. A. G. Scherer and G. Palazzo, "The New Political Role of Business in a Globalized World: A Review of a New Perspective on CSR and Its Implications for the Firm, Governance, and Democracy," *Journal of Management Studies* 2011: 48, 899–931.

71. Frynas and Stephens, ibid.

72. Robert Ackerman and Raymond Bauer, *Corporate Social Responsiveness: The Modern Dilemma* (Reston, VA: Reston Publishing Company, 1976), 6.

73. Carroll, 1979, 502–504.

74. Duane Windsor, "Corporate Citizenship: Evolution and Interpretation," in Jörg Andriof and Malcom McIntosh (eds.), *Perspectives on Corporate Citizenship* (Sheffield, UK: Greenleaf Publishing, 2001), 39–52.

75. Samuel P. Graves, Sandra Waddock, and Marjorie Kelly, "How Do You Measure Corporate Citizenship?" *Business Ethics* (March/April 2001), 17.

76. Charles J. Fombrum, "Three Pillars of Corporate Citizenship," in Noel Tichy, Andrew McGill, and Lynda St. Clair (eds.), *Corporate Global Citizenship* (San Francisco: The New Lexington Press), 27–61.

77. Archie B. Carroll, "The Four Faces of Corporate Citizenship," *Business and Society Review* (100/101, 1998), 1–7.

78. Barbara W. Altman, *Corporate Community Relations in the 1990s: A Study in Transformation*, unpublished doctoral dissertation, Boston University.

79. Andreas G. Scherer and Guido Palazzo (eds.), *Handbook of Research on Global Corporate Citizenship* (Cheltenham, UK: Edward Elgar Publishing, 2008).

80. Philip Mirvis and Bradley K. Googins, *Stages of Corporate Citizenship: A Developmental Framework* (monograph) (Boston: The Center for Corporate Citizenship at Boston College, 2006), i.

81. Ibid., 1–18.

82. For more on corporate citizenship, see the special issue "Corporate Citizenship," *Business and Society Review* (Vol. 105, No. 1, Spring 2000), edited by Barbara W. Altman and Deborah Vidaver-Cohen. Also see Jorg Andriof and Malcolm McIntosh (eds.), *Perspectives on Corporate Citizenship* (London: Greenleaf Publishing, 2001). Also see Isabelle Maignan, O. C. Ferrell, and G. Tomas M. Hult, "Corporate Citizenship: Cultural Antecedents and Business Benefits,"

Journal of the Academy of Marketing Science (Vol. 27, No. 4, Fall 1999), 455–469. Also see Malcolm McIntosh, Deborah Leipziger, Keith Jones, and Gill Coleman, *Corporate Citizenship: Successful Strategies for Responsible Companies* (London: Financial Times/ Pitman Publishing), 1998.

83. Mark S. Schwartz and Archie B. Carroll, "Integrating and Unifying Competing and Complementary Frameworks: The Search for a Common Core in the Business and Society Field," *Business and Society* (Vol. 47, No. 2, June 2008), 148–186. Also see, Schwartz, 2011.

84. One of the most important meetings held on the subject of Global CSR are the International Conferences on CSR held at Humboldt University in Berlin every other year—CSR in an Age of Digitation, Humboldt University Zu Berlin, http://www.csr-hu-berlin.org/. Accessed March 30, 2016.

85. Donna J. Wood, Jeanne M. Logsdon, Patsy G. Lewellyn, and Kim Davenport, *Global Business Citizenship: A Transformative Framework for Ethics and Sustainable Capitalism* (Armonk, NY: M. E. Sharpe, 2006), 40.

86. Dirk Matten and Jeremy Moon, "Implicit and Explicit CSR: A Conceptual Framework for Understanding CSR in Europe," *Research Paper Series, International Centre for Corporate Social Responsibility,* Nottingham University Business School, United Kingdom, 2004, 9.

87. Wayne Visser, "Corporate Social Responsibility in Developing Countries," in Andrew Crane, Abagail McWilliams, Dirk Matten, Jeremy Moon, and Donald Siegel (eds.), *The Oxford Handbook of Corporate Social Responsibility*, ibid.

88. Ioannis Ioannou and George Serafeim, "What Drives Corporate Social Performance? The Role of Nation-Level Institutions," *Journal of International Business Studies*, 43, December 2012, 834–864.

89. Fortune's Most Admired for 2016, *Fortune*, March 1, 2016, 109.

90. Fortune's 100 Best Companies to Work For, 2016, *Fortune*, March 15, 2016, 142–150.

91. CR's 100 Best Corporate Citizens for 2015, http://www.thecro.com/files/100%20Best%20List%202015.pdf. Accessed March 30, 2016.

92. See, for example, Mark Starik and Archie B. Carroll, "In Search of Beneficence: Reflections on the Connections Between Firm Social and Financial Performance," in Karen Paul (ed.), *Contemporary Issues in Business and Society in the United States and Abroad* (Lewiston, NY: The Edwin Mellen Press, 1991), 79–108; and I. M. Herremans, P. Akathaporn, and M. McInnes, "An Investigation of Corporate Social Responsibility, Reputation, and Economic Performance," *Accounting, Organizations, and Society* (Vol. 18, No. 7/8, 1993), 587–604.

93. Marc Orlitzky, Frank Schmidt, and Sara Rynes, "Corporate Social and Financial Performance: A Meta-Analysis," *Organization Studies* (Vol. 24, No. 3, 2003), 369–396. Also see Marc Orlitzky, "Payoffs to Social and Environmental Performance," *Journal of Investing* (Fall 2005), 48–51. Also see Lee E. Preston and Douglas P. O'Bannon, "The Corporate Social–Financial Performance Relationship: A Typology and Analysis," *Business and Society* (Vol. 36, No. 4, December 1997), 419–429; Sandra Waddock and Samuel Graves, "The Corporate Social Performance–Financial Performance Link," *Strategic Management Journal* (Vol. 18, No. 4, 1997), 303–319; Jennifer Griffin and John Mahon, "The Corporate Social Performance and Corporate Financial Performance Debate," *Business and Society* (Vol. 36, No. 1, March 1997), 5–31; Ronald Roman, Sefa Hayibor, and Bradley Agle, "The Relationship between Social and Financial Performance," *Business and Society* (Vol. 38, No. 1, March 1999), 121. For a reply to this study, see John Mahon and Jennifer Griffin, "Painting a Portrait: A Reply," *Business and Society* (Vol. 38, No. 1, March 1999), 126–133.

94. John Peloza, "The Challenge of Measuring Financial Impacts from Investments in Corporate Social Performance," *Journal of Management* (December 2009), 1518–1541.

95. Heli Wang and Jaepil Choi, "A New Look at the Corporate Social-Financial Performance Relationship: The Moderating Roles of Temporal and Interdomain Consistency in Corporate Social Performance," *Journal of Management*, February 2013, 416–441.

96. Orlitzky, Schmidt, and Rynes, 2005 and Peloza, 2009. For an excellent overview of this research see Marc Orlitzky, "Corporate Social Performance and Financial Performance," Chapter 5, in Crane, et al. (eds.), 2008, 113–136.

97. "Sustainability: CFOs Are Coming to the Table," 2012 Deloitte Global Services Limited, 3–4.

98. Preston and O'Bannon, 428.

99. Mercedes Rodriguez-Ferandez, "Social Responsibility and Financial Performance: The Role of Good Governance," BRQ Business Research Quarterly, September 2015.

100. Bryan Husted, "A Contingency Theory of Corporate Social Performance," *Business and Society* (Vol. 39, No. 1, March 2000), 24–48, 41.

101. "Triple Bottom Line," The Economist, November 17, 2009, http://www.economist.com/node/14301663. Accessed February 15, 2016.

102. Zadek, 105–114.

103. Sustainability, "Environmental, Social and Governance Goals," http://www.sustainability.com/. Accessed March 30, 2016.

104. Dow Jones Sustainability Indexes, http://www.sustainability-index.com/. Accessed March 30, 2016.

105. Michael E. Porter and Mark R. Kramer, ibid.

106. John Mackey, "Conscious Capitalism," http://www.consciouscapitalism.org/node/3998. Accessed February 16, 2016.

107. Ibid.

108. Susan Berfield, "The Clutter in Kip Tindell," *BloombergBusinessweek*, February 19, 2015, 41–45.

109. The Forum for Sustainable and Responsible Investment, http://ussif.org/. Accessed March 30, 2016.

110. Performance and SRI, http://www.ussif.org/content.asp?contentid=35. Accessed January 11, 2016.

111. See, for example, Lawrence A. Armour, "Who Says Virtue Is Its Own Reward?" *Fortune* (February 16, 1998), 186–189; Thomas D. Saler, "Money & Morals," *Mutual Funds* (August 1997), 55–60; and Keith H. Hammonds, "A Portfolio with a Heart Still Needs a Brain," *BusinessWeek* (January 26, 1998), 100.

112. "Key Issues in Responsible Investing, Domini Social Investments, http://www.domini.com/. Accessed March 30, 2016.

113. See Jack A. Brill and Alan Reder, *Investing from the Heart* (New York: Crown Publishers, 1992); Also see SRI Basics, http://www.ussif.org/sribasics. Accessed December 28, 2015.

114. William A. Sodeman, *Social Investing: The Role of Corporate Social Performance in Investment Decisions*, unpublished Ph.D. dissertation, University of Georgia, 1993. See also William A. Sodeman and Archie B. Carroll, "Social Investment Firms: Their Purposes, Principles, and Investment Criteria," in *International Association for Business and Society 1994 Proceedings*, edited by Steven Wartick and Denis Collins, 339–344.

115. Social Funds, "Screening Your Portfolio," http://www.socialfunds.com/page.cgi/article2.html. Accessed January 11, 2016.

116. Daniel Akst, "The Give and Take of 'Socially Responsible'," *New York Times* (October 8, 2006), 28 BU; Jia Lynn Yang, "New Rules for Do-Good Funds," *Fortune* (February 5, 2007), 109–112.

117. "Invest with Your Conscience," *Money*, July 2011, 62.

118. "Bonds for the Socially Conscious," *Kiplinger's Personal Finance*, April 2015, 45.

119. Nellie S. Huang, "Make Money and Do Good, Too," Kiplinger's Personal Finance, March 2016, 44–48.

120. Ibid.

121. Samuel B. Graves and Sandra A. Waddock, "Institutional Owners and Corporate Social Performance," *Academy of Management Journal* (Vol. 37, No. 4, August 1994), 1034–1046.

122. Alex Davidson, "How to Be a Sustainable Mutual Fund Investor," *The Wall Street Journal*, November 9, 2015, R11.

123. Report on U.S. Sustainable, Responsible, and Impact Investing Trends, http://www.ussif.org/trends. Accessed March 30, 2016.

3

The Stakeholder Approach to Business, Society, and Ethics

CHAPTER LEARNING OUTCOMES

After studying this chapter, you should be able to:

1 Identify origins of the stakeholder concept by explaining what a stake is and what a stakeholder is.

2 Explain who business's stakeholders are in primary and secondary terms.

3 Differentiate among the three stakeholder approaches—strategic, multifiduciary, and synthesis.

4 Identify and explain the three values of the stakeholder model.

5 Name and describe the five key questions that capture the essence of stakeholder management.

6 Explain major concepts in effective stakeholder management to include stakeholder thinking, stakeholder culture, stakeholder management capability, and stakeholder engagement.

7 Describe the three strategic steps toward global stakeholder management.

The business organization today, especially the modern corporation, is the institutional centerpiece of a complex society. Society today consists of many people with a multitude of interests, expectations, and demands regarding what major organizations ought to provide to accommodate people's lives and lifestyles. Business responds to many of the expectations placed on it. There has been an ever-changing social contract. There have been many assorted legal, ethical, and philanthropic expectations and demands being met by organizations willing to change as long as the economic incentives were present and honored. What was once viewed as a specialized means of providing profit through the manufacture and distribution of goods and services has become a multipurpose social institution that many people and groups depend on for their livelihoods, prosperity, and fulfillment.

Even in questionable economic times, we live in a society expecting a quality, sustainable lifestyle, with more individuals and groups every day laying claim to their share of the good life. Business organizations today have found it necessary to be responsive to individuals and groups they once viewed as powerless and unable to make such claims on them. We call these individuals and groups ***stakeholders***. The stakeholder approach to management is an accepted framework that is constantly undergoing development, especially in the business-and-society arena. In the academic and business communities, advances in stakeholder theory have illustrated the crucial development of the stakeholder concept.[1]

In terms of corporate applications, a model for the "stakeholder corporation" has even been proposed. It has been argued that "stakeholder inclusion" is the key to company success in the 21st century.[2] One book titled *Stakeholder Power* presents a "winning plan for building stakeholder commitment and driving corporate growth."[3] Another book titled *Redefining the Corporation: Stakeholder Management and Organizational Wealth* argues that the corporate model needs redefinition because of business size and socioeconomic power and the inadequacy of the "ownership" model and its implications.[4] Yet another, titled simply *Stakeholders*, a topic of primary interest in this book, traces the theory and practice of the concept and brings us up to date on both strategic and ethical perspectives on stakeholders.[5]

An outgrowth of these developments is that it has become apparent that business organizations must address the legitimate needs and expectations of stakeholders if they want to be sustainable.[6] Businesses must also address stakeholders because it is the ethical course of action. They must recognize and factor in the stakeholders' needs, expectations, claims, and rights. For sustainable development to become a reality, the stakeholder approach offers the best opportunity. It is for these reasons that the stakeholder concept and orientation have become central to the vocabulary and thinking in the study of business, society, and ethics.

3.1 Origins of the Stakeholder Concept

The stakeholder concept has become central in understanding business and society relationships. The term *stakeholder* is a variant of the more familiar and traditional concepts of *stockholders* or *shareholders*—the investors in or owners of businesses. Just as an individual might own his or her own private house, automobile, or iPhone, a stockholder owns a portion or a share of one or more businesses. Thus, a shareholder is also a type of stakeholder. However, shareholders are just one of many legitimate stakeholders that business and organizations must deal with today to be successful.

3.1a What Is the *Stake* in Stakeholder?

To appreciate the concept of stakeholders, it helps to understand the idea of a stake. A **stake** is an interest in or a share in an undertaking. If a group plans to go out to dinner and a movie for the evening, each person in the group has a stake, or interest, in the group's decision. No money has been spent yet, but each member sees his or her interests (preference, taste, priority) in the decision. A stake may also be a *claim*. A claim is a demand for something due or believed to be due. We can see clearly that an owner or a shareholder has an interest in and an ownership of a share of a business.

The idea of a stake can range from simply an interest in an undertaking at one extreme to a legal claim of ownership at the other. Between these extremes might be a "need" for something or a "right." It might be a legal right to certain treatment rather than a legal claim of ownership, such as that of a shareholder. Legal rights might include the right to fair treatment (e.g., not to be discriminated against) or the right to privacy (not to have one's privacy invaded or abridged). A right also might be thought of as a moral right, such as that expressed by an employee: "I've got a right not to be fired because I've worked here 30 years, and I've given this firm the best years of my life." Or a consumer might say, "I've got a right to a safe product after all I've paid for this."

In short, stakeholders have a stake in the "value" they expect to receive from firms with which they interact. Harrington and Wicks have contended that stakeholders, in general, desire utility associated with (1) the actual goods and services companies provide, (2) organizational justice (fair treatment), (3) affiliating with companies that exhibit practices consistent with the things they value, and (4) getting a good deal from the company based on the opportunity costs they spend compared with value received from other companies.[7] When stakeholders perceive they have shared utility in a relationship, they will be more cooperative and more inclined to govern themselves, rather than rely on the government or other institutional bodies.[8] Stakeholders, thus, have a significant stake in the value provided them by firms.

As we have seen, stakes take on a variety of different forms. Figure 3-1 summarizes various categories or types of stakes and provides examples.

3.1b What Is a Stakeholder?

It follows, then, that a **stakeholder** is an individual or a group that has one or more of the various kinds of stakes in the organization. Just as stakeholders may be *affected by* the actions, decisions, policies, or practices of the business firm, these stakeholders may also *affect* the organization's actions, decisions, policies, or practices. With stakeholders, therefore, there is an actual two-way interaction or exchange of influence. In short, a stakeholder may be thought of as "any individual or group who can affect or is affected by the actions, decisions, policies, practices, or goals of the organization."[9]

FIGURE 3-1 Types of Stakes

	An Interest	A Right	Ownership
Definitions	When a person or group will be affected by a decision, it has an *interest* in that decision.	(1) Legal right: When a person or group has a *legal claim* to be treated in a certain way or to have a particular right protected.	When a person or group has a *legal title* to an asset or a property; ownership.
Examples	This plant closing will affect the community. This TV commercial demeans women, and I'm a woman. I'm concerned about the environment for future generations.	Employees expect due process, privacy; customers or creditors have certain legal rights.	"This company is mine. I founded it, and I own it," or "I own 1,000 shares of this corporation."
Definitions		(2) Moral right: When a person or group thinks it has a *moral or ethical right* to be treated in a certain way or to have a particular right protected.	
Examples		Fairness, justice, equity.	

3.2 Who Are Business's Stakeholders?

In today's hypercompetitive, global business environment, any individuals and groups may be business's stakeholders. From the business point of view, certain individuals and groups have more *legitimacy* in the eyes of the management; that is, they have a legitimate (authentic, justified), direct interest in, or claim on, the operations of the firm. The most obvious of these groups are shareholders, employees, and customers.

However, from the point of view of a highly pluralistic society, stakeholders include not only these groups, but other groups as well. These other groups include the community, competitors, suppliers, special-interest groups, the media, and society, or the public at large. Regulators, activists, and geographic communities also have been identified as stakeholders.[10] Marc Benioff, CEO of Salesforce.com, recently said "My customers are my stakeholders. My partners are my stakeholders. My employees are my stakeholders. I have other stakeholders, too. I even consider the communities that we live in are stakeholders. The environment is a stakeholder. We cannot do our business without that."[11] And, the list of relevant stakeholders obviously extends beyond these major groups.

Since sustainability is one of the key themes in this book, special attention is called to the natural environment as stakeholder. The natural environment, along with the economic and social environments, was identified in Chapter 2 as central to the triple bottom line concept. When the concept of sustainability first became popular, however, it was the natural environment that was primarily discussed. In keeping with sustainability, it has been reasoned that the natural environment, nonhuman species, and future generations should be considered among business's important stakeholders.[12] However, one reason these groups have been neglected is that there has never been a direct spokesperson for them. Who is to speak for the mountain ranges, the biosphere, the oceans, and the flora and fauna? The answer is interest groups such as Greenpeace, Friends of the Earth, and other environmental groups.[13] But, these nonprofit organizations and nongovernmental organizations (NGOs) are *indirect* stakeholders and consequently there has been a failure to fully incorporate their concerns by some organizations. This is why explicit consideration for the natural environment needs to be emphasized in this stakeholder chapter.

3.2a Three Views of the Firm: Production, Managerial, and Stakeholder

From an historical perspective, the advancement of the stakeholder concept parallels the growth and expansion of the business enterprise. In what has been termed the traditional **production view of the firm**, owners thought of stakeholders as only those individuals or groups that supplied resources or bought products or services.[14] Later, as we witnessed the growth of corporations and the resulting separation of ownership from control, business firms began to see their responsibilities toward other major constituent groups to be essential if they were to be successful. In addition to suppliers of goods and users of goods, the owners and employees were acknowledged as stakeholders. Thus, the **managerial view of the firm** emerged. Finally, as major internal and external changes occurred in business and its environment, managers were required to undergo a radical conceptual shift in how they perceived the firm and its multilateral relationships with constituent or stakeholder groups. The result was the **stakeholder view of the firm.**[15] Figure 3-2 depicts the evolution from the production view to the managerial view of the firm, and Figure 3-3 illustrates the stakeholder view of the firm. The stakeholder view encompasses numerous different individuals and groups that are embedded

FIGURE 3-2 The Production and Managerial Views of the Firm

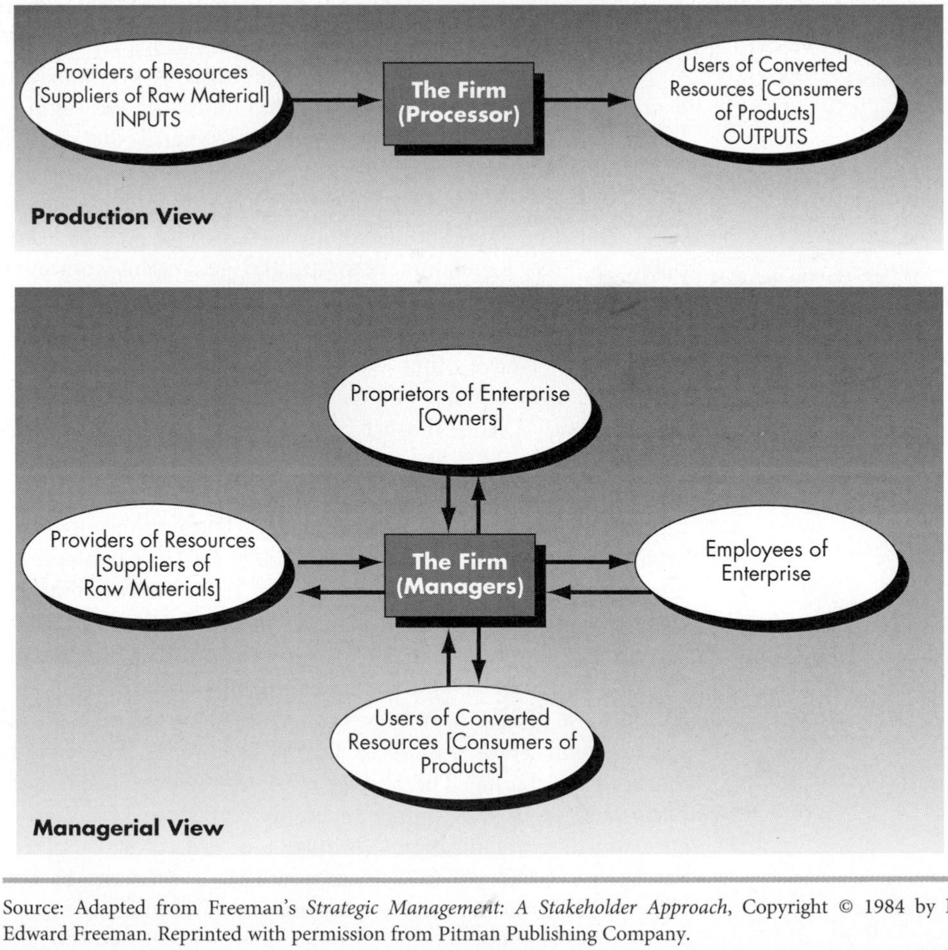

Source: Adapted from Freeman's *Strategic Management: A Stakeholder Approach*, Copyright © 1984 by R. Edward Freeman. Reprinted with permission from Pitman Publishing Company.

FIGURE 3-3 The Stakeholder View of the Firm

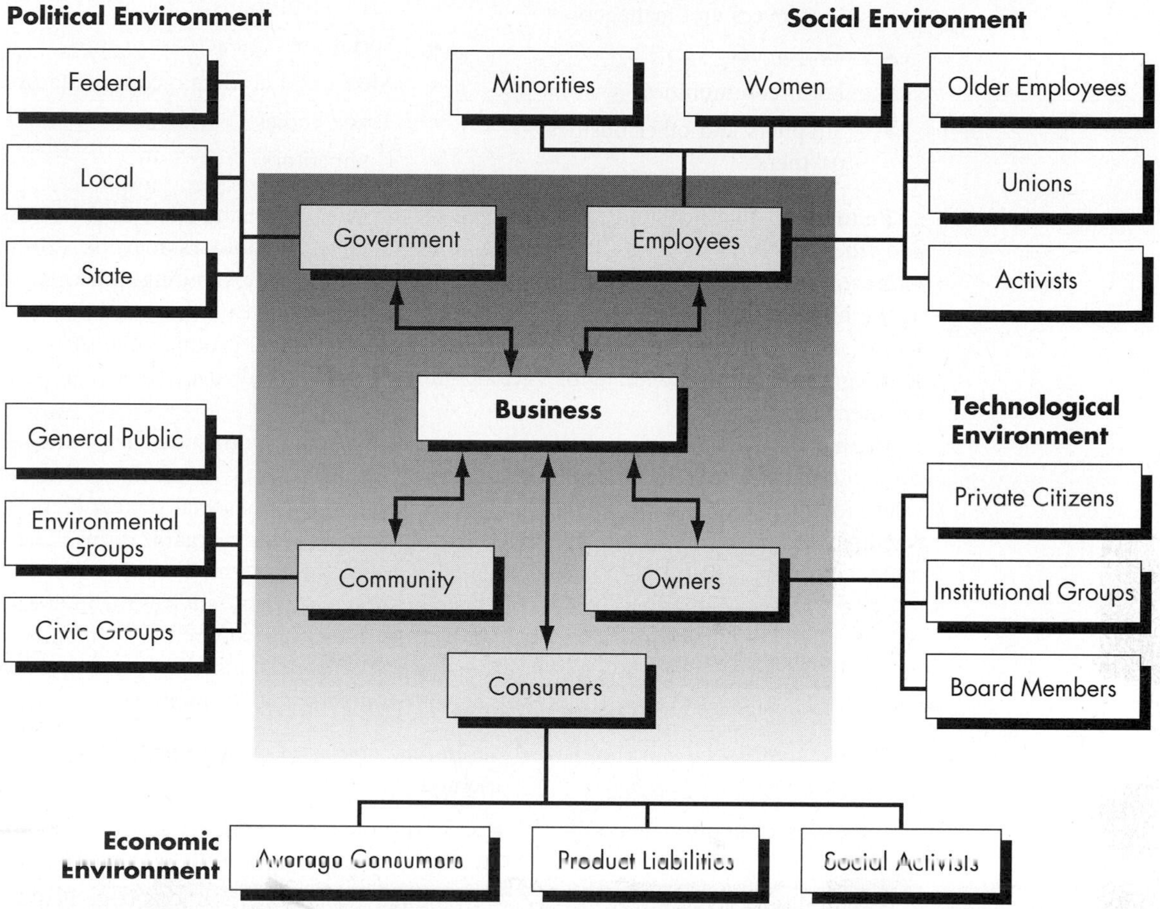

in the firm's internal and external environments. The diagram in Figure 3-3 is called a **stakeholder map** because it charts out a firm's stakeholders.

In the stakeholder view of the firm, the management must perceive as stakeholders not only those groups that the management *thinks* have some stake in the firm but also those individuals and groups that themselves think or perceive they have a stake in the firm. This is an essential perspective that the management must take, at least until it has had a chance to weigh carefully the legitimacy of the claims and the power of various stakeholders. Of particular note is that each stakeholder group may be thought of as being composed of subgroups; for example, the government stakeholder group includes federal, state, and local government subgroups as stakeholders. Similarly, employees may be classified into subgroups such as women, minorities, older workers, and union members.

3.2b Primary and Secondary Stakeholders

A useful way to categorize stakeholders is to think of them as *primary* and *secondary* as well as *social* and *nonsocial*; thus, stakeholders may be thought of as follows:[16]

Primary social **stakeholders include:**

- Shareholders and investors
- Employees and managers
- Customers
- Local communities
- Suppliers and other business partners

Secondary social **stakeholders include:**

- Government and regulators
- Civic institutions
- Social pressure/activist groups
- Media and academic commentators
- Trade bodies
- Competitors

Primary social stakeholders have a *direct* stake in the organization and its success and, therefore, are most influential. **Secondary social stakeholders** may be extremely *influential* as well, especially in affecting reputation and public standing, but their stake in the organization is more *indirect* or *derived*. Therefore, a firm's responsibility toward secondary stakeholders may be less but is not avoidable. These groups quite often represent legitimate public concerns or wield significant power, and this makes it impossible for them to be ignored.[17]

Primary nonsocial stakeholders also exist and these might include the natural environment, future generations, and nonhuman species. **Secondary nonsocial stakeholders** might include those who represent or speak for the primary nonsocial stakeholders. They might include environmental interest groups or animal welfare organizations. The secondary social and nonsocial stakeholders have also been termed *nonmarket players* (NMPs) by strategy experts, and they may include activists, environmentalists, and NGOs. Often they are hostile to the firm because they hold competing ideologies such as conflicting beliefs and attitudes regarding social, ecological, ethical, or political issues. This often puts them on a collision course with company managements.[18]

Primary nonsocial **stakeholders include:**

- Natural environment
- Future generations
- Nonhuman species

Secondary nonsocial **stakeholders include:**

- Environmental interest groups (e.g., Friends of the Earth, Greenpeace, Rainforest Alliance)
- Animal welfare organizations (e.g., People for the Ethical Treatment of Animals—PETA, Mercy for Animals, American Society for the Prevention of Cruelty to Animals—ASPCA.

The terms *primary* and *secondary* may be defined differently depending on the situation. Secondary stakeholders can quickly become primary, for example. This often occurs through the media or special-interest groups when a claim's *urgency* (as in a boycott or demonstration) takes precedence over its legitimacy. In today's business environment, the media and social media have the power to instantaneously transform a stakeholder's status within minutes or hours. Thus, it may be useful to think of primary and secondary classes of stakeholders for discussion purposes, but we should understand how easily and quickly those categories can shift.

3.2c Important Stakeholder Attributes: Legitimacy, Power, Urgency

How do managers decide which stakeholders deserve their attention? Stakeholders have attributes such as legitimacy, power, and urgency. A typology of stakeholders has been developed based on these three attributes.[19] When these three attributes are superimposed, as depicted in Figure 3-4, seven stakeholder categories may be created.

FIGURE 3-4 Stakeholder Typology: One, Two, or Three Attributes Present

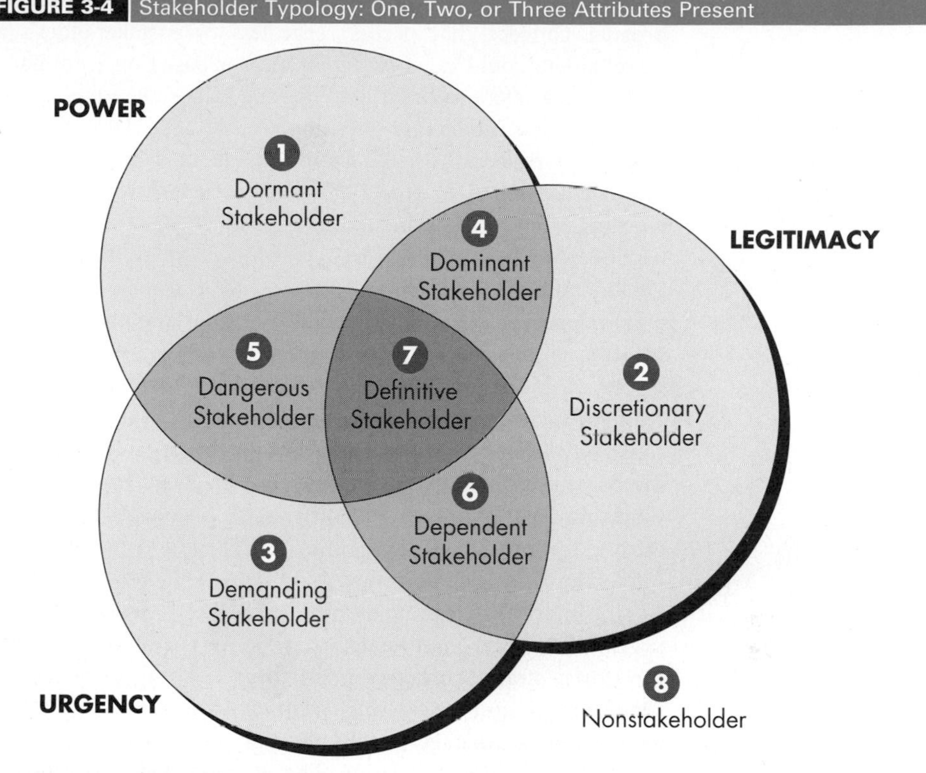

Source: Reprinted with permission of Academy of Management, PO Box 3020, Briar Cliff Manor, NY 10510-8020. Stakeholder Typology: One, Two, or Three Attributes Present (Figure), R. K. Mitchell, B. R. Agle, and D. J. Wood, *Academy of Management Review*, October 1997. Reproduced by permission of the publisher via Copyright Clearance Center, Inc.

The three attributes of legitimacy, power, and urgency help us see how stakeholders may be thought of and analyzed in terms of their characteristics. The stakeholders are more or less salient depending on these factors. **Legitimacy** refers to the perceived validity or appropriateness of a stakeholder's claim to a stake. Therefore, owners, employees, and customers represent a high degree of legitimacy due to their explicit, formal, and direct relationships with a company. Stakeholders that are more distant from the firm, such as social activist groups, NGOs, competitors, or the media, might be thought to have less legitimacy.

Power refers to the ability or capacity of the stakeholder(s) to produce an effect—to get something done that otherwise may not be done. Therefore, whether one has legitimacy or not, power means that the stakeholder could affect the business. For example, with the help of the media, a large, vocal, activist group such as the People for the Ethical Treatment of Animals (PETA) could wield extraordinary power over a business firm. In recent years, PETA has been successful in influencing the practices and policies of virtually all the fast-food restaurants regarding their suppliers' treatment of chickens and cattle.

Though not referring to it as power, several researchers have highlighted the importance of stakeholder "pressure" in implementing CSR in companies. They have defined stakeholder pressure as "the ability and capacity of stakeholders to affect an organization by influencing its organizational decisions."[20] This sounds very much like the concept of power, but they assert that the pressure they are referring to occurs regardless of the legitimacy, power, or urgency of different groups. Hence, it might be thought of as a broader concept that occurs regardless of a stakeholder's attributes. In other words, stakeholders could exert *pressure* whether based on legitimacy, power, or urgency.

Urgency refers to the degree to which the stakeholder's claim on the business calls for the business's *immediate* attention or response. Urgency may imply that something is critical—it really needs to get done. Or it may imply that something needs to be done immediately, or on a timely basis. A management group may perceive a union strike, a consumer boycott, a contaminated product, or a social activist group picketing outside headquarters as urgent. With social media today, the concept of urgency has taken on new meaning.

Other research has suggested that at least one other criterion should be considered in addition to legitimacy, power, and urgency—**proximity**.[21] The spatial distance between the organization and its stakeholders refers to proximity, and it is a relevant consideration in evaluating stakeholders' importance and priority. Stakeholders that share the same physical space or are adjacent to the organization may affect and be affected by the organization more than those further away. In a global example, nation-states may share borders, introducing spatially related stakeholders. It is evident, therefore, that the greater the proximity, the greater the likelihood of relevant and important stakeholder interactions and relationships.[22]

An interesting example of a stakeholder action that illustrated both power and urgency occurred in several dozen Home Depot stores around the country. In each of the stores, strange announcements began blaring from the intercom systems: *"Attention shoppers, on aisle seven you'll find mahogany ripped from the heart of the Amazon."* Shocked store managers raced through the aisles trying to apprehend the environmental activists behind the stunt. The activists had apparently gotten the access codes to the intercoms. After months of similar antics, Home Depot bowed to the demands of the environmental group and announced that it would stop selling wood from endangered forests and, instead, stock wood products certified by the Forest Stewardship Council (FSC).[23] This group of environmental activists was not even on Home Depot's stakeholder radar screen and then, all of a sudden, the company was "persuaded" it had to sell only FSC-certified wood. This was an awesome display of stakeholder power.

The typology of stakeholder attributes suggests that managers must attend to stakeholders on the basis of their assessment of the extent to which competing stakeholder claims reflect legitimacy, power, and urgency and are salient. Using the categories shown in Figure 3-4, the stakeholder groups represented by overlapping circles (e.g., those with two or three attributes such as Categories 4, 5, 6, and 7) are highly "salient" to the management and would likely receive priority attention. Of course, like any typology, it is important to recognize that it is a static model subject to interpretation. For example, some have argued that urgency may not be as relevant (as legitimacy and power) for identifying stakeholders, whereas "legitimacy" may be defined as "moral legitimacy."[24] Nevertheless, it is a helpful tool for assessing stakeholder claims.

3.3 Stakeholder Approaches: Strategic, Multifiduciary, and Synthesis

A major challenge embedded in the stakeholder approach is to determine whether it should be seen primarily as a way to *manage better* or as a way to *treat more ethically* those groups known as stakeholders. Both of these concerns have sustainability

ETHICS IN PRACTICE CASE

Are Plants and Flowers Stakeholders? Do They Have Rights?

Scientists in Switzerland for years have created genetically modified produce, such as rice, corn, and apples. In fact, the question has been raised as to whether they ever stopped to think that their experiments may be "humiliating" to plants. A recently passed constitutional rule came into existence after the Swiss Parliament asked a panel of philosophers, geneticists, theologians, and lawyers to establish the "meaning" of a flora's dignity. The panel wrote a lengthy treatise on the "moral consideration of plants for their own sake." The document argued that vegetation has an inherent value and that it is immoral to harm plants arbitrarily. One example of this would be the "decapitation of wildflowers at the roadside without any apparent reason."

Defenders of the new law state that it reflects a broader, progressive effort to protect the sanctity of living things and promote sustainability. Switzerland also granted new rights to all "social animals." For example, prospective dog owners now have to take a four-hour course on pet care before they can acquire a dog. Anglers now have to learn how to catch fish humanely. Goldfish can no longer be flushed down the toilet as a means of disposal. First, they must be anesthetized with special chemicals. One Swiss scientist recently exclaimed, "Where does it stop? Should we now defend the dignity of microbes and viruses?" In a related decision, the people of Ecuador passed a new constitution that is said to be the first to recognize ecosystem rights enforceable in a court of law. Now, the nation's rivers, forests, and air are right-bearing entities with "the right to exist, persist, and regenerate."

One nonprofit organization that has formed to support this point of view is "Fair Flowers Fair Plants," an independent foundation representing international stakeholders in the flower industry striving for social and environmental standards.

1. Are plants stakeholders? Are they primary or secondary stakeholders? Do flora have rights? What about dogs and goldfish?
2. Are the Swiss and Ecuadorian decisions too extreme? What are the limits of stakeholders' rights? Is this taking sustainability too far or pushing the idea to unrealistic limits?
3. What are the implications for business decisions of the Swiss and Ecuadorian decisions? Are these unique to these countries and won't apply elsewhere?

Sources: "Swiss Government Issues Bill of Rights for Plants," http://www.treehugger.com/green-food/swiss-government-issues-bill-of-rights-for-plants.html. Accessed March 31, 2016; "Do Animals (and Plants) Have Rights? The Ethics of Food, http://www.geopolitics.us/do-animals-have-rights/. Accessed March 31, 2016; Animal Ethics, "Do Plants Have Rights?" http://animalethics.blogspot.com/2004/01/do-plants-have-rights.html. Accessed March 31, 2016.

implications. This issue may be addressed by considering the stakeholder approach used. Kenneth Goodpaster has suggested three approaches: the strategic approach, the multifiduciary approach, and the stakeholder synthesis approach.[25] The **strategic approach** views stakeholders primarily as factors to be taken into consideration and managed while the firm pursues profits for its shareholders. The **multifiduciary approach** views stakeholders as more than just individuals or groups who can wield economic or legal power. This view holds that the management has a fiduciary responsibility toward stakeholders just as it has this same responsibility toward shareholders. An innovative, **stakeholder synthesis approach** is preferred because it holds that business does have moral responsibilities to stakeholders but that they should not be seen as part of a fiduciary obligation. As a consequence, the management's basic fiduciary responsibility toward shareholders is kept intact, but it is also expected to be implemented within a context of ethical responsibility toward other stakeholders.[26] The result is the same in the multifiduciary and stakeholder synthesis views. However, the reasoning or rationale is different.

As we continue our discussion of stakeholder management, it should become clear that we are pursuing it from a balanced perspective, which suggests that we are integrating the strategic approach with the stakeholder synthesis approach. We should be managing strategically and morally at the same time.[27] The stakeholder approach should not be just a better way to manage. It also should be a more ethical and sustainable way to manage.

3.4 Three Values of the Stakeholder Model

In addition to the strategic, multifiduciary, and stakeholder synthesis approaches, the stakeholder model of the firm has three aspects or *values* that should be appreciated. Although interrelated, these include the descriptive, instrumental, and normative values or aspects.[28]

3.4a Descriptive Value

First, the stakeholder model has value because it is **descriptive**; that is, it provides language and concepts to describe effectively the corporation or organization in stakeholder inclusive terms. The business organization is a constellation of cooperative and competitive interests possessing both instrumental and intrinsic value. Understanding organizations in this way allows us to have a fuller description and explanation of how they function. The language and terms used in the stakeholder model are useful in helping us understand organizations. As a result, stakeholder language and concepts are being used more and more in many fields of endeavor—business, government, politics, education, nonprofit organizations, and so on.

3.4b Instrumental Value

Second, the stakeholder model has value because it is **instrumental** in that it is useful in portraying the relationship between the practice of stakeholder management and the resulting achievement of corporate performance goals. The fundamental premise here is that practicing effective stakeholder management should lead to the achievement of important business goals, such as profitability, stability, and growth.[29] This is similar to the *strategic approach* discussed earlier. Business school courses in strategic management and human resource management often employ the instrumental model of stakeholders.

3.4c Normative Value

Third, the stakeholder model has value because it is **normative**, wherein stakeholders are seen as possessing value irrespective of their instrumental use to management. This is often considered the moral or ethical view because it emphasizes how stakeholders *should* be treated. The "principle of stakeholder fairness" has been suggested as the moral underpinning, or normative justification, for the stakeholder model.[30] Thus, the normative value of stakeholder thinking is of central importance in business ethics and business and society.

In summarizing, stakeholder theory is *managerial* in the broad sense of the term in that it not only describes or predicts but also recommends attitudes, structures, and practices that constitute effective stakeholder management. Successful stakeholder management requires simultaneous attention to the legitimate interests of all salient stakeholders in the creation of organizational structures and policies and in decision making.[31]

3.5 Stakeholder Management: Five Key Questions

The managers of a business firm are responsible for establishing the firm's overall direction (its governance, mission, strategies, goals, and policies) and ensuring implementation of these plans. As a consequence, they have some long-term responsibilities and many that are of more immediate concern. Before the stakeholder environment became as turbulent and dynamic as it now is, the managerial task was relatively straightforward because the external environment was fairly stable. As managers have had to transition to the stakeholder view of the firm, however, the managerial task has become an inevitable consequence of the changing trends and developments described in the first two chapters.

The challenge of **stakeholder management** is to see to it that while the firm's primary stakeholders achieve their objectives, the other stakeholders are dealt with ethically and are also relatively satisfied. At the same time, the firm's profitability must be ensured. This is the classic "win–win" situation. The management's second-best alternative is to meet the goals of its primary stakeholders, keeping in mind the important role of its owner-investors. Without economic sustainability, all other stakeholders' interests become unresolved.

With these perspectives in mind, it is possible to approach stakeholder management with the idea that managers can become successful stewards of their stakeholders' resources by gaining knowledge about stakeholders and using this knowledge to predict and improve their company's decisions, policies, and actions. Thus, the important functions of stakeholder management are to describe, to analyze, to understand, and, finally, to manage. The quest for stakeholder management embraces social, legal, ethical, and economic considerations. Normative as well as instrumental objectives and perspectives are essential.

Five key questions are critical to capturing the essential information needed for effective stakeholder management:

1. *Who* are our organization's stakeholders?
2. What are our stakeholders' *stakes*?
3. What *opportunities and challenges* do our stakeholders present to the firm?
4. What *responsibilities* (economic, legal, ethical, and philanthropic) does the firm have to its stakeholders?
5. What *strategies or actions* should the firm take to best address stakeholder challenges and opportunities?[32]

Figure 3-5 presents a schematic of the decision process outlining the five questions and key issues with respect to each. The feedback loop suggests that this is an ongoing process.

3.5a Who Are the Organization's Stakeholders?

To manage effectively, each firm and its management group must ask and answer this question: *Who are our stakeholders?* This stage is often called "stakeholder identification." To answer this question fully, management must identify not only *generic* stakeholder groups but also *specific* subgroups. A generic stakeholder group is a general or broad grouping, such as employees, shareholders, environmental groups, or consumers. Within each of these generic categories, there may be a few or many specific subgroups. Figure 3-6 illustrates some of the generic and specific stakeholder subgroups of a large organization.

McDonald's Continuing Experience. To illustrate the process of stakeholder identification, it is helpful to consider some events in the life of the McDonald's Corporation that resulted in their broadening significantly who were considered their stakeholders. The case study begins when the social activist group PETA, which claims over two million members and supporters, decided it was dissatisfied with some of McDonald's practices and launched a billboard and bumper sticker campaign against the hamburger giant.[33] PETA, convinced that McDonald's was dragging its feet on animal welfare issues, went on the offensive. The group announced that it would put up billboards saying "The

FIGURE 3-5 Stakeholder Management: Five Key Questions

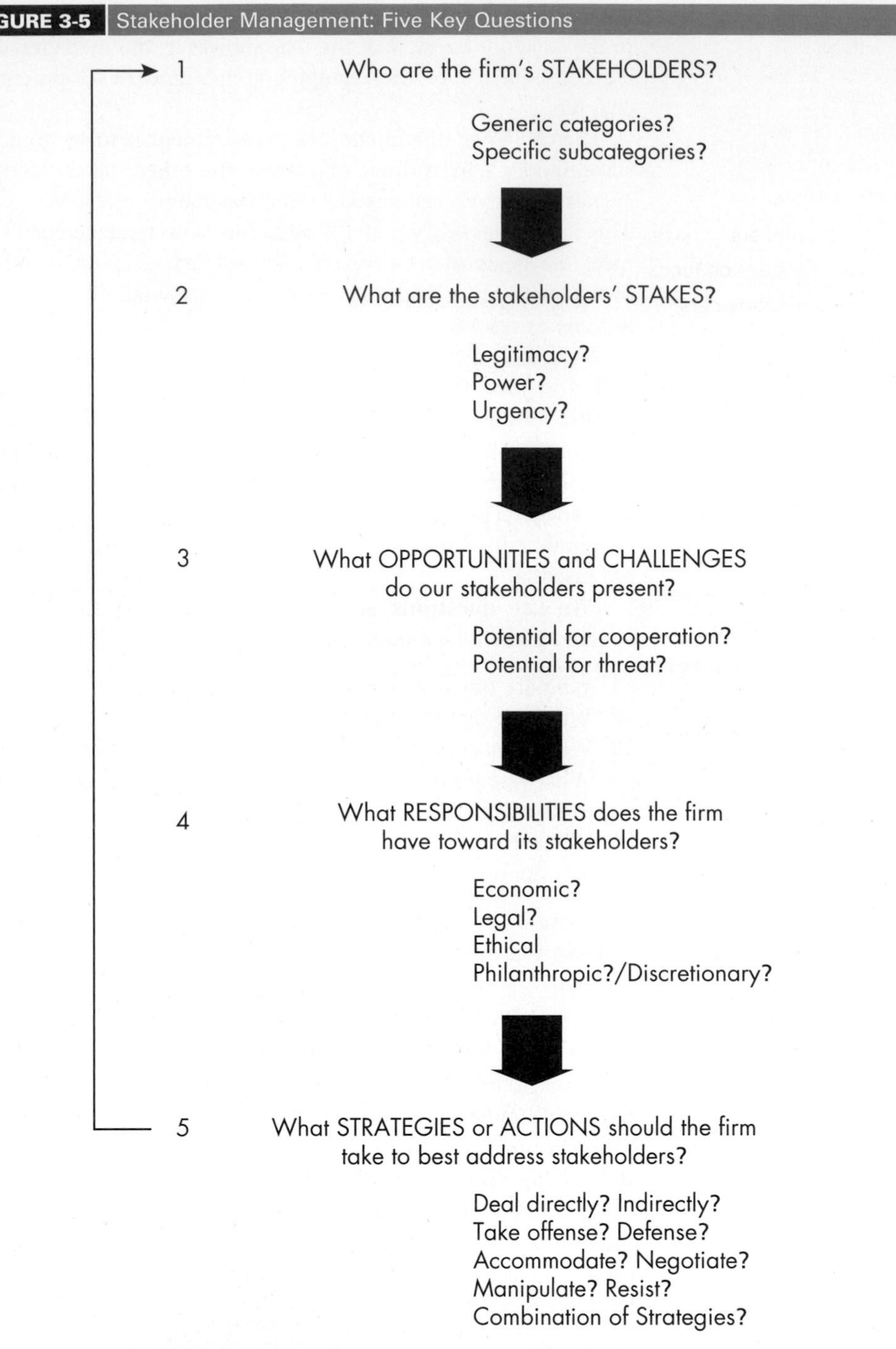

animals deserve a break today" and "McDonald's: Cruelty to Go" in Norfolk, Virginia, PETA's hometown. The ad campaign was announced when talks broke down between PETA and McDonald's on the subject of ways the company might foster animal rights issues within the fast-food industry. Using terminology introduced earlier, PETA was a secondary social or nonsocial stakeholder and, therefore, had low legitimacy. However,

FIGURE 3-6 Some Generic and Specific Stakeholders of a Large Firm

Owners	Employees	Governments	Customers
Trusts	Young employees	Federal	Business purchasers
Foundations	Middle-aged employees	• EPA	Government purchasers
Mutual funds	Older employees	• FTC	Educational institutions
Universities	Women	• OSHA	Global markets
Board members	Minority groups	• CPSC	Special-interest groups
Employee pension funds	Disabled	State	Internet purchasers
Management owners	Special-interest groups	Local	
Individual owners	Unions		

Community	Competitors	Social Activist Groups
General fund-raising	Firm A	Common Cause
United Way	Firm B	Rainforest Action Network (RAN)
YMCA/YWCA	Firm C	Public Citizen's Congress Watch
Middle schools	Indirect competition	American Civil Liberties Union
Elementary schools	Global competition	Consumers Union
Residents who live close by	Internet-based competition	People for the Ethical Treatment of Animals (PETA)
All other residents		National Farmers Union
Neighborhood associations		National Resources Defense Council
Local media		Citizens for Health
Chamber of Commerce		Greenbiz.com
Environments		

its power and urgency were extremely high as it was threatening the company with a highly visible, potentially destructive campaign that was being reported by a cooperative and empathetic media.

PETA's pressure tactics continued and escalated. In the early 2000s, McDonald's announced significant changes in the requirements it was placing on its chicken and egg suppliers. Egg suppliers were required to improve the "living conditions" of their chickens. Specifically, McDonald's insisted that its suppliers no longer cage its chickens wingtip to wingtip. Suppliers were required to increase the space allotted to each hen from 48 square inches to 72 square inches per hen. They were also required to stop "forced molting," a process that increases egg production by denying hens food and water for up to two weeks.[34]

PETA then escalated its pressure tactics against the firm by distributing "*unhappy* meals" at restaurant playgrounds and outside the company's shareholder meeting venues. The kits came in boxes similar to that of Happy Meal™, McDonald's meal for children, but were covered instead with pictures of slaughtered animals. These also depicted a bloody, knife-wielding "Son of Ron" doll that resembled the Ronald McDonald clown, as well as toy farm animals with slashed throats. One image featured a bloody cow's head and the familiar fast-food phrase "Do you want fries with that?"[35] PETA continued to aggressively pursue McDonald's and other firms, such as Burger King and KFC, for their chicken slaughter methods and other animal treatment issues. PETA had become the stakeholder that refuses to go away. Even today, PETA continues its ongoing campaign against McDonald's with its Web page proclaiming "McCruelty: I'm Hating It."[36]

As a result of this ongoing, living example, it can be seen how the set of stakeholders that McDonald's had to deal with grew markedly from its traditional stakeholders to include a powerful, special-interest group such as PETA. With the cooperation of the media, especially major newspapers, magazines, TV, and social media, PETA moved from being a secondary stakeholder to a primary stakeholder with great power and urgency in McDonald's life.

In a related example, Denny's, "America's Diner," has also been responding to pressure placed on it and others by PETA. In 2011, Denny's announced it would begin buying all its turkeys from slaughterhouses that used controlled atmosphere killing (CAK) thought to be the least cruel poultry slaughter method.[37] In 2016, Denny's ran a full page ad in *USA Today* announcing its pledge to source and serve cage-free eggs in all its U.S. restaurants by 2026. Denny's also pointed out that it already offers wild-caught, sustainable Alaska Salmon and offers seven-grain bread and gluten-free English muffins. One cannot help wonder how many of these decisions are internally driven and how many are in response to stakeholder expectations and pressure.

Wool Industry under Fire. Not only does PETA attack companies, it also takes on whole *industries* as well. Under pressure from PETA, many companies began to ban Australian wool. PETA's complaint against Australia's $2.2 billion industry has been targeted toward its use of wool from so-called mulesed merino sheep. Mulesing is a process of removing folds of skin from a sheep's hindquarters. The technique developed over 70 years ago and named after John Mules, who devised it, is performed without anesthetics. The intention is to protect the sheep against infestation by blowflies whose eggs hatch into flesh-eating maggots while in the wool. When PETA first started lobbying against this process over ten years ago, most apparel makers had never heard of the process or the issue. PETA began its attacks on Benetton, the Italian company that produces sweaters. It dispatched protestors wielding signs that read "Benetton—Baaad to Sheep" to picket stores stocking the product. In New York City, PETA also put up billboards with the question "Did your sweater cause a bloody butt?" The protests worked. Benetton soon publicly came out in favor of phasing out mulesing.

Other companies followed. As one European retailer observed, "who wants to be on PETA's radar screen?" More than 30 companies signed on to the ban, including well-known brands such as Abercrombie & Fitch, Timberland, Hugo Boss, and Adidas. Meanwhile, Australia's 55,000 sheep farmers are unhappy because they believe mulesing is the best way to protect their flocks.[38] Perhaps in response to PETA and other animal rights groups, North Face and Patagonia have been phasing out cruelty in down production and this is good news for geese who now get to live their lives free of live plucking and force feeding.[39] In two other examples of PETA's power as a stakeholder, it pressured SeaWorld in Los Angeles to dispense with its killer whales, and it has been pressuring Tesla Motors to do away with its leather seats (animal-sourced materials). In 2016, SeaWorld announced that it was phasing out its killer whale shows and their captivity. The orca shows are scheduled to end in San Diego in 2017 and in San Antonio and Orlando in 2019.[40]

These actual experiences of companies illustrate the evolving nature of the question, "Who are our stakeholders?" In actuality, stakeholder identification is an unfolding process. However, by recognizing early the potential of failure if one does not think in stakeholder terms, the value and usefulness of stakeholder thinking can be readily seen. Had McDonald's, KFC, Benetton, and other firms perceived PETA as a stakeholder with power, urgency, and some moral legitimacy, earlier on, perhaps it could have dealt with these situations earlier and more effectively. These firms should have been aware of one of the basic principles of stakeholder responsibility: "Recognize that stakeholders are real and complex people with names, faces, and values."[41]

Getting to know a company's stakeholders requires managers to go beyond simple list making of their characteristics. It means getting to know your stakeholders just like you get to know your customers. A McKinsey study found a strong positive correlation between in depth profiling of stakeholders and success at engaging them.[42] But, many businesses do not carefully identify their generic stakeholder groups, much less their specific stakeholder groups. "Who are our stakeholders?" is an essential first question, however, if the management is to be in a position to address the second major question, "What are our stakeholders' stakes?"

3.5b What Are Our Stakeholders' Stakes?

Once stakeholders have been identified, the next step is to address the question: *What are our stakeholders' stakes?* Even groups in the same generic category frequently have different specific interests, concerns, perceptions of rights, and expectations. Management's challenge is to identify the nature, legitimacy, power, urgency, and saliency of a group's stake(s) and their potential to affect the organization.

Nature or Legitimacy of a Group's Stakes. Stakeholders may possess varying types of stakes. Think about a large corporation with several hundred million shares of stock outstanding. Among the shareholder population of this corporation are these more specific subgroups:

1. Institutional owners (trusts, foundations, pension funds, churches, universities)
2. Large mutual fund organizations (Fidelity, Vanguard, Pax World)
3. Board of director members who own shares
4. Members of management who own shares
5. Millions of small, individual shareholders

For all these subgroups, the nature of stakeholder claims on this corporation is *ownership*. All these groups have legitimate claims—they are all owners. Because of other factors, such as power or urgency, however, these stakeholders may have to be dealt with differently. Increasingly, however, special interest groups are claiming moral legitimacy for the actions they take. Examples might include PETA, as described earlier, and any interest group promoting fair worker treatment or safer consumer products.

Power of a Group's Stakes. When power is considered, significant differences become apparent. Which of the groups in the previous list are the most powerful? Certainly not the small, individual investors, unless they have found a way to organize and thus wield power. The powerful stakeholders in this case are (1) the institutional owners and mutual fund organizations, because of the sheer magnitude of their investments and (2) the board and management shareholders, because of their dual roles of ownership and management (control).

Subgroups within a Generic Group. Consider a manufacturing firm in an industry in Ohio that is faced with a generic group of environmental stakeholders. Within the generic group of environmental stakeholders might be the following specific subgroups:

1. Residents living within a 25-mile radius of the plant
2. Other residents in the city
3. Residents who live in the path of the jet stream hundreds of miles away (some in Canada) who are being impacted by acid rain
4. Environmental Protection Agency (federal government)
5. Ohio's Environmental Protection Division (state government)

6. Sierra Club (environmental activist group)
7. Ohio Environmental Council (special interest group)

It would require some degree of time and care to identify the nature, legitimacy, power, and urgency of each of these specific groups. However, it could and should be done if the firm wants to better engage and manage its environmental stakeholders. Furthermore, it should be stressed that companies have an ethical responsibility to be sensitive to legitimate stakeholder claims even if the stakeholders have no power or leverage with the management.

Return for a moment to the fast-food and wool industry examples. One may conclude that PETA, as a special-interest, animal welfare group, did not have much *legitimacy* vis-à-vis these companies. It did claim animals' rights and treatment as a moral issue and thus had some moral legitimacy through the issues it represented. Unfortunately for PETA, not all of the public shares its concerns or degree of concern with these issues. However, PETA has and continues to have tremendous power and urgency. It was this power, wielded in the form of adverse publicity, media attention, and tenacity that without a doubt played a significant role in bringing about changes in these companies' policies as the companies sought to maintain their reputational capital.

3.5c What Opportunities and Challenges Do Our Stakeholders Present?

Opportunities and challenges represent opposite sides of the coin when it comes to stakeholder analysis. The opportunities are for business to build decent, productive working relationships with the stakeholders. Challenges, on the other hand, usually present themselves in such a way that the firm must handle the stakeholders acceptably or be hurt in some way—financially (short term or long term) or in terms of its public image or reputation in the community.

Stakeholder challenges typically take the form of varying degrees of expectations, demands, boycotts, or threats. In most instances, they arise because stakeholders think or believe that their needs or points of view are not being met adequately. The stakeholder groups may hold competing ideologies or conflicting beliefs. The example of PETA illustrated this point quite well. The challenges also arise when stakeholder groups think that any crisis that occurs is the responsibility of the firm or that the firm caused the crisis in some way.

Another example of a stakeholder crisis illustrates this point:[43] A campaign to transform the entire logging industry was launched by Rainforest Action Network (RAN). RAN, an environmental activist group, campaigns "for the forests, their inhabitants and the natural systems that sustain life by transforming the global marketplace though education, grassroots organizing and non-violent direct action."[44] RAN directed their campaign against Boise, Inc., an international distributor of office supplies and paper and an integrated manufacturer and distributor of paper, packaging, and building materials. As a result, Boise implemented a domestic old-growth policy and committed to "no longer harvesting timber from old-growth forests in the United States." To catch up with public values and meet the new marketplace standards, Boise became the first U.S. logging and distribution company to commit to "eliminate the purchase of wood products from endangered areas."[45] RAN's aggressive protection of rainforests continues to this day. Currently, RAN has campaigns against Chevron, Disney, Cargill, and Bank of America, among others.[46]

If one looks at the recent experiences of businesses, including the crisis mentioned here, it is evident that there is a need to think in stakeholder terms to understand fully the potential threats and challenges that businesses of all kinds face on a daily basis.

Potential for Cooperation or Threat. Opportunities and challenges might also be viewed in terms of *potential for cooperation* and *potential for threat* to enable managers to identify strategies for dealing with stakeholders.[47] In terms of potential for threat, managers need to consider stakeholders' relative power and its relevance to a particular issue facing the organization. In terms of potential for cooperation, the firm needs to be sensitive to the possibility of joining forces with stakeholders for the advantage of all parties involved. Several companies have entered into cooperative partnerships with the sustainability group Environmental Defense Fund (EDF).

Companies such as Facebook, Google, Boeing, and Procter & Gamble have participated in EDF's Climate Corps that was launched in 2008. In this program, students from leading business and public policy schools are trained and sent to major companies and organizations for summer fellowships. These Climate Corps Fellows have as their main task searching for energy savings. To date, these EDF Climate Corps Fellows have identified over $1 billion in energy savings.[48] In another example of collaboration, EDF and FedEx joined together in a cooperative relationship to launch the first "street ready" hybrid trucks ever built. Today, hundreds of these trucks are in the corporate fleets of UPS, Coca-Cola, and the U.S. Postal Service.

3.5d What Responsibilities Does a Firm Have toward Its Stakeholders?

The next logical question after identifying and understanding stakeholders' threats and opportunities is *"What responsibilities does a firm have in its relationships with its stakeholders?"* One way of answering this question might be to state what different stakeholder groups might logically expect from companies. If this is done, a list such as the following might be the result and it would certainly embrace at least one major outcome each group might expect:

- Shareholders—good return on their investment
- Employees—fair pay and good working conditions
- Customers—fair prices and safe products
- Local community—jobs and minimal disruption
- Suppliers—regular business and prompt payment[49]

Responsibilities also might be thought of in terms of the corporate social responsibility framework presented in Chapter 2. What economic, legal, ethical, and philanthropic responsibilities does management have toward each stakeholder? Because most of the firm's economic responsibilities are principally to itself and its shareholders, the analysis naturally turns to legal, ethical, and philanthropic questions. The most pressing threats are typically presented as legal and ethical issues. Often, opportunities are reflected in areas of philanthropy or "giving back" to the community.

It should be pointed out, however, that the firm itself has an economic stake in most legal and ethical issues it faces. For example, when Johnson & Johnson (J&J) faced the Tylenol poisoning crisis, it had to decide what legal and ethical actions to take and what actions were in the firm's best economic interests. In this classic case, J&J concluded that recalling the tainted Tylenol products was not only the ethical choice but also one that would preserve its reputation for being concerned about consumers' health and well-being. Figure 3-7 illustrates the **stakeholder responsibility matrix** that management might face when assessing the firm's responsibilities to stakeholders. The matrix may be seen as a template that managers might use to systematically think through its various responsibilities to each stakeholder group.

FIGURE 3-7 Stakeholder Responsibility Matrix

	Types of Responsibilities			
Stakeholders	Economic	Legal	Ethical	Philanthropic
Owners				
Customers				
Employees				
Community				
Public at Large				
Social Activist Groups				
Others				

3.5e What Strategies or Actions Should Management Take?

Once responsibilities have been assessed, an organization must contemplate strategies and actions for addressing its stakeholders. In every decision situation, a number of alternative courses of action are available, and management must choose one or several that seem best. Important questions or decision choices that management has before it in dealing with stakeholders include:

- Do we deal *directly* or *indirectly* with stakeholders?
- Do we take the *offense* or the *defense* in dealing with stakeholders?
- Do we *accommodate, negotiate, manipulate*, or *resist* stakeholder overtures?
- Do we employ a *combination of the aforementioned* strategies or pursue a *singular course* of action?[50]

In actual practice, managers need to prioritize stakeholder expectations and demands before deciding the appropriate strategy to employ.[51] In addition, strategic thinking in terms of forms of communication, degree of collaboration, development of policies or programs, and allocation of resources would need to be thought through carefully.[52] The development of specific strategies could be based on a classification of stakeholders' *potentials for cooperation and threat* discussed earlier. If these two factors are used, four stakeholder types and resultant generic strategies emerge: supportive, marginal, nonsupportive, and mixed blessing.[53]

***Type 1: Supportive* Stakeholder.** The **supportive stakeholder** is high on potential for cooperation and low on potential for threat. This is the ideal stakeholder. To a well-managed organization, supportive stakeholders might include its board of directors, managers, employees, and loyal customers. Others might be suppliers and service providers. The strategy with supporters is one of *involvement*. An example of this might be the strategy of engaging employee stakeholders through participative management or employee volunteerism.

***Type 2: Marginal* Stakeholder.** The **marginal stakeholder** is low on both potential for threat and potential for cooperation. For large organizations, these stakeholders might include professional associations of employees, inactive consumer interest groups, or shareholders—especially those that hold few shares and are not organized. The strategy here is for the organization to *monitor* the marginal stakeholder. Monitoring is especially called for to make sure circumstances do not change.

***Type 3: Nonsupportive* Stakeholder.** The **nonsupportive stakeholder** is high on potential for threat but low on potential for cooperation. Examples of this group could include competing organizations, unions, federal or other levels of government, and the media. Special-interest groups or NGOs often fall in this category. The recommended strategy here is to *defend* against the nonsupportive stakeholder.

An example of a special-interest group that many would regard as nonsupportive is the Earth Liberation Front (ELF), a movement that originated in the Pacific Northwest. It claimed responsibility for a string of arsons in the suburbs of Los Angeles, Detroit, and Philadelphia. ELF's attacks targeted luxury homes and sports utility vehicles (SUVs), the suburban status symbols that some environmentalists regard as despoilers of the Earth. Many such radical environmental groups have been called "eco-terrorists."[54] Such organizations do not seem interested in establishing positive, or supportive, relationships with companies and industries. In the examples discussed earlier, PETA and RAN typically come across as nonsupportive stakeholders because of their high potential for threat and reticence toward cooperation.

***Type 4: Mixed-Blessing* Stakeholder.** The **mixed-blessing stakeholder** is high on both potential for threat and potential for cooperation. Examples of this group, in a well-managed organization, might include employees who are in short supply, clients, or customers. A mixed-blessing stakeholder could become a supportive or a nonsupportive stakeholder. The recommended strategy here is to *collaborate* with the mixed-blessing stakeholder. By maximizing collaboration, the likelihood that this stakeholder will remain supportive is enhanced. Today, many companies regard sustainability groups as mixed blessings rather than nonsupportive. These firms are turning environmentalists into allies by building alliances with them for mutual gain.[55]

Figure 3-8 summarizes an analysis of stakeholder types and recommended strategies and actions.

FIGURE 3-8 Analyzing Stakeholders and Recommended Strategies and Actions

Stakeholder Type	Examples of Stakeholder Type	Stakeholder *Potential for Threat*	Stakeholder *Potential for Cooperation*	Strategy/Action Recommended
Supportive Stakeholder	Board of directors, some employees	Low	High	Involve; take offense, accommodate, proact; keep satisfied
Marginal Stakeholder	Professional associations, interest groups	Low	Low	Monitor; watch carefully; minimal effort; offense or defense
Nonsupportive Stakeholder	Competitors, unions, governments, some activist groups	High	Low	Defend; be prepared; guard against; negotiate
Mixed-Blessing Stakeholder	Employees, clients, customers	High	Medium-to-High	Collaborate; take offense, partnership, pool resources; keep informed

Sources: Compiled from multiple sources: Grant T. Savage, Timothy W. Nix, Carlton J. Whitehead, and John D. Blair, "Strategies for Assessing and Managing Organizational Stakeholders," *Academy of Management Executive* (Vol. V, No. 2, May 1991), 61–75; Ian C. MacMillan and Patricia E. Jones, *Strategy Formulation: Power and Politics* (St. Paul, MN: West, 1986), 66; "Stakeholder Management," http://pubs.opengroup.org/architecture/togaf9-doc/arch/chap24.html. Accessed March 31, 2016.

A summary guideline regarding these four stakeholder types might be stated in the following way:[56]

Managers should attempt to satisfy minimally the needs of marginal stakeholders and to satisfy maximally the needs of supportive and mixed blessing stakeholders, enhancing the latter's support for the organization.

The four stakeholder types and recommended strategies illustrate what was referred to earlier in this chapter as the "strategic" or instrumental view of stakeholders. It also could be argued that by taking stakeholders' needs and concerns into consideration, businesses' ethical treatment of them may be improved. It takes more than just consideration, however. Management still has an ethical responsibility toward stakeholders that extends beyond the strategic view. A fuller appreciation of this ethical responsibility is developed in Chapters 7 through 10.

Tapping Expertise of Stakeholders. Especially with "supportive" stakeholders, but potentially with the other categories as well, it has been proposed that managers can turn "gadflies into allies." Nonprofit special-interest groups, especially activist NGOs, hold great promise for cooperation if managements refrain from seeing them as "pests" and strive to get them to join in the company initiatives.[57] These NGOs have resources such as legitimacy, awareness of social forces, distinct networks, and specialized technical expertise that can be tapped by companies to gain competitive advantage.

ETHICS IN PRACTICE CASE

Chickens or Employees? Which Is the Most Important Stakeholder?

In October, 2015, Tyson Foods, Inc., the largest U.S. chicken processor, fired two of its employees at a Mississippi meatpacking plant. The firing occurred after an animal rights group, Mercy for Animals, released an undercover 2 ½-minute video that showed the workers mistreating the birds at the slaughterhouse. Mercy for Animals accused the firm of cruelty to chickens.

As a result of this disclosure, six Tyson employees and the company faced possible criminal charges of animal cruelty. A spokesman for Tyson said that the firm does not believe the behavior shown in the video represents the thousands of workers it employs across the country.

Mercy for Animals secretly recorded employees tossing, punching, throwing, and dismembering birds that had been improperly shackled and missed the blade designed to slaughter them.

The investigation at Tyson's plant was the fourth such probe by Mercy for Animals and the group was calling for Tyson to implement "meaningful animal welfare requirements" at its farms and plants.

The practice of exposing animal cruelty by way of undercover videos has become a controversial issue and some states ban the practice that some opponents call "ag-gag laws." The animal rights groups say that these videos are the only way to expose wrongdoing. Opponents of the practice say that the filmmakers get their jobs under false pretenses and that the videos misrepresent the meatpacking industry.

1. Are chickens stakeholders? Are animal rights groups stakeholders? If so what is the nature of their stake? Do they have legitimacy as stakeholders? If not, what is the nature of their stake?
2. What are the stakes of the company and employees in this type of situation? Are their stakes more important than those of the special interest groups?
3. Is it ethical for special interest groups to use undercover video techniques such as this?
4. What responsibilities does the company have toward its employees in this situation? To its chickens and special interest groups?
5. What strategies or actions should Tyson take to address the stakeholders in this case?

Sources: Mercy for Animals, Tyson Foods, 2015, http://www.mercyforanimals.org/investigations. Accessed March 31, 2016; "Tyson Fires Workers over Cruelty," *The Wall Street Journal*, October 29, 2015, B4; "Tyson Fires Two Workers after Video Shows Cruelty to Chickens," *BloombergBusiness*, October 28, 2015, http://www.bloomberg.com/news/articles/2015-10-28/tyson-fires-two-workers-after-video-shows-cruelty-to-chickens. Accessed March 31, 2016.

3.6 Effective Stakeholder Management

Effective stakeholder management is at the top of the list in terms of executive priorities today. This process requires a strong commitment on the part of managements and demands a careful assessment of the five key questions posed in this chapter. To deal successfully with those who assert claims on the organization, managers must understand these core questions. Business has been and will continue to be subjected to careful scrutiny of its actions, practices, policies, and ethics. Stakeholder management helps deal with these issues.

Criticisms of business and calls for better corporate citizenship have been the consequences of the changes in the business–society relationship, and the stakeholder approach to viewing the organization has become one needed response. To do less is to deny the realities of business's plight in the modern world, which is increasingly global in scope, and to fail to see the kinds of adaptations that are essential if businesses are to prosper now and in the future.

3.6a Stakeholder Thinking

Stakeholder thinking undergirds stakeholder management and is the process of always reasoning in stakeholder terms throughout the management process, and especially when organizations' decisions and actions have important implications for others. It is aligned with a **stakeholder mindset**, whereby managers look at the world if they start with a stakeholder "script" to create value for a wide array of stakeholders within their value chain.[58] However, some managers continue to think in shareholder terms because it is simpler. To think in stakeholder terms increases the complexity of decision making, and it is quite taxing for some managers to assess which stakeholders' claims take priority in a given situation. Despite its complexity, however, the stakeholder view is most consistent with the environment that business faces today, and "stakeholder thinking" has become a vital characteristic of effective stakeholder management.

In fairness, we should also note that there are criticisms and limitations of the stakeholder approach. One major criticism relates to the complexity and time-consuming nature of identifying, assessing, and responding to stakeholder claims, which constitute an extremely demanding process. Also, the ranking of stakeholder claims is no easy task. These challenges must be kept in mind as the approach is used in practice.

Effective stakeholder management is facilitated by a number of other useful concepts. The following concepts—stakeholder culture, stakeholder management capability, the stakeholder corporation model, and principles of stakeholder management—round out a useful approach to stakeholder management effectiveness. Each of these is considered in more detail.

3.6b Developing a Stakeholder Culture

In management circles, the importance of developing a strong, values-based corporate culture has been recognized as a key to successful enterprises. Corporate culture refers to the taken-for-granted beliefs, functional guidelines, ways of doing things, priorities, and values important to managers.[59] Within that context, developing a strong **stakeholder culture** is a major factor supporting successful stakeholder management. Stakeholder culture embraces the beliefs, values, and practices that organizations have developed for addressing stakeholder issues and relationships.

There are at least five categories of stakeholder cultures that reside on a continuum from little concern to great concern for stakeholders.[60] First is an *agency* culture, which basically is not concerned with others. Next are two cultures characterized by limited

SPOTLIGHT *on Sustainability*

Engaging Stakeholders on Sustainability

Many companies underestimate the importance of engaging their stakeholders on their sustainability initiatives. Enlightened companies have discovered that this is vitally important and have concluded there are some important guidelines for making this happen. Some of these guidelines include the following:

- Stakeholders need to be "on board" with your sustainability initiatives.
- Engage your stakeholders *sooner* rather than later. It is important to understand their perspectives and to be able to integrate them into your strategies and practices.
- Identify an *internal champion* who can help to align the interests of high priority stakeholders with high-level internal decision makers.
- Employ *internal education*. It is important to identify and prioritize internal stakeholders and to get them on board.
- Identify and engage your *most vocal critics*. It is important to find common ground early. These stakeholders can impact others both positively and negatively.
- Use *social media*. This will help engagement with stakeholders earlier and on a more timely basis.
- Use social media *openly and authentically*. Stakeholders will trust you more.
- Be accepting of *occasional disagreement and conflict*. This is bound to happen.
- Pay close attention to *consumer stakeholders*. They are frequently confused about sustainability messages. Many consumers are suspicious of green claims due to greenwashing.
- Pay close attention to *employees, NGOs, and the community stakeholders*. Employee engagement is critical to the success of engaging those outside the organization. Make it easy for them to participate.
- Face-to-face feedback and interactions are critical to success. Social media is important but not enough.

Sources: *Greenbiz*, "How to Engage Stakeholders on Sustainability," http://www.greenbiz.com/blog/2009/09/17/how-engage-stakeholders-sustainability. Accessed February 4, 2016; Ellis Roanhorse, "Effect of Sustainability on Stakeholders," *Houston Chronicle*, http://smallbusiness.chron.com/effect-sustainability-stakeholders-35892.html. Accessed February 4, 2016; "Stakeholders and Sustainability," *Business Case Studies*, http://businesscasestudies.co.uk/bt/sustainability-stakeholders-and-profits/stakeholders-and-sustainability.html#axzz3zDDiVV7L. Accessed March 31, 2016.

morality considerations—*corporate egoist* and *instrumentalist*—which focus mostly on the firm's shareholders as the important stakeholders. These cultures focus on short-term profit maximization. Finally are two cultures that are broadly moral—*moralist* and *altruist*. Both of these cultures are morally based and provide the broadest concern for stakeholders.[61] Effective stakeholder management requires the development of a robust corporate culture that broadly conceives of responsibilities to others. In the above scheme, the moralist and altruist cultures would be most compatible with stakeholder management and a stakeholder corporation.

3.6c Stakeholder Management Capability

Effective stakeholder management is also greatly affected by the extent to which the organization has developed its **stakeholder management capability (SMC)**.[62] Stakeholder management capability describes an organization's integration of stakeholder thinking into its processes and it may reside at one of three levels of increasing sophistication: rational, process, transactional. The **rational level** of SMC simply entails the company identifying who their stakeholders are and what their stakes happen to be. This is the level that would enable management to create a basic stakeholder map, such as that depicted in Figure 3-3. This represents a beginning, or entry level of SMC. This first level has also been termed by Mark Starik as the element of *familiarization* and *comprehensiveness*, because the management operating at Level 1 is seeking to become familiar with their stakeholders and to develop a comprehensive assessment of their identification and stakes.[63]

At Level 2, the **process level**, organizations go a step further than Level 1 and actually develop and implement processes—approaches, procedures, policies, and practices—by which the firm may scan the environment and gather pertinent information about stakeholders, which is then used for decision-making purposes. An applicable stakeholder principle here is "constantly monitoring and redesigning processes to better serve stakeholders."[64] This second level has been described as *planning integrativeness*, because the management does focus on planning processes for stakeholders and integrating a consideration for stakeholders into organizational decision making.[65]

The **transactional level**, Level 3, is the highest and most developed of the three levels. This is the utmost goal for stakeholder management—the extent to which managers actually engage in transactions (relationships) with stakeholders.[66] At this highest level of SMC, in which a *transformation* of the business and society relationship occurs, management must take the initiative in meeting stakeholders face to face and attempting to be responsive to their needs. The transactional level may require actual negotiations with stakeholders.[67] This Level 3 is the *communication* level, which is characterized by *communication proactiveness, interactiveness, genuineness, frequency, satisfaction*, and *resource adequacy*. Resource adequacy refers to the management actually spending resources on stakeholder transactions.[68] Regarding stakeholder communications, a relevant principle is that business must "engage in intensive communication and dialogue with (all) stakeholders, not just those who are friendly."[69]

An example of successful Level 3 SMC has been the relationship established between General Motors Corporation (GM) and the Coalition for Environmentally Responsible Economies (Ceres). Over a decade ago, these two organizations actually began to talk with one another, and the result was a mutually beneficial collaboration. The arrangement became a high-profile example of a growing trend within the sustainability movement—that of using quiet discussions, engagement, and negotiations rather than noisy protests to change corporate behavior.

3.6d Stakeholder Engagement

Recently, there has been growing interest in the topic of stakeholder engagement. **Stakeholder engagement** may be seen as an approach by which companies successfully implement the transactional level (Level 3) of strategic management capability. Companies may employ different strategies in terms of the degree of engagement with their stakeholders, but best practices suggest that interaction with stakeholders must be integrated into every level of decision making in the organization.[70]

Ladder of Stakeholder Engagement. A ladder of stakeholder engagement, which depicts a number of steps from low engagement to high engagement, represents a continuum of engagement postures that companies might follow.[71] *Lower* levels of stakeholder engagement might be used for informing and explaining. Formats at this level might include news coverage, publications, or reports. *Middle* levels of engagement would focus on communicating by way of formats such as conferences, social media, mass e-mails, newsletters, or surveys. *Higher* levels of stakeholder engagement might be active or responsive attempts to involve stakeholders in company decision making. At the highest level, terms such as *involvement, collaboration, partnership* or *joint venture* might be appropriate descriptions of the high-priority relationship established.

An example of this highest level would be when a firm enters into a strategic alliance with a stakeholder group to seek the group's opinion of a product design that would be sensitive to the group's concerns, such as environmental impact, employee safety, or product safety. This was illustrated when McDonald's entered into an alliance with the Environmental Defense Fund to eliminate polystyrene packaging that was not biodegradable.[72]

ETHICS IN PRACTICE CASE

Something's Rotten in Hondo

George Mackee thought of himself as bright, energetic, and with lots of potential. "So why is this happening to me?" he thought. George, with his wife, Mary, and his two children, had moved to Hondo, Texas, from El Paso four years earlier and was now the manager of the Ardnak Plastics plant in Hondo, a small plant that manufactured plastic parts for small equipment. The plant employed several hundred workers, which was a substantial portion of the population of Hondo. Ardnak Plastics Inc. had several other small plants the size of Hondo's. George had a good relationship with Bill, his boss, in Austin, Texas.

The Emissions Problem. One of the problems George's plant had was that the smokestack emissions were consistently above EPA guidelines. Several months ago, George got a call from Bill, stating that the EPA had contacted him about the problem and fines would be levied. George admitted the situation was a continual problem, but because headquarters would not invest in new smokestack scrubbers, he didn't know what to do. Bill replied by saying that margins were at their limits and there was no money for new scrubbers. Besides, Bill commented, other plants were in worse shape than his and they were passing EPA standards.

A Questionable Solution. George ended the conversation by assuring Bill that he would look into the matter. He immediately started calling his contemporaries at other Ardnak plants. He found they were scheduling their heavy emissions work at night so that during the day when the EPA took their sporadic readings they were within standards. George contemplated this option even though it would result in increasing air contamination levels.

The Double Bind. A month went by, and George still had not found a solution. The phone rang; it was Bill. Bill expressed his displeasure with the new fines for the month and reminded George that there were very few jobs out in the industry. That's when Bill dropped the whole thing into George's lap. Bill had been speaking to the Mexican government and had received assurances that no such clean air restrictions would be imposed on Ardnak if they relocated 15 miles south of Hondo in Mexico. However, Ardnak must hire Mexican workers. Bill explained that the reason for relocating would be to eliminate the EPA problems. Bill told George he had one week to decide whether to eliminate the fines by correcting the current problems or by relocating.

George knew that relocating the plant on the Mexican side would devastate the infrastructure of the city of Hondo and would continue to put contaminants into the air on the U.S. side. When he mentioned the possibility to Mary, she reinforced other concerns. She did not want him to be responsible for the loss of the jobs of their friends and extended families.

1. Who are the stakeholders in this situation, and what are their stakes?
2. What social responsibility, if any, does Ardnak Plastics Inc. have to the city of Hondo?
3. What are the ethical issues in this case?
4. What should George do? Why?

Source: This case was written by Geoffrey P. Lantos, Stonehill College. Permission to reprint granted by Arthur Andersen & Co., SC.

Transparency. The concept of stakeholder engagement is relevant to developing what Tapscott and Ticoll refer to as *The Naked Corporation*. In their book, they argue that in the characteristics of the open enterprise, "environmental engagement" and "stakeholder engagement" are two critical factors. Environmental engagement calls for an open operating environment: sustainable ecosystems, peace, order, and good public governance. Stakeholder engagement calls for these open enterprises to put resources and effort into reviewing, managing, recasting, and strengthening relationships with stakeholders, old and new.[73] The "open enterprise" with an emphasis on "transparency" has become crucial because of the ongoing corporate scandals of recent years. Transparency is becoming an increasingly important attribute of successful stakeholder engagements.

Engaging on Sustainability. One of the most important concerns today is engaging stakeholders on sustainability. The idea here is to involve stakeholders such as the social media, consumers, NGOs, and communities as early as possible on sustainability developments and initiatives. "Sustainability Stakeholder Engagement" conferences are now being held to facilitate this process. One of the unique aspects of these conferences has been the increasing use of social media technologies, such as Twitter, to engage stakeholders in a more timely fashion.[74]

The Coca-Cola Company recently employed stakeholder engagement on sustainability with a variety of its stakeholders. Examples of their stakeholders and how they engage them include the following:

- Bottling partners. Day-to-day interactions with business partners, joint projects, participation in Global Environment Council.
- Consumers. Hotlines, consumer Web sites, plant tours, surveys, focus groups.
- Communities. Meetings, plant visits, partnerships on common issues, sponsorships.
- Employees. Engagement surveys, town hall meetings, individual development plans, employee well-being projects.

Other stakeholders engaged in the process include governments and regulatory bodies, nongovernmental organizations (NGOs), shareholders, analysts, suppliers, and trade associations. Two of their primary engagement topics include water sustainability/stewardship and sustainable agriculture. Coke's engagement with stakeholders has helped produce their Sustainable Agriculture Guiding Principles and the company believes that their stakeholder engagement initiatives on sustainability have reaped significant benefits. Coca-Cola believes that continuous dialogue and engagement is critical to respecting human and workplace rights within their system.[75]

Stakeholder Dialogue. Another element in stakeholder engagement is stakeholder dialogue. Stakeholder dialogue is primarily focused on exchanging communications with stakeholder groups and thus it is one form of engagement. When considering stakeholder dialogue among global stakeholders, it is worth noting that different countries are characterized by different approaches. In one major study, for example, it was found that stakeholder dialogue varied among three major countries—Germany, Italy, and the United States. Both Germany and Italy employed a more *implicit* approach, whereas the U.S. used a more *explicit* approach.[76] The approaches to stakeholder dialogue were more *focused* in Germany, more *engaging* in Italy, and more *strategic* in the United States. A major conclusion of this study was that stakeholder dialogue has to be tailored to the national business system and that attempts to develop universal principles or guidelines may be imprudent.

3.6e The Stakeholder Corporation

Perhaps the ultimate form or goal of the stakeholder approach or stakeholder management might be called the "**stakeholder corporation**." The central element of this concept is **stakeholder inclusiveness**.[77] Wheeler and Sillanpää say the following about this:

> *In the future, development of loyal relationships with customers, employees, shareholders, and other stakeholders will become one of the most important determinants of commercial viability and business success. Increasing shareholder value will be best served if your company cultivates the support of all who may influence its importance.*

Advocates of the stakeholder corporation would embrace the idea of "**stakeholder symbiosis**," which recognizes that all stakeholders depend on each other for their success and financial well-being.[78] It is the acceptance of this mutuality of interests that makes the difference in a firm becoming a stakeholder corporation. As James Post has summarized, "The stakeholder corporation is characterized by leaders who understand the need to balance, prioritize, and adjust to the needs of all constituencies."[79]

3.6f Principles of Stakeholder Management

On the basis of years of observation and research, a set of "**principles of stakeholder management**" was developed for use by managers and organizations. These principles, also known as the **Clarkson Principles**, were named after the late Max Clarkson, a dedicated researcher on the topic of stakeholder management. The principles are intended to provide managers with guiding precepts regarding how stakeholders should be treated. The key words in the principles are action words that reflect the kind of cooperative spirit that should be used in building stakeholder relationships: *acknowledge, monitor, listen, communicate, adopt, recognize, work, avoid,* and *acknowledge potential conflicts.* These principles serve as guidelines for successful stakeholder management.[80]

3.7 Strategic Steps toward Global Stakeholder Management

The global competition that characterizes business firms in the 21st century necessitates a stakeholder approach, for both effective and ethical management. The stakeholder approach requires that stakeholders be moved to the center of management's vision. Three strategic steps may be taken that can lead today's global competitors toward the more balanced view that is needed in today's dynamic business environment.[81]

1. **Governing Philosophy.** *Integrating stakeholder management into the firm's governing philosophy.* Boards of directors and top management groups should move the organization from the idea of "shareholder agent" to "stakeholder trustee." Long-term shareholder value, along with sustainability, will be the objective of this transition in corporate governance.
2. **Values Statement.** *Create a stakeholder-inclusive "values statement."* Various firms have done this under various titles. Twitter calls this a "mission statement" focusing on sharing ideas instantly. Whole Foods Market has its "Higher Purpose Statement" that calls for courage, integrity, and love. L. L. Bean has a "core values statement" which focuses on customer stakeholders being treated well so they will always come back. Regardless of what such a values statement is called, such a pledge publicly reinforces the organization's commitment to stakeholders.
3. **Measurement System.** *Implement a stakeholder performance measurement system.* Such a system should be integrated, monitored, and auditable as stakeholder relations are improved. Measurement is evidence of serious intent to achieve results, and such a system will motivate a sustainable commitment to the stakeholder view. One recent example of a measurement system has been Walmart's creation of a *worldwide sustainability index.* With this initiative, the company is helping create a more transparent supply chain, driving product innovation, and ultimately providing customers with information they need to assess products' sustainability.[82]

3.7a Implementation

The acid test of effective stakeholder management is in its *implementation*. Implementation implies the following key activities: execution, application, operationalization, and enactment. Corporate social responsibility and sustainability are made operable when companies translate their stakeholder dialogue into practice.[83] After studying three large, successful companies in detail—Cummins Engine Company, Motorola, and the Royal Dutch/Shell Group—prominent researchers concluded that the key to effective implementation is in recognizing and using stakeholder management as a *core competence.*

When this is done, at least four indicators or manifestations of successful stakeholder management will be apparent. First, stakeholder management results in *survival.* Second, there are many *avoided costs.* Third, there was *continued acceptance and use* in the companies studied, implying success. Fourth, there was evidence of *expanded recognition and adoption* of stakeholder-oriented policies by other companies and consultants.[84] These indicators suggest the value and practical benefits that may be derived from implementing the stakeholder approach. Finally, it should be noted that organizations develop learning processes over time in implementing their changing or evolving stakeholder orientations.[85]

Summary

A stakeholder is an individual or a group that claims to have one or more stakes in an organization. Stakeholders may affect the organization and, in turn, be affected by the organization's actions, policies, practices, and decisions. The stakeholder approach extends beyond the traditional production and managerial views of the firm and warrants a much broader conception of the parties involved in the organization's functioning and success. Both primary and secondary social and nonsocial stakeholders assume significant roles in the eyes of management. A typology of stakeholders suggests that three attributes are especially important: legitimacy, power, and urgency. Proximity also may be a salient factor.

Strategic, multifiduciary, and stakeholder synthesis approaches help us appreciate the strategies that may be adopted with regard to stakeholders. The stakeholder synthesis approach is encouraged because it highlights the ethical responsibility business has to its stakeholders. The stakeholder view of the firm has three values that make it useful: descriptive, instrumental, and normative. In a balanced perspective, managers are concerned with both goal achievement and ethical treatment of stakeholders.

Five key questions assist managers in stakeholder management: (1) Who are the firm's stakeholders? (2) What are our stakeholders' stakes? (3) What challenges or opportunities are presented to a firm by stakeholders? (4) What responsibilities does a firm have to its stakeholders? (5) What strategies or actions should a firm take with respect to its stakeholders? Effective stakeholder management requires the assessment and appropriate response to these five questions. In addition, the use of other relevant stakeholder thinking concepts is helpful. Identifying **stakeholder utility**, or value, is important.

Approaching stakeholder relationships with a mindset to creating value, and developing a stakeholder culture, is also vital. The concept of SMC illustrates how firms can grow and mature in their approach to stakeholder management. Stakeholder engagement emphasizes carefully selecting an engagement approach—informing, communicating, or actually engaging. The stakeholder corporation is a model that represents stakeholder thinking in its most advanced form and stakeholder inclusion is the central element.

Principles of stakeholder management are helpful in guiding managers toward more effective stakeholder thinking. Although the stakeholder management approach is quite complex and time consuming, it is a way of managing that is in tune with the complex, dynamic environment that business organizations face today. Strategic steps in global stakeholder management include making stakeholders a part of the guiding philosophy, creating corporate value statements, and developing measurement systems that monitor results. In the final analysis, implementation is the key to effective stakeholder management.

Key Terms

Clarkson Principles, p. 96
Descriptive value (of stakeholder model), p. 80
Instrumental value (of stakeholder model), p. 80
Key questions (in stakeholder management), p. 81
legitimacy, p. 77
managerial view of the firm, p. 74
marginal stakeholder, p. 89
mixed-blessing stakeholder, p. 89
multifiduciary approach to stakeholders, p. 79
nonsupportive stakeholder, p. 89

normative value (of stakeholder model), p. 80
power, p. 77
primary nonsocial stakeholders, p. 76
primary social stakeholders, p. 76
principles of stakeholder management, p. 96
process level, p. 93
production view of the firm, p. 74
proximity, p. 78
rational level, p. 92
secondary nonsocial stakeholders, p. 76
secondary social stakeholders, p. 76
stake, p. 72
stakeholder, p. 71
stakeholder corporation, p. 95
stakeholder culture, p. 91
stakeholder engagement, p. 93
stakeholder inclusiveness, p. 95
stakeholder management, p. 81
stakeholder management capability (SMC), p. 92
stakeholder map, p. 75
stakeholder mindset, p. 91
stakeholder responsibility matrix, p. 87
stakeholder symbiosis, p. 95
stakeholder thinking, p. 91
stakeholder utility, p. 97
stakeholder view of the firm, p. 74
supportive stakeholder, p. 88
synthesis approach to stakeholders, p. 79
transactional level, p. 93
urgency, p. 78

Discussion Questions

1. Explain the concepts of stake and stakeholder from your perspective as an individual. What kinds of stakes and stakeholders do you have? Discuss.
2. Explain in your own words the differences between the production, managerial, and stakeholder views of the firm. Which view is best and why?
3. Differentiate between primary and secondary social and nonsocial stakeholders in a business situation. Give examples of each.
4. What are the five key questions that must be answered for stakeholder management to be successful?
5. What are the three levels of stakeholder engagement that a company might use? Explain each.
6. Is the stakeholder corporation a realistic model for business firms? Will stakeholder corporations become more prevalent in the 21st century? Why or why not?

Endnotes

1. See, for example, Jill A. Brown and William R. Forster, "CSR and Stakeholder Theory: A Tale of Adam Smith," *Journal of Business Ethics* (Vol. 112, 2013), 301–312; Robert A. Phillips, "Stakeholder Theory and a Principle of Fairness," *Business Ethics Quarterly* (Vol. 7, No. 1, January 1997), 51–66; Sandra A. Waddock and Samuel B. Graves, "Quality of Management and Quality of Stakeholder Relations," *Business and Society* (Vol. 36, No. 3, September 1997), 250–279; James P. Walsh, "Taking Stock of Stakeholder Management," *Academy of Management Review* (Vol. 30, No. 2, 2005), 426–438; Thomas Jones and Andrew Wicks, 1999, "Convergent Stakeholder Theory," *Academy of Management Review* (Vol. 20, 1999), 404–437.
2. David Wheeler and Maria Sillanpää, *The Stakeholder Corporation: A Blueprint for Maximizing Stakeholder Value* (London: Pitman Publishing, 1997).
3. Steven F. Walker and Jeffrey W. Marr, *Stakeholder Power: A Winning Plan for Building Stakeholder Commitment and Driving Corporate Growth* (Cambridge, MA: Perseus Publishing, 2001).
4. James E. Post, Lee E. Preston, and Sybille Sachs, *Redefining the Corporation: Stakeholder Management and Organizational Wealth* (Stanford: Stanford University Press, 2002).
5. Robert Phillips and R. Edward Freeman, *Stakeholders*, Edward Elgar Pub, 2010. Also see Ed Freeman, Jeffrey Harrison, Bidhan Parmar, and Simone De Colle. *Stakeholder Theory: The State of the Art*, 2010, Cambridge University Press, New York.
6. Jeanne M. Logsdon, Donna J. Wood, and Lee E. Benson, "Research in Stakeholder Theory, 1997–1998: The Sloan Foundation Minigrant Project" (Toronto: The Clarkson Centre for Business Ethics, 2000).
7. Jeffrey S. Harrison and Andrew C. Wicks, "Stakeholder Theory, Value and Firm Performance," *Business Ethics Quarterly*, January 2013, 97–124.
8. Vivek Soundararajan and Jill Brown, "Voluntary Governance Mechanisms in Global Supply Chains: Beyond CSR to a Stakeholder Utility Perspective," *Journal of Business Ethics* (2014), 1–20. DOI: 10.1007/s10551-014-2418-y.
9. This definition is similar to that of R. Edward Freeman in *Strategic Management: A Stakeholder Approach* (Boston: Pitman, 1984), 25.
10. George Kassinis, "The Value of Managing Stakeholders," in Pratima Bansal and Andrew Hoffman (eds.), *The*

Oxford Handbook of Business and the Natural Environment, Oxford: Oxford University Press, 2012.

11. "The Many Stakeholders of Salesforce.com," *The Wall Street Journal*, October 27, 2015, R2.
12. Mark Starik, "Is the Environment an Organizational Stakeholder? Naturally!" *International Association for Business and Society (IABS) 1993 Proceedings*, 466–471.
13. David Woodward, "Is the Natural Environment a Stakeholder? Of Course It Is (No Matter What the Utilitarians Might Say)," in *Critical Perspectives on Accounting Conference*, New York, April 25–27, 2002, New York: Baruch College, City University of New York.
14. Freeman, 5.
15. Freeman, 24–25. Also see James E. Post, Lee E. Preston, and Sybille Sachs, 2002. Ibid.
16. Wheeler and Sillanpää (1997), 167.
17. Ibid., 168.
18. Gideon D. Markman, Theodore L. Waldron, and Andreas Panagopoulos, "Organizational Hostility: Why and How Nonmarket Players Compete with Firms," *Academy of Management Perspectives* 2016, Vol. 30, No. 1, 74–92.
19. Ronald K. Mitchell, Bradley R. Agle, and Donna J. Wood, "Toward a Theory of Stakeholder Identification and Salience: Defining the Principle of Who and What Really Counts," *Academy of Management Review* (October 1997), 853–886.
20. Bernd Helmig, Katharina Spraul, and Diana Ingenhoff. "Under Positive Pressure: How Stakeholder Pressure Affects Corporate Social Responsibility Implementation," *Business and Society* (Vol. 55, No.2, 2016), 151–187.
21. Mark Starik and Cathy Driscoll, "The Primordial Stakeholder: Advancing the Conceptual Consideration of Stakeholder Status for the Natural Environment," in A. J. Zakhem, D. E. Palmer, and M. L. Stoll (eds.) *Stakeholder Theory: Essential Readings in Ethical Leadership and Management* (Amherst, NY: Prometheus Books, 2007), 219–222.
22. Ibid.
23. Jim Carlton, "How Home Depot and Activists Joined to Cut Logging Abuse," *The Wall Street Journal* (September 26, 2000), A1.
24. Benjamin A. Neville, Simon J. Bell, and Gregory J. Whitwell, "Stakeholder Salience Revisited: Refining, Redefining, and Refueling an Underdeveloped Conceptual Tool," *Journal of Business Ethics* (Vol. 102, No. 1, 2011), 357–378.
25. Kenneth E. Goodpaster, "Business Ethics and Stakeholder Analysis," *Business Ethics Quarterly* (Vol. 1, No. 1, January 1991), 53–73.
26. Ibid.
27. Johanna Kujala, Anna Heikkinen, and Hanna Lehtimaki, "Understanding the Nature of Stakeholder Relationships: An Empirical Examination of a Conflict Situation," *Journal of Business Ethics* (Vol. 109, 2012), 53–65.
28. Thomas Donaldson and Lee Preston, "The Stakeholder Theory of the Corporation: Concepts, Evidence, Implications," *Academy of Management Review* (Vol. 20, No. 1, 1995), 65–91.
29. Ibid.
30. Robert Phillips, *Stakeholder Theory and Organizational Ethics*, San Francisco: Berrett-Koehler Publishers, Inc., 2003, 85–118.
31. Donaldson and Preston.
32. Parallel questions are posed with respect to corporate strategy by Ian C. MacMillan and Patricia E. Jones, *Strategy Formulation: Power and Politics* (St. Paul, MN: West, 1986), 66.
33. "Animal Rights Group Aims Ad Attack at McDonald's," *The Wall Street Journal* (August 30, 1999), B7. Also see http://www.mccruelty.com/why.aspx. Accessed March 31, 2016.
34. Marcia Yablon, "Happy Hen, Happy Meal: McDonald's Chick Fix," *U.S. News & World Report* (September 4, 2000), 46.
35. Ibid.
36. "McCruelty: I'm Hatin' It," http://www.mccruelty.com/. Accessed March 31, 2016.
37. PETA, "Denny's Scores One for Animals," http://www.peta.org/blog/denny-s-scores-one-animals/. Accessed March 31, 2016.
38. Kerry Capell, "The Wool Industry Gets Bloodied," *BusinessWeek* (July 14 & 21, 2008), 40. Also see http://www.peta.org/issues/animals-used-for-clothing/wool-industry.aspx. Accessed March 31, 2016.
39. Gina-Marie Cheeseman, *Triple Pundit*, "The North Face Sources Only Cruelty-Free Down," http://www.triplepundit.com/2016/01/north-face-sources-cruelty-free/. Accessed March 31, 2016.
40. Nathan Borney, "SeaWorld to Phase Out Its Killer Whale Shows, Captivity," *USA Today*, March 17, 2016, http://www.usatoday.com/story/money/2016/03/17/seaworld-orcas-killer-whales/81900498/. Accessed March 31, 2016.
41. R. Edward Freeman, S.R. Velamuri, and Brian Moriarty, "Company Stakeholder Responsibility: A New Approach to CSR," Business Roundtable Institute for Corporate Ethics, Bridge Paper, 2006, 11.
42. John Browne and Robin Nuttall, "Beyond Corporate Social Responsibility: Integrated External Engagement," *McKinsey Quarterly*, March 2013, http://www.mckinsey.com/insights/strategy/beyond_corporate_social_responsibility_integrated_external_engagement. Accessed March 31, 2016.
43. "Does It Pay to Be Ethical?" *Business Ethics* (March/April 1997), 14. "What's Your Poison?" *The Economist* (August 9, 2003), 50. Web site of Rain Forest Action Network: http://www.ran.org/. Accessed June 25, 2010. Also see Jeanne Whalen, "Drug Giant Is Targeted by Attacks," *The Wall Street Journal* (August 5, 2009), 1.

44. Rainforest Acton Network, "Mission and Strategy," http://www.ran.org/our_mission. Accessed March 31, 2016.

45. Rainforest Action Network, "Forests," http://ran.org/forests. Accessed March 31, 2016.

46. Rainforest Action Network, http://ran.org/challenging-corporations. Accessed March 31, 2016.

47. Grant T. Savage, Timothy W. Nix, Carlton J. Whitehead, and John D. Blair, "Strategies for Assessing and Managing Organizational Stakeholders," *Academy of Management Executive* (Vol. V, No. 2, May 1991), 61–75.

48. Environmental Defense Fund, "Partnerships: The Key to Scalable Solutions," http://www.edf.org/approach/partnerships/corporate. Accessed March 31, 2016.

49. Tutor2U, "Organization: Business Stakeholders, Social Responsibility & Ethics, http://www.tutor2u.net/business/reference/organisation-business-stakeholders-social-responsibility-ethics. Accessed March 31, 2016.

50. MacMillan and Jones, 66–70.

51. John F. Preble, "Toward a Comprehensive Model of Stakeholder Management," *Business and Society Review* (Vol. 110, No. 4, 2005), 421–423.

52. Ibid., 415.

53. Savage, Nix, Whitehead, and Blair, 65.

54. Seth Hettena and Laura Wides, "Eco-Terrorists Coming Out of the Wild," *USA Today* (October 3, 2003), 22A. Also see Anti-Defamation League, "Extremism in America," http://archive.adl.org/learn/ext_us/default.html?LEARN_Cat=Extremism&LEARN_SubCat=Extremism_in_America&xpicked=1&item=0. Accessed March 31, 2016.

55. Geewax, E7.

56. Savage, Nix, Whitehead, and Blair, 72.

57. Michael Yaziji, "Turning Gadflies into Allies," *Harvard Business Review* (February 2004), 110–115.

58. Andrew C. Wicks, Adrian. C. Keevil and Bidhan Parmar, "Sustainable Business Development and Management Theories," *Business and Professional Ethics Journal* (Vol. 31, No.3/4, 2012), 375–398.

59. C. Geertz, *The Interpretation of Cultures: Selected Essays* (New York: Basic Books, 1973). See also, M. J. Hatch, "The Dynamics of Organizational Culture," *Academy of Management Review* (Vol. 18, 1993), 657–693.

60. Thomas M. Jones, Will Felps, and Gregory A. Bigley, "Ethical Theory and Stakeholder-Related Decisions: The Role of Stakeholder Culture," *Academy of Management Review* (Vol. 32, No. 1, 2007), 137–155.

61. Ibid.

62. Freeman, 53.

63. Mark Starik, "Stakeholder Management and Firm Performance: Reputation and Financial Relationships to U.S. Electric Utility Consumer-Related Strategies," unpublished Ph.D. dissertation, University of Georgia, 1990, 34.

64. Freeman, Velamur, and Moriarty (2006), 11.

65. Starik (1990), 36.

66. Freeman, 69–70.

67. Freeman, Velamur, and Moriarty (2006), 11.

68. Starik (1990), 36–42.

69. Freeman, Velamur, and Moriarty (2006), 11.

70. Browne and Nuttall, 2013, ibid.

71. Andrew L. Friedman and Samantha Miles, *Stakeholders: Theory and Practice* (Oxford: Oxford University Press, 2006), 160–179.

72. Ibid., 175. Also see Laura Dunham, R. Edward Freeman, and Jeanne Liedtka, "Enhancing Stakeholder Practice: A Particularized Exploration of Community," *Business Ethics Quarterly* (Vol. 16, 1, 2006), 23–42.

73. Don Tapscott and David Ticoll, *The Naked Corporation: How the Age of Transparency Will Revolutionize Business* (Free Press, 2003).

74. Perry Goldschein and Beth Bengston, "How to Engage Stakeholders on Sustainability," *GreenBiz.com*, http://www.greenbiz.com/blog/2009/09/17/how-engage-stakeholders-sustainability. Accessed January 25, 2016.

75. Coca-Cola Company, "Sustainability: Stakeholder Engagement," July 23, 2015, http://www.coca-colacompany.com/stories/stakeholder-engagement/. Accessed March 31, 2016.

76. Lorenzo Patelli, "Stakeholder Dialogue in Germany, Italy, and the United States," *Director Notes, The Conference Board,* New York: The Conference Board, July 2012.

77. Wheeler and Sillanpää (1997), book cover.

78. "Stakeholder Symbiosis," *Fortune* (March 30, 1998), S2–S4, special advertising section.

79. James Post, "Governance and the Stakeholder Corporation: New challenges for Global Business," Corporate Public Affairs Oration, Melbourne, 24 June 2004. Cited on http://trevorcook.typepad.com/weblog/2005/07/the_stakeholder.html. Accessed February 16, 2016.

80. *Principles of Stakeholder Management*. 1999. Toronto: The Clarkson Centre for Business Ethics, School of Management, University of Toronto, 4.

81. "Measurements," *Measuring and Managing Stakeholder Relationships* (Indianapolis: Walker Information Global Network, 1998).

82. "Sustainability Index," http://corporate.walmart.com/global-responsibility/environment-sustainability/sustainability-index-leaders-shop. Accessed March 31, 2016.

83. Esben Rahbek Pedersen, "Making Corporate Social Responsibility (CSR) Operable: How Companies Translate Stakeholder Dialogue into Practice," *Business and Society Review* (Vol. 111, No. 2, 2006), 137–163.

84. James E. Post, Lee E. Preston, Sybille Sachs, "Managing the Extended Enterprise: The New Stakeholder View," *California Management Review* (Vol. 45, No. 1, Fall 2002), 22–25.

85. Marc Maurer and Sybille Sachs, "Implementing the Stakeholder View," *Journal of Corporate Citizenship* (Vol. 17, Spring 2005), 93–107.

PART 2

Corporate Governance and Strategic Management Issues

CHAPTER 4
Corporate Governance: Foundational Issues

CHAPTER 5
Strategic Management and Corporate Public Policy

CHAPTER 6
Risk, Issue, and Crisis Management

4

Corporate Governance: Foundational Issues

CHAPTER LEARNING OUTCOMES

After studying this chapter, you should be able to:

1 Link the issue of legitimacy to corporate governance.

2 Discuss the problems that have led to the recent spate of corporate scandals and problems in corporate governance.

3 Discuss the principal ways in which companies can improve corporate governance.

4 Discuss the role of shareholders and the idea of strengthening shareholder voice. What are some of the mechanisms that enable this?

5 Discuss the role of the SEC in protecting investors.

6 Discuss the principal ways in which shareholder activists exert pressure on corporate management to improve governance.

7 Discuss investor relations and the concept of shareholder engagement.

In this second part of the book, we more closely examine how management has responded, and *should* respond, to the social, ethical, and stakeholder issues developed throughout this book. This chapter explores the ways in which the board and top managers govern the corporation. In Chapters 5 and 6, the view expands to look at how these social ethical and stakeholder issues fit into not only the strategic management and corporate public affairs functions of the firm but also the management of issues and crises.

We begin by examining the concept of legitimacy and the part that corporate governance plays in establishing the legitimacy of business. We then explore how good corporate governance can mitigate the problems created by the separation of ownership and control and examine some of the specific challenges facing those involved in corporate governance today.

4.1 Legitimacy and Corporate Governance

Corporate governance took center stage at the dawn of the 21st century. The bankruptcy of Enron, once the seventh largest company in the United States, as well as those of corporate giants WorldCom, Global Crossing, and Parmalat, sent shock waves through the corporate world. When a host of firms subsequently issued earnings restatements, investors throughout the world began wondering where they could place their trust. A few years later, the global financial crisis struck and investors were stunned as they watched their life savings shrivel. More recently, Toshiba's accounting irregularities, the Volkswagen emissions-rigging scandal, General Motor's delay in recalling faulty ignition switches, the FIFA corruption probe, and Turing and Valeant Pharmaceuticals' drug-pricing scandals further chipped away at the public's trust. Events like these threaten the institution of business as a whole by calling the legitimacy of the institution of business into question. For example, in a 2015 Gallup poll, people had more confidence in the military, the public schools, and even the television news than they had in big business.[1] As noted by one governance expert, "We can do better. And with trillions of dollars of wealth governance by these rules of the game, we must do better."[2]

To understand corporate governance, it is important to understand the idea of **legitimacy**. Legitimacy is a somewhat abstract concept, but it is vital in that it helps explain the importance of the relative roles of a corporation's charter, shareholders, board of directors, management, and employees—all of which are components of the modern corporate governance system. We utilize a slightly modified version of Talcott Parsons's definition of legitimacy. He argued, "Organizations are legitimate to the extent that their activities are congruent with the goals and values of the social system within which they function."[3] From this definition, we may see legitimacy as a condition that prevails when there is congruence between the organization's activities and society's expectations. Thus,

8 Compare and contrast the shareholder-primacy and director-primacy models of corporate governance. What are their respective strengths and weaknesses? Which do you prefer and why?

whereas legitimacy is a condition, **legitimation** is a dynamic process by which business seeks to perpetuate its acceptance. We emphasize the dynamic process aspect because society's norms and values change, and business must change if its legitimacy is to continue. It is also useful to consider legitimacy at both the micro, or company, level and the macro, or business institution, level.

At the *micro level of legitimacy*, we refer to individual business firms achieving and maintaining legitimacy by conforming to societal expectations. Companies seek legitimacy in several ways. First, a company may adapt its methods of operating to conform to what it perceives to be the prevailing standard. For example, a company may discontinue door-to-door selling if that marketing approach comes to be viewed in the public mind as a shoddy sales technique,[4] or a pharmaceutical company may discontinue offering free drug samples to medical students if this practice begins to take on the aura of a bribe. Second, a company may try to change the public's values and norms to conform to its own practices by advertising and other techniques.[5] For example, vitamin retailer GNC Holdings, Inc. has been successful at this in their promotion of nutritional supplements.[6]

Finally, an organization may seek to enhance its legitimacy by identifying itself with other organizations, people, values, or symbols that have a powerful legitimate base in society.[7] This occurs at several levels. At the national level, companies proudly announce appointments of celebrities, former politicians, or other famous people to managerial positions or board directorships. For example, a recent study found that more than 45 percent of senators who have left office since 1992 have served on the board of a publicly traded firm.[8] At the community level, a company may ask the winning local football coach to provide an endorsement by sitting on its board or promoting its products.[9]

The *macro level of legitimacy* is the level with which we are most concerned in this chapter. The macro level refers to the corporate system—the totality of business enterprises. It is difficult to talk about the legitimacy of business in pragmatic terms at this level. American business is such a potpourri of institutions of different shapes, sizes, and industries that saying anything conclusive about it is difficult. Yet, this is an important level at which business needs to be concerned about its legitimacy. What is at stake is the acceptance of the form of business as an institution in our society. William Dill has suggested that business's social (or societal) legitimacy is a fragile thing:

> *Business has evolved by initiative and experiment. It never had an overwhelmingly clear endorsement as a social institution. The idea of allowing individuals to joust with one another in pursuit of personal profit was an exciting and romantic one when it was first proposed as a way of correcting other problems in society; but over time, its ugly side and potential for abuse became apparent.*[10]

Business must now accept that it has a **fragile mandate**. It must realize that its legitimacy is constantly subject to ratification, and it must realize that it has no inherent right to exist. Business exists solely because society has given it that right.[11] In this sense, business is a public institution as well as a private entity.[12] When the legitimacy of business as an institution is in question, political and social factors may overshadow economic factors to change the future of the institution of business in profound ways.[13]

In comparing the micro view of legitimacy with the macro view, it is clear that, although specific business organizations try to perpetuate their own legitimacy, the corporate or business system as a whole rarely addresses the issue at all. This is unfortunate because the spectrum of powerful issues regarding business conduct clearly indicates that such institutional introspection is necessary if business is to survive and prosper. If business is to continue to justify its right to exist, we must remember the question of legitimacy and its operational ramifications.

4.1a The Purpose of Corporate Governance

The purpose of corporate governance is a direct outgrowth of the question of legitimacy. The word *governance* comes from the Greek word for steering.[14] The way in which a corporation is governed determines the direction in which it is steered. Owners of small private firms can steer the firm on their own; however, the shareholders who are the owners of public firms must count on boards of directors to make certain that their companies are steered properly in their absence. For business to be legitimate and to maintain its legitimacy in the eyes of the public, it must be steered in a way that corresponds to the will of the people.

Corporate governance refers to the method by which a firm is being governed, directed, administered, or controlled and to the goals for which it is being governed. Corporate governance is concerned with the relative roles, rights, and accountability of such stakeholder groups as owners, boards of directors, managers, employees, and others who have a stake in the firm's governance.

4.1b Components of Corporate Governance

This chapter focuses on the **Anglo-American model**, which we explain in detail below, is one characterized as having outside directors, following common law, with market-oriented and shareholder-centered governance. This is often contrasted with the **Continental-European** (or "Rhineland") **model**, where inside directors and civil law dominate, as well as block ownership, a bank-orientation and stakeholder-coordinated governance.[15] We focus on the Anglo-American model because forces for a global convergence on this model are notably strong, albeit debatable.[16] These forces include support from global institutional investors, as well as accountants and regulators who feel comfortable with rules-based accounting standards.[17] The Anglo-American model is a shareholder-primacy model because shareholders have primary importance. Later in this chapter, we will discuss a director-primacy model of corporate governance that is receiving increasing attention.[18]

Roles of Four Major Groups. The four major groups we need to discuss in setting the stage for the shareholder-primacy model of corporate governance are the shareholders (owner-stakeholders), the board of directors, the managers, and the employees. Overarching these groups is the **charter** issued by the state, giving the corporation the right to exist and stipulating the basic terms of its existence, including corporate governance practices. Figure 4-1 presents these four groups, along with the state charter, in a hierarchy of corporate governance authority.

Shareholders own stock in the firm and, according to the shareholder-primacy model, this gives them ultimate control over the corporation as the firm's owners. This control is manifested in the right to select the board of directors of the company and to vote on resolutions. Generally, the number of shares of stock owned determines the degree of each shareholder's right. The individual who owns 100 shares of Apple Computer, for example, has 100 "votes" when electing the board of directors. By contrast, the large public pension fund that owns 10 million shares has 10 million "votes."

Because large organizations may have hundreds of thousands of shareholders, they elect a smaller group, known as the **board of directors**, to govern and oversee the management of the business. Under the shareholder-primacy model, the purpose of the board is to ascertain that the manager puts the interests of the shareholders first. The third major group in the authority hierarchy is the **management**—the group of individuals hired by the board to run the company and manage it on a daily basis. Along with the board, the top management establishes the overall policy. Middle- and lower-level managers carry out this policy and conduct the daily supervision of the operative employees. **Employees** are those hired by

FIGURE 4-1 The Corporation's Hierarchy of Authority (Shareholder Primacy)

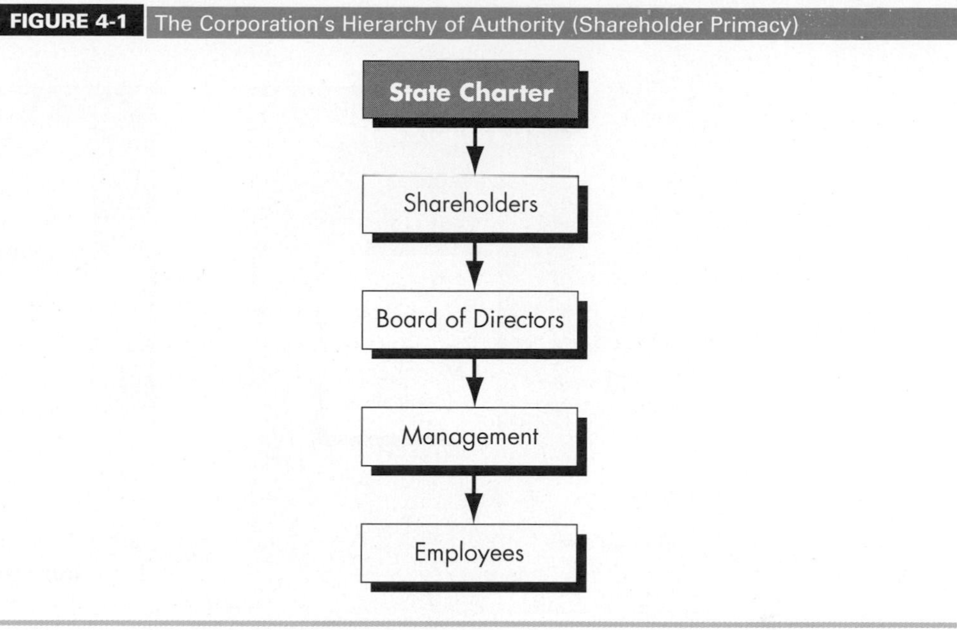

the company to perform the actual operational work. Managers are employees, too, but in this discussion, we use the term *employees* to refer to nonmanagerial employees.

Separation of Ownership from Control. The major condition embedded in the Anglo-American model of modern corporations that has contributed to the corporate governance problem has been the **separation of ownership from control**. This problem did not exist before corporations came into being. In the precorporate period, owners were typically the managers themselves; thus, the system worked the way it was intended, with the owners also controlling the business. Even when firms grew larger and managers were hired, the owners were often on the scene to hold the management group accountable. For example, if a company got in trouble, the Carnegies, or Mellons, or Morgans, were always there to fire the president.[19]

As the public corporation grew and stock ownership became widely dispersed, shareholders (owners) became more distant from managers (including the CEO) and a separation of ownership from control became the prevalent condition. Figure 4-2 illustrates the precorporate and corporate periods. The dispersion of ownership into hundreds of thousands or millions of shares meant that essentially no one person or group owned enough shares to exercise control. This being the case, the most effective control that owners could exercise was the election of the board of directors to serve as their representative and watch over the management.

The problem with this evolution was that true authority, power, and control began to rest with the group that had the most concentrated interest at stake—the management. The shareholders were owners in a technical sense, but most of them did not perceive themselves as owners. If you owned 100 shares of Walt Disney Co. and there were 10 million shares outstanding, you would be more likely to see yourself as an investor than you would be to see yourself as an owner. With just a telephone call issuing a sell order to your stockbroker, your "ownership" stake could be gone. Furthermore, with stock ownership so dispersed, no real supervision of corporate boards was possible.

The other factors that added to management's power were the corporate laws and traditions that gave the management group control over the proxy process—the method by

FIGURE 4-2 Precorporate versus Corporate Ownership and Control

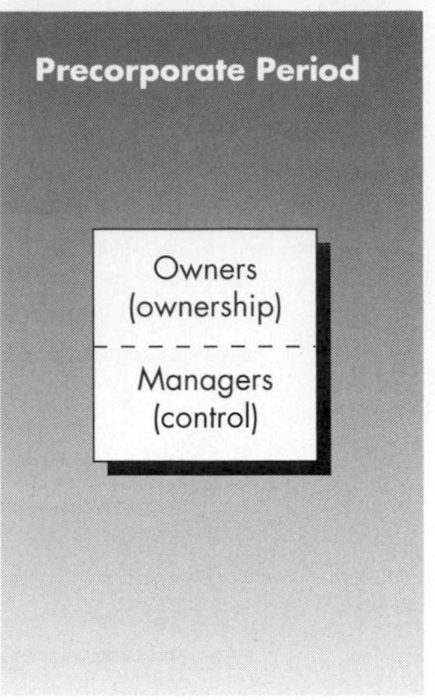

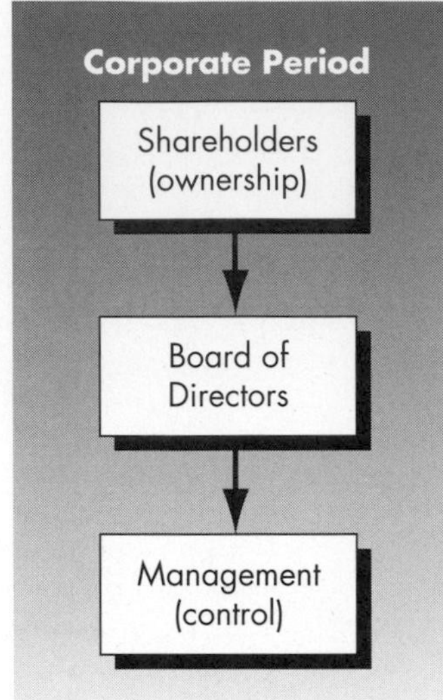

which the shareholders elected boards of directors. Technically, the board hires and fires managers, but eventually managers were able to subvert that process. Over time, managers, especially CEOs, were able to influence board member selection so that boards of directors became filled with like-minded executives who would too often defer to the management on whatever it wanted. The result of this process was the opposite of what was originally intended: power, authority, and control began to flow upward from the management rather than downward from the shareholders (owners). **Agency problems** developed when the interests of the shareholders were not aligned with the interests of the manager, and the manager (who is a hired *agent* with the responsibility of representing the owners' best interests) began to pursue self-interest instead of the owners' best interests. Agents have the ability to do this because they have more information about the workings of the organization than the shareholders do. For example, managers of the corporation may try to grow the company to avoid a firm's takeover attempt in an effort to increase his/her own job security. However, a takeover may be in the shareholders' best interests. Similarly, managers may consume corporate resources in the form of perquisites ("perks") like extra vacation time or the use of the company's jet.

4.2 Problems in Corporate Governance

It is clear from the preceding discussion that a potential governance problem is built into the corporate system because of the separation of ownership from control and the agency problems that result. The duty of the board of directors is to oversee management on behalf of the shareholders and with full regard for the stakeholders. However, this is where the system can break down. For corporate governance to function effectively, the board of directors must be an effective, potent body carrying out its roles and responsibilities. It must create a culture that does not focus too much on maximizing short-term results, and it must attract the right mix of directors that can advise, find resources, and monitor the behavior of management, including the CEO.

Surprisingly, most of the behavior that led to these crises fell within the letter of the law. Therefore, the response to them has been geared toward changing the law. The Sarbanes–Oxley Act (SOX) was a response to the problems that stemmed from Enron and WorldCom and the like, and the Dodd–Frank Wall Street Reform and Consumer Protection Act were a response to the global financial crisis. We will discuss them later in this chapter.

To be fair, corporate governance is a complex process and even a well-designed board is no guarantee of success. Nevertheless, boards have improved, and they continue to improve in many ways. In the 2015 *PwC* survey of corporate directors, director sentiment seems to have shifted toward a longer-term focus.[20] Over three-quarters of the responding boards indicated that they participated in some form of board education or training, and over two-thirds wanted some additional boardroom time and focus on strategy.[21] More than half said their company had established protocols and practices around preparing for director-shareholder interactions—a newer corporate governance issue surrounding shareholder engagement, which we discuss later in the chapter.[22] In another survey by *Spencer-Stuart* and the *New York Stock Exchange,* 96 percent of directors consider the regular evaluation of the CEO very important to company performance.[23] As we discuss the failings of corporate governance in the past decade, we must keep in mind that boards share in the blame but are not responsible for all of it. They are not superheroes, and we should not expect them to be.[24] However, even many directors themselves believe that their boards are falling short in creating value for their stakeholders.[25]

4.2a The Need for Board Independence

Board independence from management is a crucial aspect of good governance. It is here that the difference between **inside directors** and **outside directors** becomes most pronounced. Outside directors are independent from the firm and its top managers. They can come from a variety of backgrounds (e.g., top managers of other firms, academics, former government officials), but the one thing they have in common is that they have no other substantive relationship to the firm or its CEO. In contrast, inside directors have ties of some sort to the firm. They can be top managers in the firm, family members, or others with a professional or personal relationship to the firm or to the CEO. To varying degrees, inside directors may be "beholden" to the CEO and less objective in decision making; therefore, they might be hesitant to speak out when necessary. Since the implosion of Enron and its aftermath, changes in public policy and public opinion have led to an increase in the percentage of independent directors.

4.2b Issues Surrounding Compensation

The issue of executive pay is a lightning rod for those who feel that CEOs are placing their own interests over those of their shareholders. For example, people became outraged when they heard that Wall Street firms gave out $18.2 billion as bonuses in 2008 as the economy crumbled. Outrage over the widening pay gap between CEOs and rank-and-file employees continues today, with a 2015 report showing that the CEO of a Standard & Poor's 500 company was paid, on average, 216 times more than the median pay of that firm's employees—and 9 CEOs were paid 800 times more than their workers.[26] Two issues at the heart of the CEO pay controversy are (1) the extent to which CEO pay is tied to firm performance and (2) the overall size of CEO pay.

The CEO Pay–Firm Performance Relationship. The move to tie CEO pay more closely to firm performance grew in momentum when shareholders observed CEO pay rising as firm performance fell, particularly following the economic crisis in 2008/2009. Many executives had received staggering salaries, even while profits were falling, workers were being laid off, and shareholder returns were dropping. Since then, shareholders have focused not only on limiting the pay initially rewarded but also on taking back pay that, in retrospect, seems undeserved. However, the failure to link CEO pay to performance seems to continue. For example, David Zaslav, CEO of Discovery Communications was the highest paid CEO in 2014.[27] In a year when the value of the company stock dropped 24%, Zaslav received $156 million in compensation, representing a 368% increase over his compensation the year before.[28]

Efforts to strengthen the CEO pay–firm performance relationship have historically centered on the use of **stock options**. While they have improved the pay–performance relationship, they have also created a host of new problems. Stock options are designed to motivate the recipient to improve the value of the firm's stock. Put simply, an option allows the recipient to purchase stock in the future at the price it is today, that is, "at the money." If the stock value rises after the granting of the option, the recipient will make money. The logic behind giving CEOs stock options is that those CEOs will want to increase the value of the firm's stock so that they will be able to exercise their options, buying stock in the future at a price that is lower than it's worth. Of course, this logic only works if the option is granted at the true "at-the-money" price. The possibility of quick gains through misrepresentation of the pricing has led to numerous abuses. The following are the ones most frequently in the news.

Stock option **backdating** occurs when the recipient is given the option of buying stock at yesterday's price, resulting in an immediate and guaranteed wealth increase. This puts the stock option "in the money" rather than "at the money," which is where an option should be granted. Of course, backdating results in an immediate gain and is not in keeping with the purpose of stock options. This is not the only stock option abuse that has been observed. Even stock options granted "at the money" can be problematic when coupled with inside knowledge that the stock price is soon going to change. **Spring-loading** is the granting of a stock option at today's price but with the inside knowledge that something good is about to happen that will improve the stock's value. **Bullet-dodging** is the delaying of a stock option grant until right after bad news. Backdating is not inherently illegal, but can be deemed so if documents were falsified to conceal the backdating. The backdating of grant dates has considerably slowed down since the Sarbanes–Oxley Act of 2002 changed the reporting requirements for stock option grants. Additionally, stock options in general have declined as part of a CEO's total compensation, with less than half of the Standard & Poor's (S&P) 1,500 CEOs receiving options at all.[29]

To a certain extent, **restricted stock** has replaced stock option plans in attempts to incentivize CEOs, managers, and directors and align them with owners. Unlike stock options, restricted stock always has value, even in a down market, and it can deliver the same value with fewer shares than options because it does not have an exercise price. It also incentivizes executives to think for the long term, because the essence of restricted stock is that the employee must remain employed until the stock vests to receive its value. For example, since 2013 the music streaming and media company Pandora Media has shifted almost all of its stock options to restricted stock, even for rank-and-file employees, to create less risk and less dilution.[30]

Excessive CEO Pay. Concern about the size of executive compensation has been around for a long time. In ancient Greece, Plato recommended that no one in a community receives a wage higher than five times that of the lowest paid worker. Today, CEO salaries have skyrocketed while worker salaries have waned. Median pay for CEOs in the Standard & Poor's (S&P) 1,500 companies increased 7.8% in 2014, reaching $5.3 million.[31] While in the 1950's CEO average pay was just 20 times more than the average pay of workers, this has blossomed to 216 times, as we noted above.[32] Typically, the issue of excessive executive pay is a U.S. phenomenon. However, in 2013 it was reported that London's Financial Times Stock Exchange (FTSE) top 100 CEOs' total pay was 120 times the average earnings of their employees, prompting the European Commission to look at new rules over executive pay disclosures and executive/worker pay gaps.[33]

The **Say on Pay movement** evolved from concerns over excessive executive compensation and failures to link CEO pay to performance. It began in the United Kingdom in 2002, with regulations that included the requirement to put a remuneration report to a shareholder vote at each annual meeting.[34] Soon after the United Kingdom instituted its regulations, Say on Pay requirements spread through Europe and Australia, with the Netherlands making the vote binding on the company.[35] In the United States, the Dodd–Frank Wall Street Reform and Consumer Protection Act requires companies to submit their executive pay packages to a nonbinding shareholder vote at least once every three years.[36] Evidence suggests that the additional transparency has caught the eyes of shareholders, and it may be working in curbing CEO pay.[37] Two years in a row, The Wall Street Journal/Hay Group CEO Pay Survey found that pay increases were significantly lower than increases in shareholder value.[38] Executive pay also has begun to have an impact on a firm's larger reputation.[39] In Corporate Knight's ranking of the Global 100 most sustainable firms, executive pay is a part of two clean capitalism key performance indicators: the ratio of CEO to average employee pay and the linking of executive pay to clean capitalism goals.[40] Corporate Knights defines **clean capitalism** as "an economic system in which prices fully incorporate social, economic, and ecological costs and benefits, and actors are clearly aware of the consequences of their marketplace actions."[41]

When an executive's high level of pay results from dubious practices, such as financial misconduct or the exercising of options in a questionable way, shareholders have a right to try to recover those funds, but in the past, they have lacked a mechanism for doing so. This has changed due to the increasing adoption of **clawback provisions**, which are compensation recovery mechanisms that enable a company to recoup compensation funds, typically in the event of a financial restatement or executive's misbehavior.[42] *PwC* reported in 2015 that 90 percent of companies in the Fortune 100 impose clawbacks in the case of material financial restatements.[43] However, clawback provisions are not without controversy, as accountants worry that it may trigger some difficult mark-to-market accounting as companies wait for the Securities and Exchange Commission to formally implement the new rule.[44] The **Council of Institutional Investors (CII)**, a nonprofit association of corporate, public and union employee benefit funds, issued a policy that both current and former executive officers should be subject to clawback in cases of financial misstatements or fraud.[45] The CII does not have power over listings, but its members are large shareholders with voting power.[46]

Individual investors and other parties concerned do not have to wade through proxy statements to learn about CEO compensation. The AFL-CIO sponsors CEO PayWatch (http://www.aflcio.org/Corporate-Watch/Paywatch-2015) a Web site that is an "online center for learning about the excessive salaries, bonuses, and perks of the CEOs of major corporations."[47] Visitors to the Web site can enter their pay and a firm's name and find out how many years they would have to work to make what the CEO of that firm makes in one year (or how many workers are at your salary that the CEO's pay could support). The Web site also provides instructions for assessing the pay of CEOs at public corporations and beginning a campaign of shareholder activism in any company.

Executive Retirement Plans and Exit Packages. Executive retirement packages have traditionally flown under the radar, escaping the notice of shareholders, employees, and the public. However, as details of some retirement packages have become public, those packages have come under increased scrutiny. The issue took center stage when former General Electric (GE) chairman and CEO Jack Welch's retirement package was disclosed during his divorce proceedings. Country club memberships, wine and laundry services, luxurious housing, and access to corporate jets were but a few of the perks that Welch had enjoyed.[48] These packages are negotiated well in advance and so they often are unrelated to performance. The $210-million exit package Robert Nardelli received following his ouster from Home Depot inflamed shareholder activists and outraged the public.[49] After Bank of America took $45 billion in federal bailout funds and became the subject of investigation by federal and state officials, outgoing CEO Ken Lewis received nearly $64 million in retirement pay and left the firm with what some compensation analysts estimate to be $125 million.[50] Many see the CEO-worker retirement divide as an even greater contributor to the wider economic divide than basic pay—with the 100 largest U.S. CEO retirement packages worth a combined value of $4.9 billion, equal to the retirement account savings of 41 percent of American families.[51]

Part of the public's frustration is that these CEO retirement packages stand in stark contrast to the retirement packages that workers receive. Many of today's workers do not have retirement packages, and those who do are far more likely to have the less-lucrative defined contribution plans (that specify what will be put into the retirement fund) rather than the defined benefit plans (that specify the benefit the retiree will receive).[52] These defined contribution plans are more vulnerable to stock market fluctuations than defined benefit plans, and so the majority of workers saw their retirement funds plummet as the global financial crisis hit. Now top executives want to avoid that level of uncertainty and so some U.S. companies are designing supplemental retirement plans to get around ERISA, the federal pension law that falls under the Employee Retirement Income Security Act of 1974 that was intended to avoid the favoring of high-ranking managers.[53]

Outside Director Compensation. Paying board members is a relatively recent idea. Ninety years ago, it was illegal to pay nonexecutive board members. The logic was that because board members represented the shareholders, paying them out of the company's (i.e., shareholders') funds would be self-dealing.[54] Today, outside board members are paid for their efforts. From 2003 through 2015, median total outside director pay rose from $175,800 to $258,000 as the average time directors spent on the job increased 59 percent.[55] Unlike executive compensation, there is no Say-on-Pay option for shareholders to approve director compensation, but in general, there have been relatively few shareholder protests over director compensation. One exception to this has been a shareholder suit brought against Facebook directors who awarded themselves additional Facebook stock (see Ethics in Practice Case).

Transparency. SEC rules on disclosure of executive compensation are designed to address some of the more obvious problems by making the entire pay packages of top executives transparent: In the past, they have included such items as deferred pay, severance, accumulated pension benefits, and perks over $10,000.[56] There is evidence that improvements in disclosure even have an impact prior to implementation. Michael S. Melbinger, a compensation lawyer, tells the story of a CEO who had a contract provision that not only reimbursed all his medical expenses (including deductibles and co-pays) but also provided a **tax gross-up**, which reimbursed him for the taxes he would have to pay on his medical benefits. In contrast, employees in this company were required to cover their own medical expenses. Therefore, when the CEO realized how bad it would look that the company not only paid all his medical bills but also the taxes on that benefit, he quickly gave up that perk.[57]

The Dodd–Frank Wall Street Reform and Consumer Protection Act includes provisions intended to have the SEC improve the transparency of firm operations. One is an equity pay provision that requires firms to reveal the difference in salaries between executives and rank-and-file workers. The SEC adopted the **Pay-Ratio Disclosure Rule** in 2015, despite opposition from stakeholders like The Chamber of Commerce. "The ratio is not going to be a meaningful way to help investors but will be used as a political tool to attack companies," said David Hirschmann, president of the U.S. Chamber of Commerce's Center for Capital Markets.[58] Other opponents say that calculating the ratio will be cumbersome given a global marketplace with different payroll systems.[59] Proponents of the measure include labor unions and institutional investors, who believe that the requirement could slow down the high rate of growth in CEO pay, as well as motivate boards to think more often of their frontline workers.[60]

Another Dodd–Frank requirement focuses on the transparency of the compensation setting process. In 2012, the SEC approved new exchange listing standards rules to include issues such as the independence of compensation committee members, the compensation adviser hiring process, and the nature of the relationship between the compensation adviser and the committee.[61] In 2015, the SEC proposed to supplement its Dodd–Frank disclosure rules to require companies to calculate and present information highlighting the company's executive compensation practices relative to its financial performance.[62] In sum, the Dodd–Frank Act continues to provide for rules to be designed for more transparency for shareholders.

4.2c The Governance Impact of the Market for Corporate Control

Mergers and acquisitions are another form of corporate governance, one that comes from outside the corporation. The expectation from the Anglo-American shareholder-primacy perspective is that the threat of a possible takeover will motivate top managers to pursue shareholder, rather than self, interest (the expectation of the director-primacy perspective will be explained later in the chapter). The merger, acquisition, and hostile takeover craze of the 1980s motivated many corporate CEOs and boards to go to great lengths to protect themselves from these takeovers, and these continue with some of the "mega" mergers and acquisitions of the 2000s. Two of the controversial practices to emerge from the hostile takeover wave were poison pills and golden parachutes. We briefly consider each of these, and see how they fit into the corporate governance problem being discussed. Then we examine the issue of insider trading.

Poison Pills. A **poison pill** is intended to discourage or prevent a hostile takeover. It works much like its name suggests—when an acquirer tries to swallow (i.e., acquire) a company, the poison pill makes the company very difficult to ingest. Poison pills can take a variety of forms but, typically, when a hostile suitor acquires more than a certain percentage of a company's stock, the poison pill provides that other shareholders be able to purchase shares, thus diluting the suitor's holdings and making the acquisition prohibitively expensive (i.e., difficult to swallow). Poison pills have fallen out of favor, going from 2,218 such defenses in 2001 to 1,206 at the start of 2009, largely due to institutional shareholder pressure.[63] A decline in hostile takeovers has also contributed to the decline in poison pills.[64] Nevertheless, they remain within the corporate arsenal. In 2012, Netflix adopted a poison pill to fend off a corporate takeover by corporate raider, Carl Icahn.[65]

More recently, however, poison pills have taken on a new role as a strategy to fend off shareholder activists who want to change the direction of the company.[66] Poison pills adopted in response to a company being approached by an activist investor represented over one quarter of all adoptions in 2014.[67] The motivation is different from that of a hostile takeover—instead of preventing a hostile suitor that might hurt shareholders and end a company's independence, the "low-threshold" poison pill is designed to limit ownership by any single investor for a short period, subject to renewal, and the company's future survival is not in question.[68] In 2013, the auction house Sotheby's launched such a poison pill to ward off additional hedge fund ownership that might have sparked a proxy contest to replace some of its board members.[69]

Golden Parachutes. A **golden parachute** is a provision in an employment contract in which a corporation agrees to make payments to key officers in the event of a change in the control of the corporation.[70] Advocates argue that golden parachutes provide top executives involved in takeover battles with an incentive for not fighting a shareholder wealth-maximizing takeover attempt in an effort to preserve their employment. However, a study of over 400 takeover attempts found that golden parachutes had no effect on takeover resistance.[71] Critics argue that executives are already being paid sufficiently well and that these parachutes essentially reward them for failure.[72] Others argue that lavish exit packages might make CEOs too eager to accept a takeover offer.[73] The trend in the percentage of executives awarded packages is holding steady but the multiple involved (the percentage of payout relative to salary) has been declining.[74] The Council of Institutional Investors, however, has voiced its disapproval of golden parachutes by approving a policy encouraging shareholders to require that boards consider executive tenure and performance before signing off on such packages.[75] Moreover, in 2015, Chubb Corporation shareholders opposed an $80 million golden parachute payment for the CEO, John Finnegan, following the sale of the insurance company to Ace Limited.[76]

4.2d Insider Trading

Insider trading is the practice of buying or selling a security by someone who has access to material information that is not available to the public. **Material information** is information that a reasonable investor might want to use and that is likely to affect the price of a firm's stock once that information is released to the public. Although insider trading is typically thought of as illegal conduct, insider trading can be legal or illegal.[77] Whether or not insider trading is legal depends on when the trade occurs. If the trade is made while the information is still not public, then it is illegal because members of the public do not have access to that information.[78] The market system is based on trust and fair play. Investor confidence relies on fairness and integrity in the securities markets and illegal insider trading erodes that confidence (see Figure 4-3).[79]

The SEC has brought charges against people who received or revealed inside information in a variety of ways. One can be a **tipper** who provides that information or a **tippee** who receives the information. Both types are prosecutable and both have been prosecuted by the SEC.[80] It is clear that these include corporate directors, executives, and employees, but the SEC has also brought charges against friends, family members, and business associates of insiders. If an employee of a law, banking, or printing firm receives inside information in the process of providing services to a company, and then trades on that information knowing it is nonpublic, that person is prosecutable. The same is true

FIGURE 4-3 An Insider Trading Quiz

Which of the following are considered to be illegal inside trading, prosecutable by the SEC?

1. A lower-level employee of the company learns the company will have higher-than-expected earnings in the next quarterly statement and buys shares of the company's stock before the statement is released to the public. Can that employee be prosecuted by the SEC?
2. The above employee who learned the information does not trade on the information but tells his or her spouse and that spouse buys company stock shares before the information goes public. Can the spouse be prosecuted by the SEC?
3. In the above example (#2), can the employee who did not trade be prosecuted by the SEC?
4. While playing basketball on the weekend, the employee shares the information with a casual friend. That friend then buys shares of the company's stock before the statement is released to the public. Can the friend be prosecuted by the SEC?

The answer to all the questions in this quiz is "yes."

for government employees, including employees of the SEC.[81] In November 2012, cases were filed against a former portfolio manager at a leading hedge fund, a former major league baseball player accused both of trading illegally and sharing information with three friends, and six high school buddies accused of tipping while playing basketball.[82] Insider trading is prosecutable whether or not it is successful, although a defense attorney may be able to argue the information was not material if only losses occurred, or if the person disclosing the information did not receive a clear benefit.[83] Data analytics have made it much easier to catch illegal inside traders. The SEC now brings more cases in one year than it did throughout the 1990s.[84] Cases are also growing in size.

Insider trading allegations cause the general public to lose faith in the stability and security of the financial industry because **information asymmetry** (one party having information that another does not) favors one group over another. Information asymmetry can also arise if companies release information to one group before another receives it. If large investors can act on information that smaller investors do not have, the playing field is not level. To prop up investor confidence, the SEC instituted disclosure rules

ETHICS IN PRACTICE CASE

Excessive Director Compensation at Facebook?

In 2014, a shareholder derivative suit was filed in the Delaware Courts alleging that the Facebook Board of Directors violated their duties to their shareholders by paying its nonexecutive directors 43% more than "peers," despite its net income and revenues being 66% and 49% lower, respectively, than its peers. The peers named in the suit included Adobe, Amazon, Cisco, eBay, EMC, LinkedIn, Netflix, Qualcomm, SAP AG, The Walt Disney Company, VMware, and Yahoo!, Inc. The suit noted that in 2013, the Facebook Board paid its nonexecutive members an average $461,000 per director, 43%, or $140,000 higher than the average per director compensation in Facebook's Peer Group. It further noted that the Board is free to grant its board members an unlimited amount of stock as part of their annual compensation under a 2012 equity incentive plan, with the only limit a $2.5 million share limit per director in a single year (worth approximately $145 million at the time of filing).

The Facebook Board at the time consisted of eight individuals, six of whom were "outside" (i.e., nonemployee) directors including Lead Independent Director Donald Graham, and Directors Peter Thiel, Marc Andreessen, Reed Hastings, Erskine Boles and Desmond-Hellman. Inside directors included founder and CEO/Chairman Mark Zuckerberg and COO Sheryl Sandberg. The lawsuit alleged that all of the Directors approved the compensation and all of the nonexecutive directors received the compensation. The lawsuit claimed breach of fiduciary duty, waste of corporate assets, and "unjust enrichment."

The issue of director compensation accelerated in late 2014, when Jan Koum, WhatsApp cofounder and CEO, joined the board and received a salary of $1, but stock awards worth over $1.9 billion, representing a sign-on award of $25 million restricted stock units when Facebook acquired WhatsApp. However, Facebook CEO Mark Zuckerberg allegedly approved the stock grants in a written affidavit, rather than at a stockholder meeting—and with 60% of the voting power, he had the ability to approve whatever he wanted. The question remains as to whether Mark Zuckerberg failed to comply with Delaware corporate law, where the company is incorporated, in circumventing shareholders by signing off on directors' stock grants instead of presenting it at a shareholders' meeting.

1. Do you believe that directors have the right to approve their own compensation without taking it to shareholder vote? Please justify your answer and explain what might or might not warrant this.
2. Did Zuckerberg break the law by not bringing the compensation issue up in a stockholder meeting?
3. What is an appropriate level of director pay? Is the proposed compensation in the Facebook situation excessive? How might this be determined?
4. Institutional Shareholder Services, a proxy advisory firm, has noted that there is "too much work and too much time" required of directors; could this justify higher director pay?[85]

Sources: Carol Hymowitz, Caleb Melby, and Hideki Suzuki, "Nice Work If You Can Give It to Yourself," *Bloomberg Businessweek* (December 12, 2016), p.21; Jonathan Stempel, "Zuckerberg, Other Facebook Directors Are Sued over Pay Plan," *Reuters* (June 9, 2014), http://www.reuters.com/article/us-facebook-lawsuit-idUSKBN0EK1YO20140609. Accessed January 1, 2016; Paul Hodgson, "Facebook Director Pay Not Getting Many Shareholder 'Likes'," *Fortune* online (December 15, 2015), http://fortune.com/2015/12/15/facebook-director-pay/. Accessed January 1, 2016.

designed to aid the small investor who historically did not have access to the information large investors hold. **Regulation FD (fair disclosure)** set limits on the common company practice of selective disclosure. When companies disclose meaningful information to shareholders and securities professionals, they must do so publicly so that small investors can enjoy a more level playing field.[86]

4.3 Improving Corporate Governance

We first discuss legislative efforts to improve corporate governance. SOX was passed in response to the public outcry for greater protection following the financial scandals of 2001. The Dodd–Frank Wall Street Reform and Consumer Protection Act was passed in response to the global financial crisis. We then proceed to other efforts to improve corporate governance through changes in the composition, structure, and functioning of boards of directors.

4.3a Legislative Efforts

The **Accounting Reform and Investor Protection Act of 2002**, also known as the **Sarbanes–Oxley Act of 2002 (aka SOX or Sarbox)**, amended the securities laws to provide better protection to investors in public companies by improving the financial reporting of companies. According to the Senate committee report, "the issue of auditor independence is at the center of [SOX]."[87] Some of the ways the act endeavors to ensure auditor independence are by limiting the nonauditing services an auditor can provide, requiring auditing firms to rotate the auditors who work with a specific company, and making it unlawful for accounting firms to provide auditing services where conflicts of interest (as defined by the act) exist. In addition, the act enhances financial disclosure with requirements such as the reporting of off-balance-sheet transactions, the prohibiting of personal loans to executives and directors, and the requirement that auditors assess and report upon the internal controls employed by the company. Other key provisions include the requirement that audit committees have at least one financial expert, that CEOs and chief financial officers (CFOs) certify and be held responsible for financial representations of the company, and that whistle-blowers are afforded protection. Corporations must also disclose whether they have adopted a code of ethics for senior financial officers, and, if they have not, provide an explanation for why they have not.[88] The penalties for noncompliance with SOX are severe. A CEO or CFO who misrepresents company finances may face a fine of up to $1 million and imprisonment for up to ten years. If that misrepresentation is willful, the fine may go up to $5 million with up to 20 years of imprisonment.[89]

Since the passage of SOX, debate has continued regarding its costs and benefits, with attitudes becoming more positive as firms have more experience with SOX's requirements. A 2015 SOX compliance survey found that more companies continue to concentrate on strengthening their ability to leverage SOX compliance requirements to achieve improvements in their other business processes, despite the rising costs of compliance.[90]

The Dodd–Frank Wall Street Reform and Consumer Protection Act was passed in the wake of the global financial crisis and signed into law on July 21, 2010. This comprehensive legislation covers 16 major areas of reform affecting banks, credit card companies, credit rating agencies, insurance companies, hedge funds, and futures trading. Legislative efforts are important and governments have a responsibility to respond when crises such as the Enron and WorldCom bankruptcies and global economic crises occur. Government has a responsibility to protect the public interest, but no amount of legislative oversight will fully protect the public from the next crisis. In their study of the global financial crisis, Michael Santoro and Ronald Strauss acknowledge that government has a crucial role to play but conclude, "No amount of government regulation can

FIGURE 4-4 Ranking of Red Flags That Signal Board Problems and Steps to Take for Board Repair

Ranking of Red Flags	Steps to Take for Board Repair
1. Company has to restate earnings	1. Spread risk oversight among multiple committees
2. Poor employee morale	2. Seek outside help in identifying potential risks
3. Adverse Sarbanes–Oxley 404 opinion	3. Deepen involvement in corporate strategy
4. Poor customer satisfaction track record	4. Align board size and skill mix with strategy
5. Management misses strategic performance goals	5. Revamp executive compensation
6. Company is target of employee lawsuits	6. Pick compensation committee members who will question the status quo
7. Stock price declines	7. Use independent compensation consultants
8. Quarterly financial results miss analysts' expectations	8. Evaluate CEO on grooming potential successors
9. Low corporate governance quotient rating	9. Know what matters to your investors

Sources: "What Directors Think 2015," *SpencerStuart* (February 2015), https://www.spencerstuart.com/research-and-insight/what-directors-think-2015. Accessed January 13, 2016. Joanne S. Lublin, "Corporate Directors Give Repair Plan to Boards," *The Wall Street Journal* (March 24, 2009), B4.

succeed where the moral core is corrupt… Unless Wall Street itself formulates a coherent moral response to the crisis, no amount of regulatory oversight will prevent another, potentially more destabilizing, crisis from occurring."[91]

4.3b Changes in Boards of Directors

Because of the growing belief that CEOs and executive teams need to be made more accountable to shareholders and other stakeholders, boards have been undergoing a variety of changes. Here we focus on several key areas that need change as well as some of the recommendations that were set forth for improving board functioning. Figure 4-4 presents a ranked list of nine "red flags" that signal that a board member should increase his or her involvement and the National Association of Corporate Directors' nine steps that provide a roadmap for board repair.

4.3c Board Diversity

Prior to the 1960s, boards were composed primarily of white, male inside directors. It was not until the 1960s that pressure from Washington, Wall Street, and various stakeholder groups began to emphasize the concept of board diversity. Nevertheless, a significant percentage of boards are still composed of exclusively white, male directors.

In response to the lack of gender and minority diversity on boards, several groups have formed to try to organize campaigns for more representation. One organization, The Women on Boards 2020, conducted a census of the Fortune 1000 firms and found that while the number of women on boards has grown each year since 2011, women still only hold 18.8 percent of board seats—falling short of the organization's national goal dedicated to increasing the percentage of women on boards to 20 percent by 2020.[92] The Alliance for Board Diversity continues to track increases in representation for women and minorities, but sees boardroom diversity "at a standstill in Fortune 500 companies."[93] Despite some efforts by organizations to increase board diversity and ongoing academic research on how to bring change in gender diversity on boards,[94] representation of Hispanic, Asian, African American, and female directors on boards continues to grow modestly. However, as many directors reach retirement, it is predicted that pressure on boards to refresh their composition will increase.[95]

Problems with achieving board diversity are not confined to the United States. Women occupy only 15 percent of the London Stock Exchange's FTSE 100 board seats.[96] Women's share of board seats at Canadian Stock Index companies is about 20 percent, and their share at European Stock Index companies' ranges from 7.9 percent in Portugal to a high of 35.5 percent in Norway.[97] Norway's high numbers may be directly linked to a government mandate to increase the number of women on boards. The 500 publicly traded firms in Norway were told they would face closure if they did not meet a January 2008 deadline for achieving 40 percent female representation on their boards.[98] By 2008, every major Norwegian corporation was in compliance. In fact, the number of women on Norway's corporate boards almost quadrupled in five years.[99] Not surprisingly, this dramatic shift ignited a fierce debate about the use of quotas to create change and the role of women in the workplace.[100] Spain, Iceland, Italy, Belgium, the Netherlands, and France regulators have now followed Norway's lead, with their regulators making compulsory or quasi-compulsory recommendations for female representation.[101] Yet, women continue to be underrepresented on boards worldwide, with only 19 percent of board seats globally occupied by women.[102]

Do diverse boards make a difference? Given the diversity of stakeholders, a diverse board is better able to hear their concerns and respond to their needs.[103] Diverse boards are also less likely to fall prey to groupthink because they would have the range of perspectives necessary to question the assumptions that drive group decisions.[104] There is some evidence of board diversity being associated with better financial performance.[105] However, a cause–effect relationship is very difficult to determine because so many factors influence the performance of a firm.

4.3d Outside Directors

As we discussed earlier, legislative, investor, and public pressure have led firms to seek a greater ratio of outside to inside board members. Do outside board members make a difference for both shareholders and stakeholders? As with diversity, a relationship between the proportion of outside directors and financial performance is difficult to find. For that reason, scholars have looked to more targeted measures. One study found outside directors to be associated with fewer shareholder lawsuits.[106] Regarding stakeholders, researchers found that outside directors correlated positively with dimensions of social responsibility associated with both people and product quality.[107] A recent study suggests that outside directors have the ability to be objective, and therefore, it is one of the core attributes needed for a director to be an effective monitor of management.[108] Some have suggested that a lack of outside directors on the board of Volkswagen led to a "clannish board" that did not allow for the objectivity that might have stopped its engineers from purposefully circumventing U.S. emissions standards.[109] Board independence can come at a cost, however, as inside directors have greater knowledge of the firm because of their connections to it. Additionally, some observers have expressed concern that the push for more outside directors has pushed chief financial officers (CFOs) off the board. The number of CFOs on a Fortune 500 board dropped from 37 to 19 in two years.[110] Finally, it is unclear that a board made up of outsiders truly brings objectivity in decision making when the CEO often remains a powerful insider of the organization.[111]

Outside directors are a heterogeneous group and so the impact of appointing more outside directors to boards can be expected to vary with the characteristics of the directors who are appointed, such as their expertise, their experience, and the time they have available to give to their post. Arguably, the most important characteristic for outside directors is the ability to ask difficult questions and speak truthfully about concerns, without letting ties to the firm get in the way.

4.3e Use of Board Committees

The **audit committee** is responsible for assessing the adequacy of internal control systems and the integrity of financial statements. Governance scandals prior to the Sarbanes–Oxley Act, and the many companies that have subsequently needed to restate earnings, underscore the importance of a strong audit committee. SOX mandates that the audit committee be composed entirely of independent board members and that there be at least one identified financial expert, as defined in SOX.[112] The principal responsibilities of an audit committee are as follows:[113]

1. To ensure that published financial statements are not misleading
2. To ensure that internal controls are adequate
3. To follow up on allegations of material, financial, ethical, and legal irregularities
4. To ratify the selection of the external auditor

While the audit committee has taken center stage in the current corporate governance environment, other committees still play key roles. The **nominating committee**, which should be composed of outside directors, has the responsibility of ensuring that competent, objective board members are selected. The function of the nominating committee is to nominate candidates for the board and for senior management positions. The suggested role and responsibility of this committee notwithstanding, in most companies, the CEO continues to exercise a powerful role in the selection of board members. This is because the CEO is part of the upper echelon of business people that share social clubs, business groups, and government policy forums.[114]

The **compensation committee** has the responsibility of evaluating executive performance and recommending terms and conditions of employment. This committee should be composed of outside directors. Both the New York Stock Exchange (NYSE) and NASDAQ require that the compensation committee be composed of independent board members. Together, the audit, nominating, and compensation committees are considered to be the principal monitoring committees in an organization.[115] Additionally, many companies, particularly in the financial services industry, have formed board-level **risk committees** to provide oversight about risks regarding strategy and tactics across operational, financial, and compliance areas.

Finally, each board has committees that respond to the needs of their industries and that addresses public policy and social issues. They have a variety of names. For example, Johnson & Johnson has a regulatory, compliance, and governmental affairs committee as well as a science, technology, and sustainability committee.[116] Unilever has a corporate responsibility and reputation committee.[117] Most major companies today have **corporate responsibility committees** or **corporate sustainability committees** that typically deal with such issues as diversity, equal employment opportunity, environmental affairs, employee health and safety, consumer affairs, political action, and other areas in which public or ethical issues are present. Yet, surveys suggest that no more than 10 percent of U.S. public company boards have stand-alone corporate responsibility or sustainability committees.[118] The tide may be turning, however, with companies like Nike, and its active board-level corporate responsibility committee receiving much attention in the press.[119] Debate continues over the extent to which large firms really use such committees, but the fact that they have institutionalized such concerns by way of formal corporate committees is encouraging.

4.3f The Board's Relationship with the CEO

Boards of directors have always been responsible for monitoring CEO performance and dismissing poorly performing CEOs. Historically, however, CEOs were protected from the axe that hit other employees when times got rough. Post Sarbanes–Oxley, this was no longer true, with the rising vigilance of outside directors and the increasing power of large institutional investors causing average CEO tenure in the S&P 500 to hit its lowest, at 7.2 years, in 2009.[120] With current CEO tenure ratcheting back up to an average of 9.9 years across the S&P 500,[121] shareholder activists have begun pressuring boards to impose term limits and/or mandatory retirement ages for CEOs and directors alike.[122]

"You have to perform or perish," according to John A. Challenger, CEO of outplacement firm Challenger, Gray & Christmas Inc. "If you don't produce immediate results, you just don't have much room to move."[123] Research has shown that there is a considerable "CEO effect" on firm performance, supporting the idea that the CEO is ultimately responsible for the fate of the business.[124] Disciplinary CEO departures have recently declined, due to more stable economic conditions and improved corporate performance, with 16 percent of CEO turnover in the S&P 500 in 2014—the lowest level since 2005. [125] Nevertheless, the optimal time for a CEO or board member to serve on a board is a subject of much debate. As noted by one expert, "There is no simple answer to the question of CEO tenure. A firm can perform well with leaders enjoying a wide spectrum of terms of office … If there was an automatic formula we could apply we would not need boards with independent judgment."[126]

Part of the protection that CEOs once felt came from **CEO duality**, which occurs when the CEO serves a dual function, being both CEO and Chair of the board. One can only wonder how the board's responsibility to monitor the CEO can be fulfilled effectively when the CEO is heading the process, and so it is not surprising that activist shareholders have pushed to separate the CEO and board chair functions. As is true with outside directors, CEO duality is "a double-edged sword."[127] CEOs who also serve as chairs are able to act decisively in responding to a competitive marketplace; however, that comes at the cost of a reduced ability of the board to monitor effectively.[128] Activist shareholders have been succeeding in getting companies to split the CEO and board chair function. In 2015, nearly half of the S&P 500 companies split the chair and CEO role compared to 40 percent in 2010 and 29 percent in 2005.[129]

4.3g Board Member Liability

Concerned about increasing legal hassles emanating from stockholder, customer, and employee lawsuits, directors have been quitting board positions or refusing to accept them in the first place. In the past, courts rarely held board members personally liable in the hundreds of shareholder suits filed every year. Instead, the **business judgment rule** prevailed. The business judgment rule holds that courts should not challenge board members who act in good faith, making informed decisions that reflect the company's best interests instead of their own self-interest. The argument for the business judgment rule is that board members need to be free to take risks without fear of liability. The issue of good faith is central here because the rule was never intended to absolve board members completely from personal liability. In cases where the good faith standard was not upheld, board members have paid a hefty price.

The TransUnion Corporation case involved an agreement among the directors to sell the company for a price the owners later decided was too low. A suit was filed, and the court ordered that the board members be held personally responsible for the difference between the price the company was sold for and a later-determined "fair value" for the deal.[130] More recently, when Dole Food Company went private, the Delaware Court of Chancery held two directors of the company jointly and severally liable for $148 million because they breached their duty of loyalty by spinning off high-margin businesses prior to going private that did not allow for a "fairer price" for the stockholders.[131]

The Caremark case then further heightened directors' concerns about **personal liability**. Caremark, a home health-care company, paid substantial civil and criminal fines for submitting false claims and making illegal payments to doctors and other health-care providers. The Caremark board of directors was then sued for breach of fiduciary duties because the board members had failed in their responsibility to monitor effectively the Caremark employees who violated various state and federal laws. The Delaware Chancery Court ruled that it is the duty of the board of directors to ensure that a company has an effective reporting and monitoring system in place. If the board fails to do this,

ETHICS IN PRACTICE CASE

Monitoring the Monitors

News leaks seemed to plague Hewlett Packard. The first leaks surrounded the ouster of chairwoman and chief executive Carly Fiorina. In the midst of this internal turmoil, *The Wall Street Journal* published an article with details of closed-door board discussions about the planned management reorganization. An external legal counsel interviewed board members but did not succeed in identifying the leak. Evidence of more leaks appeared a year later as news organizations once again described the deliberations of closed-door board and senior management meetings in extensive detail. It was clear that someone from inside was leaking information. In addition to board members, reporters from such publications as *The New York Times*, *The Wall Street Journal*, *Businessweek*, and *CNET* became targets of the ensuing investigation into ten different leaks. The methods used to try to plug these news leaks led eventually to a board shake-up, which included the departure of nonexecutive chairwoman Patricia Dunn.

Fast forward to 2013, and another company, J. C. Penney, was involved in a story about board leaks. J. C. Penney director and activist investor William Ackman allegedly provided a news outlet information about board meetings, detailing discussions about his frustration with the CEO search process. In another example, the University of North Carolina Board of Governors in 2014 removed a trustee when he allegedly leaked information about candidates in the search for a new chancellor.

Investigating board members is a difficult proposition. Coming back to the HP example, the board could not supervise what was essentially an investigation of themselves. Neither could the employees handle the investigation because that would have put them in the untenable position of investigating their own bosses. Left with few options, HP board chairwoman Dunn turned the investigation over to a network of private investigators. According to Dunn, she could not supervise the investigation because she was a potential target. Dunn asked the head of corporate security to handle the investigation, as this was the person who handled employee investigations, but he still had conflicts of interest as an employee of the board. So the company outsourced the investigation to a network of outside investigators, telling them to conduct it within the confines of the law.

The primary source of the leaks was uncovered, but questions remained about the process of the investigations. Although no recording or eavesdropping occurred, investigators had used a form of "pretexting" to elicit phone records. Pretexting is a way of obtaining information by disguising one's identify. In this case, investigators used pretexting to obtain phone records of not only HP board members but also reporters who covered the story. In addition, investigators followed board members and journalists and watched their homes. They also planted false messages with journalists in an effort to get them to reveal their sources inadvertently through the tracking software included in the fake messages.

1. Who should be responsible for taking action when a board member engages in problematic behavior? If the chairperson is responsible, when should he or she involve the whole board? What are the costs of early full board involvement? What are the costs of late full board involvement?
2. One complaint lodged was that HP provided board members' home phone numbers to investigators. Was this out of line? Do board members have a responsibility to provide certain basic information, or was their privacy breached when their home phone numbers were given? A board member whose phone records proved he was not involved in any leaks still resigned the board in protest that his privacy was invaded by the pretexting. Was he right?
3. The law regarding pretexting is unclear. While it is illegal when used to obtain financial records, the use of pretexting in other situations—such as the phone records in this example—was not necessarily against the law. Should it be?
4. How might things have evolved differently if the ethicality rather than the legality of the practice had been the issue? Are the two synonymous or is there a difference?

Sources: Ellen Nakashima and Yuke Noguchi, "HP CEO Allowed 'Sting' of Reporter," *Washington Post* (September 21, 2006), A1; David A. Katz and Laura A. McIntosh, "Corporate Governance Update: Boardroom Confidentiality under Focus," *New York Law Journal* (Vol. 251, No. 15, January 23, 2014), p. 5, col. 2; Jane S. Shaw, "The UNC Board of Governors Takes Action on a Leak to the Press," *John William Pope Center for Higher Education Policy Commentaries*, http://www.popecenter.org/commentaries/article.html?id=3097. Accessed January 9, 2015; "JC Penney Board Erupts into a Fight over Next CEO," CNBC (August 8, 2013), http://www.cnbc.com/id/100948492. Accessed January 2, 2016.

individual directors can be held personally liable for losses that are caused by their failure to meet appropriate standards.[132]

The issue of board members paying personal liability costs from their personal funds (also known as **out-of-pocket liability**) came to the forefront following the Enron and WorldCom debacles. Twelve WorldCom directors were ordered to pay $24.75 million out of their personal funds instead of drawing on their D&O insurance.[133] Ten former Enron directors agreed to pay $13 million from their personal funds.[134] In a November 2006 decision, the Delaware Supreme Court affirmed the "Caremark Standard" that states directors can only be held liable if "1. The director utterly failed to implement any reporting or information system or controls, or 2. having implemented such a system or controls, consciously failed to monitor or oversee its operations, disabling their ability to be informed of risks or problems requiring their attention."[135] The economic meltdown raised new concerns about personal liability as directors realized they could be held personally liable when employees seek redress for the impacts of layoffs and plant closings.[136]

4.4 The Role of Shareholders

Shareholders are a varied group with a range of interests and expectations. They, however, have one aspect in common—In the Anglo-American system of corporate governance, they are the owners of the corporation. As such, they have a right to have their voices heard. Putting that right into practice, however, has presented an ongoing challenge for shareholders and managers.

Our discussion begins with an overview of the state of shareholder democracy, which relates to strengthening shareholder voice and participation in corporate governance. We then discuss shareholder activism and close with recommendations for improved shareholder relations.

4.4a Shareholder Democracy

Throughout the world, shareholders have been fighting to have their voices heard in corporate governance. This **shareholder democracy** movement stems from the lack of

SPOTLIGHT *on Sustainability*

Shareholder Impact on Sustainability

Shareholder resolutions can appear to be frustrating propositions. Boards of directors and top management usually oppose them, and, even when resolutions are put forth, they typically get only a fraction of the votes needed to pass. In spite of these discouraging statistics, shareholders often can have a greater impact than one would first believe. Erin Reid and Michael Toffel conducted a study of the results of a campaign by the Carbon Disclosure Project (CDP), a London-based NGO that represents more than 300 institutional investors. The CDP targeted firms in the S&P 500 and asked that they become transparent about greenhouse gas emissions: They then publicized the names of companies that responded as well as the companies that declined to do so. The authors found that the existence of an environmental resolution not only caused managers of the target firm to become more transparent, but it also had a spillover effect leading nontargeted firms in the same industry to become more transparent too. Apparently, being targeted by shareholder activists, or being in an industry with other firms that have been targeted "primes the pump," making firms more receptive to implementing changes and that receptivity is likely to continue as there is an upward trend in attention to environmental, social, and governance (ESG) issues. According to the *2014 Report on Sustainable, Responsible and Impact Investing Trends in the US*, more investors, both individual and institutional, are factoring their values into their investments, with 308 money managers and 880 community investing institutions incorporating ESG issues into their investment decision making.

Sources: Erin M. Reid and Michael W. Toffel, "Responding to Public and Private Politics: Corporate Disclosure of Climate Change Strategies," *Strategic Management Journal* (Vol. 30, No. 11, 2009), 1157–1178; Michael Kramer, "How Sustainable Investors Impact Industries and Corporate Policies," *Greenbiz.com* (November 26, 2012), http://www.greenbiz.com/blog/2012/11/26/how-sustainable-investors-impact-industries-and-corporate-policies. "2014 Report on Sustainable, Responsible and Impact Investing Trends," http://www.ussif.org/files/publications/sif_trends_14.f.es.pdf. Accessed January 3, 2016.

power shareholders have felt, particularly in board elections. In the United States, votes against board members have generally not been counted and corporations have been free to ignore shareholder resolutions.[137] Withholding a vote for a board member has typically had no impact because only the votes that were actually cast were counted.[138] Similarly, many European firms have not had one vote for each share issued.[139] Of course, the ability of shareholders to elect board members is central to the governance process because the elected board members will be governing the corporation.[140] However, pundits and scholars disagree over the value of the recommended reforms.

Proponents of shareholder democracy argue that if shareholders are not able to select their own representatives, the board is likely to become a self-perpetuating oligarchy.[141] They contend that increased shareholder power and involvement will lead to improved firm performance.[142] Opponents counter that shareholders are not "owners" in the traditional sense of the word because they can exit their ownership relatively easily by simply selling their shares.[143] They contend that increased shareholder power will lead to inefficient and short-term-oriented decision making, as well as infighting among competing interests.[144]

Shareholder democracy begins with board elections and so we focus our discussion there. Three key issues that have arisen are majority vote, classified boards, and proxy access.

Majority vote is the requirement that board members be elected by a majority of votes cast. This is in contrast to the previously prevailing norm of plurality voting. With plurality voting, the board members with the greatest number of "yes" votes are elected to the available seats on the board. The "no" and withheld votes are not counted. With "plurality plus," board members who receive less than a majority of votes cast must submit their resignation; however, boards of directors have not always accepted the resignations.[145]

Classified boards (also known as **staggered boards**) are those that elect their members in staggered terms. For example, in a board of 12 members, four might be elected each year, and each would serve a three-year term. It would then take three years for the entire board slate to be replaced. Classified boards are popular, with companies like Facebook and Tesla choosing to operate with such boards. Many shareholder activists oppose classified boards because of the time required to replace the board. Proponents of classified boards argue that board members need a longer period to make longer-term-oriented strategic decisions. However, it is still up for debate as to whether classified boards are better or worse for stakeholders than unitary boards, where shareholders vote on board members every year.[146]

Proxy access provides shareholders with the opportunity to propose nominees for the board of directors. This has been an issue of contention for years. In the prevailing system, shareholders must file a separate ballot if they want to nominate their own candidates for director positions. This procedure is time-consuming and costly, so shareholder groups are asking for the ability to place their candidates directly on the proxy materials. In 2010 the Dodd–Frank Act reaffirmed the authority of the SEC to issue a proxy access rule and in August that year the SEC approved it. However, a lawsuit challenging the rule succeeded and the SEC had to vacate it. Many institutional investors believe that proxy access would make boards more responsive to shareholders and more vigilant in their oversight. The CII (Council of Institutional Investors) has recommended that companies should provide access to management proxy materials for "long-term" investors owning in aggregate at least 3 percent of a company's voting stock for at least 2 years, to nominate less than a majority of directors.[147]

4.5 The Role of the SEC

The role of the SEC in the United States is clear; the Commission is responsible for protecting investor interests. However, many critics argue that the SEC often appears more focused on the needs of business than on that of investors. In the one of the worst scandals in the SEC's 75-year history, the SEC failed to stop the Bernard Madoff ponzi scheme that cost investors around the world tens of billions of dollars. A **ponzi scheme** lures investors in with the fake promise of profit but actually pays earlier investors with later investors' money until the scheme collapses.

The SEC failed to stop Madoff in spite of having been warned of the scheme nearly a decade earlier. Harry Markopolos, an independent financial fraud investigator, provided the SEC with both the reasons and the roadmap for investigating Madoff, but they failed to stop the scheme. According to Markopolos, "I gift wrapped and delivered the largest Ponzi scheme in history to them and somehow they couldn't be bothered to conduct a thorough and proper investigation because they were too busy on matters of higher priority."[148] In addition to characterizing the regulatory agency as "financially illiterate," Markopolos considers it plagued by infighting and captive to big industry.[149] It appears that Madoff might agree. In a jailhouse interview, he said he was "astonished" that the regulators did not follow simple procedures such as checking his clearinghouse accounts when complaints surfaced.[150] The first substantive complaint the SEC received about Madoff was in 1992, 16 years before the scheme imploded.[151] A 2011 movie, *Chasing Madoff,* about Markopolos's ten-year quest to catch Madoff draws heavily from his aptly named book, *No One Would Listen.*[152]

By all accounts, the failure to catch Madoff would be unlikely to happen today. The SEC may be "outmanned" and "outgunned" but, according to Bloomberg Businessweek, they are "on a roll."[153]

4.6 Shareholder Activism

One major reason that relations between management groups and shareholders have heated up is that shareholders have discovered the benefits of organizing and wielding power. **Shareholder activism** is not a new phenomenon. It goes back over 60 years to 1932, when Lewis Gilbert, then a young owner of ten shares, was appalled by the absence of communication between the New York-based Consolidated Gas Company's management and its owners. Supported by a family inheritance, Gilbert decided to quit his job as a newspaper reporter and "fight this silent dictatorship over other people's money." He resolved to devote himself "to the cause of the public shareholder."[154] Today, technology has made it easier for even the smallest investor to obtain information and share news, ideas, and any issues they have with the companies in which they invest.[155] Today, shareholder activism is thriving. Shareholder activists have put forth a record number of proposals that have led to a shift toward greater shareholder power, but have also created tensions between shareholders and board members.[156]

4.6a The History of Shareholder Activism

The major impetus for the shareholder activist movement came in the 1960s and early 1970s. The early shareholder activists were an unlikely conglomeration—corporate gadflies, political radicals, young lawyers, an assortment of church groups, and a group of physicians.[157] The movement grew out of a period of political and social upheaval—civil rights, the Vietnam War, pollution, and consumerism.

The watershed event for shareholder activism was Campaign GM in the early 1970s, also known as the Campaign to Make General Motors Responsible. Among those involved in this effort was, not surprisingly, Ralph Nader, who is discussed in more detail in Chapter 13. The shareholder group did not achieve all its objectives, but it won enough to demonstrate that shareholder groups could wield power if they worked at it hard enough. Two of Campaign GM's most notable early accomplishments were that (1) the company created a public policy committee of the board, composed of five outside directors, to monitor social performance and (2) GM appointed the Reverend Leon Sullivan as its first black director.[158]

One direct consequence of the success of Campaign GM was the growth of church activism. Church groups were the early mainstay of the corporate social responsibility movement and were among the first shareholder groups to adopt Campaign GM's strategy of raising social issues with corporations. Church groups began examining the relationship between their portfolios and corporate practices, such as minority hiring and companies' presence in South Africa. Church groups remain among the largest groups of institutional stockholders willing to take on the management and press for what they think is right. Many churches' activist efforts are coordinated by the Interfaith Center on Corporate Responsibility (ICCR), which coordinates the shareholder advocacy of about 275 religious orders with about $90 billion in investments. The ICCR was instrumental in convincing Kimberly-Clark to divest the cigarette paper business and pressuring PepsiCo to move out of Burma.[159]

Shareholder activists have historically been socially oriented; that is, they want to exert pressure to make the companies in which they own stock more socially responsive. While that remains true for many, activist shareholders are now also driven by a concern for profit. In late 2015, DuPont CEO Ellen Kullman faced a very public and controversial proxy battle against activist investor Nelson Peltz, cofounder of an $11 billion hedge fund. Peltz wanted Kullman to step down as CEO because he believed the company was underperforming, and his group had plans for dividing and spinning off parts of the company.[160] Kullman eventually won the proxy battle, at a cost of $15 million to the company in defending itself. However, Kullman resigned shortly after the battle, and within a few months, DuPont merged with Dow Chemical.[161]

The growth of shareholder activism shows no signs of abating.[162] Activist shareholders, known also as **corporate gadflies**, are no longer dismissed as nuisance and are instead viewed as credible, powerful, and a force with which to be reckoned.[163] In fact, money managers and hedge funds advertise their activist orientation in the belief that being seen as aggressive gives them an edge.[164]

4.6b Shareholder Resolutions

One of the major vehicles by which shareholder activists communicate their concerns to management groups is through the filing of **shareholder resolutions**. An example of such a resolution is, "The (company name) should name women and minorities to the board of directors." To file a resolution, a shareholder or a shareholder group must obtain a stated number of signatures to require management to place the resolution on the proxy statement so that all the shareholders can vote it on. Resolutions that are defeated (fail to get majority votes) may be resubmitted provided they meet certain SEC requirements for such resubmission.

Although an individual could initiate a shareholder resolution, she or he probably would not have the resources or means to obtain the required signatures to have the resolution placed on the proxy. Thus, most resolutions are initiated by large institutional investors that own large blocks of stock or by activist groups that own few shares of stock but have significant financial backing. Foundations, religious groups, universities, and other such large shareholders are in the best position to initiate resolutions. The issues on which shareholder resolutions are filed vary widely, but they typically concern some aspect of a firm's social performance. Resolutions have addressed such issues as executive compensation, animal testing, board structure, sustainability reporting, board diversity, and climate change. In 2015, according to one shareholder advocacy group, a record number of social and environmental resolutions were filed, with political spending and climate change at the heart of most of the activity.[165]

Most shareholder resolutions never pass, and even those that pass are typically non-binding. So one might ask why groups pursue them. Meredith Benton, research associate with Walden Asset Management, describes why she would come to the point of wanting to put forth a resolution: "The process begins when there's an issue of concern for our clients. We look at what the issue is and how it may impact the companies in our portfolio. Once we have determined what that impact might be and believe there is a long-term business case for why one of our companies should be concerned about the issue, we approach the company. They have a couple different ways they can respond to us. They can ignore us, which happens sometimes. They can constructively engage with us and sit down with us. If they're ignoring us or strongly disagreeing with our viewpoint, we have one more option, which is the shareholder resolution."[166] Benton notes that resolutions are the most public aspect of what they do but that they actually have constructive conversations far more often.[167]

4.6c Shareholder Lawsuits

An earlier reference was made to the **shareholder lawsuit** in the TransUnion case. Shareholders sued the board of directors for approving a buyout offer that the shareholders argued should have had a higher price tag. Their suit charged that the directors had been negligent in failing to secure a third-party opinion from experienced investment bankers. The case went to trial and resulted in a $23.5-million judgment against the directors.[168] The TransUnion case may have been one of the largest successful shareholder suits at that time, but it was dwarfed by the Enron settlement of $7.2 billion.[169] In 2013, Bank of America shareholders received a $2.4 billion settlement to settle claims that the bank hid crucial information from shareholders when it bought Merrill Lynch & Co. at the height of the financial crisis.[170] The **Private Securities Litigation Reform Act of 1995** was intended to rein in excessive levels of private securities litigation. There is speculation that the "gravy train" of securities class action lawsuits, particularly regarding market fraud, may be dwindling as the courts have a harder time determining what exactly might endanger economic competitiveness.[171]

4.7 Investor Relations and Shareholder Engagement

Over the years, corporate boards have neglected their shareholders. As share ownership has dispersed, there are several legitimate reasons why this separation has taken place. However, the tide seems to be turning, as boards seem to be communicating more with their major investors. **Shareholder engagement** is becoming part of a board's policy—a strategy and set of formal procedures for opening communication between shareholders and a company on a variety of issues, including executive compensation, CEO succession, and company financial and ESG performance. In response to prompting by SEC Chair Mary Jo White in 2013 that boards ought to be a "central player in shareholder engagement," the investment company Vanguard proposed "shareholder liaison committees" for the boards of its invested companies.[172] In 2014, independent directors and representatives of the world's largest institutional investors formed the **Shareholder-Director Exchange (SDX)** working group to develop protocols for director-shareholder engagement for U.S. public companies. However, despite such initiatives, the concept of shareholder engagement is still emerging, with some resistance from companies that worry about less-than-legitimate investor concerns that might require time and attention away from key issues.[173]

Public corporations have obligations to existing shareholders as well as potential shareholders. **Full disclosure** (also known as **transparency**) is one of these responsibilities.

Disclosure should be made at regular and frequent intervals and should contain information that might affect the investment decisions of shareholders. This information might include the nature and activities of the business, financial and policy matters, tender offers, and special problems and opportunities in the near future and in the longer term.[174] Of paramount importance are the interests of the investing public, not the interests of the incumbent management team. Board members should avoid conflicts between personal interests and the interests of shareholders. Company executives and directors have an obligation to avoid taking personal advantage of information that is not disclosed to the investing public and to avoid any personal use of corporation assets and influence.

Shareholder engagement and transparency can take many different forms. For example, Berkshire Hathaway Inc. is known for attending to its shareholders, and CEO Warren Buffett is praised by shareholders in return.[175] One indication of Berkshire Hathaway's relationship with shareholders is the annual meeting. Buffett calls the annual shareholders' meeting "Woodstock weekend for capitalists."[176] It is not unusual for shareholders to attend a minor league baseball game decked out in their forest green Berkshire Hathaway T-shirts and caps. Many wait in line to have a picture taken with Buffett or get his autograph.[177] Even in a difficult year, Buffett is honest with his shareholders. In his chairman's letter that followed the global financial crisis, Buffett said bluntly, "I did some dumb things in investments."[178] Of course, communicating is easier when you have Buffett's record of serving his shareholders well. Companies that have incidents to explain like Massey Energy's coal facility explosion or BP's Deepwater Horizon rig explosion make communication with shareholders more challenging.[179]

Technology has made investor relations easier to accomplish, and companies have begun to take advantage of it. Intel Corporation was the first company to let shareholders use the Internet to vote and submit questions to the annual meeting, and Walmart provides live Twitter and video updates from their annual meetings.[180] Herman Miller, the furniture company, has switched to virtual shareholder meetings, not only enhancing shareholder access but also saving money in the process.[181]

With good investor relations, greatly enhanced with stakeholder engagements, many serious problems can be averted and those that are unavoidable are less likely to fester. If shareholders are able to make their concerns heard outside the annual meeting, they are less likely to confront managers with hostile questions when the meeting is in session. If their recommendations receive serious consideration, they are less likely to put them in the form of a formal resolution. Constructive engagement is easier for all involved.[182]

In sum, holding corporations accountable requires the orchestration of many different stakeholders including the board of directors, the CEO, senior management, employees, shareholders, regulators, whistle-blowers, and other stakeholder groups—supported by legislation that helps to increase transparency. We provide a summary of these participants in Figure 4-5.

4.8 An Alternative Model of Corporate Governance

As we mentioned in the beginning of this chapter, the material presented so far is based on the Anglo-American model of corporate governance: It is one of shareholder primacy, that is, it considers shareholders to be of primary importance. As we discussed previously, the **shareholder-primacy model** asserts that maximizing share value is the ultimate firm goal and that improving corporate governance entails reducing board power, maximizing

FIGURE 4-5 Holding Corporations Accountable

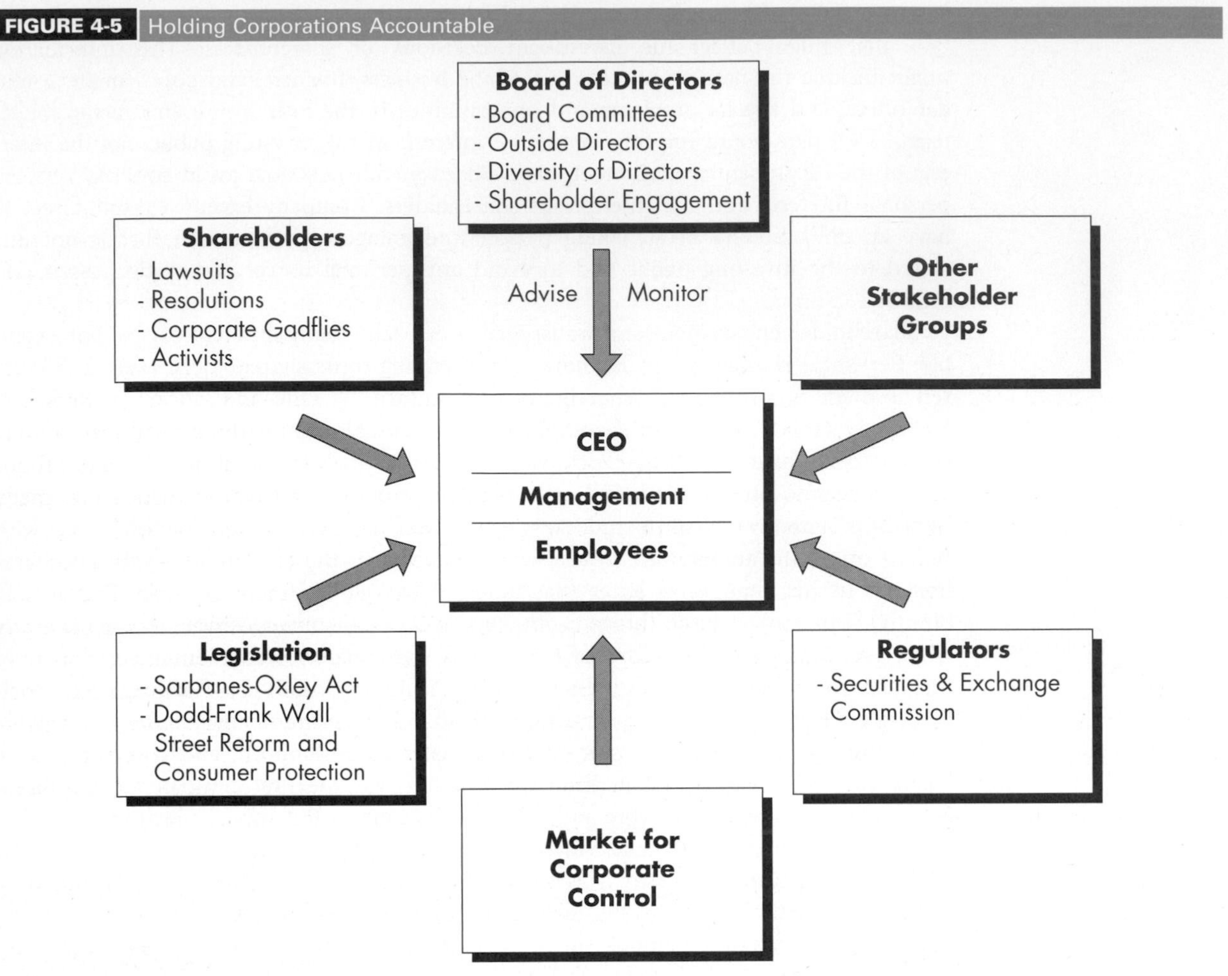

shareholder power, and tying incentives to share price. Activist shareholders have been pursuing these goals with some success, but sometimes that pursuit has strained relations between shareholders and the board.[183] A new perspective is emerging to challenge the traditional model of shareholder primacy. A **director-primacy model** of corporate governance challenges the status quo and asks whether the balance of power in corporate governance should favor shareholders or board members.[184] Some observers argue that the current push to increase shareholder power represents a sorely needed improvement in corporate governance.[185] Others express skepticism about the value of an increase in shareholder power and argue for a different conception of corporate governance.[186]

A director-primacy model of corporate governance is based on the concept of a corporation that is not owned, but instead is an independent legal entity that owns itself.[187] In it, boards are "mediating hierarchs" who are responsible for balancing the often competing interests of a variety of stakeholders. In this model, boards have a duty to shareholders but board members are the ultimate decision makers and their primary duty is to the corporation. From this perspective, board members should be given the autonomy and discretion needed to balance demands that sometimes conflict with each other.[188]

Instead of a principal-agent based model, the director-primacy view stems from a **team production model** of corporate governance: Team production notes that the work of a corporation requires the combined input of two or more individuals or groups.[189] From this perspective, corporations are cooperative teams charged with the responsibility of not only creating new wealth but also attending to the interests and needs of stakeholders—and boards should be reflective of that cooperative team.[190] Some analysts suggest that corporations will not be able to fulfill their sustainability and corporate social responsibility goals until corporate boards move away from a singular focus on shareholder wealth maximization.[191]

Many of the proponents for a director-primacy model of corporate governance come from the field of law. They argue that the laws used to support a shareholder-primacy model of corporate governance have been misinterpreted and that shareholders do not own corporations—they only own stock and thus have no legal right to control the firm.[192] Nevertheless, those in support of director-primacy place value on shareholder welfare; they simply argue that a director-primacy model of corporate governance will ultimately serve shareholders best because it provides boards of directors the autonomy needed to do what is in the long-term best interests of the corporation.[193] These proponents contend that focusing on share value promotes short-termism, which eventually can cause harm to firms and all their stakeholders, including shareholders.[194]

The pursuit of share value is coming under question by practitioners as well as academics. As noted by *PwC* in its 2015 Annual Corporate Directors Survey, "The dichotomy between long-term and short-term thinking has had a polarizing effect on corporate boardrooms and investors in recent years."[195] Recent controversies over the "myth of maximizing shareholder value" continue to be debated, and the arguments for and against shareholder primacy and director primacy continue to evolve and are not likely to be settled soon. In the meantime, awareness and understanding of both perspectives is helpful in developing a richer understanding of the complexities of corporate governance.

Summary

Recent events in corporate America have served to underscore the importance of good corporate governance and the legitimacy it is supposed to provide for business. To remain legitimate, corporations must be governed according to the intended and legal pattern. Governance debacles, such as the global financial crisis, call not only the legitimacy of individual companies into question but also that of business as a whole.

The modern corporation is a complex entity and so it is not surprising that reasonable people would differ on the model by which corporate governance should be based. The Anglo-American shareholder-primacy model has been a dominant model for years but the director primacy–based team production model is making inroads in U.S. businesses with the idea that it offers a broader stakeholder perspective. In the shareholder-primacy model, the key issue is a separation between ownership and control, which has resulted in problems with managers not always doing what the owners would rather they do. From this perspective, boards of directors are responsible for ensuring that managers represent the best interests of owners, but boards sometimes lack the independence needed to monitor management effectively. This has led to serious problems in the corporate governance arena, such as excessive levels of CEO pay and a weak relationship between CEO pay and firm performance. Of course, at times an effort to solve one problem can create another. The use of stock options in CEO compensation has helped tie CEO pay to firm performance more closely, but it has resulted in skyrocketing levels of pay, as well as in the manipulation of option timing and pricing. Other issues are lavish executive retirement plans and outside director compensation. New SEC rules for transparency may have an impact on the compensation issue in the future.

In the director-primacy model, the board is a mediating hierarch, responsible for balancing the needs of all the stakeholders. At times, the two models of corporate governance converge but more often, they diverge. The Market for Corporate Control is an example. From the shareholder-primacy perspective, the market for corporate control should rein in CEO excesses. The threat of a takeover should motivate a CEO to represent shareholders' best interests. Poison pills become problems because they can blunt the takeover threat by making it prohibitively expensive for an acquirer. In contrast, the director-primacy model would see poison pills as an opportunity to slow the speed of a hostile takeover attempt, providing an opportunity to assure that all stakeholders are well represented.

SOX was a landmark piece of legislation, drafted in response to the financial scandals of 2001. As with all efforts to improve corporate governance, it has had both costs and benefits. The demands of SOX have led many firms to go private to avoid the costs involved in compliance; however, evidence indicates that firms have adjusted to the requirements and seen positive outcomes from the requirements. The global financial crisis ushered in the Dodd–Frank Wall Street Reform Act, which brought comprehensive financial regulatory reform, and new requirements that affected the oversight of financial institutions and corporate governance practices, many of which are just being implemented.

In many ways, corporate governance has improved. CEOs no longer enjoy job security when firm performance suffers. Corporations can no longer release false or misleading reports without threat of consequences. The growth in CEO pay has tapered off, although it remains at extremely high levels. These improvements are worthy of note, but they are insufficient to protect the legitimacy of business. Steps were taken to lessen the likelihood of another Enron or another global financial crisis occurring. Continual vigilance must be maintained if corporate governance is to realize its promise and its purpose, that of being responsive to the needs of shareholders and the many individuals and groups who have a stake in the firm, as well as enabling business to be a positive force in society.

Key Terms

Discussion Questions

1. Explain the evolution of corporate governance. What problems developed? What are the current trends?
2. What are the major criticisms of boards of directors? Which single criticism do you find to be the most important? Why?
3. Explain how governance failures such as Enron and the global financial crisis could happen. How might they be avoided?
4. Outline the major suggestions that have been set forth for improving corporate governance. In your opinion, which suggestions are the most important? Why?
5. Discuss the pros and cons of the shareholder-primacy and director-primacy models of corporate governance. Which do you prefer and why?

Endnotes

1. Gallup Confidence in Institutions, http://www.gallup.com/poll/1597/confidence-institutions.aspx. Accessed January 11, 2016.
2. Guhan Subramanian, "Corporate Governance 2.0," *Harvard Business Review* (March, 2015, p. 98).
3. Cited in Edwin M. Epstein and Dow Votaw (eds.) *Rationality, Legitimacy, Responsibility: Search for New Directions in Business and Society* (Santa Monica, CA: Goodyear Publishing Co., 1978), 72.
4. Ibid., 73.
5. Ibid.
6. "Miracle Healers," *The Economist*, (September 19, 2015), 57.
7. Epstein and Votaw, 1978.
8. Maxwell Palmer and Benjamin Schneer, "How and Why Retired Politicians Get Lucrative Appointments on Corporate Boards," *Washington Post Monkey Cage Post* (February 1, 2015 https://www.washingtonpost.com/blogs/monkey-cage/wp/2015/02/01/how-and-why-retired-politicians-get-lucrative-appointments-on-corporate-boards/. Accessed December 28, 2015
9. Epstein and Votaw, 1978.
10. William R. Dill (ed.), *Running the American Corporation* (Englewood Cliffs, NJ: Prentice Hall, 1978), 11.
11. Ibid.
12. Richard C. Warren, "The Evolution of Business Legitimacy," *European Business Review* (Vol. 15, No. 3, 2003), 153–163.
13. Ibid.
14. "Special Report: Corporate America's Woes, Continued—Enron: One Year On," *The Economist* (November 30, 2002).
15. Ruth V. Aguilera and Gregory Jackson. "The Cross-National Diversity of Corporate Governance: Dimensions and Determinants," *Academy of Management Review* (2003), 28, no. 3, 447–465.
16. R.I. (Bob) Tricker, "The Cultural Dependence of Corporate Governance," (November 7, 2011), https://corporategovernanceoup.wordpress.com/page/2/. Accessed December 17, 2015.
17. Ibid.
18. Lynn Stout, *The Shareholder Value Myth* (San Francisco, CA: Berrett-Koehler Publishers, Inc., 2012).
19. Carl Icahn, "What Ails Corporate America—And What Should Be Done," *Businessweek* (October 17, 1986), 101.
20. PwC's 2015 Annual Corporate Directors Survey, *Governing for the Long Term: Looking Down the Road with an Eye on the Rear-View Mirror,* http://www.pwc.com/us/en/corporate-governance/annual-corporate-directors-survey/assets/pwc-2015-annual-corporate-directors-survey.pdf. Accessed December 17, 2015.
21. Ibid.
22. Ibid.
23. SpencerStuart and NYSE Survey, "What Do Directors Think?" (February 2015) https://www.spencerstuart.com/research-and-insight/what-directors-think-2015. Accessed December 17, 2015.
24. Jack Welch and Suzy Welch, "How Much Blame Do Boards Deserve?" *Businessweek* (January 14, 2009), http://www.businessweek.com/stories/2009-01-13/how-much-blame-do-boards-deserve. Accessed January 2, 2016.
25. Dominic Barton and Mark Wiseman, "Where Boards Fall Short," *Harvard Business Review*, (January-February 2015), https://hbr.org/2015/01/where-boards-fall-short. Accessed December 10, 2015.
26. Matt Krantz, "9 CEOs Paid 800 Times More than Their Workers," *USA Today Money* (August 6, 2015).
27. Tim Mullaney, "Why Corporate CEO Pay Is so High and Going Higher," *CNBC.com* (May 18, 2015) http://www.cnbc.com/2015/05/18/why-corporate-ceo-pay-is-so-high-and-going-higher.html. Accessed December 28, 2015.
28. Ibid.

29. Equilar, "2015 CEO Pay Strategies" (August 4, 2015), http://www.equilar.com/reports/21-2015-CEO-pay-strategies.html. Accessed December 29, 2015.

30. Emily Chasan, "Last Gap for Stock Options?" *The Wall Street Journal CFO Report* (August 16, 2013) http://blogs.wsj.com/cfo/2013/08/26/last-gasp-for-stock-options/. Accessed December 17, 2015.

31. Equilar, 2015.

32. Krantz, 2015.

33. Alex Barker, David Oakley, and Brian Groom, "EU Eyes New Rules over Executive Pay," *Financial Times*, March 8, 2014 (London Edition), 2.

34. Paul Hodgson, "A Brief History of Say on Pay," *Ivey Business Journal* (September/October 2009), http://www.iveybusinessjournal.com/topics/leadership/a-brief-history-of-say-on-pay. Accessed January 1, 2016.

35. Ibid.

36. Diane Brady, "Say on Pay: Boards Listen When Shareholders Speak," *Bloomberg Businessweek* (June 7, 2012), http://www.businessweek.com/articles/2012-06-07/say-on-pay-boards-listen-when-shareholders-speak. Accessed January 31, 2016.

37. Paul Hodgson, "Surprise Surprise: Say on Pay Appears to be Working," *Fortune* online (July 8, 2015), http://fortune.com/2015/07/08/say-on-pay-ceos/. Accessed December 15, 2015.

38. Ibid.

39. Joann Lublin, "How Much the Best-Performing and Worst-Performing CEOs Got Paid," *The Wall Street Journal* online (June 25, 2015), http://www.wsj.com/articles/how-much-the-best-and-worst-ceos-got-paid-1435104565. Accessed January 3, 2016.

40. Corporate Knights 2015 Global 100 Methodology, http://www.global100.org/methodology/selection-criteria.html. Accessed January6, 2016.

41. Corporate Knights, Clean Capitalism, http://www.corporateknights.com/us/about-us/. Accessed January 10, 2016.

42. Gretchen Morgenson, "Making Managers Pay, Literally," *The New York Times* (March 25, 2007), 1.

43. Executive Compensation Clawbacks: 2014 Proxy Disclosure Study *PwC*, http://www.pwc.com/us/en/hr-management/publications/executive-compensation-clawbacks-2014-proxy-disclosure-study.html. Accessed December 17, 2016.

44. Ibid.

45. Randy Diamond, "CII Gets Specific on Its Clawback Recommendations," *Pensions & Investments* (October 5, 2012), http://www.pionline.com/article/20121005/DAILYREG/121009896. Accessed January 1, 2016.

46. Ibid.

47. ALF-CIO. Executive PayWatch, http://www.aflcio.org/Corporate-Watch/Paywatch-2015. Accessed January 12, 2016.

48. John J. Sweeney, "Commentary: The Foxes Are Still Guarding the Henhouse," *Los Angeles Times* (September 19, 2003), B13.

49. "Relentless Activism," *Directorship* (January/February, 2007), 1–13.

50. Alyce Gomstin, "Why Bank of America's Ken Lewis Will Take Home More than Peers," *ABC News Business Unit* (October 8, 2009), http://abcnews.go.com/Business/bank-america-ceo-ken-lewis-retirement-pay-higher/story?id=8775299. Accessed December 29, 2016.

51. Kevin McCoy, "Retirement Benefit Gap: CEOs Have Platinum Pension Packages," USA Today, (October 28, 2015), http://www.usatoday.com/story/money/2015/10/28/ceo-retirement-packages-dwarf-employee-benefits/74681692/. Accessed November 10, 2015.

52. Stephanie Costo, "Trends in Retirement Plan Coverage over the Last Decade," *Bureau of Labor Statistics* (February, 2006), http://www.bls.gov/opub/mlr/2006/02/art5full.pdf. Accessed January 31, 2016.

53. Fran Hawthorne, "For Top Executives, Richer Retirement Plans," *The New York Times* (September 11, 2012), http://www.nytimes.com/2012/09/12/business/retirementspecial/companies-beef-up-retirement-plans-for-top-executives.html?pagewanted=all&_r=0. Accessed January 31, 2016.

54. Geoffrey Colvin, "Is the Board Too Cushy?" *Director* (February 1997), 64–65.

55. Sacha Pfeiffer and Todd Wallack, "Few Hours, Soaring Pay for Corporate Board Members," The Boston Globe (December 2, 2015), https://www.bostonglobe.com/business/2015/12/01/good-work-you-can-get-corporate-directors-among-highest-paid-part-time-employees-america/rYHPP7ozPXU0AG8VSo37MM/story.html. Accessed December 29, 2015.

56. Nanette Byrnes and Jane Sasseen, "Board of Hard Knocks," *Businessweek* (January 22, 2007), 35–39.

57. Ibid.

58. Leslie Kwoh, "Firms Resist New Pay-Equity Rules," *The Wall Street Journal* (June 26, 2012), http://www.wsj.com/articles/SB10001424052702304458604577490842584787190. Accessed March 12, 2016.

59. Ibid.

60. Ibid.

61. Matt Orsagh, "SEC: "More Transparency Please" on Executive Compensation," *Market Integrity Insights* (June 22, 2012), http://blogs.cfainstitute.org/market integrity/2012/06/22/sec-more-transparency-please-on-executive-compensation/. Accessed January 31, 2016.

62. Statement by SEC Commissioner Luis A. Augilar at an Open Meeting on Pay Versus Performance Disclosures (April 29, 2015), http://www.sec.gov/news/statement/improving-transparency-for-executive-pay-practices.html. Accessed December 29, 2015.

63. Heidi N. Moore, "The Demise of Poison Pills?: Why Takeover Defenses Have Been on the Wane; Shareholders vs. Boards," *The Wall Street Journal* (February 24, 2009), C4.

64. David Futrelle, "Corporate Raiders Beware: A Short History of the "Poison Pill" Defense," *Time* (November 7, 2012), http://business.time.com/2012/11/07/corporate-raiders-beware-a-short-history-of-the-poison-pill-takeover-defense/. Accessed January 31, 2016.

65. Dealbook, "Netflix Adopts Poison Pill," DealB%k (November 5, 2012), http://dealbook.nytimes.com/2012/11/05/netflix-adopts-poison-pill/. Accessed January 31, 2016.

66. Steven Davidoff Solomon, "Poison Pill's Relevance in the Age of Shareholder Activism," DealB%k (April 18, 2014), http://dealbook.nytimes.com/2014/04/18/poison-pills-relevance-in-the-age-of-shareholder-activism/?_r=0. Accessed December 29, 2015.

67. John Laide, "2014 Poison Pill Impetus: Why Are U.S. Companies Adopting Poison Pills? FactSet Insight (January 2, 2015), http://www.factset.com/insight/2015/01/2014-poison-pill-impetus-why-are-u.s.-companies-adopting-poison-pills#.VwEjl3qUQmR. Accessed January 3, 2016.

68. Solomon, 2014.

69. Ibid.

70. Philip L. Cochran and Steven L. Wartick, "Golden Parachutes: Good for Management and Society?" in S. Prakash Sethi and Cecilia M. Falbe (eds.) *Business and Society: Dimensions of Conflict and Cooperation* (Lexington, MA: Lexington Books, 1987), 321.

71. Ann K. Buchholtz and Barbara A. Ribbens, "Role of Chief Executive Officers in Takeover Resistance: Effects of CEO Incentives and Individual Characteristics," *Academy of Management Journal* (June 1994), 554–579.

72. Cochran and Wartick, 325–326.

73. Chris Gay, "Can Huge CEO Golden Parachutes Hurt You?" U.S. News Money (November 4, 2012), http://money.usnews.com/money/personal-finance/mutual-funds/articles/2012/11/14/can-huge-ceo-golden-parachutes-hurt-you. Accessed March 12, 2016.

74. Equilar Study: Change in Control Case Severance Analysis, http://www.globalequity.org/geo/sites/default/files/Equilar-Change-in-Control-August2011.pdf. Accessed January 31, 2016.

75. Lydia DePillis, "The Rise and (Maybe) Fall of the Golden Parachute," *The Washington Post* online (April 2, 2015), https://www.washingtonpost.com/news/wonk/wp/2015/04/02/the-rise-and-maybe-fall-of-the-golden-parachute/. Accessed December 29, 2015.

76. Alicia Ritcey and Katherine Chiglinsky, "Chubb Shareholders Say No to Finnegan's $80M Golden Parachute," *Insurance Journal*, (October 22, 2015), http://www.insurancejournal.com/news/national/2015/10/22/385874.htm , Accessed December 5, 2015.

77. U.S. Securities and Exchange Commission "Insider Trading," http://www.sec.gov/answers/insider.htm. Accessed January 31, 2016.

78. Josh Clark, "How Insider Trading Works," *howstuffworks*, http://money.howstuffworks.com/insider-trading.htm. Accessed January 31, 2016.

79. U.S. Securities and Exchange Commission, "Insider Trading". http://www.sec.gov/answers/insider.htm. Accessed January 31, 2016.

80. Reem Heakal, "Defining Illegal Insider Trading," Investopedia (July 26, 2013), http://www.investopedia.com/articles/03/100803.asp. Accessed January 31, 2016.

81. Ibid.

82. Peter Henning, "String of Insider Trading Cases Shows Prosecutors Casting a Wider Net," *The New York Times* (December 3, 2012), http://dealbook.nytimes.com/2012/12/03/string-of-insider-trading-cases-shows-prosecutors-casting-a-wider-net/. Accessed February 1, 2016.

83. See Greg Stohr and Patricia Hurtado, "Insider Trading Cases Imperiled as U.S. Supreme Court Spurns Appeal," *Bloomberg* (October 5, 2015), http://www.bloomberg.com/news/articles/2015-10-05/insider-trading-cases-imperiled-as-top-u-s-court-spurns-appeal. Accessed March 21, 2016; Alex Berenson, "A Deal That Lost Millions for Galleon," *The New York Times* (October 20, 2009), http://www.nytimes.com/2009/10/21/business/21insider.html. Accessed January 1, 2016.

84. "SEC Enforcement Cases Hit Record High in 2011," *Thomson Reuters Insight* (November 9, 2011), https://content.next.westlaw.com/Document/I8b6918809 56d11e19fefb85885c303b5/View/FullText.html?transitionType=Default&contextData=%28sc.Default%29. Accessed March 11, 2016; Josh Clark, "How Insider Trading Works," *howstuffworks*, http://money.howstuffworks.com/insider-trading.htm. Accessed December 29, 2015.

85. Christopher H. Schmitt, "The SEC Lifts the Curtain on Company Info," *Businessweek* (August 11, 2000).

86. Liz Moyer, "Study Finds Director Pay Rising Sharply," *DealB%k*, (December 9, 2015), http://www.nytimes.com/2015/12/10/business/dealbook/study-finds-director-pay-rising-sharply.html?_r=0. Accessed December 20, 2015.

87. Michael Schlesinger, "2002 Sarbanes–Oxley Act," *Business Entities* (November/December 2002), 42–49.

88. Ibid.

89. Jonathon A. Segal, "The Joy of Uncooking," *HR Magazine* (November 2002), 52–57.

90. SOX Compliance—Changes Abound Amid Drive for Stability and Long-term Value, *Protiviti 2015*

Sarbanes-Oxley Compliance Survey, http://www.protiviti.com/en-US/Documents/Surveys/2015-SOX-Compliance-Survey-Protiviti.pdf. Accessed January 13, 2016.

91. Michael Santoro and Ronald Strauss, *Wall Street Values: Business Ethics and the Financial Crisis,* New York: Cambridge University Press, 2013, p. 19.

92. Women on Boards 2020, Gender Diversity Study, https://www.2020wob.com/companies/2020-gender-diversity-index. Accessed January 1, 2016.

93. Alliance for Board Diversity, "Board Diversity at a Standstill in Fortune 500 Companies," (August 15, 2013), http://www.theabd.org/ABD_Missing_Pieces_Press_Release_Final_8_15.pdf. Accessed January 1, 2016.

94. See for example, Susan Adams, Patricia Flynn and Toni Wolfman, "Orchestrating the Demise of All-Male Boards," *Journal of Management Inquiry* (DOI 1056492614546264, 2014).

95. Russell Reynolds Survey on Board Diversity, http://www.russellreynolds.com/insights/thought-leadership/minority-female-representation-on-fortune-250-boards-executive-teams. Accessed January 1, 2016.

96. Johanne Grosvold, Stephen Pavelin, and Ian Tonks, "Gender Diversity on Company Boards," *Vox* (March 27, 2012), http://www.voxeu.org/article/women-boardroom. Accessed January 4, 2016

97. 2014 Catalyst Consensus: Women Board Directors (January 13, 2015), http://www.catalyst.org/knowledge/2014-catalyst-census-women-board-directors, Accessed January 1, 2016.

98. Joan Warner, "Get Ready for a Red-Hot Season," *Directorship* (December 2006–January 2007), 1–27.

99. Stephanie Holmes, "Smashing the Glass Ceiling," *BBC News* (January 11, 2008), http://news.bbc.co.uk/2/hi/business/7176879.stm. Accessed January 4, 2016.

100. Claire Cain Miller, "Women on the Board: Quotas Have Limited Success, *The Upshot* (June 19, 2014), http://www.nytimes.com/2014/06/20/upshot/women-on-the-board-quotas-have-limited-success.html?_r=0. Accessed December 30, 2015.

101. Ibid.

102. International Labour Organization, "Women on Boards: Building the Female Talent Pipeline," http://www.ilo.org/gender/Informationresources/Publications/WCMS_410200/lang–en/index.htm. Accessed March 21, 2016.

103. Thomas W. Joo, "A Trip through the Maze of 'Corporate Democracy': Shareholder Voice and Management Composition," *St. John's Law Review* (Fall, 2003), 735–767.

104. Steven A. Ramirez, "A Flaw in the Sarbanes–Oxley Reform: Can Diversity in the Boardroom Quell Corporate Corruption?" *St. John's Law Review* (Fall, 2003), 837–866.

105. Niclas L. Erhardt, James D. Werbel, and Charles B. Shrader, "Board of Director Diversity and Firm Financial Performance," *Corporate Governance: An International Review* (April 2003), 102–111.

106. Eric Helland and Michael Sykuta, "Who's Monitoring the Monitor? Do Outside Directors Protect Shareholders' Interests?" *Financial Review* (May 2005), 155–172.

107. Richard A. Johnson and Daniel W. Greening, "The Effects of Corporate Governance and Institutional Ownership Types on Corporate Social Performance," *Academy of Management Journal* (October 1999), 564–576.

108. Donald C. Hambrick, Vilmos Misangyi, and Chuljin Park, "The Quad Model for Identifying a Corporate Director's Potential for Effective Monitoring: Toward a New Theory of Board Sufficiency," *Academy of Management Review* (Vol. 40, No. 3, 2015), 323–344.

109. James B. Stewart, "Problems at Volkswagen Start at the Boardroom," *The New York Times* (September 24, 2015), B1.

110. Maxwell Murphy, "A 'Waste of a Board Seat'," *The Wall Street Journal* (October 16, 2012), B1.

111. John Joseph, William Ocasio, and Mary-Hunter McDonnell, "The Structural Elaboration of Board Independence: Executive Power, Institutional Logics, and the Adoption of the CEO-Only Board Structures in U.S. Corporate Governance, *Academy of Management Journal,* (Vol. 57, No. 6, 2014), 1834–1858.

112. The Sarbanes–Oxley Act 2002, http://www.legalarchiver.org/soa.htm Accessed January 31, 2016.

113. Charles A. Anderson and Robert N. Anthony, *The New Corporate Directors: Insights for Board Members and Executives* (New York: John Wiley & Sons, 1986), 141.

114. Sydney Finkelstein and Donald Hambrick, "Boards of Directors and Corporate Governance," In *Strategic Leadership: Top Executives and Their Effects on Organizations,* (MN: West Publishing, 1996), 216.

115. Olubunmi Faleye, Rani Hoitash, and Udi Hoitash, "The Costs of Intense Board Monitoring," *Journal of Financial Economics,* (Vol. 101, 2011), 160–181.

116. Johnson & Johnson, http://www.investor.jnj.com/governance/committee.cfm. Accessed February 1, 2016.

117. Unilever Investor Relations http://www.unilever.com/investorrelations/corp_governance/boardandmanagementcommittees/. Accessed January 28, 2016.

118. Lynn Paine, "Sustainability in the Boardroom," *Harvard Business Review* (Vol. 92, No 7/8, July–August 2014), 86–94.

119. Ibid.

120. The Conference Board, "CEO Dismissals in the U.S. at the Lowest Level in a Decade" (April 14, 2015), https://www.conference-board.org/press/pressdetail.cfm?pressid=5430. Accessed January 2, 2016.

121. Ibid.
122. Theo Francis and Joann Lublin, "Big Investors Question Corporate Board Tenures," *The Wall Street Journal* (March 23, 2016), http://www.wsj.com/article_email/big-investors-question-corporate-board-tenures-1458761857-lMyQjAxMTE2MjI2NTgyODU3Wj. Accessed March 30, 2016.
123. Nanette Byrnes and David Kiley, "Hello, You Must Be Going," *Businessweek* (February 12, 2007), 30–32.
124. Donald Hambrick and Timothy Quigley, "Toward a More Accurate Contextualization of the CEO Effect on Firm Performance," *Strategic Management Journal* (Vol. 35, No. 4, 2014), 473–491.
125. The Conference Board, 2015.
126. Jeffrey Sonnenfeld, "CEO Exit Schedules: A Season to Stay, a Season to Go," *Fortune* online, (May 6, 2015), http://fortune.com/2015/05/06/ceo-tenure-cisco/. Accessed January 2, 2016.
127. Sydney Finkelstein and Richard D'Aveni, "CEO Duality as a Double-Edged Sword: How Boards of Directors Balance Entrenchment Avoidance and Unity of Command," *Academy of Management Journal* (Vol. 37, No. 5, 1994), 1079–1106.
128. Ibid.
129. SpencerStuart, "More New Independent Directors added to S&P 500 Boards, but Turnover Remains Slow" (October 2015), https://www.spencerstuart.com/who-we-are/media-center/more-new-independent-directors-added-to-s-and-p-500-boards. Accessed January 13, 2016.
130. "A Landmark Ruling That Puts Board Members in Peril," *Businessweek* (March 18, 1985), 56–57.
131. Court of Chancery of the State of Delaware Memorandum Opinion In Re Dole Food Co., Inc Stockholder Litigation, In Re Appraisal of Dole Food Company, Inc. (August 15, 2015), http://courts.delaware.gov/opinions/download.aspx?ID=228790. Accessed January 2, 2016.
132. Paul E. Fiorella, "Why Comply? Directors Face Heightened Personal Liability after Caremark," *Business Horizons* (July/August 1998), 49–52.
133. "Liability & Litigation," *Corporate Board* (January/February 2007), 28–29.
134. J. P. Donlon. "The Flaw of Law," *Directorship* (February 2005), 3.
135. *Corporate Board*, 2007.
136. Jennifer B. Rubin, "A View from the Bar: Directors Can Be Liable for Layoffs, Plant Closings," *Corporate Board Member* (Third Quarter 2009), https://archive.boardmember.com/MagazineArticle_Details.aspx?id=3879. Accessed January 31, 2016.
137. "Ownership Matters," *The Economist* (March 11, 2006), 10.
138. Joo, 735–767.
139. "What Shareholder Democracy?" *The Economist* (March 26, 2005), 62.
140. "Who Selects, Governs," *Directorship* (May 2004), 6.
141. Dennis M. Ray, "Corporate Boards and Corporate Democracy," *Journal of Corporate Citizenship* (Winter, 2005), 93–105.
142. Lucien A. Bebchuk, "The Case for Increasing Shareholder Power," *Harvard Law Review* (January 2005), 835–914.
143. Iman Anabtawi and Lynn A. Stout, "Fiduciary Duties for Activist Shareholders," *Stanford Law Review* (February 2008), 1255–1329.
144. Lynn A. Stout, "Corporations Shouldn't Be Democracies," *The Wall Street Journal—Eastern Edition* (September 27, 2007), A17.
145. Joann S. Lublin, "Directors Lose Elections but Not Seats: Staying Power of Board Members Raises Questions about Investor Democracy," *The Wall Street Journal* (September 28, 2009), B4.
146. Ann Buchholtz and Jill Brown, "Shareholder Democracy as a Misbegotten Metaphor," in M. Goranova and L. Ryan (Eds) *Shareholder Empowerment*, New York: Palgrave-MacMillan, 81–102.
147. The Council of Institutional Investors, http://www.cii.org/proxy_access. Accessed January 3, 2016.
148. Allan Chernoff, "Madoff Whistleblower Blasts SEC," CNNMoney.com (February 4, 2009), http://money.cnn.com/2009/02/04/news/newsmakers/madoff_whistleblower/. Accessed January 31, 2016.
149. Ibid.
150. Diana B. Henriquez, "Lapses Helped Scheme, Madoff Told Investigators," *The New York Times* (October 30, 2009), A1.
151. Ibid.
152. Daniel M. Gold, "The High Human Cost of Following the Money in the Madoff Fraud Case," *The New York Times* (August 25, 2011), http://movies.nytimes.com/2011/08/26/movies/chasing-madoff-a-documentary-of-a-fraud-review.html?_r=0. Accessed February 1, 2016.
153. Devin Leonard, "Outmanned, Outgunned, and On a Roll," *Bloomberg Businessweek* (April 23–April 29, 2012), 59–66.
154. Lauren Tainer, *The Origins of Shareholder Activism* (Washington, DC: Investor Responsibility Research Center, July 1983), 2.
155. Rob Curran, "Small Investor, Bigger Voice," *The Wall Street Journal* (December 3, 2009), R8.
156. Jennifer G. Hill 2010. "The Rising Tension between Shareholder and Director Power in the Common Law World," *Corporate Governance: An International Review* (July 2010), 344–359.
157. Ibid., 1.
158. Ibid., 12–22.

159. "Religious Activists Raise Cain with Corporations," *Chicago Tribune* (June 7, 1998), Business Section, 8.

160. Jeffrey Sonnenfeld, "Another Suicidal Board? How DuPont's Directors Failed Ellen Kullman," Fortune (October 13, 2015), http://fortune.com/2015/10/13/dupont-board-ellen-kullman/. Accessed December 2, 2015.

161. Stephen Gandel, "How Dupont Went to War with Activist Investor Nelson Peltz," Fortune online (May 11, 2015), http://fortune.com/2015/05/11/how-dupont-went-to-war. Accessed December 15, 2015.

162. David Benoit, "Activism's Long Road from Corporate Raiding to Banner Year," *The Wall Street Journal Online*, (December 26, 2015), http://www.wsj.com/articles/activisms-long-road-from-corporate-raiding-to-banner-year-1451070910. Accessed January 2, 2016.

163. Duhigg, 2007.

164. Ibid.

165. *Proxy Preview*, 2015, "Record Number of Social and Environmental Shareholder Resolutions Filed in 2015," http://www.asyousow.org/wp-content/uploads/2015/03/release-record-number-of-social-and-environmental-shareholder-resolutions-filed-in-2015.pdf. Accessed January 3, 2016.

166. "How Shareholder Resolutions Influence Corporate Behavior," *Christian Science Montor Daily Online Newspaper* (May 1, 2006).

167. Ibid.

168. Thomas J. Neff, "Liability Panic in the Board Room," *The Wall Street Journal* (November 10, 1986), 22.

169. Dan Fitzpatrick, Christian Berthelson, and Robin Sidel, "BofA Takes New Crisis-Era Hit," *The Wall Street Journal* (September 29–30, 2012), B1–B2.

170. Justin Fox, "Ending the Shareholder Lawsuit Gravy Train," *Harvard Business Review* (February 27, 2014). https://hbr.org/2014/02/ending-the-shareholder-lawsuit-gravy-train/. Accessed January 3, 2016.

171. Ibid.

172. Lex Suvanto, "Should Boards of Directors Communicate with Shareholders?" Edelman Global Practices (Janary 5, 2015), http://www.edelman.com/post/boards-directors-communicate-shareholders/. Accessed January 3, 2016.

173. Matt Orsagh, "Shareholder Engagement: Bridging the Divide between Boards and Investors," CFA Institute Market Integrity Insights (March 26, 2014), https://blogs.cfainstitute.org/marketintegrity/2014/03/26/shareholder-engagement-bridging-the-divide-between-boards-and-investors/. Accessed January 3, 2016.

174. "The Responsibility of a Corporation to Its Shareholders," *Criteria for Decision Making* (C. W. Post Center, Long Island University, 1979), 14.

175. Mel Duvall and Kim S. Nash, "Auditing an Oracle: Shareholders Nearly Deify Warren Buffett for the Way He Manages His Diverse Holding Company, Bershire Hathaway of Omaha," *Baseline* (August 1, 2003), 30.

176. "Recap: The 2015 Berkshire Hathaway Annual Meeting," (May 2, 2015), *The Wall Street Journal* online Moneybeat, http://blogs.wsj.com/moneybeat/2015/05/02/live-analysis-the-2015-berkshire-hathaway-annual-meeting/. Accessed January 12, 2016.

177. Amy Kover, "Warren Buffett: Revivalist," *Fortune* (May 29, 2000), 58–60.

178. Alex Crippen, "Warren Buffet Tells Shareholders He Did 'Some Dumb Things' in 2008," *CNBC* (February 28, 2009), http://www.cnbc.com/id/29441086. Accessed January 31, 2016.

179. Michael McGinn, "Disclose No Evil," *Newsweek* (February 28, 2011), 5.

180. Curran, 2009.

181. Ibid.

182. Warner, 2007.

183. Hill, 2010.

184. Margaret M. Blair and Lynn A. Stout, "A Team Production Theory of Corporate Law," *Virginia Law Review* (March, 1999), 247–329; Stephen M. Bainbridge, "Director Primacy and Shareholder Disempowerment," *Harvard Law Review* (April 2006), 1735–1758; Luh Luh Lan and Loizos Heracleous, "Rethinking Agency Theory: The View from the Law," *Academy of Management Review* (April 2010) 223–239.

185. Lucien A. Bebchuk, Cohen A., and Ferrell A. 2009. "What Matters in Corporate Governance?" *Review of Financial Studies* (February 2009), 783–827.

186. Iman Anabtawi, "Some Skepticism about Increasing Shareholder Power," *UCLA Law Review* (February 2006), 561–599.

187. Stout, 2012.

188. Blair and Stout, 1999.

189. Ibid.

190. Allen Kaufman and Ernie Englander, "A Team Production Model of Corporate Governance," *Academy of Management Executive* (August 1, 2005), 9–22.

191. Edward E. Lawler and Christopher G. Worley, "Why Boards Need to Change," *MIT Sloan Management Review* (Fall 2012), 10–12.

192. Stout, 2010.

193. Stout, 2012.

194. Ibid.

195. PwC Annual Corporate Directors Survey (2015), http://www.pwc.com/us/en/corporate-governance/annual-corporate-directors-survey/assets/pwc-2015-annual-corporate-directors-survey.pdf. Accessed January 1, 2016.

5

Strategic Management and Corporate Public Policy

CHAPTER LEARNING OUTCOMES

After studying this chapter, you should be able to:

1 Describe the concepts of strategic management and corporate public policy.

2 Articulate the four major strategy levels and explain enterprise-level strategy, social entrepreneurship, and the Benefit Corporation.

3 Explain the strategic management process and the role that sustainability reports and integrated reports play in the process.

4 Link public affairs with the strategic management function.

5 Describe the public affairs function today, and enumerate the different activities and functions that comprise it.

In this chapter, we provide a broad overview of *strategic management* and discuss how social, ethical, and public issues fit into this concept. We introduce the term *corporate public policy* to describe that component of management decision making that embraces these issues. Then we discuss corporate public affairs, or public affairs management, as the formal organizational approach some companies use in implementing these initiatives. The overriding goal of this chapter is to focus on planning for the turbulent social/ethical stakeholder environment, and this encompasses the strategic management process, integrated social reporting, and public affairs management.

5.1 Strategic Management and Corporate Public Policy

Strategic management refers to the overall management process that strives to identify corporate purpose and position a firm to succeed in its market environment by achieving competitive advantage. A business relates to its market environment through the products and services it produces and the markets in which it chooses to participate. Strategic management therefore incorporates environmental, ethical, and social concerns, with the realization that the long-term viability of a firm is linked inextricably with its impact on the economy, society, and the environment.

Corporate public policy is about a firm's posture, stance, strategy, or position regarding the environmental, social, global, and ethical aspects of stakeholders and corporate functioning. It can also be called *corporate sustainability policy*, and it might be identified under the *corporate public affairs* function, or the concept of *corporate citizenship*. While the impact of the environmental/social/ethical/global stakeholder environment on business organizations has always been powerful, it seems to grow stronger each year. What started as a simple awareness of social issues and social responsibility in business has matured into a focus on the management of sustainability, reflected in the triple bottom line. Sustainability is now a strategic issue with far-reaching implications for organizational purpose, direction, and functioning.

Corporate policy issues run the gamut from pollution to divestment campaigns, and not a year goes by without a scandal that reminds us of the toll that corporate inattention to public matters can take. Such has been the case, for example, with General Motor's ethical failure in waiting to recall autoignition switches, which compromised consumer safety in the process and contributed to an overall mistrust of the automobile industry by consumers.[1] In contrast, when CVS Health made the decision to stop tobacco sales at all of its drugstores, it did so with the idea that tobacco sales conflicted with its image as a health-care company.[2] A year after walking away from over $2 billion of tobacco revenue per year, CVS estimates that its decision caused people to buy 95 million fewer packs of cigarettes in 13 states.[3] CVS took a stance against tobacco so it could have a real public health impact.

Later in the chapter, we discuss how many businesses formalize this concern under the rubric of **corporate public affairs**, or public affairs management. Businesses encounter several situations daily that involve highly visible public and ethical issues, including those that are subject to intensive public debate for specific periods before being institutionalized. Examples of such issues have included sexual harassment, equal employment opportunities, product safety, and employee privacy. Other issues that are more basic, more enduring, and more philosophical might include the broad role of business in society, issues of corporate governance, and the relative balance of business versus government that is best for our society.

The idea behind corporate public policy is that a firm must give specific attention to issues in which basic questions of justice, fairness, ethics, or public policy reside. Today's dynamic stakeholder environment necessitates that managers employ a policy perspective to these issues. At one time, the social environment was thought to be a relatively constant backdrop against which the real work of business took place. Today, these issues are central, and managers at all levels must address them. Corporate public policy is the process by which management addresses these significant concerns.

Corporate public policy incorporates sustainability as that part of the overall strategic management of the organization that focuses on the environmental, economic, social, and ethical stakeholder issues that are embedded in the decision processes of the firm. Therefore, just as a firm needs to develop policy on functional areas such as human resources, operations, marketing, or finance, it also must develop corporate *public* policy to address proactively the host of issues discussed throughout this book.

Citizens Bank of Canada is a company that concluded it needed a formal corporate public policy. As a company trying to build a strong reputation in the CSR area since opening its doors over a decade ago, the bank's management concluded that it needed more than the establishment of a few enlightened policies. It needed something that would set a systematic course and foundation for "doing well by doing good." Citizens' first step was the establishment of a document of guiding principles, called an *ethical policy*, which would steer the firm's practices toward its social and environmental commitments. To implement its policy and follow-up on implementation, the bank created an "ethical policy compliance" unit.[4] The Citizens' initiatives illustrate the value of a formalized public policy. It became the first North American–based bank to become carbon neutral, and it achieved this goal two years ahead of schedule.[5] In that same year, the bank donated $50,000 to Habitat for Humanity and one day of volunteering to nonprofit causes.[6]

5.1a Relationship of Ethics to Strategic Management

A consideration of ethics is implicit in corporate public policy discussions, but it is useful to make this relationship more explicit. Over the years, a growing number of observers have stressed this point. The leadership challenge of determining future strategy in the face of rising moral and ethical standards may be the most strenuous in strategic decision making, particularly stressful within the inherently amoral corporation.[7] However, a shift is taking place in business as more companies attempt to integrate ethics, social responsibility, and strategic management. In 2015, *Fortune* magazine introduced its first "Change the World List" in an effort to acknowledge this shift, ranking companies that have made an impact on major global social or environmental problems as part of their competitive strategy.[8]

The focus of linking ethics and strategy moved to center stage in the book *Corporate Strategy and the Search for Ethics*, which argued that if business ethics were to have any meaning beyond pompous moralizing, it should be linked to business strategy. The theme was that the concept of corporate strategy could be revitalized by linking ethics to strategy. This linkage permits addressing the most pressing management issues of the day in ethical terms. The book introduces the idea of *enterprise strategy* as the one that best links these two vital notions, and this concept is examined in more detail in the next section.[9]

The concept of corporate public policy and the linkage between ethics and strategy are better understood when we think about the

1. four key levels at which strategy decisions arise, and
2. steps in the strategic management process in which these decisions are embedded.

5.2 Four Key Strategy Levels

Because organizations are hierarchical, it is not surprising to find that strategic management also is hierarchical in nature; that is, the firm has several different levels at which strategic decisions are made, or the strategy process occurs. These levels range from the broadest or highest levels (where missions, visions, goals, and decisions entail higher risks and are characterized by longer time horizons, more subjective values, and greater uncertainty) to the lowest levels (where planning is done for specific functional areas and are characterized by shorter time horizons, less complex information needs, and less uncertainty). Four key strategy levels are important: (1) enterprise-level strategy, (2) corporate-level strategy, (3) business-level strategy, and (4) functional-level strategy.

5.2a Four Strategy Levels Described

Enterprise-Level Strategy. The broadest level of strategic management is known as *societal-level strategy* or *enterprise-level strategy*. **Enterprise-level strategy** is the overarching strategy level that poses such basic questions as, "What is the role of the organization in society?" and "For what do we stand?" As will be evident from the detailed discussion later, this encompasses the development and articulation of corporate public policy and may be considered the first and most important level at which ethics and strategy are linked. Corporate governance is one of the most important topics at this level.

Corporate-Level Strategy. **Corporate-level strategy** addresses what are often posed as the most defining business question for a firm, "In what business(es) should we be?" Thus, mergers, acquisitions, and divestitures, as well as whether and how to participate in global markets, are examples of decisions made at this level. A host of issues related to ethics and sustainability arise at this level as well.

Business-Level Strategy. **Business-level strategy** is concerned with the question, "How should we compete in a given business or industry?" Thus, a company whose products or services take it into many different businesses, industries, or markets will need a business-level strategy to define its competitive posture in each of them. A competitive strategy might address whether a product should be low cost or differentiated, as well as whether it should compete in broad or narrow markets and how to do so in a sustainable way.

Functional-Level Strategy. **Functional-level strategy** addresses the question, "How should a firm integrate its various subfunctional activities and how should these activities be related to changes taking place in the diverse functional areas (finance, marketing, human resources, IT and operations)?"[10] Companies need to ascertain that their functional areas conduct themselves in ways that are consistent with the values for which the firm stands.

FIGURE 5-1 The Hierarchy of Strategy Levels

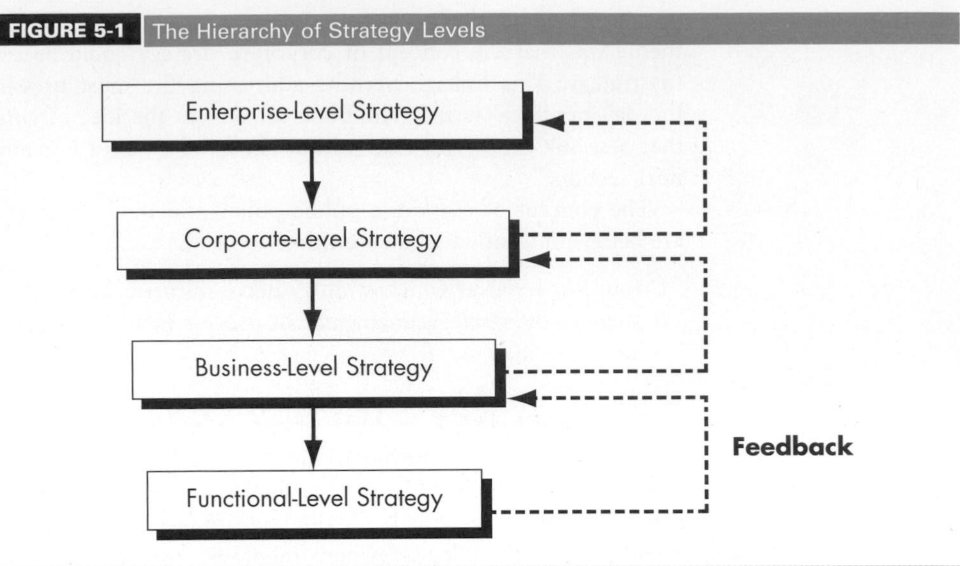

The purpose of identifying the four strategy levels is to clarify that corporate public policy is primarily a part of enterprise-level strategy, which, in turn, is but one level of strategic decision making that occurs in organizations. In terms of its implementation, however, the other strategy levels inevitably come into play and all levels play a part in fulfilling a firm's commitment to its values. Figure 5-1 illustrates that enterprise-level strategy is the broadest strategy level and that the other levels are narrower concepts that cascade from it.

5.2b Emphasis on Enterprise-Level Strategy

The term *enterprise-level strategy* is not used frequently in the business community, but it is helpful here. Although many firms address the issues with which enterprise-level strategy is concerned, use of this terminology is concentrated primarily in the academic community. This terminology describes the level of strategic thinking necessary if firms are to be fully responsive to today's complex and dynamic stakeholder environment. Most organizations today convey their enterprise or societal strategy in their vision, missions, or values statements. Others embed their enterprise strategies in codes of conduct. Increasingly, these strategies are reflecting a global level of application. For example, the 12,000+ members of the UN Global Compact, from more than 145 countries around the world, commit to abiding by ten principles in the areas of human rights, labor, environment, and anticorruption.[11]

Enterprise-level strategy needs to be thought of as a concept that more closely aligns "social and ethical concerns" with traditional "business concerns."[12] In setting the direction for a firm, a manager needs to understand the impact of changes in business strategy on the underlying values of the firm and the new stakeholder relations that will consequently emerge and take shape. Thus, at the enterprise level, the task of setting strategic direction involves understanding the role in society of a particular firm as a whole and its relationships to other social institutions. Important questions that help flesh out enterprise strategy then become:

- What is the role of our organization in society?
- How do our stakeholders perceive our organization?

- What principles or values does our organization represent?
- What obligations do we have to society, including to the world?
- What are the broad implications for our current mix of businesses and allocation of resources?

Many firms have addressed some of these questions—perhaps only in part or in an ad hoc way. The point of enterprise-level strategy, however, is that the firm needs to address these questions intentionally, specifically, and cohesively in such a way that a corporate public policy is articulated.

How have business firms addressed these questions? How are these reflected in enterprise-level thinking and corporate public policy? The manifestations show up in various ways in different companies, such as a firm's response when faced with public crises. Does it respond to its stakeholders in a positive, constructive, and sensitive way or in a negative, defensive, and insensitive way? Corporate decisions and actions reveal the presence or absence of soundly developed enterprise-level strategy. Companies also demonstrate the degree of thinking that has gone into public issues by the presence or absence and use or nonuse of codes of ethics, codes of conduct, mission statements, values statements, vision statements, or other such policy-oriented codes and statements.

Social Entrepreneurship. Although enterprise strategy is relevant for all firms, it holds special importance in **social entrepreneurship**. Social entrepreneurship is a cultural phenomenon that has been growing exponentially.[13] In spite of its popularity, it remains "a term in search of a good definition."[14] Social entrepreneurs, as discussed in Chapter 2, differ from traditional entrepreneurs in that the social enterprise has a mission of societal value creation, and that mission is its reason for being. Social entrepreneurs must create wealth to survive and thrive as well, but it is a means to an end of social value creation. The social mission is fundamental to social entrepreneurship. In contrast, socially responsible businesses may create social value en route to creating wealth but wealth creation remains that business's ultimate goal. J. Gregory Dees, Professor of the Practice of Social Entrepreneurship at Duke University, provides the following definition of social entrepreneurship:[15]

Social entrepreneurs play the role of change agents in the social sector, by:

- *Adopting a mission to create and sustain social value (not just private value)*
- *Recognizing and relentlessly pursuing new opportunities to serve that mission*
- *Engaging in a process of continuous innovation, adaptation, and learning*
- *Acting boldly without being limited by resources currently in hand*
- *Exhibiting heightened accountability to the constituencies served and for the outcomes created*

Social entrepreneurship can address a range of societal goals, including education, the environment, and the arts. However, alleviating poverty has been a central focus of many social entrepreneurs. For example, as we noted in Chapter 2, Toms Shoes founder Blake Mycoskie set out with the goal of providing shoes to impoverished children. A decade later, he continues this model by providing eyewear, drinking water, birthing kits, and more to help people in poor areas all over the world. As he noted in one interview, "I've asked people, 'What could Toms do better?' I've learned that the keys to poverty alleviation are education and jobs. And now we have the resources to put investment behind this. Maybe five years from now, we'll be able to say it's really good for business. But the motivator now is, how can we have more impact?"[16]

The **Bottom of the Pyramid (BOP)** is a term used to characterize the largest and poorest socioeconomic group of people, the billions of people who live on less than $2 a day.[17] A decade ago, C. K. Prahalad and Stuart L. Hart introduced the concept that businesses could make a fortune by engaging with this typically forgotten segment of society because it contains innovative entrepreneurs as well as value-demanding customers.[18] Prahalad and Hart envisioned large, multinational corporations (MNCs) being the ones that would be able to take advantage of the BOP concept. A review of the work that has happened in the decade since they highlighted this potential market shows that only a small number of MNCs have been involved.[19] Instead, smaller enterprises and social entrepreneurs have led the effort.[20]

Social entrepreneurship helps to highlight the enterprise strategy of business and to provide a mechanism by which entrepreneurial individuals can draw on their business-based skills to make a positive difference in the world. At the same time, social entrepreneurship holds a mirror up to traditional business, showing it the potential the marketplace has for creating societal as well as economic value. As mentioned in Chapter 2, Porter and Kramer have proposed the concept of **shared value** that holds that economic and social goals are not mutually exclusive—business can pursue profit while also promoting the common good.[21] In an interview about social entrepreneurship, Porter talked about the "crisis of purpose" that he is seeing in his work with the main CEOs in the world.[22] He said, "The profit that comes from benefitting society is a higher form of profit that corporations should aspire to," and that redefining aspirations in this way will lead to "a sense of much greater purpose."[23]

The Benefit Corporation. A new corporate form has arisen that helps companies that wish to emphasize enterprise-level strategy. This new corporate form is designed to aid companies that have found it challenging to fulfill their social good–oriented missions in traditional for-profit corporations that entail a fiduciary duty for profit maximization and shareholder primacy. The **Benefit Corporation**, as mentioned in Chapter 2, permits corporations to pursue stakeholder and societal welfare maximization as well as shareholder wealth maximization because benefit corporations have a broader mission that includes having a positive impact on society. In Benefit Corporations, that societally oriented mission does not take a backseat to shareholder wealth maximization. Benefit Corporations give managers the opportunity to build, investors the opportunity to finance, and customers the opportunity to patronize businesses that promise to make social responsibility an important goal. The law grew out of B Lab, a nonprofit group that certifies companies as **B Corporations**, based on their accountability, transparency, and social responsibility.[24] Notable B Corporations include Ben & Jerry's, Etsy, and Patagonia, which altered its bylaws and went through a rigorous assessment to reincorporate as a Benefit Corporation in 2011.[25] Patagonia made the decision to do so because the designation codified and made more transparent the company's efforts to be environmentally friendly, while also providing them access to over 1,300 global companies that share similar values.[26]

In the United States, individual states have the authority to create and charter corporations and so the benefit corporation movement is growing state by state. In 2010, Maryland and Vermont were the first states to pass Benefit Corporation legislation: By 2015, this had grown to 31 states, with five more pending legislation reviews.[27] The popularity of the B Corp certification is not just contained in the United States. In September 2015, 62 companies became Benefit Corporations in the United Kingdom as the country launched its accreditation process. The certification process is also available in South America, Canada, Australia, and other parts of Europe.[28]

Rob Thomas, founder and president of Social (k), a Springfield, Massachusetts–based retirement planning company that screens for social funds, plans to apply for Benefit Corporation status for his company. He says, "It sends a message that we take seriously the opportunity for a business to bake into its DNA that we're here for more than just

SPOTLIGHT *on Sustainability*

Enterprise-Level Strategy in Action

One of the best ways to appreciate a company's public policy or enterprise-level strategy is to examine its posture on sustainability. Wegmans, a regional U.S. supermarket chain with stores in the Mid-Atlantic region, has made a formal and effective commitment to promoting sustainability through a sustainability mission statement, a sourcing philosophy, and a sustainability coordinator.

Wegmans' mission statement begins with the Native American proverb, "We do not inherit the earth from our ancestors; we borrow it from our children." It goes on to say, "There are no simple solutions to these challenges. Still, we all have a responsibility to be aware and be accountable. We promise to take steps to protect our world for future generations—it's part of our commitment to make a difference in every community we serve."

To learn more about Wegmans' commitment to sustainability, check out its Web site: http://www.wegmans.com.

financial return."[29] Benefit Corporation status does not give firms tax or other incentives; however, it offers companies some legal protection to make decisions for reasons other than maximizing profits.[30] According to Andrew Kassoy, cofounder of B-Lab, "it expands the fiduciary duties of a business to include having a material, positive impact on society and the environment, not just value for shareholders."[31]

Patagonia has helped guide numbers other companies through the process of becoming B Corps over the years. However, the process of becoming a B Corp is not without controversy. Figure 5-2 outlines some of the pros and cons of being a B Corporation.[32]

FIGURE 5-2 The Pros and Cons of B Corporation Status

Pros:

- **Built-in Commitment**. It builds social commitment directly into governance to support the corporation and protect it.
- **Good Publicity**. It offers reputational effects with best practices.
- **Protection from Investor Pressures**. It can protect the company from pressures by capital markets to capitalize short-term profits.
- **Partners with Similar Values**. It offers the chance set a high benchmark for stakeholders with B Lab screenings for certain requirements on working conditions, supply chain management, and relationships with local communities.

Cons:

- **Lack of Oversight**. The rigorous B Corp certification process involves annual self-reports with a "third-party standard" for assessing performance, but only 10% of applicants receive on-ground verification.
- **Legal Uncertainty and Brand Erosion**. The B Corp represents a certification, whereas the Benefit Corporation is an actual legal entity. Neither is required to adhere to the same standards—inviting legal questions and this could erode the brand.
- **Investor Wariness**. Some investors could balk at the emphasis on social good over shareholder returns.

Sources: Ryan Bradley, "The Tao of Rose," *Fortune* (September 15, 2015), 155–162, Jonathan Crew, "The Good and Bad of Being a B Corp," *Fortune* (September 15, 2015), 160; James Surowiecki, "Companies with Benefits," *The New Yorker* (August 4, 2014), http://www.newyorker.com/magazine/2014/08/04/companies-benefits. Accessed January 11, 2016; Aiden Livingston, "To B or Not to B? Weighing the Benefits of Benefit Corporations," *Mashable* (March 2, 2012), http://mashable.com/2012/03/02/benefit-corporations/#GzZBM.RQskqx. Accessed January 10, 2016, Doug Bend and Alex King, "Why Consider a Benefit Corporation?," *Forbes* (May 30, 2014), http://www.forbes.com/sites/theyec/2014/05/30/why-consider-a-benefit-corporation/. Accessed January 12, 2016.

Importance of Core Values. It is crucial that firms not only have values statements that provide guidance but also that these values also "mean something." Ever since Jim Collins and Jerry Porras published *Built to Last: Successful Habits of Visionary Companies*, companies have felt they needed such statements. The authors made the case that many of the best companies adhere to a set of principles called **core values**. Core values are the deeply ingrained principles that guide all of a company's actions and decisions, and they serve as cultural cornerstones.[33] Though many companies have written publicly proclaimed values statements, many have been sullied because they are not followed. To be effective, companies need to weave core values into everything they do. If a company's core values are not upheld, they become hollow or empty and may do more harm than good.

Deeply felt and strongly held values have the power to transform. A good example of that came from when Tim Cook, the man tapped to run Apple's operations in Steve Jobs' absence, was asked by investors how the company would function without Jobs. Cook's seemingly extemporaneous response created what *Fortune's* Adam Lashinsky described as a "magical moment" when Cook referenced the power of Apple's value system surrounding innovation, deep collaboration, honesty, courage, and excellence.[34] According to Lashinsky, Cook had been considered uncharismatic and uninspiring, but he came across in this response as "forceful, eloquent, and passionate about Apple."[35]

In what do value-based companies believe? It has been argued that three basic organizational values undergird all others: transparency, sustainability, and responsibility.[36] Transparency emphasizes the company being open and honest, especially with employees. Sustainability is about conducting today's business in a way that does not rob the future, and responsibility invokes the idea of commitment to integrity and social responsibility. A good example of a values-based business is Stonyfield Farms, a small New Hampshire yogurt company. The company's mission is devoted to healthy food, healthy people, a healthy planet, and healthy business.[37] "In 1983, we had a wonderful business, just no supply and no demand, no one knew what organic was, no one ate yogurt," says CEO Gary Hirshberg.[38] Today, the company has succeeded through offering a high-quality differentiated product, focusing on customer engagement, and undertaking a variety of initiatives to lessen the impact of its operations on the planet.[39] Similarly, the enterprise-level strategy and corporate values of Unilever are reflected in their purpose and principles statement shown in Figure 5-3. Just as the character of a person will be evident in his or her actions, the values of an organization can be seen in that organization's activities.

Other Manifestations of Enterprise-Level Strategic Thinking. Enterprise-level strategic thinking is manifested in other ways. It may include the extent to which firms have established board or senior management committees. Such committees might include the following: public policy or issues committees, sustainability committees, ethics committees, governance committees, social audit committees, corporate philanthropy committees, and ad hoc committees to address specific public issues. The firm's public policy function can also reflect the firm's level of enterprise-level thinking. Does the firm have an established public affairs office? To whom does the director of corporate public affairs report? What role does public affairs play in corporate-level and strategic decision making?

Another major indicator of enterprise-level strategic thinking is the extent to which the firm attempts to identify social or public issues, analyze them, and integrate them into its strategic management processes. For many firms, it will be necessary to undergo a "**value shift**" in order to integrate environmental, ethical, and social considerations into its strategic plans. Such a value shift, according to Lynn Sharp Paine, requires firms to get back to basics and adopt a different kind of management than that often practiced

FIGURE 5-3 Unilever Purpose and Principles

Purpose & Principles

Our corporate purpose states that to succeed requires "the highest standards of corporate behavior towards everyone we work with, the communities we touch, and the environment on which we have an impact."

Always Working with Integrity

Conducting our operations with integrity and with respect for the many people, organizations, and environments, our business touches has always been at the heart of our corporate responsibility.

Positive Impact

We aim to make a positive impact in many ways: through our brands, our commercial operations and relationships, through voluntary contributions, and through the various other ways in which we engage with society.

Continuous Commitment

We're also committed to continuously improving the way we manage our environmental impacts and are working toward our longer-term goal of developing a sustainable business.

Setting out our Aspirations

Our corporate purpose sets out our aspirations in running our business. It's underpinned by our code of Business Principles, which describes the operational standards that everyone at Unilever follows, wherever they are in the world. The code also supports our approach to governance and corporate responsibility.

Working with Others

We want to work with suppliers who have values similar to our own and work to the same standards we do. Our Business Partner code, aligned to our own Code of business principles, comprises ten principles covering business integrity and responsibilities relating to employees, consumers, and the environment.

Source: https://www.unileverusa.com/about/who-we-are/purpose-and-principles/. Accessed January 27, 2016. Reproduced with kind permission of Unilever PLC and group companies.

by companies.[40] More and more, superior performers are those companies that meet both the social and financial expectations of their stakeholders, a theme we seek to develop in this chapter and book. Following is a discussion of how corporate public policy is integrated into the **strategic management process**.

5.3 The Strategic Management Process

To understand how corporate public policy is just one part of the larger system of management decision making, it is useful to identify the major steps that make up the strategic management process. Boards and top management teams are responsible for activating the process. One conceptualization includes six steps: (1) goal formulation, (2) strategy formulation, (3) strategy evaluation, (4) strategy implementation, (5) strategic control, and (6) environmental analysis.[41] Figure 5-4 graphically portrays an expanded view of this process.

The environmental analysis component requires collection of information on trends, events, and issues that occur in the stakeholder environment, and this information is then fed into the other steps of the process. Although the tasks or steps are often discussed sequentially, they are in fact interactive and do not always occur in a neatly ordered pattern or sequence. Figure 5-4 also captures the relationship between the strategic management process and corporate public policy.

FIGURE 5-4 The Strategic Management Process and Corporate Public Policy

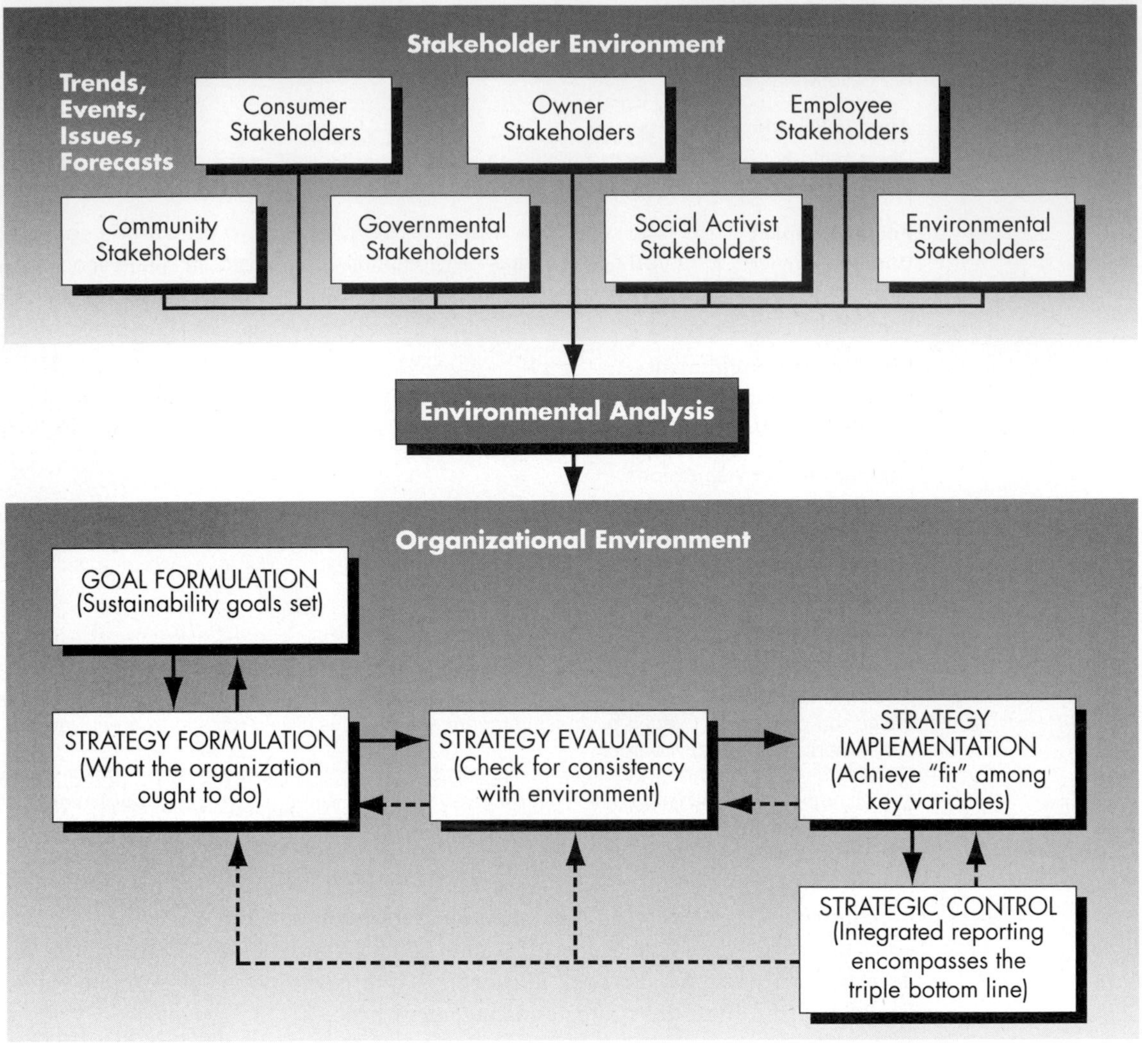

5.3a Strategic Corporate Social Responsibility

In recent years, the term *strategic corporate social responsibility* has captured the idea of integrating a concern for society into the strategic management processes of the firm.[42] Such a perspective insures that CSR is fully integrated into the firm's strategy, mission, and vision. Strategic CSR and the firm's level of strategic management reflect a firm's enterprise-level strategy discussed earlier.

Porter and Kramer Framework. The notion of strategic CSR got a huge boost when strategy expert Michael Porter began advocating the importance of the linkage between competitive advantage, a crucial strategy concept, and CSR.[43] Though Porter had been preceded by others in advocating this linkage, the strength of his reputation has furthered the cause. He and co-author Mark Kramer argued that the interdependence between business and society takes two forms: "inside-out linkages," wherein company operations affect society, and "outside-in linkages," wherein external societal forces affect companies.[44]

In order to prioritize social issues, they proceed to categorize three broad ways corporations intersect with society. First, there are "generic social issues" wherein a company's operations do not significantly affect society and the issue is not material to the firm's long-term competitiveness. Second, there are "value chain social impacts" where a company's normal operations significantly affect society. Finally, there are "social dimensions of competitive context" wherein social issues affect the underlying drivers of a company's competitiveness.[45]

Porter and Kramer next divide these three categories into two primary modes of corporate involvement. *Responsive CSR* addresses "generic social impacts" through good corporate citizenship and "value chain social impacts" by mitigating harm from negative corporate impacts on society, whereas *strategic CSR* transforms "value chain social impacts" into activities that benefit society, while simultaneously reinforcing corporate strategy, as well as advances strategic philanthropy that leverages relevant areas of competitiveness.[46]

The aforementioned ideas are integrated into a series of steps that intend to integrate business and society strategically. These steps include:

1. Identifying the points of intersection (inside-out and outside-in)
2. Choosing which social issues to address (generic, value chain social impacts, and social dimensions of competitiveness)
3. Creating a corporate social agenda (responsive and strategic)
4. Integrating inside-out and outside-in practices (getting practices to work together)
5. Creating a social dimension to the value proposition (The company adds a social dimension to its value proposition, thus making social impact integral to the overall strategy.)[47]

Whole Foods Market (WFM) is presented as an example of this final point. The value proposition of WFM is to sell natural, organic, healthy food products to customers who passionately care about the environment. Social issues are central to WFM's mission and are implemented through sourcing approaches, commitment to the environment, and use of environment-friendly policies and practices. [48]

The Porter–Kramer framework is useful because it applies strategic thinking to both leverage positive social and environmental benefits and mitigate negative social and environmental impacts in ways that enhance competitive advantage.[49] From all indications, companies are beginning to accept this way of thinking. In the Ethical Corporation's *State of Sustainability Report 2015*, companies identified "sustainable innovation" and "sustainability as a source of competitive advantage" as the two most important issues for their CSR initiative over the next five years.[50] The challenge for companies, therefore, is to find the ways in which the environmental and social dimensions can be incorporated into the business as part of the whole rather than a separate part. Integrated reporting represents a major step in that direction.

5.3b Measuring Sustainable Corporate Performance

Achieving sustainability requires performance accountability and that necessitates a change in the way many firms operate. Organizations can only perform well financially, socially, and environmentally if performance information and performance accountability reflect those goals.[51] When firms only measure financial performance and the board holds them responsible for only maximizing shareholder value, environmental and social considerations become side issues. Social or environmental initiatives might be approved if they add to corporate image or the bottom line but they are not viewed as central to the business.[52] To achieve sustainable corporate performance, corporations need a "fundamental change in their goals and how they achieve them."[53] The triple bottom line must be reflected in every aspect of the firm's operations to achieve sustainability.

Sustainability Reporting. **Sustainability reports**, also known as **social responsibility reports**, **social audits**, and **integrated reports (IRs)**, represent an effort to measure a firm's overall value creation and to spur integrated thinking that recognizes the interconnections of the range of business functions, as well as the multiple business bottom lines.[54] The movement toward sustainability reports is new but gaining momentum. The International Integrated Reporting Council (IIRC) is spearheading the development of a global framework for IR. The IIRC group is composed of regulators, investors, businesses, NGOs, standard setters, and representatives from the accounting profession.[55] According to Professor Mervyn King, Chairman of the IIRC:

> *We define Integrated Reporting as the language evidencing sustainable business. It is the means by which companies communicate how value is created and will be enhanced over the short, medium and long term... The journey towards Integrated Reporting therefore also entails a mindset change about how the company makes its money.*[56]

Global organizations like the IIRC are supported by regional organizations like the European Union Directive, the U.S.-based Sustainability Accounting Standards Board (SASB), and other organizations that guide and provide metrics for preparing sustainability reports.[57] As a result, the KPMG Survey of Corporate Responsibility Reporting 2015 concluded that over 90 percent of the world's largest 250 companies now report on corporate responsibility, with three in five companies including this information in their annual financial reports.[58]

IR does not necessarily replace other reports. Firms may still issue financial statements, environmental impact reports, social responsibility reports, and so on. However, by pulling that information together into an integrated format, decision makers become more aware of the interconnectedness of decisions and the fact that sustainability considerations cut across all the individual areas. The goal is to provide single comprehensive report that connects ESG (environmental, social, governance) metrics with the standard annual report to encourage long-term value creation.

Novo Nordisk was one of the first companies to commit to integrated reporting when they discontinued the use of separate financial, social, and environmental reports in 2004. Ranked at the top of the 2015 Global 100 list of most sustainable corporations in the world, Novo Nordisk incorporates sustainability into every decision.[59] It is the only pharmaceutical company that measures the CEO's pay relative to indicators of sustainability, and it sells insulin to some of the world's poorest countries at no more than 20 percent of the average price in the western world.[60] The company considers sustainability to be a driver or innovation and a means of engaging with stakeholders that illuminates opportunities and warns of potential trouble.[61]

Sustainability reports are important to the context of strategic control. When sustainability goals are developed, these goals serve as standards in the process of measuring, disclosing, and documenting progress on economic, environmental, social, and governance goals. Following the development of goals, actual sustainability performance results are compared to the established goals, and then corrective action is taken to make sure that actual performance and goals are aligned. For example, Adidas's 2015 sustainability report sets strategic sustainability goals for 2020 and beyond, with five-year planning cycles and reviews.[62] In the context of strategic control, the sustainability report can assume a role much like that portrayed in Figure 5-5. This figure is similar to the diagram of the strategic management process and corporate public policy shown in Figure 5-4, but it is modified somewhat to highlight sustainability goals and the first three steps in the strategic control process.

FIGURE 5-5 The Sustainability Report in the Context of Strategic Control

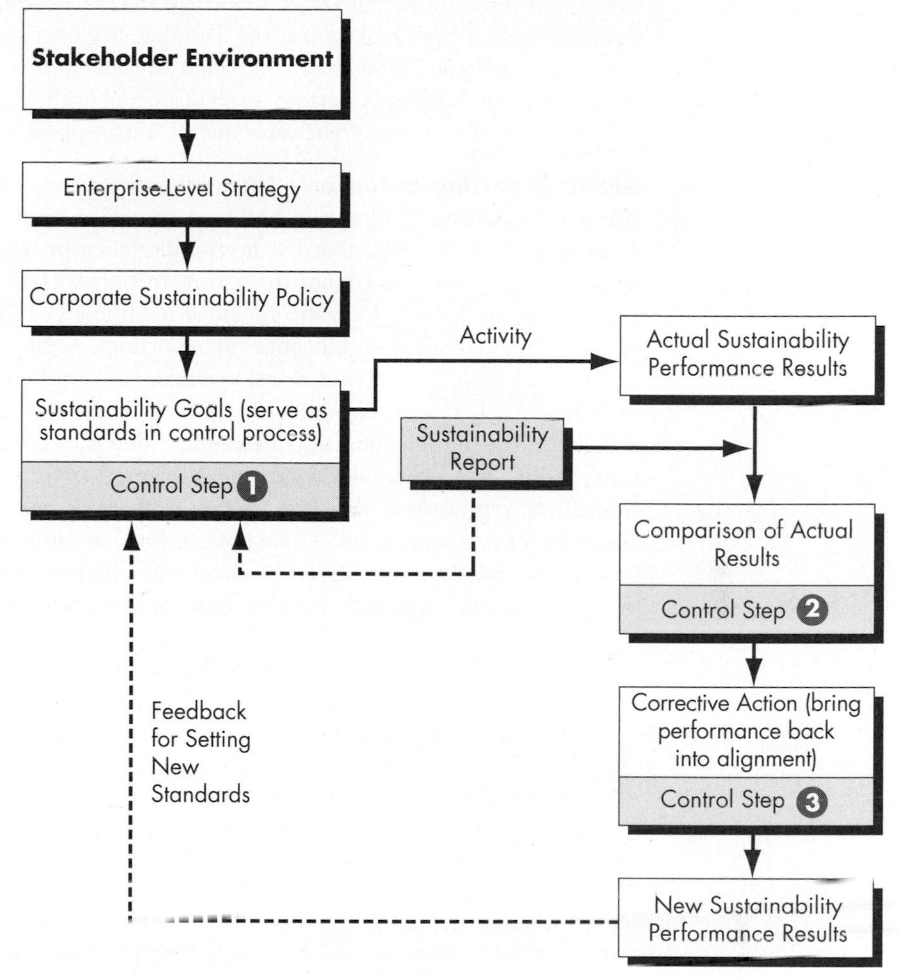

The impetus for sustainability reports in recent years has come both from inside the firm and from societal and public interest group's expectations that firms report their achievements in the triple bottom line. Such reports typically require monitoring and measuring progress, and this is valuable to management groups wanting to track their own progress as well as be able to report it to other interested parties. Globalization is another driver for sustainability reports. As more and more companies do business globally, they need to document their achievements when critics raise questions about their contributions, especially in developing countries. Companies such as Apple, Walmart, and many others have been criticized for their use of sweatshops abroad, so they have an added incentive to issue such reports. Sustainability reports can also help companies to engage with stakeholders. Ford Motor Company, for example, works with stakeholder committees to inform and shape their reporting approach and materiality analysis, but these forums have also allowed them to address problems on human rights and carbon dioxide reduction.[63]

Ceres. The nonprofit organization Ceres (pronounced "series") is a nongovernmental (NGO) national network of investors, environmental organizations, and other public interest groups working with companies and investors to address sustainability challenges and promote sustainability reporting. Ceres's mission is "mobilizing investor and business leadership to build a thriving, sustainable global economy."[64] Beginning in 2014, it got an impressive number of companies to sign onto the Climate Declaration—a call to action from leading American businesses and individuals urging policymakers and business leaders to pursue renewable energy and support national carbon reductions.[65]

Global Reporting Initiative. One of the major impediments to the advancement of effective sustainability reporting has been the absence of standardized measures. Standardization is a challenge that has been undertaken by a consortium of over 300 global organizations called the **Global Reporting Initiative (GRI)**. Ceres launched the GRI in conjunction with the U.N. Environment Programme (UNEP) with the mission of developing globally applicable guidelines for reporting on the economic, environmental, and social performance of corporations, governments, and nongovernmental organizations (NGOs).[66] GRI is now considered the de facto international standard for such reporting. It includes the participation of corporations, NGOs, accountancy organizations, business associations, and other worldwide stakeholders.[67] The GRI's Sustainability Reporting Guidelines represented the first global framework for comprehensive sustainability reporting, encompassing the "triple bottom line" of economic, environmental, and social issues. The mission of GRI is to maintain, enhance, and disseminate the guidelines through ongoing consultation and stakeholder engagement.[68]

ETHICS IN PRACTICE CASE

DuPont and Sustainability Reporting

The 2015 Sustainability Report for DuPont reads, "Between now and 2050, the world's population will climb to 9 billion, placing growing demands on our planet's scarce resources. This means the world needs plentiful, healthier food, renewably sourced materials, ample energy, and better infrastructure and transportation. We are poised to deliver." However, not too long after this report was released, an article was published that for years DuPont had been supplied with the chemical PFOA, used in the manufacture of Teflon, and it was polluting the air and drinking water near its Parkersburg, West Virginia facility, dumping the chemical into the Ohio River and digestion ponds that could seep into the ground.[69] DuPont stopped using PFOA in 2013, but the story highlighted the shortcomings in the regulatory environment, because PFOA and its newer fluorochemical substitutes are not regulated by the Environmental Protection Agency, separate from provisional limits on short-term exposure.[70]

1. To what extent does sustainability reporting address the future, rather than the past? What is a company to do when their sustainability report is positive but they later are found not to live up to their past report? Can sustainability reports work against a company in this regard?
2. In its 2015 Sustainability Report, DuPont, Chair and CEO noted, "DuPont has come a long way since the 1970s when our focus was on our environmental compliance." How can newer sustainability reports address these issues?
3. DuPont agreed to a $16.5 million settlement with the E.P.A. in 2015 for PFOA, but over 3,500 plaintiffs have since filed lawsuits against DuPont for issues that range from kidney cancer to ulcerative colitis. How can DuPont bring more consistency between its stated commitments in its Sustainability Reports and later reported violations?

Sources: Michael Kourabas, "The Case of DuPont's Pollution and the Importance of CSR" (January 11, 2016), *Triple Pundit*, http://www.triplepundit.com/2016/01/case-duponts-pollution-importance-csr/?utm_source=Daily+Email+List&utm_campaign=ddd5cb046f-RSS_EMAIL_CAMPAIGN&utm_medium=email&utm_term=0_9dedefcee3-ddd5cb046f-220417273, DuPont. Accessed January 11, 2016; *Dupont 2015 Sustainability Progress Report*, http://www.dupont.com/content/dam/dupont/corporate/our-approach/sustainability/documents/DuPont-Sustainability-Report-2015_111615.pdf. Accessed January 11, 2016.

As firms develop enterprise-level strategies and corporate public policies, the potential for sustainability reporting remains high. Sustainability reporting is best appreciated not as an isolated, periodic attempt to assess social performance but rather as an *integral part* of the overall strategic management process as it described here. Because the need to improve planning and control will remain as long as the management desires to evaluate its corporate social performance, the need for approaches such as sustainability reporting will likely be with us for some time, too. The net result of continued use and refinement should be improved sustainability and enhanced credibility of business in the eyes of its stakeholders and the public.

5.4 Public Affairs as a Part of Strategic Management

In a comprehensive management system, which this chapter describes, the overall flow of activity would be as follows: A firm engages in strategic management, part of which includes the development of enterprise-level strategy, which poses the question, "For what do we stand?" The answers to this question help the organization form a corporate public policy, which is a more specific posture on the public, social, or stakeholder environment or specific issues within this environment. Some firms call this a **public affairs strategy**.

Public affairs and **public affairs (PA) management** are umbrella terms that some companies use to describe the management processes that focus on the formalization and institutionalization of corporate public policy. The PA function is a logical component of the overall strategic management process. PA experts argue that it has grown to be one of the most important parts of strategic management and today may be seen as the strategic core business function for companies wanting to compete successfully internationally.[71] In fact, one consultant in public affairs noted that he foresaw companies in the future having two leaders working in parallel with the CEO: one to run operations and the other, to be a policy and issues manager.[72]

As an overall concept, PA management embraces corporate public policy, discussed earlier, along with **issues management** and **crisis management**, which we cover in more detail in Chapter 6. Indeed, many issues management and crisis management programs are housed in **public affairs departments** or intimately involve PA professionals. Corporate PA also embraces the broad areas of governmental relations and corporate communications. In sum, an integrated model of PA suggests that it is the interface of multiple disciplines, including business and society, ethics, CSR, ecological systems, ethics, economics, sociology, political science, reputational management, and strategic management.[73]

We now consider how the PA function has evolved in business firms, what concerns PA departments currently face, and how PA thinking might be incorporated into the operating manager's job. This last issue is crucial, because PA management is most effective when it is thought of as an indispensable part of every manager's job, rather than an isolated function or department.

5.5 The Corporate Public Affairs Function Today

PA blossomed in the United States because of four primary reasons: (1) the growing magnitude and impact of government; (2) the changing nature of the political system, especially its progression from a patronage orientation to an issues orientation; (3) the growing recognition by business that it was being outflanked by interests that were counter to its own on a number of policy matters; and (4) the need to be more active in politics outside the traditional community-related aspects, such as the symphony and art museums.[74]

Thus, the PA function as we know it today was an outgrowth of the social activism begun decades ago. Today, the Public Affairs Council (PAC), the leading professional organization of executives who do the PA work of companies, located in Washington, DC, provides the following definition of *public affairs*:

> *Public affairs represents an organization's efforts to monitor and manage its business environment. It combines government relations, communications, issues management and corporate citizenship strategies to influence public policy, build a strong reputation, and find common ground with stakeholders.*[75]

An important element of the public affairs function is the influence it has on corporate strategy and planning. If the public affairs function is to be effective in representing the "noncommercial" factors and issues affecting business decision making, it is important that public affairs has influence at the top management level. Public affairs can help to identify and prioritize issues, as well as provide input on emerging social and political trends. For public affairs to fulfill this function, it is important that they have a seat at the table for corporate planning sessions.

Another way for public affairs to have an impact on top management is to think of the CEO as the company's chief public affairs officer. The idea here is that the public affairs function needs a transformation from being reactive to being proactive, and that the best way to make this happen is to place the CEO in charge of the function.[76] This might not work as a practical reality, but the spirit of the idea is appropriate. It is an excellent idea in terms of elevating the importance of public affairs and its relationship to corporate strategy.

5.5a PA's Place at the Table

Part of the problem may be that, in today's highly specialized business world, it is easy for the day-to-day operating managers to let PA departments worry about government affairs, community relations, issues management, PR, or any of the numerous other PA functions. It is not surprising, therefore, that the PA remains a largely specialist function.[77] The problem may stem largely from ambiguity surrounding the definition of public affairs and the differences in the activities undertaken by different PA departments.[78]

5.5b Future of Corporate PA in the 21st Century

With growing worldwide sensitivity to corporate social performance, sustainability, and business ethics, it is easy to argue that corporate PA should have a bright future. With the unfortunate, but ongoing problems surrounding ethical crises in business, PA specialists have an ideal opportunity to solidify their strategic roles and help to transform companies' approaches to handling business and society relationships. Three different opportunities for PA executives have been set forth for future consideration.[79]

- First, PA executives can help develop value-based enterprises. Such enterprises actively seek out stakeholders and work cooperatively with them on social issues. As an example, Whirlpool reached agreements with the National Resource Defense Council, Friends of the Earth, and the Sierra Club to work together in solving energy efficiency challenges. By proactively engaging stakeholders, competitive advantages may be created.[80]
- Second, PA executives can assert themselves as thought leaders in their companies. As thought leaders, they should not just market the company, but actively engage academics, researchers, media, and public opinion formers, about the great issues of the day and how companies can best respond to the latest thinking about social and public issues.

- Finally, PA specialists have the opportunity to seek alternative arenas of resolution as they can broaden issues to embrace global considerations while they pay close attention to domestic matters. Today, public issues migrate across geographical boundaries and political jurisdictions, and PA executives are in a perfect position to track these issues and employ preemptive initiatives. A case in point might be their opportunities in the global debate over genetically modified organisms (GMOs) that are controversial in the United Kingdom while being largely ignored in the United States.[81]

In short, the PA function within firms is strategically positioned to wield more and better influence in the years ahead to help business build bridges between its strategic management and its corporate social performance. It must be added, however, that many firms have decided not to use traditional PA departments for these issues but have begun separate Corporate Citizenship, CSR, Sustainability and Ethics Offices to organize their corporate-level handling of these issues.

Summary

Corporate public policy is a firm's posture or stance regarding the public, social, or ethical aspects of stakeholders and corporate functioning. It is a part of strategic management, particularly enterprise-level strategy. Enterprise-level strategy is the broadest, overarching level of strategy, and its focus is on the role of the organization in society. A major aspect of enterprise-level strategy is the integration of important core values into company strategy. The other strategy levels include the corporate, business, and functional levels. The strategic management process entails six stages, and a concern for social, ethical, and public issues may be seen at each stage. In the control stage, the social audit, social performance, sustainability report is crucial.

Social entrepreneurship holds the mission of the firm as its ultimate purpose. Creating wealth is necessary for social entrepreneurs if they are to survive and thrive but wealth is more of a means to an end that benefits society. The Benefit Corporation is a new corporate form that makes it possible for social entrepreneurs and other like-minded business people to promote the social good as well as wealth creation. Sustainability reports, otherwise known as social responsibility reports, measure how well the firm achieves the triple bottom line of planet, people, and profit. Integrating Reporting is becoming increasingly prevalent as firms try to pull their reporting together into a comprehensive format.

Public affairs can be described as the management function that is responsible for monitoring and interpreting a corporation's noncommercial environment and managing its response to that environment. PA is intimately linked to corporate public policy, environmental analysis, issues management, and crisis management. The major functions of PA departments today include government relations, political action, community involvement or responsibility, issues management, global PA, and corporate philanthropy. PA executives are positioned to increase their future status and influence as they embark on such challenges as helping create values-based enterprises, exerting themselves as thought leaders in their companies, and helping seek alternative arenas of resolution as they broaden issues to embrace global considerations. Some companies do not use public affairs departments but choose to organize these activities into different departments such as Sustainability, CSR, and Ethics offices.

Key Terms

B Corporation, p. 140
benefit corporation, p. 140
bottom of the pyramid (BOP), p. 139
business-level strategy, p. 137
core values, p. 142
corporate-level strategy, p. 137
corporate public affairs, p. 136
corporate public policy, p. 135
enterprise-level strategy, p. 137
functional-level strategy, p. 137

Global Reporting Initiative (GRI), p. 148
integrated report (IR), p. 146
issues management, p. 149
crisis management, p. 149
public affairs, p. 149
public affairs departments, p. 149
public affairs (PA) management, p. 149
public affairs strategy, p. 149
shared value, p. 140
social audit, p. 146
social entrepreneurship, p. 139
social responsibility report, p. 146
strategic management, p. 135
strategic management process, p. 143
sustainability report, p. 146
value shift, p. 142

Discussion Questions

1. Which of the four strategy levels is most concerned with social, ethical, or public issues? Discuss the characteristics of this level.
2. Identify the steps involved in the strategic management process.
3. What is the difference between integrated reporting and a social performance report?
4. What is social entrepreneurship and how is it related to the Bottom of the Pyramid (BOP)?
5. Why are integrated reports increasing in popularity?
6. Describe the corporate public affairs function today. What are the three opportunities for PA executives in the future?

Endnotes

1. Nathan Bomey, "Automakers Face a Problem of Their Own Creation: Broken Trust," *USA Today* (January 10, 2016), 2A.
2. Jayne O'Donnell and Laura Ungar, "CVS Stops Tobacco Sales," *USA Today* (September 3, 2014), 3A.
3. Jayne O'Donnell, "CVS: No-Cigarette Policy a Success," *USA Today* (September 4, 2015), 2B.
4. Victoria Miles, "Auditing Promises: One Bank's Story," *CMA Management* (Vol. 74, No. 5, June 2000), 42–46.
5. https://www.citizensbank.ca/AboutUs/CorporateSocialResponsibility/. Accessed January 27, 2016.
6. Ibid.
7. Kenneth R. Andrews, *The Concept of Corporate Strategy*, 3d ed. (Homewood, IL: Irwin, 1987), 68–69.
8. Michael Porter and Mark R. Kramer, "How Companies Can Enrich Shareholders—and the Planet," *Fortune* online (August 20, 2015), http://fortune.com/2015/08/20/change-the-world-business-model/. Accessed January 31, 2016.
9. R. Edward Freeman and Daniel R. Gilbert, Jr., *Corporate Strategy and the Search for Ethics* (Englewood Cliffs, NJ: Prentice Hall, 1988), 20. Also see R. Edward Freeman, Daniel R. Gilbert, Jr., and Edwin Hartman, "Values and the Foundations of Strategic Management," *Journal of Business Ethics* (Vol. 7, 1988), 821–834; and Daniel R. Gilbert, Jr., "Strategy and Ethics," in *The Blackwell Encyclopedic Dictionary of Business Ethics* (Malden, MA: Blackwell Publishers Ltd., 1997), 609–611.
10. Charles W. Hofer, Edwin A. Murray, Jr., Ram Charan, and Robert A. Pitts, *Strategic Management: A Casebook in Policy and Planning*, 2d ed. (St. Paul, MN: West Publishing Co., 1984), 27–29. Also see Gary Hamel and C. K. Prahalad, *Competing for the Future* (Boston: Harvard Business School Press, 1994).
11. United Nations Global Compact, https://www.unglobalcompact.org/what-is-gc/mission/principles. Accessed January 27, 2016.
12. R. Edward Freeman, *Strategic Management: A Stakeholder Approach* (Boston: Pitman, 1984), 90.
13. Nicola M. Pless, "Social Entrepreneurship in Theory and Practice: An Introduction," *Journal of Business Ethics* (Vol. 111, 2012), 317–320.
14. Samer Abu-Saifan, "Social Entrepreneurship: Definition and Boundaries," *Technology Innovation Management Review* (February 2012), 22–27.
15. https://socinnovation.wordpress.com/2010/09/20/duke-case/. Accessed January 31, 2016.
16. Jeff Chu, "Toms Sets out to Sell a Lifestyle, Not Just Shoes," *Fast Company* (July/August 2013), http://www.fastcompany.com/3012568/blake-mycoskie-toms. Accessed January 23, 2016.
17. C. K. Prahalad and Stuart L. Hart. "The Fortune at the Bottom of the Pyramid," *Strategy+Business* (Vol. 20, 1998), 1–13.
18. Ibid.
19. Ans Kolk, Miguel Rivera-Santos, and Carlos R. Rufin, "Reviewing a Decade of Research on the 'Base/Bottom of the Pyramid' (BOP) Concept," *Business & Society*, Forthcoming, DOI 10.1177/0007650312474928. Available at SSRN: http://ssrn.com/abstract=2193938. Accessed January 27, 2016.

20. Ibid.
21. Michael E. Porter and Mark R. Kramer, "Creating Shared Value," *Harvard Business Review* (January /February 2011), 62–77.
22. Michaela Driver, "An Interview with Michael Porter: Social Entrepreneurship and the Transformation of Capitalism," *Academy of Management Learning and Education* (Vol. 11, No. 3, 2012), 436.
23. Ibid.
24. Shira Schoenberg, "Massachusetts Companies Create Socially Responsible "Benefit Corporations," Masslive.com (December 4, 2012), (http://www.masslive.com/politics/index.ssf/2012/12/massachusetts_companies_create.html. Accessed January 31, 2016.
25. Ryan Bradley, "The Tao of Rose," *Fortune* (September 15, 2015), 155–162.
26. Ibid.
27. The Benefit Corporation (2015), http://benefitcorp.net/policymakers/state-by-state-status. Accessed January 10, 2016.
28. Catherine Clifford, "B Corp Movement Gets Its Wings in Europe," *Entrepreneur* (April 22, 2015), http://www.entrepreneur.com/article/245403. Accessed January 10, 2016.
29. Schoenberg, 2012.
30. Clifford, 2015.
31. Schoenberg, 2012.
32. Jonathan Chew, "The Good and Bad of Being a B Corporation," *Fortune* (September 15, 2015), 160.
33. James C. Collins and Jerry I. Porras, *Built to Last: Successful Habits of Visionary Companies* (HarperBusiness, 1994).
34. Adam Lashinsky, "The Cook Doctrine at Apple," *Fortune* (January 22, 2009), http://fortune.com/2009/01/22/the-cook-doctrine-at-apple/. Accessed January 24, 2016.
35. Ibid.
36. Mark Albion, *True to Yourself: Leading a Values-Based Business* (San Francisco, CA: Berrett-Koehler, 2006).
37. http://www.stonyfield.com/about-us/our-mission. Accessed January 21, 2016.
38. http://www.triplepundit.com/2012/04/economics-stonyfield-yogurt/. Accessed January 21, 2016.
39. http://www.triplepundit.com/2012/03/starbucks-stonyfield-recycling-extended-producer-responsibility/. Accessed January 21, 2016.
40. Lynn Sharp Paine, *Value Shift: Why Companies Must Merge Social and Financial Imperatives to Achieve Superior Performance* (New York: McGraw-Hill, 2003).
41. C. W. Hofer and D. E. Schendel, *Strategy Formulation: Analytial Concepts* (St. Paul: West, 1978), 52–55. Also see J. David Hunger and Thomas L. Wheelen, *Essentials of Strategic Management* (Reading, MA: Addison-Wesley, 2000).
42. William B. Werther, Jr., and David Chandler, *Strategic Corporate Social Responsibility: Stakeholders in a Global Environment* (Thousand Oaks, CA: Sage Publications), 2006.
43. Michael E. Porter and Mark R. Kramer, "Strategy and Society: The Link between Competitive Advantage and Corporate Social Responsibility," *Harvard Business Review* (December 2006), 80–92.
44. Ibid., 84.
45. Ibid., 85.
46. Ibid., 85.
47. Ibid., 83–90.
48. Ibid., 90–91.
49. Ibid.
50. "The State of Sustainability 2015," *The Ethical Corporation* (April 2015), http://www.ethicalcorp.com/business-strategy/press-release-ethical-corporation-publish-state-sustainability-2015-report. Accessed January 11, 2016.
51. Lawler and Worley, 2012, 10–12.
52. Ibid.
53. Ibid., 10.
54. http://integratedreporting.org/. Accessed January 27, 2016.
55. Ibid.
56. Black Sun Plc, *Understanding Transformation: Building the Business Case for Integrated Reporting* (2012, 1). The report is available for download from www.theiirc.org. Accessed January 27, 2016.
57. "Sustainability and Reporting Trends in 2025—Preparing for the Future, Global Reporting Initiative First Analysis Paper (May 2015), https://www.globalreporting.org/resourcelibrary/Sustainability-and-Reporting-Trends-in-2025-1.pdf, 4. Accessed January 11, 2016.
58. "The KPMG Survey of Corporate Responsibility Reporting, 2015," KPMG http://www.kpmg.com/CN/en/IssuesAndInsights/ArticlesPublications/Documents/kpmg-survey-of-corporate-responsibility-reporting-2015-O-201511.pdf. Accessed March 26, 2016.
59. *2015 Global 100 Results*, http://www.corporateknights.com/reports/global-100/2015-global-100-results/. Accessed January 11, 2016.
60. http://www.marcgunther.com/ratings-rankings-and-the-worlds-most-sustainable-company/. Accessed January 26, 2016.
61. Ibid.
62. *The Adidas Group Sustainability Report 2014*, http://www.adidas-group.com/media/filer_public/e8/32/e832823b-8585-4e26-8990-07b80e3ae71c/2014_sustainability_report_make_a_difference.pdf. Accessed January 11, 2016.

63. http://corporate.ford.com/microsites/sustainability-report-2014-15/strategy-stakeholder-engaging.html. Accessed January 29, 2016.

64. http://www.ceres.org/about-us. Accessed January 22, 2013.

65. Andrew Winston, "The 10 Most Important Sustainable Business Stories from 2014," *Harvard Business Review* (December 19, 2014), https://hbr.org/2014/12/the-10-most-important-sustainable-business-stories-from-2014. Accessed January 11, 2016.

66. https://www.globalreporting.org/information/about-gri/Pages/default.aspx. Accessed January 22, 2016.

67. Ibid.

68. Ibid.

69. Michael Kourabas, "The Case of DuPont's Pollution and the Importance of CSR," TriplePundit (January 11, 2016), http://www.triplepundit.com/2016/01/case-duponts-pollution-importance-csr/?utm_source=Daily+Email+List&utm_campaign=ddd5cb046f-RSS_EMAIL_CAMPAIGN&utm_medium=email&utm_term=0_9dedefcee3-ddd5cb046f-220417273. Accessed January 12, 2016.

70. Ibid.

71. Phil Harris and Craig S. Fleisher (eds.), *The Handbook of Public Affairs* (Thousand Oaks, CA: Sage Publications, 2005), 561–562. Also see "Public Affairs at Heart of Corporate Strategy," *Corporate Public Affairs* (Vol. 16, No. 2, 2006), 1–2.

72. Geoff Allen, "Scholarship and Public Affairs Theory Building," *Corporate Public Affairs* (2015, Vol. 25, No. 1), 2.

73. Harris and Fleisher, 2005.

74. Craig S. Fleisher, "Evaluating Your Existing Public Affairs Management System," in Craig S. Fleisher (ed.), *Assessing, Managing and Maximizing Public Affairs Performance* (Washington, DC: Public Affairs Council, 1997), 4.

75. http://pac.org/faq. Accessed January 27, 2016.

76. "Corporate Public Affairs and Organizational Change: Towards a New Positive Model," *Corporate Public Affairs* (Vol. 17, No. 1, 2007), 12.

77. Danny Moss, Conor McGrath, Jane Tonge, and Phil Harris, "Exploring the Management of the Corporate Public Affairs Function in a Dynamic Global Environment," *Journal of Public Affairs* (Vol. 12, No. 1, 2012), 47–57.

78. Ibid.

79. Jennifer J. Griffin, Steven N. Brenner, and Jean J. Boddewyn, "Corporate Public Affairs: Structure, Resources, and Competitive Advantage," in Marc J. Epstein and Kirk O. Hanson (eds.), *The Accountable Corporation, Volume 4: Business-Government Relations* (Westport, CT: Praeger Publishers, 2006), 134–138.

80. Ibid., 135–136.

81. Ibid., 136–137.

6

Risk, Issue, and Crisis Management

CHAPTER LEARNING OUTCOMES

After studying this chapter, you should be able to:

1. Distinguish between risk management, issue management, and crisis management.
2. Describe the major categories of risk management and some of the factors that have characterized risk management in actual practice.
3. Define issue management and the stages in the issue management process.
4. Define crisis management and identify the four crisis stages.
5. List and discuss the major stages or steps involved in managing business crises.

In previous chapters, we have mentioned companies that have had challenges in managing issues and crises ranging from product safety issues to financial fraud. Enron and Toshiba created financial scandals that caused people to lose faith in business as an institution. Slow product recalls like General Motors with its ignition switches and Takata with its airbags led to consumer deaths and an overall erosion of public confidence in the automobile industry.[1] Food safety, highlighted with far-reaching *E. coli* outbreaks like that of Chipotle's in 2015, is another example of an issue that shocked consumers into being fearful of "fresh" food.[2] Other continuing issues, such as employee rights, sexual harassment, workplace safety, sweatshops, bribery, corruption, and deceptive advertising, contribute to the negative opinion many people hold of business. At the heart of these issues is the question, can the public trust business? In the past few years, business has seen the trust of consumers, employees, investors, and the public erode because of issues such as these that threaten the public's safety when they become crises.

Of course, not all issues are caused by business. External events are sometimes unavoidable, but firms must still prepare for their possibilities and manage their repercussions effectively. The World Trade Center terrorist attacks affected businesses at the site as well as around the globe. The 2011 earthquake and tsunami in Japan not only devastated a nation but also led to the world's worst nuclear accident in 25 years.[3] In 2012, Superstorm Sandy became the largest Atlantic hurricane on record, causing death and destruction throughout the northeastern United States.[4] In 2015, a 7.8-magnitude earthquake killed nearly 8,000 people and destroyed nearly 900,000 buildings in Nepal, India, debilitating an already weak economic infrastructure.[5] Each of these events posed serious challenges for businesses. Throughout this book, we discuss major social and ethical issues that have become controversies in the public domain. Some have been caused by external events, whereas the roots of others can be traced back to the businesses themselves.

Managerial decision-making processes known as **risk management**, **issue management**, and **crisis management** are three major ways by which business responds to these situations. These three approaches symbolize the extent to which the environment has become turbulent and the public sensitized to business's responses to the issues that have emerged from this turbulence. In today's environment of instantaneous and global communication, no event is too small to be noticed by everyone. In an ideal situation, risk, issue, and crisis management might be seen as the natural and logical by-products of a firm's development of enterprise-level strategy and overall corporate public policy, but this is not always the case. Some firms do not think seriously about public and ethical issues until they face a crisis. However, even those firms that have not experienced major crises themselves have seen what major business crises can do to companies. Such firms should still be concerned with risk, issue, and crisis management in preparing for an uncertain future because no company is immune from the threat of a crisis.

6.1 The Relationships between Risk, Issue, and Crisis Management

Differentiating between risk, issue, and crisis management is difficult, even for the professionals who work in those fields. Many product managers cannot differentiate between risks and issues, and the apparent inseparability of issue and crisis management has led issue management practitioner and expert Tony Jaques to label them "the Siamese twins of public relations."[6] As is true with all planning processes, risk, issue, and crisis management have many characteristics in common as well as differences. Though they are interrelated, we have chosen to treat them separately for discussion purposes.

We begin with a discussion of risk management, which involves efforts to keep issues from arising—*potential* issues that may or may not occur."[7] Then, we explore issue management, which is a process by which organizations identify issues in the stakeholder environment, analyze and prioritize those issues in terms of their relevance to the organization, plan responses to the issues, and then evaluate and monitor the results. Thus, an issue is something that already exists. Finally, crisis management is the management of issues that have become major threats—those that have escalated into a critical state. A common thread is that all three processes focus on improving stakeholder management and enabling the organization to be more ethically responsive to stakeholders' expectations. It is helpful to think of these management approaches in connection with concepts introduced in the preceding chapter, such as the sustainable strategic management process, enterprise-level strategy, corporate public policy, and integrated reporting.

6.2 Risk Management

Risk management concerns potential issues—addressing potential issues that have not yet occurred and endeavoring to keep issues from arising. The act of identifying and preparing for potential issues is difficult for the human psyche, as our bounded rationality is not geared toward envisioning the future.[8] Robert Kaplan and Annette Mikes argue that, too often, managers adopt a compliance approach to the management of risk by basing it on rules. This can be effective in controlling preventable, internal risks but not in controlling risks that stem from a company's strategy or risks caused by major disruptions in the external environment. They provide an example of Tony Hayward's tenure as CEO of BP. When he arrived at BP, he promised to make safety his priority and, to that end, he instituted new rules. These rules included the requirement that employees not text while driving and that they use lids on their coffee cups while walking. Of course, these rules may have addressed some issues, but they did not prevent the *Deepwater Horizon* from exploding three years later.[9]

Kaplan and Mikes provide a useful framework for risk management that divides it into three categories:[10]

- *Preventable risks*—internal risks that offer no strategic benefits
- *Strategic risks*—risks taken to achieve greater returns
- *External risks*—external threats that cannot be controlled

Tony Hayward's employee safety program of safe driving and covered coffee cups comes under the first category of **preventable risks**. Failing to prevent these risks can cause serious damage and so risk managers should eliminate them whenever possible. Because they are internal and foreseeable, preventable risks lend themselves to a rule-based compliance approach. A corporate mission that defines the company's values, clear boundaries for employee behavior, and effective monitoring procedures usually is effective at preventing this category of risks.[11] However, oftentimes, even the savviest of companies fails to prevent risks. For example, Uber found itself in a public relations crisis in 2016 after one of its drivers allegedly murdered six people in Kalamazoo, Michigan, and picked up fares as an Uber driver between killings.[12] The issue is why/how Uber failed to address some of the preventable risks for their riders. Uber had long resisted doing more to assure the safety of riders, including fingerprinting its drivers, putting in place panic buttons on its smartphone app, or even screening them in face-to-face interviews.[13]

Strategic risks, unlike preventable risks, are not necessarily bad. Because risk and return are related, companies might take on additional risk in order to pursue a company strategy that promises higher returns. BP took on extra risk when it decided to drill several miles below the surface of the Gulf of Mexico, because the oil and gas there held the potential of significant returns. In this instance, a two-pronged risk management approach is needed to curtail the risk:

1. Reducing the probability of the risk event occurring, and
2. Developing the capability to manage the risk event should it occur.

A strategic risk management program does not prevent a firm from taking on strategic risks; it simply enables the firm to do so more effectively.[14]

External risks are beyond the firm's control: They originate from outside the company and include events such as natural disasters and economic shocks. These usually cannot be controlled and they can be the most difficult to predict. Methods of identifying external risks should include techniques like scenario analysis and war-gaming to assist risk managers in foreseeing the unforeseeable. Some external risk events have a low probability of occurrence and so are difficult for managers to envision.[15]

6.2a Risk Management and Sustainability

Sustainability involves living in the present in a way that does not compromise the future. Risk management involves taking action today that will mitigate or prevent a problem that could arise in the future. As such, sustainability and risk management share a connection in that both are concerned with the future consequences of present-day actions. Sustainability is concerned both with not harming and with benefitting future generations. Risk management can provide a mechanism for avoiding, or at least mitigating, future harm to stakeholders and avoiding or mitigating the risk of not benefitting stakeholders in the future.[16] Such is the case, for example, of a company's environmental goals to reduce carbon emissions to address climate change. Microsoft and other companies like Disney and Shell are leading a movement to offset emissions with an internal carbon tax, called "carbon pricing," by voluntarily charging themselves and using that money to build solar panels and wind farms.[17]

Risk shifting is an issue that merits attention in this regard. In the pursuit of sustainability for the business enterprise, some managers may use management techniques that shift risk from the firm to other parties. For example, some techniques can shift risks to the customer base, eroding the economic sustainability of the consumer.[18] This underscores the importance of a holistic approach to sustainability. Risk managers must take care not to promote the sustainability of the firm in such a way that it threatens the sustainability of stakeholders.

6.3 Issue Management

The Issue Management Council defines an issue as "a gap between [a firm's] actions and stakeholder expectations" and issue management as "the process used to close that gap."[19] Many of the crises companies face today arise out of issues that are being monitored and prioritized through issue management systems. In addition, effective issue management is a vital component of post-crisis management. For example, after dealing with an oil spill crisis, a company must continue to address the issue of environmental degradation.[20] Figure 6-1 provides examples of major *issue* categories and specific *crises* that have occurred within these issue categories.

The emergence of "company issue management groups" and "issue managers" has been a direct outgrowth of the changing mix of issues that managers have had to handle. Economic and financial issues have always been an inherent part of the business process, although their complexity seems to have increased as global markets have broadened and

FIGURE 6-1 Issue Categories and Sample Crises within Categories

Issue Categories		
Food, Beverage, and Products	**Health-Related Issues**	**Corporate Fraud and Ethics**
Crises	*Crises*	*Crises*
Chipotle: *E.coli* and norovirus outbreaks closed stores nationwide (2015/16).	U.S. National Football League: Investigation into head and brain injuries from occupational hazard of the sport (2016).	Valeant Pharmaceuticals: Charged with accounting fraud and price gouging (2015/16).
Horsemeat Scandal in the United Kingdom: Millions of burgers and beef products recalled across Europe for containing horsemeat (2013).	Ebola: The largest outbreak of Ebola in history, beginning in West Africa, but with multiple countries affected (2014).	Volkswagen: Accused of "diesel dupe" in the United States with deceptive emissions testing software (2015/16).
Peanut Corporation of America: Over 125 varieties of products recalled due to salmonella contamination (2008/09).	H1N1: A possible flu pandemic led to crises for companies and questions of how to treat employees (2009).	Turing Pharmaceuticals: CEO Shkreli charged with price gouging the drug Daraprim (2015).
Taco Bell: Outbreak of *E.coli* closed outlets nationwide (2006).	Avian flu: A possible bird flu pandemic has created a crisis environment for many businesses, including mask makers who are facing short supplies (2006–2007).	Bernie Madoff: Ponzi scheme cost major foundations millions of dollars jeopardizing critical medical research (2008–2009).
Coca-Cola and Pepsi: Allegations that soft drinks in India contained pesticide residue (2004–2007).	Banned dietary supplements androstenedione and ephedra by FDA. Crisis for dozens of pharmaceutical and vitamin firms (2004).	Hewlett-Packard: Boardroom information was leaked causing a governance crisis (2006).
Coca-Cola's Dasani bottled water: High levels of bromate led to recall in Great Britain (2004).	Tobacco companies: Dangerous products and advertising. Allegations of addictions and death by cancer (1990s–2004).	Boeing: Loses CEO and top-level executive to ethics scandals (2004–2005).
Mad cow disease crisis: Outbreaks in Europe and Canada have created crises in sales and safety for meat industry (2001–2004).	Johnson & Johnson: Cyanide-tampering Tylenol poisonings (1982).	Enron: Scandal began with off-the-books partnerships, aggressive accounting, and allegations of fraud and bankruptcy (2001–2004).
Firestone and Ford: Tire tread separation outbreak (2001–2002).		WorldCom: CEO Bernard Ebbers charged with massive accounting fraud (2003–2004).
		Arthur Andersen: Involvement in Enron scandal led to dissolution of firm (2002).

competitiveness has become such a critical issue. The growth of technology, especially the Internet, has presented business with other issues to address, such as cybersecurity and data management issues. For example, during the peak of the 2013 holiday shopping season, over 40 million Target customers had their credit and debit card information stolen, and up to 70 million more people had their personal information compromised.[21] Consumer advocates simultaneously pointed out that Target was an industry leader in data mining—the practice of analyzing customers' information to find out about their shopping habits.[22] The most dramatic growth has been in social, ethical, and political issues—all public issues that have high visibility, media appeal, and interest among special-interest stakeholder groups. We should further observe that these issues become more interrelated over time.

For most firms, social, ethical, political, and technological issues are at the same time economic issues, because firms' success in handling them frequently has a direct bearing on their financial statuses, reputations, and well-being. Over time, management groups face an escalating challenge as a changing mix of issues creates a cumulative effect.

6.3a A Portfolio Approach

Firms get affected by so many issues that one wonders how they can manage them all. One way is to see no connection between the issues; that is, take things on an issue-by-issue basis. An alternative is the "**portfolio approach**."[23] In this view, experience with prior issues likely influences future issues; therefore, a portfolio view is in order. Such a view provides focus and coherence to the firm's dealing with the mix of issues it faces. Issues that might show up in Royal Dutch Shell's issue portfolio, for example, might be preventing climate change, protecting biodiversity, reducing wastewater, and operating in sensitive regions. A company such as Shell might deal with hundreds of issues, but the issue portfolio helps to prioritize and provide focus for the company's resources. The failure to adopt certain issues into the portfolio does not signal neglect, but is part of a rational process of issue management in which strategic priorities are vital.[24]

6.3b Issue Definition and the Issue Management Process

Before describing the issue management process, we should briefly discuss what constitutes an issue and what assumptions we are making about issue management. As we said previously, an **issue** is a gap between what stakeholders expect and what the firm is doing. The gap typically evokes debate, controversy, or differences of opinion that need to be resolved. At some point, the organization needs to make a decision on the unresolved matter, but such a decision does not mean that the issue is resolved. Once an issue becomes public and subject to open debate and high-profile media exposure, its resolution becomes increasingly more difficult. One of the features of issues, particularly those arising in the social or ethical realm, is that they are ongoing and therefore require ongoing responses.

Following are some of the characteristics of an "**emerging issue**"[25]:

- The terms of the debate are not clearly defined.
- The issue deals with matters of conflicting values and interest.
- The issue does not lend itself to automatic resolution by expert knowledge.
- The issue is often stated in value-laden terms.
- Trade-offs are inherent.

Examples of modern day emerging issues include "big data" issues, like the extent to which businesses should implement safeguards for privacy, or use consumer data, as in the Target example above. Other examples might be how companies monitor their global supply chains, or tackle gender inequality and wage gap issues, or the extent to which they commit resources to tackling climate change. One can even consider the issue of traumatic brain injuries in American football, a controversial issue associated with high incidences of player concussions in the National Football League, and highlighted in the movie, *Concussion*, starring Will Smith.[26]

The question of **issue definition** can be complicated because of the multiple viewpoints that come into play when an issue is considered. There are multiple stakeholders and motivations in any given management situation. Personal stakes frequently can be important factors but are often either ignored or not taken into consideration. For example, some of the affected parties may be interested in the issue from a deep personal perspective and will not compromise or give up their positions even in the face of concrete evidence that clearly refutes them.[27] This was documented, for example, in a timeline of the way the National Football League and its many stakeholders ignored experts' attention to the "concussion crisis."[28] Some issues may have an ethical dimension to them, and this may evoke differences of opinion as to what represents the right or fair action to take. Thus, the resolution of issues in organizations is not easy.

Climate change continues to emerge as a complex and controversial issue that is important to many stakeholders. We will discuss this further in Chapter 15, but it is easy to see how it is an emerging issue that involves conflicting values and interests, with little automatic resolution, and tradeoffs that often involve businesses forfeiting profits in the short-term for longer-term sustainability goals. In fact, there is much debate amongst experts regarding the measures associated with assessing climate change, contributing to uncertainty about how businesses and policymakers should address it.[29]

The following assumptions are typically made when we choose to use issue management[30]:

- Issues can be identified earlier, more completely, and more reliably than in the past.
- Early anticipation of issues widens the organization's range of options.
- Early anticipation permits better study and understanding of the full range of issues.
- Early anticipation permits the organization to develop a positive orientation toward the issue.
- The organization will have earlier identification of stakeholders.
- The organization will be able to supply information to influential publics earlier and more positively, thus allowing them to understand the issue better.

These are not only assumptions of issue management but also benefits in that they make the organization more effective in its issue management process.

Model of the Issue Management Process. The issue management process discussed here has been extracted from many of the conceptualizations previously developed. Like the strategic management process, which entails a multitude of sequential and interrelated steps or stages, many different authorities including companies, academics, consultants, and associations have conceptualized the issue management process in a variety of ways. Figure 6-2 presents a model of the issue management process that depicts the elements or stages that seem to be common to most issue management models. It is also consistent with the stakeholder orientation we have been developing and using. It contains *planning aspects* (identification, analysis, ranking or prioritization of issues, and formulation of responses) and *implementation aspects* (implementation of responses and evaluation, monitoring, and control of results). Although we discuss the stages in the issue management process as though they are discrete, in reality, they may be interrelated and overlap one another.

FIGURE 6-2 The Issue Management Process

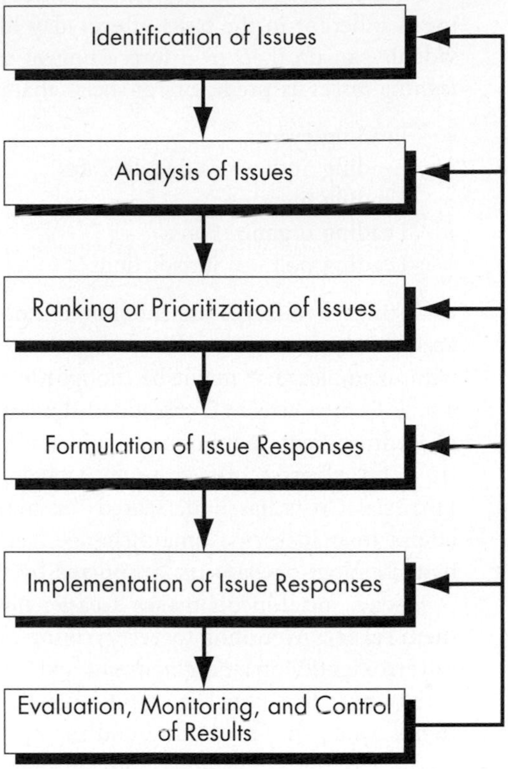

Identification of Issues

Analysis of Issues

Ranking or Prioritization of Issues

Formulation of Issue Responses

Implementation of Issue Responses

Evaluation, Monitoring, and Control of Results

Identification of Issues. Many names have been assigned to the process of issue identification. The terms *social forecasting*, *futures research*, *environmental scanning*, and *public issues scanning* have been used at various times, and many techniques have been employed too. All of these approaches or techniques are similar, but each has its own unique characteristics. Common to all of them, however, is the need to scan the environment and identify emerging issues or trends that might later be determined to have some relevance to or impact on the organization. In recent years, examples of identified issues that may have widespread ramifications for many organizations include natural disasters (e.g., the Great East Japan Earthquake), acts of terrorism (e.g., World Trade Center, the kidnapping of company executives in foreign countries), potential pandemics (e.g., Zika virus, H1N1 outbreaks), and economic events (e.g., the global financial crisis).

Issue identification, in its most rudimentary form, involves the assignment to some individual in the organization the tasks of continuously scanning social media and a variety of publications to build a comprehensive inventory of issues. Often this same person or group will also review public documents, records of congressional hearings, and other such sources of information. One result of this scanning is an internal report that is circulated throughout the organization. The next step in this evolution may be for the company to subscribe to a trend information service that is prepared by a private individual or consulting firm that specializes in environmental or issue scanning.[31]

Futurists, people who make a systematic effort to predict the future, have contributed to the body of knowledge that has helped issue identification. The field of futurism was founded over a century ago and remains strong today.[32] Futurists are common on Madison Avenue, in Washington think tanks and as corporate change experts.[33]

Futurist Graham T. T. Molitor contends, "[e]verybody is a futurist" because forecasting is inherent in the tasks of everyday life.[34] Thus by monitoring ongoing trends, individuals can do their own forecasting of the future. Molitor proposed that there are five *leading forces* as predictors of social change[35]:

- Leading events
- Leading authorities or advocates
- Leading literature
- Leading organizations
- Leading political jurisdictions

If these five forces are monitored closely, impending social change can be identified and, in some cases, predicted. Figure 6-3 presents Molitor's five leading forces, along with examples that might be thought to illustrate his points. The attacks on the World Trade Center in New York added the issue of "preparation for terrorism" to future lists of leading events portending significant social change. National security, business security, and cyber security are now vital issues for managers today. Similarly, the Global Financial Crisis has underscored the importance of corporate transparency and public affairs to managers. Climate change, genetic engineering, information technology, and biotechnology are also issues spurred by the forces of social change.

Today, social media makes it easier not only to spot emerging trends but also to spot them earlier. According to Terry Young, who is forming a new advertising agency geared toward identifying emerging trends, social media "is allowing us to do things we couldn't three, four, five years ago. We have the opportunity to identify and see pop culture trends when they're starting and incorporate our brands early in the process."[36] Social media has the same impact on the management of issues—issues can be identified as they are starting and these emerging issues can then be incorporated into issue management much earlier in the process. In fact, the Twitter response to the 2012 Hurricane Sandy included 9.7 million Sandy-related messages sent by 2.2 million people that was a better measure of local damages than federal emergency estimates.[37]

Issue Selling and Buying. Though the source of most issues is the external environment, the internal perception of and managerial treatment of issues greatly affects the issue identification process. The key in issue identification is getting the people regularly confronted with issues in touch with top managers who can do something about them. This process has two aspects. First is **issue selling**. This relates to middle managers exerting upward influence in organizations as they try to attract the attention of top managers to issues salient to them and the organization.[38] In other words, they have to sell top management on the importance of the issue. The second part of this process is **issue buying**. This involves top managers adopting a more open mind-set for the issues that matter to their subordinates.[39] In short, internal organization members and their assessments of what matters to the organization significantly affect the issue identification process. In fact, following Target's hacking incident, it came to light that Target's executives had ignored the potential for data breaches for a while—in essence, ignoring the issue of data security; this led to the subsequent resignation of Target CEO Gregg Steinhafel.[40]

Analysis of Issues. The next two steps in the issue management process (analysis and ranking of issues) are closely related. To analyze an issue means to carefully study, dissect, break down, classify, or engage in any specific process that helps management

FIGURE 6-3 Examples of Forces Leading Social Change

Leading Forces	Examples	Public Issue Realm
Events	*E. coli*/Salmonella outbreaks	Food safety
	Zika virus/H1N1 flu outbreaks	Public health/safety
	Enron, WorldCom, Toshiba	Corporate governance, fraud
	World Trade Center attacks	Terrorism as public threat
	Three Mile Island/Chernobyl	Nuclear plant safety
	Bhopal gas leak	Plant safety
	Earth Day	Environment
	Tylenol poisonings	Product tampering
	Love Canal, Flint River	Toxic waste—environment
	Bernie Madoff	Ponzi schemes; financial fraud
	Raj Rajaratnam scandal	Insider trading abuses
	Clarence Thomas hearings	Sexual harassment
	BP oil rig explosion	Environment
	Global financial crisis, subprime lending crisis	Corporate governance, regulation
Authorities/Advocates	Ralph Nader	Consumerism
	Rachel Carson	Pesticides and genetic engineering
	Rev. Martin Luther King	Civil rights
	Angelina Jolie	Refugee rights
	Malala Yousafzai	Children, women's rights
	General Colin Powell	'Volunteerism
Literature	*Global Warming* (John Houghton)	Global warming
	Unsafe at Any Speed (Ralph Nader)	Automobile safety
	Megatrends (John Naisbitt)	Issue identification
Organizations	Center for Science in the Public Interest	Food safety
	Black Lives Matter	Civil Rights
	Earth Liberation Front	Environment
	Action for Children's Television (ACT)	Children's advertising
	People for the Ethical Treatment of Animals (PETA)	Animal rights
	Mothers Against Drunk Driving (MADD)	Highway safety, alcohol abuse
Political Jurisdictions	State of Michigan—Whistle-Blower Protection Act	Employee freedom of speech
	State of Delaware	Corporate governance
	States of Connecticut, Iowa, Massachusetts, New Hampshire, Vermont	Gay marriage
	States of Arizona, California, Colorado, Connecticut, Delaware, Missouri, Nebraska, Oklahoma, Pennsylvania, Utah, Tennessee, Texas	Internet privacy and data sharing

understand the nature or characteristics of the issue. An analysis requires that you look beyond the obvious manifestations of the issue and strive to learn more of its history, development, current nature, and potential for future relevance to the organization. It is clear that this is a very important part of the issues management process, and yet, companies often fail in this step. In a 2015 study, *PwC* noted that Toyota failed to address their "sticky" accelerator defects, denying and postponing the issue, which resulted in more accidents.[41] In contrast, when Fitbit discovered that their activity-monitoring wristbands resulted in some customers experiencing irritated skin, they immediately launched an internal investigation with independent experts to analyze and address the issue.[42]

A series of key questions that focus on stakeholder groups in attempting to analyze issues has been proposed[43]:

- Who (which stakeholder) is affected by the issue?
- Who has an interest in the issue?
- Who is in a position to exert influence on the issue?
- Who has expressed opinions on the issue?
- Who ought to care about the issue?

In addition to these questions, the following key questions help with issue analysis:[44]

- Who started the ball rolling? (historical view)
- Who is now involved? (contemporary view)
- Who will get involved? (future view)

Answers to these questions place management in a better position to rank or prioritize the issues so that it will have a better sense of the urgency with which the issues need to be addressed.

Ranking or Prioritization of Issues. Issues vary in the extent to which they matter to an organization, and so determining which issues matter most is essential in determining which ones should receive the most organizational resources, such as time and money. Of the many ways to analyze issues, the two most critical dimensions of issues are *likelihood of occurrence* and *impact* on the organization. Two essential questions are (1) *How likely is the issue to affect the organization?* and (2) *How much impact will the issue have?*[45]

Once these questions are answered, it is necessary to rank issues in some form of a hierarchy of importance or relevance to the organization. Those listed as top priority will receive the most attention and resources, whereas those at the bottom may even be removed from consideration because of their low likelihood or potential impact. The prioritization stage may involve a simple grouping of issues into categories ranging from the most urgent to the least important. Alternatively, a more elaborate or sophisticated scoring system may be employed.[46] Other techniques that have been used in issues identification, analysis, and prioritization include polls or surveys, expert panels, content analysis, the Delphi technique, trend extrapolation, scenario building, and the use of precursor events or bellwethers.[47] Teams of company experts are also used. For example, Baxter International, a U.S.-based health-care and biotech firm, uses multidisciplinary teams because its main issues are in bioethics, and expertise in this subject cuts across a number of different knowledge-based lines of business.[48]

Earlier we described a simple issues identification process as involving an individual in the organization or a subscription to a newsletter or trend-spotting service. While the analysis and ranking stages could be done by an individual, more often, the company moves up to a next stage of formalization. This next stage involves assignment of the issue management function to a team, often as part of a public affairs department, which begins to specialize in the issue management function. This group of specialists can provide a wide range of issue management activities, depending on the commitment of the company to the process. Some companies have created issue management units or managers to alert the management on emerging trends and controversies and to help mobilize the companies' resources to deal with them.

Formulation and Implementation of Responses. Formulation and implementation of responses are two steps in the issue management process combined here for discussion purposes. We should observe that the formulation and implementation stages in the issue management process are quite similar to the corresponding stages discussed in the preceding chapter, which pertained to the strategic management process as a whole.

Formulation in this case refers to the response design process. Based on the analysis conducted, companies can then identify options that might be pursued in dealing with the issues, in making decisions, and in implementing those decisions. Strategy formulation refers not only to the formulation of the actions that the firm intends to take but also to the creation of the overall strategy, or degree of aggressiveness, employed in carrying out those actions. Options might include aggressive pursuit, gradual pursuit, or selective pursuit of goals, plans, processes, or programs.[49] All of these more detailed plans are part of the strategy formulation process. This is a key stage for rebuilding trust with stakeholders as well. As noted by *PwC*, a credible commitment to change, with a plan of action, can reverse any mistrust from the initial incident.[50] Again, Fitbit provides an example of a company that, while dealing with customer complaints, contracted with external dermatologists and formulated a plan to address the skin irritation issues in their wristbands and a plan for next-generation trackers.[51]

Once plans for dealing with issues have been formulated, *implementation* becomes the focus. Many organizational aspects need to be addressed in the implementation process, including the clarity of the plan itself, resources needed to implement the plan, top management support, organizational structure, technical competence, and timing.[52]

Evaluation, Monitoring, and Control. These recognizable steps in the issue management process were also treated as steps in the strategic management process in Chapter 5. In the current discussion, they mean that companies should continually evaluate the results of their responses to the issues and ensure that these actions are kept on track. In particular, this stage requires careful monitoring of stakeholders' opinions. A form of stakeholder audit—something derivative of the social audit discussed in Chapter 5—might be used. Stakeholder engagement might also be used at this stage. The information gathered during this final stage in the issue management process is then fed back to the earlier stages in the process so that changes or adjustments might be made as needed. Evaluation information may be useful at each stage in the process.

The issue management process has been presented as a complete system. In practice, companies apply the stages across various degrees of formality or informality as needed or desired. For example, because issue management is more important in some situations than in others, some stages of the process may be truncated to meet the needs of different firms in different industries. In addition, some firms are more committed to issue management than others.

It is helpful here to provide an example. The Chipotle *E. coli* outbreak case, which we discuss in our more detail in Case 4, began with Chipotle's attention to a growing issue in food quality; the need and desire to provide customers with healthier, non-artificial, high-quality food in chain restaurants. The company capitalized on an issue that had been highlighted in polls and in the media—the need for healthier fast food options—and implemented resources including relying on local farms, to create a new business model and address the issue. Of course, Chipotle's business model that began as a strength quickly became a weakness with supply chain constraints. As one columnist noted, "All of a sudden, highly processed industrial food doesn't look so bad."[53]

6.3c Issue Development Process

A vital attribute of issue management is that issues tend to develop according to an evolutionary pattern and a life cycle emerges. Figure 6-4 presents a simplified view of what an **issue development life cycle process** might look like. In the beginning, a nascent issue emerges in the press or social media, is enunciated by public interest organizations, and is detected through public opinion polling. According to a former director of corporate responsibility at Monsanto, the issue is low-key and somewhat flexible at this stage.[54] During this time, the issue may reflect a felt need, receive media coverage, and attract interest group development and growth. A typical firm may notice the issue but take no action. More issue-oriented firms may become more active in their monitoring and in their attempts to shape or help "define the issue."[55] Active firms may have the capacity to prevent issues from going any further, through either effective responses to the issues or effective lobbying. In the next stage of the cycle, national media attention may address the issue, quickly followed by leading political jurisdictions (e.g., cities, states, or countries). Quite often, federal government attention is generated in the form of studies and hearings; legislation, regulation, and litigation follow.

This is simply an example of a sequence. Issues vary, and so the stages in the process, especially the early stages, might occur in a different sequence or in an iterative pattern. Further, not all issues complete the process; some are resolved before they reach the stage of legislation or regulation. It is important not to oversimplify the issue development process. The paths issues follow vary with the nature of the issues and the intensity

FIGURE 6-4 Issue Development Life Cycle Process

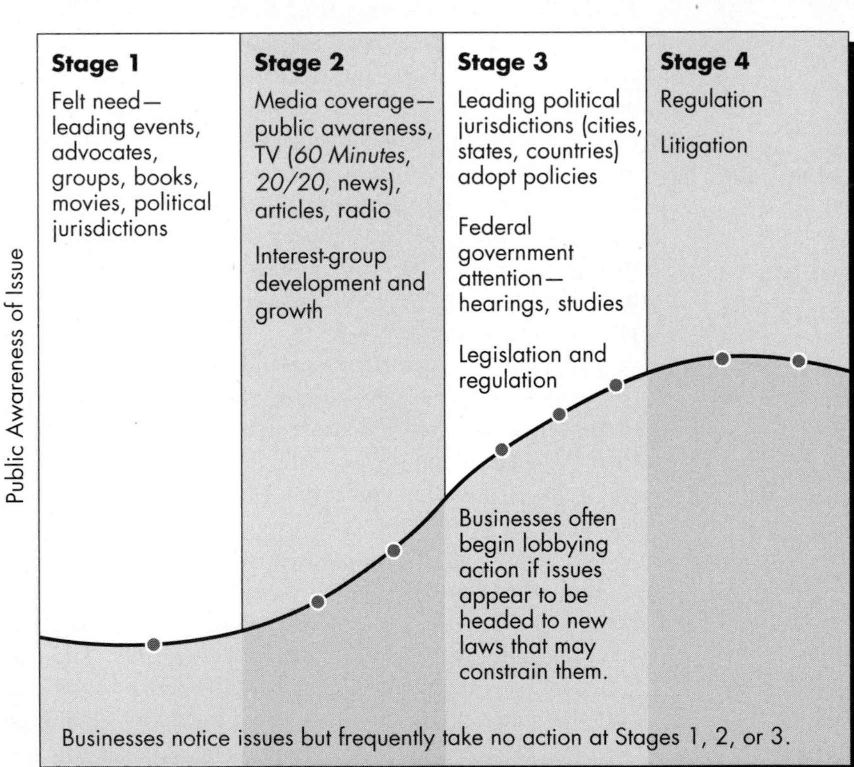

and variety of stakeholder interests and values. The complex interactions of all the variables make it unlikely issues will follow a straight line.[56]

Illustrations of Issue Development. This evolution of issue development may be illustrated through two examples. First, consider the issue of environmental protection. The social expectation was manifested in Rachel Carson's book *Silent Spring* (1963); it became a political issue in Eugene McCarthy's political platform (1968); it resulted in legislation in 1971–1972 with the creation of the Environmental Protection Agency (EPA); and it was reflected in social control by emissions standards, pollution fines, product recalls, and environmental permits in later years. Today, the important and pervasive issue of sustainability can be traced to these early roots. The second example involves product or consumer safety. The social expectation was manifested in Ralph Nader's book *Unsafe at Any Speed* (1964). It then became a political issue through the National Traffic Auto Safety Act and Motor Vehicle Safety Hearings (1966), and that resulted in legislation in 1966 with the passage of the Motor Vehicle Safety Act and mandatory seat belt usage laws in four states (1984). It was reflected in social control through the ordering of seat belts in all cars (1967), defects litigation, product recalls, and driver fines. Today, product safety is an institutionalized issue that all companies must address.[57]

More recently, facing growing public concern about the collection and trade of personal data, U.S. states have taken the lead in proposing a series of privacy laws including protecting the privacy of student data, and sharing customer data, even as they wait for federal legislation to address these issues and move through the issue development life cycle.[58] Alert companies will be proactive and take actions earlier perhaps to head off or shape future government regulations that may emerge.

6.3d Issue Management in Practice

Issue management began as a way for companies to get in front of, and not simply respond to, public policy issues that could affect the organization. Howard Chase, the father of issue management, described it as "a methodology by which the private sector can get out of the unenviable position of being at the end of the crack-the-whip political line."[59] Today, issue management covers not only public policy activities but also a full range of public relations and management activities. There is greater use of interdepartmental issue teams, with the public affairs department often serving as coordinator and strategist but with appropriate line and staff executives charged with ultimate accountability for implementation. In practice, therefore, issue management does not function as a stand-alone activity but has been subsumed into a host of functions for which modern public affairs departments take responsibility.[60]

Issue management faces a serious challenge in business today. From the standpoint of the turbulence in the stakeholder environment, issue management is sorely needed. To become a permanent part of the organization, however, issue management will have to prove itself continuously. We can talk conceptually about the process with ease, but the field remains somewhat nebulous even though it is struggling to become more scientific and legitimate. Managers want results, and if issue management cannot deliver those results, it will be destined to failure as a management process. A practitioner of issue management warned that issue management "often attracts excessive process at the expense of real progress."[61]

Research has shown that companies that adopted issue management processes developed better overall and issue-specific reputations and had better short- and longer-term financial performance than organizations not practicing issue management.[62] By tying issue management in with stakeholder management, the most successful companies used stakeholder integration techniques in their implementation. This means that the firms actively sought to establish close-knit ties with a broad range of external and internal stakeholders and successfully incorporated their values and interests into management decisions.[63]

6.4 Crisis Management

Prudential Financial became a major player in the Japanese market over time. After entering the market in 1988, the company expanded through a 2001 acquisition of Gibraltar Life Insurance, Ltd.[64] In February 2011, the company "doubled down" on its investment in Japan with a $4.8 billion purchase of Star and Edison life-insurance companies from AIG.[65] The earthquake and tsunami hit just a few weeks later, with devastating loss of life and property.[66] The first thing Prudential did was to check to make sure their 23,000 employees in Japan were safe. Then they set about responding to the crisis. The Prudential Foundation donated $6.1 million to support relief efforts: The Foundation also pledged to match individual donations that employees made.[67] Then people pitched in with volunteer efforts. In one instance, a team of volunteers, 37 people from 10 different countries and 16 different businesses, went to Japan to help with clean up in one of the worst affected areas.[68]

Prudential could not control the devastation caused by the earthquake and tsunami but the company could, and did, control its reaction to it effectively. Crises occur with regularity, making them almost routine. However, the fallout from a crisis is not routine in any way. Crises can topple organizations if top management does not respond quickly, decisively, and effectively.[69] At the same time, a strong and effective response to a crisis can strengthen an organization in the end. Masahiro Watanabe, Head of Human Resources at Prudential Corporation Asia Life in Japan, saw value in the volunteer experience, "It was a great opportunity for me to be able to support and participate in this program as a citizen of the host country. In one respect, this program is a part of the social contribution activities of a corporation. However, looking at it from a different side, it offered an occasion for training and team-building that transcended the boundaries of the local business units."[70]

Contrast this case with the crisis of the disappearance of the Malaysian flight MH370 in April 2014 following its departure form Kuala Lumpur. While this crisis was handled quite well by the Malaysia Airlines (which released five public statements during the day MH370 disappeared and communicated regularly and publicly with stakeholders), the Malaysian Government did not handle the crisis as well. They mishandled information, attacked the foreign media when journalists asked to verify conflicting statements, failed to include a senior official who could speak Mandarin, and manhandled the relative of a missing passenger with security staff that ejected the relative during a press conference.[71] The way the Malaysian Government mishandled the crisis became an international issue that created a crisis of confidence in the country itself.[72]

Several observers have suggested that the Tylenol poisonings in 1982 put crisis management "on the map." The case marked the beginning of the new corporate discipline known as crisis management because J&J's voluntary recall of some 31 million Tylenol bottles was the first highly visible example of an organization assuming responsibility for its products without being pressured.[73] Other corporate crises have included the Union Carbide Bhopal disaster, which killed over 2,000 people in India, the attacks on the World Trade Center in New York, which resulted in the deaths of approximately 3,000 people, and Firestone and Ford being implicated in massive tire recalls due to faulty tires causing tread separations and deaths. More recently, such big name companies and organizations as Volkswagen (emissions cheating), General Motors (ignition switch crisis), Uber (alleged driver abuse of passengers), Sony Pictures (massive hacking), NFL (football concussions), and FIFA (international soccer corruption) have kept crisis management in the news.

SPOTLIGHT *on Sustainability*

Sustainable Corporations Shine in Financial Crisis

An A. T. Kearney study entitled "Green Winners: The Performance of Sustainability Focused Companies in the Financial Crisis" analyzed 99 of the largest companies officially recognized as having a strong commitment to sustainable practice. The study defined sustainable practice as being "geared toward protecting the environment and promoting social well-being while achieving shareholder value." They found that sustainable companies outperformed their competitors by 15 percent in 16 of 18 industries, with the difference representing an average of $650 million more in market capitalization per company than their competitors.

The study found that sustainability involves characteristics that help firms weather a crisis. A long-term perspective, sound risk management practices, and green innovations such as reduced waste and emissions and the use of alternate energy sources were cited as factors that gave sustainable companies a competitive edge. Recognition for their sustainability efforts may also have enabled them to differentiate themselves from their competitors.

The report concluded that "the most sustainability-focused may well emerge from the current crisis stronger than ever … recognized by investors who appreciate the true long-term value of sustainability."

Sources: Robert Kropp, "Sustainable Corporations Outperform during Economic Crisis," *Social Funds*, http://www.socialfunds.com/news/article.cgi/article2628.html. Accessed February 10, 2016; Xavier University, "Sustainability and the Economic Crisis, http://www.xavier.edu/green/Sustainability-and-the-Economic-Crisis.cfm. Accessed February 10, 2016.

6.4a The Nature of Crises

There are many kinds of crises. Those mentioned here have all been associated with major stakeholder groups and have achieved high-visibility status. Hurt or killed customers, hurt employees, injured stockholders, stolen information, and unfair practices are the concerns of modern crisis management. Not all crises involve such public or ethical issues, but these kinds of crises almost always ensure front-page status. Major companies can be seriously damaged by such episodes, especially if the episodes are poorly handled.

What is a crisis? Dictionaries state that a **crisis** is a "turning point for better or worse," an "emotionally significant event," or a "decisive moment." We all think of crises as being emotionally charged, but we do not always think of them as turning points for better or for worse. The implication here is that a crisis is a decisive moment that, if managed one way, could make things worse but, if managed another way, make things better. Choice is present, and how the crisis is managed can make a difference. From a managerial point of view, a line needs to be drawn between a problem and a crisis. Problems, of course, are common in business. A crisis, however, is not as common. A useful way to think about a crisis is as follows:

> *A crisis is an extreme event that may threaten your very existence. At the very least, it causes substantial injuries, deaths, and financial costs, as well as serious damage to your reputation.*[74]

Figure 6-5 presents a "how *not* to do it" case in crisis management as experienced by golf star, Tiger Woods. Woods was under fire for allegations of serial infidelity that were at odds with the family-oriented image he had cultivated. Some have said that Tiger's golf game never fully recovered after this crisis he faced.

Types of Crises. A variety of situations leave companies vulnerable to crises. These include industrial accidents, environmental problems, union problems or strikes, product recalls, investor relations, hostile takeovers, proxy fights, rumors or media leaks, government regulatory problems, acts of terrorism, and embezzlement.[75] Other common crises

FIGURE 6-5 Crisis Management and Tiger Woods, Inc.: How Not to Do It

When Tiger Woods crashed his Cadillac Escalade into a fire hydrant and a tree in his gated Florida community, the world's media converged upon him. Allegations of serial infidelity soon arose that set the pro-golfer's personal and professional life into a tailspin. As the man behind a billion dollar financial empire and the personification of the brand it sells, Woods' personal trouble quickly developed into an organizational crisis. His management of the crisis held implications not only for him but also for the business that had been built around him.

Most crisis management experts fault his management of the crisis. Woods waited days to issue a statement, and the statement that appeared spoke only vaguely of "transgressions." Robbie Vorhaus, a crisis reputation adviser in New York, believes he should have spoken more quickly, "If you don't tell your story first, then you're letting someone else tell your story. Now he has to react and respond to what everyone else is saying." This advice is similar to the advice Woods gave in an ESPN interview when he was asked about Michael Vick's response after Vick was caught being involved in a dog-fighting ring:

> *If you made that big a mistake, you've got to come out and just be contrite, be honest and just tell the public that "I was wrong."*
>
> *Waiting a long time got a lot of people polarized.... If he would have come out earlier, he would've diffused a little more of it.*

It has been suggested that Woods broke three basic rules of crisis management when he failed to follow his own advice:

- **Rule No. 1: Don't Wait.** After the car crash, Woods issued a statement acknowledging the accident but nothing else. Two days later, Woods issued another statement, but it was vague and the story was shaped by others in the interim.
- **Rule No. 2: Don't Run from the Truth.** Woods' first statement pleaded for privacy and claimed that "false, unfounded and malicious rumors" were circulating, giving the impression that the rumors were untrue. Three days later, he changed his story but admitted only to unspecified "transgressions."
- **Rule No. 3: Don't Hide.** Woods hid away long after the accident, leaving the women who alleged that they had relationships with him as the only voices telling the story.

Sources: Dana Mattoli, "'Tiger Bungles Crisis Management 101," *The Wall Street Journal* (December 8, 2009), A31; Ryan Ballingee, "'Tiger's Own Words May Be Cause for Concern about Anthony Galea," *Waggle Room* (December 18, 2009); Blair Berstein, "Crisis Management and Sports in the Age of Social Media," http://www.studentpulse.com/articles/833/2/crisis-management-and-sports-in-the-age-of-social-media-a-case-study-analysis-of-the-tiger-woods-scandal?utm_expid=22625156-1.jO__KIIlQVuEPc9uLGsmiQ.0&utm_referrer=https%3A%2F%2Fwww.google.com%2F. Accessed February 11, 2016.

include information system hacks, product tampering, executive kidnapping, work-related homicides, malicious rumors, and natural disasters that destroy corporate offices or information bases.[76] Since September 11, 2001, we have had to add terrorism to this list.

Crises may be grouped into seven families[77]:

- *Economic crises* (recessions, hostile takeovers, stock market crashes)
- *Physical crises* (industrial accidents, product failures, supply breakdown)
- *Personnel crises* (strikes, exodus of key employees, workplace violence)
- *Criminal crises* (product tampering, kidnappings, acts of terrorism)
- *Information crises* (theft of proprietary information, cyberattacks)
- *Reputational crises* (rumormongering or slander, logo tampering)
- *Natural disasters* (earthquakes, tornadoes, floods, fires)

After major crises, companies report the following outcomes: The crises escalated in intensity, were subjected to media and government scrutiny, interfered with normal business operations, and damaged the company's bottom line. For example, as a result of the horrific attacks on the World Trade Center, companies experienced major power shifts among executives as some bosses fumbled with their responsibilities and didn't handle the crisis well. Those bosses who handled the crisis well garnered more responsibility, whereas others lost responsibilities.[78]

Reputational crises may particularly difficult for businesses to rebound from as they attempt to reintegrate and rebuild trust with their stakeholders.[79] However, it is not impossible. For example, in 2013 the FBI raided the headquarters of Pilot Flying J's—one of the largest companies operating filling stations on America's highways.[80] The affidavit accused individuals at the firm of running a scheme for a number of years to swindle small haulage firms out of millions of dollars in rebates on purchases of fuel. After the FBI raid, lenders and suppliers were nervous about the penalties, compensation payments, and departure of clients that might happen in the fallout. However, in November 2013, the company paid $83 million to settle a class action lawsuit, and then it followed up by accepting responsibility for the criminal conduct of employees and paid the U.S. Justice Department a fine of $92 million. According to one analyst, "Its prompt actions to put things right meant that most of Pilot's users stayed loyal."[81]

Four Crisis Stages. There are several ways of describing the stages through which a crisis may progress. One useful view is that a crisis may consist of as many as four distinct stages: (1) a **prodromal crisis stage**, (2) an **acute crisis stage**, (3) a **chronic crisis stage**, and (4) a **crisis resolution stage**.[82]

Prodromal Crisis Stage This is the warning stage. (*Prodromal* is a medical term that refers to a previous notice or warning.) This stage could also be thought of as a symptom stage. Although it could be called a "pre-crisis" stage, this presupposes that one knows that a crisis is coming. Some experts have suggested that a possible outbreak of Zika virus would be in this stage. It is believed that crises "send out a repeated trail of early warning signals" that managers can learn to recognize.[83] Perhaps management should adopt this perspective: Watch each situation with the thought that it could be a crisis in the making. Early symptoms may be obvious, such as in the case where a social activist group tells the management it will boycott the company if a certain problem is not addressed. On the other hand, symptoms may be more subtle, as in the case where defect rates for a particular product a company makes start edging up over time.

Acute Crisis Stage This is the stage at which the crisis has actually occurred, and there is no turning back. Damage has been done, and it is now up to management to handle or contain it. If the prodromal stage is the pre-crisis stage, the acute stage is the *actual* crisis stage. The crucial decision point at which things may get worse or better has been reached.

Chronic Crisis Stage This is the lingering period. It may be the period of investigations, audits, or in-depth news stories. For example, following investigations by the CDC into Chipotle's *E. coli* outbreaks, a federal criminal investigation began to determine the extent to which management knew about food safety issues that extended back three years.[84] Management may see it as a period of recovery, self-analysis, or self-doubt. A survey of major companies found that crises tended to linger as much as two-and-a-half times longer in firms without crisis management plans than in firms with such plans.

Crisis Resolution Stage This is the final stage—the goal of all crisis management efforts. When an early warning sign of a crisis is noted, the manager should seize control swiftly and determine the most direct and expedient route to resolution. If the warning signs are missed in the first stage, the goal is to speed up all phases and reach the final stage as soon as possible.

Figure 6-6 presents one way in which these four stages might be visualized. It should be noted that the phases may overlap and that each phase varies in intensity and duration. It is expected that management will learn from the crisis and thus will be better prepared for, and better able to handle, any future crisis.

6.4b Managing Business Crises

Five Practical Steps in Managing Crises. The following five steps, synthesized by *Businessweek* magazine from the actual experiences of companies going through crises, are summarized and discussed next. They are (1) identifying areas of vulnerability, (2) developing a plan for dealing with threats, (3) forming crisis teams, (4) simulating crisis drills, and (5) learning from experience.[85]

First: Identifying Areas of Vulnerability In this first step, some areas of vulnerability are obvious, such as potential chemical spills, whereas others are more subtle. The key seems to be in developing a greater consciousness of how things can go wrong and get out of hand. At Chipotle, following *E. coli* incidences that sickened at least 53 people in nine states, the company responded almost immediately to customers through Twitter and Facebook, issuing statements to the media, voluntarily closing restaurants, and hiring two food safety consulting firms to assess and strengthen their food safety precautions.[86] Chipotle had to act immediately; it did not have time to completely develop a plan. However, after several incidences of norovirus breakouts at restaurants in Boston and California, one critic noted that Chipotle failed to identify the areas of vulnerability in their newer business model, "If Chipotle is going to continue to provide an alternative

FIGURE 6-6 Four Stages in a Management Crisis

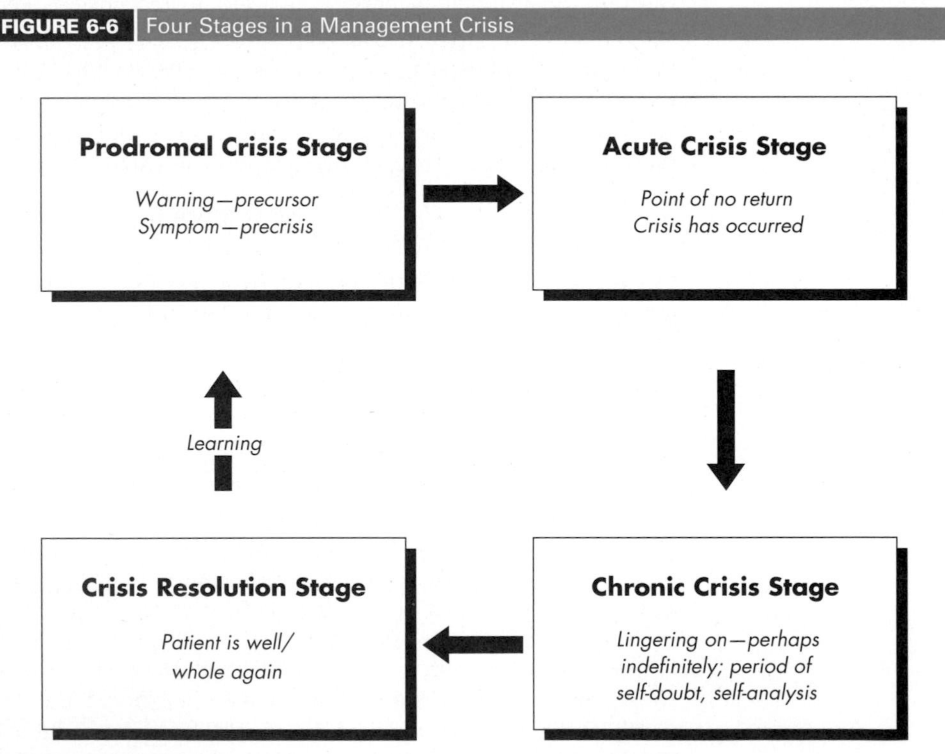

model to processed, industrial food, it needs to also be at the forefront of creating systems to support that new approach, such as offering its employees paid sick days."[87]

A key to identifying areas of vulnerability is "recognizing the threat." Recognizing low-probability but high-consequence events is a challenge, but planning for them can help a company to survive major crises.[88] Some ways that companies can identify areas of vulnerability include the following[89]:

- *Scenario planning.* Create scenarios for crises that could occur over the next two years.
- *Risk analysis.* Estimate the probabilities and costs/benefits of estimated future events.
- *Incentives.* Reward managers for information sharing.
- *Networks.* Build formal coalitions to mobilize internal and external information suppliers.

Second: Develop a Plan for Dealing with Threats A plan for dealing with the most serious crisis threats is a logical next step. One of the most crucial issues is communications planning. After a Dow Chemical railroad car derailed near Toronto, forcing the evacuation of 250,000 people, Dow Canada prepared information kits on the hazards of its products so that executives would be knowledgeable enough to respond properly if a similar crisis were to arise in the future. Dow Canada also trained executives in interviewing techniques. This effort paid off several years later when an accident caused a chemical spill into a river that supplied drinking water for several nearby towns. The company's emergency response team arrived at the site almost immediately and established a press center that distributed information about the chemicals. In addition, the company recruited a neutral expert to speak on the hazards and how to deal with them. Officials praised Dow for its handling of this crisis.[90]

Getting an entire organization trained to deal with crises is difficult and expensive, but the Dow CEO paraphrases what a car repairperson once said in a TV commercial: "You can pay now or pay a lot more later." Similarly, Chipotle founder and co-chief executive Steve Ells acknowledged that the cost of new safety programs to prevent future outbreaks of *E. coli* and norovirus were "very, very expensive," but CFO John Hartung said, "We're not trying to make this cost-effective. We're just doing it."[91] Most of us would believe that paying for something now is infinitely better for the safety and well-being of everyone.[92]

Third: Forming Crisis Teams Another step that can be taken as part of an overall planning effort is the formation of **crisis teams**, especially in large organizations. Such teams have played key roles in many well-managed disasters. A good example is the team formed at Procter & Gamble when its Rely tampon products were linked with the dreaded disease toxic shock syndrome. The team was quickly assembled, a vice president was appointed to head it, and after one week, the decision was made to remove Rely products from marketplace shelves. The quick action earned the firm praise, and it paid off for P&G in the end.

Another task in assembling crisis teams is identifying managers who can cope effectively with stress. Not every executive can handle the fast-moving, high-pressured, ambiguous decision environment that is created by a crisis, and early identification of executives who can is important.

Fourth: Simulating Crisis Drills Some companies have gone so far as to run crisis drills in which highly stressful situations are simulated so that managers can "practice" what they might do in a real crisis. As a basis for conducting crisis drills and experiential exercises, a number of companies have adopted a crisis management software package. This software allows companies to centralize and maintain up-to-date crisis management information and allows company leaders to assign responsibilities to their crisis team, target key audiences, identify and monitor potential issues, and create crisis-response processes.[93]

Fifth: Learning from Experience The final stage in crisis management is learning from experience. At this point, managers need to ask themselves exactly what they have learned from past crises and how that knowledge can be used to advantage in the future. Part of this stage entails an assessment of the effectiveness of the firm's crisis-handling strategies and identification of areas where improvements in capabilities need to be made. Without a crisis management system of some kind in place, the organization will find itself reacting to crises after they have occurred. If learning and preparation for the future are continuous, however, the firm may engage in more proactive behavior.[94]

6.4c Crisis Communications

An illustration of crisis management without effective communications occurred during the Jack in the Box hamburger disaster years ago. There was an outbreak of *Escherichia coli* bacteria in the Pacific Northwest area, resulting in the deaths of four children. Following this crisis, the parent company, San Diego–based Foodmaker, entered a downward spiral after lawsuits by the families of victims enraged the public and franchisees. Foodmaker did most of the right things and did them quickly. The company immediately suspended hamburger sales, recalled suspect meat from its distribution system, increased cooking time for all foods, pledged to pay for all the medical costs related to the disaster, and hired a food safety expert to design a new food-handling system. However, it forgot to do one thing: Communicate with the public, including its own employees.[95]

The company's **crisis communications** efforts were inept. It waited a week before accepting any responsibility for the tragedy, preferring to point fingers at its meat supplier and even the Washington state health officials for not explaining the state's new guidelines for cooking hamburgers at higher temperatures. The media pounced on the company. The company was blasted for years, even though within itself, the company was taking proper steps to correct the problem. The company suffered severe financial losses, and it took at least six years before the company really felt it was on the road to recovery. "The crisis," as it was called around company headquarters, taught the firm an important lesson. CEO Robert Nugent was quoted later as saying, "Nobody wants to deal with their worst nightmare, but we should have recognized you've got to communicate."[96]

Virtually all crisis management plans call for effective crisis communications, but they are not always effectively executed. There are a number of different stakeholder groups with whom effective communications are critical, especially the media and those immediately affected by the crisis. Many companies have failed to manage their crises successfully because of inadequate or failed communications with key stakeholder groups. It is axiomatic that *prepared* communications will be more helpful than *reactive* communications. Ten steps of crisis communication that are worth summarizing include[97]:

1. Identify your crisis communications team.
2. Identify key spokespersons who will be authorized to speak for the organization.
3. Train your spokespersons.
4. Establish communications protocols.
5. Identify and know your audience.
6. Anticipate crises.
7. Assess the crisis situation.
8. Identify key messages you will communicate to key groups.
9. Decide on communications methods.
10. Be prepared to ride out the storm.

ETHICS IN PRACTICE CASE

Crisis Management: When to Repent? When to Defend?

When facing a crisis, especially one in which the organization is implicated, many experts on crisis management take the approach that management or the firm needs to quickly repent of its malfeasance or wrongdoing, ask for forgiveness, and promise to do better in the future. This soft approach argues for engaging in careful communications and apologizing, if necessary. This approach, it is believed, is the best route to limiting damage and restoring the public's confidence in the company and its leaders.

In their book, *Damage Control: Why Everything You Know about Crisis Management Is Wrong,* authors Eric Dezenhall and John Weber argue that this soft approach is often wrong. According to the authors, if you are facing a lawsuit, a sex scandal, a defective product, or allegations of insider trading, experts may tell you to stay positive, get your message out, and everything will be just fine. But, Dezenhall and Weber conclude, this kind of cheery talk does not help much during a real crisis, and it's easy to lose sight of your genuine priorities. If your case goes to trial, for example, you might want the public to think you're a wonderful company, but all that matters is what the jury thinks.

The authors support a political model of crisis management, which means you may have to fight back and defend yourself. When the company has done wrong, repentance is in order. When the company has been wronged, a strong defense is recommended. The authors recommend not admitting guilt and meeting each accusation with a counter claim. They say this is how Martha Stewart turned her public image around after serving a jail sentence. In another example, they say this is how Merck, the pharmaceutical company, recovered from legal defeats and bad press as it began to portray plaintiffs as selfish opportunists. They also cite how successful the mobile phone industry was in mounting a defense against the consumer complaints that the phones were causing brain tumors. The key, they say, is determining when to be conciliatory and when to defend aggressively.

1. What are the relevant issues in this debate over the best response to a crisis?
2. Is it best to apologize, repent and move on, or stand firm and aggressively defend?
3. What is the downside risk of mounting a rigorous defense?
4. Do research on the Chipotle crisis. Did the company Repent or Defend?

Sources: Eric Dezenhall and John Weber, *Damage Control: Why Everything You Know about Crisis Management Is Wrong* (New York: Portfolio Hardcover, 2007); Howcast, "Damage Control and Crisis Management in PR," http://www.howcast.com/videos/508056-damage-control-crisis-management-public-relations/. Accessed February 10, 2016.

A brief elaboration on the importance of identifying key messages that will be communicated to key groups is useful (point 8). It is important that you communicate with your internal stakeholders first because rumors are often started there, and uninformed employees can do great damage to a successful crisis management effort. Additionally, with the popularity of social media and the use of outlets like Twitter to report eyewitness accounts about disasters, terrorist attacks, and other social crises, it is important to squelch misinformation and provide localized information to assist in decision making. Internal stakeholders are your best advocates and can be supportive during a crisis. Prepare news releases that contain as much information as possible, and get this information out to all media outlets at the same time. Communicate with others in the community who have a need to know, such as public officials, disaster coordinators, stakeholders, and others. Uniformity of response is of vital importance during a crisis and so it is important to have a key spokesperson (point 2).[98]

The Centers for Disease Control and Prevention (CDC) states as part of its crisis communications training that the first 48 hours of a crisis are the most important. The program's mantra is reported as "be *first*, be *right*, be *credible*."[99] This became known in their efficient handling of the Ebola outbreak in West Africa in 2014. Being first means getting your message out first, which allows you to control its accuracy and content. If a company is late in getting its message out, the media and others will fill in the blanks, and they might include rumors, their own speculations, misunderstandings, or bias. Being right means saying and doing the right thing. This is the ethical dimension of communications. This is done after the management team has gathered all the facts and understands exactly what has happened in the crisis. Being credible means being open, honest, and speaking with one consistent voice. Mixed messages from mixed sources can lead to disaster. The company's spokesperson should be sincere, be empathetic, be accountable, demonstrate competence, display expertise, and put forth consistent facts.[100] For all this to happen, of course, careful crisis communications must be a priority in the crisis plan.

6.4d Successful Crisis Management

Being Prepared for Crises. Being prepared for crises has become a primary activity in a growing number of companies. Today, most companies may be prepared for crises, but their degree of preparedness varies widely. When Hurricane Sandy hit the United States in 2012, 24 states were affected as it swept the entire eastern seaboard and west across the Appalachian Mountains—but New York City and New Jersey were hardest hit. For the first time since 1888, the New York Stock Exchange closed down, for two days, and 7.9 million businesses and homes were without power in 15 states.[101] While many businesses had crisis management plans in place, it was noted that the quality of the plans varied widely, and IT recovery capabilities, in particular, were deficient.[102] While it is certainly difficult to anticipate everything, successful crisis management requires businesses to develop a comprehensive program that includes training throughout the entire organization for many different scenarios and they need to review their needs in advance.[103]

Learning from Crises. Many businesses that failed to take the threat of Hurricane Sandy seriously learned that their crisis management plans must extend beyond what is commonly referred to as "BCP's"—business continuity plans—to include specific issues related to employees, technology, business continuity, and communication.[104] Similarly, General Electric (GE) chairman and CEO Jeff Immelt described himself as "humbler and hungrier" as a result of the global recession and credit crisis that sorely tested GE.[105] In addition to the expected responses of refocusing operations and cutting costs, Immelt has looked inward, changing his management style in response to the crisis and recession. He meets more regularly and individually with his 25 top executives, pushes more decision making to lower organizational levels, and, in a move that might not come naturally to a former applied math major, he has become more comfortable with ambiguity.[106]

A Successful Crisis Management Example. We conclude this chapter with an illustration of a successful crisis management case study of one company. Earlier, we presented the handling of the J&J Tylenol crisis as a success story. This success story started with the kind of phone call every company dreads—"Your product is injuring people; we're announcing it at a press conference today." Schwan's Sales Enterprises, Inc., got such a call from the Minnesota Department of Health at about noon one fateful day. The Health Department reported that it had found a statistical link between Schwan's ice cream and confirmed cases of salmonella. Thousands of people in at least 39 states became ill with salmonella after eating tainted Schwan's ice cream, potentially setting the company up for a decade's worth of litigation. Instead, in a little more than a year after the outbreak, the vast majority of claims had been handled outside the legal system through direct settlements or as part of a class action in Minneapolis.[107]

Schwan's knew that its image of the smiling man in the sunshine-yellow Schwan's truck (with a Swan on the side) busily hand-delivering ice cream to grateful consumers was one of its major assets. Before the company was sure of the Health Department's findings, it halted sales and production, shut down, and invited the state health department, the department of agriculture, and the FDA into the plant to investigate. It also notified all its sales offices nationwide. Also, within the first 24 hours of the crisis, the company set up a hotline to answer consumer questions, contacted employees and managers to staff the hotline, prepared for a product recall, and began working with its insurer.[108]

By placing consumer safety as its number one priority, Schwan's was able to resolve the crisis much more quickly than ever would have been possible without a carefully designed crisis management plan. Whether by coincidence or preparedness, the manager of public affairs and the company's general counsel had completed a review and rewriting of the company's crisis management manual just two months before the outbreak. One vital component of the plan was a crisis management team, which went to work as soon as the news came. The crisis management team quickly set up a process for handling consumers who had been affected. The team, working with its insurance company, quickly helped customers get medical treatment and their bills paid. Settlements to customers who suffered from salmonella symptoms included financial damages, medical expenses, and other costs, such as reimbursement for workdays missed.[109]

How did the ice cream get contaminated with salmonella? After a month's investigation that kept the Marshall, Minnesota, plant closed, it was determined that the ice cream mix supplied by a few vendors was the culprit. The mix of cream, sugar, and milk had been shipped in a tanker truck that had previously held raw, unpasteurized eggs that had the bacteria. Schwan's quietly sought and received legal damages from the suppliers but stayed focused on its customers throughout the crisis.

What did Schwan's learn from this crisis? Previously, Schwan's did not repasteurize its ice cream mix once the mix arrived at the Marshall plant. Within a few weeks of the outbreak, however, the company had broken ground to build its own repasteurization plant. The company also leased a dedicated fleet of tanker trucks to deliver the ice cream mix from the suppliers to the plant, set up a system for testing each shipment, and delayed shipping the final product until the test results were known. In summary, Schwan's planning, quick response, and customer-oriented strategy combined to retain customer loyalty and minimize the company's legal exposure.[110] It was a case of good, effective crisis management.

Undoubtedly, in the years to come, stories will be told of successful crisis management in the aftermath of major traumatic events in the lives of organizations and society. Sadly, preparation for acts of terrorism is now a vital national and business issue. Clearly, the events of the past few years have made crisis management a priority topic in boardrooms and among managers.

Summary

Risk, issue, and crisis management are key approaches by which companies may plan for the turbulent stakeholder environment. These approaches are frequently found housed in a company's department of public affairs. Risk management identifies and prepares for potential issues that have not yet occurred in order to keep the issues from arising. Issue management is a process by which an organization identifies issues in the stakeholder environment, analyzes and prioritizes those issues in terms of their relevance to the organization, plans responses to the issues, and then evaluates and monitors the results. Issue management requires knowledge of the changing mix of issues, as well as a comprehensive understanding of the issue management process, the issue development process, and the implementation of issue management. In sum, issue management serves as a bridge to crisis management.

Crisis management, like issue management, is not a panacea for organizations. In spite of well-intended efforts by management, not all crises will be resolved in the company's favor. Nevertheless, being prepared for the inevitable makes sense, especially in today's world of instantaneous global communications and obsessive media coverage. Whether thinking about the long term, the intermediate term, or the short term, managers need to be prepared to handle crises. A crisis has a number of different stages, and managing crises requires a number of key steps before, during, and after the crisis. These steps include identifying areas of vulnerability, developing a plan for dealing with threats, forming crisis teams, using crisis drills, and learning from experience. Crisis communications is critical for successful crisis management. When used in tandem, risk, issue and crisis management can help managers fulfill their economic, legal, ethical, and philanthropic responsibilities to stakeholders.

Key Terms

acute crisis stage, p. 171
chronic crisis stage, p. 171
crisis, p. 169
crisis communications, p. 174
crisis management, p. 155
crisis resolution stage, p. 171
crisis teams, p. 173
emerging issue, p. 159
external risks, p. 157
issue, p. 159
issue buying, p. 162
issue definition, p. 160
issue development life cycle process, p. 166
issue management, p. 155
issue selling, p. 162
portfolio approach, p. 159
preventable risks, p. 157
prodromal crisis stage, p. 171
risk management, p. 155
strategic risks, p. 157

Discussion Questions

1. Which of the major stages in the issue management process do you think is the most important? Why?
2. Following the approach presented in Figure 6-1, identify a new issue category not listed in Figure 6-1. Identify several examples of "crises" that have occurred in recent years under each issue category.
3. Identify one example, other than those listed in Figure 6-3, of each of the leading force categories: events, authorities/advocates, literature, organizations, and political jurisdictions.
4. Identify a crisis that has occurred in your life or in the life of someone you know, and briefly explain it in terms of the four crisis stages: prodromal, acute, chronic, and resolution.
5. Do research on the impact of Hurricane Sandy on business organizations. What have been successful and unsuccessful examples of crisis management that have come out of this research? Is terrorism a likely crisis for which business may prepare? How does preparation for terrorism (which comes from without) compare with preparation for ethical scandals (which come from within)?

Endnotes

1. Douglas Yeung, "Trust Me, I'm a Corporation," *U.S. News* (October 28, 2015), http://www.usnews.com/opinion/economic-intelligence/2015/10/28/when-public-trust-in-corporations-is-shaken. Accessed March 20, 2016.
2. Roberto Ferdman and Ana Swanson, "Chipotle Sales and Profits Plunge as Fears of Food Poisonings Grow," *The Washington Post* (February 2, 2016), https://www.washingtonpost.com/news/wonk/wp/2016/02/02/chipotle-sales-and-profits-plunge-as-fears-of-food-poisonings-grow/. Accessed March 31, 2016.
3. Danielle Demetriou, "Legacy of Nuclear Disaster in Japan's Fukushima Plant," The National (July 1, 2013), http://www.thenational.ae/business/industry-insights/economics/legacy-of-nuclear-disaster-in-japans-fukushima-plant. Accessed February 2, 2016.
4. Alan Duke, "Superstorm Sandy Breaks Records," *CNN* (October 31, 2012), http://www.cnn.com/2012/10/30/us/sandy-records/. Accessed March 30, 2016.
5. Susana Ferreira, "The Sad Economic Lessons of the Earthquake in Nepal," *Fortune* (May 13, 2015) http://fortune.com/2015/05/13/the-sad-economic-lesson-of-the-earthquakes-in-nepal/. Accessed February 2, 2016.
6. Duraideivamani Sankararajan and NK Shrivastava, "Risks vs. Issues," *PM Network* (June 2012), 28–29; Tony Jaques, "Towards a New Terminology: Optimizing the Value of Issue Management," *Journal of Communication Management* (Vol. 7, No. 2),

140–147. Cited in Tony Jaques, "Issue and Crisis Management: Quicksand in the Definitional Landscape," *Public Relations Review* (September 2009), 281.

7. Risks vs. Issues, *The Engineer Leader* (August 6 2012), http://engineeringcareercoach.com/2012/08/16/risks-vs-issues/. Accessed February 24, 2016.
8. Louis Anthony Cox, Jr., "Community Resilience and Decision Theory Challenges for Catastrophic Events," *Risk Analysis: An International Journal* (November 2012), 1919–1934.
9. Robert S. Kaplan and Anette Mikes, "Managing Risks: A New Framework," *Harvard Business Review* (June 2012), 48–60.
10. Ibid.
11. Ibid.
12. Leon Kaye, "Uber Refuses to Increase Safety Measures in Wake of Kalamazoo Tragedy, TriplePundit, http://www.triplepundit.com/2016/02/uber-refuses-to-increase-safety-measures-in-wake-of-kalamazoo-tragedy/?utm_source=Daily+Email+List&utm_campaign=1a4e7ef77e-RSS_EMAIL_CAMPAIGN&utm_medium=email&utm_term=0_9dedefcee3-1a4e7ef77e-220417273. Accessed February 24, 2016.
13. Ibid.
14. Kaplan and Mikes, 2012, 48.
15. Ibid.
16. Frank C. Krysiak, "Risk Management as a Tool for Sustainability," *Journal of Business Ethics* (April 2009, Supplement 3), 483–492.
17. David Gelles, "Microsoft Leads Movement to Offset Emissions with Internal Carbon Tax," *The New York Times* (September 26, 2015), http://www.nytimes.com/2015/09/27/business/energy-environment/microsoft-leads-movement-to-offset-emissions-with-internal-carbon-tax.html?_r=0. Accessed February 3, 2016.
18. Diane B. MacDonald, "When Risk Management Collides with Enterprise Sustainability," *Journal of Leadership, Accountability & Ethics* (January 2011), 56–66.
19. http://issuemanagement.org/learnmore/clarification-of-terms/. Accessed February 3, 2016.
20. Tony Jaques, "Issue Management as a Post-Crisis Discipline: Identifying and Responding to Issue Impacts beyond the Crisis," *Journal of Public Affairs* (February 2009), 35–44.
21. Jia Lynn Yang and Amrita Jayakumar, "Target Says That up to 70 Million More Customers Were Hit by December Data Breach," *Washington Post* (January 10, 2014), https://www.washingtonpost.com/business/economy/target-says-70-million-customers-were-hit-by-dec-data-breach-more-than-first-reported/2014/01/10/0ada1026-79fe-11e3-8963-b4b654bcc9b2 story.html. Accessed February 24, 2016.
22. Ibid.
23. Pursey P. M. A. R. Heugens, John F. Mahon, and Steve L. Wartick, "A Portfolio Approach to Issue Adoption," *International Association for Business and Society* (2004 Annual Meeting, Jackson Hole, WY).
24. Ibid.
25. Joseph F. Coates, Vary T. Coates, Jennifer Jarratt, and Lisa Heinz, *Issues Management* (Mt. Airy, MD: Lomond Publications, 1986), 19–20.
26. Jason Breslow, "New: 87 Deceased NFL Players Test Positive for Brain Disease," *Frontline*, http://www.pbs.org/wgbh/frontline/article/new-87-deceased-nfl-players-test-positive-for-brain-disease/. Accessed February 24, 2016.
27. John Mahon, "Issues Management: The Issue of Definition," *Strategic Planning Management* (November 1986), 81–82. For further discussion on what constitutes an issue, see Steven L. Wartick and John F. Mahon, "Toward a Substantive Definition of the Corporate Issue Construct," *Business & Society* (Vol. 33, No. 3, December 1994), 293–311.
28. Lauren Ezell, "Timeline: The NFL's Concussion Crisis," *Frontline* (October 8, 2013), http://www.pbs.org/wgbh/frontline/article/timeline-the-nfls-concussion-crisis/. Accessed March 31, 2016.
29. Lamar Smith, "The Climate-Change Religion," *The Wall Street Journal* (April 24, 2015), A11.
30. Coates et al., 1986, 18.
31. Ibid., 32.
32. Bernhard Warner, "Happy Birthday, Futurists! A Movement Turns 104," *Bloomberg Businessweek* (February 20, 2013), http://www.businessweek.com/articles/2013-02-20/happy-birthday futurists-a-movement-turns-104. Accessed February 3, 2016.
33. Ibid.
34. Graham T. T. Molitor, "We're All Futurists," *Vital Speeches of the Day* (November 1, 2003).
35. T. Graham Molitor, "How to Anticipate Public Policy Changes," *SAM Advanced Management Journal* (Vol. 42, No. 3, Summer 1977), 4.
36. Stuart Elliott, "Spotting the Trends before They Break Out," *The New York Times* (March 11, 2012), http://www.nytimes.com/2012/03/12/business/media/spotting-the-trends-before-they-break-out-advertising.html?_r=0. Accessed February 3, 2016.
37. Robert Lee Hotz, "Twitter Storms Gauge Damage of Real Ones," *The Wall Street Journal* (March 12/13, 2016), A3.
38. J. E. Dutton, S. J. Ashford, R. M. O'Neill, E. Hayes, and E. E. Wierba, "Reading the Wind: How Middle Managers Assess the Context for Selling Issues to Top Managers," *Strategic Management Journal* (Vol. 18, 1997), 407–425; Jennifer A. Howard-Grenville, "Developing Issue-Selling Effectiveness over Time:

Issue Selling as Resourcing," *Organization Science* (July/August 2007), 560–577.

39. Pursey P. M. A. R. Heugens, "Issues Management: Core Understandings and Scholarly Development," in Phil Harris and Craig S. Fleisher (eds.), *The Handbook of Public Affairs* (Thousand Oaks, CA: Sage Publications, 2005), 490–493.

40. Trefis Team, "Target's CEO Steps down Following the Massive Data Breach and Canadian Debacle," *Forbes* (May 8, 2014), http://www.forbes.com/sites/greatspeculations/2014/05/08/targets-ceo-steps-down-following-the-massive-data-breach-and-canadian-debacle/#34d2f45f3f56. Accessed February 24, 2016.

41. *PwC* Report, "Rebuilding Trust after Times of Crisis: A Practical Guide," (February 2015), https://www.pwc.nl/nl/assets/documents/pwc-rebuilding-trust.pdf. Accessed March 2, 2016.

42. Ibid.

43. William R. King, "Strategic Issue Management," in William R. King and David I. Cleland (eds.) *Strategic Planning and Management Handbook* (New York: Van Nostrand Reinhold, 1987), 259.

44. James K. Brown, *This Business of Issues: Coping with the Company's Environment* (New York: The Conference Board, 1979), 45.

45. Elizabeth Dougall, "Issues Management," *Essential Knowledge Project* (December 12, 2008), http://www.instituteforpr.org/issues-management/. Accessed February 3, 2016.

46. Brown, 33.

47. Coates et al., 46.

48. Cited in Heugens, 2005, 488.

49. I. C. MacMillan and P. E. Jones, "Designing Organizations to Compete," *Journal of Business Strategy* (Vol. 4, No. 4, Spring 1984), 13.

50. *PwC* Report, 8.

51. Paul Lamkin, "Fitbit Still Plagued with Skin Irritation Complaints," *Forbes* (April 27, 2015), http://www.forbes.com/sites/paullamkin/2015/04/27/fitbit-still-plagued-with-skin-irritation-complaints/#56de5a81487b. Accessed March 2, 2016.

52. Roy Wernham, "Implementation: The Things That Matter," in King and Cleland, 453.

53. Craig Giammona and Leslie Patton, "Small Suppliers, Big Problems," *Businessweek* (December 14–20, 2015), 21.

54. Earl C. Gottschalk, Jr., "Firms Hiring New Type of Manager to Study Issues, Emerging Troubles," *The Wall Street Journal* (June 10, 1982), 33, 36.

55. Mahon, 81–82.

56. Barbara Bigelow, Liam Fahey, and John Mahon, "A Typology of Issue Evolution," *Business & Society* (Spring 1993), 28. For another useful perspective, see John F. Mahon and Sandra A. Waddock, "Strategic Issues Management: An Integration of Issue Life Cycle Perspectives," *Business & Society* (Spring 1992), 19–32. Also see Steven L. Wartick and Robert E. Rude, "Issues Management: Fad or Function," *California Management Review* (Fall 1986), 134–140.

57. Thomas G. Marx, "Integrating Public Affairs and Strategic Planning," *California Management Review* (Fall 1986), 145.

58. Somini Sengupta, "No U.S. Action, So States Move on Privacy Laws," *The New York Times* (October 30, 2013), http://www.nytimes.com/2013/10/31/technology/no-us-action-so-states-move-on-privacy-law.html?_r=0. Accessed February 2, 2016.

59. W. H. Chase, "Issues and Policy," *Public Relations Quarterly* (Vol. 1, Winter 1980), 5, cited in Jaques, 2009, 282.

60. Public Affairs Council, "Public Affairs: Its Origins, Its Present, and Its Trends," http://www.pac.org (2001).

61. Tony Jaques, "Issue Management: Process versus Progress," *Journal of Public Affairs* (February 2006), 69–74.

62. Pursey P. M. A. R. Heugens, "Strategic Issues Management: Implications for Corporate Performance," *Business & Society* (Vol. 41, No. 4, December 2002), 456–468.

63. Ibid., 459. Also see Archie B. Carroll, "Stakeholder Management: Background and Advances," in Phil Harris and Craig S. Fleisher (eds.), *The Handbook of Public Affairs* (Thousand Oaks, CA: Sage Publications, 2005), 501–516.

64. Trefis Team, "Japan Is Key to Prudential's International Success," *Forbes* (September 17, 2012), http://www.forbes.com/sites/greatspeculations/2012/09/17/japan-is-key-to-prudentials-international-success/#efeb2816a940. Accessed February 3, 2016.

65. Jack Willoughby, "For Pru, Japan Is the Land of the Rising Premium," *Barrons* (August 6, 2011), http://online.barrons.com/article/SB50001424052702304183104576488413229552474.html?mod=rss_barrons_this_week_magazine. Accessed February 3, 2016.

66. Ibid.

67. http://www.news.prudential.com/article_print.cfm?article_id=5897. Accessed February 3, 2016.

68. http://2011cr.prudential.co.uk/our-people/helping-out-in-the-earthquake-zone.aspx. Accessed February 3, 2016.

69. Ken Brumfield, "Succeeding in Crisis Leadership," *Financial Executive* (October 2012), 45–47.

70. Willoughby, 2016.

71. Wayne Burns, "Off course: The Baffling Case of MH370 and the Crisis Management That Survived It," *Corporate Public Affairs* (2014, 24, 1), 1–4.

72. Ibid.
73. Ian Mitroff, with Gus Anagnos, *Managing Crises Before They Happen: What Every Executive and Manager Needs to Know about Crisis Management* (New York: AMACOM, 2001), Chapter 2.
74. Ian Mitroff, "Crisis Leadership: Seven Strategies of Strength," *Leadership Excellence* (Vol. 22, No. 1, 2005), 11.
75. Ibid., 68. For further discussion of types of crises, see Ian Mitroff, "Crisis Management and Environmentalism: A Natural Fit," *California Management Review* (Winter 1994), 101–113.
76. Pearson and Clair, 60.
77. Ian I. Mitroff and Mural C. Alpaslan, "Preparing for Evil," *Harvard Business Review* (April 2003), 3–9.
78. Steven Fink, *Crisis Management: Planning for the Inevitable* (New York: AMACOM, 1986), 69. Also see Sharon H. Garrison, *The Financial Impact of Corporate Events on Corporate Stakeholders* (New York: Quorem Books, 1990); and Joe Marconi, *Crisis Marketing: When Bad Things Happen to Good Companies* (Chicago: NTC Business Books, 1997). See also Carol Hymowitz, "Companies Experience Major Power Shifts as Crises Continue," *The Wall Street Journal* (October 9, 2001), B1; and Sue Shellenbarger, "Some Bosses, Fumbling in Crisis, Have Bruised Loyalty of Employees," *The Wall Street Journal* (October 17, 2001), B1.
79. See for example, Nicole Gillespie, Graham Dietz, and Steve Lockey, "Organizational Reintegration and Trust Repair after an Integrity Violation: A Case Study. *Business Ethics Quarterly* (Vol. 24, No. 3, 2014), 371–410, Jonathan Bundy and Michael D. Pfarrer, "A Burden of Responsibility: The Role of Social Approval at the Onset of a Crisis," *Academy of Management Review* (Vol. 40, No. 3, 2015), 345–369; Michael Pfarrer, Katherine DeCelles, Ken Smith, and M. Susan Taylor, "After the Fall: Reintegrating the Corrupt Organization," *Academy of Management Review* (No. 33, 2008), 730–749.
80. "Pilot Flying J: If the Game Goes against You," *The Economist* (February 6, 2016), 60.
81. Ibid.
82. Fink, 20.
83. Mitroff and Anagnos, 2001.
84. "Criminal Investigation of Chipotle Mexican Grill, Inc. Just Took a Turn for the Worse," *The Motley Fool* (February 9, 2016), http://www.fool.com/investing/general/2016/02/09/criminal-investigation-of-chipotle-mexican-grill-i.aspx. Accessed February 24, 2016.
85. "How Companies Are Learning to Prepare for the Worst," 76.
86. Goeff Williams, "Chipotle's E. Coli Crisis: P.R. Experts Say It's Handling It Right," *Forbes* online (November 4, 2015), http://www.forbes.com/sites/geoffwilliams/2015/11/04/can-chipotle-survive-its-e-coli-crisis-pr-experts-seem-to-think-so-and-offer-advice/#3b1269e11644. Accessed February 3, 2016.
87. Nancy Gagliardi, "A Tough Year Is Ahead for Chipotle," *Forbes* (January 6 2016), http://www.forbes.com/sites/nancygagliardi/2016/01/06/looks-like-a-tough-year-ahead-for-chipotle/#7f44395761f9. Accessed February 3, 2016.
88. Ibid.
89. Watkins and Bazerman, 2003.
90. *Businessweek,* 1985, 74.
91. Susan Berfield, "Chipotle's Crisis," *Bloomberg Businessweek* (December 28-January 10, 2016), 49.
92. Richard J. Mahoney, "The Anatomy of a Public Policy Crisis," *The CEO Series, Center for the Study of American Business* (May 1996), 7.
93. Melissa Master, "Keyword: Crisis," *Across the Board* (September 1998), 62.
94. Ian Mitroff, Paul Shrivastava, and Firdaus Udwadia, "Effective Crisis Management," *Academy of Management Executive* (November 1987), 285.
95. Robert Goff, "Coming Clean," *Forbes* (May 17, 1999), 156–160. Also see James Andrews, "Jack in the Box and the Decline of E. coli," *Food Safety News* (February 11, 2013), http://www.foodsafetynews.com/2013/02/jack-in-the-box-and-the-decline-of-e-coli/#.VruzYI-cGUk. Accessed February 10, 2016.
96. Goff, ibid.
97. Johnathan L. Bernstein, "The Ten Steps of Crisis Communications" (January 2013), http://www.crisisnavigator.org/The-Ten-Steps-of-Crisis-Communications.490.0.html. Accessed January 27, 2013.
98. Richard Wm. Brundage, "Crisis Management—An Outline for Survival," *Crisisnavigator* (January 2013), http://www.crisisnavigator.org/Crisis-Management-An-Outline-for-Survival.454.0.html?&no_cache=1&sword_list[]=Brundage. Accessed February 3, 2016.
99. Cited in Irene Rozansky, "Communicating in a Crisis," *Board Member* (March/April 2007), 2.
100. Ibid.
101. *CNN*, "Hurricane Sandy Fast Facts," (October 3, 2015), http://www.cnn.com/2013/07/13/world/americas/hurricane-sandy-fast-facts/. Accessed March 1, 2016.
102. Neil Kaufman, "Picking Up after Sandy: Resilience in the Eye of the Storm," *PwC Resilience Journal* (2015/16), http://www.pwc.com/gx/en/services/advisory/consulting/risk/resilience/publications/in-the-eye-of-the-storm.html. Accessed March 2, 2016.

103. Ibid.
104. Regina Phelps, "Lessons Learned from Hurricane Sandy," *Disaster Resource Guide*, http://www.disaster-resource.com/index.php?option=com_content&view=article&id=2328:lessons-learned-from-hurricane-sandy&catid=3:planning-and-management. Accessed March 2, 2016.
105. Paul Glader, "GE's Immelt to Cite Lessons Learned," *The Wall Street Journal* (December 14, 2009), http://www.wsj.com/articles/SB10001424052748703954904574596350792489752. Accessed February 3, 2016.
106. Ibid.
107. Bruce Rubenstein, "Salmonella-Tainted Ice Cream: How Schwan's Recovered," *Corporate Legal Times Corp.*, June 1998.
108. Ibid.
109. Ibid.
110. Ibid.

PART 3
Business Ethics and Leadership

7

Business Ethics Essentials

CHAPTER LEARNING OUTCOMES

After studying this chapter, you should be able to:

1 Describe the public's opinion of business ethics.

2 Define business ethics, explain the conventional approach to business ethics and identify the sources of ethical norms in individuals.

3 Analyze the economic, legal, and ethical aspects of a decision by using a Venn model.

4 Identify, explain, and illustrate three models of management ethics.

5 In terms of making moral management actionable, describe and discuss Kohlberg's three levels of moral development and Gilligan's ethics of care.

6 Identify and discuss six major elements of moral judgment.

Public interest in business ethics is at an all-time high. Certainly, there has been an ebb and flow of interest on society's part, but lately this interest has grown to a preoccupation or, as some might say, an obsession. With the ethics scandal tsunami of the early 2000s, beginning with Enron, we witnessed the birth and accelerated maturation of the "ethics industry."[1] The Enron scandal has been considered to be the most notorious in American history and it involved massive misrepresentations of earnings, creation of a fraudulent energy crisis, and embezzlement. The impact of the Enron scandal was so great on business ethics that it has been dubbed the "Enron Effect"[2] and it is still talked about today.

We thought we would never soon see anything like the Enron era of scandals. The Enron collapse, brought to light in 2001, ushered in an avalanche of ethics scandals that brought down WorldCom, Tyco, Arthur Andersen, and other companies. The magnitude of CEO greed and contempt for the law seemed unprecedented. Congress thought it put the problems to bed with the passage in 2002 of the Sarbanes–Oxley (SOX) Act, as we discussed in Chapter 4. The legislation did bring about improved financial controls and it did strengthen the accountability of CEOs and CFOs for the veracity of financial statements. The public had a sense of relief that government regulations had once again solved their problems. Regrettably, SOX did not "fix" the problem of financial scandals among businesses, although it did improve conditions somewhat.

The public may have been lulled into a false sense of security over the next several years. And, it wasn't until the Wall Street financial crisis beginning in 2008 that the country realized that the difficulties with corporate ethics had not been fixed. The stock market collapse in 2008 began a recession that has not been seen since the Great Depression, in terms of its effects on the world economy. It appears we have had two business ethics "eras" in two decades. First, there was the Enron Era (2001–2008) and, beginning in 2008, we found ourselves in the era of the Wall Street financial scandals that resulted in a global financial crisis.[3] This period is not yet completely behind us.

Before Enron, many thought business ethics was a problem having to do with employees and lower- and middle-level managers; that is, the lower two-thirds of the corporate pyramid. Beginning with the Enron Era, the focus turned to the top one-third of the corporate pyramid, especially CEOs and CFOs, including negligent corporate boards. After prolonged investigations and trials, some of these chief-level executives were found guilty and were sent to prison.

The Wall Street financial crisis and scandals, commencing in 2008, ushered in a new set of corporate characters, and it has been mostly companies and not CEOs or CFOs accused of questionable dealings. The new faces we began reading about were companies, not executives, and these included Fannie Mae, Freddie Mac,

Bear Stearns, Lehman Brothers, AIG, Countrywide Financial, and Merrill Lynch. Some will argue that these firms did not commit ethics violations, per se, but rather made bad judgments about risk and returns. This is still being debated today.

At a minimum, there was widespread recklessness about risk, especially with the subprime lending crisis and use of exotic financial instruments that very few experts completely understood. These firms were led by the financial wizards who had become known as "the smartest guys in the room," and they should have known better. It is unethical to lend money to customers who, in your reasonable judgment, will not be able to pay it back. It is unethical to lend money without checking people's job status, income, and assets. It can be called bad risk-return calculations, but many think that this is just a euphemism for the questionable business practices that were taking place. Many observers have argued that the firms got greedy and were driven by profits (and bonuses) without regard for the consequences.

A number of observers believe that Wall Street firms, and in particular the major banks, have deep cultural flaws that have corrupted them or, at a minimum, made it difficult for them to engage in ethical behavior. According to this view, Wall Street's problems have developed over generations by leaders who have rewarded those who cut corners and engaged in a variety of unethical behaviors.[4] In a major study of the banking industry, some researchers have concluded that there is a Wall Street culture that rewards bad behavior, that there are norms at their workplaces that induce them to cheat. One of the lead researchers reported that "the apples are good but the barrel is bad.[5] Even Federal Reserve Chairman Janet Yellen recently raised concerns about ethics and culture on Wall Street when she scolded them about pervasive shortcomings in the values of some of the large financial firms and how these values might undermine their safety and soundness.

Yellen's remarks were aligned with those of William Dudley, President of the Federal Reserve Bank of New York who mounted a public and private campaign in which he urged Wall Street to clean up its behavior.[6] William Cohan, author of three books on Wall Street, including *The Price of Silence*, believes the bankers also were able to stay out of jail because the U.S. Department of Justice had developed a lax attitude toward the banking industry, including delaying action and somewhat excusing the bankers' practices because there might be collateral consequences such as corporate instability or collapse. Cohan argued that since institutions and not real corporate leaders were held accountable by just paying fines, the leaders received the message that their behaviors were permissible.[7] The 2015 movie, The Big Short, based on a nonfiction book of the same name, revealed details as to how the Wall Street financial scandal developed and how the public's interest in these revelations remain active.

Occurring at about the same time as the Wall Street financial scandals was the exposure of Bernard L. Madoff's infamous Ponzi scheme, highlighted in Chapter 4. The world economy has improved since the Wall Street financial scandals, but it may take much longer for trust in business to be restored. With each passing day, it seems, some new business ethics scandal hits the news. Some are more serious than others. But, in recent years, companies such as Wells Fargo, with it fake account scandal, Volkswagen, with its emissions scandal, GM, with its purported defective ignitions, Toshiba, with its $1 billion in accounting irregularities, the Veteran's Administration scandal, or Takata's faulty airbags, and others, have assured us that business ethics challenges deserve their front page status and that businesses still have much to do to restore the public's trust in them.

What the scandals of the past couple decades have revealed is that the issue of business ethics has both macro and micro effects. At the macro-level, the entire business system has been polluted and called into question. This is the level of capitalism and Big Business, as an institution, maintaining its legitimacy in a complex world. At the micro-level, individual companies, managers, and employees still face the continuing onslaught of ethics challenges that occur daily. Using a managerial perspective, business ethics education is more focused on this latter category of ethics challenges. The broad environment, which deals with business and society relationships, however, continues to be a confounding backdrop against which these daily challenges occur.

Figure 7-1 summarizes some of the major business ethics scandals that have occurred since Enron. The effects of some of these continue to the present day. Many of these companies and executives have claimed their innocence, and allegations and trials are at various stages of completion. Some executives have been convicted and sent to prison.

FIGURE 7-1 Major Business Ethics Scandals

Companies Implicated	Major Executives Implicated	Legal/Ethical Charges and Convictions
Volkswagen	Top executives and board	Emissions scandal
Chesapeake Energy	Aubrey McClendon, CEO	Conspiracy to rig bids
Takata	Shigehisa Takada, chairman and CEO	Faulty airbags leading to consumer deaths/recalls
Toshiba Corp.	Hisau Tanaka, CEO	Accounting irregularities
Veteran's Administration	Eric Shinseki, VA Secretary	Manipulation and falsification of medical waiting lists and systemwide rigging to hide deception
Peanut Corporation of America	Stewart & Michael Parnell	Deadly salmonella outbreak leading to deaths; fraud
Enron	Andrew Fastow, Jeffrey Skilling, Kenneth Lay	Securities fraud, conspiracy to inflate profits, corrupt corporate culture
WorldCom	Scott Sullivan, CFO; Bernard J. Ebbers, CEO	Accounting fraud, lying, filing false financial statements
Arthur Andersen	Entire firm; David Duncan, auditor for Enron	Accounting fraud, criminal charges, obstruction
Tyco	Mark Schwartz, CFO; Dennis Kozlowski, CEO	Sales tax evasion, stealing through corruption, fraud
HealthSouth	Richard Scrushy, CEO	Found not guilty in company scandal; later convicted of bribery, conspiracy, mail fraud
Fannie Mae, Freddie Mac, Bear Stearns, Lehman Brothers, AIG, Merrill Lynch, Countrywide	Most executives were not legally charged. Upper echelon executives and board implicated in list of questionable behaviors.	Recklessness, excessive risk taking, greed, bad loan decisions, governance failures, arrogance, hubris
Bernard L. Madoff Investment Securities LLC	Bernie L. Madoff	Convicted; $17.3 billion Ponzi scheme; fraud
Barclay's Bank	Robert Diamond, CEO	False reports; Libor scandal; heavy fines
Galleon Group Hedge Fund	Raj Rajaratnam, Founder	Insider trading; securities fraud; 11 years in prison

FIGURE 7-2 Examples of Ethical Issues Businesses Face

Stakeholder Group	Examples of Ethical Issues
Customers	Product safety/healthfulness
	Advertising/marketing honestly
	Packaging fairly/accurately
	Labeling accurately/completely
	Pricing fairly relative to quality
	Protecting consumer privacy
Employees	Fair compensation practices
	Fair day's work and pay; living wage
	Compliance with employment laws
	Avoidance of employment discrimination
	Safe working conditions
	Avoiding employee theft/embezzlement
	Protecting employees' privacy
	Dealing with distracted employees
Community/Environment	Environmental protection/sustainability
	Adherence to legal mandates
	Good corporate citizenship
	Philanthropy/Supporting Causes
	Adapting to foreign cultures
	Avoidance of bribery
Shareholders	Protecting shareholders' interests
	Fair compensation for executives
	Quality boards of directors
	Protection of company assets
	Fair returns on investments
	Communicating accurately
	Transparency

Not all business ethics issues turn into major scandals. But the range of business issues within which ethical problems continue to reside are numerous. To gain an appreciation of the kinds of issues that are important on a day-to-day basis under the rubric of business ethics, Figure 7-2 presents a list of business ethics issues that companies typically have to face with select stakeholder groups. Against this backdrop, we plan to begin our business ethics discussion in this chapter and the next three chapters. This chapter introduces essential business ethics concepts. Chapter 8 extends the discussion by considering managerial and organizational ethics. Chapter 9 addresses newly emerging technology and business ethics issues. Finally, Chapter 10 turns to the international sphere as ethical issues in the global arena are examined.

7.1 The Public's Opinion of Business Ethics

The public's view of business ethics has never been very high. Anecdotal evidence suggests that many citizens see business ethics as essentially a contradiction in terms, an oxymoron, and sometimes suspect that there is only a fine line between a business executive and a crook. Each of us as consumers, employees, or citizens can easily recall some problem that occurred in our everyday lives that involved suspected unethical behavior on the part of businesses. Over many years now, public opinion polls have revealed the public's deep concerns about the honesty and ethical standards of business and other professions. The December 2015 Gallup Poll on the public's opinion of business executives, the latest available at this writing, revealed that only 17 percent of the public thought business executives had high or very high ethics. This was a decline from the 21 percent who rated them highly in the same category in 2012.[8] Specific categories of business people had even lower ethics rankings. These included stockbrokers, advertising practitioners, car salespeople, and telemarketers.[9]

The public's opinion of business ethics may be thought about at two levels. At a broad level is the general perception of business ethics by the public and at a narrower level are specific perceptions as to what is going on inside organizations. It is apparent from the aforementioned Gallup Poll that society does not consider business' ethics very highly. There can be no doubt that the endless stream of ethical scandals over the past have contributed significantly to this lack of trust.

In terms of what is going on within companies, the most recent National Business Ethics Survey (NBES) conducted by the Ethics Resource Center (ERC) had some encouraging news but presented a mixed picture of results. The NBES was a study of *employees* to determine what was going on *within* companies. Following are a few of the major findings:[10]

- *Misconduct observed.* Forty-one percent of workers reported observing misconduct. This was down slightly from two years prior.
- *Reporting bad behavior.* Sixty-three percent of the workers surveyed recounted that they had reported the bad behavior they had observed. This was down slightly over two years prior.
- *Retaliation against workers.* Retaliation against those reporting wrongdoing (whistleblowers) was at 21 percent. This was about the same as two years prior.
- *Pressure to compromise.* The percentage of employees who reported they felt pressure to compromise standards in order to do their jobs was at 9 percent, which was a decline from two years prior.

The survey revealed several other areas of concern. While misconduct is down somewhat, a relatively high percentage of the misconduct was committed by managers, the ones who are supposed to be setting a good example for everyone to follow. Employees reported that 60 percent of the misconduct involved someone with managerial authority ranging from supervisors to top managers. One-fourth of the misdeeds occurred among senior managers.[11] This is indeed troublesome when considering that the management team is supposed to be demonstrating ethical leadership for others to follow.

As we are wrapping up the second decade of the 2000s, it appears that society is clamoring for a renewed emphasis on values, morals, and ethics and that the business ethics debate of this period is but a subset of this larger societal concern. Whether the business community will be able to close the trust gap and ratchet up its reputation to a higher plateau remains to be seen. One thing is sure: There is a continuing interest in business ethics, and the proliferation of business ethics courses, blogs, and tweets, along with the revitalized interest on the part of the business community, paints an encouraging picture for the "ethics industry" of the future.

7.1a Are the Media Reporting Business Ethics More Vigorously?

Sometimes it is difficult to tell whether business ethics have really deteriorated or that the media, including social media, is doing a more thorough job of reporting on ethics violations. There is no doubt that the media are reporting ethical problems more frequently and fervently. Spurred on by the continuing supply of scandals, the media have found business ethics and, indeed, ethics questions among all institutions to be subjects of mounting and sustaining interest. Of particular interest in recent years has been the in-depth investigative reporting of business ethics on such TV shows as *60 Minutes*, *20/20*, *Dateline NBC*, and *Frontline*, as well as the growing number of such programs. As discussed earlier, social media also have entered the fray and are quick to report ethics issues in business as they occur. During the Chipotle food contamination crisis, for example, Twitter was used extensively by consumers to give people up-to-date news of the latest occurrences. Such high-profile investigations and reports keep business ethics in the public eye and make it difficult to assess whether public opinion polls are reflecting the actual business ethics of the day or simply the reactions to the latest scandals covered on a weekly or daily basis.

7.1b Is It Society That Is Changing?

As argued in Chapter 1, society is always changing. Due to affluence, education, awareness, and other factors, society is not just changing but raising its expectations of business's integrity. Many business managers subscribe to this belief—that it is society that is changing, not just them. You do not have to make a lengthy investigation of some of today's business practices to realize that a good number of what are now called questionable practices were at one time considered acceptable or tolerable; for example, the use of company perquisites, like the company-owned jet, for personal use. CEO, Jeffrey Immelt of GE, for example, was reported to have racked up almost $400,000 of expenses using the company jet for personal use in one recent year and other top-level GE executives added another $263,000 to the total. When it comes to executive perks, some top-level executives just can't let go.[12] It is questionable whether the public would consider private use of corporate jets to be an acceptable practice; most likely, they were just not aware that this was going on.

So, it may be that many business practices never really were acceptable to the public but that, because they were not known, there was no perceived moral dilemmas in the mind of people. One cannot help but believe that the greed by top-level business executives that has been exposed in the past two decades has elevated the ethics issue to new heights. Executive deception has contributed to the problem. Though corporate governance has become better in recent years, lack of careful oversight of top-echelon executives has been a problem as well. Corporate boards, in many cases, have fallen down in their duties to monitor top-executive behavior, and one consequence has been a continuing stream of ethics scandals.

Figure 7-3 illustrates one way of looking at the ethical problem in business today compared to earlier. It depicts the growing disconnect between society's expectations of business ethics and ethics in practice. Note in the figure that actual business ethics is assumed to be slightly improving but not at the same pace as public expectations are rising. In this analysis, the magnitude of the current ethics problem is seen partially to be a function of rising societal expectations about business behavior compared with smaller increases, declines or stability in actual business ethics. It is difficult to accurately say whether business ethics are getting better, worse, or staying the same, but perceptions and expectations are significantly driving businesses' reputations.

7.2 Business Ethics: Some Basic Concepts

In Chapter 2, ethical responsibilities of business were presented in an introductory way. The contrast between ethics, economics, law, and philanthropy were discussed. To be sure, we all have a general idea of what business ethics means, but now it is important to probe the topic more deeply. To understand business ethics, it is useful to comment on the relationship between ethics and morality.

FIGURE 7-3 Business Ethics Today versus Earlier Periods

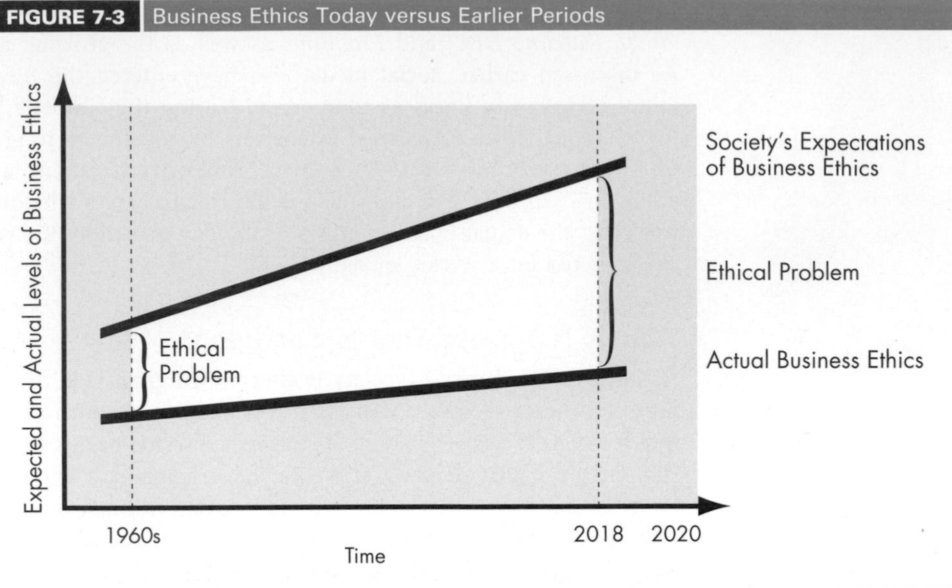

The terms *ethics* and *morals* often are used interchangeably by commentators on business ethics. Both have to do with the standards of right or wrong, fairness, or justice. One distinction holds that **ethics** are standards of conduct, which originate from some external group or source such as society, in general, or business, in particular. Ethics, in this view would be governed by society, professions or organizations and may appear as principles, standards or codes.

By contrast, **morals** are frequently seen as standards of conduct that originate within the individual. Morality, in this view, is often viewed as one's personal compass regarding right or wrong.[13] One complication is that some experts define these terms in the opposite manner to that expressed above. Another complication is that it is quite difficult for a person to sort out the origins of his or her standards of behavior or conduct; that is, whether they are coming from outside the individual or from within the individual. For this reason, we will take the position that both ethics and morality are so similar to one another that we may use the terms interchangeably to refer to the study of fairness, justice, and behavior.

Business ethics, therefore, is concerned with the rightness, wrongness, fairness or justice of actions, decisions, policies, and practices that take place within a business context or in the workplace. Business ethics is often seen as a set of principles or code of conduct by which activities are judged to be appropriate or questionable. Business ethics is a field of study in which the practices in organizations are analyzed to determine whether they are acceptable or not. Business ethics is also a field of study and topic that is of interest to the public, academics, students, and managers. Many stakeholders have much at stake in issues of business ethics.

7.2a Descriptive versus Normative Ethics

Two key branches of moral philosophy, or business ethics, are *descriptive* ethics and *normative* ethics. Each takes a different perspective that is important to understand.

Descriptive ethics is concerned with describing, characterizing, and studying the morality of people, an organization, a culture, or a society. It also compares and contrasts different moral codes, systems, practices, beliefs, and values.[14] In descriptive business ethics, the focus is on learning what *is* occurring in the realm of behavior, actions, decisions, policies, and practices of business firms, managers, or, perhaps, specific industries. The public opinion poll cited earlier gives us glimpses into descriptive ethics—what people believe is going on as the basis of their perceptions and understandings.

Descriptive ethics focuses on "what is"—the prevailing set of ethical standards and practices in the business community, specific organizations, or on the part of specific managers. The major danger in limiting our attention to descriptive ethics is that some people may adopt the view that "if everyone is doing it," it must be acceptable. For example, if a survey reveals that 70 percent of employees are padding their expense accounts, this describes what they say *is* taking place, but it does not describe what *should* be taking place. Just because many employees are participating in this questionable activity doesn't make it an appropriate practice. This is why normative ethics is important.

Normative ethics, by contrast, is concerned with supplying and justifying a coherent moral system of thinking and judging. Normative ethics seeks to uncover, develop, and justify basic moral principles that are intended to guide behavior, actions, and decisions.[15] Normative business ethics, therefore, seeks to propose some principle or principles for distinguishing what is ethical from what is unethical in the business context. It deals more with "what ought to be" or "what should be" in terms of business practices. Normative ethics is concerned with establishing norms or standards by which business practices might be guided or judged.

Normative business ethics might be based on moral common sense (be fair, honest, truthful), or it might require critical thinking and the pursuit of different types of ethical analysis (interest based, rights based, duty based, virtue based).[16] In our study of business ethics, we need to be ever mindful of this distinction between descriptive and normative perspectives. It is tempting to observe the prevalence of a particular practice in business (e.g., discrimination or deceptive marketing) and conclude that because so many are *doing it* (descriptive ethics), it must be acceptable behavior. Normative ethics would insist that a practice be justified on the basis of some ethical principle, argument, philosophy, or rationale before being considered acceptable. Normative ethics demands a more meaningful moral anchor than just "everyone is doing it." Normative ethics is our primary concern in this book, though we frequently compare "what ought to be" with "what is (really going on in the real world)" for purposes of analysis.

7.2b The Conventional Approach to Business Ethics

The **conventional approach** to business ethics is to compare a decision, practice, or policy that is being used in practice with prevailing norms of acceptability in society. We call this the conventional approach because it is thought that this is the way conventional or general society thinks. The conventional approach relies on the use of common sense and a widely held sense of what is ethical. The major challenge in this approach is answering the questions "*Whose* ethical norms do we use?" in making the ethical judgment, and "What ethical norms are *prevailing*?" This approach may be depicted by highlighting the major variables to be compared with one another:

Decisions, Behaviors, or Practices ⟷ *Prevailing Norms of Acceptability*

There is considerable room for variability on both of these questions. With respect to whose/which norms should be used as the basis for ethical judgments, the conventional approach would consider as legitimate those norms emanating from a variety of sources—family, friends, religious beliefs, the local community, one's employer, law, the profession, and so on. This approach might also employ what is in one's own judgment or best self-interest as a guideline. If one was deciding whether to deduct a certain expense on one's taxes, for example, the conventional approach might cause one to look at what the law says; or, it may lead one to ask friends how they are handling the expense. The problem arises, of course, because different decisions may be made based upon whose standard is used.

One's conscience, one's personal judgment, or one's self-interest, would be seen by many to be a legitimate source of ethical norms in the conventional approach. Two classic "Frank & Ernest" comic strips poke fun at the use of one's conscience, however. In the first panel, a sign on the wall reads "Tonight's Lecture: Moral Philosophy." Then in the second panel, it shows Frank saying to Ernest, "I'd let my conscience be my guide, but I'm in enough trouble already!" In a second comic strip, Frank says to Ernest, while they are standing at a bar, "I always use my conscience as my guide. But, fortunately, it has a terrible sense of direction." These comic strips reveal the often limiting nature of using one's conscience.

Figure 7-4 illustrates some of the sources of ethical norms that may come to bear on the individual and that might be used in various circumstances, and over time, using the conventional approach. These different sources compete in their influence on what constitutes the "prevailing norms of acceptability" in society today.

In many circumstances, the conventional approach to ethics may be useful and applicable. What does a person do, however, if norms from one source conflict with norms from another source? Also, how can we be sure that societal norms are really appropriate or defensible? Society's culture today sends us many and often conflicting messages about what is appropriate ethical conduct. We get these messages from television, movies, books, music, politics, the Internet, social media, and other sources in the culture and they do not always convey high ethical standards.

Popular TV shows such as *Survivor* and *Celebrity Apprentice* have run episodes in which questionable ethics have been depicted and sometimes celebrated. On *Survivor*, the participants are forever creating alliances (agreements of trust) with others and then breaking them (violating trust) in the interest of winning the game. On one segment of

FIGURE 7-4 Sources of Ethical Norms Transmitted to Individuals

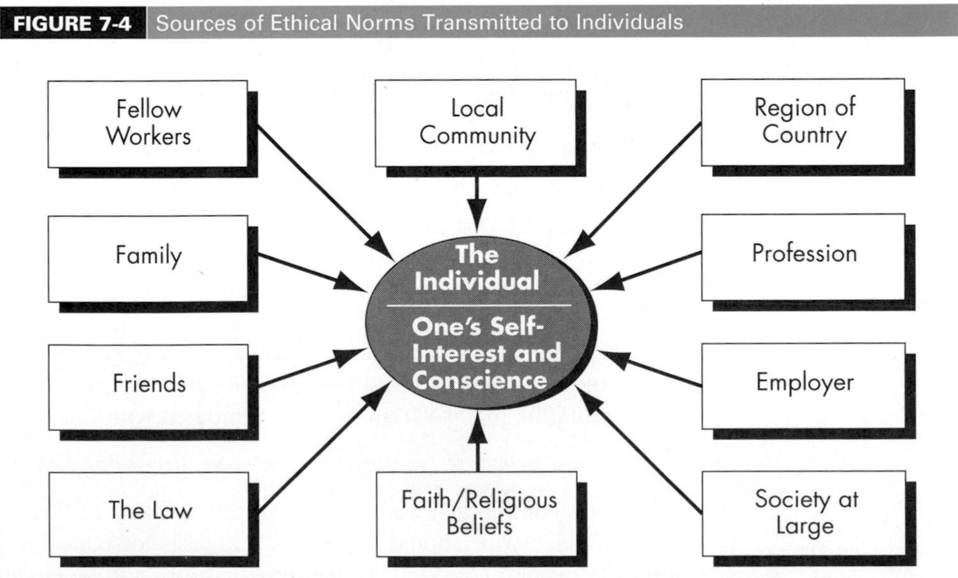

Celebrity Apprentice, Donald Trump, the host and CEO who gets to aim his deadly quip "You're fired!" at a person on the losing team, conveyed to the viewing public that loyalty was more important than honesty in business. When one celebrity was in the final board room, he expressed the opinion that the other team *did* do a better job on a commercial than his team. Trump fired him for being "disloyal" to his team. One major Web site gave Trump the Ethics Alarms Dunce of the Year Award for that example of a conflicting judgment.[17] People may differ on whether loyalty is more important than honesty.

Another example of the conflicting messages people get today from society occurs in the realm of sexual harassment in the workplace. On the one hand, today's television, movies, advertisements, and music are replete with sexual innuendo and the treatment of women and men as sex objects. This would suggest that such behavior is normal, acceptable, even desired. On the other hand, the law and the courts are stringently prohibiting sexual gestures or innuendo in the workplace. As we will see in Chapter 19, it does not take much sexual innuendo to constitute a "hostile work environment" and a sex discrimination charge under Title VII of the Civil Rights Act. In this example, we see a norm that is prevalent in culture and society clashing with a norm arising from employment law and business ethics. These examples serve to illustrate how views of

ETHICS IN PRACTICE CASE

What Would You Do?

A popular U.S. TV show is titled "*What Would You Do?*" Using actors and hidden cameras, the show presents a variety of scenarios of people acting out in situations, usually conflicts or poor treatment of someone, in a public setting. The show focuses on the reactions of the people watching what is being acted out, while not knowing that those engaged in the scenario are just actors. The reactions of those watching the scenarios are recorded and later the show's anchor, John Quinones, comes out from hiding and confronts those who have reacted and asks them why they did what they did.

Some of the show's episodes have featured situations, such as racial profiling occurring in a restaurant, parents publically disapproving of their child's interracial dating, a pompous club promoter denying people entry based on how they are dressed, teenagers taunting a homeless man on the street, and a grocery bagger being insulted because of a disability.

If you observed the following scenarios, what would you do? Why would you react the way you did?

1. Several young men and women are stealing items from an open house you are attending. You do not know the hosts very well but you know most of those who are stealing.
2. A waitress is being hassled by her supervisor who is using verbal sexual innuendo at the restaurant where you are trying to enjoy your meal. You are a regular customer but you don't know the waitress because she is new.
3. You observe a man accidentally dropping an expensive bottle of wine in a liquor store when the manager is not looking. The man turns to those around him and denies responsibility; he even tries to blame a Latino maintenance employee who is working cleaning up the store.
4. A transgender woman named Amelia works as a server at a restaurant and proceeds to inform a regular customer that she used to be a man named Bill. The customer begins to harass Amelia.
5. A good friend of yours tells you he is planning to omit certain important facts from his resume before he applies for the same job you are applying for. He says "it's not important that they know I just lived off my parents for two years after college. Hey, I needed a break."
6. At your place of employment, a customer paid too much for an order; but, your boss told you not to call it to his attention.

What would you do in each of these situations if you observed them occurring?

Would your actions reflect "conventional" thinking about business ethics? Would you react differently than most people? Why?

What would be the primary source of ethical norms that would be at work in your thinking (see Figure 7-5)?

Sources: "Primetime: what would you do?" *Wikipedia*, https://en.wikipedia.org/wiki/Primetime:_What_Would_You_Do%3F. Accessed April 22, 2016; ABC News, "What would you do?" http://abcnews.go.com/WhatWouldYouDo, Accessed February 20, 2016; A&E, "What would you do?" http://www.aetv.com/shows/what-would-you-do. Accessed April 22, 2016.

ethics that are acceptable to many in conventional society would not be accepted in more rigorous forms of ethical analysis.

7.2c Ethics and the Law

The issue of ethics versus the law arises often in discussions of business ethics. In Chapter 2, we said that ethical behavior is typically thought to reside *above* behavior required by the law. This is the generally accepted view of ethics. We should make it clear however that in many respects the law and ethics overlap and are intertwined. To appreciate this, you need to recognize that the law embodies notions of ethics. That is, the law may be seen as a reflection of what society thinks are minimal standards of conduct and behavior.

Both law and ethics have to do with what is deemed appropriate or acceptable, but law reflects society's *codified* ethics. Therefore, if a person breaks a law or violates a regulation, she or he is also behaving unethically. We should be open to the possibility, however, that in some rare cases the law may not be ethical, in which case standing up to the law might be the principled course of action. A case in point might have been when Rosa Parks, a black woman, stood up to the authorities and refused to move to the back of the bus because she thought this was racial discrimination. In retrospect, Parks was doing the principled thing and civil rights history has borne this out.

The late Ronald Dworkin, a legal scholar, always argued that laws should be understood to be part of a larger moral vision rather than as an ordinary set of rules. He held that law should not produce results that were not in harmony with ordinary morality.[18] In spite of this frequent intermixing of law and ethics, we continue to talk about desired ethical behavior as behavior that extends beyond what is required by law. The *spirit* of the law often extends beyond the *letter* of the law and often taps into the ethical dimension. Viewed from the standpoint of minimums, we would certainly say that obedience to the law is generally regarded to be a minimum standard of ethical behavior.

Following is a good business examples in which the confusion between law and ethics led to disastrous results. The Enron scandal was said to have been all about the difference between the letter of the law and the spirit of the law (ethics). Interestingly, the fraud at Enron was accompanied by obsessive and careful attention to the letter of the law. One observer stated that "the people who ran Enron did back flips and somersaults as they tried to stay within the law's lines."[19] But CEO Ken Lay and CFO Jeffrey Skilling apparently missed the main point of securities law, which is that CEOs and other high-level officials should not get rich while their shareholders go broke. So, the source of all their crimes was the basic dishonesty of trying to keep Enron's stock afloat so that they could make money.[20] Their focus on the law to the neglect of ethics was a significant part of their downfall.

In addition, it should be noted that the law does not address all realms in which ethical questions might be raised. Thus, there are clear roles for both law and ethics to play.[21] In the realm of rapidly changing technological advances, for example, it is hard for our law makers to keep laws up to date; therefore, ethics plays a very important role in situations such as this. An example of this situation occurs in the case of drones. Drone technology and their recreational uses are way ahead of laws regulating and protecting the public's safety regarding them; therefore, we all depend on the good consciences of their users until laws are passed to help protect us.

Research on illegal corporate behavior has been conducted for some time. Illegal corporate behavior, of course, comprises business practices that are in direct defiance of law or public policy. This research has focused on two dominant questions: (1) Why do firms behave illegally or what leads them to engage in illegal activities and (2) what are the consequences of behaving illegally?[22] We will not deal with these studies of law breaking in this discussion; however, we should acknowledge this body of studies and

FIGURE 7-5 Elements Involved in Making Ethical Judgments

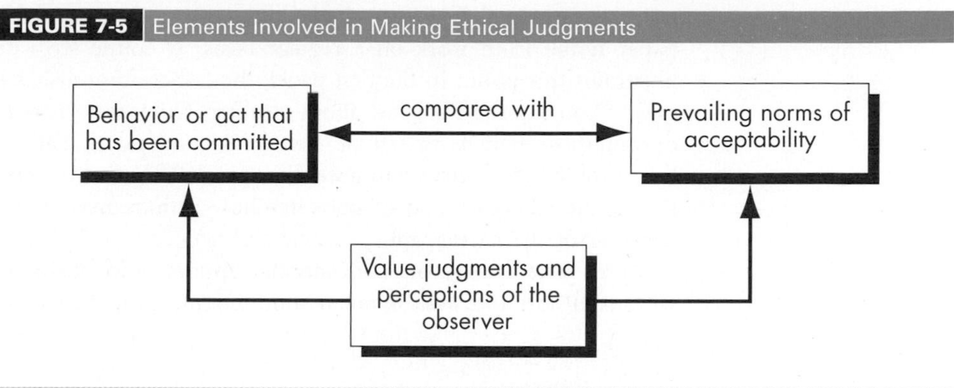

investigations as being very relevant to our interest in business ethics because it represents a special case of business ethics (illegal behavior).

7.2d Making Ethical Judgments

Making business decisions that have an ethical dimension to them is something faced by managers and employees every day. When a decision is made about what is ethical (right, just, fair) using the conventional approach, there is room for variability on several counts (see Figure 7-5). Three key elements compose such a decision. First, we observe or participate in the *decision, action,* or *practice* that has taken place in the workplace setting. Second, we *compare the practice with prevailing norms of acceptability*—that is, society's or some other group's standard of what is acceptable or unacceptable. Third, we must recognize that *value judgments are being made* by someone as to what really occurred (the actual behavior) and what the prevailing norms of acceptability actually are.

This means that two different people could look at the same behavior or practice, compare it with their beliefs of what the prevailing norms are, and reach different conclusions as to whether the behavior was ethical or not. In fact, this happens all the time and really is the basis of much ethical analysis that takes place. This judgment process becomes quite complex as perceptions of what is ethical inevitably lead to the difficult task of ranking different values against one another.

If we can put aside for a moment the fact that perceptual differences about an incident do exist, and the fact that we might differ among ourselves because of our personal values and philosophies of acceptable behavior, we are still left with the challenging task of determining society's prevailing norms of acceptability of business practice. As a whole, members of society generally agree at a very high level of abstraction that certain practices are inappropriate. However, the consensus tends to disintegrate as we move from the general situation to specific details.

This may be illustrated with a business example. We might all agree with the general belief that "You should not steal someone else's property." As a general precept, we likely would have consensus on this. But, as we look at specific situations, our consensus may tend to disappear. Is it acceptable to take home from work such things as pencils, pens, paper clips, paper, staplers, jump drives, and calculators? Is it acceptable to use the company telephone for personal long-distance calls? Is it acceptable to use company-bought gasoline for private use or to pad one's expense accounts? Is it acceptable to use company computers for personal e-mail or Web surfing? What if everyone else is doing it?

What is important in these examples is that we are more likely to reach consensus in principle than in practice. Some people who would say these practices are not acceptable might privately engage in them and rationalize them. Furthermore, a person who would not think of shoplifting even the smallest item from a local store might take pencils and paper home from work on a regular basis. A comic strip depicting the "Born Loser" illustrates this point. In the first panel, the father admonishes his son Wilberforce as follows: "You know how I feel about stealing. Now tomorrow I want you to return every one of those pencils to school." In the second panel, Father says to Wilberforce: "I'll bring you all the pencils you need from work." This, of course, is an example of the classic double standard, and it illustrates how actions may be perceived differently by the observer or the participant.

Thus, when using the conventional approach to business ethics, determinations of what is ethical and what is not require judgments to be made on at least three counts:

1. What is the *true nature* of the practice, behavior, or decision that occurred?
2. What are society's (or business's) *prevailing norms* of acceptability?
3. What *value judgments* are being made by someone about the practice or behavior, and what are that person's *perceptions* of applicable norms?

The human factor in the situation thus introduces the problem of perception, rationalization, and values and makes the decision process depicted in Figure 7-5 to be more complex than it first appears.

The conventional approach to business ethics can be valuable because we all need to be aware of and sensitive to the total environment in which we exist. We need to be aware of how society regards ethical issues. It has limitations, however, and we need to be cognizant of these as well. The most serious danger is that of falling into an **ethical relativism** where we pick and choose which source of norms we wish to apply on the basis of what will justify our current actions or maximize our freedom. A relevant comic strip illustrates this point. In a courtroom, while swearing in, one witness stated, "I swear to tell the truth … *as I see it.*"

In the next chapter, we present a principles approach that is needed to augment the conventional approach to business ethics. The **principles approach** represents *normative*

ETHICS IN PRACTICE CASE

To Hunt or Not to Hunt—That Is the Question

John Q. Expert from Enterprise Consulting Firm (ECF) has been working with City in South Georgia for approximately six months now on a study to reorganize the local government. The arrangement with City in South Georgia has generated nearly $50,000 in revenues for ECF so far.

A member of the City Council of City in South Georgia, Councilman Lotsoland, happens to be a prominent landowner and operates a 500-acre hunting & fishing preserve on the outskirts of City in South Georgia. Councilman Lotsoland uses the preserve to host prominent business and community leaders to City in South Georgia. Regular customers pay as much as $1,000 a day for use of the property.

During the course of completing the six-month study with City in South Georgia, John Q. Expert develops a friendship with Councilman Lotsoland. Councilman Lotsoland and John Q. Expert share many mutual interests especially their love for the outdoors, and in particular their unending love for quail hunting.

Toward the end of the local government reorganization study, Councilman Lotsoland offers John Q. Expert an "all expenses paid" weekend at his hunting & fishing preserve.

1. What factors must John Q. Expert consider in his decision of whether or not to accept the complimentary weekend? Are there any conflicts of interest present that ought to be considered?
2. Is it appropriate for Councilman Lotsoland to offer the "all expenses paid" weekend? What factors make it acceptable or unacceptable?
3. Is it proper for John Q. Expert to accept the offer? Why? Why not?

Contributed by Matthew L. Bishop, PhD
J. W. Fanning Institute for Leadership Development

ethics and considers general guidelines to ethical decision making that managers should consider in practice. We also present an **ethical tests approach**, which is more of a practical approach to ethical decision making.

7.3 Ethics, Economics, and Law—A Venn Model

In many business decisions, ethics, economics, and the law all come into play. When we focus on ethics and ethical decision making, it is useful to consider these primary elements that come into tension while making ethical judgments. In Chapter 2, these were introduced as part of the four-part definition of corporate social responsibility, and they were depicted in the Pyramid of CSR. When we discuss a firm's CSR, philanthropy commonly enters the discussion. This is because philanthropic initiatives are one of the primary ways many companies display their CSR in the community—through good and charitable works.

In ethical decision making, however, we tend to set aside philanthropic expectations and focus on ethical expectations and, especially, those elements that primarily come into tension with ethics—economics (the quest for profits) and law (society's codified ethics). Thus, in most decision-making situations, ethics, economics, and law become the central variables that must be considered and balanced against each other in the quest to make wise and sensible decisions.

A firm's economic, legal, and ethical responsibilities may be depicted in a Venn diagram model illustrating how certain actions, decisions, practices, or policies fulfill one, two, or three of these responsibility categories. Figure 7-6 presents this Venn diagram model, illustrating the overlapping potential of these three responsibility categories.

In Area 1 of the diagram, where the decision, action, or practice fulfills all three responsibilities, the management prescription is to "go for it." That is, the action is

FIGURE 7-6 A Venn Model for Ethical Decision Making

profitable, in compliance with the law, and represents ethical behavior. In Area 2a, the action under consideration is profitable and legal, but its ethical status may be uncertain. The guideline here is to "proceed cautiously." In these kinds of situations, the ethics of the action needs to be carefully considered. In Area 2b, the action is profitable and ethical, but perhaps the law does not clearly address the issue or is ambiguous. If it is ethical, there is a good chance it is also legal, but the guideline again is to "proceed cautiously."

In Area 3 of the diagram, the action is legal and ethical but not profitable. Therefore, the strategy here would be to avoid this action or "find ways to make it profitable." However, there may be a compelling case to take the action if it is legal and ethical and, thus, represents the right thing to do. Schwartz and Carroll have presented a three-domain approach to CSR that employs a Venn diagram format similar to that presented in Figure 7-6. They provide corporate examples to illustrate each section of the Venn diagram.[23]

By taking philanthropy out of the picture, the Venn model serves as a useful template for thinking about the more immediate expectations that society has on business in a situation in which the ethical dimension plays an important role. It illustrates clearly that many business decisions boil down to trade-offs between the influences of economics, law, and ethics.

ETHICS IN PRACTICE CASE

Is Résumé Inflation and Deception Acceptable?

According to Steven Levitt, author of *Freakonomics*, a small bit of inflation on one's résumé is universal. Levitt estimates that at least half the people engage in this deception to some degree. Typically, the small edits to one's résumé are done to disguise some unaccounted for time in between jobs. There may be nothing to hide except the fact that unexplained time period looks suspicious. On other occasions, the deceptions have been more substantial; for example, claiming an academic degree one almost acquired but didn't: "Well, I was just two courses short!" It has also been said that based on studies, the average American tells one or two lies a day, often at work. A survey of 2,500 hiring managers by CareerBuilder found that 30 percent of them find false or misleading information on applicants' résumés.

A résumé controversy with significant consequences occurred when the then-Yahoo CEO, Scott Thompson, was questioned about a statement on his company's Web site, which reported that he had a degree in computer science. A dissident shareholder went public with the revelation that Thompson couldn't have a degree in computer science because the small college he graduated from didn't have a computer science *major* until *after* he graduated. The company's regulatory filing indicated that Thompson had a degree in accounting and computer science. Thompson claimed the Web site information was an inadvertent error without providing more information. According to his college, Thompson graduated with a bachelor's of science in business administration degree.

Days after this information came out, a person close to Yahoo's board reported that in absence of information that Thompson intentionally misled, the company probably would not force him out, indicating that his importance as CEO to the company was more important than whether he had a computer science degree or not. In spite of this, CEO Scott Thompson resigned his position soon thereafter amid the controversy over his résumé discrepancy.

1. In light of the prevalence of these practices, is résumé inflation and deception acceptable? Is it okay up to a point as long as the distortion doesn't get too big? Is a small amount of puffery on one's résumé just expected as part of the game of getting a job and getting ahead? What would the conventional approach to business ethics say?
2. Some small schools don't have official majors but people sometimes claim them anyway because they took several courses in a specialized area. Is this an acceptable practice?
3. If you had been on Yahoo's board, would you have supported keeping Thompson?
4. Why do you suppose Thompson resigned?

Sources: Steven Levitt, *Freakonomics*, 2005; David Wescott, "The Truth Won't Set You Free," *Bloomberg Business Week*, February 4–10, 2013; "Imaginary Friends," *Bloomberg Businessweek*, January 21–27, 2013, 68; Amir Efrati and J. S. Lublin, "Résumé Trips Up Yahoo's Chief," *Wall Street Journal*, May 5–6, 2012, A1, A12.; Chris Smith, "Scott Thompson Quits as Yahoo CEO following 'fake degree' controversy," *Techradar*, May 12, 2012, http://www.techradar.com/us/news/internet/scott-thompson-quits-as-yahoo-ceo-following-fake-degree-controversy-1080165. Accessed February 11, 2016.

7.4 Three Models of Management Ethics

In striving to understand the basic concepts of business ethics, it is useful to think in terms of key ethical models that might describe different types of management or business ethics found in the organizational world.[24] These models provide some useful base points for discussion and comparison. The media have focused so much on immoral or unethical business behavior that it is easy to forget about the possibility of other ethical types. For example, scant attention has been given to the distinction that may be made between those activities that are *immoral* and those that are *amoral*. Similarly, little attention has been given to contrasting these two forms of behavior with ethical or *moral* management.

Believing that there is value in discussing descriptive models, or frameworks, for purposes of clearer understanding, here we describe, compare, and contrast three models or types of ethical management:

- Immoral management
- Moral management
- Amoral management

A major goal in this section is to develop a clearer understanding of the range of management postures in which ethics or morality is a defining characteristic. By seeing these approaches come to life through description and example, prospective managers will be in an improved position to assess their own ethical approaches and those of other organizational members (supervisors, subordinates, and peers). Another important objective is to identify more completely the amoral management model, which often is overlooked in the everyday rush to classify things as good or bad, moral or immoral. In a later section, we discuss the **elements of moral judgment** that must be developed if the transition to moral management is to succeed. A more detailed development of each management model is valuable in coming to understand the range of ethics that leaders may intentionally or unintentionally display. The two extremes will be considered first—immoral and moral management—and then amoral management.

7.4a Immoral Management

Using *immoral* and *unethical* as synonyms, **immoral management** is defined as an approach that is devoid of ethical principles or precepts and at the same time implies a positive and active opposition to what is ethical. Immoral management decisions, behaviors, actions, and practices are discordant with ethical norms and principles.

This model holds that the management's motives are selfish and that it cares only or primarily about its own or its organization's gains. If the management's activity is actively opposed to what is regarded as ethical, this suggests that the management understands right from wrong and yet chooses to do wrong; thus, its motives are deemed greedy or self-centered. In this model, the management's goals are profitability and organizational success at virtually any price. The management does not care about other stakeholders' claims to be treated fairly or justly.

What about the management's orientation toward the law, considering that law is often regarded as an embodiment of minimal ethics? Immoral management regards legal standards as barriers that the management must avoid or overcome to accomplish what it wants. Immoral managers would just as soon engage in illegal activity as in immoral or unethical activity. This point is illustrated in a popular Dilbert comic strip. Dogbert, the VP of Marketing, announces at a meeting: "It's my job to spray paint the road kill." In panel 2, he says: "I'll use a process the experts call 'dishonesty.' " In panel 3, Dilbert concludes: "My motto is 'If it isn't immoral, it probably won't work.' "[25]

FIGURE 7-7 Characteristics of Immoral Managers

- These managers intentionally do wrong.
- These managers are *self-centered* and *self-absorbed.*
- They care only about self or organization's profits or success.
- They actively oppose what is right, fair, or just.
- They *exhibit no concern* for stakeholders.
- These are the "bad guys."
- An ethics course probably would not help them.

Operating Strategy. The operating strategy of immoral management is focused on exploiting opportunities for personal or corporate gain. An active opposition to what is moral would suggest that managers cut corners anywhere and everywhere it appears useful. Thus, the key operating question guiding immoral management is, "Can we make money with this action, decision, or behavior, *regardless of what it takes*?" Implicit in this question is that nothing else matters, at least not very much. Figure 7-7 summarizes some of the major characteristics of immoral managers.

Illustrative Cases. Examples of immoral management abound. The Enron scandal is one that is illustrative and enduring.

Enron Few business scandals stand out as clearly as an example of immoral management as much as that of Enron Corporation. The two major players in the Enron scandal were CEO Jeffrey Skilling and president Ken Lay, now convicted felons. CFO Andy Fastow also was convicted and went to prison. Though Enron imploded in 2001, it was not until 2006 that Skilling and Lay were brought to justice and convicted.[26] Ken Lay, founder and CEO of Enron, died on July 5, 2006, before he had a chance to serve his prison sentence that would have taken him to the end of his life.[27] The Enron scandal became so famous that it produced a British play about the financial scandal that engulfed it, and in 2010, the play moved to Broadway in the United States but only lasted through 16 performances before it closed.[28] In addition, many books have been written about this infamous scandal.

Lay and Skilling were both convicted of securities fraud and conspiracy to inflate profits, along with a number of other charges. They used off-the-books partnerships to disguise Enron's debts, and then they lied to investors and employees about the company's disastrous financial situation while selling their own company shares.[29] In addition, Enron traders manipulated California's energy market to create phony shortages. This forced the state to borrow billions to pay off artificially inflated power bills. Voters in California were so fearful of brownouts, skyrocketing power bills, and rising state debt that they recalled Gov. Gray Davis and replaced him with Arnold Schwarzenegger.[30]

In 2013, Skilling, though in prison, was still trying to convince the courts that he was not given a fair trial and that his conviction should be overturned.[31] In 2016, Enron CFO, Andy Fastow, finished his prison sentence and quietly made amends but it is not clear whether the public is willing to forgive him.[32] The *Wall Street Journal* has observed that "the shadow of Enron still lingers."[33] Lay, Skilling, and Fastow were clearly immoral managers. Volkswagen's cheating on emissions testing and Wells Fargo's creation of fake consumer accounts would both be cases of immoral management.

Everyday Questionable Practices In a "Deloitte & Touche USA Ethics & Workplace" survey, respondents identified a number of questionable behaviors observed in the workplace that they thought were unacceptable. This list reveals everyday practices that would illustrate the model of immoral management:[34]

- Stealing petty cash
- Cheating on expense reports

SPOTLIGHT *on Sustainability*

Ray Anderson's Conversion Experience

Many managers have a conversion experience before they become moral managers. In other words, they had to transition from, probably, an amoral condition to a moral style. Often this comes as a result of an epiphany, a sudden realization in understanding what they experience. A prominent example is that of Ray Anderson, former CEO of Interface Carpet, who has been ranked as one of the leading sustainable CEOs in business today. Anderson had a special moment occur when he was reading Paul Hawken's *Ecology of Commerce* in which he came to the conclusion that he, personally, was an environmental villain.

"It was an epiphanic spear in my heart, a life-changing moment; a new definition of success flooded my mind," he told the U.K.'s *Guardian* newspaper about the revelation. He went on to report: "I realized I was a plunderer and it was not a legacy I wanted to leave behind. I wept."

Anderson then made it his new mission to change that legacy and proceeded to, as the *Guardian* puts it, "turn the company into a champion of environmental sustainability." By taking this courageous step, Anderson played a leadership role in getting many other companies into the conversation about sustainability. Without his ethical leadership, it is questionable when or if this would have occurred.

Anderson was a sought-after international speaker who gave nearly 100 talks each year to audiences hungry for a message about the company that was proving the business model for sustainability works. Mr. Anderson passed away in 2011 but his memory serves as a constant reminder of the importance of sustainability and moral management.

Sources: Katherine Gustafson, "A Look at America's Most 'Sustainable' CEOs," http://intentblog.com/look-americas-most-sustainable-ceos/. Accessed February 11, 2016; Also see "Ray's Legacy," http://www.interfaceglobal.com/company/leadership-team/ray-watch.aspx. Accessed February 11, 2016; Natural Profits Interview with Ray Anderson, http://www.earthsayers.com/special_collection/Ray_Anderson/41/0/. Accessed February 11, 2016.

- Taking credit for another person's accomplishments
- Lying on time sheets about hours worked
- Coming into work hung over
- Telling a demeaning joke (e.g., racist)
- Taking office supplies for personal use

In this same Deloitte & Touche survey, respondents provided what they considered to be other unethical behaviors.[35] These practices also would be characterized as immoral management:

- Showing preferential treatment toward certain employees
- Taking credit for another person's accomplishments
- Rewarding employees who display wrong behaviors
- Harassing a fellow employee (e.g., verbally, sexually, racially)

All of these are examples of immoral management wherein executives' decisions or actions were self-centered, actively opposed to what is right, focused on achieving organizational success at whatever the cost, and cutting corners where it was useful. These decisions were made without regard to the possible consequences of such concerns as honesty or fairness to others. What is apparent from the Deloitte & Touche survey findings is that immoral management can occur on an everyday basis and does not need to be in the league of the mega scandals such as Enron or Bernie Madoff to be unacceptable behavior.

7.4b Moral Management

At the opposite extreme from immoral management is **moral management**. Moral management conforms to the highest standards of ethical behavior or professional standards of conduct. Although it is not always crystal clear what level of ethical standards prevail, moral management strives to be highly ethical in terms of its focus on elevated ethical norms and professional standards of conduct, motives, goals, orientation toward the law, and general operating strategy.

In contrast to the selfish motives in immoral management, moral management aspires to succeed, but only within the confines of sound ethical precepts; that is, standards predicated on such norms as fairness, justice, respect for rights, and due process. Moral management's motives would be termed fair, balanced, or unselfish. Organizational goals continue to stress profitability, but only within the confines of legal compliance and responsiveness to ethical standards.

Moral management pursues its objectives of profitability, legality, and ethics as both required and desirable. Moral management would not pursue profits at the expense of the law and sound ethics. Indeed, the focus here would be not only on the letter of the law but on the spirit of the law as well. The law would be viewed as a minimal standard of ethical behavior because moral management strives to operate at a level above what the law mandates.

Operating Strategy. The operating strategy of moral management is to live by sound ethical standards, seeking out only those economic opportunities that the organization or management can pursue within the confines of ethical boundaries. The manager or organization assumes a leadership position when ethical dilemmas arise. The central question guiding moral management's actions, decisions, and behaviors is, "Will this action, decision, behavior, or practice be fair to all stakeholders involved as well as to the organization?"

Integrity Strategy Lynn Sharp Paine advocates an "integrity strategy" that closely resembles the moral management model.[36] The **Integrity Strategy** is characterized by a conception of ethics as the driving force of an organization. Ethical values shape management's search for opportunities, the design of organizational systems, and the decision-making process. Ethical values in the integrity strategy provide a common frame of reference and serve to unify different functions, lines of business, and employee groups. Organizational ethics, in this view, helps to define what an organization is and what it stands for. Some common features of an integrity strategy include the following,[37] which are all consistent with the moral management model:

- Guiding values and commitments make sense and are clearly communicated.
- Company leaders are personally committed, credible, and willing to take action on the values they espouse.
- Espoused values are integrated into the normal channels of management decision making.
- The organization's systems and structures support and reinforce its values.
- All managers have the skills, knowledge, and competencies to make ethically sound decisions on a daily basis.

Habits of Moral Leaders Closely related to moral management is the topic of moral leadership. Carroll has set forth what he refers to as the "Seven Habits of Highly Moral Leaders."[38] Adapting the language used by Stephen Covey in his best-selling book *The Seven Habits of Highly Effective People*,[39] these qualities would need to be so common in the leader's approach that they become habitual as a leadership approach. Helping to further flesh out what constitutes a moral manager, the seven habits of highly moral leaders have been set forth as follows.

Regarding Highly Moral Leaders:

1. They have a passion to do right.
2. They are morally proactive.

3. They consider all stakeholders.
4. They have a strong ethical character.
5. They have an obsession with fairness.
6. They undertake principled decision making.
7. They integrate ethics wisdom with management wisdom.[40]

Figure 7-8 summarizes the important characteristics of moral managers.

Positive Ethical Behaviors Drawing on the "Deloitte & Touche USA Ethics & Workplace" survey cited earlier, following are the examples of positive ethical behaviors identified by the survey respondents.[41] These represent everyday ways that managers might display moral management:

- Giving proper credit where it is due
- Always being straightforward and honest when dealing with other employees
- Treating all employees equally
- Being a responsible steward of company assets
- Resisting pressure to act unethically
- Recognizing and rewarding ethical behavior of others
- Talking about the importance of ethics and compliance on a regular basis

Illustrative Cases. A couple cases of moral management illustrate how this model of management is played out in actual practice.

Navistar Navistar is a diesel engine manufacturer. One of its plants is located in Huntsville, Alabama. Because of the sour economy, at one point the company had to cut its production from 900 engines a day to 100. The company faced imminent layoffs. Plant manager Chuck Sibley wrestled with the layoff decision and finally came up with a creative solution that saved 50 jobs. Sibley's decision was not to lay off the employees but to send them out into the community, at corporate expense, to help the needy.

Their initial assignments were to help Habitat for Humanity, the Salvation Army, and CASA, all nonprofit organizations deeply involved in community volunteerism. The employees were shocked but pleasantly surprised. They would still be paid by Navistar and they would keep all their benefits. The reassignments were expected to be for three months. Plant manager Sibley argued that the company will save money because they will avoid the costs of rehiring and training. The company expected an improvement in market conditions in three months and then the plan was to bring the 50 employees back to the plant.[42] The 50 employees were brought back to work as scheduled and they reported positive experiences about their time spent helping others.[43] This creative solution not only saved the employees from unemployment, but helped the community in a big way as well. Only a moral manager could come up with such a win–win solution.

FIGURE 7-8 Characteristics of Moral Managers

- These managers conform to a *high level of ethical or right behavior* (moral rectitude).
- They conform to a high level of personal and professional *standards*.
- *Ethical leadership* is commonplace—they search out where people may be hurt.
- Their goal is to succeed but only within the confines of *sound ethical precepts* (fairness, due process).
- *High integrity* is displayed in *thinking, speaking,* and *doing*.
- These managers embrace the letter and *spirit* of the law. Law is seen as a *minimal* ethical level. They prefer to operate *above* legal mandates.
- They possess an acute *moral sense* and *moral maturity*.
- Moral managers are the "good guys."

Merck Another well-known classic case of moral management occurred when Merck & Co., the pharmaceutical firm, invested millions of dollars to develop a drug for treating "river blindness," a Third World disease that was affecting almost 18 million people. Seeing that no government or aid organization was agreeing to buy the drug, Merck pledged to supply the drug for free forever. Merck's recognition that no effective mechanism existed to distribute the drug led to its decision to go far beyond industry practice and organize a committee to oversee the drug's distribution.[44]

It should be emphasized that not all organizations now engaging in moral management have done so all along. These companies sometimes arrived at this posture after years or decades of rising consumer expectations, increased government regulations, lawsuits, and pressure from social and consumer activists. By the same token, some moral management companies may slip from this status due to actions or practices taken. One of the most puzzling examples recently is that of the Volkswagen scandal. For years VW has been building its reputation as a socially responsible company; then, out of the blue, we learn about its emissions scandal wherein its actions were wholly inconsistent with the image and reputation it had spent years developing.

We must think of moral management, therefore, as a desirable posture that in many instances has evolved over periods of several years. If we hold management to an idealistic, 100 percent historical moral purity test, no management or company will meet the standard. Rather, we should consider moral those managements that now see the enlightened self-interest of responding in accordance with the moral management model rather than alternatives, and are able to sustain this approach.

7.4c Amoral Management

Amoral management is not just a middle position on a continuum between immoral and moral management. Conceptually it has been positioned between the other two, but it is different in nature and kind from both, and it is of two kinds: **intentional amoral management** and **unintentional amoral management**.

Intentional Amoral Management. Intentionally amoral managers do not factor ethical considerations into their decisions, actions, and behaviors because they believe business activity resides outside the sphere to which moral judgments apply. They simply think that different rules apply in business than in other realms of life. Intentionally amoral managers are in a distinct minority today. At one time, however, as managers first began to think about reconciling business practices with sound ethics, some managers adopted this stance. A few intentionally amoral managers are still around, but they are a vanishing breed in today's ethically conscious world.

Unintentional Amoral Management. Like intentionally amoral managers, unintentionally amoral managers do not think about business activity in ethical terms, but for different reasons. These managers are simply casual about, careless about, or inattentive to the fact that their decisions and actions may have negative or deleterious effects on others. These managers lack ethical perception and moral awareness. They have no "moral sense." That is, they blithely go through their organizational lives not thinking that what they are doing has an ethical dimension or facet. These managers are generally thought to be well intentioned but are either too insensitive or too self-absorbed to consider the effects of their decisions and actions on others. These managers normally think of themselves as ethical managers, but they are frequently overlooking these unintentional, subconscious, or unconscious aspects. As it turns out, they are more amoral than moral.

Unconscious Biases Sometimes amoral managers may be unconscious of hidden biases that prevent them from being objective. Researchers have found that many business people go through life deluded by the illusion of objectivity. Unconscious, or implicit biases, can run contrary to our consciously held, explicit beliefs.[45] Though most managers think they are ethical, sometimes even the most well-meaning person unwittingly allows unconscious thoughts and biases to influence what appear to be objective decisions. Four sources of unintentional, or unconscious, influences include implicit forms of prejudice, bias that favors one's own group, conflict of interest, and a tendency to over claim credit.[46]

Unconscious biases were believed to be at work among accountants in some of the major accounting scandals. Three *structural aspects* of accounting bias include ambiguity, attachment, and approval. When *ambiguity* exists, people tend to reach self-serving conclusions. For example, subjective interpretations of what constitutes a deductible expense may be made in a self-serving fashion. *Attachment* occurs when auditors, motivated to stay in their clients' good graces, approve things they might otherwise not approve. With respect to *approval*, external auditors may be reviewing the work of internal auditors, and self-serving biases may become even stronger when other people's biases are being endorsed or approved, especially if those judgments align with one's own biases.[47]

In addition, three aspects of human nature may amplify unconscious biases: familiarity, discounting, and escalation. With *familiarity*, it is noted that people may be more willing to harm strangers (anonymous investors) than individuals they know (clients). *Discounting* refers to the act of overlooking or minimizing decisions that may not have immediate consequences. Finally, *escalation* occurs when an accountant or businessperson allows small judgments to accumulate and become large and then she decides to cover up the unwitting mistakes through concealment. Thus, small indiscretions escalate into larger ones, and unconscious biases grow into conscious corruption.[48] These unconscious biases have been exposed in research within the general realm of behavioral ethics, which will be explored in further detail in Chapter 8. For now, they are considered because they can be the source of unintentional amorality.

Amoral management pursues profitability as its goal but does not consciously or cognitively attend to moral issues that may be intertwined with that pursuit. If there is an ethical guide to amoral management, it would be the marketplace as constrained by law—the letter of the law, not the spirit. The amoral manager sees the law as the parameters within which business pursuits take place but is not particularly concerned with the spirit of the law.

Operating Strategy. The operating strategy of amoral management is to not bridle managers with excessive ethical structure but to permit free rein within the supposedly unspoken but understood tenets of the free enterprise system. Personal ethics may periodically or unintentionally enter into managerial decisions, but it does not preoccupy management. Furthermore, the impact of decisions on others is an afterthought, if it ever gets considered at all.

Amoral management represents a model of decision making in which the managers' ethical mental gears, to the extent that they are present, are stuck in neutral. The key management question guiding decision making is, "Can we make money with this action, decision, or behavior?" Note that the question does not imply an active or implicit intent to be either moral or immoral.

Compliance Strategy Lynn Sharp Paine has articulated a "compliance strategy" that is consistent with the characteristics of amoral management. The **compliance strategy**, as contrasted with her integrity strategy discussed earlier, is more focused on submission to the law as its driving force. The compliance strategy is lawyer-driven and is oriented not toward ethics or integrity but more toward conformity with existing regulatory and criminal law. The compliance approach uses deterrence as its underlying assumption. This approach envisions managers as rational maximizers of self-interest, responsive to the personal costs and benefits of their choices, yet indifferent to the moral legitimacy of those choices.[49]

FIGURE 7-9 Characteristics of Amoral Managers

Intentionally Amoral Managers

- These managers don't think ethics and business should "mix."
- Business and ethics are seen as existing in *separate* spheres. Ethics is seen as too "Sunday schoolish" and not applicable to business.
- These managers are a vanishing breed. There are very few managers like this left in the world.

Unintentionally Amoral Managers

- These managers forget to consider the *ethical dimension* of decision making.
- They just don't "*think ethically.*"
- They may lack *ethical perception* or awareness; they have no "ethics buds" that help them sense the ethical dimension.
- They are well intentioned but morally casual or careless; may be morally *unconscious.*
- Their ethical gears, if they exist, are in *neutral.*

Figure 7-9 summarizes the major characteristics of amoral managers.

Illustrative Cases. Unintentionally amoral management seems to be built into many decision-making applications.

Examples When police departments first stipulated that recruits must be at least 5′ 9″ tall and weigh at least 180 pounds, they were making an amoral decision, because they were not considering the detrimental exclusion this would impose on women and other ethnic groups who do not, on average, attain that height and weight. When companies decided to use scantily clad young women to advertise autos, men's cologne, and other products, these companies were not thinking of the degrading and demeaning characterization of women that would result from what they thought was an ethically neutral decision. When Domino's initially decided to deliver pizza orders within 30 minutes or the food was free, they didn't think about how such a policy might induce their drivers to speed and, sometimes, cause auto accidents. This policy was later dropped.

Nestlé Nestlé's *initial* decision to market infant formula in Third World countries (see Chapter 10) could have been seen as an amoral decision when it was first made. Nestlé may not have considered the detrimental effects such a seemingly innocent business decision would have on mothers and babies in a land of impure water, poverty, and illiteracy. In other words, Nestlé simply wasn't factoring ethical considerations into its marketing decisions. As Nestlé continued this practice after it learned of the problems, the decision was seen by many as moving from amoral to immoral.

Sears A classic illustration of unintentionally amoral management involved the case of Sears Roebuck and Co. and its automotive service business, which spanned a decade. Paine described how consumers and attorneys general in 40 states accused the company of misleading consumers and selling them unneeded parts and services.[50] In the face of declining revenues and a shrinking market share, Sears' executives put into place new goals, quotas, and incentives for auto-center service personnel. Service employees were told to meet product-specific and service-specific quotas—sell so many brake jobs, batteries, and front-end alignments—or face consequences such as reduced working hours or transfers. Some employees spoke of the "pressure" they felt to generate business. Although Sears' executives did not set out to defraud customers, they put into place a commission system that led to Sears' employees feeling pressure to sell products and services that consumers did not need. Fortunately, Sears eliminated its quota system as a partial remedy to the problem.[51]

FIGURE 7-10 Three Models of Management Ethics

Organizational Characteristics	Immoral Management	Amoral Management	Moral Management
Ethical Norms	Management decisions, actions, and behavior imply a positive and active opposition to what is moral (ethical). Decisions are discordant with accepted ethical principles. An active negation of what is moral is implied.	Management is neither moral nor immoral, but decisions lie outside the sphere to which moral judgments apply. Management activity is outside or beyond the moral order of a particular code. May imply a lack of ethical perception and moral awareness.	Management activity conforms to a standard of ethical, or right, behavior. Conforms to accepted professional standards of conduct. Ethical leadership is commonplace on the part of management.
Motives	Selfish. Management cares only about its or the company's gains.	Well-intentioned but selfish in the sense that impact on others is not considered.	Good. Management wants to succeed but only within the confines of sound ethical precepts (fairness, justice, due process).
Goals	Profitability and organizational success at any price.	Profitability. Other goals are not considered.	Profitability within the confines of legal obedience and ethical standards.
Orientation Toward Law	Legal standards are barriers that management must overcome to accomplish what it wants.	Law is the ethical guide, preferably the letter of the law. The central question is what we can do legally.	Obedience toward letter and spirit of the law. Law is a minimal ethical behavior. Prefer to operate well above what law mandates.
Strategy	Exploit opportunities for corporate gain. Cut corners when it appears useful.	Give managers free rein. Personal ethics may apply but only if managers choose. Respond to legal mandates if caught and required to do so.	Live by sound ethical standards. Assume leadership position when ethical dilemmas arise. Enlightened self-interest.

Source: Archie B. Carroll, "In Search of the Moral Manager," *Business Horizons* (March/April 1987), 8. Copyright © 1987 by the Foundation for the School of Business at Indiana University. Used with permission.

Today, many companies do not think carefully about the effects employee rewards systems might have on customers and others. Some research has shown that the effects of rewards and recognitions often backfire and work against employee motivation and productivity.[52]

Figure 7-10 provides a summary of the major characteristics of immoral, amoral, and moral management. It compares the three in terms of ethical norms, motives, goals, orientation toward the law, and operating strategy.

7.4d Two Hypotheses Regarding the Models of Management Morality

A thorough study has not been conducted to ascertain precisely what proportions of managers each model of morality represents in the total management population. However, two plausible hypotheses regarding the moral management models are worthy of consideration.

Population Hypothesis. The **population hypothesis** is that the distribution of the three models might approximate a normal curve within the management *population*, with the amoral group occupying the large middle part of the curve and the moral and immoral categories occupying the smaller tails of the curve. It is difficult to research this question. If you asked managers what they thought they were or what others thought they were, a self-serving bias would likely enter in and you would not get an accurate, unbiased answer. Another approach would be to observe management actions. This would be nearly impossible because it is not possible to observe all management actions for any sustained period. Therefore, the supposition remains a hypothesis based on one person's judgment of what is going on in the management population.

This proposed normal curve distribution is similar to behavioral economist Dan Ariely's belief that 1 percent of people would *never* steal, 1 percent would *always* try to steal, and 98 percent would be honest as long as they were not tempted. Ariely believes that most of us are 98-percenters. One of Ariely's students told him the story about a locksmith who helped him when he locked himself out of his house. Being amazed at how easily and quickly the locksmith was able to pick the lock, the locksmith told him that the locks were there to keep the honest people from stealing. The locks remove the temptation for most people.[53] It is uncertain whether the large middle group of amoral managers would cheat or not if tempted, but the normal curve distribution pattern is strikingly similar.

Individual Hypothesis. Equally disturbing as the belief that the amoral management style is common among the managerial population today is an alternative hypothesis, the **individual hypothesis**, which holds that within each *individual* manager, these three models may operate at various times and under various circumstances. That is, the average manager himself or herself may be amoral most of the time but may slide into a moral or an immoral mode on occasion, based on a variety of impinging factors. Like the population hypothesis, this view cannot be empirically supported at this time, but it does provide an interesting perspective for managers to ponder. This perspective would be somewhat similar to the situational ethics argument that has been around for some time. Is the individual hypothesis more likely valid than the population hypothesis? Could it be that both may exist at the same time?

Amoral Management Is a Serious Organizational Problem. With the exception of the major ethics scandals witnessed in the past couple decades, it could be argued that the more insidious ethical problem in organizations today seems to be the group of managers who for one reason or another subscribe to or live out the amoral management ethic pattern. These are managers who are driven primarily by profitability or a bottom-line ethos, which regards economic success as the exclusive barometer of organizational and personal achievement. These amoral managers are not necessarily bad people, but they essentially see the competitive business world as ethically neutral. Until this group of managers moves toward the moral management ethic, we will continue to see businesses and other organizations criticized as they have been in the past.

To connect the three models of management morality with concepts introduced earlier, we show in Figure 7-11 how the components of corporate social responsibility (Chapter 2) would likely be viewed by managers using each of the three models of management morality.

FIGURE 7-11 Three Models of Management Morality and Emphases on CSR

Models of Management Morality	Components of the CSR Definition			
	Economic Responsibility	Legal Responsibility	Ethical Responsibility	Philanthropic Responsibility
Immoral management	XXX	X		
Amoral management	XXX	XX	X	X
Moral management	XXX	XXX	XXX	XXX

Weighting code:
X = token consideration (appearances only)
XX = moderate consideration
XXX = significant consideration

FIGURE 7-12 The Moral Management Models and Acceptance or Rejection of Stakeholder Thinking (SHT)

Moral Management Model	Acceptance of Stakeholder Thinking (SHT)	Explanation of Stakeholder Thinking Posture Embraced
Immoral management	SHT rejected: management is self absorbed	SHT rejected, not deemed useful. Accepts profit maximization model. Does not pursue SHT.
Amoral management	SHT accepted: narrow view (minimum number of stakeholders considered)	Instrumental view of SHT prevails. How will it help management?
Moral management	SHT enthusiastically embraced: wider view (maximum number of stakeholders considered)	Normative view of SHT prevails. SHT is fully embraced in all decision making.

Figure 7-12 displays how managers using the three models would probably embrace or reject the stakeholder concept or stakeholder thinking (Chapter 3). Recall that an acceptance of stakeholder thinking (SHT) means that the ethical management type would use the more inclusive stakeholder model in her or his decision making. It is expected that immoral managers would reject considering stakeholders. The figure also gives explanations of the SHT posture embraced by that ethical management type. It is hoped that these suggested interrelationships among these concepts will make them easier to understand and appreciate.

7.5 Making Moral Management Actionable

The characteristics of immoral, moral, and amoral management discussed in this chapter should provide some useful benchmarks for managerial self-analysis because self analysis and introspection significantly help managers recognize the need to move from the immoral or amoral ethic to the moral ethic. Organizational leaders must acknowledge that amoral management is a morally vacuous condition that can be quite easily disguised as just an innocent, practical, bottom-line philosophy—something to take pride in. Amoral management is, however, and will continue to be, the bane of the management profession until it is recognized for what it really is and until managers take steps to overcome it. Most managers are not "bad guys," as they sometimes are portrayed, but the idea that managerial decision making can be ethically neutral is bankrupt and not tenable in today's world.[54] To make moral management actionable, both immoral and amoral management must be discarded and the process of developing moral judgment begun.

7.6 Developing Moral Judgment

As a manager, it is helpful to know something about how people, whether they are managers or employees, develop moral (or ethical) judgment. Perhaps if we knew more about this maturation process, we could better understand our own behavior and the behavior of those around us and those we manage. Further, we might be able to better design reward systems for encouraging ethical behavior if we knew more about how employees and others think and process issues about ethics. A good starting point is to appreciate what psychologists have to say about how we as individuals develop morally. The major research on this issue is **Kohlberg's levels of moral development**.[55] After this discussion,

FIGURE 7-13 Kohlberg's Levels of Moral Development

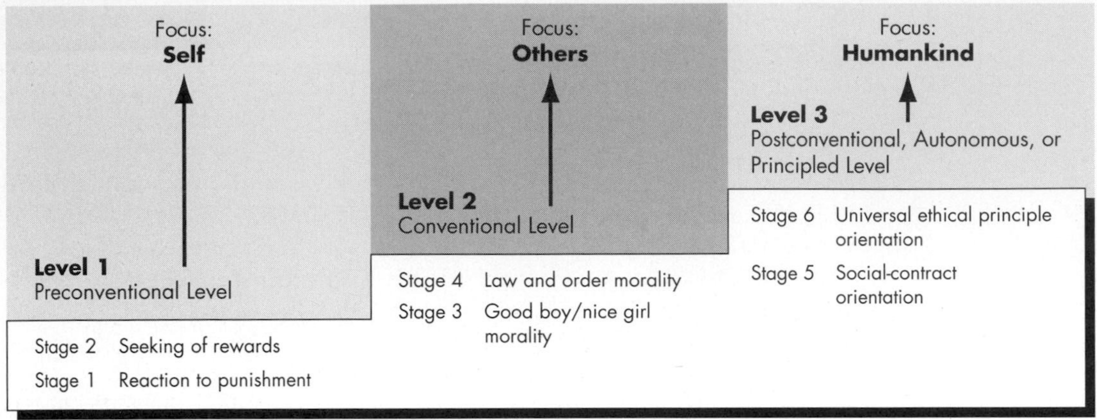

we consider other sources of a manager's values, especially those emanating from both societal sources and from within the organization itself.

7.6a Levels of Moral Development

The psychologist, Lawrence Kohlberg, conducted extensive research into the topic of **moral development**. He concluded, on the basis of over 20 years of research, that there is a general sequence of three levels (each with two stages) through which individuals progress in learning to think or develop morally. There is widespread academic and practical usage of his levels of moral development, and this suggests a general if not unanimous consensus that it is valuable. Figure 7-13 illustrates Kohlberg's three levels and six stages. There it can be seen that as one develops morally, the focus moves from the *self*, to *others*, and then *to humankind*. Understanding this progression is of great value in developing a basic foundation in business ethics and leadership.

Level 1: Preconventional Level. At the **preconventional level of moral development**, which is typically characteristic of how people behave as infants and children, the focus is mainly on the *self*. As an infant starts to grow, his or her main behavioral reactions are in response to punishments and rewards. Stage 1 is the *reaction-to-punishment stage*. If you want a child to do something (such as stay out of the street) at a very early age, scolding or disciplining often is needed. The child's orientation at this stage is toward the avoidance of pain.

As the youngster gets a bit older, rewards start to work. Stage 2 is the *seeking-of-rewards stage*. The youngster begins to see some connection between being "good" (i.e., doing what Mom or Dad wants the child to do) and some reward that may be forthcoming. The reward may be parental praise or something tangible, such as ice cream, extra TV time, or getting to use Mom or Dad's iPad. At this preconventional level, children do not completely understand the moral idea of "right" and "wrong" but rather learn to behave according to the consequences—punishments or rewards—that are likely to follow.

Though we normally associate the preconventional level with the moral development of children, many adults in organizations are significantly influenced by rewards and punishments. Consequently, the preconventional level of motivation may be observed in adults as well as children and is relevant to a discussion of adult moral maturity. Like children, adults in responsible positions react to punishments (organizational sanctions) or seek rewards (approval). In fact, some adults get stuck at this level of moral development.

Level 2: Conventional Level. As a person matures, she or he learns that there are *others* whose ideas or welfare ought to be considered. Initially, these others include family and friends. At the **conventional level of moral development**, the individual learns the importance of conforming to the conventional norms of the group or society. This is the level at which social relationships form and become dominant.

The conventional level is composed of two stages. Stage 3 has been called the *"good boy/nice girl" morality stage*. The young person learns that there are some rewards (such as feelings of acceptance, trust, loyalty, or friendship) for living up to what is expected by family and peers, so the individual begins to conform to what is generally expected of a good son, daughter, sister, brother, friend, and so on.

Stage 4 is the *law-and-order morality stage*. Not only does the individual learn to respond to family, friends, the school, and the church, as in Stage 3, but the individual now recognizes that there are certain norms in society (in school, in the theater, in the mall, in stores, in the car, waiting in line) that are expected or needed if society is to function in an orderly fashion. Thus, the individual becomes socialized or acculturated into what being a good citizen means. These "law-and-order" rules for living include not only the actual laws (don't run a red light, don't walk until the "Walk" light comes on, don't text or talk while driving) but also other, less official norms (don't break into line, be sure to tip the server, mute your cell phone in restaurants).

At Stage 4, the individual sees that she or he is part of a larger social system and that to function in and be accepted by this social system requires a considerable degree of acceptance of and conformity to the norms and standards of society. Therefore, many organizational members are strongly influenced by society's conventions as manifested in both Stages 3 and 4 as described. Most adults do reach Level 2 of Kohlberg's levels.

Level 3: Postconventional, Autonomous, or Principled Level. At this third level, which Kohlberg argues few people reach (and those who do reach it have trouble staying there), the focus moves beyond those "others" who are of immediate importance to the individual to *humankind* as a whole. At the **postconventional level of moral development**, the individual develops a concept of ethics that is more mature than the conventionally articulated situation. Thus, it is sometimes called the level at which moral principles become self-accepted, not because they are held by society but because the individual now perceives and embraces them as "right."

Kohlberg's third level consists of two stages that differ by whether the individual can just follow rules established by society or others, or engage in his or her own moral reasoning. Stage 5 is the *social-contract orientation*. At this stage, right action is thought of in terms of general individual rights and standards that have been critically examined and agreed upon by society as a whole. Social contracts have influence. There is a clear awareness of the relativism of personal values and a corresponding emphasis on fair processes for reaching consensus.

Stage 6 is the *universal-ethical-principle orientation*. Here, the individual uses his or her thinking and conscience in accord with self-chosen ethical principles that are anticipated to be universal, comprehensive, and consistent. These universal principles (e.g., the Golden Rule) might be focused on such ideals as justice, human rights, reciprocity, and social welfare. At this stage, the individual is motivated by a commitment to universal principles or guidelines for humankind.

Kohlberg suggests that at Level 3, the individual is able to rise above the conventional level where "rightness" and "wrongness" are defined by others and societal institutions and that she or he is able to defend or justify her or his actions on some higher ethical basis. For example, in our society the law tells us we should not discriminate against minorities. A Level 2 manager might not discriminate because to do so is to violate the law and social custom. A Level 3 manager would not discriminate but might offer a different reason—for example, it is wrong to discriminate because it violates universal principles of human rights and justice. Part of the difference between Levels 2 and 3, therefore, is traceable to the motivation for the course of action taken. The authenticity of one's motives is crucial at Level 3.

The discussion to this point may have suggested that we are at Level 1 as infants, at Level 2 as youths, and, finally, at Level 3 as adults. There is some approximate correspondence between chronological age and Levels 1 and 2, but the important point should be made that Kohlberg thinks many of us as adults never get beyond Level 2. The idea of getting to Level 3 as managers or employees is desirable because it would require us to think about people, products, and markets at a higher ethical level than that generally attained by conventional society. However, even if we never get there, Level 3 urges us to continually ask "What ought to be?" The first two levels tell us a lot about moral development that should be useful to us as managers. There are not many people who consistently operate according to Level 3 principles. Sometimes a manager or employee may dip into Level 3 on a certain issue or for a certain period of time. Sustaining that level, however, is quite challenging.

If we frame the issue in terms of the question, "Why do managers and employees behave ethically?" we might infer conclusions from Kohlberg that look like those presented in Figure 7-14. These conclusions attempt to generalize about people's reactions to various factors.

Ethics of Care as Alternative to Kohlberg. One of the major criticisms of Kohlberg's research was set forth by psychologist Carol Gilligan. Gilligan argued that

FIGURE 7-14 Why Managers and Employees Behave Ethically

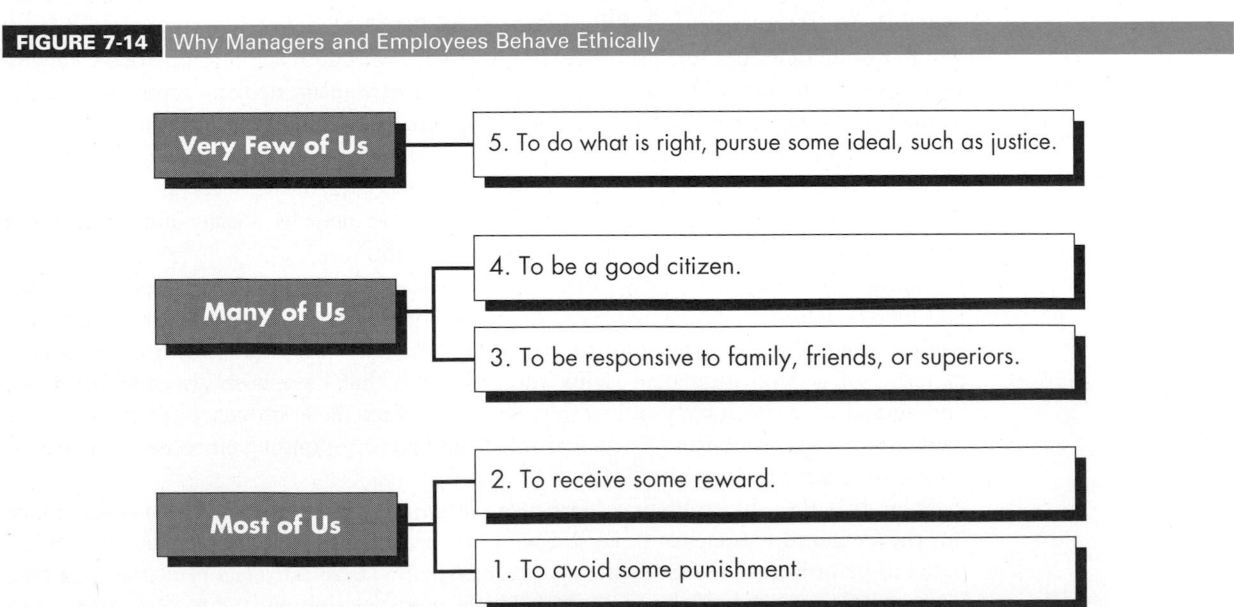

Kohlberg's conclusions may accurately depict the stages of moral development among men, whom he used as his research subjects, but that his findings are not generalizable to women.[56] According to Gilligan's view, men tend to deal with moral issues in terms that are impersonal, impartial, and abstract. Examples might include the principles of justice and rights that Kohlberg argues are relevant at the postconventional level. Women, on the other hand, perceive themselves to be part of a network of relationships with family and friends and thus are more focused on *relationship maintenance* and *hurt avoidance* when they confront moral issues. For women, then, morality is often more a matter of caring and showing responsibility toward those involved in their relationships than in adhering to abstract or impersonal principles, such as justice. This alternative view of ethics has been called the **ethics of care**.

According to Gilligan, women move in and out of three moral levels.[57] At the first level, the *self* is the sole object of concern. At the second level, the chief desire is to *establish connections and participate* in social life. In other words, maintaining relationships or directing one's thoughts toward others becomes dominant. Gilligan says that this is the conventional perception of women. At the third level, women recognize their own needs and the *needs of others*—those with whom they have relationships. Gilligan goes on to say that women never settle completely at one level. As they attain moral maturity, they do more of their thinking and make more of their decisions at the third level. This level requires care for others as well as care for oneself. In this view, morality moves away from the legalistic, self-centered approach that some say characterizes traditional ethics.

Some research does not support the view that moral development varies by gender in the fashion described by Gilligan. However, it does support Gilligan's claim that a different perspective toward moral issues is sometimes used. Apparently, both men and women sometimes employ an impartial or impersonal moral-rules perspective and sometimes they employ a care-and-responsibility perspective. This "care perspective" is still at an early stage of research, but it is useful to know that perspectives other than those found by Kohlberg are being considered.[58] More will be said about the ethics of care in the next chapter. In the final analysis, we need to exercise caution when thinking about the applicability of Kohlberg's and Gilligan's research as well as the thousands of studies that have sought to fine tune their research. The value of this research, however, is the idea that moral development levels and stages do occur and that managers need to be aware of and sensitive to this in their approaches to dealing with people and ethics challenges in their organizations. Research on this topic is ongoing.

7.6b Different Sources of a Person's Values

In addition to considering the levels of moral development as an explanation of how and why people behave ethically, it is also useful to look at the different *sources of a manager's (employee's) values*. Ethics and values are intimately related. We referred earlier to ethics as the set of moral principles or values that drives behavior. Thus, the rightness or wrongness of behavior, sense of fairness, and sense of justice really turns out to be a manifestation of the ethical beliefs held by the individual. Values, on the other hand, are the individual's concepts of the relative worth, utility, or importance of certain ideas. Values reflect what the individual considers important in the larger scheme of things. One's values, therefore, shape one's ethics. They are closely interrelated. Because this is so, it is important to understand the many different value-shaping forces that influence employees and managers.

The increasing pluralism of the society in which we live has exposed managers to a large number of values of many different kinds, and this has resulted in ethical diversity. One way to examine the sources of a manager's values is by considering both forces that originate from *outside the organization* to shape or influence the manager and those that

ETHICS IN PRACTICE CASE

Are People More Ethical When Being "Watched?"

Most people would probably say they would be more honest if they were being watched. This is human nature, isn't it? A team of researchers at Newcastle University in the United Kingdom decided to test this proposition by creating an experiment.

The setting for the experiment was the often seen coffee station set up in a department break room where faculty and staff could help themselves to coffee, tea, or milk during the day and then place their payment for the refreshments in a jar or a box. The "honor system" was requested because there was no one at the station to monitor whether people actually paid or not. The department had been using an "honesty box" for people to place their money in for years.

The researchers decided to post the prices for the coffee, tea, and milk on a poster that featured a banner across the top that contained images that were alternated without announcement from week to week. The poster was placed above the coffee station. The alternating images included a set of eyes and a picture of flowers. The image of eyes was varied in their gender and position, but they were always situated so that they appeared to be looking directly at the person.

The research team collected the money each week and recorded how much had been placed in the box. The team calculated that, on average, the amount collected when the "eyes poster" was present was 2.76 times the amount collected when the flowers poster was there. The researchers concluded that the effect of being "watched" had the subconscious effect of improving people's honesty. But, the researchers were surprised at how large an effect resulted from being watched.

Later, the question was raised whether using "watching eyes" could curb dishonest behaviors in other settings. A police department in Birmingham, U.K. decided to test whether it worked to deter crime by posting pictures of staring eyes all over the city. Time will tell whether this approach to keeping crime at bay will work.

1. Was it unethical for the research team to conduct this experiment without telling people it was going on?
2. Do the results of the experiment surprise you? What ethical phenomena were at work here?
3. Evaluate the experiment using Kohlberg's levels of moral development. Does the experiment tend to support or refute Kohlberg's findings? Do you think it would make a difference whether the coffee drinkers were men or women?
4. How could managers use the conclusions reached in this experiment?
5. Will the police department experiment work? Why? Why not?

Sources: "Big Brother Eyes Encourage Honesty, Study Shows," http://www.sciencedaily.com/releases/2006/06/060628091247.htm. Accessed February 12, 2016; "Watchful gaze that can keep you honest," http://www.independent.co.uk/news/science/watchful-gaze-that-can-keep-you-honest-6096951.html. Accessed February 12, 2016; "Big Brother Eyes Encourage Honesty," http://psychcentral.com/news/archives/2006-06/uonu-be062606.html.
Accessed February 12, 2016.

emanate from *within the organization.* This, unfortunately, is not as simply done as we would like because some sources are difficult to pinpoint. This discussion expands on and organizes some of the sources of ethical norms depicted earlier in Figure 7-4.

Sources External to the Organization: The Web of Values. The external sources of a person's values refer to those broad sociocultural values that have emerged in society over a long period of time. Although current events (scandals, fraud, deception, bribery) seem to affect these historic values by bringing specific ones into clearer focus at a given time, these values are rather enduring and change slowly. It has been stated that "every executive resides at the center of a web of values" and that there are five principal repositories of values influencing businesspeople. These five include religious, philosophical, cultural, legal, and professional values.[59] Each deserves brief consideration.

Religious Values Religion and faith have long been a basic source of morality in most societies. Religion and morality are so intertwined that William Barclay related them for definitional purposes: "Ethics is the bit of religion that tells us how we ought to behave."[60] The biblical tradition of Judeo-Christian theology forms the core for much of what Western society believes today about the importance of work, the concept of fairness, and the dignity of the individual. Other religious traditions also inform management behavior and action.[61]

Philosophical Values Philosophy and various philosophical systems are also external sources of the manager's values. Beginning with preachments of the ancient Greeks, philosophers have claimed to demonstrate that *reason* can provide us with principles or morals in the same way it gives us the principles of mathematics. John Locke argued that morals are mathematically demonstrable, although he never explained how.[62] Aristotle with his Golden Rule and his doctrine of the mean, Kant with his categorical imperative, Bentham with his pain and pleasure calculus, and modern-day existentialists have shown us the influence of various kinds of reasoning for ethical choice. Today, the strong influences of moral relativism and postmodernism have influenced some people's values.

Cultural Values Culture is that broad synthesis of societal norms and values emanating from everyday living. Culture has also had an impact on the manager's and employees' thinking. Modern sources of culture include music, movies, television, video games, social networking, and the Internet. The melting-pot culture of many countries today is a potpourri of norms, customs, and rules that defy summarization. In recent years, it has become difficult to summarize what messages the culture is sending people about ethics. In an influential book, *Moral Freedom: The Search for Virtue in a World of Choice*, by Alan Wolfe, the author argues that the United States, like other Western nations, is undergoing a radical revolution in morals and is now, morally speaking, a new society.[63] Wolfe thinks the traditional values that our culture has looked upon with authority (churches, families, neighborhoods, civic leaders) have lost the ability to influence people as they once did.

Wolfe goes on to say that as more and more areas of life have become democratized and open to consumer "choice," people have come to assume that they are free to determine for themselves what it means to lead a good and virtuous life. He says that a key element in this new moral universe is nonjudgmentalism, which pushes society to suspend judgment on much immoral behavior or interpret immoral behavior as not the fault of the perpetrator. Thus, although many people may uphold the old virtues, in principle, they turn them into personal "options" in practice.[64] These trends are clearly a departure from the past, and are likely impacting the way managers perceive the world of business. Employees, likewise, share these same perspectives and this creates challenges for managers.

Legal Values The legal system has been and continues to be one of the most powerful forces defining what is ethical and what is not for managers and employees. This is true even though ethical behavior generally is that which occurs over and above legal dictates. As stated earlier, the law represents the codification of what the society considers right and wrong or fair. Although we as members of society do not completely agree with every law in existence, there often is more consensus for law than for ethics. Law, then, "mirrors the ideas of the entire society."[65] Law represents a minimum ethic of behavior but does not encompass all the ethical standards of behavior. Law addresses only the grossest violations of society's sense of right, wrong, and fairness and thus is not adequate to describe completely all that is acceptable or unacceptable. Because it represents our official consensus ethic, however, its influence is pervasive and widely accepted.

In recent years, it has become an understatement to observe that we live in a litigious society. This trend toward suing someone to bring about justice has clearly had an impact on management decision making. Whereas the threat of litigation may make managers more careful in their treatment of stakeholders, the threat of losing tens or hundreds of millions of dollars has distorted decision making and caused many managers and companies to be running scared—never knowing exactly what is the best or fairest course of action to pursue. Therefore, it is easy to see how laws and regulations are among the most influential drivers of business ethics.[66]

Professional Values These include those values emanating from professional organizations and societies that represent various jobs and positions. As such, they presumably articulate the ethical consensus of the leaders of those professions. For example, the Public Relations Society of America has a code of ethics that public relations executives have imposed on themselves as their own guide to behavior. The National Association of Realtors has created its own code of conduct. Professional values thus exert a more particularized impact on the manager than the four broader values discussed earlier. Though there is not a generally accepted code of conduct or ethics for general managers, in recent years The Oath Project has sought to establish enhanced professionalization of management by proposing and gaining signatories to a form of a "Hippocratic oath for business" which would help integrate professional conduct and social responsibility into the culture, core values, and day-to-day operations of corporations and academic institutions.[67]

In sum, several sources of values are external to the organization and they come to bear on the manager and employees and influence their ethics. In addition to those mentioned, people are influenced by family, friends, acquaintances, and social events and current events of the day as depicted earlier in Figure 7-4. People thus come to the workplace with personal philosophies that truly are a composite of numerous interacting values that have shaped their views of the world, of life, and of business.

Sources Internal to the Organization. The external forces constitute the broad background or milieu against which a manager or an employee behaves or acts. There are, in addition, a number of more immediate factors that help to channel the individual's values and behavior. These values grow out of the specific organizational experience itself. These internal (within the organization) sources of a manager's values constitute more immediate and direct influences on one's actions and decisions.

When an individual goes to work for an organization, a *socialization process* takes place in which the individual comes to learn and adopt the predominant values of that organization. The individual learns rather quickly that to survive and to succeed, certain norms must be internalized, honored, and perpetuated. This is a process of learning and adapting to the organization's culture. Several of these "internal" norms that are prevalent in business organizations include:

- Respect for the authority structure
- Loyalty to bosses and the organization
- Conformity to principles, practices, and traditions
- Performance counts above all else
- Results count above all else

Each of these norms may take on a major influence in a person who subordinates her or his own standard of ethics to those of the organization. In fact, research suggests that these internal sources play a much more significant role in shaping business ethics than do the host of external sources we considered first. *Respect for the authority structure, loyalty, conformity, performance*, and *results* have been historically synonymous with survival and success in business. When these influences are operating together, they form a composite **"bottom-line" mentality** that is remarkably influential in its impact on individual and group behavior. These values form the central motif of organizational activity and direction.

Underlying the first three norms is the focus on performance and results. This has been called the "calculus of the bottom line."[68] One does not need to study business organizations for long to recognize that the bottom line—profits—is the sacred instrumental value that seems to take precedence over all others. "Profits now" rather than later seems to be the orientation that spells success for managers and employees alike. Respect for authority, loyalty, and conformity become means to an end, although one could certainly find organizations and people who see these as legitimate ends in themselves. The impact of the bottom-line mentality is explored further in Chapter 8 when we discuss the powerful influence leaders have over employees and peers. Only recently are some managers and organizations starting to respond to the "multiple bottom line" or "triple-bottom-line" perspective introduced in Chapter 2. From the standpoint of sustainability, managers will increasingly need to think and practice beyond that which is dictated by the short-term obsession with quarterly earnings.

7.7 Elements of Moral Judgment

A positive way to close out this chapter is to consider what it takes for moral or ethical judgment to develop. For growth in moral judgment to take place, it is necessary to appreciate the key elements involved in making moral judgments. This is a notion central to the transition from the amoral management condition to the moral management condition. Powers and Vogel have suggested that there are six major elements or capacities that are essential to making moral judgments: (1) moral imagination, (2) moral identification and ordering, (3) moral evaluation, (4) tolerance of moral disagreement and ambiguity, (5) integration of managerial and moral competence, and (6) a sense of moral obligation.[69] Each reveals an essential ingredient in developing moral judgment, which then forms the basis for managerial and organizational ethics to be examined in the next chapter.

7.7a Moral Imagination

Moral imagination refers to the ability to perceive that a web of competing economic relationships is, at the same time, a web of moral or ethical relationships. Business and ethics are not separate topics but occur side by side in organizations. Those with moral imagination are able to perceive more clearly the presence of ethical issues and develop creative ways for dealing with them. Developing moral imagination means not only becoming sensitive to ethical issues in business decision making but also developing the perspective of *searching out* subtle places where people are likely to be harmfully affected by adverse decision making or behaviors of managers. Moral imagination requires the manager to rise above the everyday stress and confusion and carefully identify the ethical issues and values conflicts that exist in the organization or for which symptoms of problems may be present.[70]

7.7b Moral Identification and Ordering

Moral identification and ordering refers to the ability to discern the relevance or nonrelevance of moral factors that are introduced into a decision-making situation. Are the moral issues actual or just rhetorical? The ability to see moral issues as issues that can be dealt with is at stake here. Once moral issues have been identified, they must be ranked, or ordered, just as economic or technological issues are prioritized during the decision-making process. A manager must not only develop this skill through experience but also finely hone it through repetition and the application of ethics principles. In this prioritizing process, for example, a manager may conclude that worker safety is more important than worker privacy, though both are important qualities.

7.7c Moral Evaluation

Once issues have been imagined, identified, and ordered, evaluations must be made. *Moral evaluation* is the practical, decision phase of moral judgment and entails essential skills, such as coherence and consistency that have proved to be effective principles in other contexts. What managers need to do here is to understand the importance of clear principles, develop processes for weighing ethical factors, and develop the ability to identify what the likely moral as well as economic outcomes of a decision will be. Important here is the foresight of likely consequences of different courses of action.

The real challenge in moral evaluation is to integrate the concern for others into organizational goals, purposes, and legitimacy. In the final analysis, though, the manager may not know the "right" answer or solution, although moral sensitivity has been introduced into the process.

7.7d Tolerance of Moral Disagreement and Ambiguity

An objection managers often have to ethics discussions is the amount of disagreement generated and the volume of ambiguity that must be tolerated. This must be accepted, however, because it is a natural part of ethics discussions. To be sure, managers need closure and precision in their decisions. But the situation is not always clear in moral discussions, just as it is in many traditional and more familiar decision contexts of managers, such as introducing a new product based on limited test marketing, choosing a new executive for a key position, deciding which of a number of excellent computer systems to install, or making a strategic decision based on instincts. All of these are risky decisions, but managers have become accustomed to making them in spite of the disagreements and ambiguity that prevail among those involved in the decision or within the individual. The *tolerance of moral disagreement and ambiguity* is simply an extension of a managerial aptitude that is present in practically all decision-making situations managers face. It includes the ability to hear, discuss and be respectful toward other people's views.[71]

7.7e Integration of Managerial and Moral Competence

The *integration of managerial and moral competence* is a necessary capability to make ethical decisions in organizations. Moral issues in management do not arise in isolation from traditional business decision making but right in the middle of it. The scandals that major corporations face today did not occur independently of the companies' economic activities but were embedded in a series of decisions made at various points in time and culminated from those earlier decisions. Therefore, moral competence is an integral part of managerial competence. Managers are learning—some the hard way—that there is a significant corporate, and in many instances, personal price to pay for their amorality. The amoral manager sees ethical decisions as isolated and independent of managerial decisions and competence, but the moral manager sees every evolving decision as one in which an ethical perspective must be integrated. This kind of future-looking view is essential to sustainable organizations.

7.7f A Sense of Moral Obligation

The foundation for all the capacities we have discussed is a *sense of moral obligation*[72] and integrity. This wisdom is the key to the process but is the most difficult to acquire. Developing a sense of moral obligation requires the intuitive or learned understanding that moral threads—a concern for fairness, justice, and due process to people, groups, and communities—are woven into the fabric of managerial decision making and are the integral components that hold systems together.

These elements of moral judgment are perfectly consistent with, and indeed are essential prerequisites to, the free enterprise system as we know it today. One can go back in time to Adam Smith and the foundation tenets of the free enterprise system and find references to moral and ethical practices as being qualities needed for the system to work.[73]

FIGURE 7-15 Elements of Moral Judgment in Amoral and Moral Managers

Amoral Managers	Moral Managers
Moral Imagination	
See a web of competing economic claims as just that and nothing more.	Perceive that a web of competing economic claims is simultaneously a web of moral relationships.
Are insensitive to and unaware of the hidden dimensions of where people are likely to get hurt.	Are sensitive to and hunt out the hidden dimensions of where people are likely to get hurt.
Moral Identification and Ordering	
See moral claims as squishy and not definite enough to order into hierarchies with other claims.	See which moral claims being made are relevant or irrelevant; order moral factors just as economic factors are ordered.
Moral Evaluation	
Are erratic in their application of ethics if it gets applied at all.	Are coherent and consistent in their normative reasoning.
Tolerance of Moral Disagreement and Ambiguity	
Cite ethical disagreement and ambiguity as reasons for forgetting ethics altogether.	Tolerate ethical disagreement and ambiguity while honestly acknowledging that decisions are not precise like mathematics but must finally be made nevertheless.
Integration of Managerial and Moral Competence	
See ethical decisions as isolated and independent of managerial decisions and managerial competence.	See every evolving decision as one in which a moral perspective must be integrated with a managerial one.
A Sense of Moral Obligation	
Have no sense of moral obligation and integrity that extends beyond managerial responsibility.	Have a sense of moral obligation and integrity that holds together the decision-making process in which human welfare is at stake.

Source: Archie B. Carroll, "In Search of the Moral Manager," *Business Horizons* (March/April 1987), 15. Copyright © 1987 by the Foundation for the School of Business at Indiana University. Used with permission.

The late Milton Friedman, our modern-day Adam Smith, even alluded to the importance of ethics when he stated that the purpose of business is "to make as much money as possible while conforming to the basic rules of society, both those embodied in the law and *those embodied in ethical custom*."[74] The moral manager develops a sense of moral obligation and integrity that is the glue that holds together the decision-making process in which human welfare is inevitably at stake. Indeed, the sense of moral obligation is what holds society and the business system together as a sustainable enterprise.

Figure 7-15 summarizes the six elements of moral judgment identified by Powers and Vogel as they might be perceived by amoral and moral managers. The contrast between the two perspectives should be helpful in understanding each element of moral judgment.

Summary

Business ethics has become a serious challenge for the business community over the past several decades. The major ethics scandals of the past couple decades affected the public's trust of executives and major business institutions. The Wall Street financial scandals brought the public's trust of business into further question. Polls indicate that the public does not have a high regard for the ethics of business or managers.

It is not easy to say whether business's ethics have declined or just seem to have done so because of increased media coverage and rising public expectations. Business ethics concerns the rightness, wrongness, and fairness of managerial practices and policies and these are not easy judgments to make. Multiple norms compete to as to which standards business behavior should be compared.

The conventional approach to business ethics was introduced as the way that average people on the street or in organizations might reason through ethical situations. One major challenge with this approach is that it is not clear which standards or norms should be used, and thus conventional thinking is susceptible to ethical relativism and misjudgment. Though conventional thinking has value, the varied sources of norms informing decision making can often result in confusion and conflicting expectations.

A Venn diagram model was presented as an aid to making decisions when economics, law, and ethics expectations compete with each other and are in tension. Three models of management ethics were presented: (1) immoral management, (2) moral management, and (3) amoral management. Amoral management is further classified into intentional and unintentional categories. There are two hypotheses about the presence of these three moral types in the management population and in individuals themselves.

Understanding how moral judgment develops is helpful to aspiring managers. A generally accepted view is that moral judgment develops similar to the pattern described by Lawrence Kohlberg. His three levels of moral development reflect how individuals progress in their thinking: (1) preconventional, (2) conventional, and (3) postconventional, autonomous, or principled. Gilligan and others have suggested that men and women use different perspectives as they perceive and deal with moral issues. Care must be exercised in generalizing about the process of moral development.

In addition to moral maturity, managers' ethics are affected by sources of values originating from external to the organization and from sources within the organization. This latter category includes respect for the authority structure, loyalty, conformity, and a concern for financial performance and results. Together, they represent the "bottom line" mentality. It is toward these values that much business ethics thinking is addressed.

Finally, six elements in developing moral judgment were presented. These six elements include (1) moral imagination, (2) moral identification and ordering, (3) moral evaluation, (4) tolerance of moral disagreement and ambiguity, (5) integration of managerial and moral competence, and (6) a sense of moral obligation. If the moral management model is to be sustained, these six elements need to be developed and successfully integrated.

Key Terms

amoral management, p. 204
bottom-line mentality, p. 216
business ethics, p. 190
compliance strategy, p. 205
conventional approach to business ethics, p. 191
conventional level of moral judgment (level 2), p. 211
descriptive ethics, p. 190
elements of moral judgment, p. 199
ethical relativism, p. 196
ethical tests approach, p. 197
ethics, p. 190
Gilligan's ethics of care, p. 213
individual hypothesis, p. 208
immoral management, p. 199
integrity strategy, p. 202
intentional amoral management, p. 204
Kohlberg's levels of moral development, p. 209
moral development, p. 210
moral management, p. 201
normative ethics, p. 191
population hypothesis, p. 207
preconventional level of moral judgment (level 1), p. 210
principles approach, p. 196
postconventional level of moral development, p. 211
unintentional amoral management, p. 204

Discussion Questions

1. Give a definition of ethical business behavior, explain the components involved in making ethical decisions, and give an example from your personal experience of the sources of ethical norms that affect you while making these determinations.
2. To demonstrate that you understand the three models of management ethics—moral, immoral, and amoral—give an example, from your personal experience, of each type. Do you agree that amorality is a serious problem? Explain.

3. Give examples, from your personal experience, of Kohlberg's Levels 1, 2, and 3. If you do not think you have ever gotten to Level 3, give an example of what it might be like.
4. Compare your motivations to behave ethically with those listed in Figure 7-14. Do the reasons given in that figure agree with your personal assessment? Discuss the similarities and differences between Figure 7-14 and your personal assessment.
5. From your personal experience, give an example of a situation you have faced that would require one of the six elements of moral judgment. Which of these six elements are most important and why?

Endnotes

1. For a history of business ethics, see Richard T. DeGeorge, "The History of Business Ethics," in Marc J. Epstein and Kirk O. Hanson (eds.), *The Accountable Corporation, Business Ethics*, Vol. 2 (Westport, CT: Praeger Publishers, 2006), 47–58.
2. Cathy Booth Thomas, "The Enron Effect," *Time* (June 5, 2006), 34–35.
3. Archie B. Carroll, "Two Scandals and the Decade Isn't over Yet," *Athens Banner Herald* (November 16, 2008), http://onlineathens.com/stories/111608/bus_356090174.shtml. Accessed April 27, 2013.
4. William D. Cohan, "Can Bankers Behave?" *The Atlantic*, May 2015, 75–80.
5. Ibid., 76.
6. Victoria McGrane, "Yellen Scolds Wall Street on Culture, Ethics," *Wall Street Journal*, March 4, 2015, C5.
7. William D. Cohan, "How the Bankers Stayed out of Jail," *The Atlantic*, September 2015, 20–21.
8. Gallup Poll, "Honesty/Ethics in the Professions," December 2–6, 2015, http://www.gallup.com/poll/1654/honesty-ethics-professions.aspx. Accessed February 8, 2016.
9. Ibid.
10. Ethics Resource Center, "The 2013 National Business Ethics Survey," https://www.ethics.org/research/eci-research/nbes/nbes-reports/nbes-2013. Accessed February 8, 2016.
11. Ibid.
12. Emily Stewart, "CEO's Just Can't Let Go of the Company Jet for Personal Use—Even When They Should," The Street, http://www.thestreet.com/story/13085659/1/ceos-just-cant-let-go-of-the-company-jet-for-personal-use-even-when-they-should.html. Accessed April 22, 2016.
13. Diffen, "Ethics vs. Morals," http://www.diffen.com/difference/Ethics_vs_Morals. Accessed February 9, 2016.
14. Richard T. DeGeorge, *Business Ethics*, 4th ed. (New York: Prentice Hall, 1995), 20–21. See also Rogene A. Buchholz and Sandra B. , *Rosenthal, Business Ethics* (Upper Saddle River, NJ: Prentice Hall, 1998), 3.
15. DeGeorge, 15.
16. Kenneth E. Goodpaster, "Business Ethics," in Patricia H. Werhane and R. Edward Freeman (eds.), *The Blackwell Dictionary of Business Ethics* (Malden, MA: Blackwell Publishers, 1997), 51–57.
17. Ethics Alarms, "The Donald's Dangerous Ethics: Loyalty Trumps Honesty on Celebrity Apprentice," http://ethicsalarms.com/2012/04/10/the-donalds-dangerous-ethics-loyalty-trumps-honesty-on-celebrity-apprentice/ April 10, 2012. Accessed January 28, 2013.
18. Stephen Miller and Joe Palazzolo, "Scholar Argued for Moral Understanding of the Law," *Wall Street Journal*, February 15, 2013, A6.
19. Mark Gimein, "The Skilling Trap," *BusinessWeek* (June 12, 2006), 31.
20. Ibid., 32.
21. For more on ethics and the law, see William A. Wines, *Ethics, Law, and Business* (Mahwah, NJ: Lawrence Erlbaum Associates, Publishers, 2006).
22. See, for example, Melissa Baucus and Janet Near, "Can Illegal Corporate Behavior Be Predicted? An Event History Analysis," *Academy of Management Journal* (Vol. 34, No. 1, 1991), 9–36; and P. L. Cochran and D. Nigh, "Illegal Corporate Behavior and the Question of Moral Agency," in William C. Frederick (ed.), *Research in Corporate Social Performance and Policy*, Vol. 9 (Greenwich, CT: JAI Press, 1987), 73–91.
23. Mark S. Schwartz and Archie B. Carroll, "Corporate Social Responsibility: A Three-Domain Approach," *Business Ethics Quarterly* (Vol. 13, Issue 4, October 2003), 503–530.
24. Most of the material in this section comes from Archie B. Carroll, "In Search of the Moral Manager," *Business Horizons* (March/April 1987), 7–15. See also Archie B. Carroll, "Models of Management Morality for the New Millennium," *Business Ethics Quarterly* (Vol. 11, Issue 2, April 2001), 365–371.
25. *Dilbert* comic strip, by Scott Adams (September 15, 2007), http://www.dilbert.com. Accessed July 6, 2010.
26. Allan Sloan, "Laying Enron to Rest," *Newsweek* (June 5, 2006), 25–30.

27. "Kenneth Lay," *The Economist* (July 8, 2006), 81.
28. Daily Finance, "Wall Street Applauds as Enron the Play Dies on Broadway," May 7, 2010, http://www.dailyfinance.com/2010/05/07/wall-street-applauds-as-enron-the-play-dies-on-broadway/. Accessed March 4, 2013.
29. Andrew Dunn, "Lay, Skilling Assets Targeted by U.S. After Guilty Verdicts" (May 26, 2006), http://Bloomberg.com. Accessed May 26, 2006.
30. Kim Clark and Marianne Lavelle, "Guilty as Charged," *U.S. News & World Report* (June 5, 2006), 44–45.
31. The Enron Blog, "Status of Jeff Skilling," January 10, 2013, http://caraellison.wordpress.com/2013/01/10/status-of-jeff-skilling/. Accessed March 4, 2013.
32. Mimi Swartz, "Forgive Those Who Trespass against Us?" Texas Monthly, April 20, 2016, http://www.texasmonthly.com/articles/andy-fastow-enron-cfo-apology-tour/. Accessed April 22, 2016.
33. Jean Eaglesham, "The Shadow of Enron Still Lingers," *Wall Street Journal*, October 17, 2012, C1.
34. "Deloitte & Touche USA 2007 Ethics & Workplace" survey, 2007, Deloitte Development LLC, 16. Also see Deloitte, Leadership Counts, http://staging.ilo.org/public/libdoc/nonigo/2009/456844.pdf. Accessed February 11, 2016.
35. Ibid., 15.
36. Lynn Sharp Paine, "Managing for Organizational Integrity," *Harvard Business Review* (March–April 1994), 106–117.
37. Ibid., 111–112.
38. Archie B. Carroll, "The Moral Leader: Essential for Successful Corporate Citizenship," in Jorg Andriof and Malcolum McIntosh (eds.), *Perspectives on Corporate Citizenship* (Sheffield, UK: Greenleaf Publishing Co., 2001), 139–151.
39. Stephen Covey, *The Seven Habits of Highly Effective People* (New York: Simon & Schuster, 1989).
40. Carroll (2001), ibid., 145–150.
41. "Deloitte & Touche USA 2007 Ethics & Workplace" survey, 15.
42. Abc news, Michael Murray and Lisa Stark, "American Heart: Volunteer and Save Your Job," http://abcnews.go.com/WN/navistar-saves-jobs-50-employees-volunteering-program/story?id=10104687. Accessed February 11, 2016; PR News, Navistar wins platinum PR award for "A boss saves jobs, helps the community," http://www.prnewsonline.com/featured/2011/09/29/navistar-wins-platinum-pr-award-for-a-boss-saves-jobs-helps-the-community-campaign/. Accessed February 11, 2016.
43. Marian Accardi, The Huntsville Times, "Navistar Employees Return to Their Plants after Nonprofit Work," April 19, 2010, http://blog.al.com/breaking/2010/04/post_271.html. Accessed April February 11, 2016.
44. Business Enterprise Trust, 1994, "The Business Enterprise Trust Awards (1991 Recipients)," unpublished announcement; Zicklin School of Business, "People, Not Profit: Merck's Battle against River Blindness," http://zicklin.baruch.cuny.edu/centers/zcci/zcci-events/the-merck-river-blindness-case. Accessed February 11, 2016.
45. Mahzarin R. Banaji, Max H. Bazerman, and Dolly Chugh, "How (Un) Ethical Are You?" *Harvard Business Review* (December 2003), 56–64.
46. Ibid.
47. Max Bazerman, George Loewenstein, and Don A. Moore, "Why Good Accountants Do Bad Audits," *Harvard Business Review* (November 2002).
48. Ibid.
49. Paine, 109–113.
50. Ibid., 107–108.
51. Ibid.
52. Dina Gerdeman, "How to Demotivate Your Best Employees," Harvard Business School Working Knowledge, http://hbswk.hbs.edu/item/how-to-demotivate-your-best-employees. Accessed April 25, 2016.
53. Dan Ariely, *The (Honest) Truth about Dishonesty*, Harper: 2012; also see Gary Belsky, "Why (Almost) All of Us Cheat and Steal," *Time Business*, June 18, 2012, 40.
54. Carroll (1987), 7–15.
55. Lawrence Kohlberg, "The Claim to Moral Adequacy of a Highest Stage of Moral Judgment," *The Journal of Philosophy* (Vol. 52, 1973), 630–646.
56. Carol Gilligan, *In a Different Voice: Psychological Theory and Women's Development* (Cambridge, MA: Harvard University Press, 1982).
57. Manuel G. Velasquez, *Business Ethics*, 3d ed. (Englewood Cliffs, NJ: Prentice Hall, 1992), 30. See also Brian K. Burton and Craig P. Dunn, "Feminist Ethics as Moral Grounding for Stakeholder Theory," *Business Ethics Quarterly* (Vol. 6, No. 2, 1996), 136–137.
58. See, for example, Robbin Derry, "Moral Reasoning in Work Related Conflicts," in William C. Frederick (ed.), *Research in Corporate Social Performance and Policy*, Vol. 9 (Greenwich, CT: JAI Press, 1987), 25–49. See also Velasquez, 30–31.
59. George A. Steiner, *Business and Society* (New York: Random House, 1975), 226.
60. William Barclay, *Ethics in a Permissive Society* (New York: Harper & Row, 1971), 13. http://www.princeton.edu/~achaney/tmve/wiki100k/docs/Ethic_of_reciprocity.html.
61. "Ethic of Reciprocity," http://www.princeton.edu/~achaney/tmve/wiki100k/docs/Ethic_of_reciprocity.html. Accessed February 20, 2016.
62. Marvin Fox, "The Theistic Bases of Ethics," in Robert Bartels (ed.), *Ethics in Business* (Columbus, OH: Bureau of Business Research, Ohio State University, 1963), 86–87.

63. Alan Wolfe, *Moral Freedom: The Search for Virtue in a World of Choice* (New York: W.W. Norton & Co., 2001).
64. John Leo, "My Morals, Myself," *U.S. News & World Report* (August 13, 2001), 10.
65. Carl D. Fulda, "The Legal Basis of Ethics," in Bartels, 43–50.
66. American Management Association, "The Ethical Enterprise: Doing the Right Things in the Right Ways, Today and Tomorrow—A Global Study of Business Ethics 2005–2015," http://www.amanet.org/images/HREthicsSurvey06.pdf. Accessed February 20, 2016.
67. "The Oath Project," http://theoathproject.org/. Accessed February 20, 2016.
68. Carl Madden, "Forces Which Influence Ethical Behavior," in Clarence C. Walton (ed.), *The Ethics of Corporate Conduct* (Englewood Cliffs, NJ: Prentice Hall, 1977), 31–78.
69. Charles W. Powers and David Vogel, *Ethics in the Education of Business Managers* (Hastings-on-Hudson, NY: The Hastings Center, 1980), 40–45. Also see Patricia H. Werhane, *Moral Imagination and Management Decision Making* (New York: Oxford University Press, 1999).
70. Patricia Werhane, "Moral Imagination," Volume 2, *Business Ethics*, Wiley Online Library, online published January 21, 2016. Accessed February 20, 2016.
71. Powers and Vogel, ibid.
72. Powers and Vogel, ibid.
73. Jill A. Brown and William R. Forster, "CSR and Stakeholder Theory: A Tale of Adam Smith," *Journal of Business Ethics* (Vol. 112, 2013), 301–312
74. Milton Friedman, "The Social Responsibility of Business Is to Increase Its Profits," *The New York Times* (September 1962), 126 [italics added].

8

Managerial and Organizational Ethics

CHAPTER LEARNING OUTCOMES

After studying this chapter, you should be able to:

1 Identify and explain the different levels at which business ethics may be addressed.

2 Enumerate and discuss the principles of managerial ethics and ethical tests for guiding ethical decisions.

3 In terms of managing organizational ethics, identify the factors affecting an organization's ethical culture and provide examples of these factors at work.

4 Describe the best practices that management may take to improve an organization's ethical culture.

5 Identify and explain concepts from "behavioral ethics" that affect ethical decision making and behavior in organizations.

6 Explain the cascading effect of moral decisions, moral managers, and moral organizations.

The ethical issues on which managers must make decisions are numerous and varied. The news media tends to focus on the major ethical scandals involving well-known corporate names. Therefore, Wells Fargo, Volkswagen, General Motors, Toshiba, Takata, and other such high-visibility firms have attracted considerable attention. As a consequence, many of the day-to-day ethical challenges that managers and employees face in medium-sized and small organizations are often overlooked or underreported.

The recent ethics scandals and the global financial crisis are not the only urgent issues facing the corporate world, though they may get the most press coverage. Managers encounter day-to-day ethical challenges in arenas such as conflicts of interest, sexual harassment, inappropriate gifts to corporate personnel, unauthorized payments, customer dealings, evaluation of personnel, and pressure to compromise their personal standards. But often these managers have no experience or training in business ethics or ethical decision making to tackle such quandaries.

People today face ethical issues in a variety of settings, but our concern in this chapter is limited to managerial and organizational ethics. David Callahan's highly influential book titled *The Cheating Culture: Why More Americans Are Doing Wrong to Get Ahead* talks at length about how these ethical issues touch organizations and managers.[1] Callahan uses the term "cheating" as a synonym for terms that are commonly accepted today, including *dishonesty, immorality, lying,* and *corrupting*—all of which characterize the kinds of managerial and organization threats we are addressing in this chapter. Callahan argues that the instances of cheating have shot up in today's society and organizations because of four essential reasons: (1) higher levels of inequality, which means larger paychecks for some and larger incentives to cut corners to succeed; (2) today's widespread insecurities, which can lead ordinary people to think they must cheat to survive; (3) a failure of oversight across many sectors, meaning that cheating often goes unpunished; and (4) America's highly individualistic culture, which glorifies wealth, status, and personal gratification.[2] Each of these factors, along with others, influences managerial and organizational ethics and thus frames the issues that need to be addressed at these levels.

The ethical challenge in business is a daunting one, and progress on this front is vital to sustainable businesses. An ethics officer for a large corporation once said that there are three types of organizations: those that *have had* ethics problems, those that *are having* ethics problems, and those that *will have* ethics problems. Ethical issues appear through all levels of management, in many different types of jobs, and in organizations of all sizes.

A study of managers' desired leadership qualities was conducted by consultant and writer Lee Ellis, who concluded that *integrity* is the quality most sought after in leaders.[3] A retired corporate executive, now business school lecturer, Bill George, former CEO at Medtronic, argued that today we need corporate leaders with integrity.[4] But how does one get personal integrity, and as a manager, how do you instill it in yourself and your organization to create an ethical organizational climate?

Following are some significant challenges managers face today: How do you keep your own managerial ethics focused in such a way that you avoid immorality and amorality? What principles, concepts, or guidelines are available to help you to be ethical? What specific strategies, approaches, or best practices might be emphasized to bring about an ethical culture in companies and organizations? How is "behavioral ethics" affecting decision making?

8.1 Ethics Issues Arise at Different Levels

As individuals and as managers, we experience ethical pressures or dilemmas in a variety of settings and at different levels of analysis, including the individual or personal level, the managerial and organizational level, the industry level, the societal level, and the global level. These levels ripple out from the individual level to the global level. Some observers believe that "ethics are ethics" regardless of whether they are applied at the personal, managerial, or organizational level. In many respects this is true. However, each level of application also introduces distinct challenges. To help understand the types of decision situations that are faced at the various levels, however, it is worth considering them in terms of the types of issues that may arise in different contexts.

8.1a Personal Level

First, we all experience *personal-level* ethical challenges. These challenges include situations we face in our personal lives that are generally outside the context of our employment but may have implications for our jobs. Questions or dilemmas that we might face at the personal level include the following examples:

- Should I cheat on my income tax return by overinflating my charitable contributions?
- Should I tell the professor I need this course to graduate this semester when I really don't?
- Should I download music from the Internet although I realize it is someone else's intellectual property?
- Should I connect this TV cable in my new apartment and not tell the cable company?

Wanda Johnson, a 34-year-old single mother of five from Savannah, Georgia, faced a personal-level ethical dilemma when temptation came knocking in the form of a bagful of money that contained $120,000. True story: Johnson, a low-paid custodian at a local hospital, was on her lunch break when she witnessed the money bag falling off an armored truck. She could have used the money to pay her outstanding bills. She had recently pawned her television set to procure enough cash to keep the bill collectors at bay. The bag contained small bills and nobody saw her find it. Johnson's experience is not uncommon. Others, in Salt Lake City, Harvey, Louisiana, and San Jose, California, have similarly found bags of money that have fallen off armored trucks. What should she do? What would you do?

Johnson later confessed that she knew she had to turn it in. After consulting with her pastor, she turned in the money to the police. Johnson reported that her religious upbringing had taught her that was the right thing to do. Later she was rewarded by the SunTrust Bank with $5,000 and was also promised an unspecified sum by EM Armored Car Service, Inc.[5] Would everyone react to this personal, ethical dilemma in the same fashion as did Johnson? We all face hundreds of such dilemmas throughout our lives.

8.1b Managerial and Organizational Levels

Individuals also encounter ethical issues at the *managerial or organizational level* (or firm level) in their roles as managers or employees. Many of these issues are similar to those we face personally. However, managerial- and organizational-level issues carry consequences for an individual's status in the organization, for the company's reputation and success in the community, and also for the kind of ethical environment or culture that will prevail on a day-to-day basis at the office. In addition, how the issue is handled may have serious managerial or organizational consequences. Examples of issues faced at the managerial level that have implications for the organizational level include the following:

- Should I set high performance goals for my work team to benefit the organization, even though I know it may cause them to cut corners to achieve such goals?
- Should I over report the actual time I worked on this project, hoping to get overtime pay or additional recognition?
- Should I authorize a subordinate to sidestep company policy so that we can close the deal and be rewarded by month's end?
- Should I misrepresent the warranty time on some product I'm selling in order to get the sale?

One August, it was revealed that months before people began dying nationwide, managers at the Bil Mar plant, a Sara Lee Corporation-owned plant in Michigan, knew they were shipping tainted hot dogs and deli meats. This was a managerial- and organization-level ethical dilemma. The consumption of tainted food caused a national outbreak of listeriosis, in which 15 people were killed, 6 suffered miscarriages, and 101 got sick. Employees of the plant later revealed that several employees, as well as the management, were aware of the shipment of contaminated meat, but kept silent.

According to a report, a USDA worker had told a Bil Mar employee at the time that the plant was running the risk of getting into trouble if it continued shipping contaminated foods, but the worker replied, "they would never know it was our product since [listeria] has about a two-week incubation period." Before these latest revelations, the company had pleaded guilty to a federal misdemeanor charge, paid a $200,000 fine, and made a $3 million grant to Michigan State University for food safety research.[6] In 2016, Dole faced this same issue and was forced to recall packaged salads in six states due to a similar listeria outbreak.[7]

When thinking about the managerial and organizational level of ethics, the presence or absence of unethical practices goes a long way toward revealing the climate or culture of ethics that exists within that organization. To illustrate the types of unethical practices that may be evident in organizations, the results of a revealing survey conducted by the Ethics Resource Center documented the situations that managers and employees often face. In this survey of employees, the following were some of the types of misconduct observed and reported along with the percentage of time these items were mentioned:[8]

- Abusive or intimidating behavior toward employees (23 percent)
- Misreporting actual time or hours worked (20 percent)
- Lying to employees, customers, vendors, or the public (19 percent)
- Withholding needed information from employees, customers, vendors, or the public (18 percent)

- Discriminating on the basis of race, color, gender, age, or similar categories (13 percent)
- Stealing, theft, or related fraud (12 percent)

Each of these categories reveals the array of questionable practices that employees and managers face every day in their work lives. How they respond to these ethical issues often carry serious consequences for themselves and their organizations.

8.1c Industry or Profession Level

A third level at which a manager or an organization might experience business ethics issues is the *industry or profession level.* The industry might be stock brokerage, real estate, insurance, manufactured homes, financial services, telemarketing, electronics, or a host of others. Related to the industry might be the *profession*, of which an individual is a member—accounting, engineering, pharmacy, medicine, journalism, or law. Examples of questions that might pose ethical dilemmas at this level include the following:

- Is this safety standard we electrical engineers have passed really adequate for protecting the consumer in this age of do-it-yourselfers?
- Is this standard contract we realtors have adopted really in keeping with the financial disclosure laws that have recently been strengthened?
- Is it ethical for telemarketers to make cold calls to prospective clients during the dinner hour when we suspect they will be at home?
- Is it ethical for accountants to allow a restatement of earnings that can cause investors to lose money and confidence in the market?

An excellent example of an industry-wide ethical problem occurred during the buildup to the Wall Street financial scandals and market collapse in 2008. The mortgage-lending industry became enthralled with subprime lending. Granting home loans to individuals who could not meet their payments unless housing prices continued to rise turned out to be a questionable and unsustainable practice. The industry became disreputable for its NINJA loans—loans to people with *N*o *In*come, *N*o *J*ob, no *A*ssets. For the sake of keeping up with the whirlwind competition, firms were granting loans just to keep up competitors and to collect commissions. This practice contributed significantly to the worldwide recession.

Many analysts believe the same type practices are now going on in the student loan industry. Educational debt today is seen by many to be a ticking time bomb inasmuch as there is now over $1 trillion in outstanding loan balances. Weak job prospects as well as rising costs for basic living expenses have meant that many college students are not earning enough to pay back their loans. Default rates have been climbing for over ten years. According to many analysts, the student loan industry is facing serious problems and they have been brought about by questionable loans in the industry.[9] The student loan situation is examined in closer detail in Case 29 at the end of the text.

8.1d Societal and Global Levels

At the *societal* and *global levels*, it becomes very difficult for the individual manager to have a direct effect on business ethics. However, managers acting in concert through their companies and industries and professional associations can certainly bring about high standards and constructive changes. Because the industry, societal, and global levels are quite removed from the actual practicing manager, in this chapter we will focus our attention primarily on the managerial and organizational levels. The manager's greatest impact can be felt through what he or she does personally or as a member of the management team.

In Chapter 9, we will deal with business ethics and technology, a major societal issue, and in Chapter 10, we will address global ethics more specifically—a crucial topic that is increasing in importance as global capitalism has come to define our commercial world.

8.2 Managerial Ethics and Ethical Principles

In discussing managerial ethics, it is anticipated that most individuals want to behave ethically or improve his or her ethical conduct in organizational situations. Each individual, whether acting on his or her own or acting in a management capacity, is a stakeholder of someone else—a friend, a family member, an associate, a colleague, or a businessperson, who is affected by that person's actions. That "someone else" has a stake in the individual's honesty; therefore, the individual person's ethics are important to that someone else too. Our discussion here focuses on those who desire to be ethical and are looking for help in doing so. All the difficulties with making ethical judgments that we discussed in the previous chapter are applicable in this discussion as well.

Managerial ethics, for the most part, entails making decisions which have ethical implications or consequences. Difficult decisions typically present the individual with a conflict-of-interest situation. A **conflict of interest** is usually present when the individual has to choose between her or his interests and the interests of someone else or some other group (his or her organization, other stakeholders). What it boils down to in the final analysis is answering the question, "What is the right or fair thing to do in this situation?" In other instances, practices that managers and organizations employ are embedded with ethical implications. Someone else most likely first introduced the practices at an earlier time, so some managers do not see that each time they continue a questionable practice, they are implicitly deciding that it is appropriate.

In answering the question about the right or fair course of action, it often seems that individuals think about the situation briefly and then go with their instincts. There are, however, guidelines for ethical decision making that one could turn to if she or he really wants to make the best ethical decisions. Some of these guidelines are discussed in this chapter.

In Chapter 7, we discussed business ethics using the conventional approach. The conventional approach entailed making a comparison between a decision, action, or policy and prevailing norms of acceptability. There are many difficulties inherent in conventional thinking. These arise from the multitude of value expectations being placed on individuals and the questions "of whose" ethics to use and which ethics are "prevailing." In this chapter, we introduce two approaches to managerial ethics or ethical decision making that serve as additional guidance: (1) the principles approach and (3) the ethical tests approach.

8.2a Principles Approach to Ethics

The principles approach to ethics or ethical decision making is based on the idea that employees and managers desire to anchor their decisions and actions on a more solid foundation than that provided with the conventional approach. Several principles of ethics have evolved over time as moral philosophers and ethicists have attempted to organize and codify their thinking and guidelines. These principles are normative in nature as they offer guidance regarding what one "ought to do" in a situation.

What Is an Ethics Principle? From a practical point of view, a principle of business ethics is an ethical concept, guideline, or rule that, if applied when you are faced with an ethical decision or practice, will assist you in taking the ethical course of action.[10] Ethics principles or guidelines have been around for centuries. The Golden Rule, presented in various forms, has been around for several millennia. In the 16th century, Miguel de Cervantes, the Spanish novelist and author of *Don Quixote*, uttered an important ethics principle that is still used today and seldom attributed to him: *Honesty is the best policy.*

Types of Ethical Principles or Theories. Moral philosophers customarily divide ethics principles or theories into two categories: teleological and deontological.

Teleological theories focus on the *consequences* or results of the actions they produce. Utilitarianism is the major principle in this category. It recommends taking the action that results in the greatest good for the greatest number. For example, it could be argued that the workplace would be better off if only college graduates were hired even though not everyone needs a college degree to do our work. **Deontological theories**, by contrast, focus on *duties*. For example, it could be argued that managers have a duty to tell the truth when they are doing business. The principles of rights and of justice, two major ethics theories we will discuss, seem to be nonteleological in character.[11]

Aretaic theories are a third, less-known category of ethics, put forth by Aristotle. The term comes from the Greek word *arete*, which means "goodness" (of function), "excellence" (of function), or "virtue." Aristotle saw the individual as essentially a member of a social unit and moral virtue as a behavioral habit, a character trait that is both socially and morally valued. Virtue theory is the best example of an aretaic theory.[12] Other principles, such as the principle of caring, the Golden Rule, and servant leadership, reflect concerns for duty, consequences, and virtue, or a combination of several principles.

Many different principles of ethics have been promulgated, but we must limit our discussion to those that have been regarded as most useful in business applications. Therefore, we will concentrate on the following major principles: *utilitarianism* (consequences based), and *Kant's categorical imperative, rights*, and *justice* (duty based). In addition, we will consider the principles of *care, virtue ethics, servant leadership*, and the *Golden Rule*—approaches that are popular and relevant today.

The basic idea behind the principles approach is that managers may improve the wisdom of their ethical decision making if they factor into their proposed actions, decisions, behaviors, and practices a consideration of certain principles or philosophies of ethics.

Principle of Utilitarianism. Many ethicists have held that the correctness or fairness of an action can be determined best by looking at its overall results or consequences. If the consequences are good, the action or decision is considered good. If the consequences are bad, the action or decision is considered wrong. An example of utilitarianism might be in the case of a pharmaceutical firm that has released a new drug that has been approved by the government but it does have side effects. But, the drug is able to help more people than are bothered by the side effects so it is considered a good drug though it has problems for some.

The **principle of utilitarianism** is therefore a *consequential* principle, or as stated earlier, a *teleological* principle. In its simplest form, **utilitarianism** asserts: "we should always act so as to produce the greatest ratio of good to evil for everyone."[13] Another way of stating utilitarianism is to say that one should take the course of action that represents the "greatest good for the greatest number." Two of the most influential philosophers who advocated this consequential view were Jeremy Bentham (1748–1832) and John Stuart Mill (1806–1873).

The attractiveness of utilitarianism is that it forces the decision maker to think about the general welfare, or the common good. It proposes a standard outside of self-interest by which to judge the value of a course of action. To make a cost-benefit analysis is to engage in utilitarian thinking. Utilitarianism forces us to think in stakeholder terms: What would produce the greatest good in our decision, considering stakeholders such as owners, employees, customers, and others, as well as ourselves? Finally, it provides for latitude in decision making in that it does not recognize specific actions as inherently good or bad but rather allows us to fit our personal decisions to the complexities of the situation.

A weakness of utilitarianism is that it ignores actions that may be inherently wrong. A strict interpretation of utilitarianism might lead a manager to fire minorities and older workers because they "do not fit in" or to take some other drastic action that contravenes public policy and other ethics principles. In utilitarianism, by focusing on the ends (consequences) of a decision or an action, one may ignore the means (the decision or action itself). This leads to a problematic situation wherein one may argue that the end justifies the means, using utilitarian reasoning. Therefore, the action or decision is considered objectionable only if it leads to a lesser ratio of good to evil.

Another problem with the principle of utilitarianism is that it may come into conflict with the ideas of justice or rights. Critics of utilitarianism say that the mere increase in total good is not good in and of itself because it ignores the *distribution* of good, which is also an important issue. Another stated weakness is that when using this principle, it is very difficult to formulate satisfactory rules for decision making. Therefore, utilitarianism, like most ethical principles, has its advantages and disadvantages.[14] Like many ethics principles, utilitarianism seems to work best when used in combination with other ethics principles.

Kant's Categorical Imperative. Immanuel Kant's **categorical imperative** is a *duty-based* principle of ethics, or as stated earlier, it is a deontological principle.[15] A duty is an obligation; that is, it is an action that is morally obligatory. The duty approach to ethics refers both to the obligatory nature of particular actions and to a way of reasoning about what is right and what is wrong.[16] Kant's categorical imperative argues that a sense of duty arises from *reason* or *rational nature*, an internal source. By contrast, the Divine Command principle maintains that God's law is the source of duties. Thus, we can conceptualize both internal and external sources of duty.

Kant proposed three formulations in his theory or principle. The categorical imperative is best known in the following form: "Act only according to that maxim by which you can at the same time *will* that it should become a universal law." Stated another way, Kant's principle is that a person should act only on rules (or maxims) that you would be willing to see everyone follow.[17] Kant's second formulation, referred to as the *principle of ends*, is "so act to treat humanity, whether in your own person or in that of any other, in every case as an *end* and never as merely a means." This has also been referred to as the *respect for person's principle*.[18] This means that each person has dignity and moral worth and should never be exploited or manipulated or merely used as a means to another end; therefore, we have a duty to respect persons.[19]

The third formulation of the categorical imperative invokes the *principle of autonomy*. It basically holds that "every rational being is able to regard oneself as a maker of universal law. That is, we do not need an external authority—be it God, the state, our culture, or anyone else—to determine the nature of the moral law. We can discover this for ourselves."[20] Kant argues that this view is not inconsistent with Judeo-Christian beliefs, his childhood heritage, but one must go through a series of logical leaps of faith to arrive at this point.[21] Like all ethical principles, Kant's principles have strengths, weaknesses, supporters and detractors. In the final analysis, it is his emphasis on *duty*, as opposed to consequences, that merits their discussion here. Further, the notion of universalizability and respect for persons are key ideas. The principles of rights and of justice, which we discuss next, seem more consistent with the duty-based perspective than with the consequences-based perspective.

Principle of Rights. One major problem with utilitarianism is that it does not handle the issue of **rights** very well. That is, utilitarianism implies that certain actions are morally right (i.e., they represent the greatest good for the greatest number) when in fact they may violate another person's rights.[22] The principle of rights maintains that persons have both moral and legal rights that should be honored and respected. **Moral rights** are important, justifiable claims or entitlements. They do not depend on a legal system to be valid. They are rights that people ought to have based on moral reasoning. The right to life or the right not to be killed by others is a justifiable claim in our society. The Declaration of Independence referred to the rights to life, liberty, and the pursuit of happiness. John Locke had earlier spoken of the right to property. Today we speak of human rights, some of which are legal rights and some moral rights. **Legal rights** are rights that some governing authority (the Constitution, the Bill of Rights, or federal, state, or local government) have formalized as rights.

An important aspect of the **principle of rights** is that a right can only be overridden by a more basic or important right. Let us consider the problem of applying the principle of utilitarianism when it collides with the principle of rights. For example, if we accept the basic right to human life, we are precluded from considering whether taking someone's life might produce the greatest good for the greatest number. To use a business example, if a person has the right to equal treatment (not to be discriminated against), we could not argue for discriminating against that person to produce more good for others (e.g., a more harmonious workplace).[23] However, some people would say that this is precisely what we did in the push for affirmative action policies in the past few decades; hence, this is a major reason they fell out of favor.

The principle of rights expresses morality from the point of view of the individual or group of individuals, whereas the principle of utilitarianism expresses morality in terms of the group or society as a whole. The rights view forces us in our decision making to ask what is due each individual and to promote individual welfare. It also limits the validity of appeals to numbers and to society's aggregate benefit.[24] However, a central question that is not always easy to answer is: "What constitutes a legitimate right that should be honored, and what rights or whose rights take precedence over others?"

Figure 8-1 provides a listing of many types of rights that are being claimed in our society today. Some of these already are legally protected, whereas others are "claimed" as moral rights but are not legally protected. Managers are expected to be attentive to both legal and moral rights, but clear guidelines are not always available to help one sort out which claimed moral rights should be protected, to what extent they should be protected, and which rights should take precedence over others. Sometimes politics gets intertwined in this determination. This is one of the limitations of the rights theory.

Rights may be subdivided further into two types: negative rights and positive rights.[25] A **negative right** is the right to be left alone. It is the right to think and act free from the

FIGURE 8-1 Some Legal Rights and Claimed Moral Rights in Today's Society

Civil rights
Minorities' rights
Women's rights
Disabled people's rights
Older people's rights
Religious affiliation rights
Employee rights
Consumer rights
Shareholder rights
Privacy rights
Right to life
Right to work
Criminals' rights
Smokers' rights
Nonsmokers' rights
AIDS victims' rights
Children's rights
Fetal rights
Embryo rights
Animal's rights
Right to burn the American flag
Right of due process
Right to choose
Right to health care
Gay rights
Transgender rights
Victims' rights
Rights based on looks
Right to free expression

coercion of others; for example, freedom from false imprisonment, freedom from illegal search and seizure, and freedom of speech are all forms of negative rights.[26] A **positive right** is the right to something, such as the right to food, to health care, to clean air, to a certain standard of living, or to education.[27] In business, as in all walks of life, both negative and positive rights are played out in both legal and morally claimed forms.

Competing Rights A special problem arises with the rights approach to ethical decision making when the situation is not a clear "right vs. wrong" but is more nearly "right vs. right." This represents the special case of dealing with the dilemma of **competing rights**.[28] We know that when right faces wrong, we need to choose that which is right. Nevertheless, sometimes the decision will be between two apparent rights and then it is harder to choose. Here are some examples of competing rights:

- It is right to tell the truth, but it is also right to be kind and considerate of people's feelings.
- It is right to offer job security, but as a manager you may have to lay off employees to balance your accounts.
- It is right to apply rules and procedures without favoritism, but it is also right to give special consideration to hard working, dependable employees.[29]

In 2016, a high-profile debate occurred between Apple Computers and the FBI. The case involved two rights—the right to homeland security (safety) and the right to data security/privacy. In this debate, the FBI wanted Apple to provide it with access to an iPhone that had been used by a terrorist but Apple didn't want to give them access arguing that their customers' security and privacy were at stake.[30] This case was very complex and we will not resolve it here, but it is an excellent example of how two apparent "rights" may compete with each other. This dilemma is discussed in detail in Case 8 at the end of the text.

In a dilemma that involves competing rights, there are no easy solutions. Two general approaches are to (1) eliminate the conflict by reframing it or (2) decide what is "more right." In deciding what is more right, identify which competing right is more in line with laws, regulations, and organizational policies; which is most in sync with organizational values; which provides the greatest good for the greatest number of stakeholders; or, which establishes the best precedent for guiding similar situations in the future.[31] In the final analysis, someone may still be dissatisfied with the resolution.

In recent years, some have argued that we are in the midst of a rights revolution in which too many individuals and groups are attempting to urge society to accept their wishes or demands as rights. The *proliferation of rights* claims has the potential to dilute or diminish the power of more legitimate rights. If everyone's claim for special consideration is perceived as a legitimate right, the rights approach will lose its power to help management concentrate on the morally justified rights. A silly example of how far rights thinking can be taken occurred in a 2016 full-page ad in the *USA Today* newspaper for "The Hot Dog Bill of Rights." This was an ad run and endorsed by 7-Eleven food stores promoting the consumers' right to buy a delicious 100 percent beef hot dog 24/7, 365 days a year and to customize it with a variety of toppings.[32] Unfortunately, not all rights issues are as humorous as this claim.

A related problem has been the *politicization of rights*. As our elected lawmakers bestow legal or protected status upon rights claims for political reasons rather than moral reasons, managers may become blinded to which rights or whose rights really should be honored in a decision-making situation. As rights claims expand, the common core of morality may diminish, and decision makers may find it more and more difficult to balance individuals' interests with the public interest.[33]

Principle of Justice (Fairness Principle). Just as the principle of utilitarianism does not handle well the idea of rights, it does not deal effectively with the principle of justice either. One way to think about the **principle of justice** is to say that it involves the fair treatment of each person. This is why it is often called the "fairness principle." Most would accept that we have a duty to be fair to employees, consumers, and other stakeholders. But how do you decide what is fair to each person? How do you decide what is "due" each person? Sometimes it is hard to say because people might be expecting their due according to their *type of work*, their *effort expended*, their *merit*, their *need*, *time spent*, or other criteria. Each of these measures could be argued to be appropriate in different situations. Today the question of what constitutes fairness has divided people to such an extent that it has been argued that we have a new culture war over fairness.[34]

To use the principle of justice, we also must ask, "What is meant by justice?" There are several kinds of justice (or fairness) that come into play in organizations. **Distributive justice** refers to the distribution of benefits and burdens in societies and organizations. **Compensatory justice** involves compensating someone for a past injustice. **Procedural justice**, or *ethical due process*, refers to fair decision-making procedures, practices, or agreements.[35]

Ethical Due Process Procedural justice, or **ethical due process**, is especially relevant to business and professional organizations. Employees, customers, owners, and all stakeholders want to be treated fairly. They want to believe that they have been treated rightly and fairly in decision situations. They want their side of the issue to be heard, and they want to believe that the managers or decision makers took all factors into consideration and weighed them carefully before making a decision that affected them. Whether the decision was who should be hired (or fired), who should get what promotion or raise, or who should get a choice assignment, employees want to know that it was fairness that prevailed and not favoritism or some other inappropriate factor.

People want to know that their performance has been evaluated according to a fair process. Ethical due process, then, is simply being sure that fairness characterizes the decision-making process. It should be noted too that ethical due process is as important as, if not more so than, outcome fairness. In other words, people can live with an outcome that was not their preferred result if they believe that the method, system, or procedure used in making the decision was fair.

The term **process fairness** has also been used to describe ethical due process.[36] Three factors have been identified that help to decide whether process fairness has been achieved. First, have people's (employees, customers) input been included in the decision process? The more this occurs, the more fair the process is perceived to be. Second, do people believe the decisions were made and implemented in an appropriate manner? People expect consistency based on accurate information. They see whether mistakes are being corrected and whether the decision-making process was transparent. Third, people watch their managers' behavior. Do they provide explanations when asked? Do they treat others respectfully? Do they actively listen to comments being made?[37] Ethical due process, or process fairness, works effectively with all stakeholders, whether they are employees, customers, owners, or others. Almost everyone responds positively to being treated fairly.

Rawls's Principle of Justice John Rawls, a political philosopher who died in 2002 at the age of 81, became well known for his own version of ethical due process.[38] He provided what some have referred to as a comprehensive principle of justice.[39] Rawls' theory is based on the idea that what we need first is a fair method by which we may choose the principles through which conflicts will be resolved. The two principles of justice that underlie his theory are as follows:[40]

1. Each person has an equal right to the most extensive basic liberties compatible with similar liberties for all others.
2. Social and economic inequalities are arranged so that they are both (a) reasonably expected to be to everyone's advantage and (b) attached to positions and offices open to all.

According to Rawls's first principle, each person should be treated equally. In other words, it holds that each person should enjoy equally a full array of basic liberties.[41] The second principle is more controversial. It is often misinterpreted to imply that public policy should raise as high as possible the social and economic well-being of society's worst-off individuals. It is criticized by both those who argue that the principle is too strong and those who think it is too weak. The former think that, as long as people enjoy equal opportunity, it is not a case of injustice if some people benefit from their own work, skill, ingenuity, or assumed risks. Therefore, such people are more deserving and should not be expected to produce benefits for the least advantaged. The latter group thinks that the inequalities that may result could be so great as to be clearly unjust. Therefore, the rich get richer and the poor get only a little less poor.[42] The "income inequality" movement that is in the news today is essentially based on this latter explanation.

In developing further his second principle, Rawls imagined people gathered behind a "veil of ignorance," unaware of whether they, personally, were rich or poor, talented or incompetent. He then asked what kind of society they would create. He reasoned that the rule everyone would be able to agree on would be to maximize the well-being of the worst-off person, partially out of fear that anyone could wind up at the bottom.[43] This view, of course, had its critics, and it represents a situation that could not likely be brought about especially in a meritocracy—a system based on ability rather than need.

Supporters of the principle of justice claim that it preserves the basic values—freedom, equality of opportunity, and a concern for the disadvantaged—that have become embedded in our moral beliefs. Critics object to various parts of the theory and would not subscribe to Rawls's principles at all. Utilitarian's, for example, think the greatest good for the greatest number should reign supreme.

Ethics of Care. The concept of **ethics of care** or the **principle of caring** is being discussed just after our discussion of utilitarianism, rights, and justice because this alternative view is critical of many traditional views. Some traditional views, it has been argued, embrace a masculine approach to perceiving the world and advocate rigid rules with clear lines.[44] The "care" perspective builds on the work of Carol Gilligan, whose criticisms of Kohlberg's theory of moral development were discussed in Chapter 7. Gilligan found that women often spoke in "a different voice" that was more reflective of responsibility to others and on the continuity of interdependent relationships.[45]

The care perspective maintains that traditional ethics like the principles of utilitarianism and rights focus too much on the individual self and on cognitive thought processes. In the traditional view, "others" may be seen as threats, so rights become important. Resulting moral theories then tend to be legalistic or contractual.

Caring theory is founded on wholly different assumptions. Proponents who advocate this perspective view the individual person as essentially relational, not individualistic. These persons do not deny the existence of the self but hold that the self has relationships that cannot be separated from the self's existence. This caring view emphasizes the relationships' moral worth and, by extension, the responsibilities inherent in those relationships, rather than in rights, as in traditional ethics.[46]

Several writers have argued that caring theory is consistent with stakeholder theory, or the stakeholder approach, in that the emphasis is on a more cooperative, caring type of relationship. In this view, firms should seek to make decisions that satisfy stakeholders, leading to situations in which all parties in the relationship gain. Robbin Derry elaborates: "In the corporate environment, there is an increasing demand for business to be attentive to its many stakeholders, particularly customers and employees, in caring ways. As organizations attempt to build such relationships, they must define the responsibilities of initiating and maintaining care. The ethics of care may be able to facilitate an understanding of these responsibilities."[47]

Jeanne Liedtka, by contrast, has questioned whether organizations can care in the sense in which caring theory proposes. Liedtka takes the position that caring people could lead to a caring organization that offers new possibilities for simultaneously enhancing the effectiveness and the moral quality of organizations.[48] The principle of caring offers a different perspective to guide ethical decision making—a perspective that clearly is thought provoking and valuable.

Virtue Ethics. The major principles just discussed have been more action-oriented. That is, they were designed to guide our actions and decisions and they involved the manager or leader "doing something." Another ethical tradition, often referred to as **virtue ethics**, merits consideration. Virtue ethics, rooted in the thinking of Plato and Aristotle, is a school of thought that focuses on the individual becoming imbued with virtues (e.g., honesty, fairness, truthfulness, trustworthiness, benevolence, respect, and nonmalfeasance).[49] Virtue ethics is sometimes referred to as an aretaic theory of ethics, as defined earlier.[50]

Virtue ethics is a system of thought that is centered in the heart of the person—the manager, the employee, the competitor, and so on. This is in contrast to the principles we have discussed, which see the heart of ethics in actions or duties being carried out. Action-oriented principles focus on *doing*. Virtue ethics emphasizes *being*. The underlying assumption of virtue ethics, of course, is that the actions of a virtuous person will also be virtuous. Traditional ethical principles of utilitarianism, rights, and justice focus on the question, "What should I do?" Virtue ethics focuses on the question, "What sort of person should I *be* or *become*?"[51]

Programs that have developed from the notion of virtue ethics have sometimes been called *character education* because this particular approach emphasizes character development. Many observers think that one reason why business and society are witnessing moral decline today is that we have failed to teach our young people universal principles of good character . The Character Counts program promotes the Six Pillars of Character as being: Trustworthiness, respect, responsibility, fairness, caring, and citizenship.[52]

It has been argued that character education is needed not only in schools but in corporations as well. Corporate well-being demands character and business leaders are a vital and necessary force for putting character back into business.[53]

Virtue ethicists have brought back to the public debate the idea that virtues are important whether they be in the education of the young or in the management training programs. Virtues such as honesty, integrity, loyalty, promise keeping, fairness, and respect for others are completely compatible with the major principles we have been discussing. The principles, combined with the virtues, form the foundation for effective ethical action and decision making.

Servant Leadership. An increasingly popular approach to organizational leadership and thinking today is **servant leadership**. It is an approach to ethical leadership and decision making based on the moral principle of *serving others first*. Can these two roles—servant and leader—be fused in one person—a manager or leader? What are the basic tenets of servant leadership?

Servant leadership is a model of ethical management—an approach to ethical decision making—based on the idea that serving others such as employees, customers, community, and other stakeholders is the first priority. The modern era of servant leadership is marked primarily by the works of Robert K. Greenleaf, who spent 38 years of his career working for AT&T. Greenleaf takes the strong position that the servant leader is "servant first." Of course, the "servant first" and the "leader first" are the two extreme types, and between them there are a number of shadings and blends that define a useful range within the notion of leadership. Carol Walker has argued recently in the *Harvard Business Review* that servant leadership is a good place for leaders to start thinking about their roles: when you have a servant mentality it's no longer about you, it's about your team and your organization.[54]

Ten key characteristics essential for the development of servant leaders have been culled from Greenleaf's writings. Each of these is worth noting because, collectively, they paint a portrait of servant leadership in terms of leader behaviors and characteristics. These characteristics are as follows:[55]

- Listening
- Empathy
- Healing
- Persuasion
- Awareness
- Foresight
- Conceptualization
- Commitment to the growth of people
- Stewardship
- Building community

Each of these characteristics is based on the ethical principle of putting the other person first—whether that other person is an employee, a customer, or some other important stakeholder. Some of these characteristics could be stated as virtues and some as behaviors. Thus, servant leadership embraces several of the ethical perspectives discussed earlier. Servant leadership builds a bridge between the ideas of business ethics and those of leadership. Joanne Ciulla has observed that people follow servant leaders because they can trust them, and this invokes the ethical dimension.[56] James Autry, a top-selling leadership author, argues that servant leadership is the right way, a better way of being a manager and part of organizational life. He adds, "it will enhance productivity, encourage creativity, and benefit the bottom line."[57] It is also clear that the servant leadership principle is quite compatible with sustainability within organizations.

The Golden Rule. The **Golden Rule** merits consideration because of its history and popularity as a basic and strong principle of ethical living and decision making. A number of studies have found it to be the most powerful and useful to managers.[58] The Golden Rule—"Do unto others as you would have them do unto you"—is a straightforward, easy-to-understand principle. Further, it guides the individual decision maker to behavior, actions, or decisions that she or he should be able to express as acceptable or not based on some direct comparisons with what she or he would consider ethical or fair.

The Golden Rule, also known as the **ethic of reciprocity**, argues that if you want to be treated fairly, treat others fairly; if you want your privacy protected, respect the privacy of others. The key is impartiality. According to this principle, we are not to make an exception of ourselves. In essence, the Golden Rule personalizes business relations and brings the idea of self-perceived fairness into business deliberations.[59]

The popularity of the Golden Rule is linked to the fact that it is rooted in history and religious traditions and is among the oldest of the principles of living. Further, it is universal in that it requires no specific religious belief or faith. Since time began, religious leaders and philosophers have advocated the Golden Rule in one form or another. It is easy to see, therefore, why Martin Luther said that the Golden Rule is a part of the "natural law," because it is a moral rule that anyone can recognize and embrace without any particular religious teaching. In three different studies, when managers or respondents were asked to rank ethical principles according to their value to them, the Golden Rule was ranked first.[60]

Leadership expert John C. Maxwell published an insightful book titled *There's No Such Thing as "Business" Ethics: There's Only One Rule for Making Decisions*. The one rule Maxwell advocates is the Golden Rule. According to Maxwell, there are four reasons why managers and all decision makers should adopt the Golden Rule.

1. The Golden Rule is accepted by most people.
2. The Golden Rule is easy to understand.
3. The Golden Rule is a win–win philosophy.
4. The Golden Rule acts as a compass when you need direction.[61]

As one considers the ethics principles and concepts presented, no single principle is recommended for use always. As one gets into each principle, one encounters a number of challenges with definitions, measurement, and generalizability. The more one gets into each principle, the more one realizes how difficult it would be for a person to use each principle consistently as a guide to decision making. On the other hand, to say that an ethical principle is imperfect is not to say that it has not raised important criteria that should be addressed in personal or business decision making. The major principles and approaches we have discussed have raised to our consciousness the importance of the collective good, individual rights, caring, character, serving others first, and fairness.

In summary, the principles approach to ethics focuses on guidelines or concepts that have been created to help people and organizations make wise, ethical decisions. Two ethical categories include the teleological (ends-based) and the deontological (duty-based). Both duty and consequences are important ethical concepts. In our discussion, we have treated the following as important components of the principles-based approach: utilitarianism, rights, justice, caring, virtue, servant leadership, and the Golden Rule. Such principles, or principle-based approaches, cause us to think deeply and to reflect carefully on the ethical decisions we face in our managerial and organizational lives. For the most part, these principles are rooted in moral philosophy, logic, and religion. On a more pragmatic level, we turn now to a series of ethical tests that constitute another major approach to ethics.

8.2b Ethical Tests Approach to Decision Making

In addition to the principles approach to ethics in guiding personal and managerial decision making, a number of practical **ethical tests** also might be set forth and used to help clarify what is the most prudent course of action to take. Whereas the principles have almost exclusively been generated by moral philosophers and business ethicists, the ethical tests presented here have been culled from the real-world experiences of many. The ethical tests are more practical or hands-on in orientation and do not require the depth of moral thinking that the principles do. The answer to the ethical tests questions should provide useful guidance. No single test is recommended as a universal answer to the question, "What action or decision should I take in this situation?" However, each person may find one or several tests that will be beneficial in helping to clarify the appropriate course of action in a decision situation.

To most of us, the notion of a test invokes the thought of questions posed that need to be answered. Indeed, each of these tests for managerial ethical decision making requires the thoughtful deliberation of a central query that gets to the heart of the ethics issue. The answer to the question should help the decision maker decide whether the course of action, practice, or decision should be pursued or not. No single test is foolproof, but each should be helpful. Often, several tests can be used in conjunction with one another.

Test of Common Sense. With this first test, the individual simply asks, "Does the action I am getting ready to take really make sense?" When you think of behavior that might have ethical implications, it is logical to consider the practical consequences. If, for example, you would surely get caught engaging in a questionable practice, the action does not pass the **test of common sense**. Many unethical practices have come to light when one is led to ask whether a person really used her or his common sense at all. This test has limitations. For example, if you conclude that you would not get caught engaging in a questionable practice, this test might lead you to think that the questionable practice is an acceptable course of action, when in fact it is not. In addition, there may be other aspects of the situation that you have overlooked. Some have called the test of commonsense the **"smell" test**. If a proposed course of action stinks, do not do it.

Test of One's Best Self. Psychologists tell us that each person has a self-concept. Most people can envision a scenario of themselves *at their best*. This ethics test requires the individual to pose the question, "Is this action or decision I'm getting ready to take compatible with my concept of myself *at my best*?" This test addresses the notion of the esteem with which we hold ourselves and the kind of person we want to be known as. Naturally, this test would not be of much value to those who do not hold themselves in high esteem. To those concerned about their esteem and reputation, however, this could be a powerful guide preventing one from taking a questionable course of action.

Test of Making Something Public (Disclosure Rule). The test of making something public, sometimes called the disclosure rule, is one of the most powerful tests.[62] If you are about to engage in a questionable practice or action, you might pose the following questions: "How would I feel if others knew I was doing this? How would I feel if I knew that my decisions or actions were going to be featured on the national evening news tonight for the entire world to see?" This test addresses the issue of whether your action or decision can withstand public disclosure and scrutiny. How would you feel if all your friends, family, and colleagues knew you were engaging in this action? If you feel comfortable with this thought, you are probably on solid footing. If you feel uncomfortable with this thought, you might need to rethink your position. A variation of this test has been called the "Grandma test." Here the question would be "If my grandmother saw what I was doing, would she approve?"

The concept of public exposure is quite powerful. A poll of managers was taken asking whether the Foreign Corrupt Practices Act would stop bribes abroad. Many of the managers said it would not. When asked what *would* stop bribes, most managers thought that public exposure would be most effective. "If the public knew we were accepting bribes, this knowledge would have the best chance of being effective," they replied. This idea gives further testimony to the strength of the transparency movement that is permeating organizations today.

Test of Ventilation. The test of ventilation is to "expose" your proposed action to others and get their thoughts on it before acting. This test works best if you get opinions from people who you know might not see things your way. The important point here is that you do not isolate yourself with your ethical dilemma but seek others' views. After you have subjected your proposed course of action to other opinions, you may find that you have not been thinking clearly or fairly. In other words, ventilate—or share—your ethical quandary, rather than keeping it to yourself. Someone else may say something of value that will help you in making your decision.

Test of Purified Idea. An idea or action might be thought to be "purified"—that is, cleansed or made acceptable—when a person with authority says or implies it is appropriate. Such a person of authority might be a supervisor, an accountant, or a lawyer. The central question here is, "Am I thinking this action or decision is right just because someone with appropriate or higher authority or knowledge says it is right?" Be careful about this type thinking. If you look hard enough, you always can find a lawyer or an accountant to endorse almost any idea if it is phrased right.[63] However, these other persons are not the final arbiter of what is right or wrong. Similarly, just because a superior says an action or a decision is ethical does not make it so. The decision or course of action may still be questionable or wrong even though someone else has sanctioned it with her or his approval. This is one of the most common ethical errors people make, and people must constantly be reminded that they themselves ultimately will be held accountable if the action is indefensible.[64]

Test of the Big Four. Another test of your ethical behavior is to question whether it has fallen victim to "the Big Four." The Big Four are four characteristics of decision making that may lead you astray or toward the unethical course of action. The four factors are greed, speed, laziness, and haziness.[65] *Greed* is the drive to acquire more and more in your own self-interest. *Speed* refers to the tendency to rush things and cut corners because you are under the pressure of time. Do not confuse "cutting corners" with efficiency. *Laziness* may lead you to take the easy course of action that requires the least amount of effort. This can lead to mental errors. *Haziness* may lead you to acting or reacting without a clear idea of what is going on. Be sure you understand the situation before taking action. All four of these factors represent temptations that, if succumbed to, might lead to unethical behavior.[66]

Gag Test. This test was provided by a judge on the Louisiana Court of Appeals. He argued that a manager's clearest signal that a dubious decision or action is going too far is when you simply "gag" at the prospect of carrying it out.[67] Admittedly, this test can capture only the grossest of unethical behaviors, but there are some managers who may need such a crude kind of test. Actually, this test is intended to be more humorous than serious, but a few might be helped by it. Figure 8-2 summarizes the practical ethical guidelines that may be extracted from these ethical tests.

FIGURE 8-2 Practical Guidelines Derived from Key Ethical Tests

Ethical Test	Practical Ethical Guideline
Common Sense	If the proposed course of action violates your "common sense," don't do it. If it doesn't pass the "smell" test, don't do it.
One's Best Self	If the proposed course of action is not consistent with your perception of yourself at your "best" don't engage in it.
Making Something Public	If you would not be comfortable with people knowing you did something, don't do it. Don't take a course of action if you think your grandma might disapprove.
Ventilation	Expose your proposed course of action to others' opinions. Don't keep your ethical dilemma to yourself. Get a second opinion.
Purified Idea	Don't think that others in authority such as an accountant, a lawyer, or a boss can "purify" your proposed action by saying they think it is okay. It still may be wrong. You will still be held responsible.
Big Four	Don't compromise your action or decision by tempting behaviors, such as greed, speed, laziness, or haziness.
Gag Test	If you "gag" at the prospect of carrying out a proposed course of action, don't do it.

Use Several Tests in Combination. None of the previously mentioned tests alone offers a perfect way to determine whether a decision, act, or practice is ethical or unethical. If several tests are used in combination, especially the more powerful ones, they do provide a means of practically examining proposed actions before engaging in them. To repeat, this assumes that the individual really wants to do what is right and fair and is looking for assistance. To the fundamentally unethical person, however, these tests would not be of much value.

Based on a five-year study of ethical principles and ethical tests, Phillip Lewis asserted that there is high agreement on how a decision maker should behave when faced with a moral choice. He presents a general process:

> *In fact, there is almost a step-by-step sequence. Notice: One should (1) look at the problem from the position of the other person(s) affected by a decision; (2) try to determine what virtuous response is expected; (3) ask (a) how it would feel for the decision to be disclosed to a wide audience and (b) whether the decision is consistent with organizational goals; and (4) act in a way that is (a) right and just for any other person in a similar situation and (b) good for the organization.*[68]

Implicit in Lewis's recommendation is evidence of stakeholder theory, virtue theory, servant leadership, the Golden Rule, the disclosure rule, and Rawls's principle of justice.

8.3 Managing Organizational Ethics

To this point, our discussion has centered on principles, guidelines, and approaches to managerial decision making. Clearly, ethical decision making is at the heart of business ethics, and we cannot stress enough the need to sharpen decision-making skills if amorality is to be prevented and moral management is to be achieved. Now we shift our attention to the *organizational context* in which decision making occurs. Actions and practices that take place within the organization's structure, processes, culture, or climate are vital in bringing about ethical business practices and results. Based on his own research, Craig VanSandt has concluded, "Understanding and managing an organization's ethical work climate may go a long way toward defining the difference between how a company does and what kind of organization it is."[69]

To manage ethics in an organization, a manager must appreciate that the organization's ethical climate is just one part of its overall corporate culture. When McNeil Laboratories, a subsidiary of Johnson & Johnson, voluntarily withdrew Tylenol® from the market immediately after the reports of tainted, poisoned products, some people wondered why they made this decision. An often cited response was, "It's the J & J way."[70] This statement conveys a noteworthy message about the firm's ethical work climate or corporate culture. It also raises the question of how organizations and managers should deal with, understand, and shape business ethics through actions taken, policies established, and examples set. The organization's moral climate is a complex entity, and we can discuss only some facets of it in this section.[71] Thomas A. Kennedy, Chairman of the Board and CEO of Raytheon, has argued that "a strong ethical culture requires work. We believe that working at ethics plays dividends, and that it gives us a competitive advantage."[72]

Figure 8-3 portrays several levels of moral climate and some of the key factors that may come to bear on the manager as he or she makes decisions. What happens within organizations, as Figure 8-3 depicts, is nested in industry's, business's, and society's moral climate. Our focus in this section is on the organization's moral climate. Regardless of the ethics of individuals, organizational factors prove to be powerful in shaping ethical or unethical behavior and practices. The following three major questions drive the consideration of managing organizational ethics:

FIGURE 8-3 Factors Affecting the Morality of Managers and Employees

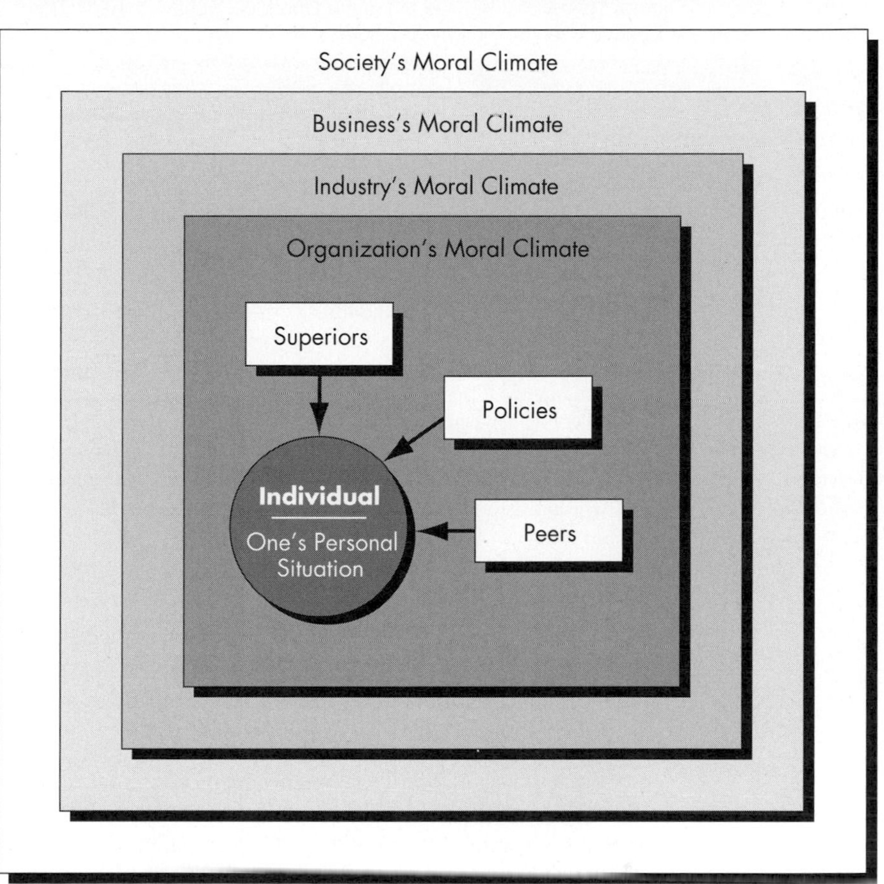

1. What factors contribute to ethical or unethical behavior in the organization?
2. What actions, strategies, or best practices might the management use to improve the organization's ethical climate?
3. What psychological and organizational processes revealed through "behavioral ethics" come into play when ethical decision making and behavior are pursued?

8.3a Factors Affecting the Organization's Moral Climate

For managers to be able to create an ethical work climate, they must first understand the factors at work in the organization that influence whether or not other managers and employees behave ethically. More than a few studies have been conducted that have sought to identify and to rank the sources of ethical behavior in organizations.

Figure 8-4 summarizes the findings of three landmark, baseline studies.

Although there is some variation in the rankings of the three studies, several findings are worthy of note:

- *Behavior of superiors* was ranked as the primary influence on unethical behavior in all three studies. In other words, the influence of bosses is powerful.
- *Behavior of one's peers* was ranked high in two of the three studies. People do pay attention to what their peers are doing and expecting.

FIGURE 8-4 Factors Influencing Unethical Behavior Question

"Listed Below Are the Factors That Many Believe Influence Unethical Behavior. Rank Them in Order of Their Influence or Contribution to Unethical Behaviors or Actions by Managers."[a]

	Posner and Schmidt Study[b] ($N = 1{,}443$)	Brenner and Molander Study[c] ($N = 1{,}227$)	Baumhart Study[d] ($N = 1{,}531$)
Behavior of superiors	2.17(1)	2.15(1)	1.9(1)
Behavior of one's organizational peers	3.30(2)	3.37(4)	3.1(3)
Ethical practices of one's industry or profession	3.57(3)	3.34(3)	2.6(2)
Society's moral climate[e]	3.79(4)	4.22(5)	
Formal organizational policy (or the lack thereof)	3.84(5)	3.27(2)	3.3(4)
Personal financial need	4.09(6)	4.46(6)	4.1(5)

[a]Ranking is based on a scale of 1 (most influential) to 6 (least influential).

[b]Barry Z. Posner and Warren H. Schmidt, "Values and the American Manager: An Update," *California Management Review* (Spring 1984), 202–216.

[c]Steve Brenner and Earl Molander, "Is the Ethics of Business Changing?" *Harvard Business Review* (January/February 1977).

[d]Raymond C. Baumhart, "How Ethical Are Businessmen?" *Harvard Business Review* (July/August 1961), 6ff.

[e]This item is not included in the Baumhart study.

- *Industry or professional ethical practices* ranked in the upper half in all three studies. These contextual factors are influential.
- *Personal financial need* ranked last in all three studies. But let's not assume it does not matter because for some people it does.

What stands out in these studies from an organizational perspective is the influence of the behavior of one's superiors and peers. Also notable about these findings is that quite often it is assumed that society's moral climate has a lot to do with managers' morality, but this factor was ranked low in the two studies in which it was considered. Apparently, society's moral climate serves as a background factor that does not have a direct and immediate impact on organizational ethics. Furthermore, it is enlightening to know that personal financial need ranked so low. But we should not assume that personal needs and wants are irrelevant. Sometimes personal financial needs and greed are at work. What these findings suggest is that there are factors at work over which managers can exercise some discretion. Thus, we begin to see the managerial dimension of business ethics.

Pressures Exerted on Employees by Superiors. One major consequence of the behavior of superiors and peers is that pressure is placed on subordinates and/or other organizational members to achieve results, and this often requires that they compromise their ethics. In one national study of this topic, managers were asked to what extent they agreed with the following proposition: "Managers today feel under pressure to compromise personal standards to achieve company goals."[73] It is insightful to consider the management levels of the 64.4 percent of the respondents who agreed with the proposition. The results by management level were:

- Top management: 50 percent agreed
- Middle management: 65 percent agreed
- Lower management: 85 percent agreed

This study revealed that the perceived pressure to compromise ethics seems to be felt most by those in lower management, followed by those in middle management. In a later study, managers were asked whether they sometimes had to compromise their personal principles to conform to organizational expectations.[74] Twenty percent of the top executives agreed, 27 percent of the middle managers agreed, and 41 percent of the lower managers agreed. In other words, the same pattern prevailed in this second study.

What is especially insightful about these findings is the *pattern of response*. It appears that the lower a manager, or employee, is in the hierarchy, the more he or she perceives pressures to engage in unethical conduct. Although there are several plausible explanations for this phenomenon, one explanation seems particularly attractive—that higher level managers do not fully understand how strongly their subordinates perceive pressures to go along with their bosses. These varying perceptions at different levels in the managerial hierarchy suggest that higher-level managers may not be tuned in to how pressure is perceived or "felt" at lower levels. This breakdown in understanding, or lack of sensitivity by higher management to how far subordinates will go to please them, can be conducive to lower-level subordinates behaving unethically out of a real or perceived fear of reprisal, a misguided sense of loyalty, or a distorted concept of their jobs.

Another study of the sources and consequences of workplace pressure[75] produced findings that were consistent with those of the studies reported earlier and provided additional insights into the detrimental consequences of workplace pressure. The following were among the key findings of this study:

- The majority of workers (60 percent) felt a substantial amount of pressure on the job. More than one out of four (27 percent) felt a "great deal" of pressure.
- Nearly half of all workers (48 percent) reported that, due to pressure, they had engaged in one or more unethical and/or illegal actions during the past year. The most frequently cited misbehavior was cutting corners on quality control.
- The sources most commonly cited as contributing to workplace pressure were "balancing work and family" (52 percent), "poor internal communications" (51 percent), "work hours/workload" (51 percent), and "poor leadership" (51 percent).

In another major survey of ethics in organizations conducted by the Ethics Resource Center, some other insights regarding pressure perceived was found:[76]

- First-line supervisors and employees were the groups most "at risk" to feel pressure.
- Organizational transitions such as mergers, acquisitions, and restructurings are associated with increased pressure on employees to compromise organizational ethics standards.
- Employees who observe unethical actions more frequently in their organization tend to feel pressure to compromise their ethical standards.
- Employees whose organizations have in place key elements of formal ethics programs feel less pressure to compromise standards.

In the 2013 National Business Ethics Survey, the most recent available at this writing, the survey revealed that employees still perceive pressure to compromise their ethics but that this has not been getting worse in the past couple years. It was also found that the ethical misconduct observed by the respondents among managers, the people who are supposed to be setting good examples of ethical conduct, revealed a troubling pattern. Of the misconduct observed among managers, the frequency of misconduct observed was senior leaders (24 percent), middle managers (19 percent), and first-line supervisors (17 percent). This pattern reflects a problematic reality of ethical issues among higher-level managers. Among nonmanagerial personnel, 41 percent of the respondents identified their peers as a source of ethical misconduct.[77]

8.3b Improving the Organization's Ethical Culture

Because the behavior of managers has been identified as the most important influence on the ethical behavior of organization members, it should come as no surprise that most

ETHICS IN PRACTICE CASE

More Sales, Lower Ethics?

At my recent job, I held a position as a Customer Service and Sales Representative for a well-recognized bank. My responsibility was to help customers solve issues and concerns they might have on their accounts, but mainly I was to concentrate on selling them bank products. I started out as a teller and worked my way up to a Sales Rep. As I went through training they instructed us to concentrate on customer service before anything else, but also mentioned that sales were an important part of the position, yet never mentioning that it would be the primary goal. The goal setting level in the bank is determined by the amount of sales the bank needs quarterly. However, these goals differ from the requirements of each individual's position. There is also a big emphasis on meeting daily sales goals to reach your numbers by the end of the quarter.

As I started working, I realized that it was difficult to meet the daily goals that are expected. The Bank sets goals that are somewhat unrealistic to most of us, particularly because we have the same customers visiting the bank. It is very difficult to sell other products to the same customers since they already have every bank product they need. By the bank setting these high goals, we are pushed to sell to some customers extra checking or savings accounts that sometimes were unnecessary for them to have. Yet, to achieve our goals we encourage them to open the new accounts by saying it would somehow benefit them. I am not pleased with doing this, since we could easily just convert the existing product to the new one without having to open another account for them. The customers have more trouble keeping track of all these other extra accounts rather than just keeping the existing ones with the new benefits. However, not selling them the new products sometimes makes it impossible to meet our sales goal for the quarter.

1. Is it ethical for the bank to keep raising our goals and expect that we keep selling these extra accounts that customers might not really need?
2. What are the ethical issues facing the company?
3. Is it right for us not to disclose to the customer the idea of keeping the same account and just covert it instead of opening a new one?
4. Should I give into the pressure of the company to meet the company's goal? What should I do?

Contributed by Catalina Vargas

actions and strategies for improving the organization's ethical culture must originate from top management and other management levels as well. Organizational ethical culture refers to the shared values, beliefs, behaviors and ways of doing things in the organization. It has been found that positive corporate cultures help a company's bottom line but the reverse is not necessarily true—a company's success is not enough to ensure a positive culture.[78] Therefore, intended initiatives to improve the organization's culture are needed; it does not just happen because the business is successful.

The process by which managers strive to improve upon the organization's ethical culture has sometimes been referred to as "institutionalizing ethics" into the organization.[79] According to the Ethics Resource Center, critical aspects of an organization's ethical culture include management's trustworthiness, whether managers at all levels talk about ethics and model ethical behavior, and the extent to which employees value and support ethical conduct, accountability and transparency. Ethics culture includes the tone set by top management leaders, supervisor reinforcement of ethical behavior, and peer commitment—supporting one another in doing the right thing.[80]

The Ethics Resource Center has found that misconduct declines as the company's ethical culture improves. Their research found that misconduct was less observed as ethical cultures transitioned from weak, weak-leaning, strong-leaning, to strong. It was found that strong ethical cultures were ones in which managements and supervisors:

- Communicated ethics as a priority
- Set a good example of ethical conduct
- Kept commitments
- Provided information as to what was going on
- Supported following organization's standards[81]

In short, an organization's ethical culture has been found to be one of the most important factors in influencing and producing sound ethical results.

Compliance versus Ethics Orientation. Another factor important to an ethical culture is whether the organization has a compliance or an ethics orientation. An organization with a culture of ethics is most likely a mixture of an emphasis on compliance and on such values as integrity or ethics. Early efforts of companies were to avert corporate crime. Compliance emphases took a huge step forward when the Organizational Sentencing Guidelines were introduced in 1991 and were revised in 2004 in response to the Sarbanes–Oxley Act. Their most recent revision came in 2015. These guidelines began a partnership between companies and the federal government to prevent and deter corporate illegal/unethical practices.[82] These guidelines were created by the U.S. Sentencing Commission, which is an independent agency of the judicial branch of the federal government. The guidelines gave companies incentives for creating strong compliance and ethics programs. It is little wonder, then, that we have seen such programs increase in number and become vital parts of companies' corporate cultures.

An ongoing discussion today is whether a **compliance orientation** or an **ethics orientation** should prevail in companies' **ethics programs.**[83] Historically, more emphasis has been placed on legal compliance than on ethics. More recently, much concern has been raised about the restrictiveness of a compliance focus. Several concerns articulated about a compliance focus have been identified.[84]

- First, a pure *compliance focus* could undermine the ways of thinking or habits of mind that are needed in ethics thinking. Ethics thinking is more principles based, while compliance thinking is more rule bound and legalistic.
- Second, it has been argued that compliance can squeeze out ethics. An organization can become so focused on following the law that ethics considerations no longer get factored into discussions.
- Third, the issue of "false consciousness" has been raised. This means that managers may become accustomed to addressing issues in a mechanistic, rule-based way, and this may cause them to not consider tougher issues that a more ethics-focused approach might require.[85]

Because of the rule of law and growing litigation, a compliance focus cannot be eliminated. This is so even though some lawyers have claimed that the United States has experienced a "national drift" from the rule of law beginning with the 2008 financial crisis.[86] The approach recommended here is toward developing organizational cultures and programs that aspire to be ethics-focused. The importance of both has been emphasized in the observation that the ethics perspective is needed to give a compliance program "soul," while compliance features may be necessary to give ethics programs more "body."[87] In short, both are essential.

8.4 Best Practices for Improving an Organization's Ethics

Best practices are those approaches, programs, policies, or guidelines that experience has shown produce the most effective results. In the following sections, we will discuss some of the best practices that experts have concluded are vital to improving an organization's ethical culture or climate. Figure 8-5 summarizes a number of best practices for creating such an ethical organization. Top management leadership in the pursuit of moral management is at the hub of these initiatives. Board of Directors' Oversight has become especially vital in recent years as corporate governance has been discovered to be an integral part of an ethical culture.

FIGURE 8-5 Best Practices for Improving an Organization's Ethical Culture

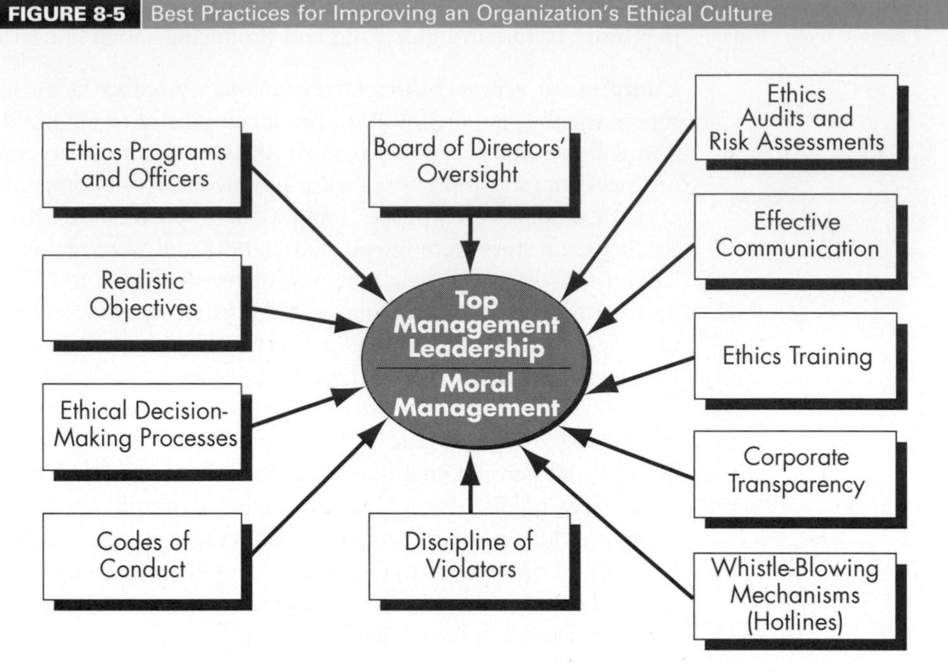

There are three key elements that must exist if an ethical organizational culture is to be developed and sustained. These include the following:

1. The continuous presence of **ethical leadership** reflected by the board of directors, senior executives and managers
2. The existence of a set of **core ethical values** infused throughout the organization by way of policies, processes, and practices
3. A **formal ethics program** that includes a code of ethics, ethics training and ethics officer and ethics training.[88] These and other considerations are discussed below.

8.4a Top Management Leadership (Moral Management)

It has become an established principle of ethical leadership that the **moral tone** of an organization is set by top management. One poll of communication professionals found that over half believed that top management is an organization's conscience.[89] This is because managers and employees look to their bosses for cues regarding acceptable practices and policies. A former chairman of a major steel company stated it well: "Starting at the top, management has to set an example for all the others to follow."[90] Although the concept of moral tone is not always completely defined, it is intended to capture the ethical messages that are conveyed by persons in leadership positions.[91] Researcher D. M. Mayer and colleagues explain that "leaders set the tone of an organization by enacting practices, policies, and procedures that help facilitate the display of ethical behavior and reduce the likelihood of misconduct."[92]

Top management, through its capacity to set a personal example and to shape policy, is in the ideal position to provide a highly visible role model. The authority and ability to shape policy, both formal and implied, forms one of the vital aspects of the job of any leader in any organization. This aspect of becoming a moral manager has been referred to as "role modeling through visible action." Effective moral managers recognize that

ETHICS IN PRACTICE CASE

Fired for Cheating on Employer Tests

In October 2015, Goldman Sachs Group, Inc. fired about 20 new employee analysts for cheating on tests during their training period . The employees had been working with the investment bank's securities division and included analysts from its New York and London offices. The topics on the tests were the employees' knowledge of important industry and regulatory information, including information about compliance, gift-giving policies, and anti-money laundering policies. JPMorgan Chase had fired 10 employees a month earlier for similar violations.

Goldman Sachs is one of the most selective employers on Wall Street, and during the previous year the company hired only 3 percent of its 267,000 applicants. The firm's CEO has called his company the employer of choice in their industry. They typically recruit the best and the brightest from some of the nation's most elite business schools. One observer said that getting a job at Goldman was harder than being accepted into Harvard.

Seemingly, the tests had never been received well by the new employees. The tests are seen as time consuming, repetitive and annoying and some of the test takers saw them as a waste of time and put them off until the last minute. Some observers remarked that cheating on these types of tests had been an accepted part of finance training in the industry.

How the employees got caught cheating was somewhat surprising in its lack of complexity. The employees who cheated used their Goldman-issued computers to look up terms that appeared on the exam . They took their tests on these computers and also used them to Google search for some of the answers. The company was able to trace the cheating activity on their computers. Some of the cheaters shared answers, a practice said to be a routine way to save time during the hectic workweek.

The tests they took were not seen as difficult and a person had to score a 70 to pass on the one hour test. If they failed, they would have been given another chance to take the test and they would not have been fired (at least the first time). However, they might have evoked disappointment and ire by their supervisors.

A Goldman Sachs spokesperson said "this conduct was not only a clear violation of the rules, but completely inconsistent with the values we foster at the firm."

1. If these were bright, young employees who had survived a very competitive hiring process, why do you think they risked it all by cheating?
2. Did the topics covered by the test make firing a more likely outcome? Should the test takers have seen this?
3. Was firing a fair consequence in this situation? Should the company have used some other penalty? If so, what?

Sources: Julia La Roche, "This is how the Goldman Sachs analysts who got fired cheated," Business Insider, October 19, 2015, http://www.businessinsider.com/goldman-sachs-analysts-fired-for-cheating-2015-10, Accessed February 9, 2016; Justin Baer, "Goldman to fire workers for cheating," Wall Street Journal, October 17-18/2016, B2, Sofia Horta E Costa and Ruth David, "Goldman, JPMorgan said to fire 30 analysts for cheating on tests," BloombergBusiness, October 16, 2015, http://www.bloomberg.com/news/articles/2015-10-16/goldman-sachs-said-to-dismiss-20-analysts-for-cheating-on-tests, Accessed February 9, 2016.

they live in a fishbowl and that employees are watching them for cues about what's important.[93] There is a striking contrast between weak and strong ethical leadership in business practice today. Indeed, weak leaders are often called "bad" leaders and, according to researchers Gini and Green, they could be called "*mis-leaders*."[94]

Weak Ethical Leadership An example of weak ethical leadership (or role modeling) was found in one of the authors' consulting experiences in a small company where a long-time employee was identified as having embezzled about $20,000 over a 15-year period. When the employee was questioned as to why she had done this, she explained that she thought it was all right because the president of the company had led her to believe it was okay by actions he had taken. She further explained that any time during the fall, when the leaves had fallen in his yard and he needed them raked, he would simply take company personnel off their jobs and have them do it. When he needed cash, he would take it out of the company's petty cash box or get the key to the soft drink machine and raid its coin box. When he needed stamps to mail his personal Christmas cards, he would take them out of the company stamp box. The woman's perception was that it was okay for her to take the money because the president did it frequently.

Therefore, she thought it was an acceptable practice for her as well. When later questioned, the president admitted this was all true and he thought the woman should not be dealt with too harshly.

Strong Ethical Leadership An example of strong, positive ethical leadership was seen in the case of a firm that was manufacturing modern vacuum tubes. One day the plant manager called a hurried meeting to announce that a sample of the tubes in production had failed a critical safety test. This meant that the safety and performance of the batch of 10,000 tubes was highly questionable. The plant manager wondered out loud, "What are we going to do now?" Ethical leadership was shown by the vice president for technical operations, who looked around the room at each person and then declared in a low voice, "Scrap them!" According to an employee who worked for this vice president, that act set the tone for the corporation for years, because every person present knew of situations in which faulty products had been shipped under pressures of time and budget.[95]

These cases provide a vivid example of how a leader's actions and behavior communicated important messages to others in the organization. In the absence of knowing what to do, most employees look to the behavior of their leaders for cues as to what conduct is acceptable. In the second case, another crucial point is illustrated. When we speak of management providing ethical leadership, it is not just restricted to top management. Vice presidents, plant managers, supervisors, and, indeed, all managerial personnel share the responsibility for ethical leadership. This was reinforced in one ethics survey when employees were asked to identify their "leaders" and quite often they identified their direct supervisors as top management more often than the CEO or president.[96] This finding reinforces the critical role that all managers play in ethical leadership. To workers, what all their superiors in the organization do is important.

Two Pillars of Leadership It has been argued that a manager's reputation for ethical leadership is founded on two pillars: perceptions of the manager both as a moral person *and* as a moral manager. Being a *moral person* requires three major attributes: traits, behaviors, and decision making. Important traits are stable personal attributes, such as integrity, honesty, and trustworthiness. Critical behaviors—what you do, not what you say—include doing the right thing, showing concern for people, being open, and being personally ethical. Decision making by the moral person needs to reflect a solid set of ethical values and principles. In this activity, the manager would hold to values, be objective/fair, demonstrate concern for society, and follow ethical decision rules.[97]

The idea of the second pillar, being a *moral manager*, was developed and discussed in the previous chapter. According to researchers, moral managers recognize the importance of proactively putting ethics at the forefront of their ethical agenda. To them, good leadership necessarily consists of a moral ingredient.[98] Putting ethics at the forefront involves three major activities. First, the moral manager must engage in *role modeling* through visible action. Second, the moral manager *communicates about ethics and values*. Third, the moral manager needs to *use rewards and discipline effectively*. This is a powerful way to send signals about desirable and undesirable conduct in the workplace.[99]

In a period in which the importance of a sound corporate culture has been strongly advocated, ethical leaders must stress the primacy of integrity and morality as vital components of the organization's culture. There are many different ways and situations in which management needs to do this. In general, management needs to create a climate of moral consciousness. In everything it does, it must stress the importance of sound ethical principles and practices. The leader must infuse the organization's climate with values and ethical consciousness, not just run a one-person show. This point is made vividly clear in the following observation: "Ethics programs which are seen as part of one manager's management system, and not as a part of the general organizational process, will be less likely to have a lasting role in the organization."[100] In short, ethics is more about leadership than about programs.

8.4b Effective Communication of Ethical Messages

Management also carries a profound burden in terms of providing ethical leadership in the area of effective communication. We have seen the importance of communicating through acts, principles, and organizational climate. Later we will discuss further the communication aspects of setting realistic objectives, codes of conduct, and the decision-making process. Here, however, we want to stress the importance of communicating principles, techniques, and practices. If organization members do not clearly understand what the ethical standards, values and expectations are, this creates a major impediment to their use.

Conveying the importance of ethics through communication includes both written and verbal forms of communication. It also includes nonverbal communications. In each of these settings, management should operate according to certain key ethical principles. Candor, fidelity, and confidentiality are three very important communication principles. *Candor* requires that a manager be forthright, sincere, and honest in communication transactions. It requires the manager to be fair and free from prejudice and malice in the communication. *Fidelity* in communication means that the communicator should be faithful to detail, should be accurate, and should avoid deception or exaggeration. *Confidentiality* is another principle that ought to be stressed. The ethical manager must exercise care in deciding what information she or he discloses to others. Trust can be easily shattered if the manager does not have a keen sense of what is confidential in a communication.

8.4c Ethics and Compliance Programs and Officers

One of the most important strategies in creating an ethical workplace culture is the use of ethics and compliance programs along with officers to lead them in their initiatives and responsibilities. Ethics and compliance programs are typically organizational units, people or departments that have been assigned the responsibility for monitoring and improving ethics in the organization. There are several certification programs for ethics and compliance officers. One of the most popular is the LPEC—Leading Professional in Ethics and Compliance—which is available through the Ethics and Compliance Initiative. Recognized at the international level, LPEC-certified professionals represent over 60 countries and range across all industries.[101]

Based upon common practice, ethics and compliance programs typically include the following features:[102]

- Written standards of ethical workplace conduct (e.g., codes of conduct/ethics)
- Ethics training on the standards
- Mechanisms to seek ethics advice or information
- Methods or means for reporting misconduct anonymously
- Performance evaluations of ethical conduct
- Systems to discipline violators
- A set of guiding values or principles

In addition to this list of common practices, other important features of successful ethics and compliance programs include the ethical tone set at the top, and the organization's culture, risk assessments, and ethics testing.[103]

A key finding in business ethics research has been that ethics and compliance programs are increasing in number and that they do make a difference. A major survey disclosed that the impact of ethics programs depends somewhat on the culture in which they are implemented. The study found that the more formal are the program elements, the better it is; formal programs make more of a difference in weak ethical cultures, and, once a strong culture has been established, the formal programs do not have as much impact on results.[104] It has also been estimated that companies with effective programs face half the rules violations as those without effective programs. CEO Patricia Harned of the Ethics Resource Center says "companies that invest in ethics reap an enormous return." She goes on to say that "better workplace ethics cuts business risks by reducing the chance that serious ethics problems will throw companies off course and distract them from their core business."[105]

Figure 8-6 summarizes the elements that ought to exist in companies' ethics programs in order to comply with the U.S. Sentencing Commission's Organizational Guidelines for effective programs. Two major benefits accrue to organizations that follow these guidelines. First, following the guidelines mitigates severe financial and oversight penalties. Second, some prosecutors are choosing not to pursue some actions when the companies in question already have sound programs in place if they follow these guidelines.[106]

In 2016, the Ethics and Compliance Initiative released a report intended to be a road map for companies wanting to establish programs that moved beyond the U. S. Sentencing Commission's guidelines.[107] The report was compiled by a team of chief compliance

FIGURE 8-6 Essential Elements in an Effective Ethics and Compliance Program

The U.S. Sentencing Commission has identified seven key elements that companies should have in their ethics and compliance programs to satisfy the commission's review . If a company has these important elements, it will be dealt with less harshly should violations arise. If companies follow the guidelines they may receive reduced fines, reduced sentences, or deferred prosecutions. Organizations should consider adopting Governance, Risk Management and Compliance (GRC) software applications to serve as foundations for their programs.

STRUCTURE. Establish Policies, Procedures, and Controls. Organizations must establish these to serve as standards to prevent and detect unethical conduct.

OVERSIGHT. Exercise Effective Compliance and Ethics Oversight. Multiple layers of management need to be involved to ensure the effectiveness of programs. Designated individuals at the various levels must be knowledgeable of the program.

DUE DILIGENCE. Exercise Due Diligence to Avoid Delegation of Authority to Unethical Individuals. Reasonable efforts need to be made to be sure that individuals with a history on unethical behavior are avoided.

COMMUNICATION. Communicate and Educate Employees on Programs. Practical steps must be taken periodically by the organization to be sure that all employees understand the policies, procedures, and standards.

MONITORING. Monitor and Audit Programs for Effectiveness. Mechanisms must be created for ensuring that the ethics and compliance program is being followed by all employees and that the program is effective.

PROMOTION & ENFORCEMENT. Ensure Consistent Promotion of Program and Enforcement of Violations. Organizations should reward those actions that demonstrate adherence to an ethical culture and discipline violators of ethical standards.

RESPONSE. Respond to Incidents and Take Steps to Prevent Future Incidents. Organizations should take appropriate investigative actions to look into possible violations and should preserve the confidentiality of such investigations.

Sources: U. S. Sentencing Commission, 2015 USSC Guidelines Manual, http://www.ussc.gov/guidelines-manual/2015/2015-ussc-guidelines-manual. Accessed February 29, 2016; Compliance 360. White Paper: The Seven Elements of an Effective Compliance and Ethics Program, http://compliance360.com/downloads/case/Seven_Elements_of_Effective_Compliance_Programs.pdf. Accessed February 29, 2016; "New Requirements for an Effective Ethics and Compliance Program," Jones Day Publications, http://www.jonesday.com/new_requirements_for_effective_compliance/. Accessed February 29, 2016.

officers, former regulators and lawmakers, and other thought leaders. The report presented five key tenets for the best compliance and ethics programs:

- Ethics and compliance are a central component to a company's business strategy.
- Ethics and compliance risks are owned, managed and mitigated and it's not just the job of the compliance people to do this; risks of noncompliance must be considered when companies conduct risk assessments.
- Leaders at all levels are involved in building and sustaining a culture of integrity.
- The organization should project its values and encourage the reporting of concerns or suspected wrongdoing.
- The organization will take action and hold itself accountable when wrongdoing takes place.[108]

The Ethics and Compliance Initiative has said that it will later make available a self-assessment tool to help organizations gauge where they are in the process of developing a strong program.[109]

Ethics and Compliance Officers Ethics and compliance programs are often headed by an individual with the title **ethics and compliance officer**, **ethics officer**, or **compliance officer**, who is in charge of implementing the array of ethics and compliance initiatives in the organization. In some cases, the creation of ethics programs and designation of ethics and compliance officers has been in response to the Federal Sentencing Guidelines, which reduced penalties to those companies with ethics programs that were found guilty of ethics violations.[110] Many companies have created ethics and compliance programs and hired officers to lead them because of the Sarbanes–Oxley law or because they were seeking to improve the organization's ethics.

Ethics and compliance programs often are established as an effort to centralize the coordination of ethics-related initiatives. Many ethics programs and ethics officers initially got started with compliance issues. Only later, in some cases, did ethics or integrity become a focal point of the programs. As suggested earlier, most ethics programs and ethics officers have major corporate responsibility for both legal compliance and ethics practices, and there is some debate as to whether they should be called compliance programs or ethics programs.[111] Major companies that do a lot of their business with the government, such as defense contractors, continue to emphasize compliance. Others strive more for a balance between compliance and ethics.

Just as ethics programs have proliferated in companies, the number of ethics officers occupying important positions in major firms has grown significantly. In addition, they are now scrutinized more carefully because some have been found personally liable for mistakes taking place within their firms.[112] These officers are increasingly getting a direct line to their company's boss as many companies are now responding more assertively to government enforcement efforts. Recently, major firms such as Johnson & Johnson, Alcatel-Lucent, Pfizer, and Tenet Healthcare have decided that their chief compliance officer would report directly to the CEO and Board rather than the chief legal or finance officer.[113] The purpose of such moves is to elevate their importance and authority over compliance and ethics matters.

There are two major professional organizations that ethics and compliance officers may join: (1) Ethics and Compliance Initiative (ECI), and (2) the Society of Corporate Compliance and Ethics (SCCE). The ECI is comprised of three nonprofit organizations: the Ethics Research Center; the Ethics and Compliance Association; and the Ethics and Compliance Certification Institute.[114] The SCCE is a member-based association for regulatory compliance professionals that provide training, certification, networking and other resources.[115]

As valuable as ethics and compliance programs and officers are, there is some possible downside danger in their existence. By holding individuals and organizational units responsible for the company's "ethics and compliance," there is some possibility that managers may tend to "delegate" to these persons/units the responsibility for the firm's ethics. Ethics is everyone's job, however, and specialized units should not be used as a substitute for the assumption of ethical responsibility by everyone in leadership positions.

8.4d Setting Realistic Objectives

Closely related to all ethics initiatives and programs being implemented by top management is the necessity that managers at all levels set realistic objectives or goals. A manager may quite innocently and inadvertently create a condition leading to unethical behavior on a subordinate's part. Take the case of a marketing manager setting a sales goal of a 20 percent increase for the next year when a 10 percent increase is all that could be realistically and honestly expected, even with outstanding performance. In the absence of clearly established and communicated ethical norms, it is easy to see how a subordinate might believe that she or he should go to any lengths to achieve the 20 percent goal. With the goal having been set too high, the salesperson faces a situation that is conducive to unethical behavior in order to please the superior.

Fred T. Allen, a former executive, strongly reinforced this point:

> *Top management must establish sales and profit goals that are realistic—goals that can be achieved with current business practices. Under the pressure of unrealistic goals, otherwise responsible subordinates will often take the attitude that "anything goes" in order to comply with the chief executive's target.*[116]

Managers need to be keenly sensitive to the possibility of unintentionally creating situations in which others may perceive a need or an incentive to cut corners or do the wrong thing. Unrealistic expectations are the primary driver of employees perceiving excessive pressure to achieve goals. This kind of knowledge is what justifies business ethics being a management and leadership topic.

8.4e Ethical Decision-Making Processes

Decision making is at the heart of the management process. If there is any practice or process that is synonymous with management, it is decision making. Decision making usually entails a process of stating the problem, analyzing the problem, identifying the possible courses of action that might be taken, evaluating these courses of action, deciding on the best alternative, and then implementing the chosen course of action.

Ethical decision making is not a simple process but rather a multifaceted one that is complicated by multiple alternatives, mixed outcomes, uncertain and extended consequences, and personal implications.[117] It would be nice if a set of ethical principles was readily available for the manager to "plug in" and walk away from, with a decision to be forthcoming. However, that was not the case when we discussed principles that help managerial decision making in Chapter 7, and it is not the case when we think of organizational decision making. The ethical principles discussed earlier are useful here, but there are no simple formulas revealing easy answers. The key here is that managers establish decision-making processes that will yield the most appropriate ethical decisions.

An Ethics Screen Although it is difficult to portray graphically the process of ethical decision making, it is possible as long as we recognize that such an effort cannot totally capture reality. Figure 8-7 presents one conception of the ethical decision-making process. In this model, the manager is asked to identify the action, decision, or behavior that is being considered and then work through the steps in the model. The decision maker is asked to subject the proposed course of action to an **ethics screen**, which

FIGURE 8-7 A Process of Ethical Decision Making Using an Ethics Screen

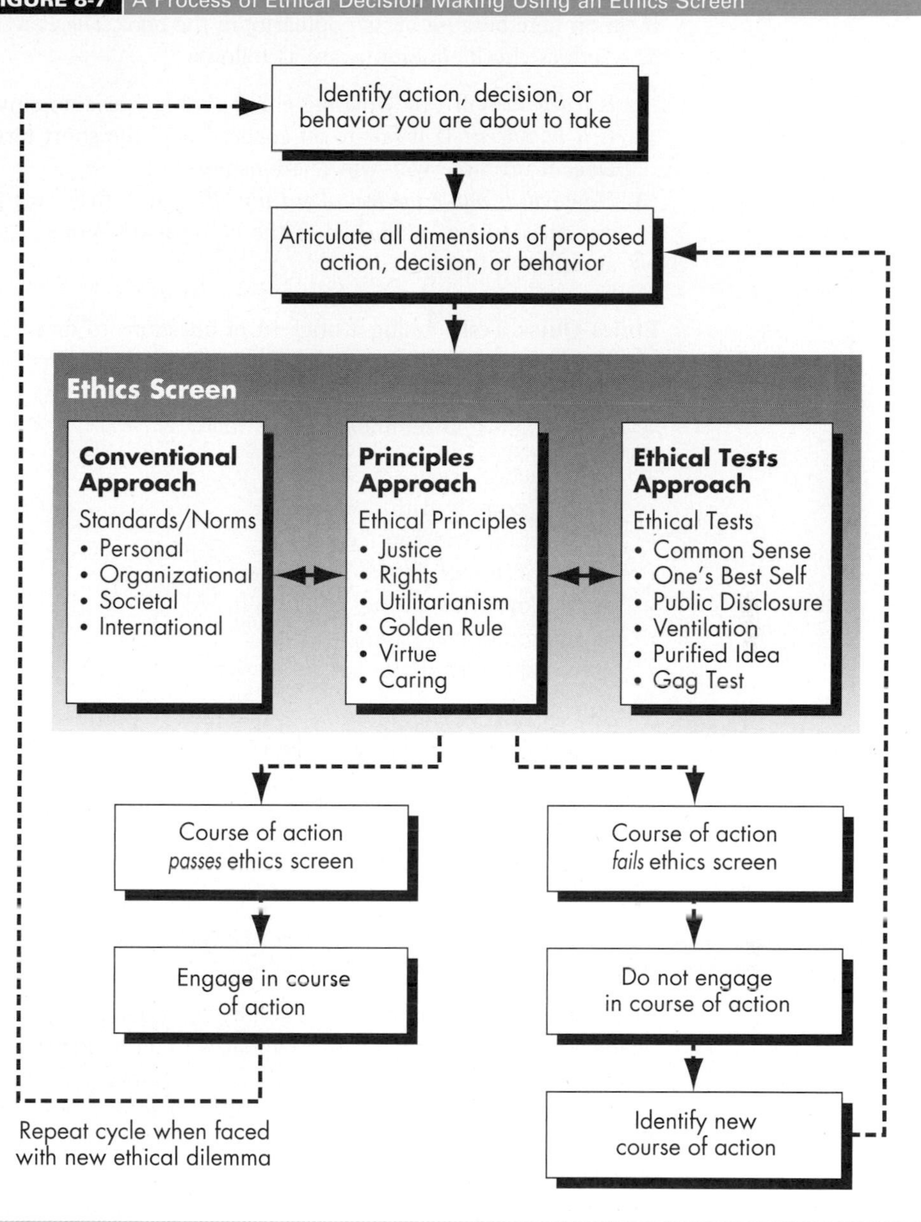

consists of several select standards against which the proposed course of action is to be compared. The idea is that unethical alternatives will be "screened out" and ethical ones will be "screened in." In the ethics screen presented in Figure 8-7, we reference our earlier discussion of the conventional approach (embodying societal standards/norms), the principles approach, and the ethical tests approach to ethical decision making. By using all or a combination of these ethical standards, it is expected that more ethical decisions will be made than would have been made otherwise.

Another useful approach to making ethical decisions is to systematically ask and answer a series of simple questions. This approach is similar to the Ethical Tests Approach presented earlier in the chapter.

Ethics Check One well-known set of questions to guide ethical decision making merits mention here because of its popularity in the book *The Power of Ethical Management.*[118] The "ethics check" questions are as follows:

1. *Is it legal*? Will I be violating either civil law or company policy?
2. *Is it balanced*? Is it fair to all concerned in the short term as well as the long term? Does it promote win–win relationships?
3. *How will it make me feel about myself*? Will it make me proud? Would I feel good if my decision was published in the newspaper? Would I feel good if my family knew about it?

Ethics Quick Test Using a brief set of questions to make ethical decisions has become popular in business. For example, for years now Texas Instruments has used and printed its seven-part "Ethics Quick Test" on a wallet card for its employees to carry. The test's seven questions and reminders are as follows:[119]

- Is the action legal?
- Does it comply with our values?
- If you do it, will you feel bad?
- How will it look in the newspaper?
- If you know it's wrong, don't do it.
- If you're not sure, ask.
- Keep asking until you get an answer.

This set of practical questions is intended to produce a process of ethical inquiry that is of immediate practical use and understanding to a group of employees and managers. Many of the items are similar or identical to points raised earlier in the Ethical Tests Approach. These questions help ensure that ethical due process takes place. Answers to these questions cannot tell us for sure whether our decisions are ethical or not, but they can help us be sure that we are raising the appropriate issues and genuinely attempting to be ethical.

8.4f Codes of Ethics or Conduct

Top management has the responsibility for establishing standards of behavior and for effectively communicating those standards to all managers and employees in the organization. The most formal way by which companies and ethics officers have fulfilled this responsibility is through the use of **codes of ethics** or **codes of conduct**. According to Joan Dubinsky, a former ethics officer and now ethics consultant, "a Code of Conduct is the single most important element of your ethics and compliance program. It sets the tone and direction for the entire function. Often, the Code is a standalone document, ideally only a few pages in length. It introduces the concept of ethics and compliance and provides an overview of what you mean when you talk about ethical business conduct."[120]

Virtually all major corporations have codes of conduct today, and the central questions in their usefulness or effectiveness revolve around the managerial policies and attitudes associated with their use.[121] Levi Strauss & Co. and Caterpillar have worldwide codes of ethics. Johnson & Johnson has a worldwide credo. McDonald's has worldwide standards of best practices. Firms that operate in the domestic market have codes that reflect more local concerns.[122] Some ethics codes are rather simple and straightforward. Take the case of Costco's Code of Ethics. According to the company's co-founder and former CEO, Jim Sinegal, the Costco code requires them to – (1) obey the law, (2) take care of your customers and your employees, (3) respect your suppliers, and if you systematically do these, you will (4) reward your shareholders.[123] Hasbro CEO Brian Goldner emphasizes the idea that an ethics code is essential: "Fundamentally, it starts with high ethical standards and a strong corporate code of conduct. We have a set of personal 'guideposts' around what it means to be ethical, responsible, transparent, and credible."[124]

Some corporate codes are designed around stakeholders. Others are designed around issues.[125] The content of corporate codes typically addresses the following topics: employment practices; employee, client, and vendor information; public information/ communications; conflicts of interest; relationships with vendors; environmental issues; ethical management practices; and political involvement.[126] Increasingly, corporate codes of conduct are addressing global issues and relationships with other firms, communities, and governments.[127] Recent research has found that the *quality of code content* plays a crucial role in the effectiveness of codes of conduct and in their ability to transform organizational cultures. Those companies maintaining high quality codes were found to be more often associated with high rankings of corporate social responsibility, ethical behavior, sustainability and public perception.[128]

Both successes and failures have been reported with organizational codes of conduct, but the acid test seems to be whether or not such codes actually become "living documents," not just platitudinous public relations statements that are put into a file drawer upon dissemination. Codes may not be a panacea for management, but when properly developed, administered, and communicated, they serve to raise the level of ethical behavior in the organization by clarifying what is meant by ethical conduct, encouraging moral behavior, and establishing a standard by which accountability may be measured.

Metaphors for Perceiving Codes A major study of corporate codes by Mark Schwartz revealed that there are a number of different ways that employees perceive or understand codes of conduct.[129] Schwartz's research yielded eight themes or metaphors that helped to explain how codes influence ethical behavior within organizations.

1. As a *rule book*, the code acts to clarify what behavior is expected of employees.
2. As a *signpost*, the code can lead employees to consult other individuals or corporate policies to determine the appropriateness of behavior.
3. As a *mirror*, the code provides employees with a chance to confirm whether their behavior is acceptable to the company.
4. As a *magnifying glass*, the code suggests a note of caution to be more careful or engage in greater reflection before acting.
5. As a *shield*, the code acts in a manner that allows employees to better challenge and resist unethical requests.
6. As a *smoke detector*, the code leads employees to try to convince others and warn them of their inappropriate behavior.
7. As a *fire alarm*, the code leads employees to contact the appropriate authority and report violations.
8. As a *club*, the potential enforcement of the code causes employees to comply with the code's provisions.[130]

In summary, the code metaphors provide insights into a number of ways in which codes are perceived or viewed by organizational members. In each case, the metaphor emphases an important dimension or value of codes of conduct.

8.4g Disciplining Violators of Ethics Standards

To instill an ethical climate that all organizational members will believe in, management must discipline violators of its accepted ethical norms and standards. A major reason the

ETHICS IN PRACTICE CASE

The New Ethics Code–Sign or Resign

Barclay's PLC, the major U.K. bank, was fined £290 million by regulators in the United Kingdom and United States after it was found guilty of manipulating the interbank lending rate Libor. In August 2012, a new CEO, Anthony Jenkins, took over after his predecessor Bob Diamond resigned in the wake of the allegations and fines.

As an early order of business, Jenkins decided it was time to change the ethics culture of the bank and to improve the bank's ethics. Jenkins sent a memo to the bank's 140,000 employees informing them that from now on employee performance would be evaluated on a set of ethical standards. The new standards would be part of the bank's code of conduct, and it would be built around five key values: respect, integrity, service, excellence, and stewardship. Jenkins was quoted as saying that "We must never again be in a position of rewarding people for making the bank money in a way which is unethical or inconsistent with our values."

Jenkins said that the bank's culture has been "too short-term focused, too aggressive and on occasions too self-serving." Some of the changes being introduced include the following: the reward structure will be altered so that it upholds the company's values; a new code of conduct will be issued and expected to be signed off on by everyone; a new role called head of compliance will help redesign the bank's compensation policies.

Jenkins' message to those who don't desire to make the changes is simple—Barclay's is not the place for you—the rules have changed and you will no longer feel comfortable at Barclay's and we will not be comfortable with you as our colleagues.

1. What is your evaluation of Jenkin's proposed approach to changing the ethics culture at Barclays?
2. Can an ethics culture change of the magnitude desired be initiated effectively by a memo ? What else is necessary and why?
3. Is a threat of discharge the best way to frame a desire for new, ethical values? How would you recommend the bank take on such its gargantuan ethics program?

Sources: Margot Patrick, "Barclays Vows Culture Shift," *Wall Street Journal*, February 6. 2013, C3 ; "Barclays Boss Anthony Jenkins Tells Staff to Sign up to Ethical Code or Quit," *HuffPost Business United Kingdom*, January 17, 2013, http://www.huffingtonpost.co.uk/2013/01/17/barclays-ethical-code-anthony-jenkins-quit-libor-_n_2494463.html?view=screen, Accessed February 29, 2016; "The rules have changed: Barclays new boss tells new staff to sign up new ethics code or quit the bank," This is money.co.uk, http://www.thisismoney.co.uk/money/saving/article-2263903/Barclays-new-boss-tell-staff-sign-new-ethics-code-quit-bank.html, Accessed February 29, 2016.

general public, and even employees in many organizations, have questioned business's sincerity in desiring a more ethical environment has been business's unwillingness to discipline violators. There are numerous cases where top management officers have behaved unethically and yet were retained in their positions. At lower levels, there have been cases of top management overlooking or failing to penalize unethical behavior of subordinates. This evidence of inaction on management's or the board's part signals implicit approval of the individual's behavior . To be fair, organizations need to communicate their ethics standards clearly and convincingly before taking disciplinary action. But then, an organization needs to respond forcefully to the individual who is guilty of deliberately or flagrantly violating its code of ethics.

Based on their research, Treviño, Hartman, and Brown have argued: "The moral manager consistently rewards ethical conduct and disciplines unethical conduct at all levels in the organization, and these actions serve to uphold the standards and rules."[131] The effort on the part of management has to be complete in communicating to all, by way of disciplining offenders, that unethical behavior will not be tolerated in the organization.

A stark example of this point was the discharge by the Boeing Company of its chief financial officer—Michael Sears—and another senior manager for engaging in unethical behavior. Sears, a 34-year veteran of the industry, had been considered to be a possible successor to then chairman and CEO Phil Condit. The company said that Mr. Sears and the other senior manager had been dismissed when they tried to conceal their alleged misconduct from a team of lawyers hired by the firm to investigate their actions. At the time of the firing, the CEO said, "When we determine there have been violations of our standards, we will act swiftly to address them, just as we have today."[132] In another case, Nortel Networks, North America's largest telecommunications equipment maker, fired its chief executive officer, chief financial officer, and controller for their involvement in accounting problems that had been under scrutiny. The accounting irregularities resulted in the company having to restate its earnings.[133] In the past decade or so, we have witnessed more and more corporate boards taking disciplinary action with respect to CEO and top management wrongdoing.

8.4h Ethics "Hotlines" and Whistle-Blowing Mechanisms

One problem that frequently leads to the covering up of unethical acts by people in an organization is that they do not know how to respond when they witness or suspect a questionable practice. An effective ethical culture is contingent on employees having a mechanism for, and top management support of, reporting violations or "blowing the whistle" on wrongdoers. One corporate executive summarized this point as follows: "Employees must know exactly what is expected of them in the moral arena and how to respond to warped ethics."[134] According to the Ethics Resource Center's 2013 National Business Ethics Survey, whistle-blowing among those who have observed wrong behavior has remained steady in about the 63–65 percent range over the past three surveys.[135] Most employees try to report observed wrong doing to their supervisors, higher management, or the human resources department. Only about 16 percent have used a hotline to report wrongdoing but they think it is an important mechanism that needs to be available. [136]

The Association of Certified Fraud Examiners report that Ethics Hotlines are the most frequent way employees blow the whistle on fraud or related infractions.[137] Such hotlines may be telephone, Web, or e-mail based. In addition, they are typically used without alerting anyone in management about the problem ahead of time. The fraud examiners report that anonymous tips they receive on ethics hotlines are by far the most common way that fraud is detected in organizations. In their survey, 37.8 percent of frauds were detected based on these anonymous tips, while only 17 percent were identified through management reviews and 14 percent by management audits. They conclude that ethics hotlines are clearly one of the best practices for detecting fraud and helping to create an ethical work culture.[138]

Ethics hotlines can have a downside risk, however. Ethicist Barbara Ley Toffler has argued that ethics hotlines have the potential to do harm. She suspects that many of the reported wrongdoings are false accusations and that if the company does not handle these issues carefully, it may do a lot of damage to employee morale.[139]

8.4i Business Ethics Training

Today, business ethics training and training programs are considered to be one of the most important best practices in improving organizational ethics. Thomas A. Kennedy, Chairman of the Board and CEO of Raytheon Company, has stated "We invest in ethics and provide employees with robust, award-winning ethics education to reinforce how important doing the right thing in business is to our success."[140] What are the goals of ethics training? Different companies set different goals, but a typical set of goals for ethics training includes the following:

- To learn the fundamentals of business ethics
- To learn to solve ethical dilemmas
- To learn to identify causes of unethical behavior
- To learn about common managerial ethical issues

ETHICS IN PRACTICE CASE

Sometimes Ethics Hotlines Don't Work

Ethics and compliance "hotlines" are designed to give employees an opportunity to internally "blow the whistle" on wrongdoing. Many of them are designed by corporate compliance and ethics offices and some of them are contracted out to independent firms to give employees a greater sense of confidentiality when they report what they see or think is going wrong in the company.

A major corporation that created such a compliance hotline was Olympus Corp., the Japanese camera maker. Olympus Corp. started its compliance hotline (now called an Integrity Hotline) soon after Japan passed a whistleblower protection law. The hotline office was to handle the receipt of phone calls, letters, e-mails and other forms of reporting from employees. These were to be reports of violations of the law or the company's code of conduct.

Upon investigation, the *Wall Street Journal* learned that the company created an independent panel to look into the use of the hotline and other company irregularities. It was discovered that there were significant problems with how the hotline was being used. It was found, for example, that the two executives who were in charge of the company's hotline were also allegedly behind the concealment of $1.5 billion in company losses.

The panel's report noted that the company's corporate culture was characterized by serious problems. The panel observed a suffocating atmosphere that inhibited employees from speaking openly. The panel concluded that compliance systems were significantly disabled. One employee who used the hotline to report on wrongdoing claimed he was transferred to a less desirable job after issuing a complaint via the hotline. The hotline required employees to report their names in case complaints needed to be investigated further.

When the hotline was initially set up, some recommended that it be administered by external parties so that those reporting complaints would feel more secure about their anonymity. The manager in charge strongly opposed using an outside party to administer the hotline. It was later revealed by a Japanese consumer affairs agency that about two-thirds of the large firms did use outside parties to administer their hotlines.

1. What ethics issues do you see in this company's culture and administration of the hotline?
2. As an employee, would you feel uncomfortable filing an ethics complaint in a system run by the company itself? Could anything be done to ensure your confidentiality?
3. What principles should be followed in designing a company ethics or compliance hotline?

Sources: Juro Osawa, "Olympus Hotline Didn't Blow Whistle," *Wall Street Journal*, January 4, 2012, http://www.wsj.com/articles/SB10001424052970203899504577129863418959828, Accessed February 29, 2016 ; "Ethics Hotlines," In Touch, http://getintouch.com/solutions/compliance-hotlines/, Accessed February 29, 2016; Olympus, Ethics and Corporate Compliance, http://www.olympusamerica.com/corporate/ethics_corporate_compliance.asp, Accessed February 29, 2016.

- To learn whistle-blowing criteria and risks
- To learn to develop a code of ethics and execute an internal ethical audit[141]

Though it is not easy designing ethics training programs, and there are limits to how much ethics may be taught, a set of recommendations set forth by AccountingWeb for designing an effective ethics training program include the following nine steps:[142]

- Make it specific. Be sure specific behaviors are targeted.
- Make it a two-way conversation. There must be Q & A between employees and managers.
- Make it interactive. This is so employees may learn firsthand how to make ethical decisions.
- Make it memorable and situational. Use quizzes targeted towards specific situations.
- Make it relatable. Use examples of good and bad behavior that employees can relate to.
- Reinforce training. This is an important role for ethics trainers to continue communicating with trainees.
- Repeat the program. Ongoing programs that are repeated annually or quarterly will be most effective and memorable.

- Make it a visible program. Principles should be highlighted during strategic planning sessions and also during employee performance reviews.
- Enforce the ethics hotline. Employees need to be armed with the proper tools for when they observe questionable behaviors or have questions themselves.

A well-designed ethics training program will help embed the company's code of conduct into the culture of the organization. A well-implemented program will strive to align an employee's personal and professional ethics with the expected business ethics of his or her employer.

Materials and formats typically used by firms in their ethics training include the following: codes of ethics (as a training device), lectures, workshops/seminars, case studies, CDs/discussions, and articles/speeches. One major firm, Lockheed Martin, introduced some humor into its ethics training by creating the Dilbert and Dogbert-inspired board game, "The Ethics Challenge," to promote engagement for company-wide ethics training. To play the game, players (employees) move around the board by answering "Case File" questions, such as "You've been selected for a training course in Florida, and you want to go only for the vacation." Among the answers and their respective points are "Go, but skip the sessions" (0 points), "Ask your supervisor if it would be beneficial" (5 points), and, the Dogbert answer, "Wear mouse ears to work and hum 'It's a Small World After All' all day." Sessions for the company's 185,000 employees were led by supervisors, not ethics officers. The chairman of the company kicked off the training by leading the training of those who reported to him directly.[143]

One former ethics officer of a major corporation has criticized much ethics training done by companies. He said that most of this training is being done in the form of a mandatory annual compliance exercise, typically one hour in duration. Often, it is a "check the box" exercise in that management can check off that it is completed for the year. He goes on to say that if such training is not done well, it turns out to be indistinguishable from all the other meetings employees have to attend.[144]

In terms of the effectiveness of ethics training, research has shown that exposure to lengthy programs (e.g., ten weeks) resulted in significant improvements in moral development.[145] In one recent study of formal ethics training with bankers, the researchers found that two years after a single training session, there were sustained, positive effects on the ethics of the organizational culture. The indicators of the ethical organizational culture included observing unethical behavior, intentions to behave ethically, and perceptions of organizational usefulness in managing ethics.[146] Though brief ethics training does not always yield noticeable results, some approaches have demonstrated that improved moral reasoning can be learned in just a few weeks.[147]

Business Roundtable Institute for Corporate Ethics One of the major limitations of business ethics training has been the exemption of the CEO and other top-level managers from it. This has been changing. The Business Roundtable, an organization of CEOs, developed a business ethics institute targeted toward CEOs.[148] The CEOs who comprise the Business Roundtable are involved. The main office for the institute is located at the Darden School at the University of Virginia. The goal of the institute is to help restore public confidence in the marketplace in light of the ongoing scandals in business. Through the institute, research is conducted, courses created, and executive seminars offered on business ethics. Some skeptics wonder whether this will truly make a difference or not. Some say that CEOs are pretty set in their ways by the time they reach the pinnacle of their organizations. Optimists are withholding judgment until experience indicates whether the new institute will add significant value or not.[149] Regardless, it is encouraging that CEOs are finally planning to subject themselves to the same kind of training they have always wanted for their subordinates. If ethical leadership truly begins at the top, the institute should provide a useful resource for these organization leaders.

8.4j Ethics Audits and Risk Assessments

In increasing numbers, companies today are beginning to appreciate the need to follow up on their ethics initiatives and programs. Ethics audits are mechanisms or approaches by which a company may assess or evaluate its ethical climate or programs. **Ethics audits** are intended to carefully review ethics initiatives such as ethics programs, codes of conduct, hotlines, and ethics training programs to determine their effectiveness and results. Ethics audits are similar to social audits discussed in Chapter 5. In addition, they are intended to examine other management activities that may add to or subtract from the company's ethics initiatives. This might include management's sincerity, communication efforts, incentive and reward systems, and other activities. Ethics audits may employ written instruments, committees, outside consultants, and employee interviews.[150] A popular variation on the ethics audit is the **sustainability audit**. More companies today are employing this approach for identifying and managing sustainability issues within their organizations. They want to improve the credibility of their sustainability reports and provide greater confidence to all stakeholders.[151]

Spurred on by the revised Federal Sentencing Guidelines and more recent legislation, companies are increasingly designing and conducting fraud risk assessments of their operations. **Fraud risk assessments** are the review processes designed to identify and monitor conditions and events that may have some bearing on the company's exposure to compliance/misconduct risk and to review company's methods for dealing with these concerns. Risk, in this context, is typically focused on the company's exposure to possible compliance, misconduct, and ethics issues. According to recent surveys, the top five subjects of ethics program risk analyses include internal policies and processes, employee awareness and understanding of compliance and ethics issues, anonymous reporting systems, disciplinary systems as prevention tools, and employee intent or incentives.[152] Typically arising from outside the firm, but becoming an important fraud issue today, has been *cyber risk*. Hacks at Target, Sony, JPMorgan and Anthem have surfaced as dramatic examples of technology-based vulnerabilities to fraud companies face today.[153] Since companies have a legal and ethical responsibility to keep information secure and private, this is an important reason why fraud risk assessments are crucial.

In additional to providing benefits for legal reasons, the conduct of periodic risk assessments provides internal benefits to management. Some of these include the following: detecting compliance and ethics threats and permitting companies to correct problems before they occur or become worse. If problems are not detected and corrected, they may be discovered by regulators, investors, the media, or potential plaintiffs.[154]

8.4k Corporate Transparency Policies

One of the most important best practices in the improvement of ethics programs and ethical conduct in the organization is that of **transparency**. **Corporate transparency** refers to a quality, characteristic, or state in which activities, processes, practices, and decisions that take place in companies become *open or visible to the outside world.* A common definition of transparency is the degree to which an organization

- Provides public access to information
- Accepts responsibility for its actions
- Makes decisions more openly
- Establishes incentives for leaders to uphold these standards[155]

The three characteristics that seem to dominate the concept of transparency are: openness, ongoing communication, and accountability.[156] The opposite of transparency is **opacity**, or an opaque condition in which activities and practices remain obscure or hidden from outside scrutiny and review.

Pressures toward transparency have come both from the outside and from within companies. From the outside, various stakeholders such as consumers, environmentalists, government, and investors want to know more clearly what is going on within the organizations. Over the years, business scandals have served as an added outside force. The Sarbanes–Oxley Act also mandated greater transparency. The importance of transparency is that it leads to accountability. From the perspective of the inside, companies are increasingly seeing how transparency makes sense as an ethics best practice. In their book *The Transparency Edge: How Credibility Can Make or Break You in Business*, Pagano and Pagano state that a transparent management approach—"what you see is what you get" code of conduct—will increase your company's credibility in the marketplace, build loyalty, and help you gain the trust and confidence of those with whom you work.[157] One major study found that management transparency is the most important factor determining employee engagement. It puts employees in a positive mindset and they generally become more committed to the organization and productive.[158]

Several examples of successful corporate transparency are worth noting. On the GM Blog, the company has written about the repayments it made to the government. It reported on a CEO resignation and the hiring of some new executives.[159] This is information seldom made available to the public. Salesforce.com runs Trust Site, a Web site that reports any outages with its online CRM services. On this site, you are able to check to see if the service you depend upon for your customer data is up and running. This type information is seldom provided. AT&T used Twitter to put out the news that it had experienced a fiber cut in the San Francisco Bay area. They then sent out more tweets to keep people informed of the repair status.[160] McDonald's Canada used its digital platform to encourage customers to ask them questions. McDonald's promised and provided clear and concise answers.[161] Transparency such as this will continue to provide dividends for the companies and the brands as they strive to stay relevant in a world in which more openness is expected.

8.4l Board of Directors Leadership and Oversight

One would think that oversight and leadership of ethics initiatives by the boards of directors of businesses would be a "given." That has not been the case, however, in many instances.[162] The primary impetus for board involvement in and oversight of ethics programs and initiatives has been the mega scandals of the past couple decades that have impacted many major companies. This has been coupled with the passage of the Sarbanes–Oxley Act, which has overhauled federal securities laws to improve corporate governance. Corporate governance was discussed in detail in Chapter 4, but here we want to emphasize the board's role in oversight of corporate ethics, one of the most urgent issues in recent years.

Corporate boards, like top managers, should provide strong ethical leadership. Former SEC Chair William Donaldson said that it is not enough for a company to profess a code of conduct. According to Donaldson, "the most important thing that a board of directors should do is determine the elements that must be embedded in the company's moral DNA."[163] In other words, strong leadership from the board and CEOs is still the most powerful force in improving the company's ethical culture.

According to an ethics and compliance benchmarking survey conducted by the Conference Board, board involvement in ethics programs has risen significantly in the companies surveyed.[164] According to another survey of 165 company boards, it is reported

SPOTLIGHT ***on Sustainability***

The Keys to Successful Transparency

The importance of transparency in developing ethical business cultures has been established. But, how is this done? There are several important criteria that are needed to be sure transparency is done right. Lorraine Smith has proposed six essential criteria for successful transparency. First, there is the need to get and make available the right information. Accurate information about organizational practices is essential. Second, the right stakeholders need to be reached. Whether the stakeholders are customers or special interest groups, the right information needs to be targeted to the right stakeholders. Third, the right format for organizing and presenting information need to be selected. Reports, news releases, text messages, Facebook pages, Web pages—there are many options for making information available. Communicating information in the right format is essential for effective transparency.

Fourth, the right time for release of information is essential. Historically, yearly or monthly publication of information once was adequate. This is no longer true in a high-tech, high-communications world. Stakeholders expect information on a more timely basis now—this week, today, right now! Rumors can get started quickly if companies are not transparent in the time frame people expect today. Fifth, the right frequency is essential and this is related to the right format and the right time. This means more than issuing weekly or monthly e-mail blasts. It means carefully assessing when and how often stakeholders expect information to be available and then making it available. The standard issuances of the public relations department may no longer be adequate to have a successful transparency operation.

Finally, the right intentions must be at work. Management needs to be genuine about why information is being made available. Is it in reaction to an issue or a demand? Has someone requested the information? Is it a proactive response to a set of standards the company is now following, such as the Global Reporting Initiative or the Caux Principles? Is management striving to create an authentic culture of transparency? Stakeholders can figure motive out so it is best if management has the best intentions to begin with.

All in all, companies need to pay close attention to scope, disclosure, and timing in their transparency efforts. Giving stakeholders fair and equitable access will help build a culture of integrity. Following standards of professionalism, a culture of transparency may be developed. If these recommendations are used, companies will be in a stronger position to convey their honesty and trustworthiness with respect to transparency. In the long term, such a strategy will make the overall culture of the organization more sustainable.

Sources: Olympus, "Principle of Transparency Guidelines," http://www.olympus-global.com/en/csr/integrity/fairness/transparency/policy.jsp, Accessed April 25, 2016; OECD, "Principles for Transparency," http://www.oecd.org/corruption/ethics/Lobbying-Brochure.pdf, Accessed April 25, 2016 ; Sustainability, Lorraine Smith, "Six Elements of Effective Transparency," http://www.sustainability.com/blog/six-elements-of-effective-transparency#.Vx556PkrKUk, Accessed April 25, 2016;

that although corporate scandals and Sarbanes–Oxley Act have been strong forces in bringing about more board involvement in ethics, other factors have motivated it as well. In the United States, general legal developments have increased board scrutiny of ethics programs, but in the United Kingdom, India, and Western Europe, "enhancement of reputation" has often been cited as a reason for closer board scrutiny of corporate ethics. There is also widespread enthusiasm for training board members in ethics, but such enthusiasm does not often result in action.[165]

8.5 Behavioral Ethics–Toward a Deeper Understanding

In this chapter, we have discussed managerial ethics and the challenges involved in managing organizational ethics. At this point, it is helpful to focus on a relatively new field of thought that has been termed **behavioral ethics**. For the most part, our discussions to this point have been normative in nature. Behavioral ethics, by contrast, helps us to understand at a deeper level many of the behavioral processes that research has shown actually are taking place in people and organizations. Thus, most of these learnings are *descriptive* in nature as they strive to capture insights into processes that have been observed to be taking place in actual practice. An awareness of these behavioral phenomena greatly adds to our understanding of business ethics and should help us to better design ethics initiatives in organizations.

Bazerman and Gino have defined behavioral ethics as "the study of systematic and predictable ways in which individuals make ethical decisions and judge the ethical decisions of others that are at odds with intuition…."[166] The approach embraces both intentional and unintentional unethical behaviors. Treviño, Weaver and Reynolds note that behavioral ethics embraces individual, group and organizational influences.[167] Behavioral ethics gives us insights into how people actually behave in organizations as a result of psychological processes or as a consequence of organizational factors at work. These insights help us overcome problems or better design organizations to offset detrimental consequences.

Some of the phenomena that have been observed that would fit into the category of behavioral ethics are worth briefly noting. **Bounded ethicality** tends to occur when managers and employees find that even when they aspire to behave ethically it is difficult due to a variety of organizational pressures and psychological tendencies that intervene.[168] There are limits on people's abilities to be ethical. Tendencies toward bounded ethicality might include claiming credit for a group's work without realizing you are doing it, engaging in implicit discrimination and in-group favoritism, and falling prey to the influence of conflicts of interest.[169]

Conformity bias is a behavioral pattern that has also been observed. This is the tendency people have to take their cues for ethical behavior from their peers rather than exercising their own independent ethical judgment. Another predisposition is **overconfidence bias**. This is the tendency for people to be more confident of their own moral character or behavior than they have objective reason to be. **Self-serving bias** is similar; this is the propensity people have to process information in a way that serves to support their preexisting beliefs and their perceived self-interest.[170]

Other important behavioral ethics patterns include framing, incrementalism, role morality, and moral equilibrium. **Framing** refers to the fact that people's ethical judgments are affected by how a question or issue is posed (framed). It has been found, for example, that when people are prompted to think of an issue as an "ethical" issue they will tend to make more ethical decisions than if they had been prompted to think of the issue as a "business" issue.[171] **Incrementalism** is the predisposition toward the slippery slope. It has been noted that there is a tendency toward making a series of minor ethical misjudgments that can lead to major ethical mistakes.

Role morality is the tendency some people have to use different ethical standards as they move through different roles in life. For example, a person might make more questionable decisions at work when job and profits are at stake than they would at home or in their family. Finally, **moral equilibrium** has been observed. This is the penchant for people to keep an ethical scoreboard in their heads and use this information when making future decisions. While seeking equilibrium, for example, a person might take moral license on an issue if they think they are running a moral surplus in their overall behavior.[172] While seeking balance, people may rationalize future behavior rather than judging each decision situation on its own merits.

Related to some of these concepts, Bazerman and Tenbrunsel describe ethical breakdowns or barriers that organizational members may experience even as they see themselves as "good people" striving to do what is right.[173] Their five barriers to an ethical organization include the following: **Ill-conceived goals** are poorly set goals that encourage negative behaviors such as sales goals emphasized too much or set too high. **Motivated blindness** is the process of overlooking the questionable actions of others when it is in one's own best interest. This is the self-serving bias described earlier. **Indirect blindness** occurs when one holds others less accountable for unethical behaviors when they are carried out through third parties. The **slippery slope**, mentioned earlier as incrementalism, causes people to not notice others' unethical behavior when it gradually occurs in small increments. Finally, **overcoming values** is the act of letting questionable behaviors pass if the outcome is good. This can occur when managers over emphasize results rather than how the results were achieved. It could be played out as the ends justifying the means.

Research into behavioral ethics gives us deeper and richer insights into the challenges of being ethical within our managerial and organizational roles and the difficulties of creating an ethical organizational culture while implementing many of the best practices and principles discussed earlier. Behavioral ethics may be seen as an overlay of real-world experience on the normative strategies of improving business ethics using ethics training, ethics principles and other decision-making approaches. Consequently, they must be taken into consideration when striving to manage business ethics.

8.6 Moral Decisions, Managers, and Organizations

In the last two chapters, we have discussed ethical or moral acts, decisions, practices, managers, and organizations. Though the goal of ethics initiatives is to develop moral organizations, sometimes all we get are isolated ethical acts, decisions, or practices, or, if we are fortunate, a few moral managers. Achieving the status of moral standing in organizations is a goal, whatever the level on which it may be achieved. Sometimes all we can do is bring about ethical acts, decisions, or practices. A broader goal is to create moral managers, in the sense in which they were discussed in Chapter 7 and this chapter. Finally, the highest level goal for managers may be to create moral organizations, for which many of the best practices discussed in this chapter will need to be successfully implemented. As ethicist Kenneth Goodpaster has reminded us, "The depths of a company's *cultural* commitment to ethical values in the pursuit of economic values are a mark of corporate *moral* development."[174]

The important point here is to emphasize that the goal of managers should be to create *moral decisions*, *moral managers*, and ultimately, *moral organizations* while recognizing that what we frequently observe in business is the achievement of moral standing at only one of these levels. The ideal is to create a moral organization that is fully populated by moral managers making moral decisions (and practices, policies, and behaviors), but this is seldom achieved. Figure 8-8 depicts the sequencing and goals of each of these

FIGURE 8-8 Moral Decisions, Moral Managers, and Moral Organizations

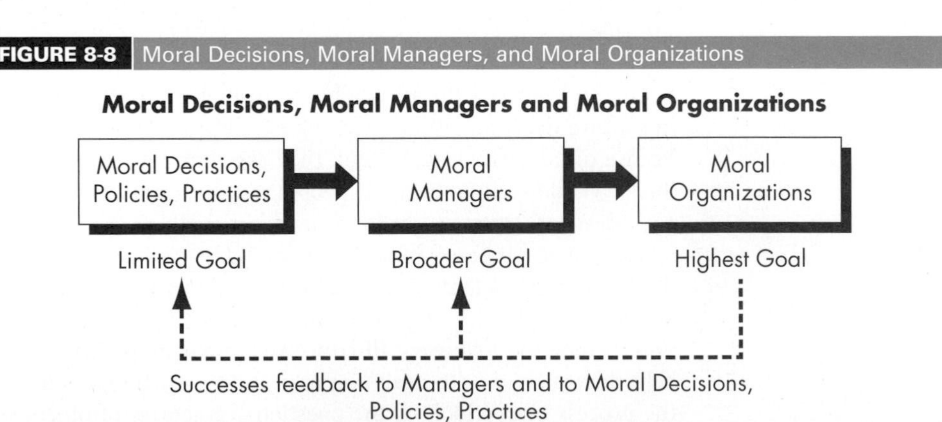

levels. Once moral organizations are achieved, the stories and successes feed back in such a way that they augment the creation of moral managers and moral decisions. Over time, the overall level of moral development and maturity should rise when this process is repeated over several cycles. These challenges become even more specialized when we consider business ethics and technology in Chapter 9 and ethical issues in the global arena in Chapter 10.

Summary

The subject of business ethics may be addressed at several different levels: personal, managerial–organizational, industrial, societal, and international. This chapter focuses on the managerial and organizational levels—the levels at which managers can have the most impact. The chapter concludes with insights from the newly emerging field of behavioral ethics.

A number of different ethical principles serve as guides to managerial decision making. Ethics principles may be categorized as teleological (ends-based), deontological (duty-based), or Aretaic (virtue-based). One of the major deontological principles is the categorical imperative. Major philosophical principles of ethics include utilitarianism, rights, and justice. The Golden Rule was singled out as a particularly powerful ethical principle among various groups studied. Virtue ethics was identified as an increasingly popular concept. Servant leadership was presented as an approach to management that embraced an ethical perspective of putting others first. Seven practical tests were proposed to assist the manager in making ethical decisions: the test of common sense, the test of one's best self, the test of making something public, the test of ventilation, the test of purified idea, the test of the Big Four, and the gag test.

At the organizational level, factors were discussed that affect the organization's moral culture or climate. It was concluded that the behavior of one's superiors and peers and industry ethical practices were the most important influences on an organization's ethical culture. Society's moral climate and personal needs were considered to be relevant factors but less important. Best practices for improving the firm's ethical climate include providing leadership from management, ethics and compliance programs, and ethics and compliance officers; setting realistic objectives; infusing the decision-making process with ethical considerations; utilizing codes of conduct; disciplining violators; creating whistle-blowing mechanisms or hotlines; training managers in business ethics; using ethics audits and risk assessments (which often include sustainability audits); adopting the concept of transparency, and board of director oversight of ethics initiatives.

Behavioral ethics is a maturing field based upon empirically observed phenomena describing psychological processes that occur when managers and employees strive to do the right thing in their decision making and in their design of an ethical organizational culture. Our knowledge from behavioral ethics serves as a reality check on the implementation of normative processes in business ethics.

The goal of ethics initiatives is to achieve a status that may be characterized not just by isolated and intermittent moral decisions but also by the presence of moral managers and the ultimate achievement of a moral organization. When a moral organization is achieved, the successes will feed back into the process and greatly improve decisions, practices, and managers themselves.

Key Terms

aretaic theories, p. 229
behavioral ethics, p. 262
bounded ethicality, p. 263
categorical imperative, p. 230
codes of conduct, p. 254
codes of ethics, p. 254
test of common sense, p. 238
compensatory justice, p. 233
competing rights, p. 232
compliance officer, p. 251
compliance orientation, p. 245
conflict of interest, p. 228
conformity bias, p. 263
core ethical values, p. 246
corporate transparency, p. 260
deontological theories, p. 229
distributive justice, p. 233
ethical due process, p. 233
ethic of reciprocity, p. 236
ethical leadership, p. 246
ethical tests, p. 237
ethics and compliance officer, p. 251
ethics audits, p. 260

ethics of care, p. 234
ethics officer, p. 251
ethics orientation, p. 245
ethics programs, p. 245
ethics screen, p. 252
formal ethics programs, p. 246
framing, p. 263
fraud risk assessments, p. 260
Golden Rule, p. 236
Ill-conceived goals, p. 263
incrementalism, p. 263
indirect blindness, p. 263
legal rights, p. 231
moral rights, p. 230
moral tone, p. 246
motivated blindness, p. 263
moral equilibrium, p. 263
negative right, p. 231
opacity, p. 261
overcoming values, p. 264
overconfidence bias, p. 263
positive right, p. 232
principle of caring, p. 234
principle of justice, p. 233
principle of rights, p. 231
principle of utilitarianism, p. 229
procedural justice, p. 233
process fairness, p. 233
rights, p. 230
role morality, p. 263
self-serving bias, p. 263
servant leadership, p. 235
slippery slope, p. 264
"smell" test, p. 238
sustainability audit, p. 260
teleological theories, p. 229
transparency, p. 260
utilitarianism, p. 229
virtue ethics, p. 235

Discussion Questions

1. From your personal experience, give two examples of ethical dilemmas you have experienced as a member of an organization.
2. Using the examples you provided for question 1, identify one or more of the guides to decision making or ethical tests that you think would have helped you resolve your dilemmas. Describe how it would have helped.
3. Which is most important in ethics principles—consequences or duty? Discuss.
4. Assume that you are in your first managerial position. Identify five ways in which you might provide ethical leadership. Rank them in terms of importance, and be prepared to explain your ranking.
5. What do you think about codes of conduct? Give three reasons why an organization ought to have a code of conduct and three reasons why an organization should not have a code of conduct. On balance, how do you assess the value of codes of conduct?
6. An ongoing debate concerns whether business ethics can and should be taught in business schools. Do you think ethics can be taught in B-school? Substantiate your point with reasons. Can top managers and board members be taught business ethics?
7. Identify and prioritize the best practices for improving the organization's ethical climate. What are the strengths and weaknesses of each?
8. Which three of the concepts under the field of behavioral ethics appear to be the most powerful? Explain why and give examples.

Endnotes

1. David Callahan, *The Cheating Culture: Why More Americans Are Doing Wrong to Get Ahead* (New York: Harcourt, Inc., 2004).
2. David Callahan, "About Cheating Culture," http://www.cheatingculture.com/about/. Accessed February 29, 2016.
3. Lee Ellis, *Leading Talents, Leading Teams* (Chicago: Northfield Publishing, 2003), 201–204.
4. Bill George, *Authentic Leadership: Rediscovering the Secrets to Creating Lasting Value* (San Francisco: Jossey-Bass, 2003).
5. Dan Chapman, "Woman Rewarded for Act of Honesty," *The Atlanta Journal-Constitution* (September 8, 2001).
6. Jennifer Dixon, "Bosses Knew Shipped Meat Was Tainted, Workers Say," *Chicago Tribune* (August 30, 2001).
7. FoxNews, "Dole Voluntarily Withdraws Packaged Salads Amid 6-State Listeria Outbreak," January 25, 2016, http://www.foxnews.com/health/2016/01/25/dole-voluntarily-withdraws-packaged-salads-amid-6-state-listeria-outbreak.html. Accessed February 20, 2016.
8. Ethics Resource Center, *National Business Ethics Survey 2003: How Employees View Ethics in Their Organizations* (Washington, DC: Ethics Resource Center, 2003), 28; also see https://www1.toronto.ca/inquiry/inquiry_site/cd/gg/add_pdf/77/Conflict_

of_Interest/Electronic_Documents/Research_orgs /NBE_Survey.PDF. Accessed February 20, 2016.

9. Dollars & Sense, "The Student Loan Crisis and the Debtfare State," May/June 2015, http://www.dollarsandsense.org/archives/2015/0515soederberg.html. Accessed February 20, 2016.
10. Archie B. Carroll, "Principles of Business Ethics: Their Role in Decision Making and an Initial Consensus," *Management Decision* (Vol. 28, No. 28, 1990), 20–24.
11. John R. Boatright, *Ethics and the Conduct of Business,* 7th ed. (Pearson Higher Education, 2012).
12. Tom L. Beauchamp, *Philosophical Ethics: An Introduction to Moral Philosophy,* 3rd ed. (New York: McGraw-Hill, 2001).
13. William H. Shaw and Vincent Barry, *Moral Issues in Business,* 12th ed. (Cengage Learning, 2013).
14. Ibid., 45–46.
15. I. Kant, *Groundwork of the Metaphysic of Morals,* trans. H. J. Paton (New York: Harper and Row, 1964).
16. Victoria S. Wike, "Duty," in Patricia H. Werhane and R. Edward Freeman (eds.), *The Blackwell Encyclopedic Dictionary of Business Ethics* (Malden, MA: Blackwell Publishers, Ltd, 1997), 180–181.
17. Boatright, 53.
18. Scott J. Reynolds and Norman E. Bowie, "A Kantian Perspective on the Characteristics of Ethics Programs," *Business Ethics Quarterly* (Vol. 14, No. 2, April 2004), 275–292.
19. Louis P. Pojman, *Ethics: Discovering Right and Wrong,* 7th ed. (Cengage Learning, 2012).
20. Ibid., 150.
21. Ibid., 152–153.
22. Manuel C. Velasquez, *Business Ethics: Concepts and Cases,* 7th ed. (Pearson Education Limited, 2014).
23. Richard T. DeGeorge, *Business Ethics,* 5th ed. (Upper Saddle River, NJ: Prentice Hall, 1999), 69–72.
24. Velasquez, 73.
25. "Rights: What Are They Anyway?" http://dspace.dial.pipex.com/town/street/pl38/rights.htm. Accessed July 18, 2007.
26. "Negative and Positive Rights," http://www.globalization101.org/negative-vs-positive-rights/. Accessed February 22, 2016.
27. Ibid.
28. "How to Balance Competing Rights?" http://www.casselsbrock.com/CBNewsletter/How_to_Balance_Competing_Rights. Accessed February 23, 2016.
29. Eric Harvey and Scott Airitam, Ethics 4 Everyone, Walk the Talk Company, 2002, 24–27.
30. Jon Swartz, "Split Opinion on Apple-FBI Standoff," *USA Today,* February 22, 2016, 4B.
31. Harvey and Airitam, 26–27.
32. "The Hot Dog Bill of Rights," *USA Today,* February 22, 2016, 8A.
33. See the following sources for a discussion of these points: David Luban, "Judicial Activism and the Concept of Rights," *Report from the Institute for Philosophy & Public Policy* (College Park, MD: University of Maryland, Winter/Spring, 1994), 12–17; George F. Will, "Our Expanding Menu of Rights," *Newsweek* (December 14, 1992), 90; John Leo, "The Spread of Rights Babble," *U.S. News & World Report* (June 28, 1993), 17; and William Raspberry, "Blind Pursuit of Rights Can Endanger Civility," *The Atlanta Journal* (September 14, 1994), A14; "Are There Too Many Rights With Too Few Responsibilities," http://mic.com/articles/3811/are-too-many-rights-with-too-few-responsibilities-creating-our-nation-s-problems#.UdJqxXybs. Accessed February 22, 2016.
34. Jonathan Haidt, "The New Culture War Over Fairness," *Time,* October 22, 2012, 25.
35. Ibid; also see "Four Types of Justice," http://changingminds.org/explanations/trust/four_justice.htm. Accessed February 22, 2016.
36. Joel Brockner, "Why It's So Hard to Be Fair," *Harvard Business Review* (March 2006), 122–129.
37. Ibid., 123.
38. "John Rawls," *The Economist* (December 7, 2002), 83.
39. John Rawls, *A Theory of Justice* (Cambridge, MA: Harvard University Press, 1971).
40. DeGeorge, 69–72.
41. Michael M. Weinstein, "Bringing Logic to Bear on Liberal Dogma," *The New York Times* (December 1, 2002), 5.
42. Ibid., 72.
43. Ibid., 5.
44. Dahlia Lithwick, "Women: Truly the Fairer Sex," *Newsweek* (April 20, 2009), 13.
45. Robbin Derry, "Ethics of Care," in Werhane and Freeman (1997), 254.
46. Brian K. Burton and Craig P. Dunn, "Feminist Ethics as Moral Grounding for Stakeholder Theory," *Business Ethics Quarterly* (Vol. 6, No. 2, 1996), 133–147; see also A. C. Wicks, D. R. Gilbert, and R. E. Freeman, "A Feminist Reinterpretation of the Stakeholder Concept," *Business Ethics Quarterly* (Vol. 4, 1994), 475–497; "Care Ethics," Internet Encyclopedia of Philosophy, http://www.iep.utm.edu/care-eth/. Accessed February 22, 2016.
47. Derry (1997), 256.
48. Jeanne M. Liedtka, "Feminist Morality and Competitive Reality: A Role for an Ethic of Care?" *Business Ethics Quarterly* (Vol. 6, 1996), 179–200. See also John Dobson and Judith White, "Toward the Feminine Firm," *Business Ethics Quarterly* (Vol. 5, 1995), 463–478.
49. Alasdair MacIntyre, *After Virtue* (University of Notre Dame Press, 1981); see also Louis P. Pojman, *Ethics:*

Discovering Right and Wrong, 7th ed. (Cengage Learning, 2012).

50. Beauchamp, 2001.
51. Pojman, 161; see also Bill Shaw, "Sources of Virtue: The Market and the Community," *Business Ethics Quarterly* (Vol. 7, 1997), 33–50; and Dennis Moberg, "Virtuous Peers in Work Organizations," *Business Ethics Quarterly* (Vol. 7, 1997), 67–85; "Virtue Ethics," Internet Encyclopedia of Philosophy, http://www.iep.utm.edu/virtue/. Accessed February 22, 2016.
52. Character Counts! "Six Pillars of Character," https://charactercounts.org/program-overview/six-pillars/. Accessed February 22, 2016.
53. "Aspects of Leadership: Good Character and Good Choices," Josephson Institute, http://business.josephsoninstitute.org/blog/2016/02/02/build-your-future-by-building-your-character-character-is-a-matter-of-choices-not-fate/. Accessed February 22, 2016.
54. Carol Walker, "New Managers Need a Philosophy about How They'll Lead," *Harvard Business Review,* September 15, 2015, https://hbr.org/2015/09/new-managers-need-a-philosophy-about-how-theyll-lead. Accessed April 25, 2016.
55. Larry C. Spears (ed.), *Reflections of Leadership* (New York: John Wiley & Sons, 1995), 4–7.
56. Joanne B. Ciulla (ed.), *Ethics: The Heart of Leadership,* 3rd ed. (Praeger Publishers, 2014), 17.
57. James A. Autry, *The Servant Leader* (Penguin Random House, 2004), flyleaf.
58. Carroll, 1990, 22; also see Archie B. Carroll, "One Rule Can Best Guide Practices," in Archie B. Carroll, *Business Ethics: Brief Readings on Vital Topics* (New York and London: Routledge Publishers, 2009), 170–171.
59. Barry, 50–51.
60. Carroll, 1990, 22.
61. John C. Maxwell, *There's No Such Thing as "Business" Ethics: There's Only One Rule for Making Decisions* (Warner Books, 2003), 24–29.
62. Gordon L. Lippett, *The Leader Looks at Ethics,* (Washington, DC: Leadership Resources, 1969), 12–13.
63. "Stiffer Rules for Business Ethics," *BusinessWeek* (March 30, 1974), 88.
64. Lippett, 12–13.
65. Eric Harvey and Scott Airitam, *Ethics 4 Everyone: The Handbook for Integrity-Based Business Practices* (Dallas, TX: The Walk the Talk Company, 2002), 31.
66. Ibid., 31.
67. Frederick Andrews, "Corporate Ethics: Talks with a Trace of Robber Baron," *The New York Times* (April 18, 1977), C49–C52.
68. Phillip V. Lewis, "Ethical Principles for Decision Makers: A Longitudinal Study," *Journal of Business Ethics* (Vol. 8, 1989), 275.
69. Craig V. VanSandt, "The Relationship between Ethical Work Climate and Moral Awareness," *Business & Society* (Vol. 42, No. 1, March 2003), 144–151.
70. Cited in John B. Cullen, Bart Victor, and Carroll Stephens, "An Ethical Weather Report: Assessing the Organization's Ethical Climate," *Organizational Dynamics* (Autumn 1989), 50.
71. For an excellent discussion, see Deborah Vidaver Cohen, "Creating and Maintaining Ethical Work Climates: Anomie in the Workplace and Implications for Managing Change," *Business Ethics Quarterly* (Vol. 3, No. 4, October 1993), 343–355; see also B. Victor and J. Cullen, "The Organizational Bases of Ethical Work Climates," *Administrative Science Quarterly* (Vol. 33, 1988), 101–125; and H. R. Smith and A. B. Carroll, "Organizational Ethics: A Stacked Deck," *Journal of Business Ethics* (Vol. 3, 1984), 95–100.
72. Thomas A. Kennedy, *Introduction to the Raytheon Lectureship in Business Ethics* (Waltham, MA: Center for Business Ethics, Bentley University, March 26, 2015), 3.
73. Archie B. Carroll, "Managerial Ethics: A Post-Watergate View," *Business Horizons* (April 1975), 75–80.
74. Posner and Schmidt, 211.
75. American Society of Chartered Life Underwriters & Chartered Financial Consultants and Ethics Officer Association, "Sources and Consequences of Workplace Pressure: A Landmark Study," unpublished report (1997); see also Del Jones, "48% of Workers Admit to Unethical or Illegal Acts," *USA Today* (April 4–6, 1997), 1A–2A.
76. Ethics Resource Center (2003), 33.
77. Ethics Resource Center, "2013 National Business Ethics Survey of the U. S. Workforce" (Arlington, VA, 2013), 20.
78. Alina Dizik, "Corporate Culture Affects a Company's Results—But in Surprising Ways," *Wall Street Journal* (February 22, 2016), R6.
79. T. V. Purcell and James Weber, *Institutionalizing Corporate Ethics: A Case History, Special Study No. 71* (New York: The President's Association, American Management Association, 1979); see also James Weber, "Institutionalizing Ethics into Business Organizations: A Model and Research Agenda," *Business Ethics Quarterly* (Vol. 3, No. 4, October 1993), 419–436.
80. Ethics Resource Center, 2013, ibid. 19.
81. Ibid.
82. Ronald Berenbeim, "Universal Conduct: An Ethics and Compliance Benchmarking Survey," The Conference Board, 2006, 7; United States Sentencing Commission, http://www.ussc.gov/guidelines-manual/2015/2015-ussc-guidelines-manual. Accessed February 22, 2016.

83. Archie B. Carroll, "Ethics Programs Go Beyond Compliance Strategy," *Business Ethics: Brief Readings on Vital Topics* (New York and London: Routledge Publishers, 2009), 184–185.

84. Ronald E. Berenbeim and Jeffrey M. Kaplan, "Ethics and Compliance … The Convergence of Principle- and Rule-Based Ethics Programs: An Emerging Trend," *The Conference Board, Executive Action Series*, No. 231, March 2007.

85. Ibid., 2.

86. David Skeel, "A Nation Adrift from the Rule of Law," *Wall Street Journal* (August 22, 2012), A11.

87. Berenbeim and Kaplan, 4.

88. Mark S. Schwartz, "Developing and Sustaining an Ethical Corporate Culture: The Core Elements," *Business Horizons*, January 2013, Vol. 56, No. 1, 39–50.

89. "The Big Picture: Ethics," *BusinessWeek* (June 19, 2006), 13.

90. L. W. Foy, "Business Ethics: A Reappraisal," *Distinguished Lecture Series, Columbia Graduate School of Business* (January 30, 1975), 2.

91. Danielle E. Warren, Marietta Peytcheva, and Joseph P. Gaspar, "When Ethical Tones at the Top Conflict: Adapting Priority Rules to Reconcile Conflicting Tones," *Business Ethics Quarterly* (Vol. 25, Issue 4, October 2015), 559–582.

92. D. M. Mayer, M. Kuenzi, and R. L. Geenbaum, "Examining the Link between Ethical Leadership and Employee Misconduct: The Mediating role of Ethical Climate," *Journal of Business Ethics* (Vol. 95, 2010), 9.

93. Linda Klebe Treviño, Laura Pincus Hartman, and Michael Brown, "Moral Person and Moral Manager: How Executives Develop a Reputation for Ethical Leadership," *California Management Review* (Vol. 42, No. 4, summer 2000), 134.

94. Al Gini and Ronald M. Green, *Ten Virtues of Outstanding Leaders: Leadership and Character,* (Malden, MA: Wiley-Blackwell, 2013).

95. Harvey Gittler, "Listen to the Whistle-Blowers Before It's Too Late," *The Wall Street Journal* (March 10, 1986), 16.

96. Ethics Resource Center. "National Business Ethics Survey of the U. S. Workforce--Ethical Leadership: Every Leader Sets a Tone," Ethics Resource Center, 2013.

97. Treviño, Hartman, and Brown, 128–142.

98. Gini and Green, 2013, ibid.

99. Treviño, Hartman, and Brown, ibid., 133–136.

100. Steven N. Brenner, "Influences on Corporate Ethics Programs" (San Diego, CA: International Association for Business and Society, March 16–18, 1990), 7.

101. Ethics & Compliance Initiative, "Leading Professional in Ethics & Compliance (LPEC)," http://www.ethics.org/certification/lpec. Accessed April 25, 2016.

102. 2013 National Business Ethics Survey, 16.

103. "Five key features of a Good Ethics and Compliance Program," http://www.ethicalsystems.org/content/five-key-features-good-ethics-and-compliance-program. Accessed February 24, 2016.

104. National Business Ethics Survey, 2003, ibid.

105. "Large companies can boost ethical performance and cut business risk," Corporate Board, May–June 2015, 27. Business Insights: Essentials. Web. 2 March 2016.

106. Bruce A. Hamm, "Elements of the US Federal Sentencing Guidelines," http://www.refresher.com. Accessed April 29, 2004; United States Sentencing Commission Guidelines Manual, November 2012, http://www.ussc.gov/sites/default/files/pdf/guidelines-manual/2012/manual-pdf/TitlePage_Citation_ToC.pdf. Accessed February 24, 2016.

107. Ben Dipietro, "How to Create a Topnotch Compliance Program," *Wall Street Journal* (April 25, 2016), http://blogs.wsj.com/riskandcompliance/2016/04/25/how-to-create-a-top-notch-compliance-program/?mod=djem_jiewr_BE_domainid. Accessed April 29, 2016.

108. Ibid.

109. Ibid.

110. Susan Gaines, "Handing Out Halos," *Business Ethics* (March/April 1994), 20–24.

111. Roy J. Snell, "Should We Call It an Ethics Program or a Compliance Program?" *Journal of Health Care Compliance* (March/April 2004), 1–2.

112. Emily Glazer, "Now in the Cross Hairs: Compliance Officers," *Wall Street Journal* (February 5, 2016), C1.

113. Gregory Millman and Ben DiPietro, "For Compliance Chiefs, Who's the Boss?" *Wall Street Journal* (January 16, Vol. 214), B7.

114. Ethics and Compliance Initiative (ECI), https://www.ethics.org/about/mission-statement. Accessed April 25, 2016.

115. Society of Corporate Compliance and Ethics, http://www.corporatecompliance.org/AboutSCCE/AboutSCCE.aspx. Accessed April 25, 2016.

116. Fred T. Allen, "Corporate Morality: Is the Price Too High?" *The Wall Street Journal* (October 17, 1975), 16.

117. LaRue T. Hosmer, *The Ethics of Management,* 7th Revised ed. (McGraw Hill Book Company, 2011), 12–14.

118. Kenneth Blanchard and Norman Vincent Peale, *The Power of Ethical Management* (New York: Fawcett Crest, 1988), 20.

119. Texas Instruments, "The TI Ethics Quick Test," http://www.ti.com/corp/docs/company/citizen/ethics/quicktest.shtml. Accessed February 24, 2016.

120. Joan Dubinsky, "Code Redux Part One: Tips for Writing and Updating Your Corporate Code of Conduct," Corporate Compliance Insights, March 2009, http://corporatecomplianceinsights.com/corporate-code-of-conduct-guidelines-policy-tips-writing-updating/. Accessed February 24, 2016.

121. Institute for Global Ethics, "Building a Code of Ethics," https://www.globalethics.org/What-We-Do/Consulting/Code-of-Ethics.aspx?gclid=Cj0KEQiAxrW2BRCFidKbqKyq1YEBEiQAnMDWxp4IF7magQPsr5iP9fhgvb8iNvXFl0eWzFdWAMrVYxoaAiiq8P8HAQ. Accessed February 24, 2016.

122. "Codes of Ethics," by Leon V. Ryan, in Patricia Werhane and R. Edward Freeman (eds.), *The Blackwell Encyclopedic Dictionary of Business Ethics* (Malden, MA: Blackwell Publishing, 1997), 114.

123. Jim Sinegal, "Costco: How Our Ethics Evolved Over the First 30 Years," Raytheon Lectureship in Business Ethics, (Waltham, MA: Center for Business Ethics, Bentley University, March 26, 2015), 6–12.

124. "A Sense of Responsibility–CEO Interview with Brian Goldner, CEO of Hasbro," *CR: Corporate Responsibility Magazine*, January–February 2016, 14.

125. Institute of Business Ethics, "Nine Steps for Preparing a New Code," http://www.ibe.org.uk/index.asp?upid=61&msid=11, Accessed February 29, 2016.

126. "Common Ethics Code Provisions," http://www.ethics.org/eci/research/free-toolkit/code-provisions. Accessed March 11, 2016.

127. Cynthia Stohl, Michael Stohl, and Lucy Popova, "A New Generation of Corporate Codes of Ethics," *Journal of Business Ethics* (2009: 90), 607–622.

128. Patrick Erwin, "Corporate Codes of Conduct: The Effects of Code Content and Quality on Ethical Performance," *Journal of Business Ethics* (April 2011, Vol. 99 Issue 4), 535–548.

129. Mark Schwartz, "The Nature of the Relationship between Corporate Codes of Ethics and Behavior," *Journal of Business Ethics* (Vol. 32, 2001), 247–262.

130. Ibid., 255.

131. Treviño, Hartman, and Brown, op. cit., 136.

132. J. Lynn Lunsford and Anne Marie Squeo, "Boeing Dismisses Two Executives for Violating Ethical Standards," *The Wall Street Journal* (November 25, 2003). http://www.wsj.com/articles/SB106968087463716900. Accessed February 29, 2016.

133. "Nortel fires top exec amid financial probe," *Computer Weekly*, http://www.computerweekly.com/news/2240055788/Nortel-fires-top-exec-amid-financial-probe. Accessed February 29, 2016.

134. Allen, 16.

135. 2013 National Business Ethics Survey, 14.

136. Ibid., 30.

137. Lighthouse, "Why Ethics Hotlines are Considered a Best Practice," https://www.lighthouse-services.com/documents/Why%20Ethics%20Hotlines%20Are%20Considered%20a%20Best%20Practice.pdf. Accessed April 25, 2016.

138. Ibid.

139. Toffler, 22–23.

140. Thomas A. Kennedy, *Introduction to Raytheon Lectureship in Business Ethics* (Waltham, MA: Center for Business Ethics, Bentley University, March 25, 2015), 3.

141. "Business Ethics Training," Webucator, https://www.webucator.com/management-training/course/business-ethics-training.cfm. Accessed February 29, 2016.

142. AccountingWeb, "Nine steps to make your company's ethics training program stick," http://www.accountingweb.com/practice/practice-excellence/nine-steps-to-make-your-companys-ethics-training-program-stick. Accessed February 29, 2016.

143. "Humor in Compliance and Ethics," http://compliance-toolbox.wikispaces.com/Humor+in+Compliance+and+Ethics. Accessed February 29, 2016.

144. Francis J. Daly, "An Ethics Officer's Perspective," in Marc J. Epstein and Kirk O. Hanson (eds.), *The Accountable Corporation: Business Ethics,* Vol. 2 (Westport, CT: Praeger Publishers, 2006), 186.

145. Thomas M. Jones, "Can Business Ethics Be Taught? Empirical Evidence," *Business & Professional Ethics Journal* (Vol. 8, 1989), 86.

146. Danielle E. Warren, Joseph P. Gaspar, William S. Laufer, "Is Formal Ethics Training Merely Cosmetic? A Study of Ethics Training and Ethical Organizational Culture," *Business Ethics Quarterly* (Vol. 24, Issue 1, January 2014), 85–117.

147. David Allen Jones, "A Novel Approach to Business Ethics Training: Improving Moral Reasoning in Just a Few Weeks," *Journal of Business Ethics* (2009, Vol. 88), 367–379.

148. Business Roundtable Institute for Ethics, http://www.corporate-ethics.org/about/. Accessed February 29, 2016.

149. Katherine S. Mangan, "Business Schools and Company CEOs to Create Ethics Center," *Chronicle of Higher Education* (January 30, 2004), A9; also see Louis Lavelle and Amy Borrus, "Ethics 101 for CEOs," *BusinessWeek* (January 26, 2004), 88.

150. Eric Krell, "How to Conduct an Ethics Audit," *HR Magazine*, April 2010, 55:4, 48–51; also see David Ingram, "How to Conduct an Ethics Audit," *Chron*, http://smallbusiness.chron.com/conduct-ethical-audit-16101.html. Accessed February 29, 2016.

151. *Environmental Leader*, "Big Four Audit Firms Lead Sustainability Assurance Services," June 22, 2011, http://www.environmentalleader.com/2011/06/22/big-four-audit-firms-lead-sustainability-assurance-services/. Accessed February 29, 2016.

152. Ronald E. Berenbeim, "Ethics Programs and Practices: A 20-Year Retrospective," The Conference Board, https://www.conference-board.org/publications/publicationdetail.cfm?publicationid=1207. Accessed February 29, 2016; Association of Certified Fraud Examiners, "Fraud Risk Assessment Tool," http://www.acfe.com/frat.aspx?id=6797. Accessed February 29, 2016.

153. The Conference Board, "Emerging Practices in Cyber Risk Governance," https://hcexchange.conference-board.org/topics/publicationdetail.cfm?publicationid=5040&topicid=30&subtopicid=250. Accessed February 29, 2016.

154. Marcia Narine, "Conducting a Risk Assessment—One Approach," Risk Assessments and Compliance Program Benchmarking, The Conference Board, Webcast, V0060-05-CH, November 2, 2005.

155. Ethics Resource Center, 2009 National Business Ethics Survey 20–21; Ben McClure, *Investopedia*, "The Importance of Transparency," http://www.investopedia.com/articles/fundamental/03/121703.asp#axzz2MhVHuZYp. Accessed February 29, 2016.

156. Peter Levesque, "What Do We Mean by Transparency?" Institute for Knowledge Mobilization, http://www.knowledgemobilization.net/archives/603. Accessed February 29, 2016.

157. Barbara Pagano and Elizabeth Pagano, *The Transparency Edge: How Credibility Can Make or Break You in Business* (New York: McGraw Hill Trade, 2003); also see Elizabeth Pagano, *The Transparency Edge* (New York: McGraw Hill, 2005).

158. Victor Lipman, "New Study Shows Transparency Isn't Just Good Ethics—It's Good Business," Forbes, December 11, 2013, http://www.forbes.com/sites/victorlipman/2013/12/11/new-study-shows-transparency-isnt-just-good-ethics-its-good-business/#68dd5dcb5798. Accessed February 29, 2016.

159. Vertical Response Blog, Janine Popick, "Five Examples of How Being Transparent is Good for Business," http://www.verticalresponse.com/blog/5-examples-of-how-being-transparent-can-help-your-business/. Accessed April 26, 2016.

160. Ibid.

161. Vision Critical, Matt Kleinschmit, "Five Brands That Employed Transparency and Won," https://www.visioncritical.com/5-brands-employed-transparency-marketing-and-won/?lb=1. Accessed April 26, 2016.

162. Archie B. Carroll, "Slack Corporate Governance Costs Us All," *Business Ethics: Brief Readings on Vital Topics* (New York and London: Routledge Publishers, 2009), 86–87.

163. Quoted in Curtis C. Verschoor, "Unethical Workplace Is Still with Us," *Strategic Finance* (April 2004), 16.

164. Ronald E. Berenbeim, *Ethics Issues and Programs: The Role of the Board*, https://www.conference-board.org/publications/publicationdetail.cfm?publicationid=2063. Accessed February 29, 2016.

165. "Boards of Directors Getting More Involved in Companies" Ethics Programs," *PR Newswire*, http://www.prnewswire.com/news-releases/boards-of-directors-getting-more-involved-in-companies-ethics-programs-58812907.html. Accessed February 29, 2016.

166. Max H. Bazerman and Francesca Gino, "Behavioral Ethics: Toward a Deeper Understanding of Moral Judgment and Dishonesty," *Annual Review of Law and Social Science, December 2012,* http://www.hbs.edu/faculty/Pages/item.aspx?num=42452. Accessed February 29, 2016.

167. Linda Treviño, Gary Weaver, and Scott Reynolds, "Behavioral Ethics in Organizations: A Review," *Journal of Management* (2006, Vol. 32) 951.

168. Robert S. Benchley, "Answering an Ethical SOS," *McCombsToday.org/Magazine*, Fall 2012, 16–21, http://www.today.mccombs.utexas.edu/2012/10/answering-an-ethical-sos. Accessed February 29, 2016.

169. Ann E. Tenbrunsel, Kristina A. Diekmann, Kimberly A. Wade-Bezoni, Max H. Bazerman, "The Ethical Mirage: A Temporal Explanation as to Why We Are Not as Ethical as We Think We Are," *Research in Organizational Behavior* (Vol. 30, 2010) 153–173.

170. Benchley, 2012, 21.

171. Benchley, 2012, 21.

172. Benchley, 2012, 21.

173. Max H. Bazerman and Ann E. Tenbrunsel, "Ethical Breakdowns," *Harvard Business Review* (April 2011), 58–65.

174. Kenneth E. Goodpaster, "Examining the Conscience of the Corporation," in Marc J. Epstein and Kirk O. Hanson (eds.), *The Accountable Corporation: Business Ethics*, Vol. 2 (Westport Connecticut: Praeger Publishers, 2006), 102.

9

Business Ethics and Technology

CHAPTER LEARNING OUTCOMES

After studying this chapter, you should be able to:

1. Identify and describe what the new world of Big Data is all about and the implications it holds for businesses.
2. Explain how social media have changed the world of business and technology.
3. Discuss how surveillance is a new dimension to being a consumer and an employee and what its implications are for stakeholders.
4. Articulate an understanding of technology and the technological environment.
5. Identify the characteristics of technology to include their benefits, side effects, and challenges in business.
6. Comment on the relationship between technology and ethics.
7. Define information technology and discuss the issues relating to e-commerce in business.
8. Define biotechnology. Identify the ethical issues involved in genetic engineering and genetically modified organisms (GMOs).

We live in an age dominated and driven by rapidly advancing technology. As Nancy Gibbs, editor of *Time* magazine recently observed, "technology ... accelerates and complicates."[1] Each new generation experiences technological advances that were not seen by previous generations. Businesses have realized it as well. A study of Fortune 500 CEOs recently reported that "technology" was their greatest challenge, especially the rapid technological changes they now are facing. A close second to the rapid pace of technological change was cybersecurity. Today's CEOs recognize that new technologies are radically changing the way they do business and they need to figure it out before their competitors do.[2]

The new generation comprising young people, called the iGeneration, is said to have no "off switch" when it comes to technology. For this new group of post-Millennials, technology is said to be a "part of their DNA."[3] To understand the present and to see the future, we need to pay attention to the findings of Common Sense Media, which has recently reported that "screen addiction" is now a real phenomenon among young people. On average, more than six and a half hours a day are spent by youth on devices using screens—TVs, tablets, phones, video games, computers—for nonschool purposes. Digital citizenship is now a topic being discussed in schools.[4] Now and in the future, we live in a world driven by technology—for consumers, employees, and life, in general.

Technology is how we sustain life and make it comfortable. Technology is at the core of most businesses, whether it is used to pursue new products, processes, or services, or as a means to achieve other worthwhile ends. But technology, as many have observed, is a two-edged sword. Many positive benefits flow from technological advances. By the same token, many new problems or challenges are posed by advancing technology, especially in the arena of business ethics. Futurist John Naisbitt, for example, has questioned whether advancing technology has the potential to be a "liberating" or "destructive" force in society. He has said that, at best, technology supports and improves human life, and at its worst it alienates, isolates, distorts, and destroys.[5]

In either case, dynamic technological advances have become such a central part of our lives and doing business in the 21st century that they must be carefully considered. More and more ethical issues for business and for society have arisen as a result of technological advances. Many believe that technology has developed at a speed that significantly outstrips the capacity of society, government, or business to grasp its consequences or ethical implications. In this chapter, we will explore some of these issues, knowing full well that other aspects related to technology will be touched upon in other chapters as specific stakeholder groups are considered in more detail.

It is interesting and challenging to brainstorm about what new technologies may have in store for business. And, they are all embedded in a new, complex world of data proliferation and overload. One observer has even called it an "idolatry of data," which has been enabled by the almost unimaginable data-gathering capabilities of new technology.[6]

9.1 The New World of Big Data

Experts now call this new information universe "Big Data"—an "infinite sea of facts, products, books, maps, conversations, references, opinions, trends, videos, advertisements, surveys" and it is "literally at your fingertips, 24-7, every day from now on."[7]

The term **Big Data** describes the tons of information that are out there and how businesses are striving to put it to work. This information comes from many more sources than ever before and businesses can get access to it as quickly as it is generated.[8] Using powerful computers, ubiquitous sensors, monitoring devices, and the Web, it is now possible to analyze mountains of raw data, which yields previously unknown insights that increasingly are being used by business, government, and others.[9] Big Data is characterized by the 3Vs—high *v*olume, high *v*elocity, and high *v*ariety. It has been in the commercial world where Big Data has seen its greatest impact to date. A 2016 survey by NewVantage Partners found that the number of U.S. firms using Big Data in the past three years has increased 58 percentage points such that 70 percent of firms now report that Big Data is of critical importance to their firms. Its impact can now be found everywhere—products and services that can predict the unique needs of customers, significantly improved credit precision, and merchants who can offer special deals to consumers and send them to their smartphones as they are walking through the door.[10] As one Chief Information Officer (CIO) put it: "We are drowning in Data."[11] For companies, the advantages of Big Data have been accompanied by a host of new issues, among them, data security, privacy, and cybercrime, which have become huge threats to, and responsibilities of, business.

Technology has driven new and growing fields, which have significant implications for businesses and the ethical issues they eventually will face. In addition to Big Data, among these new arenas are the "Internet of things," (IoT) data analytics, cloud computing and artificial intelligence, just to name a few of the growing applications.[12]

9.1a Social Media

In the sea of Big Data, one of the hottest topics in technology these days is social media. Social media represent the cutting edge of business communication based on technology. Consumers want to use it and companies want to exploit it. A relevant question is what possible social and ethical implications will tools such as Facebook, Twitter, LinkedIn, Snapchat, Pinterest, Reddit, Google Plus+, WhatsApp, and Instagram have?[13] On the positive side, most popular tools in social networking provide a cyber-meeting space for people wanting to network. Networking tools provide a space where individuals can describe themselves and connect with others.

But, social media has a dark side in which social and ethical issues arise as companies and others try to take advantage of the technology. For example, many Web sites as well as individuals have become wary of Facebook's tracking techniques.[14] Others have objected to Facebook, in collaboration with researchers, attempting to manipulate news feeds to gauge emotional reactions of users. Some have felt they were being treated by Facebook as "lab rats."[15] Twitter has also raised some ethical issues that appear to be ongoing. The company has tried to scrub sensitive content from its Web sites but it walks a fine line between free expression and an aversion to being held legally responsible for the actions of its users.[16]

For companies, unfair reviews of products or services and how to respond to these pose a constant challenge. The public should expect accurate information about companies and products, but often this does not happen when "tweets" are flying based upon emotional reactions rather than facts. Social media frequently places more emphasis on instantaneous rather than accurate information and this can unfairly put companies on the defensive, sometimes for reasons based on inaccurate information.[17] The challenge of social media as a technology is to promote freedom within an ethical context of responsibility. More information is good, but only if it promotes truth-telling.[18]

9.1b Surveillance

Another relentless issue in the realm of ethics and technology has been the rising extent to which companies are using video camera surveillance mounted in stores to monitor customers' and employees' actions. We know we are being watched, but do we know how smart these technologies have become? For example, a few Macy's, CVS, and Babies 'R' Us stores have used a system called the Video Investigator. This advanced surveillance software can monitor a customer's movements and compare them between video images and recognize any type of unusual activity. If the shopper removes ten items at once from a shelf, for example, or opens a case that is normally kept closed and locked, the system alerts security guards of the activity. The system can also predict where a shoplifter is likely to hide (e.g., at the end of aisles or behind floor displays).[19] In short, surveillance provided by technological advances now address a variety of business issues—theft, substance abuse, vandalism, corporate espionage, and other illegal, unethical or unauthorized activities.[20] We are, indeed, being watched and recorded—more and more. Much of this is for the good. But there can be possible abuses as well.

In this chapter, we explore the subject of technology and business ethics—a deep and wide subject that we can examine only in a limited fashion. Technology has become such an integral aspect of our work and consumer lives, however, that special treatment of these topics is warranted. First, we will consider what technology embraces and some of its characteristics, benefits and challenges. Second, we will discuss the subject of ethics and technology. Finally, we will consider business ethics issues that arise in connection with two major spheres of technology: (1) computers and information technology and (2) biotechnology.

9.2 Technology and the Technological Environment

Technology means many things to many people. In this chapter, **technology** will refer to the "totality of the means employed to provide objects necessary for human sustenance and comfort."[21] It is also seen as a scientific method used in achieving a practical purpose.[22] Technology refers to all the ways people use or apply their inventions, discoveries, data, and information to satisfy their needs and desires. Taken together, these technological advances have made work easier and more productive.[23] But, technology has also introduced new challenges, many of them social or ethical in nature.

In Chapter 1, we discussed the macroenvironment of business and how this total environment was composed of several significant and interrelated segments such as the social, economic, political, and technological. The **technological environment**, our current topic of concern, represents *the total set of technology-based advancements or progress taking place in society*. Pertinent aspects of this segment include new products, processes, materials, states of knowledge, and scientific advancements in both theoretical and applied senses.

ETHICS IN PRACTICE CASE

Twitter Ethics in Business

Twitter is one of the most frequently used social media. It may be because it is so easy and fast to use. Maybe it's because tweets are so brief. Knocking out a few tweets does not take much time or thought.

Twitter has been used for a number of nefarious and malicious uses. Though most people who tweet do it responsibly, there are thousands of misleading, deceptive, criminal, or maligned tweets that go out daily. Though young people use social media more than anyone, Twitter has caught on in business too. Many business people, especially entertainment and sports personalities, use Twitter extensively. Regular business people and employees use Twitter also—often to promote a product or a cause their employer wants to rally support for. Public relations business people use Twitter often and they are business people who ought to subscribe to some form of ethical behavior.

Angela Dwyer has suggested that there are at least four categories of tweeters and they all face ethical challenges. First, there are *Paid Tweeters*. Sometimes these are celebrities or sports stars that are paid by companies to tweet as a form of advertising. They typically do not disclose that they are being paid to tweet. The FTC has said that celebrities in this category should disclose their relationships with advertisers when making endorsements but it is hard to enforce.

Second, there are *Company Tweeters*. These individuals write reviews or tweets about promotional offers for their own companies. Some company tweeters are enthusiastic about their own companies and products and want the world to know. Others are tweeting because their boss has asked them to do so or they want to be viewed favorably come raise and promotion time.

Third, there are *Out-of-Context Tweeters*. Sometimes while attending events, these tweeters tweet hurried reactions or impressions that contain unverified or false information. Or, they do not present the context in which something was said or done. In other words, they do not provide the big picture. Tweets such as this have the potential to misinform or distort. To make matters worse, they are often retweeted before fuller or more accurate information is given.

Fourth, there are *Ghost-Tweeters*. When someone is paid to write tweets on behalf of someone else, the ghostwriter, or Ghost-Tweeter may put out information without any confidence about whether the information is factual or accurate. Politicians, executives, sports stars, and other highly placed business people may use Ghost-Tweeters who are simply following a script without knowing for sure of the accuracy of its information.

In short, there are many opportunities and ways by which social media such as Twitter may be abused, misused, or be implicated in questionable practices by businesses and business people.

1. Are these forms of tweeting ethical? How do you draw the fine line between ethical and unethical in each of these categories of tweeting? Which category faces the most ethical challenges in business?
2. Are there other categories of tweeters you can think of? Do they face ethical challenges?
3. Some people may say "hey, don't sweat it, it's only a tweet! You need to be on guard yourself!" Is this a reasonable response to business use of Twitter or other social media? Who agrees?!
4. Are there other forms of social media that business uses that are more ethically challenging than Twitter? Describe them.
5. Should companies that use Twitter have a code of conduct for guidance in what represents ethical tweets? What key ethical principles should guide the use of Twitter?

Sources: "Twitter is Your Window to the World," Twitter.com, https://about.twitter.com/; Charlie Warzel, "Scientists May Have Figured Out Twitter Ethics," BuzzFeed News, http://www.buzzfeed.com/charliewarzel/scientists-may-have-figured-out-twitter-ethics#.saA4r2dnN; Angela Dwyer, "Twethics": A Brief Analysis of Twitter Ethics in Public Relations, Commpro, http://www.commpro.biz/pr-roi/twethics-a-brief-analysis-of-twitter-ethics-in-public-relations/. Accessed April 24, 2016; The Establishment, "The Dubious Ethics of Twitter Mining," http://www.theestablishment.co/2015/11/04/the-dubious-ethics-of-twitter-mining/. Accessed April 24, 2016.

The rate of change and complexity of the technological environment have made it of special interest to business today. In the exploding information technology realm and the burgeoning field of biotechnology, the shape of how we are living, what products we are using, and what processes we are being exposed to is changing at an accelerating pace.

9.3 Characteristics of Technology

At the 2016 World Economic Forum held in Davos, Switzerland, CEOs met to discuss the sweeping changes in the world of business. A major takeaway from this meeting was that we have entered the latest industrial revolution, one characterized by artificial intelligence, Big Data, sensors, robotics, and more to come. This new revolution has taken us beyond that, which began 50 years ago when automated production, electronics and computers arrived on the scene.[24] We have moved from a world characterized by industrial technology to one dominated by mobile computing, the proliferation of inexpensive sensors collecting terabytes of data, and the rise of machine learning that can use data in a way that will fundamentally change the way the global economy is organized and functions.[25] Whatever the technological level of advancement, there are general benefits and undesirable side effects of technology, and ethical challenges inherent in these technological advancements.

9.3a Benefits, Costs, and Challenges

Few would dispute that society has benefited greatly from technology and innovation. We live better lives today as employees, consumers, and members of the community due to technology. Technology has helped us gain control over nature and to build for ourselves a civilized life. Through the ages, technology has benefited society in four main ways.[26] It has increased society's production of goods and services; it has reduced the amount of labor needed to produce goods and services; it has made labor easier and safer; and higher standards of living have been a direct result of laborsaving technology.[27] The potential of the IoT has been unlocked. We now have sensors and actuators connected by networks to computing systems and these have received enormous attention over the past five years. McKinsey & Company has estimated that IoT has a total potential economic impact of $4 trillion to $11 trillion a year by 2025.[28]

Though technologies have benefited people in many ways, there have also been some unanticipated costs and side effects as well—problems, issues, or effects not anticipated before technologies were designed and implemented. One major reason for this is that technologies are often implemented before much thought is given to possible costs, side effects, ethical problems, or downside risks. In fact, almost "every technology is used before it is completely understood. There is always a lag between an innovation and the apprehension of its consequences" and we are living in that lag.[29] A major problem during this lag is that ethical issues and challenges are only later perceived and faced.

Four categories of undesirable side effects of technology are representative of the issues we face in business today. First, there is *environmental pollution*. Second, there is *depletion of natural resources*. Third, there is *technological unemployment*. The most common form of technological unemployment occurs when machines take the place of humans, as we experienced in the automation phase of industrial development and now in the robotic movement. Fourth, there are the *creation of unsatisfying jobs* due to technology as jobs are broken down into smaller components and workers are further removed from the finished product that might provide a greater sense of fulfillment and pride. Monotony and boredom can easily set in when jobs are significantly shaped by certain technological processes.[30]

Another cost or side effect of new and growing technology use has been termed **digital amnesia**. In a digital economy, this forgetfulness phenomenon has affected young and old, consumers and employees, as we are outsourcing our brainwork to digital devices.[31] A study by Kapersky Labs concluded that the majority of digital consumers are no longer able to recall critical contact information even for those closest to them; they suggest there is now a direct link between data available at the click of a button and a failure to remember that information anymore. Related to this, our average attention spans have fallen from 12 seconds in 2000 to 8.25 seconds today.[32]

This is similar to the **Google Effect**, which holds that just knowing that some bit of data can easily be retrieved on the Internet makes us less likely to now remember it. In fact, one report on the Google Effect concludes that losing our Internet connection has become more and more like losing a friend. In addition, there is an amazing amount of research now going on about the effects of communications technology on our brains, nervous systems, social abilities, relationships, mental health, physical health, and family structures.[33] To these undesirable effects, we can surely add others, many of which are replete with ethical issues.

9.4 Technology and Ethics

Technology unquestionably has many benefits for humankind. Our perspective at this juncture, however, is to raise the ethical questions that may be related to business development and use of technology and innovation. To do so does not mean that one is against technology. It simply means that one is concerned about the ethical use and implications of technology. Like management decision making and globalization of business, the actions of the business community with respect to technology have ethical implications that should be identified, discussed, and factored into decision making. Management needs to ask "who will be hurt and in what ways" by technology; what are the downside risks and problems that may arise? Management's goal should be to avoid immoral and amoral practices with respect to technology and to move toward an ethically sustainable posture with respect to this potent business resource.

Applying business ethics analysis to questions involving technology is essentially an extension of our discussions of business ethics up to this point. The goal of managers and businesses striving to be ethical should be to avoid harm and to do what is morally justified and fair. In making ethical judgments, the prevailing norms of acceptability regarding technology must be tested by the principles of fairness and justice, protection

SPOTLIGHT *on Sustainability*

The Field of Technoethics

It is not surprising that the field of study known as *technoethics* has arrived and become popular and important. **Technoethics** is an interdisciplinary field concerned with ethical issues and the ethical dimension of technology in society. Technoethics conceives of technology and ethics as socially embedded fields that specialize in the ethical use of technology, guarding against the misuse of technology, and striving to develop principles to guide new technological developments and applications that will be beneficial to society. Technology and ethics are perceived as interconnected topics that are ever present in life and society. Technoethics describes a wide range of ethical issues revolving around technology that include people working and shopping in organizations to broader concerns such as the social, ethical and legal aspects of technology and its use in society.

Just a few of the issues in which technoethics is concerned today include digital copyrights, cybercriminality, privacy versus security, GPS technologies and privacy, genetically modified organisms (GMOs), surveillance cameras at work and at stores, computer monitoring devices, biotech issues, and information and communication issues.

Organizational technoethics is a rapidly growing subfield. This subfield focuses on how information spreads within organizations and is shared among managers and colleagues around the world in global organizations. The technological means by which organization members communicate with one another today have proliferated and have raised many ethical concerns. As a consequence there is a growing need for more study and analysis of its implications.

Figuring out what is ethical in the Internet age has added impetus to the expansion of technoethics. Companies that are on the leading edge are finding that they can quickly find themselves in trouble with some offended public. It could be about privacy, free speech, marketing tactics, or a range of other issues.

Sources: "Technoethics," Wikipedia, https://en.wikipedia.org/wiki/Technoethics. Accessed March 14, 2016; R. Luppicini, Technoethics and the Evolving Knowledge Society (Hershey: Idea Group Publishing), 2010; "New Forms of Communication, New Ethical Dilemmas," The Western Front, http://www.westernfrontonline.net/news/news_photo/article_8188b94c-c3c8-11e4-bcc6-cb047be98e85.html. Accessed March 14, 2016; David Freedman, Inc., "The Technoethics Trap," http://www.inc.com/magazine/20060301/column-freedman.html. Accessed March 14, 2016.

of rights, utilitarianism, and other applicable ethical guidelines. The goal should be to reconcile and build bridges over the gap between "what is" and "what ought to be." Beyond this, the challenge of business ethics and technology is to identify the major issues in which an ethical dimension may reside, and apply ethical analysis to them. Many of these issues arise in chapters throughout the book. Here, however, our focus is on taking a closer look at technology, in general, and issues that arise due to technology in business.

Two Key Ethical Issues. There are two key ethical issues in the realm of technology that seem to drive everything. First is the idea of technological determinism. **Technological determinism** is the imperative that "what *can* be developed *will* be developed." When someone once asked, "why do we want to put men on the moon?" the answer was always "because we *can* put men on the moon." In other words, scientists and those who work with advanced technologies are driven to push back the frontiers of technological development without consideration of ethical issues, social problems, or side effects.

The second important concept is that of ethical lag. **Ethical lag** occurs when the speed of technological change far exceeds that of ethical development.[34] As stated earlier, we always seem to be living in the condition of ethical lag. Throughout our consideration of technology and ethics, these two phenomena are evident and influential.

There are a number of arenas in which specific issues of business ethics and technology might be explored. Research over the past few years reveals two broad categories of issues that now merit consideration in this chapter: **information technology** and **biotechnology**. Each is broad and deep, so we can consider them only in an introductory way in this chapter. Each, however, significantly involves business, either directly or indirectly. Within each, there are thousands of technologies that raise ethical questions. Our purpose, therefore, will be to focus on a few that give us a representative sampling of ethical issues we face with technology.

9.5 Information Technology

Information technology (IT) is the use of computers, storage, networking, and other physical devices, infrastructure, and processes to create, process, store, secure, and exchange all forms of electronic data.[35] Information technology is deeply entrenched in all businesses and stakeholders involved in those businesses. Businesses and people both are affected by technology and are directly involved in pursuits based on technology. We will consider them both. We will discuss two broad business areas in this section: *electronic commerce*, or Web-based marketing, and *computer technology in the workplace*, including telecommunications. These areas overlap significantly and are interdependent, so our separate discussion of each is to lend some structure to the discussion.

9.5a E-Commerce as a Pervasive Technology

Electronic commerce, often referred to as *e-commerce*, *e-business*, or *Web-based marketing*, is one of the most significant technological phenomena of our day. It primarily affects consumer stakeholders and competitors of the e-commerce firms. Most experts today are convinced that the Internet has reshaped the way business is conducted around the world. Part of this is firms selling products and services online. Beyond this, companies are integrating the Internet into every aspect of their businesses and many products are being interconnected through the IoT. The IoT refers to the development of the Internet in which everyday objects (computers, thermostats, appliances, smartphones, etc.) have network connectivity allowing them to receive and send data.[36]

Business transactions via e-commerce are a multiple trillion dollar business, and the majority of it comes from business-to-business (B2B) sales.[37] Consumer transactions are huge and growing. The pull of e-business is powerful and many companies are responding by moving their operations to the Internet. Companies are spending billions of dollars linking customers, sales, and marketing over the Web, increasingly through social networking. In short, electronic commerce is a flourishing business, and the opportunity for questionable practices arises along with this growth.

Online Scams. Along with the growth of electronic commerce, business ethics problems have arisen as well. The major category of problems for consumers is **online scams**. According to Fraud!Alert, a project of the National Consumer League, con artists are taking advantage of the Internet's growth in popularity to scam the unwary. During one recent year, for example, the top frauds over the Internet included fake check scams, prizes/sweepstakes/free gifts, phishing/spoofing, advance fee loans, friendship scandals, Nigerian money offers, Internet auctions, family/friend imposters, and scholarships /grants.[38] Other scams included credit card fraud, travel and vacation scams, pyramid schemes, and bogus investment opportunities. Virtually all of these scams are delivered via technology: World Wide Web, telephone, and e-mail using technologies such as wire transfers, credit cards, bank account debits, and bank debit cards.[39]

9.5b Ongoing Issues in E-Commerce Ethics

Many of the ongoing issues in e-commerce ethics include the following[40]: access, intellectual property, privacy and informed consent, protection of children, security of information, and trust. These ethical issues are not restricted to e-commerce. They also occur in brick-and-mortar businesses. The manifestations and scope of these issues, however, differ from those of traditional businesses.

Access refers to the differences in computer access between the rich and the poor. *Intellectual property*, in e-commerce, is illustrated by the ethics of downloading music or books. *Privacy and informed consent* differ in e-commerce. An illustration is the novel ways companies place cookies on our computers without informed consent. In addition, firms collect online information and merge it with offline information. *Protection of children* is an ongoing ethical issue, and it is illustrated in the issue of pornography and the dangers of children getting hooked up with sexual predators. E-commerce makes porn more accessible than through traditional businesses. *Security* is such a major issue that even today some are reluctant to do business on the Web for fear their credit card numbers will be intercepted by someone not associated with the e-commerce business. Finally, *trust* is the basis for practically all business transactions, and it is especially crucial in e-commerce.[41]

9.5c Invasion of Consumer Privacy via E-Commerce

The average person encounters two forms of Internet electronic commerce: business-to-consumer (B2C) transactions and business-to-business (B2B) transactions. Most of us are quite familiar with B2C transactions when we do personal business on the Internet—buying products and services, arranging credit cards, accessing travel Web sites, and doing financial business such as personal banking. As employees, we also encounter B2B transactions, which are anticipated to be the greatest area of e-commerce growth in the coming years. One reason for this is the rapid globalization of commerce. In terms of Web-based marketing to consumers, consumer stakeholders are primarily affected by such issues as database sharing, identity theft, and invasion of privacy. Invasion of privacy is a legitimate concern in all business transactions; however, the special case of e-commerce deserves special attention because of the ease with which data can be accessed, stored and transmitted in electronic form. The new world of Big Data has accelerated this trend.

One of the most important ethical issues with respect to doing business over the Internet is the question of invasions of consumer privacy.[42] Business executives and private citizens alike are spending more time today worrying about consumer privacy. Figure 9-1 summarizes some of the concerns that privacy advocates and law enforcement experts have about the Internet's threat to privacy.

Some of the most prevalent technological means by which companies invade consumers' privacy include the use of cookies and spam. **Cookies** are identification tags that Web sites drop on our personal computer hard drives so they can recognize repeat visitors the next time we visit their Web sites.[43] Surveys show that some consumers don't know what cookies are; others are aware of them but don't even think about blocking them.[44]

Spam, which crowds our inboxes daily, is unsolicited commercial e-mail. It is sent through "open-relays" to millions of persons. It takes a toll on Internet users' time, their resources, and the resources of Internet service providers (ISPs). Another problem is that spammers have begun to send advertisements via text messages to cell phones.[45] Most consumers interpret the receipt of *spam* as a rude invasion of their privacy. Opening our e-mail mailboxes only to find a few dozen unsolicited ads is annoying, at the least, and an invasion of privacy to many. Also, some companies experiment with pop-up pulsing background ads that never go away. Interestingly, dozens of companies make programs that protect our e-mail privacy, block cookies, and filter spam and porn, but very few consumers bother to use them.[46]

Collection and use of personal information is a serious invasion of privacy with respect to electronic commerce. Though non-Internet companies have engaged in this practice for years, everything seems magnified in the e-world in which we now live. None of us really knows how much personal information is collected, saved, swapped, or sold in e-commerce. Thousands of retailers, from department stores to catalog companies, collect and store personal information, from asking customers for their zip codes to collecting names, addresses, household income, and purchasing patterns through a store credit card. Retailers also share, exchange, and even sell their customer databases to other companies. In short, the average consumer has very little control over what is done with his or her personal data once it is collected.[47] An ongoing concern is **identity theft** or someone tampering with one's financial accounts. Less serious is the inundation of marketing attempts, both online and offline, which consumers are subjected to as a result of information being distributed.

Phishing One of the most common and serious problems in the realm of computer scams against consumers and companies continues to be the ongoing scam identified as **phishing**. Phishing is a an attempt to obtain financial or other confidential, personal information from Internet users, typically by way of an e-mail that looks like it is from a legitimate organization, such as a financial institution, but contains a link to a fake Web site that replicates the real one.[48] An example of this occurred when a hacker who goes by the cyber name of Robotector sent an e-mail with the subject line "I still love you" to three million people. Within the message had been planted a small computer virus that, when executed, began to record user names and passwords each time their owner visited more than 30 online banks or payment Web sites. Then, this information was secretly e-mailed back to Robotector. This technique is called "phishing" because it lures prey (computer users) with convincing bait into revealing passwords and other private data. The Anti-Phishing Working Group, an industry association, reports that in one month in 2015, there were 90,000 reports of phishing scams that had occurred.[49]

Botnet scams, one of the latest techniques by which hackers get access to personal and corporate information, are exploding in numbers. *Bots* are computers that have been compromised by unethical hackers. A network of bots, called a *botnet*, is created by e-mails that get distributed by these compromised computers, and these are controlled by

FIGURE 9-1 Examples of Threats to Consumers' Privacy Posed by the Internet

Threats to Privacy	Description
Social networks	Social networks allow individuals to establish connections and store information remotely. Default privacy settings provide too much personal information online. This information creates a field day for identity thieves, hackers, scammers, debt collectors, employers, marketers, data miners, and governments.
Hackers	Organized cybercriminals known as hactivists participate in phishing, online shopping fraud, banking fraud, and other deceptions.
Behavioral advertising	Behavioral advertising is a technique used by advertisers to present targeted ads to consumers by collecting information about their browsing behavior. These techniques create a behavioral profile of you that is then used for exploitation.
Data stealing	Done through rogue applications on social networking sites—computers that harbor botnets (Coreflood) and smartphone malware (DroidDream) are a couple that may be after you.
Facial-recognition technology	Once used for security and surveillance. Now in the public realm with apps such as Social Camera and Scene Tap. Facebook deployed Facial-recognition software allows Facebook to gather data or recognize your face. Then people can be searched for using a picture.
GEO-Tags	Used when photos or videos are taken with a GPS-equipped device (e.g., smartphone). Photos are embedded with a geo-tag revealing exact location of where taken. Revelation of geo-locational data on social networking sites creates danger of social surveillance and stalking.

Source: Wired, "Privacy and Security in the Internet Age," http://www.wired.com/insights/2015/01/privacy-and-security-in-the-internet-age/. Accessed March 16, 2016: "The Top Ten Online Privacy Threats," https://www.mywot.com/en/blog/156-the-top-10-online-privacy-threats. Accessed March 25, 2016; Reputation.com, "The Top Five Threats to Your Online Privacy, https://www.reputationdefender.com/blog/general/top-five-threats-your-online-privacy. Accessed March 25, 2016.

a central computer called the command-and-control server.[50] Experts have said that on any given day now, 40 percent of the 800 million computers hooked up to the Internet are infected and made a part of botnets that continue to distribute e-mail spam and malware, steal sensitive data, bombard Web sites, and spread fresh infections.[51] It has been estimated that 73 percent of e-mails contain spam, one in 106 e-mails contain a virus, and one in 99 e-mails contain some form of a phishing attack. These numbers increase every year. **Botnets** are not only the way our personal information is compromised, but they represent the greatest threat to data security for businesses and governments today.[52]

At a personal level, many individuals are losing their privacy through the use of *social networking sites* such as Facebook, Twitter, LinkedIn, Pinterest, Periscope, Meerkat, Tumblr, Snapchat, Slack, Blab, and others.[53] We should also acknowledge social networking sites in other countries; for example, Weibo in China. Cybercriminals are now accessing social networking accounts and stealing personal information. Social networks provide a rich repository of information that cybercriminals can use to fine-tune their other computer attacks. Twitter accounts are likewise vulnerable to data theft. Once stolen credentials occur, they often appear on eBay-like hacking forums where they are sold in batches of 1,000. Cyber scammers can acquire e-mail addresses, contact lists, birthdates, home towns, and mothers' maiden names, which all then become useful for targeting specific victims.[54]

Government's Involvement in Consumer Privacy Protection. The federal government has gotten involved in protecting consumers' privacy, but many observers believe it is not doing enough.[55] The Financial Services Modernization Act of 1999 was the breakthrough legislation that permitted banks, insurers, and brokers to join forces. Under the law, it is now possible for consumers to get their credit cards, checking accounts, investments, home loans, and health insurance from one company. This is convenient for consumers. However, the law also empowered these companies to develop exceptionally detailed profiles of their customers just by merging files about their income, assets, debts, health, spending habits, and other personal data. Increasingly, this sensitive data is becoming a public commodity.[56]

Over the past several years, a number of different bills designed to protect consumer privacy on the Internet have been filed but have not yet been passed. Many of the legislators have been uncertain whether a broad privacy bill is even needed or what it should look like. Some progress has been made on the subject of consumer privacy, however. In February 2012, the White House issued a proposed Consumer Privacy Bill of Rights.[57] Figure 9-2 summarizes its provisions. Like so many proposals, the proposed Privacy Bill of Rights has not been adopted into law by Congress. However, it does contain some important privacy principles that ethical companies should consider. A proposed Consumer Privacy Protection Act of 2015 was still in committee as of this writing.[58]

The Federal Trade Commission annually reports its summary of consumer complaints. Many of the complaints involve the Internet and invasion of privacy. In its 2015 report, the most frequent consumer complaints were debt collection, identity theft, and imposter scams. Other categories of complaints included shop-at-home and television and electronic media.[59] The FTC is the primary government agency concerned with protecting consumers' privacy today. Under the FTC Act, the commission guards against unfairness and deception. The primary legislation now governing consumers' privacy includes the Financial Services Modernization Act (Gramm–Leach–Bliley Act), concerned with financial privacy; the Fair Credit Reporting Act; and the Children's Online Privacy Protection Act.[60] Other legislation regulating consumer and employee privacy may come soon, but Congress seems preoccupied with other priorities.

FIGURE 9-2 Proposed Consumer Privacy Bill of Rights

The proposed Consumer Privacy Bill of Rights would apply to personal data and contain the following provisions:

1. INDIVIDUAL CONTROL: Consumers have a right to exercise control over what personal data companies collect from them and how they use it.
2. TRANSPARENCY: Consumers have a right to easily understandable and accessible information about privacy and security practices.
3. RESPECT FOR CONTEXT: Consumers have a right to expect that companies will collect, use, and disclose personal data in ways that are consistent with the context in which consumers provide the data.
4. SECURITY: Consumers have a right to secure and responsible handling of personal data.
5. ACCESS AND ACCURACY: Consumers have a right to access and correct personal data in usable formats, in a manner that is appropriate to the sensitivity of the data and the risk of adverse consequences to consumers if the data is inaccurate.
6. FOCUSED COLLECTION: Consumers have a right to reasonable limits on the personal data that companies collect and retain.
7. ACCOUNTABILITY: Consumers have a right to have personal data handled by companies with appropriate measures in place to assure they adhere to the Consumer Privacy Bill of Rights.

Source: Consumer Data Privacy in a Networked World: A Framework for Protecting Privacy and Promoting Innovation in the Global Digital Economy, February 23, 2012, Washington, DC: The White House, http://www.whitehouse.gov/sites/default/files/privacy-final.pdf. Accessed March 16, 2016.

The FTC has issued a report on what it considers to be the "best practices" companies should follow in protecting consumer privacy. Each of these recommended best practices are just one part of the FTC's suggested privacy framework[61]:

1. *Privacy by Design.* Companies should "build in" privacy at every stage of product development.
2. *Simplified Choice for Consumers and Businesses.* Consumers should be given the ability to make decisions about their data at a relevant time and context, including a Do Not Track mechanism, while reducing the burden on businesses of providing unnecessary choices; and
3. *Greater Transparency.* Make information collection and use practices transparent.

With this report, the FTC has called on companies to take action to implement best practices in protecting consumers' privacy. The FTC argues that privacy protection should be the default setting for commercial data practices and has again called on Congress to enact baseline privacy legislation.[62]

Business Initiatives with Consumer Privacy Protection. There are a number of different ways companies are striving to protect the privacy of their customers in electronic commerce.

Ethical Leadership First, business needs to recognize the potential ethical issues involved in electronic commerce and be committed to treating customers and all affected stakeholders in an ethical fashion. This commitment and ethical leadership from the top undergirds all other initiatives. Ethical leadership must begin with the board of directors, the CEO, and top management. Every principle discussed in Chapter 8 about top management leadership applies to this discussion as well.

Privacy Policies Companies may take the initiative with their own carefully crafted privacy policies designed to protect customers. An example of this might be a company deciding to do more than the law requires. A company that has gone to great lengths to explain its privacy policy to customers and guests is the Walt Disney Company. On its Web site, it provides the following statement regarding its privacy policy:

> *Our privacy policy is designed to provide transparency into our privacy practices and principles, in a format that our guests can navigate, read and understand. We are dedicated to treating your personal information with care and respect.*[63]

One of the most significant advances in privacy policies has been made by Microsoft. Microsoft has amended its privacy policies so that consumers will have greater control over what the company does with information it gathers about their online purchasing behavior.[64]

One of the most important consumer privacy issues involving technology is being played out in the ongoing debate between Apple and the FBI regarding the security of its iPhones and the FBI wanting access so that it can track down terrorists. Apple thinks it is important to take a stand for privacy as a feature that is critical to its brand.[65] One writer observed that this case is more broadly a fight over the future of high-tech surveillance, the trust infrastructure undergirding the global software ecosystem and just how far technology companies will have to go to meet government's desire to get access to companies' technology.[66] Clearly, electronic privacy of consumers is a primary issue at stake. The *Apple iPhone* case may be explored further in Case 8 at the end of the text.

Chief Privacy Officers An innovative approach to protecting consumers' privacy has been the increasing use of a **chief privacy officer (CPO)** in a number of major companies. Companies like American Express, Sony Corporation, Citigroup, IBM, and Facebook have appointed their own privacy chiefs.[67] In other companies, these responsibilities are falling under the administration of a chief technology officer.

It is the primary responsibility of the CPO to keep a company out of trouble, whether in a court of law or in the court of public opinion. This includes developing Internet policies, helping their companies avoid consumer litigation, creating methods of handling and resolving consumer complaints, and assessing the risk of privacy invasion of company activities and practices. Because the position is relatively new at most companies, these newly appointed individuals are still trying to figure out what they need to be doing.[68] The job is a challenging one. CPOs must balance their customers' right to privacy with their employer's need for information for financial purposes.[69]

CPOs also play a critical role in ensuring employee as well as consumer privacy. CPOs are relevant to the section of this chapter on the workplace and they are brought up again in Chapter 18, where employees' rights to privacy are discussed further.

Data Security One of the clearest ways companies can protect the information of their customers is through data security systems and practices. Yet, data breaches (also called "hacks") are on the rise. In 2014, the cyber invasion of Sony Pictures occurred in what has been called the "Hack of the Century." The hack not only stole massive quantities of documents and e-mails but it also erased all the data on half the company's computers and servers.[70] Similarly, in 2015, a massive cybertheft scheme at JPMorgan Chase was revealed and it was reported that data on more than 100 million people had been stolen using a vast network of accomplices to turn it into hundreds of millions of dollars in illegal profits.[71] Major data breaches hitting companies in 2015 included firms such as Anthem, eBay, Adobe, Home Depot, and Target.[72] It is obvious that data security and cybercrime are among the biggest threats companies face today. Some believe that cyber-espionage and computer crime could soon surpass terrorism as the primary threat facing Americans and developed nations.[73]

Data breaches that have occurred in recent years point out the strong need for companies, governments, and individuals to make data security a number one priority. Companies have an ethical responsibility to protect data in spite of the lack of severe penalties for failing to do so.

Questionable Businesses and Practices. Several questionable businesses and practices have been made possible by electronic commerce and the use of the Internet. Three business categories that are viewed as questionable by many include Web-based pornography, Internet gambling, and Web-based downloading of music, movies, books, and other copyrighted digital materials.

Illegal Downloading The illegal or uncompensated downloading of music, movies, television shows and other copyrighted works continues to be a serious, questionable practice because it represents theft of intellectual property. Bringing this problem to the public's attention in 2015, Taylor Swift made headlines with her social media assault on Apple in response to the company's failure to pay her and others for their music during the free trial period downloads. After Ms. Swift's tirade, Apple changed its position and said it would pay artists for streaming even during customer's free trial period.[74]

In response to the illegal or uncompensated downloading practice, the Copyright Alert System was created by the film and music industries to catch consumers who may be engaging in theft using peer-to-peer software. Under the system, complaints will trigger Internet service providers—for example, Verizon, AT&T, Comcast—to notify a customer whose Internet address has been detected sharing files illegally. Then, the individual will be given a limited number of chances to stop before the Internet provider will take more extreme steps, such as temporarily slowing their connection.[75] Time Warner Cable has stated that after the first four notifications, it will lock down the offenders' browser until they call and show that they understand what they have done and will agree to stop.[76] Proponents of the new technology claim the focus is on educating consumers and they admit that it is unlikely to deter extreme violators. Already, five Internet Service Providers have agreed to participate in the program.[77]

For the past several years, university students in the United States have been a leading target of a litigation campaign carried out by the Recording Industry Association of America (RIAA). RIAA is the music industry trade group that has found university campuses to be hotbeds of file-sharing activity. The mission of RIAA is to protect the intellectual property and First Amendment rights of artists and music labels.[78] In reflecting on this issue, one student observed that downloading was so easy and there is so much free content on the Internet that it's hard to discriminate between illegal downloading, streaming free content, and just copying something from a friend's laptop. The student went on to observe that when a product is digital, it doesn't feel like stealing. Over the

ETHICS IN PRACTICE CASE

Copyright Infringement?

Spotify, the music streaming company, faces a $150 million class action lawsuit led by David Lowery, the frontman for Cracker, the alternative rock band, and Camper Van Beethoven, an American rock band. The musicians maintain that Spotify has not been securing the proper licenses for all of the music it offers and has not been paying royalties to all of the appropriate parties. The implication emerging from the lawsuit is that the company that claims to be providing an alternative to online piracy is not living up to its own legal obligations. In short, it's a case of copyright infringement and some might say it involves stealing another person's intellectual property.

A license for a piece of music involves two separate copyrights. First is the recording, which is typically owned by the performer's label and second is the underlying composition, which is often owned by the songwriter or his or her publisher. So, to use a recording, a streaming company such as Spotify would have to get two licenses. This is done by negotiating with the publisher or by sending the rights holder a notice and paying a royalty.

Lowery claims that Spotify frequently skips the second part. He claims that there may be hundreds or thousands of artists who have not been paid for their work including him. Spotify does not argue against this but does say that tracking down the proper rights holders is a complex process and hard to do. The company says it has royalties set aside for cases where royalty rights are not clear, and it stands ready to pay the royalties if the affected artists make a rightful claim. But, one of Lowery's lawyers argues that artists should not have to track down royalties owed them but that it is Spotify's responsibility to secure the license and pay the royalty.

Spotify, in its defense, says that the laws and copyright infrastructure that currently exist do not fully factor in the scope and speed with which digital music services operate. The company maintains that securing advance permissions for each track is inefficient and possibly crippling for a company trying to stay competitive. In January 2016, Spotify was hit with a second lawsuit over the alleged and systemic and willful copyright infringement.

Questions

1. Who are the stakeholders affected and what are the ethical issues in this case?
2. Is Spotify justified in saying it is prepared to pay but claimants will have to come to them and present a rightful claim? Or, does Spotify have the responsibility to find the artists and secure permission and pay the appropriate royalty before they stream the music?
3. How do you evaluate the company's claim that the system is too complex and that the laws and copyright infrastructure are the problem in the digital music industry?
4. Is the issue in this case that the law is not keeping up with the high-tech music streaming industry or that Spotify is using this as an excuse to take short cuts and engage in a questionable practice?

Sources: Adrian Covert, Vocativ, "Spotify is Facing a $150 Million Lawsuit Over Unpaid Royalties," http://www.vocativ.com/news/265949/spotify-is-facing-a-150-million-lawsuit-over-unpaid-royalties/. Accessed March 25, 2016; "Spotify Isn't Laughing Off This Lawsuit," *Bloomberg Businessweek*, January 14, 2015, 30; Ed Christman, Billboard, "Spotify Hit with Second Lawsuit Over Copyright Infringement," http://www.billboard.com/articles/business/6836439/spotify-hit-with-second-copyright-infringement-lawsuit-melissa-merrick-david-lowery. Accessed March 25, 2016.

past decade, peer-to-peer technology companies have transformed continuously and speedily, making it ever more complicated to police.[79] In spite of this, laws and ethics are being violated and these examples illustrate how Internet technology has threatened legitimate businesses.

But, it is not only individuals who are taking advantage of the creative works of others. In 2004, Google entered into an agreement with major libraries to take about 20 million books, make digital copies of them, and make them available online to users. Google made no payments to authors of these works. The Authors Guild filed suit against Google, but in October 2015, a New York Court of Appeals ruled that Google was protected in doing this under the doctrine of fair use.[80]

Monitoring Technology Another practice that has raised many questions is the use of technology by companies to monitor consumers as they use a company's products. An example of the monitoring technology was illustrated when an individual rented a vehicle from Acme Rent-a-Car in New Haven, Connecticut, only to find out later that he was the unwitting victim of a global positioning system (GPS) device planted in the minivan he leased. The surveillance device recorded him speeding in three states at the rates from 78 to 83 mph, and each violation, digitally recorded, automatically added a $150 charge to his bill.[81]

Unbeknownst to most car owners today, black boxes, officially called Event Data Recorders (EDR) are being installed in virtually all recent model cars and these track your seat belt use, speed, steering, braking and other data. These EDRs are about the size of a deck of cards. They were initially designed to analyze the cause and effects of crashes to improve safety, but their data has many other potential uses by insurance companies, police, lawyers, and others. Ninety-six percent of all new cars already have them.[82] The use of GPS, EDR and other technologies is becoming commonplace and consumers need to be aware of how they are being tracked.

These are just a sampling of the kinds of controversial ethical and legal issues that arise in connection with electronic commerce. As the Smart Revolution takes over all our consumer products, there will be plenty to worry about in the realm of consumer privacy.[83]

9.5d The Workplace and Computer Technology

Whereas computer-based information technology creates ethical issues for consumer stakeholders with respect to electronic commerce and Web-based marketing, employee stakeholders also are significantly affected by technology in the workplace. We will discuss these issues in more detail, especially employee surveillance and privacy, in Chapter 18. Though computers have provided workers with countless benefits and easier access to information, there also have been some adverse effects. Included among these have been communication breakdowns, increased stress, distractions, disconnectedness, and health issues.[84]

In this section, we will discuss several workplace technology issues: biometrics, robotics, artificial intelligence, cell phone use and texting, unethical employee activities, and company actions.

Biometrics. The newly emerging field of biometrics is starting to take off, especially in commercial applications. **Biometrics** is the use of body measurements, such as eye scans, fingerprints, or palm prints for determining and confirming identity. The technology of biometrics typically conjures up images of Big Brother surveillance tactics and it has met resistance in cases where the government has wanted to use it for identification purposes. What seems to be speeding up its use, however, are commercial applications that provide assistance for consumers.[85] Popular types of biometric devices in use today include face scanners, hand scanners, finger scanners, retina or iris scanners, and voice scanners.[86]

ETHICS IN PRACTICE CASE

Using Personal Technology in the Workplace

Increasingly, especially in small businesses, companies are permitting employees to use their own personal technology devices on the job. Smartphones, laptops, and tablets are the primary technologies being used. This has started a social movement known as BYOD—"bring your own device" to work.

The benefits to small businesses are several. If companies allow personal technologies at work this means they have to spend much less on technology resources themselves. Plus, many employees are more comfortable using their own equipment and it is portable so they can take it with them. Companies also benefit because the employees in possession of their personal devices are "always working." Some productivity gains may be expected.

But, the use of many gadgets leads to many risks. One major risk is the lost or stolen devices, which can lead to huge headaches for companies. Once lost or misplaced, others can access company information, some of which may be confidential or proprietary. Most companies do not implement basic policies such as requiring lock codes on the personal devices when they are used at work.

Another big issue is misappropriation of information. Personal devices make it much easier for employees to take information when they leave. Thus, private information may get in the hands of competitors or thieves. Viruses and other malware is another troubling issue. Frequently, employees do not keep virus protection on their personal devices up to date and an infected device could create problems throughout a company's network. Other issues include ownership, ability to monitor, technical challenges, and unanticipated costs.

As work steadily spills into personal lives and companies continue to allow personal devices to be used on the job, the dividing line between work lives and personal lives is beginning to blur. This will pose additional problems for organizations and their staff in the future.

1. What are the ethical issues at stake when companies permit employees to use personal technologies on the job? What are the implications for all stakeholders?
2. On balance, should companies continue to allow personal technological devices on the job or should they disallow them? If they allow them, what policies should be put in place?

Sources: Tekedia Editors, "The Pros and Cons of Having Personal Technology in the Office," January 26, 2015, http://tekedia.com/50565/pros-cons-personal-technology-office. Accessed March 16, 2016; Oasis Blog, "Technology in the Workplace: Should Employees Use Personal Devices for Work?" http://www.oasisadvantage.com/blog/technology-in-the-workplace-should-employees-use-personal-devices-for-work. Accessed March 16, 2016; PCWorld, "Pros and Cons of Bringing your Own Device to Work," http://www.pcworld.com/article/246760/pros_and_cons_of_byod_bring_your_own_device_.html. Accessed March 16, 2016.

Only in the past several years, there has been an explosion of applications in the commercial use of biometrics.[87] In some businesses now, consumers can scan their fingers or wave their palms over a scanner to gain access to accounts, safe deposit boxes, or to make purchases. Already one can purchase laptop computers and mobile phones that come with built-in finger scanners. Other domestic applications include biometric door locks, garage locks, and safe locks. Even online services now respond to the rhythm and other characteristics of a person's typing, using a template of your "keystroke dynamics." There are flash drives that work only when activated by your thumbprint.[88] In short, biometrics is revolutionizing the way business is conducted and is expected to grow in the future.

Like most technologies, biometrics has many advantages and some possible downside risks. At the moment, the focus has not been on the legal and ethical risks associated with biometrics, but this is an issue that companies, consumers, and employees will need to watch carefully in the future. The potential abuses and invasions of privacy are many, and must be factored into decisions about the treatment of employees.

Robotics. Worldwide industrial robot installations began to take off in 2012 and it is estimated that that number may approach doubling by 2018.[89] Recently, workers in escalating numbers believe they have been losing their jobs due to the growth in the usage of robots in more and more industries. At one time, it was thought that the automation rage would create more jobs than it would displace but that assumption is being called into question today. Some experts are now saying that the stubbornly high unemployment rates in the United States and Europe are at least partially due to the rise of the machines.[90]

There is an ongoing and continuing debate as to whether robots will decrease employment or not. Both sides of the argument have made legitimate points. Some argue that the use of robots can lead to better living.[91] Others argue robots are keeping workers up at night wondering whether or when they will be displaced. One factor that complicates measures of productivity changes due to robotics is global competition and the increasing use of low cost labor in developing countries of the world.

A Pew Research study found that two-thirds of Americans think that by 2066 robots and computers will "definitely" or "probably" do much of the work currently done by humans. At the same time, 80 percent of them expect their jobs will continue to exist in their current form during this time.[92] Oxford researchers have forecast that machines might be able to take half of all U.S. jobs within two decades.[93]

One of the most visible businesses being hit by automation today are restaurants. You may not have a robot waiting your table, but technology is beginning to replace certain functions. For example, touch screens are already transforming the way food is ordered in many establishments. Whether it be via robot or other form of technology, increased automation is making it harder to develop a company culture; there are maintenance costs, and the business has to hire IT specialists to service the technology.[94] In short, robotic takeovers and automation of much employment is expected but the timing still appears to be in the future.

An important editorial in *The Economist* argues that society needs to move quickly in developing ways of dealing with the ethics of robotics. It points out three areas where progress is needed in regulating the development and use of autonomous robots.[95] First, laws are needed to clarify who is at fault if a robotic device causes harm—the designer, programmer, manufacturer, or operator. Second, when ethical systems are embedded into robots, they need to be decision-making schemes that would seem right to most people. Third, collaboration is needed among engineers, ethicists, lawyers, and policymakers who left to their own might come up with widely divergent rules.[96] The rise of robotics and its impact on the workplace will need to be monitored closely in the years to come.

Artificial Intelligence. The growing field of artificial intelligence is closely aligned with robotics. **Artificial intelligence** (AI) embraces software technologies that make a computer or robot perform equal to or better than normal human computational ability in terms of accuracy, capacity, and speed.[97] Software built by Google shocked the field early in 2016 when its AI easily defeated the world's best player of the Asian board game "Go" in a five-game match. Go resembles chess in the deep, complex problems it poses but is even harder to play and has resisted AI researchers longer. It requires a mastery of strategy and tactics while concealing its own plans and trying to read its opponents. AI experts envision wider availability of humanlike intelligence within a few decades.[98]

Microsoft has already had troubles with an artificially intelligent chatbox it brought online in early 2016. Microsoft's product, Tay, is an artificially intelligent software chatbox that communicates through messages on social media services including Twitter, Facebook, and Snapchat. Right after being launched, Tay started spewing offensive rants, which Twitter users collected and posted on social media. Microsoft one day later took Tay offline and said it occurred because users had fed Tay the offensive comments.[99] Clearly, AI will need to be monitored closely for its implications for ethical business practices.

Cell Phones and Texting. It has been estimated that citizens have been mashing out over six billion text messages a day in the United States and probably a few billion more on services like WhatsApp and Facebook Messenger.[100] Although e-mail and the Internet most often create ethical problems in the workplace, the use of company-sponsored cell phones by employees represents one of the fastest growing technologies with increasing ethical and legal implications. The use of a cell phone is no longer a private matter as job pressures are tempting more and more employees to use the phones while driving. Because some companies now make cell phones available to their employees, this issue spills over into the business arena and becomes a business ethics and legal topic.

Actually, cell phone use while driving is a public matter because it significantly raises the risk of harm to others on the streets.[101] Increasingly, states are cracking down on drivers using cellphones and texting while driving. According to Distraction.gov, the broader issue is distracted driving and it includes texting while driving, using a smartphone, using a navigation system, talking to passengers, watching videos, and adjusting music. Smartphone use and texting are the two primary problems. Already most states ban texting while driving and many states restrict cell phone use.[102]

A trend with enormous implications for employers is the growing number of employees—managers, salespeople, consultants, lawyers, ad executives, and others—who are questionably using cell phones for talking and texting while driving and chalking up sales or billable hours. Research has documented that motorists who use cell phones while driving are four times as likely to get into crashes serious enough to injure themselves or others. Text messaging creates a crash risk 23 times worse than driving while not distracted.[103] There are two primary problems with people using such devices while driving. First, drivers have to take their eyes off the road while driving and second, they can become so absorbed in their conversations that their concentration is severely impaired. This jeopardizes the safety of not only the vehicle's occupants but also that of pedestrians and other vehicles.[104]

Plaintiffs are more frequently claiming that the employer is partly to blame because it presses employees to work long hours from distant locations, often encouraging them to use cell phones without setting safety guidelines. Research is increasingly documenting the dangers of cell phone talking and texting while driving. A study by an insurance company found that chatty drivers suffered slower reaction times, took longer to stop, and missed more road signs than drivers who were legally drunk. A new term has already been coined for accidents caused by cell phone-using drivers—DWY (driving while yakking).[105]

Cell phone use—linked to technology—is raising red flags for employers and individuals concerned about their careers. Not enough companies have the needed policies on cell phone use at this time. It appears that as high-tech tools extend the workplace into every corner of life, too many companies have been leaving the responsibility entirely up to the employees. These cases are tragic examples of what can happen when employees, using technology, become too distracted, pressured, or over focused on their work.[106]

Already, at least 40 countries restrict or prohibit the use of cell phones while driving. Supporters of restrictions on cell phone use while driving contend with the belief that cell phone distraction is far greater than other distractions while driving because of the greater continuous concentration needed, which diverts the driver's eyes from the road and his or her mind from driving. In the realm of technology, several companies are developing devices that will prevent people from receiving calls and texting while driving.[107] Companies are facing new challenges as employees walking while texting is also being revealed as a deadly combination.[108]

Unethical Activities by Employees. In most of the instances described to this point, the employer has had responsibility for the use of technology and its implications. There is another area that should be identified: questionable activities involving technology that originate from the employees. In a major study of workers, the following are unethical activities employees said they had engaged in during the previous year.[109] All these items were related to technology.

- Created a potentially dangerous situation by using new technology while driving
- Wrongly blamed an error the employee made on a technological glitch
- Copied the company's software for home use
- Used office equipment to shop on the Internet for personal reasons
- Used office equipment to network/search for another job
- Accessed private computer files without permission
- Used new technologies to intrude on coworkers' privacy
- Visited porn Web sites using office equipment

As can be seen by the activities in this list, employee related issues involving the use or misuse of technology is another significant category of challenges that must be monitored by management.

Company Actions. Companies have many options for addressing the kinds of ethical issues described to this point. A major survey of *Fortune* 500 nonmanagement employees revealed that management should clearly define guidelines for ethical computer use by employees. Options for doing this include company management making these decisions, using the Information Systems Society's code of ethics, and involving employees and users in a collaborative attempt to decide upon computer ethics policies.[110] Beyond this, companies should carefully think about the ethical implications of their use of technology and integrate decisions designed to protect employees into their policies and practices, especially their codes of conduct.

The technologies discussed to this point have been computer facilitated. Therefore, guidelines for employee computer use are helpful in many of the applications described. Several professional societies offer guidelines for computer use. Computer Professionals for Social Responsibility (CPSR) has set forth what it calls its "Ten Commandments of Computer Ethics." These guidelines are informative and useful, and are summarized in Figure 9-3. In addition to codes of conducts, companies may issue policies, guidelines or rules related to technology use. At a minimum, companies should develop and implement

FIGURE 9-3 Ten Commandments of Computer Ethics

The Computer Ethics Institute has set forth the following ten commandments of computer ethics. These should prove useful to employees and employers alike concerning the appropriateness of computer usages.

- Thou shalt not use a computer to harm other people.
- Thou shalt not interfere with other people's computer work.
- Thou shalt not snoop around in other people's computer files.
- Thou shalt not use a computer to steal.
- Thou shalt not use a computer to bear false witness.
- Thou shalt not copy or use proprietary software for which you have not paid.
- Thou shalt not use other people's computer resources without authorization or proper compensation.
- Thou shalt not appropriate other people's intellectual output.
- Thou shalt think about the social consequences of the program you are designing.
- Thou shalt always use a computer in ways that ensure consideration and respect for your fellow humans.

Sources: Computer Ethics Institute, Computer Professionals for Social Responsibility, "Ten Commandments of Computer Ethics," http://cpsr.org/issues/ethics/cei/. Accessed March 21, 2016; Association for Computing Machinery, "Code of Ethics," http://www.acm.org/about/code-of-ethics. Accessed March 21, 2016.

a technology acceptable-use policy to be followed by employees. On their behalf, employees have the responsibility to become knowledgeable and aware of acceptable and unacceptable technology use.[111]

9.6 Biotechnology

The 20th century's revolution in information technology is merging with the 21st century's revolution in biotechnology. Indeed, Walter Isaacson labeled the 2000s as the "biotech century."[112] The field of Biotechnology involves "using biology to discover, develop, manufacture, market, and sell products and services."[113] At this time, we are undergoing the most significant breakthrough of all time—deciphering the human genome, tens of thousands of genes encoded by 3 billion chemical pairs in our DNA. Among other achievements, this accomplishment will lead to the next medical revolution, which will not only increase the natural life span of healthy human beings but will also help to conquer cancer, grow new blood vessels, block the growth of blood vessels in tumors, create new organs from stem cells, and much more.[114]

The field of biotechnology carries with it significant implications for business and for business ethics, and we can only touch upon these issues here. In fact, we now have a burgeoning growth industry—the biotechnology industry. The biotech industry today consists of small entrepreneurial start-up companies funded largely by venture capitalists, along with dozens of larger, more established companies. Most of the applications of biotechnology are in health care, the pharmaceutical industry, and agriculture.[115] From a sustainability perspective, biotechnology is striving to *heal*, *fuel*, and *feed* the world.[116]

In this section, we will discuss bioethics, genetic engineering, and genetically modified organisms (GMOs).

9.6a Bioethics

The field of **bioethics** deals with the ethical issues embedded in the commercial use of biotechnology, especially in medicine. As new biotech products are developed, thorny

SPOTLIGHT *on Sustainability*

Is Biotech Agriculture Sustainable?

When we think of sustainable agriculture, we typically think of food products that have been organically grown. But, sustainable agriculture is not limited to organic production according to the Biotechnology Industry Organization (BIO). According to BIO, there is currently a new standard being developed under the auspices of the American National Standards Institute that will incorporate any technology that will increase agriculture sustainability. In BIO's perspective, biotech crops are sustainable and also good for the environment. They require fewer pesticides and employ farming techniques that improve soil health and retention of water. Through biotechnology, global pesticide use is down, soil erosion has been reduced, and fuel consumption has been reduced.

According to the Seed Biotechnology Center, Genetically engineered (GE) crop varieties offer promising traits that will help increase health and nutrition, sustain farming on marginal lands, and decrease concerns with pests and disease. Currently, there are more than 100 agricultural crops that have been genetically modified in research stations around the world, and five of the most promising traits that are being analyzed in numerous crops include herbicide tolerance, insect resistance, stress tolerance, nitrogen use efficiency, and nutritional traits.

Sources: "The Sustainability of Biotechnology," Biotechnology Industry Organization, http://www.bio.org/articles/sustainability-biotechnology. Accessed March 21, 2016; "Biotechnology for Sustainability," Seed Biotechnology Center, http://sbc.ucdavis.edu/files/191415.pdf. Accessed March 21, 2016; "Sustainable Biotechnology," https://sustainablebiotech.wordpress.com/. Accessed March 21, 2016.

ethical issues inevitably arise. In recent years, the question has arisen regarding the federal government's role in bioethics. This topic is so important that a Presidential Commission for the Study of Bioethical Issues was created and is functioning today. The advisory panel consists of experts in medicine, ethics, science, religion, and law. Some of its recent projects have addressed the intersection of neuroscience, ethics, and society; ethics and Ebola; and safeguarding children.[117]

On the business front, some biotechnology companies have adopted the idea of bioethics to guide them in their decision making. One prominent example is Johnson & Johnson, which in 2015 employed a nationally known bioethicist and created a panel that will be advisory on issues about patient's requests for life saving medicines. Emotional debates arise over the issue of whether companies should allow desperately ill patients to have access to drugs before they are approved.[118] Other companies have created such advisory boards and appointed bioethicists as well. A question that is being continually raised, however, is whether bioethical decision making is really taking place or whether the companies are using the bioethicists for public relations purposes.

According to William Saletan, who has written extensively about bioethics, the primary tool bioethicists use is *proceduralism*. This involves elaborate protocols being established that ensure that certain classical worries, such as informed consent, are not violated. The focus is on being sure that appropriate procedures are being followed rather than on the actual ethical content of the decisions. This sounds similar to the concept of ethical due process discussed in an earlier chapter. The worry continues, however, over whether corporate executives and scientists are deceiving their own consciences by focusing on the *how* rather than the *why*, or the *means* rather than the *end*.[119]

Both critics and supporters say that the use of bioethicists lends companies an air of credibility. The real question is "can they really be objective if they are on a company's payroll?" Supporters say "yes," they function like a newspaper ombudsperson that gets paid by the paper to criticize coverage and prevent potential conflicts. Detractors say "no," there's no way around a conflict of interest if money is changing hands. A real danger is that the participation of bioethicists may be interpreted as a stamp of approval. [120] If properly used, bioethicists can significantly add to the effectiveness of decision making in the biotechnology arena, just as ethics and compliance officers can add value in other organizations.

Figure 9-4 lists several nonprofit bioethics organizations that may be found on the Web.

Of special interest in this section are two broad realms of biotechnology that help us appreciate some of the challenges in business ethics: genetic engineering and genetically modified organisms (GMOs). Genetic engineering, primarily of humans, and genetic engineering of agricultural and food products are both part of genetic science and have significant implications for business. For discussion purposes, however, we will treat them separately. Genetic testing and profiling is another important issue that merits consideration.

9.6b Genetic Engineering

Genetic engineering is defined as "the development and application of scientific methods, procedures, and technologies that permit direct manipulation of genetic material in order to alter the hereditary traits of a cell, organism, or population."[121] The most controversial aspect of genetic engineering involves the applications to human beings. Two major areas of genetic engineering, or genetic science, seem to capture the public's

FIGURE 9-4 Web Sites of Nonprofit Bioethics Organizations

Bioethics is an expansive topic and there are many different organizations, especially public action organizations, that provide information regarding specific topics via the World Wide Web. Some of these include the following:

American Society for Bioethics + Humanities (http://www.asbh.org/)

The American Society for Bioethics and Humanities (ASBH) is a professional society of more than 1,500 individuals, organizations, and institutions interested in bioethics and humanities. The purpose of ASBH is to promote the exchange of ideas and foster multidisciplinary, interdisciplinary, and interprofessional scholarship, research, teaching, policy development, professional development, and collegiality among people engaged in all the endeavors related to clinical and academic bioethics and the health-related humanities.

Non-GMO Project (http://www.nongmoproject.org/)

The Non-GMO Project is a nonprofit organization committed to the preserving and building of the non-GMO food supply, educating consumers, and providing verified non-GMO choices. The Project believes that all consumers have a right to an informed choice about whether or not to consume GMOs.

Do No Harm: The Coalition of Americans for Research Ethics (http://www.stemcellresearch.org/)

This organization is a national coalition of researchers, health-care professionals, bioethicists, legal professionals, and others dedicated to the promotion of scientific research and health care that does no harm to human life.

Council for Responsible Genetics (http://www.councilforresponsiblegenetics.org/)

The council fosters debate on social, ethical, and environmental implications of new genetic technologies. CRG works through the media and concerned citizens to distribute accurate information and represent the public interest on emerging issues in biotechnology. The council publishes "GeneWATCH," a national bulletin on the implications of biotechnology.

Bioethics.net (http://www.bioethics.net/)

This Web page is quite extensive. It hosts the *American Journal of Bioethics.* In service to anyone interested in bioethics, the Web site publishes information on the latest journal publications, events, job opportunities and current news, as well as being a one-stop-shop of popular bioethics blogs.

National Human Genome Research Institute (http://www.genome.gov/A/)

This Web site hosts the Ethical, Legal, and Social Implications (ELSI) Research Program. This program supports basic and applied research that identifies and analyzes the ethical, legal, and social issues surrounding human genetics research.

imagination today. One is stem cell research and the second is cloning. Both pose enormous and interesting challenges for business and business ethics.

Stem Cell Research. **Embryonic stem cells** are the raw materials with which a human body is built. Since their isolation, stem cell research has been proliferating around the world. Until recently, the only way to get pluripotent stem cells for research was to remove the inner cell mass of an embryo and put it in a dish. However, the thought of destroying a human embryo was troubling for many people. As a result, stem cell research has raised the following ethical questions, which society has been grappling with for years now: When does life begin—at fertilization, in the womb, or at birth? Is a human embryo equivalent to a human child? Does a human embryo have any rights? And might the destruction of an embryo be justified if it provides a cure for countless other patients?[122]

The value of stem cells is that they offer the greatest hope for developing treatments for diseases such as cancer, Alzheimer's, Parkinson's, and juvenile diabetes.[123] Stem cells can actually be used to replace other cells in the body that are abnormal or have been destroyed by disease.[124]

In spite of mixed public opinion, companies, nonprofit organizations, and countries continue to push this issue. Companies want to develop cures for diseases and to have bragging rights about their technological superiority. This aggressive competition can lead to unethical practices, even fraud, and this is all the more reason why these issues have to be carefully watched.[125] To inject professionalism into stem cell research, a number of different nonprofit organizations have developed seeking to monitor and advance stem cell research. One example is the International Society for Stem Cell Research (ISSCR). Its purpose is to promote and foster the exchange of information and ideas relating to stem cells, and to promote professional and general education in all areas of research and application.[126] ISSCR also focuses on ethics and public policy dimensions of stem cell research.

Most of the ethical debate over stem cell research has occurred in the public and political arenas, not business. Businesses are moving forward now even though the societal debate is not settled.[127] This is an excellent example of the concept of technological determinism discussed earlier in the chapter. The pharmaceutical industry is one of the best illustrations of how companies are already moving on research. Three high profile companies that are investing heavily in stem cell research include Novartis, Johnson & Johnson, and Celgene Corporation.[128]

Cloning. Stem cell research is well under way. Now, **cloning** continues to be in the news. Some scientists say human cloning is a distant project; however, according to some reports, a few citizens are already lining up to freeze the DNA of their dead loved ones, including pets and racehorses. Several different groups have claimed they are attempting to clone a human being.

Actually, there are at least two debates surrounding cloning and genetic science. First, there is the issue of cloning human beings. Second, there is the issue of cloning animals and plants and using genetics to identify and fight diseases. This second quest is currently the primary focus of science. The ethics of cloning continues to be debated. According to Gallup polls conducted and published in 2015, 81 percent of those surveyed thought it was morally unacceptable to clone human beings and 60 percent thought it was morally unacceptable to clone animals.[129] The ethics of these biotech issues remain under constant scrutiny.

A variation of human cloning is known as **therapeutic cloning**. Therapeutic cloning uses the same laboratory procedures as reproductive cloning, but its aim is not procreation but rather the creation of a source of stem cells whose properties make them a possible source of replacement tissue for a wide range of degenerative diseases. Opponents of therapeutic cloning are opposed to the creation and destruction of human life for utilitarian ends. In addition, opponents fear the exploitation of women, especially in poor countries, for their eggs. On the other side of the issue, supporters want to give therapeutic cloning a chance because of its possible health advantages.[130]

Possible scenarios of therapeutic cloning have raised nightmare reactions in the minds of some. The chemicals in the human body were once estimated to be worth 89 cents. Later, however, according to the authors of a provocative, and some would say shocking, book, body parts in people and in corpses may be worth millions. In *Body Bazaar: The Market for Human Tissue in the Biotechnology Age*, Lori Andrews and Dorothy Nelkin talk optimistically about the commercialization of the human body in pursuit of new pharmaceuticals, organ transplants, and genetic research on individuals alive or dead.

The book has ethicists again asking important questions: Do individuals have "rights" to their blood and tissue? Should body parts be bought and sold? Whose body is it, anyway?[131]

Andrews and Nelkin write, "Whole businesses are developing around the body business. Companies have sprung up to make commercial products out of corpses' bones. Some grind up the bones into powder that, when sprinkled on broken live bones, will help them mend." They argue that body parts from the living and the dead are gold mines for pharmaceutical research. Some of the authors' writings raise provocative ethical questions that business must face: Who owns the rights to a corpse? What ethical considerations need to be evaluated when a researcher seeks to do genetic testing on long-deceased individuals? What are the ethical considerations associated with the morbid practice of using human body parts as a means of "expression"?

In an intended humorous insight into where cloning may be heading, a cartoon by Tom Toles depicted a man in an office sticking his head into the office copier; off to the side, there were cloned copies of him coming out of the machine. A sign on the wall stated, "July 2018. The ethical debate, part 2,473,561," and the question posed beneath the cartoon read: "Should employees be allowed to use the office cloning machine for personal business?"[132]

Cloning Animals for Food. An important issue on the cloning front is that of companies wanting to clone animals for food. Scientists and consumer experts in the United States have been debating whether the country should become the first in the world to allow food from cloned animals onto supermarket shelves. Scientists and companies strongly support cloning for food, indicating they see the technology as an effective, important way to produce higher quality, healthier food. Based on its research and risk assessment, FDA scientists issued a report in 2008 in which it concluded that meat and milk from cow, pig, and goat clones and the offspring of any animal clones are as safe as food we eat every day and this remains their latest position on the subject.[133] The FDA does continue to supervise regulations pertaining to this process. A related issue is whether food from cloned animals should be labeled as such. The FDA does not seem to think such labeling is necessary, but opponents say such labels are essential.

Opponents of cloning animals for food come from a large number of different consumer and scientific groups. Consumer advocate organizations such as the Center for Food Safety, Consumers Union, and the Consumer Federation of America, along with environmental and animal welfare groups, have protested the idea. They think there is inadequate data regarding the safety of such a practice and that there needs to be more review of the potential consequences of such a decision. A minority of scientists agree with the consumer groups that cloned animals should not enter the food supply.[134] The European Commission has said it is ready to ban animal cloning but said that it has to go further to conclude that all imports of cloned products should be banned to ease consumer's concerns about food safety.[135] This is likely to be an emotionally debated ethical for some time.

Genetic Testing and Profiling. One of the most questionable applications of biotechnology is in **genetic testing**. Genetic testing has many downside risks, especially from both a legal and an ethical perspective.[136] It has been said that someday each of us will have implanted in our bodies a DNA chip that contains all our genetic information. There are some positives associated with this. It will help each person manage his or her own personal health risks. It will also help a physician predict how well a patient will respond to various therapies. Future drugs will be developed using genetic information so that the therapy will be coupled with the DNA information. The privacy invasion implications are staggering, however, and this continues to be a debated topic. One result of genetic testing can be genetic profiling. **Genetic profiling** involves the use of biotechnology in identification of the unique characteristics of a person's DNA for forensic or diagnostic purposes.[137] This provides a perfect means for identifying a person and thus raises questions of privacy and possible discrimination based on genetic factors.[138]

In 2008, then President George Bush signed into law the *Genetic Information Nondiscrimination Act (GINA)* that was intended to protect Americans against discrimination based on their genetic information when it comes to health insurance and employment.[139] Its implementation has been taking effect for several years now.

9.6c Genetically Modified Organisms (GMOs)

Another highly debated category of biotechnology that carries important and more frequent ethical implications and debates for business is that of **genetically modified foods (GMFs)**, more frequently referred to as **genetically modified organisms (GMOs)**. GMOs are plants or animals created through the gene splicing techniques of biotechnology (also called genetic engineering).[140] Products that are not used with GMOs are typically referred to as "organic." GMOs have been deeply embedded in the global food supply for decades. In the United States, for example, almost all corn, cotton, and soybeans have been genetically modified or engineered.[141] Also, the vast majority of canola and sugar beets grown in the United States are genetically modified and they are often found as ingredients in processed foods.[142] Some alfalfa, potatoes, papaya, and other crops grown in the United States have also been genetically engineered, either to produce higher yields or resist pests and drought.[143]

In November, 2015, the FDA approved genetically modified salmon, the first altered animal allowed for human consumption in the United States.[144] After almost 20 years of regulatory scrutiny and political wrangling, the salmon that was approved, known as the AquAdvantage salmon, was said by scientists to be more beneficial than farmed salmon because it grows to adult size twice as fast, requires 20 percent less feed, and requires no antibiotics unlike conventionally farmed salmon.[145] In Spring 2016, however, environmental groups filed a lawsuit against the FDA challenging the agency's authority to approve genetically modified animals used for food.[146]

Also in 2015, the Agriculture Department approved the first genetically modified apple, known as the Artic apple, which has been designed to resist browning when sliced or cut open, making it helpful to restaurants, grocery stores, airlines and other companies that market pre-sliced fruit.[147] In other words, it is readily apparent that most of us are consuming GMOs on a regular basis and that various other species of animals or fish may be next.

It is interesting how so much opposition to GMOs has arisen in the past decade and how differences in opinions are common. Sometimes it is just the "thought" of consuming GMOs that raises questions for consumers. In one recent survey, consumers were asked if they avoided eating them, and 47 percent said yes and 53 percent said no.[148] When asked why consumers avoided GMOs, 39 percent said "GMOs don't sound like something I should eat" and 36 percent said "they are harmful to my health." Of those who did not avoid GMOs, the common responses were "GMOs are in almost everything" (27 percent) and the "FDA says they are safe" (22 percent).[149]

A major question behind the controversy, of course, is whether GMOs are safe or bad for one's health. Supporters of GMOs have emphasized that consumers have been eating foods containing them for more than 15 years and that there has been no credible evidence that people have been harmed. Critics say that just because there is no evidence of harm is not the same as saying they have been proved safe.[150] The U.S. Food and

Drug Administration (FDA) has not determined that GMOs are unsafe but they continue to be monitored. Therefore, it appears that there are two schools of thought and both sides of the issue have been able to marshal support for their views.

Extreme critics of GMOs call them "Frankenfoods" calling attention to the parallels with the mythical character Frankenstein. Opponents point to possible health risks not yet identified, environmental risks, and risks to farmers of organic products.[151] Supporters of GMOs claim that no one seems to have been "hurt" by GMOs and that there is just a lot of wild speculation as well as ignorance or indifference at work in their opposition.

In addition to consumers who have a stake in GMOs, the multibillion dollar agribusiness industry has very much at stake. What decisions are made regarding GMOs have significant implications for them and their investors as well.

For several years, there has been developing opposition to GMOs in Europe. As recently as 2015, over half of the European Union countries have decided to opt out of GMOs.[152] Their arguments have been similar to the arguments raised by GMO opponents in the United States. In addition, it may be that the European countries are trying to be more sensitive to their publics and to environmental and consumer activists. In 2015, Germany signaled that it would take a stronger stance as it indicated it would prohibit the cultivation of GMO crops there even if the crops have been approved by European scientific bodies and an attempt by Brussels to legalize them. Environmentalists and politicians in Germany support their position as an expression of "food democracy" as they acknowledge widespread opposition to GMOs in their country.[153]

Will there be more of a consumer backlash against biotechnology in food production when the public becomes more familiar with it? Recently, more concern has been expressed about questionable food products, including seafood and vegetables being imported, than GMOs. It is a business issue that merits continued close examination for both real and perceived reactions. The debate seems to hinge on whether the perceived pros or cons of GMOs will win out as the arguments are presented and experience is gained.

Labeling of GMOs. Since the safety of GMOs does not seem to be in question by scientific research, the more urgent issue has become the question of whether foods that contain GMOs should be labeled or not when they are sold in grocery stores or served elsewhere. Many consumer activists think that, at a minimum, foods that contain genetically modified ingredients ought to be labeled as such. The Consumer Federation of America Foundation, for example, issued a report recommending mandatory labeling and other ways to improve U.S. biotech food regulations. To date, the FDA has not mandated labeling of GMOs but it has issued a position statement regarding voluntary labeling.[154]

In spite of inaction on the part of the FDA, the labeling issue will not go away. Proponents of mandatory labeling argue that the consumer has a right to full disclosure about product contents and that the consumers' right to safety argues that such knowledge should be available to them. Of special concern, the organic and natural foods market segment fears that genetically modified crops may be slipping into its products. This market segment strongly supports the Non-GMO Project.[155] The Non-GMO Project is a nonprofit collaboration of manufacturers, retailers, processors, distributors, farmers, seed companies, and consumers. The project's shared belief is "that everyone deserves an informed choice about whether or not to consume genetically modified products and our common mission is to ensure the sustained availability of non-GMO choices."[156]

Several of the states have been debating bills requiring GMO labeling for years. Finally, Vermont's new bill, that went into effect on July 1, 2016, is the country's first law requiring mandatory GMO labels. Though the U.S. food industry has fought the

ETHICS IN PRACTICE CASE

Whole Foods: GMO Transparency or Clever Marketing?

Whole Foods Market, long known to be a reformist, sustainability-oriented, supermarket chain selling natural products, startled the industry in early 2013 by announcing that it was embarking on a five-year plan to require labeling of genetically modified foods (GMFs) in its stores by 2018. Its decision came months after Proposition 37 in California was narrowly defeated in November 2012. Proposition 37 would have required disclosure labels on all foods that contained genetically engineered ingredients.

The Food and Drug Administration in the United States has found no research to support allegations that genetically engineered ingredients raise safety concerns greater than those found in traditionally grown products. And, the FDA has not issued any regulations requiring GMF labeling. The World Health Organization and the National Academy of Sciences have found no evidence that GMFs are unsafe. But, critics persist and say that there still may be some unknown harmful effects that in time will be revealed.

In the California battle, large mainstream companies such as Pepsico, Kraft Foods, Coca-Cola, Nestle, General Mills and Hershey opposed the labeling measure. Supporters included smaller, natural foods companies such as Stonyfield Farm, Annie's, Clif Bar, Nature's Path Foods, and Whole Foods. Opponents of GMO labeling fear that such labeling will cause many consumers to think their products containing GMOs are unsafe.

Whole Foods has taken the position that the consumer has a right to know how its foods were produced and whether GMOs are present in any of its foods. The company already has seven stores in the United Kingdom, which already require GMO labeling. In 2016, Whole Foods reported that it was well on the way to meeting its 2018 deadline. It reported 25,000 certified organic items and about 11,500 Non-GMO Project Verified products in its stores. The company also supports animal welfare, eco-friendliness, and sourcing origins.

1. Is the Whole Food's decision a sustainable decision? Explain.
2. Do consumers have a right to know whether GMOs are present in products even if research has never found dangers associated with them?
3. Will GMO labeling unfairly raise fears among consumers that such foods are unsafe when research has shown them not to be?
4. Do you believe Whole Foods honestly thinks GMO labeling is ethically justified or is the company doing this as a strategic, marketing decision to promote its sustainability image and reputation?

Sources: Whole Foods Market, http://www.wholefoodsmarket.com/site_search/gmo%20labeling. Accessed March 25, 2016; Boston Business Journal, http://www.bizjournals.com/boston/blog/mass_roundup/2013/03/whole-foods-label-gmo.html. Accessed March 25, 2016; "Our commitment to GMO Transparency," http://www.wholefoodsmarket.com/our-commitment-gmo-transparency. Accessed March 25, 2016.

regulatory battle against labeling for years, it has finally lost to Vermont and other states may follow. Vermont's new law would mandate fines up to $1,000 a day per product. Though it is a relatively small market, several of the major food suppliers such as General Mills said it would put GMO labels on its packaged food nationwide because it would be too complex and expensive to create a separate distribution network for the 626,000 residents of Vermont. But, the company says it is still firmly against mandatory labeling.[157]

Companies and opponents of the new Vermont law say that such labeling has consequences that its backers seldom acknowledge. Opponents think it validates the notion that GMOs are dangerous, which they do not believe has been proven to be true, and that consumers will steer away from them. If consumers begin to shun GMOs because they think they are dangerous when they are not, the food industry says it will have to respond by producing less of them and this could have a harsh impact on the world food supply, especially in poorer parts of the world where food is already scarcer and more expensive. The industry has argued that a state rule to label GMOs will raise costs nationwide, and that consumers already have a choice—they can opt for voluntarily labeled products, which are increasingly being promoted as "100% organic" or "GMO free."[158,159]

The issues of safety and labeling of GMOs continue unabated. Special-interest activist groups on both sides of the debate continue to be energetic in advocating their points of view. The agribusiness industry continues to argue that the foods are safe and that mandatory testing and labeling are not necessary and is needlessly expensive. The FDA does not seem inclined to impose any new requirements on producers. Consumer activists, however, have brought together environmentalists, organic farmers, chefs, and religious leaders, and they continue to lobby for rigorous safety testing and labeling.[160]

Whole Foods Market has announced it will require GMO labeling by 2018. Whether other companies follow and how quickly remains to be seen. States other than Vermont may elect to mandate GMO labeling. The federal government, at some point, may take a stand. To be sure, all consumer stakeholders are potentially affected by the outcome of these debates, so it is likely that this issue will be with us for some time. As the economy improves, the organic and natural foods market segment will start to grow again, and with it is likely to continue the expectation that these products will be differentiated by their non-GMO characteristic.

Summary

Business use of technology today is so dramatic that the topic merits this separate chapter. Big Data, social media, and surveillance have become prominent issues. Basic concepts such as technology and the technological environment were introduced and defined. The benefits, side effects, and costs of technology were discussed. Questions regarding the ethics of technology were raised in two broad domains: information technology and biotechnology.

In the realm of information technology, characterized by Big Data, the category with the most widespread current impact in business, topics included electronic commerce, invasion of privacy via e-commerce, government's involvement in Internet privacy invasion, and business initiatives. Questions about practices and uses of technology were raised, including particular industries such as the porn industry, Internet gambling, and Web-based downloading services. Computer technologies in the marketplace and workplace have had significant application, influence, and impact. Questions regarding the ethics of new technologies such as cell phones were also raised. The field of biometrics merits close watch in the future.

The field of biotechnology was discussed with respect to social and ethical implications. A key topic in this sphere included the new field of bioethics. Arenas of biotechnology were identified and discussed. Included were the topics of genetic engineering, which included a discussion of stem cell research, cloning, and genetic testing and profiling; also discussed was the topic of GMOs. It is anticipated that the debate over food safety and labeling will continue for years as different interest groups raise questions about the appropriateness and safety of GMOs and whether labels on such foods should be ethically expected or required by legislation. The new Vermont law is likely to expedite GMO labeling in the United States.

Key Terms

artificial intelligence, p. 288
Big Data, p. 273
bioethics, p. 291
biometrics, p. 286
biotechnology, p. 278
botnets, p. 281
botnet scams, p. 280
chief privacy officer (CPO), p. 283
cloning, p. 294
cookies, p. 280
digital amnesia, p. 276
electronic commerce, p. 278
embryonic stem cells, p. 293
ethical lag, p. 278
genetic engineering, p. 292
genetic profiling, p. 296
genetic testing, p. 295
genetically modified foods (GMFs), p. 296
genetically modified organisms (GMOs), p. 296
Google Effect, p. 276
information technology, p. 278
identity theft, p. 280
online scams, p. 279
phishing, p. 280
spam, p. 280
technoethics, p. 277
technological determinism, p. 278
technological environment, p. 274
technology, p. 274
therapeutic cloning, p. 294

Discussion Questions

1. Are there any benefits or negative side effects of technology in business that have not been mentioned in this chapter? Discuss.
2. Is society intoxicated with technology? Does this pose special problems for business with respect to the ethics of technology? Will such intoxication blind people to ethical considerations in business?
3. Do you think business is abusing its power with respect to invasion of privacy of consumers? Is surveillance of consumers in the marketplace a fair and justified practice? Which particular practice do you think is the most questionable?
4. Is it an exaggeration to question the ethical implications for business of cell phone and text-messaging use? Discuss both sides of this issue.
5. Do you think genetically modified organisms (GMOs) raise a legitimate safety hazard? Should government agencies such as the FDA take more action to require safety testing? Do you think labeling unfairly stigmatizes GMOs and make consumers question their safety?

Endnotes

1. Nancy Gibbs, "The privacy debate," *Time*, March 28, 2016, 6.
2. Alan Murray, "Greatest Challenge?" *Fortune*, June 15, 2015, 16.
3. Sharon Jayson, "iGeneration Has No Off Switch," *USA Today* (February 10, 2010), 1D.
4. "Spotlight: Kids and Technology," *Time*, November 16, 2015, 25.
5. John Naisbitt, Nana Naisbitt, and Douglas Phillips, *High Tech/High Touch: Technology and Our Search for Meaning* (Nicholas Brealey Publishing Co, 1999).
6. Leon Wieseltier, "Among the Disrupted," *New York Times Magazine* (January 18, 2015), 14.
7. Chuck Raasch, "Instant Information Upends the World," *USA Today* (December 13, 2012), 1A.
8. Steven Rosenbush and Michael Totty, "How Big Data Is Changing the Whole Equation for Business," *Wall Street Journal* (March 11, 2013), R1.
9. Michael S. Malone, "The Big-Data Future Has Arrived," *Wall Street Journal* (February 23, 2016), A17.
10. Ibid., A17.
11. John Bussey, "A Transformative Time for Companies—and Their CIOs," *Wall Street Journal* (January 22, 2013), B11.
12. Kia Kokalitcheva, "How to Invest in the 21st Century Corporation," *Fortune*, December 15, 2015, 164–167.
13. CampusQuad, "The Evolution of Social Media Use among College Students," http://www.campusquad.co/evolution-social-media-use-among-college-students-2/. Accessed March 14, 2016.
14. Reed Albergotti, "Websites Wary of Facebook Tracking," *Wall Street Journal* (September 24, 2014), B1.
15. Reed Albergotti and Elizabeth Dwoskin, "Facebook Study Spurs Ethical Questions," *Wall Street Journal* (July 1, 2014), B1.
16. Yoree Koh and Reed Albergotti, "Twitter Faces Free-Speech Dilemma," *Wall Street Journal* (August 22, 2014), B1.
17. Jeremy Harris Lipschultz, *Huffpost Business*, "The Ethics of Social Media Accuracy," http://www.huffingtonpost.com/jeremy-harris-lipschultz/the-ethics-of-social-media_b_7489280.html. Accessed March 14, 2016.
18. Ibid.
19. Elizabeth Woyke, "Attention Shoplifters: With $30 Billion in Theft, There's a Revolution in Surveillance Systems," *Business Week* (September 11, 2006), 46; also see Cognitech, https://www.cognitech.com/. Accessed March 11, 2016.
20. "Ethics and Morality of Video Surveillance," http://felenasoft.com/xeoma/en/articles/video-surveillance-ethics/. Accessed March 14, 2016.
21. *Webster's Ninth New Collegiate Dictionary* (Springfield, MA: Merriam-Webster, Inc., 1983), 1211
22. Ibid.
23. *"Technology,"* Dictionary.com, http://www.dictionary.com/browse/technology. Accessed March 11, 2016.
24. Alan Murray, "Oracles of Davos: CEOs Foresee Sweeping Changes to the World of Work," *Fortune*, March 1, 2016, 20.
25. Ibid.
26. "Technology," The World Book Encyclopedia (Chicago, WorldBook, Inc., 2016).
27. Ibid.
28. McKinsey & Company, "Unlocking the Potential of the Internet of Things," Report of the McKinsey Global Institute, June 2015.
29. Wieseltier, 2015, 15.
30. "Technology," ibid., 80.

31. Dick Meyer, "Technology Creating World of 'Digital Amnesiacs' for All Ages," *Athens Banner Herald* (October 10, 2015), A4.

32. Ibid.

33. Ibid.

34. Beverly Kracher and Cynthia L. Corritore, "Is There a Special E-Commerce Ethics?" *Business Ethics Quarterly* (Vol. 14, Issue 1, January 2004), 77.

35. TechTarget, "Information Technology (IT)," http://searchdatacenter.techtarget.com/definition/IT. Accessed March 16, 2016.

36. Google, "Internet of Things," https://www.google.com/search?hl=en&gl=us&tbm=nws&authuser=0&q=internet+of+things+definition&oq=internet+of+things+de&gs_l=news-cc.1.2.43j0l2j43i53.228370.232473.0.235216.21.16.0.5.5.0.69.611.16.16.0...0.0...1ac.1.fvFpTHBgVn0#q=internet+of+things+definition&hl=en&gl=us&authuser=0. Accessed April 27, 2016.

37. TechTarget, "E-Commerce," http://searchcio.techtarget.com/definition/e-commerce. Accessed March 16, 2016.

38. Fraud!Org, "Learn about Scams," http://fraud.org/learn. Accessed March 16, 2016.

39. Ibid.

40. Kracher and Corritore, 71–94.

41. Ibid., 78–82.

42. To appreciate the different issues in which privacy arises, go to the Web site of Privacy Rights Clearinghouse, https://www.privacyrights.org/. Accessed March 16, 2016.

43. The EPIC Cookies Page: http://epic.org/privacy/internet/cookies/. Accessed March 16, 2016.

44. "Privacy Options Are a Blur," *USA Today* (April 10, 2001), 3D.

45. Spam, http://epic.org/. Accessed March 16, 2016.

46. Ibid.

47. TED Blog, "What Data Is Being Collected on You? Some Shocking Information," http://blog.ted.com/what-data-is-being-collected-on-you-some-shocking-info/. Accessed March 21, 2016.

48. "Phishing," Dictionary.com, http://www.dictionary.com/browse/phishing. Accessed March 16, 2016.

49. APWG: Unifying the Global Response to Cybercrime, http://www.antiphishing.org/. Accessed March 16, 2016.

50. Webroot, "Fake Security Scams 2015 Edition," http://www.webroot.com/blog/2015/04/27/fake-security-scams-2015-edition/. Accessed March 16, 2016.

51. Byron Acohido, "An Invitation to Crime," *USA Today* (March 4, 2010), 2A.

52. Bryon Acohido and Jon Swartz, "Botnet Scams Are Exploding," *USA Today* (March 17, 2008), 1B–2B; also see, Webroot, "Fake security scams: 2015 Edition," http://www.webroot.com/blog/2015/04/27/fake-security-scams-2015-edition/. Accessed March 21, 2016.

53. Amy Kraft, "Social Media Sites You'll Be Seeing More of in 2016," CBSNews, http://www.cbsnews.com/news/social-media-sites-youll-be-seeing-more-of-in-2016/. Accessed April 27, 2016.

54. Acohido, 1A–2A.

55. "Protecting Citizens and Their Privacy," *New York Times* (December 19, 2013), http://www.nytimes.com/2013/12/20/opinion/protecting-citizens-and-their-privacy.html. Accessed March 16, 2016.

56. Investopedia, "Financial Services Modernization Act of 1999," http://www.investopedia.com/terms/f/financial-services-act-of-1999.asp?layout=infini&v=4A&adtest=4A. Accessed March 16, 2016.

57. "Consumer Data Privacy in a Networked World," The White House, February 23, 2012, http://www.whitehouse.gov/sites/default/files/privacy-final.pdf. Accessed March 16, 2016.

58. Congress.gov, "S.1158 Consumer Privacy Protection Act of 2015," https://www.congress.gov/bill/114th-congress/senate-bill/1158. Accessed March 16, 2016.

59. Federal Trade Commission, "Consumer Protection and Privacy," March 2016, https://www.ftc.gov/policy/international/ftc-international-monthly/march-2016. Accessed March 16, 2016.

60. Federal Trade Commission, http://business.ftc.gov/documents/bus53-brief-financial-privacy-requirements-gramm-leach-bliley-act. Accessed March 16, 2016.

61. *Protecting Consumer Privacy in an Era of Rapid Change: Recommendations for Businesses and Policy Makers*, FTC Report, March 2012, Report available at http://ftc.gov/os/2012/03/120326privacyreport.pdf. Accessed March 16, 2016.

62. Ibid.

63. The Walt Disney Company Privacy Center, https://disneyprivacycenter.com/. Accessed April 27, 2016.

64. Microsoft Privacy Practices, http://www.microsoft.com/privacy/principles.aspx. Accessed March 16, 2016.

65. Katie Benner and Paul Mozur, "Apple Sees Taking a Stand for Privacy as Crucial to Its Brand," *New York Times* (February 21, 2016), 1Y; also see Apple's Privacy Policy, http://www.apple.com/privacy/privacy-policy/. Accessed March 16, 2016.

66. Julian Sanchez, "Viewpoint: The Real Meaning of Apple's Battle with the FBI over Encryption," *Time* (March 7, 2016), 32.

67. Michelle Kessler, "Position of Privacy Officer Coming into Public Eye," *USA Today* (November 30, 2000), 1B; also see Roger Grimes, "Why Your Company Needs a Chief Privacy Officer," Infoworld, http://www.infoworld.com/article/2881793/security/why-your-company-needs-a-chief-privacy-officer.html. Accessed March 16, 2016.

68. The Conference Board, "Chief Privacy Officers Council," https://www.conference-board.org/councils/councildetail.cfm?councilid=296. Accessed March 16, 2016.

69. Ibid.
70. Peter Elkind, "Inside the HACK of the Century," Fortune, July 1, 2015, 64–89.
71. Nicole Hong, "Massive Cybertheft Scheme Is Alleged," *Wall Street Journal* (November 11, 2015), A1.
72. Information is Beautiful, "World's Biggest Data Breaches," February 2016, http://www.informationisbeautiful.net/visualizations/worlds-biggest-data-breaches-hacks/. Accessed March 16, 2016.
73. "The Defense Never Rests," *Business Week* (March 19–25, 2012), 70.
74. John Jurgensen and Barbara Chai, "Apple to Pay Artists after Taylor Swift's Protests," *Wall Street Journal* (June 22, 2015), http://www.wsj.com/articles/taylor-swift-withholds-album-from-apple-music-1434916050. Accessed April 27, 2016.
75. LifeHacker, Thorin Klosowski, "The Copyright Alert System: How the New Six Strikes Anti-Piracy Program Works," http://lifehacker.com/5986961/the-copyright-alert-system-how-the-new-six-strikes-anti-piracy-program-works. Accessed March 16, 2016.
76. C. S. Stewart and S. Ramachandran, "Warning: Closer Watch on Illegal Downloads," *Wall Street Journal* (February 26, 2013), B1.
77. Yahoo News, "Net Providers Begin Warning of Illegal Downloads," http://news.yahoo.com/net-providers-begin-warning-illegal-232015855.html. Accessed March 16, 2016.
78. RIAA, "About RIAA," https://www.riaa.com/about-riaa/. Accessed March 16, 2016.
79. Ibid.
80. Roxana Robinson, "How Google Stole the Work of Millions of Authors," *Wall Street Journal* (February 8, 2016), A13.
81. Margaret Carlson, "Someone to Watch over Me," *Time* (July 16, 2001).
82. Carfax "Decoding What's in Your Car's Black Box," http://www.edmunds.com/car-technology/car-black-box-recorders-capture-crash-data.html. Accessed March 16, 2016.
83. "Is Smart Technology Making Us Dumb?" *Science Daily* (October 6, 2015), https://www.sciencedaily.com/videos/664faf0d67f8ea00d505a1ab8f232b68.htm. Accessed March 16, 2016.
84. Miki Markovich, "Negative Effects of Computers in the Workplace," *Chron.* http://smallbusiness.chron.com/negative-effects-computers-workplace-22023.html. Accessed March 16, 2016.
85. "Biometrics Gets Down to Business," *The Economist* (December 2, 2006), http://www.economist.com/node/8312246. Accessed March 16, 2016.
86. Computer Hope, "Biometrics," http://www.computerhope.com/jargon/b/biometri.htm. Accessed March 16, 2016.
87. "Biometrics: Wobbly ID," *The Economist* (April 2, 2009).
88. Ibid.
89. Timothy Aeppel, "Jobs and the Clever Robot," *Wall Street Journal* (February 25, 2015), A1.
90. Sam Grobart, "Robot Workers: Coexistence Is Possible" *Bloomberg Businessweek* (December 13, 2012), http://www.bloomberg.com/news/articles/2012-12-13/robot-workers-coexistence-is-possible. Accessed March 21, 2016.
91. "Better Living through Robots," *Bloomberg Businessweek* (January 18–24, 2016), 45.
92. Elizabeth Weise, "Looming Job Fear: Robots Keep Us Up at Night," *USA Today* (March 11, 2016), 2B.
93. Derek Thompson, "A World without Work," *The Atlantic* (July/August 2015), 51–61.
94. Andy Puzder, "Why Restaurant Automation is on the Menu," *Wall Street Journal* (March 25, 2016), A11.
95. "Morals and the Machine," *The Economist* (June 2, 2012), http://www.economist.com/node/21556234. Accessed March 21, 2016.
96. Ibid; also see Jerry Kaplan, "Is It Possible to Create an Ethical Robot?" *Wall Street Journal* (July 25–26, 2015), C3.
97. "Artificial Intelligence," BusinessDictionary.com, http://www.businessdictionary.com/definition/artificial-intelligence.html. Accessed March 21, 2016.
98. David Gelernter, "Machines That Will Think and Feel," *Wall Street Journal* (March 19–20, 2016), C1.
99. Jay Greene, "Microsoft Muzzles Artificially Intelligent Chatbox," *Wall Street Journal* (March 25, 2016), B4.
100. Clive Thompson, "OMG! We've Been Here B4," *Smithsonian*, March 2016, 23.
101. Insurance Information Institute, "Cellphones and Driving," http://www.iii.org/media/hottopics/insurance/cellphones/. Accessed February 11, 2010.
102. Distraction.gov, "State Laws," http://www.distraction.gov/stats-research-laws/state-laws.html. Accessed April 27, 2016.
103. Risk Management Stay Focused, PCT Market Leadership, http://www.pctonline.com/pct0213-safety-attention-driving.aspx. Accessed March 21, 2016.
104. "Distracted Driving," January 2016, http://www.iii.org/issue-update/distracted-driving. Accessed March 21, 2016; also see Archie B. Carroll, "Ethical Companies Curb Phone Use While Driving," *Athens Banner Herald* (October 31, 2009).
105. Trish Worron, "Cellphones Don't Ring My Chimes," *The Toronto Star* (January, 2004).
106. Ibid; also see Anahad O' Conner, "The Distracted American Driver," *New York Times* (March 15, 2013), http://well.blogs.nytimes.com/2013/03/15/the-distracted-american-driver/. Accessed March 18, 2013.
107. "Distracted Driving," January 2016, ibid.

108. Marissa Horn, "Walking + Texting: Deadly Combo," *USA Today* (March 9, 2016), 3A.

109. Amanda Mujica, Edward Petry, and Dianne Vickery, "A Future for Technology and Ethics," 286, http://philpapers.org/rec/MUJAFF, Accessed March 21, 2016.

110. Thomas Hilton, "Information System Ethics: A Practitioner Survey," *Journal of Business Ethics* (December, 2000), 279–284.

111. James C. Bourke, Jr. "Monitoring Employee Technology Use," SmartPros, http://accounting.smartpros.com/x62672.xml. Accessed April 27, 2016.

112. Walter Isaacson, "The Biotech Century," *Time* (January 11, 1999), 42–43.

113. Alison Taunton-Rigby, "Bioethics: The New Frontier" (Waltham, MA: The Sears Lectureship in Business Ethics, Center for Business Ethics, Bentley College, April 19, 2000), 7.

114. Ibid.

115. Ibid., 7–8.

116. Biotechnology Industry Organization, "What Is Biotechnology?" http://www.bio.org/articles/what-biotechnology. Accessed March 21, 2016.

117. U.S. Department of Health and Human Services, Presidential Commission for the Study of Bioethical Issues, http://bioethics.gov/about. Accessed March 21, 2016.

118. Katie Thomas, "Company Creates Bioethics Panel on Trial Drugs," *The New York Times* (May 7, 2015), http://www.nytimes.com/2015/05/07/business/company-creates-bioethics-panel-on-trial-drugs.html?_r=0. Accessed March 21, 2016.

119. "Bioethics: Wanna Buy a Bioethicist?" *Christianity Today* (October 1, 2001), 32–33, http://www.christianitytoday.com/ct/2001/october1/24.32.html. Accessed March 21, 2016.

120. Nell Boyce, "And Now, Ethics for Sale," Mindfully.org, http://www.mindfully.org/GE/GE2/Bioethicists-For-Sale.htm. Accessed March 21, 2016.

121. "Genetic Engineering," Dictionary.com, http://www.dictionary.com/browse/genetic-engineering. Accessed April 27, 2016.

122. "The Stem Cell Debate: Is It Over?" http://learn.genetics.utah.edu/content/stemcells/scissues/. Accessed March 23, 2016.

123. Tim Friend, "The Stem Cell Hard Sell," *USA Today* (July 17, 2001), 6D.

124. "The Value of Stem Cells," LifeBankUSA, http://www.lifebankusa.com/cord-blood/value.php. Accessed March 11, 2013.

125. "Value Conflicts in Stem-Cell Research: Governments Struggle with Bioethical Issues," *The Futurist* (January–February, 2007), 8–9.

126. International Society for Stem Cell Research, http://www.isscr.org/visitor-types/public/ethics-and-stem-cells. Accessed March 25, 2016.

127. Alice Park, "The Quest Resumes," *Time* (February 9, 2009), 36–43.

128. Yahoo Finance! "Three Companies Investing in Stem Cell Research," http://finance.yahoo.com/news/3-companies-investing-stem-cell-203426117.html. Accessed March 25, 2016.

129. Gallup, "Cloning," http://www.gallup.com/poll/6028/cloning.aspx. Accessed March 25, 2016.

130. "Pregnant Pause," *The Economist* (January 22, 2004); also see "What is Therapeutic Cloning," http://www.wisegeek.org/what-is-therapeutic-cloning.htm. Accessed March 25, 2016.

131. Quoted in Elizabeth M. Whelan, "Biomedical Prostitution?" *Insight* (May 28, 2001), 27.

132. For more on Tom Tole's cartoons, see http://www.gocomics.com/tomtoles. Accessed March 25, 2016.

133. Food and Drug Administration, "Animal Cloning" http://www.fda.gov/ForConsumers/ConsumerUpdates/ucm148768.htm. Accessed March 25, 2016.

134. Center for Food Safety, "Animal Cloning and Human Health," http://www.centerforfoodsafety.org/issues/302/animal-cloning/human-health-257. Accessed March 25, 2016.

135. "Biotechnology: Cloning Animals for Food to Be Banned in the E.U." September 8, 2015, http://news.discovery.com/tech/biotechnology/cloning-animals-for-food-to-be-banned-in-eu-150908.htm. Accessed March 25, 2016.

136. Medscape, "Ethical Issues in Genetic Testing," http://www.medscape.com/viewarticle/505222_4. Accessed March 25, 2016.

137. *BusinessDictionary.com*, "Genetic Profiling," http://www.businessdictionary.com/definition/genetic-profiling.html. Accessed March 25, 2016.

138. Taunton-Rigby, 18–19.

139. U.S. Department of Labor, "Genetic Information Nondiscrimination Act of 2008 (GINA)" http://www.dol.gov/ebsa/newsroom/fsGINA.html. Accessed April 27, 2016.

140. Green America, "What Are GMOs?" http://action.greenamerica.org/p/salsa/web/common/public/signup?signup_page_KEY=7626&4tag=adwords&gclid=CjwKEAjww9O3BRDp1tq0jIP023YSJAB0-j1SZxBSj8jACuymz1ee6UPf9q7g96nLmIZ04_aYaRDrkhoCUIXw_wcB. Accessed March 25, 2016.

141. "Should Companies Be Required to Label Genetically Modified Foods?" *Wall Street Journal* (July 13, 2015), R16.

142. "FAQs about GMOs," *Consumer Reports*, March 2015, 12–14.

143. Alice Park, "The First Genetically Altered Animal Is Approved for Eating," *Time* (December 14, 2015), 40.

144. Ibid.

145. Michael Shellenberger, "Frankenfish: Good for Your Nature," *USA Today* (November 23, 2015), 9A.

146. Jacob Bunge, "FDA Challenged on GMO Animals," *Wall Street Journal* (April 1, 2016), B3.

147. Tennile Tracy, "Gene-Altered Apple Approved," *Wall Street Journal* (February 14–15, 2015), A3.

148. Ibid.

149. Ibid.

150. Ibid., 13.

151. Green America, "Why Should Be Concerned about GMOs?" http://action.greenamerica.org/p/salsa/web/common/public/signup?signup_page_KEY=7626&tag=adwords&gclid=CjwKEAjww9O3BRDp1tq0jIP023YSJAB0-j1SZxBSj8jACuymz1ee6UPf9q7g96nLmIZ04_aYaRDrkhoCUIXw_wcB. Accessed March 25, 2016.

152. Alexandra Sifferlin, "Over Half of E.U. Countries Are Opting Out of GMOs," *Time* (October 3, 2015).

153. "Germany versus Science," *Wall Street Journal* (August 31, 2015), A12.

154. U.S. Food and Drug Administration, "Guidance for Industry: Voluntary Labeling Indicating Whether Foods Have or Have Not Been Derived from Genetically Engineered Plants," http://www.fda.gov/food/guidanceregulation/guidancedocumentsregulatoryinformation/ucm059098.htm. Accessed March 25, 2016.

155. Non-GMO Project, http://www.nongmoproject.org/about/who-we-are/. Accessed March 25, 2016.

156. Non-GMO Project, ibid.

157. Annie Gasparro and Jacob Bunge, "GMO Labeling Law Roils Food Companies," *Wall Street Journal* (March 21, 2016), B1.

158. "GMO Labels Feed Unwarranted Fears," *USA Today* (March 11, 2016), 9A.

159. "Vermont Invades Your Kitchen," *Wall Street Journal* (March 7, 2016), A16.

160. For an interesting discussion of the environmentalists' viewpoint, see Jonathan Rauch, "Will Frankenfood Save the Planet?" *The Atlantic Monthly* (October 2003), 103–108.

10

Ethical Issues in the Global Arena

CHAPTER LEARNING OUTCOMES

After studying this chapter, you should be able to:

1. Describe the ethical and social challenges faced by multinational corporations (MNCs) operating in the global environment.
2. Summarize the key implications for managers of the following ethical issues: infant formula controversy, Bhopal tragedy, factory collapses, sweatshops, and human rights abuses.
3. Define corruption and differentiate between bribes and grease payments, and outline the major features of the Foreign Corrupt Practices Act.
4. Identify and discuss strategies companies may employ for improving global business ethics.

In 2016 it was revealed that many global leaders and business people had been implicated in secret offshore companies in which they have been hiding their wealth from the world and from taxation. This disclosure was made in document leaks, now known as the "Panama Papers," reporting that there have been secret financial dealings of some of the world's richest and most powerful executives, and, in some cases, outright corruption.[1] The Panama Papers, revealing information about what was going on from the 1970s until the spring of 2016, documented an extensive network of offshore shell companies in which a number of mega-rich, high-level politicians and business people engaged in deception, corruption or fraud. Among those named have been some American business people accused of or convicted of financial crimes or Ponzi schemes. One bookmaker was even taking bets as to who would be the next world leader to step down.[2] The Panama Papers have publicized yet another adverse blow to the state of global business-government relations, and the implications for global business ethics are yet to be fully determined.

The growth of global business as a critical element in the world economy is one of the most important developments of the past half century, and from the Panama Paper's revelations, it is being seen as an increasingly fertile ground for corruption and ethical challenges. This has been set up during the past two decades, in particular, by the growth of foreign direct investment globally by the United States, by countries in Western Europe, by Japan, and by other developing countries as well, such as China, India, and Russia. Many emerging economies have joined the mix. In the United States and elsewhere, domestic issues have been made immensely more complex by the escalating international growth of commerce. At the same time, the **internationalization** of business has created unique challenges of its own. With the rise of global business, international markets have been seen as natural extensions of an ever-expanding global marketplace that must be pursued if firms are to remain competitive.

Peter Drucker referred to the expanded global marketplace as the **transnational economy**.[3] One useful definition of this transnational or global economy is as follows: trade in goods, a much smaller trade in services, the international movement of labor, and international flows of capital and information.[4]

Most observers have assumed that international business would continue its rapid growth of the past two decades and that, increasingly, companies and countries would become more integrated with the rest of the world. Global trade statistics, however, suggest that after a burst of **globalization** in the pre-2008 period, world business has been more in a period of consolidation, possibly even retrenchment.[5]

Time magazine recently observed that after decades of consensus on the value of global free trade, it is now being contested by some as to whether globalization has been good or bad for the American economy.[6] Some business experts have begun to think that the globalization moment is over. Why, for example, would one want to offshore jobs to China when Chinese workers are demanding and getting large pay raises? Why would a company want to expand its supply chain when it might be interrupted by terrorists?[7] These and other important questions are being asked.

Not only has world economic growth slowed, but global instability in the form of geopolitics has become more intense than in any recent period.[8] Geopolitical issues that have now intertwined governments with business include terrorism, global migration patterns, and corruption. The managing director of McKinsey recently stated that he has not seen as much volatility since World War II. He observed that while businesses have not significantly pulled back from their globalized operations they are now wondering, "what's next?"[9]

Some companies are beginning to question the breadth of their operations and are worried about their vulnerability to regional instabilities.[10] Not only has business growth slowed in the global economy, but it has also been getting more complex and subject to increasing disruptive changes. Researchers at the McKinsey Global Institute have observed that there are four trends or forces that are transforming the nature of the global economy and, hence, global business: the rise of emerging markets, the accelerating rate of technological change on market competition, an aging world population, and greater connectedness in movements of trade, capital, people, and data.[11] These trends have been ushering in a dynamic, new phase of globalization.

The complexity and intricacies of the transnational economy and the globalization of business are seen visibly when social or ethical issues arise. At best, business ethics is difficult when we are dealing with one culture. Once we bring two or more cultures into consideration, along with the rapid changes in each of them, it gets extremely complex. Managers have to deal not only with differing customs, protocols, and ways of operating but also with differing concepts of law and standards of acceptable business practices. All of this is then exacerbated by the fact that world political issues become intertwined. What might be intended as an isolated corporate attempt to bribe a foreign government official, in keeping with local custom, could explode into major international political tensions between two or more countries.

10.1 Business Challenges in a Global Environment

Firms face two major underlying challenges as they operate in a multinational, global business environment. One challenge is that of achieving *corporate legitimacy* as the **multinational corporation (MNC)**, or **multinational enterprise (MNE)**, seeks to be recognized and accepted in an unfamiliar society. A related problem is the fundamentally *differing philosophies* that may exist between the firm's home country and the host country in which it seeks to operate.[12] For firms to be perceived as legitimate in the eyes of a host country, they must fulfill their social responsibilities and be good corporate citizens abroad just as they were expected to do so at home. Sometimes being socially responsible has different meanings in different countries.

Closely related to the legitimacy issue is the dilemma of MNCs that have quite different cultural or philosophical perspectives from those of their host countries. The philosophy of Western industrialized nations, and thus their MNCs, has focused on economic growth, efficiency, specialization, free trade, and comparative advantage. By contrast, many developing countries or emerging economies have different priorities. Other important objectives for them might include a more equitable income distribution or increased economic self-determination. In this context, the economically advanced nations may appear to be inherently exploitative in that their presence may perpetuate the dependency of the poorer nation.[13] Very large MNCs have budgets that exceed those of many small countries. Thus, critics of MNCs say they have too much power and undue political influence over governments and can exploit developing nations.[14] These basic challenges set the stage for examining how ethical problems arise in the global environment.

Another issue that has come up in recent years has to do with the different views about corporate social responsibility (CSR) relative to business–government relationships that occur in different regions of the world. For example, Andreas Scherer and Guido Palazzo have noted that under conditions of globalization, the strict division of responsibilities between private businesses and nation-state governments do not hold as much everywhere.[15] They observe that many business firms have begun to assume social and political responsibilities that extend beyond legal requirements and fill some vacuums in global governance. That is, there is a growing politicized concept of CSR that is occurring in some parts of the world.[16] Though this changing relationship between business and government is not occurring everywhere, it is a factor that needs to be considered in some parts of the world. This notion of Political CSR was introduced in Chapter 2. It is in the global business environment where it has become most applicable.

One could well argue that social and ethical tensions are built into global business. MNCs attempt to bridge the cultural gaps between two cultures; yet, as they attempt to adapt to local customs and business practices, they are assailed at home for not adhering to the standards, practices, laws, or ethics of their home country.

Figure 10-1 graphically depicts the dilemma of MNCs caught between the characteristics and expectations of their home country and those of one or more host countries.

FIGURE 10-1 The Dilemma of the Multinational Corporation

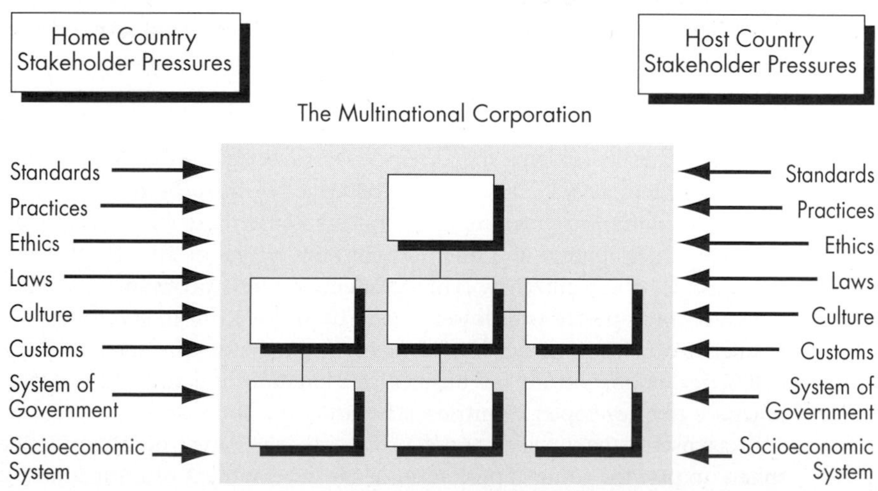

SPOTLIGHT *on Sustainability*

Earth Hour: A Global Ethical Sustainability Movement

Earth Hour was started in Australia in 2007 by the World Wide Fund for Nature (WWF). The organization's mission is to stop degrading Earth's natural environment and to create a low-carbon future for planet Earth.

Earth Hour is a global sustainability movement that was initiated with the hope that each year will bring about a continued celebration. The first Earth Hour was held in Australia, and after national acclaim, it gained high international interest, with more and more cities beginning to sign up for the next Earth Hour campaign.

Earth Hour has now come to be known as the world's largest global climate change initiative. The event is recognized by millions switching off their lights for one hour. Iconic buildings such as Sydney Harbur Bridge, the CN Tower in Toronto, Rome's Colosseum, India Gate, the Golden Gate Bridge in San Francisco, and many more stood in darkness in contemplation of the world's ethical responsibility to planet Earth. Earth Hour in 2016 was held on March 19, 2016.

Earth Hour now inspires a global community of millions of people across 178 countries to switch their lights off to demonstrate a massive support for environmental sustainability. You can discover the Earth Hour events in your country by going to: http://www.earthhour.org/.

Sources: Earth Hour, http://www.earthhour.org/. Accessed April 29, 2016; "Earth Hour City Challenge," WWF, http://worldwildlife.org/pages/earth-hour-city-challenge. Accessed April 29, 2016.

They often find themselves in an almost unmanageable situation, but cannot be deterred from finding sustainable solutions if they desire to expand markets abroad.

10.2 Ethical Issues in the Global Business Environment

The challenges for companies operating in the global business environment include issues of corporate social responsibility, generally, and business ethics, specifically. Our primary focus in this chapter will be on business ethics, but the issues related to other dimensions of CSR should not be forgotten. For many companies, most of the ethical problems that arise in the global environment are in the same categories as those that arise in their domestic environments. These ethical issues reside in all of the functional areas of business: production/operations, marketing, finance, accounting, and management. These issues concern the fair treatment of stakeholders—employees, customers, the community, and competitors—and involve product safety, plant safety, advertising practices, human resource management, human rights, environmental problems, business practices, and so on.

These ethical problems may seem to be somewhat fewer in developed countries, but they exist there as well. The ethical challenges seem to be more acute in less-developed countries (LDCs), or emerging economies because these countries are at earlier stages of economic development and often do not have a legal or ethical infrastructure in place to help protect their citizenry. This situation creates an environment in which there is temptation to operate with lower standards, or perhaps no standards, because fewer government regulations or activist groups exist to protect the stakeholders' interests. In the LDCs, the opportunities for business exploitation and the engagement in questionable practices (by developed countries' standards) are abundant.

It is useful to consider some prominent categories of ethical issues in the global sphere to provide some appreciation of the development of these kinds of issues for business. First, we will discuss questionable marketing and manufacturing safety practices. Then, we will address the issue of human rights and labor abuses often found in "sweatshops" (the use of cheap labor in developing countries)—a topic that has dominated international business discussions for the past couple decades. Then, we will consider the special challenges of corruption, bribery, and questionable payments. From these prominent examples, we should be able to develop an appreciation of the kinds of ethical challenges that confront all MNCs doing business globally. Finally, we will consider some strategies for companies seeking to improve their global business ethics.

10.2a Questionable Marketing and Plant Safety Practices

The process of marketing either domestically or abroad creates many ethical and legal challenges for businesses. The most obvious marketing issues are those embedded in the product itself and its promotion. A classic example of a *questionable marketing practice* is the now-infamous infant formula controversy that spanned most of the 1970s, 1980s, and 1990s and remains an issue today. The *plant safety issue* is best illustrated by considering the Union Carbide Bhopal crisis that began in 1984, continued into the 1990s, and is not completely resolved today. These plant safety issues have continued with fires and building collapses in Bangladesh.

These issues are significant because they illustrate the endless problems companies can face as a result of mistakes made in global business ethics and how their effects can be felt for decades. It is easy to now predict that BP's oil spill in the Gulf of Mexico may be in this classic category someday as its repercussions are likely to last for decades.

The Infant Formula Controversy. The **infant formula controversy** is a classic example that illustrates ethical questions that can arise while marketing products abroad.[17] For decades, there was this realization among physicians working in tropical lands (many of which were LDCs) that severe health risks were posed to infants from bottle-feeding as opposed to breast-feeding. Such countries typically had neither refrigeration nor sanitary conditions. Water supplies were not pure, and therefore, powdered infant formula mixed with bacteria-infected water likely led to disease and diarrhea in the bottle-fed infant.

Because people in these developing countries are typically poor and often uneducated, mothers tended to over dilute the powdered formula, trying to make it last longer, thus diminishing significantly the amount of nutrition the infant receives. Once a mother begins bottle-feeding, her capacity for breast-feeding quickly diminishes. Poverty also leads the mother to put less-expensive substitute products such as powdered whole milk and cornstarch in the bottle. These products are nutritionally inadequate and unsatisfactory for the baby's digestive system.

It later became apparent that in LDCs there was increased bottle-feeding, decreased breast-feeding, and a dramatic increase in the numbers of malnourished and sick babies because of this. The problems began when several of the infant formula companies, aware of the conditions just described, were promoting their products and, therefore, promoting bottle-feeding in an intense way. Such marketing practices as mass advertising, billboards, radio jingles, and free samples became commonplace. These promotional devices typically portrayed the infants who used their products as healthy and robust, in sharp contrast with the reality that was brought about by the conditions mentioned.

One of the worst marketing practices entailed the use of "milk nurses"—women dressed in nurses' uniforms, walking the halls of maternity wards, and urging mothers to get their babies started on formula. In reality, these women were sales representatives employed by the companies on a commission basis. Once the infants began bottle-feeding, the mothers' capacity to breast-feed diminished, and they became hooked on the formula.[18]

Although several companies were engaging in these questionable marketing practices, the Swiss conglomerate Nestlé was singled out by a Swiss social activist group in an article entitled "Nestlé Kills Babies." At about the same time, an article appeared in Great Britain entitled "The Baby Killers."[19] From this point on, a protracted controversy developed, with Nestlé and other infant formula manufacturers on one side and a host of organizations on the other side filing shareholder resolutions and lawsuits against the company.

Among the groups that were actively involved in the controversy were church groups such as the National Council of Churches and its Interfaith Center on Corporate Responsibility (ICCR), UNICEF, the World Health Organization (WHO), and the Infant Formula Action Coalition (INFACT). Nestlé was singled out because it had the largest share of the world market and because it aggressively pushed sales of its infant formula in developing countries, even after the WHO developed a sales code to the contrary.[20]

INFACT and ICCR organized and led a national boycott in 1977 against Nestlé that continued for almost seven years.[21] In 1984, after spending tens of millions of dollars resisting the boycott, Nestlé finally reached an accord with the protesters. The company agreed to make some changes in its business practices. The protesters, in return, agreed to end their boycott but to continue monitoring Nestlé's performance.[22] The infant formula controversy continued well into the 1990s and 2000s.

The infant formula controversy illustrates the character of questionable business practices by firms pursuing what might be called normal practices were it not for the fact that they were being pursued in foreign countries where local circumstances made them suspect.[23] The infant formula controversy also illustrates the endurance of certain ethical issues, particularly in the global arena.

Later, the AIDS crisis, especially in Africa, put an unusual twist on the infant formula debate. Some have said that UNICEF, the UN agency charged with protecting children, today may be indirectly responsible for thousands of African babies being infected with the deadly AIDS virus. AIDS entered the picture since the early boycotts of Nestlé and others, and it was discovered that HIV-infected mothers could transfer the disease through breast-feeding to their own children. In response to this problem, Nestlé and formula maker Wyeth-Ayerst Labs said they stood ready to donate tons of free formula to the infected women. However, UNICEF refused to give the green light to these gifts.[24]

Even today, the International Baby Food Action Network (IBFAN) (http://www.ibfan.org/) continues to advocate safety in feeding babies and lobbies against companies that continue engaging in questionable business and marketing practices.[25] By 2013, the infant formula issue was flaring anew in China where it has been alleged that formula makers pay doctors and medical staff to motivate them to get newborns hooked on infant formula.[26] In addition, because many more well-to-do families in China do not trust the quality and safety of their own brands, they have been buying up infant formula from Australia that because of its proximity the product can be delivered more quickly.[27]

Plant Safety and the Bhopal Tragedy. The Union Carbide **Bhopal tragedy** brought into sharp focus the challenges of multinationals conducting manufacturing operations in a foreign, particularly less-developed, business environment. On December 3, 1984, the leakage of methyl isocyanate gas caused what many have termed the "worst industrial accident in history." The gas leak killed more than 2,000 people and injured 200,000 others. The tragedy has raised numerous legal, ethical, social, and technical questions for MNCs.[28] Observers who have studied this tragedy say the death toll and destruction are many times greater than the "official" numbers indicate. One report is that more than 3,500 were killed in the accident.[29] Over 30 years later, many issues related to the Bhopal disaster remain unresolved.[30]

Interviews with experts just after the accident revealed a belief that the responsibility for the accident had to be shared by the company and the Indian government.

According to Union Carbide's own inspector, the Bhopal plant did not meet U.S. standards and had not been inspected in over two years. In addition, the Indian government allowed thousands of people to live dangerously near the plant, and there were no evacuation procedures.[31]

Many important questions that have implications for manufacturing abroad have been raised by the Bhopal disaster. Among the more important of these issues are the following[32]:

1. To what extent should MNCs maintain identical standards at home and abroad regardless of how lax laws are in the host country?
2. How advisable is it to locate a complex and dangerous plant in an area where the entire workforce is basically unskilled and uneducated, and where the populace is ignorant of the inherent risks posed by such plants?
3. How wise are laws that require plants to be staffed entirely by local employees?
4. What is the responsibility of corporations and governments in allowing the use of otherwise safe products that become dangerous because of local conditions? (This question applies to the infant formula controversy also.)
5. After reviewing all the issues, should certain kinds of plants even be located in developing nations?

At the heart of these questions is the issue of differing safety standards in various parts of the world.

The complexity and tragedy of the Bhopal gas leak case for its victims, the Indian government, and Union Carbide are attested to by the fact that this issue remains a topic of discussion today. In 1989, Union Carbide extricated itself from relief efforts by agreeing to pay the Indian government $470 million to be divided among victims and their families. Dow Chemical Co. bought Union Carbide in 2001. Over 30 years later after the accident, the Union Carbide tragedy continues to haunt Dow Chemical. Survivors of the accident and their supporters continue to push Dow to pay more than $1 billion in additional damages for what they claim are unmet medical bills and toxic cleanup.[33] Dow continues to argue that the $470 million settlement it paid in 1989 resolved its outstanding liabilities.[34]

In 2012, the Madhya Pradesh, India, high court finally lifted a five-year stay that prevented the summoning of Dow Chemical in the ongoing criminal case in connection with the gas tragedy. Activists in India insist they will continue to pursue this case until Dow Chemical is held accountable.[35] The ghosts of Bhopal continue to haunt multinational firms as they contemplate locating in a developing country. When the Bhopal disaster occurred, it was a less media-saturated, pre-Twitter world so many Americans were unaware of the disaster. Today, companies would experience significant media, activist, and political pressure that did not weigh on the Union Carbide officials back then.[36] Current Web pages (http://www.bhopal.org) document that the Bhopal tragedy continues to be of deep concern even today. Like the infant formula controversy, it is an ethical issue that will not be forgotten.

Factory Fire and Building Collapse in Bangladesh In a factory fire reminiscent of the Bhopal tragedy, 112 workers were killed in a Tazreen Fashions, Ltd., factory near Dhaka, Bangladesh, in November 2012. This disaster was especially newsworthy because more than 500 Bangladeshi garment workers had died in fires in the previous six years according to labor groups. The fire has been called the country's worst industrial accident and it received high-profile news coverage when it was discovered that garments for Wal-Mart Stores' were being manufactured there at the time.[37]

Wal-Mart says it had found serious fire-safety concerns at the plant in an inspection conducted in 2011 and that it had removed Tazreen from its list of authorized factories "months ago" but that one of its suppliers used the plant without its authorization.[38]

A Bangladesh government committee investigation found that the incident was an act of sabotage. In addition, the committee's report disclosed that three mid-level executives from Tazreen Fashions were suspected of stopping workers from leaving during the fire because they wanted to prevent employee theft.[39] Companies such as Wal-Mart were under the gun even more so to police the safety concerns of factories used. Although 45 cases were filed against the Tazreen Fashions factory owners, as of 2016 no action had been taken against them.[40]

In April 2013, a garment factory known as the Rana Plaza Building collapsed in Bangladesh killing more than 1,100 workers and injuring some 3,000 more. The building housed 5,000 workers in five textile firms. This incident has continued the spotlight on Western companies that use factories for low-cost clothes manufacturing though these companies have not been identified as the guilty parties.[41] The building that collapsed was owned by a local politician who had the building built six years earlier without the required permits.

The public in Bangladesh had been upset over the lack of safety regulations governing buildings and the ease with which politicians get these structures built.[42] In 2015, police finally filed homicide charges against 42 people, including the building owner, former mayor of the local council, owners of the five garment factories located in the complex, and dozens of council officials and engineers. This was considered to be a remarkable legal step in a country where past industrial accidents were rarely pursued or prosecuted.[43]

After the 2013 disaster, global corporations not held to be responsible in the disaster formed two parallel, corporate-backed groups to address safety issues in Bangladesh's garment industry. Twenty-six North American–based companies formed the Alliance for Bangladesh Worker Safety. One hundred eighty-nine mostly European retailers and global workers' unions formed the Accord on Fire and Building Safety in Bangladesh.[44] These groups were formed to help monitor and improve working conditions in the Bangladeshi garment industry.

The lessons from Bhopal, Tazreen Fashions, and Rana Plaza are many and will continue to be debated. In companies around the globe, these disasters have stimulated continued discussions in the debate about how to operate abroad. To be sure, legal and ethical issues are central to the discussions. What are at stake, however, are not just the practices of businesses abroad but also the very question of their presence. Depending on the final outcome of the Union Carbide case, MNCs may decide that the risks of doing certain types of business abroad are just too great.

10.2b Human Rights, Sweatshops, and Labor Abuses

No issue has been more consistently evident in the global business ethics debate than the use and alleged abuse of women, children, and workers in cheap-labor factories, often called "sweatshops," in developing countries. In a report by the Associated Press (AP) released in 2015, for example, labor abuses in the Thai shrimp industry were reported. The AP found that slavery persists in this industry though Thai businesses and government have repeatedly vowed to clean up the nation's $7 billion seafood exporting industry. One factory was found to be housing dozens of enslaved workers and runaway migrants. Children and their parents were found to be working side by side in a warehouse that had overflowing toilets and the stench of sewage.[45]

The AP found shrimp peelers who were working 16 hour days for little or no pay while the company monitored them to prevent their escape. They also found that the farmed shrimp entered the supply chains of major food stores and retailers including Walmart, Whole Foods, and Target, as well as the supply chains of popular restaurant

ETHICS IN PRACTICE CASE

Is the Fair Trade Movement Sustainable?

The Fair Trade Movement began with coffee. Starbuck's was one of the first companies to sign on to the idea of fair trade coffee to help farmers and workers in less-developed countries. But, after the collapse of the Rana Plaza factory in Bangladesh, killing over 1,100 workers, the fair trade movement for apparel and home furnishings took off. Fair trade is an alternative approach to conventional trade and is based on partnerships being developed between producers and traders, businesses and consumers. The global fair trade system is represented by Fair Trade International (FTI) and its member organizations.

FTI carries out its mission of empowering producers and combating poverty by certifying factories that meet certain standards that include employee safety and health, acceptable wages and working conditions, environmental impact, worker's rights, and other pertinent criteria.

Fair Trade USA (FTUSA) audits and certifies transactions between U.S. companies and their international suppliers to ensure that rigorous Fair Trade standards have been met. Fair Trade USA is a 501 (c) (3) nonprofit organization that seeks to inspire the rise of conscious consumers and eliminate exploitation. Fair Trade USA now certifies 20 brands and includes companies such as Patagonia, Williams-Sonoma, and Bed Bath & Beyond. Before Rana Plaza, FTUSA only certified a handful of brands. Whole Foods Market got into apparel when it began carrying Fair Trade Certified T-shirts made by Pact Apparel.

Fair trade does not come without higher costs. The average total cost to the brands to get certification including third-party factory audits comes to about 1 to 5 percent of what the brands pay to factories. Brands are also expected to pay more based on the volume of purchases from factories.

In its concept, the Fair Trade Movement appears to be the epitome of CSR. The Fair Trade Movement has its detractors, however. Among the criticisms are that: (1) little money actually reaches the developing world, (2) less money actually reaches the farmers and workers, (3) evidence of impact has not been adequately assessed, (4) fair trade is profitable to traders in rich countries, (5) fair trade hurts other farmers and producers, (6) fair trade criteria presuppose a set of political values that everyone does not agree with, (7) some supporters of fair trade use bullying and misleading selling techniques, (8) people who volunteer to work on free trade are misled, (9) there is failure to monitor standards, and (10) corruption is in the process. In another criticism of fair trade, it was pointed out that it may increase revenues to some farmers, but it is mostly about redistribution rather than expanding the overall amount of value created.

1. Do consumers continue to support the idea of paying more for a product just to help workers in emerging economies?
2. Why did the Fair Trade movement explode in popularity after the Rana Plaza collapse? Will the movement continue to grow once working conditions get better?
3. What are the global ethical issues embedded in the concept and implementation of fair trade?
4. Do the "certified" companies really care or are they simply interested in their reputations?
5. Is the Fair Trade Movement sustainable? Or, will it plateau and decline over time?

Sources: Fair Trade USA, http://fairtradeusa.org/about-fair-trade-usa. Accessed April 19, 2016; Fair Trade International, http://www.fairtrade.net/. Accessed April 19, 2016; Andria Cheng, "Fair Trade Becomes a Fashion Trend," *The Wall Street Journal*, July 8, 2015, B7; "Fair Trade Debate," Wikipedia, https://en.wikipedia.org/wiki/Fair_trade_debate. Accessed April 19, 2016; "Criticisms of Fair Trade," http://money.howstuffworks.com/fair-trade2.htm. Accessed April 19, 2016; Bizzy Resource, "Michael Porter's Creating Shared Value Concept—Summary Notes," January 21, 2011, http://www.bizzyresource.com/2011/01/michael-porters-creating-shared-value.html. Accessed April 29, 2016.

chains such as Red Lobster and Olive Garden. Although most of these companies denied that this was happening, they condemned the reported labor practices and said they were striving to eliminate human rights and labor abuses that were taking part in the industry.[46]

In the Tazreen factory fire described earlier it was reported that even though Bangladesh has become the world's second largest exporter of garments behind China, it also pays some of the lowest wages in the world.[47] It was recently reported that workers in Bangladesh now earn about $67 a month.[48] The major players in this controversy, large corporations, have highly recognizable names—Nike, Wal-Mart, Gap, Kmart, Reebok, J. C. Penney, and Disney, to name just a few. The countries and regions of the world that have been involved are also recognizable—Southeast Asia, Pakistan, Indonesia, Honduras, Dominican Republic, Thailand, China, Bangladesh, the Philippines, Mexico, and Vietnam. Sweatshops have not been totally eliminated in the United States either, but the most serious problems seem to be in the developing countries.[49]

The search for cheap labor has led many firms to Africa, called the final frontier in the global rag trade—the last untapped continent with plentiful and cheap labor. In Ethiopia, for example, the garment industry has no minimum wage as workers there start at about $21 a month. These moves are being made because labor costs have been rising in China, with Chinese garment workers said to be earning from $155 to $297 a month.[50]

Though **sweatshops**, characterized by child labor, low pay, poor working conditions, worker exploitation, and health and safety violations, have existed for decades, they have grown in number in the past couple decades as global competition has heated up and corporations have gone to the far reaches of the world to lower their costs and increase their productivity.

The Nike Corporation became an early lightning rod for social activists concerned about overseas manufacturing conditions, standards, and ethics. A major reason for this was the company's high profile and visibility, extensive advertising using athletic superstars, as well as the stark contrast between the tens of millions of dollars Nike icons Michael Jordan and Tiger Woods were earning and the several dollars of daily wage rate the company's subcontractors once paid their Indonesian workers.[51] The continuing challenges faced by Nike are developed further in Case 15 in the Case section at the end of the book.

Critics of sweatshop labor practices, including social activist groups, labor unions, student groups, and grassroots organizations, have been speaking out, criticizing business abusers, and raising public awareness for decades. These critics claim many businesses are exploiting children and women by paying them poverty wages, working them to exhaustion, punishing them for minor violations, violating health and safety standards, and tearing apart their families. Many of these companies counter that they offer the children and women workers a superior alternative. They say that although their wage rates may be embarrassing by developed-world standards, those rates frequently equal or exceed local legal minimum wages, or average wages.

Defenders of the system that has produced sweatshops further say that because so many workers in developing countries work in agriculture and farming, where they make less than the average wage, the low but legal minimums in many countries put sweatshop workers among the higher-paid ones in their areas.[52] A study conducted by economists found that MNCs generally paid more, often a lot more, than the wages offered by locally owned companies. In one study, it was found that affiliates of U.S. MNCs pay a wage premium that ranges from 40 percent to 100 percent higher than the local average pay in low-income countries.[53] When these wages are compared to the developed world, however, they seem embarrassing and abusive.

A number of different programs, organizations, and initiatives have begun seeking to redress these problems in sweatshops. Two that merit closer consideration include The Fair Labor Association and SA8000.

Fair Labor Association (FLA). The **Fair Labor Association (FLA)** has been working to improve sweatshop conditions and human rights violations for 20 years. FLA claims that its mission "is to combine the efforts of business, civil society organizations, and colleges and universities to promote and protect workers' rights and to improve working conditions globally through adherence to international standards."[54] Some of its participating companies include well-known names such as Adidas Group, Cutter & Buck, Patagonia, and Under Armor. FLA uses a multi-stakeholder approach to improving workers' lives. They have employed a three-step process that entails setting standards through a code of conduct, monitoring and reporting, and supporting compliance.[55]

In addition to the work of FLA, there have been a number of other proposals aimed at eliminating or improving sweatshops. Some call for clothing firms and their contractors to impose a code of conduct that would prohibit child labor, forced labor, and worker abuse; establish health and safety regulations; recognize workers' right to join a union; limit the workweek to 60 hours (except in exceptional business circumstances); and insist that workers be paid at least the legal minimum wage (or the "prevailing industry wage") in every country in which garments are made. Such proposals have some drawbacks, however. For example, the legal minimum wage in many developing countries is below the poverty line. In addition, the "prevailing industry wage" could prove to be a convenient escape clause.

Some groups are also concerned that some initiatives, in effect, have sanctioned 60-hour workweeks and that it will still allow 14-year-olds to work if local laws do. Another big issue also includes monitoring the agreements abroad. For example, at one time Liz Claiborne alone had 200 contractors in over 25 countries. Furthermore, in some countries, like the Philippines, Malaysia, Thailand, and Vietnam, sweatshops go to great lengths to hide their business dealings by "fronting" businesses using false documents to "prove" they pay minimum wages and by intimidating workers to keep quiet.[56]

Social Accountability 8000 (SA8000). Another major initiative to improve sweatshop and human rights conditions was created by **Social Accountability International (SAI)**. SAI is a nongovernmental, multi-stakeholder organization whose mission is to advance the human rights of workers around the world. SAI convenes key stakeholders in an effort to develop consensus-based standards, conduct cost-benefit research, accredit auditors, provide training and technical assistance, and assist corporations in improving social compliance in their supply chains.[57]

SAI has developed one of the world's preeminent social standards—Social Accountability 8000 or SA8000—designed to piggyback on the ISO8000 quality-auditing system of the International Standards Organization (ISO).

The SA8000 initiative involves a broad spectrum of U.S. and international companies, such as Gucci, General Mills, Walt Disney Company, Chiquita Brands, VF, and Carrefour, plus a number of labor and human rights groups. The current standards for SA8000 may be summarized as follows[58]:

1. *Child Labor:* No use or support of child labor.
2. *Forced or Compulsory Labor:* No use of forced or compulsory labor.
3. *Health and Safety:* Provide a safe and healthy work environment; prevent potential occupational accidents.
4. *Freedom of Association and Right to Collective Bargaining:* Respect the right to form and join trade unions and bargain collectively.
5. *Discrimination:* No discrimination in hiring, remuneration, access to training, promotion, termination, or retirement based upon many different factors.
6. *Discipline:* No corporal punishment, mental or physical coercion, or verbal abuse. No harsh or inhumane treatment is allowed.
7. *Working Hours:* Comply with the applicable law but, in any event, no more than 48 hours per week with at least one day off for every seven-day period; voluntary overtime paid at a premium rate and not to exceed 12 hours per week on a regular basis.
8. *Remuneration:* Respect right of personnel to living wage; all workers paid at least the minimum wage; wages sufficient to meet basic needs and provide discretionary income.

9. *Management Systems:* Facilities seeking to gain and maintain certification must go beyond simple compliance to integrate the SA8000 standard into their management systems and practices.[59]

The SA8000 process offers companies the opportunity to be certified. To certify conformance with SA8000, every facility seeking certification must be audited. Thus auditors will visit factories and assess corporate practices on a wide range of issues and evaluate the state of a company's management systems, necessary to ensure ongoing acceptable practices. Once an organization has implemented any necessary improvements, it can earn a certificate attesting to its compliance with SA8000.

This certification provides a public report of good practice to consumers, buyers, and other companies and is intended to be a significant milestone in improving workplace conditions.[60] However, like other multi-stakeholder initiatives that are cooperative in nature, the SA8000 faces challenges in implementing best practices, particularly in bringing sustained improvements to workers' conditions in developing countries.[61]

Campaigns to create **ethical supply chains** have proliferated in recent years as companies have sought to improve working conditions in factories.[62] Richard Locke of MIT decided to study how things really worked and he convinced four major companies to share with him six years of data from their factory audits. After analyzing the data, Locke reached four conclusions. First, codes of conduct, compliance programs, and audits do not deliver sustained improvements in labor conditions over time. These help to highlight the problems but don't remedy them. Second, investments in helping factories improve their managerial and technical capabilities did benefit in improved working conditions. Third, for significant and sustained improvements to occur, the company and the suppliers needed to function in a more collaborative way. Fourth, many firms use business models such as just-in-time manufacturing that prevent improved working conditions from occurring.[63]

Individual Company Initiatives. In addition to the initiatives by such industry organizations as the FLA and the SAI (SA8000), it is important to note that some individual companies are striving on their own behalf to address the issues surrounding sweatshops. A number of companies have developed *global outsourcing guidelines* and codes and have made important strides in attempts at self-monitoring of their production facilities in developing countries. Companies such as Nike, Levi Strauss & Co., and Gap are notable examples.[64]

Despite the best of efforts by some companies to improve factory conditions in emerging countries, there is growing evidence that some suppliers have learned how to conceal abuses and continue to get away with unacceptable practices. In a major report, *Businessweek* disclosed that many factories, especially in China, have learned how to "game the system" through questionable practices. Some of these practices include keeping double sets of books; scripted responses wherein managers and employees are tutored how to answer auditor's questions about hours, pay, and safety practices; and hidden production, whereby plants meet U.S. demands by secretly shifting work to subcontractors that violate pay and safety standards, but these subcontractors are hidden from the auditors.[65]

Sweatshops and labor abuses sharply contrast the "haves" and the "have-nots" of the world's nations. Consumers in developed countries have benefited greatly from the lower prices made possible by cheap labor. It remains to be seen how supportive those consumers will be when prices rise because MNCs improve wage rates and conditions in developing countries. The MNCs face a continuing and volatile ethical issue that will not go away. Their profits, public image, and reputations will hinge on how well they respond. The MNCs must be prepared to handle increased scrutiny in their age-old quest to balance shareholder profits with the desires of expanded, global stakeholders

ETHICS IN PRACTICE CASE

Helping Factories to Pass Sweatshop Audits—Using Cheating Consultants

A new group of consulting firms in China now advertise that they can help Chinese factories pass labor audits being conducted by Western companies. These firms claim they can help generate two sets of books—real ones and fake ones. These consultants are part of a growing cottage industry in China that help factories "appear" to pass the increasingly stringent audits being used to help clean up sweat shops and labor abuses in that country.

Auditors of working conditions in low-wage plants have also said they have found documents that might have been used in factories to prep workers with the answers the factory wanted the auditors to hear—this is according to the Fair Labor Association (FLA) that conducted an investigation.

The director of the Ethical Trading Initiative, a London-based group, has said that audit fraud is a serious problem. Fake payroll books have become so common that auditors now assume there are (at least) two sets of books. China Labor Watch, a New York–based advocacy group, alleged that one toy factory in China may have bribed its auditor in addition to forging employee time sheets and salary records.

One Chinese consulting firm even advertised on the Internet that it has software available to generate fake factory books. The software also allows the factories to adjust their employee data to present the type of profile the auditors are expecting. The demand for the services of these consulting firms seems to be rising as factories seek to pass the sometimes difficult audit standards.

In their defense, some factory owners in China say it's impossible to meet the MNC's demands for better working conditions while also keeping prices low.

1. Is it ethical to operate a consulting firm that helps factories to lie, cheat, and deceive auditors seeking to monitor working conditions? Could you imagine firms such as this succeeding in your country?
2. What are the implications for the business system in countries that permit this to occur? What happens to the business and society relationship?
3. Should the MNCs striving to create ethical supply chains attempt to interact with and lobby the Chinese government to outlaw consulting firms such as these?
4. Is it possible that we have now reached the point that working conditions cannot be improved while keeping prices low? If so, what comes next?

Sources: Ethical Trading Initiative, "Auditing Working Conditions," http://www.ethicaltrade.org/in-action/issues/auditing-working-conditions. Accessed April 13, 2016; Kathy Chu, "Some Chinese Factories Lie to Pass Western Audits," *USA Today*, April 30, 2012, 4B; China Labor Watch, http://chinalaborwatch.org/home.aspx. Accessed April 13, 2016.

who want better corporate social performance. In the age of transparency, we should expect more revelations in the years to come.

Alien Tort Claims Act and Human Rights Violations. Looking beyond possible human rights violations in sweatshops, claims that companies may have violated the human rights of foreign nationals could come back to haunt firms that have been accused of more serious human rights abuses. What is at stake is the U.S. courts' interpretation of an obscure piece of legislation known as the **Alien Tort Claims Act (ATCA)**. Though researchers cannot determine why Congress passed this little-known act in 1789, recently it has been the centerpiece of a controversy that may have widespread implications for American firms operating abroad.

In the past decade, efforts have been made to use the ATCA to sue transnational companies for violations of international law in countries outside the United States. Plaintiffs have argued that ATCA could be used by foreign individuals seeking to sue U.S. firms in U.S. courts for companies' actions abroad. If these suits were to succeed, the ATCA could become a powerful tool to increase corporate accountability around the globe.[66] Some of the companies that have been targeted under this law include Occidental Petroleum of Los Angeles, Del Monte, Chevron, Caterpillar, Ford, IBM, and GM.

Many of the companies have said that they have been unfairly targeted by activists who are using the law to try to remedy the injustices of foreign governments. Many of the lawyers for these companies also say the companies are being blamed for crimes they deplore and know nothing about. The president of the National Foreign Trade Council observed that the ATCA statute was being misused and that it was being exploited by trial lawyers who have seized the law as their new "asbestos" litigation and are hoping to get rich by hitting the jackpot.[67]

In a significant 2013 judgment, the U.S. Supreme Court reined in the scope of the Alien Torts Act. The Court held that the statute cannot be applied to actions that take place overseas thus weakening a device some human rights groups have used against alleged violators in their home countries. The Court held that the ATCA only applies to actions that take place in the United States. The Supreme Court's ruling will shut down many cases that have been ongoing for decades. Several justices expressed the concern that affirming liability in events which took place overseas would make American courts a magnet for distressed foreign plaintiffs for acts unrelated to the United States and could invite foreign courts to encourage judging U.S. corporations for actions outside their own borders.[68] This court ruling was upheld in a Connecticut U.S. District Court as recently as 2016.[69]

10.2c Corruption, Bribery, and Questionable Payments

The most frequent and highly publicized ethical problems with respect to global business have most recently been corruption, bribes, and questionable payments. These acts of fraud are as old as history itself, but in the past decade governments around the world have escalated their attempts to eliminate them. In the United States alone, the Justice Department enforcement actions related to bribery and corruption have increased dramatically in recent years.[70]

Corruption in global business continues to be an overarching problem. It starts with outright bribery of government officials and the giving of questionable political contributions. Beyond these, there are many other corrupt activities: the misuse of company assets for political favors, kickbacks and protection money for police, free junkets for government officials, secret price-fixing agreements, and insider dealing, just to mention a few. All of these activities have one thing in common—they are attempts to influence the outcomes of decisions in cases when the nature and extent of the influence are not made public. In essence, these activities are abuses of power.[71]

Corruption afflicts virtually every country in the world, especially developing countries. It has been observed that the scale of corruption is mind-boggling, especially in countries such as Argentina, China, India, Pakistan, Russia, Turkey, and many African nations as well.[72] It has also been argued that corruption is more of a symptom than a disease. To eliminate corruption, institutions in these countries will need to rebuild and strengthen, especially their legal and political institutions.

Corruption does not just occur; it is the predictable result of economic and political institutions that permit some to take power and others to be shut out. The absence of accountability and checks and balances such as the rule of law and media freedom are typically the root causes. **Institutional voids** exist in these settings such that multinational businesses are left trying to enforce the rules and regulations of their home countries without virtually any guidance or support from legal, judiciary, or even cultural norms.[73] And, global poverty will not be defeated until corruption is defeated.[74]

Though one seldom hears an official definition of corruption, such synonyms as dishonesty, sleaze, fraud, deceit, and cheating are typically invoked. Two definitions of corruption that are useful include the following[75]:

- *Behavior on the part of officials in the public sector, whether politicians or civil servants, in which they improperly and unlawfully enrich themselves, or those close to them, by the misuse of the public power entrusted to them. This would include embezzlement of funds, theft of corporate or public property as well as corrupt practices such as bribery, extortion or influence peddling.* (Transparency International [TI])

- *Corruption involves behavior on the part of officials in the public and private sectors, in which they improperly and unlawfully enrich themselves and/or those close to them, or induce others to do so, by misusing the position in which they are placed.* (World Bank)

Corruption comes in many forms, some petty and some grand. Though hugely lucrative to a few, corruption is incredibly damaging in terms of its effects on stakeholders and their countries. It corrodes the rule of law, the legitimacy of government, the sanctity of property rights, and incentives to invest and accumulate. Corruption also is a drag on a country's growth. In fact, corruption has become the biggest problem for developing economies.[76] A major problem, of course, is that those who benefit from corruption most will resist attempts to curb it, and often these are politicians who play decision-making roles.

Bribery is the primary form of corruption found in global business, and its practice merits closer examination. Simply speaking, bribery is the practice of offering something (usually money, but also other monetary benefits) in order to gain an illicit advantage. Bribes, of course, are illegal in most places and generally held to be unethical, but it is informative to consider the debate about bribery that has been ongoing. Some businesspeople continue to contend that bribery is necessary in some parts of the world, and some countries of the world continue to assert that they are culturally obligatory or defensible.

Debates about Bribery. Opinions typically given in favor of permitting bribery have included the following: (1) they are necessary for profits in order to do business; (2) everybody does it—it will happen anyway; (3) it is an accepted practice in many countries—it is normal and expected; and (4) bribes are forms of commissions, taxes, or compensation for conducting business between cultures.

Reasons frequently cited against giving bribes include the following: (1) bribes are inherently wrong and cannot be accepted under any circumstances; (2) bribes are illegal in the United States and most developed nations and, therefore, unfair elsewhere; (3) one should not compromise her or his own beliefs; (4) managers should not deal with corrupt governments; (5) such demands, once started, never stop; (6) one should take a stand for honesty, morality, and ethics; (7) those receiving bribes are the only ones who benefit; (8) bribes create dependence on corrupt individuals and countries; and (9) bribes deceive stockholders and pass on costs to customers.[77]

The costs of bribes and other forms of corruption are seldom fully understood or described. Several studies suggest the huge economic costs of such corrupt activities. The World Bank estimates that more than $1 trillion of bribes are paid worldwide each year. The World Economic Forum estimates that the cost from global graft is more than 5 percent of world domestic product and this probably underestimates it. In addition, bribes and corruption retard economic growth, especially in emerging economies.[78]

When government officials accept "speed" money or "grease payments" to issue licenses, the economic cost is 3 to 10 percent above the licensing fee. When tax collectors permit underreporting of income in exchange for a bribe, income tax revenues may be reduced by up to 50 percent. When government officials take kickbacks, goods and services may be priced 20 to 100 percent higher than they actually could have been. In addition to these direct economic costs, there are many indirect costs—demoralization and cynicism and moral revulsion against politicians and the political system. Due to bribery and corruption, politicians have been swept from office in many countries including Brazil, Italy, Japan, and Korea.[79]

The Foreign Corrupt Practices Act (FCPA). One of the first initiatives by a major government to address the problem of corruption and bribery in international business was the passage of the U.S. **Foreign Corrupt Practices Act (FCPA)** in 1977. Before this, many of the payments and bribes made by U.S.-based MNCs were not illegal. Even so, firms could have been engaging in illegal activities depending on whether and how the payments were reported to the Internal Revenue Service (IRS).

With the passage of the FCPA, however, it became a criminal offense for a representative of an American corporation to offer or give payments to the officials of other governments for the purpose of getting or maintaining business. The FCPA specifies a series of fines and prison terms that can result if a company or management is found guilty of a violation.[80] The legislation was passed not only for legal and ethical reasons but also out of a concern for the image and reputation of the United States abroad.

The FCPA differentiates between bribes and facilitating payments, also called **grease payments**. The law does not prohibit so-called grease payments, or minor, facilitating payments to officials, for the primary purpose of getting them to do whatever they are supposed to do anyway. Such payments are commonplace in many countries. The real problem with questionable payments is that some forms of payments are prohibited (e.g., bribes), but other payments (e.g., grease payments) are not prohibited. The law is sometimes ambiguous on the distinctions between the two.[81]

To violate the FCPA, payments (other than grease payments) must be made corruptly to obtain business. This suggests some kind of *quid pro quo*. The idea of a corrupt *quid pro quo* payment to a foreign official may seem clear in the abstract, but the circumstances of the payment may easily blur the distinction between what is acceptable "grease" (e.g., payments to expedite mail pickup or delivery, to obtain a work permit, border crossings, or to process paperwork) and what is illegal bribery. The safest strategy for managers to take is to be careful and to seek a legal opinion when questions arise. It also is helpful for companies to have clear policies on such payments.

Figure 10-2 presents a basic distinction, with examples, between bribes (which are prohibited) and grease (or facilitating) payments (which are not prohibited) based on the FCPA.

The FCPA was intended to have and has had a significant impact on the way American and many developed country's firms do business globally. A number of firms that paid

FIGURE 10-2 Bribes Compared to Grease Payments

Definitions	Examples
Grease Payments	
Relatively small sums of money given for the purpose of getting minor officials to: • Do what they are supposed to be doing • Do what they are supposed to be doing faster or sooner • Do what they are supposed to be doing better than they would otherwise do	Money given to minor officials (clerks, attendants, or customs inspectors) for the purpose of expediting. This form of payment helps get goods or services through red tape or administrative bureaucracies.
Bribes	
Relatively large amounts of money given for the purpose of influencing officials to make decisions or take actions that they otherwise might not take. If the officials considered the merits of the situation only, they might take some other action.	Money given, often to high-ranking officials. Purpose is often to get these people to purchase goods or services from the bribing firm. May also be used to avoid taxes, forestall unfavorable government intervention, secure favorable treatment, and so on.

bribes to foreign officials have been the subject of criminal and civil enforcement actions, resulting in large fines and, sometimes, suspension and debarment from federal procurement contracting. Sometimes their employees and officers have been imprisoned as well.[82] The Department of Justice (DoJ) has been cracking down on bribery at an accelerating pace in recent years. The DoJ's crackdown on corrupt practices has been broadened in that it is now attempting to catch both U.S. and foreign-based companies. Beginning in the late 1990s, the antibribery provisions of the FCPA now apply to foreign firms and persons doing business in the United States. Further, foreign companies whose securities are publicly traded in the United States now are also subject to the FCPA.[83]

The costs that companies have to pay when found guilty of FCPA violations can be staggering even for large corporations. In addition, these companies have to spend huge amounts defending themselves against charges. For example, as of 2015 Walmart had spent $800 million so far in defending itself against 2012 alleged bribery charges in Mexico. This sum is expected to settle down somewhere between $1 and $2 billion when all is completed. To this can be added whatever fines may be levied, bills for settling related private litigation, and the hard-to-calculate thousands of man-hours managers and employees have spent on what has turned out to be a huge distraction from conducting everyday business.[84]

In other cases, Siemens, the German industrial group, spent more than $3 billion on bribery-related fines and costs over an eight-year period. In addition, Avon, the American cosmetics firm, was caught bribing in China and it spent $350 million on a variety of legal and compliance fees.[85] A recent trend on the part of companies to reduce their costs has been to self-report bribery issues with the hope that the government might not punish them with larger fines. Some lawyers have said that self-disclosure can be a huge factor in settling cases faster and less costly.[86] It is no wonder that with this kind of approach to corruption, companies that have high incidences of corruption have been found to embark in other areas of social irresponsibility.[87]

Figure 10-3 summarizes some of the key features of the antibribery provisions of the FCPA.

FIGURE 10-3 Antibribery Provisions of the Foreign Corrupt Practices Act—Key Features

- In general, the FCPA prohibits American companies from making corrupt payments to foreign officials for the purpose of obtaining or keeping business.
- The Department of Justice is the chief enforcement agency, with a coordinate role played by the Securities and Exchange Commission (SEC).
- The FCPA's antibribery provisions extend to two types of behavior: making bribes (1) directly and (2) through intermediaries.
- The FCPA applies to any individual firm, officer, director, employee, or agent of the firm and any stockholder acting on behalf of the firm.
- The person making or authorizing the payment must have a corrupt intent, and the payment must be intended to induce the recipient to misuse his or her official position to direct business wrongfully to the payer or to any other person.
- The FCPA prohibits paying, offering, promising to pay, or authorizing to pay or offer money or anything of value.
- The prohibition extends only to corrupt payments to a foreign official, a foreign political party or party official, or any candidate for foreign political office, or anyone acting in an official capacity.
- The FCPA prohibits corrupt payments through intermediaries.
- An explicit exception is made to the bribery provisions for "facilitating payments" for "routine governmental action."
- The following criminal penalties may be imposed: firms are subject to a fine of up to $2 million; officers, directors, stockholders, employees, and agents are subject to a fine of up to $100,000 and imprisonment for up to five years. Fines imposed on individuals may not be paid by the firm.

Source: "Foreign Corrupt Practices Act Antibribery Provisions," U.S. Department of Justice, http://www.osec.doc.gov/ogc/occic/fcparev.html. Accessed April 18, 2016.

The Growing Anticorruption Movement. Corruption and bribery in global business is a significant and ongoing topic. With substantial increases in global trade and competition, free markets, and democracy over the past decade, this comes as no surprise.[88] Several powerful developments are worthy of mention. Each has contributed to what has been called a growing **anticorruption movement**. By all accounts, the fight against corruption has been a long and continuing march but progress is being made.[89]

The following programs and initiatives constitute the major players in the anticorruption movement: Transparency International, OECD Antibribery Initiatives, UN Convention against Corruption, and individual country initiatives.

Transparency International An innovative special-interest group—**Transparency International (TI)**—was modeled after the human rights group Amnesty International. TI has established itself as the world's foremost anticorruption organization. TI states its vision in the following way: *Our Vision: A world in which government, politics, business, civil society and the daily lives of people are free from corruption."*[90]

TI maintains over 100 national chapters run by local activists.[91] TI has established two simple principles for businesses striving to root out corruption:

- The enterprise shall prohibit bribery in any form, whether direct or indirect.
- The enterprise shall commit to implementing a program to counter bribery.

According to TI, "These Business Principles are based on a Board commitment to fundamental values of integrity, transparency and accountability. Enterprises should aim to create and maintain a trust-based and inclusive internal culture in which bribery is not tolerated."[92]

There are two primary tools that TI uses to combat corruption worldwide—its Corruption Perception Index and its Bribe Payers Index.

Corruption Perception Index (CPI). One of the most important tools TI uses to combat corruption is its now-famous annual **Corruption Perception Index (CPI)**. The annual CPI has been widely credited with putting TI and the issue of corruption on the international policy agenda. The CPI ranks more than 175 countries by their perceived levels of corruption, as determined by expert assessments and opinion surveys. The result of the ranking is a list of countries in the world ranging from "highly clean" (least corrupt) to "highly corrupt."[93]

In TI's 2015 rankings, the most recent available, the "highly clean" countries included Denmark, Finland, Sweden, and New Zealand. The most "highly corrupt" countries included Somalia, Afghanistan, and North Korea. The United States was ranked 16th from the top. TI makes the point that in spite of excellent records, no country is exempt from corruption. They have reported that many "clean" countries have dodgy records overseas.[94]

Bribe Payers Index (BPI). In addition to the CPI, TI also publishes what it calls the **Bribe Payers Index (BPI)**. The BPI ranks leading exporting countries in terms of the degree to which international companies with their headquarters in those countries are likely to pay bribes to senior public officials in key emerging market economies. In that sense, the BPI measures the supply side of bribery in the countries where the bribes are paid. Countries are ranked on a mean score from the answers given by respondents to the following statement: "In the business sectors with which you are most familiar, please indicate how likely companies from the following countries are to pay or offer bribes to win or retain business in this country."[95]

Among the major exporting countries of the world, the countries that are perceived to pay more bribes include Russia, China, Mexico, Indonesia, United Arab Emirates, and

Argentina.[96] The countries least likely to pay bribes include Netherlands, Switzerland, Belgium, and Germany. The United States ranked tenth from the top in a list of 28 exporting countries studied.[97] It should be pointed out that Transparency International does not conduct its BPI as often as it does its CPI so the rankings are only approximate. Transparency International hopes and expect that public exposure to its corruption ratings will bring pressure to bear on countries and companies to become less corrupt.

OECD Antibribery Initiatives Another major ongoing program in the anticorruption movement is an antibribery treaty and initiative that the 29 industrialized nations of the Organization for Economic Cooperation and Development (OECD) and five other countries agreed to in late 1997. By 2016, 34 OECD member countries and seven non-member countries were subscribed to the OECD Antibribery Convention.[98] The OECD member nations agreed to ban international bribery and to ask each member nation to introduce laws patterned after the U.S. FCPA in its country. The main thrust of the treaty was to criminalize offering bribes to foreign officials who have sway over everything from government procurement contracts and infrastructure projects to privatization tenders.

In spite of good intentions, the OECD has been criticized for not doing enough quickly enough. It has also been criticized for dramatically failing to live up to its own governance and anti-sleaze standards. The broader criticism is that the OECD antibribery signatories have failed to follow through on their plans. Implementation and execution, often problems in effective management, have been serious issues for the OECD initiatives. According to one critic's report, only four of the OECD nations are major enforcers of their laws and only six are moderate enforcers.[99]

It may be some years to come before the OECD Antibribery Convention is fully implemented. However, the OECD represents a noteworthy initiative by a number of major countries in the global battle to eliminate corruption from commercial transactions.

UN Convention against Corruption (UNCAC) Another major initiative to combat corruption around the world is the **UN Convention against Corruption (UNCAC)**, which was implemented in December 2005.[100] It created the opportunity to develop a global language about corruption and a coherent implementation strategy. A multitude of international anticorruption agreements already exist; however, their implementation has been uneven and only moderately successful. The UNCAC gives the global community the opportunity to address both of these weaknesses and begin establishing an effective set of benchmarks for effective anticorruption strategies.[101]

From a business perspective, UNCAC claims to hold the potential to become the global framework for combating corruption, which will pave the way for the establishment of a level playing field for all market participants. A central objective of UNCAC is to bring a higher degree of uniformity in the formulation and application of anticorruption rules across the world. For companies doing business in multiple jurisdictions, this agreement aspires to improve legal certainty and facilitate their global compliance efforts, thereby allowing them to fully compete in open markets without being exposed to extortion or unfair practices by their competitors.[102] UNCAC builds on the UN Global Compact, which presents ten principles of conduct in the areas of human rights, labor standards, and environment. The most recent principle of the Global Compact states that "Businesses should work against corruption in all its forms, including extortion and bribery."[103] To date, 140 countries have become signatories to UNCAC.[104]

Individual Country Initiatives In addition to the antibribery initiatives discussed, some individual countries have begun antibribery campaigns on their own. Great Britain has its Bribery Act, and France has its Paris-based Financial Action Task Force that monitors member states for their effectiveness in implementing anti-money-laundering

ETHICS IN PRACTICE CASE

Violations of the Foreign Corrupt Practices Act or Not?

Following are some hypothetical situations that involve payments while doing international business. Do these represent bribes, which are illegal under the Foreign Corrupt Practices Act (FCPA) or are they "grease payments" intended to facilitate work getting done?

Situation 1

Healthy Forever, an infant formula manufacturer, has a subsidiary in Korea. The subsidiary makes payments to health-care professionals to get them to recommend Healthy Forever's products to new and expectant mothers.

Has a violation of the FCPA occurred in this situation?

Situation 2

QualityCom, a Phoenix-based technology company, hired several relatives of Chinese officials who were deciding whether to select the company's products.

Has a violation of the FCPA occurred in this situation?

Situation 3

Dynamic Products Co. (DP) of Atlanta, Georgia, is attending a trade show in Beijing, China, because it wants to penetrate the Asian market. While at the trade show, a DP manager takes some prospective customers out for dinner and drinks and picks up the tab. The customers were mid-level managers at several different companies that were regulated by the government of China.

Have violations of the FCPA occurred in this situation?

Situation 4

While at the trade show in Beijing, Dynamic Products Co. decides it wants to invite some executives from one of China's state-owned utilities to the United States to engage in talks about a lucrative contract with the utility on which it plans to make a bid. DP desperately wants the contract and offers to fly the officials and their wives first class to the United States and put them up at Augusta, Georgia's nicest hotel for a week and offers them tickets to The Master's, one of the premier golf events in the world. On the final day of their visit, DP organizes a meeting at which they discuss the possible contract.

Have violations of the FCPA occurred in this situation?

Situation 5

Big Mining Corp. (BMC), a major company listed on the New York Stock Exchange, recently discovered a quartz deposit in Kuwait. To get access to the deposit, BMC needs to construct a road from the deposit site to the nearest port. BMC hires an agent to help it get this job done, especially the securing of the required permits and documents from government officials. The agent informed BMC that he will need to make a small cash payment to an administrative clerk in Kuwait so that he will process the permit application speedily. In their previous experiences, BMC learned that permit approvals such as this could take months to get approved. BMC's director of projects is anxious to get the road permit approved, so she gives the agent permission to make the payment to the clerk.

Is this payment a violation of the FCPA?

Sources: U.S. Securities & Exchange Commission, "Spotlight on Foreign Corrupt Practices Act," http://www.sec.gov/spotlight/fcpa.shtml. Accessed April 20, 2016; "Is it a Bribe…or Not?" *The Wall Street Journal*, July 22, 2013, R3; U.S. Department of Justice, "Foreign Corrupt Practices Act," https://www.justice.gov/criminal-fraud/foreign-corrupt-practices-act. Accessed April 20, 2016; *The FCPA Blog*, http://www.fcpablog.com/blog/2016/2/19/heres-our-new-top-ten-list-with-vimpelcom-landing-sixth.html. Accessed April 20, 2016.

laws.[105] Interestingly, many other countries that have begun antibribery campaigns are those that typically do not score very highly on business ethics surveys, for example, Mexico and China. Perhaps they were motivated by Transparency International's rankings of them.

Mexico has dabbled in its anticorruption fight though it continues to say it is trying. After three years in office, Mexican President Enrique Pena Nieto has not yet fulfilled his campaign promises to fight corruption. Apparently, Mexico's Congress has also been dragging its feet on important legislation. Mexico was hurt badly in real estate scandals in 2014. In 2015 its Congress passed important constitutional changes to create a new anticorruption task force, an independent prosecutor, and specialized courts, but in 2016 the enabling legislation was stalled in the legislature.[106]

On a positive note, in early 2016 a group of college students began collecting signatures to support an anticorruption bill that could be the first legal initiative proposed directly by the people. Though the initiative seems to indicate growing power of civil society in Mexico in responding to disillusionment with the country's politicians, many citizens are skeptical that such a bill would make a difference if passed.[107]

China is another country that seems to be working to eliminate graft. In its broadest crackdown launched in late 2012, the government of President Xi Jinping has been campaigning against corruption and has even appointed one of its most savvy and efficient senior leaders to be its top enforcer. President Xi is focusing on the culture of bribery and kickbacks among the country's political and corporate elites and more than 70,000 officials were reported to have been punished in one year for violating anticorruption rules.[108] In 2016, Xi Jinping was still aggressively trying to root out corruption.

Regardless of what various countries do, the best way to deal with bribes is to stem the practice before it starts. A major paradox is that the very people who often benefit from illicit payments—the politicians—are the ones who must pass the laws and set the standards against bribes and corruption in the first place. Another factor is that bribes and corruption, whenever possible, need to be exposed. Public exposure, more than anything else, has the potential to bring questionable payments under control. This means that practices and channels of accountability need to be made public.[109]

Transparency International's CPI and BPI are especially valuable in making the issue public. Beyond these steps, managers need to understand that corruption and bribery are not in their best interests. Not only do bribes debase the economic system, but they corrupt business relationships as well and cause business decisions to be made on the basis of factors that ultimately destroy all the institutions involved. The OECD treaty and individual country efforts suggest that many countries now understand this important point. Their efforts will not totally eliminate bribery, but they do represent a significant step toward reducing bribery and bringing it under control.

We have by no means covered all the areas in which ethical problems reside in the global business environment. The topics treated have been major ones subjected to extensive public discussion. Examples of other issues that have become important and will probably increase in importance include the issues of international competitiveness, protectionism, industrial policy, political risk analysis, outsourcing, and antiterrorism.

Also vital will be the dangers of developed countries importing dangerous products from some of the less-developed ones. These issues are of paramount significance in discussions of business's relations with international stakeholders. Other issues that include an ethical dimension are national security versus profit interests, dealing with rogue nations, the use of internal transfer prices to evade high taxes in a country, mining of the ocean floor, stealing intellectual property, offshoring, and harboring of terrorists. Space does not permit us to discuss these issues in detail.

10.3 Improving Global Business Ethics

It is clear from the discussion up to this point that business ethics is much more complex at the global level than at the domestic level. The complexity arises from the fact that a wide variety of value systems, stakeholders, cultures, forms of government, socioeconomic conditions, and standards of ethical behavior exist throughout the world. Recognition of diverse standards of ethical behavior is important, but if we assume that firms from developed countries should operate in closer accordance with developed countries' ethical standards than with those of developing countries, the strategy of ethical leadership in the world will indeed be a challenging one.

Because the United States and European multinationals have played such a leadership role in world affairs—usually espousing fairness and human rights—these firms have a heavy responsibility, particularly in underdeveloped countries and developing nations.

The power–responsibility equation and the Iron Law of Responsibility (Chapter 1) suggest that these firms have a serious ethical responsibility in global markets. That is, the larger sense of ethical behavior and social responsibility derives from the enormous amount of power these countries have.

In the following section, we will first discuss the challenge of honoring and balancing the ethical traditions of a business's home country with those of its host country. Next, we will discuss four recommended strategies for conducting business in foreign environments.[110] We will conclude by taking a look at some other steps companies are taking to improve their global ethics.

10.3a Balancing and Reconciling the Ethics Traditions of Home and Host Countries

One of the greatest challenges that businesses face while operating globally is achieving some kind of reconciliation and balance in honoring both the cultural and moral standards of their home and host countries. Should a business adhere to its home country's ethical standards for business practices or to the host country's ethical standards? There is no simple answer to this question. The diagram presented in Figure 10-4 frames the extreme decision choices businesses face when they consider operating globally. At one extreme, firms may engage in ethical imperialism by adhering to their home country's

FIGURE 10-4 Ethical Choices in Home versus Host Country Situations

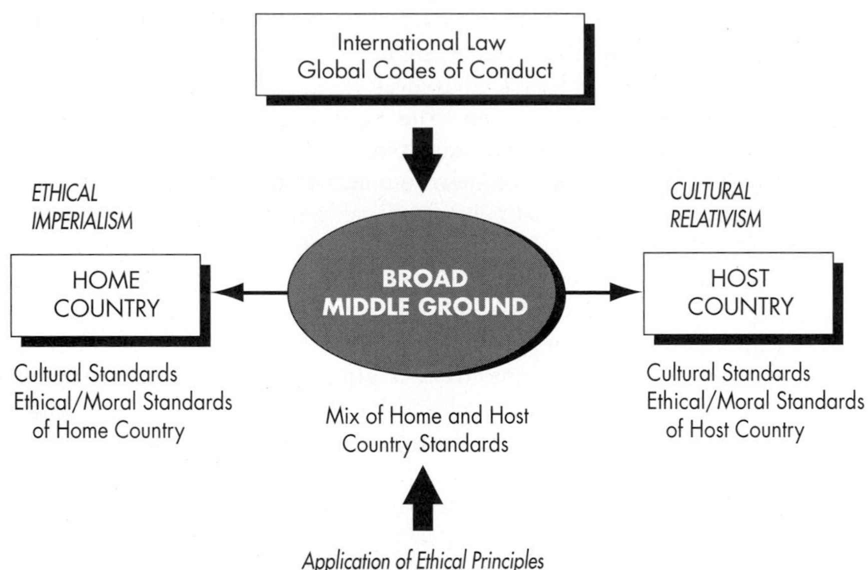

standards. At the other extreme, they may engage in cultural relativism by adapting to the host country's standards. These extreme alternatives deserve further discussion.

Ethical Imperialism. At one extreme in Figure 10-4 is a position often called **ethical imperialism**. This position holds that the business firm should continue to follow its home country's ethical standards even while operating in another country. Because U.S. and Western standards for treating employees, consumers, and the natural environment are quite high relative to the standards in many developing countries, it is easy to see how managers might find this posture appealing.

As reliance on foreign factories has soared in recent years and harsh conditions have been documented by the media, an increasing number of companies, such as Levi Strauss, Nordstrom, Inc., Wal-Mart, and Reebok, have espoused higher standards for foreign factories that cover issues such as wages, safety, and workers' rights to organize. Such higher standards could be seen by other countries, however, as the United States and the Western world attempting to impose its standards on the host country—thus the name "ethical imperialism" resides at one end of the continuum. Fortunately, the business world seems to be moving in the direction of eliminating corruption and operating according to higher ethical standards.

Cultural Relativism. At the other extreme in Figure 10-4 is a position often called **cultural relativism**. This position is characterized by foreign direct investors such as MNCs following the host country's ethical standards. This is the posture reflected in the well-known saying "When in Rome, do as the Romans do." This position would maintain that the investing firm should set aside its home country's ethical standards and adopt the ethical standards of the host country. For example, if Saudi Arabia holds that it is illegal to hire women for most managerial positions, the investing MNC would accept and adopt this standard, even if it runs counter to its home country's standards. Or if the host country has no environmental protection laws, this position would argue that the multinational need not be sensitive to environmental standards.

It has been argued that cultural relativism holds that no culture's ethics are better than any other's and that there are, therefore, no international rights or wrongs. If Thailand tolerates the bribery of government officials, then Thai tolerance is no worse than Japanese or German intolerance. If Switzerland does not find insider trading morally repugnant, then Swiss liberality is no worse than American restrictiveness.[111] Most ethicists find cultural relativism to be a case of moral or ethical relativism and, therefore, an unacceptable posture for companies to take.

Presented in Figure 10-4 is a series of questions management needs to ask to help determine its stance on home versus host country ethics. Depending on the issue (e.g., worker safety versus minimum pay), companies may be more inclined to follow their home country's ethics. Key questions that must be posed and answered include the following: Which ethical standards will be used? Which ethical standards will transcend national boundaries? What constitutes moral minimums with respect to each category of ethical issue?

It may sound like a simplistic solution to say that the MNC needs to operate in some broad middle ground where a mix of home and host country ethical standards may be used. The challenge for managers will be to determine what mix of ethical standards should be used and how this decision should be made. As mentioned earlier, managers will need to ask themselves which moral standards are applicable in the situations they face. Which ethical standards best protect stakeholders and their rights?

Use of ethical principles such as those articulated in the previous chapters—rights, justice, utilitarianism, and the Golden Rule—still apply. Managers will need to decide which ethical standards should transcend national boundaries and thus represent **hypernorms** (transcultural values).[112] Hypernorms can be thought of as standards that are so basic that they are universally accepted. Examples might be health, safety, and freedom—but some cultures would not accept these examples. Donaldson and Dunfee have argued that for hypernorms to be established to help guide global business ethics, certain evidences are needed to confirm their legitimacy. For example, they maintain that hypernorms are more justified or confirmed when they meet some of the following conditions:

- widespread consensus that the principle is universal;
- a component of well-known global industry standards;
- supported by prominent NGOs;
- supported by regional governmental organizations such as the European Community, the OECD or the Organization of American States;
- supported by global business organizations such as the Caux Round Table and the International Chamber of Commerce.[113]

When it is not possible to identify hypernorms that may guide ethical practices, the safest course of action would be to operate based upon the higher of home versus host ethical standards though this is not always easy to determine especially when a host country invokes a standard as being part of its culture. The home and host country's stage of maturity on economic development and culture are also important factors that must be considered.[114]

Managers also need to decide what will represent their **moral minimums** with respect to these and other issues. It would be nice to think that international laws and global codes of conduct will make these decisions easier. Though several such sets of codes and principles are available, they may be challenging to apply. In the interim, managers will need to be guided by the ethical concepts at their disposal, possibly with help from some of the strategies to which we now turn.

10.3b Strategies for Improving Global Business Ethics

In many instances, major companies work to improve their global business ethics through their global social responsibility programs. Often, however, additional strategies must be used when operating globally. Four major strategies or categories of action that could help MNCs conduct global business while maintaining an ethical sensitivity in their practices include the following and each deserves some explanation:

1. global codes of conduct,
2. linking ethics with global strategy,
3. suspension of business activities in certain countries, and
4. ethical impact statements and audits.[115]

(1) Global Codes of Conduct. Global codes of conduct seek to establish universal principles or guidelines that should be followed while doing business around the world. These would be closely related to the hypernorms discussed in the previous section. There are two types of global codes of conduct of interest here. First, there are specific corporate global codes that individual companies have developed. Second, there are global codes or guidelines that have been developed by various international organizations. Each of these deserves some consideration.

Corporate Global Codes In Chapter 8, we discussed codes of conduct, and that discussion applies in the global sphere as well. While operating on the world stage, MNCs have been severely criticized for employing divergent ethical standards in different countries, thus giving the impression that they are attempting to exploit local circumstances. A growing number of MNCs, for example, Chiquita Brands International, Caterpillar Tractor, Allis Chalmers, Coca-Cola, Johnson's Wax, Medtronic, and others, have developed and used codes geared toward worldwide operations.

One of the first and most well-known of the corporate global codes is that of Caterpillar Tractor Company. It is now titled "Our Values in Action: Caterpillar's Worldwide Code of Conduct."[116] Caterpillar has been building work machines that have been used the world over for over 80 years. The company asserts that its code sets a high standard for honesty and ethical behavior for every employee. The code goes into considerable detail and has major sections that cover the following important values that Caterpillar aspires toward: integrity, excellence, teamwork, and commitment. In addition, on its Web site, its code of conduct is presented as downloads in 18 different languages.[117]

Other companies have specific categories of ethical issues in their codes of conduct in which they address global considerations. For example, Chiquita Banana's Code of Conduct says the following regarding *bribery and corruption:* "Chiquita policy prohibits employees from using improper, unethical, or questionable business practices while conducting business on its behalf. We abide by all international laws, treaties and regulations that forbid bribery of foreign officials, including the U.S. Foreign Corrupt Practices Act."[118]

The GBS Codex Four researchers have published what they have called a Global Business Standards (GBS) Codex.[119] The **GBS Codex** was not intended to be a model code of conduct for global business, but a *benchmark* for companies wanting to develop their own world-class code. The researchers studied 5 well-known global codes put together by international organizations and 14 codes of the world's largest companies and extracted the underlying ethical principles they felt the different codes had in common.

The researchers found eight principles, representing worldwide ethical standards that they thought were basic to the codes studied. The eight principles identified and described standards of conduct in the following categories: *fiduciary, property, reliability, transparency, dignity, fairness, citizenship*, and *responsiveness*.[120] The researchers argued that companies that wanted to assess their current codes of conduct or to create new codes of conduct would find their eight principles useful as a standard by which comparisons could be made.

Company designed codes of conduct are usually just the starting point for companies in dealing with global business ethics. The acid test is whether these codes become living documents that the companies actually use on a daily basis. Beyond this, most companies will need to further develop their global ethics programs if they are to be successful.

Global Codes Created by International Organizations In addition to individual corporate codes, global codes or standards have been developed by a number of international organizations that anticipate companies will adopt and follow. Some of these codes focus on one specific issue; many provide standards across a number of issue areas. Two of the most recent global codes have been developed by the International Standards Organization (ISO), an independent NGO with a membership of 161 national standards bodies, with its headquarters in Geneva, Switzerland.

In 2010, the ISO activated **ISO 26000–Social Responsibility**. ISO 26000 provides guidance on how businesses and organizations can operate in a socially responsible way. This encompasses acting in an ethical and transparent way that contributes to the health and welfare of society.[121] The standard was launched after five years of work by many different stakeholders including governments, NGOs, industry, consumer groups, and labor organizations. The core subjects and issues addressed in ISO 26000 included human rights, labor practices, the environment, fair operating practices, consumer issues, and community involvement.[122]

In 2016, ILO was preparing to launch **ISO 37001 - Anti-Bribery Management Systems**, a new standard designed to specifically address bribery and corruption. In addition to addressing bribery and corruption, the new standard was designed to help companies instill a culture of honesty, transparency, and integrity. The draft version of the new standard received 91 percent support and endorsement from the ISO members involved in its creation. ISO 37001 proposes a series of measures to help organizations prevent, detect, and address bribery. The steps include adopting an antibribery policy, appointing a person to oversee compliance, training, risk assessments, and due diligence.[123]

Figure 10-5 summarizes brief information about some of the more prominent of the global codes and principles that have been created by international organizations. Among them are the UN Global Compact, Caux Round Table Principles, Global Sullivan Principles, OECD Guidelines for Multinational Enterprises, Global Reporting Initiatives, and ILO standards.

Two of the most widely used global standards are the **UN Global Compact** and the **Caux Round Table Principles.** In 2015, the UN Global Compact took another important step by issuing its Sustainable Development Goals that lay out a 15-year path to

FIGURE 10-5 Global Ethics Codes and Standards Developed by International Organizations

Codes, Standards, or Guidelines	Brief Description and Web Site
UN Global Compact	The Global Compact's operational phase was launched at UN headquarters in New York on July 26, 2000. Today, thousands of companies from all regions of the world and international labor and civil society organizations are engaged in the Global Compact, working to advance ten universal principles in the areas of human rights, labor, the environment, and anticorruption. http://www.unglobalcompact.org/. Accessed April 18, 2016.
Caux Round Table Principles for Business	The CRT Principles for Business are a worldwide vision for ethical and responsible corporate behavior and serve as a foundation for action for business leaders worldwide. As a statement of aspirations. The CRT Principles aim to express a world standard against which business behavior can be measured. http://www.cauxroundtable.org/index.cfm?menuid=8. Accessed April 18, 2016.
Global Sullivan Principles of Social Responsibility	The objectives of the Global Sullivan Principles are to support economic, social, and political justice by companies where they do business; to support human rights and to encourage equal opportunity at all levels of employment, including racial and gender diversity on decision-making committees and boards; and to train and advance disadvantaged workers for technical, supervisory, and management opportunities. https://www1.umn.edu/humanrts/links/sullivanprinciples.html. Accessed April 18, 2016.
OECD Guidelines for Multinational Enterprises	The guidelines are recommendations addressed by governments to multinational enterprises operating in or from adhering countries. They provide voluntary principles and standards for responsible business conduct in a variety of areas including employment and industrial relations, human rights, environment, information disclosure, combating bribery, consumer interests, science and technology, competition, and taxation. http://www.oecd.org/daf/inv/mne/48004323.pdf. Accessed April 18, 2016.
Global Reporting Initiative Guidelines	GRI's guidelines have been updated over the years. They address three major categories of reporting: Human Rights and Reporting, Reporting on Community Impacts, and Gender Reporting. https://www.globalreporting.org/Pages/default.aspx. Accessed April 18, 2016.
ISO Standards	ISO 26000 addresses Social Responsibility and ISO 37001 addresses corruption and bribery. ISO 26000 was launched in 2010 and ISO 37001 was set to launch late in 2016. http://www.iso.org/iso/iso26000, http://www.iso.org/iso/home/news_index/news_archive/news.htm?refid=Ref2069. Accessed April 18, 2016.

FIGURE 10-6 UN Global Compact and Caux Round Table Principles

UN Global Compact	Caux Round Table Principles
Human Rights Businesses should • Principle 1: support and respect the protection of internationally proclaimed human rights. • Principle 2: make sure that they are not complicit in human rights abuses. **Labor Standards** Businesses should uphold • Principle 3: the freedom of association and the effective recognition of the right to collective bargaining. • Principle 4: the elimination of all forms of forced and compulsory labor. • Principle 5: the effective abolition of child labor. • Principle 6: the elimination of discrimination in respect of employment and occupation. **Environment** Businesses should • Principle 7: support a precautionary approach to environmental challenges. • Principle 8: undertake initiatives to promote greater environmental responsibility. • Principle 9: encourage the development and diffusion of environmentally friendly technologies. **Anticorruption** Businesses should • Principle 10: work against corruption in all its forms, including extortion and bribery.	1. Respect Stakeholders beyond Shareholders 2. Contribute to Economic, Social, and Environmental Development 3. Respect the Letter and the Spirit of the Law 4. Respect Rules and Conventions 5. Support Responsible Globalization 6. Respect the Environment 7. Avoid Illicit Activities

Source: UN Global Compact, "The Ten Principles," http://www.unglobalcompact.org/AboutTheGC/TheTenPrinciples/index.html. Accessed April 18, 2016; Caux Round Table, "Principles for Responsible Businesses," http://www.cauxroundtable.org/index.cfm?menuid=8. Accessed April 18, 2016.

end extreme poverty, fight injustice and inequality, and protect the planet. The 17 Sustainable Development Goals (Agenda 2030) are intended to address the most important economic, social, environmental, and governance challenges of our time.[124] The Caux Round Table Principles were launched over 20 years ago and are seen as the precursor to the UN Global Compact that was developed soon after.[125]

Figure 10-6 summarizes the major specific principles in each.

(2) Ethics and Global Strategy. The major recommendation regarding ethics and global strategy is that the ethical dimensions of multinational corporate activity should be considered as significant inputs into top-level strategy formulation and implementation.[126] At the top level of decision making in the firm, corporate strategy is established. At this level, commitments are made that will define the underlying character and identity of the organization. The overall moral tone of the organization and all decision making and behaviors are set at the strategic level, and management needs to ensure that social and ethical factors do not get lost in the preoccupation with market opportunities and competitive factors.

A more proactive stance is needed for dealing with ethical issues at the global level. Strategic decisions that may be influenced by ethical considerations in the global sphere include, but are not limited to, product/service decisions, plant location, operations policy, supply chain, marketing policy and practices, and human resource management policies. More and more companies are employing departments and strategies with respect to global corporate social responsibility and global business citizenship.[127] Two companies illustrate how ethical considerations may be factored into global business decisions: Levi Strauss & Co. and Starbucks.

Levi Strauss & Co. A valuable illustration of ethics being factored into strategic decision making is provided by Levi Strauss & Co. Because the company operates in many countries and diverse cultures, it believes that it must take special care in selecting its contractors and the countries where its goods are produced in order to ensure that its products are being made in a manner consistent with its values and reputation. Years ago, the company developed a set of *global sourcing guidelines* that established standards its contractors must meet.[128]

More recently, Levi Strauss took the unprecedented action of publishing on its Web site a list of all active owned-and-operated and contract factories producing the company's branded products. The company's senior vice president for Global Sourcing said, "We believe that greater transparency within the supply chain will provide additional momentum for our efforts to improve working conditions in apparel factories worldwide. Our hope is that this level of transparency will become standard across the apparel sector, fostering greater collaboration among brands in shared factories."[129] Levi Strauss & Co.'s *Sustainability Guidebook* discusses the company's core values that it employs as it strives to be socially and ethically responsible in its global operations.[130]

Starbucks Another example of a company integrating ethical concerns into its corporate strategies is that of Starbucks Coffee Co., the Seattle-based firm. In an innovative pilot program initiated over a decade ago, Starbucks began paying a premium above market price for coffee, with the bonus going to improve the lives of coffee workers. The initial payments were made to farms and mills in Guatemala and Costa Rica, which co-funded health-care centers, farm schools, and scholarships for farm workers' children. Starbucks's incentive program was part of a larger "Framework for Action," its plan for implementing its code of conduct.[131] Starbucks began purchasing Fair Trade Certified coffee in 2000. The company has been recognized for helping grow the market for Fair Trade Certified coffee in the United States and bringing it to consumers. By 2012, the company had reached the 93 percent level of ethical sourcing (responsible purchasing practices, farmer loans, and forest conservation). Starbucks states that it is committed to 100 percent ethical sourcing in its relationships with farmers. The company has created what it calls Coffee and Farmer Equity (C.A.F.E.) Practices, which is one of the coffee industry's first set of sustainability standards verified by third-party experts. C.A.F.E. Practices include guidelines in four areas—product quality, economic accountability and transparency, social responsibility, and environmental leadership.[132]

(3) Suspension of Activities. A multinational enterprise may sometimes encounter unbridgeable gaps between the ethical values of its home country and those of its host country. When this occurs, and reconciliation does not appear to be in sight, the responsible company might consider suspending activities in the host country. For example, years ago IBM and Coca-Cola established a precedent for this activity by suspending their activities in India because of that country's position on the extent of national ownership and control.[133] In a fight against corruption, Procter & Gamble even closed a Pampers diaper plant in Nigeria rather than pay bribes to customs inspectors.[134]

In 2010, Google decided to move its search engine out of China because it no longer thought it to be appropriate to censor searches at the request of the Chinese government. Google is credited with a clever, strategic decision by moving its search engine to Hong Kong, which is a special administrative region that has broader free-speech protections. This decision allowed Google to adhere to its own privacy principles while also allowing the Chinese government to save face.[135] By 2016, however, Google was planning to return to China while thinking of ways it could live with local laws and yet still provide some services.[136] Other technology companies such as Twitter and Facebook have also faced challenges working in repressive regimes and they are seeking balances between their standards and those of their host countries that will allow them to expand their markets.

Suspension of business in a foreign country is not a decision that can or should be taken too hastily, but it must be regarded as a viable option for those firms that desire to travel on the higher moral road of free trade. Each country is at liberty to have its own standards, but this does not mean that other country's firms must do business in that country. What does ethical leadership mean if it is not backed up by a willingness to take a moral stand when the occasion merits?

(4) Ethical Impact Statements and Audits. MNCs need to be constantly aware of the impacts they are having on society, particularly foreign societies. One way to do this is to periodically assess the company's impacts. Companies have a variety of impacts on foreign cultures, and ethical impacts represent only a few of these. The impact statement idea derived, in part, from the practice of environmental impact statements pioneered years ago. **Ethical impact statements** are an attempt to assess the underlying moral justifications for corporate actions and the consequent results of those actions. The information derived from these actions would permit the MNCs to modify or change their business practices if the impact statement suggested that such changes would be necessary or desirable.

One form of ethical impact assessment is some firms' attempts to monitor their compliance with their companies' global ethics codes. For example, Mattel Toy Company developed an independent audit and monitoring system for its code. Mattel's monitoring program was headed by an independent panel of commissioners who selected a percentage of the company's manufacturing facilities for annual audits. In one audit, for example, Mattel terminated its relationship with three contractor facilities for refusing to meet company-mandated safety procedures.[137] Mattel claims to be continuing its auditing of compliance to its code of conduct through its Global Manufacturing Principles.[138]

A major problem with Mattel's and others' auditing processes of their operations is that maintaining them in the face of competitors who are not doing the same gets to be time consuming and expensive. In a major report examining Mattel's experience, a group of researchers concluded that the company's efforts began to fade or decline once Mattel had reached its easy audit targets of auditing its company-owned plants. But then, when the company had to take on the gargantuan task of monitoring vendor's plants, a new set of challenges were presented and management no longer pursued the program as vigorously as it once did. The researchers concluded that Mattel's management did not see the advantage to their proactive stance when competitors were not following suit.[139] The Mattel example highlights the challenges involved in monitoring a company's social impact in international markets.

Many companies today are issuing sustainability audits and reports in which they attempt to report on their global activities. For the most part, however, these reports cover the positive impacts and do not carefully examine the questionable practices of the firm. The major challenge in global business today is monitoring supply chains. This is where unethical practices are likely to occur. And, though there are some violators, many companies today are doing a better job of monitoring their global operations and working environments. As consumers and the public are becoming better educated and aware of overseas operations, companies are sensing greater pressure to build more sustainable supply chains.[140]

10.3c Corporate Action against Corruption

An enlightening study conducted by the Conference Board disclosed some details on companies' anticorruption campaigns within their organizations. When asked what was the single most important factor in their company's decision to develop an anticorruption program, the most frequent responses were "senior management leadership and personal convictions," "bribe payments being illegal under their home country laws," the belief that "bribe payments are wrong," and the impact of "Sarbanes–Oxley Section 404."[141]

The report revealed that there were five vital steps among anticorruption programs that seemed to work best for companies[142]:

1. High-level commitment by top management
2. Detailed statements of policies and operating procedures
3. Training and discussion of policies and procedures
4. Hotlines and help lines for all organizational members
5. Investigative follow-up, reporting, and disclosure

These essential steps, which mirror ethics programs discussed in Chapter 8, when combined with the strategies for improving global business ethics discussed earlier, go a long way toward establishing a solid foundation for fighting bribery and corruption, the most insidious issues in global business ethics. The good news is that companies are now very much aware of these issues and most are moving to address them.

Summary

Ethical dilemmas pose difficulties, in general, for businesses, and those arising in connection with doing business in global markets are among the most complex. An examination of major issues that have arisen in global business ethics over the past several decades shows that they rank right up there with the most well-known news stories about business performance. The infant formula controversy, the Bhopal tragedy, factory fires and collapses in Bangladesh, corruption and bribery, concern about human rights and sweatshops, and the exploits of MNCs in Third World countries have all provided an opportunity for business critics to assail corporate ethics in the international sphere. These problems arise for a multiplicity of reasons, but differing cultures, value systems, forms of government, socioeconomic systems, and underhanded and ill-motivated business exploits have all been contributing factors.

Steps taken by the United States and other major countries to address the issues of corruption and bribery include the Foreign Corrupt Practices Act, the OECD Antibribery Convention, and the UN Convention against Corruption (UNCAC). Individual country initiatives also have been vital, as are the efforts of nonprofit organizations such as Transparency International. A number of different approaches to improving global business ethics were presented. The balancing of home and host country standards were discussed with the extreme options of ethical imperialism or cultural relativism presented and contrasted.

Four strategies for improving global business ethics were set forth: (1) global codes of conduct, encompassing corporate codes, the GBS Codex, and global codes created by international organizations; (2) the integration of ethical considerations into corporate strategy; (3) the suspension of activities in the host country; and (4) the use of ethical impact statements and audits. These strategies offer some hope that global business can be better managed. A major study by the Conference Board indicates that companies are taking important actions against corruption within their organizations. Five vital steps being taken against corruption were presented, and these were headed up by high-level commitment by top management.

In spite of the worldwide economic recession and questions being raised about the future of international business, current trends point to a growth in business activity in the transnational economy, and though there is some evidence of a backlash against globalization, these issues will become more rather than less important in the future. Indeed, it could easily be argued that business's greatest ethical challenges in the future will be on the global stage.

Key Terms

Alien Tort Claims Act (ATCA), p. 317
anticorruption movement, p. 322
Bhopal tragedy, p. 310
Bribe Payers Index (BPI), p. 322
bribery, p. 319
Caux Round Table Principles, p. 330
corruption, p. 318
Corruption Perception Index (CPI), p. 322
cultural relativism, p. 327
ethical impact statements, p. 333
ethical imperialism, p. 327
ethical supply chains, p. 316
Fair Labor Association (FLA), p. 314
Foreign Corrupt Practices Act (FCPA), p. 320
GBS Codex, p. 329
globalization, p. 305
grease payments, p. 320
hypernorms, p. 328
infant formula controversy, p. 309
internationalization, p. 305
institutional void, p. 318
ISO 26000–Social Responsibility, p. 329
ISO 37001 - Anti-Bribery Management Systems, p. 330
moral minimums, p. 328
multinational corporations (MNCs), p. 306
Multinational enterprises (MNEs), p. 306
Social Accountability International (SAI), p. 315
sweatshops, p. 314
transnational economy, p. 305
Transparency International (TI), p. 322
UN Convention against Corruption (UNCAC), p. 323
UN Global Compact, p. 330

Discussion Questions

1. Drawing on the notions of moral, amoral, and immoral management introduced in Chapter 7, categorize your impressions of (a) Nestlé, in the infant formula controversy; (b) Union Carbide, in the Bhopal tragedy; and (c) Google, in moving its search engine out of China. Why is Google planning to return to China?
2. As an MNC seeks to balance and honor the ethical standards of both the home and host countries, conflicts inevitably will arise. What criteria do you think managers should consider as they try to decide whether to use home or host country ethical standards? Does the use of hypernorms help? Explain.
3. Differentiate between a bribe and a grease payment. Give an example of each.
4. Conduct research, for purposes of updating the latest rankings of Transparency International and the activities of the OECD, UNCAC, and individual country initiatives. How could countries such as China, India, and Russia most effectively improve their TI rankings?
5. What are the major strategies companies might employ in improving global business ethics? What are the key steps research has shown are important to successful company anticorruption efforts?

Endnotes

1. "The Panama Papers in Perspective," *The Wall Street Journal*, April 5, 2016, A12.
2. Kim Hjelmgaard, "Panama Papers: Bookmaker Takes Bets on Next World Leader to Step Down," USA Today, April 7, 2016, 8A.
3. Peter F. Drucker, "The Transnational Economy," *The Wall Street Journal* (August 25, 1987), 38. See also Tammie S. Pinkston and Archie B. Carroll, "Corporate Citizenship Perspectives and Foreign Direct Investment in the U.S.," *Journal of Business Ethics* (Vol. 13, 1994), 157–169.
4. Paul Krugman, cited in Alan Farnham, "Global—Or Just Globaloney?" *Fortune* (June 27, 1994), 97–98.
5. William Mauldin, "Worries Rise over Global Trade Slump," *The Wall Street Journal*, September 14, 2015, http://www.wsj.com/articles/worries-rise-over-global-trade-slump-1442251590. Accessed April 6, 2016.
6. Rana Foroohar, "After Decades of Consensus, the Value of Global Free Trade Is Being Contested by the Left and the Right: What Every Voter Needs to Know," *Time*, April 11, 2016, 32–35.
7. Adrian Woolridge, "Made Everywhere and Nowhere," *The Wall Street Journal*, April 19, 2016, A11.
8. Chrystia Freeland, "Globalization Bites Back," The Atlantic, May 2015, 82.
9. Quoted in Freeland, ibid.
10. Ibid.
11. Richard Dobbs, James Manyika, and Jonathan Woetzel, *No Ordinary Disruption: The Four Forces Breaking All the Trends*, Public Affairs, 2015.
12. John Garland and Richard N. Farmer, *International Dimensions of Business Policy and Strategy*, 2d ed. (Boston: Kent Publishing Company, 1990), 166–173.
13. Ibid., 172.
14. Investopedia, "What Is a Multinational Corporation (MNC)?" http://www.investopedia.com/terms/m/multinationalcorporation.asp. Accessed April 6, 2016.
15. Andreas Scherer and Guido Palazzo, "The New Political Role for Business in a Globalized World: A Review of the New Perspective on CSR and Its Implications for the Firm, Governance, and Democracy," *Journal of Management Studies* 48:4 (2011), 899–931.
16. Ibid.
17. James E. Post, "Assessing the Nestlé Boycott: Corporate Accountability and Human Rights," *California Management Review* (Winter 1985), 115–116.
18. Ibid., 116–117.
19. Rogene A. Buchholz, William D. Evans, and Robert Q. Wagley, *Management Response to Public Issues* (Englewood Cliffs, NJ: Prentice Hall, 1985), 80.
20. Ibid., 81–82.
21. Oliver Williams, "Who Cast the First Stone?" *Harvard Business Review* (September–October, 1984), 155.
22. "Nestlé's Costly Accord," *Newsweek* (February 6, 1984), 52.
23. For further discussion, see S. Prakash Sethi, *Multinational Corporations and the Impact of Public Advocacy on Corporate Strategy: Nestlé and the Infant Formula Case* (Boston: Kluwer Academic, 1994).
24. Alix M. Freedman and Steve Stecklow, "As UNICEF Battles Baby-Formula Makers, African Infants Sicken," *The Wall Street Journal* (December 5, 2000).
25. The International Baby Food Action Network, http://www.ibfan.org/index.html. Accessed April 11, 2013.
26. Laurie Burkitt, "Infant Formula Issue Flares Anew in China," *The Wall Street Journal*, September 17, 2013, B4.
27. Alex Janin, "China Is Buying up Australia's Supply of Baby Formula," Takepart, http://www.takepart.com/article/2016/03/01/why-china-buying-up-australia-baby-formula. Accessed April 8, 2016.
28. Stuart Diamond, "The Disaster in Bhopal: Lessons for the Future," *The New York Times* (February 5, 1985), 1. See also Russell Mokhiber, "Bhopal," *Corporate Crime and Violence* (San Francisco: Sierra Club Books, 1988), 86–96.
29. Deepti Ramesh and Ian Young, "Tata Boss Proposes Cleanup of Bhopal Site; Survivors Protest," *Chemical Week* (January 17, 2007), 13.
30. IBT, "30 Years after the Bhopal Disaster, India Has Not Learned the Lessons of the World's Worst Industrial Tragedy, http://www.ibtimes.com/30-years-after-bhopal-disaster-india-has-not-learned-lessons-worlds-worst-industrial-1731816. Accessed April 29, 2016.
31. Stuart Diamond, "Disaster in India Sharpens Debate on Doing Business in Third World," *The New York Times* (December 16, 1984), 1.
32. Ibid.
33. Jim Carlton and Thaddeus Herrick, "Bhopal Haunts Dow Chemical," *The Wall Street Journal* (May 8, 2003), B3.
34. David Bogoslaw, "Dow Chem Face Holder Proposal on Bhopal Risk at Annual Meeting," *The Wall Street Journal* (May 13, 2004). Matt Kovac, "Dow Chemical: Shareholder Resolutions a Reality of Life," *ICIS Chemical Business Americas* (April 30–May 6, 2007), 10. Accessed August 16, 2007. "Dow Chemical: Liable for Bhopal?" *Businessweek* (June 9, 2008), 61–62.
35. "Gas Activists Plead Court to Summons Dow Officials," *The Times of India*, March 6, 2013, http://timesofindia.indiatimes.com/city/bhopal/Gas-activists-plead

-court-to-summon-Dow-officials/articleshow/18821423 .cms. Accessed April 11, 2013.

36. Paul M. Barrett, "The Ghosts of Bhopal," *Bloomberg Businessweek*, December 1–7, 2014, 12–13.
37. Miguel Bustillo, Tom Wright, and Shelly Banjo, "Tough Questions in Fire's Ashes," *The Wall Street Journal*, November 30, 2012, B1.
38. Syed Al-Mahmood, Tripti Lahiri, and Dana Mattioli, "Fire Warnings Went Unheard," *The Wall Street Journal*, December 11, 2012, B1.
39. Syed Zan Al-Mahmood, "Bangladesh Probe Calls Fatal Fire Act of Sabotage," *The Wall Street Journal*, December 18, 2012, B4.
40. Sushmita S. Preetha, "A Lesson on Lessons Not Learnt," The Daily Star, April 11, 2016, http://www .thedailystar.net/op-ed/politics/lesson-lessons-not -learnt-1207150. Accessed April 11, 2016.
41. Syed Zain Al-Mahmood and Shelly Banjo, "Deadly Collapse," *The Wall Street Journal*, April 25, 2013, A1.
42. Syed Zain Al-Mahmood and Tom Wright, "Collapsed Factory Was Built without Permit," *The Wall Street Journal*, April 26, 2013, A9.
43. Syed Zain Al-Mahmood, "Bangladeshi Police Charge 42 in Collapse of Factory Complex," *The Wall Street Journal*, June 2, 2015, B6.
44. Syed Zain Al-Mahmood, "Alliance to Help Bangladeshi Plants," *The Wall Street Journal*, December 8, 2014, B3.
45. Kevin McCoy, "Slave-Peeled Shrimp Exported to U.S. Stores," *USA Today*, December 15, 2015, 4B.
46. Ibid.
47. Syed Zain Al-Mahmood, Kathy Chu, and Tripti Lahiri, "After Fire, Pressure on Bangladesh," *The Wall Street Journal*, December 15–16, 2012, B1.
48. Christina Passariello and Suzanne Kapner, "Search for Cheaper Labor Leads to Africa," *The Wall Street Journal*, July 13, 2015, B1.
49. Mark Clifford, Michael Shari, and Linda Himelstein, "Pangs of Conscience: Sweatshops Haunt U.S. Consumers," *Businessweek* (July 29, 1996), 46–47. See also Keith B. Richburg and Anne Swardson, "Sweatshops or Economic Development?" *The Washington Post National Weekly Edition* (August 5–11, 1996), 19.
50. Ibid.
51. Mark Clifford, Michael Shari, and Linda Himelstein, "Pangs of Conscience: Sweatshops Haunt U.S. Consumers," *Businessweek* (July 29, 1996), 46–47.
52. Ibid.
53. Ronald Baily, "Sweatshops Forever," *Reason* (February 2004), 12–13.
54. Fair Labor Association, "Mission & Charter," http:// www.fairlabor.org/mission-charter. Accessed April 11, 2016.
55. Ibid.
56. Baily, Ibid.
57. Social Accountability International, "About SAI," http://www.sa-intl.org/index.cfm?fuseaction=Page .ViewPage&pageId=490. Accessed April 11, 2016.
58. SA8000 Standards. http://www.sa-intl.org/index.cfm? &pageid=937#childlabor. Accessed April 11, 2013.
59. Details maybe found at Social Accountability 8000, June 2014, http://sa-intl.org/_data/n_0001/resources /live/SA8000%20Standard%202014.pdf. Accessed April 11, 2016.
60. SA 8000, http://www.sa-intl.org/index.cfm?fuseaction=Page.ViewPage&pageId=472. Accessed April 11, 2016.,
61. Vivek Soundararajan and Jill Brown, "Voluntary Governance Mechanisms in Global Supply Chains: Beyond CSR to a Stakeholder Utility Perspective," *Journal of Business Ethics* (Vol. 134, No. 1, 2016), 83–102.
62. Tarun Wadhwa, "Using Technology to Create Safe and Ethical Retail Supply Chains," Forbes, January 8, 2016, http://www.forbes.com/sites/tarunwadhwa/2016/01/08 /the-ongoing-struggle-to-use-technology-to-create-safe -and-ethical-retail-supply-chains/#4bfeba735293. Accessed April 11, 2016.
63. *The Economist*, "Working Conditions in Factories: When the Job Inspector Calls," March 31, 2012.
64. Levi Strauss & Company, Global Sourcing and Operating Guidelines, http://www.levistrauss.com /wp-content/uploads/2014/01/Global-Sourcing-and-Operating-Guidelines.pdf. Accessed April 13, 2016; Gap, Inc. "UN Guiding Principles on Business and Human Rights," http://www.gapinc.com/content/csr /html/human-rights/un-guiding-principlesonbusiness humanrights.html. Accessed April 13, 2016; Nike, Inc. "Sustainable Business Performance Summary," http:// www.nikeresponsibility.com/report/search/524d264 9f5adcd74f66348908fb5f1e9/. Accessed April 13, 2016.
65. Dexter Roberts, Pete Engardio, Aaron Bernstein, Stanley Holmes, and Xiang Ji, "Secrets, Lies, and Sweatshops" (cover story), *Businessweek* (November 27, 2006), 50–58. Also see Kathy Chu, "Some Chinese Factories Lie to Pass Western Audits," *USA Today*, April 30, 2012, 4B.
66. "Alien Tort Claims Act," *Global Policy Forum*, http:// www.globalpolicy.org/international-justice/alien-tort -claims-act-6-30.html. Accessed April 13, 2016; Also see "Alien Tort Claims," *International Law Update* (Vol. 13, April 2007), 66–67.
67. Ibid.
68. Jess Bravin, "High Court Reigns in Scope of Alien Torts Act," *The Wall Street Journal*, April 17, 2013. For further information, see EarthRights International, "The Alien Tort Statute," https://www.earthrights.org /legal/alien-tort-statute. Accessed April 29, 2016.
69. Connecticut Law Tribune, April 7, 2016, http://www .ctlawtribune.com/id=1202754419182/Conn-Judge

-Says-Journalist-Cant-Be-Sued-for-Critical-Coverage-of-Religious-Sect?mcode=0&curindex=0. Accessed April 13, 2016.

70. "Cracking Down: A U.S. Anticorruption Drive Makes Waves," *The Wall Street Journal*, June 24, 2014, C10; Kara Scannell, "US Redoubles Efforts on Foreign Bribery Cases," *Financial Times*, February 10, 2016, http://www.ft.com/intl/cms/s/0/cdb01524-cb8b-11e5-be0b-b7ece4e953a0.html#axzz45iorIihT. Accessed April 13, 2016.

71. Bruce Lloyd, "Bribery, Corruption and Accountability," *Insights on Global Ethics* (Vol. 4, No. 8, September 1994), 5.

72. Daron Acemonglu and James A. Robinson, "Corruption Is Just a Symptom," *The Wall Street Journal*, December 5–6, 2015, C3.

73. Cynthia Clark and Jill A. Brown, "Multinational Corporations and Governance Effectiveness: Toward an Integrative Board," *Journal of Business Ethics* (Vol. 132, No. 3, 2015), 565–577.

74. Soundararajan and Brown, 2016.

75. "Corruption on the Agenda, "What Is Corruption?" http://www.corruption-agenda.org/getting-started/what-is-corruption. Accessed April 13, 2016.

76. Geoff Colvin, "The Biggest Problem for Developing Economies: Corruption," *Fortune*, May 2, 2011, 48.

77. Ian I. Mitroff and Ralph H. Kilmann, "Teaching Managers to Do Policy Analysis: The Case of Corporate Bribery," *California Management Review* (Fall 1977), 50–52. Also see Debatepedia, "Debate: Is Bribery Ever Acceptable?" http://dbp.idebate.org/en/index.php/Debate:Bribery_or_Corruption. Accessed April 13, 2016.

78. Acemonglu and Robinson, 2015, ibid.

79. "The Destructive Costs of Greasing Palms," *Businessweek* (December 6, 1993), 133–138. See also Henry W. Lane and Donald G. Simpson, "Bribery in International Business: Whose Problem Is It?" (Reading 12) in H. W. Lane, J. J. DiStefano, and M. L. Maznevski (eds.), *International Management Behavior*, 4th ed. (Oxford: Blackwell Publishers, 2000), 469–487.

80. "Foreign Corrupt Practices Act," *Department of Justice*, http://www.justice.gov/criminal/fraud/fcpa/. Accessed April 13, 2016.

81. FCPA and Ethics Blog, "When Does a Grease Payment Become a Bribe under the FCPA?" February 2, 2011, http://tfoxlaw.wordpress.com/2011/02/02/when-does-a-grease-payment-become-a-bribe-under-the-fcpa/. Accessed April 13, 2016.

82. "DOJ and SEC Release Long Anticipated FCPA Guidance," http://www.sidley.com/en/news/doj–sec-release-long-anticipated-fcpa-guidance-11-15-2012. Accessed April 13, 2016.

83. U. S. Department of Justice, "Foreign Corrupt Practices Act," https://www.justice.gov/criminal-fraud/foreign-corrupt-practices-act. Accessed April 13, 2016.

84. "The Anti-Bribery Business," *The Economist*, http://www.economist.com/news/business/21650557-enforcement-laws-against-corporate-bribery-increases-there-are-risks-it-may-go. Accessed April 13, 2016.

85. Ibid.

86. Rachel L. Ensign, "Why Companies Might Opt to Self-report Bribery Issues," *The Wall Street Journal*, November 3, 2014, B4.

87. Dawn Keig, Lance Eliot Brouthers, and Victor Marshall, "Formal and Informal Corruption Environments and Multinational Enterprise Social Irresponsibility," *Journal of Management Studies* (Vol. 52, No. 1, 2015), 89–116.

88. Daniel Henniger, "Capitalism's Corruptions," *The Wall Street Journal*, April 4, 2013, A13.

89. *The Economist*, "The Fight against Corruption: Naming and Shaming," October 30, 2010, 65 http://www.economist.com/node/17361580. Accessed April 13, 2016.

90. Transparency International, "Our Vision," http://www.transparency.org/whoweare. Accessed April 13, 2016.

91. Ibid.

92. Ibid.

93. Ibid.

94. TI's Corruption Perception Index, http://www.transparency.org/cpi2012/press. Accessed April 13, 2016.

95. Transparency International's Bribe Payers Index, http://www.transparency.org/bpi2011. Accessed April 13, 2016.

96. Ibid.

97. Ibid.

98. OECD, http://www.oecd.org/corruption/oecdantibriberyconvention.htm. Accessed April 13, 2016.

99. Huffpost Politics, "Inside the Battle against Global Corruption," http://www.huffingtonpost.com/entry/unaoil-corruption-enforcement_us_56fb04b4e4b0daf53aedee71. Accessed April 13, 2016.

100. UNOD, "UNOD's Action against Corruption and Economic Crime," http://www.unodc.org/unodc/en/corruption/index.html?ref=menuside. Accessed April 13, 2016.

101. UNODC, "UN Convention against Corruption, Signature and Ratification Status as of 1 December 2015," http://www.unodc.org/unodc/en/treaties/CAC/signatories.html. Accessed April 13, 2016.

102. UN Convention against Corruption, http://www.unodc.org/unodc/en/treaties/CAC/. Accessed April 13, 2016.

103. UN Global Compact, "The Ten Principles of the UN Global Compact," https://www.unglobalcompact.org/what-is-gc/mission/principles/principle-10. Accessed April 13, 2016.

104. UNODC, "UN Convention against Corruption," http://www.unodc.org/unodc/en/treaties/CAC/signatories.html. Accessed April 13, 2016.

105. *The Economist*, "The Politics of Corruption: Squeezing the Sleazy," December 15, 2012, 61.

106. Juan Montes, "Mexico's Anticorruption Fight Wilts," *The Wall Street Journal*, January 28, 2016.

107. Juan Montes, "A Grass-roots Debut in Mexico," *The Wall Street Journal*, March 14, 2016.

108. *Bloomberg Businessweek*, "Collateral Damage from China's Antigraft Drive," February 12, 2015, http://www.bloomberg.com/news/articles/2015-02-12/china-gift-cards-are-casualty-of-anticorruption-drive. Accessed April 13, 2016. Also see Lingling Wei and Bob Davis, "Meet China's Top Enforcer," *The Wall Street Journal*, August 21, 2014, A1.

109. Lloyd, 5.

110. Gene R. Laczniak and Jacob Naor, "Global Ethics: Wrestling with the Corporate Conscience," Business (July–September 1985), 3–10.

111. Tom Donaldson, "Global Business Must Mind Its Morals," *The New York Times* (February 13, 1994), F-11. See also Tom Donaldson, "Ethics Away from Home," *Harvard Business Review* (September–October, 1996).

112. Tom Donaldson and Thomas W. Dunfee, "When Ethics Travel: The Promise and Peril of Global Business Ethics," *California Management Review* (Vol. 41, No. 4, Summer 1999), 48–49.

113. T. Donaldson and T. Dunfee, "Toward a Unified Conception of Business Ethics: Integrative Social Contracts Theory," *Academy of Management Review* 19, 1994, 252–284.

114. Clark and Brown, 2015, ibid.

115. Laczniak and Naor, 3–10.

116. Caterpillar, "Our Values in Action: Caterpillar's Worldwide Code of Conduct," http://www.caterpillar.com/en/company/code-of-conduct.html. Accessed April 18, 2016.

117. Ibid.

118. Chiquita Code of Conduct, http://www.chiquita.com/Code-of-Conduct-PDF/ChiquitaCode-FINAL-EN.aspx. Accessed April 18, 2016.

119. Lynn Paine, Rohit Deshpandé, Joshua Margolis, and Kim Eric Bettcher, "Up to Code: Does Your Company's Conduct Meet World-Class Standards?" *Harvard Business Review* (December 2005), 122–133. Also see http://arson04.blogspot.com/2011/07/global-business-standards-codex-gbs-and.html. Accessed April 18, 2016.

120. Ibid.

121. ISO, "ISO 26000," http://www.iso.org/iso/iso26000. Accessed April 18, 2016.

122. ISO, "ISO 26000 in the Post-2015 Development Agenda," http://www.iso.org/iso/home/news_index/news_archive/news.htm?refid=Ref2039. Accessed April 18, 2016.

123. ISO, "ISO 37001–Anti-Bribery Management Systems," http://www.iso.org/iso/iso37001. Accessed April 18, 2016.

124. UN Global Compact, "Agenda 2030: the Sustainable Development Goals," https://www.unglobalcompact.org/what-is-gc/our-work/sustainable-development/sdgs. Accessed April 29, 2016.

125. CSRWire, "Reflections on the 20th Anniversary of the Caux Round Table Principles for Business," July 31, 2014, http://www.csrwire.com/press_releases/37271-Reflections-on-the-20th-Anniversary-of-the-Caux-Round-Table-Principles-for-Business. Accessed April 29, 2016.

126. Laczniak and Naor, 7–8.

127. Donna J. Wood, Jeanne M. Logsdon, Patsy G. Lewellyn, and Kim Davenport, *Global Business Citizenship: A Transformative Framework for Ethics and Sustainable Capitalism* (Armonk, NY: M.E Sharpe), 2006.

128. Robert D. Haas, "Ethics in the Trenches," *Across the Board* (May 1994), 12–13.

129. CSRWire, "Levi Strauss & Co. Publishes List of Active Suppliers," http://www.csrwire.com/press_releases/18753-Levi-Strauss-Co-Publishes-List-of-Active-Suppliers. Accessed April 18, 2018.

130. Levi Strauss & Co., *Sustainability Guidebook*, http://lsco.s3.amazonaws.com/wp-content/uploads/2014/01/LSCO-Sustainability-Guidebook-2013-_-December.pdf. Accessed April 18, 2016.

131. "Starbucks Pays Premium Price to Benefit Workers," *Business Ethics* (March/April 1998), 9.

132. Starbuck's, "Ethical Sourcing: Coffee," http://www.starbucks.com/responsibility/sourcing/coffee. Accessed April 18, 2016.

133. Laczniak and Naor, 8.

134. "The Short Arm of the Law," *The Economist* (March 2, 2002), 63–65.

135. L. Gordon Crovitz, "Google's Search Result: Hong Kong," *The Wall Street Journal* (March 29, 2010), A21.

136. Kaveh Waddell, "Why Google Quit China—and Why Its Heading Back," The Atlantic, January 19, 2016.

137. Mattel press release (November 20, 1997).

138. Mattel's Global Manufacturing Principles, http://corporate.mattel.com/about-us/GMP-PrinciplesOverview.pdf. Accessed April 18, 2016.

139. S. Sethi, Emre Veral, H. Jack Shapiro, and Olga Emelianova, "Mattel, Inc.: Global Manufacturing Principles (GMP)–A Life Cycle Analysis of a Company-Based Code of Conduct in the Toy Industry," Journal of Business Ethics, April 1, 2011, https://www.deepdyve.com/lp/springer-journals/mattel-inc-global

-manufacturing-principles-gmp-a-life-cycle-analysis-oO03uYk0mg. Accessed April 18, 2018.

140. SupplyChainBrain, "Ethics Issues Are at the Heart of Supply-Chain Management," http://www.supplychainbrain.com/content/general-scm/education-professional-development/single-article-page/article/ethics-issues-are-at-the-heart-of-supply-chain-management-1/. Accessed April 18, 2016.

141. Ronald E. Berenbeim, *Resisting Corruption: How Company Programs Are Changing, Research Report R-1397-06-RR* (New York: The Conference Board, 2006). http://www.conference-board.org/publications/publicationdetail.cfm?publicationid=1239. Accessed April 18, 2016.

142. Ibid.

PART 4
External Stakeholder Issues

11

Business, Government, and Regulation

CHAPTER LEARNING OUTCOMES

After studying this chapter, you should be able to:

1. Articulate a brief history, and changing nature of the government's role in its relationship with business.
2. Appreciate the complex roles of government and business.
3. Identify the elements in the complex interactions among business, government, and the public.
4. Identify and describe the government's nonregulatory influences, especially the concepts of industrial policy and privatization.
5. Identify and describe the government's regulatory influences on business including the major reasons for regulation, the types of regulation, and issues arising out of deregulation.

How can business and government work effectively together? The last decade swung the pendulum of government involvement in business from minimal intervention to active participation. The depth, scope, and direction of government's involvement in business have made the relationship of government to business one of the most hotly debated issues today. Issues of privatization, government monitoring of e-mails and phone calls, tax rates, regulation and deregulation, the scope of state versus federal laws, and so on: these are some of the hot-button issues in the business/government relationship that businesses face today. Some argue that government interferes too much in the process of value creation and hinders, rather than helps business, whereas others argue that business is a "ravenous predator" that the government needs to control.[1] In a recent U.S. Gallup poll, generally more Americans say government regulation of business is too much (49 percent), and a near-low percentage say it regulates too little (21 percent).[2]

Yet business and government need each other, as pointed out in a special issue in *The Economist* magazine. Governments rely on businesses to drive economic growth and create jobs while businesses need government for legal systems and security. The government also educates workers, creating infrastructure that supports a market system. It is important to understand that the government is also a customer of business—the typical government spending in a developed country represents around 40 percent of GDP.[3] Therefore, the government is a major stakeholder with which business must establish an effective working relationship if it is to survive and prosper.

The increased level of government involvement in business is likely to remain for some time. The seriousness of the global economic crisis revealed systemic weaknesses that have led many to call for structural change with greater protections.[4] At the same time, many worry about the impact of increased government involvement on business's innovation and growth.[5] This chapter and the next examine the relationship between business and government, with the public assuming an important role in the discussion as well. Exploring this relationship carefully will provide an appreciation of the complexity of the issues surrounding business or government interactions. From a manager's standpoint, one needs an understanding of the forces and factors involved in these issues before beginning to talk intelligently about strategies for dealing with them. This chapter discusses how government influences business and the next chapter discusses how business influences government.

11.1 The Pendulum of Government's Role in Business

To be certain, the government involvement pendulum has swung back and forth for years. Business has never been fond of government having an activist role in establishing the ground rules under which it operates. In contrast, public sentiment has been cyclical, going through periods when it has thought that the federal government had too much power and other periods when it has thought that government should be more activistic in its business dealings. As an exemplar of a free market economy, the United States serves as a case in point. There have been periods of strong government intervention. In 1791, while serving as Secretary of the U.S. Treasury, Alexander Hamilton pushed for tariffs to protect domestic manufacturers. The purpose was to protect fledgling industries. Then, in the 1860s, President Abraham Lincoln expanded federal powers by opening the American West to settlement.[6] By the 1860s, industrialists like John D. Rockefeller dominated the steel, oil, and banking industries, swinging the pendulum back toward business autonomy.[7]

At the same time, government gave large land grants as incentives for private business to build railroads. Several railroads had grown large and strong through mergers, and people began to use them because their service was faster, cheaper, and more efficient. This resulted in a decline in the use of alternative forms of transportation, such as highways, rivers, and canals. Many railroads began to abuse their favored positions. They charged higher rates for shorter hauls and gave preference to large shippers over smaller shippers. Public criticism of these practices led to the passage of the Interstate Commerce Act of 1887, therein marking the beginning of extensive federal government regulation of interstate commerce. The Act created the Interstate Commerce Commission, which became the first federal regulatory agency and a model for future agencies.[8]

Many large manufacturing and mining firms also began to abuse consumers during the late 1800s. Typical actions included the elimination of competition and the charging of excessively high prices. During this period, several large firms formed organizations known as *trusts*. A trust was an organization that brought all or most competitors under a common control that then permitted them to eliminate most of the remaining competitors by price-cutting, an act that forced the remaining competitors out of business. Then, the trusts would restrict production and raise prices. As a response, Congress passed the Sherman Antitrust Act (Sherman Act) in 1890, which became the first in a series of actions intended to control monopolies in various industries. The Sherman Act outlawed any contract, combination, or conspiracy in restraint of trade, and it also prohibited the monopolization of any market. In the early 1900s, the federal government used the Sherman Act to break up the Standard Oil Company, the American Tobacco Company, and several other large firms that had abused their economic power.[9]

The Clayton Antitrust Act was passed in 1914 to augment the Sherman Act. It addressed other abusive practices that had arisen. It outlawed price discrimination that gave favored buyers preference over others and forbade anticompetitive contracts, whereby a company would agree to sell only to suppliers who agreed not to sell the products of a rival competitor. The act prohibited an assortment of other anticompetitive practices. Also in 1914, Congress formed the Federal Trade Commission, which was intended to maintain free and fair competition and to protect consumers from unfair or misleading practices.[10]

Then the Great Depression (roughly 1929–1939) led to President Franklin Roosevelt's New Deal and the creation of more regulatory agencies.[11] Significant legislation included the Securities Act of 1933 and the Securities and Exchange Act of 1934. These laws were aimed at curbing abuses in the stock market, stabilizing markets, and restoring investor confidence in order to prevent a second depression. Significant labor legislation during this same period signaled government involvement in a new area. Several examples were the 1926 Railway Labor Act, the 1932 Norris–LaGuardia Act, and the 1935 Wagner Act. During the New Deal period in the 1930s, government also took on a new dimension in its relationship with business, actively assuming responsibility for restoring prosperity and promoting economic growth through public works programs. In 1946, this new role of government was formalized with the passage of the Full Employment Act. Prior to the mid-1950s, most congressional legislation affecting business was economic in nature. The 1960s and 1970s continued the trend of government involvement but the concern was largely with the quality of life.[12] Several examples of this included the Civil Rights Act of 1964, the Water Quality Act of 1965, the Occupational Safety and Health Act of 1970, the Consumer Product Safety Act of 1972, and the Warranty Act of 1975.

The pendulum swung back when President Ronald Reagan came into office in 1980. The public was growing somewhat weary of an active federal role. Throughout the 1980s, the federal government assumed a smaller and smaller role, especially in terms of monitoring and regulating business. It was not without reason, therefore, that in late 1989 *Time* magazine ran a cover story entitled "Is Government Dead?"[13] The "Reagan Revolution" of an inactive federal government had left the public with a desire for government to become active again. It was against this backdrop that George Herbert Walker Bush was elected president in 1988. During the first Bush administration (1988–1992), the country witnessed a growth in the rate of federal government spending.

The Clinton administration (1992–2000) then sought a middle ground, advocating a more activist role for the government in international politics and social concerns, while launching other initiatives to control federal spending. As the economy rebounded in the early 1990s, the peace dividend bore fruit, cost-cutting initiatives took hold, and the rate of government spending slowed dramatically.[14] With the exception of the Americans with Disabilities Act of 1990, the 1990s were characterized by financial deregulation. The repeal of the Glass–Steagall Act, the Commodity Futures Modernization Act, and the revisions to the Community Reinvestment Act all created a more permissive lending environment that, many argue, led to the financial crisis of 2008.[15]

George W. Bush came into office in 2001 on a platform of a reduced role for federal government; however, the attack on the World Trade Center changed everything.[16] Repercussions of the attack, such as the bailout of the troubled airline industry, relief for other distressed industries, the increase in military spending, and the federalization of airport security, expanded dramatically both government spending and governmental intervention in business activities.[17] Key examples of this are the USA Patriot Act of 2001 and the Homeland Security Act. In addition, the passage of Sarbanes–Oxley Act in 2002 brought stricter regulation to publicly traded businesses.

By the end of G.W. Bush's second term, the financial crisis prompted bailouts of the financial services and auto industries that were supported by both then-President Bush and President-elect Obama. When Barack Obama became President in 2009, the economic crisis was in full swing and government was involved in business operations at historically high levels. He continued that trend through a variety of initiatives such as efforts to institute new banking regulations through the Dodd–Frank Wall Street Reform and Consumer Protection Act, which we discuss in Chapter 5. In addition, fees to recoup the bailout money and plans to institute a community bank-lending fund to encourage loans to small businesses were instituted. The Obama administration passed new regulations establishing credit card rules, health-care reform in the name of the Affordable Care Act, consumer financial protection, and financial regulatory reform.

The changing areas in which government has chosen to initiate legislation have been accompanied by cries for less or more regulation—with many of these messages on the "less" side. For example, Philip K. Howard, author of "The Rule of Nobody," writes about how regulations have programmed government officials to follow rules so detailed, rigid, and obsolete that they leave little room for human judgment. He cites the example of a tree falling into a stream and causing flooding during a winter storm. The New Jersey township where it occurred was barred from pulling the tree out until it had spent 12 days and $12,000 for permits and engineering work required under a state environmental rule.[18] In a similar vein, author Charles Murray notes that in 2013, the Code of Federal Regulations was over 175,000 pages, and some of the laws about businesses are so complicated that, "Only lawyers, working in teams, know everything that the law requires."[19] He goes on to say that, "No individual can know how to 'obey' laws such as Sarbanes-Oxley (810 pages), the Affordable Care Act (1,024 pages) or Dodd–Frank (2,300 pages). We submit to them."[20]

It is not surprising that businesses often argue for fewer regulations, citing the additional costs and administrative burdens of compliance. However, even some small business operators acknowledge that the benefits from regulation can often outweigh the costs. Responding to the news of a possible hike in the minimum wage in his locale, one entrepreneur noted, "Having a healthy, balanced workforce is in our best long-term interests, even if it costs us some short-term labor dislocation."[21] One of the challenges in assessing the ideal level of involvement of government in business is that the arguments are often couched in partisan politics.

The multiplicity of roles that government has assumed has increased the complexity of its relationship with business. Government is not only a regulator of business that can determine the rules of the game but also a major purchaser with buying power that can affect a business or industry's likelihood of survival. It can elevate some businesses and industries while devaluing others through the setting of government policy. For example, fees on crude oil production may facilitate government support for new climate change initiatives.[22] The government can even create new businesses and industries through subsidization and privatization. Take, for example, the advent of new business opportunities for U.S. businesses after diplomatic relations were renewed with Cuba in 2015. A handful of companies like Verizon and Netflix were able to expand into the Cuban market immediately, but with a Cuban trade embargo still in force, most U.S. companies will not be able to set up shop in Cuba until Congress lifts the embargo.[23] The range of government roles illuminates the crucial interconnectedness between business and government and the difficulty both business and the public have in fully understanding (much less prescribing) what government's role ought to be in relation to business.

11.2 The Roles of Government and Business

We do not intend to philosophize in this chapter on the ideal role of government in relation to business, because this is outside our stakeholder frame of reference. However, we will strive for an understanding of current major issues as they pertain to this vital relationship. For effective management, government's role as a stakeholder must be understood.

The fundamental question underlying our entire discussion of business and government relationships is, "What should be the respective roles of business and government in our socioeconomic system?" More specifically, we can ask, "Given all the tasks that must be accomplished to make our society work, which of these tasks should be handled by government and which by business?" This poses the issue clearly, but other questions remain unanswered. If we decide, for example, that it is best to let business handle the production and distribution roles in our society, the next question becomes "How much autonomy are we willing to allow business?" If our goals were simply the production and distribution of goods and services, we would not have to constrain business severely. In modern times, however, other goals have been added to the production and distribution functions—a safe working environment for those engaging in production, equal employment opportunities, fair pay, clean air, safe products, employee rights, and so on. When we superimpose these goals on basic economic goals, the tasks of business become much more complex and challenging.

Because businesses do not automatically factor these more socially oriented goals into their decision making and processes, it often falls on the government to ensure that those goals that reflect social concerns be achieved. Thus, whereas the marketplace dictates economic production decisions, government becomes one of the citizenry's designated representatives charged with articulating and protecting the public interest. Of course, the concepts of corporate social responsibility, sustainability and business ethics, urge businesses to factor these considerations into their practices so that it is not left to government alone to deal with these issues. In spite of this, some measure of government involvement is typically needed.

11.2a A Clash of Ethical Belief Systems

A clash of emphases partially forms the crux of the antagonistic relationship that has evolved between business and government over the years. Although this clash will vary between different countries and cultures, the underlying tension between business and government still holds true. This problem has been termed "a clash of ethical systems." The two ethical systems (systems of belief) are the **individualistic ethic of business** and the **collectivistic ethic of government**. Figure 11-1 summarizes the characteristics of these two philosophies.[24]

The clash of these two ethical systems partially explains why the business or government relationship is adversarial in nature. In elaborating on the adversarial nature of the business or government relationship, Neil Jacoby offered the following comments:

> *Officials of government characteristically look upon themselves as probers, inspectors, taxers, regulators, and punishers of business transgressions. Businesspeople typically view government agencies as obstacles, constraints, delayers, and impediments to economic progress, having much power to stop and little to start.*[25]

The business–government relationship not only continues to be adversarial but also is more complicated in the 21st century. The goals and values of a pluralistic society continue to be complex, numerous, interrelated, and difficult to reconcile. At the same time, economic conditions compel governments around the world to take a more active role in the economy.[26] As the conflicts among diverse interest groups increase, it becomes more difficult to reconcile trade-off decisions and establish social priorities. An NBC/*The Wall*

FIGURE 11-1 The Clash of Ethical Systems between Business and Government

Business Beliefs	Government Beliefs
• Individualistic ethic	• Collectivistic ethic
• Maximum concession to self-interest	• Subordination of individual goals and self-interest to group and group interests
• Minimizing the load of obligations society imposes on the individual (personal freedom)	• Maximizing the obligations assumed by the individual and discouraging self-interest
• Emphasizes inequalities of individuals	• Emphasizes equality of individuals

Street Journal poll of adults in the United States underscores the underlying tensions in the relationship. When asked about the role of government in business following the economic crisis, 49 percent said that the government was doing too many things and 45 percent said that the government should do more.[27] Establishing social priorities also involves staying current with sociocultural and demographic issues. In a *Shriver Report* bipartisan poll of 3,500 adults about whether U.S. government policies and business practices are out of touch with the changing state of American families, the majority of respondents said "yes," with the idea that the government needs to adapt to the new realities of single-parent families, working mothers, and equal pay for equal work.[28] In sum, the relative pros and cons of government intervention in business continue to serve as fuel for debates.[29]

11.3 Interaction of Business, Government, and the Public

This section offers a brief overview of the influence relationships among business, government, and the public. This should be helpful in understanding both the nature of the public policy decision-making process and the current problems that characterize the business–government relationship. Figure 11-2 illustrates the interactive pattern of these influence relationships.

One might rightly ask at this point, "Why include the public? Isn't the public represented by government?" In an ideal world, perhaps this would be true. To help us appreciate that government functions somewhat apart from the public, we depict it separately in the diagram. In addition, the public has its own unique methods of influence that we also depict separately.

11.3a Government–Business Relationship

Government influences business through regulations, taxation, and other forms of persuasion that we will consider in more detail in the next section. Business, likewise, has

FIGURE 11-2 Interaction among Business, Government, and the Public

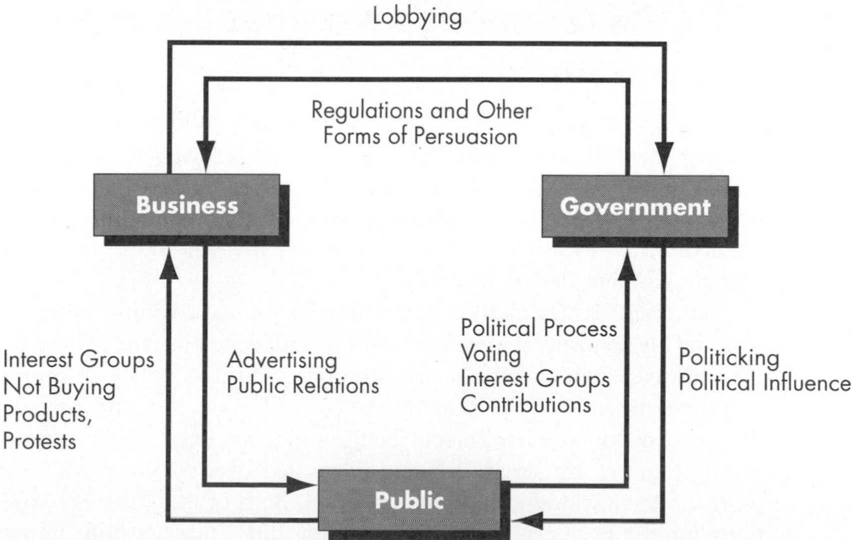

its approaches to influencing government, which we will deal with in Chapter 12. Lobbying, in one form or another, is business's primary means of influencing government.

11.3b Public–Government Relationship

The public uses the political processes of voting and electing officials (or removing them from office) to influence government. It also exerts its influence by forming special-interest groups (farmers, small business owners, educators, senior citizens, truckers, manufacturers, etc.) to wield more targeted influence. Government, in turn, uses politicking, public policy formation, and other political influences to have an impact on the public.

11.3c Business–Public Relationship

Business influences the public through advertising, public relations, and other forms of communication. The public influences business through the marketplace or by forming special-interest groups (e.g., AARP, Friends of the Earth, American Civil Liberties Union) and protest groups.

Earlier we raised the question of whether government really represents the public. This question may be stated another way: "Who determines what is in the public interest?" In our pluralistic society, determining the public interest is not a simple matter. Whereas government may be the official representative of the public, we should not assume that representation occurs in a straightforward fashion. As we saw in Figure 11-2, the public takes its own initiatives both with business and with government. The three major groups, therefore, are involved in a dynamic interplay of influence processes that strive to define the current public interest.

Our central concern in this chapter is with government's role in influencing business, and we now turn our attention to that topic. We will begin to see more clearly how government is a major stakeholder of business. Government's official priority is in representing the public interest as it sees and interprets the public's wishes. However, like all large bureaucratic organizations, government also takes on a life of its own with its own goals and agenda.

11.4 Government's Nonregulatory Influence on Business

Broadly speaking, we may categorize the kinds of influence government has on business as *nonregulatory* and *regulatory*. We limit our treatment to the federal government's influence on business, but we must remain mindful of the presence and influence of state, local, and other governments as well. In the next section, we focus on government regulation, but in this section, let us consider the wide range of *nonregulatory* influences that government has on business.

Two major issues merit consideration before we examine some of the specific policy tools or mechanisms government uses to influence business. These two major issues are (1) industrial policy and (2) privatization. Industrial policy is concerned with the role that government plays in shaping the national economy, and privatization zeroes in on the question of whether current public functions (e.g., public education, public transit, social security, fire service) should be turned over to the private (business) sector for more effective and efficient administration. Both of these issues have important implications for the business–government relationship. They are both important, because they seem to come into and out of popularity on a regular basis.

11.4a Industrial Policy

Industrial policy is "every form of state intervention that affects industry as a distinct part of the economy."[30] Industrial policy has differed over time and across countries in both its philosophy and its actions, but it has generally addressed ailing industries.[31] A newer form of industrial policy is characterized by Robert Reich in his book *The Next American Frontier*, wherein he argues for a national industrial policy that attempts to identify winning (or sunrise) industries and foster their growth while redirecting resources from losing (or sunset) industries.[32] Current examples of this new form of industrial policy abound in the United States today. For example, over the past few years the U.S. government has supported the development and growth of the electric car industry. This followed President Obama's goal for the United States to become the first country to have one million electric vehicles on the road by 2015.[33] To support this growth, his administration pledged $2.4 billion in federal grants to support the development of electric vehicles (also known as "plug-in hybrids") and batteries, with companies like Tesla Motors, Inc., benefiting from such subsidies.[34] Similarly, the U.S. federal government also provides grants or tax credits to cover a percentage of the cost of solar installations, benefiting companies like SolarCity, which reported receiving $497.5 million in direct grants from the Treasury Department.[35] This type of industrial policy is not limited to the United States of course. The European Union, for example, provides subsidies to support various sectors of the energy industry, with the largest amounts going to renewables such as solar, onshore wind, biomass, and hydropower.[36]

The appropriate trade policy for the United States is an intensely debated topic.[37] However, this is not new, as the United States has always had strong reactions to any form of industrial policy because it conflicts with widely held views on the role of government in the economy.[38] During the Reagan (1980–1988) and first Bush (1988–1992) administrations, the notion of industrial policy was not looked upon with great favor. Both these administrations advocated a free market posture rather than government activism via industrial policy. President Bill Clinton, however, supported several actions that typified an active industrial policy. For example, the Clinton administration took an activist stance in promoting the Internet by creating a Framework for Global Electronic Commerce. This framework outlined key principles for supporting the evolution of electronic commerce, identified where international efforts were needed, and designated the U.S. governmental agencies responsible for leading the effort. The administration did this because businesses were wary of becoming involved in the then-new Internet because they were unsure of the legal environment, and they feared government intervention would stifle electronic commerce.[39] Amazon, for example, is a company made possible by this deregulation, with access at the time to unregulated transportation and a flexible delivery system.

The George W. Bush administration entered office intending to follow in the footsteps of the early Reagan and Bush administrations by adopting a free market posture and minimizing government intervention. However, the tragic events of September 11, 2001, prompted extensive new regulations in the areas of homeland security, and the Enron meltdown, as well as the other financial scandals that followed, prompted new regulations in corporate governance. That trend continued with the Obama administration that entered office during a deep global recession and spent the first four years focused on digging out of an economic hole. These events prompted a stronger industrial policy in areas such as financial services and led to auto industry bailouts, student and mortgage loan intervention, and high-tech investments in non-carbon-based energies. Even the Internet became a hotbed area for more regulation in 2015, as the U.S. Federal Communications Commission (FCC) adopted new regulations under a "net neutrality" plan to monitor broadband use. This put the Internet in the same regulatory camp as a public utility, where providers would have to act in the "public interest" when providing services.[40] After a drone landed on the lawn of the White House in early 2015, safety concerns over their use prompted the passage of new laws requiring registration of their use and monitoring by the Federal Aviation Association.[41]

The global financial crisis compelled governments around the world to take an active part in reviving economic growth and restoring financial stability.[42] To do this, governments needed not only to focus on economic reform but also on ways to make government more efficient and effective.[43] Figure 11-3 provides an example of how industrial policy can be affected by economic crises that may require bailouts, subsidies, and other forms of government assistance. In sum, while nonregulatory influences continue in industrial policy, economic and safety concerns often swing the pendulum of government intervention toward more regulation.

FIGURE 11-3 Industrial Policy Following Economic Crises

In Chapter 6, we discussed economic crises as one type of crises that can leave companies vulnerable. Historically, the U.S. government has opted to minimize government involvement in business, but crises (and politics) can always change that stance. The global financial crisis beginning in 2008 led to bailouts in the auto, banking, and insurance industries. After the September 11, 2001, terrorist attacks, the crippled airline industry requested bailouts of about $24 billion. Congress passed a bailout program of $15 billion—$5 billion in immediate cash assistance and $10 billion in loan guarantees. Other affected industries soon made requests as well.

There is a long history of government stepping in to rescue industries in distress:

- In 1971, the Lockheed Corporation received $250 million in loan guarantees from Congress.
- In 1976, the federal government merged seven failing Northeast railroads and then spent about $7 billion to keep the combined entity afloat.
- In 1979, the Chrysler Corporation received up to $1.5 billion in loan guarantees.
- In 1989, Congress addressed the Savings and Loan Crisis by closing more than 1,000 S&Ls at a cost of $124 billion.

In the past, some government interventions have been successes while others have faltered. Chrysler paid off its loan seven years early, and the government received a profit of $350 million. However, the Lockheed bailout was rocky from the start. When it was revealed that Lockheed had paid foreign bribes, the government ousted two top executives and proceeded to give Lockheed activities closer scrutiny. In the case of airlines, the U.S. government made $119 million from their equity ownership in the shares of airlines like Frontier. One key to success is for the government to require equity in return for aid: The U.S. government made their profit from the Chrysler bailout due to such an arrangement. It would seem logical then that all government bailouts would include an equity arrangement; however, corporate lobbyists typically block the way.

One of the largest and most controversial bailouts was the $152 billion rescue of the American International Group (AIG). Their debt was repaid, with $22.7 billion profit for the government, but Maurice Greenberg, former CEO of AIG, sued the federal government arguing that the bailout was unconstitutional and cheated shareholders. In 2015 Greenberg won his case and the government was chastised for its harsh treatment of AIG including taking control and forcing the company to sell off assets. However, shareholders did not receive any monetary damages because the judge ruled that if not for the government's intervention, AIG would have filed for bankruptcy.

It is estimated that the U.S. government closed its books on the Troubled Asset Relief Program (TARP) for the 2008 bailout of U.S. banks and the auto industry with a total of $428 billion spent and a profit of $15.3 billion. However, it can be difficult to assess the outcome from the news as the bailouts were politically charged events, and different metrics may be used. ProPublica, an independent nonprofit newsroom, is keeping a running tab of the status of the payment to the U.S. bailout recipients (http://projects.propublica.org/bailout/list). Each recipient is listed separately and an overall tally is kept at the top. By 2016, 956 recipients received $618 billion in total disbursements. At this writing, $390 billion was returned and the government has made a profit of $65.3 billion from dividends, interest, and other fees.

Sources: Paul Magnusson, "Suddenly, Washington's Wallet Is Open," *Businessweek* (October 1, 2001), 34; Michael Arndt, "What Kind of Rescue?" *Businessweek* (October 1, 2001), 36–37; Jon Birger, "The Bailout Bounty," *Fortune* (March 5, 2007), 24–26; Chris Isidore, "Ex-AIG Chief Wins Bailout Suit against Feds, but Gets Zero Damages," CNN Money (June 15, 2015), http://money.cnn.com/2015/06/15/news/companies/aig-greenberg-bailout-verdict/. Accessed February 27, 2016; Chris Isidore, "U.S. Ends TARP with $15.3 Billion Profit," CNN Money (December 19, 2014), http://money.cnn.com/2014/12/19/news/companies/government-bailouts-end/index.html?iid=EL. Accessed February 27, 2016; http://projects.propublica.org/bailout/list. Accessed February 23, 2016.

Few observers today would argue that a strong industrial policy helps firms compete in a fast-moving global economy. Government is not known for being nimble. However, a country without an industrial policy can find itself losing out to countries that are willing to invest in industries they value and in companies they want to have operating within their borders.[44] Additionally, there is some evidence that firm-level advantages exist when industrial policy is accompanied by the right combination of global production networks, government capabilities, and geographic advantages.[45] Yet, most developed countries are not seeking to institute a strong industrial policy, if they can avoid doing so.[46] Nevertheless, government intervention in business continues, sometimes in ways that are appropriate and sometimes not. Various interventions such as "voluntary" restrictions on imports, occasional bailouts for nearly bankrupt companies, and a wide array of subsidies, loan guarantees, and special tax benefits for particular firms and industries constitute an industrial policy by default.[47] Thus, it is important to think carefully about the role of government in business so that a default industrial policy does not emerge.

Interest in the concept of industrial policy ebbs and flows, depending on the political philosophy of the presiding administration and on events in the external environment. Many of the problems that started the current debate are still with us, whereas new problems have arisen to add further complexity to the issue. Industrial policy (whether coordinated or by default) is a powerful nonregulating approach by government to influence business that is certain to be debated for years to come.

11.4b Privatization

Privatization, generally speaking, refers to the process of changing a public organization to private control or ownership.[48] It is the second major, nonregulatory means by which government might influence business. The intent of privatization is to capture both the discipline of the free market and a spirit of entrepreneurial risk-taking.[49] However, it is a highly contested issue, as we discuss below. To understand privatization, we need to differentiate two functions government might perform: (1) *producing* a service and (2) *providing* a service.[50]

Producing versus Providing a Service. A city government would be *providing* a service if it employed a private security firm to work at the coliseum during the state basketball play-offs. This same city government would be *producing* a service if its own police force provided security at the same basketball tournament. The federal government is providing medical care to senior citizens with a national Medicare program. The "production" of medical care would be coming from private physicians. The government would be providing and producing medical care if it employed its own staff of doctors, as, for example, the military does. The terminology can be very confusing, but the distinction must be made, because sometimes government provides a service (has a program for and actually pays for a service) and at other times it also produces a service (has its own employees who do it).[51]

The Privatization Debate. Proponents of privatization in both the United States and Europe suggest that the functions of entire bureaucracies need to be contracted out to the private sector. They maintain that government at all levels is involved in thousands of businesses in which it has no real comparative advantage and no basic reason for being involved. They also argue that publicly owned enterprises are less efficient and less flexible than are competitive private firms.[52] This argument has played out recently in legislation introduced to privatize the U.S. air traffic control system.[53] Citing the safe, but "incredibly inefficient" operations of the system under the Federal Aviation

Administration, the proposal sets up the air traffic control system as a nonprofit corporation governed by an 11-member board including representatives appointed by the government, airlines, general aviation, and both the pilots' and controllers' unions.[54] In another example, Atlanta's Hartsfield-Jackson International Airport, one of the world's busiest airports, is considering privatizing the security screening process to deal with staffing problems and long passenger wait times.[55] Screening at U.S. airports was done by private contractors until Congress created the Transportation Security Administration (TSA) to manage it in response to the 9/11 attacks. However, commercial airports can apply through the TSA's Screening Partnership Program to hire screeners through an outside firm, although they must use TSA procedures.[56] Opponents of privatization contend that certain activities cannot be handled safely or effectively by the private sector.[57] For example, many point to the **federalization** of airport security (the return of airport security to the government sector) following the attack on the World Trade Center.

Successful privatization can achieve both financial efficiency and broad social goals. When Argentina privatized its national water system, the results were impressive. Service expanded to reach areas that were previously underserved.[58] Furthermore, far fewer children died from infections and parasitic diseases, and investment in this endeavor soared.[59] When things go badly, however, a public backlash can stunt privatization efforts. In February 2015, almost a full year before the news of widespread lead poisoning in the drinking water in Flint, Michigan, the city of Flint contracted with a private water company, Veolia North America.[60] The company assessed the water situation, made some recommendations to improve water color and quality, and deemed it to be safe and "in compliance with State and Federal regulations."[61] By 2016, however, it was clear that the privatization initiatives there did not work. In another example, the privatization of New Jersey halfway houses has been a subject of investigative scrutiny: From 2005 to 2012, 5,100 inmates escaped, some of whom committed murder and other violent crimes shortly thereafter.[62] In contrast, escapes from the state prisons are in single digits each year, if they occur at all.[63]

Privatization efforts are always undertaken with the hope that they will lead to improvements in efficiency and overall performance. In some cases, these hopes are realized, but in others, they are not. However, differences in post-privatization performance can also result from differences in the ways that firms implement privatization programs. The nature of top management, the functioning of the board, and the strategic actions the firms undertake will all contribute to the likelihood of a privatization strategy's success.[64] This was supported by the findings of a study on the efficiency and effectiveness of privatized urban transit services after 25 years of operation. They found no difference between public and private provision of services and concluded that the situation specifics are better predictors of performance than whether the service was public or private.[65]

The two issues, industrial policy and privatization, are largely unresolved and so they continue to be discussed and debated. As we have seen, the success of these efforts is largely dependent on their context—both the environments in which they are adopted and the ways in which they are implemented. Regardless, they both illustrate the nonregulatory influences that government can have on business. We now return to our discussion of the ways in which government uses various policies and mechanisms for influencing business.

11.4c Other Nonregulatory Governmental Influences on Business

Government has a significant impact on business by virtue of the fact that it has a large payroll and is a *major employer* itself. At all levels, government employs millions of people who, as a consequence of being government employees, see things from the government's perspective. Government is also in the position of being a standard setter; for example, the eight-hour workday began in the federal government.

Government is one of the largest *purchasers* of goods and services produced in the private sector. Some key industries, such as aerospace, electronics, and shipbuilding, are very dependent on government purchasing. Government can exert significant influence over the private sector by its insistence that minorities be hired, depressed areas be favored, small businesses be favored, and so on. Changes in government policy can dramatically change a firm's business environment.[66] For some firms in narrow markets, such as defense, the government dominates and controls whether or not those firms have a good year—indeed, whether or not they survive at all.[67]

Government influences the behavior of business by using *subsidies* in a variety of ways. Subsidies are made available to industries such as agriculture, fishing, transportation, nuclear energy, and housing and to groups in special categories, such as minority-owned enterprises and businesses in depressed areas. Quite often, these subsidies have special qualifications attached. Government also influences business, albeit indirectly, by virtue of its *transfer payments*. Government provides money for social security, welfare, and other entitlement programs that totals hundreds of billions of dollars every year. These impacts are indirect, but they do significantly affect the market for business's goods and services.[68]

Government also is a major *competitor* of business. Organizations such as the TVA compete with private suppliers of electricity, the Government Printing Office competes with private commercial publishers and printing firms, and the U.S. Postal Service competes with private delivery services. In areas such as health, education, recreation, and security, the competition between government and private firms runs the gamut of levels—federal, state, and local.

Government loans and *loan guarantees* are sources of influence as well. Government lends money directly to small businesses, housing providers, farmers, and energy companies. Often such loans are made at lower interest rates than those of private competitors. During the global financial crisis, the U.S. Federal Reserve loaned money to undercapitalized banks and the Department of Education essentially acquired the private student loan market.[69]

Taxation is another example of a nonregulatory government influence. Tax deductibility, tax incentives, depreciation policies, and tax credits are tools that are all at the disposal of the government. International tax policy can increase or decrease competitiveness for business. It can make a country more attractive, relative to other countries as a site for new investment and new jobs. For example, a controversial issue in the United States is that of "tax inversions," where U.S.-operating companies can choose to re-incorporate in another country like Ireland where corporate tax rates are lower. The United States is one of the few countries in the world where U.S. domiciled companies must pay taxes on all their global income—not just the income earned in the United States. Hence, a tax inversion is a strategy companies employ to reduce their tax burden. It is highly controversial, with critics pointing to issues of "fairness," lack of patriotism, and inability for U.S. companies to compete globally.[70] Yet, it is a plausible alternative for companies that are trying to remain competitive in a global economy where investing abroad is attractive and easier than ever.

Monetary policy can have a profound effect on business. In the United States, the Federal Reserve System is independent of the executive branch; however, it often responds to presidential leadership or initiatives. Hence, there are concerns of increasing government influence over the Federal Reserve in areas of balance sheet and financial market operations and, particularly, interest rate setting, which affects business. Many have called for

SPOTLIGHT *on Sustainability*

Utilities and the Costs of Going Green

As consumers and green activists push for investments in renewables, energy charging stations and the closing of coal plants, many utility companies find themselves bargaining with state lawmakers to reach compromise and cover costs. Recently, large electric utilities in Oregon forestalled a referendum from green activists by promising to close plants within two decades and expand renewable energy alternatives to 50 percent of the power supply by 2040. However, in return, power consumers would essentially buy out power companies for their remaining investment in coal plants, as well as cover the projected cost of decommissioning. How does this happen? Utility regulation is meant to simulate a competitive market, but utilities typically enjoy a "cost of service" revenue model where expenditures are recaptured from the captive base of customers over time, along with an annual return on the undepreciated amount of their investment. Hence, consumers will most likely see an increase in their rates to cover the costs. Additionally, many electric utilities are trying to change the way they charge customers, shifting more of their fixed costs to monthly fees in the wake of reduced energy consumption. The irony here is that high monthly fees reduce the proportion of the total bill that a customer can lower by conserving energy, reducing the incentive for consumers to embrace alternative energy sources and cut usage. The challenge for utilities and consumers going forward will be figuring out how to manage the costs of renewable energy alternatives while also incentivizing consumers to "go green."

Sources: Travis Kavulla, "How Utilities Team Up with Greens against Consumers," *The Wall Street Journal* (February 26, 2016), A14; Rebecca Smith, "As Conservation Cuts Electricity Use, Utilities Turn to Fees," *The Wall Street Journal* (October 20, 2015), http://www.wsj.com/articles/as-conservation-cuts-electricity-use-utilities-turn-to-fees-1445297729. Accessed March 1, 2016.

pressures—either setting the rates lower when elections are coming up or setting the rates higher as part of partisan politics.[71]

Finally, *moral suasion* is a tool of government. This refers to the government's attempts to "persuade" business to act in the public interest by taking or not taking a particular course of action. These public interest appeals might include a request to roll back a price hike, show restraint on wage and salary increases, or exercise "voluntary" restraints of one kind or another. For example, the U.S. Education's Department Office for Civil Rights has been using moral suasion through "Dear Colleague" letters to colleges asking them to review procedures for disciplinary proceedings for allegations of sexual assault. [72] Moral suasion tactics are often controversial, with some believing that they become like "bullying," particularly when they are framed under some authority.[73]

11.5 Government's Regulatory Influences on Business

In many ways, government regulation has been the most controversial issue in the business–government relationship. Government regulation has affected virtually every aspect of how business functions. It has affected the terms and conditions under which firms have competed in their respective industries. It has touched almost every business decision ranging from the production of goods and services to packaging, distribution, marketing, and service. Most people agree that some degree of regulation has been necessary to ensure that consumers and employees are treated fairly and are not exposed to unreasonable hazards and that the environment is protected. However, they also think that government regulation has often been too extensive in scope, too costly, and inevitably burdensome in terms of paperwork requirements and red tape. One thing is clear; the level of regulation continues to rise.

The annual page count in the *Federal Register* is an imperfect measure of regulatory intensity, but the overall upward trend tells us something about the nature of government and business in the United States. The *Federal Register* celebrated its 90th birthday in 2016. In 1936, it contained 2,620 pages; by 2015, the page count had grown more than 30-fold to a staggering 81,611 pages.[74] The page count seems to stay high irrespective of the party in office. The highest count was 83,294 in 2010 at the end of the Clinton presidency.

11.5a Regulation: What Does It Mean?

Generally, **regulation** refers to the act of governing, directing according to rule, or bringing under the control of law or constituted authority. Although there is no universally agreed-upon definition of federal regulation, we can look to the definition of a federal regulatory agency proposed years ago by the Senate Governmental Affairs Committee.[75] It described a federal regulatory agency as one that:

1. Has decision-making authority.
2. Establishes standards or guidelines conferring benefits and imposing restrictions on business conduct.
3. Operates principally in the sphere of domestic business activity.
4. Has its head and/or members appointed by the president (generally subject to Senate confirmation).
5. Has its legal procedures generally governed by the Administrative Procedures Act.

The commerce clause of the U.S. Constitution grants to the government the legal authority to regulate. Within the confines of a regulatory agency as outlined here, the composition and functioning of regulatory agencies differ. Some are headed by an administrator and are located within an executive department—for example, the Federal Aviation Administration (FAA). Others are independent commissions composed of a chairperson and several members located outside the executive and legislative branches—such as the Interstate Commerce Commission (ICC), the Federal Communications Commission (FCC), and the Securities and Exchange Commission (SEC).[76]

11.5b Reasons for Regulation

Regulations have come about over the years for a variety of reasons. Some managers probably think that government is just sitting on the sidelines looking for reasons to butt into their business. There are several legitimate reasons why government regulation has evolved, although these same businesspeople may not entirely agree with them. For the most part, government regulation has arisen because some kind of **market failure** (failure of the free enterprise system) has occurred and government, intending to represent the public interest, has chosen to take corrective action. We should make it clear; however, that many regulations resulted from special-interest groups lobbying successfully for them. Four major reasons or justifications for regulations are typically offered: (1) controlling natural monopolies, (2) controlling negative externalities, (3) achieving social goals, and (4) other reasons.

Controlling Natural Monopolies. One of the earliest circumstances in which government felt a need to regulate occurred when a natural monopoly existed. A **natural monopoly** exists in a market where the economies of scale are so great that the largest firm has the lowest costs and thus is able to drive out its competitors. Such a firm can supply the entire market more efficiently and cheaply than can several smaller firms. Local telephone service is a good example, because parallel sets of telephone wires would involve waste and duplication that would be much more costly. The same is true for railroads. Monopolies such as this may seem "natural," but when left to their own devices could restrict output and raise prices. This potential abuse justifies the regulation of monopolies. Therefore, we see public utilities, for example, regulated by a public utility commission. This commission determines the rates that the monopolist may charge its customers.[77]

Related to the control of natural monopolies is the government's desire to intervene when it thinks companies have engaged in anticompetitive practices, often called "antitrust" cases that are in violation of the Sherman Antitrust Act. Many of these circumstances arise when companies vertically integrate and make their companies dependent on them, or when there has been considerable consolidation in an industry, sparking concerns over limiting competition.[78] For example, in 2016 concerns over a proposed merger between AB InBev and SABMiller centered on AB InBev's control over beer distribution to consumers that would restrict the distribution of rival products.[79] Similarly, in 2011, the U.S. Justice Department and the Federal Communications Committee blocked the merger between AT&T and T-Mobile with concerns over AT&T being the largest provider of wireless service; this scenario was repeated in 2015 with the proposal, and defeat, of a T-Mobile and Sprint merger.[80] As another example, Staples faced regulatory hurdles in its quest to buy Office Depot.[81] Recent concerns over online platforms like Amazon, Google, Uber, and Airbnb that connect buyers and sellers through the Internet "sharing economy" have sparked concerns over natural monopolies that may need to be regulated in the future.[82]

Controlling Negative Externalities. Another important rationale for government regulation is that of controlling the **negative externalities** (or spillover effects) that result when the manufacture or use of a product gives rise to unplanned or unintended side effects on third parties (the producer and the consumer are first and second parties). Examples of these negative externalities are air pollution, water pollution, and improper disposal of toxic wastes. The consequence of such negative externalities is that neither the producer nor the consumer of the product directly "pays" for all the "costs" that are created by the manufacture of the product. The "costs" that must be borne by the public include an unpleasant or a foul atmosphere, illness, and the resulting health-care costs. These also have been called **social costs**, because they are absorbed by society rather than incorporated into the cost of making the product.

Preventing negative externalities is enormously expensive, and few firms are willing to pay for these added costs voluntarily. This is especially true in an industry that produces an essentially undifferentiated product, such as steel, where the millions of dollars needed to protect the environment would only add to the cost of the product and provide no benefit to the purchaser. In such situations, therefore, industry incumbents may even welcome government regulation because it requires all firms competing in a given industry to operate according to the same rules. By forcing all firms to incur the costs, regulation can level the competitive playing field.

Just as companies do not voluntarily take on extra expenditures for environmental protection, individuals often behave in the same fashion. For example, automobile emissions are one of the principal forms of air pollution; but, how many private individuals would voluntarily request an emissions control system if it were offered as optional equipment? In situations such as this, a government standard that requires everyone to adhere to the regulation is much more likely to address the public's concern for air pollution.[83]

Achieving Social Goals. Government not only employs regulations to address market failures and negative externalities but also seeks to use regulations to help achieve certain **social goals** it deems to be in the public interest. Some of these social goals are related to negative externalities in the sense that government is attempting to correct problems that might also be viewed as negative externalities by particular groups. An example of this might be the harmful effects of a dangerous product or the unfair treatment of minorities resulting from employment discrimination. These externalities are not as obvious as air pollution, but they are just as real.

Another important social goal of government is to keep people informed. One could argue that inadequate information is a serious problem and that government should use its regulatory powers to require firms to reveal certain kinds of information to consumers. Thus, the Consumer Product Safety Commission requires firms to warn consumers of potential product hazards through labeling requirements. Other regulatory mandates that address the issue of inadequate information include grading standards, weight and size information, truth-in-advertising requirements, and product safety standards.

Other important social goals that have been addressed include preservation of national security (deregulation of oil prices to lessen dependence on imports), considerations of fairness or equity (employment discrimination laws), protection of those who provide essential services (farmers), allocation of scarce resources (gasoline rationing), and protection of consumers from excessively high price increases (natural gas regulation).[84]

Other Reasons. One rationale for regulation is to deal with **excessive competition**. The basic idea behind this rationale is that excessive competition will lead to prices being set at unprofitably low levels. This action will force firms out of business and ultimately will result in products that are too costly because the remaining firm will raise its prices to excessive levels, leaving the public worse off than before.[85] Another rationale for regulation occurs when a company or companies are deemed important to the general health of the national economy. For example, in 2008, the U.S. government entered a conservatorship with the Federal National Mortgage Association (Fannie Mae) and the Federal Home Loan Mortgage Corporation (Freddie Mac), two federally chartered but privately owned companies that required bailout money following the economic crisis in 2008. Under the **conservatorship** of the U.S. government, the two mortgage/financing behemoths received $187.5 billion and, by 2012, the companies were making money for their shareholders. However, the government's position became controversial with the announcement by the U.S. Treasury Department and the conservator agency, the Federal Housing Finance Agency (FHFA), that there would be an annual dividend to the government at 100 percent of its net worth.[86] There were no terms to repay the principal, effectively nationalizing the two companies and, in the words of some, "wiping out the shareholders."[87] Overall, while there are many reasons to regulate, the process and justification for doing so is often controversial.

11.5c Types of Regulation

Broadly speaking, government regulations address two basic types of goals, economic and social; therefore, it has become customary to identify two different types of regulation: economic regulation and social regulation.

Economic Regulation. The classical or traditional form of regulation that dates back to the 1800s in the United States is **economic regulation**. This type of regulation is best exemplified by old-line regulatory bodies such as the Interstate Commerce Commission (ICC), which was created in 1887 by Congress to regulate the railroad industry; the Civil Aeronautics Board (CAB), which was created in 1940; and the Federal Communications Commission (FCC), which was established in 1934 to consolidate federal regulation of interstate communications and, later, the radio, telephone, and telegraph. These regulatory

ETHICS IN PRACTICE CASE

The Marijuana Regulatory Dilemma

In the United States in 1996, California's voters legalized the sale of marijuana for medical use. Since then, over 25 more states have done the same; however, it has yet to be approved on the federal level. This provides a dilemma for businesses in those states that regularly test employees for substance abuse. In *Coats v. Dish Network*, a Colorado employee who is quadriplegic and used medical marijuana outside of working hours sued for wrongful termination of his job after he tested positive for marijuana. The confusing legal landscape led to his claim that Colorado labor laws (i.e., state laws) deemed his use of marijuana legal and thus his termination illegal. The Colorado Supreme Court ruled against Mr. Coats, however, because Mr. Coats broke the law by using a product that is illegal under the federal Controlled Substances Act.

This case highlights the confusing and complex issues of drug policy and law in the United States. Contradictions between state and federal statutes also cross over to the sales of recreational marijuana. In 2014 in the United States, the states of Colorado and Washington began selling it for recreational use and Oregon and Alaska recently approved its sale. Proponents for the legalization of marijuana at the federal level note that regulated markets protect consumers, raise revenues, reduce the costs of enforcement, and put criminals out of business. Arguments against it capture those from the states who have opposed it up-to-date: the public-health effects of marijuana, the increased tax burden, the danger of cannabis "edibles" with young children, and its potentially addictive nature. The legalization of marijuana has been more of a debate in the United States than in other countries, particularly because of the contradictions between state and federal laws. Much of Europe has embraced the sale of medical marijuana, and Australia recently announced similar plans. Jamaica has legalized "ganja" for broadly defined religious purposes and Spain allows users to grow and buy it through small collectives. At the time of this writing, Canada had plans to legalize it for recreational use in 2017.

1. What are the ethical issues in this case? Who are the stakeholders, and what are their stakes?
2. How are the two issues different—the legalization of marijuana for medical use versus the legalization of marijuana for recreational use?
3. U.S. state versus federal law makes this issue particularly complex. What are other examples of industries where U.S. state and federal law are seemingly at odds?
4. What actions should the federal government take to help resolve this conflict between federal and state laws?

Sources: David McNew, "The Conflict between Federal and State Marijuana Laws Claims a Victim," Newsweek (June 20, 2015), http://www.newsweek.com/conflict-between-federal-and-state-marijuana-laws-claims-victim-345099. Accessed February 27, 2016; "Reefer Regulatory Challenge," *The Economist* (February 13, 2016), 18.

bodies divide along industry lines: They regulate business behavior through the controlling and influencing economic or market variables such as prices (maximum and minimum), entry to and exit from markets, and types of services offered.[88]

In the federal regulatory budget, the major costs of economic regulation are for (1) finance and banking (e.g., Federal Deposit Insurance Corporation and Comptroller of the Currency), (2) industry-specific regulation (e.g., Federal Communications Commission and Federal Energy Regulatory Commission), and (3) general business (e.g., Department of Commerce, Department of Justice, Securities and Exchange Commission, and Federal Trade Commission).[89] Again, many of these economic regulations are accompanied by some controversy and debate. For example, one of the criticisms of the Dodd–Frank Consumer Financial Protection Act (discussed in detail in Chapter 5), is that it empowers regulators like the Securities and Exchange Commission, the Federal Trade Commission, the Financial Stability Oversight Council and the Consumer Financial Protection Bureau to set rules on their own, rather than implement requirements set by Congress.[90]

Later we discuss deregulation, a trend that has significantly affected the old-line form of economic regulation that dominated business–government relations in the last century.

Social Regulation. The 1960s ushered in a new form of regulation that has come to be known as **social regulation**, because its major thrust is the furtherance of societal objectives quite different from the earlier focus on markets and economic variables. While economic regulation focuses on markets, social regulation focuses on business's impacts on people. This emphasis on people addresses the needs of people in their roles as employees, consumers, and citizens.

Two major examples of social regulations having specific impacts on people as employees were (1) the Civil Rights Act of 1964, which created the Equal Employment Opportunity Commission (EEOC) and (2) the creation of the Occupational Safety and Health Administration (OSHA) in 1970. The goal of the EEOC is to provide protection against discrimination in all employment practices. The goal of OSHA is to ensure that the nation's workplaces are safe and healthy. Examples of major social regulations protecting people as consumers were the 1972 creation of the Consumer Product Safety Commission (CPSC), and the 2011 creation of the Consumer Financial Protection Bureau (CFPB). More recently, social regulations run the gamut from reducing exposure limits to silica, a chemical used in construction and fracking, to requiring more small-scale gun sellers to perform background checks, to more disclosure about how much sugar is disclosed on product labels.[91] In fact, amid a general climate of distrust with the U.S. government, a 2015 Pew research survey found that over 50 percent of respondents thought that the federal government was doing well in the following social areas[92]:

- Responding to natural disasters
- Setting standards for workplaces
- Keeping the country safe from terrorism
- Ensuring safe food and medicine
- Protecting the environment
- Ensuring access to health care
- Maintaining infrastructure
- Ensuring access to education

However, the survey also noted that less than 50 percent of respondents felt good about the government's role in providing for social needs in the areas of ensuring basic income for the elderly, helping people get out of poverty and managing the immigration system.[93]

Figure 11-4 summarizes the nature of economic versus social regulations along with pertinent examples. Whereas economic regulation aims primarily at companies

FIGURE 11-4 Comparison of Economic and Social Regulations

	Economic Regulations	Social Regulations
Focus	Market conditions, economic variables (entry, exit, prices, services)	People in their roles as employees, consumers, and citizens
Industries affected	Selected (railroads, aeronautics, communications)	Virtually all industries
Examples	Civil Aeronautics Board (CAB)	Equal Employment Opportunity Commission (EEOC)
	Federal Communications Commission (FCC)	Occupational Safety and Health Administration (OSHA)
		Consumer Product Safety Commission (CPSC)
		Environmental Protection Agency (EPA)
Current trend	Reregulation (e.g., Financial Stability Oversight Board)	Reregulation (e.g., Consumer Financial Protection Bureau)

ETHICS IN PRACTICE CASE

Banning the Big Gulp

New York City Mayor Michael Bloomberg created a firestorm when he proposed a ban on large sugary soft drinks. The proposed ban limited sugary drinks (including sodas, energy drinks, and presweetened iced teas) to cups no larger than 16 ounces. It does not apply to diet drinks and customers would have been allowed to get refills. The ban only applied to restaurants, movie theaters, stadiums, and arenas. It did not apply to grocery stores, drug stores, or convenience stores because those are regulated by New York State rather than the city.

The purpose of the ban was to stem a rising tide of obesity that has been linked to sugary drinks. The protests did not question the motivation; they attacked the ban on other grounds. Some argued that the ban oversteps the role of government and interferes in a personal decision. Others argued that it would create unfair competition because someone who wants a 20-ounce drink can simply go to a convenience store and buy a bottle there. The NAACP entered a lawsuit against the ban on the grounds that it generates racial discrimination because the smaller establishments to which the ban applies are more likely to be owned by people of color. At the same time, people of color have a higher incidence of obesity and so proponents argue the N.A.A.C.P. should welcome the ban.

1. Who are the stakeholders in this case, and what are their stakes?
2. The ban received approval from the New York City Board of Health, but a state Supreme Court judge subsequently halted it. Mayor Bloomberg vowed to appeal. Irrespective of the legal wrangling, was the ban appropriate? Should the city, as local government, ever be allowed to institute it?
3. Did the ban represent racial discrimination? Was the N.A.A.C.P. right to join in the lawsuit?
4. Where should government (federal, state, or local) draw the line on what it regulates and what it leaves to the marketplace?

Sources: Chris Dolmetsch, "NYC Judge Told Big-Soda Ban Is Unfair to Small Business," *Bloomberg.com* (January 23, 2013), http://www.bloomberg.com/news/2013-01-23/nyc-judge-told-big-soda-ban-is-unfair-to-small-business.html. Accessed February 29, 2016; Michael M. Grynbaum," "In N.A.A.C.P., Industry Gets Ally against Soda Ban," *The New York Times* (January 23, 2013), http://www.nytimes.com/2013/01/24/nyregion/fight-over-bloombergs-soda-ban-reaches-courtroom.html?_r=0. Accessed February 29, 2016.

competing in specific industries, the social regulation tends to addresses business practices affecting all industries. However, there are social regulations that are industry specific, such as the National Highway Traffic Safety Administration (automobiles) and the Food and Drug Administration (food, drugs, medical devices, and cosmetics).

11.5d Issues Related to Regulation

It is important to consider some of the issues that have arisen out of the increased governmental role in regulating business. In general, managers have been concerned with what might be called "regulatory unreasonableness."[94] We could expect that business would just as soon not have to deal with these regulatory bodies; therefore, some of business's reactions are simply related to the nuisance factor of having to deal with a complex array of restrictions. However, other legitimate issues that have arisen over the past few years also need to be addressed.

To be certain, there are benefits of government regulations. Businesses treat employees more fairly and provide them with safer work environments. Consumers are able to purchase safer products and receive more information about them. Citizens from all lifestyles have cleaner air to breathe and cleaner water in lakes and rivers. These benefits are real, but their exact magnitudes are difficult to measure. Costs resulting from regulation also are difficult to measure. The **direct costs** of regulation are most visible when we look at the number of new agencies created, aggregate expenditures, and growth patterns of the budgets of federal agencies responsible for regulation. There were 14 major regulatory agencies prior to 1930, over two dozen in 1950, and 57 by the early 1980s.

FIGURE 11-5 Regulatory Spending in the United States

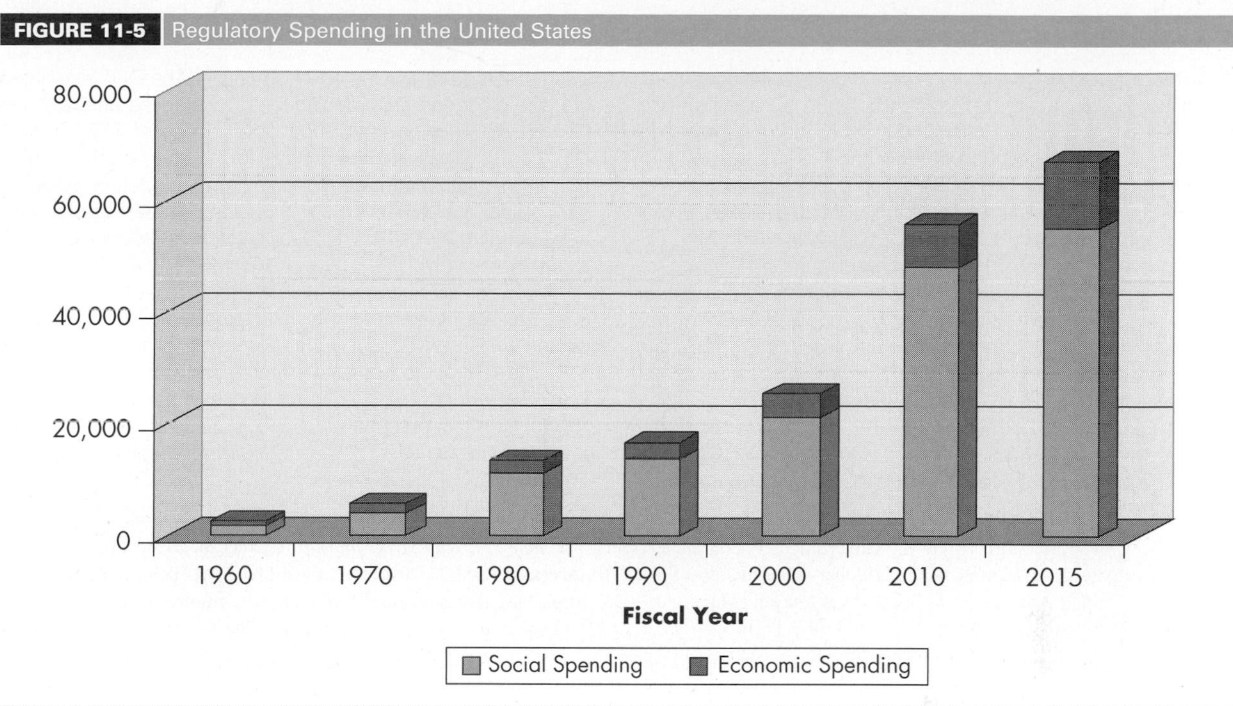

Source: Susan E. Dudley and Melinda Warren, "2016 Regulators' Budget: Increases Consistent with Growth in Fiscal Budget," Weidenbaum Center, Washington University and the George Washington University Regulatory Studies Center,https://regulatorystudies.columbian.gwu.edu /2016-regulators-budget-increases-consistent-growth-fiscal-budget. Accessed March 1, 2016.

The most rapid expansion in the number of agencies came in the 1970s, whereas the most rapid increase in spending came in the 2000s. Figure 11-5 shows the rise in spending for both economic and social regulation in millions of constant 2,000 dollars.

Interestingly, government agencies in the U.S. are required to conduct a cost-benefit analysis for every regulation expected to cost $100 million or more in a year. They do this with something called the value of statistical life (VSL) estimate. Read more about this technique in Figure 11-6.

In addition to the direct costs of administering the regulatory agencies, there are **indirect costs** such as forms, reports, and questionnaires that business must complete to satisfy the requirements of the regulatory agencies. These costs of government regulation are passed on to the consumer in the form of higher prices. There are also **induced costs**. The induced effects of regulation are diffuse and elusive, but they constitute some of the most powerful consequences of the regulatory process. Truly, then, these induced effects are also costs. Three induced effects are worthy of elaboration.[95]

1. *Innovation may be affected.* When corporate budgets must focus on "defensive research," certain types of innovation are less likely to take place. To the extent that firms must devote more of their scientific resources to meeting government requirements, fewer resources are available to dedicate to new product and process research and development and innovation. However, the relationship is anything but clear. A study showed that deregulation actually had a dramatic negative impact on public interest environmental research by public utilities, whereas regulation can have a positive impact on pollution abatement research by profit maximizing firms.[96] The moral of these findings seems to be that organizations will pursue their own interests. Regulation can require firms to lower their pollution and pursue greater

FIGURE 11-6 What Is the Value of Statistical Life?

When the U.S. government considers a new regulation that is expected to cost over $100 million or more a year, they are required to perform a cost/benefit analysis to assess the amount of money the public is willing to spend on one life. This is done through a technique called the Value of Statistical Life (VSL), where legislators and regulators attempt to answer questions of spending for consumer safety, food labeling, airline equipment, or other regulatory issues by calculating the value of a human life relative to the cost. In a recent example of how this works, *The Wall Street Journal* described how the Department of Transportation considered the decision to mandate that truckers and bus drivers record their hours of driving electronically (instead of by paper) with the hopes of reducing the number of crashes related to driver fatigue. The DOT valued the statistical life at $9.2 million, well within the $7 million to $10 million range that the U.S. Office of Management and Budget puts for the value of a human life. The DOT estimated that the electronic records would save 26 lives annually and prevent 562 injuries for a total safety value of $572 million, plus cost savings of $2.4 billion, for a total benefit of over $3 billion. With estimated annual implementation costs of $1.8 billion, the DOT decided to implement the regulation for a net benefit of $1 billion—a seemingly easy decision through cost/benefit analysis.

While the VSL seems to make sense, it is also controversial. After all, who is really qualified to put a dollar figure on a person's life? In addition, what about those potential regulatory issues that do not easily factor into cost/benefit analysis? However, the VSL is based on estimates from surveys and market data on consumer choices, and some see that as a better alternative to arbitrary numbers selected by the government.

Sources: Jo Craven McGinty, "Why the Government Puts a Dollar Value on Life," *The Wall Street Journal* (March 26, 2016), http://www.wsj.com/articles/why-the-government-puts-a-dollar-value-on-life-1458911310. Accessed April 30, 2016; Jo Craven McGinty, "Behind the Numbers: VSL in Cost-Benefit Analyses," *The Wall Street Journal* (March 20, 2016), http://blogs.wsj.com/numbers/behind-the-numbers-vsl-in-cost-benefit-analyses-2186/. Accessed April 23, 2016; Frank Partnoy, "The Cost of Human Life, Statistically Speaking," The Globalist (July 21, 2012), http://www.theglobalist.com/the-cost-of-a-human-life-statistically-speaking/. Accessed April 30, 2016.

expenditures on research to lower emissions. In contrast, utilities that once received reinforcement for doing research in the public interest may find they no longer have an incentive for that research once they begin to compete on the basis of profits.

2. *New investments in plant and equipment may be affected.* To the extent that corporate funds must be used for regulatory compliance purposes, these funds are diverted from uses that are more productive. Environmental and job safety requirements lessen productivity and uncertainty about future regulations diminishes motivation for introducing new products and processes.[97] Once again, the incentives will play a major part. Investments that aid the firms in complying with regulations are likely to be continued or increased, whereas those that are beyond the scope of the regulation are likely to diminish.
3. *Small business may be adversely affected.* Although it is not intentional, federal regulations can have a disproportionately adverse effect on small firms because of economies of scale. Large firms have more money, personnel, and resources with which to get the work of government done than do small firms do. They can spread the costs over a larger base, whereas small companies can find their resources drained from their efforts to comply.

Robert Reich's advice to executives who feel the government is breathing down their necks has been, "Get used to it."[98] That advice is true today, as companies worldwide will be dealing with regulatory concerns for the foreseeable future. In financial services, governments in the United States, Europe, and Japan now hold equity in banks. In housing, the U.S. government has taken over a large portion of outstanding mortgage loans. The controversial bailout of insurance giant AIG made the United States a major participant in insurance markets. In the auto industry, the United States, Canada, Germany, Sweden, and Japan provided tens of billions of dollars in loans and equity. The United States, Europe, and Japan are all subsidizing non-carbon-based energy development. The United States is enacting health-care reforms that will affect both the health-care and pharmaceutical industries and it is investing in greater broadband coverage that will affect the telecom industry.

11.6 Deregulation

Quite frequently, trends and countertrends overlap with one another. Such is the case with regulation and its counterpart, **deregulation**. From an economic perspective, a continual striving for the balance of freedom and control for business will be best for society. From a political perspective, there is an ongoing interplay of different societal goals and means for achieving those goals. The outcome is a mix of economic and political decisions that seem to be in a constant state of flux. Thus, in the economy at any point in time, trends that appear counter to one another can coexist. These trends are the natural result of competing forces seeking some sort of balance or equilibrium.

This explains how the trend toward deregulation evolved in a highly regulated environment. Deregulation represents a counterforce aimed at keeping the economy in balance. It also represents a political philosophy that prevailed during the period of its origin and growth.

Deregulation is one kind of regulatory reform. It is unique and quite unlike the regulatory reform measures discussed earlier, so we treat it separately. Deregulation has taken place primarily with respect to economic regulations, and this, too, helps to explain its separate treatment.

11.6a Purpose of Deregulation

The basic idea behind deregulation has been to remove certain industries from the old-line economic regulations of the past. The purpose of this deregulation, or at least a reduced level of regulation, has been to increase competition with the expected benefits of greater efficiency, lower prices, and enhanced innovation. These goals are not always met and so debate continues regarding whether deregulation works as a method of maximizing society's best interests. The positives of deregulation include that it allows more innovation while allowing the free market to set prices. The negatives include that it can allow asset bubbles to build and burst (like a housing crisis) and industries that have large initial infrastructure costs may have a difficult time getting started.[99]

11.6b The Changing World of Deregulation

A trend toward deregulation began in the 1980s, most notably exemplified in the financial industry, the telecommunications industry, and the transportation (trucking, airline, railroad) industry represented business's first major redirection in 50 years.[100] The result seemed to be a mixed bag of benefits and problems. On the benefits side, prices fell in many industries, and better service appeared in some industries along with increased numbers of competitors and innovative products and services.

Several problems arose also. Although prices fell and many competitors entered some of those industries, more and more of those competitors were unable to compete with the dominant firms. They were failing, going bankrupt, or being absorbed by the larger firms. Entry barriers into some industries were enormous and had been greatly underestimated. Deregulation is generally blamed for the savings and loan industry crisis, which resulted in an unprecedented $124 billion bailout by the U.S. government. Most dramatically, deregulation in the repeal of the Depression-era Glass–Steagall Act has been accused of causing the global recession that began in 2008.[101] Figure 11-7 outlines the debate surrounding the Glass–Steagall Act, a banking act dating back to 1933, which

FIGURE 11-7 The Glass–Steagall Act: To Regulate, or Not to Regulate?

The Glass–Steagall Act (GSA), also known as the Banking Act of 1933, prohibited commercial banks from operating as investment banks. In the wake of the stock market crash of 1929, it was considered prudent to curb overenthusiastic banking activity in stock market investment. In 1956, Congress and the Federal Reserve Board extended the Glass–Steagall to the Bank Holding Company Act, further separating banking and the underwriting of insurance, with the rationale extending to issues of antitrust and fear that the banks might become too big and controlling. However, the GSA at the time continued to spark debate over how much restriction is healthy for the banking industry. A strong argument against the GSA was that it did not offer the banking industry the opportunity to reduce potential risk through diversification. Perhaps in response to this argument, Congress repealed the GSA in 1999 with the Gramm-Leach Bliley Act, allowing banks to provide more services including underwriting and investment banking.

Since then, the repeal of the Glass–Steagall Act has come under fire, usually during times of economic strain. While many thought that the Sarbanes–Oxley Act of 2002, and its mandate for transparency, would plug the whole left when the GSA went away, that comfort fell away in the wake of the economic crisis of 2008/2009. In fact, the repeal of the Glass–Steagall Act became the "sine qua non" of the financial crisis for many. Senator Elizabeth Warren from Massachusetts, for example, sent an e-mail to her constituents pressing to bring back the law, which she said, "Stopped investment banks from gambling away people's life savings for decades—until Wall Street successfully lobbied to have it repealed in 1999." In response to this, analysts like Andrew Ross Sorkin pointed out that GSA would not have prevented the financial crisis, as the fall of both Bear Stearns and Lehman Brothers (both investment banks with no commercial business), as well as the issues surrounding Merrill Lynch, would not have been applicable under the GSA. Still, many feel that financial reforms like the Dodd–Frank Act of 2010 do not go far enough to prevent the too-big-to-fail mentality of U.S. banks that led to the 2009 bank bailouts. It remains to be seen whether current financial reforms are working, but Glass–Steagall will continue to pop up in political debates about whether it would have, and might still, prevent financial crises.

Sources: Robert Schmidt and Jesse Westbrook, "Wall Street Rules May Fall Short of Glass-Steagall," *Bloomberg Businessweek* (May 26, 2010), http://www.bloomberg.com/news/articles/2010-05-26/history-suggests-new-wall-street-regulations-won-t-prevent-the-next-crisis. Accessed March 11, 2016; Andrew Ross Sorkin, "Reinstating an Old Rule Is Not a Cure for Crisis," *Dealb%k* (May 21, 2012),http://dealbook.nytimes.com/2012/05/21/reinstating-an-old-rule-is-not-a-cure-for-crisis/?_r=0. Accessed March 11, 2016; Ream Heakal, "What Was the Glass Steagall Act?" *Investopedia*, http://www.investopedia.com/articles/03/071603.asp. Accessed March 11, 2016; Tracey Samuelson, "Why Do So Many People Love Glass-Steagall?" Marketplace, (January 5, 2016), http://www.marketplace.org/2016/01/05/world/glass-steagall. Accessed March 6, 2016.

prohibited retail banks from using deposits to fund risky stock market purchases. It was repealed in 1999; however, many believe that its repeal contributed to U.S. bank failings and the subsequent economic crisis in 2008.

Another problem that developed with deregulation in the 1980's was that a few firms began to dominate key industries. This trend was obvious in transportation, where the major railroad, airline, and trucking companies boosted their market shares considerably during that time. The top six railroads went from about 56 percent of market share to about 90 percent during this time. The top six airlines went from about 75 percent of market share to about 85 percent. The top ten trucking firms went from about 38 percent of market share to about 58 percent. Prior to its breakup, AT&T enjoyed about an 80 percent share of the domestic market and a virtual monopoly in the huge toll-free, big business, and overseas markets.[102]

The dilemma with deregulation is how to enhance the competitive nature of the affected industries without sacrificing the applicable social regulations, that is, to allow for freer competition without lowering health and safety requirements. Unfortunately, the dog-eat-dog competition unleashed by economic deregulation can force many companies to cut corners in ways that endanger the health, safety, and/or welfare of their customers. For example, the trucking industry spent about $37 million on lobbying for rules that industry officials said would save the industry billions.[103] The transportation department then issued rules that increased the maximum allowable hours of driving from 60 to 77 over seven consecutive days and from 70 to 88 hours over eight consecutive days. Maximum daily work hours (which includes loading) were set at 14.[104]

Congress provided very little scrutiny of trucking standards but the courts were less reticent. Concerned about the relaxed standards, several safety organizations brought a lawsuit to a federal appeals court. A three-judge panel ruled that the Federal Motor Carrier Safety Administration was guilty of "ignoring its own evidence that fatigue causes many truck accidents."[105] They went on to say that "the agency admits that studies show that crash risk increases, in the agency's words, 'geometrically' after the eighth hour on duty" and questioned the legality of the "agency's passive regulatory approach."[106] The American Trucking Association supported the rules, whereas the Teamsters Union opposed them. The Obama administration reduced drivers' maximum allowable hours of work per week from 82 hours to 70 hours and made comparable reductions in other fatigue-related issues such as breaks required.[107]

Financial services in the United States were one of the most heavily regulated industries until the passage of the Depository Institutions Deregulation and Monetary Control Act of 1980. It removed caps on deposit interest rates. Gradually, Congress then began to take apart the regulatory barriers that had been in place for decades. The Federal Deposit Insurance Improvement Act of 1991 loosened restrictions on deposit insurance premiums; the Neal–Riegle Interstate Banking Act of 1994 removed geographic restrictions on branches; and the Gramm–Leach–Bliley Act of 1999, as noted in Figure 11-7, created financial holding companies and removed enforced separation of insurance companies and commercial and investment banks.[108] It appeared that the deregulation of financial services would continue until two events, the World Trade Center attacks and the Enron financial scandals, changed the tide.

In response, a variety of agencies within the U.S. government began to issue new financial rules and regulations; The Internal Revenue Service, the FBI, the Justice Department, the Financial Crimes Enforcement Network, and the Federal Reserve each contributed to financial service **reregulation**.[109] The global financial recession motivated the Credit Card Act of 2009 and the Dodd–Frank Wall Street Reform and Consumer Protection Act of 2010. The landmark Dodd–Frank financial reform legislation created the Financial Stability Oversight Council (FSOC), which will determine which firms are critical to the financial system and thus should have higher capital requirements. It also created the Consumer Financial Protection Bureau, which allows consumers to sue credit rating agencies that recklessly overlook relevant information.[110]

Summary

Any discussion of business and society must consider the paramount role played by government. Although the two institutions have opposing systems of belief, they interconnect in their functioning in our socioeconomic system. In addition, the public assumes a major role in a complex pattern of interactions among business, government, and the public. Government exerts a host of nonregulatory influences on business. Two influences with a macro orientation include industrial policy and privatization. A more specific influence is the fact that government is a major employer, purchaser, subsidizer, competitor, financier, and persuader. These roles permit government to affect business significantly.

One of government's most controversial interventions in business is direct regulation. Government regulates business for several legitimate reasons, and social regulation has now become more dominant than economic regulation. There are many benefits and various costs of government regulation. A response to the problems with regulation has been deregulation. However, bad experiences in key industries such as trucking, airlines, telecommunication, financial services, and utilities have led to some reregulation and caused many to wonder what the optimal mix of regulation and deregulation should be.

Key Terms

collectivistic ethic of government, p. 346
conservatorship, p. 357
deregulation, p. 363
direct costs, p. 360
economic regulation, p. 357
excessive competition, p. 357
federalization, p. 352
indirect costs, p. 361
individualistic ethic of business, p. 346
induced costs, p. 361
industrial policy, p. 349
market failure, p. 355
natural monopoly, p. 355
negative externalities, p. 356
privatization, p. 351
regulation, p. 355
reregulation, p. 365
social costs, p. 356
social goals, p. 356
social regulation, p. 359

Discussion Questions

1. Briefly explain how business and government represent a clash of ethical systems (belief systems). With which do you find yourself identifying most? Explain. With which would most business students identify? Explain.
2. Explain why the public is treated as a separate group in the interactions among business, government, and the public. Doesn't government represent the public's interests? How should the public's interests be manifested?
3. What is regulation? Why does government see a need to regulate? Differentiate between economic and social regulation. What social regulations do you think are most important, and why? What social regulations ought to be eliminated? Explain.
4. Outline the major benefits and costs of government regulation. In general, do you think the benefits of government regulation exceed the costs? In what areas, if any, do you think the costs exceed the benefits?
5. What are the trade-offs between privatization and federalization? When would one or the other be more appropriate? What problems might you foresee and what future events would merit a shift in the current mix?
6. What are deregulation and reregulation? Under what circumstances should each be considered?

Endnotes

1. Philip Coggan, "A World of Robber Barons," *The Economist* (Vol. 410, No. 8875, February 22, 2014).
2. "In U.S., Half Still Say Government Regulates Too Much," Gallup (September 18, 2016), http://www.gallup.com/poll/185609/half-say-gov-regulates-business.aspx. Accessed March 1, 2016.
3. Coggan, 2014.
4. Curtis Verschoor, "Can Government Manage More Ethically than Capitalism?" *Strategic Finance* (October 2009), 15–16, 63.
5. Ibid.
6. Bob Davis, Damian Paletta, and Rebecca Smith, "Sour Economy Spurs Government to Grab a Bigger Oversight Role," *The Wall Street Journal* (July 25, 2008), A12.
7. Ibid.
8. "Antitrust Laws," *The World Book Encyclopedia*, Vol. 1 (Chicago: World Book, 1988), 560. See also "The Interstate Commerce Act" (Vol. 10), 352–353.
9. Ibid.
10. Ibid.
11. Ibid.
12. Alfred L. Seelye, "Societal Change and Business-Government Relationships," *MSU Business Topics* (Autumn 1975), 5–6.
13. "Is Government Dead?" *Time* (October 23, 1989).
14. Michael J. Mandel, "Rethinking the Economy," *Businessweek* (October 1, 2001), 28–33.
15. "25 People to Blame for the Financial Crisis," *Time* (November 24, 2009), http://content.time.com/time/specials/packages/article/0,28804,1877351_1877350_1877339,00.html. Accessed February 26, 2016.
16. Paul Magnusson, "Suddenly, Washington's Wallet Is Open," *Businessweek* (October 1, 2001), 34.
17. Mandel, 30.
18. Stuart Taylor, "Book Review: 'The Rule of Nobody by Philip K. Howard'," *The Wall Street Journal* (April 8, 2014), A13.

19. Charles Murray, "Fifty Shades of Red: A Modest Proposal for Rejecting the Rules," *The Wall Street Journal* (May 9/10, 2015), C1.
20. Ibid.
21. Leigh Buchanan, "How Successful CEOs Really Feel about 2016," Inc. (December 2015/January 2016), http://www.inc.com/magazine/201512/leigh-buchanan/2015-state-of-small-business-health-care-cost-regulations.html. Accessed February 26, 2016.
22. Amy Harder, "Obama Proposes Tax on Oil Firms," *The Wall Street Journal* (February 5, 2016), A2.
23. Jason Ankeny, "The Challenges of Doing Business in Cuba," *Entrepreneur* (December 15, 2015), http://www.entrepreneur.com/article/252795. Accessed February 26, 2016.
24. L. Earle Birdsell, "Business and Government: The Walls Between," in Neil H. Jacoby (ed.), *The Business—Government Relationship: A Reassessment* (Santa Monica, CA: Goodyear, 1975), 32–34.
25. Neil H. Jacoby, *Corporate Power and Social Responsibility* (New York: Macmillan, 1973), 167.
26. Nancy Killefer, "The New Business of Government," *McKinsey Quarterly* (Issue 3, 2009), 7.
27. Naftali Bendavid, "Rage at Government for Doing Too Much and Not Enough," *The Wall Street Journal* (October 13, 2009), A5.
28. Dan Balz, "Survey: America Has Changed. Have Government and Business?" *The Washington Post* (January 12, 2014), https://www.washingtonpost.com/politics/survey-america-has-changed-have-government-and-business/2014/01/11/f0fdf194-7a35-11e3-b1c5-739e63e9c9a7_story.html. Accessed February 26, 2016.
29. "Should the Government Intervene with Free Market and Save Failing Businesses?," *Debate.org*, http://www.debate.org/opinions/should-the-government-intervene-with-the-free-market-and-save-failing-businesses. Accessed February 26, 2016.
30. James Foreman-Peck and Giovanni Frederico, *European Industrial Policy: The Twentieth-Century Experience* (Oxford University Press, 1999).
31. Karl Aiginger, "Industrial Policy: A Dying Breed or a Reemerging Phoenix?" *Journal of Industry, Competition & Trade* (December 2007), 297–323.
32. Robert B. Reich, *The Next American Frontier* (New York: Penguin Books, 1983).
33. Sharon Silke Carty, "Obama Pushes Electric Cars, Battery Power This Week," *USA Today* (July 14, 2010), http://content.usatoday.com/communities/driveon/post/2010/07/obama-pushes-electric-cars-battery-power-this-week-/1#.VtMJbuaUQmQ. Accessed February 28, 2016.
34. U.S. Department of Energy, "Recovery Act Announcement: President Obama Announces $2.4 Billion for Electric Vehicles" (March 19, 2009), http://apps1.eere.energy.gov/news/progress_alerts.cfm/news_id=19814. Accessed February 28, 2016.
35. Jerry Hirsch, "Elon Musk's Growing Empire Is Fueled by $4.9 Billion in Government Subsidies," Los Angeles Times (May 30, 2015), http://www.latimes.com/business/la-fi-hy-musk-subsidies-20150531-story.html. Accessed February 28, 2016.
36. European Commission Interim Report on Energy Costs and Subsidies for EU28 across Power Generation Technologies (October 13, 2014), European Commission Press Release, http://europa.eu/rapid/press-release_IP-14-1131_en.htm. Accessed February 28, 2016.
37. Clyde Prestowitz, "America's Industrial Policy," *Foreign Policy* (March 6, 2012), http://prestowitz.foreignpolicy.com/posts/2012/03/06/americas_industrial_policy. Accessed February 28, 2016.
38. Ibid.
39. Anonymous, "The Clinton Administration's Framework for Global Electronic Commerce: Executive Summary (July 1, 1997)," *Business America* (Vol. 119, No. 1, January 1998), 5–6.
40. Jonathan Weisman, "F.C.C. Net Neutrality Rules Clear Hurdle as Republicans Concede to Obama," *The New York Times* (February 24, 2015), http://www.nytimes.com/2015/02/25/technology/path-clears-for-net-neutrality-ahead-of-fcc-vote.html?_r=0. Accessed February 26, 2016.
41. See Victor Luckerson, "Obama Calls For Drone Regulation after White House Crash," Time (January 27, 2015) http://time.com/3683923/obama-drone-regulation/. Accessed February 28, 2016; Jim Fisher, "Drone Regulations: What You Need to Know," *PC Magazine* (December 24, 2015), http://www.pcmag.com/article2/0,2817,2491507,00.asp. Accessed March 1, 2016.
42. Killefer, 7.
43. Ibid.
44. Tom Cohen, "President Obama Unveils $3.8 Trillion Budget," *CNN Politics* (February 13, 2012), http://www.cnn.com/2012/02/13/politics/obama-congress-budget/. Accessed May 1, 2016.
45. Sergio Lazzarini, "Strategizing by the Government: Can Industrial Policy Create Firm-Level Competitive Advantage?" *Strategic Management Journal* (Vol. 36, No. 1, January 2015), 97–112.
46. Jeffrey Kutler, "Financial Industrial Policy," *Security Industry News* (April 30, 2007), http://www.securitiesindustry.com/issues/20070429/20313-1.html. Accessed February 9, 2013.
47. Ira C. Magaziner and Robert B. Reich, *Minding America's Business: The Decline and Rise of the American Economy* (New York: Vintage Books, 1983), 255.
48. http://www.merriam-webster.com/dictionary/privatize. Accessed February 9, 2013.

49. Shaker A. Zahra, R. Duane Ireland, Isabel Gutierrez, and Michael A. Hitt, "Privatization and Entrepreneurial Transformation: Emerging Issues and a Future Research Agenda," *Academy of Management Review* (July 2000), 509–524.
50. Ted Kolderie, "What Do We Mean by Privatization?" (St. Louis: Center for the Study of American Business, Washington University, May 1986), 2–5.
51. Ibid., 3–5.
52. John B. Goodman and Gary W. Loveman, "Does Privatization Serve the Public Interest?," *Harvard Business Review* (Vol. 69, No. 6, 1990), 26–36.
53. Bart Jansen, "Controversial Bill Aims to Privatize Air-Traffic Control," *USA Today* (February 3, 2016), B1.
54. Ibid.
55. Kelly Yamanouchi, "Hartsfield-Jackson May Seek Private Screeners" *Atlanta Journal Constitution* (February 19, 2016), http://www.myajc.com/news/business/hartsfield-jackson-may-seek-private-screeners/nqS5s/. Accessed February 26, 2016.
56. Ibid.
57. Ann Markusen, "The Case against Privatizing National Security," *Governance* (Vol. 16, No. 4, 2003), 471–501.
58. Eduardo Porter, "When Public Outperforms Private in Services," *The New York Times* (January 15, 2013), http://www.nytimes.com/2013/01/16/business/when-privatization-works-and-why-it-doesnt-always.html. Accessed March 30, 2016.
59. Ibid.
60. Donald Cohen, "Is the Tragedy in Flint an Opening for Privatization?" *Huffington Post* (January 28, 2016), http://www.huffingtonpost.com/donald-cohen/is-the-tragedy-in-flint-a_b_9103320.html. Accessed March 1, 2016.
61. Ibid.
62. Sam Dolnick, "As Escapees Stream Out a Penal Business Thrives," *The New York Times* (June 16, 2012), http://www.nytimes.com/2012/06/17/nyregion/in-new-jersey-halfway-houses-escapees-stream-out-as-a-penal-business-thrives.html?_r=2. Accessed April 9, 2016.
63. Ibid.
64. Alvaro Cuervo and Bélen Villalonga, "Explaining the Variance in the Performance Effects of Privatization," *Academy of Management Review* (July 2000), 581–590.
65. Suzanne Leland and Olga Smirnova, "Reassessing Privatization Strategies 25 Years Later: Revisiting Perry and Babitsky's Comparative Performance Study of Urban Bus Transit Services," *Public Administration Review* (September/October 2009), 855–867.
66. Richard Reed, David J. Lemak, and W. Andrew Hesser, "Cleaning Up after the Cold War: Management and Social Issues," *Academy of Management Review* (Vol. 22, No. 3, July 1997), 614–642.
67. Murray L. Weidenbaum, *Business, Government and the Public*, 3rd ed. (Englewood Cliffs, NJ: Prentice Hall, 1986), 5–6.
68. Ibid., 6–8.
69. "Did the Federal Reserve's Lending during the Recession Violate the Law?," *Monthly Labor Review* (September 2012), 35–36; Elizabeth Dwoskin and Karen Weise, "The Government Takes Aim at Risky Student Loans," *Bloomberg Businessweek* (July 20, 2012), http://www.businessweek.com/articles/2012-07-20/the-government-takes-aim-at-risky-student-loan. Accessed March 15, 2016.
70. See James Surowiecki, "Why Firms Are Fleeing," The New Yorker (January 11, 2016), http://www.newyorker.com/magazine/2016/01/11/why-firms-are-fleeing. Accessed March 11, 2016; Chris Matthews, "Why Washington Is Tackling the Tax Inversion Problem All Wrong," Fortune (November 25, 2015), http://fortune.com/2015/11/25/why-republicans-democrats-tax-plans-inversion-problem/. Accessed March 10, 2016.
71. "Why Giving Politicians Influence over Monetary Policy Is a Bad Idea," *The Economist* (March 10, 2016), http://www.economist.com/blogs/economist-explains/2016/03/economist-explains-7. Accessed April 30, 2016.
72. Jacob E. Gersen, "How the Feds Use Title IX to Bully Universities," *The Wall Street Journal* (January 24, 2016), http://www.wsj.com/articles/how-the-feds-use-title-ix-to-bully-universities-1453669725, April 30, 2016.
73. Ibid.
74. *Federal Register*, "Federal Register Pages Published Annually," https://www.federalregister.gov/index/2015. Accessed March 1, 2016.
75. *Congressional Quarterly's Federal Regulatory Directory*, 5th ed. (1985–1986), 2.
76. Ibid., 2–3.
77. Ibid., 9.
78. Lina Khan, "The Next President Should Break Up Some Big Companies," *The Washington Post* (October 28, 2015), https://www.washingtonpost.com/posteverything/wp/2015/10/28/the-next-president-should-break-up-some-big-companies/. Accessed March 1, 2016.
79. David McLaughlin, "AB InBev Faces In-Depth U.S. Antitrust Review on SABMiller Deal," *Bloomberg Businessweek* (January 14, 2016), http://www.bloomberg.com/news/articles/2016-01-14/ab-inbev-faces-in-depth-u-s-antitrust-review-on-sabmiller-deal. Accessed March 1, 2016.
80. "Sprint, T-Mobile Could Combine Network Assets into a New Company, Analysts Argue," *FierceWireless* (September 22, 2015). Accessed March 1, 2016. http://www.fiercewireless.com/story/sprint-t-mobile-could-combine-network-assets-new-company-analysts-argue/2015-09-22

81. Shelly Banjo, "Forget that Staples-Office Depot Deal," *Bloomberg* (January 20, 2016), http://www.bloomberg.com/gadfly/articles/2016-01-20/staples-office-depot-merger-will-fail. Accessed March 11, 2016.
82. Lina Khan, 2015.
83. *Congressional Quarterly's Federal Regulatory Directory*, 10–11.
84. Ibid., 12.
85. Stephen Breyer, *Regulation and Its Reform* (Cambridge, MA: Harvard University Press, 1982), 31–32.
86. Roger Parloff, "Uncle Sam's $130 Billion Money Grab," *Fortune* (December 1, 2015), 112.
87. Ibid.
88. Weidenbaum, 178–179.
89. Melinda Warren, "Federal Regulatory Spending Reaches a New Height: An Analysis of the Budget of the U.S. Government for the Year 2001" (St. Louis, Missouri: Center for the Study of American Business, June 2000); derived from the budget of the U.S. government.
90. Phill Gramm, "Dodd-Frank's Double Whammy," *The Wall Street Journal* (July 24, 2015), http://www.wsj.com/articles/dodd-franks-nasty-double-whammy-1437692851. Accessed February 22, 2016.
91. Timothy Noah, "Obama Pushing Thousands of New Regulations in Year 8," *Politico* (January 14, 2016), http://www.politico.com/agenda/agenda/story/2016/1/obama-regulations-2016. Accessed March 1, 2016.
92. Pew Research Foundation, "Beyond Distrust: How Americans View Their Government" (November 23, 2015), http://www.people-press.org/2015/11/23/3-views-of-governments-performance-and-role-in-specific-areas/. Accessed February 26, 2016.
93. Ibid.
94. Graham K. Wilson, *Business and Politics: A Comparative Introduction*, 3d ed. (Chatham, NJ: Chatham House, 2003).
95. Ibid., 12–14.
96. Paroma Sanyal, "The Effect of Deregulation on Environmental Research by Electric Utilities," *Journal of Regulatory Economics* (June 2007), 335–353.
97. Ibid., 12.
98. Reich, 98.
99. Kimberly Amadeo, "Deregulation: Definition, Pros, Cons, Examples," *AboutNews* (February 8, 2016). http://useconomy.about.com/od/glossary/g/deregulation.htm. Accessed March 12, 2016.
100. "Deregulating America," *Businessweek* (November 28, 1983), 80–89.
101. Alison Vekshin, "U.S. Senators Propose Reinstating Glass–Steagall Act," *Bloomberg.com* (December 16, 2009), http://www.bloomberg.com/apps/news?pid=newsarchive&sid=aQfRyxBZs5uc. Accessed April 9, 2016.
102. Ibid., 52.
103. Stephen Labaton, "As Trucking Rules Are Eased, a Debate on Safety Intensifies," *The New York Times* (December 3, 2006), 1, 30.
104. Ibid.
105. Ibid., 30.
106. Ibid., 30.
107. https://www.fmcsa.dot.gov/newsroom/new-hours-service-safety-regulations-reduce-truck-driver-fatigue-begin-today. Accessed March 9, 2016.
108. "Financial Deregulation," Chapter 21, *Cato Handbook for Congress: Policy Recommendations for the 108th Congress* (2003), http://object.cato.org/sites/cato.org/files/serials/files/cato-handbook-policymakers/2003/9/hb108-63.pdf. Accessed April 29, 2016.
109. Richard W. Rahn, "Regulatory Malpractice," *The Cato Institute* (March 27, 2004), http://www.cato.org/publications/commentary/regulatory-malpractice. Accessed April 30, 2016.
110. David Lawder, "Timeline: Long Road to Implement Financial Reform Bill," *Reuters.com* (July 21, 2010), http://www.reuters.com/article/idUSTRE66K49320100721. Accessed February 7, 2016.

12

Business Influence on Government and Public Policy

CHAPTER LEARNING OUTCOMES

After studying this chapter, you should be able to:

1 Describe the evolution of corporate political participation, including the different levels at which business lobbying occurs.

2 Discuss corporate political spending and the arguments for and against it.

3 Describe the different types of political action committees (PACs), in terms of their historical growth, and the magnitude of their activity.

4 Describe the agency issues involved with corporate political spending and some of the contexts where these might arise.

5 Discuss the issues of corporate political accountability and disclosure.

6 Outline the types of strategies for corporate political activity.

As our previous discussion of industrial policy showed, government is a central stakeholder of business. Government's interest, or stake, in business is broad and multifaceted, and its power is derived from its legal and moral right to represent the public in its dealings with business. Today, because of the multiple roles it plays in influencing business activity, government poses significant challenges for business owners and managers. Government not only establishes the rules of the game for business functions but also influences business in its roles as competitor, financier, purchaser, supplier, watchdog, and so on. Opportunities for business and government to cooperate in a mutual pursuit of common goals are present to some extent, but the major opportunity for business is in developing strategies for effectively working with government in such a way that businesses achieve their own objectives. In doing this, business has the responsibility of obeying the laws of the land and of being ethical in its responses to government expectations and mandates. To do otherwise raises the specter of abuse of power.

However, the active interaction of businesses and government in the United States is also considered by many to be an issue of **political corporate social responsibility (PCSR)**, as we noted in Chapter 2. The logic behind PCSR is that if citizens expect companies to be socially responsible, then businesses *need* to be political actors and take on responsibilities traditionally left to governments in order to meet societal expectations. It goes beyond corporate citizenship because it entails those responsibilities that turn corporations into political actors.[1] This is a newer concept for businesses in the United States relative to European or other contexts where businesses have historically assumed a larger political role in society. Of course, there are many challenges to managing political corporate social responsibility—the dynamics, the different national settings and institutional contexts, the role of business leaders in engaging in different strategies, and even the role of digital technologies and the way businesses frame their political responsibilities.[2] PCSR is a growing issue that businesses around the world must consider.

Attempts by business to influence government are a major and accepted part of the public policy process in the United States. The active participation of interest groups striving to achieve their own objectives drives the U.S. political system. The business sector is behaving, therefore, in a normal and expected fashion when it assumes an advocacy role for its interests. Other groups, be they labor organizations, consumer groups, farmers' groups, doctors' organizations, real estate broker organizations, military groups, women's rights organizations, environmental groups, church groups, and so on, also strive to pursue their special interests with government. Today's pluralism necessitates that all of these groups take advantage of their opportunity to influence government.

Society would be best served if the system maintained a balance of power; however, business's power to drive the political agenda in Washington is now virtually unchecked with over 12,000 Washington lobbyists, including the U.S. Chamber of Commerce, which has been coined the "influence machine" of business by author Alyssa Katz.[3] During election years, the influence of business may also be seen in the amount of money spent on elections. For example, spending by businesses and unions on presidential and congressional races more than doubled from 2000 to 2014.[4] In the 2014 midterm elections, the U.S. Chamber of Commerce alone spent $35 million from undisclosed sources.[5] These numbers speak to the staggering amounts that help businesses to gain access to legislators and agencies. Throw in the other monies that businesses plow into lobbying—an estimated $2.78 billion in 2015—and it is obvious that business has tremendous influence on government.[6] Power comes with the duty to use it responsibly and so the need for business to be mindful in its approach to influencing government is greater than ever. Given its inherent wealth and power, business must navigate the political waters thoughtfully, taking care to understand the range of corporate political activity's consequences, for society as well as for business. This qualifies as enlightened self-interest because business too needs a healthy and balanced society to thrive.

12.1 Corporate Political Participation

Political involvement is broadly defined as participation in the formulation and execution of public policy at various levels of government. As decisions about the current and future shape of society and the role of the private sector shift from the marketplace to the political arena, corporations, like all interest groups, find it imperative to increase their political involvement and activity.[7]

Historically, companies entered into debates in Washington only on an issue-by-issue basis and with no overall sense of a purpose, goal, or strategy. Companies tended to be reactive; that is, they dealt with issues only after they became threats. For example, in its early days Microsoft did not take political participation seriously. While other companies had suites of offices filled with lobbyists looking out for their interests, Microsoft simply had a man traveling around in his Jeep. Then an antitrust case from the U.S. Justice Department convinced the company of the importance of corporate political activity.[8] Today, Microsoft's lobbying expenditures total around $8.5 million annually, but tech rivals Google, Facebook, and Amazon spend even more, posting 2015 numbers of $16.7 million, $9.8 million, and $9 million, respectively.[9] Microsoft and its rivals have learned the hard way that political strategies could be as important as competitive strategies in today's marketplace.[10]

In this chapter, we focus on the following major approaches to corporate political activity: (1) lobbying and (2) political spending. As we begin, our perspective will be largely descriptive as we seek to understand these approaches, their strengths and weaknesses, and business's successes and failures with them. We will then explore normative issues in corporate political activity, highlighting areas where there are possible abuses of power and violations of sound ethics.

12.2 Business Lobbying

Lobbying is the process of influencing public officials to promote or secure the passage or defeat of legislation. Lobbyists are intensely self-interested. Their goals are to promote legislation that is in their organizations' interests and to defeat legislation that runs

ETHICS IN PRACTICE CASE

The NRA and the CDC

Trade associations exist to support their member organizations and the industries in which they operate. If another organization begins work that can potentially undermine that industry and lead to a decrease in sales, the trade association will naturally respond and try to put a stop to the work that threatens its industry. This is true across industries but when the trade association is the National Rifle Association (NRA) and the organization posing a threat is the Center for Disease Control and Prevention (CDC)'s National Center for Injury Prevention and Control (NCIPC), a variety of ethical issues arise.

Prior to the mid-1990s, the NCIPC published a variety of studies that analyzed gun-related injuries and deaths, but then the public health scientists clashed with the NRA and the NRA fought back by lobbying sympathetic lawmakers to take action. The lawmakers first tried to close the NCIPC but, when that failed, they successfully put forth an amendment that removed $2.6 million from their budget—the same amount used the previous year to fund gun-related research—and stipulated that money may not go to research that advocates gun control. Today, the CDC asks funded researchers to let them know if the studies they are conducting involve firearms and then the CDC forwards that information to the NRA as a courtesy. Arthur Kellermann of the Rand Corp notes, "The (NRA) strategy of shutting down the pipeline of science was effective. It is almost impossible today to get federal funding for firearm injury prevention research."

1. Do you think the NRA is justified in its actions toward the CDC?
2. Do you think the CDC should pursue gun-related injury research?
3. The NRA contends that the CDC had an anti-gun agenda and that they were doing politics instead of medicine. Does this alter your assessment of the NRA's approach to lobbying?
4. Where do you draw the line regarding lobbying by industry groups? The NRA's actions promote shareholder wealth—is that not the responsibility of a trade group? Are there lines that trade associations should not cross when they lobby and, if so, what are they?

Sources: "CDC: Politics Affected Gun Violence Research," *The Atlanta Journal Constitution* (December 19, 2012), http://www.ajc.com/news/news/cdc-politics-affected-gun-violence-research/nTZnf/. Accessed March 16, 2016; James Swift, "Former CDC Director Says NRA 'Terrorized' Gun Violence Researchers," *Juvenile Justice Information Exchange* (January 1, 2013), http://jjie.org/former-cdc-director-says-nra-terrorized-gun-violence-researchers/101449. Accessed March 16, 2016.

counter to that. Business interests, labor interests, ethnic and racial groups, professional organizations, and those simply pursuing ideological goals they believe to be in the public interest are lobbying at the federal, state, and local levels. Our focus is on business lobbying at the federal level, although we must remember that this process is also occurring daily at the state and local levels.

Lobbying has been defined as the professionalization of the art of persuasion.[11] Lobbying serves several purposes. It is not just a technique for gaining legislative support or institutional approval for some objective such as a policy shift, a judicial ruling, or the modification or passage of a law. Lobbying may be directed toward the reinforcement of established policy or the defeat of proposed policy shifts. As a tool to get the votes they want, lobbyists can also target the election or defeat of national, state, and local legislators.[12] A lobbyist may be a lawyer, a public relations specialist, a former head of a public agency, a former corporate executive, or a former elected official. In this sense, there is no typical lobbyist.[13] It is clear, however, that more and more businesses, as well as other special-interest groups, are turning to lobbyists to facilitate their involvement in the public policy process.

Lobbying has been called "one of America's most despised professions," and sometimes the label fits.[14] Jack Abramoff was at the center of a corruption and influence peddling investigation that netted 21 people, including legislators, White House officials, lobbyists, and congressional aides.[15] In addition to corruption and tax offenses, the

Court found he defrauded Native American tribes of millions of dollars.[16] His crimes were so notorious that he became the subject of a 2010 documentary *Casino Jack and the United States of Money* as well as a feature film that same year, *Casino Jack*, with Kevin Spacey in the title role. Given the large amounts of money involved, it is not surprising that people will cross the legal and ethical line. In 2015, over 11,000 lobbyists spent $3.21 billion advocating for a range of interests.[17] One study examined lobbying for multinational tax breaks and found that the return on investment was 22,000 percent.[18]

We should note, however, that lobbying is not inherently evil. Some lobbyists work for nonprofit organizations, supporting causes about which the public would forget without someone representing them in Washington. They become involved in issues surrounding education, for example, like the lobbyist groups who square off in debate about the best ways to increase the quality of education.[19] Other lobbyists work for companies that care about doing the right thing and creating a marketplace in which responsible companies can thrive. Some for-profit lobbyists are doing pro bono work in an effort to remake the profession's tainted image.[20] Lobbyists can serve as educators, providing needed information to elected officials and the public. Lawrence Lessig, who conducts research on public corruption, puts it well, "There's all the difference in the world between a lawyer making an argument to the jury and a lawyer handing out $100 bills to the jurors. That's a distinction the system doesn't understand right now."[21] A look at some of the top lobbying issues in the 2016 U.S. presidential election year provides some insight into the range of issues that may be involved in lobbying[22]:

- Trans-Pacific Partnership—A trade deal between the United States and 11 other Pacific Rim nations involving many special-interest groups, including environmental activists who believe it encourages fossil fuel production.
- Puerto Rico—Efforts to allow Puerto Rico to restructure its debts in bankruptcy involving interest groups like bondholders and investors.
- Criminal Justice Reform—Efforts to reduce minimum sentences for drug offenders, involving social justice groups and businesses.
- Mega Mergers—Proposed mergers that bring up antitrust issues and have lobbyists on both sides—some arguing for approvals for big business, others arguing that the mergers squelch competition.
- Environmental Regulations—Regulations including the "Waters of the U.S." rule (meant to protect waterways from pollution), the Clean Power Plan (meant to reduce carbon emissions from power plants), and tougher ozone standards.

12.2a Organizational Levels of Lobbying

The business community engages in lobbying at several organizational levels. At the broadest level are **umbrella trade associations**, which represent the collective business interests of the United States. The best examples of umbrella trade associations are the Chamber of Commerce of the United States and the National Association of Manufacturers (NAM). Other umbrella organizations represent subsets of business in general, such as the Business Roundtable, which represents the largest firms in America, and the National Federation of Independent Businesses (NFIB), which represents smaller firms.

At the next level are **sectoral trade associations**, which are composed of many firms in a given industry or line of business. Examples include the National Automobile Dealers Association, the National Association of Home Builders, the National Association of Realtors, PhRMA, the American Bankers Association, the American Chemistry Council, and the American Council of Life Insurers. In addition, there are individual **company**

lobbying efforts. Here, firms such as IBM, AT&T, Ford, and Delta Airlines lobby on their own behalf. Typically, companies use their own personnel, establish Washington offices for the sole purpose of lobbying, or hire professional lobbying firms or consultants located in Washington or a state capital. To the extent that limited transparency allows, interest groups now rate companies on the nature of their lobbying. For example, in their *Guide to Greener Electronics*, Greenpeace, the independent environment campaigning organization, rated electronics companies on whether they "showed climate leadership" by supporting cuts in global emissions.[23] Finally, companies sometimes form **ad hoc coalitions** to address a particular issue for a period. For example, the Coalition of Gulf Shrimp Industries, an ad hoc coalition of vessel owners and shrimp processors in the United States and Mexico, joined together to petition the U.S. Department of Commerce and the International Trade Commission for relief from unfair trade involving subsidized shrimp from other countries.[24]

It should be noted, however, that there is some opportunity for all levels of lobbying to come together for a specific purpose. Take, for example, the moves by Monsanto Corporation in defense of genetically modified foods (a.k.a. GMOs, which we also discuss in Chapter 9). In this case, Monsanto formed an alliance with the (umbrella organization) Biotechnology Industry Organization, as well as the (sectoral) Grocery Manufacturers Association and various (ad hoc coalitions) universities to make their case in the safety debate surrounding GMOs.[25]

Figure 12-1 depicts examples of the broad range of lobbying and political interest organizations used by businesses.

It is now useful to discuss lobbying in greater detail, beginning with the use of professional lobbyists.

FIGURE 12-1 Examples of the Range of Lobbying Organizations Used by Businesses

Broad Representation: Umbrella Trade Associations

- Chamber of Commerce of the United States
- National Association of Manufacturers (NAM)
- Business Roundtable
- National Federation of Independent Businesses (NFIB)
- State Chambers of Commerce
- City Chambers of Commerce

Midrange Representation: Sectoral Trade Associations and Coalitions

- National Automobile Dealers Association
- National Association of Realtors
- American Petroleum Institute American Trucking Association
- National Association of Medical Equipment Suppliers
- Tobacco Institute
- Health Benefits Coalition
- United States Telecom Association

Narrow/Specific Representation: Company-Level Lobbying

- Washington and State Capital Offices
- Law Firms Specializing in Lobbying
- Public Affairs Specialists
- Political Action Committees (PACs)
- Grassroots Lobbying
- Company-Based Coalitions
- Former Government Officials

SPOTLIGHT *on Sustainability*

What Green Rankings Don't Tell You

A corporation's political activities can have a greater impact on the environment than the work it does to make its operations greener. Green rankings can be misleading because they focus on operational impacts, compliance with regulations and overall practices, while ignoring the firm's political advocacy activities. A recent study compared companies' green rankings to their ranking on political transparency and noted a weak correlation: some of the companies with higher-than-average green rankings had lower-than-average political transparency rankings.

Companies with higher environmental transparency rankings include Duke Energy, Halliburton, Hess, and Newmont Mining. These firms are in the highly environmentally regulated mining, chemical, and energy industries. Firms in those industries typically lobby for more relaxed regulations and so some question whether these companies have environmentally friendly political activity to match their environmental transparency. Because disclosure of corporate political activity is not required, there is no way to know the nature of their efforts. What is the solution? Some suggest that future green rankings should include voluntary disclosure of environment-related lobbying and donations. Otherwise, firms may receive credit for being green when, behind closed doors, they are working against the interests of the environment with their corporate political activity.

Sources: Aaron Chatterji and Michael Toffel, "What Green Rankings Don't Tell You," *Newsweek* (October 22, 2012), http://www.hbs.edu/faculty/Publication%20Files/Chatterji%20Toffel%202012%20DailyBeast_c01da612-2a82-462c-ad67-33cea6af3d2b.pdf. Accessed March 20, 2016; Auden Schendler and Michael Toffel, "The Factor Environmental Ratings Miss." *MIT Sloan Management Review* 53.1 (Fall 2011): 17–18.

Professional Lobbyists. Lobbyists, sometimes derisively referred to as "influence peddlers," operate under a variety of formal titles and come from a variety of backgrounds. Officially, they are lawyers, government affairs specialists, public relations consultants, or public affairs consultants. Some are on the staffs of large trade associations based in Washington. Others represent specific companies that have Washington-based offices dedicated to the sole purpose of representing those companies in the capitol city. Still others are professional lobbyists who work for large law firms or consulting firms in Washington that specialize in representing clients to the lawmakers.

The Washington lobbyist is frequently a former government official. Called **revolving door lobbyists**, some are former congressional staff members or former members of Congress.[26] Others are former presidential staff assistants or other highly placed government officials. In 2007, President George W. Bush passed the "Honest Leadership and Open Government Act" that prohibited many of these individuals from lobbying for a year after leaving office in an effort to stem conflicts of interest and other potential ethics issues. In 2009, President Obama signed an Executive Order extending this time frame to two years.[27] However, attempts to constrain this practice have fallen short of the mark for several reasons. First, a two-year time frame is still a relatively short apprenticeship for people who are likely to increase their former salaries many times over. Second, the classification of individuals as lobbyists can be hard to determine. To be formally considered a lobbyist, an ex-legislator must be engaged in lobbying activities for 20 percent or more of his or her time for an individual client. By spreading services among many clients, or by providing "strategic advice" rather than "lobbying services," any ex-lawmaker can effectively evade the ban.[28] This practice has given rise to the term **stealth lobbying** or **shadow lobbying**. Finally, the "cooling off" periods between government and lobbying work apply only to the agency where an ex-official used to work—so contacting other agencies during that time is still allowable.[29]

For example, after serving as chief architect of the Medicare prescription drug law, former Rep. Billy Tauzin (R-Louisiana) received a lucrative job offer to lobby for the pharmaceutical industry. Pundits suggested that he had already earned his salary when he walked in the door because the Medicare bill provided huge profits for drug makers.[30] Tauzin began his job as Chairman and CEO of the drug industry trade group, Pharmaceutical Research and Manufacturers of America (PhRMA).[31] He did not register to lobby until after the one-year waiting period mandated by the Ethics Reform Act of 1989. During that waiting year, however, he was able to advise other lobbyists on how to proceed and he was able to call on his former chief of staff who joined PhRMA with him. Since then, the House Ethics Code added a provision known as "The Tauzin Rule," which prohibits lawmakers from negotiating future employment deals while still working as representatives.[32] Tauzin became the highest-paid health-care lobbyist when he earned $11.6 million for brokering a deal with the Obama administration over health-care reform: He left his position as head of PhRMA after the law was signed.[33]

The revolving door between Congress and lobbying firms may have contributed significantly to the global financial crisis. Deniz Igan and Prachi Mishra followed the track of financial regulation bills in the five-year period before the crisis, classifying them as to whether they promoted deregulation or not.[34] In the years leading up to the financial crisis, they found that bills that were friendlier to the financial industry (i.e., promoted deregulation) were three times more likely to become law; furthermore, the more money lobbyists spent, the more likely legislators were to vote for the bill.[35] What mattered most, however, was the influence of connections—the greatest influence on the likelihood of a legislator voting for a bill was whether or not the lobbyist promoting it has worked for that legislator in the past.[36]

What do business lobbyists actually do? Lobbyists offer a wide range of services that include drafting legislation, creating slick advertisements and direct-mail campaigns, consulting, and, most importantly, getting access to lawmakers. Access, or connections, seems to be the central product that the new breed of lobbyist is selling—the returned phone call, the tennis game with a key legislator, or lunch with the Speaker of the House. Social media, of course, has made it a little easier to gain access, with sites like LinkedIn facilitating connections.[37] With so many competing interests in Washington today, the opportunity for businesses to get their points across to regulators in any format is a significant advantage. Lobbyists also play the important role of showing busy legislators the virtues and pitfalls of complex legislation.[38] Figure 12-2 summarizes some of the various activities that business lobbyists accomplish for their clients.

Grassroots Lobbying. In addition to lobbying directly through the use of professional lobbyists, firms and trade associations use what is called **grassroots lobbying**, which refers to the process of mobilizing the "grassroots"—individual citizens who might be most directly affected by legislative activity—to political action. An estimated 40 percent

FIGURE 12-2 What Business Lobbyists Do for Their Clients

- Get access to key legislators (connections)
- Monitor legislation
- Establish communication channels with regulatory bodies
- Protect firms against surprise legislation
- Draft legislation, slick ad campaigns, direct-mail campaigns
- Provide issue papers on anticipated effects of legislative activity
- Communicate sentiments of association or company on key issues
- Influence outcome of legislation (promote helpful legislation, defeat harmful legislation)
- Assist companies in coalition building around issues that various groups may have in common
- Help members of Congress get reelected
- Organize grassroots efforts

of Fortune 500 companies use grassroots consultants.[39] The better corporate grassroots lobbying programs usually arise in companies whose leaders recognize that people are a firm's most potent political resource. Although firms cannot direct or require people to become politically involved, they persuade and encourage them. Trade associations often use grassroots support by asking their members to contact their representatives and maintaining contact through social media. They also organize rallies and develop instant advertisements.[40]

Grassroots lobbying has become such an effective tool for such a wide range of individual firms and associations that the Public Affairs Council holds an annual National Grassroots Conference.[41] The 2015 agenda included participation from companies as diverse as Allstate, Caterpillar, Eli-Lilly, and Wal-Mart, as well as trade groups such as the American Insurance Association, the National Restaurant Association, and the National Retail Federation.

Other forms of grassroots lobbying have emerged with the growth of technology. For example, **cyberadvocacy** is a computer-based form of grassroots campaigning. Computers and the Internet have made communication, and thus grassroots lobbying, infinitely easier. Books and consulting services have sprung up to assist organizations in using the Internet to both amass grassroots support and enable grassroots supporters to contact their legislators. Social media platforms have taken this a step further, creating the opportunity for companies to launch populist social media assaults at the click of an app. For example, the livery service Uber used their app to rally riders to go to City Hall and challenge New York City Mayor Bill de Blasio's proposal to cap the number of livery vehicles.[42] Uber offered free rides to the venue, and then got customers to send 17,000 e-mails in opposition to the new rules. Competitor Lyft also mobilized users to support less-restrictive regulations, as did home-sharing company Airbnb, and e-commerce company eBay, which was fighting online sales taxation.[43]

Grassroots lobbying can be highly effective, but the grassroots response should be genuine. Some organizations and trade associations have created fake groups that appear to be grassroots but are largely created and funded by an organization or trade association. These phony "**astroturf lobbying**" efforts give the impression of being the result of a genuine public groundswell but are actually orchestrated and funded by professional organizations. The practice once involved the sending of hundreds of phone calls or thousands of identical postcards, letters, or e-mails that arrived on the same day and was rarely effective.[44] Over time, astroturfing has grown more sophisticated and is estimated to be a billion-dollar industry in Washington.[45]

Today's astroturf organizations are more subtle and less likely to be show their true origins without investigation from an outside source. Even professional journalists have been duped by astroturf organizations.[46] Until transparency requirements are in place, consumers of information will have to be vigilant in expecting lobbying groups to be transparent and accountable.

Trade Associations. Lobbying at the association level is frequent today. Trade associations are established by individual industries to help businesses in the same industry to interact with each other and benefit from those interactions. One successful experience worth noting has been the pharmaceutical industry's continued success at blocking Congress's efforts to impose prescription drug price controls and to allow the importation of less-expensive drugs. In a true show of the trade association's strength, the pharmaceutical industry was able to have passage written into law that barred the federal government from negotiating the prices of prescription drugs supplied through Medicare Part D. Economist Dean Baker estimates that, even using a conservative scenario, the United States loses about $50 billion each year due to the government's inability to negotiate drug prices in Medicare.[47] President Obama had vilified the costly provision when on the campaign trail; however, his perspective changed during the health-care reform process. PhRMA was able to protect the provision in the health-care reform package in return for other considerations. The pharmaceutical industry agreed to provide $80 billion to close the "doughnut hole" coverage gap for seniors and people with disabilities and subsequently advertised in support of the health-care reform legislation.[48]

Newer and smaller trade associations, like the Fantasy Sports Industry Association, have more of an uphill battle in promoting their interests. This industry involves daily-fantasy sports where customers pay entry fees to draft virtual teams that compete against each other for prize money. In 2015, industry revenues were about $290 million, with two large players, FanDuel, Inc., and DraftKings, Inc., dominating market share.[49] Despite the initiation of a lobbying blitz to get legal protections for fantasy-sports operators, the businesses are under scrutiny for operating in violation of some states' gambling laws, as well as federal issues of money movement.[50] At the time of this writing, it was still up in the air as to whether the companies could continue to take entries in states like New York, pending the outcome of legal action by that state's attorney general.[51]

Trade associations sometimes find themselves in the undesirable role of battling with each other in their attempts to lobby Congress. An example of these types of battles occurred between the credit union and the banking industries regarding the scope of services supplied by credit unions. Credit unions argued that they provide services to individuals and small businesses that traditional banks shun. They contended that they should be able to expand the services they provide to this generally underserved population. Banks countered that credit unions enjoy an unfair competitive advantage by virtue of their exemptions from both taxes and the Community Reinvestment Act (CRA) obligations required of banks. They maintained that large, multiple-employer credit unions should be subject to the same taxes, CRA rules, and safety requirements as banks. Ultimately, the House passed H.R. 1151—the Credit Union Membership Access Act, which relaxed restrictions on credit union membership.[52]

Umbrella Organizations. The umbrella organizations are trade associations, too; however, an umbrella organization has a broad base of membership that represents businesses in several different industries of various sizes. Historically, the two major umbrella organizations in the United States have been the Chamber of Commerce of the United States and the National Association of Manufacturers. Two other prominent organizations include the Business Roundtable and the National Federation of Independent Businesses. Each of these groups has political action as one of its central objectives.

Chamber of Commerce of the United States The national chamber of commerce was founded in 1912 as a federation of businesses and business organizations. In addition to firms, corporations, and professional members, the chamber has thousands of local, state, and regional chambers of commerce; American chambers of commerce abroad; and several thousand trade and professional associations. Its diversity of membership shows why it is referred to as an umbrella organization.

Historically, the U.S. Chamber of Commerce had been a legislative powerhouse in its ability to influence public policy. When Thomas Donohue became the Chamber president, he promised to awaken the "sleeping giant, missing in action from many important battles." One tactic he used to great success was to dispense favors to individual businesses that might not want their company name associated with lobbying efforts. The Chamber established the Institute for Legal Reform (ILR) to fight for tort reform: The ILR is funded by large donations from companies like chemicals and insurance that are typically subject to lawsuits but do not want to make their support for tort reform public.[53] Having spent nearly a billion dollars from 1998 through 2015, the Chamber's lobbying expenditures dwarf those of other individual business groups.[54]

Recently, the Chamber has been at odds with many of its former associates. Since 2009, 60 local Chambers of Commerce have either quit or publicly denounced the U.S. Chamber due to its positions.[55] The Chamber's reputation for supporting legacy industries like tobacco, firearms, and oil has been particularly controversial as these industries' interests often collide with other industries.[56] The Chamber's position on climate change led Apple to resign from the organization and Nike to withdraw from the board, remaining as a member to "debate climate change from within."[57] Nevertheless, if pay is an indication, some members appreciate Donohue's efforts greatly as his compensation is now closer to that of a multinational CEO than a head of a trade association.[58]

Business Roundtable Formed in 1972, the Business Roundtable (BRT) is often regarded as an umbrella organization, although it has a more restricted membership. It is an association of chief executive officers of leading corporations with a combined workforce of more than 16 million employees in the United States and $7.3 trillion in revenues.[59] The Business Roundtable is different from most groups, such as the U.S. Chamber of Commerce and NAM, in the limitation of participation to chief executive officers (CEOs). Rather than pushing narrow issues that benefit narrow interests, the organization generally selects broader concerns on which to focus. The BRT was once regarded as a sleeping giant, but its former president John Castellani turned the organization into a "lobbying juggernaut."[60]

One of the targets for that lobbying activity is the shareholder empowerment movement. Not surprisingly, this association of CEOs prefers that the decision-making power reside in top management. The BRT was active in fighting efforts to empower shareholders through proxy access, a provision included in the Senate's financial regulation bill.[61] Castellani referred to this as the BRT's "highest priority" and noted, "Nearly all of our members have called about this."[62] Recently, companies like Whole Foods, eBay, and Citigroup have the support of the BRT in blocking shareholder proposals, much to the chagrin of the Securities and Exchange Commission.[63]

The push against shareholder democracy has resulted in some criticism of BRT. In *Corpocracy: How CEOs and the Business Roundtable Hijacked the World's Greatest Wealth Machine*, Robert Monks describes a meeting between Castellani and John Connolly of Institutional Shareholder Services (ISS). Castellani went to the ISS office to berate Connolly personally for ISS's recommendation that shareholders withhold proxy votes from compensation committee members who approved a controversial CEO pay package. In 2011, Castellani left BRT to head PhRMA and John Engler, former three-term governor of Michigan, became President of BRT.

National Association of Manufacturers (NAM) NAM describes itself as "the preeminent US manufacturers association as well as the nation's largest industrial trade association."[64] Although the membership of NAM has historically been tilted toward the larger smokestack industry firms, it now includes small- and medium-sized firms as well as member associations. The membership of NAM encompasses every industrial sector and all 50 U.S. states.[65] Current issues for manufacturers include the costs of reducing greenhouse gas emissions, which the NAM argues imposes an unfair burden on manufacturers as consumers of one-third of the nation's energy.[66]

National Federation of Independent Businesses (NFIB) During the end of the 20th century, the growth of small businesses came to dominate the business news. It should not be surprising, therefore, that the NFIB, as a small business association, also came into a position of power. Although their businesses are small, their influence in Washington is not. When *Fortune* magazine last conducted its ranking of the Power 25 Lobbying, the NFIB ranked third overall and top in business organizations for clout.[67]

The NFIB is able to speak with one voice due to the homogeneity of their membership and the many issues that small businesses share because of their size. For this reason, the NFIB avoids the problems faced by the NAM and the U.S. Chamber of Commerce. For example, its monthly Index of Small Business Optimism is often used for insight into economic growth and job creation.[68] However, like other umbrella organizations, its political activities can often cost its influence with different presidential administrations. For example, the NFIB joined the lawsuit against health-care reform and subsequently lost when the Supreme Court upheld the constitutionality of the law.[69] According to NFIB President and CEO Dan Danner, "It's been a long two-year effort, but I think, certainly from where I am, we'd do it again in a heartbeat."[70]

Coalitions A noteworthy and growing mechanism of political involvement in the public policy process is the creation and use of **coalitions** to influence government processes. A coalition forms when distinct groups or parties realize they have something in common that might warrant their joining forces, at least temporarily, for joint action. More often than not, an issue that various groups feel similarly about creates the opportunity for a coalition. For example, the Coalition for an Airline Passengers Bill of Rights (now called "FlyersRights.org") was formed when a family was stranded for nine hours on the tarmac in Austin, Texas. Today, with more than 40,000 members, it is the largest nonprofit consumer organization in the United States representing airline passengers.[71] One of its more recent causes is the fight to get airlines to stop "shrinking" the airline seats.[72] As people have gotten larger, the coalition suggests, there are new consumer safety issues associated with the smaller seats including increased risk of blood clots and the ability for passengers to safely evacuate a plane in an emergency.[73] A coalition can work cooperatively with government or it can lobby government when that government does not share the coalition's priorities.

Coalition formation has become a standard practice for firms interested in accomplishing political goals or influencing public policy. If a company or an association wants to pass or defeat particular legislation, it can strengthen its position by enlisting support from an individual or organization that has a similar position on the issue. Coalitions enable members to share their resources and pool their energies when they confront difficult issues. Coalitions also can provide cover for a company that wants to push for its own agenda without necessarily having its name attached to the campaign.

One example of coalition building around a specific issue is the Global Business Coalition against Human Trafficking. Members include Carlson, Delta Air Lines, Exxon Mobil, LexisNexis, ManpowerGroup, Microsoft, NXP, and Travelport.[74] These corporations have joined to share their resources and expertise to work with business and government to fight the growing problem of modern-day slavery.[75] The International Labour Organization estimates that almost 21 million people are victims of forced labor, with 5.5 million younger than 18.[76] The companies' supply chains may contain forced labor, and travel and tourism facilities can unknowingly facilitate sex trafficking.[77] The coalition plans to develop training modules for employees and best practices guidelines for corporate leaders.[78] More than 12,000 private employers have signed the Athens Accord, a voluntary agreement developed at a meeting of the Business Community against Human Trafficking, held in Athens, Greece.[79] By signing the Accord, companies promise to uphold a zero-tolerance policy toward working with any entity that benefits from human trafficking.[80]

ETHICS IN PRACTICE CASE

Double Irish with a Dutch Sandwich

One way that business affects government is by avoiding taxes by exploiting (and sometimes creating) loopholes. Doing this improves corporate profits, meeting one of business's responsibilities. However, businesses also have responsibility to contribute financially to the governments whose resources enable them to grow and prosper. Those contributions are needed to maintain and promote a sustainable world, as evidenced by tax payments being included as a key performance indicator in determining the Global 100 most sustainable corporations. A key question is—where should business draw the line between retaining profits to enhance shareholder wealth and contributing its fair share to government?

As the U.S. government looks for ways to deal with a growing deficit, greater attention is being paid to the issue of corporate taxation. The Center for Investigative Reporting evaluated the earnings and assets of Silicon Valley tech companies and compared them to taxes paid. They concluded that Silicon Valley giants, such as Apple, eBay, Google, and Yahoo, were paying effective global tax rates well below the top U.S. corporate tax rate of 35 percent. Non-tech companies such as General Electric, Coca-Cola, and Procter and Gamble also reduce their taxes with offshore holdings. However, because they deal with intellectual property, tech companies are most easily able to shift their intellectual property to tax havens.

Years ago, Apple pioneered an accounting method that sent profits to the Caribbean by way of Irish subsidiaries and the Netherlands—hence the name "Double Irish with a Dutch Sandwich." In 2014, the Irish government said it would phase out rules that let companies use the Double Irish, but it grandfathered in companies including Google and LinkedIn until 2021. In 2016, European regulators began investigating whether individual countries' tax breaks for certain companies, like Apple and Amazon, violate rules against excessive "state aid."

1. Who are the stakeholders and how are they affected by these corporate tax-saving strategies?
2. Do companies have a responsibility to pay a fair share of income tax to local, state, and federal governments? Who determines what that fair share should be?
3. Where do you draw the line on tax savings by corporations?
4. The U.K. government has declared that corporate tax avoiders will no longer be able to bid on government contracts. Critics believe that corporations will find a way to work around it. If it were possible to design a foolproof system, would you support the UK policy? Would you recommend it to other governments?

Sources: Richard Rubin, "U.S. Treasury's Lew Challenges EU on Corporate Tax Investigations," *The Wall Street Journal* (February 11, 2016), http://www.wsj.com/articles/u-s-treasurys-lew-challenges-eu-on-corporate-tax-investigations-1455177782. Accessed April 30, 2016; Kyung Song and Janet Tu, "Hearing: Microsoft (Legally) Avoided $6.5B in Taxes over 3 Years," *Scattle Times* (September 20, 2013), http://www.seattletimes.com/business/hearing-microsoft legally avoided-65b-in-taxes-over-3-years/. Accessed March 23, 2016; Matt Orange, "Silicon Valley Firms Shelter Assets Overseas, Avoid Billions in U.S. Taxes," *Center for Investigative Reporting* (February 13, 2013), http://cironline.org/reports/silicon-valley-firms-shelter-assets-overseas-avoid-billions-us-taxes-4203. Accessed March 20, 2016; Prem Sikka, "Big UK Tax Avoiders Will Easily Get Round New Government Policy," The Guardian (February 15, 2013), http://www.guardian.co.uk/commentisfree/2013/feb/15/uk-tax-avoiders-wont-stop-new-policy. March 20, 2016; Jesse Drucker and Zachary Mider, "Tax Inversion: How U.S. Companies Buy Tax Breaks," *Bloomberg* (January 2015), http://www.bloombergview.com/quicktake/tax-inversion. Accessed March 23, 2016; Jesse Drucker, "Google Isn't Paying 'Google Tax'," Bloomberg (February 18, 2016), 37.

12.3 Corporate Political Spending

To this point, our discussion of lobbying has focused primarily on interpersonal contact and powers of persuasion. We now turn our attention to corporate political spending and its implications for businesses and their stakeholders. The channels through which corporations can make political contributions are many and varied. In addition to the traditional **political action committee (PAC)**, companies can contribute corporate funds to trade associations and other tax-exempt groups that will subsequently support a particular candidate or cause. Companies can also contribute to Super PACs, political parties, and political committees, both connected and nonconnected to candidates.

In the United States, the Federal Election Campaign Act (FECA) prohibits corporations from making direct contributions to candidates.[81] However, the law has always permitted corporations to form PACs. The U.S. Federal Elections Commission (FEC) differentiates between PACs that are connected and nonconnected. A **connected PAC**, also known as a separate segregated fund, is associated with a specific group or organization and can only raise money from that group. The FEC permits the company or organization sponsoring the PAC to absorb the cost of soliciting contributions, as well as administrative overhead.[82] A **nonconnected PAC** can accept funds from any individual or organization, as well as from a connected PAC—as long as those contributions are legal.[83] Nonconnected PACs are typically formed around a specific issue or by specific political leaders. **Leadership PACs** are nonconnected PACs formed by political leaders to support other candidates for office.[84]

Unlike PACs formed by legislation, **Super PACs** resulted from judicial decisions.[85] The first decision occurred in 2010 when the U.S. Supreme Court ruled in ***Citizens United v. FEC*** that corporations and labor unions could use the funds from their treasuries to support or oppose political candidates as long as spending is independent, that is, not coordinated with a candidate.[86] The Court upheld the prohibition against corporations donating directly to candidates.[87] We should note, however, that money spent independently to support or oppose a candidate is as effective as money given to a candidate to spend. The Federal Court in ***Speechnow v. FEC*** further clarified the implementation of *Citizens United* by ruling that any government restrictions on the amount corporations can spend would be unconstitutional.[88]

Those two rulings spurred the creation of Super PACs, new entities that have transformed the political landscape. Super PACS, officially known as **independent expenditure-only committees**, may raise unlimited amounts of money to support or oppose political candidates.[89] Their financial contributions are unlimited; however, they may not coordinate with or donate directly to a political candidate.[90] Of course, many people question the actual independence of the Super PAC expenditures. Typically, Super PACS are headed by former aides and associates who know the candidate well and so do not need to confer with the candidate to know what he or she would want the Super PAC to do. In addition, the candidate can simply speak to the media and then the Super PAC can simply follow the news for clues as to where to spend the money.

With this range of options and few meaningful restrictions on corporate involvement, corporate political spending has become "dangerous terrain."[91] Instead of just worrying about contributions to candidates and political parties, firms must now deal with requests from Super PACs, trade associations, and 501(c)(4) "social welfare" associations, and they must do so carefully.[92] As Bruce Freed and Karl Sandstrom explain[93]:

> *Political spending should not be a casual decision, a choice defaulted to companies' government-relations managers—or to trade associations or c4s. The spending, whether done directly or through third-party groups, needs to reflect the deliberate choices of senior managers and the board. When it comes to political engagement, a company must adhere to its values, keep its broader interests in mind, and understand that giving money to candidates or entities whose behavior is uncertain or at odds with those values and long-term business interests ultimately harms the company and its shareholders. To understand political spending fully is to understand its full consequences.*

Target Corporation, the huge retailer, did not understand the full consequences of its political spending and ended up paying a price. The company contributed to Minnesota Forward, a pro-economic growth political action group, in order to help it support pro-growth political candidates.[94] However, one of those candidates opposed gay marriage, a position that neither Target nor Minnesota Forward endorsed: This led to a boycott of Target stores by gay-marriage activists.[95] Target later apologized for the contribution, noting that the company endorsed the candidate's stance on economic issues and not social issues.[96] The company also said it would do a strategic review of its political donations before moving forward with any more.[97] Supporting a pro-growth candidate was consistent with creating value for Target's shareholders.[98] Minnesota Forward's stance on gay marriage was unrelated to the reason that Target contributed funds to the organization. However, the resultant boycott threatened to harm the company and its shareholders.[99] Target learned the hard way that corporate political spending contains repercussions that extend beyond any single issue.

12.3a Arguments for Corporate Political Spending

The most visible and ultimately influential defenders of corporate political spending are the five U.S. Supreme Court justices who shared in the majority opinion in *Citizens United*, the controversial 2010 U.S. Supreme Court ruling that declared government may not restrict independent corporate political expenditures. The logic behind the ruling is that the First Amendment establishes the right to free speech and that not only individuals, but also groups of individuals, have that right. From this perspective, limiting a group's right to political advocacy would violate the free speech of the people who belong to that group. It follows from this logic then that corporations, as well as unions and other groups of people, have the right to express their political opinions and their candidate preferences. Business has an important part to play in society and part of that is speaking up for the needs of business and sharing an economic perspective. In this pluralistic society, business provides a counterbalance to other interest groups who express their own agendas.

12.3b Arguments against Corporate Political Spending

Senator John McCain (R-AZ) became one of the most often quoted critics of corporate campaign spending when he called the *Citizens United* decision "one of the worst decisions I have ever seen.… I predict to you that there will be huge scandals associated with this huge flood of money."[100] Senator McCain's comments crystallize one of the key arguments against corporate political spending: Corporations have access to large amounts of money and that creates a serious imbalance of power. Another concern is the possibility of agency problems as managers may promote their own interests rather than the shareholders' interests, or the interests of stakeholders, when promoting candidates or issues.

Even when promoting shareholder welfare, the innate self-interest of business gives people pause as business is not likely to focus on the common good. Justice Stevens shared these apprehensions in the dissenting opinion on *Citizens United*, "The financial resources, legal structure and instrumental orientation of corporations raise legitimate concerns about their role in the electoral process. Our lawmakers have a compelling constitutional basis, if not also a democratic duty, to take measures designed to guard against the potentially deleterious effects of corporate spending in local and national races."[101] The **Golden Rule of Politics** sums up the concerns of those who argue against corporate political spending: "He who has the gold, rules."[102]

12.4 Political Action Committees

Political action committees (PACs) are committees that are organized to raise and spend money for political candidates, ballot initiatives, and proposed legislation. Figure 12-3 shows the top ten PAC contributors to federal candidates. Most PACs have a political point of view, either conservative or liberal, but many simply focus on a specific issue and try to do so in a nonpartisan manner.[103]

FIGURE 12-3 Top Ten PAC Contributors to Candidates (2015–2016)

PAC	Total Amount ($)	Democratic Percentage	Republican Percentage
Honeywell International	1,911,582	36	64
AT&T, Inc.	1,825,500	38	62
Lockheed Martin	1,694,750	34	65
National Beer Wholesalers	1,609,700	40	60
National Association of Realtors	1,518,380	39	61
Northrup Grumman	1,482,200	39	61
Credit Union National Association	1,443,350	46	54
Blue Cross/Blue Shield	1,432,350	32	67
International Brotherhood of Electrical Workers	1,426,800	96	4
American Bankers Association	1,278,958	21	79

Source: The Center for Responsive Politics, http://www.opensecrets.org/pacs/toppacs.php, based on data released by the FEC on April 21, 2016.

12.4a The Impact of Super PACs

Super PACs have facilitated outside spending in politics and the effect of outside spending has been huge. In the five years since the *Citizens United* ruling there has been an "explosion" of political money, much of it Super PAC money supporting future candidates that one expert called "a system that is pretty close to no holds barred."[104,105] By the end of January before the presidential election in 2016, the top three candidates had raised over $388 million, and their affiliated Super PACs had raised over $100 million.[106] Super PACS are still relatively new and so their full effect is not yet known but sums of money that large are certain to have a profound impact.

Regardless of how you feel about corporate political spending campaigns, it is clear that "money matters." Particularly during presidential elections, money is a "necessary but not a sufficient condition" for winning an election because while money might not buy elections, it allows the candidates to stay in the race.[107]

It is important to note that we focus on corporate contributions because the purpose of this chapter is to explore the impact of business on government. However, Super PACS do not stem only from business—unions and other interested organizations may also form them.

12.4b Agency Issues

As we discussed in Chapter 4, agency problems arise when the actions of managers are not in the shareholders' best interests. Corporate political spending, like all corporate spending, should have the best interests of the firm, its shareholders, and its stakeholders in mind. Political spending should not provide an opportunity for managers to pursue their personal preferences because the money those managers are spending is not their own. Political spending should have a clear association with the firm's best interests rather than the managers' personal points of view.

Agency problems can also arise when managers give the firm's money to a third party, such as a trade association or nonprofit group. These organizations might donate to a candidate whose actions do not serve the interests of the firm's shareholders and stakeholders. Several major drug companies found themselves in this predicament after donating money to PhRMA, the trade association that represents their industry after a

Bloomberg report shed light on PhRMA's political donations.[108] The trade association gave $4.8 million to two 501(c)(4) associations that subsequently used that money to support 23 congressional candidates successfully. After being elected, all 23 voted to limit access to and cut federal funding for birth control, as well as to cut medical research funds on which pharmaceutical companies rely.[109] Bayer AG, Johnson & Johnson, Merck, and Pfizer are all leading manufacturers of contraceptives. As members of PhRMA, these companies had contributed part of the money that got those congressional candidates elected.[110] In essence, through the trade association, they had inadvertently supported politicians who voted both to shrink their market and to reduce funding on which they depend. Angry investors berated the firms' managers for belonging to a trade association that used "its members' payments against those same members' best interests."[111]

12.5 Political Accountability and Transparency

Political accountability is an assumption of responsibility for political actions and a willingness to be answerable for them. In *Man's Search for Meaning*, Victor Frankl suggests that in addition to the Statue of Liberty on the East Coast of the United States, there should be a Statue of Responsibility on the West Coast because "freedom is only part of the story and half of the truth." He goes on to say, "Freedom is but the negative aspect of the whole phenomenon whose positive aspect is responsibleness. In fact, freedom is in danger of degenerating into mere arbitrariness unless it is lived in terms of responsibleness."[112] In today's political landscape, corporations have unprecedented freedom to pursue their political agendas. Restrictions on the money they can spend are virtually gone and multiple opportunities exist to hide the nature of their activities from public view. This freedom, and the power it gives, brings forth a duty for corporations to be responsible and, to that end, a movement to promote corporate political accountability has formed.

Some efforts are aimed at putting limits on what companies can spend; these include shareholder resolutions and lawsuits against big spenders. Since the *Citizens United* decision, investors have filed more than 500 resolutions calling for more transparency in corporate political activity.[113] Other efforts involve companies exerting self restraint. In a 2015 evaluation of the top 300 companies in the S&P 500, the Center for Political Accountability found that more than 6 out of 10 companies either disclose political spending or do not make such contributions.[114] Almost half disclose at least some information about payments to trade associations like the U.S. Chamber of Commerce.[115] Interestingly, the impact of shareholder engagement on political disclosure has been very positive for future transparency. Companies with a history of shareholder resolutions on political disclosure, and who subsequently reach an agreement with shareholders, have significantly better disclosure policies, according the CPA-Zicklin Index of Political Disclosure and Accountability at the Center.[116] Figure 12-4 is the Center for Political Accountability's list of the key elements of corporate disclosure and accountability.

Transparency has become a major issue in political accountability because much corporate political activity today is outside the public view. The Sunlight Foundation coined the term **dark money** to refer to the political contributions from undisclosed donors.[117] Well over $300 million was spent by dark money donors in the 2012 presidential election, without accounting for money not reported to the Federal Election Commission.[118] In the 2016 cycle, $4.88 million in dark money expenditures had been made in the year before the election—more than ten times the money that was spent at that point during the 2012 cycle.[119] The *Citizens United* ruling made it easier for donors to stay hidden, and this can occur several different ways:

FIGURE 12-4 Key Elements of Corporate Political Disclosure and Accountability

1. Policies
   a. Ways in which we participate in the political process
   b. Who makes spending decisions
   c. Our commitment to publicly disclose all of our expenditures, indirect and direct
2. Disclosure
   a. Itemized Direct Expenditure
      i. State-level candidates and committee contributions
      ii. Ballot measure spending; and
      iii. Independent expenditures
   b. Itemized Indirect Expenditures
      i. Trade association dues and other payments, including special assessments used for political purposes
      ii. Payments to other tax-exempt organizations [527 groups, Super PACs, and 501 (c)(4) "social welfare" organizations] used for political purposes
3. Oversight
   a. Board of directors regularly reviews our spending, direct and indirect, and existing policies.

Source: The Center for Political Accountability, http://politicalaccountability.net/. Accessed April 30, 2016.

- Tax-exempt "social welfare organizations," known as **501(c)(4)** groups, are not required to disclose their donors and so it is impossible to trace the money candidates receive from them back to the source.[120]
- Tax-exempt **527 groups** are groups organized under section 527 of the Internal Revenue Code to raise money for political activities, but they are only required to file with the FEC if it is a PAC or political party that expressly advocates for or against a federal candidate.[121]
- Super PACs are required to disclose their donors but often their donors hide behind other nonprofit groups, creating a vicious cycle of secrecy.[122]
- **Hybrid PACs** are also called **Carey Committees**, named after Retired Rear Admiral James Carey who brought suit against the Federal Election Commission (FEC) in 2011. These are hybrid political actions committees not affiliated with a candidate and can operate both as a traditional PAC (contributing funds to a candidate's committee) and as a super PAC, which makes independent expenditures. It can collect unlimited contributions from almost any source for its independent expenditure account.[123]
- Trade associations are another conduit for dark money. In *Hidden Rivers*, the Center for Political Accountability dubbed trade associations "the Swiss bank accounts of American politics." This in-depth examination of the nation's trade associations showed how they have become conduits for unlimited corporate political spending of dark money. Of major concern is the fact that trade associations "are subject to even less disclosure than the much criticized spending of independent political committees (527s)."[124]

The arguments against dark money are undeniable. Advocacy is best understood when one knows the motives of the person making the arguments. Voters have a right to know who is putting forth arguments for and against a candidate or an issue, and dark money denies them that right. In addition, it is a well-known fact that people behave more ethically when their actions are visible to others. As former U.S. Supreme Court Justice, Louis D. Brandeis famously explained, "Sunlight is said to be the best of disinfectants; electric light the most efficient policeman."[125] It is not surprising, therefore, that ads funded by dark money tend to be "the most vicious," with nearly 90 percent being negative.[126] According to an Annenberg Public Policy Center study, 26 percent of the ads funded by dark money are deceptive.[127]

Advocates of transparency at the federal level have tried repeatedly to enact legislation to require that donors be identified. Getting a handle on dark money is not easy because dark money spending often comes in layers. In California, state law requires nonprofit organizations to disclose donors who give money in order to fund political activities. Americans for Responsible Leadership (ARL), a 501(c)(4) based in Arizona, donated $11 million to assist the Small Business Action Committee (SBAC) to support its effort to defeat two pending propositions. Because the donations were for political activities, the California Fair Political Practices Commission filed suit when ARL refused to disclose its donors saying, "Under California law, the failure to disclose this initially was campaign money laundering."[128] When ARL disclosed its donor, no meaningful light was shed. The donation came from another dark money nonprofit called Americans for Job Security (AJS), whose money came through another nonprofit, The Center to Protect Patient Rights (CPPR).[129] As Brendan Fischer of the Center for Media and Democracy's PR Watch observed, "California managed to peel back one layer of the dark money onion, but discovered little information about who is really bankrolling the operation—they only found more of the dark money onion."[130]

12.6 Strategies for Corporate Political Activity

We have discussed the two principal approaches by which business has become politically active—lobbying and political spending. To be sure, there are other approaches, but these are the major ones. In our discussion, we have unavoidably referred to the use of these approaches as part of a strategy. To develop the idea of strategy for political activism, it is important to understand that managers must not only identify useful approaches but also address when and under what conditions these various approaches should be used or would be most effective. We do not want to carry this idea too far, because it is beyond the scope of this book. On the other hand, as managers devise and execute political strategies, it is useful to see political strategy as consistent with their development of stakeholder management capabilities.

The purpose of political strategy is "to secure a position of advantage regarding a given regulation or piece of legislation, to gain control of an idea or a movement and deflect it from the firm, or to deal with a local community group on an issue of importance."[131] As with all strategies, it is important to approach political activity in a well-thought-out manner, paying attention not only to the procedures to follow but also to the values inherent in the sought-after outcomes and any repercussions that could follow. As we discussed in Chapters 1 and 2, business is often accused of abusing its power and its political power is enormous. Companies therefore need to watch carefully that their power is not abused or used unethically.

Amy Hillman and Michael Hitt offer three distinct types of strategies that companies use to interact with decision makers in the political arena.[132] They are:

- *Information Strategy*—providing information to policymakers through activities such as lobbying, research projects, position papers, and being an expert witness
- *Financial Incentives Strategy*—making direct financial contributions, providing desired services, reimbursing travel, or paying fees to policymakers
- *Constituency Building Strategy*—mobilizing grassroots or business cohort to work together through public relations, political education, press conferences, and advertising

Firms may use any or all of them at any given time. These are all proactive strategies, in which the firm makes a conscious decision to be politically active.[133] They also align with the concept of political corporate social responsibility, discussed earlier. For example, in a recent study examining the relationship between corporate community programs and corporate political activity, researchers found that businesses could gather more information and engage in more constituency-building political strategies through community programs that enhance a firm's human, organizational, and geographic capital.[134] Of course, firms can also sit by the sidelines and passively react to changes in political environment but that strategy is unlikely to serve the business world in today's rapidly changing political environment. What Murray Weidenbaum wrote over 30 years ago is even truer for business today: Public policy is "no longer a spectator sport for business."[135]

12.6a Financial Performance Outcomes

Many studies have been conducted to calculate whether corporate political spending influences political decisions and, ultimately, firm performance. These studies have mixed results. Some find strong support, others find none, and a third group has mixed or marginal findings.[136] A recent meta-analysis found that corporate political activity had a consistent positive relationship with firm financial performance.[137] However, generic results are of limited value because the outcomes of corporate political activity occur in a variety of contexts and so researchers have looked for contingencies that might explain differences in returns. For example, another study shows that corporate donations to political campaigns are associated with an increase in firm value of 3.5 percent.[138] The authors speculate that the increase in firm value stems from the economic benefits accruing to the companies from legislation they supported. The return is greatest for firms in the candidate's home state.[139]

Evidence suggests that corporations are aware of the context in which they operate and adjust their corporate political activity accordingly. Universities do more lobbying when congressional appropriations committee members serve the districts in which they are located.[140] This targeted lobbying is a successful strategy. The universities who engage in lobbying appropriations committee members receive more federal funds for specific projects.[141]

The mixed results of these studies make it difficult to draw a definite connection between corporate political activity and firm performance. Clearly, context matters and so strategies that work in one situation will not necessarily transfer to another. We should even remember that corporate political activity can worsen performance. In a 2013 study of the corporate political activity of 943 firms over a ten-year period, Michael Hadani and Douglas Schuler found very little good news: They likened the hope of reaping corporate profits from corporate political activity to the famously unsuccessful search for El Dorado, the city of gold.[142] They found a negative association between political investments and market performance, with cumulative political investments worsening both market and accounting performance.[143] The only good news was for firms in regulated industries. For them, corporate political activity was positively associated with market performance. Yet, despite the uncertainty of results, companies seem to believe that political activity pays off because they keep doing it at unprecedented levels.

Summary

The world is still feeling the after-effects of the global financial meltdown. As a weak-but-improving economy struggles to get on its feet, items that were once at the forefront of the legislative agenda have been shelved to deal with issues such as joblessness and business failures. In this challenging environment, corporate political participation and political corporate social responsibility have taken on renewed importance.

We discussed the different levels of lobbying, the different types of PACs, and how each can be used responsibly. The 2010 Supreme Court ruling in *Citizens United v. Federal Election Commission* has changed the rules significantly, particularly in terms of corporate political spending. In the midst of these ebbs and flows in restrictions, lobbying and corporate political spending remain a permanent part of the political landscape. Business advocating for its interests is an important part of maintaining the balance of power needed in a pluralistic society. To maintain a true balance of power, however, businesses must advocate in a way that is both ethical and legal. Business has a duty to temper the freedom it now has with responsibility, accountability, and transparency.

Two major ways companies seek to influence government action include lobbying and corporate spending. While we describe these strategies at a macro level, they each contain a variety of different ways for corporations to take political action. We should remember that politically active firms are inclined to combine various strategies.[144] Companies make political contributions, set up their own lobbyists in Washington offices, contract with outside lobbyists to represent their interests, and join like-minded organizations to push for change through trade associations and coalitions. Corporate political spending and lobbying are not separate strategies; they are part of an overall approach.[145]

Business's political activity continues to be controversial with the public. As we discussed in Chapters 1 and 2, business often receives criticism for using and abusing its power. Nowhere is this more evident than in corporate lobbying and its outcomes. Efforts are underway to rein in some of the power that business now holds in the political action process. As new excesses develop, new regulations and rulings come to address the problems they present. In the meantime, responsible businesses are focused on determining how they can pursue an ethical approach to political participation. This is the ongoing "back and forth" that characterizes the political process.

Key Terms

501(c)(4)s, p. 386
527 groups, p. 386
ad hoc coalitions, p. 374
astroturf lobbying, p. 377
Carey committees, p. 386
Citizens United v. FEC, p. 382
coalitions, p. 380
company lobbying, p. 373
connected PAC, p. 382
cyberadvocacy, p. 377
dark money, p. 385
Golden Rule of Politics, p. 383
grassroots lobbying, p. 376
hybrid PACs, p. 386
independent expenditure-only committee, p. 382
Leadership PAC, p. 382
lobbying, p. 371
nonconnected PAC, p. 382
political accountability, p. 385
political action committees (PACs), p. 383
political corporate social responsibility (PCSR), p. 370
political involvement, p. 371
revolving door lobbyists, p. 375
sectoral trade associations, p. 373
shadow lobbying, p. 375
stealth lobbying, p. 375
Speechnow v. FEC, p. 382
Super PACs, p. 382
trade associations, p. 372
transparency, p. 385
umbrella trade associations, p. 373

Discussion Questions

1. Explain lobbying in your own words. Describe the different levels at which lobbying takes place. Why is there a lack of unity among the umbrella organizations?
2. What is a PAC? How is it different from a Super PAC? What are the major arguments in favor of PACs? What are the major types of PACs and how do they differ? In your opinion, are PACs a good way for business to influence the public policy process? What changes would you recommend for PACs?
3. Discuss *Citizens United* and *Speechnow* and their likely effect on future elections. What, if any, reforms would you recommend?
4. What does corporate accountability mean to you? How important is corporate political transparency?
5. What are the limits of corporate political strategy? Are there lines that companies should not cross?

Endnotes

1. Andreas G. Scherer, Andreas Rasche, Guido Palazzo, and Andre Spicer, "Managing for Political Corporate Social Responsibility: New Challenges and Directions for PCSR 2.0," *Journal of Management Studies* (Vol. 53, No. 3, May 2016), 273–298.
2. Ibid.
3. Alyssa Katz, *The Influence Machine* (New York, NY: Penguin Random House, 2015).
4. See George Melloan, "The Devil's Advocate," Review of The Influence Machine by Alyssa Katz, *The Wall Street Journal* (August 7, 2015), A9; "Who's Buying Elections? Shine Light on Dark Money," *USA Today* (January 28, 2016), 7A.
5. Ibid.
6. Tory Newmyer, "So Why Can't the Business Roundtable Get Anyone in Washington to Take It Seriously?" *Fortune* (February 20, 2015), 117–124.
7. S. Prakash Sethi, "Corporate Political Activism," *California Management Review* (Spring 1982), 32.
8. Jeffrey H. Birnbaum, "Microsoft's Capital Offense," *Fortune* (February 2, 1998), 84–86; Dan Carney, "Microsoft's All-Out Counterattack," *Businessweek* (May 15, 2000), 103–106.
9. John M. Simpson, "Google's 2015 Spending on Lobbying Tops $16 Million for Second Year," *Consumer Watchdog* (January 21, 2016), http://www.consumerwatchdog.org/newsrelease/google%E2%80%99s-2015-spending-lobbying-tops-16-million-second-year-leading-16-tech-and-communic. Accessed March 17, 2016.
10. David B. Yoffie and Sigrid Bergenstein, "Creating Political Advantage: The Rise of the Corporate Political Entrepreneur," *California Management Review* (Fall 1985), 124. See also John F. Mahon, "Corporate Political Strategy," *Business in the Contemporary World* (Autumn 1989), 50–62.
11. H. R. Mahood, *Interest Group Politics in America* (Englewood Cliffs, NJ: Prentice Hall, 1990), 52.
12. David D. Kirkpatrick, "Lobbyists Get Potent Weapon in Campaign Ruling," *The New York Times* (January 21, 2010), http://www.nytimes.com/2010/01/22/us/politics/22donate.html?_r=0. Accessed February 12, 2016.
13. Ibid., 53–54.
14. Elizabeth Dwoskin, "Lobbyist on Incremental Mission to Restore Lobbying's Good Name," *Bloomberg Businessweek* (June 7, 2012), 78.
15. Keith Matheny, "Abramoff Lists 8 Tips to Overhaul Lobbying Laws," *USA Today* (January 28, 2013), http://www.usatoday.com/story/news/nation/2013/01/28/abramoff-lobby-reform-tips/1870507/. Accessed February 24, 2016.
16. Michael Crowley, "A Lobbyist in Full," *The New York Times* (June 24, 2010), http://www.nytimes.com/2005/05/01/magazine/01ABRAMOFF.html?pagewanted=all. Accessed February 24, 2016.
17. Lobbying Database, OpenSecrets.org, https://www.opensecrets.org/lobby/index.php. Accessed March 17, 2016.
18. Raquel Meyer Alexander, Stephen W. Mazza, and Susan Scholz, "Measuring Rates of Return for Lobbying Expenditures: An Empirical Case Study of Tax Breaks for Multinational Corporations," *Journal of Law and Politics* (Vol. 25, No. 401, 2009), 401.
19. Peter Elkind, "Business Gets Schooled," *Fortune* (January 1, 2016), 49
20. Erich Lichtblau, "Tired of 'Tainted' Image, Lobbyists Try Makeover," *The New York Times* (May 3, 2012), http://www.nytimes.com/2012/05/04/us/politics/tired-of-tainted-image-lobbyists-try-makeover.html?pagewanted=all. Accessed February 24, 2016.
21. Dwoskin, 78.
22. Catherine Ho, "The Five Biggest Lobbyist Fights to Watch in 2016," *The Washington Post* (December 29, 2015), https://www.washingtonpost.com/news/powerpost/wp/2015/12/29/the-five-biggest-lobbying-fights-to-watch-in-2016/. Accessed March 23, 2016
23. "Greenpeace Rates Electronics Firms on Lobbying," *EnvironmentalLeader.com* (January 7, 2010), http://www.environmentalleader.com/2010/01/07/greenpeace-rates-electronics-firms-on-lobbying/. Accessed March 25, 2016.
24. "Coalition of Gulf Shrimp Industries Files for Relief from Subsidized Shrimp Imports," https://globenewswire.com/news-release/2012/12/28/513975/10016720/en/Coalition-of-Gulf-Shrimp-Industries-Files-Petitions-for-Relief-From-Subsidized-Shrimp-Imports.html. Accessed March 20, 2016.
25. Eric Lipton, "Emails Reveal Academic Ties in a Food War," *The New York Times* (September 6, 2015), 1.
26. Michael Hiltzik, "The Revolving Door Spins Faster," The Los Angeles Times (January 6, 2015) (http://www.latimes.com/business/hiltzik/la-fi-mh-the-revolving-door-20150106-column.html. Accessed March 21, 2016.
27. Ibid.
28. Ibid.
29. Josh Gerstein, "How Obama Failed to Shut Washington's Revolving Door," *Politico* (December 31, 2015), http://www.politico.com/story/2015/12/barack-obama-revolving-door-lobbying-217042. Accessed March 23, 2016.

30. "The Glint of the Revolving Door," *The New York Times* (February 5, 2004).

31. M. Asif Ismail, "Spending on Lobbying Thrives: Drug and Health Products Industries Invest $182 Million to Influence Legislation," *Center for Public Integrity Report* (April 1, 2007), http://www.publicintegrity.org/2007/04/01/5780/spending-lobbying-thrives. Accessed March 20, 2016.

32. David Kirkpatrick and Duff Wilson, "Health Reform in Limbo: Top Drug Lobbyist Quits," *The New York Times* (February 11, 2010), http://www.nytimes.com/2010/02/12/health/policy/12pharma.html?_r=0. Accessed March 20, 2016.

33. Alex Wayne and Drew Armstrong, "Tauzin's $11.6 Million Made Him Highest Paid Health-Law Lobbyist," Bloomberg.com (November 20, 2011), http://www.bloomberg.com/news/2011-11-29/tauzin-s-11-6-million-made-him-highest-paid-health-law-lobbyist.html. Accessed March 20, 2016.

34. Deniz Igan and Prachie Mishra, "Making Friends," *Finance and Development* (June 2011), http://www.imf.org/external/pubs/ft/fandd/2011/06/Igan.htm. Accessed March 20, 2016.

35. Ibid.

36. Ibid.

37. Deanna Fox, "Social Media Powers Young Lobbyists," *Timesunion* (January 13, 2016), http://www.timesunion.com/tuplus-local/article/Social-media-powers-young-lobbyists-6753277.php. Accessed April 28, 2016.

38. Evan Thomas, "Peddling Influence," *Time* (March 3, 1986), 27.

39. Kieron Monks, "The Lucrative Business of Crowds for Hire," *CNN* (October 20, 2015), http://www.cnn.com/2015/10/16/business/crowds-for-hire/. Accessed March 20, 2016.

40. Jane M. Keffer and Ronald Paul Hill, "An Ethical Approach to Lobbying Activities of Businesses in the United States," *Journal of Business Ethics* (September 1997), 1371–1379.

41. http://pac.org/conferences/grassroots. Accessed March 20, 2016.

42. Edward T. Walker, "The Uber-ization of Activism," *The New York Times* (August 6, 2015), http://www.nytimes.com/2015/08/07/opinion/the-uber-ization-of-activism.html. Accessed March 23, 2016.

43. Ibid.

44. Jeffrey H. Birnbaum, "Washington's Power 25," *Fortune* (December 8, 1997), 145–158.

45. Daniel Stone, "The Browning of Grassroots," *Newsweek* (August 20, 2009), http://www.newsweek.com/id/212934. Accessed March 8, 2013.

46. http://www.sourcewatch.org/index.php/Journalists_who_have_been_taken_in_by_astroturfing. Accessed April 28, 2016.

47. Joseph E. Stiglitz, *The Price of Inequality: How Today's Divided Society Endangers Our Future* (W.W. Norton Company, 2012).

48. Peter Baker, "Obama Was Pushed by Drug Industry, E-Mails Suggest," *The New York Times* (June 8, 2012), http://www.nytimes.com/2012/06/09/us/politics/e-mails-reveal-extent-of-obamas-deal-with-industry-on-health-care.html. Accessed April 30, 2016.

49. Alexandra Berzon, "Fantasy Sports Industry Mounts Lobbying Blitz," *The Wall Street Journal* (February 15, 2016), http://www.wsj.com/articles/fantasy-sports-industry-mounts-lobbying-blitz-1455585446. Accessed March 1, 2016.

50. "Fantasy Sports Trade Association Gets Subpoena from U.S. Prosecutor," *The Wall Street Journal* (October 16, 2015), http://www.wsj.com/articles/fantasy-sports-trade-association-gets-subpoena-from-u-s-prosecutor-1445030125. Accessed March 1, 2016.

51. Julia Marsh, "Daily Fantasy Sports Sites Allowed to Operate during Appeal," *The New York Post* (January 11, 2016), http://nypost.com/2016/01/11/daily-fantasy-sports-sites-allowed-to-operate-during-appeal/. Accessed April 30, 2016.

52. Jeffrey Marshall, "Credit Union Battleground Shifts," *US Banker* (April 1998), 10–11. See also Jill Wechsler, "Employers, Healthcare Industry Lash Back at White House, Congress," *Managed Healthcare* (February 1998), 8.

53. "The Chamber of Secrets," *The Economist* (April 21, 2012), 77–79.

54. https://www.opensecrets.org/lobby/clientsum.php?id=D000019798. Accessed March 1, 2016.

55. http://www.fixtheuschamber.org/issues/local-chambers-vs-us-chamber. Accessed April 24, 2016.

56. See Danny Hakim, "Big Tobacco's Staunch Friend in Washington: U.S. Chamber of Commerce," *The New York Times* (October 9, 2015), http://www.nytimes.com/2015/10/10/business/us-chamber-of-commerces-focus-on-advocacy-a-boon-to-tobacco.html?rref=collection%2Ftimestopic%2FChamber%20of%20Commerce%2C%20U.S.&action=click&contentCollection=timestopics®ion=stream&module=stream_unit&version=latest&contentPlacement=8&pgtype=collection&_r=1. Accessed March 20, 2016; David Brodwin, "The Chamber's Secrets," US News (October 22, 2015), http://www.usnews.com/opinion/economic-intelligence/2015/10/22/who-does-the-us-chamber-of-commerce-really-represent. Accessed March 20, 2016.

57. Jane Sasseen, "Who Speaks for Business?" *Businessweek* (October 19, 2009), 22–24.

58. "The Chamber of Secrets," 79.

59. *Business Roundtable*, http://businessroundtable.org/about. Accessed March 20, 2016.

60. Louis Jacobson, "The Roundtable's Turnaround," *National Journal* (June 28, 2003), 2120.
61. Jia Lynn Yang, "CEOs from Far and Wide Band against Financial Bill Provision," *Washington Post* (May 14, 2010), http://www.washingtonpost.com/wp-dyn/content/article/2010/05/13/AR2010051305288.html. Accessed March 23, 2016.
62. Ibid.
63. Kaja Whitehouse, "Shareholders Threaten Boards over 'Proxy Access'," USA Today (January 27, 2015), http://www.usatoday.com/story/money/business/2015/01/27/proxyaccess-investors-businessroundtable-wholefoods/22234271/. Accessed March 20, 2016.
64. http://www.nam.org/About-Us/About-the-NAM/US-Manufacturers-Association.aspx. Accessed March 20, 2016.
65. Ibid.
66. Mallory Micetich, "Manufacturers Continue to Look to Courts on Clean Power Plan," *National Association of Manufacturers* (January 21, 2016), http://www.nam.org/Newsroom/Press-Releases/2016/01/Manufac-turers-Continue-to-Look-to-Courts-on-Clean-Power-Plan/. Accessed March 20, 2016.
67. Jeffrey H. Birnbaum, "Washington's Power 25," *Fortune* (May 28, 2001), 95.
68. William Dunkelberg, "Small Business Is Contributing More to Economic Growth and Job Creation," *Forbes* (June 3, 2015), http://www.forbes.com/sites/william-dunkelberg/2015/06/03/small-business-is-contributing-more-to-economic-growth-and-job-creation/#545a1b0b1746. Accessed March 23, 2016.
69. Kent Hoover, "NFIB Has No Regrets about Lawsuit Challenging Obamacare," *The Business Journals* (June 28, 2012), http://www.bizjournals.com/bizjournals/washingtonbureau/2012/06/28/nfib-has-no-regrets-about-lawsuit.html?page=all. Accessed March 23, 2016.
70. Ibid.
71. http://www.flyersrights.org/. Accessed March 20, 2016.
72. Stephanie Rosenbloom, "Fighting the Incredible Shrinking Airline Seat," *The New York Times* (February 29, 2016), http://www.nytimes.com/2016/02/29/travel/shrinking-airline-seats.html. Accessed March 1, 2016.
73. Ibid.
74. Dori Meinert, "Businesses Target Human Trafficking." *HR Magazine* 57, no. 12 (December 2012): 20.
75. Ibid.
76. Ibid.
77. Ibid.
78. Ibid.
79. http://www.ungift.org/doc/knowledgehub/events/Luxor_End_Human_Trafficking_Now.pdf. Accessed March 14, 2016.
80. Dori Meinert, "Modern-day Slavery," *HR Magazine* 57.5 (2012): 22–27.
81. "Court Won't Hear Campaign Contributions Appeal," *Boston Herald* (February 25, 2013), http://www.bostonherald.com/news_opinion/us_politics/2013/02/court_wont_hear_campaign_contributions_appeal Accessed February 26, 2016.
82. http://www.fec.gov/pages/brochures/ssfvnonconnected.shtml. Accessed February 26, 2016.
83. Federal Election Commission Record, *Nonconnected committees* (May 2008), http://www.fec.gov/pdf/record/2008/may08.pdf. Accessed March 20, 2016.
84. Ibid.
85. R. Sam Garrett, "Super PACs" in Federal Elections: Overview and Issues for Congress," *Congressional Research Service* (April 4, 2013), http://www.fas.org/sgp/crs/misc/R42042.pdf. Accessed February 26, 2016.
86. Adam Liptak, "Courts Take on Campaign Finance Decisions," *The New York Times* (March 26, 2010), http://www.nytimes.com/2010/03/27/us/politics/27campaign.html. Accessed February 26, 2016.
87. Ibid.
88. Ibid.
89. http://www.opensecrets.org/pacs/superpacs.php?cycle=2012. Accessed March 4, 2016.
90. Ibid.
91. Bruce F. Freed and Karl J. Sandstrom, "Dangerous Terrain: How to Manage Corporate Political Spending in a Risky New Environment," *The Conference Board Review* (Winter 2012), 20–27.
92. Ibid.
93. Bruce F. Freed and Karl J. Sandstrom, "Navigating Politics," *The Conference Board Review* (Winter 2013), http://www.tcbreview.com/tcbr-leadership/navigating-politics.html. Accessed March 20, 2016.
94. J. W. Verret, "The SEC Ponders Circumventing Citizens United," *The Wall Street Journal* (January 8, 2013), A5.
95. Ibid.
96. Brian Bakst, "Target Apologizes for Political Donation in Minnesota," *USA Today* (August 8, 2010), http://usatoday30.usatoday.com/money/industries/retail/2010-08-05-target-campaign-donation_N.htm. Accessed March 23, 2016.
97. Ibid.
98. Verret, A5.
99. Ibid.
100. Staff, "McCain Raps High Court's Campaign Finance Ruling," *Associated Press* (January 12, 2012), https://www.yahoo.com/news/mccain-raps-high-courts-campaign-finance-ruling-123521384.html. Accessed March 24, 2016.
101. Michael Beckel,"Supreme Court Gives Corporations, Unions Power to Spend Unlimited Sums on Political Messaging," *OpenSecretsblog* (January 21, 2010), http://www.opensecrets.org/news/2010/01/supreme-court-gives-corporatio.html. Accessed March 24, 2016.

102. Larry J. Sabato, "PAC-Man Goes to Washington," *Across the Board* (October 1984), 16.
103. http://www.sourcewatch.org/index.php/Political_action_committee. Accessed February 26, 2016.
104. Peter Overby, "5 Years after 'Citizens United,' Super PACs Continue to Grow," NPR Georgia Public Broadcasting (January 13, 2015), http://www.npr.org/2015/01/13/377024687/five-years-after-citizens-united-superpacs-continue-to-grow. Accessed March 20, 2016.
105. Spencer MacColl, "Citizens United Decision Profoundly Affects Political Landscape," *OpenSecretsblog* (May 5, 2011), http://www.opensecrets.org/news/2011/05/citizens-united-decision-profoundly-affects-political-landscape.html. Accessed March 24, 2016.
106. "Which Presidential Candidates Are Winning the Money Race," *The New York Times* (February 22, 2016), http://www.nytimes.com/interactive/2016/us/elections/election-2016-campaign-money-race.html?_r=0. Accessed March 23, 2016.
107. Kirby Goidel and Keith Gaddie, "Money Matters (in Presidential Elections)," *Huffington Post* (February 8, 2016), http://www.huffingtonpost.com/kirby-goidel/money-matters-in-presiden_b_9190198.html. Accessed March 23, 2016.
108. Freed and Sandstrom, 2013.
109. Ibid.
110. Ibid.
111. Ibid., 26.
112. Viktor Emil Frankl, *Man's Search for Meaning,* Beacon Press (1956), 132.
113. See Kelly Ngo, "Political Spending Shareholder Resolutions: The Big Ten," Citizenvox (April 22, 20150, http://www.citizenvox.org/2015/04/22/political-spending-shareholder-resolutions-the-big-ten/ Accessed March 20, 2016; Sustainable Investments Institute Special Report (July 2, 2014) https://si2news.files.wordpress.com/2014/07/corporate-political-activity-shareholder-proposals-2010-2014-as-of-7-2-14.pdf. Accessed January 5, 2016.
114. Eduardo Porter, "Corporations Open up about Political Spending," *The New York Times* (June 9, 2015), http://www.nytimes.com/2015/06/10/business/corporations-open-up-about-political-spending.html?_r=0. Accessed March 24, 2016.
115. Ibid.
116. The 2015 CPA-Zicklin Index of Corporate Political Disclosure and Accountability, http://files.politicalaccountability.net/index/CPA-Zicklin_Index_Final_-with_links.pdf. Accessed March 20, 2016.
117. Sunlight Foundation, http://sunlightfoundation.com/. Accessed March 24, 2016.
118. See Paul Steiger and Stephen Engelberg, "Dark Money and the 2012 Election," *ProPublica* (November 6, 2012), http://www.propublica.org/article/dark-money-and-the-2012-election-we-need-your-help. Accessed March 25, 2016; Tom Kertscher, "Ten Times More 'Dark Money' Has Been Spent for 2016 Elections," *Politifact* (November 5, 2015), http://www.politifact.com/wisconsin/statements/2015/nov/05/tammy-baldwin/ten-times-more-dark-money-has-been-spent-2016-elec/. Accessed March 23, 2016.
119. Kertscher, 2015.
120. Brian C. Mooney, "Ruling Allows Major Political Donors to Hide Identities," *The Boston Globe* (February 15, 2012), http://www.bostonglobe.com/news/nation/2012/02/15/major-political-donors-can-hide-identities/JrQx1lLgLQNJ1Mfuz5LbjN/story.html?camp=pm. Accessed March 25, 2016.
121. http://www.opensecrets.org/527s/types.php. Accessed March 25, 2016.
122. John Dimsdale, "Required Super PAC Disclosures Don't Reveal All," *Marketplace* (February 1, 2012), http://www.marketplace.org/topics/elections/campaign-trail/required-super-pac-disclosures-dont-reveal-all. Accessed March 25, 2016.
123. https://www.opensecrets.org/527s/types.php. Accessed March 25, 2016.
124. Center for Political Accountability, "Hidden Rivers (2006): How Trade Associations Conceal Corporate Political Spending, Its Threat to Companies, and What Shareholders Can Do," http://politicalaccountability.net/reports/cpa-reports. Accessed March 23, 2016.
125. http://www.brandeis.edu/legacyfund/bio.html. Accessed March 24, 2016.
126. Michael Scherer, "Dark Money: The Rise of Outside Spending in 2012," *Time* (November 1, 2012), http://swampland.time.com/2012/11/01/dark-money/#ixzz2FX0K5omj. Accessed March 20, 2016.
127. Ibid.
128. Eliza Newlin Carney, "DISCLOSE Advocates Renew Fight," *Roll Call* (January 4, 2013), http://atr.rollcall.com/disclose-advocates-renew-fight/. Accessed March 24, 2016.
129. Ibid.
130. Ibid.
131. Mahon, 1989.
132. Amy J. Hillman and Michael A. Hitt, "Corporate Political Strategy Formulation: A Model of Approach, Participation, and Strategy Decisions," *Academy of Management Review* (Vol. 24, No. 4, 1999), 825–842.
133. Ibid.
134. Douglas A. Schuler and Kathleen Rehbein, "Linking Corporate Community Programs and Political Strategies," *Business & Society* (Vol. 54, No. 6, 2015), 794–821.
135. Murray L. Weidenbaum, "Public Policy: No Longer a Spectator Sport for Business," *Journal of Business Strategy* (Vol. 1, No. 1, 1980), 46.
136. Sean Lux, T. Russell Crook, and Terry Leap. "Corporate Political Activity: The Good, the Bad, and the

Ugly." *Business Horizons*, May 2012, 307–312; Frank R. Baumgartner and Beth L. Leech, *Basic Interests: The Importance of Interest Groups in Politics and Political Science* (Chicago: University of Chicago Press, 1995), cited in Jeffrey E. Cohen and John A. Hamman, "Interest Group PAC Contributions and the 1992 Regulation of Cable Television," *The Social Science Journal* (2003), 357–369.

137. Sean Lux, T. Russell Crook, and David J. Woehr, "Mixing Business with Politics: A Meta-Analysis of the Antecedents and Outcomes of Corporate Political Activity," *Journal of Management* (Vol. 37, No. 1, 2011), 223–236.

138. Daniel Fisher and William P. Barrett, "All Follow the Money," *Forbes* (April 16, 2007), 48; Michael J. Cooper, Huseyin Gulen, and Alexei V. Ovtchinnikov, "Corporate Political Contributions and Stock Returns," *Journal of Finance* (Vol. 65, No. 2, 2010), 687–724.

139. Ibid.

140. De Figueiredo, John M., and Brian S. Silverman, "Academic Earmarks and the Returns to Lobbying." *Journal of Law & Economics*, 49.2 (2006): 597–625.

141. Ibid.

142. Michael Hadani and Douglas A. Schuler. "In Search of El Dorado: The Elusive Financial Returns on Corporate Political Investments." *Strategic Management Journal* (Vol. 34, No. 2, February 2013), 165–181.

143. Ibid.

144. Douglas A. Schuler, Kathleen Rehbein, and Roxy D. Cramer, "Pursuing Strategic Advantage through Political Means: A Multivariate Approach," *Academy of Management Journal* (August 2002), 659–672.

145. Ibid.

13

Consumer Stakeholders: Information Issues

CHAPTER LEARNING OUTCOMES

After studying this chapter, you should be able to:

1 Describe the consumer movement and identify the consumer's Magna Carta and explain its meaning.

2 Identify product information issues that are affected by business's social and ethical responsibilities. Identify the major abuses of advertising and discuss specific controversial advertising issues.

3 Describe the role and functions of the Federal Trade Commission (FTC).

4 Explain recent consumer-related legislation that has been passed—Credit Card Act (CARD) and the Consumer Financial Protection Bureau (CFPB).

5 Discuss the strengths and weaknesses of self-regulation of advertising.

6 Identify the three moral models and their likely perspectives on consumer stakeholders.

As businesses are striving to come out of the worldwide economic malaise, they all have been fighting for the hearts and minds of consumers. By virtually all measures, consumer spending has been stable to modestly higher over the past five years and consumers have become more cautious and selective about their spending on the entire gamut of products and services.[1] Even as the economy is trying to perk up, some observers say it may be years before consumers return to their prerecession levels of spending. Other analysts are more optimistic. Some think the new consumer is "down" but "not out." By all measures, however, it is clear that businesses need to be paying careful attention to customer stakeholders if they expect to survive and grow.

How important are consumers as stakeholders? According to management expert Peter Drucker, there is only one valid definition of business purpose: *to create a customer*.[2] *Retaining* customers is essential, too. In fact, small increases in customer retention rates can lead to dramatic increases in profits.[3] Clearly, businesses must create and retain customers if they are to succeed in today's competitive marketplace. It is not surprising, therefore, that **customer relationship management (CRM)** has become an important mantra of marketing.[4] Customer relationship management is "the ability of an organization to effectively identify, acquire, foster, and retain loyal profitable customers."[5]

Recently, the Gallup Poll has been tracking business–customer relationships by way of the concept of **customer engagement**.[6] Customer engagement is all about the emotional connection companies are able to establish between their customers and the company. Gallup uses a scale that focuses on three assessments that customers make: whether the company always delivers what it promises, the pride the customer feels by being a company's customer, and the judgment made that the company is a good match for the customer.[7] Research has shown that simply satisfying customers is no longer the key to increasing sales. Engaging them is the key. Fully engaged customers bring in 30 to 45 percent more annual revenues.[8]

With CRM and a concern for customer engagement guiding businesses in their customer relations, one would expect consumers to be pleased, or at least satisfied, with the way they have been treated. Unfortunately, this seldom has been the case. The consumer still feels "often ignored"[9] and, in practice, CRM has been said to be "an awful lot of bland talk and not a lot of action."[10] In practice, some think the customer care revolution is largely considered a failure.[11] Most statistics seem to indicate that although product and service quality has improved somewhat, the treatment of customers has been weak.

In practice, a focus on customer satisfaction seems to be more prevalent than a focus on customer engagement. As an important book has told us, "satisfied customers tell three friends, but angry customers tell 3,000."[12] There are many reasons why customers are not satisfied today. One reason seldom gauged is that consumers are not satisfied today because they are exhausted at all the choices they face and the decisions they must make in their roles as consumers. Whether the consumer is attempting to buy a new mobile device or a cup of coffee, the choices are dizzying. And, when it comes to paying for products and services, there is too much fine print to read, much less understand. In short, as companies have sought to satisfy customers, they have frustrated them with too much complexity whether it be in the products or services offered or the information related to the decision and after purchase experience. Exhausted customers are seldom satisfied customers.

The business-and-consumer stakeholder issue is at the forefront of discussions about business and its relationships with and responsibility to the society in which it exists because we are all consumers and companies are not sustainable without us. Products and services are the most visible manifestations of business in society. For this reason, the whole issue deserves careful examination. We devote two chapters to consumer stakeholders. In this chapter, we focus on the consumer movement and product/service information issues—most notably, advertising.

13.1 The Consumer Movement

In Chapter 14, we consider product and service issues, especially product safety and liability, and business's response to its consumer stakeholders. The basic expectations of the modern consumer movement were found in the **consumer's Magna Carta**, or the four basic consumer rights spelled out by President John F. Kennedy in his "Special Message on Protecting the Consumer Interest."[13] Those rights included the right *to safety*, the right *to be informed*, the right *to choose*, and the right *to be heard*.

The **right to safety** concerns many products (insecticides, foods, drugs, automobiles, appliances) that are dangerous. The **right to be informed** is marketing and advertising related and refers to the consumer's right to know about a product, its use, and the cautions to be exercised while using it. This right includes the whole array of marketing: advertising, warranties, labeling, and packaging. The **right to choose**, although not a great concern today, refers to the assurance that competition is working effectively and that choices are available. The fourth, the **right to be heard**, was proposed because of many consumers' belief that they could not effectively communicate to business their desires and, especially, their grievances.[14]

In addition to the basic rights, consumers today want "fair value" for money spent, a product that will meet "reasonable" expectations, a product (or service) with full disclosure of its specifications, a product (or service) that has been truthfully advertised, and a product that is safe and has been subjected to appropriate product safety testing. Consumers also expect that if a product is too dangerous, it will be removed from the market or some other appropriate action will be taken.

For decades, there have been outcries that business has failed in these responsibilities to consumers, leaving them often neglected or mistreated.[15] The roots of consumer activism in the United States date back to 1906, when Upton Sinclair published *The Jungle*, his famous exposé of unsanitary conditions in the meatpacking industry.[16] The contemporary wave of consumer activism, however, has been growing for many decades, although in a variety of forms.[17] Today it is called consumerism, consumer activism, or the consumer movement.

The following definition of **consumerism** captures the essential nature of the consumer movement:

> *Consumerism is a social movement seeking to augment the rights and powers of buyers in relation to sellers.*[18]

Although the modern consumer movement is often said to have begun with the publication of Ralph Nader's criticism of General Motors in his book *Unsafe at Any Speed*,[19] the impetus for the movement was actually a complex combination of circumstances. Doubtless, the factors of affluence, education, awareness, and rising expectations mentioned in Chapter 1 also have been at work.

13.1a Ralph Nader's Consumerism

Ralph Nader's contribution to the birth, growth, and nurturance of the consumer movement cannot be overstated. Nader arrived on the scene over 50 years ago, and he is still the acknowledged father of the consumer movement. The impact of Nader's auto safety exposé, *Unsafe at Any Speed*, was momentous. His book not only gave rise to auto safety regulations and devices (safety belts, padded dashboards, stronger door latches, head restraints, air bags, etc.) but it also created a new era—that of the consumer. Nader, personally, was thrust into national prominence.

Nader put his money to work and built an enormous and far-reaching consumer protection empire. His legions of zealous activists became known as "Nader's Raiders." Nader popularized public interest law and his activism generated significant growth in the popularity of law schools. Nader and the consumer movement were the impetus for consumer legislation being passed in the 1970s.

In the late 1980s, however, Nader began what *Businessweek* dubbed his "second coming." Nader successfully campaigned to roll back car insurance rates in California and to squelch a congressional pay raise. These victories vaulted him to a prominence he had not enjoyed in years.[20] In 2000, Nader ran as the Green Party candidate for U.S. president with a campaign that focused on establishing a viable third party, attacking corporate wealth, and protecting the environment. He was unsuccessful in his goal of getting 5 percent of the total popular vote so that the Green Party would be eligible to receive federal matching funds in the 2004 presidential election.[21] When he announced a second run for the presidency in February 2004, the Green Party disavowed him, and a poll found that two-thirds of Americans did not want him to run again.[22]

Ralph Nader continues to be a controversial man and a strong activist for the consumer voice. His articles appear regularly on CommonDreams, a nonprofit news center.[23] He also continues to weigh in on business and politics.[24] Nader has been the source of considerable progress for consumers. Consumer complaints did not disappear with the advent of Ralph Nader's activism; instead, they intensified. One of Nader's greatest contributions is that he made consumer complaints respectable. In 2016, Nader opened a museum in his hometown of Winsted, Connecticut, celebrating class action lawsuits and tort law.[25]

13.1b Consumerism Today

Many groups make up the loose confederation known today as the consumer movement. Consumerism involves grassroots organizations, social media activism, and the rise of many different nonprofit organizations and Web sites that increasingly specialize in one aspect of consumer products or services. At a broad level, the consumer movement is represented by organizations such as the Consumer Federation of America, Public Citizen, American Council on Consumer Interests, and Consumer's Union of United States,

FIGURE 13-1 Consumer Organizations Today

Consumer Organization	Information about Organization
American Council on Consumer Interests http://www.consumerinterests.org/	ACCI is a leading consumer policy research and education organization consisting of a world-wide community of researchers, educators, and related professionals dedicated to enhancing consumer well-being. ACCI promotes the consumer interest by encouraging, producing, and communicating policy-relevant research.
Consumerist http://consumerist.com/	Founded in 2005, Consumerist is an independent source of consumer news and information published by Consumer Media LLC, a not-for-profit subsidiary of Consumer Reports.
Consumer Federation of America http://www.consumerfed.org/	The Consumer Federation of America (CFA) is an association of non-profit consumer organizations that was established in 1968 to advance the consumer interest through research, advocacy, and education.
Consumer Reports http://www.consumerreports.org/cro/index.htm	Consumer Reports is an expert, independent, nonprofit organization whose mission is to work for a fair, just, and safe marketplace for all consumers and to empower consumers to protect themselves.
Consumer Action http://www.consumer-action.org/	Through multilingual financial education materials, community outreach, and issue-focused advocacy, Consumer Action empowers underrepresented consumers nationwide to assert their rights in the marketplace and financially prosper.
Public Citizen http://www.citizen.org/Page.aspx?pid=2306	Public Citizen serves as the people's voice in the nation's capital. Since its' founding in 1971, it has delved into an array of areas, but its' work on each issue shares an overarching goal: To ensure that all citizens are represented in the halls of power.
Center for Science in the Public Interest http://www.cspinet.org/about/mission.html	CSPI is a consumer advocacy organization whose twin missions are to conduct innovative research and advocacy programs in health and nutrition and to provide consumers with current and useful information about their health and well-being.

Inc., which publishes *Consumer Reports* a highly respected magazine focused on evaluating products and services in the marketplace. Some of the more specialized organizations that focus on specific consumer issues include Center for Auto Safety, Center for Science in the Public Interest, and the Better Business Bureau.

Figure 13-1 presents information about some of the leading consumer organizations today.

The consumer movement is driven by consumer problems and consumer complaints. Figure 13-2 lists some of the most frequently cited examples of consumer's problems with business. In addition to this list of general consumer problems, the Consumer Federation of America each year lists its top ten consumer complaints, by category, and its most recent listing included issues related to the following[26]:

- Autos—misrepresentations in advertising, lemons, faulty repairs
- Home improvement/construction—shoddy work, failure to start/complete
- Credit/debit—billing/fee disputes, predatory lending, abusive collection
- Retail sales—false advertising, deceptive practices, problems with rebates and coupons
- Services—misrepresentations, shoddy work, failure to perform
- Landlord/tenant—unhealthy/unsafe conditions, failure to make repairs, deposits
- Home solicitations—misrepresentations, telemarketing, do-not-call violations
- Health products/services—misleading claims, unlicensed practitioners
- Fraud—bogus sweepstakes, work-at-home scams, fake check scams
- Household goods—misrepresentations, failure to deliver, faulty repairs

FIGURE 13-2 Examples of Consumer Problems with Business

- The high prices of many products
- The poor quality of many products
- Misleading and deceptive advertising, often on social media
- Hidden fees
- Poor quality of after-sales service
- Too many products breaking or going wrong after you bring them home
- Misleading packaging or labeling
- Slack filling
- The feeling that it is a waste of time to complain about consumer problems because nothing substantial will be achieved
- Inadequate guarantees and warranties
- Failure of companies to handle complaints properly
- Too many products that are dangerous or unsafe
- The absence of reliable information about various products and services
- Not knowing what to do if something is wrong with a product you have bought

Before we consider more closely the corporate response to the consumer movement and the consumer stakeholder, it is fruitful to examine some of the issues that have become prominent in the business–consumer relationship and the role that the major federal regulatory bodies have assumed in addressing these issues. Broadly, we may classify the major kinds of issues into two groups: *product/service information* and the *product/service itself.* As stated earlier, in this chapter we focus on product/service information issues such as advertising, warranties, packaging, and labeling. The next chapter focuses on the product or service itself.

13.1c Product/Service Information Issues

Why have questions been raised about business's social and ethical responsibilities in the area of product/service information? Most consumers know the answer. Companies understandably want to portray their products in the most flattering light. However, efforts to paint a positive portrait of a product can easily cross the line into misinformation or deception regarding the product's attributes. Consumer Reports conducts independent tests of products and report their findings in their print and online editions of *Consumer Reports (CR).*[27] "Selling It" is a segment in the print edition of *Consumer Reports*; it is designed to "memorialize the excesses in the world of marketing." Quite often the ads are contradictory. The following items are examples of the often humorous absurdities they chronicle:

- On a Subway sandwich shop sign, the print read "Subway New Management Everyday $2.50 6 inch sub." Did they really mean new management every day? Or, did they mean Subway is under new management; every day you can get a 6-inch sub for $2.50?[28] So, who's in charge today?
- A resident in Sacramento, California, received an advertisement for an oil change from Pep Boys. Printed on the card was his "closest Pep Boys"; it was San Juan, Puerto Rico.[29] By the time he gets home, he'll need another oil change!
- A banner hung outside the Dunkin' Donuts restaurant. It read "CLOSED to better serve you." How so, by causing you to go to Starbuck's?[30]
- The ad implores you to "switch to Verizon high-speed internet at a super-low price that'll never go up." The ad repeats again "Guaranteed to Never Go Up." Then, when you read the fine print on the same page, it says "Rates increase after two years."[31] What part of "never go up" do they fail to understand?

The box of pudding and pie filling claims boldly to be Pistachio and the photo of it is green. When you read the ingredients list, however, it says the nuts are diced *almonds*, the flavor is artificial, and the green color is yellow and blue dyes![32] These cases are actual examples of the questionable and careless use of **product information**, usually in an ad, flyer, or on a sign. It is doubtful whether the firms that created these communications were intending to deceive, but the information they provided did not match the reality of the product or service. Business has a legal and an ethical responsibility to provide fair and accurate information about its products or services.

The primary ethical issue with product or service information falls in the realm of advertising. Other information-related areas include warranties or guarantees, packaging, labeling, instructions for use, and the sales techniques used by direct sellers. Information about after-sale service is also a critical issue.

13.1d Advertising Issues

The advertising industry represents the face of big business to consumers. In 2015, global advertisers spent around $538 billion and this figure rises annually.[33] As a result of its huge impact, the debate over the role of advertising in society has been going on for decades. Most observers have concentrated on the economic function of advertising in our market system, but opinions vary as to whether advertising is beneficial or detrimental as a business function. Critics charge that it is a wasteful and inefficient tool of business and that our current standard of living would be even higher if we could be freed from the negative influences of advertising.[34]

In response, others have claimed that advertising is a beneficial component of the market system and that the increases in the standard of living and consumer satisfaction may be attributed to it. They argue that, in general, advertising is an efficient means of distributing information because consumers need to know about the enormous and ever-changing array of products. From this perspective, advertising is an effective and relatively inexpensive way of informing consumers of new and improved products.[35]

The debate over whether advertising is a productive or wasteful business practice will undoubtedly continue. As a practical matter, however, advertising has become the lifeblood of the free enterprise system. It stimulates competition and makes available information that consumers can use in comparison shopping. It also provides competitors with information with which to respond in a competitive way and contains a mechanism for immediate feedback in the form of sales response. So, despite some criticisms, advertising does provide social and economic benefits to consumers.

With the availability of tens of thousands of products and their increasing complexity, the consumer today has a real need for information that is clear, accurate, and adequate. **Clear information** is that which is direct and straightforward and on which neither deception nor manipulation relies. **Accurate information** communicates truths, not half-truths. It avoids gross exaggeration and innuendo. **Adequate information** provides potential purchasers with enough information to make the best choice among the options available.[36]

Whereas *providing information* is one legitimate purpose of advertising in our society, another legitimate purpose is *persuasion*. Most consumers today expect that business advertises for the purpose of persuading them to buy their products or services, and they accept this as a part of the commercial system. Indeed, many people enjoy companies' attempts to come up with interesting ways to sell their products. It is commonplace for people to talk with one another about the latest appealing or entertaining advertisement they have seen but at the same time complain about others.

Awards are given for outstanding advertisements. The most famous ones today seem to be the ranking of the top ads that appear on Super Bowl Sunday. They generate considerable interest and talk before, during and after the big game. But, just as excellent ads

ETHICS IN PRACTICE CASE

What Do We Tell the Customer?

While working as a customer service representative at a bank, a huge part of our job is to sell financial products to customers. We have to meet our goal every quarter by opening as many accounts as we can and to sell the bank's products. The branch manager is very tough and we can be written up if we don't reach our goal; then, eventually we can be terminated from the job if it continues.

As part of our jobs we are supposed to make sure the customer is aware of the banking products they are getting or the accounts they are opening. Also, the customer service representative needs to explain the product fully to the customer and leave it up to them to decide if they want to open the account or not.

Some of my coworkers don't explain everything in detail to the customer unless the customer asks. However, I have overheard the whole conversation of one of my coworkers—telling a customer to open a lot of accounts combined together because they come as a package. This means the customer will have to open Checking, Savings, Debit Card, Apply for Overdraft Protection, and Credit Card.

My coworker didn't give the customer an option to choose from but told her she had to open everything because it's a package—which is not true. The customer had no option because she trusted the employee because he knows better than her. The employee is the one that has more knowledge of what he/she is doing. The customer ended up opening all the accounts.

I was really in shock because I knew what was going on and what I have heard is totally wrong. I also knew that we are supposed to explain the products to the customer and leave the decision up to them as to what accounts they would like to open. I felt so bad that the customer just went by what the employee had said and opened everything, even though she didn't want it, but she believed she had to. In addition, the same coworker always got recognized for selling a lot of products and always reaching his goal. I was in shock and I didn't know how to react.

1. Is it fair to miscommunicate to the customer in this way? Are we being accurate, unambiguous, and clear? What's the harm if the customer opens all the accounts?
2. Should I have gone over to my coworker's desk while he was with the customer and stopped what was going on and made sure the customer got the correct information? Or, should I have waited until the customer leaves and then go to my coworker and tell him that what he had done is wrong and unethical?
3. Is this misinformation given to the customer important enough for me to approach my manager and tell her everything I heard even though the manager pushes us to sell accounts and do whatever it takes?
4. Is it possible the coworker felt pressure from management to meet unrealistic goals and that this pressure was behind the deception?

Contributed by Haidy Elfarra

are recognized, so are the bad ones.[37] Ethical issues in advertising arise as companies cross over the line in their attempts to inform and persuade, and sometimes entertain, consumer stakeholders. The frequently heard phrase "the seamy side of advertising" alludes to the economic and social costs that derive from advertising abuses, such as those mentioned earlier in the chapter, and of which the reader is probably able to supply ample personal examples.

Advertising Abuses. There are four general types of advertising abuses in which ethical issues surface. These include situations in which advertisers are ambiguous, conceal facts, exaggerate, or employ psychological appeals.[38] These four types cover most of the common criticisms leveled at advertising.

Ambiguous Advertising One of the simplest ways that companies deceive is through **ambiguous advertising**, in which something about the product or service is not made clear because it is stated in a way that may mean several different things.

An ad can be made ambiguous in several ways. One way is to make a statement using **weasel words**, which leaves it to the viewer to infer the message. Weasel words are inherently vague and the company could always claim it was not misleading the consumer. An example of a weasel word is *help*. Once an advertiser uses the qualifier "help," almost anything could follow, and the company could claim that it was not intending to deceive. We see ads that claim to "help us keep young," "help prevent cavities," or "help keep our houses germ free." Think how many times you have seen expressions in advertising such as "helps stop," "helps prevent," "helps fight," "helps you feel," "helps you look," or "helps you become."[39] Other weasel words include *like*, *virtually*, and *up to* (e.g., stops pain "up to" eight hours—which simply means it won't stop pain for more than eight hours). The use of such words makes ads ambiguous. Another way to make an ad ambiguous is through use of legalese, or other excessively complex and ambiguous terminology. To make matters worse, often the legalese and complex language is found in the fine print, which consumers are not inclined to read anyway.

Concealed Facts A type of advertising abuse called **concealed facts** refers to the practice of not telling the whole truth or deliberately not communicating information the consumer ought to have access to in making an informed choice. Another way of stating this is to say "a fact is concealed when its availability would probably make the desire, purchase, or use of the product less likely than its absence."[40] This is a difficult area because few would argue that an advertiser is obligated to tell "everything," even if that were humanly possible. For example, a pain reliever company might claim the effectiveness of its product in superlative terms without stating that there are dozens of other products on the market that are just as effective.

Ethical issues arise when a firm, through its advertisements, presents facts in such a selective way that a false belief is created. As consumers, it is up to us to be informed about factors such as competitors' products and prices. Of course, judgment is required in determining which ads have and have not created false beliefs. This makes the entire realm of deceptive advertising a challenge. At times it can be considered harmless. For example, a burrito restaurant in a college town ran a humorous newspaper ad with "FREE BEER" in large block letters; underneath in small letters were the words "will not be served." No one accused this company of unlawful deception; however, not all instances of concealed facts are considered benign. Other concealed facts often occur with respect to hidden fees or surcharges on services. Today, you have to be a sophisticated consumer willing to do timely detective work to root out the rules and policies governing fees companies charge.

An increasingly popular form of concealed advertising is **product placement**, the practice of embedding products in movies and TV shows. Critics call this "stealth advertising." Product placements are everywhere—an Apple store in the background, an iPhone, a Coke, a Pepsi, Reebok shoes, Nike sweats, a GM car, and so on. One prominent example finds James Bond sipping a Heineken beer in the movie *Skyfall*.[41] Nonprofit activist groups have called this practice of sneaking in product pitches egregious and deceptive.[42] In a variation of product placement, termed **plot placement**, sponsors have paid to make their products integrated into the plotline of a TV show. In one episode of *Biggest Loser*, the dieting contestants hiked from one Subway sandwich shop to another to get a meal as part of the contest rules. The product placement of the Apple iPad on *Modern Family* may have gone too far. The Dunphys went on a family mission to get Phil an iPad. At the end of the show, Phil was shown stroking his new iPad while uttering "I love you" to his new gadget.[43]

Product and plot placement as forms of advertising are in part a response to the "TiVo effect." The popularity of digital video recorders (DVRs) such as TiVo and video streaming has lessened the time that consumers spend watching commercials. The fact that DVRs make it easy and convenient for TV watchers to zap through commercials has advertisers looking for new ways to make customers take notice.[44] Even advertising stalwarts, like Coca-Cola with its advertising budget of more than $3 billion per year, are relying less on traditional ads and more on product placement in DVDs and video games.[45]

Exaggerated Claims Companies can also mislead consumers by exaggerating the benefits of their products and services. **Exaggerated claims** are claims that simply cannot be substantiated by any kind of evidence. An example of this would be a claim that a pain reliever is "50 percent stronger than aspirin" or "superior to any other on the market." The Food and Drug Administration has taken several companies to task for exaggerated claims. The FDA rebuked L'Oréal's Lancôme subsidiary for claiming that its antiwrinkle products do more than it can document. Rather than just claiming its products reduce wrinkles, the company claimed that one product "boosts the activity of genes and stimulates the production of youth proteins." The FDA argued that this ad confuses a cosmetics product with a new drug that would require FDA approval. If the company does not comply and change its ads, the FDA may issue injunctions or seize the company's products.[46] In another case, Merck & Co. was ordered to stop using the term *waterproof* in its Coppertone advertising. The company also agreed to stop using the terms *sunblock* and *all day protection* in its adverting because these were considered to be exaggerations of the products' benefits. Merck will pay fines to settle the case.[47]

A general form of exaggeration is known as **puffery**, a euphemism for hyperbole or exaggeration that usually refers to the use of general superlatives. Is Budweiser really the "King of Beers"? Is Wheaties the "Breakfast of Champions"? Does "better ingredients" mean Papa John's has "Better Pizza"? Normally, a claim of general superiority is considered puffery and is allowable. However, companies walk a fine line when engaging in puffery. They need to be certain that no direct comparison is being made.

Most people are not too put off by puffery, because the claims usually are so general and so frequent that any consumer would know that the firm is exaggerating and simply doing what many do by claiming their product is the best. One study found that consumers actually have mixed reactions to puffery, and that they don't always react positively to it.[48]

Psychological Appeals In advertising, **psychological appeals** are those designed to persuade on the basis of human emotions and emotional needs rather than reason. There is perhaps as much reason to be concerned about ethics in this category as in any other category. One reason is that the products can seldom deliver what the ads promise (i.e., power, prestige, sex, masculinity, femininity, approval, acceptance, and other such psychological satisfactions).[49] Another reason is that psychological appeals can stir emotions in a way that is manipulative and appears designed to take advantage of the consumer's vulnerability. For example, many home security salespeople will watch the newspapers for reports of home break-ins and then call the home owner with a sales pitch for a new home security system (appeal to fear).

Studies have demonstrated that emotional and psychological appeals resonate with consumers more than product functions or features. Thus, ads that employ a psychological aspect typically outsell others that focus on product functions. Demonstrating how a new computer will change your life for the better generally sells more computers than ads that explain how the computer works. Fear, uncertainty, and doubt are often used by businesses to motivate consumers to change their behavior.[50]

Though most advertising strives to appeal to our sight, an increasingly popular form of sensual advertising has been focusing on consumers' hearing. Neuromarketers have concluded, on the basis of research, that the most effective sounds in terms of their psychological appeals are babies giggling, cell phones vibrating, ATM machines dispensing cash, steaks sizzling on a grill, and a soda being popped and poured.[51] Whether such ploys represent unethical uses of psychological persuasion is debatable.

13.1e Specific Controversial Advertising Issues

We have considered four major kinds of deceptive advertising—ambiguous advertising, concealed facts, exaggerated claims, and psychological appeals. There are many other

ETHICS IN PRACTICE CASE

Should the Word *Free* Be Banned in Advertising?

A recent article brought home a very significant point. It said the "best things in life are free—unless they're not." What is your reaction when you see the word "free" in advertisements? Unless you are an inexperienced novice, you are probably uttering "what's the catch?" In other words, consumers today are skeptical when they are told something is free and yet marketers continue to find clever ways to make us "think" something is free.

Many different industries use the "free" offer as a key part of their advertising. One prominent industry that does this is the travel industry. Many of their advertisements include phrases such as "free tickets," "free checked bags," "free upgrades," and "kids eat free." One woman checked into a hotel that told her she had "free internet." Turns out she did have free internet but it was a basic, sluggish internet connection and she kept getting pop up ads asking her to upgrade to a premium version at an added charge. The woman did not believe she had gotten anything free though the ad had drawn her in to this hotel.

The airlines are famous for their "free" offers. It turns out that no matter what you end up paying for what you are getting—it's costing you tons of miles from your frequent flyer plan; it's costing you taxes and fees you never anticipated; and, so on. You apply for a "free" item online and all they want, you find out, is all of your personal information along with complete contact information. Is this free? Or, will the advertiser be using or selling your personal information to a third-party advertiser?

Chip Bell, author of *9½ Principles of Innovative Service*, has explained three types of "free." The first type is "truly free." This you get without any preconditions. You can walk into the store, pick it up, and walk out. A second type is "free with purchase." You buy this item and you'll get one of these. The third type is "free with strings." The internet provider offers you a "free" $300 rewards card to spend as you like. All you have to do is to convert to their service. The Big Print offers you a free printer. The Small Print says you have to buy your printer ink from their company for a year.

1. What questions should you ask yourself as you strive to understand a "free" offering?
2. Describe an experience you have had on social media where you thought you were getting something free, but it was not? If you pursued it, how did it turn out?
3. What ethical guidelines should an advertiser use to not be accused of exploiting the word *free*?
4. Is the word *free* so abusive in advertising that it should be banned by the FTC?

Sources: Directory Journal, "Is There Anything Really Free Out There?" http://www.dirjournal.com/shopping-journal/is-there-anything-really-free-out-there/. Accessed May 7, 2016; Chip Bell, "9½ Principles of Innovative Service," 2013; Christopher Elliott, "Best Things in Life Are Free—Unless They're Not," *USA Today*, August 4, 2014, 3B; Federal Trade Commission, "What Makes an Advertisement Deceptive?" https://www.ftc.gov/tips-advice/business-center/guidance/advertising-faqs-guide-small-business. Accessed May 7, 2016.

variations on these themes, but these are sufficient to make our point. Later in this chapter, we will discuss the FTC's attempts to keep advertising honest. But even in that discussion, we will see that the whole issue of what constitutes deceptive advertising is an evolving and amorphous concept, particularly when it comes to the task of proving deception and recommending appropriate remedial action. This is why the role of business responsibility is so crucial if business honestly desires to deal with its consumer stakeholders in a fair and truthful manner.

There are several specific advertising issues that have become particularly controversial in recent years because of borderline and questionable ethics. These merit further consideration: comparative advertising, use of sex in advertising, advertising to children, marketing to the poor, advertising of alcoholic beverages, cigarette advertising, health and environmental claims, **ad creep**, and social media advertising.

Comparative Advertising. One of the earliest forms of advertising that became controversial and threatened to affect advertising adversely is **comparative advertising**. This refers to the practice of directly comparing a firm's product or service with the product or service of a competitor—typically going so far as to name the competitor's brand or product. Some classic examples of past high-profile comparative campaigns include Coke versus Pepsi, Whopper versus Big Mac, Subway versus Quiznos, Avis versus Hertz, and Papa John's versus Pizza Hut.

SPOTLIGHT *on Sustainability*

Are Consumers Willing to Pay More for Sustainability?

Two companies recently joined together to publish a report on how consumers viewed the concept of sustainability. Consumers were asked about sustainability with respect to four product categories: purchased food and beverages, household cleaning products, personal care products, and over-the-counter medications. Consumers most often said that sustainability meant "the ability to last over time" and "the ability to support oneself." Consumers also linked the concept with "environmental concerns." The consumers also said that terms such as *eco-conscious* and *green* unduly limited the concept of sustainability because they do not account for the variety of economic, social, and environmental issues that real people believe are important in sustaining themselves, their communities, and society as a whole.

The consumers surveyed went on to say that they would pay a 20 percent premium for sustainable products. In another study, 40 percent of consumers said they would not purchase a product if the company did not communicate its sustainability results.

In another study, Nielsen found that consumers are trying to be responsible citizens when it comes to purchasing. Consumers are increasingly doing their homework before buying. They are checking labels, checking Web sites, and paying attention to public opinion. Nielsen found that 66 percent of global respondents were willing to pay more for sustainable products. They especially sought out fresh, natural, or organic ingredients. They also sought out companies that were environmentally friendly.

Sources: "Sustainability, Through Consumers' Eyes," http://www.highbeam.com/doc/1G1-214713138.html. Accessed May 2, 2016; "Consumers Demand Sustainability Results, Survey Says," Environmental Leader, October 24, 2012, http://www.environmentalleader.com/2012/10/24/consumers-demand-sustainability-results-survey-says/. Accessed May 2, 2016. 2013 Cone Communications Green Gap Trend Tracker, http://www.conecomm.com/research-from-cone. Accessed May 2, 2016; Nielsen, The Sustainability Imperative, October 12, 2015, http://www.nielsen.com/us/en/insights/reports/2015/the-sustainability-imperative.html. Accessed May 2, 2016.

Though comparative advertising is not used as much as it once was, a memorable and successful example was the "Get a Mac" campaign. The ads featured two men, Mac and PC, standing in front of a white background. PC is in an ill-fitting jacket and tie, whereas Mac is in comfortable jeans. The banter between the two characters is a running comparison of the two machines. The cultural icon campaign struck a nerve with the public: In 2009, *U.S. News & World Report* named the "Get a Mac" campaign one of the best marketing schemes in recent times.[52] It was also named Ad of the Decade by *Adweek*.[53]

Comparative advertising sometimes generates unexpected and undesirable conflicts among companies. Whether out of pride or general business interest, more and more companies are fighting back when they think the competition has gone too far. Companies may take their adversaries to court, before the FTC, or before voluntary associations, such as the National Advertising Division of the Council of Better Business Bureaus, that attempt to resolve these kinds of disputes. Though there can be good reasons to launch comparative ads, they sometimes come at a cost.

Use of Sex Appeal in Advertising. The use of sex appeal in U.S. advertising has been an ongoing ethical issue for decades. It took center stage years ago when several women's groups were offended by a series of television commercials sponsored by a major airline. Today, sexual references and innuendos in advertising have become commonplace, featuring men as well as women, and the issue continues to spark controversy. Though many companies have transitioned to promoting healthier food options, Hardee's and Carl, Jr., still believe that sex sells as they depict a Sports Illustrated swimsuit model frolicking in a bikini in a hot tub in the back of a pickup truck to sell its latest high-caloric burger. They explain this decision by saying that their target market is "young, hungry guys."[54] Of course, companies can go too far. Consumer behavior professor Bruce Stern has observed: "We're moving into an arena that we are becoming numb to things that would have offended us a few years ago."[55]

ETHICS IN PRACTICE CASE

Do These "Advertising Traps" Represent Ethical Advertising?

There are many declarations and promises companies make in their advertising. These occur in magazines, newspapers, online Web sites, and social media. In most cases they represent deceptive or misleading promotions of a product or a service. Sometimes they represent only partial truths. Some of the most frequently used ad traps are discussed below.

"We will not be undersold"

This declaration is commonly understood to mean that the company promoting the product or service is making an offer that cannot be beat by anyone else. Sometimes the declaration means that the company will lower its price to meet that of any competitor. Sometimes not. Sometimes there are exclusions such as "does not include online offers and prices." Usually the true meaning of this expression cannot be found without significant effort on the consumer's part.

"Satisfaction Guaranteed"

This expression can mean many different things. Sometimes companies will advertise to give you your money back if you are not "satisfied." Often, there are limitations on the "satisfaction guaranteed" promise. You must return the product in ten days; in original packaging; only for an exchange, not a refund; money back after we deduct a re-stocking fee; and so on. Again, the truth is often in the fine print, sometimes not easily available.

"Lifetime Warranty"

Whose or what lifetime is being referred to here? The purchaser's lifetime? The product's lifetime? Only as long as the company stocks the product? Only with the original receipt? (Who keeps those?) Is the offer "unconditional?" Are there strings attached? Maybe the product has to be registered online first? Maybe a shipping fee is required when returning the product.

"Going out of Business" Sale

What does "going out of business" really mean? In some retail sectors it is not uncommon to go out of business under one company name only to open up soon thereafter in the same location under a different name. Does "going out of business" mean you will get a better price? Not always. Are products sold under these terms still "guaranteed" once the company goes out of sale? Researchers have learned that sometimes prices go up during a sale of this type.

"Free"

Is there any offer that has been abused more than being offered something "free?" This ubiquitous offer has been misused and abused probably more than any other ad trap. "Free" is one of those "gotcha" offers that may be qualified in many different ways. The FTC has said that if the word "free" is used in an ad then it must be absolutely free without condition. But, how many times have you wondered if related products have been jacked up to cover the cost of the free item? Or, what about the offer of "buy one, get one free?" Has the one you bought been overpriced? What if you only want one? Will it be half priced?

Other Abused Words Used as "Ad Traps"

Other words that are often used as ad traps include the following: *New, Save, Proven, Results,* and *You,* as in "let's talk about *you*" or "this will make *you* rich."

Questions

1. Which of the above advertising traps have you been caught in? Explain how it happened.
2. Does use of these ad traps represent deceptive advertising? What would make each one of them a fair advertisement?
3. Should agencies like the FTC, FDA, Consumer Product Safety Commission, and others have official definitions of these terms before they may be used?
4. How should companies monitor themselves to be sure they are treating consumers fairly when using these marketing terms?
5. What steps should you take as a consumer to make sure you are not being deceived by these terms?

Sources: Federal Trade Commission Act Section 5: Unfair or deceptive acts or practices, http://www.federalreserve.gov/boarddocs/supmanual/cch/ftca.pdf. Accessed May 15, 2016; Money, "Why Prices at Going out of Business Sales Can Be Ripoffs," March 9, 2016, http://time.com/money/4252250/sports-authority-sales-stores-closing/. Accessed May 15, 2016; "Don't Let These Ad Traps Catch You," *Consumer Reports*, March 2014, 13; Better Business Bureau, "Are You Advertising a Guarantee?" September 9, 2015, https://www.bbb.org/greater-maryland/news-events/business-tips/2015/Advertising-Guarantees/. Accessed May 15, 2016; About Money, Paul Suggett, "The Ten Most Powerful Words in Advertising," http://advertising.about.com/od/copywriting/a/The-10-Most-Powerful-Words-In-Advertising.htm. Accessed May 15, 2016.

A troubling trend in using sex appeal advertising campaigns is to target younger and younger girls and boys with the idea that they can be sexy too. Ads are targeting younger and younger girls to diet, get hair extensions, eye-lash extensions, and push-up bras. Critics say this is subtly training girls to focus on their external appearance at the expense of developing a fuller identity. It is argued that girls are being overly sexualized in our culture long before they are cognitively and emotionally prepared.[56] In addition, boys are being sexualized in ads too at a younger and younger age.[57]

Most studies have shown that the use of sex in advertising works. One study looked at the use of sex in magazines over a 30-year period and found that the numbers were up and the conclusion has been that's its effective.[58] Studies seem to show, however, that though many oppose the use of sex appeal in ads, their purchasing decisions reflect that sex appeal works. However, one recent study has raised questions about the effectiveness of the "sex sells" mantra. This study found that sexual content within an ad causes consumers to have a less favorable attitude toward the brand but it does not result in a decline in sales.[59] Recently, brands such as Abercrombie & Fitch and American Apparel have announced they plan to desexualize their ads in a quest to increase sales.[60] The result seems to be that some questions are being raised about the effectiveness of using sex as an advertising theme.

Research has also shown that ads that portray young women as sex objects can have a serious impact on the physical and mental health of girls. A task force report from the American Psychological Association (APA) studied this issue and found that the media's sexualization of young women can lead to a lack of confidence with their bodies as well as depression, eating disorders, and low self-esteem.[61] In spite of the fact that sex in advertising is widespread today, the practice still carries serious ethical questions about its appropriateness, and responsible companies must be careful and sensitive to these concerns.

Advertising to Children. A hotly debated ethical issue over the past several decades has been advertising to children, especially on television. This practice has sometimes been called "kid-vid" advertising. A typical weekday afternoon or Saturday morning in America finds millions of kids sprawled on the floor, glued to the TV, or staring at the computer. According to one study, the average child in the United States watches 25,000 to 40,000 commercials each year and advertisers spend $15 to $17 billion annually marketing products to children.[62] The statistics in other countries are staggering as well. Of course, today, the kids are being exposed to questionable advertising at an escalating rate through computers, handheld devices, games, and social media.

Children are the consumers of the future, and companies are eager to get their foot in the door of their spending habits. Merchandisers are trying to instill brand loyalty at a young age. Mattel, with its iconic Barbie doll, is a case in point. Mattel has long been criticized for its Barbie doll's unrealistic body proportions—a young woman who appears impossibly thin, tall, and busty.[63] Mattel took advertising to a new level when Mattel's "Cool Shopping Barbie" was given her own personal toy MasterCard, with a cash register that had the MasterCard logo, and a terminal through which Barbie could swipe her card to make a purchase. By 2013, Mattel was continuing Barbie's consumption habits with "Barbie Shopping Games" including "Shopaholic Best Friends," "Barbie Christmas Shopping," and "School Shopping Day."[64]

Mattel's most recent strategy, announced in 2016, is to make Barbie available in different body shapes and different skin tones. Mattel has been trying to put Barbie through a transformation that would bring their dolls into more realistic body standards and reflective of the diversity of the kids playing with the dolls.[65] This latest move has not been criticized as much as some of the earlier Barbie ads. According to William

F. Keenan of Creative Solutions, an advertising and marketing agency, "[If you] set the brand by age seven, they will favor the brand into adulthood. One of the smartest places to plant marketing seeds in the consumer consciousness is with kids."[66]

This is particularly troubling given an APA finding that children under the age of eight do not have the cognitive development to understand persuasive intent, making them easy targets.[67] Children have proved to be receptive targets as well. A phenomenon called **age compression** or "kids getting older younger" (KGOY) has marketers targeting eight- and nine-year-olds with products once meant for teenagers. With the overabundance of ads to which they are exposed, children are tiring of toys much earlier and looking for products that they see teenagers using.[68]

The Children's Advertising Review Unit (CARU) of the Council of Better Business Bureaus was established to respond to public concerns. CARU developed "Self-Regulatory Guidelines for Children's Advertising."[69] The function of the CARU guidelines is to delineate those areas that need particular attention to help avoid deceptive and/or misleading advertising messages to children. The basic activity of CARU is the review and evaluation of child-directed advertising in all media. When advertising to children is found to be misleading, inaccurate, or inconsistent with the guidelines, CARU seeks changes through the voluntary cooperation of advertisers. It does not always get cooperation and sometimes the advertiser appeals to the National Advertising Review Board (NARB).

Recently, the advertising to children of food products that contain sweets and unhealthy ingredients has become a burning issue. One recent report found that kids get 12 percent of their calories from fast-food restaurants.[70] As the obesity epidemic among children has become widely known and debated, special interest groups have been criticizing companies for their marketing of these products to children. In addition, the Federal Trade Commission is now watching ads to children more carefully.[71] Today, childhood favorites such as Cinnamon Toast Crunch, Honey Nut Cheerios, Fruit Loops, Reese's Puffs, and other cereals are being labeled a public health menace by the Rudd Center for Food Policy and Obesity at Yale University. The center is trying to expose the marketing tactics companies use that make kids clamor for a sugary, calorie-laden start to each day. Obesity researchers now say they have data documenting that the least healthy cereals are the ones that are marketed most aggressively to children. The obesity crisis among children in the United States is now established and researchers believe that TV advertising is a significant contributing factor.[72]

To their credit, some leading cereal makers have responded by reducing calories, fat, and sugar and increasing fiber and vitamins. Kellogg, General Mills, and Quaker's parent company, PepsiCo, are among about 12 of the largest food companies that have promised to market only "better for you" foods to kids under age 12. Skeptics are concerned because the companies themselves are deciding what constitutes "better for you" standards.[73]

Regulatory bodies have been trying for decades to get greater supervisory authority with respect to children's advertising. In 1990, the **Children's Television Act (CTA)** was passed. A grassroots activist group known as Action for Children's Television claimed credit for getting this legislation passed. This act prohibited the airing of commercials about products or characters during a show about those products or characters and limited the number of commercial minutes in children's shows. Much has changed since that act was passed. With the rise of the Internet, social media, and smart toys, companies have found new ways to advertise to children. More than two-thirds of the children and teen Internet sites rely on advertising for their revenue. Banner ads were not successful in reaching children, and so these Internet sites have employed games,

ETHICS IN PRACTICE CASE

Should Food Advertising to Children Be Banned?

There continues to be an ongoing battle between those who think marketing food and beverages to children should be halted and those who think it's up to parents to make these decisions not Big Government. Some companies have been attempting to come up with their own standards to decrease unhealthy ingredients and make kids' foods more nutritious.

It is now estimated that one-third of children in the United States are overweight or obese. It has been argued by a number of experts that sugar in soft drinks and fast foods are the major culprits.

We live in a country where cartoon characters tempt kids to eat the wrong foods, where children don't get enough exercise, where parents don't say "no" often enough, and where childhood diabetes is escalating. Commercial advertising assaults children with TV commercials, ads in schools, product placements, and digital marketing. Research shows that this advertising works.

Founded in the year 2000, a nonprofit organization Campaign for a Commercial Free Childhood (CCFC) is seeking to address the rapidly escalating problem of commercialism encroaching on the lives of children. Starting out as a small group of concerned parents, health professionals, and educators, CCFC has grown into a powerful force seeking to end what it calls the exploitative practice of child-targeted advertising.

CCFC has taken on the following issues: marketing to children, advertising in schools, commercializing toys and play, food marketing and childhood obesity, marketing to babies and toddlers, sexualizing childhood, and media violence.

1. Should food and beverage advertising to children be banned? What about for other types of products as well?
2. Is it unethical for food companies to target their ads toward children? In a period when most parents are working, how are children to be protected?
3. Should the federal or state government begin restricting food ads targeted at children? What about for other products?
4. Can companies do enough on their own to adequately address these problems?
5. Of the list of issues CCFC has taken on (listed above), which do you see as the most serious and why?

Sources: Campaign for a Commercial Free Childhood, http://www.commercialfreechildhood.org/. Accessed May 4, 2016; Josh Golin, "Ban Food Marketing to Kids," *USA Today*, October 17, 2013, 10A; Diane Levin and Christina Asquith, "As Marketing to Children Intensifies, What Can Society Do?" Solutions Magazine, April 12, 2013, http://www.thesolutionsjournal.com/node/6641. Accessed May 4, 2016; American Psychological Association, "The Impact of Food Advertising on Childhood Obesity," http://www.apa.org/topics/kids-media/food.aspx. Accessed May 4, 2016.

e-mail, and wireless technology in creative ways. The FCC has added new regulations over the last decade that address cable and Internet Web pages.[74]

The issue of obesity and advertising to children continues to pick up steam. New York Mayor Michael Bloomberg introduced an anti-obesity campaign that sought to ban large-serving sugary drinks, especially sodas, but this law was struck down in the courts.[75] Both Coca-Cola and Disney have embarked on strategies to reduce calories in products they sell.[76] Time will tell whether these programs will work and be copied by others, but the trend has definitely begun.

Marketing to the Poor. A variety of businesses have found that significant profits can be obtained from advertising and marketing to poor people. In the subprime credit industry, businesses provide financing to high-risk borrowers at high interest rates. While this gives poorer people greater access to cars, credit cards, computers, and homes, it often ends with the borrower buried under a mountain of debt. The past several years have been the worst ever in home mortgage foreclosures and loan defaults. Many of these have come from the subprime mortgage market where relatively poor people were lured into loans they had little hope of repaying. Several of the deceptive marketing practices mentioned earlier have been involved in these loans: concealed facts, ambiguous advertising, and psychological appeals.

Another technique by which business profits from the poor is in the form of *payday loans*, loans that provide the borrower with an advance on his or her paycheck. As the FTC warns, these loans represent costly cash; for example, a borrower might write a personal check for $115 to borrow $100 for up to two weeks. The payday lender agrees to hold the check until the person's next payday. Then, depending on the plan, the lender deposits the check, which the borrower can redeem by paying the $115 in cash. Alternatively, the borrower can roll over the check by paying a fee to extend the loan for another two weeks. In this example, the cost of the initial loan is a $15 finance charge and 391 percent annual percentage rate (APR). If they roll over the loan three times, the finance charge would climb to $60 to borrow $100.[77] The special case of payday loans is explored further in Case 10 at the end of the text. Similar tactics are used by many credit card companies, rent-to-own outfits, and used car dealers.

Tax preparation services provide another way of making money from the poor. Many firms provide quick tax refund services for a fee. Advertising "Money Now," they will prepare your tax return and provide you with an advance on your refund. Low-income tax payers have access to a variety of free tax preparation services, but many still use this expensive service because they do not understand the price they will pay for receiving an early refund.[78]

Bloomberg Businessweek tells the story of a single mother with five children who was making ends meet on $8,500 a year until she was laid off. She borrowed $400 for rent and food from Advance America, a payday loan service; then she renewed the loan every two weeks, eventually paying more than $2,500 in fees before she paid it off. Two months after paying it off, she was anxious for her $4,500 tax refund and so she took out a refund-anticipation loan from Jackson Hewitt. It cost her $453 (10.4 percent) to get that short-term loan.[79] When asked about the price she paid for these loans, the young mother sounded confused, replying, "What do you call it—interest?"[80]

The issue with marketing and advertising to the poor is the vulnerability of this consumer segment. All consumers are vulnerable to a certain extent because business has more information about its product or service than does the consumer. However, poor people are especially vulnerable because they are likely to be less educated and thus less aware of the true price of the products or services being advertised to them. Nevertheless, businesses continue to push these products. Another vulnerable group of consumers is the elderly, and some of the same tactics are used on them that are used on the poor.[81]

Advertising Alcoholic Beverages. The issue of advertising alcoholic beverages, especially to a younger demographic profile, has been an issue for decades.[82] In addition to the concern for the health effects, critics have argued that many alcohol ads link drinking with valued personal attributes such as sociability, elegance, and physical attractiveness that might relate to outcomes such as success, romance, relaxation, and adventure.[83] It has been found that, in general, adolescents are drawn to alcohol ads especially those with celebrity endorsers, humor, animation, and popular music. Further, it has been shown that lifestyle or image advertising results in more favorable attitudes toward alcohol when compared with strictly product-oriented or informational advertising.[84]

The primary focus of concern today about the advertising of alcoholic beverages has been the rise of underage alcohol consumption and binge drinking. Along with this has been a rise in the targeting of youth by advertising. It is believed that this advertising focus has had a negative impact on the demographic.[85] Though it is not certain that reducing the number of alcohol ads targeted at teenagers will decrease the number of young drinkers, it is believed that it might be a step closer to achieving that goal.[86]

Around 2011, the broadcasters started easing their decades-old voluntary bans that limited their national alcohol advertising to beer and wine on network TV. This reflected more consumer acceptance—or at least less consumer resistance to the ads. Today, many liquor companies are starting to increase their TV marketing budgets by double-digit percentages. The broadcasters have not opened their doors completely; liquor ads for the most part run after 11 P.M. But, since they have been running on cable TV for years, critics say that youth exposure to liquor ads on TV already has increased 30-fold or more. Today, their advertising also enters into film, music, and social media. The liquor companies continue to argue that there ought to be a level playing field in their competition with beer and wine. The Federal Trade Commission has said that there is no basis for treating liquor ads differently than ads for beer and wine.[87]

Although efforts to curb advertising abuses of alcohol continue, consumer advocates may find they face an uphill battle. There seems to be less public opposition today to alcohol advertising but the industry will need to remain vigilant because any attempts at exploitation of youth, for example, are likely to meet considerable criticism and resistance. A newly emerging issue is the advertising of marijuana in states where it is legal. This will be an issue to watch carefully in the days ahead.

Cigarette Advertising. No industry has been under greater criticism and regulation than the cigarette industry for its products and its marketing and advertising practices. Cigarette makers have been under fire from all sides for decades. Two particularly important issues dominate the debate about cigarettes and their advertising. First, there has been general opposition to the promotion of a dangerous product. As the World Health Organization (WHO) puts it, "Cigarettes remain the only legal product that kills half of its regular users when consumed as intended by the manufacturer."[88] Smoking accounts for more than 480,000 deaths each year in the United States or about one in every five deaths, according to the Centers for Disease Control and Prevention (CDC). In addition, another 16 million Americans live with a smoking-related disease.[89]

The second issue concerns the ethics of the tobacco industry's longstanding advertising to young people and to less-educated consumer markets. The classic examples of these ads were when R. J. Reynolds (RJR) was publicly taken to task by several consumer groups for its Joe Camel campaign targeted toward youth, and Philip Morris used the rugged Marlboro Man in its ads. Although Joe Camel and the Marlboro Man are gone, the issue of advertising to young people and less-educated consumers remains.

In 2009, Congress gave the Food & Drug Administration (FDA) oversight of the tobacco industry when it passed the Tobacco Control Act. The Tobacco Control Act was intended to protect the public and to create a healthier future for all citizens.[90] This act authorized the FDA to regulate the manufacture, distribution, and marketing of tobacco products. Among other actions, the FDA decided to restrict tobacco marketing and sales to youth, require smokeless tobacco products to carry warning labels, and require disclosures of ingredients in tobacco products.[91]

In the past several years, electronic-cigarettes (e-cigs) have become all the rage and the tobacco companies have been working hard to promote them. E-cigarette sales have skyrocketed in the past five years.[92] In fact, they are now a $3.5 billion industry.[93] E-cigs vaporize nicotine without burning tobacco and are a fast-growing rival to traditional cigarettes (over 45 million users).[94] The CDC is concerned about how e-cigs are attracting more teenagers and the rate of increase has doubled or tripled in recent years. The CDC is particularly concerned about addiction and the effect on the developing brains of youth.[95]

Some researchers claim e-cigs are less harmful than regular cigarettes, but this is a continuing debate. As e-cigarette sales increase among youth, they are attracting significant attention by regulators and state legislatures.[96] In May 2016, the FDA finally announced it would extend its authority to all tobacco products, including e-cigarettes, cigars, hookah tobacco, and pipe tobacco among others.[97] The FDA claimed that this decision will allow it to better protect the public against the dangers of tobacco and will help it prevent misleading claims by tobacco companies, evaluate the ingredients of tobacco products, and communicate their risks.[98]

Opponents of tobacco and tobacco-related products continue their campaigns against cigarettes and e-cigarettes and their advertising. The Campaign for Tobacco-Free Kids, an advocacy group, is concerned about the growing popularity of e-cigarettes and have been urging the FDA to take more decisive regulation over them.[99] They are also concerned that smokeless tobacco products are gaining in popularity with high school students and that this is dangerous. Some think the flavored versions are specifically targeted toward young people and getting them hooked on the addictive products.[100] Although the industry seems to be striving to make products that are more palatable and appealing, there is still the concern that the smokeless varieties carry significant health risks.

The future will be somewhat determined by what actions and decisions the FDA decides to take regarding existing products and whatever new products come on the market. In 2016, the FDA also announced its first ad campaign on the dangers of smokeless tobacco. Its "The Real Cost" campaign focused on educating teenagers about the negative health consequences of smokeless tobacco to include nicotine addiction, gum disease, tooth loss, and multiple types of cancer. Their central message is "smokeless doesn't mean harmless."[101] The ethical issues surrounding tobacco products and their advertising show no signs of abating, and this will likely be a controversial advertising issue into the foreseeable future.

Health and Environmental Claims. Advertising and labeling practices that make claims about health and environmental safety have taken on growing importance in the past decade. One reason that these issues have come to the forefront is the renewed enforcement activities of the Food and Drug Administration (FDA), the Federal Trade Commission (FTC), and state attorneys general in cracking down on misleading or unsubstantiated claims. In 2016, the FDA announced it was taking a fresh look at "healthy" labeling as many of the regulations governing it date back to the 1990s.[102]

We now live in a health-conscious and environmentally aware society, and consumers' interest in products that are healthful and sustainable has grown significantly, and so it is not too surprising that these issues have gained so much attention. Because health and environmental sustainability claims attract customers, marketers are tempted to tout claims that are not really true. Consumers today are undoubtedly bewildered as they scan health claims on so many products. The fronts of boxes are shouting out claims about different nutrients—sugar free, extra fiber, all natural, zero transfats, multi-grain, organic, free range, gluten free, added vitamins, fat free, and healthy for your heart.

Perhaps the best example of a health-related product characteristic that is being advertised aggressively today is "gluten free." A decade ago virtually no one knew what gluten free meant. Today, many people still do not know what it is but it has exploded into a $1 billion U.S. market with all kinds of positive health claims being made about it.[103] In 2015, even Cheerios cereal joined the gluten-free food craze because it had become so popular.[104] General Mills had a rough start with Cheerios, however, because almost 2 million boxes had wheat flour inadvertently added and had to be recalled.[105]

Gluten free may carry some modest health advantages for the average person, but the population of consumers with celiac disease who have to avoid gluten number about 1 percent of the population. Experts who have studied this topic have concluded that it is mostly health-marketing hype and some say just a fad. Dismayed by the proliferation of gluten free everything, Alan Levinovitz wrote a book titled *The Gluten Lie* in which he takes aim at many different fad health diets often based on shoddy science. Levinovitz claims we are living in a period in which there is one-at-a-time demonization of individual food ingredients and gluten is just one of them.[106]

In 2010, the FDA embarked on a quest to clean up misleading and deceptive advertising regarding the health claims of food products. The FDA has become concerned that the food claims companies make are not backed by strong enough scientific evidence to support the claims. By 2013, the FDA had issued guidelines for food producers for nutrient claims and health claims.[107]

Regulators in the United States and Europe have become more concerned about a new category of foods that are being called "functional foods," which make claims to improve your health functioning in specific ways. For example, all supermarkets today carry probiotic yogurts that claim to ease constipation, improve regularity, and fight infections. Or, you might be interested in butter substitutes that declare they reduce your cholesterol, or tomato extracts that claim they can keep your skin young while warding off cancer. Sales growth of these products have been increasing fast, and Nestlé, the world's largest food company, has predicted that functional foods will be a primary source of future sales growth. All this activity has caught the attention of regulators, and they are beginning to investigate whether the health claims are supported or misleading.[108] The temptation for unethical advertising in this sector is significant.

The market for more healthy food products is growing, and a few companies have been taking it upon themselves to progressively plan for the future. One highly visible example is that of PepsiCo, led by CEO Indra Nooyi. Nooyi made it known that she wants PepsiCo to be "seen as one of the defining companies of the first half of the 21st century." She wants her company to be "a model of how to conduct business in the modern world."[109] With respect to her company's products, she wants to help customers wean off of sugar, salt, and fat. Nooyi unveiled a series of goals to improve the healthiness of PepsiCo products. By 2015, the company planned to reduce the salt in its leading brands by 25 percent. By 2020, the company plans to reduce the amount of sugar in its drinks by 25 percent and the amount of saturated fat in certain snacks by 15 percent. In 2016, PepsiCo announced it had met its 2020 goal of reduction in foods with saturated fats in the United States, the United Kingdom, and Turkey.[110]

Astutely, Nooyi observed that she wants to prevent the food companies from going the way of the tobacco firms.[111] In addition to actions by the FDA, the Federal Trade Commission (FTC) has also cracked down on false advertising in health-related products, including vitamin supplements, weight-loss plans, and beauty products.[112] The FTC has noted that Americans spend billions of dollars each year on foods, supplements, and devices that claim to improve their health and fitness. Many of these products do not live up to their advertising claims that they can help people lose weight, combat disease, or improve their cognitive abilities. The FTC also tried to monitor truth in advertising for tanning salons, personal care products, disinfectant devices, and body slimming creams.[113]

Organic food claims is another arena in which deceptive advertising claims are often made. One of the most challenging questions to answer pertains to what exactly does organic mean? Organic foods or ingredients are generally defined to be those that meet certain criteria. The USDA, for example, claims that to be "Certified Organic" or carry the "USDA Organic" label, the item must have an ingredients list and the contents should be at least 95 percent or more "certified organic," which means free of synthetic additives like pesticides, chemical fertilizers, and dyes and must not be processed using industrial solvents, irradiation, or genetic engineering.[114]

If you see the alternative label, "100% organic," it must meet the standards listed above. Or, it could say "Made with Organic" in which case it means the ingredients must contain 70 percent of more organic ingredients.[115] The volume of organic products now available and the low penalties assessed for violations has led to some skepticism as to whether the USDA is fully enforcing its own requirements. Some now worry that *organic* has turned into a marketing and advertising term with little meaning.[116] If this is the case, consumers will have to shop carefully and hope that the reputation of the seller is high enough to be conveying the truth.

Closely related to organic products are a set of products that claim to be "natural." Many natural food companies also promote their products as environmentally friendly, or "green." What is the difference between organic and natural? Unfortunately, organic and natural do not mean exactly the same thing and this poses more challenges for consumers trying to understand various health claims of products. **Natural products** are generally meant to be foods that are minimally processed and do not contain any hormones, antibiotics, or artificial flavors or colors.[117] In the United States, the FDA and the USDA do not have rules for products that claim to be natural. By contrast, for a food to be labeled organic, it must meet more tightly regulated standards. The result has been some confusion between organic and natural, and many natural product claims turn out to be murky.[118]

Green advertising is another major controversial advertising practice wherein companies are claiming that their products and/or their product packages are environmentally friendly, sustainable, or safe. For some time now, many companies have been ramping up their advertising claims about the environmental friendliness of their products—that their products are "green." A survey by Cone Communications revealed what consumers think a "green/environmentally friendly" message is all about: 54 percent said it is a product that has "a positive or neutral impact on the environment" and 28 percent said it's a product that has "a lighter impact than similar/older products."[119] But, another poll asked consumers whether "green eco" labels are misleading. Sixty-three percent said *yes* and 37 percent said *no*.[120] These findings support the idea that some consumers think questionable practices are involved in the green advertising industry.

In late 2012, the Federal Trade Commission issued their most updated guidelines for "eco-friendly" labeling saying that companies better be able to back up their claims.[121] The FTC called these their **Green Guides**.[122] The FTC's Green Guides are intended to help marketers avoid making environmental claims that are misleading to consumers. The guidance they provide include (1) general principles that pertain to all environmental marketing claims, (2) information on how consumers are likely to interpret particular claims and how companies can substantiate their claims, and (3) how marketers can qualify their claims to avoid deceiving consumers.[123]

One of the latest violations today involving green advertising pertains to Volkswagen's "clean diesel" vehicle advertising. In addition to facing issues of criminal fraud and deception regarding its product wherein it admitted it rigged more than half a million vehicles with software to cheat emissions regulations, the FTC has added to VW's legal problems by filing a complaint that the company's advertising falsely claimed its diesel vehicles were environmentally friendly.[124] The FTC filing alleges the company falsely advertised "clean diesel" vehicles, purchased by about 550,000 buyers, and is seeking more than $15 billion in what could be one of the largest false advertising cases in U.S. history.[125] Volkswagen did reach a deal with consumers in which it would agree to buy back the cars affected and the buyback could cost VW more than $7 billion. VW is also being required to invest funds to "promote green automotive" initiatives and establish an environmental remediation fund after years of cars spewing harmful nitrogen oxide emissions.[126]

There have been contradictory studies about whether consumers are willing to pay more for environmentally friendly products. Some studies say yes and others say no. Some studies indicate that customers are willing to pay more up to a point but that they are not willing to trade off a product's "green" qualities for product performance. According to a poll released by Nielsen, 55 percent of the world's consumers would pay extra for products when companies are committed to positive social and environmental impact.[127]

It is incontrovertible that the green economy is huge. It has been estimated to be in excess of $1.04 trillion and growing. This is a gigantic market segment, and the temptation for companies to promote questionable claims is strong. The major consumer challenge is the difficulty in assessing the reliability of the claims that products are environmentally friendly or safe.

To offset much of the green advertising, an industry of what might be called **green watchdogs** has been growing also. Certification groups claiming to verify eco-friendly claims have arrived on the scene. One example is Green-e, a San Francisco-based non-profit.[128] Oxfam America ranks food brands on the sustainability of their supply chains and the League of Conservation Voters scores elected officials on their voting records.[129] Another green watchdog, The Forest Stewardship Council, promises to verify that the wood in your new furniture was actually harvested from a sustainably managed forest. Sustainable Travel International watches to make sure the hotel you stay at is minimizing its garbage.[130]

Other groups claiming to certify the green aspects of products include Energy Star, which is one of the best-known eco-labels, evaluating energy savings, EcoLogo, which monitors 150 product categories, EPEAT (Electronic Product Assessment Tool), which covers computers and monitors, and Eco Options, which covers 3,500-plus products sold at Home Depot. Even though these groups are emerging, even some of them use looser standards than others and it is difficult knowing how much due diligence each one of them has behind their eco-seals.[131] The fact that these monitoring groups are actively at work, however, suggests this is an issue that needs to be watched closely by consumers lest they be duped about the eco-friendliness of products they buy.

Advertisers have come on so fast and strong with their environmental friendly claims that there is a growing sense of **green fatigue** developing among some consumers who are growing weary of environmental claims.[132] The evidence seems to be that being green is not enough. Products need to be wallet-friendly as well, especially as the economy has been struggling. Some marketers even have noticed a green backlash among consumer attitudes.[133] Companies and advertisers will need to watch carefully the quality of their claims or a real cynicism about environmental claims may develop.

One recent trend is that companies are striving to transition from **green marketing** to marketing for environmental sustainability.[134] Part of this challenge is to create a stronger case along with documentation. Four insights along these lines have been presented. First, more reliable metrics are needed to translate environmental commitments into customer value. Second, verifiable product standards and certifications help to communicate this value. Third, these standards need to be developed in concert with multiple stakeholders if they are to be trustworthy. Fourth, environmental sustainability brand value needs to be embedded in sincere, systemic, and organization-wide commitments.[135] It will be challenging for companies to make this transition, and the opportunities for questionable practices will be present all along the way.

Ad Creep. **Ad creep** refers to the way that advertising can increasingly be found everywhere one looks. Both produce placement and plot placement, discussed earlier, are special cases of ad creep. Ads are now going into places that once were not considered acceptable for advertisements. School buses, textbooks, doctors' offices, ATMs, garbage cans, and historical monuments have all been festooned with advertisements. The traditional term for advertising that is located in nontraditional places is **ambient advertising**, but *ad creep* reflects both the way the ads have grown and the way people often feel about its creators.[136]

A variety of factors contribute to ad creep. A declining network TV audience and increased dispersion from cable and Internet outlets combine with soaring network television rates to make it difficult to blanket the population with an advertising message. The arrival of digital video recorders such as TiVo and those of cable TV providers has made it easier for viewers to speed through ads without watching them. One response to ad-skipping technologies such as TiVo has been companies inserting ads into video games. Since most PCs and an increasing number of video games are connected to the Internet, it will be possible to update advertisements when required.[137]

Furthermore, ad creep generates more ad creep because people become numb to messages in traditional places and so unique new venues are sought—just to get the consumer's attention.[138] Some of the ad creep examples of recent years have been quite bizarre. One extreme example has been the appearance of ads on Japanese girls' thighs. A Japanese PR agency began paying young women to wear advertising stickers on their thighs, between the edge of their miniskirts and their high socks. After choosing a sticker ad, the woman has to wear it for at least eight hours a day for a set period of time in order to receive payment. In another interesting example of ad creep, Papa John's delivery boy ads were placed outside the peep hole in people's apartments and then the door bell was rung. When the resident peeped out he or she saw a Papa John delivery boy offering up a box of pizza with a phone number on it.[139]

Social Media Advertising. Though **social media advertising** is used in virtually all the advertising issues discussed above, special consideration should be given to it as a controversial category on its own because of its rapid growth in recent years and some of the questionable uses to which it has been employed. Traditional TV ads will continue, but today consumers seem to be more interested in social media advertising and the industry is taking notice. Social media as an approach to marketing and advertising is exploding and the industry was expected to reach $34 billion by 2016 and continuing to grow.[140]

As social media advertising grows, so does the opportunity for deceptive advertising via social media rise as well. In fact, Social Media & Marketing Daily has called social media and deceptive advertising the "new frontier."[141] Companies that communicate using social media face legal, ethical, and reputational risks in the realms of false and deceptive advertising just like traditional companies.

Advertising Agency, Deutsch L.A., Inc., came under scrutiny by the FTC in a social media campaign for its Sony Playstation Vita. The advertising agency launched a campaign in which it encouraged consumers to tweet positive reviews of the PS Vita using the hashtag #gamechanger. The FTC investigated and eventually charged Deutsch with encouraging its own employees to also tweet on their personal accounts. The FTC concluded that the agency's failure to disclose their employee's connection with their employer was deceptive. They entered into a settlement agreement with the FTC for deceptive advertising.[142]

In another important case, Lord & Taylor settled charges with the FTC for deceiving customers when it paid for Instagram posts. The department store chain gave 50 popular trendsetters a free dress and paid them as much as $4,000 to post a picture of them wearing it. The posts reached 11 million Instagram users and the dress sold out. Lord & Taylor said it was not trying to deceive customers and that it corrected the posts.[143] Critics ask — could anyone reasonably assume the company was not trying to deceive customers? There are many more examples of deceptive advertising via social media and we see them daily. But, the FTC has warned that all the laws and regulations that apply to traditional forms of advertising media also apply to social media advertising. This will be a category of controversial advertising that will require special attention in the years ahead.

The eight controversial advertising issues discussed above are simply the tip of the iceberg. Issues have been raised about the marketing of pharmaceutical drugs directly to patients through magazine and television ads. These ads encourage patients to ask their doctor for the prescription drug, to the frustration of doctors everywhere. Concerns have also been raised about the marketing of guns and ammunition, particularly in family stores like Walmart and Kmart. Channel One, a television station that beams educational programming to schools across the country, has been sharply criticized for its commercials, which students end up watching along with the educational programming. Ads have crept onto smartphones and social media apps as well, and as handheld devices grow in popularity, this will be yet another burgeoning area where advertisers may run the risk of raising questionable issues.

Audiences in movies everywhere have bemoaned the inclusion of commercials in the preview clips, as they are captive audiences, unable to change the channel. There is no end to the list of concerns about the advertising practices undertaken today. Businesspeople must tread carefully to make certain they do not cross the line where their customers become more annoyed with their practices than be attracted to their products. Further, serious ethical questions may arise about the types and placements of advertising in the future.

13.1f Warranties and Guarantees

From the glamorous realm of advertising, we now proceed to the less glamorous issues of warranties and guarantees. Warranties were initially used by manufacturers to limit the length of time they were expressly responsible for products. Over time, they came to be viewed by consumers as mechanisms to protect the buyer against faulty or defective products. Most consumers have had the experience of buying a cell phone, a hair dryer, a stereo, a computer, a refrigerator, an automobile, a washing machine, a chain saw, or any of thousands of other products only to find that it did not work properly or did not work at all. That is when warranties and guarantees take center stage.

Warrantees and guarantees are promises made to consumers by manufacturers or sellers. A **warranty** is usually a written, contractual promise that attests to the quality or durability of a product purchased for a period of time. Should a product become defective while it is still under warranty for some limited time, say a year, the company agrees to repair or replace the product.[144] A **guarantee** is also a promise regarding product quality, but guarantees are less likely to be written. Vendors will sometimes verbally guarantee a product with unsatisfied customers getting a full or a partial refund. Warrantees and guarantees are very similar, but usually the warranty is the written contract that is legally enforceable.[145] But, not all types of warrantees are in writing.

The law recognizes two types of warranties—implied and express. An **implied warranty** is an unspoken promise that there is nothing significantly wrong with the product and that the product can be used for the purposes intended. An **express warranty** is explicitly offered at the time of the sale. The nature of express warranties can range from advertising claims to formal certificates, and they may be oral or written.

The passage of the Magnuson–Moss Warranty Act (1975) helped clarify the nature of warranties for consumers. It is still the basic law of the land, although the FTC has amended, clarified, and interpreted it over the years.[146] This act was aimed at clearing up a variety of misunderstandings about manufacturers' warranties—especially whether a **full warranty** was in effect or whether certain parts of the product or certain types of defects were excluded from coverage, resulting in a **limited warranty**.[147] The Warranty Act set standards for what must be contained in a warranty and the ease with which consumers must be able to understand it. If a company, for example, claims that its product has a full warranty, it must contain certain features, including repair "within a reasonable time and without charge."[148] The law holds that anything less than this unconditional assurance must be promoted as a limited warranty.

With the rise of e-commerce, warranties have become a much more important issue to consumers. Companies find that warranties or guarantees are essential when marketing by mail.

Another issue of increasing ethical concern is **extended warranties**, service plans that lengthen the warranty period and are offered at an additional cost. Consumer advocates advise against buying most extended warranties because they often cost as much as the original item bought would eventually cost to replace. Eric Antum, editor of *Warranty Week*, explains that retailers might make only $10 on a $400 television, but will then make $50 on a $100 extended warranty.[149] Not surprisingly, the lure of big profits has led to some hardball sales tactics.

Consumers spend billions of dollars on extended warranties.[150] They have become very popular with car purchases, perhaps because customers are keeping their cars longer. Some customers view the warranties to be insurance, and they are willing to take the risk. A serious problem today are third-party vendors who are selling extended warranties on products such as autos, and some of them may go out of business when you try to collect, and some represent scams that never intend to pay off for anyone.[151] Opponents of extended warranties offer the following reasons not to buy them: the manufacturer's warranty is usually sufficient; extended warranties are not always effective; the necessity of repairs is rare; warranties are not cost-effective; and credit cards can offer better protection.[152]

Of course, if companies simply offer complete satisfaction, with no fine print, the warranty problem is not such a problem. Few companies accomplish this, but one that does is L.L.Bean, whose guarantee says, "Our products are guaranteed to give 100 percent satisfaction in every way. Return anything purchased from us at any time if it proves otherwise. We will replace it, refund your purchase price, or credit your credit card, as you wish. We do not want you to have anything from L.L.Bean that is not completely satisfactory."[153]

Closely related to warranties and guarantees are the **returns policies** that merchants use to provide customers with a chance to return the product if they are not satisfied. The returns policy is often a part of the warranty, but it could be a separate document. The returns policy usually spells out the terms under which the merchant will accept returns and how that process should be handled.[154] Most merchants use reasonable returns policies, but the consumer should always check carefully as to what the policy is before making a purchase. In recent years, customer abuses of returns policies have become a huge issue for merchants. One estimate is that **return fraud** is costing American merchants about $9 billion annually.[155]

13.1g Packaging and Labeling

Abuses in the packaging and labeling areas were fairly frequent until the passage of the Federal Packaging and Labeling Act (FPLA) of 1967. The purpose of this act was to prohibit deceptive labeling of certain consumer products and to require disclosure of certain important information. This act, which is administered by the Federal Trade Commission, requires the FTC to issue regulations regarding net contents disclosures, identity of commodity, and name and place of manufacturer, packer, or distributor. Both the FTC and the Food and Drug Administration (FDA) have direct responsibilities under this act. The act authorizes additional regulations when necessary to prevent consumer deception or to facilitate value comparisons with respect to the declaration of ingredients, slack filling of packages, "downsizing" of packaging, and use of "cents off" designations. The act gives the FTC responsibility for consumer commodities. The Food and Drug Administration (FDA) administers the FPLA with respect to foods, drugs, cosmetics, and medical devices.[156]

As mentioned in an earlier section, the packaging and labeling issue is drawing renewed interest because of health and environmental claims and advertising law in specific product categories such as pharmaceuticals, food, tobacco, alcohol, and advertising directed at children. Consumer interest groups as well as lawsuits have been bringing the

ETHICS IN PRACTICE CASE

Return Fraud—A Growing Business

Consumers love warranties, guarantees, and excellent return policies on the products they purchase. From the merchant's perspective, these policies help to keep customers satisfied and coming back. But, a problem merchants are facing more and more is the burgeoning business of return fraud. Return fraud typically occurs when consumers purchase a product, use it for some limited period of time, and then return it wanting their money back. One estimate is that return fraud is costing American businesses almost $9 billion annually.

One type of return fraud occurs with merchants such as L.L.Bean or REI, Inc., when they offer lifetime warranties with the privilege of returning anything, anytime, for any reason. Recently, REI, the privately held sporting goods chain, has had to change its return policy because so many people took unreasonable advantage of it. At one REI store, a customer returned a 9-year-old backpack that he had used for mountain climbing because it was getting old and dirty and the customer didn't like it any more. In another case, a woman returned a worn pair of sandals designed for hiking and wading in rivers because she had concluded they were not sexy enough.

Customers have returned clothing or shoes that have been torn, charred in a fire, or otherwise abused in extreme sports and have expected and gotten refunds. Some stores have gotten shredded clothing returned that was cut loose from customers when rescue workers had to cut through the fabric while saving them from a mishap. Though REI has concluded it must put restrictions on its returns policies, L.L.Bean, Patagonia, and Orvis have claimed they have no current plans to change their policies.

Another form of returns fraud also has been occurring, often in high-end clothing stores such as Bloomingdales, when women purchase fancy dresses, wear them once to a wedding or party, and then return them, sometimes soiled with sweat and want their money back. Jewelry purchases are also being abused. The merchants call this practice "wardrobing" and are starting to take a firmer stand with respect to returns because of all the returns abuse they have been experiencing. In one recent year, 65 percent of retailers reported they were victims of wardrobing.

Bloomingdale's finally started a policy of placing a 3-inch black tag in a highly visible place, such as on the hemline of dresses costing $150 or more, as they are being purchased. Then, the customer can try the dress on at home without disturbing the tag and return it if it doesn't fit. Once the customer removes the tag to wear the dress in public, however, the garment cannot be returned. The company says it is using the "b-tags" to reinforce their policy that once garments have been worn, washed, damaged, used or altered, they cannot be returned.

Stores such as Victoria's Secret and Bath & Body Works claim they are keeping returns data bases so they can detect patterns of returns abuse and be able to refuse future return privileges on serial returners.

1. How do excellent customers, ones who do not abuse return policies, regard what merchants are currently having to face today?
2. Is it unethical for customers to take advantage of returns policies or is this just the cost of doing business today? Is it unethical for companies to take the actions they are taking?
3. What is your appraisal of some of the actions companies have to take with respect to their return policies? Are they justified? Is the consumer no longer "always right?"

Sources: "Credit Card and Returns Fraud Causing Soaring Losses for Retailers," Professional Jeweller, April 15, 2016, http://www.professionaljeweller.com/credit-card-and-returns-fraud-causing-soaring-losses-for-retailers/. Accessed May 6, 2016; "Don't Even Think about Returning That Dress," *Bloomberg Businessweek*, September 30–October 6, 2013, 29–31; Kathy Allen, "Retailers Estimate Holiday Returns Fraud Will Cost $2.2 Billion in 2015," National Retail Federation, December 17, 2015, https://nrf.com/media/press-releases/retailers-estimate-holiday-return-fraud-will-cost-22-billion-2015. Accessed May 6, 2016; Kirsten Grind, "Unsportsmanlike Conduct: Retailer Ends Era of Many Happy Returns," *The Wall Street Journal*, September 16, 2013, A1.

issue of labeling and packaging to the forefront in recent years. It should be added that the advertising of products with labeling or packaging issues also represents the additional charge of deceptive advertising, a topic discussed earlier.

The most important issue in labeling today is ingredient labeling. Consumers now want to know more about what ingredients are in the products they are using, especially food and health-related products. We discussed the consumer's desire for GMO labeling in Chapter 9 because it was an ethical issue being raised in the realm of biotechnology and business ethics. But, GMO labeling certainly falls within the purview of this discussion as well. GMO labeling will likely come quickly due to Vermont's new law requiring

GMO disclosure, but food companies still resist the idea. General Mills and Campbell Soups have argued that such labeling would be perceived as a warning label and would mislead consumers into thinking the product is unsafe when regulators say they are not. At a minimum, the Grocery Manufacturers Association (GMA), an industry group, is urging Congress to pass legislation establishing a uniform national standard so companies will not have to deal with various state laws.[157]

With respect to ingredients labeling, generally, more transparency is now expected by consumers. In response, the FDA is in the process of revising its Nutrition Facts label panel that has been standard on most food products since 1994. The FDA's proposed changes will include a redesign to make calorie information more prominent and also a change to what is considered a single serving size to reflect the increase in portion sizes that people have begun eating over the past two decades.[158] Some researchers have said that the proposed labels are an improvement but still are not clear enough to convey what the net value of a food may be.[159]

As consumers are demanding to know more about food ingredients, the Grocery Manufacturers Association (GMA) recently announced its *SmartLabel* initiative that is supported by more than 30 companies including Hershey, PepsiCo, and General Mills among others.[160] As part of this initiative, the companies are planning to use smartphone scanning technology so that shoppers can quickly get a detailed picture of their product's ingredients.

The proposed SmartLabel would use a Quick Response (QR) code that shoppers can scan while in the stores and using an app this will take them to the company's Web site where more nutrition information regarding ingredients will be available. The GMA says they have a survey that reveals that 75 percent of consumers would likely use the new label.[161] The Center for Food Safety, an environmental-and-health nonprofit, however, has said that conveying information in this way is insufficient because some consumers cannot afford smartphones. They say the QR code labeling discriminates against the poor, minorities, rural populations, and the elderly.[162]

In the area of product packaging, the issue of slack fill has been the topic of much recent criticism. Slack fill, known in regulatory terms as *nonfunctional slack fill*, is the practice of companies putting less product in the package while often keeping the container size the same but raising the price.[163] In toilet paper packaging, the practice has been called "de-sheeting" as the number of sheets on a roll are reduced. The slack fill practice has been going on for years in products such as cereal, candy bars, deodorants, and virtually all consumer products.

One prominent example that was in the news in 2015 was when McCormick, the spice company, reduced the amount of black pepper from 4 ounces to 3 ounces in its signature red-and-white tins but the container remained the same size.[164] This issue came to a head when a competitor, Watkins, Inc., claimed in a lawsuit that McCormick was engaging in a deceptive practice that put it at a competitive disadvantage. Watkins alleges that McCormick's reduction in pepper volume violates federal laws that govern slack fill.[165] In 2016, another consumer filed a similar lawsuit against McCormick for slack fill.[166] The outcome of these cases will be important in the realm of product packaging as thousands of products are potentially affected. In a related case, Procter & Gamble's Olay skin-care products entered into a settlement when a California prosecutor accused the company of misleading consumers by selling jars of face cream in packaging that was at times much larger than the contents. P&G agreed to change its packaging and paid an $850,000 settlement in civil penalties and costs.[167]

Prominent companies that often carry strong social responsibility records are not exempt from charges of deceptive packing. In 2015, Whole Foods Market was accused of overcharging customers in New York after officials discovered the company had mislabeled weights of freshly packaged foods like vegetable platters and chicken tenders that lead to overcharges of $1 to $15 per item.[168] In 2016, Starbuck's faced a lawsuit from a woman in Chicago who claimed Starbucks regularly overfills its cold drinks with ice instead of using the advertised amount of coffee or other liquid in its plastic cups. The lawsuit alleged that an iced beverage advertised at 24 ounces contains about 14 ounces of product and the rest is ice. The lawsuit seeks class action status so it could include customers from the past decade to join in.[169] The Starbucks case could be viewed as both a deceptive advertising and packaging example. Both Starbuck's and Whole Foods have had strong CSR records, so these examples illustrate how no companies are exempt from close scrutiny and have to watch carefully their own practices.

13.1h Other Product Information Issues

It is difficult to catalog all the consumer issues in which product information is a key factor. Certainly, advertising, warranties, guarantees, packaging, and labeling constitute the bulk of the concerns. In addition to these, however, we must briefly mention several others. Sales techniques in which direct sellers use deceptive information must be mentioned. Some other major laws that address information disclosure issues include the following:

1. *Equal Credit Opportunity Act,* which prohibits discrimination in the extension of consumer credit.
2. *Truth-in-Lending Act,* which requires all suppliers of consumer credit to fully disclose all credit terms and to permit a three-day right of rescission in any transaction involving a security interest in the consumer's residence (e.g., in the case of home equity loans).
3. *Fair Credit Reporting Act,* which ensures that consumer-reporting agencies provide information in a manner that is fair and equitable to the consumer.
4. *Fair Debt Collection Practices Act,* which regulates the practices of third-party debt collection agencies.

13.2 The Federal Trade Commission (FTC)

We have discussed three main areas of product information—advertising, warranties & guarantees, and packaging and labeling. Both the FTC and the FDA are actively involved in these issues. It is important now to look more closely at the federal government's major instrument, the FTC, for ensuring that business lives up to its responsibilities in these areas. Actually, the FTC has broad and sweeping powers, and it delves into several other areas that we refer to throughout the book. The Consumer Product Safety Commission and the FDA are major regulatory agencies, too, but we consider them more carefully in the next chapter, where we discuss products and services more specifically.

The FTC was created in 1914. Its purpose was to prevent unfair methods of competition in commerce as part of the battle to "bust the trusts." Over the years, Congress passed additional laws giving the agency greater authority in the policing of anticompetitive prices. In 1938, Congress passed a broad prohibition against "unfair and deceptive acts or practices." Since then the FTC has also been directed to administer a wide variety of other consumer protection laws including Truth-in-Lending, Fair Packaging and Labeling, Fair Credit Reporting, and Equal Credit Opportunity Acts.[170] Over the course of its history, the FTC has been more or less active depending on the administration that was in office and the zeal of the Chairperson. Figure 13-3 provides additional information about the FTC's mission, vision, and how it helps consumers.

FIGURE 13-3 The Federal Trade Commission

FTC's Mission	To prevent business practices that are anticompetitive or deceptive or unfair to consumers; to enhance informed consumer choice and public understanding of the competitive process; and to accomplish this without unduly burdening legitimate business activity.
FTC's Vision	A U.S. economy characterized by vigorous competition among producers and consumer access to accurate information, yielding high-quality products at low prices and encouraging efficiency, innovation, and consumer choice.
FTC's Strategic Goals	1. *Protect Consumers*: Prevent fraud, deception, and unfair business practices in the marketplace. 2. *Maintain Competition*: Prevent anticompetitive mergers and other anticompetitive business practices in the marketplace. 3. *Advance Performance*: Advance the FTC's performance through organizational, individual, and management excellence.
FTC's Benefits to Consumer	As a consumer or business person, you may be more familiar with the work of the Federal Trade Commission than you think. The FTC deals with issues that touch the economic life of every American. The FTC is the only federal agency with both consumer protection and competition jurisdiction in broad sectors of the economy. The FTC pursues vigorous and effective law enforcement; advances consumers' interests by sharing its expertise with federal and state legislatures and U.S. and international government agencies; develops policy and research tools through hearings, workshops, and conferences; and creates practical and plain-language educational programs for consumers and businesses in a global marketplace with constantly changing technologies.

Sources: Federal Trade Commission, "About the Federal Trade Commission," http://www.ftc.gov/ftc/about.shtm. Accessed May 6, 2016; FTC Consumer Information, http://www.consumer.ftc.gov/. Accessed May 6, 2016.

13.2a The FTC in the 21st Century

In addition to carrying out its ongoing responsibilities, the FTC has had a number of successes in carrying out its mission in the 2000s.[171] An early accomplishment was the creation of the National Do-Not-Call Registry. The registry opened to consumers in 2003 and forbade telemarketers from calling consumers who sign up with the registry. The FTC also instituted a requirement that all companies placing marketing calls have their information available for consumers' caller ID systems. Consumers could then report companies that make calls in violation.[172]

Beginning in 2004, the FTC extracted millions of dollars in settlements from firms that made misleading claims for weight-loss products, but opted not to require disclosure of the existence of product placement or the sources of word-of-mouth advertising.[173] The FTC preference has been that business would self-regulate when possible and that the police action of the FTC would be a court of last resort.[174] Beginning in 2009, the FTC argued for a more vigorous enforcement of the FTC Act and moved more aggressively on issues such as health care; advertising and marketing to children; Internet, telecom, and technology; energy; and competition enforcement beyond the Sherman Act. Under the Obama administration, the FTC and other federal consumer protection agencies assumed a more active role than in the recent past. The FTC has been dealing with such issues as robocalls, telemarketers, phone spam, pyramid schemes, Google's antitrust case, children's online privacy, and data brokers.

Currently, the FTC is playing a more active role as government's consumer data watchdog. Though it has long used computer scientists and technically knowledgeable lawyers, in 2010 the FTC embarked on yet another mission in its quest to keep current with rapid changes in technology. The agency created a new position, that of chief technologist, and in the past several years it has been investigating whether companies truly are keeping customers' personal data secure and private.[175] The FTC's most recent chief technologist has challenged the tracking of shoppers online and in stores, though this has drawn criticism from an online-advertising trading group.[176]

The FTC recently has created a new unit called the Office of Technology Research and Investigation so that it can keep on top of new technologies and ensure that consumers are better protected from invasive approaches.[177] The FTC expects the new unit will enable it to investigate a wider array of emerging technologies including Internet-connected automobiles, connected home devices, and mobile payment systems, and in particular, their implications for data security and privacy.[178] In one of their recent projects, the agency filed a complaint against a retail-tracking company that uses mobile phone signals to track shoppers' movements in stores but has failed to live up to its commitment to inform shoppers about the in-store surveillance and permit them to opt out.[179]

In another recent action, the FTC has sued DeVry Education Group for allegedly running false TV and online advertisements about the employment successes and earnings of its graduates. The FTC's lawsuit also seeks to bar DeVry and other for-profit colleges from using faulty statistics in its advertisements. Corinthian Colleges, Inc., liquidated in bankruptcy in 2015 after charges it had engaged in similar practices.[180]

13.2b Consumer Financial Protection Bureau

Though the FTC supervises most consumer regulations with respect to product and service information and advertising, and other laws have been passed that address specific issues, it is useful to briefly consider the most recent federal consumer legislation that has been passed in the last few years. As we noted in Chapter 11, the Dodd–Frank Wall Street Reform and Consumer Protection Act of 2010 (Dodd–Frank Act) established the **Consumer Financial Protection Bureau (CFPB)**. Congress established the CFPB to protect consumers by implementing and enforcing federal consumer financial laws. Among other activities, the CFPB:

- Writes rules, supervises companies, and enforces federal consumer financial protection laws
- Restricts unfair, deceptive, or abusive acts or practices
- Takes consumer complaints
- Promotes financial education
- Researches consumer behavior
- Monitors financial markets for new risks to consumers
- Enforces laws that outlaw discrimination and other unfair treatment in consumer finance

The new agency had considerable support due to the belief by many consumers and political leaders that such an agency was needed in light of the financial misdealings and deceptions of the previous decade. One aim of the bill was that it would police and write rules for financial firms' retail products such as mortgages, bank accounts, and credit cards. In fact, the CFPB was given authority to administer the **Credit Card Act of 2009** that spelled out new regulations governing credit cards. Officially, the act was named the *Credit Card Accountability, Responsibility, and Disclosure Act 2009 (CARD)* and it was passed by Congress and enacted in February 2010.[181] The law had two purposes—fairness and transparency. With respect to fairness, CARD would prohibit certain practices that are unfair and abusive such as hiking up the rate on an existing balance or allowing a customer to go overlimit and then imposing an overlimit fee. With respect to transparency, CARD would make the rates and fees on credit cards more transparent so that consumers can better understand how much they are paying for their credit card and can compare credit cards.[182]

The relatively new Consumer Financial Protection Bureau, patterned in concept after the Consumer Product Safety Commission, which will be discussed in the next chapter, was a key element in financial reform legislation that had been debated in Congress for several years. The basic motivation for the legislation had been that greedy banks had exploited naïve consumers, and this led up to the credit crisis the country has been experiencing.[183] While much of the debate centered on banks and their role in the financial crisis, lawmakers were also concerned about how to handle other financial consumer businesses such as payday lenders, debt collectors, check-cashing businesses, title and installment lenders, and pawnbrokers.[184]

Critics of the relatively new CFPB included those who philosophically opposed more government regulation and the business community, which saw the new regulator as unnecessary. Lobbying by business associations was vigorous. The U.S. Chamber of Commerce, as well as many of the financial service firms themselves, fought the proposed bureau since the beginning.[185] The majority of consumers and consumer advocacy groups were in favor of the proposed legislation, and business associations that were likely to be impacted were against the new agency.

According to statistics gathered by CFPB, the agency produced the following results that they state were accurate as of January 2016. The CFPB held companies accountable for illegal practices and gave $11.2 billion in relief to consumers due to their enforcement actions. Twenty-five million consumers were served. The CFPB claimed it handled 800,000 complaints from consumers and 98 percent of consumers received timely replies when their complaints are sent to companies.[186]

The CFPB has not been without its critics. One of the primary criticisms relate to its governing structure. When first conceived, the bureau was intended to be governed by five bipartisan commissioners. When the proposal was passed by Congress, however, it came out with a single-director structure. This would be one person who reports to the president and favors whichever political party is in office. A commission structure would promote predictability in rule-making by preventing the director from unilaterally and abruptly reversing the decisions made under the previous director.[187]

An example of what critics have called the bureau's biased decision making occurred in the case of its auto loan regulation that critics say was based on "shamefully flawed" information. Documents have been revealed showing that the bureau officials knew their information was flawed and that they even discussed ways to prevent people from outside the bureau from knowing about it.[188] Apparently, the bureau had been guessing the race and ethnicity of car loan borrowers based on their last names and addresses and then suing banks whenever it looked like borrowers the bureau guessed were white appeared to be getting better deals than the people it guessed were minorities. This decision-making method was the reason a bipartisan House supermajority voted to roll back the bureau's auto loan rules.[189] When the bureau and its authority were being debated in Congress, critics warned that it would not have adequate accountability and would tend to overreach. There is concern that this has been happening.[190] In March 2015, the House passed a bill along party lines that would replace the single director with a commission and give Congress direct control over its budget, but that bill does not appear to be succeeding in the Senate.[191] In spite of its criticisms, everyone hopes that the CFPB will be able to succeed in its primary mission that is to protect consumers.

13.3 Self-Regulation in Advertising

Cases of deceptive or unfair advertising in the United States are handled primarily by the FTC. In addition to this regulatory approach, however, self-regulation of advertising has become an important business response. Under the regulatory approach, advertising behavior is controlled through various governmental rules that are backed by the use of penalties. **Self-regulation**, on the other hand, refers to the control of business conduct and performance by the business itself, or business associations, rather than by government or by market forces.[192] The idea behind self-regulation is that companies will carefully monitor their own advertising for legal and ethical issues and take the initiative in correcting deficient advertising without the regulatory agencies having to get involved. It is a proactive strategy rather than a reactive one.

13.3a The National Advertising Division's Program

The most prominent instance of self-regulation by business in the advertising industry is the program sponsored by the National Advertising Division (NAD) of the Council of Better Business Bureaus, Inc.[193] The NAD and the National Advertising Review Board (NARB) were created to help sustain high standards of truth and accuracy in national advertising and still serves today in an active manner. NAD only reviews national advertisements. It leaves to state and city jurisdictions the responsibility for local advertisements.[194]

The NAD initiates investigations, determines issues, collects and evaluates data, and makes decisions as to whether an advertiser's claims are substantiated. When the NAD determines that an advertiser's claims are unsubstantiated, the advertiser is asked to undertake modification or permanent discontinuance of the advertising. If an advertiser disagrees with NAD's decision, it can file an appeal with the NARB, which has a reservoir of dozens of professionals representing national advertisers, advertising agencies, and the public sector. The chairman of the NARB selects an impartial panel of five members for each appeal. The parties involved, including NAD, submit briefs expressing their views for discussion at an oral hearing, after which the panel issues a public report.[195] If an advertiser is unwilling to abide by the NARB panel's decision, the advertising at issue may be referred to the FTC.[196] NAD is a low-cost alternative to litigation, and it reaches determinations regarding the truth and accuracy of advertising in a fair, impartial, and expeditious manner.[197]

13.4 Moral Models and Consumer Stakeholders

It is useful to conclude this chapter by providing insights into how the three types of moral manager models, introduced in Chapter 7, would view consumer stakeholders. Figure 13-4 presents a brief statement as to the likely orientations of immoral, amoral, and moral managers to this vital stakeholder group. As it can be seen in these descriptions, the moral management model best represents the highest ethical standards of consumer treatment and is, therefore, the recommended model for business to follow.

FIGURE 13-4 Three Moral Management Models and Their Orientations toward Consumer Stakeholders

Model of Management Morality Orientation to Consumer Stakeholders

Immoral Management Customers are viewed as opportunities to be exploited for personal or organizational gain. Ethical standards in dealings do not prevail; indeed, an active intent to cheat, deceive, and/or mislead is present. In all marketing decisions—advertising, pricing, packaging, distribution, warrantees—the customer is taken advantage of to the fullest extent.

Amoral Management Management does not think through the ethical consequences of its decisions and actions. It simply makes decisions with profitability within the letter of the law as a guide. Management is not focused on what is fair from the perspective of the customer. The focus is on management's rights. No consideration is given to ethical implications of interactions with customers.

Moral Management Customers are viewed as equal partners in transactions. The customer brings needs and expectations to the exchange transaction and is treated fairly. Managerial focus is on giving the customer fair value, full information, fair guarantee, and satisfaction. Consumer rights are liberally interpreted and honored.

Summary

Consumer stakeholders have always been at the top of the list of business's stakeholders. Some of the newer challenges, such as social media advertising, advertising and labeling for more healthy food options, the expanding use of E-cigarettes, and new government agencies that are beginning to have influence, are important features of this chapter.

The issue of consumer stakeholders has come to the forefront during the recent economic recovery. More and more, businesses are realizing that the economy is built upon consumer spending and that they need to do all they can do to get consumers spending again. In a consumption-driven society, business must be especially attentive to the issues that arise in its relationships with consumers. It is a paradox that consumerism arose during the very period that the business community discovered the centrality of the marketing concept to business success. The consumer's Magna Carta includes the rights to safety, to be informed, to choose, and to be heard. Consumers, however, expect more than this, and hence the consumer movement, or consumerism, was born. Ralph Nader, considered the father of this movement, made consumer complaining respectable. Since then, the consumer movement has been among the most active of the stakeholder categories and promises to be important in the future.

Product and service information issues comprise a major area in the business–consumer stakeholder relationship. Foremost among these is advertising. Many issues have arisen because of perceived advertising abuses, such as ambiguity, concealed facts, exaggerations, and psychological appeals. Specific controversial spheres have included, but are not limited to, comparative advertising, use of sex appeal in advertising, advertising to children, marketing to the poor, advertising of alcoholic beverages, advertising of cigarettes, health and environmental claims, ad creep, and social media advertising.

Other product information issues include warranties, guarantees, packaging, and labeling. The major governmental body for regulating product information issues is the FTC. The FDA and the state attorneys general have become active as well. Recent consumer protection legislation has included the Credit Card Act and the Consumer Financial Protection Bureau, intending to give consumers greater protection, especially with financial service industry products. On its own initiative, business has introduced a variety of forms of self-regulation with respect to its product and service information, especially advertising. The National Advertising Division coordinates self-regulation in the advertising industry. Moral models with respect to consumer stakeholders were presented, and the moral management model in which customers are viewed as equal partners in transactions was held out to be the best practice.

Key Terms

accurate information, p. 400
ad creep, p. 404
adequate information, p. 400
age compression, p. 408
ambient advertising, p. 415
ambiguous advertising, p. 401
Children's Television Act (CTA), p. 408
clear information, p. 400
comparative advertising, p. 404
concealed facts, p. 402
Consumer Financial Protection Bureau (CFPB), p. 423
consumerism, p. 397
consumer's Magna Carta, p. 396
Credit Card Act of 2009, p. 423
Customer engagement, p. 395
customer relationship management (CRM), p. 395
exaggerated claims, p. 402
express warranty, p. 417
extended warranties, p. 417
full warranty, p. 417
green advertising, p. 414
green guides, p. 414
green marketing, p. 415
green fatigue, p. 415
green watchdog, p. 415
guarantees, p. 417
implied warranty, p. 417
limited warranty, p. 417
natural products, p. 414
organic food, p. 413
plot placement, p. 402
product information, p. 400
product placement, p. 402
psychological appeals, p. 403
puffery, p. 403
right to be heard, p. 396
right to be informed, p. 396
right to choose, p. 396
right to safety, p. 396
return fraud, p. 418
returns policies, p. 418
self-regulation, p. 424
social media advertising, p. 416
warranties, p. 417
weasel words, p. 401

Discussion Questions

1. In addition to the basic consumer rights expressed in the consumer's Magna Carta, what other expectations or rights do you think consumer stakeholders have of business? Do consumers have some moral rights that have not yet been articulated in law?
2. What is your opinion of the consumerism movement? Is it "alive and well" or is it fading away? Why has consumerism been such an enduring movement for so long?
3. Give an example of a major abuse of advertising via social media from your own observations and experiences. How do you feel about this as a consumer?
4. Are companies genuinely interested in marketing sustainable products or is this just a marketing strategy that is popular today. Do you think "green fatigue" has set in? If so, what should companies now do?
5. Does the new Consumer Financial Protection Bureau make sense? How do you keep politics out of government agencies? In a free market, why shouldn't consumers be left to fend for themselves with respect to consumer financial products?

Endnotes

1. Gallup, "U.S. Consumer Spending Increases in April, to $95," May 2, 2016, http://www.gallup.com/poll/191222/consumer-spending-average-increases-april.aspx?g_source=Economy&g_medium=newsfeed&g_campaign=tiles. Accessed May 2, 2016.
2. Peter F. Drucker, *Management: Tasks, Responsibilities, Practices* (New York: Harper & Row, 1973), 61.
3. Frederick F. Reichheld, *The Loyalty Effect* (Cambridge, MA: Harvard Business School Press, 1996).
4. Russell S. Winer, "A Framework for Customer Relationship Management," *California Management Review* (Summer 2001), 89–105; also see "Customer Relationship Management," BusinessDictionary.com, http://www.businessdictionary.com/definition/customer-relationship-management-CRM.html. Accessed May 2, 2016.
5. "The Customer Is Often Ignored," *Marketing Week* (September 27, 2001), 3.
6. Gallup, "Customer Engagement," http://www.gallup.com/services/169331/customer-engagement.aspx?g_source=CUSTOMER_ENGAGEMENT&g_medium=topic&g_campaign=tiles. Accessed May 2, 2016.
7. Ibid.
8. Ibid.
9. Camilla Ballesteros, "Don't Talk about CRM; Do It," *Marketing Week* (September 27, 2001), 49.
10. Ibid.
11. Scott M. Broetzmann, "Why the Customer Care Revolution Has Failed: How Companies Misuse the Telephone When Responding to Customers" (May 31, 2006), http://www.tmcnet.com/news/2006/04/18/1581418.htm. Accessed August 9, 2010.
12. Pete Blackshaw, *Satisfied Customers Tell Three Friends, Angry Customers Tell 3,000*, Crown Business, 2008.
13. Robert J. Holloway and Robert S. Hancock, *Marketing in a Changing Environment*, 2d ed. (New York: John Wiley & Sons, 1973), 558–565.
14. Ibid., 565–566.
15. Robert O. Herrmann, "Consumerism: Its Goals, Organizations, and Future," *Journal of Marketing* (October 1970), 55–60.
16. Ruth Simon, "You're Losing Your Consumer Rights," *Money* (Vol. 25, No. 3, 1996), 100–111.
17. For more on the history of the consumer movement, see Archie B. Carroll, Kenneth J. Lipartito, James E. Post, Patricia H. Werhane, and Kenneth E. Goodpaster, executive editor, 2012, *Corporate Responsibility: The American Experience*, Cambridge: Cambridge University Press.
18. Philip Kotler, "What Consumerism Means for Marketers," *Harvard Business Review* (May–June 1972), 48–57.
19. Ralph Nader, *Unsafe at Any Speed* (New York: Grossman Publishers, 1965).
20. Rich Thomas, "Safe at This Speed," *Businessweek* (August 22, 1994), 40; Douglas Harbrecht and Ronald Grover, "The Second Coming of Ralph Nader," *Businessweek* (March 6, 1989), 28.
21. Paul Magnusson, "The Punishing Price of Nader's Passion," *Businessweek* (November 20, 2000), 44.
22. Gary Fields, "Leading the News: Nader to Run for President Again; Democrats Fear a Reprise of 2000," *The Wall Street Journal* (February 23, 2003), A3.
23. CommonDreams, http://www.commondreams.org/about-us. Accessed May 2, 2016.
24. John Nichols, "Ralph Nader on 2016, Wall Street, and our Broken Political System," The Nation, December 1, 2015, http://www.thenation.com/article/ralph-nader-on-2016-wall-street-and-our-broken-political-system/. Accessed May 11, 2016.

25. "Ralph Nader's New Museum; Old Soapbox, *Fortune*, January 1, 2016, 24.

26. Consumer Federation of America, "Nation's Top Ten Consumer Complaints," July 29, 2015, http://consumerfed.org/press_release/nations-top-ten-consumer-complaints-2014/. Accessed May 2, 2016.

27. Consumer Reports, http://www.consumerreports.org/cro/index.htm. Accessed May 2, 2016.

28. "Selling It," *Consumer Reports*, January 2016.

29. Consumer Reports, April 2016, 99.

30. *Consumer Reports*, December 2012, 75.

31. "Never Say Never," http://www.ConsumerReports.org (September 2009), 63.

32. *Consumer Reports*, September 2012, 63.

33. Chuck Klosterman, "Try This at Home," *The New York Times Magazine*, January 18, 2015, 17.

34. William Leiss, Stephen Kline, and Sut Jhally, *Social Communication in Advertising* (Toronto: Methuen, 1986), 13.

35. Ibid.

36. William Shaw and Vincent Barry, *Moral Issues in Business*, 12th ed. (Cengage Learning, 2012), 389–414.

37. *The Federalist*, "The 3 Worst Superbowl Ads…and Why They Are Bad for America," February 2, 2015, http://thefederalist.com/2015/02/02/the-3-worst-superbowl-ads-and-why-theyre-bad-for-america/. Accessed May 11, 2016.

38. Shaw and Barry, ibid.

39. Ibid., 404.

40. Shaw and Barry, ibid.

41. Justine Goodman, "5 Hilariously Blatant Examples of Product Placement," November 14, 2012, http://www.maxim.com/movies/5-hilariously-blatant-examples-of-product-placement. Accessed April 30, 2013.

42. Tom Lowry and Burt Helm, "Blasting Away at Product Placement," *Businessweek* (October 26, 2009), 60.

43. Ingela Ratledge, "Modern Product Placement," *TVGuideMagazine.com* (April 12, 2010).

44. Ronald Grover, Tom Lowry, Gerry Khermouch, Cliff Edwards, and Dean Foust, "Can Mad. Ave. Make Zap-Proof Ads?" *Businessweek* (February 2, 2004), 36–37.

45. *Investopedia*, "A Look at Coca-Cola's Advertising Expenses," http://www.investopedia.com/articles/markets/081315/look-cocacolas-advertising-expenses.asp.

46. Jennifer C. Dooren and Emily Glazer, "FDA Rebukes Lancome on Marketing," *The Wall Street Journal*, September 12, 2012, B3; Alexander Gaffney, "Cosmetic Companies, Watch Out: FDA Cracking Down on Improper Claims," December 3, 2014, http://www.raps.org/Regulatory-Focus/News/2014/12/03/20881/Cosmetic-Companies-Watch-Out-FDA-Cracking-Down-on-Improper-Claims/. Accessed May 2, 2016.

47. Ben Fox Rubin, "Coppertone to Stop Using 'Waterproof' in Marketing," *The Wall Street Journal*, September 26, 2012, B10.

48. "Consumers Have Mixed Reactions to Puffery in Advertising" (January 19, 2010), Phys.Org, http://phys.org/news183128214.html. Accessed May 2, 2016.

49. Shaw and Barry.

50. Fast Company, "Five Psychological Tactics Marketers Use to Influence Consumer Behavior," http://www.fastcompany.com/3032675/hit-the-ground-running/5-psychological-tactics-marketers-use-to-influence-consumer-behavior. Accessed May 2, 2016.

51. Jeffrey Kluger, "Now Hear This," *Time* (March 1, 2010).

52. Nicole Martinelli, "Get a Mac Campaign Named One of the Best Marketing Jobs Ever" (January 15, 2009), http://www.cultofmac.com/7091/get-a-mac-campaign-named-one-of-best-marketing-jobs-ever/7091/. Accessed May 9, 2013.

53. Academy of Art University, "Academy Alums 'Get a Mac' Campaign Named Ad of the Decade," http://www.academyart.edu/news/articles/academy-alums-get-mac-named-campaign-decade.html. Accessed May 1, 2013.

54. Suzanne Vranica, "For Hardee's and Carl's, Jr., Sex Sells," *The Wall Street Journal*, May 26, 2015, http://blogs.wsj.com/cmo/2015/05/26/for-hardees-and-carls-jr-sex-sells/. Accessed May 11, 2016.

55. Hillary Chura, "Spirited Sex; Alcohol Ads Ratchet Up the Sex to Woo Jaded Customers," *Advertising Age* (July 9, 2001), 1.

56. Jill Weber, "Sexy Teen Lingerie Sends All the Wrong Messages," *USA Today*, March 13, 2013, 8A.

57. Mary Bailey, *The Watchful Eye*, "The Sexualization of Boys: The Other Half of the Story," http://www.mcmdnow.org/Sexualization-of-Boys.pdf. Accessed May 11, 2016.

58. Jeanette Mulvey, BusinessNewsDaily, "Why Sex Sells… More than Ever," http://www.businessnewsdaily.com/2649-sex-sells-more.html. Accessed May 4, 2016.

59. About-Face, "Does Sex Really Sell?" September 23, 2015, http://www.about-face.org/does-sex-really-sell/. Accessed May 4, 2016.

60. Ibid.

61. American Psychological Association, "Sexualization of Girls," http://www.apa.org/pi/women/programs/girls/report.aspx. Accessed May 4, 2016.

62. "The Ethics of Advertising Aimed at Children," HubPages, http://brandconsultant.hubpages.com/hub/advertisingtochildren. Accessed May 4, 2016.

63. Mary Bowerman and Hadley Malcolm, "New Barbies Are Tall, Petite, Curvy," *USA Today*, January 29, 2016, 3B.

64. DressUpGamesite.com, "Barbie Shopping Games," http://www.dressupgamesite.com/games/barbie-shopping-games-2013.htm. Accessed May 1, 2013.

65. Bowerman and Malcolm, ibid.

66. "Barbie Gets Her First Credit Card," *Credit Card Management* (January 1998), 6–8.

67. American Psychological Association, http://www.apa.org/topics/children/index.aspx. Accessed May 4, 2016.

68. Jayne O' Donnell, "As Kids Get Savvy, Marketers Move the Age Scale," http://www.usatoday.com/search/jayne%20o'donnell/. Accessed May 4, 2016.

69. Children's Advertising Review Unit, Better Business Bureau, "Self-Regulatory Program for Children's Advertising," 2009, http://www.caru.org/guidelines/guidelines.pdf. Accessed May 4, 2016.

70. Liz Szabo, "Kids Consume 12% of Their Calories from Fast Food," *USA Today*, September 15, 2015, 3A.

71. Anton Troianovski, "FTC Shines Light on Food Ads, Kids," *The Wall Street Journal*, September 19, 2012, B6.

72. "Food Fight over Marketing to Kids Misses Key Ingredient," *USA Today*, October 17, 2011, 10A.

73. Bonnie Rochman, "Sweet Spot: New Data on How the Least Healthy Cereals Do the Most Marketing," *Time* (November 2, 2009), 55–56, http://content.time.com/time/magazine/article/0,9171,1931730,00.html. Accessed May 4, 2016.

74. U.S. Government Accountability Office, "Children's Television Act," July 14, 2011, http://www.gao.gov/products/GAO-11-659. Accessed May 4, 2016.

75. Michael L. Marlow, "The Skinny of Anti-Obesity Soda Laws," *The Wall Street Journal*, April 1, 2013, A11.

76. Holman W. Jenkins, Jr., "Coke and the Calorie Wars," *The Wall Street Journal*, January 30, 2013, A11; Nanci Hellmich, "Disney Cuts Junk from Its Diet," *USA Today*, June 5, 2012, 1B.

77. Federal Trade Commission, "Payday Loans," http://www.consumer.ftc.gov/articles/0097-payday-loans. Accessed May 4, 2016.

78. HUB, Jill Rosen, "Income Tax Preparation Chains Target Low Income Filers, Study Suggests," April 14, 2016, http://hub.jhu.edu/2016/04/14/tax-companies-exploit-working-poor. Accessed May 4, 2016.

79. Brian Grow and Keith Epstein, "The Poverty Business," *Bloomberg Businessweek*, http://www.bloomberg.com/news/articles/2007-05-20/the-poverty-business. Accessed May 4, 2016.

80. Ibid.

81. Huff/Post50, Martha T. S. Laham, "One in 5 Seniors Has Fallen Prey to a Financial Swindle, but This Is Just the Tip of the Iceberg," August 11, 2015, http://www.huffingtonpost.com/martha-ts-laham-/1-in-5-seniors-has-fallen-prey-to-a-financial-swindle-but-this-is-just-the-tip-of-the-iceberg_b_7961978.html. Accessed May 11, 2016.

82. Dana Silversteen, "The Ethics behind Advertising Alcohol to the Teenage Demographic," Business Government and Society, https://bizgovsoc2.wordpress.com/2012/04/09/the-ethics-behind-advertising alcohol-to-the-teenage-demographic/. Accessed May 4, 2016.

83. NCBI, Joel W. Grube, "Alcohol in the Media: Drinking Portrayal, Alcohol Advertising, and Alcohol Consumption by Youth," http://www.ncbi.nlm.nih.gov/books/NBK37586/. Accessed May 4, 2016.

84. Ibid.

85. Silversteen, ibid.

86. Ibid.

87. Mike Esterl, "Liquor Ads Win Airtime," *The Wall Street Journal*, August 24, 2012, B6.

88. WHO, "Regulation Urgently Needed to Control Growing List of Deadly Tobacco Products" (May 30, 2006), http://www.who.int/mediacentre/news/releases/2006/pr28/en/. Accessed May 3, 2013.

89. "Are E-Cigarettes a Healthy Way to Quit Smoking?" *The Wall Street Journal*, April 11, 2016, R1.

90. U.S. Food and Drug Administration, "Tobacco Control Act," http://www.fda.gov/TobaccoProducts/Labeling/RulesRegulationsGuidance/ucm246129.htm. Accessed May 4, 2016.

91. Ibid.

92. "Weigh Potential Risks, Benefits of E-cigarettes," USA Today, December 18, 2014, 6A.

93. Tripp Mickle, "FDA to Regulate E-cigarette Industry," *The Wall Street Journal*, May 6, 2016.

94. "A Quitter's Market: Electronic-Cigarette Sales Are Up and Big Tobacco Wants In," *Time*, January 21, 2013, 19.

95. Liz Szabo, "CDC Report: More Teens Toke from E-cigarettes," USA Today, April 17, 2015, 2A.

96. Mike Esterl and John Kell, "Big Tobacco Embraces E-Cigs," *Wall Street Journal*, April 26, 2013, B3; Trip Mickle, "States Dash to Regulate E-cigarettes," *The Wall Street Journal*, January 31–February 1, 2015, B4.

97. Food and Drug Administration, "FDA Takes Significant Step to Protect Americans from Dangers of Tobacco through New Regulation," May 5, 2016, http://www.fda.gov/NewsEvents/Newsroom/PressAnnouncements/ucm499234.htm. Accessed May 6, 2016.

98. Ibid.

99. "Campaign for Tobacco Free Kids," http://www.tobaccofreekids.org/facts_issues/tobacco_101/. Accessed May 4, 2016.

100. Ibid.

101. U.S. FDA, "Tobacco Products," April 19, 2016, http://www.fda.gov/TobaccoProducts/NewsEvents/ucm496722.htm. Accessed May 4, 2016.

102. Annie Gasparro, "Healthy Labeling on Food Gets New Scrutiny," *The Wall Street Journal*, May 11, 2016, B1.

103. Siobhan O'Conner, "The Gluten Wars," *Time*, June 15, 2015, 54.

104. Sarah Nassauer, "Cheerios Joins Gluten-Free Food-Label Craze," *The Wall Street Journal*, February 18, 2015, B5B.

105. Annie Gasparro, "General Mills Recalls Some Gluten-Free Cheerios," October 5, 2016, http://www.wsj.com/articles/general-mills-recalls-some-gluten-free-cheerios-that-may-contain-wheat-1444078360. Accessed May 11, 2016.

106. Alan Levinovitz, *The Gluten Lie: And Other Myths about What You Eat*, Regan Arts, 2015.

107. U.S. Food and Drug Administration, "Guidance for Industry: A Food Labeling Guide and Claims," http://www.fda.gov/Food/GuidanceRegulation/GuidanceDocumentsRegulatoryInformation/LabelingNutrition/ucm064908.htm. Accessed May 4, 2016.
108. "Regulating Health Food: The Proof Is in the Pudding," *The Economist* (October 31, 2009), 17–18; NCBI, "Health Claim Regulation of Probiotics in the US and EU: Is There a Middle Way?" March 1, 2013, http://www.ncbi.nlm.nih.gov/pubmed/23257017. Accessed May 4, 2016.
109. "Pepsi Gets a Makeover: Taking the Challenge," *The Economist* (March 27, 2010), 67.
110. Pepsico, http://www.pepsico.com/Purpose/Human-Sustainability/Product-Choices. Accessed May 4, 2016.
111. *The Economist*, 2010, ibid.
112. Federal Trade Commission, "Truth in Advertising: Health Claims," https://www.ftc.gov/news-events/media-resources/truth-advertising/health-claims. Accessed May 4, 2016.
113. Ibid.
114. Alan Henry, "What Does Organic Really Mean, and Is It Worth My Money?" http://lifehacker.com/5941881/what-does-organic-really-mean-and-should-i-buy-it. Accessed May 4, 2016.
115. Ibid.
116. Ibid.
117. "Natural vs. Organic," http://www.organicitsworthit.org/natural/natural-vs-organic. Accessed May 4, 2016.
118. Serena Ng, "Natural Product Claims Can Be Murky," *The Wall Street Journal*, March 30, 2016, B1.
119. USA Today Snapshots, *USA Today*, May 29, 2012, B1.
120. USA Today Snapshots, *USA Today*, March 8, 2012, 1B.
121. Edward Wyatt, "FTC Issues Guidelines for 'Eco-friendly' Labels," *The New York Times*, October 1, 2012, http://www.nytimes.com/2012/10/02/business/energy-environment/ftc-issues-guidelines-for-eco-friendly-labels.html. Accessed May 4, 2016.
122. Federal Trade Commission, "Green Guides," https://www.ftc.gov/news-events/media-resources/truth-advertising/green-guides. Accessed May 4, 2016.
123. Ibid.
124. Sara Randazzo, "FTC Sues Volkswagen over Its Clean Diesel Vehicle Advertising," *The Wall Street Journal*, March 30, 2016, B3.
125. Nathan Bomey, "Feds Seek $15B for VW Diesel Claims," *USA Today*, March 29, 2016, 1A.
126. Nathan Bomey, "Volkswagen Reaches Deal with Consumers," *USA Today*, April 22, 2016, B1.
127. Mashable, "Consumers Are Willing to Pay more for Sustainability," http://mashable.com/2014/06/30/sustainability-consumers/#si9J28i3gkqp. Accessed May 4, 2016.
128. Green-e, http://www.green-e.org/. Accessed May 5, 2016.
129. Nonprofit Chronicles, Marc Gunther, "Who's Watching the Environmental Watchdogs?" https://nonprofitchronicles.com/2015/05/17/whos-watching-the-environmental-watchdogs/. Accessed May 5, 2016.
130. "The Green Watchdogs," *Smartmoney* (April 2010).
131. Ibid.
132. Hank Campbell, "Climate Hype Gives Way to Green Fatigue," March 4, 2013, http://www.realclearpolitics.com/2013/03/04/climate_hype_gives_way_to_quotgreen_fatiguequot_303214.html. Accessed May 5, 2016.
133. Megan Basham, "Green Fatigue," *World* (March 27, 2010), 59–60.
134. Debra L. Scammon and Jenny Mish, "From Green Marketing to Marketing for Environmental Sustainability," in Pratima Bansal and Andrew J. Hoffman (editors), *The Oxford Handbook of Business and the Natural Environment*, 2012 (Oxford: Oxford University Press), 347–402.
135. Ibid., 353.
136. Carrie McLaren, "Ad Creep," *Print* (November/December 2000), 102–107.
137. "Inserting Advertisements into Video Games Holds Much Promise," *The Economist* (June 9, 2007), 73–74.
138. Ibid.
139. "Ad-Creep Creep Is Getting Creepier," March 17, 2013, http://www.buzzfeed.com/copyranter/ad-creep-creep-is-getting-creepier. Accessed May 5, 2016.
140. MediaPost, "The New Frontier: Social Media and Deceptive Advertising," May 11, 2015, http://www.mediapost.com/publications/article/249403/the-new-frontier-social-media-and-deceptive-adver.html. Accessed May 13, 2016.
141. Ibid.
142. Ibid.
143. AP The Big Story, "Lord & Taylor Settles Charges of Deception Instagram Posts," March 15, 2016, http://bigstory.ap.org/article/167017a757c0425bbe35903c702070e0/lord-taylor-settles-charges-deceptive-instagram-posts. Accessed May 13, 2016.
144. Diffen, "Guarantee vs. Warrantee," http://www.diffen.com/difference/Guarantee_vs_Warranty. Accessed May 5, 2016.
145. Ibid.
146. "A Businessperson's Guide to Federal Warranty Law," Federal Trade Commission, http://business.ftc.gov/documents/bus01-businesspersons-guide-federal-warranty-law. Accessed May 5, 2016.
147. "The Guesswork on Warranties," *Businessweek* (July 15, 1975), 51; "Marketing: Anti-Lemon Aid," *Time* (February, 1976), 76.
148. Ibid.
149. "Stores Make Big Profits on Warranties You Don't Need. Here's a Look at Some of the Hooey You Shouldn't Heed," *Consumer Reports Buying Guide* (2007), 8.
150. Ibid.

151. Neal Templin, "Please Spare Me the Extended Warranty," *The Wall Street Journal* (October 14, 2009), D1.
152. US News Money, "6 Reasons Why You Should Never Purchase an Extended Warranty," April 24, 2012, http://money.usnews.com/money/blogs/my-money/2012/04/24/6-reasons-why-you-should-never-purchase-an-extended-warranty. Accessed May 6, 2016.
153. L.L.Bean, http://www.llbean.com/. Accessed May 6, 2016.
154. PrestaShop, Kate Robinson, "The Ins and Outs of Warranties and Return Policies for Ecommerce Stores," September 1, 2015, https://www.prestashop.com/blog/en/ins-outs-warranties-returns-policies-ecommerce-stores/. Accessed May 6, 2016.
155. "Don't Even Think about Returning That Dress," *Bloomberg Businessweek*, September 30–October 6, 2013, 29.
156. "Fair Packaging and Labeling Act," *Federal Trade Commission*, https://www.ftc.gov/enforcement/rules/rulemaking-regulatory-reform-proceedings/fair-packaging-labeling-act. Accessed May 6, 2016.
157. Annie Gasparro, "Food Firms Tackle Labeling," *The Wall Street Journal*, December 3, 2015, B3.
158. Priya Anard, "A hunger for Better Food Labels," *The Wall Street Journal*, February 16, 2016, R5.
159. Ibid.
160. Annie Gasparro, "Food Firms Tackle Labeling," *The Wall Street Journal*, December 3, 2015, B3.
161. Ibid.
162. Ibid.
163. Paul Ziobro, "Same Package, Same Price, Less Product," *The Wall Street Journal*, June 12, 2015, B1.
164. Ibid.
165. Ibid.
166. Carrie Bradon, "Consumer Sues McCormick & Co. Alleging Slack Filling and Unfair Trade Practices," Penn Record, January 6, 2015, http://pennrecord.com/stories/510655023-consumer-sues-mccormick-co-inc-alleging-slack-filling-and-unfair-trade-practices. Accessed May 6, 2016.
167. Serena Ng, "P&G Backs Off Puffed-up Packages," *The Wall Street Journal*, July 8, 2015, B1.
168. Annie Gasparro, "Whole Foods Sales Sour after Pricing Scandal," *The Wall Street Journal*, July 30, 2016, B1.
169. Associated Press, "Lawsuit: Starbuck's Overfills Cold Drinks with Ice," Atlanta Journal Constitution, May 3, 2016, A2.
170. Federal Trade Commission, "History of the FTC," http://www.ftc.gov/ftc/about.shtm. Accessed May 6, 2016.
171. Ibid.
172. Ibid.
173. Jim Edwards, "FTC Chief Majoras Offers a (Laissez) Faire Deal," *Brandweek* (February 5, 2007), 9.
174. Ibid.
175. Natasha Singer, "The Government's Consumer Data Watchdog," *The New York Times*, May 24, 2015, 3 BU.
176. Ibid.
177. Federal Trade Commission, Jessica Rich, "BCP's Office of Technology Research and Investigation: The Next Generation in Consumer Protection," https://www.ftc.gov/news-events/blogs/business-blog/2015/03/bcps-office-technology-research-investigation-next. Accessed May 6, 2016.
178. Singer, ibid.
179. Ibid.
180. Josh Mitchell and Brent Kendall, "FTC Sues DeVry over Ads," *The Wall Street Journal*, January 28, 2016, B2.
181. Consumer Financial Protection Bureau, "The Credit Card Act," http://www.consumerfinance.gov/credit-cards/credit-card-act/. Accessed May 6, 2016.
182. Ibid.
183. "First, Slap Limits on Bank Leverage," *Bloomberg Businessweek* (March 22, 29, 2010), 26–27.
184. Sewell Chan, "Consumer Groups Urge Regulation of Nonbank Financial Institutions," *The New York Times* (March 6, 2010), B3.
185. Bob Herbert, "Derailing Help for Consumers," *The New York Times* (March 27, 2010), A17.
186. Consumer Financial Protection Bureau, "Standing up for You," http://www.consumerfinance.gov/. Accessed May 6, 2016.
187. Kyrsten Sinema and Randy Neugebauer, "Depoliticizing Elizabeth Warren's Pet Project," *The Wall Street Journal*, October 15, 2015, A13.
188. "The Consumer Bureau Cover-Up," *The Wall Street Journal*, December 10, 2015, A14.
189. Ibid.
190. Ramesh Ponnuru, "CFPB Proves Its Critics Right," February 25, 2015, *Bloomberg View*, http://www.bloomberg.com/view/articles/2015-02-25/cfpb-proves-its-critics-right. Accessed May 7, 2016.
191. Massimo Calabresi, "The Agency That's Got Your Back," *Time*, August 24, 2015, 40–47.
192. John F. Pickering and D. C. Cousins, *The Economic Implications of Codes of Practice* (Manchester, England: University of Manchester Institute of Science and Technology, Department of Management Sciences, 1980), 17. Also see J. J. Boddewyn, "Advertising Self-Regulation: Private Government and Agent of Public Policy," *Journal of Public Policy and Marketing* (1985), 129.
193. Better Business Bureau, "National Advertising Division," https://www.bbb.org/council/the-national-partner-program/national-advertising-review-services/national-advertising-division/. Accessed May 7, 2016.
194. Ibid.
195. Advertising Industry Self-Regulation, http://www.asrcreviews.org/supporting-advertising-industry-self-regulation/. Accessed May 7, 2016.
196. Edwards, 9.
197. Better Business Bureau, 2016, ibid. Accessed May 7, 2016.

14

Consumer Stakeholders: Product and Service Issues

CHAPTER LEARNING OUTCOMES

After studying this chapter, you should be able to:

1. Describe and discuss the two major product/service issues—quality and safety.
2. Explain the role and functions of the Consumer Product Safety Commission (CPSC).
3. Explain the role and functions of the Food and Drug Administration (FDA).
4. Outline business's responses to consumer stakeholders, including customer service programs, and quality initiatives such as Total Quality Management (TQM), Six Sigma, Lean Six Sigma, Kaizen, and ISO 9000.

Sam Walton, founder of Walmart, got it right when he said, "There is only one boss. The customer. And he can fire everybody in the company from the chairman on down, simply by spending his money somewhere else." This is why important new books such as *The Customer of Tomorrow* (2016) are gaining in popularity. As the authors point out, customers today have more access to information and, at a click or a swipe, they may make their decisions.[1] Therefore, the consumer is more empowered than they have ever been before to weigh in on the quality and safety of products.

Product information, as discussed in the previous chapter, is a pivotal issue between business and consumer stakeholders, but product and service issues such as *quality* and *safety* are more central to consumers' concerns. In other words, the product or service *itself* is a more compelling issue than information about it. The quest to improve product and service quality has been driven by the demands of a competitive global marketplace and an increasingly sophisticated consumer base. With product safety, an additional driving force has been the threat of product liability lawsuits and the damage these can inflict upon both the balance sheet and the reputation. The marketers' challenge has been to meet these market-driven needs as well as the social and ethical expectations consumers have of them.

Two recent cases illustrate how the issue of product safety can become urgent to consumers and costly to companies. First is the case of Takata air bag ruptures, and, second is the case of Johnson & Johnson's talc powder being implicated in cancer cases.

Japanese auto supplier, Takata, has not historically been a high-profile name known to the average consumer. But, now it is becoming so. Many of today's autos are equipped with Takata manufactured air bags, which have taken on monumental importance because of the safety issues involved. The defective air bags have been seen to be at risk of rupturing violently in collisions and throwing fiery shrapnel into drivers and passengers.[2] In early 2016, bursting air bags were linked to 10 deaths (9 in the United States) and dozens of injuries worldwide.[3] First, 29 million air bags were implicated and recalled. Then, another 40 million rupture-prone air bags were ordered to be recalled. The Takata recall is being called the biggest in U.S. history.[4]

In a recent analysis of the Takata crisis, Knowledge@Wharton observed that Takata has a "broken safety culture."[5] The National Highway Traffic Safety Administration is estimating that 24 million vehicles are affected by the recall involving more than 14 different auto makers. In short, we are now talking about a large percentage of the air bags in the U.S. vehicle population possibly being recalled as dangerous and needing replacement. The escalating numbers of recalls are causing experts to say that Takata's corporate survival is at stake.[6]

Lawsuits against Johnson & Johnson's talc powder seem to be increasing as well. J&J is appealing two lawsuits in which a total of $127 million in jury verdicts have been awarded to women who have blamed their ovarian cancer on the use of the company's iconic baby power.[7] Though still under appeal, the verdicts point to the possible linkage between use of the product and ovarian cancer. The link to date has yielded mixed results, but when juries get the evidence presented, they often are inclined to side with the alleged injured party. In May 2016, J&J reported that it is facing 1,400 lawsuits involving its baby power. For J&J, the threats that have been posed by current and future lawsuits are significant. Though the company has long had a record of outstanding corporate social responsibility, the recent lawsuits are coming on the heels of other product liability lawsuits involving off-label prescription drug marketing, faulty hip and knee parts, and consumer product recalls of children's Tylenol.[8]

The Takata and J&J cases illustrate vividly how a company's products can cause serious life and health consequences for consumers and financial and reputational harm to the company that may take years to overcome. And, most relevant here, it was all because of quality and safety issues in their widely respected products.

Consumers face many issues with companies, their products, and their marketing, but this chapter focuses the discussion on product quality and safety issues. Product quality is both a business and an ethical issue. In connection with safety, we examine the product liability issue and the ongoing calls for tort reform. The Consumer Product Safety Commission (CPSC) and the Food and Drug Administration (FDA) are the government's primary regulatory bodies with respect to these issues and they are also discussed. Finally, business's responses to consumer stakeholders regarding the manufacturing and marketing issues introduced both in Chapter 13 and in this chapter are considered.

14.1 Two Central Issues: Quality and Safety

The two central issues—quality and safety—in this chapter represent the overwhelming attention given to product and service issues over the past decade. As the Takata and J&J examples so clearly suggest, quality and safety are not separate concepts—safety is one aspect of quality. Its importance, however, merits separate attention.

14.1a The Issue of Quality

The concept of *product* quality means different things to different people. Some consumers are interested in the composition and design of a product. Others are more concerned with the product's features, functionality, and durability. All are essential aspects of quality. In general, quality is considered the totality of characteristics and features of a product and may embrace both reality and perceptions of excellence, conformance to specifications, value, and the degree to which the product meets or exceeds the consumer's expectations.

With respect to *service* quality, customers are typically concerned that the service is performed the way expected or advertised, that it is completed on time, that all that was promised has been delivered, that courtesy was extended by the provider, and that the service was easily obtained and consistent from use to use. Some of these issues involve personal judgment and perception, and so one can see how difficult it often is to judge quality.

There are several important reasons for the current and ongoing obsession with product and service quality. A concern for quality has been driven by the average consumer household's family income and consequent demand for good value. With both adults often working outside the home, consumers expect a higher lifestyle. In addition, no one has surplus time to hang around repair shops or wait at home for service representatives to show up. This results in a need for products to work as they should, to be durable and long lasting, and to be easy to maintain and fix.

The Internet, and social media in particular, has also made it possible for customers to communicate immediately with other customers about their satisfaction, or dissatisfaction, with a product, and this has heightened consumers' exchange of information and expectations. Companies such as TripAdvisor, Yelp, and Citysearch depend heavily on consumer reviews as part of their quest to keep quality up and to inform consumers interested in other customer's experiences. One downside to this has been revelations that an industry of fibbers and promoters has arisen to sell positive recommendations and raves for a price.

Closely related to rising household expectations is the global competitiveness that has dominated business transactions for the last decade or more. Businesses now compete in a hypercompetitive landscape in which multinational strategies have given way to global strategies, and the solutions that once worked no longer will.[9] As firms jockey for position in these hypercompetitive markets, they vie to attract customers by increasing the value of the product or service.

Value can be a subjective calculation, but it typically refers to a comparison of the quality received for the price spent. A set of Bose Quiet Comfort Noise Cancelling Headphones that sell for $399 at some shops are expected to be of proportionally higher quality than the Monster Inspiration Noise Cancelling Headphones sold at Walmart for $75. To increase value, firms try to provide higher quality than their competitors for the same price, offer the same quality at a lower price, or some combination of the two.

Each time a competitor raises the quality and/or lowers the price, other competitors scramble to catch up, and the bar is raised.[10] The greater the competition, the more firms will be jockeying for position and the more often the bar will be raised. Firms that do not continually improve their quality are certain to be left behind. The above-mentioned stories about Takata and J&J show how quickly, in this highly competitive atmosphere, well-respected companies can derail. Once derailed, it is difficult to catch up because of a lag in reputations. Chipotle's food contamination case discussed earlier in the book illustrates clearly how long it can take for a company to snap back from a product safety or quality crisis. Often, consumer perceptions of quality do not catch up to actual changes in quality for years after the quality improvements have been made.[11]

Service Quality. It should be underscored that our discussion of quality here includes service as well as products. However, we will discuss service quality as a separate issue as well. The United States and many developed nations have visibly become more service-based in their economies, and poor quality of service has become one of the great consumer frustrations of all time. The American Customer Satisfaction Index measures customer satisfaction with purchasing, and this index has declined noticeably between 2013 and 2015 with the future uncertain.[12]

If we rely on anecdotal evidence, there seems to be more complaining about service quality than ever before. Obviously, this varies by industry sector but very few comments about excellent service quality seem to be heard today. In one outrageous case of customer dissatisfaction, an irate man returned his cell phone to the store where he bought it after he had proceeded to shoot it full of holes as he was angered over the store's unwillingness to fix a cracked screen that they said was not covered in his service plan.[13]

When returning his shot up phone, the customer could not get anyone to wait on him, so he left his phone in a bag on the counter, left the store, and sat and watched to see what would happen next. The store called the police, they came, and the customer admitted it was a stupid thing to do but he was upset and mad at the store for their lack of service.[14] No charges were filed.

On the front line of the new economy, service—fast and customized—is now the ultimate strategic business imperative. Consumers today often swap horror stories about poor service as a kind of ritualistic, cathartic exercise. Consider the following typical examples: repeated trips to the car dealer; poor installation of refrigerator ice makers, resulting in several visits from repair people; poor customer service from the cable company; fouled-up travel reservations; poorly installed carpeting; no clerk at the shoe department of your favorite department store; and on and on. Shoddy service comes at a price. One study showed that 54 percent of the people interviewed would lose all loyalty to a company that had rude or unhelpful staff. One in ten said they would walk away if a company did not seem to listen.[15]

When business executives are asked about the quality of their customer service, they generally indicate they think they are doing a good job, but only about 20 to 30 percent think they are doing an excellent job.[16] According to a 2015 *Forbes'* survey, a few of the key findings in the arena of customer service were as follows[17]:

- Modern customer service is entrenched in most companies—and many think they are doing it really well, better than their peers.
- At the same time, serving customers is not given the weight it deserves. Organizations may not be fully grasping its full importance and impact as part of a corporate strategy beyond customer retention.
- Companies may be reluctant to move outside their customer service comfort zone.
- Companies are using newer technologies and striving to provide a seamless multichannel experience, but still feel most comfortable with traditional channels.

The survey's findings seem to suggest there is a gap between how companies think they are performing and how the consumer thinks they are responding. One "blind spot" pointed out in the report itself was that the companies report a contradictory desire to learn about customer needs while at the same time spending as little time with them as possible.[18]

ETHICS IN PRACTICE CASE

The Pirated Popcorn

Last year, I worked in a local movie theater to earn money during the summer. Part of my job was to clean the theater between showings, collecting discarded cups, napkins, and popcorn tubs. I thought it was odd when my manager asked that I empty and then bring him discarded popcorn tubs that were in fairly good shape. He would then reuse them—refilling them with popcorn for unsuspecting customers.

I soon learned that the theater paid for its popcorn concession by the number of tubs it used. By reusing the tubs, the theater was able to lower its costs. However, I was fairly certain that customers would have been upset if they knew what was happening (I knew that I would be).

1. How would you characterize the practice in which the movie theater engaged? Does this practice represent fair customer service? How are customers hurt or adversely affected?
2. Should I have followed my manager's orders and gone along with his request? Was it really such a terrible thing to do?

Dimensions of Quality. At least eight critical dimensions of product or service quality must be understood and acted upon if business is to respond strategically to this factor.[19] These include (1) performance, (2) features, (3) reliability, (4) conformance, (5) durability, (6) serviceability, (7) aesthetics, and (8) perception. *Performance* refers to a product's primary operating characteristics. For an automobile, this would include such items as handling, steering, and comfort. *Features* are the "bells and whistles" of products that supplement their basic functioning. *Reliability* reflects the probability of a product malfunctioning or failing. *Conformance* is the extent to which the product or service meets established standards.

Durability is a measure of product life. *Serviceability* refers to the speed, courtesy, competence, and ease of repair. *Aesthetics* is a subjective factor that refers to how the product looks, feels, tastes, and so on. Finally, *perceived quality* is a subjective inference that the consumer makes on the basis of a variety of tangible and intangible product characteristics. It should be emphasized that these quality dimensions are not distinct. Depending on the industry, situation, type of contract, or specification, several dimensions may be interdependent.[20] To address the issue of product or service quality, a manager must be astute enough to appreciate these different dimensions of quality and the subtle and dynamic interplays among them.

Ethical Underpinnings. An important question is whether quality is a social or an ethical issue or just a competitive factor that business needs to emphasize to be successful in the marketplace. For many consumers, quality is seen to be something more than just a business issue although it is definitely a business issue. Three ethical theories based on the concept of duty that informs our understanding of the ethical dimensions of quality include (1) contractual theory, (2) due care theory, and (3) social costs view. The **contractual theory** focuses on the contractual agreement between the firm and the customer. Firms have a responsibility to comply with the terms of the sale, inform the customers about the nature of the product, avoid misrepresentation of any kind, and not coerce the customers in any way. The **due care theory** focuses on the relative vulnerability of the customer, who has less information and expertise than the firm, and the ethical responsibility that places on the firm or its sales person. Customers must depend on the firm providing the product or service to live up to the claims about it and to exercise due care to avoid customer injury. The third view, **social costs view**, extends beyond contractual theory and due care theory to suggest that, if a product causes harm, the firm should pay the costs of any injury, even if the firm had met the terms of the contract, exercised all due care, and taken all reasonable precautions. This perspective serves as the underpinning for strict liability and its extension into absolute liability, which is discussed later.[21]

14.1b The Issue of Safety

Business clearly has a duty to consumer stakeholders to sell them safe products and services. The concept of safety, in a definitional sense, means "free from harm or risk" or "secure from threat of danger, harm, or loss."[22] Practically speaking, however, the use of virtually any consumer product or service entails some degree of risk or some chance that harm will come to the consumer who uses the product or service. Today, it is thought to be important that even financial services do not cause damage or financial harm. It is for this reason that the Consumer Financial Product Bureau discussed in Chapter 13 was passed. An important question that never goes away is "how safe" should a product be made? Difficult judgments about this question often thrust the issue of safety into the ethical category by many consumers.

SPOTLIGHT *on Sustainability*

Sustainable Products Meet Long-Term Market Needs

Companies today are seeking to develop sustainable products. Sustainable products are made to last for an indefinite period and have the least damaging effects on the environment. They are products providing environmental, social, and economic benefits as compared with other commercial products. An excellent example are the Levi's® Eco jeans by Levi Strauss Europe designed to tap into the consumers' interest in organic and sustainable products. Levi's also brought out a line of RECYCLED blue jeans.

Another example of a company that is promoting its sustainable products is Unilever. Unilever's *Sustainable Living Brands* are promoted as having both purpose and product in action. Unilever says that its program provides more growth, less cost, less risk, and more trust. Examples of products that the company promotes as sustainable brands include Dove soap, one of the first brands to offer compressed aerosol deodorants that reduce carbon food print; Knorr sauces, soups, and seasonings that use 100 percent sustainable sourcing; and Lipton teas that are sourced from Rainforest Alliance Certified estates. Unilever is striving to embed sustainability into its products, and the company is counting on its *Sustainable Living Brands* to drive current and future growth. Unilever has led its sector in the Dow Jones Sustainability World Indexes for 13 consecutive years.

Sources: "Levi's RECYCLED Blue Jeans," Maidsoftampa Blog, http://maidsoftampa.wordpress.com/2010/04/21/levis-recycled-blue-jeans/. Accessed May 8, 2016; Greenliving, "Levi's Recycled Blue Jeans," http://www.greenlivingonline.com/article/levi%E2%80%99s-recycled-blue-jeans. Accessed May 8, 2016; Unilever, Embedding Sustainability, https://www.unilever.com/sustainable-living/the-sustainable-living-plan/our-strategy/embedding-sustain ability/. Accessed May 13, 2016; Sustainable Brands, "Unilver," http://www.sustainablebrands.com/solution providers/unilever. Accessed May 13, 2016.

Throughout most of history the legal view that prevailed has been ***caveat emptor*** ("let the buyer beware"). The basic idea behind this concept was that the buyer had as much knowledge of what she or he wanted as the seller and, in any event, the marketplace would punish any violators. The caveat emptor doctrine gradually lost its favor and rationale, because it was frequently impossible for the consumer to have complete knowledge about manufactured goods.[23] In addition, the explosive increase in the number of lawyers and the emergence of a litigious society ensured that those harmed by products would have their day in court. Today, businesses are held responsible for all products placed on the market. Thus, we have the doctrine known as ***caveat vendor*** (or ***caveat venditor***)—"let the seller beware."[24]

Through a series of legal developments as well as changing societal values, business has become increasingly and significantly responsible for product safety. Court cases and legal doctrine now hold companies financially liable for harm to consumers. Yet this still does not answer the difficult question, "How safe are manufacturers obligated to make products?" It is not possible to make products totally "risk free"; experience has shown that consumers seem to have an uncanny ability to injure themselves in novel and creative ways, many of which cannot be anticipated. The challenge to management, therefore, is to make products as safe as possible while at the same time making them affordable and useful to consumers. And consumers today expect that if products are found to be unreasonably dangerous, they will be removed from market.

Figure 14-1 presents the top ten ways companies can emphasize safety and avoid product recalls.

Today the public is concerned about a variety of potential or perceived hazards, such as the rise in genetically modified foods and the dangers of living near toxic waste dumps or nuclear plants. Food and drug scares, both real and imagined, have occupied much of the public's attention in the past several years as questions have been raised about food safety all over the world.

FIGURE 14-1 Top Ten List of Product Safety Principles

The following product safety principles are straight-forward. These principles can be used by corporate decision makers and officials to give direction to their employees who have responsibility for product safety. These principles may also provide impetus to middle managers and all employees to suggest creative safety improvements for their company.

The Top Ten Product Safety Principles are:

1. Build safety into product design.
2. Do product safety testing for all foreseeable hazards.
3. Keep informed about and implement latest developments in product safety.
4. Educate consumers about product safety.
5. Track and address your products' safety performance.
6. Fully investigate product safety incidents.
7. Report product safety defects promptly.
8. If a defect occurs, promptly offer a comprehensive recall plan.
9. Work with the Consumer Product Safety Commission (CPSC) to make sure your recall is effective.
10. Learn from mistakes—yours and others'.

Source: U.S. Consumer Product Safety Commission, "Top Ten Product Safety Principles," http://www.cpsc.gov/en/Newsroom/News-Releases/2001/CPSC-Chairman-Ann-Brown-Unveils-Product-Safety-Initiative/. Accessed May 8, 2016.

Food Safety. In the United States, food safety issues, especially tainted or contaminated foods, have dominated the news for years recently and have been the safety issue most troubling to consumers.

In 2009, salmonella in peanut butter was blamed for nine deaths and Peanut Corporation of America (PCA) was charged with crimes linked to an alleged cover-up. In 2015, Stewart Parnell, the former CEO of PCA, received a 28-year prison sentence for his role in the salmonella-peanut case. The judge said the defendant broke the trust society places in food companies to assure that consumers are safe.[25] This was the toughest punishment in U.S. history for a food-borne illness case.[26] Since then, food recalls involving salmonella in eggs, listeriosis linked to cantaloupes, and peanut butter tainted by salmonella poisoning have been in the news.

One of the most recent and highly visible food recalls occurred with Blue Bell Creameries after a deadly listeria outbreak forced a massive recall of ice cream. As of 2016, the company claims that it only partly knew what went wrong. Blue Bell has stated that it now has programs in place to effectively control for the bacteria.[27] On top of these reports, Chipotle has been struggling to survive a food safety nightmare for quite some time now and its efforts to get back on track have been highly visible.[28]

In a special report titled "Contamination Nation," it has been stated that food-borne illness still gets 49 million consumers sick each year and this is costing the food industry billions of dollars annually.[29] The annual cost of treatment, lost productivity, and mortality has been estimated to be $56 billion. There has been a significant increase in both meat and nonmeat recalls in the past couple years. The main reasons for the recalls have been microbiological contamination, labeling issues, processing defects, physical contamination, chemical contamination, and unapproved ingredients.[30]

The government's regulation of food safety is primarily driven by the **Food Safety Modernization Act (FSMA) of 2011**, the most sweeping reform of U.S. food laws in 70 years. The FSMA is enforced by the FDA. The purpose of the legislation is to ensure that the food supply is safe by shifting from responding to contaminations to preventing them.[31] After a two-year delay in getting approvals, the FDA in 2015 tightened its food safety rules so that the above-mentioned FSMA could be more fully implemented.[32] The rule tightening focused on requiring companies to create and implement written plans for keeping food safe. Companies will have to identify hazards in manufacturing, create measures to reduce the risk of contamination, and design methods to verify that the controls are working. If they do not comply, then the FDA is authorized to access a company's plans and take action.[33]

Food safety advocates have complimented the new rules of the FDA because they attempt to transform a regulatory system that used to be mostly reactive to one that is focused on prevention of food contamination. The new rules were announced shortly after the Blue Bell ice cream company resumed sales following its recall earlier in the year. According to FDA records, Blue Bell did not have in place safety practices that might have prevented the listeria outbreak, including the implementation of a comprehensive food safety program that food manufacturers will now have to have in place because of the tighter FDA rules.[34]

In spite of the new FDA rules, it has been argued that the new regulations alone will not completely solve the problem because of the following four major issues[35]:

- Health officials can identify only a fraction of those who get food poisoning.
- Regulators have new tools but industry does not trust them.
- The consumer's food pantry is global and so are the chances for contamination.
- It is partially the fault of the consumers, too.

One writer on public health has argued that the rise in food contamination reports is actually a good thing because it means that the more we hear about it, the more the food supply will be getting safer.[36] The speed with which outbreaks have been identified, along with public notifications, has risen significantly. This is partially attributable to advances in the government's pathogen-tracking system, known as *PulseNet. PulseNet* has allowed regulators to get information faster and more accurately. The Blue Bell outbreak was only one of a number of different contaminations that were speeded up because of *PulseNet*. Previously, some contaminations took much longer or were not solvable without the new technology.[37]

Figure 14-2 lists some of the food safety issues that have been in the news. In some cases, these products were recalled voluntarily.

Other Safety Issues. Manufacturing is a high-profile industry for which product safety is of paramount concern, as the Takata and J&J recalls discussed earlier illustrate.

FIGURE 14-2 Food Safety Issues in the News

Company/Product	Food Safety Issue
Peanut Corporation of America	Deadly salmonella outbreak
Chipotle Mexican Grill	*E. coli* outbreak
Blue Bell Ice Cream	*Listeria* infections
Husi Foods (Shanghai meat supplier to many U.S. restaurants)	Repackaging expired meat (beef, chicken) products and selling to restaurants
Multiple suppliers	Arsenic in rice, juice, and beer
Pilgrim's Pride	Chicken contamination with multiple materials
Twin City Foods	Frozen organic peas and mixed vegetables possibly contaminated with Listeria
CRF Frozen Foods	Frozen fruits and vegetables contaminated with strains of listeria
4 Frendz Beef Jerky	Possible undercooking; possible bacteria
General safety issues	Foodborne illnesses, food contaminants, pesticide exposure, antibiotic resistance, environmental effects

ETHICS IN PRACTICE CASE

Was "Pink Slime" a Victim of Social Media Frenzy?

The "pink slime" case has been called a cautionary tale of what can happen to a company that gets involved in a hot button issue when challenged by a contingent of online tweeters with social media accounts.

In the early 1990s, Eldon Roth started a meat processing company named Beef Products, Inc. (BPI). The company would buy tons of fatty meat scrap that was left over after cattle were carved into steaks and roasts. Roth developed a centrifuge that would spin the fat away. The remaining product was then treated with a puff of ammonia hydroxide as a safety measure to kill bacteria. Then he would quick freeze the remaining meat into a pink pulp that when mixed in with ground beef made it leaner. This product became known as "lean finely textured beef" or LFTB in the industry. Roth's company would then package the product in the form of frozen bricks and sell them to companies as an additive to ground beef, making the resulting beef leaner and cheaper. Among others, McDonald's, Burger King, Taco Bell, Kroger, and Wal-Mart would then use the product.

Roth's company was so successful that it opened plants in Kansas, Texas, Iowa, and Nebraska, employing about 1,500 workers. In fall, 2011, Roth was inducted into the Meat Industry Hall of Fame. Roth had been called a genius who ran a company that was on the vanguard of food safety.

In March 2012, someone labeled Roth's product "pink slime" and a food blogger launched an online petition to have it removed from the federal lunch program. ABC News and other media jumped on the story and soon the product was being assailed as unsafe and gross as the story went viral on the blogosphere. On Twitter, uses of the term *pink slime* rapidly occurred and went on for several months. As the social media frenzy increased, many customers quickly abandoned his product and Roth was forced to suspend production at three plants and lay off half his workers. After the ABC News reports, BPI initiated an extensive PR campaign seeking to get the truth out. BPI also filed a $1.2 billion lawsuit against ABC News and the reporters. The company claimed over 200 false or disparaging statements were made about BPI.

In the United States, pink slime eventually came back in favor as beef prices soared and retailers began seeking cheaper trimmings.

For the record, LFTB is not an unsafe product even in the eyes of food safety advocates. It is an ingredient we have all eaten many times. The USDA insisted the product was safe but would let schools choose whether to buy meat with or without the textured beef. Iowa Governor Terry Branstad, whose state hosts a BPI plant, said he would call for a congressional investigation of the "smear campaign" against BPI.

1. How can a product that has been characterized as "lean" and less expensive be treated in this way?
2. Do you think LFTB and Roth's company has been treated fairly? Has this product gotten a bad rap by overzealous social media critics?
3. Should those who labeled the product "pink slime" and questioned it unfairly be disciplined in any way? Or, is this just the social media "market at work" and nothing should be done?
4. What should Roth and his company do now? What further action should the USDA, state governors, or other officials take to ensure fair treatment?
5. Should Beef Products, Inc., ramp up its online presence and become more adept at social media defense before this happens again?

Sources: "'Pink slime' uproar overshadows more serious food safety threats," USA Today, April 17, 2012, 8A; "Was a Food Innovator Unfairly Targeted?" *Bloomberg Businessweek*, April 16–April 22, 2012, 18–20; Josh Sanburn, "One Year Later, the Makers of 'Pink Slime' Are Hanging on and Fighting Back," *Time*, March 6, 2013, http://business.time.com/2013/03/06/one-year-later-the-makers-of-pink-slime-are-hanging-on-and-fighting-back/. Accessed May 9, 2016; Jacob Bunge and Kelsey Gee, "Pink Slime Back in Favor as Prices Soar for U.S. Beef," *The Wall Street Journal*, May 24–25, 2014, A1; Kristin Runge, "Pink Slimed: The Beef Industry Learns the Importance of Social Media Literacy," Wisconsin Public Radio, March 23, 2016, http://www.wpr.org/pink-slimed-beef-industry-learns-importance-social-media-literacy. Accessed May 9, 2016.

Other recent recalls have involved medical-device flaws such as defibrillator wires, surgical vaginal mesh, and metal hip joints.[38] Manufactured products create hazards not only because of unsafe product design but also as a result of consumers being given inadequate information regarding the hazards associated with using the products. Consequently, in product liability claims, it is not surprising to find charges based on one or more of several allegations. First, may be the charge that the product was *improperly manufactured*, wherein the producer failed to exercise due care in the product's production, which contributed directly to the accident or injury. Second, could be the charge that, though manufactured properly, the product's *design could have been defective*, in that alternative designs or devices, if used at the time of manufacture, may have prevented the accident. Third, could be that the producer failed to provide *satisfactory instructions and/or warnings* that could have helped avert accident or injury. Fourth, may be that the producer failed to *foresee a reasonable and anticipated misuse* of the product and warn against such misuse.[39]

To appreciate the "big picture" of dangerous products, it should be noted that the Consumer Product Safety Commission keeps track of injuries treated in hospital emergency rooms and has identified the following categories of consumer products as being the most frequently associated with hospital-treated injuries[40]:

- Sports and Recreation
- Toys and Children's Products
- Fuel, Lighters, and Fireworks
- Furniture & Décor
- Home Maintenance and Construction
- Kitchen & Dining

Whether we deal with consumer products (where there is potential for harm following accidents or misuse) or with food products (where not-so-visible threats to human health may exist), the field of product safety is a significant responsibility and a growing challenge for the business community. No matter how careful business is with regard to these issues, the threat of product liability lawsuits has become an industry unto itself and intimately linked with product safety discussions. Therefore, we now turn our attention to this vital topic. Product liability has been a monumental consumer issue in the United States for many decades.

14.1c Product Liability

In recent years, the product liability issue (sometimes called products liability), has been one of the most important legal and ethical responsibilities businesses have faced. What is at stake is the responsibility for harm caused by products. **Product liability**, as a legal concept, includes the liability of any or all parties in the chain of manufacture and sale of a product and for any damage caused by that product. This includes the manufacture, assembly, wholesaling, and retailing of the product. Products containing defects that result in harm to a consumer or someone to whom the product was loaned or given are the subjects of product liability lawsuits.[41]

Reasons for Concern about Product Liability. Product, or products, liability has become a major issue because of the *sheer number of cases* involving products that have resulted in illness, harm, or death. More than in other countries, U.S. residents tend to file lawsuits and pursue litigation when faced with situations in which they are harmed or dissatisfied.

Another cause for concern has been the *size of the financial awards* that have been given by the courts. Some of the largest U.S. product liability cases in recent years have included the following well-known companies. General Motors, in response to several of its automobiles being manufactured with faulty ignition switches leading to accidents and deaths, has faced liability lawsuits exceeding $400 million and is still involved in one class action lawsuit that is asking for $10 billion.[42] Another huge product liability lawsuit was against Philip Morris, now known as Altria Group. The company was sued for $28 billion by a woman claiming its cigarettes had caused her sickness and that her tobacco addiction was the company's fault. The company settled for $28 million after fighting the case for nine years.[43]

Dow Corning reached a settlement in which it agreed to pay $2 billion as part of a larger $4.5 billion class action lawsuit filed by customers who claimed their silicone breast implants were rupturing, causing bodily injury, bodily damage, scleroderma, and death.[44] It has been estimated that litigation's *cost to society* is over $250 billion per year, more than half of which goes to legal fees and costs, some of which could be spent to hire more teachers, police officers, and fire fighters.[45] The cost of litigation to companies has been said to represent approximately 30 percent of a stepladder's price, 50 percent of a football helmet, and 95 percent of the price of a childhood vaccine. The problem is largely confined to the United States, which is a litigious society.[46] One major study showed that the money firms now pay on lawsuit settlements, damage awards, insurance lawyers, and legal defense costs is money they no longer have available to spend on improvements in their processes and products. This *decrease in innovation* due to tort litigation carries lasting consequences for competitiveness.[47]

Doctrine of Strict Liability. Though one should consult law books and lawyers for all of the intricacies and complexities of legal concepts, it is useful to have an overview of what the basic concepts mean. The key legal concept in product liability cases is the **doctrine of strict liability**. In its most general form, the doctrine of strict liability holds that anyone in the value chain of a product is liable for harm caused to the user if the product as sold was unreasonably dangerous because of its defective condition. This applies to anyone involved in the design, manufacture, or sale of a defective product. Beyond manufacturing, courts have ruled against plaintiffs from a broad array of functions, such as selling, advertising, promotion, and distribution.[48]

As an example, the department of transportation (DOT) holds warehouses liable for violations of hazardous materials regulations even when the warehouse relied on information provided by the customer (the depositor) when documenting the shipment.[49] In short, there is no legal defense for placing on the market a product that is dangerous to a consumer because of a known or knowable defect, unless the strict liability is imposed by a statute that allows for an argument of due diligence.[50] To prove due diligence, a company must take every possible precautionary step and follow all industry standards.

The doctrine of strict liability and the expansion of this concept in the courts have been at the heart of the litigation explosion in the United States. As mentioned previously, the social costs view of product quality underlies the concept of strict liability and its extensions. In addition, some hold the strict liability view as utilitarian; that is, society has made a determination that it is better to hold persons responsible for certain actions even without a showing of negligence because the benefits derived (e.g., safety, improved products, accountability) outweigh the burden placed on the defendant in a strict liability lawsuit. In the area of consumer product development, strict liability laws have fostered meaningful safety developments that have prevented innumerable deaths and injuries. Strict liability is not without its cost, however, and the price of consumer goods today reflects this cost-shifting consequence.[51]

Extensions of Strict Liability Rule. Courts in several states and certain countries have established a standard that is much more demanding than strict liability. This concept is known as **absolute liability**. The ruling that established this concept was handed down by the New Jersey Supreme Court in *Beshada v. Johns Manville Corporation* (1982). The plaintiffs in the Beshada case were employees of Johns Manville and other companies who had developed asbestos-related diseases as a result of workplace exposure.[52] The court ruled in this case that a manufacturer could be held *strictly liable* for failure to warn of a product hazard, even if the hazard was scientifically unknowable at the time of manufacture and sale. Therefore, a company cannot use as its defense the claim that it did its best according to the state of the art in the industry at that time. Under this ruling, the manufacturer is liable for damages even if it had no way of knowing that the product might cause a problem later. This led to what *The Wall Street Journal* termed the *asbestos tort blob*, named for the movie *The Blob* that devours everything in its path.[53] Although the United States has been rightly termed the litigation nation, other countries struggle with the issue as well. For example, the Supreme Court of India upheld the absolute liability of a common carrier, in this case Patel Roadways Ltd., for goods destroyed by fire. The court ruled that, in the case of damage or loss, it is not necessary for the plaintiff to establish negligence.[54]

Another extension of strict liability is known as **market share liability**. This concept evolved from **delayed manifestation cases**—situations in which delayed reactions to products appear years later after consumption of, or exposure to, the product.[55] Market share liability was derived from the California case in which a group of women with birth defects claimed that the defects had been caused by the drug DES, which their mothers had taken while pregnant years earlier. The women could not name the company that had made the pills their mothers had taken. But, the California Supreme Court upheld a ruling that the six drug firms that made DES would be held responsible in proportion to their market shares of DES sales unless they could prove that they had not made the actual doses the women had taken.[56] Market share liability is not used much today, but it is a constant threat for firms in situations in which it might apply. One reason it is not used as often now is because, in market share liability cases, the awarding of punitive damages is not permitted.[57]

Product liability law can be extremely complex and managers should seek legal advice when faced with uncertain situations. The recommended course of action, of course, is to create safe products and be guided by law and ethics in all phases of the design, production, and distribution process. As part of their social and ethical responsibilities, companies might elect to develop a **product liability risk management program**.[58] Five steps may be followed in such a program.

- First, transfer risk through management of suppliers. This helps the business avoid financial vulnerability to damages and claims due to liabilities caused or contributed by others.
- Second, manage supplies and imported goods. Companies that import products and components later provided to an end user may bear responsibility for safety requirements. The company may be responsible for assuring that the imported product complies with applicable industry standards and government regulations and documenting that proper safety warnings, labels, and instructions are provided to the end user.[59]
- Third, companies should build safety into the product's design. Hazards may often be eliminated in the product design stage.
- Fourth, the company should keep essential records for documentation purposes should product liability issues arise.
- Fifth, enable and review customer feedback. If the company makes it easy for customers to share their concerns, they will have information that may improve on product exposures and issues.[60]

Product Tampering and Product Extortion. Two other concerns that have contributed to the product liability risks that companies face are *product tampering* and *product extortion*. The most well-known case of product tampering involved Tylenol in the 1980s—first in 1982, when seven Chicago people died from taking tainted Tylenol® Extra Strength capsules, and again in 1986, when cyanide-laced bottles of Tylenol were found in New York, and one woman died. James Burke, J&J chairperson at the time, characterized the case as "terrorism, pure and simple."[61] In response to these and other incidents, firms began to employ tamper-evident packaging. Although improvements in packaging have slowed the rate of pharmaceutical product tampering, they have not stopped it. In addition to the Tylenol case, other notable cases of product tampering have involved Jell-O pudding, bottled water, oranges, candy, baby food, and Girl Scout cookies.[62] In addition to invading packaging, there are other approaches to product tampering as well. In 2016, a man walked into a Michigan Whole Foods Market and sprinkled a mysterious substance on the grocery store's buffet. An observant employee saw the incident and all of the food was thrown away. The FBI is still seeking the perpetrator.[63]

After the 9/11 terrorist attacks, product-tampering concerns centered on anthrax and the possible ways it could be used for extortion and terror. When attorneys at Stoel Rives in Portland, Oregon, mailed 50,000 cards in envelopes with bumpy seeds, some recipients became so scared they dialed 911. Publisher's Clearinghouse mailed packages of powdered detergent to customers, causing alarm in the process.[64] Now that the furor over mail has subsided, attention has shifted to ways in which terrorists might tamper with the food or water supply. Since the 9/11 attacks, food companies have spent hundreds of millions of dollars to upgrade security, institute employee background checks, and install lights and video cameras.[65] In spite of these efforts, some incidents continue to occur.[66]

Product extortion occurs when someone threatens to damage, destroy, or contaminate products in an effort to leverage ransom monies from the affected companies.[67] Though there have not been many recent cases in the United States, product extortions have occurred around the world in a variety of markets. The problem has occurred frequently enough, however, that insurance companies now exist that specialize in product extortion insurance.[68] Unlike product tampering and contamination, product extorters do not try to do reputational harm to the company. They are typically just interested in ransom from the company.[69]

Product Liability Reform. The problems discussed up to this point have combined to generate calls from many groups for **product liability reform**, also known as **tort reform**. A tort is an act that injures someone in some way and for which the injured person may sue the wrongdoer for damages. Legally, torts are civil wrongs, not criminal wrongs.[70] The U.S. tort system costs Americans hundreds of billions of dollars every year. Built into the price of every product is a component to pay for liability insurance and lawsuit defense. Tort risks are the second most important factor when a company decides where to relocate or expand operations or build a new plant or introduce a new product.[71]

With the recent changes in health-care law, many experts believe that changes in tort law are also needed as part of the process of bringing health-care costs under control. However, not everyone agrees that tort reform is needed. On one side are business groups, medical associations, local and state governments, and insurance companies that want to change the system that they claim gives costly and unfair advantage to plaintiffs in liability suits. On the other side are consumer groups and trial lawyers who defend the current system as one that protects the constitutional rights of wrongfully injured parties.[72]

The business community's criticisms of the current system illustrate some of the aspects of the controversy. Currently, there is a patchwork of state laws, with the law varying significantly from state to state. Business wants a uniform federal code to govern product liability. It also argues for no punitive damages unless the plaintiff meets tougher standards of proof because meeting government standards is no defense in most states. Business thinks it should have an absolute shield against punitive damages for drugs, medical devices, and aircraft that meet government regulations. Business also wants a cap placed on how high punitive awards can be. Finally, business wants victorious plaintiffs to be able to recover damages only to the extent that defendants are liable.[73]

On the other side of the issue are consumer and citizen groups and others who support the current system and say the critics of the product liability laws have exaggerated the problems. These supporters of the current system point out that some of the most infamous injuries inflicted on consumers were remedied mainly through lawsuits, not regulatory action. Examples include the Dalkon Shield, a contraceptive device that made thousands of women infertile; the Pinto's exploding gas tank; the damage to workers exposed to asbestos; tobacco cases; and many lesser-known cases.[74] To be sure, the health-care arena is one of the primary stages upon which the tort system's reform is being played out. According to Ralph Nader, trial lawyers are "all that is left to require wrongdoers to be held accountable."[75]

The debate over product liability reform is ongoing. Business claims the current system is inherently inefficient, raises the costs of litigation, and imposes a hidden tax on consumers because it inhibits innovation and dampens competitiveness. Consumer groups argue that the current system has forced companies to make safer products and listen to their customers. Studies show that both sides have valid arguments. The laws have spurred some safety improvements, but they have also hampered innovation.[76] The American Tort Reform Association (ATRA) has been working for decades to bring about modifications in product liability legislation. ATRA is an organization that represents a nationwide network of state-based liability reform coalitions back by many grassroots supporters. The issue of tort reform is so heated, controversial, and complex, however, that very little progress seems to be made.[77] From an ethical perspective, if businesses internalize the notion of product safety and take responsibility for the products and services they sell, the need for legal redress is precluded and the entire business–consumer relationship is far better served.

There are two major government agencies that are dedicated to product safety and both of them have become more activist in recent years—the Consumer Product Safety Commission and the Food and Drug Administration.

14.2 Consumer Product Safety Commission

The **Consumer Product Safety Commission (CPSC)** is an independent regulatory agency that was created by the Consumer Product Safety Act of 1972. CPSC works to reduce the risk of injuries and deaths from consumer products by[78]:

1. developing voluntary standards with industry,
2. issuing and enforcing mandatory standards,
3. banning consumer products if no feasible standard would adequately protect the public,
4. obtaining the recall of products or arranging for their repair,
5. conducting research on potential product hazards, and
6. informing and educating consumers through the media, state and local governments, private organizations, and by responding to consumer inquiries.

Figure 14-3 summarizes the Mission, Vision, and Goals of the CPSC for the period 2011–2016. This strategic plan represents the initiatives the CPSC has in place and continues to implement.

FIGURE 14-3 Consumer Product Safety Commission (CPSC) Strategic Plan–2011-2016

MISSION	Protecting the public against unreasonable risks of injury from consumer products through education, safety standards activities, regulation, and enforcement.
VISION	The CPSC is the recognized global leader in consumer product safety.
	GOALS
Goal 1	**Leadership in Safety** Take a leadership role in identifying and addressing the most pressing consumer product safety priorities and mobilizing action by our partners.
Goal 2	**Commitment to Prevention** Engage public and private sector stakeholders to build safety into consumer products.
Goal 3	**Rigorous Hazard Identification** Ensure timely and accurate detection of consumer product safety risks to inform agency priorities.
Goal 4	**Decisive Response** Use the CPSC's full range of authorities to quickly remove hazards from the marketplace.
Goal 5	**Raising Awareness** Promote a public understanding of product risks and CPSC capabilities.

Source: U.S. Consumer Product Safety Commission Strategic Plan–2011-2016, http://www.cpsc.gov//PageFiles/123374/2011strategic.pdf. Accessed May 11, 2016.

The CPSC was created at the zenith of the consumer movement as a result of initiatives taken in the late 1960s. Over the decades, the CPSC has experienced ups and downs and various degrees of activism as various administrations came into office. During some administrations, it was significantly bolstered in its power and budget, and during other administrations, it was downplayed and underemphasized. As with all government agencies, their directors are appointed by the presidents in office at the time and their powers are greatly affected by the budgets given them by Congress.

During the Obama Administration, the CPSC has been more activist and has introduced a number of new priorities including an official blog titled *OnSafety* (http://www.cpsc.gov/onsafety/) that reports the latest product safety information that consumers might need. By 2016, some of the product safety issues being carefully monitored by the CPSC included defective humidifiers, portable hook-on chairs for children, architectural glazing materials, pool and spa drain entrapments, harmful toys, and other dangerous children's products.[79] On a regular basis, the CPSC is actively engaged in product recalls, safety education, regulations, laws, and standards.[80] Consumers may now connect with CPSC safety warnings and other information on YouTube, Twitter, and GooglePlus, as well as through RSS Feeds, Podcasts, and the OnSafety blog.[81]

The **Consumer Product Safety Improvement Act (CPSIA) of 2008** is the most recent and comprehensive piece of legislation given to the CPSC for enforcement. This act provided the CPSC with new regulatory and enforcement tools. CPSIA addresses, among other things, lead, phthalates, toy safety, third-party testing and certification, imports, ATVs, civil and criminal penalties, and SaferProducts.gov. It also repeals a funding limitation on the number of CPSC commissioners.[82] In 2011, CPSIA was updated to provide stronger regulatory and enforcement tools.[83]

The CPSC continues to play an important role in protecting consumers from unsafe products. Since the passage of CPSIA, the cap on civil penalties has been increased from just under $2 million to $15 million for violations of the consumer safety laws.[84] Up until 2016, no penalty higher than $5 million had been issued. But, in 2016, CPSC entered into an agreement with several non-U.S. companies that agreed to payments in the range of $15 million. The huge penalty was a way of sending a message to non-U.S.

companies that if they sell, manufacture, or distribute consumer goods in the United States, they must meet their reporting and product certifications that must be accurate and up-to-date under the U.S. consumer protection laws or face record high consequences.[85]

14.3 Food and Drug Administration

The **Food and Drug Administration (FDA)** grew out of experiments with food safety by one man—Harvey W. Wiley—chief chemist for the agricultural department in the late 1800s.[86] Wiley's most famous experiments involved feeding small doses of poisons to human volunteers. The substances fed to the volunteers were similar to those found in food preservatives at the time. The volunteers became known as the "Poison Squad," and their publicity generated a public awareness of the dangers of eating adulterated foods. The **Food and Drugs Act of 1906** was a direct result of the publicity created by Wiley's experiments. The act was administered by Wiley's Bureau of Chemistry until 1931, when the name "Food and Drug Administration" first was used.[87] Today, the FDA is responsible for protecting public health by assuring the safety, efficacy, and security of human and veterinary drugs, biological products, medical devices, the nation's food supply, cosmetics, tobacco products, and products that emit radiation.[88] The scope of the FDA's regulatory authority is very broad and is closely related to some other regulatory agencies. As a result, it is often frustrating and confusing to consumers to determine the appropriate regulatory body to contact.[89] The FDA conducts an enormous amount of business as it carries out its mission, and like the CPSC it has been controversial over the decades and its zeal in pursuing its mission has varied widely depending on the administration in office.

Figure 14-4 provides information about the FDA and its strategic priorities.

FIGURE 14-4 U.S. Food & Drug Administration (FDA)—Overview, Mission, and Strategic Priorities—2014–2018

FDA Overview	The U.S. FDA is the agency within the U.S. Department of Health and Human Services (HHS) responsible for ensuring the safety and effectiveness of products that account for about 20 cents of every dollar spent by American consumers each year—products that touch the lives of every American every day. These include human and animal drugs, 80 percent of the food supply, biological products, medical devices, cosmetics, radiation-emitting products, and tobacco products.
Five Crosscutting Strategic Priorities	Regulatory Science Globalization Safety and Quality Smart Regulation Stewardship
Core Mission Goals and Objectives	Goal 1—Enhance oversight of FDA-regulated products Goal 2—Improve and safeguard access to FDA-regulated products to benefit health Goal 3—Promote better informed decisions about the use of FDA-regulated products Goal 4—Strengthen organizational excellence and accountability
Implementation	FDA will implement these strategic priorities through a tiered planning framework. Most importantly, FDA senior leadership will integrate them into the annual budget priority setting and formulation process. Progress will be monitored by aligning annual executive and employee performance metrics with long-term objectives and strategies.

Source: U.S. Food & Drug Administration, "FDA Strategic Priorities, 2014–2018," http://www.fda.gov/downloads/AboutFDA/ReportsManuals Forms/Reports/UCM416602.pdf. Accessed May 11, 2016; "About FDA," http://www.fda.gov/AboutFDA/default.htm. Accessed May 11, 2016.

14.4 Business's Response to Consumer Stakeholders

Business's response to consumerism and consumer stakeholders has varied over the years. It has ranged from poorly conceived public relations ploys at one extreme to well-designed and implemented programs focusing on customer relations, customer satisfaction, customer engagement, and customer relationship management at the other extreme. Business's response has also included programs focusing on quality and continuous improvement initiatives such as Total Quality Management (TQM), Kaizen, ISO Certification, and Lean Six Sigma programs, although there is some indication that these are falling out of favor, as passing "fads."[90] Though particular programs may become less fashionable to businesses, the core activities that are involved in being responsive to consumers remain.

The history of business's response to consumers parallels its perceptions of the seriousness, pervasiveness, effectiveness, and longevity of the consumer movement. When the consumer movement first began, business's response was casual, perhaps symbolic, and hardly effective. Today, the consumer movement has matured, and formal interactions with consumer stakeholders have become more and more institutionalized. Business has realized that consumers today are more persistent than in the past, more assertive, and more likely to use or exhaust all appeal channels before being satisfied. Armed with considerable power, consumer activists have been a major stimulus to more sincere efforts on behalf of business to provide consumers with a forum. These efforts have included the creation of toll-free hot lines, user-friendly Web sites, consumer service representatives, and more extensive customer service training. Today, virtually all successful companies have customer service programs, irrespective of whether they are selling products or services.

14.5 Customer Service Programs

It is ironic that the United States is said to now be a service economy and yet poor customer service seems to be a topic on every consumer's minds today. In recent years, retailers of all types have been pushing the idea of self-service and many consumers continue to be upset with how businesses' keep pushing this concept whether it be checking out your own groceries, following a computer voice protocol to fix your own cable TV or internet connection problem, printing your own boarding pass at the air terminal kiosk, or pumping your own gas (except in New Jersey and Oregon where pumping your own gas is forbidden by state law). One writer recently exclaimed "Are we entering a dark, deeply un-American era when we literally have to do everything for ourselves?"[91]

But, the other type of consumer dissatisfaction is simply with the way merchants and retailers who claim they are providing good service do not do a very good job and sometimes they behave unethically. Even McDonald's Corporation has said its own service is broken (rude and unfriendly employees, slow service) and is tackling a major repair job.[92] Companies seem to always be finding new ways to stick the consumer with lousy service.[93]

In one recent study, 66 percent of consumers switched brands or business due to poor customer service. Eighty-two percent of those who switched said the brand could have done something to stop them.[94] In spite of customer frustrations with poor to erratic service, consumers today continue to expect high-quality, safe products and responsive customer service regarding the products and services they buy. Nothing is more frustrating than spending money on a product only to encounter after-sale problems or issues that are not quickly and easily remedied. Experts today argue that companies should strive to develop loyal customers who will always come back and that the key to customer retention is customer service. Building life-long devotion among customers takes serious commitment and hard work. It also requires that a company create a culture and employees who are motivated and committed to delivering outstanding service.

One major factor that holds out hope for better customer service is the fact that there are a number of companies that not only give good customer service but have become well known for excellence in customer service. One notable example is Zappos, the e-commerce company, led by Tony Hsieh, their passionate CEO.[95] Zappos has become a model for how to build a culture of employees that know how to serve their customer base while also enjoying their work. One of the keys to Zappos success is the careful hiring process they use to make sure the employees will fit in with and can adapt to the customer-centric culture.[96]

Companies address customer service in a variety of ways, and it is often dependent on the nature of the products or services and the competitiveness of the market that drive commitment on the part of companies. Companies provide customer service through money-back guarantees, warranties, and offices of consumer affairs in which are found customer service representatives whose full-time job is to make customers happy. The effective execution of customer service depends on a host of factors, but it is absolutely critical that top management be committed to providing a service as part of its ongoing relationship with the consumer. Management's job is to attract, maintain, and retain customers, and this requires a high degree of dedication and commitment.

One merchant that has done a fine job at customer service is The Vermont Country Store. It has built its high-level customer service around its own "Customer's Bill of Rights." Its first two customer's rights include (1) the right to expect polite and courteous service and (2) the right to always be treated as a priority. Its other customer's rights pretty much cover any possible concern a customer might have.[97]

Under Armour is another company that is well known for its strong customer service. Under Armour employs customer service agents that actually use the products it sells. The company believes that by using agents who have experience with their products, they will better be able to talk with customers in a more meaningful way. Under Armour works with live chat provider Needle, Inc., to find prospective agents from among the company's 1.7 million Facebook fans.[98]

There are many principles that drive high-quality customer service and many guidelines for creating a customer-oriented company. Figure 14-5 presents some key customer service principles and guidelines for developing customer-oriented companies. If companies followed these, customers would justifiably think they have been treated fairly.

A recent trend report on customer service argued that there were five trends helping to define and improve customer service now and into the future.[99] First, always have a Plan B. When BMW launched its BMWi3 electric vehicle, purchasers were given access to petrol vehicles to ease their "range anxiety." This was their Plan B. Second, provide video valets. Forward thinking brands will now provide Webcam-enabled face-to-face interaction with customer service representatives.[100] For example, the Amazon Mayday button connects Kindle Fire HDX tablet owners with an Amazon customer service representative via Webcam. Third, deliver (more than) the goods. Be prepared for a smartphone-fueled rush of delivery innovations. In 2014, Pizza Hut Panama began delivering pizzas that were cooked in transit in special mobile ovens to ensure freshness.[101]

Fourth, customer-focused brands will promote a sixth sense—info-sense. Using smart sensors and face-and-object technologies, it is now possible to gather information about

FIGURE 14-5 Customer Service Principles and Customer-Oriented Companies

Seven Principles of Customer Service[a]

1. **Keeping your word is where it all begins.** Keeping your word builds trust. Trust is the foundation of all successful relationships.
2. **Always be honest and tell it like it is.** By being honest and telling your customers the truth, you are much more likely to get a positive response to any situation.
3. **Always think proactively, looking around the corner.** Thinking proactively when it comes to customer service boils down to addressing concerns prior to you having to hear from the customer that something needs to be done.
4. **Deal with problems as best you can yourself, never passing the buck.** The more authority employees have to address customer problems, the better it is because nothing upsets customers more than being passed from department to department.
5. **Do not argue with a customer because it is a lose/lose situation.** The best question to ask yourself is: What can be done to make the customer feel happy and cared for?
6. **Accept your mistakes, learn from them, and do not repeat them.** Accept that you have made a mistake, evaluate the situation, learn the lesson, and move on. Don't get stuck in an indefinite state of denial.
7. **Consistency is the name of the game for lasting success.** When the customer service principles discussed above are practiced consistently, customers realize over time that the integrity of how you choose to run your business is not to be compromised.

Creating a Customer-Oriented Company[b]

1. Top–down culture and commitment are essential.
2. Identify internal champions and uphold them.
3. Commit resources to the task.
4. Hire the right people.
5. Empower your employees.
6. Make customer service training a priority.

[a]Summarized from Imran Rahman, "Seven Service Principles Guaranteed to Create Raving Fans," http://www.dreammanifesto.com/service-principles-guaranteed-create-raving-fans.html. Accessed May 11, 2016.
[b]Summarized from John Allen, "Creating a Service-Oriented Company Takes Commitment," *Houston Business Journal* (April 10, 2009), http://www.gnapartners.com/system/files/private/Creating%20a%20service%20oriented%20company%20takes%20commitment.pdf. Accessed May 11, 2016.

consumers in real time and use this information to enhance personal service.[102] Fifth, remember that politeness pays. Customer relationships are a two-way street. McDonald's and Coca-Cola in the Philippines introduced an app that would reward diners for not using their phones while eating. Another restaurant initiated a pricing policy that rewarded customer's politeness.[103] These ideas are just some of the innovative thinking on customer service that is taking place today.

Customer service programs are very important. In addition, programs such as Total Quality Management (TQM) and Six Sigma have become important strategic responses to product quality and safety issues. Lean Six Sigma, Kaizen, and ISO 9000 are also popular quality enhancement programs. These responses merit brief consideration.

14.6 Total Quality Management Programs

Total Quality Management (TQM) has many different characteristics, but it essentially means that all of the functions of the business are blended into a holistic, integrated philosophy built around the concepts of quality, teamwork, productivity, customer understanding, and satisfaction.[104] The purpose of TQM is to satisfy customers by focusing on product quality and safety issues. To be successful, a strong TQM program needs to employ principles, practices, and techniques that focus on the customer, use continuous improvement, and employ teamwork.[105] It should be noted that the customer, or consumer stakeholder, is at the center of the process. The positive impact TQM can have on safety in the workplace has been established.[106]

According to the American Society for Quality (ASQ), a global community of people interested in quality, TQM has a number of established benefits. Some of these include strengthened competitive position, elimination of defects and waste, reduced costs, enhanced market position, and improved customer focus and satisfaction.[107] To be successful, TQM must emphasize eight key elements—Ethics, Integrity, Trust, Training, Teamwork, Leadership, Recognition, and Communication. The first three—Ethics, Integrity, and Trust—constitute the foundation on which all else is built. These three elements foster openness, fairness, and sincerity, and they create the foundation for involvement by everyone.[108]

A vital assumption and premise of TQM is that the customer is the final judge of quality. Therefore, the first part of the TQM process is to define quality in terms of customer expectations and requirements. Quality means different things to different people, and this makes its achievement challenging, but the four attributes of quality that most often seem to be used include *excellence, value, conformance to specifications*, and *meeting and/or exceeding expectations*.[109] It is important to remember that customers' *perception* of quality is not always the same as *actual* quality and so firms may have to wait for customers to realize that genuine quality improvements have been made.[110]

Opportunities for recognition have helped to propel quality efforts. In the United States and the rest of the industrialized world, the Malcolm Baldrige Award, ISO 9000, and the Deming Quality Award have enhanced the reputations of firms that undertake quality initiatives and complete them successfully. As often occurs with new management approaches, TQM became a management buzzword, and many of its slogans, such as "Getting it right the first time," became viewed as clichés. It is against this backdrop that other tools developed and became popular, such as Just in Time (JIT) strategy and Business Process Reengineering (BPR). Recently, some analysts have argued that sustainability and TQM are intimately related. And, TQM is often characterized as a predecessor to Six Sigma and other approaches though it is still practiced in its fundamental principles.

The need for a more rigorous definition of quality was part of the appeal of Six Sigma, and other approaches, which are briefly described.

14.7 Six Sigma Strategy and Other Processes

Six Sigma is a development within TQM that has become a way of life for many corporations. *Sigma* is a statistical measure of variation from the mean; higher values of sigma mean fewer defects. The six-sigma level of operation is 3.4 defects per million. Most companies operate around the four-sigma level, that is, 6,000 defects per million.[111]

Six Sigma also is viewed as a general heading under which is grouped a body of strategies, methodologies, and techniques. Six Sigma continues as a popular way of improving quality and reducing costs.[112] IBM, Motorola, Amazon, GE, Nokia, and Sony are but a few of the major corporations that have adopted the Six Sigma methodology.[113] Although some observers deride Six Sigma as "TQM on steroids," it has brought new commitment and energy to the quest for quality in the new millennium. It is even said to have brought "more prominence to the quality world than it has enjoyed since the glory days of the mid-1980s."[114]

Motorola first developed Six Sigma, and Allied Signal later experimented with it, but most observers believe that GE perfected it. One of Six Sigma's strengths has been the clarity of the process and the steps companies must take to adopt it. However, Six Sigma is more than a toolbox with clear instructions. The program also represents a philosophy or strategy that stresses the importance of customers as well as careful

FIGURE 14-6 A Consumer Stakeholder Satisfaction Model

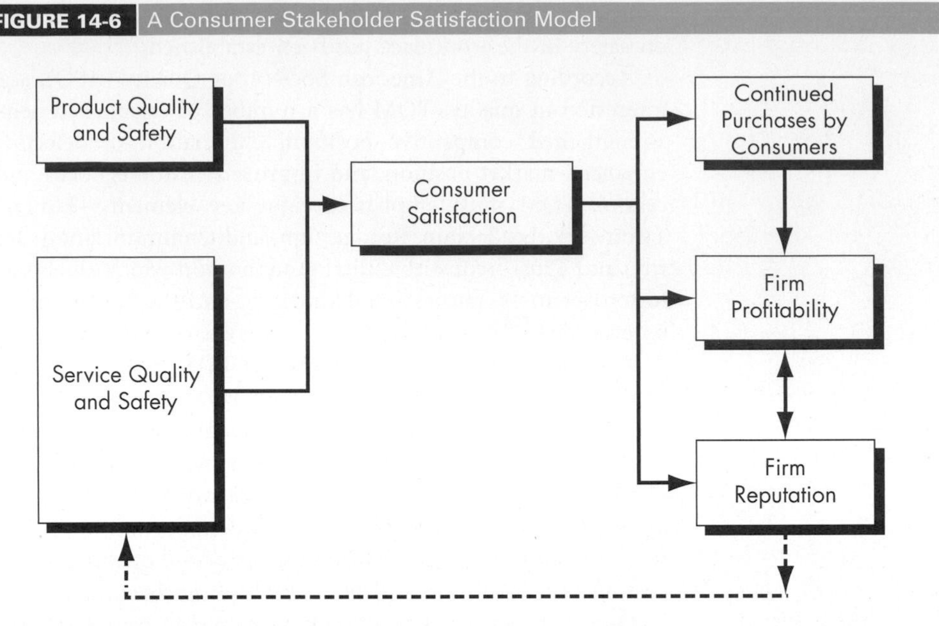

measurement. Six Sigma practitioners look for facts rather than opinions, and they believe in fixing the process rather than the product.[115] Of course, these underlying principles are the foundation of TQM and most other quality efforts.

Whereas Six Sigma is a comprehensive quality program, a newer program, **Lean Six Sigma (LSS)** began being practiced in conjunction with it. Whereas Six Sigma focused on improving quality, Lean Six Sigma focused on removing waste. As a combined quality management approach, LSS amplifies the strengths and minimizes the weaknesses of both approaches.[116] TQM and Six Sigma are often used in conjunction with the Japanese concept of **Kaizen**, which means "improvement," and refers to activities that are continuously involving all employees, management, and workers toward process improvement. Kaizen is also seen as a company-wide improvement mindset that is focused on customer satisfaction.[117] Accompanying these approaches to quality improvement, **ISO 9000** is often used as well. ISO 9000 is a set of international standards on quality management and quality assurance that have a customer focus. The standards are based on quality management principles that senior management can apply for organizational improvement.[118]

The basis for all of these quality or safety approaches is the satisfaction of the consumer. Figure 14-6 outlines a **consumer stakeholder satisfaction model** that depicts how product and service quality and safety lead to consumer satisfaction and the consequences for the firm's profitability, reputation, and continued purchasing by consumers.

Summary

Consumer stakeholders have become concerned with product quality and safety, largely because businesses have failed to meet their needs reliably on these two fronts. The situation has been the same with both manufacturing and services. One major challenge has been to identify and understand the different dimensions of the quality issue. Today, quality may mean performance, features, reliability, conformance, durability, serviceability, aesthetics, perceived quality, or some combination of these dimensions. Product and service quality is both a business and an ethics issue.

An extremely important legal and ethical issue has been the consumer's right to safety. Product safety, especially food safety, has become one of the most crucial consumer issues for firms. The product liability crisis has been an outgrowth of business's lack of attention to this issue. Other factors contributing to the product liability crisis have been the number of harmful-product cases, our increasingly litigious society, the size of financial awards given by the courts, and rising insurance rates. A major consequence of these phenomena has been calls for product liability reform or tort reform.

Discussions of tort reform are ongoing, but few changes in these laws have recently occurred. There are many stakeholders on both sides of the tort reform issue. Product tampering and product extortion have also become safety-related issues. In recent years, the health and safety issues related to foods, drugs, tobacco, and medical devices have propelled the CPSC and the FDA into prominent roles, fueled by supplementary regulations like the CPSIA and the FSMA to help provide protocols and enforce regulations. The CPSC and FDA play vital roles in product safety, but strong business ethics remains the best practice for dealing with these issues.

Companies today employ a host of different customer service programs, all of which are aimed at creating satisfied customers who will demonstrate loyalty and will return for future purchases. In addition, firms use a variety of approaches that specifically address the issue of quality, primarily in the production process, and these embrace safety as one significant feature. Quality improvement initiatives such as TQM, Six Sigma, Lean Six Sigma, Kaizen, and ISO 9000 are being used systematically, but they have not solved all the problems; however, they and other techniques have the potential for addressing the problems in a significant way if they are properly formulated and implemented.

In addition to these specific responses, a consumer focus and orientation needs to permeate management decision making if the concerns of consumers are to be handled effectively. In today's business environment, consumers have many choices. Consequently, companies have no alternative but to internalize the consumer focus if they are to succeed.

Key Terms

absolute liability, p. 442
caveat emptor, p. 437
caveat vendor, p. 437
caveat venditor, p. 437
Consumer Product Safety Commission (CPSC), p. 445
Consumer Product Safety Improvement Act (CPSIA) of 2008, p. 446
consumer stakeholder satisfaction model, p. 452
contractual theory, p. 436
delayed manifestation cases, p. 443
doctrine of strict liability, p. 442
due care theory, p. 436
Food and Drugs Act of 1906, p. 447
Food and Drug Administration (FDA), p. 447
Food Safety Modernization Act (FSMA) of 2011, p. 438
ISO 9000, p. 452
Kaizen, p. 452
Lean Six Sigma (LSS), p. 452
market share liability, p. 443
product extortion, p. 444
product liability reform, p. 444
product liability risk management program, p. 443
product (products) liability, p. 441
Six Sigma, p. 451
social costs view, p. 436
tort reform, p. 444
Total Quality Management (TQM), p. 450

Discussion Questions

1. Identify the major dimensions of quality. Give an example of a product or service in which each of these characteristics is important.
2. What ethical theories can help us to better understand the issue of quality? Discuss.
3. Identify the principal reasons why we have a product liability crisis. Have any reasons been omitted? Discuss.
4. Differentiate the doctrine of strict liability from the doctrines of absolute liability and market

share liability. What implications do these views have for the business community and for future products and services that might be offered?

5. Given the current business and consumer climate, what do you anticipate the future to be for the CPSC and the FDA? What role does politics play in your answer?
6. What is your assessment of business's response to product and service quality and safety? Have they done enough? What is missing from their approaches?

Endnotes

1. Knowledge@Wharton Essentials, *The Customer of Tomorrow*, 2016, http://wdp.wharton.upenn.edu/book/customer-tomorrow/?&utm_medium=email&utm_source=kw051116&utm_campaign=customer-tomorrow&utm_content=ad. Accessed May 11, 2016.
2. Nathan Bomey, "Takata Recall Now Biggest in U.S. History," USA Today, May 5, 2016, 2B.
3. Mike Spector, "Group Pinpoints Takata Defects," *The Wall Street Journal*, February 24, 2016, B2.
4. Ibid.
5. Knowledge@Wharton, "What Caused Takata's Airbag Problem?" February 2, 2016, http://knowledge.wharton.upenn.edu/article/dasher-macduffie-takata-airbags/. Accessed May 13, 2016.
6. Mike Spector, "U.S. Doubles Size of Takata Air Bag Recall," *The Wall Street Journal*, May 5, 2016, B3.
7. Jonathan D. Rockoff, "J&J Appeals $127 Million in Awards in Talc Cancer Cases," *The Wall Street Journal*, May 4, 2016, B3.
8. Ibid.
9. Hermelo, Francisco Diaz, and Roberto Vassolo. "Institutional Development and Hypercompetition in Emerging Economies." *Strategic Management Journal* 31.13 (2010): 1457–1473.
10. Rajaram Veliyath and Elizabeth Fitzgerald, "Firm Capabilities, Business Strategies, Customer Preferences, and Hypercompetitive Arenas," *Competitiveness Review* (Vol. 10, 2000), 56–82.
11. Debanjan Mitra and Peter N. Golder, "Quality Is in the Eye of the Beholder," *Harvard Business Review* (April 2007) 26–28.
12. "ACSI Quarterly Scores," *American Customer Satisfaction Index*, http://www.theacsi.org/acsi-results/acsi-commentary-november-2012. Accessed May 8, 2016.
13. Mike Longaecker, Grand Forks Herald, "Angry T-Mobile Customer Guns down His Cellphone in Wisconsin," January 21, 2016, http://www.grandforksherald.com/news/region/3929875-angry-t-mobile-customer-guns-down-his-cellphone-wisconsin. Accessed May 13, 2016.
14. Ibid.
15. "Customers Turned Off by Poor Service Levels," *Marketing Week* (March 5, 1998), 11.
16. Forbes Insights, "Modern Customer Service," New York: New York 2015.
17. Ibid., 3.
18. Ibid., 10.
19. Chris Akins, "8 Dimensions of Quality," Lean Six Sigma Academy, http://lssacademy.com/2008/05/28/8-dimensions-of-quality/. Accessed May 8, 2016.
20. Ibid.
21. Manuel G. Velasquez, *Business Ethics: Concepts and Cases* (Upper Saddle River, NJ: Prentice Hall, 2002), 335–344.
22. Merriam Webster, "Safety," http://www.merriam-webster.com/dictionary/safety. Accessed May 8, 2016.
23. Yair Aharoni, *The No Risk Society* (Chatham, NJ: Chatham House Publishers, 1981), 62–63.
24. "Caveat Venditor," BusinessDictionary.com, http://www.businessdictionary.com/definition/caveat-venditor.html. Accessed May 8, 2016.
25. Leon Stafford, "After Dramatic Day, Ex-CEO Gets 28 Years," *The Atlanta Journal-Constitution*, September 22, 2015, A1.
26. Kevin McCoy, "Exec Gets 28 Years in Salmonella-Peanut Case," USA Today, September 22, 2015, 1A.
27. Jesse Newman, "Blue Bell: Outbreak's Sources Partly Known," *The Wall Street Journal*, April 4, 2016, B3.
28. Alexandra Sifferlin, "Why the Rise in Food-Poisoning Reports Is Actually a Good Thing," *Time*, March, 28, 2016.
29. Beth Kowitt, "Contamination Nation," Fortune, October 1, 2015, 119–126.
30. Ibid., 121.
31. FDA, "FDA Food Safety and Modernization Act (FSMA)" http://www.fda.gov/Food/GuidanceRegulation/FSMA/default.htm. Accessed May 9, 2016.
32. Jesse Newman, "FDA Tightens Its Food Safety Rules," *The Wall Street Journal*, September 15, 2015, B3.
33. Ibid.
34. Ibid.
35. Kowitt, 120–121.
36. Sifferlin, 2016, Ibid.
37. Ibid.
38. Thomas M. Burton, "FDA Plans ID-Tag System to Detect Faulty Devices," *The Wall Street Journal*, April 26, 2012, B3.
39. E. Patrick McGuire, "Product Liability: Evolution and Reform" (New York: The Conference Board, 1989), 6.

40. "U.S. Consumer Product Safety Commission, "Research & Statistics," http://www.cpsc.gov/en/Research–Statistics/. Accessed May 10, 2016.

41. Cornell University Law School, Legal Information Institute, "Products Liability Law: An Overview," http://www.law.cornell.edu/wex/Products_liability. Accessed May 10, 2016.

42. Investopedia, "The 5 Largest Product Liability Lawsuits," http://www.investopedia.com/slide-show/5-largest-us-product-liability-cases/. Accessed May 10, 2016.

43. Ibid.

44. Ibid.

45. Matt Kibbe, "America's Ongoing Tort Litigation Nightmare," http://www.forbes.com/sites/mattkibbe/2012/01/19/americas-ongoing-tort-litigation-nightmare/#ca3c1a770dc6, Accessed May 10, 2016.

46. Ibid.

47. Kara Sissell, "Study Tallies Tort Litigation's Effect on Innovation," *Chemical Week* (April 4, 2007), 43.

48. Fred W. Morgan and Karl A. Boedecker, "A Historical View of Strict Liability for Product-Related Injuries," *Journal of Macromarketing* (Spring 1996), 103–117.

49. Ann Christopher, "Avoiding a Hazardous Violation," *Warehousing Management* (August 2001), 20.

50. Kerry Powell, "Liability Language: Know the Difference between Strict and Absolute," *On-Site* (March 2004), 46.

51. Curt Ward, "What Is Strict Liability?" http://buteralaw.com/attorneys/n-curtis-ward/. Accessed May 10, 2016.

52. Terry Morehead Dworkin and Mary Jane Sheffet, "Product Liability in the 1980s," *Journal of Public Policy and Marketing* (1985), 71.

53. "The Asbestos Blob, Cont.," *The Wall Street Journal* (April 6, 2004), A16.

54. "Business Line: India Supreme Court Ruling on Damage Liability of Common Carrier," *Businessline* (June 30, 2000), 1.

55. Dworkin and Sheffet, 69.

56. Clemens P. Work, "Product Safety: A New Hot Potato for Congress," *U.S. News & World Report* (June 14, 1982), 62. Also see "What Is Market Share Liability?" Rottenstein Law Group, http://www.rotlaw.com/legal-library/what-is-market-share-liability/. Accessed May 10, 2016.

57. "What Is Market Share Liability?" ibid.

58. Travelers, "Five Steps for Product Liability Risk Management," https://www.travelers.com/resources/product-service-liability/5-steps-for-product-liability-risk-management.aspx. Accessed May 10, 2016.

59. Ibid.

60. Ibid.

61. "Tampering with Buyers' Confidence," *U.S. News & World Report* (March 3, 1986), 46.

62. ListVerse, "Ten Notorious Cases of Product Tampering," http://listverse.com/2010/12/27/10-notorious-cases-of-product-tampering/. Accessed May 10, 2016.

63. New York Daily News, "FBI Looks for Man Suspected of Attempting to Contaminate Whole Foods Products with Unknown Liquid," May 3, 2016, http://www.nydailynews.com/news/national/fbi-man-suspected-contaminating-foods-buffet-article-1.2622702. Accessed May 10, 2016.

64. Dean Foust, Brian Grow, and Sheridan Prasso, "Evolution of the Envelope," *Businessweek* (November 5, 2000), 14.

65. Thomas Lee, "Food Service Is on Front Line of Terror War," *St. Louis Post-Dispatch* (September 23, 2002), 8.

66. Daniel Schwartz, "Five Major Product Tampering Cases," CBC News, August 2, 2012, http://www.cbc.ca/news/world/story/2012/08/02/f-product-tampering-list.html. Accessed May 10, 2016.

67. "Product Extortion Insurance," http://www.koeberich-fl.com/grobritannien-uk/financial-lines/produkterpressung/index.html. Accessed May 10, 2016.

68. Ibid.

69. Product Extortion Insurance, http://www.alphags.com.my/product-extortion-insurance/. Accessed May 10, 2016.

70. "Tort," *The Lectric Law Library's Lexicon*, http://www.lectlaw.com/def2/t032.htm. Accessed May 10, 2016.

71. Matt Kibbe, "America's Ongoing Tort Litigation Nightmare," *Forbes*, January 19, 2012, http://www.forbes.com/sites/mattkibbe/2012/01/19/americas-ongoing-tort-litigation-nightmare/2/#224d32583434. Accessed May 10, 2016.

72. Asia-Pacific Economics Blog, "Tort Reform Pros and Cons," http://apecsec.org/tort-reform-pros-and-cons/. Accessed May 11, 2016.

73. Michele Galen, "The Class Action against Product Liability Laws," *Businessweek* (July 29, 1997), 74. Also see Amy Buttell Crane, "The ABCs of Tort Reform," Bankrate.com, http://www.bankrate.com/brm/news/pf/20050727a1.asp. Accessed May 11, 2013.

74. Robert Kuttner, "How Tort Reform Will Hurt Consumers," *San Diego Union Tribune* (June 24, 1994), B7. See also Jerry Phillips, "Attacks on the Legal System: Fallacy of Tort Reform Arguments," *Trial* (February 1992), 106–110; Emma Gallimore, "Former Ark. Lawmaker Attempting to Gain Signatures for Tort Reform Ballot Measure," Legal News Line, May 5, 2016, http://legalnewsline.com/stories/510722833-former-ark-lawmaker-attempting-to-gain-signatures-for-tort-reform-ballot-measure. Accessed May 11, 2016.

75. Stuart Taylor and Evan Thomas, "Civil Wars," *Newsweek* (December 15, 2003), 47.

76. "The Defects in Product-Liability Laws," *Businessweek* (July 29, 1991), 88. Also see W. Kip Viscusi, "Does Product Liability Make Us Safer?" Regulation, Spring 2012, http://www.cato.org/sites/cato.org/files/serials/files/regulation/2012/4/v35n1-4.pdf. Accessed May 11, 2016.

77. American Tort Reform Association, "ATRA–At a Glance," http://www.atra.org/about. Accessed May 11, 2016.

78. U.S. Consumer Product Safety Commission, http://www.cpsc.gov/. Accessed May 11, 2016.

79. U.S. Consumer Product Safety Commission, "News Releases," http://www.cpsc.gov/en/Newsroom/News-Releases/. Accessed May 11, 2016.

80. Ibid.

81. "Connect with Us," http://www.cpsc.gov/. Accessed May 11, 2016.

82. Consumer Product Safety Improvement Act of 2008, http://www.cpsc.gov/en/Regulations-Laws–Standards/Statutes/. Accessed May 11, 2016.

83. Ibid.

84. Baker & McKenzie, "CPSC Signals Civil Penalties Will Reach New Heights after Chinese Entities Agreed to Pay a Landmark $15.45 Million Settlement," April 11, 2016, http://www.lexology.com/library/detail.aspx?g=ff3db2a3-6d2a-4b44-b4b6-73ed2f9d2265. Accessed May 11, 2016.

85. Ibid.

86. John P. Swan, "FDA's Origins," http://www.fda.gov/AboutFDA/WhatWeDo/History/Origin/ucm124403.htm. Accessed May 11, 2016.

87. Ibid.

88. FDA, "What We Do," http://www.fda.gov/AboutFDA/WhatWeDo/default.htm. Accessed May 11, 2016.

89. Ibid.

90. Mike Collins, "Why So Many Management Strategies Become Fads That Fade Away," Forbes, June 11, 2015, http://www.forbes.com/sites/mikecollins/2015/06/11/why-so-many-management-strategies-become-fads-that-fade-away/#54bf6486cf68. Accessed May 13, 2016.

91. Joe Queenan, "Die, Die, DIY! Enough of the Self-Service," *The Wall Street Journal*, October 27–28, 2012, C11.

92. Julie Jargon, "McDonald's Says 'Service Is Broken,' Tackles Repair," *The Wall Street Journal*, April 11, 2013, B1.

93. Bill Saporito, "Staying Power: New Ways Companies Are Getting Us to Stick with Lousy Service," *Time*, February 4, 2013, 56.

94. TrendWatching, "The Future of Customer Service," http://trendwatching.com/trends/future-customer-service/. Accessed May 11, 2016.

95. Buzz Knight, RadioInk, "Culture Breeds Excellent in Customer Service," April 25, 2016, http://radioink.com/2016/04/25/culture-breeds-excellence-in-customer-service/. Accessed May 13, 2016.

96. Ibid.

97. The Vermont Country Store, "Customer Bill of Rights," http://www.vermontcountrystore.com/store/company/static/About-Us/Customer-Bill-of-Rights. Accessed May 11, 2016.

98. Internet Retialer, Zak Stambor, "Under Armour Gains Sales via Live Chat Experience," https://www.internetretailer.com/2012/07/11/under-armour-gains-sales-live-chat-expertise. Accessed May 13, 2016.

99. TrendWatching, 2016, ibid.

100. Ibid.

101. Ibid.

102. Ibid.

103. Ibid.

104. K. Ishikawa, *What Is Total Quality Control?* (Milwaukee, WI: Quality Press, 1985).

105. James W. Dean, Jr., and David E. Bowen, "Management Theory and Total Quality: Improving Research and Practice through Theory Development," *Academy of Management Review* (Vol. 19, No. 3, July 1994), 395.

106. I. Salaheldin Salaheldin and Zain Mohamed, "How Quality Control Circles Enhance Work Safety: A Case Study," *TQM Magazine* (2007), 229–244.

107. ASQ, "Total Quality Management Benefits," http://asq.org/learn-about-quality/total-quality-management/overview/tqm-gets-results.html. Accessed May 11, 2016.

108. "The Eight Elements of TQM," i*Six Sigma*, http://www.isixsigma.com/methodology/total-quality-management-tqm/eight-elements-tqm/. Accessed May 11, 2016.

109. Carol A. Reeves and David A. Bednar, "Defining quality: Alternatives and Implications," *Academy of Management Review* (Vol. 19, No. 3, July 1994), 437.

110. Debanjan Mitra and Peter N. Golder, "Quality Is in the Eye of the Beholder," *Harvard Business Review* (April 2007), 26–28.

111. *iSixSigma*, "What Is Six Sigma?" http://www.isixsigma.com/new-to-six-sigma/getting-started/what-six-sigma/. Accessed May 11, 2016.

112. Michael Hammer and Jeff Godling, "Putting Six Sigma in Perspective," *Quality* (October 2001), 58–62.

113. Asixsigma, "Who Uses Six Sigma?" http://asixsigma.com/ss_why.php. Accessed May 11, 2016.

114. Hammer and Godling, 58.

115. Ibid.

116. "New to Six Sigma?" https://www.moresteam.com/new-to-lean-six-sigma.cfm. Accessed May 13, 2016.

117. "Kaizen and Total Quality Management," http://www.1000ventures.com/business_guide/mgmt_kaizen_tqc_main.html. Accessed May 13, 2016.

118. ASQ, "What Is the ISO 9000 Standards Series," http://asq.org/learn-about-quality/iso-9000/overview/overview.html. Accessed May 13, 2016.

15

Sustainability and the Natural Environment

CHAPTER LEARNING OUTCOMES

After studying this chapter, you should be able to:

1. Discuss the concept of sustainability and its imperative.
2. Describe the natural environment, the impact of business on the natural environment, and the ten major natural environment issues.
3. Identify and discuss the issues that arise for businesses in their responsibility for the environment and sustainability.
4. Discuss the role of governments in environmental and sustainability issues.
5. Describe other environmental stakeholders, including interest groups, employees, and investors.
6. Discuss business environmentalism, sustainability goals, and the future of the business/environment relationship.

What does it mean for a company to be sustainable? There are so many definitions and measures of sustainability that it can be hard to answer that question. In fact, one article pointed out that in one year, a large company was recognized as a top ten sustainable company by one data provider and a bottom ten performer by another.[1] However, assessing the sustainability of a company involves understanding how it is broadly defined, how it is important to business, how it translates into sustainability goals and measures, and what stakeholders might be involved. All of these things are important to understanding the concept of sustainability and business.

There are many definitions of **sustainability**. For our purposes, we borrow from the Brundtland Commission (formerly the World Commission on Environment and Development [WCED]) to define sustainable business as "business that meets the needs of the present without compromising the ability of future generations to meet their own needs."[2] The focus of sustainability is the creation of a good quality of life for both current and future generations of humans and nonhumans by achieving a balance between economic prosperity, ecosystem viability, and social justice.[3] The concept is akin to walking lightly on the earth, taking only what is needed, and leaving behind enough for future generations to have access to the same resources. Sustainability is not just about cutting back and limiting waste, rather it is a philosophy that embraces a new type of abundance—one that can inspire greater levels of business creativity.[4]

As the sustainability movement grows, creative business people are developing new ways of doing business that benefit all aspects of the **triple bottom line**—people, planet, and profits. The growth of sustainability has been swift as businesses become more and more convinced that it is not only the right thing to do but also something that can drive revenues, savings, and be a source of competitive advantage. In a recent survey by *The Ethical Corporation*, 79 percent of executives polled said that their CEO is convinced of the value of sustainability—additionally, they noted that most of their sustainability teams are headed up by senior executives.[5] While consulting companies have explored the idea of sustainability for years, many have even developed separate centers to help businesses manage a variety of sustainability issues like global supply chains and ecosystems.[6]

The growth of attention to sustainability is not surprising when one considers the strong business case for sustainability. In fact, a recent survey by McKinsey & Company of over 3,000 executives indicated there has been a shift in the way they view sustainability. In past surveys, when asked about their companies' reasons for pursuing sustainability, respondents most often cited cutting costs or managing their company's reputation; however, 43 percent of respondents now see it as aligning with their company's business goals, mission, or values.[7] In *Green to Gold*, Daniel Esty and Andrew Winston offer three basic reasons for incorporating sustainability into a business's core strategy.[8] First, there are upside benefits. Sustainability requires innovation and entrepreneurship that can help a firm to move ahead of competitors through new ideas, lower costs, and stronger intangibles such as trust and credibility. Sustainable companies can even carry less risk, resulting in lower lending rates. Second, companies that ignore the sustainability imperative run the risk of incurring society's wrath once they step over the line. Companies like DuPont Chemical and BP Oil, as well as the City of Flint, Michigan, experienced significant stakeholder backlash following their pollution issues. AT&T faced shareholder resolutions from outraged shareholders when they did not set company-wide quantitative targets to increase renewable energy sourcing and/or production.[9] Finally, sustainability is the right thing to do. As the sign in Patagonia headquarters says, "There is no business to be done on a dead planet."[10]

This chapter begins by discussing the concept of sustainability and its importance to business. An overview of the growth of the sustainability movement and the drivers of corporate sustainability will follow. We highlight Unilever, a company that continues to be named as a top leader in sustainability, and the principles that guide them. We then narrow the focus to environmental sustainability and the top environmental issues facing business today. The section on environmental ethics begins a discussion of individual and collective responsibility for sustaining the environment. We then explore the role of the government and environmental interest groups in effecting change, look at companies that are leaders in environmentally sustainable business practices, and offer ways in which businesses can develop a strategy aimed at achieving environmental sustainability.

15.1 The Sustainability Imperative

Several years ago, a discussion of sustainability would have had to include strong arguments about why businesses would benefit from sustainable practices. Today, the need for sustainability is increasingly taken as a "given" and businesses must simply determine how best to respond. As noted by Carroll, "Sustainability seems so logical—take care of the present, take care of the future—that virtually no one opposes it (anymore) as a concept."[11] According to *TriplePundit*, the business case for sustainability has become increasingly easier to make, that is, an "easier sell" for companies of all sizes.[12] This movement has been accompanied by large-scale initiatives like the U.N. Sustainable Development Goals launched in New York in late September 2015, as well as news media attention to companies who "do well by doing good," like those highlighted in *Fortune* magazine's 2015 launch of their first Change the World (CTW) rankings.[13] In sum, the concept of sustainability has been institutionalized as a form of CSR, with a critical mass of supporters that point to its benefits.[14]

CERES' Roadmap to Sustainability identifies several key drivers that underscore the movement toward sustainability, presenting both risks and opportunities:[15]

1. Competition for Resources—Demand for resources is growing more quickly than they can be replaced.

2. Climate Change—Businesses must be prepared to not only respond to new policies and regulations regarding emissions but also take advantage of opportunities to profit from new technologies that reduce emissions or create solutions.
3. Economic Globalization—Wide disparities in social and environmental standards bring risks as well as opportunities.
4. Connectivity and Communications—Stakeholders can monitor and react to sustainability efforts more quickly and effectively. Reputations are more easily and quickly built and destroyed.

The attention to sustainability inevitably begins at the top ranks of any organization. For example, Anne Sheehan, director of Corporate Governance at the California State Teachers' Retirement System (CalSTRS), notes, "Given the role of corporate boards we pay very close attention to what the board is and is not doing on sustainability."[16] According to the *GreenBiz Group*, corporate engagement at the executive levels will be the key to move beyond the "low hanging fruit" of finding control inside their operations, such as facilities and fleets, which have attractive financial paybacks.[17]

One of the foremost advocates of corporate sustainability is Paul Polman, CEO of Unilever. While many business executives are at odds with government, he contends that business, government, and nonprofit/nongovernmental organizations should be working together to tackle the world's challenges.[18] Since taking the reins of Unilever in 2009, Polman has been charting a dramatic new direction for the company. Concerned that a focus on shareholder wealth maximization would lead to a short-term outlook at odds with the long-term perspective needed for sustainability, he banned quarterly earnings reports, which lowered his percentage of hedge fund investors from 15 percent to 5 percent in three years.[19] Not sorry to see the hedge fund investors go, he then actively courted more long-term-oriented investment funds. In his words, "Historically, too many CEOs have just responded to shareholders instead of actively seeking out the right shareholders. Most CEOs go to visit their existing shareholders; we go to visit the ones we don't yet have."[20]

Shortly after Polman took over, Unilever embarked on an ambitious ten-year "Sustainability Living" plan to halve the greenhouse gas impact of its deodorants, food, detergents, and other products between 2010 and 2020. Further, in 2015 they announced a commitment to be **carbon positive** in its operations by 2030. This means that 100 percent of its energy across operations will come from renewable sources, enabling them, with partners, to generate more renewable energy than they need for their own operations and making the surplus available to the markets and communities in which they operate.[21]

The Sustainability Living plan is detailed in Figure 15-1. However, the challenge has been that more than two-thirds of greenhouse emissions and half the water in Unilever products' life cycle come from consumer use, and convincing consumers to cut their environmental impact is tough.[22] Nevertheless, the environmental targets directly within the company's control have been achieved, including slashing the carbon emissions impact of its manufacturing processes by 32 percent since 2008. Additionally, they have taken a very public stance against suppliers who have not embraced sustainability targets. For example, Unilever recently discontinued business with its major palm oil supplier after the company failed to comply with standards for palm oil production designed to address deforestation issues.[23] It is important to note that Unilever is doing well by traditional measures, as well as by the goals of the Sustainable Living Plan. Unilever's revenues and operating income have risen steadily since Polman took charge, and 50 percent of its growth in recent years has from sustainable living brands.[24] Moreover, share price has outperformed the industry average, enabling Polman to move forward without criticism.[25]

FIGURE 15-1 The Unilever Sustainable Living Plan

The Unilever Sustainable Living Plan (USLP) sets out to decouple our growth from our environmental impact, while at the same time increasing our positive social impact. It has three big goals to achieve by 2020—to improve health and well-being, reduce environmental impact, and enhance the livelihoods of people across our value chain. Supporting these goals are seven commitments underpinned by targets spanning our social, environmental, and economic performance across the value chain—from the sourcing of raw materials all the way through to the use of our products in the home.

Improving Health and Well-Being

- Health & Hygiene
  - By 2020 we will help more than a billion people to improve their hygiene habits and we will bring safe drinking water to 500 million people. This will help reduce the incidence of life-threatening diseases like diarrhea.
- Improving Nutrition
  - We will continually work to improve the taste and nutritional quality of all our products. By 2020 we will double the proportion of our portfolio that meets the highest nutritional standards, based on globally recognized dietary guidelines. This will help hundreds of millions of people to achieve a healthier diet.

Reducing Environmental Impact

- Greenhouse Gases
  - Halve the greenhouse gas impact of our products across the life cycle by 2020.
- Water
  - Halve the water associated with the consumer use of our products by 2020.
- Waste
  - Halve the waste associated with the disposal of our products by 2020.

Enhancing Livelihoods

- Sustainable Sourcing
  - By 2020 we will source 100% of our agricultural raw materials sustainably.
- Better Livelihoods
  - By 2020 we will engage with at least 500,000 smallholder farmers and 75,000 small-scale distributors in our supply network.

Sources: Unilever Sustainable Living Plan, http://www.unileverusa.com/sustainable-living/uslp/#PillarGroup3Pillar1. Accessed March 27, 2016; Edie.net, "Unilever's Sustainable Living Plan Drives Business Growth," May 15, 2015, http://www.edie.net/news/5/Unilever-s-Sustainable-Living-Plan-drives-business-growth/. Accessed April 15, 2016; *Brandchannel*, "Unilever Makes Progress on Sustainable Living Plan," November 24, 2015, http://www.brandchannel.com/2015/11/24/unilever-sustainability-112415/. Accessed April 15, 2016.

15.2 The Natural Environment

For years, businesses conducted their operations with little concern about environmental consequences. Virtually every sector of business in every country was responsible for consuming significant amounts of materials and energy and causing waste accumulation and resource degradation. For instance, forestry firms and companies that process raw materials, such as uranium, coal, and oil, have caused major air, water, and land pollution problems in their extraction, transportation, and processing stages. Manufacturing firms, such as those in steel, petrochemicals, and paper products, have been major sources of air and water pollution. Most major industry sectors have contributed significant levels of pollution with relatively little concern. Businesses have looked the other way, simply labeling the negative consequences of their actions as *externalities*.[26] **Externalities** are side effects or by-products of actions that are not intended and often disregarded.

By labeling the environmental consequences as external to the process, businesses in the past were able to both acknowledge and dismiss the problems they created. The few business environmentalism efforts that existed tended to come from two sources—compliance and efficiency.[27] Environmentalists had one approach available for getting most businesses to treat the environment with greater respect, "mandate, regulate, and litigate." Businesses would stop damaging the environment only when it became illegal and/or unprofitable to do so.[28] In some ways, those days are ending. Companies that were once infamous for the damage they did to the environment are now scrambling to lead the way in environmental initiatives as they realize that such initiatives not only increase efficiency but also satisfy stakeholders and perhaps even help to invent entirely new businesses. Companies like Tesla (electric cars), First Solar (utility-scale solar energy), and Everlane (ethical fashion) are examples of businesses that were developed from environmental initiatives like alternative energy and ethical sourcing.

Nevertheless, businesses still pose hazards to the environment, as evidenced by recent large-scale pollution examples. These include the decades-long damage to the air and drinking water in West Virginia due to chemical giant DuPont's use of the toxin PFOA for manufacturing Teflon and the Southern California Gas Company methane leak that had the largest-ever recorded leak at over 200 million pounds outside of Los Angeles, California.[29] It is no wonder that in a recent poll by *Just Capital* of over 20,000 adults in the United States, respondents felt that of all stakeholders, businesses fell particularly short in meeting their obligations to the environment.[30]

15.3 A Brief Introduction to the Natural Environment

Similar to other broad terms, **environment** means many things to many people—trees in the backyard, a family's favorite vacation spot, a mare and her colt in a pasture, a trout stream in the mountains, earth and the other planets, and space objects in our solar system. This chapter focuses on the natural environment—specifically, what it is, why it is important, how it has become a major concern, and what businesses and other organizations have done both to and for it. It identifies what we mean when we use the term *environment* and why it has become one of the most significant societal issues of our time. The chapter also describes the variety of responses human organizations, including businesses, have developed to ad dress this issue. Throughout the chapter, the emphasis is on two themes: that humans are a part of their natural environment, and that the environment itself, as well as the issues and human responses related to it, is extremely complex, defying simple analyses.

To assist in making business environmental decisions in the future, this chapter presents data, some of which are technical and scientific, related to environmental issues and responses. These data are included to help understand the complexities involved in the business and public environmental issues of today. Because of the influence of business, government, and environmental interest groups and individuals, these and many other technical terms and concepts are discussed in the media and, increasingly, in business and society and business ethics texts. Environmental literacy, whether for business, government, or individual decision making, requires, at minimum, some rudimentary knowledge of environmental issues. Without at least some basic technical information, would-be stakeholder managers abdicate their responsibility to make wise choices, which are potentially critical to the survival of their organizations, as well as to the survival of humans and other species in the natural environment. Figure 15-2 presents definitions of a few of the most important environmental terms that might be helpful to you now and in the future.

FIGURE 15-2 Glossary of Important and Helpful Environmental Terms

Term	Definition
Bio-Based Product	A product (other than food or feed) that is composed, in whole or in significant part, of biological products or renewable agricultural or forestry materials.
Environment	Broadly, anything that is external or internal to an entity. For humans, the environment can include external living, working, and playing spaces and natural resources, as well as internal physical, mental, and emotional states.
Carbon Footprint	The total amount of greenhouse gases a person, product, or company emits directly or indirectly.
Carbon Neutral	The maintenance of a balance between producing and using carbon dioxide.
Carrying Capacity	The volume of and intensity of use by organisms that can be sustained in a particular place and at a particular time without degrading the environment's future suitability for that use. A resource's carrying capacity has limits that need to be respected for continued use.
Circular Economy	A system of keeping resources and extracting value from them for as long as possible and then recovering and regenerating the resources and products at the end of each life cycle. More than just recycling, it is an alternative to a "take-make-dispose" approach that requires less energy than recycling.
Entropy	A measure of disorder of energy, indicating its unavailability for recycling for the same use. Energy tends to break down into lower quality with each use. For instance, a kilowatt of electricity, once it is produced and consumed, can never be used as electricity again and, if stored, will allow far less than 1 kW to be consumed.
Ecosystem	All living and nonliving substances present in a particular place, often interacting with others.
Internal Carbon Tax	A tax on individual business units within the company based on energy usage that goes into a common fund that invests in environmental sustainability projects.
Irreversibility	The inability of humans and nature to restore environmental conditions to a previous state within relevant time frames. Human environment-related actions that appear irreversible are the destruction of a rainforest or wilderness area and the extinction of a species.
Threshold	The point at which a particular phenomenon, previously suppressed, suddenly begins to be activated. For instance, when a population's carrying capacity threshold is exceeded, the population tends to decrease or even crash as a result of increased morbidity and mortality.

15.4 The Impact of Business on the Natural Environment

Following is a list of ten fundamental environmental issues that merit consideration. They are:

1. Climate change
2. Energy
3. Water
4. Biodiversity and land use
5. Chemicals, toxics, and heavy metals
6. Air pollution
7. Waste management
8. Ozone layer depletion
9. Oceans and fisheries
10. Deforestation

Each is discussed briefly to provide a sense of the issue's complexity and its current status.

15.4a Climate Change

No environmental issue has been more contentious than has the subject of **climate change**, which is also known as **global warming** because it is associated with the precipitation of **greenhouse effects** (i.e., the prevention of solar heat absorbed by our atmosphere from returning to space) that can persist in the atmosphere for centuries.[31] The debate about climate change's existence poses "alarmists against deniers"[32] in the realm of climate science, which has been termed "a veritable cornucopia of unanswered questions."[33] Debated issues include the evidence and rate of global warming, the extent to which human activity contributes to it, as well as the resolutions and safeguards that might be put in place to thwart forecasted warming trends. Melting glaciers, the decline of crop yields, and the effects of sea-level rise are presented as evidence of climate change. While some debate the science, the reality is that climate change is a hot-button issue for businesses, with over 72 percent of American adults reported to believe that there is "solid evidence" of global warming.[34] In a 2016 survey of 750 members of the *World Economic Forum*, including CEOs, industry experts, and global business leaders, environmental concerns were ranked the #1 area of concern, over regional conflicts, pandemics, and water shortage.[35]

New regulations and initiatives, like the Environmental Protection Agency's Clean Power Plan, introduced in 2015 by President Obama under his Clean Air Act, have been put forward to address climate change issues. The Plan was designed to lower carbon emissions from U.S. power plants by 2030 to 32 percent below 2005 levels.[36] However, it has met with some resistance in the U.S. court systems with concerns over the boundaries of EPA enforcement.[37] On a global scale, the 2016 Paris Agreement on Climate Change brought together 190 countries with an overall aim to limit global warming to below 2 degrees Celsius above preindustrial levels. While the countries agreed to submit voluntary plans focusing on shifting to renewable energy sources, the hope is that the plans legally bind countries to a periodic review that should keep them focused on reducing greenhouse gas emissions.[38]

In an effort to address these concerns, businesses like Microsoft are leading a movement to offset emissions with an **internal carbon tax**—a tax on individual business units within the company based on energy usage that goes into a common fund that invests in environmental sustainability projects.[39] Also known as **carbon pricing**, the tactic seems to be working, as Microsoft reduced its emissions by $7.5 million metric tons of carbon dioxide and saved more than $10 million through reduced energy consumption.[40] Microsoft is not the only company to do this, with 437 companies, including Disney and Shell voluntarily charging themselves in 2015.[41]

Figure 15-3 shows growth in global carbon dioxide emissions, measured in million metric tons, from 1900 to 2010.

15.4b Energy

A major environmental issue is **energy inefficiency**, or the wasting of precious nonrenewable sources of energy. Nonrenewable energy sources, such as coal, oil, and natural gas, were formed millions of years ago under unique conditions of temperature, pressure, and biological phenomena (hence the term **fossil fuels**). Once these are depleted, they will be gone forever. In addition, because these fuels are not equally distributed around the world, they are the cause of significant power imbalances worldwide, with associated armed conflicts that are typically disastrous for both humans and the natural environment in general.[42] As India, China, and other fast-growth areas in the developing world increase their demand for energy, the depletion of fossil fuels is occurring at a quickening pace.

FIGURE 15-3 Global Carbon Dioxide Emissions

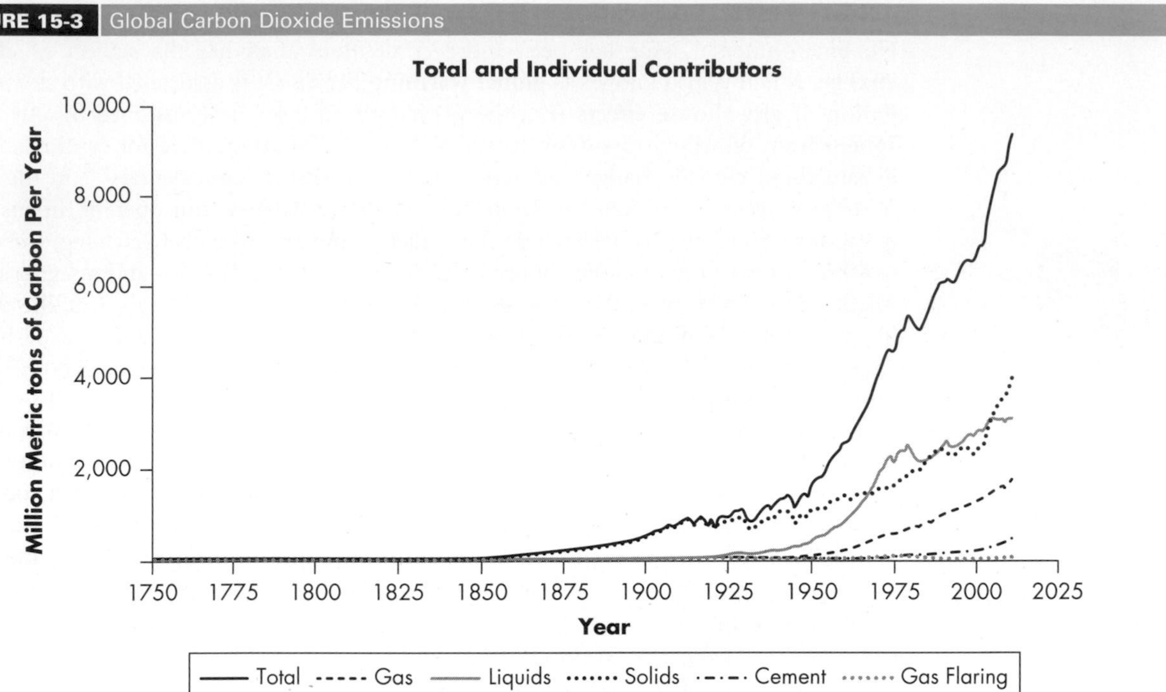

The answer to the nonrenewability problem is to use as little as possible of these energy sources through implementation of sound energy conservation practices, while also shifting to renewable energy sources. Several technologies for tapping these renewable, low-polluting energy sources are becoming economically competitive with nonrenewable sources and so, for business, the energy issue represents not only a challenge but also an opportunity.[43] Companies like Facebook, Google, Amazon, and Apple have successfully invested in renewable energy technology, in part due to a boost in government incentives and declining systems costs.[44] Many states now mandate that utilities obtain a minimum percentage of their energy supply through renewable energy sources, and companies ranging from Johnson & Johnson to Fed Ex and Starbucks have committed to buying a portion of their energy from renewable sources.[45] With the money now flowing into "clean tech" funds that focus mainly on renewable sources of energy like hydropower, wind, and solar, firms are scrambling to determine how to capitalize on this sustainability trend. Not every firm will succeed in this arena but those that do stand to reap big profits.

15.4c Water

Water presents problems in both quality and quantity. The developed world has made significant progress in the quality of water—no longer are waterways so polluted that they risk catching on fire as the Cuyahoga River did in Cleveland in 1969.[46] However, recent incidence like the Flint, Michigan, water contamination crisis, which identified lead poisoning in the community as a result of changing the water supply from Detroit's system to the Flint River, is evidence of ongoing problems with water pollution that can affect the health and welfare of communities for decades.[47] We discuss this in more detail below.

Municipal sewage, industrial wastes, urban runoff, agricultural runoff, atmospheric fallout, and overharvesting all continue to contribute to the degradation of the world's oceans and waterways. So, too, do dam sedimentation, deforestation, overgrazing, and over-irrigation. The quality of the developing world's water quality is in far worse shape than that in the developed world. A staggering 90 to 95 percent of sewage and 70 percent of industrial waste is untreated as it flows into rivers, lakes, and the ocean.[48] More than a billion people worldwide lack clean water, and the problem shows no signs of abating.[49]

Beyond the problem with pollution, experts now warn that the world is facing a "water bankruptcy."[50] Over four billion people, or two-thirds of the world's population, face severe water shortages during at least one month every year.[51] In the United States, the state of California has faced severe droughts for many years in a row. As a result, the state developed its own Web site (http://drought.ca.gov/) and developed conservation actions and recovery efforts to address dry conditions and devastating wildfires.

The earth is a closed system with a water supply that is fixed, so as populations grow and crop irrigation increases, supplies become depleted. Pollution renders existing water unusable, further diminishing the supply. A global water crisis brought on by a combination of drought, pollution, mismanagement, and politics has thus developed.[52] No country, no matter how big, is immune from this crisis. In the United States, the giant Ogallala Aquifer, which lies under parts of eight states, is diminishing dramatically due to heavy demand.[53]

In China, the Yangtze River is so heavily polluted that a recent World Wildlife Fund report declared the damage to the river's ecosystem to be largely irreversible.[54] The Yellow River has slowed to a trickle for much of the year, leaving nearly 400 million Chinese people, one-third of the country's population, without access to clean water.[55] In India, two-thirds of the 1.1 billion population lack clean water, and the water table drops six to ten feet each year. More than half the people in the world could be living in severely water-stressed areas by 2030 if current trends continue.[56] This water bankruptcy poses an even bigger threat than the global financial crisis.[57]

World Water Day, first launched by the United Nations Conference on Environment and Development in 1992, is held annually to draw attention to these issues, as governments and companies around the world unveil their latest plans to tackle water quality and scarcity.[58] One hundred fifty companies and organizations in the United States gathered at the White House Water Summit and pledged over $5 billion to improve drinking water quality and systems in the United States.[59] Simultaneously, the jeans company, Levi's, announced that it would make its innovative, trademarked "Water < Less™" technology for manufacturing denim open source, leading the way to help other businesses across the world use less water in their manufacturing and design processes.[60] As more companies sign on to invest in water technologies, improve water protections, and address groundwater depletion, the hope is that developed and developing countries can work together to address some of these issues. Researchers point out that water quality and quantity are not only important to basic human needs but also to the safety and security of agriculture, industry, and ecosystems that can even undermine national security.[61]

15.4d Biodiversity and Land Use

An ecosystem's **biodiversity**, that is, the variation of life forms inside the system, serves as a key indicator of its health. According to H.E. Dr. Ali Abdussalam Treki, President of the United Nations General Assembly, "Biodiversity continues to be lost at an unprecedented rate, thus threatening the capacity of the planet to provide the required goods and services. Throughout most of time, species died off at a natural rate of one to five in a year; now dozens become extinct each day."[62] Ecosystem and habitat destruction through agricultural and urban development activities and, of course, pollution have put at risk both wildlife and beneficial plants. Excesses in individual and organizational activities may be responsible for significant and tragic ecosystem and species degradation.

Another disturbing environmental issue that human populations face is land degradation. Degradation includes such different multiple facets as desertification, deforestation, overgrazing, salinization, and alkalization. Soil acidification, urban sprawl, and soil sealing, or industrial soil contamination, are part of land degradation as well. According to Dr. Treki, "Seventy per cent of the world's poor live in rural areas. They depend directly on biological resources for as much as 90 per cent of their needs such as food, fuel, medicine, shelter, and transportation. Over three billion people depend on marine and coastal biodiversity, while more than 1.6 billion rely on forests and non-timber forest products for their livelihoods. The degradation of habitat and the loss of biodiversity are threatening the livelihoods of more than one billion people living in dry and subhumid lands, particularly in Africa, the continent most affected by drought and desertificatication."[63]

What does this mean for business? In a recent McKinsey study, a majority of executives see biodiversity as more of an opportunity than a risk.[64] Preserving biodiversity through new products from renewable natural resources and communicating with stakeholders about these ideas were noted to boost their company's reputation. Nevertheless, they also identified areas of concern for companies in the areas of water scarcity, infectious disease, food insecurity, flooding, droughts and desertification, and soil degradation. As the population of the world continues to grow, the problems created by these issues will only increase.

15.4e Chemicals, Toxics, and Heavy Metals

The production of **toxic substances**, whether as constituents of intended products or as unwanted by-products, is an important issue because of its potential for harm. The U.S. Environmental Protection Agency (EPA) defines toxic substances as chemicals or compounds that may present an unreasonable threat to human health and the environment: Human exposure to toxic substances can cause a variety of health effects, including

ETHICS IN PRACTICE CASE

Water Scoring: A Way to Push for Better Water Stewardship?

CDP, formerly known as the Carbon Disclosure Project, is a nonprofit organization that works with investors, corporations, and policymakers on sustainability issues. In 2015 they partnered with South Pole Group to launch a "water scoring" system. The main objective of the scoring is to "catalyze" companies to improve water quality. Since 2009, CDP has been actively gathering water management data for large institutional investors. The data covers self-reported corporate water risk assessments, water risk exposure, mitigation activities, and governance strategies. CDP and South Pole Group will evaluate the water practices of companies operating in 112 countries across the "most water dependent industry sectors" and score them for investors, policymakers, and consumers to see. They promote their services to institutional investors with the idea that if water scarcity prevails, companies will not be able to grow and may not even be able to provide their core products or businesses.

1. CDP and South Pole make the business case for corporate water stewardship, do you agree?
2. How does water scoring help to push companies to do more to address water stewardship?
3. What company stakeholders might be concerned about the risks of water scarcity and quality?

Sources: Renaut Heuberger, "Water Scoring: Managing the Risks of Having Big Fish Stuck in Polluted Ponds," *HuffPost Green* (August 5, 2015), http://www.huffingtonpost.com/renat-heuberger/water-scoring-managing-the-risk-of-having-big-fish-stuck-in-polluted-ponds_b_7930904.html. Accessed March 30, 2016; Renaut Heuberger, "The Business Case for Corporate Water Stewardship," *HuffPost Impact* (July 29, 2015), http://www.huffingtonpost.com/renat-heuberger/the-business-case-for-cor_1_b_7887590.html. Accessed March 20, 2016.

damage to the nervous system, reproductive and developmental problems, cancer, and genetic disorders.[65]

Two problems are central to the toxic substances issue. First, we are not always aware of the effects, especially the long-term and interactive effects, of exposure to the thousands of chemicals produced each year. Hence, the DuPont chemical dump of PFOA waste in Virginia, which we discussed in Chapter 5, went unnoticed for years, because the substance itself was not regulated, and it was unknown exactly how much PFOA was safe to ingest.[66] As we discussed in the previous chapter, strict and absolute liability doctrines hold firms to a high degree of accountability for the effects of toxic substances. Second, toxic substances can be associated with industrial accidents, causing unforeseen widespread biological damage. The Bhopal, India, chemical plant leak; the Chernobyl nuclear power plant meltdown in the former Soviet Union; the BP oil rig explosion; and the more recent Flint Michigan lead water poisonings are known environmental disasters involving toxic substances. Not so well known are the thousands of spills, leaks, fires, and explosions reported to the EPA that can average 18 a day.[67]

15.4f Air Pollution

The short- and long-term effects of both outdoor and indoor **air pollution** are wide-ranging and severe.[68] Air pollution leads to acid rain, global warming, smog, the depletion of the ozone layer, and other serious conditions. It also causes serious respiratory and other illnesses, so it is not surprising that it rates high in concern according to public opinion polls.[69] In addition to causing human health problems, ambient air pollution is also responsible for a condition called **acid rain**. Acid rain refers broadly to a mixture of wet and dry deposition (deposited material) from the atmosphere containing higher than normal amounts of nitric and sulfuric acids.[70]

Both natural sources, such as volcanoes and decaying vegetation, and artificial sources, primarily emissions of sulfur dioxide and nitrogen oxides from fossil fuel combustion, can lead to acid rain.[71] Acid rain causes acidification of lakes and streams, contributes to the damage of trees at high elevations, and accelerates the decay of building materials and paints, including irreplaceable buildings and statues. Before falling to the earth, acid rain degrades visibility and harms public health.[72]

Indoor air pollution is another environmental problem that is becoming an increasing concern, because most people spend the majority of their lives indoors. Indoor air pollution comes from a variety of sources, including oil, gas, kerosene, coal, wood, and tobacco products, and building materials and furnishings such as asbestos-containing insulation, damp carpets, household cleaning products, and lead-based paints.[73] In 2016 the company Lumber Liquidators had to pay $2.5 million to settle claims that some of its products violated California air standards. Its laminate flooring made in China had high levels of the carcinogen formaldehyde that violated California's air standards.[74] The immediate effects of indoor air pollution are typically short term and treatable; these include irritation of the eyes, nose, and throat, headaches, dizziness, and fatigue. However, longer-term effects that might show up years after exposure can be severely debilitating or fatal. These effects include some respiratory diseases, heart disease, and cancer.[75]

15.4g Waste Management

Reduce, Reuse, and Recycle is the waste management mantra. The first goal is to *reduce* the amount of waste discarded, which is source reduction; this is the best form of waste management because in this case the waste is never generated in the first place. The next best option is to *reuse* containers and products—either repairing anything that is broken or giving it to someone who can repair it. Reusing is preferable to recycling because it does not require reprocessing to make the item usable again. *Recycling* is the third best option but still very valuable. **Recycling** transforms what once might have been waste into a valuable resource. Business can profit greatly from the boon in recycling. By recycling, businesses are able to cut costs—producing less garbage means lower landfill fees. Apple is a company that embraces the recycling process with strict factory standards for recycling the iPhone—both to protect its technology and benefit the bottom line. They have a "full-destruction" policy that partners them with a network of recyclers to grind the iPhone to bits and allows recycling partners to share in the sale of extracted materials like gold and copper.[76]

Recognizing these advantages, companies like Gap have developed lofty goals for diverting waste away from landfills, with the goal of diverting 80 percent away from landfills by 2020—a significant increase from their 2014 numbers that only tallied 29 percent.[77] The company is trying to reduce packaging weight and even change the produce materials to allow for greater recycling. Similarly, Coca-Cola decided that it was time to change the materials in its plastic bottle. In 2015 it produced its first 100 percent plant-based PET plastic bottle that converts Brazilian sugar cane into recyclable plastic.[78] Even the Danish toy maker Lego, which has been making building blocks from petroleum-based plastic since 1963, is searching to reduce its carbon footprint with bio-based plastics.[79] Efforts like these also present new business opportunities for the entrepreneur.

The term **circular economy** is a term applied to the system that businesses use to recycle—it involves keeping resources and extracting value from them as long as possible and then recovering and regenerating the resources and products at the end of each life cycle.[80] It is an alternative to a "take-make-dispose" approach for lower energy use. Patagonia is a company that uses a circular economy strategy. Through an initiative called Worn Wear, they provide support for their customers to repair damaged clothing and equipment themselves.[81] Alternatively, they provide a way for customers to send clothing to the company for repair or recycling. They also urge their customers to buy only what they need and avoid "relentless consumption." At the same time, Patagonia established a fund to invest in other "circular leaning" companies and they support secondary markets for their products through partnerships with eBay in the United States and United Kingdom and through investment in Yerdle, an app that lets people give away items.[82] Figure 15-4 provides a diagram of how the circular economy works.

FIGURE 15-4 The Circular Economy

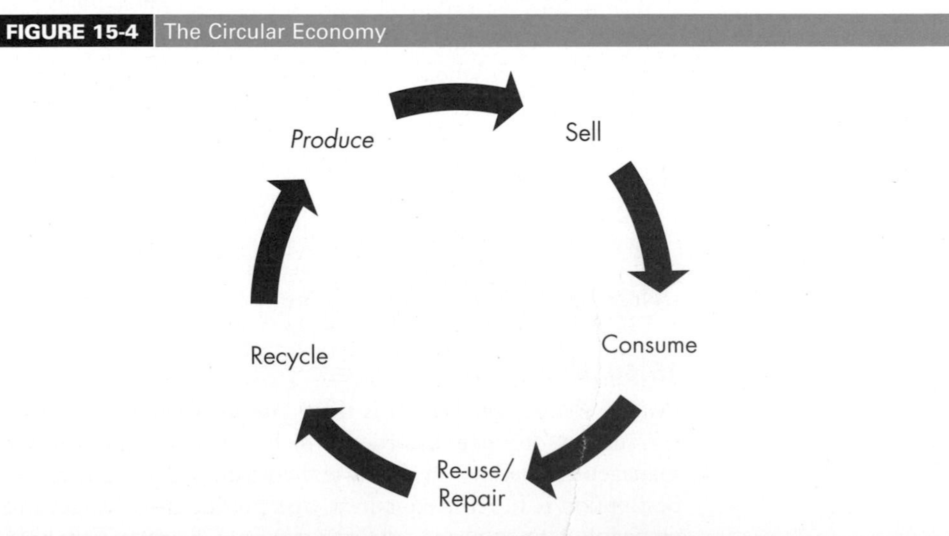

Special consideration must be given to waste that is hazardous. Hazardous waste has properties that make it harmful or potentially harmful to human health or the environment. As defined by the EPA, the large and diverse world of hazardous waste includes liquids, solids, contained gases, or sludges.[83] Hazardous wastes can be generated by manufacturing processes, or they can simply result from discarded commercial products, such as cleaning fluids or pesticides.[84] The risk posed by these wastes creates countless causes for concern. Exposure to these wastes in the environment, whether in air, water, food, or soil, can cause cancer, birth defects, and a host of other problems.[85] Another concern is the toxicological effects of a number of new chemicals coming onto the market. Because they are new, we know less about their effects and the measures needed to protect human health and the environment from possible contamination.[86]

15.4h Ozone Depletion

Ozone is an oxygen-related gas that is harmful to life near the earth's surface but is vital in the stratosphere in blocking dangerous ultraviolet radiation from the sun. Over 20 years ago, NASA scientists observed a huge decrease in ozone over Antarctica. They then discovered a "hole" in the ozone layer that had grown as large as the North American continent. Their measurements showed that the flow of ultraviolet light had increased directly under the ozone hole. This phenomenon was attributed to human-produced chemicals—chlorofluorocarbons (CFCs), used in refrigeration, and halons, used in fire extinguisher systems, as well as other ozone-depleting chemicals. A thinner layer of ozone is associated with a higher rate of skin cancer and other illnesses, as well as an increase in problems with agricultural production.

Ozone hole observers were cautiously optimistic in 2013 when the hole in the ozone layer was at its second smallest point in 20 years.[87] However, ongoing concerns with the impact of ozone holes led the Obama administration to tighten the federal ozone standard from 75 parts per billion (ppb) to 70 parts per billion, with ramifications for businesses as they adapt to new standards.[88] For those interested in observing the hole in process, NASA provides "Ozone Watch" (ozonewatch.gsfc.nasa.gov), a Web site with pictures created from satellite images that enable observers to check on the latest status of the ozone layer over the South Pole.

15.4i Oceans and Fisheries

The EPA expresses it well by saying we all live in a **watershed**—an area that drains to a common waterway, such as a stream, lake, estuary, wetland, aquifer, or even the ocean.[89] Our actions affect the oceans and other waterways, and so far, it has not been for the better. Many of the same factors that affect fresh water have an impact on the marine environments. Each year, trillions of gallons of sewage and industrial waste are dumped into marine waters. These and other pollutants, such as oil and plastics, have been associated with significant damage to a number of coastal ecosystems, including salt marshes, mangrove swamps, estuaries, and coral reefs. The result has been local and regional shellfish bed closures, seafood-related illnesses, and reduced shoreline protection from floods and storms.

Once it would have been inconceivable that the vast oceans would ever run short of fish to meet human needs. However, a 2008 report found that 85 percent of the world's fisheries were either at capacity, over capacity, or had collapsed.[90] Fast forward to 2016, and the issue still remains. As the *Economist* magazine noted, overfishing has led to "catastrophic" falling fish stock levels.[91] Although more work is needed, efforts to reclaim the waters have met with some success. The return of the Chesapeake Blue Crab is an example. A variety of efforts such as shortening the crabbing season, instituting a crabber license buyback program, and not permitting the raking of hibernating pregnant females from the bay floor have yielded promising results over the years.[92]

SPOTLIGHT *on Sustainability*

There's an App for That

Sustainability software has become a huge growth market. With increased interest in sustainability reporting and major buyers such as Walmart requiring suppliers to show proof of sustainable practices, companies are looking for ways to improve and monitor their environmental impacts. At the same time, individuals are increasingly interested in achieving a more sustainable lifestyle. Software manufacturers have been designing apps for smartphones to make that task easier. The following apps are free and available for both iPhone and Android users.

Paper Karma:

Use your phone to stop unwanted paper mail (coupons, flyers, catalogs, magazines, yellow pages, etc.). Simply take a photo of the mail you do not want and Paper Karma takes care of the rest. Paper Karma contacts the mailer and asks to have your name removed from the distribution list.

GoodGuide:

GoodGuide helps consumers find products that are safe, healthy, green, and ethical. The app has the capability to scan bar codes, enabling consumers to decide between products based on their environmental, health, and social impact. Main ratings are provided by qualified scientists, but users may also comment on and review products.

Locavore:

Eating local food is not only a way to enjoy the freshest food available but also a way to reduce one's carbon footprint by minimizing transportation. Locavore identifies the foods that are currently in season, as well as those that are coming into season soon. They also provide information about the food, in season recipes, and directions to local farmer's markets.

FoodKeeper:

Knowing how to store your food properly is a subject many people are not well educated in. USDA FoodKeeper is a free app by USDA Food Safety and Inspection Service that provides information about how you can buy food at its peak quality so you can reduce food waste.

iRecycle:

Local recycling options can be hard to locate. iRecycle provides users with the collection points for recycling a range of materials, as well as directions, hours, and the materials collected at each location. Interested users can also connect with other recyclers through Facebook and Twitter.

Seafood Watch:

This project of the Monterey Bay Aquarium strives to inform consumers about the fishing practices that are depleting fish populations, destroying habitats, and polluting the oceans. The Seafood Watch app lets consumers search for seafood and sushi so that they can make sustainable seafood choices. It also provides alternatives to seafood on the "Avoid" list. Project Fishmap lets users add names of restaurants and stores where they found sustainable seafood and find out where others have found it.

Sources: https://www.paperkarma.com/; http://www.goodguide.com/; http://www.getlocavore.com/; http://www.earth911.com/eco-tech/food-waste-foodkeeper-app/; http://www.earth911.com/eco-tech/irecycle-now-on-android/; http://www.seafoodwatch.org/seafood-recommendations/our-app. Accessed March 30, 2016.

15.4j Deforestation

Although humans depend on forests for building materials, fuel, medicines, chemicals, food, employment, and recreation, the world's forests can be quickly depleted by a variety of human factors. **Deforestation** adds to soil erosion problems and is a major cause of the greenhouse effect. Felled trees are no longer able to absorb carbon dioxide and are sometimes burned for land clearing and charcoal, thereby releasing rather than absorbing carbon dioxide. Moisture and nutrient ecosystem cycles can also be severely damaged in deforesting activities, negatively affecting adjacent land and water ecosystems.

Deforestation plays a key role in global warming. Few would be able to guess which country makes the third greatest greenhouse gas emissions after China and the United States. Most would guess Germany because of its industry or Japan because of its cities and high technology. The right answer is Indonesia; it releases 3.3 billion tons of carbon dioxide a year because of deforestation.[93] Trees absorb carbon dioxide when they are alive and when they die they release it into the air. As a result, deforestation accounts for 20 percent of global carbon emissions—more than the world's trains, boats, and planes combined.[94]

15.5 Responsibility for Environmental and Sustainability Issues

Environmental problems such as smog, toxic waste, and acid rain can be described as "**wicked problems**"—that is, problems with characteristics such as interconnectedness, complexity, uncertainty, ambiguity, conflict, and societal constraints. Every wicked problem seems to be a symptom of another problem.[95] Responsibility for such messy situations is difficult to affix, because solutions to wicked problems are seldom complete and final and, therefore, credit for these solutions is seldom given or taken. *Chlorofluorocarbons*, or *CFCs*, for example, were once considered safe alternatives to other, more toxic refrigerants, which is why these ozone destroyers are so ubiquitous in our society's technologies.

When no one takes responsibility for adverse environmental effects, a phenomenon called the **tragedy of the commons** is likely to occur.[96] A "commons" is a plot of land available to all. When the commons is large enough to accommodate the needs of everyone, no problems occur. However, as herders continue to add animals to their herds, the carrying capacity of the commons becomes strained. It is in the self-interest of each herder to allow the animals to graze, even though the cumulative grazing will inevitably destroy the commons. The analogy of a "commons" can be applied to the environment as a whole as well as its many constituent parts. For example, public parks experience unconstrained use (e.g., vehicles driving anywhere or unrestrained picking of vegetation) that can damage them, as a shared resource. As Garrett Hardin points out in his classic article on the tragedy of the commons in the environment, constraints must also be placed on the use of the commons (i.e., our environment) because in the absence of constraints, self-interest is likely to lead individuals and organizations to behave in ways that will not sustain our shared resources.[97]

15.5a Environmental Ethics

Nature itself is a polluter and destroyer. The earth's core is continually polluting many bodies of water and airsheds with a full range of toxic heavy metals. Species have been going extinct since life evolved as, in a continuous cycle of life and death, nature acts as its own destroyer. Given this fact, there are many questions to be raised regarding the environment. For example:

- What does absolute human environmental sensitivity mean? Humans must consume at least some plants and water to survive. If humans and their organizations need to pollute and destroy at least some of nature for their survival, what is the relative level of degradation that is ethical?
- Do nonhuman species have any "rights," and, if so, what are they, and how can they be reconciled with human rights?
- Concerning human rights and the environment, how do we assess the claims of indigenous cultures to the use of their respective environments? Is there any connection between the domination of humans by humans (e.g., the domination of one nation, race, or gender by another) and the domination of nature by humans? This latter question is especially central to several schools of environmental ethical thought, including social ecology, ecofeminism, and environmental justice.

- Whose standards will determine what is or is not ethical? How clean do the air and water need to be, and how much is the public willing to pay to meet these standards? As in our earlier discussion of business ethics, values play a major role and can be highly variable in breadth and depth across perspectives, situations, and time.

Following the ethical models and concepts discussed in Chapters 7 and 8, we can develop a better idea of what environmental ethics is and how it can be practiced. Kohlberg's model of moral development, for instance, can be used to identify environment-related attitudes and behaviors by developmental level. At the preconventional (infant) level in environmental ethics, humans and human organizations can be perceived as being concerned only with self or with their own species and habitats. A conventional (adolescent) level might entail some appreciation of nature, but only when and where such appreciation is commonplace or "in." A postconventional (adult) environmental ethic might include more mature attitudes and behaviors that are more universal (including all species and habitats), of greater duration (including unborn generations), and more consistent (if we humans have a right to survive as a species, why don't all species have that right?).

Similarly, the ethical principle of utilitarianism—the greatest good for the greatest number—could be expanded in environmental ethics to the greatest good for the greatest numbers of species and ecosystems. The Golden Rule could read, "Do unto other species as you would have them do unto you." From a virtue ethics perspective, a "Best Self" ethical test could include the question, "Is this action or decision related to the natural environment compatible not only with my concept of myself at my best but also with my concept of myself as a human representing my species at its best?"

In *Who Speaks for the Trees*, authors Sama, Welcomer, and Gerde show that integrating sustainability into a firm's philosophy is a natural extension of stakeholder theory.[98] They expand the concept of the natural environment beyond living things to the entire ecological system from which the firm obtains resources and to which it bears responsibility for the impacts, both positive and negative, that firm actions have on it. They invoke the ethic of care, discussed in Chapter 8, and explain that organizations that follow a practice of care would treat the natural environment, which they call the "silent stakeholder," with respect.[99] Many other ethics concepts and principles discussed earlier apply to the natural environment and sustainability discussions.

15.5b The NIMBY Problem

The acronym, **NIMBY**, can often be found on bumper stickers and conference agendas and in newspaper articles, college courses, and many other communication vehicles. It stands for the "Not in My Back Yard" phenomenon, and it reflects human denial of responsibility for the misuse of the environment. The growth of the NIMBY attitude can be seen in the proliferation of other acronyms describing it. *NOTE* or "Not Over There Either," *BANANA* or "Build Absolutely Nothing Near Anything," and *NOPE* or "Not On Planet Earth" were all coined by observers frustrated with the human tendency to avoid assuming responsibility for societal costs.

Essentially, NIMBY is an attitude or behavior set based on avoidance or denial of responsibility, and examples of NIMBY abound regarding environmental issues. One is the community that uses ever-increasing amounts of electricity but decides it does not want a power plant that produces electricity to locate near its homes and schools. Another is a company that generates increasing amounts of waste but is unwilling to pay the full cost of proper disposal. The cost of NIMBY with delays, cancellations, and inflated expenses on issues that range from housing construction caps in San Francisco to port expansion in Savannah, Georgia, is estimated to be more than $1 trillion annually

ETHICS IN PRACTICE CASE

A Little Green Lie

I work for Telecommunication Company as a sales consultant. The environment is very competitive and as "salespeople," we are always required to surpass our quotas and "make money." Lately the company has decided to "go green," which is good for the environment. However, the true motive behind the company's initiative is to save money on paper bills, as the managers have confessed to us. As a way of making us convert customers to paperless billing, they have factored paperless billing conversion into our metrics, which means that if we do not perform, we can be reprimanded or fired. One of the area managers suggested we tell customers that the company is no longer sending paper bills and that if they wish to still receive a paper bill, they will be charged a fee (which is completely false, paper bills are free to customers). I usually see customers fall for it and go paperless in order to save money, and the sales consultants who have applied this method are usually our top rankers. The manager said it is not really lying especially if you are helping selfish customers to help the environment.

1. Global warming and environmental issues have become serious problems. Keeping this in mind, is it right deceive customers if your main motive is to save the environment and help save trees?
2. Is it ethical for the area manager to demand that sales representatives lie?
3. Would it be ethical for the sales representative to follow the directions of the manager?
4. What would you do if you were in this position and what would be your motive behind it?

Contributed Anonymously

by *Forbes* magazine.[100] The obvious difficulty with the NIMBY syndrome is that the entities (human individuals, organizations, or both) causing environmental pollution or degradation are not identified as the sources of the problem, and therefore no action is taken to reduce the problem. The NIMBY phenomenon avoids or denies the root cause of the damage and addresses only the symptoms with an attitude of nonresponsibility characterized by an approach of "I'll create an environmental problem, but I want to have as little as possible to do with solving it." One popular cartoon characterizing the NIMBY problem pictures a stream of polluting, honking cars passing along a highway in front of a huge billboard that reads "Honk if you love the environment!"

15.6 The Role of Governments in Environmental and Sustainability Issues

As mentioned earlier, governments have played major roles in environmental matters since the inception of such issues. Governments have procured, distributed, and developed habitable lands and other resources; protected, taxed, and zoned natural environment-based areas; and, more recently, exercised regulatory control over how those environments could be used. This section looks at how governments in the United States have dealt with environmental challenges and then identifies what has been done in several other countries and at the international level.

15.6a Responses of Governments in the United States

Although the U.S. federal government has influenced environmental policy since at least 1899, with its permit requirement for discharge of hazardous materials into navigable waters, the major entrance of the U.S. government into environmental issues occurred in 1970 with the signing of the National Environmental Policy Act (NEPA). The second section of this act spells out its purposes: "To declare a national policy which will encourage productive and enjoyable harmony between man and his environment; to promote efforts which will prevent or eliminate damage to the environment and biosphere and stimulate the health and welfare of man; and to enrich the understanding of the ecological systems and natural resources important to the Nation."[101]

In addition to establishing these broad policy goals, this legislation requires federal agencies to prepare **environmental impact statements (EISs)** for any "proposals for legislation and other major federal action significantly affecting the quality of the human environment." Environmental impact statements are reports of studies explaining and estimating the environmental impacts of questionable practices and irreversible uses of resources and proposing detailed, reasonable alternatives to these practices and uses.

Business is affected by the NEPA in several ways. First, the federal government pays private consultants to conduct tens of billions of dollars' worth of EISs each year. Second, because the federal government is the largest landholder in the United States, private businesses wishing to secure licenses and permits to conduct timber, grazing, mining, and highway, dam, and nuclear construction operations likely will be parties to the preparation of EISs. Third, private businesses working under federal government contracts are typically obliged to participate in EIS preparation. Fourth, the NEPA has been used as a model by many state governments, and therefore businesses heavily involved in significant state and local government contracts are likely to be involved in the EIS process.

Also in 1970, the U.S. **Environmental Protection Agency (EPA)** was created as an independent agency to research pollution problems, aid state and local government environmental efforts, and administer many of the federal environmental laws. These laws can be categorized into three areas—air, water, and land—even though a specific problem of pollution and/or degradation, such as acid rain, often involves two or more of these categories. The roles and responsibilities of the EPA include a wide range of functions to protect the environment, but it is also important to remember that it is a federal agency that must work with state agencies. This can often be difficult in enforcing pollution and other environmental problems, which can cross over state and federal jurisdictions. This challenge is evidenced in the Flint City, Michigan, water crisis, mentioned earlier, and outlined in the Ethics in Practice Case: Who Failed to Protect the Community in Flint, Michigan?

Air Quality Legislation. The key piece of federal air quality legislation is the **Clean Air Act.**[102] The overall approach of this act is similar to that used in other areas of federal regulation, such as safety and health legislation, in that standards are set and timetables for implementation are established. The EPA has set primary standards (based on health effects) and secondary standards (based on environmental effects) for a variety of air pollutants. Businesses that directly produce these substances, such as electric utilities, and those whose products when used cause these substances to be produced, such as automobiles, must reduce their emissions to within the set standards.[103] Fines levied under the Clean Air Act can be pretty substantial. In 2014, the largest-ever civil penalty under the Act was imposed on Hyundai and Kia, who agreed to pay $100 million to settle an investigation into its misstatements of gas mileage estimates on about 1.2 million vehicles.[104]

The Clean Air Act introduced the concept of **emissions trading** (i.e., "**cap and trade**") to the United States. This approach is intended to reduce a particular pollutant over an entire industrial region by treating all emission sources as if they were all beneath one bubble. A business can increase its emissions of sulfur dioxide in one part of a plant or region if it reduces its sulfur dioxide pollution by as much or more in another part of the plant or region. In addition, and as an extension of this bubble analogy, businesses that reduce their emissions can trade these rights to other businesses that

ETHICS IN PRACTICE CASE

Who Failed to Protect the Community in Flint, Michigan?

In April 2014, the city of Flint, Michigan, switched its water supply from Detroit's system to the Flint River under the control of a state-appointed emergency manager. The decision was made as a cost-saving measure because of Flint's dire economic situation. But, not too long after the switch was made, residents began complaining about the taste, color, and odor of the water. Some began to have concerns about the water quality. By October 2014, coliform bacteria had been detected in some of the tap water, but the Michigan Department of Environmental Quality blamed it on cold weather, aging pipes, and a population decline. Over the next few months, there were rising concerns about the water quality, including statements from the local General Motors factory about the water's corrosive effects on auto parts and statements from local residents and private testing companies about higher levels of lead in the water. The City of Detroit offered to reconnect to Flint to its system in January 2015, waiving the reconnection fee, but the Flint emergency manager declined the offer.

In September 2015, a professor at Virginia Tech reported that the corrosiveness of the river water was causing lead to leach into the supply, and shortly thereafter, a group of doctors in Flint urged the city to stop using the river water after finding high levels of lead in the blood of local children, which could cause learning disabilities, behavior problems, and additional illness. The results of tests showed lead levels running from 11 parts per billion to as high as 397 parts per billion. At this point, the "blame game" began.

An official at the U.S. Environmental Protection Agency said her department knew as early as April 2015 about the lack of corrosion controls in Flint's water supply, but she said she could not bring the information to the public and override state control. EPA Administrator Gina McCarthy blamed Flint's lead problems on state regulators who prescribed the wrong chemical treatments to keep corrosive river water from leaching the lead pipes. She said she did not have enough evidence of state delays that EPA needed to move in and take control. Some observers point out that the EPA did everything it was required to do under the law because there is no policy or regulation that required the EPA to tell the public what it knew about the lead in Flint's drinking water system.

In October 2015, Flint reconnected to Detroit's water supply after the Governor got involved; however, residents still could not drink the water unfiltered. While the blame game continued, residents of Flint were waiting to see what the long-term health effects would be for those who ingested the lead-tainted water.

1. Who are the stakeholders in this case and what are their stakes?
2. Where does the responsibility for the Flint, Michigan, water crisis belong?
3. When would it have been the appropriate time for the EPA to notify Flint residents? Would it have mattered?
4. What would you have done if you were the "official" at the EPA who knew about the problem back in April 2015?
5. How is this an example of the tensions between law and ethics? Explain.
6. How can sustainability be a state and federal objective if cases such as the Flint River are permitted to occur?

Sources: Emily Atkin, "Does the EPA Bear Responsibility for Flint?" *ThinkProgress* (January 26, 2016), http://thinkprogress.org/politics/2016/01/26/3741139/epa-flint-water-crisis/. Accessed May 6, 2016; Michael Bastasch, "EPA Named in Blistering Report on Flint Water Crisis," *The Daily Caller* (March 24, 2016), http://dailycaller.com/2016/03/24/epa-named-in-blistering-report-on-flint-water-crisis/. Accessed May 6, 2016; Lenny Bernstein, "EPA's McCarthy Stands up to Claims Her Agency Is Responsible for Flint Water Crisis," *The Washington Post* (March 17, 2016), https://www.washingtonpost.com/national/health-science/epas-mccarthy-stands-up-to-claims-her-agency-is-responsible-for-flint-water-crisis/2016/03/17/b928f562-ec6f-11e5-bc08-3e03a5b41910_story.html; Jim Lynch, "EPA Stayed Silent on Flint's Tainted Water," *The Detroit News* (January 12, 2016). http://www.detroitnews.com/story/news/politics/2016/01/12/epa-stayed-silent-flints-tainted-water/78719620/; Flint Water Advisory Task Force Report (March 21, 2016), http://mediad.publicbroadcasting.net/p/michigan/files/201603/taskforce_report.pdf?_ga=1.147700144.609033213.1458749402. Accessed May 6, 2016.

want to increase their emissions. Proponents of emissions credit trading hail these policies as free market environmentalism, whereas opponents ridicule them as licenses to pollute. In the Hyundai/Kia settlement noted above, the companies had to also give up greenhouse gas emissions credits—estimated at $200 million—because the lower mileage ratings added up to 4.75 million more metric tons of greenhouse gases.[105] The emissions trading system is part of the Kyoto Protocol, an international agreement that set legally binding targets and deadlines for cutting the greenhouse gas emissions of industrialized countries.[106] In 2015, these targets were amended at the Paris Climate Change Conference, as we discussed earlier in the chapter, and again below.

Water Quality Legislation. U.S. government involvement in water quality issues has followed a pattern similar to that of air quality issues. The **Clean Water Act** (also known as the Federal Water Pollution Control Act) was passed in the early 1970s with broad environmental quality goals and an implementation system, involving both the federal and state governments, designed to attain those goals. The ultimate purpose of the Clean Water Act was to achieve water quality consistent with protection of fish, shellfish, and wildlife and with safe conditions for human recreation in and on the water. The more tangible goal was to eliminate discharges of pollutants into navigable waters, which include most U.S. rivers, streams, and lakes. These goals were to be accomplished through a pollution permit system, called the National Pollutant Discharge Elimination System, which specifies maximum permissible discharge levels, and often timetables for installation of state-of-the-art pollution control equipment.

In August 2015, the Clean Water Act was updated with the Clean Water Rule. The Rule, to be jointly enforced by the U.S. EPA and the U.S. Army, more precisely defines the streams and wetlands to be protected as well as the permitting requirements for agriculture.[107] Another act—the Marine Protection, Research, and Sanctuaries Act of 1972—sets up a similar system for control of discharges into coastal ocean waters within U.S. territory. A third water quality law administered by the EPA, the Safe Drinking Water Act of 1974, establishes maximum contaminant levels for drinking water.[108]

Land-Related Legislation. Land pollution and degradation issues differ from air and water quality issues, because land by definition is far less fluid and therefore somewhat more visible than air and water and is more amenable to local or regional problem-solving approaches. Consequently, the U.S. federal government, in the Solid Waste Disposal Act of 1965, recognized that regional, state, and local governments should have the main responsibility for nontoxic waste management. The EPA's role in this area is limited to research and provision of technical and financial assistance to these other government levels. However, a 1976 amendment to this act, called the Resource Conservation and Recovery Act, set up a federal regulatory system for tracking and reporting the generation, transportation, and eventual disposal of hazardous wastes by businesses responsible for creating these wastes.[109]

The U.S. government has staked out a much larger role for itself in the area of toxic wastes. The 1976 **Toxic Substances Control Act** requires manufacturing and distribution businesses in the chemical industry to identify any chemicals that pose "substantial risks" of human or other natural environment harm. This act also requires chemical testing before commercialization and the possible halting of manufacture if the associated risks are unreasonable. Because there are over 70,000 chemicals already in use in the United States and more than 1,000 new chemicals introduced every year, the EPA has prioritized the substances that must be tested to focus on those that might cause cancer, birth defects, or gene mutations.[110]

The other major U.S. government activity in toxic wastes is known as **Superfund**, or, more formally, the Comprehensive Environmental Response, Compensation, and Liability Act of 1980 (CERCLA). Superfund is an effort to clean up more than 2,000 hazardous waste dumps and spills around the country, some dating back to the previous century. Funded by taxes on chemicals and petroleum, this program has established a National Priorities List to focus on the most hazardous sites and places legal and financial responsibility for the proper remediation of these sites on the appropriate parties. In addition, CERCLA also requires that unauthorized hazardous waste spills be reported and can order those responsible to clean up the sites.[111] The General Electric Company, as we discuss in Case 22, is a company who has been involved in the Hudson River PCBs Superfund Site, and its cleanup, for over a decade. The first five-year review for the Hudson River dredging project occurred in 2012 and concluded that the cleanup is meeting, or is expected to meet, the goals that were set by the EPA for the project. The next five-year review is expected to be completed by April 2017.[112]

One of the most important amendments to the Superfund law, the Emergency Planning and Community Right-to-Know Act of 1986, requires manufacturing companies to report to the federal government annually all of their releases into the environment of any of more than 500 toxic chemicals and chemical compounds. The EPA accumulates these reports and makes them available to the public (at https://iaspub.epa.gov/triexplorer/tri_release.chemical) with the intention that an informed public will pressure manufacturers to reduce these toxic releases.[113]

Endangered Species. The world's species are disappearing at an alarming rate, according to the World Conservation Union, which releases an annual Red List of endangered species.[114] Their 2015 report shows that nearly 20,000 species are now considered threatened with extinction—a quarter of the total number of species they assessed.[115]

In the United States, responsibility for endangered species is shared by two agencies, the U.S. Interior Department's Fish and Wildlife Service and the Commerce Department's National Marine Fisheries Act. They administer the 1973 **Endangered Species Act (ESA)**. This federal law assigns the responsibility of preventing harm to species considered "endangered" (i.e., facing extinction) or "threatened" (likely to become endangered).[116] Protection of species sometimes means moving them to safe areas when their original habitats have been destroyed by human activities, but it can also mean prevention of these activities, such as mining, construction, and fishing, before such habitat deprivation occurs. This restriction of business activities can be expected to continue as the extinction rate for species climbs, resulting in sometimes intense political conflicts between business interests and environmental groups.[117]

15.6b International Government Environmental and Sustainability Responses

The *United Nations Environment Programme (UNEP)* has led the way in identifying global environmental and sustainability problems and in working toward their resolution. As early as 1977, UNEP was studying the ozone problem and began to lay the groundwork for the 1987 **Montreal Protocol** in which most of the CFC-producing and CFC-consuming nations around the world agreed to a quick phase-out of these ozone-destroying substances. In 2009, the Montreal Protocol achieved universal ratification, the first United Nations treaty to do so.[118] Observers believe that, thanks to the Protocol, the ozone layer should return to pre-1980 levels by 2050 to 2075.[119] The ozone reduction brought by the Protocol has helped the world to avoid millions of cases of fatal skin cancer and tens of millions of cases of nonfatal skin cancer and cataracts.[120]

Another United Nations initiative is the **Global Compact**, discussed in Chapter 10. It brings thousands of companies from across the world society to support universal environmental and social principles. The Global Compact works to advance ten universal principles and seventeen sustainability goals. Three of the principles are targeted toward businesses' responsibilities for the environment, including that businesses should support a precautionary approach to environmental challenges (#7), undertake initiatives to promote greater environmental responsibility (#8), and encourage the development and diffusion of environmentally friendly technologies (#9)."[121] The **Global Reporting Initiative (GRI)**, also discussed in Chapter 10, is a collaborating center of the UNEP. GRI spearheaded the development of a sustainability reporting framework that has become the most widely used standard in the world. The reporting framework outlines the principles and indicators that organizations can use to measure and report their economic, environmental, and social performance.[122]

The U.N.'s Paris Climate Conference (otherwise known as **COP21**), which took place in December 2015, is considered to have created an "unprecedented global mandate to arrest climate change."[123] With approximately 190 countries committing to reducing greenhouse gas emissions through "Nationally Determined Contributions" (NDCs), the nations agreed to meet every five years to revise their pledges toward the goal of limiting global temperature increases. Following up on commitments made at earlier COP conferences, developed countries agreed to provide $100 billion annually through 2020, as a "floor" of financial assistance for developing countries to adapt to climate change and reduce emissions while growing their clean energy economies.[124] The Paris Climate Conference also made permanent the **Warsaw International Mechanism**, established at **COP19** to help address the loss and damage associated with impacts of climate change, including extreme events and slow onset events, in developing countries that are particularly vulnerable to the adverse effects of climate change. The loss and damage provision in the agreement does not create any "new legal liability" for high emitting countries.

However, challenges remain to accomplishing the goals established at COP21. As noted by several international energy officials, these challenges include:[125]

- Managing policy risk
- Figuring out how to price carbon
- Deciding the role of natural gas
- Providing sources of baseload power to support renewables
- Closing the gap between the costs of renewables and traditional energy sources.

In addition, there are a number of "practical market considerations" that will determine whether or not nations can deliver on the promises made in Paris.[126] Nevertheless, most agree that the Paris Climate Change Conference made significant movement forward in addressing the issues of reducing greenhouse gas emissions.[127]

15.7 Other Environmental and Sustainability Stakeholders

15.7a Environmental Interest Groups

Perhaps no force in today's society is more responsible for the "greening" of nations around the world than are the many environmental interest groups making up what has come to be known as "the environmentalist movement." This collection of nonprofit membership and think-tank organizations has been credited with moving the world's governments and businesses, as well as publics, in the direction of environmental responsibility through a host of activities, including demonstrations, boycotts, public education, lobbying, and research.

The history of the environmental movement is instructive. Whereas a few U.S. groups (the National Audubon Society, the Izaak Walton League, and the Sierra Club) were formed in the early 1900s during the first green wave of the century, many of the largest national and international environmental groups, such as the Environmental Defense Fund (now called Environmental Defense), Greenpeace, and the National Resources Defense Council, were created during the second environmental wave, in the late 1960s and early 1970s. Since that time, all of these groups and hundreds of other smaller, more locally focused environmental organizations have grown in size and clout. It was the century's third wave of environmentalism, beginning in the late 1980s, however, that gave many of these groups the power and legitimacy to become credible players in environmental policy-making around the globe.

Environmental interest groups have been instrumental in significantly influencing business environmental policy in this third wave. For example, Environmental Defense is working with Federal Express on building a new generation of vehicles, with DuPont on developing nanotech standards, and with PHH Arval on becoming the first carbon neutral fleet.[128] Other outcomes of relationships between environmental interest groups and business stakeholders have included corporate selection of environmental group representatives for corporate boards and top management positions, mutual participation in environmental "cleanup" projects, and corporate donations of time and money to environmental groups for their environmental conservation programs. This trend toward cooperation between otherwise adversarial groups is a characteristic of the third environmental or green wave that sets this wave apart from the two previous environmental eras. That collaboration is discussed in more detail in the section on business environmentalism.

The former chair of the Sierra Club identified three types of major U.S. environmental organizations based on this criterion of cooperation with business. He labeled groups characterized by confrontational behaviors as "radicals," groups that seek pragmatic reform through a combination of confrontation and cooperation as "mainstreamers," and groups that avoid confrontation and are more trusting of corporations as "accommodators."[129] As we mentioned, the differences between the types of groups are beginning to blur as business and environmental activists collaborate increasingly on shared goals. Nevertheless, it is instructive to look at some of the groups that have taken and still sometimes take a more radical approach.

One group that falls into the radical camp is the Rainforest Action Network (RAN). RAN has been particularly successful in getting large corporations to change their ways. The ways in which RAN has accomplished their goals are described in Figure 15-5. RAN

FIGURE 15-5 The Mosquito in the Tent Strategy

Street Theater	During the holiday season, RAN carolers sang "Oil Wells" to the tune of "Jingle Bells" in front of the Citigroup headquarters on Park Avenue. RAN obtained the access code to the Home Depot intercom and announced to shoppers that they should step carefully, because the wood on Aisle 13 had been ripped from the Amazon Basin and there might be blood on the floors. They had actors, dressed up as Minnie and Mickey Mouse, locked to Walt Disney headquarters with a banner that read, "Disney is destroying Indonesia's rainforest.
Celebrity Endorsements	The night before Citigroup's annual shareholder meeting, RAN began airing commercials showing Ed Asner, Susan Sarandon, Darryl Hannah, and Ali MacGraw cutting up their Citibank credit cards.
Coalitions	RAN doesn't go it alone. They work with other environmental organizations, socially responsible investors, liberal philanthropists, and even sympathetic insiders (which is how they got the Home Depot access code).
Internet Organizing	RAN uses the Internet to both launch their own initiatives and support those of other groups. They urge individuals to contact those whose behavior they want to change and thank those who responded to RAN's requests for action.

Sources: Marc Gunther, "The Mosquito in the Tent," *Fortune* (March 31, 2004), 158–162; Lisa Gerwitz, "It's Not Easy Being Green," *Deal.com* (March 8, 2004), 1. Dan Murphy, "Stunning Reversal? Why 'Big Paper' Just Went Green in Indonesia," *Christian Science Monitor* (February 19, 2013), http://www.csmonitor.com/Environment/2013/0219/Stunning-reversal-Why-big-paper-just-went-green-in-Indonesia. Accessed March 30, 2016. See also http://www.ran.org/take-action-online. Accessed March 30, 2016.

ETHICS IN PRACTICE CASE

Slow Fashion

Fast fashion is a term that has been applied to clothing that goes from the high fashion catwalk to mainstream clothing stores in record time, enabling the average buyer to wear the latest trends. Zara and H&M are examples of retailers that have made their mark with fast fashion identities, but other retailers have joined the rush to fast fashion in order to provide their customers with the trendiest clothes to wear at moderate prices. The consumer can then afford to get new clothes in the next season when fashion trends inevitably change. Because the expected lifespan is short, fast fashion clothing tends to be made with less care and lower quality materials, cutting corners to make it cheaply and quickly. Of course, when new trends arrive, last year's trends become obsolete and ready for disposal. Making clothing consumes natural resources, and yet, because they are made more cheaply, they tend to be thrown out after a year, if not after a few washes. They then find their way to landfills where textiles are posing a serious problem. In North America alone, 12 million tons of textile waste (68 pounds of waste per family) was generated each year.

Slow fashion has entered the scene and is endeavoring to change consumer habits. Show fashion uses traditional methods of sewing and weaving, quality materials that are natural in origin, and quality handcrafting. As noted by cofounder of the slow fashion line, Zady: "It's about understanding the process or the origins of how things are made.... Where our products come from, how they're constructed and by whom. Slow fashion is really indicative of a movement of people who want to literally slow down." The clothing is made to last and consumers repair rather than replace clothing that is slightly damaged. Like the slow food movement, slow fashion promotes a more thoughtful approach to living on the earth in a sustainable way.

1. Is the criticism of fast fashion fair? Should an industry be held accountable for the waste its consumers generate?
2. Do you think slow fashion will become "fashionable" in the way that fast fashion has? If it does, will its popularity persist or just end up being another fashion trend?
3. What responsibilities do consumers have for sustainability?

Sources: *http://www.hearts.com/ecolife/join-slow-fashion-movement/*. Accessed April 2, 2016; Maureen Dickson, Carlotta Cataldi, and Crystal Glover, "The Show Fashion Movement: Reversing Environmental Damage, http://www.notjustalabel.com/editorial/the_slow_fashion_movement. Accessed April 1, 2016. Elizabeth Blair, *NPR* (April 24, 2015), "Slow Fashion Shows Consumers What It's Made Of," http://www.npr.org/2015/04/24/401764329/slow-fashion-shows-consumers-what-its-made-of. Accessed April 1, 2016.

is a small organization, with a budget of only $2.4 million and a staff of just 25. Nevertheless, they have managed to garner the attention of big business in a way that the larger, more established environmental organizations have never managed. They have been described as a mosquito in a tent, "just a nuisance when it starts, but you can wake up later with some serious welts."[130]

Most recently, RAN has been involved in the fight against some of the abuses taking place on palm oil farms in Malaysia. In 2015, an investigative report by *The Wall Street Journal* found instances of human trafficking, forced labor, and withholding of wages for migrant workers at Malaysian grower Felda Global Venture's plantations.[131] When RAN found out that Felda was a member of the Roundtable for Sustainable Palm Oil (RSPO), they immediately went into action, launching a media campaign and calling for a full investigation by the RSPO.[132]

In addition to environmental groups, businesses are paying more attention to sustainability's green wave because of at least three other stakeholder groups: green consumers, green employees, and green investors.

15.7b Other Sustainability Interest Groups

Green Consumers. Individuals referred to as green consumers are actual and potential customers of retail firms, usually in the developed countries, who express preferences for products, services, and companies that are perceived to be more environment friendly than other competitive products, services, and firms. For example, a rise in "eco-athleisure" workout gear has been embraced by consumers who look for environmentally friendly fibers and logos.[133] Of course, brands like Nike and Patagonia belong to trade groups like the **Sustainable Apparel Coalition** that follow brand-specific sustainability indices that consumers know about. However, green consumers purchasing sportswear will also look for logos like *Recycled PET,* which show that materials like plastic bottles have been recycled for fabrics. Additionally, *organic cotton labeling*, certifying that the cotton has not been treated with toxins, is popular with green consumers, as well as *Cradle-to-Cradle Fashion Positive certification*, which points to reuse and recycling opportunities.[134]

It seems that consumers, overall, are willing to pay more for green products—or at least products from companies who are committed to sustainability. In a 2015 report, Nielsen revealed that almost two-thirds of consumers are willing to pay extra for products and services that come from companies who are committed to positive social and environmental impact.[135] This represented a sizable jump from 50 and 55 percent, in the prior two years.[136]

Why consumers tend not to buy green when they hold such green philosophies is a paradox that has confounded companies. Consumers say that they want environmentally responsible products, but sales of those products are often disappointing when they hit the market. Andrew Gershoff and Julie Irwin explored this paradox and found that several issues arise for consumers as they do a **cost and benefit analysis** of using green products. One is that consumers question whether green actions will lead to green outcomes: The benefits are hard to observe and marketers are not believed because they are not considered worthy of much trust.[137] Consumers also question whether it is worth paying a cost today for a benefit that will not occur until the future.[138] Consumers also tend to believe that there is "a catch" somewhere and may infer tradeoffs that don't even exist.[139] Finally, consumers would prefer to let others bear the costs, knowing that the individual bears the cost but the benefits are shared.[140]

Green Employees. A second stakeholder group with which most businesses are concerned is green employees. Although the popular press has not focused as much attention on green employees as it has on green consumers, there is evidence that employees are playing a major role in promoting environmentalism at work. In addition to union and general employee environmental concerns with plant, warehouse, and office safety and health, employees in many companies have assisted management in going beyond these traditional concerns into areas such as pollution prevention, recycling, energy and environmental audits, and community environmental projects. In fact, a recent study about "millennials" (i.e., newer generation employees) notes that they want to work for organizations that are transparent about how they use their technology, their resources, and their talent to make positive social and environmental changes.[141]

Green Investors. Another important business stakeholder involved in environmental issues is the green investor. As we mentioned in Chapter 2, these are investors who are interested in advancing social causes. These individuals and organizations want to put their money where their environmental values are by identifying and utilizing financial instruments that are associated with environmentally oriented companies. A growing number of mutual funds, stock and bond offerings, money market funds, and other financial instruments have included environmental components in recent years. For example, in 2015, top-performing mutual funds designed to address climate change outperformed the market, and none of them included investments in fossil fuels.[142]

Shareholder resolutions address concerns that range from toxic emissions to recycling and waste to nuclear power plants and climate change. According to *Proxy Preview*, shareholder resolutions regarding environmental and sustainable governance resolutions

SPOTLIGHT *on Sustainability*

Living "The Other Low-Carb Life"

Have you calculated your Personal Carbon and/or Ecological Footprint? Many individuals have begun to make a commitment to the "carbon neutral" life by tracking and paying for the CO_2 that they spend. Carbon neutrality can be achieved through a combination of minimizing carbon emissions where possible (it is possible to book a carbon neutral flight or have carbon neutral groceries delivered to your home) and then purchasing offsets for the emissions that remain. For example, environmental consultant Guy Dauncey tallies his annual carbon spending when he tallies his taxes. He found that his personal activities caused 13.5 tons of carbon emissions. The going rate for carbon was $10 a ton, and so he arranged to do $135 of work for the Solar Electric Light Fund, a group that helps African villagers use solar power instead of kerosene.

The Nature Conservancy (http://www.nature.org) provides a free carbon footprint calculator that measures how many tons of carbon dioxide and greenhouse gasses are generated by the different choices an individual makes each year. They provide advice on how to evaluate carbon offset options, and they offer carbon offset options, such as contributing to the Tensas River Basin Project on the Mississippi River. Their Web site also provides a range of information on global warming along with ways in which individuals can become involved in the issue.

Even organizations like the National Hockey League have embraced the idea of reducing of its carbon footprint. Citing its deep connection to the natural environment, the NHL was named the Environmental Protection Agency's Green Partner of the Year in 2015 after successful implementation of LED lighting in its arenas, among other initiatives.

Sources: "The 50 Best Inventions of the Year," Time (November 23, 2009), 57–92; Danylo Hawaleshka, "The Other Low-Carb Life," *Maclean's* (June 21, 2004), 54; http://www.nature.org. Accessed April 27, 2013; Skinner Bachs, "NHL Green Week Highlights Initiatives to Reduce Hockey's Carbon Footprint, http://www.inquisitr.com/2891425/nhl-green-week-highlights-initiatives-to-reduce-hockeys-carbon-footprint/. Accessed April 1, 2015.

combined represented 40 percent of the proxies filed in 2016, with a focus on greater use of renewable energy at utilities and concerns about what will happen to fossil fuel producers following the Paris Climate treaty talks.[143] Perhaps as a result of this attention from shareholders, tech companies like Apple have begun to issue "green bonds" to finance clean energy projects across its global business operations. As noted by Apple's vice president of environment, policy, and social initiatives, "This will allow investors to show they will put their money where their hearts and concerns are."[144]

15.8 Business Environmentalism and Sustainability

Now that caring for the natural environment has become good business, there are countless examples of firms demonstrating that sustainable business practices can not only help the planet but also be a source of competitive advantage. *TriplePundit* recently identified companies that are "shaking up" sustainability, and we briefly discuss a few below. These companies—Patagonia, Apple, CVS Health, and Tesla—are considered to have taken "principled stances" and/or led innovative programs for better social and environmental conditions. We outline their sustainability initiatives below.

15.8a Patagonia

Patagonia founder and owner Yvon Chouinard has received a variety of accolades, including TriplePundit.com's Most Sustainable CEO award.[145] This is not surprising because one cannot discuss business sustainability without mentioning Patagonia, the outdoor lifestyle company that is said to be "arguably one of the most environmentally focused companies in the world."[146] Decades before most businesses considered the possibility of recycling, Patagonia had made it an integral part of operations.[147] The company used the mail-order catalog to send messages about the problems of overfishing and genetically modified foods. After discovering they could make their outdoor gear out of discarded plastic soda bottles, founder-owner Yvon Chouinard set about to do an environmental assessment of all their materials. He found that cotton was particularly damaging due to its dependencies on pesticides, insecticides, and defoliants. "To know this and not switch to organic cotton would be unconscionable," says Chouinard.[148] Today, it is considered a prime example of how the circular economy works, as we noted above.[149]

15.8b Apple

In 2014, Apple CEO Tim Cook made some bold statements to investors about how Apple does not pursue environmental improvements solely for return on investments.[150] He was angered by questions at the annual meeting about the profitability of investing in renewable energy.[151] Along with Apple's commitment to recycling, noted above, Apple partners with multiple initiatives to avoid conflict minerals and unfair labor conditions in the production chain. Although it receives some criticism for the short life cycle of its products, Apple is the electronics brand with the highest use of renewable energy, according to one sustainability ranking group.[152]

15.8c CVS Health

As we noted in Chapter 5, CVS Health, the nation's largest pharmacy company, took the impressive stance of stopping the sale of tobacco products in their stores and even going further to offer smoking cessation programs. In 2015 it announced the *Be The First* program, a five-year $50 million initiative to help people lead tobacco-free lives through comprehensive education, advocacy, tobacco control, and healthy behavior programming, in partnership with several other organizations.[153]

15.8d Tesla

Tesla is well known for its innovation in the development of the electric vehicle. However, its sustainable reach goes beyond this mission. Like Apple, Tesla is building what is generally called an **ecosystem** of sustainable brands—a group of interconnected elements, formed by interactions with others in its community and environment. Tesla's commitment to sharing technology under a "common, rapidly-evolving technology platform," is almost unprecedented, as Tesla announced in 2014 that it would not pursue lawsuits against anyone who wants to use their technology to improve transport.[154] Most recently, it developed a Powerwall battery pack for home renewable energy that is anticipated to double the battery pack usage and allow enough energy to be stored to power an entire house. It is anticipated that it will be tested and deployed in Ireland in 2017.[155]

15.8e Business and Environmental Partnerships-Activists, NGOs, and Interest Groups

In the past several years, a shift in the relationship between business and environmental activists, nongovernmental organizations (**NGOs**), and interest groups has occurred. Accommodation is replacing antagonism as the parties begin to recognize their mutual dependence. Business needs environmental partners to both inform and validate their environmental efforts and activists, NGOs, and interest groups need business to change the way it operates in order to protect the planet.[156]

More and more, businesses are partnering with these groups to accomplish their sustainability objectives. For example, a recent GreenBiz survey showed that large corporations view NGO partners in four ways, as:[157]

- Trusted Partners—Corporate-friendly, highly credible, long-term partners.
- Useful Resources—Highly credible organizations known for creating helpful frameworks and services for corporate partners.
- Brand Challenged—Credible, but not influential, organizations.
- The Uninvited—Less broadly known groups, or those viewed more as critics than partners.

Despite the obvious challenges of working with the "brand challenged" and the "uninvited," the corporations acknowledged that all four types of partners need to be addressed—to get their perspectives and attempt to address their concerns, particularly regarding climate change, community engagement, and energy (both renewables and efficiency).[158]

15.9 The Future of Business: Greening and/or Growing?

The salient environmental question we all may need to address in the future: "How much is enough?" A common business and, indeed, public policy goal in most human societies has been economic growth. Typically, businesses and societies have needed increasing amounts of either materials or energy, or both, to achieve that economic growth. Limits on growth, similar to limits on human reproduction, at either the macro or micro level, have not been widely popular. This has led to what one magazine called, "The Environmentalists' Civil War," with "pro-energy, pro-density humanists" on the one side and "anti-energy, pro-sprawl absolutists" on the other.[159]

However, one potential problem with unrestrained economic growth worldwide is that, unless technology or people change significantly within a generation, environmental problems change in degree from significant to severe. Individual governments and international organizations like the United Nations can certainly help to identify and address environmental problems, but businesses must be proactive in caring for the environment, and they will need to work with various partners to accomplish sustainability goals.

The pressures on the environment come from many directions. World population is projected to continue to grow, creating greater demands on food and fuel resources. Large countries such as China and India are industrializing and so they will use increasing amounts of materials and energy. The already industrialized countries continue to maintain the highly consumptive lifestyles that have strained the environment already. As the name implies, the sustainability imperative is of the essence. Business no longer has the luxury of deciding whether or not to respond to it—society in general and the environment in particular cannot wait.

Summary

We began by discussing the concept of sustainability and its importance to business. We then outlined the top environmental issues facing business today and some of the newer initiatives in sustainability that include concepts of the circular economy and renewable energy initiatives. Environmental ethics began our discussion of individual and collective responsibility for sustaining the environment. We explored the role of governments and environmental interest groups in effecting change and then looked at companies that are leaders in practicing sustainable business practices. Lastly, we offered ways in which businesses can act toward achieving sustainability.

Although there is a growing consensus about the importance of sustainability, there remain significant differences of opinion on how problems will develop in the future and what should be done to resolve them. The natural environment is crucial for human survival and a number of complex and interconnected human-induced activities are threatening this environment. Problems such as those profiled in this chapter are potentially endangering nonhuman species and ecosystems and reducing the quality of human life. Individuals and their organizations, including businesses, are directly or indirectly responsible for this situation.

The recent growth in partnerships between business and environmental activists, NGOs, and interest groups is a promising sign but more changes must come. A minimum baseline of sustainability—meeting the needs of the present without compromising the ability of future generations to meet their needs—should be the bottom line for business as it moves into the future.

Key Terms

acid rain, p. 467
air pollution, p. 467
biodiversity, p. 465
COP19, p. 478
COP21, p. 478
cap and trade, p. 474
carbon neutral, p. 462
carbon positive, p. 459
Carbon pricing, p. 463
CERES' Roadmap to Sustainability, p. 458
Clean Air Act, p. 474
Clean Water Act, p. 476
circular economy, p. 468
climate change, p. 463
cost–benefit analysis, p. 481
deforestation, p. 470
ecosystems, p. 483
emissions trading, p. 474
Endangered Species Act (ESA), p. 477
energy inefficiency, p. 463
environment, p. 461
environmental impact statements (EISs), p. 474
Environmental Protection Agency (EPA), p. 474
externalities, p. 460
fossil fuels, p. 463
Global Compact, p. 477
Global Reporting Initiative (GRI), p. 477
global warming, p. 463
greenhouse effect, p. 463
internal carbon tax, p. 463
Montreal Protocol, p. 477
NGOs, p. 483
NIMBY, p. 472
ozone, p. 469
recycling, p. 468
Superfund, p. 476
Sustainable Apparel Coalition, p. 481
sustainability, p. 457
toxic substances, p. 466
Toxic Substances Control Act, p. 476
tragedy of the commons, p. 471
triple bottom line, p. 457
Warsaw International Mechanism, p. 478
watershed, p. 469
wicked problems, p. 471

Discussion Questions

1. What is sustainability? How does sustainability relate to environmentalism?
2. What are several of the most important environmental issues now receiving worldwide attention?
3. Who has responsibility for addressing environmental issues?
4. How can ethics be applied in response to environmental issues?
5. Should businesses and societies continue to focus on unlimited economic growth?

Endnotes

1. Alex Davidson, "What's a Sustainable Company? It's Hard to Define," *The Wall Street Journal* (April 3, 2016), http://www.wsj.com/articles/whats-a-sustainable-company-its-hard-to-define-1459735511. Accessed May 6, 2016.

2. "Report of the World Commission on Environment and Development," http://www.un.org/documents/ga/res/42/ares42-187.htm. Accessed April 30, 2016.
3. W. Edward Stead and Jean Garner Stead with Mark Starik, *Sustainable Strategic Management* (Armonk, NY: M. E. Sharpe, Inc., 2004).
4. William McDonough and Michael Braungart, *Cradle to Cradle: Remaking the Way We Make Things* (New York: North Point Press, 2002).
5. "Sustainability in USA-Top Trends 2015," *The Ethical Corporation*, http://s3.amazonaws.com/cms_assets/accounts/690b848f-131d-4af6-a319-824db8c89e5b/site-50109/cms-assets/documents/225084-527072.sustainability-usa-trends-2015.pdf. Accessed March 20, 2016.
6. The McKinsey Center for Business and Environment, http://www.mckinsey.com/business-functions/sustainability-and-resource-productivity/how-we-help-clients/mckinsey-center-for-business-and-environment. Accessed March 20, 2016.
7. Sustainability's Strategic Worth: McKinsey Global Survey Results (July 2014), http://www.mckinsey.com/business-functions/sustainability-and-resource-productivity/our-insights/sustainabilitys-strategic-worth-mckinsey-global-survey-results. Accessed March 25, 2016.
8. Daniel C. Esty and Andrew S. Winston, *Green to Gold: How Smart Companies Use Environmental Strategy to Innovate, Create Value, and Build Competitive Advantage* (New Haven, CT: Yale University Press, 2006).
9. Ceres, "AT&T Renewable Energy Targets 2016," http://www.ceres.org/investor-network/resolutions/at-t-renewable-energy-targets-2016. Accessed March 30, 2016.
10. Susan Casey, "Éminence Green," Fortune (April 2, 2007), 62–70.
11. Archie Carroll, "Corporate Social Responsibility: The Centerpiece of Competing and Complementary Frameworks," *Organizational Dynamics* (February 2015), 93.
12. Leon Kaye, "The Business Case for Sustainability Is Becoming Easier to Make," *Triple Pundit* (March 15, 2013), http://www.triplepundit.com/2013/03/business-case-for-sustainability/. Accessed April 27, 2016.
13. "As Good as It Gets? Fortune's 'Change the World' 2015 Ranking," *TriplePundit* (September 10, 2015), http://www.triplepundit.com/2015/09/good-gets-fortune-change-world-2015-ranking/. Accessed March 26, 2016.
14. Kareem Shabana, Ann Buchholtz, and Archie Carroll, "The Institutionalization of Corporate Social Reporting," *Business & Society* (2016), doi 10.007/0007650316628177, 1–16.
15. "The 21st Century Corporation: The CERES Roadmap for Sustainability," *Ceres* (Boston, MA: 2010), http://www.ceres.org/resources/reports/ceres-roadmap-to-sustainability-2010/view. Accessed March 30, 2016.
16. Veena Ramani, "View from the Top: How Corporate Boards Can Engage on Sustainability Performance," *Ceres* (October 2015), http://www.ceres.org/resources/reports/view-from-the-top-how-corporate-boards-engage-on-sustainability-performance. Accessed March 20, 2016.
17. Joel Makower, "The State of Green Business 2015," (February 23, 2015), *GreenBiz Report*, https://www.greenbiz.com/article/state-green-business-2015. Accessed May 6, 2016.
18. See Jo Confino, "Unilever's Paul Polman: Challenging the Corporate Status Quo," *The Guardian* (April 24, 2012), http://www.guardian.co.uk/sustainable-business/paul-polman-unilever-sustainable-living-plan. Accessed March 25, 2016: Paul Polman, "Why Sustainability Is No Longer a Choice," *LiveScience* (March 1, 2016), http://www.livescience.com/53897-exclusive-unilever-ceo-on-sustainability-as-team-effort.html. Accessed March 20, 2016.
19. Ibid.
20. Ibid.
21. https://www.unilever.com/news/news-and-features/2015/Unilever-to-become-carbon-positive-by-2030.html. Accessed April 2, 2016.
22. Jessica Shankleman, "Unilever Struggles to Sell Customers on Sustainable Living," *Greenbiz* (April 29, 2014), https://www.greenbiz.com/blog/2014/04/29/unilever-struggles-sell-customers-sustainable-living. Accessed March 25, 2016.
23. Leon Kaye, "Unilever Severs Ties with Major Palm Oil Supplier," *TriplePundit* (April 4, 2016), http://www.triplepundit.com/2016/04/unilever-severs-ties-major-palm-oil-supplier/?utm_source=Daily+Email+List&utm_campaign=02d3e551c5-RSS_EMAIL_CAMPAIGN&utm_medium=email&utm_term=0_9dedefcee3-02d3e551c5-220417273. Accessed April 3, 2016.
24. Jessica Lyons Hardcastle, "How Unilever, GE, Ikea Turn a Profit from Sustainability," *Environmental Leader* (January 7, 2016), http://www.environmentalleader.com/2016/01/07/how-unilever-ge-ikea-turn-a-profit-from-sustainability/. Accessed March 20, 2016.
25. "Captain Planet," *Harvard Business Review* (June 2012), 112–118.
26. Paul R. Ehrlich, Anne H. Ehrlich, and Gretchen C. Daily, *The Stork and the Plow: The Equity Answer to the Human Dilemma* (New Haven, CT: Yale University Press, 1997), 24.

27. Marc Gunther, "Going Green," *Fortune* (April 2, 2007), 44.
28. Ibid., 44.
29. Karen Weise, "How Do You Stop the Biggest Gas Leak Ever?", *Bloomberg Businessweek* (February 10, 2016), 51–53.
30. *JUST Capital* 2015 Survey, http://justcapital.com/american-perceptions. Accessed March 20, 2016.
31. William Collins, Robert Colman, James Haywood, Martin R. Manning, and Philip Mote, "The Physical Science behind Climate Change," *Scientific American* (August 2007), 64–71.
32. James Huffman, "Getting Overheated," *The Wall Street Journal* (April 24, 2014), A13.
33. John Steele Gordon, "The Unsettling, Anti-Science Certitude on Global Warming," *The Wall Street Journal* (July 21, 2015), A11.
34. Amy Harder, "Climate Change Builds as 2016 Campaign Issue," *The Wall Street Journal* (August 31, 2015), A4.
35. See *World Economic Forum*, "What Are the Top Global Risks for 2016?," https://www.weforum.org/agenda/2016/01/what-are-the-top-global-risks-for-2016. Accessed March 30, 2016; Steven Gandel, "Here's What the World Leaders Think Is the Greatest Risk for 2016," *Fortune* (January 16, 2016), http://fortune.com/2016/01/16/davos-risk-report-world-economic-forum/. Accessed March 30, 2016.
36. "Climate Change and President Obama's Action Plan," https://www.whitehouse.gov/climate-change. Accessed March 30, 2016.
37. Paul Adler, "Supreme Court Puts the Brakes on the EPA's Clean Power Plan," *The Washington Post* (February 9, 2016), https://www.washingtonpost.com/news/volokh-conspiracy/wp/2016/02/09/supreme-court-puts-the-brakes-on-the-epas-clean-power-plan/. Accessed March 30, 2016.
38. Carol Lee and Colleen McCain Nelson, "Climate Deal Leaves Hard Decisions to Countries," *The Wall Street Journal* (December 14, 2015), A1.
39. David Gelles, "Microsoft Leads Movement to Offset Emissions with Internal Carbon Tax," *The New York Times* (September 26, 2015), http://www.nytimes.com/2015/09/27/business/energy-environment/microsoft-leads-movement-to-offset-emissions-with-internal-carbon-tax.html?_r=0,m Accessed March 30, 2016.
40. Ibid.
41. Ibid.
42. "How a Market Heats Up," *Fortune* (May 29, 2006), 74–75.
43. Wolfram Krewitt, Sonja Simon, Wina Graus, Sven Teske, Arthouros Zervos, and Oliver Schafer, "The 2°C Scenario: A Sustainable World Energy Perspective," *Energy Policy* (October 2007), 4969–4980.
44. Claire Groden, "The New Power Added to U.S. Grids in 2015 Was Mostly Renewable," *Fortune* (February 4, 2016), http://fortune.com/2016/02/04/electricity-renewable-energy/. Accessed March 31, 2016.
45. Ibid.
46. Ibid.
47. See Jeremy C.F. Lin, Jean Rutter, and Haeyoun Park, "Events That Led to Flint's Water Crisis," *The New York Times* (January 21, 2016), http://www.nytimes.com/interactive/2016/01/21/us/flint-lead-water-timeline.html?_r=0. Accessed April 26, 2016; Jonathan Lapook, "Doctors Explain the Long-Term Health Effects of the Flint Michigan Crisis," *CBS News* (January 19, 2016), http://www.cbsnews.com/news/doctors-explain-the-long-term-health-effects-of-flint-water-crisis/. Accessed May 6, 2016.
48. Esty and Winston.
49. MaAlex Garofalo, "World Water Day 2016: 12 Facts and Things to Know," *International Business Times* (March 22, 2016), http://www.ibtimes.com/world-water-day-2016-12-facts-things-know-2340534. Accessed March 31, 2016.
50. Geoffrey Lean, "Water Crisis Now Bigger Threat than Financial Crisis," *The Independent* (March 15, 2009), http://www.independent.co.uk/environment/climate-change/water-scarcity-now-bigger-threat-than-financial-crisis-1645358.html. Accessed April 1, 2016.
51. Nicholas St. Fleur, "Two-Thirds of the World Faces Severe Water Shortages," *The New York Times* (February 12, 2016), http://www.nytimes.com/2016/02/13/science/two-thirds-of-the-world-faces-severe-water-shortages.html?_r=0. Accessed March 31, 2016.
52. Carmichael, Schafer, and Mazumdar, 52–56.
53. Esty and Winston.
54. Carmichael, Schafer, and Mazumdar, 52–56.
55. Ibid.
56. Lean, 2009.
57. Ibid.
58. Mary Mazzoni, "3p Weekend: Governments, Companies Tackle Water Scarcity," *TriplePundit* (March 25, 2016), http://www.triplepundit.com/2016/03/3p-weekend-governments-companies-tackle-water-scarcity/. Accessed March 31, 2016.
59. Ibid.
60. Alexander C. Kaufman, "Why Levi's Is Giving Away Its Trade Secrets," *Huffington Post* (March 16, 2016), http://www.huffingtonpost.com/entry/levis-water_us_56f15f91e4b09bf44a9e79ee. Accessed March 20, 2016.
61. Julie Padowski, Steven Gorelick, Barton Thompson, Scott Rozelle, and Scott Fendorf (2015). Assessment of Human–Natural System Characteristics Influencing Global Freshwater Supply Vulnerability. Environmental Research Letters (Vol. 10(10), 104014, 2015).

62. Center for Biological Diversity, http://www.biologicaldiversity.org/programs/biodiversity/elements_of_biodiversity/extinction_crisis/. Accessed May 6, 2016.
63. Ibid.
64. "The Next Environmental Issue for Business: McKinsey Global Survey Results," http://www.mckinsey.com/business-functions/sustainability-and-resource-productivity/our-insights/the-next-environmental-issue-for-business-mckinsey-global-survey-results. Accessed March 30, 2016.
65. http://nationalatlas.gov/mld/efct17x.html. Accessed March 30, 2016.
66. Michael Kourabas, "The Case of DuPont's Pollution and the Importance of CSR," *TriplePundit* (January 11, 2016), http://www.triplepundit.com/2016/01/case-duponts-pollution-importance-csr/. Accessed March 30, 2016.
67. Armen Keleyian, "Oil & Gas Industry Spills Happen 'all the time'," *CBS Evening News* (April 12, 2011), http://www.cbsnews.com/8301-18563_162-20053283.html. Accessed March 30, 2016.
68. "Air Pollution Effects," https://www.epa.gov/air-research/research-health-and-environmental-effects-air-quality. Accessed March 30, 2016.
69. Mark Dolliver, "Environmental Worries Will Never Be Extinct," *Adweek* (March 26, 2007), 35.
70. "What Is Acid Rain?," https://www.epa.gov/acidrain. Accessed April 30, 2013.
71. Ibid.
72. Ibid.
73. "Air Pollution: Current and Future Challenges," https://www.epa.gov/clean-air-act-overview/air-pollution-current-and-future-challenges. Accessed March 30, 2016.
74. "Lumber Liquidators to Settle Air Safety Allegations," *The New York Times* (March 23, 2016), B2.
75. Air Pollution: Current and Future Challenges.
76. Tim Culpan Olga Kharif, "Where Phones Go to Die," *Bloomberg Businessweek* (March 7–13, 2006), 35.
77. Gina Marie Cheeseman, "Gap Wants to Halve Its Greenhouse Gas Emissions by 2020," *TriplePundit* (January 27, 2016), http://www.triplepundit.com/2016/01/gap-wants-halve-greenhouse-gas-emissions-2020/?utm_source=Daily+Email+List&utm_campaign=5ca7092b82-RSS_EMAIL_CAMPAIGN&utm_medium=email&utm_term=0_9dedefcee3-5ca7092b82-220417273. Accessed March 30, 2016.
78. Lauren Loudermilk, "Share a Coke with Mother Nature," *Atlanta Magazine* (August 2015), 26.
79. Loretta Chao, "Lego Tries to Build a Better Brick," *The Wall Street Journal* (July 14, 2015), B4.
80. See Marcus Zils, "Moving towards a Circular Economy," *McKinsey & Company Report 2014*, http://www.mckinsey.com/business-functions/sustainability-and-resource-productivity/our-insights/moving-toward-a-circular-economy. Accessed March 31, 2016.
81. The Ethical Corporation, "Patagonia Circular Economy Strategy: A Case Study," http://1.ethicalcorp.com/LP=8770?utm_source=Abhishek%20&utm_medium=Abhishek%20&utm_campaign=Abhishek. Accessed March 15, 2016.
82. Ibid.
83. http://www.epa.gov/wastes/. Accessed March 31, 2016.
84. Ibid.
85. Ibid.
86. Ibid.
87. Linda Marsa, "Is the Ozone Hole Shrinking?" *Discover Magazine* (April 5, 2013), http://discovermagazine.com/2013/may/02-is-the-ozone-hole-shrinking. Accessed April 28, 2016.
88. Ben Wolfgang, "EPA Tightens Ozone Standard, Sets off Fight with Business Groups," The Washington Post (October 2, 2015), http://www.washingtontimes.com/news/2015/oct/1/epa-tightens-ozone-standard-sets-fight-business-gr/. Accessed April 1, 2016.
89. http://www.epa.gov. Accessed April 3, 2016.
90. B. Freitas, L. Delagran, E. Griffin, K.L. Miller, and M. Hirshfield, M., "Too Few Fish: A Regional Assessment of the World's Fisheries," *May 2008, Oceana*, http://oceana.org/sites/default/files/reports/toofewfish41.pdf. Accessed May 6, 2016.
91. "How to Catch the Overfishermen," *The Economist* (January 24, 2015), http://www.economist.com/news/leaders/21640350-big-data-allow-fish-be-protected-never-governments-should-take-advantage. Accessed May 6, 2016.
92. http://www.chesapeakebay.net/issues/issue/blue_crabs#inline. Accessed May 6, 2016.
93. Toni Johnson, "Deforestation and Greenhouse-Gas Emissions," *Backgrounder: Council on Foreign Relations* (December 21, 2009), http://www.cfr.org/natural-resources-management/deforestation-greenhouse-gas-emissions/p14919. Accessed April 2, 2016.
94. Bryan Walsh, Zamira Loebis, and Jason Tedjasukmana, "Getting Credit for Saving Trees," *Time* (July 23, 2007), 58–60.
95. David C. Wagman, "Wicked Problems," *Power Engineering* (May 2006), 5.
96. Garrett Hardin, "The Tragedy of the Commons," *Science* (Vol. 162, 1968), 1243–1248.
97. Ibid.
98. Linda M. Sama, Stephanie A. Welcomer, and Virginia W. Gerde, "Who Speaks for the Trees? Invoking an Ethic of Care to Give Voice to the Silent Stakeholder," in S. Sharma and M. Starik (eds.), *Stakeholders, the Environment and Society* (Cheltenham, UK: Edward Elgar, 2004), 140–165.
99. Ibid.

100. Christopher Helman, "Nimby Nation: The High Cost to America of Saying No to Everything," *Forbes* (August 17, 2015), http://www.forbes.com/sites/christopherhelman/2015/07/30/nimby-nation-the-high-cost-to-america-of-saying-no-to-everything/#2f88dbd25945. Accessed May 6, 2016.

101. Public Law 91-190 (1969), 42 U.S.C. Section 4331 et seq.

102. Overview of the Clean Air Act and Air Pollution, http://www.epa.gov/air/caa/. Accessed May 6, 2016.

103. Ibid.

104. Chris Woodyard, "Hyundai, Kia Pay $100M," *USA Today* (November 4, 2014), B1.

105. Ibid.

106. "Kyoto Protocol," http://unfccc.int/kyoto_protocol/items/2830.php. Accessed March 30, 2016.

107. https://www.epa.gov/cleanwaterrule. Accessed May 6, 2016.

108. T. McAdams, *Law, Business & Society*, 3d ed. (Homewood, IL: Irwin, 1992), 784–787, http://www.epa. gov. Accessed April 30, 2016.

109. Summary of the Toxic Substances Control Act, http://www2.epa.gov/laws-regulations/summary-toxic-substances-control-act. Accessed April 3, 2016.

110. Ibid.

111. Summary of Superfunds, http://www.epa.gov/superfund/. Accessed April 3, 2016.

112. Hudson River Cleanup, https://www3.epa.gov/hudson/cleanup.html. Accessed May 6, 2016.

113. Superfunds, http://www.epa.gov/superfund/. Accessed May 7, 2016.

114. IUCN 2010. IUCN Red List of Threatened Species. Version 2010.1. http://www.iucnredlist.org/. Accessed April 1, 2016.

115. Ibid.

116. http://www.epa.gov/lawsregs/laws/esa.html. Accessed April 3, 2016.

117. Ibid.

118. UNEP Ozone Secretariat, http://ozone.unep.org/en/treaties-and-decisions. Accessed April 3, 2016.

119. Ibid.

120. Ibid.

121. UN Global Compact, https://www.unglobalcompact.org/what-is-gc/our-work/social/human-rights. Accessed April 30, 2016.

122. Ibid.

123. Carlos Pascual and Antonia Bullard, "Impact of Paris 2015," *The Wall Street Journal* (February 23, 2016), A12.

124. Thomas Schueneman, "COP21, the Paris Agreement and the Art of the Possible," *TriplePundit* (December 15, 2015), http://www.triplepundit.com/2015/12/cop21-paris-agreement-art-possible/#. Accessed May 7, 2016.

125. Pascual and Bullard.

126. Ibid.

127. Center for Climate and Energy Solutions, http://www.c2es.org/international/negotiations/cop21-paris/summary. Accessed May 7, 2016.

128. The Environmental Defense Fund, "Partnerships: The Key to Scalable Future," http://www.edf.org/approach/partnerships/corporate. Accessed April 3, 2016.

129. M. E. Kriz, "Shades of Green," *National Journal* (July 28, 1990).

130. Mark Gunther, "The Mosquito in the Tent," *Fortune* (March 31, 2004), 158–162; Lisa Gerwitz, "It's Not Easy Being Green," *Deal.com* (March 8, 2004), 1.

131. Syed Zain Al-Mahmood, "Palm Oil Migrant Workers Tell of Abuses on Malaysian Plantations," http://www.wsj.com/articles/palm-oil-migrant-workers-tell-of-abuses-on-malaysian-plantations-1437933321. Accessed April 1, 2016.

132. Emma Rae Lierley, "Joint NGO Statement: Modern Day Slavery Found on RSPO Member Felda Global Venture's Plantations," http://www.ran.org/joint_ngo_statement_modern_day_slavery_found_on_rspo_member_felda_global_venture_s_plantations. Accessed April 1, 2016.

133. Lauren Newton, "The Rise of Eco-Athleisure," *TriplePundit* (April 15, 2016), http://www.triplepundit.com/2016/04/rise-eco-athleisure/. Accessed May 7, 2016.

134. Ibid.

135. Nielsen 2015 Report, The Sustainability Imperative (October 12, 2015), http://www.nielsen.com/us/en/insights/reports/2015/the-sustainability-imperative.html. Accessed May 7, 2016.

136. Ibid.

137. Andrew D. Gershoff and Julie R. Irwin (2012), "Why Not Choose Green? Consumer Decision Making for Environmentally Friendly Products," in Pratima Bansal and Andrew J. Hoffman (eds.) *The Oxford Handbook of Business and the Natural Environment* (Oxford University Press), 366–383.

138. Ibid.

139. Ibid.

140. Ibid.

141. The Deloitte Millenial Survey 2016, http://www2.deloitte.com/global/en/pages/about-deloitte/articles/millennialsurvey.html. Accessed May 7, 2016.

142. Anum Yoon, "Heads up, Green Investors: Climate-Focused Mutual Funds Have Stakes in Oil," *TriplePundit* (December 30, 2015), http://www.triplepundit.com/2015/12/climate-focused-mutual-funds-stakes-oil/. Accessed May 7, 2016.

143. http://www.proxypreview.org/proxy-preview-2016/. Accessed April 1, 2016.

144. Reuters, "Apple Just Issued $1.5 Billion in Bonds to Help the Environment," *Fortune* (February 17, 2016), http://fortune.com/2016/02/17/apple-green-bonds/. Accessed April 1, 2016.

145. http://www.triplepundit.com/2010/01/top-tensustainable-ceos/. Accessed April 30, 2013.
146. Esty and Winston, 25.
147. Susan Casey, "Éminence Green," *Fortune* (April 2, 2007), 62–70.
148. Ibid, 67.
149. Anne Brock, "Patagonia Leads by Example in the Circular Economy," *TriplePundit* (February12, 2016), http://www.triplepundit.com/2016/02/patagonia-leads-example-circular-economy/. Accessed May 7, 2016.
150. "Tim Cook Tells Climate Change Sceptics to Ditch Apple Shares," *The Guardian* (March 3, 2014), http://www.theguardian.com/environment/2014/mar/03/tim-cook-climate-change-sceptics-ditch-apple-shares. Accessed May 7, 2016.
151. Ibid.
152. http://rankabrand.org/electronics/Apple. Accessed May 7, 2016.
153. "CVS Health Makes $50 Million Five-Year Commitment," (March 10, 2016), *Sustainable Brands*, http://www.sustainablebrands.com/press/cvs_health_makes_50_million_five-year_commitment_deliver_nations_first_tobacco-free_generation. Accessed May 7, 2016.
154. Geoff Ledford, "Powered by Purpose: What Tesla's Model 3 Says about the Future of Sustainability," *TriplePundit*, http://www.triplepundit.com/2016/04/tesla-model-3-sustainability/. Accessed May 7, 2016.
155. Ibid.
156. John Carey and Michael Arndt, "Hugging the Tree-Huggers," *Businessweek* (March 12, 2007), 66–68.
157. GreenBiz, "How Companies Rate Activists as Partners," (2014) http://info.greenbiz.com/rs/greenbizgroup/images/greenbiz-ngo-report.pdf. Accessed May 7, 2016.
158. Ibid.
159. Robert Bryce, "The Environmentalists' Civil War," *National Review* (April 17, 2015), http://www.nationalreview.com/article/417070/environmentalists-civil-war. Accessed May 7, 2016.

16

Business and Community Stakeholders

CHAPTER LEARNING OUTCOMES

After studying this chapter, you should be able to:

1 Discuss reasons for community involvement, various types of community projects, and management of community stakeholders.

2 Explain the pros and cons of corporate philanthropy, provide a brief history of corporate philanthropy, and explain why and to whom companies give.

3 Differentiate between strategic philanthropy, cause-related marketing, and cause branding.

4 Characterize the loss of jobs in the contexts of offshoring, reshoring, and plant closings.

There are many definitions of the word *community*; however, they all share an underlying theme of commonality. A shared geographic locale, a shared profession, a shared ideology, or even a shared recreational pastime can join communities. The actions of business affect a range of communities, and it is important that managers be aware of these impacts to manage them in a way that respects the interests of community stakeholders. This chapter focuses typically on the business's immediate locale—the town, city, or state—in which a business resides. We should remember, however, that instant communication, speedy travel, and social networking often expand the relevant community to include the region, the nation, the world, and even the virtual world.

The company, Reddit, for example, created a community of users and an online bulletin board where registered community members can submit content, such as text posts or direct links. Top Reddit users have the ability to shape or close large parts of the Web site, beyond their own personal pages or profiles. Content entries are organized by areas of interest called "subreddits." The subreddit topics include news, gaming, movies, music, books, fitness, food, and photosharing, among many others. In essence, Reddit has created an online virtual community that may also affect and be affected by business.[1] As an example of how powerful this type of community can be, Reddit's volunteer users/moderators shut down large portions of the link-sharing Web site to protest the sudden firing of a popular Reddit employee.[2]

When we think of business and its community stakeholders, two major kinds of relationships come to mind. One is the positive contribution business can make to the community. Examples of these positive contributions include volunteerism, company contributions, and support of programs in education, culture, urban development, the arts, civic activities, and health and welfare endeavors. On the other hand, business can also cause harm to community stakeholders. It can pollute the environment or put people out of work by offshore outsourcing or closing a plant. Business can abuse its power and exploit consumers and employees. When business causes harm, as with the global financial crisis, it is incumbent upon business to work harder to have a positive impact on the community. In a *Bloomberg Businessweek* report, Michael Porter opined, "As high unemployment, rising poverty, and dismay over corporate greed breed contempt for the capitalist market system.... Serving the intersecting needs of business and the community is the only path to winning back respect for Corporate America."[3] To this point, each year *The Civic 50*, an initiative of the Points of Light (in partnership with Bloomberg LP) honors the 50 most community-minded companies based on the results from a survey of employees in the United States.[4] The four levels of criteria for the award include:[5]

- Investment—How extensively the company applies its resources, like employee time, skills, cash, and in-kind giving and leadership to community engagement
- Integration—How the company "does well by doing good" through its business functions.
- Institutionalization—How the company supports community engagement through its institutional policies, systems, and incentives
- Impact—How the company measures the social and business impact of its engagement program.

It is easy to see that the companies that make this list are those which strategically integrate community engagement into their strategies. Companies like Comcast Corporation, AT&T, Dr Pepper Snapple Group, and The Hershey Company have historically held spots on the list. On the other side, companies who are not community minded either ignore members of the community, or, worse, harm them. This chapter concentrates on community involvement and corporate philanthropy as community stakeholder issues. In addition, it discusses the topics of offshore outsourcing and business or plant closings as community stakeholder concerns. This discussion should provide us with an opportunity to explore both the positive and the detrimental effects that characterize business–community relationships. It begins with the positive.

In addition to being profitable, obeying the law, and being ethical, a company may create a positive impact in the community by giving in two ways: (1) donating the time and talents of its managers and employees and (2) making financial contributions. The first category, **community involvement**, manifests itself in a wide array of voluntary activities in the community. The second category involves **corporate philanthropy** or business giving. We should note that there is significant overlap between these two categories, because companies quite frequently donate their time and talent and give financial aid to the same general projects. First, we discuss community involvement and the various ways in which companies enhance the quality of life in their communities.

16.1 Community Involvement

Business must—not only for a healthier society but also for its own well-being—be willing to give the same serious consideration to human needs that it gives to its own needs for production and profits. These sentiments are echoed in the thoughts and actions of Salesforce CEO Marc Benioff, who is pushing fellow tech giants in the San Francisco area to give back to the community by donating money, funding research grants, and subsidizing housing rents for underprivileged families.[6] Noting that "we no longer live in a world that can tolerate maximizing shareholder values," Benioff notes that Salesforce pursues a "stakeholder value" approach with consideration to balancing the interests of investors with the welfare of "employees, the people in the community and the city's children."[7] Salesforce's community engagement plan is particularly timely as the San Francisco community is trying to adapt to the tech boom influx of young, wealthy individuals who have contributed to rising housing prices and subsequent high eviction rates. Additionally, Benioff cites the fact that his industry "has a history of stinginess," and he is determined to change that.[8]

Business involvement in the community represents enlightened self-interest because businesses are in a position to help their companies in the process of helping others. The dual objectives of business clearly illustrate that making profits and addressing social concerns are not mutually exclusive endeavors. When companies draw upon their strengths, they can make deep and lasting contributions to the communities they serve.

Furthermore, when they make community service part of their identities, they can develop greater trust and community. John Lechleiter, Eli Lilly Chairman, President, and Chief Executive Officer, drives this point home:

> *The business community can—and must—play a vital role in addressing complex societal problems. It's clear that writing a check or donating product alone doesn't have a lasting impact. A growing body of evidence demonstrates that when a company engages with partners in an area in which the company has deep expertise and a vested interest, society benefits and the company enhances its own performance.*[9]

In fact, research has shown that employees receive tremendous satisfaction from community involvement, allowing them to achieve a sense of identification with the organization through social exchange with the community that translates into better productivity and ultimately better firm performance.[10] Other rationales for business involvement in community affairs provide moral justification, beyond that of enlightened self-interest. For example, utilitarian arguments can support corporate giving in that improvement of the social fabric creates the greatest good for the greatest number. This need not contradict the mandates of self-interest, because the corporation is one of the community members that will benefit.[11]

Although justifications for corporate involvement in the community are possible from various perspectives, one thing is clear: Business has a moral responsibility to build a relationship with the community and to be sensitive to its impacts on the world around it. The Center for Corporate Citizenship at Boston College has developed a set of seven management practices, processes, and policies that represent a global standard of excellence in community involvement. These are listed in Figure 16-1.

FIGURE 16-1 Standards of Excellence in Corporate Community Involvement

Standard 1: Leadership

My company actively and purposefully helps to define needs, set direction, and initiate meaningful change around community or societal issues.

Standard 2: Strategy

My company plans its community involvement and leverages its capacities and strengths to deliver meaningful value to society and to the business.

Standard 3: Integration

My company engages all facets of the business to contribute to and realize the benefit from community involvement.

Standard 4: Infrastructure

My company consistently provides the resources and support needed to ensure the successful execution of its community involvement strategy.

Standard 5: Performance Measurement

My company assesses the effectiveness and impact of its community involvement and uses the results for continuous improvement.

Standard 6: Communication

My company actively and openly communicates in order to inform, influence, and engage internal and external stakeholders.

Standard 7: Community Relationships

My company engages and collaborates with external stakeholders to advance its community involvement strategy.

Sources: Center for Corporate Citizenship at Boston College, http://www.bcccc.net/index.cfm?pageId=2096. Accessed April 7, 2016; Boston College Center for Corporate Citizenship, "Updating the Standards of Excellence," http://corporatecitizenship.bc.edu/blog/2009/01/updating-the-standards-of-excellence. Accessed April 17, 2016.

16.1a Volunteer Programs

One of the most pervasive examples of business involvement in communities is a volunteer program. Corporate volunteer programs reflect the resourcefulness and responsiveness of business to communities in need of increasing services. They also have become essential for attracting and retaining the best talent in the workforce.[12] Employees not only want to work for "the good guys," they want to be the good guys too.[13] According to Kellie McElhaney of the Haas School of Business, "For today's millennials entering the workforce, engagement in sustainability is a must-have, not a nice-to-have. They don't want to be told what the company is doing. They want to do it."[14]

In their tenth anniversary edition of "Giving in Numbers," a coalition of more than 150 CEOs in the world's largest companies called the **CECP** (the Committee Encouraging Corporate Philanthropy) issued a report in conjunction with the Conference Board about the impact of community engagement and philanthropy. According to their survey of 271 companies, 81 percent reported having at least one domestic formal employee volunteer program and 58 percent reported having at least one available for international employees.[15] However, a range of employee volunteer programs exists.

According to the CECP, **Paid Release Time** is the most common type of service program.[16] This is supported by companies like Deloitte Consulting, whose philosophy of community engagement and unlimited hours of paid time off for employee volunteering contributed to their being voted one of the "100 Best Companies to Work For" by *Fortune* magazine.[17] Another popular volunteer option is a **Company-Wide Day of Service**, where employees mobilize volunteers for a day. For example, each year Timberland organizes two global days of service: Earth Day in April and the company signature program: "Serv-a-palooza" in the fall.[18] **Skills-based Pro Bono Service** allows employees to volunteer with their specific skills—like tax accountants from KPMG and Deloitte who volunteer to help seniors prepare tax returns. Finally, **Dollars for Doers** involve contributions in recognition of a certain level of employee volunteer service.

This last type of volunteer program is worth mentioning in detail. The Dollars for Doers program magnifies the service contributions of the employee by matching employee volunteer hours with a corporate donation.[19] Unlike the traditional matching grant that matches employee donations with corporate funds, Dollars for Doers matches hours of service. For example, Campbell Soup donates $500 to nonprofits for every 25 hours an employee volunteer and IBM provides nonprofits with equipment and services to match employee volunteer hours.[20] In return, companies are likely to get healthier and happier employees.

There are numerous examples of corporations making a difference in communities through volunteer activities. The Longaberger Company has a long-standing commitment to the American Cancer Society to make and sell "Horizon of Hope" baskets, stuffed with breast cancer literature: The campaign has raised millions of dollars for research and education to combat breast cancer.[21] AT&T has had success with their Aspire Mentoring Academy, with over 700,000 hours of mentoring by AT&T employees with at-risk high school students.[22] While companies may spend on average $416 on each person that participates in a volunteer program, many companies consider that a bargain when compared to the $1,200 that it costs per employee for an average training program.[23] As noted by one expert, "These programs are an excellent way for businesses to create real impact in their communities and to foster a legacy of philanthropic storytelling that prompts employees to get and stay inspired … and professionally engaged."[24]

Big Data has also been helpful in making employee community engagement more beneficial for both employees and the community. For example, Capital One uses volunteerism data to help link employees to the best experience and also identify gaps in participation rates and build targeted strategies. When they identify an employee who has

FIGURE 16-2 Benefits of Employee Volunteerism

For the Employee
- Improves morale
- Increases meaningfulness of work
- Develops teamwork and leadership skills
- Improves mental and physical health

For the Corporation
- Builds company image and reputation
- Improves employee attraction and retention
- Develops employee skills
- Builds relationship with and loyalty from consumers

For the Community
- Addresses community needs
- Saves community resources
- Builds pool of future volunteers and contributors
- Builds awareness of community needs

not logged in volunteer hours or participated in a company-sponsored program, they send those employees a targeted message on how to sign up to volunteer. They also use the data to personalize volunteerism options.[25] The overall benefits derived from employee volunteerism are summarized in Figure 16-2.

16.1b Managing Community Involvement

For discussion purposes, we are separating our treatment of *managing community involvement* from that of *managing corporate philanthropy*. In reality, however, this separation is impossible to achieve because there are significant overlaps between these two areas. Corporate philanthropy involves primarily the giving of financial resources. Community involvement focuses on other issues in the business–community relationship, particularly the contribution of managerial and employee time and talent. This section addresses these broader community issues; a later section of this chapter deals with the more specific issue of managing corporate philanthropy.

Business Stake in the Community. When one speaks with corporate executives in the fields of community and civic affairs and examines community affairs manuals and other corporate publications, one sees a broad array of reasons why companies need to keep abreast of the issues, problems, and changes expressed as community needs. Self-interest and self-preservation provide one rationale. Companies typically have a significant physical presence in the community and so they want to protect that investment. Issues of interest to companies include zoning regulations, the threat of neighborhood deterioration, corporate property taxes, the community tax base, and the availability of an adequately trained workforce. For example, when J.C. Penney began to sell its 1.8 million-square-foot office headquarters and downsize its 20-year-old offices and 40 surrounding acres in Plano, Texas, it was careful in its rezoning request to preserve a small pond and suggest an urban village mixed-use project like one that was already popular with locals.[26]

Companies can support their communities through their daily activities in a variety of ways, including sourcing from local businesses, joining public policy debates, investing in local banks, serving on local business-government committees, and locating facilities in places that benefit community development. In addition, companies can develop community action programs that transcend daily operations. For global corporations, the world is the community and so involvement must be at both the global and the local level. Figure 16-3 presents the results of a survey of businesses, identifying businesses' perceptions of the most important issues affecting communities as well as the methods those businesses use to address them.

FIGURE 16-3 Corporate Community Involvement: The Most Important Issues and the Most Common Methods of Addressing Them

Community Investment Issues		Community Investment Methods	
K–12 Education	71%	Volunteerism	86%
Workforce Development	68%	Cause-Related Partnerships	75%
Business Development and Growth	48%	Executive Participation in Community	71%
Higher Education	47%	Nonprofit or Community Board Participation	71%
Transportation or Public Infrastructure	38%	Cash Contributions	65%
Housing	38%	Advocacy	52%
Health and Wellness	38%	Community Advisory Panels	48%
Arts, Parks, Sports	24%	Pro Bono Work	31%
Crimes or Public Safety	22%	Donated Property or Equipment	30%
Other	19%	Community Management	28%

Sources: U.S. Chamber of Commerce Survey—Summary of Findings Presented at the 2007 National Partnership Conference: Corporate Community Investment, U.S. Chamber of Commerce; U.S. Chamber of Commerce Foundation, Report on the State of Corporate Community Investment, October 13, 2011, https://www.uschamberfoundation.org/report/report-state-corporate-community-investment. Accessed April 17, 2016.

Developing a Community Action Program. The motivation for developing a **community action program** is evident when one considers the stake a firm has in the community. Likewise, the community represents a major stakeholder of business. Therefore, business has an added incentive to be systematic about its relationship with the community. First, the business must *get to know the community* in which it intends to become involved. The next step is then *to assess the company's resources* to determine what the company is best able to give. Then the company can *design a community action program* by matching the community needs to the resources the company has available. Finally, as with all corporate endeavors, management should *monitor the performance* of the community action program carefully and make adjustments where needed.

An excellent example of a community project that follows these guidelines is the Ronald McDonald House Charities (RMHC) program sponsored by McDonald's Corporation. The three core programs of RMHC—the Ronald McDonald House, Ronald McDonald Family Room, and Ronald McDonald Care Mobile—are focused on helping families in need. The well-known Ronald McDonald House program provides a "home away from home" for families of seriously ill children receiving treatment at nearby hospitals. Since its inception over 38 years ago, millions of families around the world have received shelter and solace through the program.[27]

16.2 Corporate Philanthropy or Business Giving

The word *philanthropy* comes from the Greek *philien*, which means "to love," and *anthropos*, which means "mankind."[28] Thus, **philanthropy** is defined as "a desire to help mankind as indicated by acts of charity; love of mankind."[29] Corporate philanthropy is also called "business giving." In this section, we concentrate on the voluntary giving of financial resources by business. One problem with the dictionary definition of philanthropy is that the motive for the giving is characterized as charitable, benevolent, or generous. In actual practice, it is difficult to assess the true motives behind businesses'—or anyone's—giving of themselves or their financial resources. Some companies give out of a true sense of benevolence or altruism and many companies give for

ETHICS IN PRACTICE CASE

Matters of Good Intentions

A high-level finance computer programmer is sitting at his cubicle working on an upgrade that his management assigned to him. As he works on his project, he overhears one of his co-workers talking to his wife, who has a major role at an important charity organization in the community. He hears how his fellow co-worker is explaining about how he had created an account dedicated to funding a charity because the company does not make any contributions at all. He hears his co-worker also say that he did this without getting any approval from his senior-level management and explain that the way the program works is that it takes very small fractions of cents that have been rounded off and over multiple transactions dumps the fractions of cents into this account made for charity. As he hears his co-worker explain this to his wife, he wonders to himself, "What should I do? Should I tell management? He is my friend and technically it is for a good cause... right?"

1. Who are the stakeholders in this situation and what are their stakes?
2. Should the listener report the conversation he overheard to management?
3. Is your answer affected by the fact that the money is going to a good cause?
4. Is your answer affected by the fact that the company gives no money to charity?
5. Is there some alternative way this situation should be handled?

Contributed by Steve Coiscou

practical reasons—just to be good corporate citizens in the community and to enhance their reputational capital.

Not surprisingly, corporate philanthropy took a downturn when the global financial crisis occurred. However, as the economy has rebounded, corporate giving has increased. Again, according to the CECP survey, total giving in 2015 reached a high of $18.5 billion in cash and in-kind giving, growing over 50 percent in a two-year period.[30] Corporate giving is becoming increasingly focused with companies giving in a way that is consistent with their core business strategies, skills, and resources.[31] Yet, the motivations and drivers of corporate giving are still debated by academics, as these can range from the motivations of individual top-level executives, to organizational- and industry-level drivers.[32]

Of course, the use of Big Data is also helping companies to be more strategic in their philanthropy. One company, Mission Measurement, helps companies quantify the business benefit they get from philanthropy and community engagement.[33] Companies like Coke and Disney have taken advantage of this data. Coke has been in business in Africa for years, but through mining data, they figured out a way to create a program where local women could buy Coke products at wholesale prices and take the products to sell by carts, bicycles, and mopeds.[34] Similarly, Disney is using consumer data research to help identify social causes connected to the families that visit their theme parks.[35] Even churches have been able to increase their tithing numbers with mobile apps that make it easier to collect donations.[36] In sum, philanthropy has gotten more strategic and easier to do.

16.2a A Brief History of Corporate Philanthropy

Business philanthropy of one kind or another can be traced back to the 1920s when the most significant effort to "translate the new social consciousness of management into action" emerged in the form of organized corporate philanthropy.[37] Before World War I, steps had been taken toward establishing systematic, federated fund-raising for community services. The early successes of the YMCA, the War Chests, welfare federations, Community Chests, colleges and universities, and hospitals provided impetus for these groups to organize their solicitations. The business response to the opportunity to help community needs varied. At one extreme, large enterprises such as the then Bell

Telephone system, with branches, offices, and subsidiaries in thousands of communities, contributed to literally thousands of civic and social organizations. Smaller firms, such as the companies in small mill towns of North Carolina, supported schools, housing projects, religious activities, and community welfare agencies with a degree of enthusiasm that exceeded most 19th-century paternalism.

From 1918 to 1929, the Community Chest movement dominated corporate giving. In the period from 1929 to 1935, there was an attempt to allow business to deduct up to 5 percent of its pretax net income for its community donations. During the years 1935 to 1945, marked by the Great Depression and World War II, business giving did not expand, but it began to grow again from 1945 to 1960. Since about 1960, corporate giving has grown to encompass a variety of initiatives. Now in the 21st century, broader social initiatives continue, but the nature of business giving has taken a turn. The corporate philanthropy watchword is now strategic philanthropy, philanthropy that benefits both society and the corporation that is giving.

Recent trends in philanthropy also include newer communities of philanthropists. For example, a group of self-described "**philanthropy hackers**" has evolved with the enrichment of social media and a new group of very wealthy individuals from that domain. As explained by Sean Parker, the founding president of Facebook, a board member of Spotify and the chairman of the Parker Foundation, this group shares common values that translate easily into charity: "An antiestablishment bias, a belief in radical transparency, a nose for sniffing out vulnerabilities in systems, a desire to "hack" complex problems using elegant technological and social solutions, and an almost religious belief in the power of data to aid in solving those problems."[38] Rather than favoring gifts to well-established institutions like major universities, they want to interact directly with the scientists, field workers, and academics through tools like GiveDirectly that allow them to send cash payments to worthy causes directly through cellphones.[39]

16.2b A Call for Transparency in Corporate Philanthropy

A major debate has arisen over proposals for legislation that would require companies to disclose which charities they support and how much money they give. Although companies are required to disclose the money they give through foundations because of the tax benefits derived from the foundation's tax-exempt status, companies need not disclose direct donations. This has renewed the age-old debate about the role of business in society. Proponents of disclosure contend that the money belongs to the shareholders and they alone have the right to determine where it will go. Law professors often argue that philanthropy often only serves to glorify corporate managers and that, unless the philanthropy clearly benefits the company, it represents a waste of corporate assets. A few nonprofits, such as the American Red Cross, also agree that disclosure would be good public policy. Surprisingly, the National Society of Fundraising Executives even supports disclosure, arguing that it would help the image of philanthropy, which has been hurt by scandals in recent years.[40]

This broad-based support notwithstanding, most corporations and nonprofits have expressed concern that disclosure would have a chilling effect on corporate donations. Their arguments include that charitable giving is a business decision, that it would provide competitors with information about a firm's strategy, that it might incite controversy with special-interest groups, and that the paperwork would become an administrative burden.[41] No real closure on the issue of corporate philanthropy transparency has been achieved; however, concerns about knowing the source of political donations has given the issue new life.

The fact that corporations are under no obligation to report their charitable donations has led to the rise of "dark money," that is, political funding received from undisclosed sources, an issue that was discussed in Chapter 12. Shareholder rights advocates, public pension systems, and the AFL-CIO advocate for greater transparency, while a coalition of the Chamber of Commerce, the Business Roundtable, and the National Association of Manufacturers, as well as other conservative groups, continue to lobby against it.[42]

16.2c Giving to the "Third Sector": The Nonprofits

According to philanthropist John D. Rockefeller III, business giving is necessary to support what has been called the **third sector**—the nonprofit sector. The first two sectors—business and government—receive support through profits and taxes. The third sector (which includes hundreds of thousands of churches, museums, hospitals, libraries, private colleges and universities, and performing arts groups) depends on corporate and personal philanthropy for support. Philanthropy gives these institutions the crucial margin that assures them of their most precious asset—their independence.[43]

Why Do Companies Give? Perhaps it would be more worthwhile to know why companies give to charitable causes rather than to know how much they give. There are several ways to approach this question. We get initial insights when we consider the three categories of corporate contributions programs identified by the CECP.[44] The motivations are:

- *Charitable*: Community giving for which there is little or no expected benefit for the business,
- *Community Investment*: Gifts that support long-term strategic business goals while also meeting a critical community need, and
- *Commercial*: Giving that benefits the business wherein the benefit is its primary motivation. CECP's annual report showed an increase in community investment giving and a decrease in charitable giving.[45]

As economic pressures and increased international competitiveness force companies to be more careful with their earnings, we should not be surprised to see the profit motive coexisting with loftier goals in corporate contributions programs. In a subsequent section of this chapter, we illustrate more fully how philanthropy can be "strategic," and the ways in which corporate giving can be aligned with the firm's economic or profitability objectives.

To Whom Do Companies Give? During the course of any budget year, companies receive numerous requests for contributions from a wide variety of applicants. Companies must then weigh both quantitative and qualitative factors to arrive at decisions regarding the recipients of their gifts. By looking at the beneficiaries of corporate contributions, we can estimate the value business places on various societal needs in the community. However, we should note that, because of the lack of transparency in corporate giving which we discussed earlier in the chapter, our figures for giving are simply estimates, and estimates from different sources will vary.

According to the Conference Board, the majority of business giving is distributed mostly among four major categories of recipients in the following order of emphasis: (1) health and human services, (2) education, (3) civic and community activities, and (4) culture and the arts.[46] A very small percentage of giving goes to the environment, with the recipients being environmental interest groups such as the World Wildlife Fund, the Nature Conservatory, and Greenpeace.[47] The small percentage of contributions does not mean business is unconcerned about environmental issues but that its commitment to the environment is less likely to show up in corporate philanthropy and more likely to be found in daily operations, as discussed in Chapter 15. In addition, environmental issues may end up under other categories such as community improvement. A brief discussion of each of these four categories will help explain the nature of business's involvement in philanthropy.

Health and Human Services Health and human services are critical to the welfare of a community, whether it is the local community in which a business operates, or the global community to which we all belong. Major recipients in this category include hospitals, youth agencies, and other local health and welfare agencies. Hospitals represent an obviously important need in most communities. They receive financial support for capital investments (new buildings and equipment), operating funds, and matching employee gifts. Youth agencies include such groups as the YMCA, YWCA, Boy Scouts, Girl Scouts, and Boys and Girls Clubs. These children will grow to be attending college and moving on to employment opportunities, so it is logical for business to include youth as a prominent part of its health and welfare contributions.

Another reason that health and human services are among the largest categories of business giving is the amount donated to federated drives such as the United Way. Dating back to the Community Chest movement, business has traditionally cooperated with federated giving mechanisms. Organizations such as the United Way spend the year evaluating nonprofit programs and determining where dollars would be best spent with much of the money going to the local community. This saves businesses, particularly smaller local ones, the effort of not only trying to assess the various agencies to which they could make donations but also explaining to stakeholders why they chose one over another. Business hopes, just as the community does, that the consolidated efforts of federated drives will lend some order to the requests of major recipients in the community that business has chosen to support.

Education Corporate contributions in this category go to higher education and K–12 programs.[48] Educational recipients include capital grants (including endowments), unrestricted operating grants, departmental and research grants, scholarships and fellowships, and employee matching gifts. Also included in this category are contributions to educational groups (e.g., the United Negro College Fund and the Council for Financial Aid to Education) and to primary and secondary schools.

As noted earlier, business has a very good reason for supporting higher education—to increase the pool of trained personnel. This has obvious credibility, because higher education institutions do form the resource base from which business fills its managerial and professional positions. K–12 institutions feed into higher education, and so strong preparation at those levels is critical to a strong professional pool down the road. In addition, many workers in the front lines will receive their education primarily from K–12 institutions, and so it is vital that they too be in a position to provide business with a strong and capable workforce.

However, we should note that in the realm of education, businesses are doing more than just passively giving money. Bill Gates, through his charitable foundation The Bill and Melinda Gates Foundation, has spent more than $220 million on the Common Core education standards designed to boost the educational performance of American children.[49] With the support of the Business Roundtable, Gates has been lobbying businesses to participate in education reform.[50] However, the cause has been politically controversial, despite the adoption of its standards by 45 states by late 2015. With a political storm over the idea of national standards leading up to the 2016 U.S. presidential election, companies like GE became increasingly uncomfortable with the concept and appeared to be backing away from supporting the Common Core standards at the time of this writing.[51]

Civic and Community Activities This category of business giving represents a wide variety of philanthropic activities in the community. The dominant contributions in

SPOTLIGHT ***on Sustainability***

Corporate Philanthropy through Greening the Workforce

Community colleges have always been skilled at preparing two-year graduates to enter practical professions because their close ties with industry enable them to be more responsive to industry's needs. These attributes make the two-year college the perfect venue for preparing students to enter green-economy jobs. Recognizing the fit between community colleges and eco-economy job training, businesses are entering into partnerships with community colleges to prepare workers to meet their growing eco-workforce demands. For example, GE donated a small wind turbine to Mesalands Community College in Tucumcari, New Mexico, for their wind energy technician program and promised to hire their first three years of graduates. Johnson Controls constructed a 2,500 solar panel farm at Milwaukee Area Technical College, enabling students there to be trained as the photovoltaic designers and installers that Johnson Controls needs to hire. Experts predict that the expected expansion of environmental policies could increase renewable energy jobs from 9 million in 2007 to 19.5 million in 2030.

Sources: Mina Kimes, "Get a Green Job in Two Years," *Fortune* (November 23, 2009), 32; Jim Morgan, "Mesalands Community College Capitalizes on Wind Resource to Transform a Rural Town," SEED Center (2011), http://www.theseedcenter.org/Colleges-in-Action/Success-Stories/Mesalands-Community-College-Capitalizes-on-Wind-Re. Accessed April 7, 2016.

this category are those given in support of community improvement activities, environment and ecology, nonacademic research organizations (e.g., the Brookings Institution, the Committee for Economic Development, and the Urban League), and neighborhood renewal.

General Mills saw the importance of community involvement when the nickname of Minneapolis went from the "City of Nice" to "Murderapolis." General Mills executives hired a consultant to analyze crime data and found that Hawthorne, just five miles from the company headquarters, was one of the city's most violent neighborhoods. They devoted thousands of employee hours and $2.5 million to ridding Hawthorne of its problems. As it turned out, the initiatives of General Mills along with a number of other prominent Minneapolis firms led to the development of a program known as Minnesota HEALS (Hope, Education, Law, and Safety) that has grown from a handful of people to dozens of corporate, community, and government groups convening to reduce violence and create hope. Today, Minneapolis is one of the leading cities in America in which business support of the community has become legendary.[52]

Also faced with a city in need of help, Prudential has focused significant philanthropic efforts on supporting the rebuilding of Newark, New Jersey, its headquarters since 1875. In 2012, the Prudential Foundation donated $1.25 million to Newark nonprofit organizations serving low-income families and at-risk children, as well as $250,000 to the Newark Trust for Education.[53] After Superstorm Sandy devastated Northern New Jersey, the foundation donated $3 million in relief funds to nonprofit agencies assisting the victims, and it pledged to match employee contributions to the cause.[54]

Culture and the Arts Business support for the arts has been decreasing, and the future news is not good. Americans for the Arts predict a "dire drop" in future funding because of the global economic recession.[55] Companies faced with layoffs may feel they cannot afford to support the arts, but that outlook is shortsighted. The arts provide brand recognition, ensure community development, and are key to promoting the community as a great place to live and work. Figure 16-4 tells the story of the City of Detroit, where the Detroit Institute of Arts (DIA) played a central role in the City's recovery from its 2013 bankruptcy.

Americans for the Arts conducted a recent economic impact study of the nonprofit arts and culture industry in the United States and found good reason for business to

FIGURE 16-4 The Motor City and the Arts

When the city of Detroit declared Chapter 9 bankruptcy in 2013, the Detroit Institute of Arts (DIA) played a central part in its recovery plan. The DIA was a municipal department linked to the finances of the city. The Bankruptcy Court formed a "grand bargain" plan supported by $800 million from foundations, the Detroit Institute of Arts (DIA), private donors, and the state of Michigan —to protect the DIA from having to auction off its art. Foundations and others saw the importance of preserving Detroit's historical art pieces and agreed to make contributions to the grand bargain to reduce public employee pension cuts if the DIA's survival could be guaranteed.

It worked. One year later, Detroit was out of bankruptcy. The first grand bargain payment of $23.3 million was paid to the General Retirement System and the Police and Fire Retirement Systems in December 2014, including $18.3 million from foundations and $5 million from the DIA. A total of 20 payments will ultimately be made to the City of Detroit from the Foundation for Detroit's Future. Twelve foundations are committed a total of $366 million over 20 years to the grand bargain. In addition to contributing $100 million to the grand bargain, the DIA also became an independent charitable trust, like most large American museums, instead of being owned by the city.

The grand bargain also helped Detroit out of bankruptcy by creating a new entity, called the Foundation for Detroit's Future, governed by a five-member board of directors. Going forward, money from foundations, private donors, and the state of Michigan will go through The Foundation for Detroit's Future and the foundation will then funnel the money to the city. This novel and creative way to approach a city's bankruptcy and preserve its art may pave the way for other cities to see business and the arts as true partners in a community.

Sources: Jocelyn O'Rourke, "One Year Later: Reflecting on Detroit's Philanthropy-Driven 'Grand Bargain'," *Philamplify*, http://philamplify.org/2015/12/21/one-year-later-reflecting-on-detroits-philanthropy-driven-grand-bargain/. Accessed April 10, 2016; Randy Kennedy, "'Grand Bargain' Saves the Detroit Institute of Arts," *The New York Times*, http://www.nytimes.com/2014/11/08/arts/design/grand-bargain-saves-the-detroit-institute-of-arts.html.

support the arts as part of supporting the community. Using findings from 182 regions representing all 50 states and the District of Columbia, they found that U.S. nonprofit arts and culture organizations generated $61.1 billion of economic activity on top of the $74.1 billion in event-related expenditures by their audiences.[56] As they note, this yield is far greater than the $4 billion they receive in collective arts allocations.[57] In a follow-up survey of over 600 businesses, the four most highly cited reasons that businesses contribute to the arts include:[58]

- They improve the quality of life in the community,
- They help create a vibrant community and society,
- They improve academic performance for students, and
- They offer education opportunities that benefit the community.

In sum, advocates for the arts continue to engage businesses to support the arts with a combination of both economic and social arguments.

Giving in Times of Crisis In addition to the four categories previously mentioned, firms are expected to make charitable donations when crises occur in the firm's community, the nation, or the world at large. We covered the general issues related to responding to a crisis in Chapter 6, noting that some firms are able to respond so well to a crisis that they can be counted on to lend a hand to others in need. For example, Walmart and Home Depot stood out in their ability to bring some relief following the devastation of Hurricane Katrina, as did Fed Ex for providing the Federal Emergency Management Agency (FEMA) with a radio antenna to set up communications. We also discussed Prudential's response to the havoc that the 2011 earthquake off the Pacific coast of Tohoku wreaked on Japan and the different responses of the Malaysian country officials and Malaysian Airlines to the Malaysian air flight disaster in 2014.

According to the U.S. Chamber of Commerce, U.S. businesses donated $566 million to help communities suffering from the effects of the Indian Ocean tsunami.[59] Corporations also stepped up when Superstorm Sandy ravaged the Northeastern United

States. According to the Business Civic Leadership Center of the U.S. Chamber of Commerce, businesses pledged over $141 million in support of recovery efforts, with two-thirds in the form of monetary donations to organizations like the Red Cross and Feeding America.[60] However, donors for disaster relief have not always been satisfied with the use of their monies. Recent attention to poor administration of donor funds for post-earthquake relief in Haiti as well as funds for those affected by Superstorm Sandy led *ProPublica* to suggest five tips for donating after disasters:[61] (1) research before you give, (2) demand meaningful transparency, (3) work with local organizations if possible, (4) look at options beyond traditional charities, and (5) think beyond the next disaster.

Some observers worry that in times of crisis, corporate philanthropy becomes a zero-sum game in that contributions that go to alleviate the crisis then do not go to other causes that need them as well. Typically, giving has increased from year to year irrespective of external events; however, one statistic should give us pause. In the two weeks following the attack on the World Trade Center, corporations gave over $120 million to relief funds—an unprecedented level of corporate giving.[62] According to a survey by the *Chronicle of Corporate Philanthropy*, however, corporate giving subsequently declined.[63] Other concerns surround the possibility of *donor fatigue* following crises for which corporations and individuals open their checkbooks. There has been some evidence of this. Just one month after a 7.8-magnitude struck Nepal, India, in April 2015, donor fatigue appeared to set in. The United Nations appealed for $423 million to be able to provide up to two million survivors with basic relief such as tents or tarpaulin sheets, dry food rations, safe drinking water, and toilets, but one month after the crisis, only 22 percent of the required funds had been raised. The U.N. resident coordinator attributed the slow response due to donor fatigue where governments and businesses were being torn between competing humanitarian crises across the world.[64]

16.2d Managing Corporate Philanthropy

As performance pressures on business have continued and intensified, companies have had to turn their attention to *managing* corporate philanthropy. Early on, managers did not subject their contributions to the same kinds of rigorous analysis given to expenditures for plants and equipment, inventory, product development, marketing, and a host of other budgetary items. This began to change in the early 1980s because cutbacks in federal spending on charitable causes created an increasing need for contributions by business. At the same time, however, the economy was struggling through its worst recession in 50 years. It became increasingly clear that business had to reconcile its economic and social goals, both of which were essential.[65]

Now, even as we are recovering from the global recession, the pressure on businesses to be more businesslike in its philanthropy remains. There are two aspects to this. The first is to base giving on business skills, resources, and capabilities to enhance philanthropic outcomes. The second is to focus on philanthropy that will enhance corporate profitability while also making a positive difference in the community at large. To facilitate this process, most large companies today have an executive and a department dedicated to corporate giving. Those who are leading these efforts usually carry titles such as vice president for corporate giving, director for corporate philanthropy, or manager for corporate relations.

This strategic approach to managing philanthropy follows an ethic of enlightened self-interest and is clearly on the rise. In the most recent CECP survey, the data show that companies are engaging in more focused giving, targeted to their core strategic interests.[66] That trend will only grow as recovery from the recession makes it more necessary to align philanthropic goals with strategic priorities.[67]

Community Partnerships. As a broad response to this growing need to reconcile financial and social goals, the concept of **community partnerships** evolved. A community partnership occurs when a for-profit business enters into a cooperative arrangement with a nonprofit organization for their mutual advantage. Businesses see in community partnerships the opportunity for simultaneous achievement of economic and philanthropic objectives. Business skills and resources are often exactly what a community nonprofit organization needs to achieve its mission. A good example of that is National Safe Place.

National Safe Place is a youth outreach program with two purposes: (1) educating young people about the dangers of running away or trying to resolve difficult, threatening situations on their own and (2) providing safe havens and resources for youth in crisis.[68] They have created a variety of Safe Place locations (e.g., schools, fire stations, libraries, grocery and convenience stores, public transit, YMCAs, and other appropriate public buildings) where young people can get help and be safe. The locations display the yellow and black diamond-shaped Safe Place sign. Corporations that have skills and resources that can help with the Safe Place programs have partnered with the nonprofit. These include Sprint, CSX Movers, Southwest Airlines, QT, and the National Association of Convenience Stores.[69]

Community partnerships take on many different forms. Partnership options include sponsorships, vendor relationships, licensing agreements, and in-kind donations.[70] Other ways of building alliances are based on strategic philanthropy and cause-related marketing. We consider strategic philanthropy and cause-related marketing in more detail.

Strategic Philanthropy. **Strategic philanthropy** is an approach by which corporate giving and other philanthropic endeavors of a firm are designed in a way that best fits with the firm's overall mission, goals, or objectives. This implies that the firm has some idea of what its overall strategy is and that it is able to articulate its missions, goals, or objectives. One goal of all firms is profitability. Therefore, one requirement of strategic philanthropy is to make as direct a contribution as possible to the financial goals of the firm. Philanthropy has long been thought to be in the long-range economic interest of the firm. Strategic philanthropy simply presses for a more direct or immediate contribution of business giving to the firm's economic success.

An important way to make philanthropy strategic is to bring contribution programs into sharper alignment with business endeavors. This means that each firm should pursue those social or community programs that have a direct rather than an indirect bearing on its success. Thus, a local bank should logically pursue people-oriented projects in the community in which it resides; a manufacturer might pursue programs having to do with environmental protection or technological advancement.

A third way to make philanthropy strategic is to ensure that it is well planned and managed rather than handled haphazardly and without direction. Planning implies that it has clearly delineated goals, is properly organized and staffed, and is administered in accordance with certain established policies. Figure 16-5 presents recommendations for best practices in the implementation of a philanthropy program.

FIGURE 16-5 Attributes of an Effective Strategic Philanthropy Program

An effective strategic philanthropy program should have the following attributes:

1. The program should fit with the company's strategic goals and mission.
2. The program should be connected with the community involvement programs.
3. The budget and infrastructure should be sufficient to meet goals.
4. Company policies and guidelines for should be made clear.
5. Employees should be involved in philanthropy-related activities.
6. Stakeholders should be made fully aware of the program.
7. Long-term business–nonprofit partnerships should be developed.

Strategic philanthropy must find the place of overlap where the philanthropy provides both social and economic benefits. In an important *Harvard Business Review* article, Michael Porter and Mark Kramer argued that few companies have effectively taken advantage of the competitive advantage corporate philanthropy can provide. They consider strategic philanthropy to be a myth—simply semantics that help companies to rationalize their contributions. Similarly, Pablo Eisenberg, a *Chronicle of Philanthropy* columnist wrote in *The Chronicle* in 2013: "Strategic philanthropy might be less worrisome if it were not practiced so often by very large foundations run by small, insular boards that do little to tell the public how they make decisions."[71]

To be truly strategic, philanthropy must be congruent with a company's competitive context, which consists of four interrelated elements: factor conditions, demand conditions, the context for strategy and rivalry, and related and supporting industries.[72]

Factor (Supply) Conditions These are the available inputs for production. Porter and Kramer point to DreamWorks as an example of a company that uses strategic philanthropy to improve its factor conditions effectively. They created a program that provides training to low-income and disadvantaged youth in the skills needed to work in the entertainment industry. Of course, the societal benefits of an improved educational system are clear. While providing these social benefits, DreamWorks also enhances the labor pool from which they can draw. This not only strengthens the company but the industry as a whole as well.[73] The Clorox example of improving the community surrounding their headquarters through partnership with the community foundation also addresses factor conditions by improving the general quality of life and the local infrastructure.

Demand Conditions These are concerned with the nature of the company's customers and the local market. Philanthropy can influence the local market's size and quality. Porter and Kramer point to Apple's long-held policy of donating computers to public schools. By introducing young people and their teachers to computers, Apple expands their market. They also increase the sophistication of their customer base, which benefits a differentiated product such as the ones Apple sells.[74] Similarly, Burger King focuses its philanthropic efforts on highly focused programs to help students, teachers, and schools.[75] This program enhances name recognition in its target population of consumers.

The demand for capitalism with a conscience is growing. In response to a global survey by public relations firm, Edelman, 47 percent of respondents said that every month they buy a product from a company that supports a good cause: That is a 47 percent increase in two years.[76] In another study, 84 percent of consumers globally say they seek out responsible products whenever possible, though 81 percent cite availability of these products as the largest barrier to not purchasing more.[77] The upsurge in social consciousness is partly in response to the influence of Millennials, people born from 1982 to 2004, who were burned by the recession and have learned to use social media to be more informed consumers.[78] An indication of their influence is that Rolling Stone and Participant Media are creating a new cable network, Pivot TV that is aimed at Millennials to "spark conversations and inspire change."[79]

Whole Foods has developed a strategic philanthropy program that affects both factor and demand conditions, enabling the company to reap benefits along the length of the value chain. In the factor market, Whole Foods has designed a system for sourcing products from developing countries while maintaining product standards. It developed a strict set of criteria for its suppliers to adhere to and contracted with TransFair USA and the Rainforest Alliance, two respected third-party certifiers, to ensure the suppliers met these criteria. These certified products receive a Whole Trade logo so that customers know which products come from the developing world and meet the criteria. Its customers value these attributes and so Whole Foods' demand conditions also improve as a result of their efforts.[80]

Context for Strategy and Rivalry The business's context, or environment, can be influenced by strategic philanthropy. Porter and Kramer point to the many corporations that support Transparency International as examples of firms using philanthropy to create a better environment for competition. As discussed in Chapter 10, Transparency International's mission is to deter and disclose corporate corruption around the world. The organization measures and publicizes corruption while pushing for stricter codes and enforcement. By supporting Transparency International, corporations are helping to build a better competitive environment—one that rewards fair competition.[81]

Related and Supporting Industries These can also be strengthened through strategic philanthropy, thereby enhancing the productivity of companies. American Express provides an excellent example of a firm that uses philanthropy to strengthen its related and supporting industries. For almost 20 years, American Express has funded travel and tourism academies in secondary schools. The program trains teachers, supports curricula, and provides both summer internships and industry mentors. A strong travel industry translates into important benefits for American Express.[82]

Now let us turn our attention to a special kind of strategic philanthropy that has become quite prevalent in recent years: cause-related marketing.

Cause-Related Marketing. There is some debate as to whether cause-related marketing is really philanthropy. It could be seen as a form of strategic philanthropy. Porter and Kramer argue that it is marketing and nothing more.[83] However, because cause marketing represents a close linkage between a firm's financial objectives and corporate contributions, it is discussed here. Stated in its simplest form, **cause-related marketing** is the direct linking of a business's product or service to a specified charity. Each time a consumer uses the service or buys the product, a donation is given to the charity by the business.[84] Thus some observers refer to cause-related marketing as "quid pro quo strategic philanthropy."

The term cause-related marketing was coined by the American Express Company to describe a program it began in 1983 in which it agreed to contribute a penny to the restoration of the Statue of Liberty every time a customer used one of its credit cards to make a purchase. The project generated $1.7 million for the statue restoration and a substantial increase in usage of the American Express card.[85] Since that time, companies have employed this same approach to raise millions of dollars for a wide variety of local and national causes.

Recently, cause-related marketing has given way to a new concept, **cause branding**. Cause branding represents a longer-term commitment than cause marketing. It also relates more directly to the firm's line of business and the target audience. Avon Products, Inc., has become a recognized leader in cause branding. Its target audience is women, and so it has developed an array of programs to raise awareness of breast cancer, a disease that mostly affects women. The company raises money for programs that provide low-income women with education and free screening. Avon sells products featuring the pink ribbon that is worn for breast cancer awareness and then donates the proceeds from these products to nonprofit and university programs.[86]

Cause branding has become a successful marketing tool. In a recent Cone Communications/Ebiquity survey, 90 percent of U.S. consumers say they would switch brands to one associated with a cause, given comparable price and quality.[87] The benefits do not apply only to consumers: Employees react to cause branding as well. In companies with cause programs, 87 percent of employees indicate they feel strong loyalty, while only 67 percent feel strong loyalty in firms that do not have cause programs.[88] Cause branding strengthens internal corporate cultures and has a dramatic influence on employee pride, morale, and loyalty.[89]

ETHICS IN PRACTICE CASE

Competition in the Nonprofit Workplace

I have been interning for a multibillion-dollar nonprofit organization since January. As a supply chain intern, my primary responsibility is to analyze potential suppliers. I use data to determine the cheapest supplier that can properly provide my organization with a product or service. These analyses have saved my organization thousands of dollars each year. This money can be placed back into our grant-making program to help people who are in need of our assistance.

Recently, my boss hired a second intern to assist with the supplier analyses. My boss split my desk in half and told me that I would be sharing my office with the new intern. I welcomed the notion of having someone to work with and discuss ideas.

My boss instructed that we share supplier information with each other, but not our opinions. Instead, he preferred that we come to our own separate conclusions. When the analyses are due, the other intern and I present our findings to my boss. If we come to different conclusion and choose different suppliers, my boss carefully weighs both options and chooses the best supplier.

When my co-intern first started at the foundation, I willingly shared all of my supplier research such as the price, capabilities, references, and financial status. Although the other intern had not shared information with me, I merely thought he was still growing accustomed to his new position. However, when presenting our findings to my boss, my co-intern used data and statistics that he had *never* shared with me. My boss often asked why I had not included this data in my analyses.

On several occasions, I would ask my co-intern why he had withheld information from me. He would ignore or avoid the question each time. I know that my co-intern is withholding information from me because he is competitive and wants to impress my boss.

I feel that my co-intern is taking advantage of my research in order to outperform me. I often want to withhold my research as well, but I do not want to hinder potential cost savings for my nonprofit organization. I do not want to sacrifice possible grant-making money for my own benefit, but I also do not want my boss to think my work is below average.

1. Is it productive to have competition in the workplace, especially in a nonprofit that focuses on helping others?
2. Is my boss right in assigning the same project to my co-intern and me? Are there better options to increase our productivity?
3. Should I sacrifice my performance for the benefit of my organization?
4. What actions do you recommend I should take to resolve this issue?

Contributed by Zachary Greytsman

Proponents of cause-related marketing argue that everyone involved in it comes out a winner. Business enhances its public image by being associated with a worthy cause and increases its sales at the same time. Nonprofit organizations get cash for their programs as well as enhanced marketing and public visibility made possible by business's expertise. Critics of cause-related marketing fear that the needs of capitalism will overshadow the cause. However, the criticism has not hurt the cause branding movement. Corporate cause marketing is expected to hit $2 billion by the end of 2016.[90] Firms are getting more and more creative in cause branding. Some firms are now going blue for autism awareness month. Brands are encouraged to shine a blue light to show their support. Build-A-Bear Workshop is making a blue Teddy Bear in honor of the cause and the Empire State Building was lit in all blue. Jet Blue, which already has the color in its name, initiated a "Wings for Autism" program that helps families to familiarize their autistic children with the sights and sounds of air travel so that they can be more comfortable flying.[91]

Global Philanthropy. The size of a company's workforce in international markets is the greatest determinant of the size of their charitable contributions to that market. It should come as no surprise then that as corporate operations have become increasingly globalized, so has corporate philanthropy. Firms responding to a 2015 CECP survey indicated that their global philanthropic giving has grown as their involvement in global operations had grown.[92] Approximately two-thirds (65 percent) of companies give internationally, and those that do typically allocate 21 percent to international giving.[93]

Businesses want to protect the communities in which they operate, keeping them healthy and environmentally sound. Businesses also develop infrastructure to facilitate the flow of goods and services. According to Stephen Jordan of the U.S. Chamber of Commerce Business Civic Leadership Center, companies are increasing their corporate philanthropy to "create a culture of opportunity" in the developing world. He said, "Ninety-six percent of opportunity is outside our borders.… Increasingly, companies … want to grow their customer base in emerging markets."[94]

16.3 Detrimental Impacts on Communities

Firms not only have positive, constructive impacts on communities, but they can have detrimental impacts as well. Most often this occurs when a business decides to close down, downsize, or close a plant or branch. Among the most important impacts is the issue of job losses in the community and we will focus on that primarily. Other losses include all the positive benefits discussed in the first part of the chapter—most importantly, community involvement, volunteerism, and corporate philanthropy.

In turning our attention to the loss of jobs, which represent the most direct and significant detrimental impact, we see a most pervasive example of these negative effects when mass job layoffs occur because jobs are moved elsewhere or when a business or plant closes and management does not carefully consider the community stakeholders affected. We will address the issue of offshoring first, because many of the recent job losses are attributable to this issue, and then we take a more in-depth look at business and plant closings.

16.3a Offshoring and Reshoring

The word **outsourcing** refers to the relocation of business processes to a different company. **Offshoring** refers to the relocation of business processes to a different country, whereas **reshoring** is the returning of business processes to their original location. Offshoring became popular when new technologies such as high-speed data links and the Internet have made it easier to do white-collar work overseas, where labor was cheaper. In the late 19th century, the advent of railroads had just as transforming an effect. A writer for Scribner's in 1888 said that life had changed more in the past 75 years than it had since Julius Caesar, "and the change has chiefly been made by railways."[95] Railroads destroyed industries and whole towns, in addition to jobs. There was no longer a need for icehouses or local meatpacking plants and so they closed. While new markets opened for U.S. grain, cotton farmers lost market share to cheaper Egyptian and Indian cotton. Steamboat towns faded, and struggling farmers began to resent their dependence on the wealthy railroads.[96]

Some decades ago, concerns over offshore outsourcing focused on blue-collar occupations, primarily factory workers, and it was mostly a problem in the United States. Then the Internet Boom of the 1990s made it a white-collar issue with information technology workers being particularly hard hit.[97] A programmer who made $11,000 in India or $8,000 in Poland and Hungary could do the work of a programmer who made $80,000 in the United States.[98] This represented huge savings for firms dealing with global competition. In addition, it was global competition that came to rule the day for businesses beginning in the 1990s and moving forward to today.

Lest we think that reshoring will solve the job loss problem in America, it should be emphasized that especially since the North American Free Trade Agreement (NAFTA) was passed in 1994, many American companies and jobs have moved to Mexico. A good example of this that is still in the news is the relocation of the A.O. Smith electric motor factory that closed down eight years ago in the small Kentucky town of Scottsville (population 4,226). A.O. Smith moved its factory to Acuna, Mexico, just across the Rio Grande. The impact on Scottsville was devastating. One couple, who each made $16.10 an hour and were living what they thought was the American dream, are now working in low-paying jobs where their combined income does not add up to one of their old factory wages.[99]

By 2015, the United States was posting a $60 billion trade deficit with Mexico, most of it attributed to NAFTA. One expert at the Economic Policy Institute estimates that the deficit with Mexico alone has cost 850,000 American jobs. It is little wonder that the free-trade issue became such a hotly debated issue in the 2016 presidential election year. The problem has become so severe that a Bloomberg Politics national poll conducted in March 2016 found that two-thirds of Americans are now favoring restrictions being place on imports.[100]

Though the town of Scottsville, Kentucky, was devastated by the relocation of A. O. Smith, to across the border, the town of Acuna, Mexico, was reaping the benefits of the move. One woman, put in charge of payroll there, is now making about $1.75 an hour, a small fraction of the U.S. minimum wage. She says the income has been a life-changing experience for her. Now, next door to the electric motor plant, which was sold to another buyer in 2011, there resides several other factories that also have moved to Mexico resulting in job losses somewhere else, typically from the United States.[101] In short, just as some large firms are deciding to reshore and return to their home countries, the reality of businesses closing and moving offshore or elsewhere and impacting communities detrimentally continues.

In spite of the savings involved with offshoring, it has not been a panacea for all companies. The problems that developed from shipping jobs overseas often ended up outweighing the cost savings. Capital One ended a contract for a 250-person call center in New Delhi when they found that workers would boost their sales by offering unauthorized lines of credit.[102] Similarly, Dell brought a tech support center back to the United States after customers complained of thick accents and poor service.[103] Stanley Furniture moved its manufacturing facilities back to the United States after a recall of cribs made in Slovenia.[104]

Even GE, the pioneer of offshoring, has found that the costs of offshoring often outweigh the benefits. GE Chairman and CEO Jeff Immelt refers to outsourcing as "yesterday's model."[105] GE has returned production of refrigerators, washing machines, and heaters from China back to Kentucky and shifted much of its IT work back to the United States. It is also hiring hundreds of new IT engineers at a new center in Michigan.[106] Google, Caterpillar, Ford Motor Company, and Apple are all planning to bring some production back or add new capacity to the United States.[107]

In a special issue on outsourcing and offshoring, the *Economist* identified some reasons why the offshoring trend has shifted toward reshoring:[108]

- **Cost advantages diminished**—Labor costs in China and India have risen 10 to 20 percent a year for the past decade, while more automation has reduced labor's share of the cost of operations.
- **Distance brings disadvantages**—Shipping goods long distances is increasingly expensive and takes time to complete. Distance from R&D can hamper innovation.
- **Proximity to customers is key**—Companies need to be close to customers to customize production and respond quickly to changes in demand.

Current trends indicate that reshoring will continue, most likely for industries that have access to global markets and can take advantage of cheaper natural gas—as well as those industries that have products that change rapidly, like fashion apparel and technology that uses relatively little labor.[109] Despite the popularity of reshoring, many companies in the United States and in other developed nations continue to relocate plants to other countries where labor costs are significantly less. And, due to these continuing relocations and job losses, our next section on business and plant closings is still relevant today.

16.3b Business and Plant Closings

Although the right to close a business or plant has long been regarded as a management prerogative, the business shutdowns of the past two decades—especially their dramatic effects—have called attention to the question of what rights and responsibilities business has in relation to employee and community stakeholders. The literature on business social responsibility and policy has documented corporate concern with the detrimental impact of its actions. Indeed, business's social response patterns have borne this out. Management expert Peter Drucker suggested the following business position regarding social impacts of management decisions:

> *Because one is responsible for one's impacts, one minimizes them. The fewer impacts an institution has outside of its own specific purpose and mission, the better does it conduct itself, the more responsibly does it act, and the more acceptable a citizen, neighbor, and contributor it is.*[110]

This raises the question of whether business's responsibilities in the realm of plant closings and offshoring and their impacts on employees and communities are any different from the host of responsibilities that have already been assumed in areas such as employment discrimination, employee privacy and safety, honesty in advertising, product safety, and concern for the environment. From the perspective of the employees affected, their role in plant and business closings might be considered an extension of the numerous employee rights issues.

Business essentially has two opportunities to be responsive to employee and community stakeholders in shutdown situations. It can take certain actions *before the decision* to close is made and other actions *after the decision* to close has been made.

Before the Decision to Close Is Made. Before a company makes a decision to close down, it has a responsibility to itself, its employees, and its community to thoroughly and diligently study whether the closing is the only or best option available. A decision to leave a community that has come to depend on them should be preceded by critical and realistic investigations of economic alternatives.

Diversification Sometimes it is possible to find other revenue streams to help the company cope with the slim margins of manufacturing. SRC Holdings was making only 2 to 3 percent a year but needed a profit of 4 percent to compete effectively. SRC chief executive John P. Stack explains, "We took our manufacturing discipline into the service sector to develop new sources of revenue…. Without creating these other businesses, we couldn't have survived. Manufacturing has very slim margins but if a company innovates the margins can be incredible."[111] In 2016, having weathered multiple economic storms, SRC took pride in being "the oldest employee-owned remanufacturer to OEM's in North America."[112]

New Ownership After a careful study of alternatives has been made, it may be concluded that finding new ownership for the plant or business is the only feasible alternative. Two basic options exist at this point: (1) find a new owner or (2) explore the possibility of employee ownership.[113] A company has an obligation to its employees and the community to try to sell the business as a going unit instead of shutting down. This is often not possible, but it is an avenue that should be explored. Quite often, the most promising new buyers of a firm are residents of the state who have a long-term stake in the community and are willing to make a strong commitment. Ideally, local organizations and the government will be able to offer incentives to companies willing to bring jobs to the areas.

For example, when the Grumman Olson facility closed in Lycoming County, Pennsylvania, several parties joined together to bring jobs back to the area. The local chamber of commerce worked with the state to develop an incentive package that included job creation tax credits and customized job training at the local college. Specialized Vehicles Corporation (SVC) bought the facility, promising to offer jobs first to the displaced workers of Grumman Olson.[114]

Employee Ownership The idea of a company selling its business or a plant to the employees as a way of avoiding a closedown is appealing at first glance. In the United States, over a thousand companies are **employee owned**. Most of these companies are very small. The National Center for Employee Ownership (NCEO) lists the 100 largest employee-owned companies, defined as having over 50 percent employee ownership, and, in 2015, the smallest on the list only have about 1,000 employees.[115] Although employee ownership is not a major trend in the current environment, it is instructive to understand its history and record of success and failure to appreciate fully the pros and cons of employee ownership.

Employee ownership experiences have not always been favorable.[116] In numerous cases, employees have had to take significant wage and benefit reductions to make the business profitable. Some companies, however, have met with better success. Publix Supermarkets is "the largest employee owned grocery chain in the U.S."[117] Most observers credit their employee ownership with earning Publix the number one supermarket ranking on the American Customer Satisfaction Index for many years.[118] Publix employees are known for bending over backward to please customers.[119]

After the Decision to Close Is Made. There are a multitude of actions that a business can take once the decision has been made that a closedown or relocation is unavoidable. The overriding concern should be that the company seriously attempts to mitigate the social and economic impacts of its actions on employees and the community. Regardless of the circumstances of the move, some basic planning can help alleviate the disruptions felt by those affected. There are several actions that management can take, including:[120]

- Conducting a community-impact analysis;
- Providing advance notice to the employees or community;
- Providing transfer, relocation, and outplacement benefits;
- Phasing out the business gradually; and
- Helping the community attract replacement industry.

Community-Impact Analysis Because management is responsible for its impacts on employees and the community, a thorough community-impact analysis of a decision to close down or move is always in order. The initial action should be to identify realistically those aspects of the community that would be affected by the company's plans. This entails asking questions, such as:[121]

- What groups will be affected?
- How will they be affected?
- What is the timing of initial and later effects?
- What is the magnitude of the effect?
- What is the duration of the impact?
- To what extent will the impact be diffused in the community?

FIGURE 16-6 The Worker Retraining and Adjustment Act (WARN)

The Worker Adjustment and Retraining Notification Act (WARN) seeks to protect workers, their families, and communities by requiring most employers with 100 or more employees to provide notification 60 calendar days in advance of plant closings and mass layoffs.

Employees entitled to notice under WARN include managers and supervisors, as well as hourly and salaried workers. WARN requires that notice also be given to employees' representatives, the local chief elected official, and the state dislocated worker unit.

Advance notice gives workers and their families some transition time to adjust to the prospective loss of employment, to seek and obtain other jobs, and, if necessary, to enter skill training or retraining that will allow these workers to compete successfully in the job market.

- Generally, WARN covers employers with 100 or more employees, not counting those who have worked less than six months in the last 12 months and those who work an average of less than 20 hours a week.
- Employees entitled to advance notice under WARN include managers and supervisors as well as hourly and salaried workers.
- Regular federal, state, and local government entities that provide public services are *not* covered by WARN.

The Department of Labor's (DOL) Employment and Training Administration (ETA) administers WARN at the federal level, and some states have plant closure laws of their own. DOL has no enforcement role in seeking damages for workers who did not receive adequate notice of a layoff or received no notice at all. However, they can assist workers in finding a new job or learning about training opportunities that are available.

Source: The United States Department of Labor, https://www.doleta.gov/programs/factsht/warn.htm. Accessed April 8, 2016.

Once these questions have been answered, management is better equipped to modify its plans so that negative impacts can be minimized and favorable impacts, if any, can be maximized.

Advance Notice One of the most often discussed responsibilities in business- or plant-closing situations is the provision of advance notice to workers and communities. The national advance-notice law is called the **Worker Adjustment and Retraining Notification Act (WARN)**. Figure 16-6 provides an overview of WARN.

Companies will sometimes try to get around the WARN requirements. In 2014, when the Crumbs Bake Shop announced it was closing all of its stores, its 400 employees found out that day that they would be out of a job the next.[122] While in theory mass layoffs are not supposed to work that way under WARN, the reality is that it is not restrictive enough. Crumbs Bake Shop was able to provide short notice because layoff thresholds (at least 50 employees who make up at least 33 percent of the workforce) must be met at a single company location—and Crumbs' employees were scattered at multiple locations. There is a fine line between staggering employee layoffs legally and doing it to avoid the notice requirements of WARN. Courts try to determine what employers knew at the time of the layoffs. If they deem that the employers knew they would be laying off more than 50 employees at a time, the firm is considered to be in violation of WARN.

Employees who sue successfully under WARN may get back pay and benefits for up to 60 days. The penalty for not giving adequate notice is $500 per day. The only acceptable reasons for not providing a 60-day notice are (1) action being taken by the employer, which, if successful, would have postponed or eliminated the need for layoffs, (2) unforeseen business circumstances that the employer could not reasonably have foreseen, and (3) natural disasters.[123]

Since the bill's inception, legislators have tried to strengthen the law by closing loopholes and giving it some teeth. One key problem is that the Labor Department has no enforcement power over the WARN Act and so displaced employees must hire their own attorneys to hold their former employers accountable.[124]

Good communication is critical when a company is thinking about a business closing and subsequent layoffs. Communication expert Hugh Braithwaite offers important advice on communicating with employees being laid off.[125]

- **Be complete.** Employees will try to fill any holes in your story, and that is how rumors begin.
- **Be consistent**. Information will become muddled if the story keeps changing.
- **Inform affected employees first.** Provide a thorough "exit kit" that provides all information the employee might need to smooth their transition.
- **Inform retained employees.** Recognize that survivors have challenges too and provide ample opportunity for their questions to be asked and answered.

Transfer, Relocation, and Outplacement Benefits Enlightened companies are increasingly recognizing that the provision of separation or outplacement benefits is in the long-range best interest of all parties concerned. Everyone is better off if disruptions are minimized in the lives of the firm's management, the displaced workers, and the community. Outplacement benefits have been used for years as companies have attempted to remove redundant or marginal personnel with minimum disruption and cost to the company and maximum benefit to the individuals involved. Now these same benefits are being used in business and plant closings.

Gradual Phase-Outs Another management action that can significantly ameliorate the effects of a business shutdown is the gradual phasing out of the business. A gradual phase-out buys time for employees and the community to adjust to the new situation and to solve some of their problems. Unfortunately, these types of programs are few and far between. The tech industry, for example, has a history of doing major layoffs too frequently and with poor execution.[126] As one exception, when the semiconductor industry took a deep downturn, Sony Electronics found it necessary to close its plant in San Antonio. They let their employees go in phases as they gradually wrapped up their customer orders. Affected workers were given 60 days' notice. This did not come as a surprise because, as one worker noted, "It was fairly well-known that the company was sick for a quite a while."[127] When asked about worker reactions, one employee said, "There were a few who were upset but some of them actually requested to be included in Phase 1 (job cuts). They wanted to get their severance packages and get on with their lives."[128] Sony provided workers with severance pay based on years on the job. They also extended benefits packages, outplacement services, and job transfers, where possible, to other Sony plants in the United States.

Helping to Attract Replacement Industry The principal responsibility for attracting new industry falls on the community, but the management of the closing firm can provide cooperation and assistance. The closing company can help by providing inside information on building and equipment characteristics and capabilities, transportation options based on its experience, and contacts with other firms in its industry that may be seeking facilities. Helping the community attract replacement industry has the overwhelming advantage of rapidly replacing large numbers of lost jobs. In addition, because attracted businesses tend to be smaller than those that closed, this strategy enables the community to diversify its economic base while regaining jobs.[129]

Survivors: The Forgotten Stakeholders. When job losses occur, attention is understandably placed on the workers who lose their employment and the many repercussions that loss holds for them. Their needs must come first because they withstand the worst of the impact. However, those who retain their jobs—whether they are the remaining employees at a downsized plant or the workers at a plant that survived consolidation—are in need of support as well. Even the managers who conducted the layoffs will not emerge unscathed. One study of managers who issued WARN notices found that they had an increase in health and sleep problems: They reported feelings of depersonalization, and a greater intent to quit, with emotional exhaustion playing a role in their difficulties.[130]

All survivors are likely to evidence a variety of negative actions, perceptions, and behaviors. These include depression, guilt, stress, uncertainty, decreased loyalty, and lower enthusiasm.[131] Firms must attend to these concerns of survivors if they are to emerge stronger after job cuts. They can do this by providing:[132]

1. Emotional support—assuring employees that they are important.
2. Directional support—communicating the direction the company is going and the employees' place in that journey.
3. Tactical support—presenting new goals and objectives for the employees.
4. Informational support—answering all questions about the layoff and future plans.

One of the most important actions a firm can take when providing informational support is to answer employees' questions clearly and completely. Michael Fox, senior vice president of Ogilvy Public Relations, has worked with firms that are conducting layoffs. He says, "You've got a good chance at preserving loyalty and lessening anxiety if you've always been pretty open and transparent with information. Inform (remaining employees) how the decision was made, the layoffs were based on performance reviews, or longevity or the loss of a big customer. If a decision seems arbitrary or unclear, it will only make resentment worse."[133] It is also important that the survivors believe the laid-off employees were treated well. When United Technologies paid for a year of college courses for laid-off employees, the remaining employees felt better about staying on the job.[134]

We are only just touching the surface of the stakes and stakeholders involved in the plant-closing issue, the impacts that business closings have on employees and communities, the public's reaction to the problem, and types of corresponding actions that management might take. It is important for businesses to take positive steps to be responsive to their employees and communities. Furthermore, business closings and their adverse consequences are issues that business should continue to address in the future, lest yet another public problem culminates in new laws or another knotty regulatory apparatus.

Summary

Community stakeholders are extremely important to companies and the global economic recession has heightened the importance of business's attending to community stakeholder needs. In many ways, business can provide support in difficult times. Companies may donate the time and talents of managers and employees (volunteerism). Because business has a vital stake in the community, it engages in a variety of community projects. Community action programs are a key part of managing community involvement.

Business also contributes to community stakeholders through philanthropy. The third sector, or nonprofit sector, depends on business's support. Companies give for a variety of reasons—some altruistic, some self-interested. Major recipients of business giving include health and welfare, education, civic activities, and culture and the arts. Giving in times of crisis also is important to companies and communities.

As companies have attempted to manage their philanthropy, two major types of corporate giving have been emphasized: (1) strategic philanthropy, which seeks to improve the overall fit between corporate needs and charitable programs, and (2) cause-related marketing, which tightens the linkage between a firm's profits and its contributions. Cause-related marketing represents a unique joining of business and charity with the potential for great benefit to each. Cause branding also has become an important element of philanthropy.

Just as firms have beneficial effects on community stakeholders, they can have detrimental effects as well. Businesses offshoring and then reshoring can wreak havoc for employees, although most stakeholders recognize that these decisions are not made lightly. Business or plant closings are another example of these detrimental effects. Loss of jobs is the primary way in which these effects are manifested. They frequently occur due to offshoring decisions. Plant closings have a pervasive influence in the sense that a multitude of community stakeholders—employees, local government, other businesses, and the general citizenry—are affected. There is no single reason why these closings occur, but among the major reasons are economic conditions, consolidation of company operations, outsourcing, outmoded technology or facilities, changes in corporate strategy, and international competition. Reshoring has been a recent trend, but it has not offset the number of firms that continue to relocate in other countries.

Before management makes the decision to close a facility, it has a responsibility to itself, its employees, and the community to study thoroughly whether closing is the only or the best option. Finding a new owner for the business and pursuing the possibility of employee ownership are reasonable and desirable alternatives. After the decision to close has been made, responsible actions include community-impact analysis; giving advance notice; providing transfer, relocation, or outplacement benefits; phasing out operations gradually; and helping the community attract replacement industry. Finally, the needs of survivors must be met as the firm continues operations. Companies have an added incentive to be responsive to the business-closing issue, because state and federal governments are closely watching the manner in which firms are handling this problem.

Key Terms

CECP, p. 494
cause branding, p. 506
cause-related marketing, p. 506
community action program, p. 496
community involvement, p. 492
community partnerships, p. 504
corporate philanthropy, p. 492
Company-Wide Day of Service, p. 494
Dollars for Doers, p. 494
employee owned, p. 511
offshoring, p. 508
outsourcing, p. 508
Paid Release Time, p. 494
philanthropy, p. 496
philanthropy hackers, p. 498
reshoring, p. 508
Skills-based Pro Bono Service, p. 494
strategic philanthropy, p. 504
third sector, p. 499
Worker Adjustment and Retraining Notification Act (WARN), p. 512

Discussion Questions

1. Have you participated in community involvement at work? What type of program did the company endorse? Outline what you experienced to be the benefits of employee volunteerism.
2. Explain the pros and cons of corporate philanthropy, provide a brief history of corporate philanthropy, and explain why and to whom companies give.
3. Differentiate among strategic philanthropy, cause-related marketing, and cause branding. Provide an example of each not discussed in the text.
4. Identify and discuss briefly what you think are the major trade-offs that firms face as they think about offshoring and reshoring. When substantial layoffs are involved, what are firms' responsibilities to their employees and their communities?
5. In your opinion, why does a business have a responsibility to employees and community stakeholders in a business- or plant-closing decision?

Endnotes

1. Jeff Elder, "Reddit Revolt Shows Challenge of Harnessing Community of Volunteers," *The Wall Street Journal* (July 6, 2015), http://blogs.wsj.com/digits/2015/07/06/reddit-revolt-shows-challenge-of-harnessing-opinionated-users/. Accessed April 12, 2016.
2. Ibid.
3. "Michael Porter on Inner City Business," *Bloomberg Businessweek* (May 27, 2010), http://www.business week. com/smallbiz/content/may2010/sb20100526_383016.htm.
4. Ryan Scott, "50 Companies That Crush Giving Back," *Forbes* (February 19, 2015), http://www.forbes.com/sites/causeintegration/2015/02/19/the-50-companies-that-crush-giving-back/#696fe6921b5b. Accessed April 6, 2016.
5. The Civic 50, *Points of Light* (2015), http://www.pointsoflight.org/corporate-institute/corporate-offerings/civic-50. Accessed April 6, 2016.
6. Ashlee Vance, "Pay Up You Stingy Nerds," *Bloomberg Businessweek* (December 14–January 11, 2015), 48–51.
7. Ibid.
8. Ibid.
9. http://www.lilly.com/Responsibility/our-approach/Pages/our-approach.aspx. Accessed April 7, 2016.
10. David Jones, "Does Serving the Community Also Serve the Company? Using Organizational Identification and Social Exchange Theories to Understand Employee Responses to a Volunteerism Programme," *Journal of Occupational and Organizational Psychology*," 83(4), 857–878.
11. Bill Shaw and Frederick Post, "A Moral Basis for Corporate Philanthropy," *Journal of Business Ethics* (October 1993), 745–751.
12. J. B. Rodell, H. Breitsohl, M. Schröder, and D. J. Keating, "Employee Volunteering a Review and Framework for Future Research," *Journal of Management* (Vol. 1, No. 42, 2016), 55–84.
13. Susanne Gargiulo, "Why Everyone Wants to Work for the 'Good Guys'," CNN.com (November 8, 2012), http://edition.cnn.com/2012/11/07/business/global-office-csr-volunteer/index.html?c=&page=1. Accessed April 7, 2016.
14. Ibid.
15. CECP 2015, "Giving in Numbers," the 10th Annual Analysis of Corporate Giving, http://cecp.co/measurement/benchmarking-reports/giving-in-numbers.html. Accessed April 6, 2016.
16. Ibid.
17. Benjamin Snyder, "These 10 Companies Offer Big Incentives for Volunteering," *Fortune* (March 21, 2015), http://fortune.com/2015/03/21/companies-offer-incentives-for-volunteering/. Accessed April 6, 2016.
18. Points of Flight, "Corporate Days of Service," http://www.pointsoflight.org/sites/default/files/resources/files/stp_corporate_days_of_service.pdf. Accessed April 6, 2016.
19. Ryan Scott, "Is Your Company Doubling Down on Its Employee Volunteers?" *Forbes* (October 9, 2012), http://www.forbes.com/sites/causeintegration/2012/10/09/is-your-company-doubling-down-on-its-employee-volunteers/. Accessed April 13, 2016.
20. Ibid.
21. http://www.longaberger.com/horizonofhope//. Accessed April 7, 2016.
22. AT&T, "Engaging Employees in Their Communities," http://about.att.com/content/csr/home/issue-brief-builder/people/engaging-employees-in-their-communities.html. Accessed April 6, 2016.
23. Ryan Scott, "7 Steps to Employee Volunteering Success," *Forbes* (April 11, 2016), http://www.forbes.com/sites/causeintegration/2015/04/11/7-steps-to-employee-volunteering-success/#2f366e59587e. Accessed April 12, 2016.
24. Ibid.
25. CECP 2015.
26. Steve Brown, "J.C. Penney seeks approval for big Plano office and retail complex at Legacy," *The Dallas Morning News* (March 7, 2016), http://bizbeatblog.dallasnews.com/2016/03/penney-seeks-approvals-for-big-plano-office-and-retail-complex-at-legacy.html/. Accessed April 2, 2016.
27. Ronald McDonald House of Charities, "Who We Are," http://www.rmhc.com/who-we-are/ (2016). Accessed April 7, 2016.
28. Cecily Railborn, Antoinette Green, Lyudmila Todorova, Toni Trapani, and Wilborne E. Watson, "Corporate Philanthropy: When Is Giving Effective," *The Journal of Corporate Accounting and Finance* (November/December 2003), 47–54.
29. *Webster's New World Dictionary* (Cleveland: World Publishing Company, 1964), 1098.
30. CECP 2015.
31. Ibid.
32. Arthur Gautier and Ann Claire Pache, "Research on Corporate Philanthropy: A Review and Assessment," *Journal of Business Ethics* (Vol. 126, Issue 3, 2015), 343–369.
33. Matt Krantz, "Coke, Disney Are Using Data to Donate Smarter," *USA Today* (March 15, 2016), 6B.
34. Ibid.
35. Ibid.

36. Rebecca Greenfield, "I Gave Online," *Bloomberg Businessweek* (March 14–20, 2016), 82.

37. Morrell Heald, *The Social Responsibilities of Business: Company and Community 1900–1960* (Cleveland: Case Western Reserve University Press, 1970), 112.

38. Sean Parker, "Philanthropy for Hackers," *The Wall Street Journal* (June 25, 2016), http://www.wsj.com/articles/sean-parker-philanthropy-for-hackers-1435345787. Accessed April 12, 2016.

39. Ibid.

40. Adam Bryant, "Companies Oppose Disclosure of Details on Gifts to Charity," *The New York Times* (April 3, 1998), A1.

41. Ibid.

42. Nicholas Confessore, "S.E.C. Gets Plea: For Companies to Air Donations," *The New York Times* (April 24, 2013).

43. John D. Rockfeller III, "In Defense of Philanthropy," *Business and Society Review* (Spring 1978), 26–29.

44. Giving in Numbers 2011, *Committee to Encourage Corporate Philanthropy*, http://www.corporatephilanthropy.org/pdfs/giving_in_numbers/GIN2012_finalweb.pdf. Accessed April 7, 2016.

45. Ibid.

46. Ibid.

47. Ibid.

48. Ibid.

49. Peter Elkind, "Business Gets Schooled," *Fortune* (January 1, 2016), 49–60.

50. Ibid.

51. Ibid.

52. Wilfred Bockelman, *Culture of Corporate Citizenship: Minnesota's Business Legacy for the Global Future* (Lakeville, MN: Galde Press, Inc., 2000), 15–16.

53. . http://philanthropynewsdigest.org/news/prudential-foundation-announces-1.25-million-in-grants. Accessed April 13, 2016.

54. http://www.dailyfinance.com/2012/11/05/prudential-donates-3-million-for-immediate-support/ Accessed April 13, 2016.

55. Bob Diddlebock, "To Give or Not to Give," *Time* (May 11, 2009), 10.

56. http://www.artsusa.org/information_services/research/services/economic_impact/iv/national.asp. Accessed April 7, 2016.

57. Ibid.

58. BCA Survey of Business Support for the Arts, http://www.partnershipmovement.org/research/. Accessed April 1, 2016.

59. Elizabeth Kelleher, "U.S. Companies Step Up the Business of Giving Overseas," http://iipdigital.usembassy.gov/st/english/article/2006/04/20060411182239berehellek0.1802027.html#axzz45j3GYZWg. Accessed April 7, 2016; https://www.uschamberfoundation.org/corporate-citizenship-center/hurricane-sandy-corporate-aid-tracker. Accessed April 7, 2016.

60. U.S. Chamber of Commerce November 1, 2012, https://www.uschamber.com/press-release/us-business-community-contributes-more-38-million-hurricane-sandy-response-efforts Accessed September 12, 2016.

61. *ProPublica*, "5 Tips for Donating after Disasters," (June 19, 2015), https://www.propublica.org/article/5-tips-for-donating-after-disasters. Accessed April 1, 2016.

62. Louis Lavelle, "Giving as Never Before," *Businessweek* (October 1, 2001), 10.

63. Ian Wilhelm, "Corporate Giving Takes a Dip," *Chronicle of Philanthropy* (July 24, 2003).

64. Nita Bhalla, "Donor Fatigue Hits Nepal One Month after Mega Earthquake: U.N.," *Business Insider* (May 25, 2015), http://www.businessinsider.com/r-donor-fatigue-hits-nepal-one-month-after-mega-earthquake-un-2015-5. Accessed April 12, 2016.

65. James J. Chrisman and Archie B. Carroll, "Corporate Responsibility: Reconciling Economic and Social Goals," *Sloan Management Review* (Winter 1984), 59–65.

66. CECP 2015.

67. Carolyn Cavicchio, "The 2010 Philanthropy Agenda: Is the Pressure Easing?" *The Conference Board* (March 2010).

68. http://nationalsafeplace.org/what-is-safe-place/. Accessed April 7, 2016.

69. http://nationalsafeplace.org/about-us/our-partners/. Accessed April 9, 2016.

70. Richard Steckel and Robin Simons, *Doing Best by Doing Good* (New York: Dutton Publishers, 1992); Also see "Types of Partnerships," http://www.aapcho.org/wp/wp-content/uploads/2012/02/Giachello-MakingCommunityPartnershipsWorkToolkit.pdf. Accessed April 16, 2016.

71. Tom Watson, "Philanthropy Is on a Collision Course with Presidential Campaign Politics," *The Chronicle of Philanthropy* (January 12, 2016), https://philanthropy.com/article/Opinion-Philanthropy-Is-on-a/234886. Accessed April 13, 2016.

72. Michael Porter and Mark Kramer, "The Competitive Advantage of Corporate Philanthropy," *Harvard Business Review* (December 2002), 56–69.

73. Ibid.

74. Ibid.

75. http://benefitforyourcause.com/programdetails/. Accessed April 9, 2016.

76. Bruce Horovitz, "Be Kind and They Will Come," *USA Today International Edition* (March 27, 2013), A1–A2.

77. 2015 Cone Communications/Ebiquity, "Global CSR Study," http://www.conecomm.com/2015-cone-communications-ebiquity-global-csr-study. Accessed April 16, 2016.

78. Ibid.

79. http://www.usatoday.com/story/money/business/2014/05/13/pivot-network-millennials/9049929/. Accessed April 13, 2016.

80. Jenny McTaggart, "Whole Foods Steps Up Sourcing Standards," *Progressive Grocer* (April 15, 2007), 12–13.

81. Porter and Kramer, 56–69.

82. Ibid.

83. Ibid.

84. Patricia Caesar, "Cause-Related Marketing: The New Face of Corporate Philanthropy," *Business and Society Review* (Fall 1986), 16.

85. Martin Gottlieb, "Cashing In on a Higher Cause," *The New York Times* (July 6, 1986), 6–F.

86. Michelle Wirth Fellman, "Cause Marketing Takes a Strategic Turn," *Marketing News* (April 26, 1999), 4–8.

87. Cone Communications/Ebiquity 2015.

88. 1999 Cone/Roper Cause-Related Trends Report.

89. Public Service Advertising Research Center, http://www.psaresearch.com/causebranding.html. Accessed April 9, 2016.

90. IEG Sponsorship Report, "Growth of Cause Marketing," http://www.causemarketingforum.com/site/c.bkLUKcOTLkK4E/b.6449067/k.71C8/IEG_Sponsorship_Report.htm. Accessed April 11, 2016.

91. Sheila Shayon, "Brands Go Blue for Autism Awareness Month," *brandchannel* (April 5, 2013), http://www.brandchannel.com/home/post/2013/04/05/Brands-Autism-Awareness-040513.aspx. Accessed April 7, 2016.

92. CECP 2015. Accessed April 7, 2016.

93. Ibid.

94. Kelleher, 2006. Accessed April 7, 2016.

95. Bob Davis, "Wealth of Nations: Finding Lessons of Outsourcing in Four Historical Tales," *The Wall Street Journal* (March 29, 2004), A1.

96. Ibid.

97. "Where America's Jobs Went," *The Week* (March 18, 2011), http://theweek.com/article/index/213217/where-americas-jobs-went. Accessed April 8, 2016.

98. Dale Kasler, "Outsourcing Reaps Winners, Losers in U.S. Economy," *The Sacramento Bee* (April 26, 2004).

99. Thomas Black Isabella Cota, "A Tale of Two Nafta Towns," *Bloomberg Businessweek*, April 11–April 24, 2016, 12–13.

100. Ibid.

101. Ibid.

102. Brad Stone, "Should I Stay or Should I Go," *Newsweek* (April 19, 2004), 52–53.

103. Ibid.

104. Sarah Kabourek, "Back in the USA," *Fortune* (September 28, 2009), 30.

105. "Welcome Home," The Economist (January 19, 2013), http://www.economist.com/news/leaders/21569739-outsourcing-jobs-faraway-places-wane-will-not-solve-wests. Accessed April 8, 2016.

106. Ibid.

107. "Here, There, and Everywhere," *The Economist* (January 19, 2013), http://www.economist.com/news/special-report/21569572-after-decades-sending-work-across-world-companies-are-rethinking-their-offshoring. Accessed April 8, 2016.

108. Ibid.

109. Bill Conerly, "Reshoring or Offshoring: U.S. Manufacturing Forecast 2015-2016," *Forbes* (September 2, 2014), http://www.forbes.com/sites/billconerly/2014/09/02/reshoring-or-offshoring-u-s-manufacturing-forecast-2015-2016/#66402d8d7419. Accessed April 12, 2016.

110. Peter F. Drucker, *Management: Tasks, Responsibilities, Practices* (New York: Harper & Row, 1974), 327–328.

111. Susan Diesenhouse, "To Save Factories, Owners Diversify," *The New York Times* (November 30, 2003), 5.

112. http://srcholdings.com/. Accessed April 9, 2016.

113. Archie B. Carroll, "When Business Closes Down: Social Responsibilities and Management Actions," *California Management Review* (Winter 1984), 131.

114. Vincent J. Matteo, "The Chamber View," *Williamsport Sun-Gazette* (July 7, 2003), 2.

115. The Employee Ownership 100: America's Largest Majority Employee-Owned Companies (August 2015), https://www.nceo.org/articles/employee-ownership-100. Accessed April 8, 2016.

116. Terri Minsky, "Gripes of Rath: Workers Who Bought Iowa Slaughterhouse Regret That They Did," *The Wall Street Journal* (December 2, 1981), 1.

117. http://corporate.publix.com/about-publix/company-overview/facts-figures. Accessed May 7, 2016.

118. "The Opposite of Wal-Mart," *The Economist* (May 5, 2007), 79.

119. Ibid.

120. Carroll, 132.

121. Grover Starling, *The Changing Environment of Business* (Boston: Kent, 1980), 319–320.

122. Claire Zillman, "How Crumbs Was Able to Lay Off All Its Workers in One Fell Swoop," *Fortune* (July 17, 2014), http://fortune.com/2014/07/17/crumbs-layoffs/. Accessed May 8, 2016.

123. Loretta W. Prencipe, "Impending Layoffs Need Warning," *Info World* (April 9, 2001), 15.

124. James Drew and Steve Eder, "Different Workers Face the Same Problem with the WARN Act," *The Blade* (July 17, 2007), http://www.toledoblade.com/business

/2007/07/17/Different-workers-face-the-same-problem-with-the-WARN-Act.html. Accessed April 9, 2016.

125. Kelly M. Butler, "Going above and beyond Advance WARNing," *Employee Benefit News* (February 2009), 7.

126. Rob Enderle, "How to Do Layoffs Right (When You Absolutely Have To)," *CIO.com* (September 18, 2015), http://www.cio.com/article/2984682/layoffs/how-to-do-layoffs-right-when-you-absolutely-have-to.html. Accessed April 11, 2016.

127. Greg Jefferson, "Sony Lays Off 120 Workers, Moves Closer to Closing San Antonio Plant," *San Antonio Express-News* (August 8, 2003), 1.

128. Ibid.

129. Cornell University Workshop Report, 28–30.

130. Leon Grunberg, Sarah Moore, and Edward S. Greenberg, "Managers' Reactions to Implementing Layoffs: Relationship to Health Problems and Withdrawal Behaviors," *Human Resource Management* (Summer 2006), 159–178.

131. Suzanne M. Behr and Margaret A. White, "Layoff Survivor Sickness," *Executive Excellence* (November 2003), 18.

132. Ibid.

133. "Survivor Guilt: How the Corporate Ax Affects Remaining Employees," *PR News* (March 12, 2001), 1.

134. Ibid.

PART 5
Internal Stakeholder Issues

17

Employee Stakeholders and Workplace Issues

CHAPTER LEARNING OUTCOMES

After studying this chapter, you should be able to:

1 Outline the characteristics of the new social contract between employers and employees.

2 Explain the concept of employee engagement and the actions companies are taking to make the workplace friendlier.

3 Explain the employee rights movement and its underlying principles.

4 Describe what is entailed with the right not to be fired without cause and discuss the employment-at-will doctrine and its role in employee rights.

5 Discuss the right to due process and fair treatment.

6 Elaborate on the freedom-of-speech issue and whistle-blowing.

Although external stakeholders such as government, consumers, the environment, and the community continue to be major facets of business's concern for the social environment, considerable attention is now being paid to employee stakeholders—their status, their treatment, their rights, and their satisfaction. This should come as no surprise. Employees are essential to the creation of firm value and the financial success it provides, and so companies have a moral responsibility to create value for employees in their workplace experience and lives. Doing so is also cost effective because increasing morale and reducing turnover improves the bottom line.[1] In fact, former Xerox CEO Anne Mulcahy attributes much of her successful reign at Xerox to her experience in Human Resources and her understanding of the importance of motivated employees, "I was determined not to do traditional HR—imposing process for process' sake. I focused on impact ... getting every right person in the right job, defined and evaluated the right way. It was building and upgrading an overall talent management system.[2]

A renewed focus on employee stakeholder issues has been a direct outgrowth of the kinds of social changes that have brought other societal issues into focus. Today's issues are quite unlike the historical concerns of higher pay, shorter hours, more job security, and better working conditions. These expectations still exist, but they now embrace more complex workplace trends and issues. A continued economic recovery, an influx of Millennial talent, flatter organizations, the growth of the "sharing economy," and the expectation of a 24/7 work environment have created new challenges for employee engagement in the workforce.[3] Combined with macroenvironmental issues like globalization, automation, a declining labor movement, and the growing number of part-time workers, it becomes obvious that the relationship between employees and employers has evolved to one that can be fractious at times.[4] These issues highlight the continued importance of pay levels and employee health-care and retirement benefits, particularly as companies try to reduce costs to stay competitive and employees strive to maintain their standard of living. In sum, employee stakeholders and workplace issues are complex, challenging, and vital to effective stakeholder management.

Three major themes or trends characterize the modern relationship between employees and their employers: the evolution of the social contract, the practice of employee engagement, and the expansion of employee rights. First, we will discuss the evolving social contract between organizations and workers, which is different from contracts of the past. Second, we will consider the continuing trend toward more and better employee engagement in the workforce. Third, we will examine the concept of employee rights, and we will describe how the changes in the workplace have precipitated a renewal in the employee rights movement. In particular, we focus on the right not to be fired without good cause, the right to due process and fair treatment, and the right to freedom of speech in the workplace.

Because the subject of employee stakeholders and workplace issues is very extensive, we dedicate three chapters to these topics. In Chapter 18, we will extend our discussion to the expectations and rights of employees to privacy, safety, and health. In Chapter 19, we discuss employment diversity and discrimination. These three chapters should be considered a continuous discussion of employee stakeholders wherein economic, legal, and ethical responsibilities are all taken into consideration.

17.1 The New Social Contract

In Chapter 1 we discussed the concept of the **social contract**—a set of reciprocal understandings that characterize the relationship between business and society. We noted that the social contract has been changing to reflect society's expanded expectations of business, and this may certainly be seen in the expectations surrounding employer–employee relationships. Fifty years ago, the trend was that employees stayed in the same job in the same company for years and those companies rewarded employees' loyalty by offering job stability, a decent wage, and good benefits.[5] Today, the average "baby boomer" person born in the United States between 1957 and 1964 has held 11.7 jobs, and they continue to have a large number of short-duration jobs.[6]

The workforce of today is more mobile, less loyal, and more diverse. From CEOs to factory workers, employees have come to know that their jobs are vulnerable, and so they have come to view themselves as free agents, bearing sole responsibility for their own careers.[7] As a result, there has been a shift away from conventional jobs and into more distant employer–employee relationships as employees seek "alternative work arrangements," including working for temporary help agencies, or as an independent contractor, either "on call" or through formal short-term contracts.[8] One study noted that these alternate work arrangements rose 9.4 million from 2005 to 2015—even greater than the rise in overall employment.[9]

The percentage of workers in alternative work arrangements in the fall of 2015 was 15.8 percent, up from 10.1 percent a decade earlier.[10] The trend has even given rise to a new term: the **gig economy**, characterized by work consisting of a series of short-term jobs coordinated through a mobile app.[11] A recent gathering of experts, policymakers, and activists at the Aspen Institute sought to understand the new social contract, captured in what they call the "**1099 economy**" of contingent workers.[12] The "1099" refers to one of several tax forms used for reporting income other than wages to the Internal Revenue Service; those who are self-employed use it. The concern is that workers will not be able to earn a living wage under this new social contract, without access to stable and adequate incomes, protections from abuse, and basic benefits like health care and retirement.[13]

Even today's full-time employees do not look for a promise for lifetime employment. Instead, they seek competitive pay and benefits coupled with opportunities for professional growth. At the same time, they want meaningful work, a vision they can share with the company, clear performance feedback, and a strong, supportive organizational culture.[14] Some analysts argue that a key driver of an organization's ability to survive and thrive into the future will be the social contract that firm has with its employees.[15] Figure 17-1 presents some of the characteristics of the old and new social contract between employers and employees.

FIGURE 17-1 The Changing Social Contract between Employers and Employees

Old Social Contract	New Social Contract
Job security; long, stable career and employment relationships	Few tenure arrangements; jobs constantly "at risk"; employment as long as you "add value" to the organization
Lifetime careers with one employer	Fewer life careers; changing employer common; careers more dynamic
Stable positions/job assignments	Temporary project assignments
Loyalty to employer; identification	Loyalty to self and profession; diminished identification with employer
Paternalism; family-type relationships	Relationships far less warm and familial; no more parent–child relationships
Employee sense of entitlement	Personal responsibility for one's own career/job future
Stable, rising income	Pay that reflects contributions; pay for "value added"
Job-related skill training	Learning opportunities; employees in charge of their own education and updating
Focus on individual job accomplishments	Focus on team building and projects
Personal face-to-face communication	Communication through technologies

Surveys of the **Millennial Generation** of workers born between 1980 and 2000 reflect the expectations of the new social contract. In a *Deloitte* study of over 7,000 Millennials from 29 countries, 44 percent say, if given the choice, they would like to leave their current employers in the next two years—reflecting a lack of loyalty.[16] The reasons for this include a perceived lack of leadership, feelings of being overlooked, as well as larger issues around work–life balance, the desire for flexibility, and a conflict of values.[17] However, *Deloitte* also notes that there is a positive aspect to retaining these employees because they respond to organizational traits and behaviors that promote a sense of positivity. For example, they are more likely to report high levels of satisfaction where there is a creative, inclusive working culture (76 percent) rather than a more authoritarian, rules-based approach (49 percent). Additionally, Deloitte suggests that organizations can promote loyalty from this generation of workers through providing good mentorship, developmental opportunities, and a job environment that offers good work-life balance over and above adequate compensation.[18]

In another study of Millennials by *PwC*, good opportunities for career progression was the top response for what makes an employer attractive, and companies whose corporate responsibility behaviors aligned with their own values were also most attractive.[19] Taken together, it is possible that although Millennials do not profess to have much loyalty to their employers, they *want* to be loyal to their employers. Therefore, businesses must figure out a way to retain and foster their talents.

It is difficult to say whether the new social contract is bad or good. More than anything else, it represents an adaptation to the changing world of work and changing business circumstances. In some respects, workers may prefer the new model, which supports more flexible work schedules, the opportunity for work–life balance and the ability to create one's own career path. Whatever turns out to be the case, we can expect free agent employees to be more proactive about their work environments than the loyal employees of the past once were. Therefore, businesses will need to be proactive as well with employee engagement programs that foster loyalty and dedication. It is likely that employee stakeholders' expectations of fair treatment will also continue to rise, and we will witness the continuing growth in the employee rights movement.

17.2 Employee Engagement

Engaged employees are those who identify and have an emotional commitment to the organization. They consistently bring an extra effort to their roles in the organization in support of its goals. Companies that support **employee engagement** through mentoring programs, career development training, and annual employee surveys that result in actions have notable key outcomes, including outperforming companies who do not have active employee engagement programs in areas of customer ratings, profitability, and productivity.[20] Additionally, they have significantly less turnover, less shrinkage, less absenteeism, fewer safety incidents, and fewer quality defects.[21] It is easy to see how this aligns with good stakeholder management, and specifically the Supportive Stakeholder approach, which we discussed in Chapter 3.

Companies like CarMax have led the way with employee engagement initiatives, and the result is that it has won top awards over the years, including the Gallup Great Workplace Award.[22] CarMax has a sophisticated employee engagement program that involves training and development programs that help employees earn raises and advancements. They supplement this program with strong employee recognition programs, the latest IT equipment and services, and corner office décor, which contributes to employee satisfaction.[23] Mars, Inc., is another example of a company that has participated in employee engagement initiatives. Known as a "sweet company to work for," its employee engagement program includes mentorships, generous bonuses, paid time off for community service, and competitive internal internships that have helped them keep their turnover to around 5 percent.[24]

Despite such successes in employee engagement, a recent Gallup poll found that the majority of U.S. workers surveyed (50.8 percent) said they were not engaged with their jobs. Perhaps even more alarming is that employee engagement has not experienced large year-over-year improvements in Gallup's 15-year history of measuring and tracking the metric, with employee engagement consistently averaging less than 33 percent.[25]

What is the problem? Some say that employee engagement surveys do not get enough buy-in from executives in organizations. One survey of Inc. 5,000 firms found that fewer than 2 percent of CEOs look at employee engagement survey results more than once.[26] Some say that the feedback data from employee surveys is often unwieldy and does not take into account employee sentiments.[27] The irony of this is that thanks to technology and Big Data, it is easier to identify key employee issues that could affect performance—new, sophisticated, sentiment-analysis software can allow companies to drill deeper into what other motivations might be behind their survey comments.[28] Despite these obstacles, employee engagement is a concept that is central to most business's employee stakeholder management. It is particularly important as businesses deal with an increasingly distal workforce while still trying to instill a sense of identity with the organization that might inspire loyalty and commitment.

17.3 The Employee Rights Movement

In our discussion of employee rights, we focus on employees in the private sector because of the underlying public sector–private sector dichotomy. The public sector is subject to constitutional control of its power, and so government employees have more protections. In contrast, the private sector generally has not been subject to constitutional control because of the concept of **private property**, which holds that individuals and private organizations are free to use their property as they desire. As a result, private corporations historically and traditionally have not had to recognize employee rights to the same degree because society honored the corporation's private property rights. The underlying issues for the private sector and its stakeholders then become why and to what extent the private property rights of business should be changed or diluted.

A brief comment on the role of labor unions is appropriate here. In general, although labor unions have been quite successful in improving the material conditions of life at work in the United States—pay, fringe benefits, and working conditions—they have not been as active in pursuing civil liberties. We must give unions credit for the gains they have made in converting what were typically regarded as management's rights or prerogatives into issues in which labor could participate. However, we should note that labor unions seem to be disappearing from the U.S. business scene. In 1953, union representation reached its highest proportion of the private employment workforce, at 36 percent.[29] By 2015, the proportion of union members in the private sector had fallen to 6.7 percent, with workers in education, training, library occupations, and protective service occupations holding the highest unionization rates.[30] Although the public sector union rate has a fivefold higher rate of 35.2 percent, it does not have a significant impact on the private sector employee rights we are discussing here.[31] Compared to other countries, the U.S. unionization rate is very low, but OECD statistics suggest that union membership is declining worldwide as well.[32]

17.3a The Meaning of Employee Rights

Before we consider specific employee rights issues, we should discuss briefly, what we mean by **employee rights**. A lawyer might look at employee rights as claims that one can enforce in a court of law. For many economists as well, rights are only creations of the law. For our purposes, we will approach employee rights from the "principle of rights" perspective, and viewed from this perspective, rights are justifiable claims that utility cannot override. While we will focus on employee ethical rights, we will also consider employee legal rights. Of course, the current recessionary environment has influenced discussion of employee rights. If a right is truly a moral right, it is not contingent on business's ability to provide it. However, the deep cutbacks that arose from the recession have stimulated renewed discussion of the parameters of employee rights.

Employee rights can be positive or negative. Said differently, they can focus on achieving desired outcomes or on prohibiting unwanted outcomes. Richard Edwards has grouped employee rights into three categories based on the fact that these rights find their source in law, union contracts, or employers' promises. Rights provided by the law are called **statutory rights**. These include, for example, the rights established by the Civil Rights Act of 1964 (at a national level) or by the Massachusetts Right to Know Law (at the state level), which grant production workers the right to be notified of specific toxic substances they may be exposed to in the workplace. Union contracts, by contrast, provide workers with rights established through the process of **collective bargaining**. Examples of these rights are seniority preferences, job security mechanisms, and grievance procedures.[33]

Employer promises are the third source of employees' rights categorized by Edwards. These employer grants or promises are called **enterprise rights**. Typical examples of such enterprise rights might include the right to petition beyond one's immediate supervisor, the right to be free from physical intimidation, the right to a grievance or complaint system, and the right to due process in discipline. Other enterprise rights include the right to have express standards for personnel evaluation, the right to have one's job clearly defined, the right to a "just cause" standard for dismissal, and the right to be free from nepotism and unfair favoritism.[34]

Management provides and justifies enterprise rights, and so the rationale for those rights can be as varied as the managers who implement them. They might reflect the prevailing customs and norms of a company's industry. They might extend above and

ETHICS IN PRACTICE CASE

Should I Say Something?

I was hired as a temporary employee of a toy manufacturing company, and the department I was assigned to was going through some rough changes. Their director had recently quit and the new director, from a similar company that had just recently filed bankruptcy, took her place. She said she had about 20 years in the imports business and knew it like the back of her hand. Naturally, her new employees were relieved and hoped that business would continue as usual.

Months passed and I learned a lot about the imports aspect of our company. In those months, my co-workers and I noticed that our boss was not doing much work. We were used to a hands-on director who was not afraid to pull back her sleeves and dive into the deepest piles of papers. Soon, work that we thought our new director was supposed to handle started piling up. We also gained a huge customer whose orders were the task equal to the amount of work we had already. She also put me, the temporary employee, in charge of the new customer. Because huge amounts of work were getting cranked out of our department, we worked ten-hour shifts and Saturdays to get it all done. Then my co-workers started complaining. "All she does is watch YouTube videos all day," one said. "She's always talking on her cell phone," another co-worker said. Another temp was hired to help us out so that we wouldn't have to work on Saturdays.

I was finally hired as a permanent employee. I was elated for about two months to have a job that I could call "home" and co-workers that I could get to know. However, alas, the company started laying off employees. They began to fire most of the temporary employees; then, they fired 11 regular employees. In all, we lost both of our temps and a regular employee in our department. I can't help but feel that it was our director's fault that we had to lose these employees.

1. The reason I was hired was my director's strong push to keep me. Should I let her continue to neglect her responsibilities just because I owe her some kind of thanks? Should my loyalty be with my company in general or to the person that hired me?
2. Even after one of my co-workers spoke to our director about her wasteful spending, she continued to do so. Should my co-worker have gone above her to let her boss know what was going on?
3. As an employee, do I have any rights in this situation? If so, what would they be?
4. What would you have done in this situation? Why?

Contributed Anonymously

beyond those offered by competing firms and thus be used as a type of recruiting tool. They may also be given on the basis of some normative ethical principle or reasoning (e.g., "This is the way workers ought to be treated"). In this situation, the ethical principles of justice, rights, and utilitarianism, as well as notions of virtue ethics, may be the rationales.

To summarize, employee rights may be based on economic, legal, and/or ethical sources of justification. In this way, management may provide the employee rights as part of an effort to be socially responsible or to display moral management, as discussed in Chapter 7. To illustrate this point further, Figure 17-2 characterizes how moral managers, as well as amoral and immoral managers, might view employee stakeholders.

Following are the job-related rights that are claimed often and thus merit further discussion here: (1) the *right not to be fired without good cause*, (2) the *right to due process and fair treatment*, and (3) the *right to freedom, particularly freedom of expression and freedom of speech*. In Chapter 18, we will consider the rights to privacy, safety, and health in the workplace.

17.4 The Right Not to Be Fired without Cause

A **good cause norm**, the belief that employees should be discharged only for good reasons (i.e., just cause dismissal), prevails in the United States today. This normative belief persists in spite of the fact that it does not match the descriptive reality of what often happens. From a legal perspective, most U.S. employees can be fired for any reason, or for no reason, as long as the firing is not in violation of any discrimination laws. A range

FIGURE 17-2 Three Models of Management Morality and Their Orientations toward Employee Stakeholders

Model of Management Morality	Orientation toward Employee Stakeholders
Moral Management	Employees are a human resource that must be treated with dignity and respect. Employees' rights to due process, privacy, freedom of speech, and safety are maximally considered in all decisions. Management seeks fair dealings with employees. The goal is to use a leadership style, such as consultative/participative, that will result in mutual confidence and trust. Commitment is a recurring theme.
Amoral Management	Employees are treated as the law requires. Attempts to motivate focus on increasing productivity rather than satisfying employees' growing maturity needs. Employees are still seen as factors of production, but a remunerative approach is used. The organization sees self-interest in treating employees with minimal respect. Organization structure, pay incentives, and rewards are all geared toward short- and medium-term productivity.
Immoral Management	Employees are viewed as factors of production to be used, exploited, and manipulated for gain of individual manager or company. No concern is shown for employees' needs/rights/expectations. Managers pursue a short-term focus in a coercive, controlling, and alienating environment.

of studies have shown the good cause norm to be widely held in a variety of situations, with respondents including undergraduate and graduate students as well as both blue- and white-collar workers.[35] Belief in the good cause norm stands in direct opposition to the employment-at-will doctrine, which many private employers believe is their right based upon current laws. With employers and employees holding such contradictory views, it is easy to see why so many disputes occur, and terms like *unjust dismissals* and *wrongful discharge* have become part of today's employment language.

17.4a Employment-at-Will Doctrine

The central issue in the movement to protect workers' job-related rights involves changing views of the **employment-at-will doctrine**. In the industrialized world, the United States is unique in adhering to this doctrine, which is based on the private property rights of the employer and the principle that the relationship between employer and employee is a voluntary one that can be terminated at any time by either party. This doctrine holds that just as employees are free to quit a company any time they choose, employers can discharge employees for any reason, or no reason, as long as they do not violate federal discrimination laws, state laws, or union contracts. What this doctrine means is that unless you are protected by a union contract (the vast majority of the workforce is not) or by one of the discrimination laws, your employer is free to let you go anytime, for any reason. This doctrine is not widely understood by the workforce. As previously mentioned, most employees in the United States believe that employment law not only should follow a good cause norm but also does so in practice.[36] However, most private employees in the United States are in an at-will employment relationship and could be discharged at any time by their employers.[37]

This lack of awareness about at-will employment may provide the answer to a question Louis Uchitelle poses in *The Disposable American*—why is the United States so tolerant of large-scale layoffs?[38] Uchitelle, who writes on economics for the *New York Times*, details the human costs of a system that allows employers to fire or lay off employees at will. Layoffs are traumatic events that inflict significant mental health damage. Uchitelle poses the following question to the American Psychiatric Association, "Why don't you put a warning label on layoffs?[39]

Legal Challenges to Employment-at-Will. Three broad categories of issues that illustrate the legal challenges that have arisen with regard to employment-at-will discharges are (1) public policy exceptions, (2) contractual actions, and (3) breach of good faith actions.[40] States vary in their adoption of exceptions to employment-at-will, creating a patchwork of employment situations around the country. Only three states: Florida, Georgia, and Rhode Island have never adopted an exception.[41]

A major exception to the long-standing employment-at-will doctrine is known as the **public policy exception**; 43 states recognize this exception.[42] This exception protects employees from being fired because they refuse to commit crimes or because they try to take advantage of privileges to which they are entitled by law. The courts have held that management may not discharge an employee who refuses to commit an illegal act or performs a public obligation, such as serving on a jury or supplying information to the police. This exception sometimes covers whistle-blowers. We will further discuss the case of whistle-blowers later in the chapter.

Workers who believe they have contracts or implied contracts with their employers are protected in the 42 states that recognize the **implied contract exception**.[43] In some instances, the courts hold employers to promises they do not even realize they have made. For example, statements in employee handbooks or personnel manuals, job-offer letters, and even oral assurances about job security can be interpreted as implied contracts that the management is not at liberty to violate. If an employee can prove in court that the hiring manager said, "We do not fire people without a good reason," that can be enough to create an implied contract. Even the use of the term *permanent employee* to mean an employee who had worked beyond a six-month probationary period may be construed as a promise of continuous employment.

ETHICS IN PRACTICE CASE

The Pocketed Purse

At work, we have a warehouse and an office in the building. During the Holiday season, we have a program to assemble gift sets, which requires hiring extra help for the season. About two to three months ago, a lady from the warehouse working on this project told me during a conversation that $30 was missing from her purse, which she left in the cafeteria because there was no other place for seasonal help to put their belongings. She did not make a big deal about it because she had no proof of who took the money. In addition, she did not speak English and so she did not know how to communicate to management what had happened. I asked her if she wanted me to explain the situation to management, but she told me not to do that because she had no proof of who did it.

Only a few people in the office knew that the company has surveillance cameras in the cafeteria. If I spoke up, it meant that the culprit would lose their job when caught. I had no idea who took the money; it could have been one of my close friends at work or it might have been a person to whom I barely speak. I had an ethical dilemma because if I chose to just let it go, the person who took the money would get to keep their job, but it bothered me that someone could be going into someone else's belongings and stealing from them. In the end, I went up to management and told them about the situation. They reviewed the cameras, and in fact, we were able to see who took the money. The young woman who stole the money was fired on the spot.

1. Was it right for me to report the problem to management? Considering all the facts, would you have done the same?
2. In making your decision, were you affected by the fact that the thief could have been one of your friends? Do you have any moral obligations to friends?
3. Did the fact that the woman who was robbed asked you not to say anything affect your decision? Do you feel she had any rights not to be observed via surveillance without her knowledge?
4. What else could you do to rectify the situation?

Contributed by Natalia Santos

SPOTLIGHT *on Sustainability*

Employees Are Key to Sustainability

A study by the National Environmental Education Foundation (NEEF) found educating employees in environmental and sustainability (E&S) initiatives can attract and retain good talent while also increasing profitability and reducing environmental impact. The study presents a variety of case studies including eBay. eBay's green team convinced the company to build San Jose, California's largest commercial solar installation. They reduced CO2 emissions by over one million pounds a year and saved well over $100,000. In a statement, Diane Wood, president of NEEF, said that past environmental education programs focused on employees involved in safety and health. Now they realize they must involve the entire workforce. Human resource management has a critical role to play through the recruitment and selection of the right people and the establishment of policies and incentives that support a sustainability orientation.

This idea is also supported by sustainability experts at *TriplePundit*, a global media platform committed to sustainability: "We engage stakeholders because their feedback can provide insight into the core values of the company and the core sustainability issues facing the company. When employees are engaged, and their ideas are being implemented, it makes it much easier for sustainability initiatives to succeed."

Sources: Greenbiz Staff, "Why Bringing Employees on Board Helps Sustainability Projects Succeed," *Greenbiz.com* (February 22, 2010), http://www.greenbiz.com/news/2010/02/22/bringing-employees-board-makes-sustainability-projects-success#ixzz0pS7n8RUA. Accessed May 9, 2016; Linda C. Forbes and John M. Jermier, "The New Corporate Environmentalism and the Symbolic Management of Corporate Culture," in Pratima Bansal and Andrew J. Hoffman (eds.) *The Oxford Handbook of Business and the Natural Environment* (New York: Oxford University Press, 2012); *Triple Pundit*, Employee Engagement, http://www.triplepundit.com/topic/employee-engagement/#. Accessed May 22, 2016.

Courts have also recognized that employers should hold themselves to a standard of fairness and good faith dealings with employees. This concept is the broadest restraint on employment-at-will terminations. The **good faith principle** suggests that employers may run the risk of losing lawsuits to former employees if they fail to show that employees had every reasonable opportunity to improve their performance before termination. Only 20 states recognize the good faith principle.[44] As previously noted, however, the good faith principle reflects what many already believe is the responsibility of businesses toward their employees. The principle is not a problem for companies if they simply introduce fair ways of taking disciplinary measures and mechanisms for reviewing grievances that provide employees with due process. We will discuss such due-process mechanisms later in the chapter.

Moral and Managerial Challenges to Employment-at-Will. As previously mentioned, the United States is unique in its adherence to the employment-at-will doctrine and most people in the United States believe a norm of good cause applies to employment decisions, so it is not surprising that employment-at-will has been criticized on moral as well as legal grounds. The argument generally used in favor of employment-at-will is that employers invoke their property rights when they terminate an employee. In an interesting rebuttal, Werhane, Radin, and Bowie suggest that the fruits of an employee's labor are that employee's property and so property rights can also be invoked to argue against the appropriateness of employment-at-will.[45]

Using the concept of employee property rights as a foundation, Werhane et al. derive three objections to employment-at-will. First, they argue that employees deserve respectful treatment, which includes explaining the reasons for termination when it occurs. Second, employees do not have the option of being arbitrary or capricious with employers, and so employers should bear the same responsibility in their treatment of employees. A third issue is based on the concept of reciprocity: Employees are expected to be trustworthy, loyal, and respectful in their interactions with employers, and so employers should show employees the same consideration.[46]

Employment-at-will can present managerial problems as well. We should not forget the impact that an employment-at-will environment can have on the culture of an organization. Most bad reasons for firing employees, such as discrimination, are already illegal, and managers can always fire an employee for good justifiable reasons. From this perspective, employment-at-will is not needed because it simply protects the right of the employer to fire an employee for no reason at all. This creates an odd dynamic. Trust and loyalty are important to effective workplaces, but they are reciprocal relationships. For managers to be able to trust their employees, they must be willing to be trustworthy in return.[47]

17.4b Dismissing an Employee with Care

With respect to employee dismissals, management needs to be aware not only of the content of the decision to dismiss but also of the *process* for doing it. Treating employees with care is important not only to the terminated employee but also to the survivors of the process, who then know they will be treated with care if they face a similar situation. A positive corporate culture can be preserved even in difficult times with thoughtful treatment of employees. Steve Harrison offers some do's and don'ts for dismissing employees in a responsible manner. The following are some specific recommendations for actions:[48]

1. *Fire employees in a private space.* Do not terminate an employee in a way that enables co-workers to see what is happening or that forces them to "walk a gauntlet" in front of them.
2. *Be mindful of employees' logistics.* How will they get closure on their projects? How will they get home that day?
3. *Preserve employees' dignity.* If you must lay off a trusted and valuable employee for economic reasons, don't confiscate IDs and cell phones immediately or cancel passwords immediately.
4. *Choreograph the notification in advance.* The purpose of the meeting should not be a surprise.
5. *Use transparent criteria for layoffs.* The rationale for terminations should be clear both to those laid off and to the survivors.

The following are some of the actions managers should *not* take when dismissing employees:[49]

1. *Do not fire on a Friday.* Terminated employees would not have access to support services on weekends and so would have to cope on their own.
2. *Do not say that downsizing is finished.* It is impossible to know for sure that the downsizing has ended and being wrong about that would make subsequent layoffs more difficult for all concerned.
3. *Do not terminate an employee via e-mail.* Although this advice seems obvious, firms have done so to the detriment of employees as well as their reputations.
4. *Stick to the topic and avoid platitudes.* For example, do not say, "This is as hard for me as it is for you"—it isn't.
5. *Do not rush through the meeting.* Being willing to give a person time is a way of communicating that the person matters. Not to give the employee the time needed for the termination puts salt in the wound.

For effective stakeholder management, organizations must always consider their obligations to employee stakeholders and their rights and expectations with respect to their jobs. Companies that aspire to emulate the tenets of the moral management model will need to reexamine continuously their attitudes, perceptions, practices, and policies with respect to this issue and take care to dismiss employees only for solid economic-related or performance-related reasons, not arbitrary reasons. Further, if employee discharges are handled carefully and in accordance with the above recommendations, employees are more likely to believe they received fair treatment, a topic we address next, and this will benefit everyone in the organization.

17.5 The Right to Due Process and Fair Treatment

One of the most frequently proclaimed employee rights issues of the past decade has been the right to due process. **Due process** is the right to receive an impartial review of one's complaints or opinions and to be dealt with fairly. In the context of the workplace, the right to due process involves the rights of employees to have impartial third parties review the decisions that adversely affect them. Of course, the right not to be fired without just cause would fall into this category of fair treatment; however, in this section we will expand on this concept and discuss other applications.

One major obstacle to the due-process idea is that to some extent it is a bit contrary to the employment-at-will principle discussed earlier. Due process is consistent with the democratic ideal that undergirds the universal right to fair treatment, and so one can argue that without due process, employees do not receive fair treatment in the workplace. Furthermore, the fact that the courts are gradually eroding the employment at-will principle might serve as an indication that employment-at-will is thought to be unfair. If this is true, the due-process concept makes more sense.

17.5a Due Process

Patricia Werhane, a leading business ethicist, contends that, procedurally, due process extends beyond simple fair treatment and should state, "Every employee has a right to a public hearing, peer evaluation, outside arbitration, or some other open and mutually agreed-upon grievance procedure before being demoted, unwillingly transferred, or fired."[50] Due process can range from the expectation that the company treat employees fairly to the position that employees deserve a fair system of decision making when their status in the organization is at stake.

Sometimes unfair treatment happens in such a subtle way that it is difficult to know that it has taken place. What do you do, for example, if your supervisor refuses to recommend you for promotion or permit you to transfer because she or he considers you to be exceptionally good at your job and doesn't want to lose you? How do you prove that a manager has given you a low performance appraisal because you resisted sexual advances? The issues over which due-process questions may arise can be quite difficult and subtle and often challenging to prove.

Due process, when formalized, is a system for ascertaining that organizational decisions have been fair.[51] As such, it aligns closely with the concept of procedural justice, or ethical due process, that we discussed in Chapter 8.[52] The following are the main requirements of a due-process system in an organization:[53]

1. It must be a procedure; it must follow rules. It must not be arbitrary.
2. It must be sufficiently visible and so well known that potential violators of employee rights and victims of abuse are aware of it.
3. It must be predictably effective.
4. It must be institutionalized—a relatively permanent fixture in the organization.
5. It must be perceived as equitable.
6. It must be easy to use.
7. It must apply to all employees.

Procedural due process is a concept derived from the Fifth and Fourteenth Amendments of the U.S. Constitution. In law, due process requires a balancing act between the interests of the government and those of the individual. In organizations, a similar balancing act occurs. The challenge is to balance the interests of the individual employee with those of the organization.[54]

The increased use of contract workers puts another spin on the concept of due process in the workforce. As we noted earlier, the U.S. contingent, or temporary workforce, is growing at an alarming rate and is creating a new form of the social contract between employers and employees. The concern is that employers are avoiding the costs of full-time workers (health care, retirement) by using temporary workers. U.S. Department of Labor (DOL) Wage and Hour Division director David Weil calls this trend **fissuring.**[55] He believes that many of the companies using temporary workers should really be considered "joint employers" together with the contractors that sign the checks, making them liable for violations.[56]

In response to these concerns, the DOL in July 2015 issued a warning to employers about this practice.[57] Employers who make the wrong classification about their workers face potential liabilities for state or federal minimum wage and overtime pay, workers' compensation insurance, and federal and state taxes (including unemployment benefits). The DOL noted that the vast majority of workers classified as independent contractors are invalidly classified and that companies engaging their services are violating the law. In the memo, they declared that most workers are legal employees under the Fair Labor Standards Act (FLSA), under their interpretation of the "suffer or permit to work" language that defines employment under the FLSA.

According to the memorandum (and most courts), the proper analysis is the "economic realities test," which analyzes whether a worker is operating a business of their own (an independent contractor) or economically dependent on the employer, regardless of skill level (an employee).[58] In sum, the DOL is now taking an active position to ensure that contingent workers are treated fairly and subject to due process in their employment.

17.5b Alternative Dispute Resolution

Companies can and do provide due process for their employees in several ways. **Alternative dispute resolution (ADR)** is a term that refers to ways of resolving disputes that avoid litigation. It is a popular, and yet controversial, form of conflict resolution that the International Institute for Conflict Prevention and Resolution (CPR) calls the "dispute resolution divide," because there are constant calls for more standardization in ADR approaches.[59] Yet, it is a popular choice for businesses—a recent Cornell survey of large firms showed that almost 50 percent of large U.S. corporations are now using ADR as their *main* vehicle for resolving workplace dispute.[60] The approaches described here represent some of the ADR methods that have been employed by companies.

Common Approaches. One of the most often-used mechanisms to resolve differences is the **open-door policy**. This approach typically relies on a senior-level executive who asserts that her or his "door is always open" for those who think they have been treated unfairly. Alternatively, the organization might assign to an executive of the human resources department the responsibility for investigating employee grievances and either handling them or reporting them to higher management.

From the employee's standpoint, the major problems with these approaches are that (1) the process is closed (seldom reviewed by someone else), (2) one person is reviewing what happened, and (3) there is a tendency in organizations for one manager to support another manager's decisions. The process is opened up somewhat by companies that use a **hearing procedure**, which permits employees to be represented by an attorney or another person, with a neutral company executive deciding the outcome based on the evidence. Similar to this approach is the use of a management *grievance committee*, which may involve multiple executives in the decision process.

The Ombudsman. A developing due-process mechanism that has become popular for dealing with employee problems is the use of a corporate **ombudsman**, also known as *ombud* or *ombudsperson*. "Ombudsman" is a Swedish word that refers to one who investigates reported complaints and helps to achieve equitable settlements. The ombudsman approach has been used in Sweden since 1809 to curb abuses by government against individuals. In the United States, the corporate version of the ombudsman entered the scene over 35 years ago, when the Xerox Corporation named an ombudsman for its largest division. General Electric and the Boeing Vertol division of Boeing were quick to follow.[61]

Most major corporations have ombudsmen, with many joining after Sarbanes–Oxley (SOX) was passed.[62] SOX contains a lesser known provision that encourages employees to report wrongdoing and prohibits corporate retaliation against those employees.[63] The Dodd–Frank Wall Street Reform and Consumer Protection Act took the role of the ombudsman to a newer context—creating a Securities and Exchange Commission (SEC) ombudsman under the Office of the Investor Advocate.[64] Under **Section 919D**, the SEC ombudsman acts as a liaison between the Commission and any retail investor in resolving problems that retail investors may have with the Commission or with self-regulatory organizations regarding compliance with the securities laws.

The ombudsman's task is quite different from that of the human resources manager. Hiring, firing, setting policy, and keeping records are all the responsibilities of the human resources department; the ombudsman does none of these.[65] In contrast, he or she is formally and officially neutral and promises client confidentiality.[66] Ombuds can handle the concerns of employees who believe they have witnessed wrongdoing and do so in a way that keeps the problem from getting out of hand.[67]

The financial crisis was difficult for ombud offices. Charles L. Howard, author of "The Organizational Ombudsman," explains that senior management views ombud offices as non-revenue centers, and so when times are tight they are often cut.[68] Nevertheless, the use of ombuds, while still small, is growing. The aforementioned Cornell survey reported that within the prior three years, 77 percent of companies had used employment arbitration to resolve at least one dispute, a marked increase over a previous survey which showed only 36 percent usage.[69]

The Peer Review Panel. The **peer review panel** is another due-process mechanism currently in use. Eastman Kodak (now Kodak) made good use of the peer review concept when it dealt with a planned workforce reduction of 4,500 to 6,000 people.[70] The Society for Human Resource Management (SHRM) notes that it can be an effective way to resolve workplace conflict, providing that the aggrieved employee presents his or her side of a dispute to a small panel of employees and supervisors are selected from a pool of employees trained in dispute resolution.[71] As Ann Reesman, former general counsel of the Equal Employment Advisory Council, put it, "The benefit of using peer review rather than some external decision maker is that the peer review panel is well-versed in the company culture and how the company operates."[72] In addition, peers tend to find decisions handed down by peers to be trustworthy.[73]

The key to a successful peer review committee is to make sure that the people involved in the process are respected members of the organization. Election rather than appointment of committee members helps participants to trust the independence of the process. Ideally, everyone involved in peer review should receive training in relevant areas such as dispute resolution, discrimination, fairness, legalities, and ethics. Representatives of both employees and management should be involved in the decision-making process.[74]

The Future of ADR. The trend toward using ADR is growing, with no end in sight. This growth is spurred partly by the time and money saved by avoiding costly litigation. KBR (formerly Kellogg Brown & Root), a Houston-based construction and engineering firm, estimates that its legal fees dropped 30 to 50 percent since employing ADR, and 70 to 80 percent of the firm's cases were settled within eight weeks (40 percent within a month). Further, the proportion of adverse settlements and the size of the judgments were no different from when they went through the court system.[75] Viewed from the "ethics of care" standpoint, alternative dispute resolution is preferable to the adversarial strategies that preceded it.[76]

ADR is not without problems. In particular, many observers have expressed concern that some employers were requiring new hires to sign contracts, waiving their right to sue the firm and accepting pre-dispute **mandatory arbitration** as the alternative. Arbitration is a process where a neutral party resolves a dispute between two or more parties and the resolution is binding. In mandatory arbitration, the parties must agree to arbitration prior to any dispute. Critics of this practice argue that this robs employees of their right to due process. They say that the structure of mandatory arbitration favors the organization and not the employee.

And without the strict judicial rules against conflicts of interest, companies can steer cases to friendly arbitrators. In turn, interviews and records show that some arbitrators cultivate close ties with companies to get business.[77] In one investigation into the use of arbitration by businesses for both consumers and employees, investigators discovered what they called "an alternate system of justice."[78] Reporters found that when it comes to federal class actions, arbitration clauses come into play most often in employment cases. Most of these involve wage disputes, but companies are also pursuing arbitration in discrimination claims.[79]

Supporters contend that the arbitration process is just as fair as a jury trial while costing much less in time and money. The war against mandatory arbitration continues to wage. President Obama signed into law bills that limit mandatory arbitration in certain circumstances.[80] At this writing, the Arbitration Fairness Act of 2015 is working its way through the U.S. Congress.[81] However, the popularity of ADR to resolve employee disputes continues, and employees are often unaware that they agree to this form of conflict resolution when they sign their employment documents. To avoid this, one attorney advises that employees do the following when they sign their employment documents:[82]

- Read all documents carefully. The handbook may be lengthy, but when you sign something, you agree to all the terms of the document. Protect yourself from unwittingly giving up your rights.
- Negotiate. You can refuse to sign, but the employer can opt to fire-at-will and rescind the offer. However, you can negotiate several points (with an attorney involved), including:
  - Choice of arbitrator—Ask for equal say in the choice.
  - Disclosure of information—Ask for information about the arbitrator and his/her relationship to the company.
  - Costs of arbitration—Make sure that costs are covered by the employer.
  - Right to an attorney—Make sure this is clear in the agreement.
  - Remedies—Make sure that you can receive through arbitration all of the remedies that you would have gotten if you had filed your claim in a court of law (e.g., the agreement should not prohibit you from seeking punitive damages or damages for emotional distress).

ETHICS IN PRACTICE CASE

A Whistle-Blower's Windfall

Bradley C. Birkenfeld was a private banker at the Swiss bank, UBS. In 2007, he began giving U.S. authorities detailed descriptions of the ways in which UBS was promoting tax evasion. He also confessed to smuggling a client's diamonds inside a tube of toothpaste. According to Birkenfeld, he decided to become an informant when he learned that the bank's activities were illegal and reporting it to the compliance office had no effect. In 2008, he was convicted of conspiracy for having withheld information about his top client, a property developer, and was sentenced to 40 months in prison.

While still in jail, Birkenfeld was awarded $104 million for the role he played in exposing UBS. To date that is the largest amount awarded by the Internal Revenue Service (IRS). The UBS paid a $780 million dollar fine and agreed to give the IRS thousands of names of individuals suspected of evading U.S. taxes. The IRS expects to recoup billions of dollars in unpaid taxes as a result of the information that Birkenfeld provided.

1. Is it appropriate for a convicted felon to reap rewards from reporting someone else's crimes?
2. Should the IRS continue to offer rewards for providing information about tax evaders?
3. Was this record-setting reward too big? Was it too small? Support your answer.

Sources: Eamon Javers, "Why Did the U.S. Pay This Former Swiss Banker $104M?" CNBC (April, 30, 2015), David Kocieniewski, http://www.cnbc.com/2015/04/30/why-did-the-us-pay-this-former-swiss-banker-104m.html. Accessed June 1, 2016; "Get Out of Jail Free? No, It's Better," *The New York Times* (September 12, 2012), A1; Laura Saunders, "Whistleblower Gets $104 Million," *The Wall Street Journal* (September 12, 2012), C1.

17.6 Freedom of Speech in the Workplace

According to a recent *Bloomberg Businessweek* article, the workplace is a place where "free speech goes to die.[83] In the United States, people are free to say whatever they like, unless they are at work."[84] Political speech is an example. The U.S. Constitution protects an individual's political free speech from governmental interference. However, in the absence of a state law prohibiting it, no such protection exists to stop an employer's interference. In all but eight states and the District of Columbia, bosses can insist that employees contribute money or time to their favorite candidate and they can fire employees for expressing views that are inconsistent with their own.[85]

In such a restrictive environment, it is easy to see how much courage is needed for employees to speak up when they see something wrong. However, private employers may also feel that they have a duty to speak up and monitor the free speech of their employees. In 2016, a few high-profile cases highlighted the delicate balance between the right of free speech for employees and the rights of other individuals when an employee acts and speaks on behalf of a private corporation, or even appears to do so.[86] For example, in 2016, Donald Sterling, the owner of the Los Angeles Clippers basketball team was fined and banned from the National Basketball Association for remarks he made that were deemed racist.[87]

As one attorney explained, the concept of free speech is particularly tricky when it comes to management because the employer must consider how the statements have an actual and material effect on its employees and on the workplace.[88] This explains why the CEO of Mozilla Corporation resigned from his position after mounting pressure from internal and external stakeholders when he donated to California's Proposition 8, which banned same-sex couples from marrying.[89] At issue is that private employers may feel they have a duty to curb free speech that is potentially discriminatory; however, by putting restrictions on employee speech, they may themselves be discriminatory.

Speaking truth to power is a Quaker phrase for speaking honestly and openly even when powerful parties would prefer that you keep quiet. For an employee, this can be difficult, even with some protections that exist for the right to speak freely. For an employer, they must be careful not to interfere with employee rights under the **National Labor Relations Act**. Even social media postings may be protected from retaliation for employees of private employers if the discussions involve terms and conditions of their employment.[90] The bottom line is that employees have ideas, opinions, and voices about things that are going on at work. They often possess valuable information that can actually improve the operations, the morale, and the ethical climate of a company. Good employers will be receptive to constructive feedback from their employees; in the end, it is the fair and ethical thing to do.[91]

17.6a Whistle-Blowing

As stated earlier, the current generation of employees has a different concept of loyalty to and acceptance of authority than that of past generations. The result is unprecedented numbers of employees "blowing the whistle" on their employers. A **whistle-blower** is a former or current organization member who discloses "illegal, immoral, or illegitimate practices under the control of their employers, to persons or organizations that may be able to effect action."[92] Four key elements comprise the whistle-blowing process: the whistle-blower, the act or complaint about which the whistle-blower is concerned, the party to whom the complaint or report is made, and the organization against which the complaint is made.[93]

What is at stake is the employee's right to speak out in cases where she or he thinks the company or management is engaging in an unacceptable practice. Whistle-blowing is contrary to the cultural tradition that an employee does not question a superior's decisions and acts, especially in public. The former view held that the employee owes loyalty, obedience, and confidentiality to the corporate employer; however, the current view of employee responsibility holds that the employee has a duty not only to the employer but also to the public and to her or his own conscience. Whistle-blowing, in this latter situation, becomes an important option for the employee should management not be responsive to expressed concerns. Figure 17-3 depicts these two views of employee responsibility.

FIGURE 17-3 Two Views of Employee Responsibility in a Potential Whistle-Blowing Situation

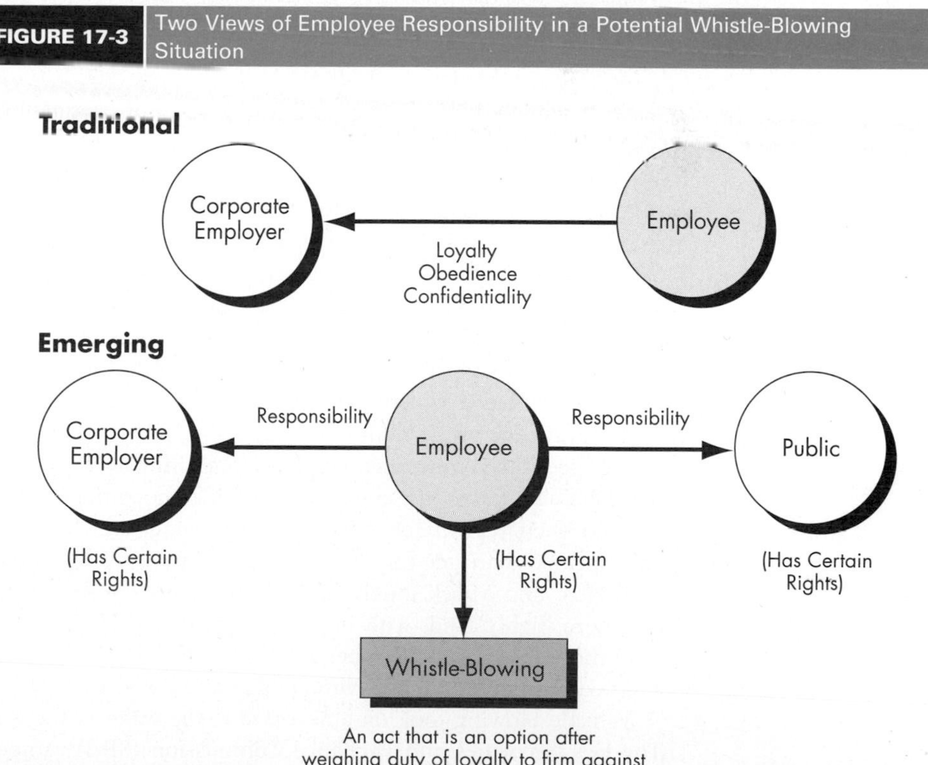

ETHICS IN PRACTICE CASE

The Serial Whistle-Blower: Have the Incentives Gone Too Far?

When the False Claims Act was instituted in 1863, the motivations of the government were pretty clear: penalize companies or people who defraud the government. When the government enacted higher potential rewards and easier filing procedures in 1986 and then again in 2009, the number of whistle-blower filings exploded, with annual filings nearly doubling over five years from 2009 to 2013. However, something else exploded as well—the growth of serial whistle-blowers.

Serial whistle-blowers file suit after suit in the hopes of landing the "big one." Often these are health-care–related cases. Since 1986, over 25 people or groups fall into this category of serial whistle-blowers with five suits or more filed in the last two decades. The phenomenon is also reflected in the number of frivolous lawsuits that do not result in any settlement or judgment, which were 74 percent of suits filed from 1987 to 2010, according to the Justice Department.

One investigation into a serial whistle-blower found that a physician who received $38 million, and was praised by a federal prosecutor for this "good citizenry," had filed 12 suits against different laboratories with a string of allegations surrounding unfair drug pricing practices and false performance claims. While the physician claims that all his filings were based on "nonpublic" documents and his original sources, many have been thrown out or abandoned because of deficient allegations. In 2016, that same physician was due to receive another $59 million from another price-fixing allegation against a large pharmaceutical company. However, the government continues to see value in the whistle-blowing incentives, particularly in the health-care industry. From 2009 to 2013, it collected $12.3 billion in civil recoveries.

1. Is it appropriate to file more than one whistle-blower claim?
2. Are the incentives too high for whistle-blowers, thus putting some people into the whistle-blowing "business?"
3. Beyond the whistle-blower, who benefits from the pursuit and settlement of these claims?

Sources: Debra Cassens Weiss, "Repeat Whistleblowers Reap Millions of Dollars in False-Claim Suits," *ABA Journal* (July 24, 2014), http://www.abajournal.com/news/article/repeat_whistleblowers_reap_millions_of_dollars_in_false_claims_suits/. Accessed June 2, 2016; Peter Loftus, "Meet the Serial Whistleblowers," *The Wall Street Journal* (July 24, 2014), A1; Andrew Ward, "Pharma Whistleblower Takes Total Payouts close to $100m," *Financial Times* (February 16, 2016), http://www.ft.com/cms/s/0/25277046-d4c3-11e5-8887-98e7feb46f27.html#axzz49Tc2Y0IY. Accessed May 22, 2016.

Most whistle-blowers engage in these acts out of a genuine or legitimate belief that certain actions in their organizations are wrong and that they are doing the right thing by reporting them. They may have learned of the wrongful acts by being asked or coerced to participate in them, or through observation or examination of company records. For example, in 2016 an executive at Oracle accused the company of terminating her in retaliation for her complaining about improper accounting practices in Oracle's cloud services business.[94] She said that her bosses instructed her to add millions of dollars of accruals for expected business that was unsubstantiated, and she complained about it. After she was terminated following a positive performance review, she filed a whistle-blower lawsuit under the anti-retaliation provisions of the Sarbanes–Oxley and Dodd–Frank laws.[95]

The genuinely concerned employee may initially express concern to a superior or to someone else within the organization. Other potential whistle-blowers may be planning to make their reports for the purpose of striking out or retaliating against the company or a specific manager for some reason. In a survey of studies of whistle-blowers, however, Near and Miceli found the latter to be uncommon. Whistle-blowers were on average more highly paid, with higher job performance than inactive observers were. They were more likely to hold supervisory or professional status, and they have both the role and responsibility to report wrongdoing and the knowledge of channels for doing so.[96]

Whistle-blowing took on a new face in the wake of the economic and financial crisis. The U.S. Securities and Exchange Commission (SEC) ramped up their whistle-blowing procedures and protections in 2011. Since that time, the SEC's whistleblower program

FIGURE 17-4 A Checklist to Follow before Blowing the Whistle

The following things should be considered before you blow the whistle:

1. Is there any alternative to blowing the whistle? Make sure you have tried to remedy the problem by reporting up the normal chain of command and have had no success.
2. Does the proposed disclosure advance public interest rather than personal or political gain? Don't act out of frustration or because you feel mistreated.
3. Have you thought about the outcomes of blowing the whistle for yourself and your family? Be prepared for the possibility of disapproval from friends, family, and fellow workers.
4. Have you identified the sources of support both inside and outside the organization on which you can rely during the process? Make sure you know your legal rights and have enlisted the help of others.
5. Do you have enough evidence to support your claim? Even more evidence is needed if you plan to remain anonymous. Be thorough but do not break the law.
6. Have you identified and copied all supporting records before drawing suspicion to your concerns? Remember to keep a factual log both before and after blowing the whistle.

Sources: The Government Accountability Center, http://www.afscmeinfocenter.org/blog/2008/06/courage-without-martyrdom-the.htm#.V0Q7rY-cHIU. Accessed May 23, 2016.Kenneth K. Humphreys, "A Checklist for Whistleblowers to Follow," *Cost Engineering* (October 2003), 14; Stephen Martin Kohn, *A Whistleblower's Handbook* (Lyons Press: Guilford, CT, 2011).

has paid more than $55 million to 23 whistle-blowers.[97] In 2014, four whistle-blowers collected a total of $170 million for helping investigators get a record $16.6 billion penalty against Bank of America for misdeeds and fraud that inflated the value of mortgage properties and loans in the 2008/2009 financial crisis.[98] Even after an appeals court threw out the penalty, whistle-blowers were still able to keep their reward money.[99] In 2015 alone, the SEC paid more than $37 million to whistle-blowers, representing a 30 percent increase for claims filed with the office, primarily due to an expansion of efforts on the international front and effective reporting of illegal bribery in violation of the Foreign Corrupt Practices Act.[100] According to the report, whistle-blowers from 61 foreign countries filed claims with the SEC in 2015.

Figure 17-4 depicts a checklist to be followed by whistle-blowers before blowing the whistle.

17.6b Consequences of Whistle-Blowing

Speaking truth to power is a Quaker phrase for speaking honestly and openly even when powerful parties would prefer that you keep quiet. Doing so is not often easy and, unfortunately, whistle-blowers are not always rewarded for their contributions to the public interest. Although they are now more likely to get some form of protection than they were in the past, whistle-blowers can still pay dearly for their actions.

Various types of corporate retaliation are often taken against whistle-blowers by their employers. The Business Ethics Resource Center recently surveyed 4,800 employees, who reported the following top forms of retaliation and their incidence.[101]

• Excluded from decisions and work activity	64%
• Cold shoulder from co-workers	62%
• Verbal abuse from management	62%
• Almost lost job	56%
• Not given promotion or raise	55%
• Verbal abuse from co-workers	51%
• Cut in hours or pay	46%
• Relocated or reassigned	44%

Whistle-blowing is not easy, and despite regulatory protections, retaliation can occur. One postal worker, a safety specialist, advised a co-worker to call the U.S. Department of Labor's Occupational Safety and Health Administration about her workplace health concerns. Soon after, the safety specialist found himself working in an increasingly hostile work environment that included being transferred to another office, forced to work in an unheated storage room, demoted, restricted on his movements, publicly humiliated, and subjected to four openly antagonistic interviews as part of workplace investigations.[102] He was also issued a disciplinary letter and refused a promotion. After filing a complaint with the Office of Safety and Health Administration (OSHA), the worker was awarded $229,228 in damages and the Postal Service was required to promote him to the same pay rate he would have had if he had he not been denied a promotion.[103] Many whistle-blowing episodes do not end this favorably, however, and employees need to be aware of this from the beginning. Employees who believe that they have been retaliated against for engaging in protected conduct may file a complaint with the secretary of labor to request an investigation by OSHA's Whistleblower Protection Program.

Figure 17-5 chronicles Hollywood's treatment of some famous whistle-blowers.

FIGURE 17-5 Whistle-Blowers Get the Hollywood Treatment

Movie	Stars	Story	Inspiration
The Snowden Files (2016)	Joseph Gordon-Levitt	Chronicles the life of NSA whistle-blower Edward Snowden.	Directed by Oliver Stone and titled after the book by Guardian journalist Luke Harding.
The Whistleblower (2010)	Rachel Weisz Vanessa Redgrave	Nebraska police officer serves as peacekeeper post-war Bosnia and blows whistle on U.N. cover-up of sex trafficking scandal.	Based on the experiences of Kathryn Bolkovac who worked with the U.N. International Police at a U.K. security company.
The Informant! (2009)	Matt Damon Scott Bakula Joel McHale	Mark Whitacre, an employee at Archer Daniels Midland (ADM), blows the whistle on the lysine price-fixing conspiracy.	This dark comedy is based on *The Informant*, a book by journalist Kurt Eichenwald.
The Insider (1999)	Russell Crowe Al Pacino Christopher Plummer	A successful scientist is fired from major tobacco company for taking a principled stand. *60 Minutes* is due to report the story, but they cave to corporate pressure.	Based on a *Vanity Fair* article, "The Man Who Knew Too Much." The movie tells the true story of Jeffrey Wigand, who was fired from Brown & Williamson tobacco company.
Silkwood (1983)	Meryl Streep (title role) Kurt Russell Cher Craig T. Nelson	Whistle-blowers try to expose unsafe practices at an Oklahoma nuclear parts factory. A worker becomes contaminated.	Based on the true story of Karen Silkwood, who was a chemical technician at the Kerr-McGee plutonium fuels production plant in Crescent, Oklahoma. As a union member and activist, she was critical of plant safety.
Serpico (1973)	Al Pacino (title role)	Frank Serpico is a nonconformist "hippie cop" in New York City who tries to report graft and corruption to his superiors. When they don't listen, he goes to *The New York Times*.	Based on Peter Maas's book, the movie tells a true story from Serpico's perspective. In the true story, another whistle-blower (David Durk) played a critical role, which is downplayed in the movie.

17.6c Government's Protection of Whistle-Blowers

Just as employees are beginning to get some protection from the courts through the public policy exception to the employment-at-will doctrine, the same is true for whistle-blowers. The U.S. federal government was one of the first organizations to attempt to protect its own whistle-blowers. A highlight of the **1978 Civil Service Reform Act** was protection for federal employees who expose illegal, corrupt, or wasteful government activities. Unfortunately, this effort has had only mixed results.[104]

It is difficult to protect whistle-blowers against retaliation because so often the reprisals are subtle. An added boost for federal employees came in 1989, when Congress passed the **Whistleblower Protection Act** and the president signed it into law. The effect of this act was to reform the Merit System Protection Board and the Office of General Counsel, the two offices that protect federal employees.[105]

Protection for private employees began to arrive at that point. The U.S. Congress introduced a range of protections for workers in various industries.[106] Typically, the whistle-blower protections were contained in various pieces of legislation that dealt with a range of issues, of which whistle-blowing was just one. As a result, no one piece of legislation provides an umbrella of protection for all whistle-blowers across the country. Even the most recent whistle-blower protections are limited. The Sarbanes–Oxley (SOX) whistle-blower protections apply only to employees in publicly held firms. The Dodd–Frank Wall Street Reform and Consumer Protection whistle-blower protections apply only to employees in the financial industry.

Current legislation attempts to address these limitations. In 2016, President Obama signed into law the **Defend Trade Secrets Act**, which includes strong and much needed protections for corporate whistle-blowers, establishing clear procedures for immunity for employees who disclose trade secrets to the government as part of a whistle-blower case.[107] In April 2016, the U.S. Senate Judiciary Committee approved the **FBI Whistleblower Protection Enhancement Act** providing compensatory damages for whistle-blowers, expanding the scope of protected activity, ending bureaucratic delays in processing cases, and allowing for case review by independent administrative law judges. At this writing, the bill was going to the Senate for approval. The motivation for this bill stemmed from the case of whistle-blower Jane Turner, who fought for 15 years for justice after reporting theft from Ground Zero and the victims of the 9/11 attacks by FBI agents.[108] Figure 17-6 lists the federal laws that include whistle-blower protections.

Of all these, SOX whistle-blower protections are the most stringent in preventing wrongful discharge. In addition to protecting employees who were fired, the law has four other important whistle-blower protections for employees in publicly traded corporations:[109]

1. The corporations are required to form independent audit committees and develop confidential procedures for whistle-blowers to follow.
2. The law establishes new ethical standards for attorneys who practice before the SEC that include specification for when the attorney is required to blow the whistle on the client.
3. In a provision that applies to all employees, not only those in publicly held corporations, SOX criminalized retaliation against whistle-blowers who give truthful information to a law enforcement officer by amending the federal obstruction of justice statute.
4. SOX gives the SEC jurisdiction over every aspect of the law, including the whistle-blower provisions, and allows for criminal penalties.

The states vary even more widely in the whistle-blower protections they provide. **Michigan's Whistleblowers Protection Act of 1981** was the first state law designed to

FIGURE 17-6 Federal Laws with Whistle-Blower Protections

Affordable Care Act	International Safe Container Act
Asbestos Hazard Emergency Response Act	Longshore and Harbor Workers' Compensation Act
Clean Air Act	Migrant and Seasonal Agricultural Worker Protection Act
CERCLA (Superfund Act)	Moving Ahead for Progress in the 21st Century Act
Commercial Motor Vehicle Safety Act	National Transit Security Act
Consumer Product Safety Act	Occupational Safety and Health Act
Department of Defense Authorization Act	Pipeline Safety Improvement Act
Dodd–Frank Wall Street Reform and Consumer Protection Act	Safe Drinking Water Act
Energy Reorganization Act	Sarbanes–Oxley Act
Fair Labor Standards Act	Seaman's Protection Act
FDA Food Safety Modernization Act	Solid Waste Disposal Act
Federal Mine Safety and Health Act	Surface Mining and Control Act
Federal Railroad Safety Act	Toxic Substances Control Act
Federal Water Pollution Control Act	Wendell H. Ford Aviation Investment and Reform for the 21st Century Act

Sources: John O. Shimabukoro and L. Paige Whitaker, "Whistleblower Protections under Federal Law: An Overview," Congressional Research Service (September 13, 2012), 1–21; Occupational Safety and Health Administration Directorate of Whistleblower Programs (DWPP), Whistleblower Statutes Desk Aid, http://www.whistleblowers.gov/whistleblower_acts-desk_reference.pdf. Accessed June 1, 2016.

protect any employee in private industry against unjust reprisals for reporting alleged violations of federal, state, or local laws to public authorities. The burden was placed on the employer to show that questionable treatment was justified based on proper personnel standards or valid business reasons.[110] The Michigan Act spurred similar laws in other states but the progress has been slow. Most state courts have recognized a public policy exception to employment at-will, and therefore whistle-blowers have some limited protection from discharge.

The normal remedy for wrongful discharge of employees is reinstatement with back pay, with some sympathetic juries adding compensatory damages for physical suffering.[111] The crazy quilt of whistle-blower protections makes it very difficult for employees to shed light safely on corporate wrongdoing. In some states, whistle-blowers could be fired at will; in other states, they would have to sort through a bewildering assortment of statutes to determine what, if any, protection existed for them. People vary in their need to know they have protection before blowing the whistle. Figure 17-7 describes a study that looks at the differences between people who do the right thing in spite of great personal danger and others who choose not to act.

17.6d False Claims Act

A provocative piece of federal legislation that was passed to add an incentive for whistle-blowers in the public interest is the **False Claims Act (FCA)**. The act has *qui tam* (Latin shorthand for "he who sues for the king as well as himself") provisions that allow employees to blow the whistle about contractor fraud and share with the government in any financial recoveries realized by their efforts. It dates back to the Civil War, when the army wanted to find and prosecute profiteers who sold the same horse twice or sold boxes of sawdust while claiming they were guns. Citizens were permitted to sue on the government's behalf and receive 50 percent of the recovery. In 1943, Congress reduced

FIGURE 17-7 Giving Voice to Values

Giving Voice to Values, spearheaded by Professor Mary Gentile, is an innovative curriculum development designed to help business students and practitioner to strengthen their abilities to voice their values when situations call them into conflict. The focus is not on determining what the right thing to do is, but rather on determining how to do it. Giving Voice to Values is designed to help students build a tool kit that will enable them to voice their values when ethical challenges arise.

Gentile cites a study of World War II rescuers that shows that moral courage can be strengthened through anticipating ethical challenges that might occur and formulating a response to them. In this study, researchers looked for commonalities among individuals who protected others from the Nazis even when they put their own lives at risk by doing so. They found that people who acted with moral courage when confronted with real danger tended to have earlier life experiences where they anticipated situations in which their values would be challenged and had a respected listener with whom they discussed how they would handle that situation. This act of practicing a response before being put in the difficult situation seemed to strengthen their subsequent ability to handle ethical challenges that occurred.

Sources: Mary C. Gentile, *Giving Voice to Values: How to Speak Your Mind When You Know What's Right* (New Haven: Yale University Press, 2010); Mary C. Gentile, "Giving Voice to Values: Way of Thinking about Values in the Workplace," The Aspen Institute Center for Business Education (September 2008); Perry London, "The Rescuers: Motivational Hypotheses about Christians Who Saved Jews from the Nazis," in J. Macaulay and L. Berkowitz (eds.), *Altruism and Helping Behavior: Social Psychological Studies of Some Antecedents and Consequences* (New York: Academic Press, 1970); Douglas H. Huneke, *The Moses of Rovno* (New York: Dodd, Mead, 1985).

the potential payout dramatically, and so it was seldom used.[112] The act was revised in 1986 to make recoveries easier to obtain and payouts more generous, thereby encouraging whistle-blowing against government contractor fraud.[113] The 1986 act grew out of outrage in the mid-1980s over reports of fraud and abuse on the part of military contractors, such as the infamous $600 toilet seats and country club memberships billed to the government.[114]

What is particularly controversial about the FCA is the magnitude of the financial incentives that individual employees may earn as a result of their whistle-blowing efforts. The law allows individuals to be awarded as much as 15 to 25 percent of the proceeds in cases where the government joins in the action and from 15 to 30 percent of the proceeds in actions that the government does not join.[115] Even with these incentives, however, whistle blowing is never easy, as the experiences of James Alderson illustrate.

James Alderson had been the chief financial officer of the North Valley Hospital for 17 years when Quorum, a former division of HCA, took over management of the hospital. Quorum created a second set of books and told Alderson to use these secret books to report higher-than-average expenses to the government for reimbursement. Knowing this would be both illegal and unethical, Alderson refused and five days later he was fired. After learning that other Quorum hospitals were cooking the books, too, Alderson went to Washington and talked to the U.S. Department of Justice. He took documentation with him of the false claims being filed and sued Quorum and HCA under the federal FCA.

HCA eventually paid a total of $840 million, consisting of $745 million in civil damages and $95 million in criminal penalties. They later paid another $881 million to settle all remaining fraud charges and other overpayment claims against the company. Thirteen years after Alderson was fired, the final settlement agreement between HCA and the U.S. Department of Justice was approved. The government received $1.5 billion from those payments, thanks to the efforts of Alderson and other whistle-blowers involved.[116]

There aren't many hospitals in Whitefish, Montana, so Alderson was forced to leave Whitefish to find work in hospital finance. For the next ten years, Alderson tried to earn a living while continuing to gather evidence. Federal officials had told him that he needed evidence that the practices at North Valley were widespread, and the collection of that evidence was his responsibility. Collecting that evidence consumed Alderson's time and money. In addition to the financial drain, Alderson had made many personal sacrifices, from missing his son's football games to not being at his mother's side when she died.[117]

Alderson and his wife Connie kept a low profile. According to Connie, it was just like being in the witness protection program, "the only difference is that we weren't receiving any protection or money to keep us going."[118] Their low profile ended when the television show *60 Minutes* did a profile of Alderson. After the show aired, Alderson became a pariah in the health-care industry. Says Alderson, "Even though I had a major impact in reducing health-care fraud by $10 billion annually, I had one hospital CEO tell me to my face that I had ruined the industry and that I had given it a black eye."[119]

Under the FCA, Anderson received $20 million in one settlement and split $100 million with another whistle-blower in another. Alderson commented, "I won't deny that money provided an incentive, but it was only part of the motivation. What Quorum and HCA were doing was wrong, and it took me 13 years and my career to prove it. Fortunately, I received enough money from the settlement to retire."[120] However, Connie Alderson says, "Knowing what I know now and knowing how long it's been, I'm not sure I would have agreed to pursuing the case. I don't think any amount of money is going to take care of what we've been through."[121]

Unfortunately, the Alderson case is not unique. Similar stories have been told about whistle-blowers at JPMorgan, the UK bank, HBOS, and Olympus.[122] Yet, whistle-blowers have been instrumental in identifying and assisting the recovery of funds, particularly in the health-care area, where fraud has been rampant. Since 1987, the U.S. federal government has recovered over $35 billion due to the FCA, with an additional $7 billion recovered in fines, and $6 billion returned to state Medicaid programs.[123] The FCA has also inspired other similar programs. Twenty-nine states, three large cities, and one country have FCAs that are modeled after the federal law.

The SEC, the IRS, and the CFTC (Commodities Future Trading Commission) all have programs that are modeled on the FCA.[124] The proceeds continue to grow. In 2015 alone, the FCA facilitated the recovery of $3.5 billion, with $1.9 billion coming from companies and individuals in the health-care industry for allegedly providing unnecessary or inadequate care, paying kickbacks to health-care providers to induce the use of certain goods and services, or overcharging for goods and services paid for by Medicare, Medicaid, and other federal health-care programs.[125] The $1.9 billion reflects federal losses only. In many of these cases, the department was instrumental in recovering additional millions of dollars for consumers and state Medicaid programs.

17.6e Management Responsiveness to Potential Whistle-Blowing Situations

Normally, employees pursue whistle-blowing options after regular, less dramatic, channels of communication have failed. Ideally, employees should always feel free to open up to management about any concerns they have. Even in the best of organizations, however, people hesitate to speak up. Employee self-censorship is common, particularly surrounding ethical issues. As noted by Professor James Detert, "Ethical situations at work can be cause for alarm, *and* are also a normal part of doing business. The key is to not let either of those realities prevent you from making a rational decision."[126]

In a study of whistle-blower protections, workers in a leading high-technology organization were asked if they felt safe speaking up about problems in the firm. In spite of the fact that this organization had a variety of formal mechanisms as ombudsperson and grievance procedures, half the employees indicated that they did not feel safe speaking up.[127] Their overall concern was with self-preservation. They perceived a risk to speaking up that lead them to conclude, "When in doubt, keep your mouth shut."[128]

In rare instances, employees were afraid to speak out because they had experiences with managers who responded badly to past suggestions. More often, the reticent employees were simply responding to a vague perception of a threat in the work environment. Sometimes they were put off by organizational stories about people who had spoken up and then suddenly were no longer there. Typically, their silence stemmed from untested assumptions.[129]

The findings of this study have clear implications for encouraging free and open speech in the workplace. It is not enough to remove barriers or put formal mechanisms in place. Significant changes in the organizational culture must occur if organizations want to deal fairly with employee stakeholders. The following are suggestions for how to accomplish that goal:[130]

1. Managers must be clear not only to accept suggestions—they must also invite them. Managers cannot implement all suggestions, but it is important for managers to acknowledge each one.
2. Managers must refute commonly held assumptions and organizational myths that discourage communication. For example, they can counter the commonly held belief that employees should give managers suggestions in private by explaining that openly discussed ideas are likely to be useful.
3. Managers should tailor rewards so that employees share more directly in any cost savings or sales increase from ideas they offer. Tangible rewards can help employees to overcome intangible concerns.

In an ideal world, employees would automatically speak freely to managers if they saw something wrong happening or had an idea to improve operations. Unfortunately, the work world is not ideal. It can be instructive to turn back to Enron, one of the classic cases of corporate malfeasance and ask what went wrong. Former Enron executive Lynn Brewer suggests that there may be "a little Enron in all of us." The problem at Enron was not "dirty secrets hidden well below the surface, but an open secret."[131] She estimates that about two thirds of the employees at Enron were aware at some time of unethical behavior in the middle ranks and believes if Enron employees had been asked if the company was ethical or not, 90 percent would have rated the company "highly unethical." [132] In the name of solving business problems, good people will often do bad things. It is incumbent upon managers to design organizations that enable and empower employees to come forward with information that will either stop wrongdoing or improve company operations long before whistle-blowing is needed.[133]

Summary

Employee stakeholders today are more sensitive about their roles and their rights for a variety of reasons. Underlying this new concern are changes in the social contract between employers and employees that have been driven by global competition and a changing economy, including more contingent workers and a new generation of workers called the Millennials. This has spurred the growth of employee engagement programs to assist employees in their personal and career development. Employee engagement efforts help both the employee and the employer. Central among the growing employee rights issues discussed in this chapter are (1) the right not to be fired without good cause, (2) the right to due process and fair treatment, and (3) the right to freedom of speech.

The basis for the argument that we may be moving toward an employee's right not to be fired is the erosion by the courts of the employment-at-will doctrine. More and more, the courts are making exceptions to this long-standing common-law principle. Three major exceptions are the public policy exception, the idea of an implied contract, and breach of good faith. Society's concept of what represents fair treatment to employees is constantly changing.

The employees' right to due process is concerned primarily with fair treatment. Common approaches for management responding to this concern such as the open-door policy and traditional grievance procedures have been disappointing, and so newer methods such as the ombudsman approach and peer review are becoming more prevalent; however, freedom of speech issues continue to challenge employers and employees alike. Thanks to the passage of SOX, whistle-blowers in the private sector now enjoy some of the protections once accorded only to public sector employees; however, those protections are not a guarantee. Whistle-blowers continue to face a slew of obstacles as they seek to speak out on their concerns. Managers should be genuinely attentive to employees' rights in this realm if they wish to avert major scandals and prolonged litigation. A stakeholder approach that emphasizes ethical relationships with employees can create an organizational environment in which employees feel freer to express their concerns openly, lessening the need to blow a whistle.

Key Terms

1099 economy, p. 523
1978 Civil Service Reform Act, p. 541
alternative dispute resolution (ADR), p. 533
collective bargaining, p. 526
Defend Trade Secrets Act, p. 541
due process, p. 532
employee engagement, p. 525
employee rights, p. 526
employment-at-will doctrine, p. 528
enterprise rights, p. 526
False Claims Act (FCA), p. 542
FBI Whistleblower Protection Enhancement Act, p. 541
fissuring, p. 533
gig economy, p. 523
good cause norm, p. 527
good faith principle, p. 530
hearing procedure, p. 533
implied contract exception, p. 529
mandatory arbitration, p. 535
Michigan Whistle-Blowers Protection Act of 1981, p. 541
Millennial generation, p. 524
National Labor Relations Act, p. 536
ombudsman, p. 534
open-door policy, p. 533
peer review panel, p. 534
private property, p. 525
public policy exception, p. 529
Section 919D, p. 534
social contract, p. 523
statutory rights, p. 526
whistle-blower, p. 537
Whistle-Blower Protection Act, p. 541

Discussion Questions

1. Rank the various changes that are occurring in the workplace in terms of their importance to the growth of the employee rights movement. Briefly explain your ranking.
2. Explain the employment-at-will doctrine, and describe how it is being eroded. Do you think its existence is leading to a healthy or an unhealthy employment environment in the United States? Justify your reasoning.
3. In your own words, explain the right to due process. What are some of the major ways management is attempting to ensure due process in the workplace?
4. If you could choose only one, which form of alternative dispute resolution would be your choice as the most effective approach to employee due process? Explain.
5. How do you feel about whistle-blowing now that you have read about it? Are you now more sympathetic or less sympathetic to whistle-blowers? Explain.
6. What is your assessment of the value of the False Claims Act? What is your assessment of the value of the whistle-blower protections under the Sarbanes–Oxley Act?
7. What other steps can managements take to be responsive to potential whistle-blowing situations?

Endnotes

1. "Taking Steps to Motivate Your Workers Improves Productivity," *Business Owner's Toolkit* (May 24, 2012), http://www.bizfilings.com/toolkit/sbg/office-hr/managing-the-workplace/motivating-workers-for-productivity.aspx. Accessed May 31, 2016.
2. Brook Manville, "How a Stint in 'Dead-End HR' Made Anne Mulcahy a Better CEO," *Forbes* (April 3, 2016), http://www.forbes.com/sites/brookmanville/2016/04/03/how-a-stint-in-dead-end-hr-made-anne-mulcahy-a-better-ceo/2/#5414c9cd25a0. Accessed May 21, 2016.
3. Josh Bersin, "Unlocking the Secrets of Employee Engagement," CFO Journal, *The Wall Street Journal* (September 4, 2015), http://deloitte.wsj.com/cfo/2015/09/04/unlocking-the-secrets-of-employee-engagement/. Accessed May 21, 2016.
4. Kim Phillips-Fein, "Why Workers Won't Unite," *The Atlantic* (April 2015), 88–98.
5. Diane Lewis, "Out in the Field: Workplace Want Loyal Workers? Then Help Them Grow," *Boston Globe* (July 15, 2001), H2.
6. Number of Jobs Held, Labor Market Activity, and Earnings Growth among the Youngest Baby Boomers, *Bureau of Labor Statistics News Release* (July 25, 2012), http://www.bls.gov/news.release/pdf/nlsoy.pdf. Accessed May 21, 2016.
7. Michelle Conlin, "Job Security, No. Tall Latte, Yes," *Businessweek* (April 2, 2001), 62–64.
8. Neil Irwin, "With 'Gigs' Instead of Jobs, Workers Bear New Burdens," *The New York Times* (March 31, 2016), http://www.nytimes.com/2016/03/31/upshot/contractors-and-temps-accounted-for-all-of-the-growth-in-employment-in-the-last-decade.html. Accessed May 21, 2016.
9. Lawrence F. Katz and Alan B. Krueger, " The Rise and Nature of Alternative Work Arrangements in the United States 1995-2015" (March 29, 2016), http://krueger.princeton.edu/sites/default/files/akrueger/files/katz_krueger_cws_-_march_29_20165.pdf?version=meter+at+2&module=meter-Links&pgtype=article&contentId =&mediaId=&referrer=https%3A%2F%2Fwww.google.com%2F&priority=true&action=click&content Collection=meter-links-click. Accessed May 21, 2016.
10. Ibid.
11. Irwin, 2016.
12. "The 1099 Economy: Exploring a New Social Contract for Employers, Employees, & Society," The Aspen Institute (September 10, 2015), http://www.aspeninstitute.org/video/1099-economy-exploring-new-social-contract-employers-employees-society-0. Accessed May 21, 2016.
13. Ibid.
14. Marla Gottschalk, "Big Idea 2013: A New Social Contract between Employer and Employees," *LinkedIn.com* (December 11, 2012), http://www.linkedin.com/today/post/article/20121211110842-128811924-big-idea-2013-a-new-social-contract-between-employer-and-employees. Accessed May 17, 2016.
15. Ibid.
16. "The Deloitte Millennial Survey 2016: Winning over the Next Generation of Leaders," http://www2.deloitte.com/global/en/pages/about-deloitte/articles/millennialsurvey.html. Accessed May 21, 2016.
17. Ibid.
18. Ibid.
19. PwC Millennials Survey 2016, "Millennials at Work: Reshaping the Workplace," http://www.pwc.com/gx/en/issues/talent/future-of-work/millennials-survey.html. Accessed May 21, 2016.
20. *Gallup Business Journal*, "Five Ways to Improve Employee Engagement Now" (January 7, 2014), http://www.gallup.com/businessjournal/166667/five-ways-improve-employee-engagement.aspx. Accessed May 22, 2016.
21. Ibid.
22. Ed O'Boyle and Jim Harter, "40 Organizations Leading the World in Employee Engagement," *Gallup* (April 15, 2015), http://www.gallup.com/opinion/gallup/182432/organizations-lead-world-employee engagement.aspx. Accessed May 20, 2016.
23. Andrew Greenburg, "Employee Engagement: Companies That Got It Right," The Recruiting Division (September 28, 2015), http://www.recruitingdivision.com/employee-engagement-got-it-right/. Accessed May 20, 2016.
24. Ibid.
25. Gallup Poll 2015, "Employee Engagement in U.S. Stagnant 2016," http://www.gallup.com/poll/188144/employee-engagement-stagnant-2015.aspx. Accessed May 21, 2016.
26. Richard Carufel, "Corporate Culture Crisis: New Study Reveals 98% of CEOs Ignore Annual Employee Engagement Survey Results," *PR Web* (January 4, 2016), https://www.bulldogreporter.com/corporate-culture-crisis-new-study-reveals-98-of-ceos-ignore-annual-employee-engagement-survey-results/. Accessed May 22, 2016.
27. Rachael King, "How Do Employees Really Feel about Their Companies?," *The Wall Street Journal* (October 13, 2015), http://www.wsj.com/articles/how-do-employees-really-feel-about-their-companies-1444788408. Accessed May 21, 2016.
28. Ibid.

29. Leo Troy, *The End of Unionism: An Appraisal* (St. Louis: Center for the Study of American Business, Washington University, September 1994), 1–2.

30. "Union Members Summary," *Bureau of Labor Statistics* (January 28, 2016), http://www.bls.gov/news.release/union2.nr0.htm. Accessed May 18, 2016.

31. Ibid.

32. "Trade Union Density," OECD (2016), https://stats.oecd.org/Index.aspx?DataSetCode=UN_DEN. Accessed May 18, 2016.

33. Richard Edwards, *Rights at Work* (Washington, DC: The Brookings Institution, 1993), 25–26.

34. Ibid., 33–35.

35. Mark V. Roehling, "The 'Good Cause Norm' in Employment Relations: Empirical Evidence and Policy Implications," *Employee Responsibility and Rights Journal* (September 2002), 91–104.

36. Ellen Dannin, "Why At-Will Employment Is Bad for Employers and Just Cause Is Good for Them," *Labor Law Journal* (Spring 2007), 5–16.

37. Tara J. Radin and Patricia H. Werhane, "Employment-At-Will, Employee Rights, and Future Directions for Employment," *Business Ethics Quarterly* (April 2003), 113–130.

38. Louis Uchitelle, *The Disposable American* (New York: Knopf, 2006).

39. Uchitelle, Battenberg, and Kochan, 7.

40. David H. Autor, John J. Donohue III, and Stewart J. Schwab, "The Employment Consequences of Wrongful-Discharge Laws: Large, Small, or None at All?" *American Economic Review* (May 2004), 440–446.

41. "Employment at Will Exceptions by State," *National Conference of State Legislatures* (April 2008), http://www.ncsl.org/research/labor-and-employment/at-will-employment-exceptions-by-state.aspx. Accessed May 18, 2016.

42. Ibid.

43. Ibid.

44. Ibid.

45. Patricia H. Werhane, Tara J. Radin, and Norman E. Bowie, *Employment and Employee Rights* (Malden, MA: Blackwell Publishing, 2004).

46. Ibid.

47. Dannin, 5–16.

48. Steve Harrison, *The Manager's Book of Decencies: How Small Gestures Build Great Companies* (Columbus, OH: McGraw-Hill, 2007).

49. Ibid.

50. Patricia H. Werhane, *Persons, Rights and Corporations* (Englewood Cliffs, NJ: Prentice Hall, 1985), 110.

51. William M. Haraway, "Employee Grievance Programs: Understanding the Nexus between Workplace Justice, Organizational Legitimacy and Successful Organizations," *Public Personnel Management* (Winter 2005), 329–342.

52. Richard A. Posthuma, "Procedural Due Process and Procedural Justice in the Workplace: A Comparison and Analysis," *Public Personnel Management* (Summer 2003), 181.

53. David W. Ewing, *Freedom inside the Organization: Bringing Civil Liberties to the Workplace* (New York: McGraw-Hill, 1977), 11.

54. Posthuma, 181–195.

55. Lydia DePillis, "Department of Labor Sends Warning Shot to Clients of Temp Staffing Agencies," *The Washington Post* (January 20, 2016), https://www.washingtonpost.com/news/wonk/wp/2016/01/20/department-of-labor-sends-warning-shot-to-clients-of-temp-staffing-agencies/. Accessed May 22, 2016.

56. Ibid.

57. Michael Groebe, "Top Labor and Employment Issues to Watch in 2016," *WardsAuto* (March 9, 2016), http://wardsauto.com/industry/top-labor-and-employment-issues-watch-2016. Accessed May 22, 2016.

58. Ibid.

59. "CPR Takes on 'The Dispute Resolution Divide': Harmonizing Global Approaches," at 2016 Annual Meeting, https://www.cpradr.org/Portals/0/CRPA-DR16annualmtg.pdf. Accessed May 22, 2016.

60. Helena Tavares Erickson, "Cutting Edge Companies Use Dispute Resolution Techniques to Address Workplace Conflict," *Inside Counsel* (April 21, 2015), http://www.insidecounsel.com/2015/04/21/cutting-edge-companies-use-dispute-resolution-tech. Accessed May 22, 2016.

61. "Where Ombudsmen Work Out," *Businessweek* (May 3, 1976), 114–116.

62. Allen Church, "Ombudsmen Ease Governance Compliance," *Claims* (December 2004), 63–65.

63. Jonathan A. Segal, "The Joy of Uncooking," *HR Magazine* (November 2002), 52–57.

64. SEC, "About the Ombudsman," https://www.sec.gov/ombudsman. Accessed May 22, 2016.

65. Carolyn Hirschman, "Someone to Listen," *HR Magazine* (January 2003), 46–50.

66. Ibid.

67. Ibid., 46–51.

68. Andrew Singer, "On the Evolving Corporate Ombudsman," *Ethikos* (March/April 2010), 10–12.

69. Erickson, 2016.

70. Margaret M. Clark, "Jury of Their Peers," *HR Magazine* (January 2004), 54.

71. Society for Human Resource Management, "Problem Resolution and Peer Review Policy, *SHRM* (July 3, 2014), https://www.shrm.org/templatestools/samples/policies/pages/cms_000515.aspx. Accessed May 22, 2016.

72. Ibid.

73. Ibid.

74. "Peer-Review Policy Provides Protection," *Credit Union Directors Newsletter* (April, 2004), 7–8.

75. Kay O. Wilburn, "Employment Disputes: Solving Them out of Court," *Management Review* (March 1998), 17–21. Marc Lampe, "Mediation as an Ethical Adjunct of Stakeholder Theory," *Journal of Business Ethics* (May 2001), 165–173.

76. Marc Lampe, "Mediation as an Ethical Adjunct of Stakeholder Theory," *Journal of Business Ethics* (May 2001), 165–173.

77. Jessica Silver-Greenburg and Michael Corkery, "In Arbitration, a 'Privatization of the Justice System," *The New York Times* (November 1, 2015), http://www.nytimes.com/2015/11/02/business/dealbook/in-arbitration-a-privatization-of-the-justice-system.html. Accessed May 22, 2016.

78. Ibid.

79. Ibid.

80. Jon Hyman, "Congress Employment Law Agenda: 7 Bills to Watch Closely," *HR Specialist* (March 2010), 7.

81. See Arbitration Fairness Act, http://www.franken.senate.gov/files/documents/150429AFABillText.pdf. Accessed May 22, 2016; Ashlee Kieler, "Arbitration Fairness Act Would Reinstate Consumers' Right to Sue in Court," Consumerist (April 30, 2015), https://consumerist.com/2015/04/30/arbitration-fairness-act-would-reinstate-consumers-right-to-sue-in-court/. Accessed May 22, 2016.

82. Lisa Guerin, "Signing an Arbitration Agreement with Your Employer," *NOLO.com* http://www.nolo.com/legal-encyclopedia/signing-arbitration-agreement-with-employer-30005.html. Accessed May 22, 2016.

83. Michael Dolgow, "Where Free Speech Goes to Die. The Workplace," *Bloomberg Businessweek* (August 3, 2012), http://www.cnbc.com/2015/04/30/why-did-the-us-pay-this-former-swiss-banker-104m.html. Accessed June 1, 2016.

84. Ibid.

85. Ibid.

86. Martin Berman-Gorvine, "Employer Ability to Silence Employee Speech Narrowing in Private Sector," *Bloomberg BNA* (May 19, 2014), http://www.bna.com/employer-ability-silence-n17179890580/. Accessed June 1, 2016.

87. Ibid.

88. Ibid.

89. Ibid.

90. Douglass Lee, "NLRB Bolsters Private-Employee Speech," *First Amendment Center* (September 14, 2011), http://www.firstamendmentcenter.org/nlrb-bolsters-private-employee-speech. Accessed June 2, 2016.

91. Shari Lava, "Voicing Your Opinion in the Workplace," *Chron.com*, http://work.chron.com/voicing-opinion-workplace-4397.html. Accessed June 1, 2016.

92. Marcia P. Miceli and Janet P. Near, *Blowing the Whistle: The Organizational and Legal Implications for Companies and Employees* (New York: Lexington Books, 1992), 15.

93. Janet P. Near and Marcia P. Miceli, *The Whistle-Blowing Process and Its Outcomes: A Preliminary Model* (Columbus, OH: The Ohio State University, College of Administrative Science, Working Paper Series 83–55, September, 1983), 2. See also Miceli and Near, 15.

94. "Oracle Hit with Whistleblower Lawsuit over Cloud Accounting," Reuters (June 1, 2016), http://www.reuters.com/article/us-oracle-lawsuit-whistleblower-idUSKCN0YN604. Accessed June 5, 2016.

95. Ibid.

96. Janet P. Near and Marcia P. Miceli, " Whistleblowing—Myth and Reality," *Journal of Management* (1996 Special Issue), 507–526.

97. National Whistleblowers Legal Defense and Education Fund, "SEC Awards Company Outsider $700,000," http://www.whistleblowersblog.org/2016/01/articles/news/sec-awards-company-outsider-700000/. Accessed May 23, 2016.

98. Christina Rexrode and Timothy Martin, "Whistle-blowers Score Big," *The Wall Street Journal* (December 20/21, 2014), B1.

99. Christina Rexrode and Aruna Viswanatha, "Bank of America Tipster Gets to Keep His Reward," *The Wall Street Journal* (May 24, 2016), http://www.wsj.com/article_email/bank-of-america-tipster-gets-to-keep-his-reward-1464131120-lMyQjAxMTA2NjI1NTgyODU2Wj. Accessed June 4, 2016.

100. Mary Jane Wilmoth, "SEC Annual Report Highlights Success of International Whistleblower Program," *Whistleblowers Protection Blog*, http://www.whistleblowersblog.org/2015/11/articles/corporate-whistleblowers/sec-annual-report-highlights-success-of-international-whistleblower-program/. Accessed May 23, 2016.

101. "National Business Ethics Survey: Workplace Ethics in Transition," *Business Ethics Resource Center* (2012), www.ethics.org/nbes. Accessed May 22, 2016.

102. United States Department of Labor, "OSHA Regional News Release" (February 26, 2015), https://www.osha.gov/pls/oshaweb/owadisp.show_document?p_table=NEWS_RELEASES&p_id=27471. Accessed May 23, 2016.

103. Ibid.

104. Joann S. Lublin, "Watchdog Has Hard Time Hearing Whistles," *The Wall Street Journal* (October 17, 1980), 30.

105. Ana Radelat, "When Blowing the Whistle Ruins Your Life," *Public Citizen* (September/October 1991), 16–20.

106. Jon O. Shimabukuro and L. Paige Whitaker, "Whistleblower Protections under Federal Law: An Overview," Congressional Research Service (September 13, 2012), 1–21.

107. National Whistleblowers Legal Defense and Education Fund, "Obama Strengthens Key Corporate Whistleblower Protections" (May 11, 2016), http://www.whistleblowersblog.org/2016/05/articles/corporate-whistleblowers/obama-strengthens-key-corporate-whistleblower-protections/. Accessed May 23, 2016.

108. National Whistleblower Center, "Senate Judiciary Committee Unanimously Approves FBI Whistleblower Reform" (April 14, 2016), http://www.whistleblowers.org/press-room/in-the-news/1613-senate-judiciary-committee-unanimously-approves-fbi-whistleblower-reform. Accessed May 23, 2016.

109. Stephen M. Kohn, "Sarbanes-Oxley Act: Legal Protection for Corporate Whistleblowers," National Whistleblower Center, http://www.whistleblowers.org/index.php?option=com_content&task=view&id=27. Accessed May 19, 2016.

110. Alan F. Westin, "Michigan's Law to Protect the Whistle Blowers," *The Wall Street Journal* (April 13, 1981), 18. Also see Daniel P. Westman, *Whistleblowing: The Law of Retaliatory Discharge* (Washington, DC: The Bureau of National Affairs, 1991); Robert L. Brady, "Blowing the Whistle," *HR Focus* (February 1996), 20.

111. Todd Wilkinson, "After Eight Years, an Insider Gets His Reward," *Christian Science Monitor* (July 24, 2001), 1.

112. Michael W. Sculnick, "Disciplinary Whistle-Blowers," *Employment Relations Today* (Fall 1986), 194.

113. Miceli and Near, 247.

114. Andrew W. Singer, "The Whistle-Blower: Patriot or Bounty Hunter?" Across the Board (November 1992), 16–22.

115. Tax Payers against Fraud Education Fund, http://www.taf.org/resource/fca/faq#faq12. Accessed May 24, 2016.

116. Grover L. Porter, "Whistleblowers: A Rare Breed," *Strategic Finance* (August 2003), 51–53.

117. Kurt Eichenwald, "He Blew the Whistle, and Health Giants Quaked," *The New York Times* (October 18, 1998), 1.

118. Porter, 52.

119. Ibid., 53.

120. Ibid.

121. Ibid.

122. Donna Boehme, "3 Accidental Whistleblowers," The National Whistleblowers Legal Defense and Education Fund (August 3, 2015), http://www.whistleblowersblog.org/2015/08/articles/corporate-whistleblowers/3-accidental-whistleblowers-fired-for-doing-their-jobs-well/. Accessed May 24, 2016.

123. http://www.taf.org/node/455. Accessed May 19, 2016.

124. Ibid.

125. U.S. Department of Justice, "Justice Department Recovers Over $3.5 Billion from False Claims Act Cases in Fiscal Year 2015" (December 3, 2015), https://www.justice.gov/opa/pr/justice-department-recovers-over-35-billion-false-claims-act-cases-fiscal-year-2015. Accessed May 24, 2016.

126. Amy Gallo, "How to Speak Up about Ethical Issues at Work," *Harvard Business Review* (June 4, 2015), https://hbr.org/2015/06/how-to-speak-up-about-ethical-issues-at-work. Accessed June 4, 2016.

127. James R. Detert and Amy C. Edmondson, "Why Employees Are Afraid to Speak," *Harvard Business Review* (May 2007), 23–25.

128. Ibid., 24.

129. Ibid., 23–25.

130. Ibid.

131. Lynn Brewer, "Is There a Little Bit of Enron in All of Us?" *Journal for Quality & Participation* (Spring 2007), 26.

132. Ibid.

133. Ibid.

18

Employee Stakeholders: Privacy, Safety, and Health

CHAPTER LEARNING OUTCOMES

After studying this chapter, you should be able to:

1 Articulate the concerns surrounding the employee's right to privacy in the workplace.

2 Understand the issues surrounding workplace monitoring, including concerns with technology and the effects of being monitored.

3 Elaborate on the right to safety and health in the workplace, with particular reference to violence in the workplace, smoke-free workplaces, and family-friendly workplaces.

In this chapter, we extend the concept of employee rights and discuss employees' rights to privacy, safety, and a healthy work environment. As we discussed in Chapter 17, macro environmental and social issues like the growing number of part-time workers and the expectation of a 24/7 work environment has shifted the balance of power from employees to employers. Despite the continued U.S. economic recovery, a recent *Gallup Poll* found that 13 percent of employed adults in the United States think it is "very" or "fairly" likely that they will be laid off in the next year.[1] This is down from a heightened period of job concerns from 2010 to 2013, when 18 percent were worried about being laid off, but it is accompanied by some pessimism about the economy's direction, which has been mostly negative for several years, according to *Gallup's* Confidence Index.[2]

With concerns over job security, employees may be more hesitant to ask that their rights be respected because they fear losing their jobs and not finding another. One study estimates that 34 percent of employees in the United States do not speak up about their rights because of fear of retribution, including job loss.[3] Another study suggests that even in more open job environments that encourage anonymous feedback, employees worry that nothing will be done, so they withhold their ideas instead.[4]

In this chapter, we continue our consideration of social and ethical issues that have become important to employee stakeholders in recent years. If managers are to be successful in dealing with employees' needs and treating them fairly as stakeholders, they must address these concerns now and in the future. For example, the status of an employee's right to privacy in the workplace today is ill defined at best and particularly challenging with regard to workplace surveillance and the use of Big Data. Constitutional protection of privacy, such as the prohibition of unreasonable searches and seizures, applies only to the actions of government, not to those of private sector employers. From a legal standpoint, the meager amount of privacy protection that exists, as with so many employee rights, is a collection of diverse statutes, varying from issue to issue and from state to state. Hence, there is a genuine need for management groups to apply ethical thinking and standards to this increasingly important area.

Employee rights to safety and health are issues of growing intensity, too. In the United States alone, approximately 4,600 employees die from fatal injuries on the job each year, while nearly three million occupational injuries and illnesses are reported.[5] Across the world, there were 2.3 million people killed at work, 6,300 per day.[6] Today's workplace, whether in a manufacturing facility or in an office complex, can expose workers to a variety of hazards, risks of accidents, and occupational diseases. If normal workplace hazards were not enough, the phenomenon of violence is a serious threat to workplace peace and stability that requires managerial attention. Management should also be aware of the issues affecting employee health in the workplace, as well as the need for family-friendly workplaces and the legal rights employees have under the Family and Medical Leave Act (FMLA).

18.1 Privacy in the Workplace

If your workplace were in a private space behind partitions and you knew there was no one in the outer office, would you change into either gym clothes or formal evening attire at the end of the day? That is what administrative assistant Gail Nelson did, and then she subsequently found out that her employer had secretly videotaped her for months with no apparent justification for doing so.[7]

Nelson's supervisor and coworkers knew she sometimes changed clothes in her office cubicle, and this was an accepted practice in her office. Nelson was concerned about her privacy and so only did this when nobody was in the outer office. She ensured herself of this by listening carefully for the sound of approaching footsteps. The videotaping never revealed any illegal or unauthorized activity; nevertheless, her employer continued to do it. Furthermore, numerous employees at her workplace had viewed the videotapes. The incident became known only when a co-worker discovered it accidentally and informed her.[8] Even after appeal, the higher court upheld the legality of her employer's surveillance, saying that she did not have a reasonable expectation of privacy because other people were able to walk into the outer office.[9] Even though employees may not have legal rights to privacy in various circumstances, managers should understand that employees have some ethical expectations of privacy and that these expectations, whenever possible, should be honored as well.

Technological developments have made surveillance simpler and less expensive—not only in public places but also in the workplace. What was once only an option for large corporations now is available to practically every work environment, along with the ethical issues it brings. With this growth in workplace monitoring come new ethical considerations. **Privacy in the workplace** is in flux as the implications of new technological options are considered. At this stage, the private employee has few privacy rights in (and sometimes out of) the workplace. In the words of one privacy advocacy group, "Technology allows employers to monitor many aspects of their employees' workplace activities. While employees may feel that such monitoring is a violation of their privacy rights, many types of monitoring are allowed under the law.

A majority of employers monitor their employees. They are motivated by concern over litigation and the increasing role that electronic evidence plays in lawsuits and government agency investigations."[10] There are no clear legal definitions of what constitutes privacy or invasion of privacy, but everyone seems to have an opinion when one personally experiences such a situation. Most experts say that privacy means the right to keep personal affairs to oneself and to know how information about one is being used.[11] Business ethicist Patricia Werhane opts for a broader definition. She says that privacy includes (1) the right to be left alone, (2) the related right to autonomy, and (3) the claim of individuals and groups to determine for themselves when, how, and to what extent information about them is communicated to others.[12]

Defining privacy, however, does not settle the issue. In today's world, achieving these ideals is extremely difficult and fraught with judgment calls about our own privacy rights versus other people's rights. This problem is exacerbated by our increasingly computerized, technological world. We gain great efficiencies from computers and new technologies, but we also pay a price. Part of that price is that information about us is stored in dozens of places, including federal agencies (the Internal Revenue Service and the Social Security Administration), state agencies (courts and motor vehicle departments), and many local departments and businesses (school systems, credit bureaus, banks, life insurance companies, and direct-mail companies).

The circumstances for workplace surveillance have also created challenges around privacy rights. Some companies, worried about employee theft, have employed what one employee called a "digital sentinel" to track every movement, every resource, and patterns that might suggest employee theft.[13] Other companies, concerned with productivity, find that tracking movements and employee behaviors can lead to better solutions to increase sales.[14] Additionally, capturing such information on worker traits and behaviors can help to estimate how he or she will perform in the future, a technique called "predictive analytics."[15] Employee wellness firms and insurers are working with companies like Walmart to identify employees found to be at risk for a given condition, to predict their individual health needs and recommend treatments.[16]

As we discussed in Chapter 9, the use of technology and Big Data has tremendous ethical implications for society, and the movement shows no signs of abating. Tracking employees in particular is an expanding niche in the security industry, with at least 20 companies marketing software for tracking and analyzing employee behavior from e-mail habits to database access.[17]

ETHICS IN PRACTICE CASE

Employee Health and the Use of Big Data

Companies like Walmart and J.P. Morgan are more actively involving themselves in employee wellness. They are paying firms to collect and crunch employee data to identify employee health problems and guide them toward doctors or services like weight-loss programs. Although health-privacy laws do not give employers the authority to view workers' personal health information, they are able to get aggregated data on employees through wellness firms who have access to workers' health data. For example, Cigna Corporation analyzed claims data for J.P. Morgan to identify employees who lacked primary-care physicians.

Another company, Castlight, can identify segments of an employee population and tell an employer how many women are currently trying to have children through data that tracks women who have stopped filling birth-control prescriptions and/or who have made fertility-related searches on their app. While employees have to "opt in" to its services, some say that this option is hidden because it is linked to the use of a search function for in-network doctors and the ability to track health-care spending. Nevertheless, some employees see the benefit of being alerted to "at-risk" situations, like rising glucose levels that might indicate diabetes, or options to surgery for a given condition. In sum, the use of employee data to track employee health issues continues to be controversial.

1. What are the pros and cons of the use of employee data for health tracking?
2. Are you comfortable with the idea of employers using your data to predict your future? Is this an invasion of your privacy?
3. What, if any, health areas would you consider "off-limits" to employee wellness firms and employers?
4. Is there any potential conflict of interest between the wellness firms and employers?
5. Is there a utilitarian logic to the collection of health information (i.e., for the greater good)?

Sources: Rachel Emma Silverman, "Bosses Tap Big Data to Flag Workers' Ills," *The Wall Street Journal* (February 15, 2016), B1; Valentina Zarya, "Employers Are Quietly Using Big Data to Track Employee Pregnancies," *Fortune* (February 17, 2016), http://fortune.com/2016/02/17/castlight-pregnancy-data/. Accessed May 26, 2016; Aimee Picchi, "The 'Big Data' App That Predicts Employees' Health," CBS News (February 18, 2016), http://www.cbsnews.com/news/the-big-data-app-that-predicts-employees-health/. Accessed May 28, 2016; Erika Morphy, "It's Open Season on Employees' Health Data," *Forbes* (February 7, 2016), http://www.forbes.com/sites/erikamorphy/2016/02/07/its-open-season-on-employees-health-data/2/#5b19f06e1c70. Accessed May 20, 2016.

In the realm of employee privacy, the following four important issues stand out as representative of the major workplace privacy issues:

1. Collection and use of employee information
2. Integrity testing
3. Drug testing
4. Monitoring of employee work, behavior, conversations, and location by electronic means

Other issues also involve protection or invasion of privacy, but the four identified here account for the majority of today's concerns relative to employee stakeholders. Therefore, they merit separate consideration.

18.1a Collection and Use of Employee Information by Employers

The collection, use, and possible abuse of employee information are serious public policy issues that warrant scrutiny. Today's government databases, with various agencies mixing and matching data, form a cohesive web of information on individual citizens. In the United States, the **Privacy Act of 1974** set certain controls on the right of the government to collect, use, and share data about individuals. These restrictions were relaxed when the **USA Patriot Act** was signed into law in 2001 in response to the attack on the World Trade Center towers. Although many people express concern that the Patriot Act gives the government too much latitude, restrictions still remain on how the government can collect, use, and share personal data. In contrast, very few laws protect the privacy of individuals in the workplace as monitoring of employees in the workplace grows. Many privacy advocates say, "You check your privacy rights at the door when you enter the workplace."[18]

The necessity for guidelines regarding the collection of information became abundantly clear when the Equal Employment Opportunity Commission (EEOC) sued Burlington Northern Santa Fe Corporation for conducting secret genetic tests on workers who filed carpal tunnel syndrome claims. The tests came to light when one of the workers, Gary Avery, went to a mandatory medical exam as a follow-up to his successful carpal tunnel surgery. His wife, Janice, a registered nurse, became suspicious when he was asked to give seven vials of blood, more than would be needed for traditional tests. She later learned that the blood was for tests to determine whether her husband had a genetic trait that made him susceptible to the syndrome.[19] Burlington Northern ended up paying $2.2 million to settle the charges.[20]

Some companies claim that there are nobler intentions to the gathering of data than just an attempt to lower costs—particularly regarding health care. These include identifying health risks for workers, encouraging them to join weight-loss programs, and helping them find treatment. However, there are also risks in the safeguarding of consumer data, as hackers continue to raid data. The Identity Theft Resource Center noted that in the first month of 2016, 21 breaches of medical/health-care providers had occurred, compromising more than 1.1 million records.[21]

Background checks of both applicants and current employees have become a source of concern for privacy advocates. States vary in the latitude they allow employers when checking employee backgrounds, but most states, with the notable exception of California, give employers relatively free rein. Several jurisdictions—including California, Colorado, Connecticut, Delaware, Hawaii, Illinois, Maryland, Nevada, Oregon, Vermont and Washington, and now New York City—limit the use of credit history in employment decisions.[22] Some state and local laws also limit the use of criminal history in employment decisions. Hawaii, Illinois, Massachusetts, Minnesota, New Jersey, and Rhode Island, and approximately a dozen cities and localities, support "**ban-the-box**"—that is, banning the check box on employment applications asking whether the candidate has ever been convicted of a crime.[23] It is okay, however, for employers to inquire about criminal history (within limits) later in the hiring process.[24]

The overriding principle that should guide corporate decision making with regard to the collection and use of employee information is that companies should collect only necessary information from employees and use it only in ways that are appropriate. Companies should be careful not to misuse this information by employing it for purposes for which it was not intended. Employers have a duty to treat their employee's private information with care, not releasing it to others nor allowing it to become public through careless management. Employers also have a responsibility to allow employees to correct any inaccurate information.

The requirements of the **Fair Credit Reporting Act (FCRA)** as it pertains to employers are detailed in Figure 18-1. The Federal Trade Commission (FTC) is responsible for monitoring employer use of consumer reports in the United States. **Consumer reports** is the official term for employment background checks. They can include credit reports, criminal background reports, and other information from a range of sources. Two significant loopholes exist in the protections that allow employers to bypass the FCRA. First, employers can opt to do the background checks themselves instead of using outside providers. If so, the restrictions do not apply.[25] Second, the restrictions do not apply if an adverse employment decision was made for reasons other than the contents of the background check and so employers can bypass the requirements by citing different reasons.[26]

FIGURE 18-1 Consumer Reports Used for Employment

Employers in the United States may use consumer reports both to hire new employees and to evaluate current employees as long as they comply with the sections of the Fair Credit Reporting Act (FCRA). Consumer reports are prepared by consumer reporting agencies (CRAs), and they contain private information about not only credit characteristics but also personal characteristics such as the applicant's or employee's character, reputation, and lifestyle. The reports may include credit payment records, driving records, criminal histories, and even interviews with neighbors, friends, or any associates. The FCRA covers only reports prepared by agencies. For example, if the employer checks references directly, the FCRA does not apply; however, verification by an employment or reference-checking agency is covered. The following are the key provisions as written by the Federal Trade Commission (FTC) to employers.

Key Provisions of the FCRA Amendments

Written Notice and Authorization. Before you can get a consumer report for employment purposes, you must notify the individual in writing—in a document consisting solely of this notice—that a report may be used. You also must get the person's written authorization before you ask a CRA for the report—and special procedures apply to the trucking industry.

Adverse Action Procedures. If you rely on a consumer report for an "adverse action"—denying a job application, reassigning or terminating an employee, or denying a promotion—be aware of the following:

Step 1: *Before* you take the adverse action, you must give the individual a pre-adverse action disclosure that includes a copy of the individual's consumer report and a copy of "A Summary of Your Rights Under the Fair Credit Reporting Act"—a document prescribed by the FTC. The CRA that furnishes the individual's report will give you the summary of consumer rights.

Step 2: *After* you have taken an adverse action, you must give the individual notice—orally, in writing, or electronically—that the action has been taken in an adverse action notice. It must include:

- The name, address, and phone number of the CRA that supplied the report;
- A statement that the CRA that supplied the report did not make the decision to take the adverse action and cannot give specific reasons for it; and
- A notice of the individual's right to dispute the accuracy or completeness of any information the agency furnished, and his or her right to an additional free consumer report from the agency upon request within 60 days.

Certifications to Consumer Reporting Agencies. Before giving you an individual's consumer report, the CRA will require you to certify that you are in compliance with the FCRA and that you will not misuse any information in the report in violation of federal or state equal employment opportunity laws or regulations.

Source: Federal Trade Commission, "Using Consumer Reports: What Employers Need to Know," https://www.ftc.gov/tips-advice/business-center/guidance/using-consumer-reports-what-employers-need-know. Accessed June 1, 2016.

Another problem is that the FCRA does not cover the interview process and so an employer can obtain some information by simply asking. For example, a background check may not contain information on an arrest that happened more than seven years earlier. However, nothing prevents an employer from asking the employee, verbally or in writing, "Have you *ever* been arrested?"[27] In addition, if a background check is inaccurate, the employee affected can dispute its contents; however, an employer is not obligated to act upon a corrected report and reinstate a job offer.[28] Finally, the FCRA does not apply when salaries are $75,000 or more.[29] It is important to note that this discussion refers to federal laws. Some states, such as California, have instituted protections that go beyond the federal requirements.

There is no doubt that the details behind the FCRA make it challenging for businesses and employees alike. Companies like Whole Foods, Dollar General, Publix, and Panera have all been sued over their use of background checks. Most often, the "clear and conspicuous" contingency is the problem. This means that the notice of a background check must stand out from the rest of the job application.[30] In October 2014, Dollar General agreed to pay $4 million to settle claims that it did not properly notify more than 200,000 applicants of background checks.[31]

The **Equal Employment Opportunity Commission (EEOC)** monitors employer use of background checks too, stepping in when discriminatory practices are thought to have occurred. Two background check practices have caused the most problems for the EEOC and, by extension, the employers who are brought into court: (1) blanket no-hire policies based on criminal records or negative credit scores and (2) lack of a correlation between the information from the background check and the actual job for which the person would have been hired.[32]

Although there are still few guidelines for the collection of information in most professions, the health-care industry has developed stronger guidelines for the way that collected information is handled in general, and those guidelines cover the use of medical information in employment. Medical information supplied to employers must be relevant to the job and requires the applicant's specific written consent.[33] An employer may require a pre-employment physical, but the Americans with Disabilities Act (ADA) requires that the physical exam be requested only *after* a job offer. The act requires employers to protect the confidentiality of applicant and employee medical information, while also making it illegal to base employment decisions on a medical condition that does not affect the employee's ability to perform the essential functions of the job. We will discuss the ADA in more detail in Chapter 19.

Background screening has become a big part of business decision making. The Society for Human Resource Management (SHRM) has been surveying employers about background checks and they find that over the last five years, fewer employers are using them, particularly as ban-the-box legislation grows at the state and local levels.[34] Even with this downward trend, employee screening is a big and very profitable business.[35] Screening often goes beyond the checking of public records to include interviews with friends and associates, some of which may be disgruntled; the resulting information can contain errors or even outright lies.[36] According to industry veteran Lester Rosen, commenting on employment screening, "Essentially, it's the Wild, Wild West. It's an unregulated industry with easy money and not a huge emphasis on compliance or on hiring quality people to do the screening."[37]

The U.S. federal government is beginning to make moves toward shoring up screening practices. In 2012, the EEOC issued guidance regarding the use of criminal background checks in hiring. People with criminal backgrounds are not a protected class, that is, federal anti-discrimination laws do not protect them. However, minorities account for a disproportionate percentage of the jail population and so the EEOC is concerned that criminal background checks will have a disparate impact on minority applicants.[38] In one of the first cases filed by the EEOC following its updated guidance, a federal court in South Carolina approved a settlement in which BMW Manufacturing agreed to pay $1.6 million and offer jobs to aggrieved African American former employees and applicants. The EEOC argued that BMW's prior screening for arrest and conviction records disproportionately screened out African Americans from employment.[39]

The EEOC guidance asks employers to make an individualized assessment of each case, considering the following three factors:[40]

1. The nature and seriousness of the offense,
2. How long ago the offense occurred, and
3. The nature of the job.

Businesses have expressed multiple concerns regarding the EEOC's guidance. They cite studies that show that businesses are actually less likely to hire minority applicants when background checks are banned.[41] The biggest problem for businesses is that they are conflicted because they are still subject to EEOC lawsuits if they require background checks in circumstances where state law requires that the firm not hire someone with a felony conviction.[42] One law group recommends that employers carefully review their background screening policies to ensure that their requirements are job related and consistent with business necessity, and be prepared to demonstrate the existence of a legitimate business reason that justifies the policy should it result in a disproportionate disqualification of minority applicants.[43]

18.1b Integrity Testing

Integrity testing, sometimes referred to as honesty testing, is another area in which employee privacy issues need careful consideration. Early efforts to judge a person's integrity focused on uncovering a lack of integrity, such as might be evidenced when a person lies. The notion of a "lie detector," historians tell us, is nothing new. The Bedouins of Arabia knew that certain physiological changes, triggered by guilt and fear, occurred when a person lied. The outstanding change they observed was that a liar would stop salivating. They developed a simple test in which a heated blade was passed across the tongue of a suspected liar. If innocent, the suspect would be salivating normally and the tongue would not be burned; if the person were lying, the tongue would be scorched. The ancient Chinese used dry rice powder. Someone suspected of lying was forced to keep a handful of rice powder in the mouth. If the powder was soggy when spat out, the person was telling the truth; if it was dry, the person was lying.[44]

In the invasion-of-privacy arena, one of the most controversial issues has been the use of the **polygraph**, or lie detector, in business. The polygraph machine measures changes in blood pressure, respiration, and perspiration, sometimes called *galvanic skin response*. The theory behind polygraphy is that the act of lying causes stress, which in turn is manifested by observable physiological changes. The examiner, or machine operator, then interprets the subject's physiological responses to specific questions and makes inferences about whether or not the subject's answers indicate deception.[45]

The **Employee Polygraph Protection Act (EPPA)** of 1988 banned most uses in the private sector of the lie detector, but it can still be used by private employers that provide security services, protection of nuclear facilities, shipment or storage of radioactive or toxic waste, public water supply facilities, public transportation, precious commodities, or propriety information. In addition, employers that manufacture, distribute, or dispense controlled substances may use polygraph tests for some of their positions.

Government employers are also exempt from the prohibitions on polygraph testing. The federal government may also use polygraph tests for private consultants or experts under contract to various government departments, agencies, or bureaus.[46] In 2010, the polygraph requirement was expanded to U.S. Customs and Border Protection.[47] It is noteworthy that Aldrich Ames, an American CIA agent, turned KGB mole, wrote from the prison that he passed the polygraph test with flying colors while selling U.S. secrets to Russia.[48]

The issue of lie detection is unlikely to diminish as new technologies are created. Research is progressing on the use of magnetic resonance imaging (MRI) brain scans to separate truth from fiction.[49] Some scientists are developing a more robust "full body motion" technique for detecting deception from body movement.[50] Other scientists are exploring the use of computers to analyze speech pattern and determine if someone is telling the truth.[51] Still others believe that Google Glass, Google's wearable computer with a head-mounted display, may be able to incorporate an advanced digital lie detector.[52] When these or other new technologies for lie detection develop, new protections for employees will be needed to address them. For now, the ability to detect lies through technology remains an elusive goal.[53]

Many companies now use question-and-answer **integrity tests** (also known as *honesty tests*), which are a specific type of **personality test**. Integrity tests receive the same kinds of criticisms that led to severe restriction of lie detector testing. However, faced with the elimination of the polygraph and the unavailability of a trustworthy technology option, integrity tests seemed to be a convenient alternative. In fact, the Society for Industrial and Organizational Psychology cites more advantages than disadvantages to the administration of such tests.[54] Critics of integrity tests claim they are intrusive and invade privacy by the nature of their inquiries. Some critics also say that they are unreliable and that employers use them as the sole measure of the fitness of an applicant. Even when these tests are properly administered, opponents charge that employers end up rejecting many honest applicants in their efforts to screen out the dishonest ones.

Management and testing companies claim the tests are very useful in weeding out potentially dishonest applicants, particularly when they are combined with cognitive ability assessments.[55] They claim that each question asked has a specific purpose. They also argue that hiring by "gut feeling" is problematic, and integrity tests provide a more objective assessment.[56] In fact, the U.S. Office of Personnel Management endorses integrity/honesty tests as valid measures of overall job performance.[57]

There is some evidence that integrity tests provide useful information. According to one security consultant, a major U.S. retailer used integrity tests in 600 of their 1,900 locations to reduce turnover and shrinkage.[58] After one year, they saw inventory shrinkage fall by more than 35 percent in the stores that used the test, while it rose by 10 percent in the stores that did not. Even though turnover was not a goal of the test administration, they noted a 13 percent decrease in turnover at stores that did use the test and a 14 percent increase in turnover at stores that did not.[59] A large hotel chain found that integrity testing reduced worker's compensation claims significantly, more than compensating for the costs of test administration.[60]

Integrity tests are subject to the same kinds of legal hurdles and ethical considerations that affect polygraph and drug tests. The Civil Rights Act (discussed in Chapter 19) makes it unlawful for any test to have a particularly negative impact on a protected subgroup. From the ADA perspective, medical examinations can be given only after a conditional offer of employment has been made. The EEOC has ruled that integrity tests are not medical examinations, and so they can be given to applicants.[61] Most states apply the federal laws to selection tools. However, Massachusetts and Rhode Island have extended the polygraph statutes to integrity tests, so there are limits on how they can be used in employment decisions.[62]

Companies are increasingly turning to the use of broader personality tests, of which the integrity test is a specific form: Personality tests cover areas such as conscientiousness, sociability, introversion, extraversion, emotional stability, maturity, and openness to new ideas.[63] They are widely used by companies like Amtrak, which hires about 2,300 new workers nationally each year.[64] Some experts estimate that as many of 60 percent of all workers are being asked to take personality assessments, either in the selection process or for career development.[65] The wide use of personality tests is raising new concerns about employment discrimination and, as a result, the EEOC has reported that it plans to pay more attention to them in the future.[66]

Even when legal issues surrounding integrity and personality tests are resolved, ethical issues are likely to remain. A test that will identify many of those who would behave unethically at a cost to the firm will also yield "false positives," people labeled as unethical who would have been good, honest employees. In statistics, this is called a **type 1 error**, finding an innocent person to be guilty. In contrast, a **type 2 error** finds a guilty person to be innocent. The nature of testing is such that an effort to decrease one type of error will lead to an increase in the other. In other words, the more strictly a test is used to rule out any person who would be guilty of unethical behavior, the greater is the chance that innocent people will be judged unethical. One human resource expert suggests the following attributes of strong personality assessments:[67]

1. They measure stable traits that will not change once the candidate has been working for some length of time.
2. They are normative in nature, which allows you to compare one candidate's scores against another.
3. They have a "candidness" or "lie detector" scale so you understand how likely it is that the results accurately portray the test-taker.
4. They have high reliability and have been shown to be valid predictors of job performance.

It is important, therefore, that integrity tests be used judiciously and that they not be the primary criterion on which employment is based.

ETHICS IN PRACTICE CASE

Co-Workers versus Friendship

I worked in retail for a handful of years, and during that time, I have made great lifelong friends. Because I am a hardworking, committed employee, my boss/owner took notice and she promoted me to manager at age 17. My fifth year working at the store, we hired a new employee, Lindsey, and we instantly became great friends. We became so close that we were hanging outside of work, and Lindsey introduced me to her group of friends. My new group of friends and I became super close, where I would see them every day.

Lindsey had a lot of health problems, and she would frequently call out sick. Being a manager, I had to take responsibility and cover her shifts, even though I would have other obligations. I requested the Fourth of July weekend off to go to my lake house with my family. At the last minute, however, Lindsey called out sick, and I received a phone call from my boss begging me to cover her shifts, which I did.

On July 3, my friend Rob invited me to come over to his family BBQ, because he knew I was missing my family BBQ. He told me all of our friends would be there as well, so I planned to head over there after I got out of work. I worked ten hours that day, I was exhausted, but I wanted to see my friends. I pulled up to his house, and I saw Lindsey's car there, I was extremely confused because Lindsey called out sick for the whole weekend, so why was she there?

Lindsey did not seem the least bit sick; in fact, she was socializing and having the time of her life. I could not believe Lindsey just put me in this horrible position—I missed my family vacation because she did not "feel" like working that weekend. If I ratted her out, I would lose the new friends with whom I had become extremely close. As her manager, should I tell my boss that Lindsey was faking it, even though we are friends outside of work? Where does the line end between friends and employees?

1. What are the ethical issues in this case?
2. Should I have just gone on my family vacation and not have covered the shift?
3. Should I report Lindsey's behavior? Is there some other action I should take?
4. How should I deal with Lindsey in the future?

Contributed by Madeline Meibauer

18.1c Drug Testing

Drug testing is an umbrella term intended to embrace drug and alcohol testing and employer testing for any suspected substance abuse. The issue of drug testing in the workplace has many of the same characteristics as the lie detector and integrity testing issues. Companies say they need to do such testing to protect themselves and the public, but opponents claim that drug tests are not accurate and invade the employee's privacy. Concerns about drug testing include the implications for employee privacy, the inaccuracy of tests, and the impact of drug testing on employee morale. If management desires to create a favorable workplace for employee stakeholders, they should pay close attention to the legalities and ethics of drug testing, which could be perceived as privacy invasions by their employees if not judiciously used.

Quest Diagnostics, a major provider of employment-related drug-testing services, releases an annual index that shows a recent spike in positive drug tests, reversing a trend in decades' long decline in the abuse of illicit drugs in the U.S. workforce.[68] From 2013 to 2015, the positivity rate for approximately 6.6 million urine drug tests in the general U.S. workforce increased overall by 9.3 percent, to 4.7 percent in 2014.[69] Marijuana continues to have the highest positivity rates and that trend is likely to continue. Various state marijuana legalization developments have created a confusing situation for companies, as we noted in Chapter 11.

The U.S. Drug Enforcement Administration continues to consider marijuana to be a Schedule 1 controlled substance, but the Department of Justice is reviewing the states that have legalized marijuana and is reviewing recommendations on how to monitor the effects of state legislation.[70] However, Quest researchers found that marijuana positivity increased at about the same rate in Colorado and Washington, two states with recreational marijuana-use laws, as the rest of the United States in 2014.[71] As the issue of state versus federal law about marijuana use continues to evolve, companies will have to sort out how best to respond to the continuous shifts in the legal landscape.

Arguments for Drug Testing. Proponents of drug testing argue that the costs of drug abuse on the job are staggering. The consequences range from accidents and injuries to theft, bad decisions, and ruined lives. The greatest concern is in industries where mistakes can cost lives—for example, the railroad, airline, aerospace, nuclear power, and hazardous equipment and chemicals industries. Thus, the primary ethical argument for employers conducting drug tests is the responsibility they have to their own employees and to the general public to provide safe workplaces, secure asset protection, and safe places in which to transact business. This is an example of the trade-offs that are often at the core of ethical decisions, as we noted in Chapter 8. In this case, drug testing places the employee's right to privacy against everyone else's right to safety.

Arguments against Drug Testing. Opponents of drug testing see it as both a due-process issue and an invasion-of-privacy issue. The due-process issue relates to the sometimes-questionable accuracy of drug tests. Common foods and medications can lead to a false positive, giving the appearance of drug use when the person being tested is innocent. This can create a downward spiral for that employee, causing reputational damage, lost income, and considerable expense to try to rebut the allegation of drug use.[72]

Beyond the rights issues of drug testing, many employers are finding it a difficult hurdle in hiring because they cannot find enough workers to pass a drug test, particularly in areas that enjoy low-to-moderate unemployment levels.[73] With one in 10 Americans age 12 or older reporting in 2014 that they had used drugs within the last month, employers are facing some real challenges in hiring drug-free workers.[74]

Many legitimate questions arise in the drug-testing issue. Do employers have a right to know if their employees use drugs off the job? Are employees performing on the job satisfactorily? Obviously, a delicate balance is necessary, because employers and employees alike have legitimate interests that must be protected. If companies are going to engage in some form of drug testing, they should think carefully about developing policies that not only will achieve their intended goals but also will be fair to the employees and will minimize invasions of privacy. Such a balance will not be easy to achieve but must be sought. To do otherwise will guarantee decreased employee morale, more and more lawsuits, and new government regulations.

Guidelines for Drug Testing. If management perceives the need to conduct a drug-testing program to protect other stakeholders, it should carefully design and structure the program so that it will be minimally intrusive of employees' privacy rights. Guidelines have been developed by the American College of Occupational and Environmental Medicine (ACOEM) to reflect the ethical aspects of drug testing. These are included in Figure 18-2.[75]

State and Federal Legislation. Some states and cities have enacted laws or are considering doing so to restrict workplace drug testing. Generally, these laws restrict the scope of testing by private and public employers and establish privacy protections and procedural safeguards. Some states do not completely ban drug testing but restrict the circumstances (e.g., for reasonable cause) under which it may be used. They may also restrict drug testing to reasonable suspicion and place limits on the disciplinary actions

FIGURE 18-2 Guidelines for Drug Testing

Guidelines for drug testing shift over time, and so exceptions to these might be considered and/or new guidelines may develop. The major point is that management needs to think through its policies and their consequences very carefully when designing and conducting drug-testing programs. The following are suggested guidelines from the American College of Occupational and Environmental Medicine (ACOEM):

1. Companies should have written policies and procedures, which should be applied impartially.
2. Companies should provide clear documentation of the reason for conducting drug testing (e.g., employee safety, public safety, security).
3. Any employees or applicants who will be affected should be informed in advance of the company's drug use, misuse, and testing policies, as well as their right to refuse to be tested and the consequences of refusal.
4. If testing is conducted on an unannounced and random basis, employees should be made aware of the special safety or security needs that justify this procedure.
5. All tests should be done in a uniform and impartial manner.
6. A licensed physician (MD/DO) should supervise the collection, transportation, and analysis of the specimens, as well as the reporting of results. Stringent legal, technical, and ethical requirements should be observed when reporting results.
7. A licensed and appropriately qualified physician should be designated as the medical review officer (MRO) and should evaluate positive results before a report is made to the employer.
8. An employee or applicant who tests positive should be informed of the positive results by the physician and should have the opportunity to explain and discuss the results before the employer is notified. The procedure for this should be clearly outlined.
9. Any report to the employer should provide only the information needed for work placement purposes or as required by government regulations. The employer should not be told of the specific types or levels of drug found unless required by law. A trained and qualified physician should make that report.

Source: ACOEM, "Ethical Aspects of Drug Testing" (February 4, 2009), https://www.acoem.org/EthicalAspectsOfDrugTesting.aspx. Accessed May 28, 2016.

employers may take. Other states provide discounts on worker's compensation and/or incentives of another kind to organizations that implement drug testing. This patchwork of incongruous state laws complicates drug testing for employers.

At the federal level, the **Americans with Disabilities Act (ADA)** must be considered, because the definition of disability applies to drug and alcohol addiction. The ADA prohibits companies from giving applicants medical exams before they extend those applicants' conditional offers of employment. Pre-hire drug tests, however, are permitted. Philadelphia employment lawyer Jonathan Segal advises employers to extend conditional offers before drug testing, because an innocent question on a drug test could easily become a medical question. He recommends conducting the drug test immediately after making the conditional offer and then waiting before beginning employment until the test results are back.[76] Employers would also be well advised to use physicians who are trained to review drug test results to evaluate claims of false positive readings.[77]

Employee Assistance Programs. One of the most significant strategies undertaken by corporate America to deal with the growing alcohol- and drug-abuse problem in the workplace has been **Employee Assistance Programs (EAPs)**. EAPs extend into a variety of employee problem areas such as compulsive gambling, financial stress, emotional stress, marital difficulties, aging, legal problems, AIDS, and other psychological, emotional, and social difficulties. The term **broad brush EAP** describes this comprehensive model.[78] A recent major concern of EAPs has been to integrate them into the company's general health management strategy so that it can become a core strategic component.[79]

EAPs represent a positive and proactive step companies can take to deal with these serious problems. EAPs are designed to be confidential and nonpunitive, and they affirm three important propositions: (1) employees are valuable members of the organization, (2) it is better to help troubled employees than to discipline or discharge them, and (3) recovered employees are better employees. Recent attention has been given to the successes of EAP programs—often in industries where you might least expect it. For example, the construction industry has become industry leaders in mental health awareness and the use of EAPs after the realization that the industry had high risks of suicide, with seasonal unemployment, long hours, and exhaustion.[80] It is encouraging that in an era when employees are increasingly exerting their workplace rights, enlightened companies are offering EAPs in an effort to help solve their mutual problems. More information on EAPs can be found at the Employee Assistance Professionals Association Web site, http://www.eap-association.org.[81]

18.1d Workplace Monitoring

In the old days, supervisors monitored employees' work activities by peeking over their shoulders and judging how things were going. Technology changed all that as cameras and listening devices gave way to computers and satellites as options for employee monitoring. Privacy advocates are concerned about the use of technology to gather information about workers on the job and with good reason. In its most recent survey, the American Management Association (AMA) found that the vast majority of mid- to large-sized firms participate in some type of **employee monitoring**.

In some cases, the method is passive, such as installing video cameras in a lobby. However, most companies use active methods of monitoring their workers, such as recording their phone calls or voice mail, reading their computer files, monitoring e-mail or Web access, and videotaping them. Employer monitoring of employees has

ETHICS IN PRACTICE CASE

Amazon: Using the Digital Bulletin Board to Shame Employees into Good Behavior

Amazon is a company with warehouses full of small, valuable items and a workforce that has relatively high turnover. In an effort to curb theft, Amazon has put up flatscreen TVs that display examples of alleged on-the-job theft, including silhouettes of employees stamped with the words "terminated" or "arrested" with details about how they stole, how much they stole, and how they got caught. In addition, Amazon is reported to display information about firings related to workplace violence, and "cheerier" announcements about updates on incentive bonuses and holidays. In warehouses without flatscreens, firings are posted on sheets of paper on a bulletin board or taped to the wall.

Some have accused Amazon of having "two faces," with a customer-focused, revolutionizing e-commerce platform on one side and a tougher, internal-focused workplace with punishing hours and stressful conditions on the other side. However, nobody disputes that loss prevention is a persistent concern for Amazon, and extra vigilance may be required, as a result.

1. There is nothing illegal with Amazon's method of broadcasting bad behavior. Is it unethical or unadvisable? Why?
2. How would you feel about this as an employee of Amazon?
3. Are you more comfortable with broadcasts about theft than violence in the workforce? Are there any other employee behaviors that should or should not be broadcast this way?

Sources: Josh Eidelson, "Amazon's Story Time Is Kind of a Bummer," *Bloomberg Businessweek* (March 14, 2016), 40–41; BBC News, "Amazon Uses Shock Tactic to Stop Thefts at Warehouses," http://www.bbc.com/news/technology-35763908. Accessed May 26, 2016; Emily Jane Fox, "Amazon Reportedly Has Scorecards to Shame Its Workers," *Vanity Fair* (March 8, 2016), http://www.vanityfair.com/news/2016/03/amazon-warehouse-theft. Accessed May 26, 2016.

become the norm in businesses today. The consequence is that millions of workers are laboring under the relentless gaze of electronic supervision. For example, as noted in the above Ethics in Practice Case, Amazon uses digital bulletin boards and videotapes to shame workers fired for alleged theft and to warn other employees to behave.

What Can Be Monitored? According to the most recent American Management Association survey, 78 percent of employers monitor their employees' Internet visits in order to prevent inappropriate surfing and 63 percent block Internet site connections they consider to be off-limits. The sites of concern to employers include adult sites, games, social networking, entertainment, shopping and auctions, sports, and external blogs.

E-mail is monitored by 47 percent of companies, with more than a quarter of companies surveyed firing employees for misusing office e-mail or the Internet, and 65 percent of companies surveyed disciplining workers for such practices.[82] However, the debate surrounding monitoring employees' social media continues as advocates say that it can help companies protect themselves, while dissenters believe that companies should monitor only when there is a solid reason to suspect employee wrongdoing.[83] However, according to one survey of over 2,000 human resource managers, more than half of their employers are using social networking sites to research job applicants.[84] The reasons why employers are doing this include looking for support of the applicant's qualifications, as well as looking for reasons *not* to hire the candidate.[85]

As was discussed in Chapter 9, the introduction of new technologies creates new opportunities for surveillance by employers. For example, the advent of global positioning system (GPS) technology has made it possible to monitor worker location and movement patterns. Of course, the advent of technology works both ways. Webcams and phone cams can possibly serve as a tool that employees can use to monitor their employers. Some companies have moved to ban them from the workplace due to fear of corporate espionage.[86]

The problems with camera spying really came to light in 2014 when a school in suburban Philadelphia provided 2,300 MacBooks to their students and installed spy software on them that snapped pictures of the students at home, in bed, and sometimes partially clothed, leading to a lawsuit and settlement that paid two students $610,000.[87] What emerged is that while it is perfectly legal to sell spy software, it is illegal to use it without permission outside of the workplace, or in this case, the school setting. However, it is legal for parents to use it to spy on their minor children, although this "permission" is also fraught with difficulty, given that other people may be monitored in the course of monitoring one's own children.[88]

The only federal level of privacy protection in the United States is the **Electronic Communication Privacy Act (ECPA)** of 1986. The interception or unauthorized access of a wire, oral, or electronic communication where there is a reasonable expectation of privacy is illegal under this act unless it is covered by one of the statutory exceptions or required by government compulsion. One of the statutory exceptions is the business use exception: The act does not apply if the interception or access occurs as part of the "ordinary course of business." It also does not apply if the person gives consent. An employee working for a company that has disclosed that it will monitor its employees is considered to have given implicit consent.

With these broad exceptions, it is not surprising that the ECPA has been ineffective in regulating the monitoring of employees in the workplace.[89] The one clear protection for employees is that employers may not listen to purely personal phone conversations; however, they can monitor a conversation for the time required to determine that the call is personal.[90] States have tried to enact laws to strengthen workplace privacy but with limited success, resulting in a patchwork of state laws.[91]

Efforts to enact a U.S. law specifically geared toward workplace privacy have always been stymied. However, recent court cases may have implications for workplace privacy in the future. One of the key issues is the phrase "reasonable expectation of privacy." In one case, the New Jersey Supreme Court ruled in favor of an employee whose company read e-mails that she sent to her attorney using her personal, password-protected, Yahoo e-mail account on the company's computer.[92] The court unanimously found that the use of a password that she did not save on the employer's hard drive, as well as the attorney client privilege, gave her a reasonable expectation of privacy.[93] The Justices further noted that the company's e-mail policy said, "Occasional personal use is permitted."[94] In another case, the Federal Appeals Court ruled against one man when he tried to get the content of workplace e-mails exchanged between him and his wife rendered inadmissible due to spousal privilege.[95] The court ruled that by not taking steps to protect the e-mails' privacy, he had waived the marital privilege and thus had no reasonable expectation of privacy.[96]

The workplace privacy issue creates dilemmas that are not easily resolved. At this writing, nearly half of the states have enacted laws that protect employee privacy by prohibiting employers from demanding that employees provide them with Facebook and other social media usernames and passwords, and other states are considering similar bills.[97] While this is a positive move in terms of employee privacy, the increased privacy may come at a price. According to the Financial Industry Regulatory Authority (FINRA), these laws may conflict with security rules, thereby decreasing investor protection and increasing the risk of securities fraud.[98] To date, efforts to reconcile the two concerns have not been successful.

Effects of Being Monitored. Invasion of privacy is one major consequence of employee monitoring. Another is potential unfair treatment. Employees working under

ETHICS IN PRACTICE CASE

Sick Day Snoops

In their "Working in America: Absent Workforce" study, Kronos Inc. found that nearly 40 percent of employees have taken sick days when they are not actually sick, and 61 percent of the respondents said their work did not get done when they were absent. In an effort to curb the resultant losses, some businesses are hiring detectives to spy on employees who have called in sick but might be playing hooky. Investigators are looking to determine if the illness or injury actually exists and, if it does, whether it is serious enough to justify the absence.

Rick Raymond is a private detective who has taken on a variety of these cases. He tracked one woman to a Theme Park where they take rider pictures as they round a sharp turn. He bought the pictures as proof she was there. He has tracked others to bowling alleys, pro football games, and weddings. He estimates that about 80 to 85 percent of the people he is hired to follow end up being guilty.

1. The courts have ruled that this practice is legal. Is it ethical?
2. Should limits be placed on the use of private detectives in following employees when they are outside of the office? Explain what these might be.
3. How would you react if your boss had you followed?
4. If you were an employer or a manager, would you hire a private detective to follow one of your employees?

Sources: "Working in America: Absent Workforce," *Kronos*, http://www.workforceinstitute.org/wp-content/themes/revolution/docs/Working-in-Amer-Survey.pdf. Accessed May 20, 2016; Thomas Chan, "Employers and Insurers Hire Private Eyes to Probe Sick Leave Scams," *South China Morning Post* (May 2, 2013), http://www.scmp.com/news/hong-kong/article/1227821/employers-and-insurers-call-private-investigators-root-out-sick-leave. Accessed May 20, 2016; Eric Spitznagel, "The Sick Day Bounty Hunters," *Bloomberg Businessweek* (December 8–December 12, 2010), 93–95.

such systems complain about stress and tension resulting from their being expected and pressured to be more productive now that their efforts can be observed. The pressure of being constantly monitored is also producing low morale and a sense of job insecurity in many places. Employees have good reason to be concerned. Companies are now going so far as to install productivity-monitoring software to analyze the time workers spend creating reports and downloading files versus scrolling through Facebook or searching for vacation rentals during work hours.[99] Hence, one technology research firm estimates that the $200 million industry will more than double to $500 million in the next four years.[100]

18.1e Policy Guidelines on the Issue of Privacy

During our discussion of various privacy issues, we have indicated steps that management might consider taking in an attempt to be responsive to employee stakeholders and to treat them fairly. Frederick S. Lane III, a law and technology expert and author of *The Naked Employee: How Technology Is Compromising Workplace Privacy*, offers an "Employee Privacy Bill of Rights" that sets forth guidelines for developing privacy policies and procedures that uphold the dignity of the employee.[101] He maintains that to preserve employee rights, firms should:

1. Obtain informed consent from employees and applicants before acquiring information about them
2. Disclose the nature of any surveillance that will occur
3. Set controls so as to avoid casual and unauthorized spread of information
4. Limit the collection and use of medical and health data to that which is relevant to the job
5. Require reasonable suspicion before doing drug tests
6. Respect and preserve the boundary between work and home

Business's concern for protection of the privacy of its employees, customers, and other stakeholders is increasing. It is not surprising, therefore, that a new form of corporate executive came on the horizon. As we discussed in Chapter 9, **chief privacy officers (CPOs)** are high-ranking executives responsible for monitoring and protecting the private information held by firms. They differ from security personnel in that they determine what data should be protected while the security department determines how it will be protected. The CPO is responsible for ensuring that the privacy of individuals is respected.

18.2 Workplace Safety

Workers Memorial Day is sponsored by the U.S. union organization, the AFL-CIO, and it is observed every year on April 28 to honor those workers who have died on the job. That date is the anniversary of the Occupational Safety and Health Administration and the Federal Coal Mine Health and Safety Act. Sadly, every 15 seconds around the world, a worker dies from a work-related incident or disease.[102] In the United States, workplace fatalities have hit their highest levels since 2008, with over 4,600 fatal worker injuries in 2014.[103] Fatality rates particularly increased in construction, agriculture, manufacturing, and mining.[104]

The primary law that protects the safety and health of workers in the United States is the Occupational Safety and Health Act. This act requires the Secretary of Labor to set safety and health standards that protect employees and their families. Every private employer who engages in interstate commerce is subject to the regulations promulgated under this act.[105] The federal agency responsible for overseeing the safety and health of America's workers is the **Occupational Safety and Health Administration (OSHA)**. Figure 18-3 provides OSHA's list of employer responsibilities for safeguarding employee health and safety.

We will begin by examining the workplace safety problem and the right-to-know laws that have evolved from it. We will look at the issue of workplace violence, which is a serious concern in today's workplace. Then, we will turn to the issue of smoking in the workplace and end with a discussion of the family-friendly workplace.

FIGURE 18-3 OSHA's List of Employer Responsibilities

Employers have the responsibility to provide a safe workplace. Employers *must* provide their employees with a workplace that does not have serious hazards and follow all relevant OSHA safety and health standards. Employers must find and correct safety and health problems. OSHA further requires employers to try to eliminate or reduce hazards first by making changes in working conditions rather than just relying on masks, gloves, earplugs, or other types of personal protective equipment. Switching to safer chemicals, implementing processes to trap harmful fumes, and using ventilation systems to clean the air are examples of effective ways to get rid of or minimize risks. Employers must also:

- Inform employees about chemical hazards through training, labels, alarms, color-coded systems, chemical information sheets, and other methods;
- Keep accurate records of work-related injuries and illnesses;
- Perform tests in the workplace, such as air sampling, required by some OSHA standards;
- Provide hearing exams or other medical tests required by OSHA standards;
- Post OSHA citations, injury and illness data, and the OSHA poster in the workplace where workers will see them;
- Notify OSHA within eight hours of a workplace incident in which there is a death or when three or more workers go to a hospital; and
- Not discriminate or retaliate against workers for using their rights under the law.

Source: "We Are OSHA We Can Help," *OSHA*, http://www.osha.gov/Publications/3334we-can-help-sm.pdf. Accessed May 31, 2016.

18.2a The Workplace Safety Problem

Two events stand out as forerunners of the workplace safety problem. The first ranks among the landmark cases on job safety. In Elk Grove Village, Illinois, Film Recovery Systems operated out of a single plant that extracted silver from used hospital x-ray and photographic film. To extract the silver, the employees first had to dump the film into open vats of sodium cyanide and then transfer the leached remnants to another tank. Employee Stefan Golab staggered outside and collapsed, unconscious. Efforts to revive him failed, and he was soon pronounced dead from what the local medical examiner labeled "acute cyanide toxicity."[106]

An intensive investigation by attorneys in Cook County, Illinois, revealed a long list of incriminating details: (1) Film Recovery workers seldom wore even the most rudimentary safety equipment, (2) workers were laboring in what amounted to an industrial gas chamber, and (3) company executives played down the dangers of cyanide poisoning and removed labeling that identified it as poisonous. The prosecutors took action under an Illinois homicide statute that targets anyone who knowingly commits acts that "create a strong probability of death or serious bodily harm."

Three executives at Film Recovery Systems—the president, the plant manager, and the foreman—were convicted of the murder of Stefan Golab and were sentenced to 25 years in prison. This marked the first ever conviction of managers for homicide in a corporate matter such as an industrial accident.[107] The Film Recovery Systems case marked a new era in managerial responsibility for job safety. Other prosecutions of managers have followed this case. What this clearly signals is not only that employees have a legal and moral right to a safe working environment but also that managers can face prosecution if they do not ensure that employees are protected.

The second forerunner event, which we also discussed in Chapter 10, was the dramatic and catastrophic poisonous gas leak at the Union Carbide plant in Bhopal, India. The death toll topped 2,000, and tens of thousands more were injured. People around the globe were startled and shocked at what the results of one major industrial accident could be. Lawsuits sought damages that quickly exceeded the net worth of the company.[108] As we noted in Chapter 10, more than 30 years after the disaster, survivors of the accident and their supporters continue to push for damages for unmet medical bills

SPOTLIGHT *on Sustainability*

It's All Connected

Workplace safety is not always mentioned in discussions of business sustainability, but that is beginning to change. Sustainability initiatives encompass environmental, social, and economic considerations—and safety hinges on all three. The lean and green movement combines eliminating waste with respecting people and the environment. For example, a recent study of ergonomics discovered that the muscle pain and stress experienced by workers in one department of the company stemmed from root causes in another department. Furthermore, factors that were the source of the muscle pain had also affected employees in still other departments.

Sustainability's focus on system-wide thinking lends itself to seeing the connections in complex systems and recognizing the resulting interactions and their consequences. However, employee safety and health have received relatively little attention in the sustainability movement, and so the Center for Safety and Health Sustainability launched in June 2011 with the purpose of bringing safety and health into the discussion and practice of sustainability.

Sources: Ash M. Genaidy, Reynold Sequeira, Magda M. Rinder, and Amal D. A-Rehim, "Determinants of Business Sustainability: An Ergonomics Perspective," *Ergonomics* (March 2009), 273–301; Michael A. Taubitz, "Lean, Green, and Safe," *Professional Safety* (May 2010), 39; Center for Safety and Health Sustainability, http://centershs.org/index.php. Accessed May 30, 2016.

and toxic cleanup. Together, the Film Recovery and Bhopal incidents foreshadowed the need to take steps to protect worker health and safety.

18.2b Workplace Safety Today

It is almost unbelievable that we still have to be concerned about workplace safety with all of the protections that employers must provide for their employees. However, an examination of OSHA reports reveals that many accidents are deemed "preventable workplace tragedies."[109] These include such incidences as the strangulation death of a bowling center mechanic working on an automatic bowling pinsetter, the crushing of an auto parts worker inside a stamping machine and the fatal fall of a construction worker on a building site.[110] Mark Twain once said, "It is better to be careful 100 times than to get killed once." One safety group cites this quote and provides the following seven most common causes of workplace accidents:[111]

1. Shortcuts
2. Overconfidence
3. Poor, or Lack of Housekeeping
4. Starting a Task Before Getting All Necessary Information
5. Neglecting Safety Procedures
6. Mental Distractions
7. Lack of Preparation

Beyond a legal obligation, it is an employer's duty and obligation to provide a safe work environment, free of any conditions or activities that might cause harm. Each of these seven causes is preventable, and so it is the obligation of businesses to provide training and development to ensure the safety of its employees.

18.2c Right-to-Know Laws

Prompted by the Union Carbide tragedy in Bhopal and other, less dramatic industrial accidents, workers have demanded to know more about the thousands of chemicals and hazardous substances they are being exposed to daily in the workplace. Experts argue that employers have a duty to provide employees with information on the hazards of workplace chemicals and to make sure that workers understand what the information means in practical terms.

To address this concern, many states have passed **right-to-know laws** and expanded public access to this kind of information by employees and even communities. Although the states took the initiative on the right-to-know front, OSHA followed suit by creating a Hazard Communication Standard that preempted state regulations. This standard requires covered employers to identify hazardous chemicals in their workplaces and to provide employees with specified forms of information on such substances and their hazards. Specifically, manufacturers, whether they are chemical manufacturers or users of chemicals, must take certain steps to achieve compliance with the standard.[112] These steps include the following:

1. Update inventories of hazardous chemicals present in the workplace.
2. Assemble material safety data sheets (MSDSs) for all hazardous chemicals.
3. Ensure that all containers and hazardous chemicals are properly labeled.
4. Provide workers with training on the use of hazardous chemicals.
5. Prepare and maintain a written description of the company's hazard communication program.
6. Consider any problems with trade secrets that may be raised by the standard's disclosure requirements.
7. Review state requirements for hazard disclosure.

Of course, despite such right-to-know laws, companies have been known to withhold information from employees. In Chapters 6 and 15, we discussed the issue of high concentrations of the toxin PFOA, used for manufacturing Teflon by DuPont, and its impact on the health of residents in communities near its manufacturing facilities. However, in the 1970's, DuPont discovered that there were high concentrations of PFOA in the blood of factory workers at their Washington Works facility and they did not tell their workers this.[113] In 1981, their PFOA supplier, 3M, found that the ingestion of the chemical caused birth defects in rats, prompting DuPont to test the children of pregnant employees in their Teflon division. Even after noting that out of seven employee births, two children had eye defects, they did not make the information public.[114]

Employees have certain workplace rights with respect to safety and health on the job that OSHA provides by law. As in our discussion of the public policy exceptions to the employment-at-will doctrine in the preceding chapter, it should be clear that workers have a right to seek safety and health on the job without fear of punishment or recrimination.

18.2d Workplace Violence

Another issue that has become a major problem and is posing challenges to management is escalating violence in the workplace. **Workplace violence** is one of the four leading causes of death in the workplace and the leading cause of death for women.[115] It falls into two categories: (1) violence from an outside source and (2) violence stemming from coworkers. Workplace violence from co-workers cuts across all industries, while certain industries have a greater likelihood of workplace violence from the general public.[116] Most recently, issues of Uber and Lyft drivers being assaulted have highlighted the violence that employees of ride sharing services are subject to, and the limitations of the protections afforded to them because they are considered to be independent contractors.[117]

In the United States, nearly two million workers report that they are victims of workplace violence each year, and many more victims never report it.[118] The leading cause of death for women in the workplace is homicide.[119] Overall, companies are making few

ETHICS IN PRACTICE CASE

When External Stakeholders Attack

Both customers and employees are primary stakeholders and so when one begins to attack the other, stakeholder management becomes even more challenging. The problem of customer violence is real and appears to be growing. Although workplace homicides in the United States have declined in general, one form of workplace homicide is on the rise—assaults on employees by customers. The number is relatively low in terms of overall workplace fatalities, but the upward trend is a concern. In a recent survey of workplace violence, the Institute of Finance and Management (IOFM) found that 61 percent of the 307 organizations surveyed believe that abuse of employees by customers has become significantly worse in the past year. Sometimes the abuse is simply verbal but other times it can result in serious injury and sometimes death.

1. Business cannot refer a customer to an EAP as it can with an employee. It also is not possible to screen and select, much less train, customers as one does for employees. What can a business do to protect its employees from violent customers?
2. Why is customer violence on the increase? Is it the fault of the customer, the organization, and/or society?
3. What do you recommend that managers do to stem this growing problem?

Sources: http://www.bls.gov/iif/oshwc/cfoi/work_hom.pdf. Accessed May 21, 2016. "The Customer Isn't Always Right," *Security Director's Report* (June 2013), 1–11. "Master Guide to Workplace Violence," *IOFM* (2013), http://www.iofm.com/research/view/master-guide-to-workplace-violence (cited in *Security Director's Report*, 2013). Accessed May 21, 2016; James Alan Fox, "When Disgruntled Customers Kill," *The Boston Globe* (August 26, 2011), http://boston.com/community/blogs/crime_punishment/2011/08/when_disgruntled_customers_kil.html. Accessed May 21, 2016.

efforts to address it. Despite the seriousness of this issue, nearly 70 percent of workplaces do not have a formal program that addresses workplace violence.[120]

The problem of workplace violence shows no sign of abating. Experts note that a variety of factors promote continued violence including an overall greater tolerance for violence, easily available weapons, economic stress, a difficult job market, and insufficient support systems.[121] In the United States, gun law battles are complicating an already difficult situation. Businesses have historically been able to keep guns out of the workplace with a posted sign, but gun advocates have been testing that in the courts.[122]

Additionally, 44 states have passed open-carry laws that allow residents with a concealed handgun license to openly carry a gun in a belt or shoulder holster without a new license or additional training.[123] As is often the case, companies cannot satisfy all stakeholders on this issue. Companies like Starbucks, Target, Chipotle, Panera Bread, Chili's, and Sonic have asked customers to refrain from bringing their guns into their stores.[124] Kroger, on the other hand, supports the open carry because they claim to have never had any problems with it.[125]

Who Is Affected? Although no workplace is immune from workplace violence, some workers are at increased risk of workplace violence from the general public. According to OSHA, the workers who are more likely to experience workplace violence include:[126]

- Workers who exchange money with the public
- Workers who deliver passengers, goods, or services
- Workers who work alone or in small groups
- Workers who work late at night or very early in the morning
- Workers who work in community settings and homes where they have extensive contact with the public
- Workers who work in high-crime areas

The workers who are direct targets of the violence are not the only people affected. Not only are the family and friends of the victims impacted, but also those employees in the workplace who escaped the violence also experience long-term effects. These survivors often spend years dealing with the after-effects.[127] Many fear returning to work and some never do. They will often play the event over in their minds, unable to forget what happened. Victoria Spang is a marketing director who hid in the personnel office when a client of her law firm came in with assault weapons, killing eight people and wounding six. "No one ever forgets. You'd walk by people's cubicles, and they would keep pictures of the victims up. It's a moment in life you'll always remember."[128]

Corporate image can also suffer long-term effects from worker rage. The term *going postal* is a thorn in the side of the U.S. Postal Service. It became part of the urban slang lexicon after a series of post office shootings. The phrase continues even after a study commissioned by the post office found that postal workers are no more likely to commit violence than employees in other professions are.[129] In fact, workplace violence can occur in the most unexpected locations. Quiet Huntsville, Alabama, was shocked when a biology professor shot three of her colleagues due to a dispute over her denial of tenure. University spokesperson Ray Garner commented, "This is a very safe campus.... This town is not accustomed to shootings and having multiple dead."[130]

Prevention. The federal Occupational Safety and Health Act (OSHA) has a "general duty clause" that mandates employers to provide safe workplaces; however, it does not set forth specific standards or requirements addressing violence and has stated it will not try to regulate "random antisocial acts."[131] OSHA will apply the general duty clause to determine whether the violent act arose from events that should have been

FIGURE 18-4 OSHA's Recommendations for Preventing Workplace Violence

The best protection employers can offer is to establish a zero-tolerance policy toward workplace violence against or by their employees. The employer should establish a workplace violence prevention program or incorporate the information into an existing accident prevention program, employee handbook, or manual of standard operating procedures. It is critical to ensure that all employees know the policy and understand that all claims of workplace violence will be investigated and remedied promptly. In addition, employers can offer additional protections such as the following:

1. Provide safety education for employees so they know what conduct is not acceptable, what to do if they witness or are subjected to workplace violence, and how to protect themselves.
2. Secure the workplace. Where appropriate to the business, install video surveillance, extra lighting, and alarm systems and minimize access by outsiders through identification badges, electronic keys, and guards.
3. Provide drop safes to limit the amount of cash on hand. Keep a minimal amount of cash in registers during evenings and late-night hours.
4. Equip field staff with cellular phones and hand-held alarms or noise devices, and require them to prepare a daily work plan and keep a contact person informed of their location throughout the day. Keep employer-provided vehicles properly maintained.
5. Instruct employees not to enter any location where they feel unsafe. Introduce a "buddy system" or provide an escort service or police assistance in potentially dangerous situations or at night.
6. Develop policies and procedures covering visits by home health-care providers. Address the conduct of home visits, the presence of others in the home during visits, and the worker's right to refuse to provide services in a clearly hazardous situation.

Source: "What Can These Employers Do to Help Protect These Employees," *Workplace Violence OSHA Fact Sheet*. http://www.osha.gov/OshDoc/data_General_Facts/factsheet-workplace-violence.pdf. Accessed May 20, 2016.

foreseen by the company. Specifically, the company will be liable when (1) the employer neglected to keep the workplace free from a hazard, (2) the hazard was one that is generally recognized by the employer or the industry, (3) the hazard was already causing or was likely to cause serious harm, and (4) elimination or removal of the hazard was feasible.[132]

Management has both the legal and moral duty to address the problem of workplace violence. Companies have barely begun to put meaningful safety measures into place, but such measures will become more important in the future. Programs that deal with crises, and long-range efforts to bring about safer workplace environments, will be essential. Figure 18-4 lists OSHA's recommendations for what employers can do to protect their employees from workplace violence. Beyond this, there are a number of different recommended actions companies may take to anticipate and prevent workplace violence before it occurs.[133]

18.3 Health in the Workplace

As the public has become more health conscious in recent decades, it is not surprising that companies in the United States have become much more sensitive about health issues. While 81 percent of employers with 200 or more workers that offer health insurance also offer weight loss, smoking cessation, or lifestyle coaching programs, the results are mixed.[134] For example, roughly four out of five large employers in the United States now offer some sort of financial incentive to employees to improve their health.[135] However, workers who are promised lower health insurance premiums in the long run do not seem to lose the weight.[136] Rather, research has shown that the incentives need to be large, unbundled from the insurance premium, and offered in increments to keep employees motivated.[137]

Smoking has been a controversial issue related to health in the workplace and so it merits special attention. Like other issues we have examined, smoking in the workplace has employee rights, privacy, and due-process ramifications.

18.3a Smoking in the Workplace

Most states regulate smoking in the workplace to some degree, but there is no federal law that governs smoking at work. The issue of **smoking in the workplace** began in the 1980s in the United States. The idea that smoking ought to be curtailed or restricted in the workplace is a direct result of the growing antismoking sentiment in society in general. Much of the antismoking sentiment crystallized when U.S. Surgeon General C. Everett Koop called for a smoke-free society. He proclaimed that smokers were hurting not only themselves but also the nonsmoking people around them, who were being harmed by secondary, or passive, smoke in the air they breathed. Koop argued that the evidence "clearly documents that nonsmokers are placed at increased risks for developing disease as the result of exposure to environmental tobacco smoke."[138] To substantiate his point, he noted that a National Academy of Science study estimated that in one year, passive smoke was responsible for 2,400 lung cancer deaths in the United States.[139]

Evidence of the need to control smoking in the workplace continues to mount. The U.S. Environmental Protection Agency (EPA) classifies secondhand smoke involuntarily inhaled by nonsmokers from other people's cigarettes as a known human carcinogen: secondhand smoke is responsible for approximately 3,000 lung cancer deaths and an average of 46,000 heart disease deaths in adult nonsmokers annually in the United States.[140] The World Health Organization calls secondhand smoke a health hazard that kills and declares that every individual has the right to breathe smoke-free air.[141] Worldwide, comprehensive national smoke-free laws protect only 7 percent of people, but the number of people protected is increasing each year.[142]

Research has also demonstrated that allowing smoking in the workplace has several strong disadvantages that relate to health and safety that management's need to consider. Among these are:[143]

- Higher rates of absenteeism among smoking employees
- Shortened equipment life
- Higher cleaning and maintenance costs
- Higher health, life and property insurance costs
- Loss of worktime due to smoking activities
- More fires and other accidents
- Difficulty hiring employees who are sensitive to smoke

It is not surprising, therefore, that many companies have adopted smoke-free workplace programs and are continuing to do so. Not only are the programs an increased protection for all employees, but the employers receive many benefits as well.[144]

18.3b The Family-Friendly Workplace

One of the most notable trends among employers for making the workplace a more desirable and healthy venue is the movement toward family friendliness. Employees are increasingly less willing to spend every waking hour at work and are more committed to having time to spend at home with family. However, despite an increase in family-friendly policies at businesses, the pressure of a round-the-clock work culture has taken its toll on the workforce. One study shows that Americans work an average 1,836 hours a year, up 9 percent from the hours worked in 1979.[145]

Another study labeled the United States as a "no-vacation nation" as the U.S. workforce, despite steady gains in productivity, has given up a full week of vacation over the years to their employer, with no associated wage growth.[146] Perhaps more disturbing is that family-friendly policies like flexible work schedules and allowing people to work from home seem to impact low-wage and higher-wage workers differently, as well as men and women. For low-wage earners, the problem is not too many hours but too few, in addition to a lack of parental leave.[147] For high-wage earners, the challenge is that long hours have become a "status symbol" and women are looked down on for working the hours necessary to succeed.[148]

Despite the challenges of a 24/7 workplace culture, companies are searching for more and more ways to help employees achieve **work–life balance**, which is defined as "a state of equilibrium where the demands of a person's personal and professional life are equal."[149] For example, *Working Mother Magazine* released its annual 100 Best Companies list by choosing the best employers based on flexibility, paid time off, advancement, and child care.[150] IBM and Johnson & Johnson are the only two companies to make the list every year since its inception.

The 2015 Society for Human Resource Management (SHRM) Employee Benefits Survey showed that companies are endeavoring to maintain **family-friendly** benefits while striving to reduce costs. However, the survey reflected a five-year decline in the percentage of firms permitting employees to bring their child to work in an emergency, offering child care referral services, and on-site parenting seminars.[151] Additionally, the percentage of firms offering family-friendly benefits remained static.[152] Some of the most popular family-friendly benefits and the percentage of firms offering them are:

1. Dependent care flexible spending accounts 66%
2. Bring a child to work in an emergency 22%
3. On-site mother's room 35%
4. Child care referral service 9%
5. Domestic partner benefits for same-sex partners 17%

Although not everyone thinks that companies are becoming as family friendly as they are claiming to be, it is clear that workers are talking more and more about the importance of family-friendly policies, and many leading companies are responding. Even through the economic slump, many companies continued to offer family-friendly environments, and these have become an important part of "best places to work" surveys, which have become popular in recent years. Directly and indirectly, family-friendly workplaces positively contribute to the physical and mental health of employees.

It is in the context of organizations becoming more "friendly" on their own that we want to discuss a law aimed at health-related issues in the workplace—the FMLA. The FMLA is important to the health and well-being of employees because it helps employees to take care of their families and health situations while still maintaining their job and career.

Family and Medical Leave Act. The **Family and Medical Leave Act (FMLA)** was made into law in 1993. This act was designed to make life easier for employees with family or health problems. In 2010, the law was expanded to include employees with family members on active military duty.[153] The new amendments extend "qualifying exigency leave" protections to families of active duty service members deployed abroad so that the families can have time to manage the service member's personal affairs while she or he is on active duty. In addition, family members who provide care for injured veterans can receive 26 weeks of leave.[154] Other changes to the FMLA include a revised definition of "spouse" in 2015 to include same-sex married couples in all 50 states.[155] Figure 18-5 provides details about the rights that the FMLA grants employees.

A study by the Department of Labor showed that the corporate views on the FMLA are mixed—generally positive but with some issues that merit concern. The good news is

FIGURE 18-5 The Family Medical Leave Act

The Family Medical Leave Act (FMLA) entitles eligible employees of covered employers to take unpaid, job-protected leave for specified family and medical reasons.

- An employee may take up to 12 weeks of unpaid leave in any 12-month period for the birth or adoption of a child or for the care of a child, spouse, or parent with a serious health condition that limits the employee's performance.
- Employees must be reinstated in their old jobs or be given equivalent jobs upon returning to work; the employer does not have to allow employees to accrue seniority or other benefits during the leave periods.
- Employers must provide employees with health benefits during leave periods.
- Employees are protected from retaliation in the same way as under other employment laws; an employee cannot be discriminated against for complaining to other people (even the newspapers) about an employer's family leave policy.

Employers also have rights under the FMLA. These rights include the following:

- Companies with fewer than 50 workers are exempt.
- Employers may demand that employees obtain medical opinions and certifications regarding their needs for leave and may require second or third opinions.
- Employers do not have to pay employees during leave periods, but they must continue health benefits.
- If an employee and a spouse are employed at the same firm and are entitled to leave, the total leave for both may be limited to 12 weeks.

Source: The U.S. Department of Labor, "Family Medical Leave Act," https://www.dol.gov/whd/fmla/. Accessed June 2, 2016.

that the law seems to work well when employees take up to 12 weeks of unpaid leave for a close relative's sickness or the birth or adoption of a child. Problems arise when employees take unscheduled intermittent leave. In addition, defining a *serious medical condition* has been a challenge.[156]

In summary, the FMLA has not been the major problem that many envisioned, and it has accomplished much good for employees' psychological health. However, clarifying terminology is important if it is to continue to provide workers with the opportunity to fulfill their family responsibilities without sacrificing their careers. Efforts to pass additional family-friendly workplace legislation continue, but in an environment of global recession, it is doubtful that major changes will occur in the near future. Efforts to streamline and clarify the FMLA are more likely to influence the direction corporate policies will take.

Summary

Critical employee stakeholder issues include the rights to and expectations of privacy, safety, and health. These issues should be seen as extensions of the issues and rights outlined in Chapter 17.

With the development of new technologies, workplace privacy has increasingly become a serious issue. The wealth of available technology presents new challenges for companies as they weigh the importance of knowing their workers' activities against the importance of maintaining trust and morale. Of equal, if not more, importance to employee stakeholders are the issues of workplace safety and health. The workplace safety problem, when it was more fully realized, led to the creation of OSHA.

OSHA is the federal government's major instrument for protecting workers on the job. State-promulgated right-to-know laws, as well as federal statutes, have been passed in recent years to provide employees with an added measure of protection, especially against harmful effects of exposure to chemicals and toxic substances, as happened with the DuPont PFOA disaster. However, existing laws and regulations deal only with known problems. As the world changes, so do the threats to worker health and safety. Unexpected or undetected threats to workers' health and safety are certain to occur and will represent new challenges for managers. Socially responsible companies will strive to move beyond what is being required by law and to do what is right and fair for their employee stakeholders.

The new 24/7 workplace culture poses additional challenges to maintaining work–life balance, even in the midst of family-friendly policies. Other major health issues in the current business–employee relationship are smoking and workplace violence. Smoking in the workplace raises issues of employee rights, those of both smokers and nonsmokers. Violence in the workplace is exacting a heavy toll, and businesses must be responsive. The need for employees to take family leave also impacts the work environment. Wise managers will develop policies for dealing with these issues, as well as their privacy and due-process implications.

Key Terms

Americans with Disabilities Act (ADA), p. 562
background checks, p. 554
ban-the-box, p. 554
broad brush EAP, p. 562
chief privacy officers (CPOs), p. 566
consumer reports, p. 555
drug testing, p. 560
Electronic Communication Privacy Act (ECPA) of 1986, p. 564
Employee Assistance Programs (EAPs), p. 562
employee monitoring, p. 562
Employee Polygraph Protection Act (EPPA), p. 557
Equal Employment Opportunity Commission (EEOC), p. 556
Fair Credit Reporting Act (FCRA), p. 555
Family and Medical Leave Act (FMLA), p. 573
family-friendly, p. 573
integrity tests, p. 558
Occupational Safety and Health Administration (OSHA), p. 566
Personality tests, p. 559
polygraph, p. 557
Privacy Act of 1974, p. 554
privacy in the workplace, p. 552
right-to-know laws, p. 568
smoking in the workplace, p. 572
type 1 error, p. 559
type 2 error, p. 559
USA Patriot Act, p. 554
work–life balance, p. 573
workplace violence, p. 569

Discussion Questions

1. In your own words, describe what privacy means and what privacy protection companies should give employees.
2. Enumerate the strengths and weaknesses of the polygraph as a management tool for decision making. What polygraph uses are legitimate? What uses of the polygraph are illegitimate?
3. What are the two major arguments for and against integrity (honesty) testing by employers? Under what circumstances could management most legitimately argue that integrity testing is necessary?
4. How has technology affected workplace privacy? What are the implications for the social contract between firms and their employees?
5. How has the World Trade Center tragedy affected workplace privacy? What are the long-term implications of that?
6. Which two of the six policy guidelines on the issue of privacy presented in this chapter do you think are the most important? Why?
7. Identify the privacy, health, and due-process ramifications of violence in the workplace.

Endnotes

1. *Gallup Poll*, "U.S. Workers' Job-Loss Fears Back to Pre-Recession Levels" (April 23, 2015) http://www.gallup.com/poll/182840/workers-job-loss-fears-back-pre-recession-levels.aspx. Accessed May 26, 2016.
2. *Gallup Poll*, "U.S. Economic Confidence Index Remains Steady at -4" (March 30, 2016), http://www.gallup.com/poll/182189/economic-confidence-index-remains-steady.aspx?utm_source=economic%20confidence&utm_medium=search&utm_campaign=tiles. Accessed May 26, 2016.
3. Paul Warner, "DecisionWise Benchmark Study," https://www.decision-wise.com/decisionwise-benchmark-study/?cat=all. Accessed May 26, 2016.
4. James Detert and Ethan Burris, "Can Your Employees Really Speak Freely?" *Harvard Business Review* (January–February 2016), https://hbr.org/2016/01/can-your-employees-really-speak-freely. Accessed May 26, 2016.

5. U.S. Department of Labor, Bureau of Labors Statistics (June 3, 2016), http://www.bls.gov/home.htm. Accessed May 20, 2016.
6. Center for Safety and Health Sustainability, http://centershs.org/index.php. Accessed May 20, 2016.
7. "NWI Surveillance Bill Enacted—Additional Efforts Underway," *Workrights News* (Fall-Winter 2005/2006).
8. Ibid.
9. Electronic Privacy Information Center, "Nelson v. Salem State College" (May 4, 2006), http://www.epic.org/privacy/nelson/. Accessed May 29, 2016.
10. Privacy Rights Clearinghouse, https://www.privacyrights.org/workplace-privacy-and-employee-monitoring. Accessed May 26, 2016.
11. "Big Brother, Inc., May Be Closer than You Think," *Businessweek* (February 9, 1987), 84.
12. Patricia H. Werhane, *Persons, Rights, and Corporations* (Englewood Cliffs, NJ: Prentice Hall, 1985), 118.
13. Steve Lohr, "Unblinking Eyes Track Employees," *The New York Times* (June 22, 2014), 1.
14. Ibid.
15. Rodd Wagner, "How Your Boss Could Be Spying on You," USA Today (January 12, 2016), 7A.
16. Rachel Emma Silverman, "Bosses Harness Big Data to Predict Which Workers Might Get Sick," *The Wall Street Journal* (February 16, 2016), http://www.wsj.com/articles/bosses-harness-big-data-to-predict-which-workers-might-get-sick-1455664940. Accessed May 29, 2016.
17. Dune Lawrence, "Tracking the Enemy Within," *Bloomberg Businessweek* (March 16–22, 2015), 39–41.
18. Privacy Rights Clearinghouse, "Privacy Today: A Review" (May 5, 2016), http://www.privacyrights.org/ar/Privacy-IssuesList.htm#D. Accessed May 29, 2016.
19. Steve Bates, "Science Friction," *HR Magazine* (July 2001), 34–44.
20. Joanne Wojcik, "Wired into Workplace Privacy," *Business Insurance* (September 15, 2003), 28.
21. Erika Morphy, "It's Open Season on Employees' Health Data," *Forbes* (February 17, 2016), http://www.forbes.com/sites/erikamorphy/2016/02/07/its-open-season-on-employees-health-data/3/#7e3cdd1f21c0. Accessed May 28, 2016.
22. Joel Greenwald, "Legal Issues with Background Checks," *Forbes* (July 10, 2015), http://www.forbes.com/sites/entrepreneursorganization/2015/07/10/legal-issues-with-background-checks/#93691337e69c. Accessed May 28, 2016.
23. Ibid.
24. Ibid.
25. Privacy Rights Clearinghouse, "Fact Sheet 16: Employment Background Checks" https://www.privacyrights.org/topics/2 (updated May 2016). Accessed May 22, 2016.
26. Ibid.
27. Ibid.
28. Ibid.
29. Ibid.
30. Claire Zillman, "Why Whole Foods, Dollar General, and Panera Have All Been Sued over a Tiny Hiring Technicality," *Fortune* (January 16, 2015), http://fortune.com/2015/01/16/whole-foods-dollar-general-panera-hiring-lawsuit/. Accessed May 28, 2016.
31. Ibid.
32. Jim Giuliana, "Recruiting: EEOC Warns about Background Checks," *HR Morning* (January 6, 2010), http://www.hrmorning.com/recruiting-eeoc-warns-aboutbackground-checks/. Accessed May 22, 2016.
33. Privacy Rights Clearinghouse, 2016.
34. Roy Maurer, "Know before You Hire: 2015 Employment Screening Trends," *SHRM* (January 27, 2015), https://www.shrm.org/hrdisciplines/staffingmanagement/articles/pages/2015-employment-screening-trends.aspx. Accessed May 29, 2016.
35. Chad Terhune, "The Trouble with Background Checks," *Businessweek* (June 9, 2008), 54–57.
36. Ibid.
37. Ibid., 56.
38. Judy Greenwald, "Background check policies under review by employers." *Business Insurance 46*, no. 43 (November 5, 2012), 11.
39. Rachel Burke, "The Use of Background Checks to Make Employment Decisions Is Not without Peril," Employer Law Report (October 14, 2015), http://www.employerlawreport.com/2015/10/articles/eeo/the-use-of-criminal-background-checks-to-make-employment-decisions-is-not-without-peril/. Accessed May 20, 2016.
40. Privacy Rights Clearinghouse, 2016.
41. James R. Bovard, "Perform Criminal Background Checks at Your Peril," *The Wall Street Journal* (February 13, 2013), A15.
42. Ibid.
43. Burke, 2015.
44. Kenneth F. Englade, "The Business of the Polygraph," *Across the Board* (October 1982), 21–22.
45. James H. Coil III and Barbara Jo Call, "Congress Targets Employers' Use of Polygraphs," *Employment Relations Today* (Spring 1986), 23.
46. David E. Terpstra, R. Bryan Kethley, Richard T. Foley, and Wanthanee Limpaphayom, "The Nature of Litigation Surrounding Five Screening Devices," *Public Personnel Management* (Spring 2000), 43–54.
47. Martin Kaste, "Trial of Polygraph Critic Renews Debate over Tests' Accuracy," South Carolina Public Radio (January 2, 2015), http://www.npr.org/2015/01/02/371925732/trial-of-polygraph-critic-renews-debate-over-tests-accuracy. Accessed May 29, 2016.

48. Diana Ray, "Can They Fool the Polygraph?" *Insight* (July 2–9, 2001), 18–19.

49. Shalisa Ladd and Jeff L. Berry, "The Potential Role of fMRI in Lie Detection," eRadimaging (January 1, 2013), http://www.eradimaging.com/site/article.cfm?ID=792. Accessed May 20, 2013.

50. Ewn MacAskill, "British and Dutch Researchers Develop New Form of Lie-Detector Test," *The Guardian* (January 4, 2015), https://www.theguardian.com/science/2015/jan/04/british-dutch-researchers-new-form-lie-detector-test-polygraph. Accessed May 30, 2016.

51. Anne Eisenberg, "Software That Listens for Lies," *The New York Times* (December 3, 2011).

52. James Hirsen, "Privacy Concerns over Google Glass," *Newsmax* (March 18, 2013), http://www.newsmax.com/Hirsen/Privacy-Google-Glass-software/2013/03/18/id/495158. Accessed May 20, 2013.

53. Nick Barron, "Honest to Goodness," *SC Magazine: For IT Security Professionals* (June/July 2009), 17.

54. Society for Industrial and Organizational Society, http://www.siop.org/workplace/employment%20testing/testtypes.aspx. Accessed May 28, 2016.

55. Dori Meinert, "What Do Personality Tests Really Reveal?" *Society for Human Resource Management*, (June 1, 2015), https://www.shrm.org/publications/hrmagazine/editorialcontent/2015/0615/pages/0615-personality-tests.aspx. Accessed May 29, 2016.

56. Gregory M. Lousig-Nont, "Seven Deadly Hiring Mistakes," *Supervision* (April 2003), 18–19.

57. U.S. Office of Personnel Management, https://www.opm.gov/policy-data-oversight/assessment-and-selection/other-assessment-methods/integrityhonesty-tests/. Accessed May 28, 2016.

58. Crimcheck, "Employment Integrity, Personality and Job Skill Testing," https://crimcheck.net/resources/employment-integrity-personality-and-job-skill-testing. Accessed June 4, 2016.

59. David W. Arnold and John W. Jones, "Who the Devil's Applying Now?" *Security Management* (March 2002), 85–88.

60. Michael Sturman and David Sherwyn, "The Utility of Integrity Testing for Reducing Worker's Compensation Costs," *Cornell Hospital Quarterly* (November 2009), 432–445.

61. Larry R. Seegull and Emily J. Caputo, "When a Test Turns into a Trial," *ABA Business Law Section* (January/February, 2006), http://apps.americanbar.org/buslaw/blt/2006-01-02/caputo.html. Accessed May 29, 2016.

62. FindLaw, "Personality Testing in Employment," http://corporate.findlaw.com/human-resources/personality-testing-in-employment.html. Accessed May 29, 2016.

63. Bill Roberts, "Your Cheating Heart," *SHRM HR Magazine* (June 1, 2011), https://www.shrm.org/publications/hrmagazine/editorialcontent/2011/0611/pages/0611roberts.aspx. Accessed May 29, 2016.

64. Meinert, 2015.

65. Ibid.

66. Joseph Walker, "Do New Job Tests Foster Bias?," *The Wall Street Journal - Eastern Edition*, September 20, 2012, B2.

67. Whitney Martin, "The Problem with Using Personality Tests for Hiring," *Harvard Business Review* (August 27, 2014), https://hbr.org/2014/08/the-problem-with-using-personality-tests-for-hiring. Accessed May 28, 2016.

68. Quest Diagnostics, "Illicit Drug Positivity Rate Increases Sharply in Workplace Testing" (June 9, 2015), http://www.questdiagnostics.com/home/physicians/health-trends/drug-testing. Accessed May 28, 2016.

69. Ibid.

70. U.S. Government Accountability Office, GAO-16-1, http://www.gao.gov/products/GAO-16-1. Accessed May 29, 2016.

71. http://www.questdiagnostics.com/home/physicians/health-trends/drug-testing. Accessed May 28, 2016.

72. Marc D. Greenwood, "FALSE Positives," *Fire Chief* (April 2003), 48–53.

73. Kevin Lyles, "Hiring Hurdle: Finding Workers Who Can Pass a Drug Test," *The New York Times* (May 17, 2016), http://www.nytimes.com/2016/05/18/business/hiring-hurdle-finding-workers-who-can-pass-a-drug-test.html?_r=0. Accessed May 28, 2016.

74. Ibid.

75. ACOEM, "Ethical Aspects of Drug Testing," https://www.acoem.org/EthicalAspectsOfDrugTesting.aspx (February 4, 2009). Accessed May 20, 2016.

76. Jane Easter Bahls, "Dealing with Drugs: Keep It Legal," *HR Magazine* (March 1998), 104–116.

77. "ADA Claim Fails to Disturb Refusal to Hire Based on Positive Test Results," *Venulex Legal Summary* (2009) 1–3.

78. Eileen Smith, "How to Choose the Right EAP for Your Employee," *Employee Benefit News* (November 1, 2000).

79. Sean Fogarty, "EAPs New Role: A Core Strategic Element," *Employee Benefits Advisor* (April 2010), 40–46.

80. Amy Morin, "What Construction Workers Could Teach Other Industries about Mental Health Awareness," *Forbes* (May 21, 2016), http://www.forbes.com/sites/amymorin/2016/05/21/what-construction-workers-could-teach-other-industries-about-mental-health-awareness/#482746e39a23. Accessed May 29, 2016.

81. Fogarty, 2010.

82. Romy Ribitzky, "Active Monitoring of Employees Rises to 78%," *ABC News* (April 18, 2016), http://abcnews.go.com/Business/story?id=88319&page=1. Accessed May 28, 2016.

83. See Nancy Flynn, "Yes: Keeping an Eye on Employees Helps Companies Protect Themselves," and Lewis Maltby, "No: It Too Often Becomes a Fishing Expedition Unrelated to Work Issues," *The Wall Street Journal* (May 12, 2014), R1.
84. Olivera Perkins, "More than Half of Employers Now Use Social Media to Screen Job Candidates," Cleveland.com (May 14, 2015), http://www.cleveland.com/business/index.ssf/2015/05/more_than_half_of_employers_no_1.html. Accessed June 4, 2016.
85. Ibid.
86. John P. Mello, Jr., "Camera Phones a Flashpoint of Concern," *Boston Works* (April 11, 2004), G7.
87. Rebecca Abrahams and Stephen Bryen, "Your Computer and Your Cameras Are On—Beware!," *The Huffington Post* (July 27, 2014), http://www.huffingtonpost.com/rebecca-abrahams/your-computer--phone-came_b_5398896.html. Accessed May 29, 2016.
88. Ibid.
89. Nancy J. King, "Electronic Monitoring to Promote National Security Impacts Workplace Privacy," *Employee Responsibilities and Rights Journal* (September 2003), 127–147.
90. Ibid.
91. Electronic Privacy Information Center, "Workplace Privacy," http://www.epic.org/privacy/workplace. Accessed May 20, 2013.
92. Susan K. Livio, "N.J. Supreme Court Upholds Privacy of Personal E-Mails Accessed at Work," *NJ.com* (March 30, 2010), http://www.nj.com/news/index.ssf/2010/03/nj_supreme_court_sets_new_ruli.html. Accessed June 1, 2016.
93. Ibid.
94. Ibid.
95. Electronic Privacy Information Center, "United States v Hamilton" (December 13, 2012) http://epic.org/amicus/hamilton/. Accessed June 1, 2016.
96. Ibid.
97. Gauri Punjabi, "Main Social Media Employee Privacy Law Goes into Effect October 15, 2015," Mintz Levin (September 20, 2015), https://www.employmentmattersblog.com/2015/09/maine-social-media-employee-privacy-law-goes-into-effect-october-15-2015/. Accessed May 28, 2016.
98. Jessica Goldenberg, "Protecting Privacy or Enabling Fraud? Employee Social Media Password Protection Laws May Clash with FINRA Rules" (May 8, 2013), http://privacylaw.proskauer.com/2013/05/articles/california/protecting-privacy-or-enabling-fraud-employee-social-media-password-protection-laws-may-clash-with-finra-rules/. Accessed May 29, 2016.
99. Katie Johnson, "Firms Step up Employee Monitoring at Work," Boston Globe (February 16, 2016), https://www.bostonglobe.com/business/2016/02/18/firms-step-monitoring-employee-activities-work/2l5hoCjsEZWA0bp10BzPrN/story.html. Accessed May 30, 2016.
100. Ibid.
101. Frederick S. Lane, III, *The Naked Employee* (New York: AMACOM, 2003).
102. International Labor Organization, "Safety and Health at Work," http://www.ilo.org/global/topics/safety-and-health-at-work/lang--en/index.htm. Accessed June 1, 2016.
103. Alexandra Berzon, "U.S. Workplace Fatalities Likely at Highest Level Since 2008," *The Wall Street Journal* (September 17, 2015), http://www.wsj.com/articles/u-s-workplace-fatalities-likely-at-highest-level-since-2008-1442502439. Accessed May 27, 2016.
104. Ibid.
105. Legal Information Institute, "Workplace Safety," http://www.law.cornell.edu/wex/workplace_safety. Accessed June 1, 2016.
106. Joseph P. Kahn, "When Bad Management Becomes Criminal," *Inc.* (March 1987), 47.
107. David R. Spiegel, "Enforcing Safety Laws Locally," *The New York Times* (March 23, 1986), 11F.
108. "Union Carbide Fights for Its Life," *Businessweek* (December 24, 1984), 52–56.
109. National Council for Occupational Safety and Health, "Not an Accident: Preventable Deaths 2015," http://www.coshnetwork.org/sites/default/files/Not-an-Accident-2015.pdf. Accessed June 3, 2016.
110. OSHA Regional News Release (September 2, 2015), https://www.osha.gov/pls/oshaweb/owadisp.show_document?p_table=NEWS_RELEASES&p_id=28662. Accessed June 4, 2016.
111. Safety Partners, "7 Most Common Causes of Workplace Accidents," http://www.safetypartnersltd.com/7-most-common-causes-of-workplace-accidents/#.V1TJYOSUQmR. Accessed June 4, 2016.
112. U.S. Department of Labor, OSHA, "Hazard Communication," http://www.osha.gov/pls/oshaweb/owadisp.show_document?p_table=FEDERAL_REGISTER&p_id=13349. Accessed June 4, 2016.
113. Nathaniel Rich, "Poisoned Ground," *The New York Times Magazine* (January 10, 2016), 36.
114. Ibid.
115. Cole A. Wist and Hugh C. Thatcher, "Workplace Violence: An American Secret," *Labor Employment and Law* (Winter 2010), 6.
116. Ibid.
117. Molly McHugh, "Uber and Lyft Drivers Work Dangerous Jobs—But They're on Their Own," *Wired* (March 10, 2016), http://www.wired.com/2016/03/uber-lyft-can-much-keep-drivers-safe/. Accessed June 4, 2016.
118. U.S. Department of Labor, OSHA, "Workplace Violence," http://www.osha.gov/SLTC/workplaceviolence/. Accessed May 31, 2016.

119. Ibid.
120. Cammie Chaumont Menendez and Bobbie L. Dillon. "Workplace Violence: Impact, Causes, and Prevention." *Work* 42.1 (2012): 15–20.
121. Wist and Thatcher, 6.
122. "Workplace Violence: New Regulation, Threats and Best Practices," *Security Director's Report* (May 2010), 1–11.
123. Law 360, "Addressing Open Carry Challenges for Texas Employers," http://www.law360.com/articles/771090/addressing-open-carry-challenges-for-texas-employers. Accessed May 30, 2016.
124. Andrew Lord, "7 Companies That Don't Want Guns in Their Stores," *The Huffington Post* (July 16, 2015), http://www.huffingtonpost.com/2015/07/16/open-carry-guns-restaurants-companies_n_7802468.html. Accessed May 31, 2016.
125. John Lott, "Open Carry Comes to Texas: They the Lone Star Will Be Safer in 2016," *FoxNews* (December 30, 2015), http://www.foxnews.com/opinion/2015/12/30/open-carry-comes-to-texas-why-lone-star-state-will-be-safer-in-2016.html. Accessed May 30, 2016.
126. OSHA Fact Sheet, http://www.osha.gov/OshDoc/data_General_Facts/factsheet-workplace-violence.pdf. Accessed May 31, 2016.
127. Stephanie Armour, "Companies, Survivors Suffer Years after Violence at Work," *USA Today* (July 9, 2003), 3A.
128. Ibid., 3A.
129. Ibid.
130. Sarah Wheaton and Shaila Dewan, "Professor Said to Be Charged after 3 Are Killed in Alabama," *The New York Times* (February 12, 2010), http://www.nytimes.com/2010/02/13/us/13alabama.html. Accessed May 31, 2016.
131. Wist and Thatcher, 6.
132. Ibid.
133. Prevent Violence at Work, "Basic Recommendations for Preventing Violence in the Workplace," http://www.prevention-violence.com/en/int-210.asp. Accessed June 1, 2016.
134. Michelle Andrews, "Why Employers' Incentives for Weight Loss Fall Flat with Workers," South Carolina NPR (January 8, 2016), http://www.npr.org/sections/health-shots/2016/01/08/462380096/why-employers-incentives-for-weight-loss-fall-flat-with-workers. Accessed May 31, 2016.
135. Mitesh Patel, David Asch, and Kevin Volpp, "Paying Employees to Lose Weight," *The New York Times* (March 6, 2016), 10.
136. Andrews, 2016.
137. Mitesh, Asch, and Volpp, 2016.
138. Otto Friedrich, "Where There's Smoke," *Time* (February 23, 1987), 23.
139. Lois Therrien, "Warning: In More and More Places, Smoking Causes Fines," *Businessweek* (December 29, 1986), 40.
140. U.S. Environmental Protection Agency, "Secondhand Tobacco Smoke and Smoke-free Homes," https://www.epa.gov/indoor-air-quality-iaq/secondhand-tobacco-smoke-and-smoke-free-homes. Accessed June 1, 2016.
141. See Christian Nordqvist, "Second Hand Smoke Kills Says World Health Organization," *Medical News Today* (May 31, 2010), http://www.medicalnewstoday.com/articles/ 190429.php. Accessed May 21, 2013; World Health Organization Global Health Observatory, http://www.who.int/gho/phe/secondhand_smoke/en/. Accessed May 31, 2016.
142. Ibid.
143. Joe Chemo, "Clearing the Air at Work," http://www.joechemo.org/business.htm. Accessed June 1, 2016.
144. Stradley Ronon, "Light My Fire: Steps for Controlling the High Cost of Employees Who Smoke," http://www.stradley.com/insights/publications/2014/04/employment-newsflash-april-2014. Accessed June 1, 2016.
145. Claire Cain Miller, "The Problem with Work Is Overwork," *The New York Times* (May 31, 2015), 4.
146. Jack Dickey, "Who Killed Summer Vacation?" *Time* (June 1, 2015), 46.
147. Miller, 2015.
148. Ibid.
149. Nancy R. Lockwood, "Work/Life Balance: Challenges and Solutions," *HR Magazine* (June 2003).
150. Kathryn Vasel, "The Best Companies for Working Moms," *CNN Money* (September 22, 2015), http://money.cnn.com/2015/09/22/pf/jobs/best-companies-working-mothers/. Accessed May 31, 2016.
151. https://www.shrm.org/Research/SurveyFindings/Articles/Documents/2015-Employee-Benefits.pdf. Accessed May 31, 2016.
152. Ibid.
153. "Military Expansions in FMLA Are Now Law," *HR Focus* (January 2010), 2.
154. Ibid.
155. U.S. Department of Labor, "Family Medical Leave Act," https://www.dol.gov/whd/fmla/spouse/. Accessed May 29, 2016.
156. Mark Schoeff, "Department of Labor Study Reveals FMLA Challenges," *Workforce Management* (July 23, 2007), 8–10.

19

Employment Diversity and Discrimination

CHAPTER LEARNING OUTCOMES

After studying this chapter, you should be able to:

1 Discuss the concept of diversity management in the workforce and the evolution of its current paradigm.

2 Chronicle the U.S. civil rights movement and minority progress in the past 50 years.

3 Outline the essentials of the federal discrimination laws.

4 Define and provide examples of the expanded meanings of employment discrimination including disparate treatment and disparate impact, and issues in employment discrimination relating to race, color, national origin, sex, age, religion, sexual orientation, and disability.

5 Discuss the concept of affirmative action and current issues related to diversity management.

In the two preceding chapters, we discussed employee rights issues that affect virtually everyone in the workplace. In this chapter, we explore the concept of diversity in the workforce and then focus on that group of stakeholders whose employment rights and circumstances are protected by discrimination laws. In the United States, we have **protected groups** who have federal legal protection from discrimination based on aspects such as race, color, religion, national origin, sex (including pregnancy), age, or disability.[1] In addition to these federal protections, 19 states and the District of Columbia have laws that protect individuals from employment discrimination based on sexual orientation and gender identity.[2] Many of the issues we treat in this chapter have grown out of the general belief that certain employees may possibly face discrimination because of the above-listed attributes and that they have workplace rights that should be protected.

Managing diversity in the workforce continues to evolve from the days when diversity was approached from an idea of promoting people from groups that continue to be affected by a legacy of discrimination (i.e., affirmative action). Diversity and inclusion is a top priority in businesses today because it is not only the right thing to do from ethical and stakeholder management perspectives, but it is also good business. While most people know this intuitively, the numbers back this up. For example, a recent *McKinsey* study shows that gender-diverse companies are 15 percent more likely to outperform their peers, and ethnically diverse companies are 35 percent more likely to do the same.[3] Research has shown that in the United States, for every 10 percent increase in racial and ethnic diversity on senior executive teams, earnings before interest and taxes (EBIT) rise 0.8 percent.[4] We examine this phenomenon of diversity in the workforce and its effective management in this chapter, including the legal, moral, and ethical issues related to discrimination.

In the United States, federal antidiscrimination laws date back to the U.S. Constitution—in particular, the First, Fifth, and Fourteenth Amendments, which were designed to forbid religious discrimination and deprivation of employment rights without due process. There were also the Civil Rights Acts of 1866, 1870, and 1871, which were based on these amendments. However, none of these acts was ever effective. Most authorities agree that the Civil Rights Act of 1964 was the effective beginning of the employee protection movement, particularly for those special groups that we will be discussing in this chapter.

In recessionary times, we must use the term *protected* with utmost care. It is true that the protected groups are protected from discrimination by the law. However, we must remember that legal protection is often not enough. It is very difficult to identify and prove discrimination even though there are laws prohibiting it.

Civil rights issues among protected groups are subjects of intense debate. Although there is basic acceptance of the idea of groups' workplace rights being protected, the extent of this protection and the degree to which governmental policy should act to accelerate the infusion of protected groups into the workforce and into higher-paying jobs remain controversial topics. To explore these and related issues, we will cover the following major topics in this chapter: diversity in the workforce, the civil rights movement, federal laws that protect against employment discrimination, the meaning of discrimination, a variety of issues related to employment discrimination, and, finally, affirmative action in the workplace.

19.1 Diversity in the Workforce

Workplace diversity refers to the variety of differences between people in an organization. It encompasses race, gender, ethnicity, age, religion, personality, tenure, education, and more. Most businesses refer to **diversity management** as assembling and then retaining workers from different backgrounds and experiences that together create a more innovative and productive workforce. However, over the years, there have been paradigm shifts in managing diversity. Researchers Thomas and Ely identified the shifts over the past three decades and have documented them as follows: (1) **discrimination-and-fairness**, (2) **access-and-legitimacy**, and (3) **integration-and-learning**.[5]

In the early 1970s, the focus was on looking at diversity with a focus on equal opportunity, fair treatment, recruitment, and federal EEOC compliance, which researchers have categorized as the "discrimination-and-fairness" paradigm.[6] The focus was on recruitment and retention goals with an emphasis on equal treatment, without a focus on the many perspectives that diversity in the workforce could bring to the fold.

In the 1980s, an "access-and-legitimacy" paradigm developed with an emphasis that diversity is not just fair, but it also makes business sense.[7] The market-based goal of diversity was to match the demographics of an organization to critical stakeholder groups, acknowledging the cultural differences in people and recognizing value in the differences. Like the discrimination-in-fairness paradigm, however, this paradigm tended to focus on the role of cultural differences without analyzing the differences to see the connection to how work is performed. While it supported a managerial view of the firm (outlined in Chapter 3), it fell short of fully integrating and synthesizing these stakeholders in business.

In the 1990s, businesses began making the connection of diversity to work perspectives through an integration-and-learning paradigm.[8] The focus was on integrating the goals of equal opportunity, acknowledgment of cultural differences and value, as well as letting the organization internalize differences, learn, and grow because of them in a long-term transformative process.

This paradigm is said to be in place still today, with a philosophy of "we are the same, *with* our differences not in spite of them."[9] The focus of businesses regarding diversity management is on providing inclusive corporate cultures that, according to the Society for Human Resource Management, "foster ways to accommodate, empower and motivate each employee."[10] Recruitment of diverse employees has also increased over the past few years, with more organizations providing staff exclusively dedicated to this function.[11] It is easy to see how the integration of diverse employees into a workplace culture under the integration-and-learning paradigm is part of good stakeholder management that is both strategic, legal, and morally managed.

Despite progress in managing a diverse workforce, challenges abound. With most companies providing diversity training programs and actively recruiting for diverse employees, there is some thought that there is "**diversity fatigue**" when companies fail to rethink their management styles and simply engage in "box-ticking."[12] In addition, despite increases in workforce diversity, many companies are setting discrete goals and tying those numbers to pay and performance, particularly regarding hiring and retaining women.[13] While there is still a stigma associated with quotas in the United States, this is not the case in other countries, as we discussed in Chapter 4. Therefore, companies like Twitter and Pinterest have made diversity goals public.[14] Additionally, companies like BASF expect managers to interview at least one woman or minority candidate for all open jobs; at least one of the interviewers must also be a woman or minority.[15] Such are the examples of diversity management techniques today.

Despite all of the inroads made in diversity management, discrimination still exists in the workforce. According to a recent *CNN/Kaiser Family Foundation* poll on race in America, 26 percent of Blacks and 15 percent of Hispanics say they had been treated unfairly because of their race or ethnicity at their place of work in the prior 30 days.[16] Additionally, 69 percent of Blacks and 57 percent of Hispanics say past and present discrimination is a major reason for the problems facing people of their racial or ethnic group.[17] In 2015 and 2016, issues of gender and race discrimination in Hollywood made the news when a federal investigation showed that women directed less than 7 percent of top movies and about 14 percent of TV shows in 2015.[18] Additionally, protests ensued when minorities were slighted in the Oscar nominations at the 2016 Academy Awards.[19] With these issues in mind, it is helpful to review the history of the Civil Rights Movement in the United States, and the protections afforded to individuals from discrimination by federal law.

19.2 The Civil Rights Movement

It would take volumes to trace thoroughly the historical events that led ultimately to passage of the first significant piece of civil rights legislation in the modern period—the Civil Rights Act of 1964. The act grew out of conflict that had been apparent for years but that erupted in the 1950s and 1960s in the form of protests and boycotts.[20]

Equal opportunity was supposed to be everyone's birthright but not everyone shared this American dream. Things began to change because of individuals who had the courage to stand up for their rights as U.S. citizens.

On December 1, 1955, Mrs. Rosa Parks, a black department store worker, was arrested for refusing to yield her bus seat to a white man. Out of that brave act grew another—a bus boycott by African Americans. One of the leaders of the boycott was a young minister, Dr. Martin Luther King, Jr. After the bus boycott came years of demonstrations, marches, and battles with police. Television coverage depicted scenes of civil rights demonstrators being attacked by officials with cattle prods, dogs, and fire hoses. Along with the violence that grew out of confrontations between protestors and authorities came the stark awareness of the economic inequality between the races that existed in the United States at that time.[21] Against this backdrop of African Americans and other minorities being denied access to the American ideal of equal opportunity in employment, it should have been no surprise that Congress finally acted in a dramatic way passing the Civil Rights Act of 1964.[22]

The women's movement began in the 1970s. Women's groups began to see that the workplace situation was little better for women than for African Americans and other minorities. Despite the fact that the labor participation rate for women was growing, women were still occupying low-paying jobs. They were making some minor inroads into managerial and professional jobs, but progress was very slow. Women, for the most part, were still in the lower-paying "women's jobs," such as bank teller, secretary, waitress, and laundry worker.[23] The 1990s then began with the next major civil rights movement, the disability rights movement. The Americans with Disabilities Act (ADA) of 1990 was designed not only to stop discrimination against people with disabilities but also to open up access to buildings and transportation, which in turn opened up access to employment.

Now, in the 21st century, one of the most significant issues arising in the new millennium has been the changing workforce composition. The U.S. Bureau of Labor Statistics projects that by 2024, every race and ethnicity will grow but Hispanics are projected to be nearly one-fifth of the labor force.[24] White, non-Hispanics are still projected to make up about 60 percent of the labor force.[25] The labor force will be older, with workers between the ages of 25 and 54 expected to be nearly 64 percent of the labor force in 2024, and composed of more women.[26] The Lesbian, Gay, Bisexual, and Transgender (LGBT) workforce is estimated to grow, with 1.6 percent of the U.S. population between the ages of 18 and 59 in this category.[27] However, a recent *Catalyst* study estimates that in 2015, one in 10 LGBT employees left a job because the environment was unwelcoming.

The challenge for business going forward will be to assimilate this increasingly diverse workforce. Additionally, businesses must determine how to respond to changing social values and new technologies. Sexual orientation and gender identity are increasingly receiving protected status from states and large organizations, while not being protected at the federal level. This creates challenges for firms with operations throughout the country. Genetic testing has opened the door to other forms of discrimination; federal law now prohibits employers from using genetic information when making hiring, firing, promotion, or job placement decisions. Diversity issues will continue to evolve with time and employers must stay aware of shifts in this changing landscape.

One way to understand the changing public policy with respect to employment discrimination is to examine the evolution of federal laws prohibiting discrimination. Once we have a better appreciation of the legal status of protected groups, we can more completely understand the complex issues that have arisen with respect to the evolving meaning of discrimination and its relationship to related workforce issues.

19.3 Federal Laws Prohibiting Discrimination

This section provides an overview of the major laws that have been passed in the United States to protect workers against discrimination. We will focus our discussion on legislation at the federal level that has been created in the past 60 years. We will discuss issues arising from the various forms of discrimination in more detail later in this chapter. We should keep in mind that there are state and local laws that address many of these same topics, but lack of space does not permit their consideration here. Our purpose in this section is to provide an overview of antidiscrimination laws and the major federal agencies that enforce those laws.

19.3a Title VII of the Civil Rights Act of 1964

Title VII of the Civil Rights Act of 1964, as amended, prohibits discrimination in hiring, promotion, discharge, pay, fringe benefits, and other aspects of employment on the basis of race, color, religion, sex, or national origin. It was extended to cover federal, state, and local employers and educational institutions by the Equal Employment Opportunity Act of 1972. The amendment to Title VII also gave the Equal Employment Opportunity Commission (EEOC) the authority to file suits in federal district court against employers in the private sector on behalf of individuals whose charges had not been successfully conciliated. In 1978, Title VII was amended to include the Pregnancy Discrimination Act, which requires employers to treat pregnancy and pregnancy-related medical conditions in the same manner as any other medical disability with respect to all terms and conditions of employment, including employee health benefits.[28]

Title VII also prohibits firms from retaliating against employees who file discrimination claims. In 2006, the U.S. Supreme Court strengthened the anti-retaliation provisions of Title VII. The High Court ruled that an employee could establish a retaliation claim even when they were not terminated or demoted. Any action that would "cause a worker to think twice" about lodging a discrimination complaint is sufficient (e.g., being transferred to a less desirable position at the same pay).[29] The High Court determined that lower courts had established a "jump off the page and slap you in the face" standard that was unacceptable.[30]

In 2010, the U.S. Supreme Court ruled unanimously that the lawsuit clock does not begin when a biased hiring test is administered. Instead, it resets each time an employer uses the biased tests to make hiring decisions. The alternative, as Justice Scalia noted when he wrote the court's opinion, would be unending ongoing discrimination: "If an employer adopts an unlawful practice and no timely charge is brought, it can continue using the practice indefinitely, with impunity, despite ongoing disparate impact."[31]

While the parameters of Title VII have not changed much in recent years, the applications of Title VII have changed in response to social changes. In 2015, the EEOC officially declared that it now considers Title VII's prohibition on sex discrimination to apply to discrimination based on sexual orientation or gender identity.[32] In 2015, the EEOC received 1,412 charges that included allegations of sex discrimination related to sexual orientation and/or gender identity/transgender status, and they resolved 1,135 of these charges through voluntary agreements and approximately $3.3 million in monetary relief for workers.[33]

Figure 19-1 presents an overview of Title VII's coverage.

FIGURE 19-1 Title VII of the Civil Rights Act of 1964

EMPLOYMENT discrimination based on race, color, religion, sex, or national origin is prohibited by Title VII of the Civil Rights Act of 1964.

Title VII covers private employers, state and local governments, and educational institutions that have 15 or more employees. The federal government, private and public employment agencies, labor organizations, and joint labor–management committees for apprenticeship and training also must abide by the law.

It is illegal under Title VII to discriminate in:

- Hiring and firing;
- Compensation, assignment, or classification of employees;
- Transfer, promotion, layoff, or recall;
- Job advertisements;
- Recruitment;
- Testing;
- Use of company facilities;
- Training and apprenticeship programs;
- Fringe benefits;
- Pay, retirement plans, and disability leave; or
- Other terms and conditions of employment.

Under the law, pregnancy, childbirth, and related medical conditions must be treated in the same manner as any other non-pregnancy-related illness or disability.

Title VII prohibits retaliation against a person who files a charge of discrimination, participates in an investigation, or opposes an unlawful employment practice.

Employment agencies may not discriminate in receiving, classifying, or referring applications for employment or in their job advertisements.

Labor unions may not discriminate in accepting applications for membership, classifying members, referrals, training and apprenticeship programs, and advertising for jobs. It is illegal for a labor union to cause or try to cause an employer to discriminate. It is also illegal for an employer to cause or try to cause a union to discriminate.

Source: U.S. Equal Employment Opportunity Commission, http://www.eeoc.gov/laws/statutes/titlevii.cfm. Accessed June 2, 2016.

19.3b Age Discrimination in Employment Act of 1967

This law protects workers aged 40 years and older from arbitrary age discrimination in hiring, discharge, pay, promotions, fringe benefits, and other aspects of employment. It is designed to promote employment of older people based on ability rather than age and to help employers and workers find ways to meet problems arising from the impact of age on employment. The Act does not protect employees under age 40 from age discrimination, but it does protect anyone from retaliation for complaining about age discrimination or being closely associated with someone who does.[34]

Like the provisions of Title VII, the **Age Discrimination in Employment Act (ADEA)** does not apply where age is a **bona fide occupational qualification (BFOQ)**—a qualification that might ordinarily be argued as being a basis for discrimination but for which a company can legitimately argue that age is job related and necessary. For example, there are mandatory retirement ages for bus drivers and airline pilots for safety reasons.[35] The act also does not bar employers from differentiating among employees based on reasonable factors other than age.[36] To prove unlawful discrimination, an employee must prove that his or her age was a determining factor in the employer's decision to take an adverse employment action. For example, courts and the federal Equal Employment Opportunity Commission (EEOC) have found that an employer's use of age-related code words such as "energetic," "new blood," "fresh," and "set in their ways" when describing candidates and employees may be examples of age discrimination.[37] Unfortunately, many employers might not even realize that they are being discriminatory with such language. This could be an example of **ethical blindness** that occurs when decision makers behave unethically without even being aware of it—a temporary inability to see the ethical dimension of a decision at stake.[38] Nevertheless, the law in this case protects against the phenomenon of ethical blindness.

19.3c Equal Pay Act of 1963

As amended, this act prohibits sex discrimination in payment of wages to women and men who perform substantially equal work in the same establishment. Passage of this landmark law marked a significant milestone in helping women, who were the chief victims of unequal pay, to achieve equality in their paychecks.[39] Figure 19-2 summarizes other details of the **Equal Pay Act of 1963**.

The Equal Pay Act received a great deal of attention in 2007, when the U.S. Supreme Court heard the *Ledbetter v. Goodyear Tire & Rubber Co.* case, in which the plaintiff, Lilly Ledbetter, alleged that she had been paid less than her male counterparts but was unaware of the discrimination until years after the decision on her pay had been made. The question at hand was whether the clock on the statute of limitations began ticking with the original pay decision or whether it was reset each time a paycheck was made.[40] The Supreme Court, decided that the statute of limitations began running from the time of the original pay decision, and so an employee must file a complaint within 180 days of the action that first sets the discriminatory pay, irrespective of its ongoing impact on the employee.[41]

The problem with this requirement is that it often takes time for an employee to learn that her pay is lower than her male counterparts. The **Lilly Ledbetter Fair Pay Act of 2009** effectively undid the Court's decision, stipulating that the clock reset each time a discriminatory paycheck was issued.[42]

Since the Lilly Ledbetter legislation, there has been much more attention to gender pay equity, with new state laws attempting to close the gender wage gap, which we also discussed in Chapter 4. While proposed federal legislation surrounding a Paycheck Fairness Act continues to stall, several states like California, Connecticut, Delaware, North Dakota, and Oregon have passed new laws designed to repair pay discrimination, or at

FIGURE 19-2 Equal Pay Act of 1963

The Equal Pay Act (EPA) prohibits employers from discriminating between men and women on the basis of sex in the payment of wages where they perform substantially equal work under similar working conditions in the same establishment. The law also prohibits employers from reducing the wages of either sex to comply with the law.

A violation may exist where a different wage is paid to a predecessor or successor employee of the opposite sex. Labor organizations may not cause employers to violate the law.

Retaliation against a person who files a charge of equal pay discrimination, participates in an investigation, or opposes an unlawful employment practice also is illegal.

The law protects virtually all private employees, including executive, administrative, professional, and outside sales employees who are exempt from minimum wage and overtime laws. Most federal, state, and local government workers also are covered.

The law does not apply to pay differences based on factors other than sex, such as seniority, merit, or systems that determine wages based on the quantity or quality of items produced or processed.

Many EPA violations may be violations of Title VII of the Civil Rights Act of 1964, which also prohibits sex-based wage discrimination. Such charges may be filed under both statutes.

Sources: *Information for the Private Sector and State and Local Governments: EEOC* (Washington: Equal Employment Opportunity Commission), 9. Also see U.S. Department of Labor, Equal Pay Act of 1963, as amended, http://www.dol.gov/oasam/regs/statutes/equal_pay_act.htm. Accessed June 2, 2016.

least prohibit employers from discriminating or retaliating against employees who discuss wages.[43] However, these laws are not without controversy. Some critics say that they are based on false accounting of the pay gap, which, when controlled for many factors that explain earnings differences like hours worked, career choice, and family roles, goes away.[44] Other critics see that there will be unintended consequences of rising compliance costs and checklisting that, in the end, will only hurt women.[45] However, what is not disputable is that businesses must do everything that they can to ensure that women are treated fairly in the workforce, and they need to address and remove any obstacles to equal treatment. We discuss this further in the section on Issues in Employment Discrimination below.

19.3d Rehabilitation Act of 1973, Section 503

This law, as amended, prohibits job discrimination on the basis of a disability. It applies to employers holding federal contracts or subcontracts. In addition, it requires these employers to engage in affirmative action to employ the disabled, a concept we will discuss later in this chapter. Related to this act is the Vietnam Era Veterans Readjustment Assistance Act of 1974, which also prohibits discrimination and requires affirmative action among federal contractors or subcontractors.[46]

19.3e Americans with Disabilities Act

The **Americans with Disabilities Act (ADA)** of 1990, as amended in 2008, prohibits discrimination based on physical or mental disabilities in private places of employment and public accommodation, in addition to requiring transportation systems and communication systems to facilitate access for the disabled. The ADA was modeled after the Rehabilitation Act of 1973, which applies to federal contractors and grantees.[47] The basic provisions of the ADA are detailed in Figure 19-3.

Essentially, the ADA gives individuals with disabilities civil rights protections similar to those provided to individuals based on race, sex, national origin, and religion. The ADA applies not only to private employers but also to state and local governments, employment agencies, and labor unions. Employers of 15 or more employees are covered.

The ADA prohibits discrimination in all employment practices, including job application procedures, hiring, firing, advancement, compensation, training, and other terms, conditions, and privileges of employment. If a person's disability makes it difficult for him or her to function, firms are expected to make **reasonable accommodations** if doing so does not represent an **undue hardship** for the firm. The act covers qualified individuals with disabilities. Qualified individuals are those who can perform the **essential functions** of the job.[48] The definition of essential function is sometimes difficult to determine. A case in point occurred with golfer Casey Martin, when he applied to the PGA for permission to ride a cart in PGA tournaments when other players were walking the course. Much controversy ensued over whether walking the golf course was an essential function of playing professional golf. The Supreme Court subsequently ruled that he could use a cart because providing the cart was a reasonable accommodation and his use of the cart would not fundamentally alter the game.

The definition of disability includes people who have physical or mental impairments that substantially limit one or more **major life activities**, such as "caring for oneself, performing manual tasks, seeing, hearing, eating, sleeping, walking, standing, sitting, reaching, lifting, bending, speaking, breathing, learning, reading, concentrating, thinking, communicating, interacting with others, and working."[49] A disability is defined using a three-pronged approach, with respect to an individual who:[50]

- has a physical or mental impairment that substantially limits one or more major life activities, or
- has a record of a physical or mental impairment that substantially limited a major life activity, or
- is perceived of as having a disability.

As the world of work changes, so do the obligations of companies to protect worker rights. While companies' sense of social responsibility and sound ethics should drive these decisions, the legal responsibility is always there. The ADA requires that firms make their places of business accessible to people with disabilities as long as doing so does not create an undue hardship. Recently, ride hailing services Uber and Lyft have found themselves named as defendants in a number of lawsuits alleging they violated the ADA by failing to make their cars handicapped accessible.[51] Several suits cite drivers refusing to pick up blind customers accompanied by dogs, or refusing to help people with their wheelchairs. While Uber has apologized to some of their customers, they argue that as a technology company they are not subject to laws regulating public transit and other transportation providers. Hence, the Department of Justice is getting involved to ensure that discrimination accusations are being given due process.[52]

As businesses have moved their sales online, advocates for people with disabilities have filed suits to require them to make those Web sites accessible for people who are blind or deaf. They are seeking "the digital version of wheelchair ramps and self-opening doors."[53] In 2016, a blind man in California won a suit against Colorado Bag'n Baggage because he could not shop online for the retailer's products because of missing Web site features that would allow him to order online, like screen-reading software.[54] This type of litigation is anticipated to increase following the Department of Justice's 2014 issuance of new compliance standards for accessibility for the disabled on commercial Web sites.[55] In sum, new technology has brought new opportunities for the disabled, while also challenging businesses to make sure that they are staying up-to-date with their legal and moral obligations to those who need protection from discrimination.

Pregnancy discrimination and genetic information nondiscrimination are two issues that also fit under the issue of disabilities discrimination. Of course, only women get pregnant and so it would seem logical to categorize pregnancy under gender discrimination, but the law treats pregnancy as a temporary disability. Fetal protection policies are similar in that they represent a concern that unborn children might have future

FIGURE 19-3 The Americans with Disabilities Act

Title I of the Americans with Disabilities Act of 1990 prohibits private employers, state and local governments, employment agencies, and labor unions from discriminating against qualified individuals with disabilities in job application procedures, hiring, firing, advancement, compensation, job training, and other terms, conditions, and privileges of employment. The ADA covers employers with 15 or more employees, including state and local governments. It also applies to employment agencies and to labor organizations. The ADA's nondiscrimination standards also apply to federal sector employees under Section 501 of the Rehabilitation Act, as amended, and its implementing rules.

An individual with a disability is a person who:

- Has a physical or mental impairment that substantially limits one or more major life activities;
- Has a record of such an impairment; or
- Is regarded as having such an impairment.

A qualified employee or applicant with a disability is an individual who, with or without reasonable accommodation, can perform the essential functions of the job in question. Reasonable accommodation may include, but is not limited to:

- Making existing facilities used by employees readily accessible to and usable by persons with disabilities;
- Restructuring jobs (for parallelism), modifying work schedules, and reassigning to a vacant position;
- Acquiring or modifying equipment or devices; adjusting or modifying examinations, training materials, or policies; and providing qualified readers or interpreters.

An employer is required to make a reasonable accommodation to the known disability of a qualified applicant or employee if it would not impose an "undue hardship" on the operation of the employer's business. Reasonable accommodations are adjustments or modifications provided by an employer to enable people with disabilities to enjoy equal employment opportunities. Accommodations vary depending on the needs of the individual applicant or employee. Not all people with disabilities (or even all people with the same disability) will require the same accommodation. For example:

- A deaf applicant may need a sign language interpreter during the job interview.
- An employee with diabetes may need regularly scheduled breaks during the workday to eat properly and monitor blood sugar and insulin levels.
- A blind employee may need someone to read information posted on a bulletin board.
- An employee with cancer may need leave for radiation or chemotherapy treatments.

An employer does not have to provide a reasonable accommodation if it imposes an "undue hardship." Undue hardship is defined as an action that requires significant difficulty or expense when considered in light of factors such as an employer's size, financial resources, and the nature and structure of its operation.

An employer generally does not have to provide a reasonable accommodation unless an individual with a disability has asked for one. If an employer believes that a medical condition is causing a performance or conduct problem, it may discuss with the employee how to solve the problem and ask if the employee needs a reasonable accommodation. Once a reasonable accommodation is requested, the employer and the individual should discuss the individual's needs and identify the appropriate reasonable accommodation. Where more than one accommodation would work, the employer may choose the one that is less costly or is easier to provide.

It is also unlawful to retaliate against an individual for opposing employment practices that discriminate based on disability or for filing a discrimination charge, testifying, or participating in any way in an investigation, proceeding, or litigation under the ADA.

Sources: EEOC Facts about the Americans with Disabilities Act https://www.eeoc.gov/eeoc/publications/fs-ada.cfm. Accessed June 2, 2016. Also see Department of Justice, Americans with Disabilities Act of 1990, as amended, http://www.ada.gov/. Accessed June 2, 2016.

disabilities. Genetic information nondiscrimination is not a protected class per se; however, the protection of that private information guards people from discrimination based on possible future disabilities and so we will discuss it in the context of disabilities as well.

Pregnancy Discrimination. For some time, maternity leave has been an issue for women. In 1987, the Supreme Court upheld a California law that granted pregnant workers four months of unpaid maternity leave and guaranteed that their jobs would be waiting for them when they returned. Justice Thurgood Marshall argued, "By taking pregnancy into account, California's statute allows women, as well as men, to have families without losing their jobs."[56]

The **Pregnancy Discrimination Act of 1978**, an amendment to Title VII, requires employers to treat pregnancy and pregnancy-related medical conditions the same way as any other medical disability with respect to all terms and conditions of employment. Because of the Pregnancy Discrimination Act (PDA), the concept of maternity leave is outdated. In fact, companies are advised to make sure they do not have "maternity leave" policies. By using the term *maternity leave*, companies imply that maternity is somehow different from other temporary disabilities.[57]

New ethical and legal issues have surfaced relative to the application of the Pregnancy Discrimination Act in the workforce. These issues were prompted by a recent Supreme Court case, *Young v. UPS*, which we discuss in the Ethics-in-Practice case, as well as studies that found pregnancy discrimination claims continue to increase to over 5,000 claims a year.[58] As a result, the EEOC continues to provide guidance in situations where employers have accommodation obligations under the PDA—essentially importing the ADA's accommodation obligations into the PDA.[59]

For example, new EEOC guidelines say that employers must treat an employee temporarily unable to perform the functions of her job because of her pregnancy-related

ETHICS IN PRACTICE CASE

What Is Reasonable Accommodation for Pregnancy?

In 2008, Peggy Young worked for UPS as a pickup and delivery driver. When she became pregnant, her doctor restricted her from lifting more than 20 pounds during her first 20 weeks of pregnancy and 10 pounds for the remainder. UPS placed Young on leave without pay because her job required her to be able to lift parcels weighing up to 70 pounds. UPS said they followed a "pregnancy-blind" policy that is nondiscriminatory by nature when they put her on leave. Young filed suit, claiming that her co-workers were willing to help her, and that UPS had a policy of accommodating other, non-pregnant drivers who suffered from disabilities, or who lost their Department of Transportation certifications. She brought suit against UPS under the Pregnancy Discrimination Act of 1987 and the Americans with Disabilities Act of 1990.

The U.S. Supreme Court found in Young's favor after two lower courts had taken UPS's side; however, they did not completely agree with her logic. Young said that employers are required to accommodate pregnant women when they provide an accommodation to any other non-pregnant employee who is similar in ability to work. The Court, however, said that under a "disparate treatment" theory of liability, the employee must show that she was intentionally discriminated against. They said that Young must demonstrate that the employer's policies impose a "significant burden" on pregnant workers, and that the employer has not raised a "sufficiently strong" reason to justify that burden. In Young's case, she had to show that UPS accommodates most non-pregnant employees with lifting limitations while categorically failing to accommodate pregnant employees with lifting limitations.

The Court clarified, however, that there is a high legal burden employers will have to meet in order to justify their policies or practices that provide accommodations to some categories of employees, but not to pregnant women. While the Supreme Court remanded the case to the lower court to determine whether UPS can meet this burden, the ramifications from the case have already changed EEOC guidelines for applying the Pregnancy Discrimination Act. What this means for businesses is that employers will have to be very careful if they accommodate some groups of employees without also accommodating pregnant employees.

1. Why do you think some employers are still refusing to comply with pregnant workers' requests for temporary accommodations?
2. How is this an example of the integration of ethics and the law? What ethical principles are at stake here?
3. What would you have done if you were Peggy Young?

Sources: *Young v. United Parcel Service, Inc.*, (n.d.)., *Oyez*. https://www.oyez.org/cases/2014/12-1226. Accessed June 3, 2016; Claire Zillman, "Yes Pregnancy Discrimination at Work Is Still a Huge Problem," *Fortune* (July 15, 2014), http://fortune.com/2014/07/15/pregnancy-discrimination/. Accessed June 2, 2016; *Young v. United Parcel Service, Inc.* Supreme Court of the United States (Argued December 3, 2014–Decided March 25, 2015, http://www.supremecourt.gov/opinions/14pdf/12-1226_k5fl.pdf. Accessed June 4, 2016; U.S. EEOC, "Enforcement and Guidance: Pregnancy Discrimination and Related Issues," https://www.eeoc.gov/laws/guidance/pregnancy_guidance.cfm.

condition in the same manner as it treats other employees similar in their ability or inability to work.[60] They can do this by providing modified tasks, alternative assignments, or fringe benefits such as disability leave and leave without pay. Additionally, parental leave that is offered to new parents so that they may bond with or care for a new child must be provided to men and women on equal terms.[61] These are just a few of the new guidelines designed to ensure that pregnant women and their families are treated respectfully and fairly—which is the right thing to do, both legally and ethically.

Fetal Protection Policies. Another related form of discrimination was identified when the Supreme Court ruled that **fetal protection policies** constituted sex discrimination. The decisive case was *UAW v. Johnson Controls, Inc.* Johnson Controls, like a number of other major firms, developed a policy of barring women of childbearing age from working in sites in which they, and their developing fetuses, might be exposed to such harmful chemicals as lead. Johnson Controls believed it was taking an appropriate action in protecting the women and their unborn children from exposure to chemicals.

Eight current and former employees and the United Auto Workers (UAW) union, who argued that the policy was discriminatory and illegal under Title VII of the Civil Rights Act, brought a class-action lawsuit against Johnson Controls. A U.S. district court ruled in the company's favor, and the Chicago-based U.S. Court of Appeals for the Seventh Circuit affirmed that decision. The U.S. Supreme Court later reversed the appellate court, arguing that the policy was on its face discriminatory and that the company had not shown that women were more likely than men to suffer reproductive damage from lead.[62]

Even though the Supreme Court ruled that injured children, once born, would not be able to bring lawsuits against the company, several experts think it is possible that such lawsuits will indeed be filed in the future. OSHA has identified reproductive health hazards as an area likely to experience an increase in litigation over time.[63] One thing is clear; companies must take care to assure that their employees are fully informed of all potential risks in the workplace.[64]

Genetic Information Nondiscrimination Act. The **Genetic Information Nondiscrimination Act (GINA)** is unique in that it is the first *preemptive* civil rights law in U.S. history.[65] Antidiscrimination laws typically respond to discrimination that has already happened. Genetic testing is so new that there is no significant history of discrimination; instead, GINA represents an effort to prevent genetics-based discrimination before it occurs. The EEOC knew that employers might discriminate against employees, spouses, and children because of concerns about health-care costs, so the GINA was put in place to protect employees and their families.

GINA prohibits employers from requiring, requesting, purchasing, or disclosing employees' genetic information; however, it does not prohibit employees from voluntarily disclosing genetic information to co-workers or to superiors.[66] GINA protects former employees as well as current ones and applies only to employers with 15 or more employees.[67] Genetic information is defined broadly and so it includes not only the information from employee genetic tests and medical history but also information from family members' tests and medical history.[68] Family members need not be blood relatives.

While over 700,000 Americans have had their DNA sequenced, many people avoid the test because of a major omission in the 2008 GINA law that allows life, disability, and long-term insurers to access the results of genetic testing.[69] Even if most insurers are not asking for the genetic tests specifically, they can seek out medical records and can use genetic test results listed there.[70] Therefore, issues of privacy and the potential that employees could be discriminated against because of their genetic makeup have sparked concerns from employee and consumer activists. Time will tell if these issues will be addressed by the EEOC with additional guidelines in the future.

19.3f Civil Rights Act of 1991

The primary objective of the **Civil Rights Act of 1991** was to provide increased financial damages and jury trials in cases of intentional discrimination relating to sex, religion, race, disability, and national origin. Under the original Title VII, monetary awards were limited to such items as back pay, lost benefits, and attorney fees and costs. This 1991 act permitted the awarding of both compensatory and punitive damages. In addition, charges of unintentional discrimination were more difficult for employers to defend, because the act shifted the burden of proof back to the employer.[71] Note that the act refers only to protected groups under Title VII and does not reference age or the Age Discrimination in Employment Act. When Congress amended Title VII of the Civil Rights Act, it did not make a similar amendment for the ADEA and that has been a source of confusion in the courtroom since then.[72]

In 2010, the U.S. Supreme Court further raised the standard of proof for age discrimination cases in their decision regarding *Gross v. FBL Financial Services*. The court's opinion in *Gross* raised the standard of proof for employees charging age discrimination by disallowing "mixed motives" defenses. In other words, employees must do more than prove age was a motivating factor. Employees must show that "but for" age, the discrimination would not have occurred.[73] Efforts by Congress to enact legislation that would supersede the *Gross* decision have stalled. Speaking in favor of that proposed legislation, EEOC Chair Jacqueline Berrien said, "The *Gross* decision was a startling departure from decades of settled precedent developed in federal district and intermediate appellate courts. It erected a new, much higher (and what will often be an insurmountable) legal hurdle for victims of age-based employment decisions. Indeed, recent case law reveals that *Gross* already is constricting the ability of older workers to vindicate their rights under the ADEA, as well as other anti-discrimination statutes."[74] As one headline recently noted, "Claims of age bias rise, but standards of proof are high."[75]

19.3g Equal Employment Opportunity Commission

As the major federal body created to administer and enforce U.S. job bias laws, the **Equal Employment Opportunity Commission (EEOC)** deserves special consideration. Several other federal agencies also are charged with enforcing certain aspects of the discrimination laws and executive orders, but we will restrict our discussion to the EEOC because it is the major agency.

The EEOC has five commissioners and a general counsel appointed by the president and confirmed by the Senate. The five-member commission is responsible for making equal employment opportunity policy and approving all litigation the commission undertakes. The EEOC staff receives and investigates employment discrimination charges/complaints. If the commission finds reasonable cause to believe that unlawful discrimination has occurred, its staff attempts to conciliate the charges/complaints. When conciliation is not achieved, the EEOC may file lawsuits in federal district court against employers.[76] In 2015, the EEOC received 89,385 private sector workplace discrimination charges: Retaliation (39,757), race (31,027), and sex discrimination, including sexual harassment and pregnancy (26,396), represented the charges that were filed most frequently.[77] However, race and discrimination were down significantly from highs in 2010 and 2012, respectively.[78]

SPOTLIGHT *on Sustainability*

Are Sustainability Advocates a New Protected Class?

As head of sustainability for Grainger, one of Britain's largest property firms, Tim Nicholson would sometimes get in conflicts with other executives at the firm. For example, when one top executive left his BlackBerry in London and then ordered a staff person to get on a plane, retrieve it, and bring it back to him, Nicholson believed that wasting jet fuel to return a BlackBerry and other such environmentally inappropriate actions were evidence of contempt for his sustainability beliefs. When he was later laid off, Nicholson filed suit.

The judge decided that if one genuinely holds a belief in man-made climate change, and its alleged resulting moral imperatives, that it could be considered a "philosophical belief." Grainger contended that Nicholson was let go when organizational restructuring made his position redundant. In the United Kingdom, it is unlawful to discriminate against a person on the grounds of their religious or philosophical beliefs. After a judge ruled he could use employment equality (religion and belief) regulations to make his claim, he reached a settlement with the company. In the words of Mr. Nicholson's solicitor, "He is pleased to have created an important point of law to support those individuals, like him, who hold a strong belief in the urgent need to combat climate change."

Sources: Karen McVeigh, "Judge Rules Activist's Belief on Environment Akin to Religion," *guardian.co.uk* (November 9, 2009), http://www.theguardian.com/environment/2009/nov/03/tim-nicholson-climate-change-belief. Accessed June 1, 2016. Richard Heap, "Beyond Belief," *Property Week* (June 5, 2009), http://www.propertyweek.com/beyond-belief/3142268.article. Accessed June 1, 2016; "Climate Change Worker Tim Nicholson Reaches Settlement," *BBC News* (April 15, 2010), http://news.bbc.co.uk/2/hi/uk_news/england/oxfordshire/8621703.stm. Accessed June 1, 2016.

19.4 Expanded Meanings of Employment Discrimination

Over the years, it has been left to the courts to define the word *discrimination*, because it was not defined in Title VII. Over time, it has become apparent that two specific kinds of discrimination exist: **disparate treatment** and **disparate impact**.

19.4a Disparate Treatment

Initially, the word *discrimination* meant the use of race, color, religion, sex, or national origin as a basis for treating people differently or unequally. This form of discrimination is known as unequal treatment or disparate treatment. Examples of disparate treatment might include refusing to consider African Americans for a job, paying women less than men are paid for the same work, or supporting any decision rule with a racial or sexual premise or cause.[79] According to this simple view of discrimination, the employer could impose any criteria so long as they were imposed on all groups alike.[80] This view of discrimination equated nondiscrimination with color-blind decision making. In other words, to avoid this direct kind of discrimination, one would simply treat all groups or individuals equally, without regard for color, sex, or other characteristics.[81]

While the message of disparate treatment is clear, businesses continue to face different contexts where this kind of discrimination might occur. Take the case of Samantha Elauf, a job applicant for Abercrombie & Fitch. When she applied for a job in 2008, the clothier refused to hire her because she was wearing a hijab, or head scarf, which A&F said was at odds with the company's "neutral look policy" and dress code that forbade caps.[82] The Council on American-Islamic relations filed a complaint on her behalf with the EEOC, who tried to resolve the issue with Abercrombie informally, but ended up suing the retailer for religious discrimination. Abercrombie claimed that Elauf was not turned down because of her faith; rather, she was in violation of the dress code and she did not specifically ask for any religious accommodation. This case went all the way to the

Supreme Court, where in 2015 the Court ruled that companies could not discriminate against job applicants or employees for religious reasons, even if an accommodation is not requested. As noted by Justice Scalia, "The rule of disparate-treatment claims based on a failure to accommodate a religious practice is straightforward. An employer may not make an applicant's religious practice, confirmed or otherwise, a factor in employment decisions."[83] Justice Thomas dissented by noting that the company's "neutral look policy" did not constitute intentional discrimination; however, the other eight Justices disagreed.

19.4b Disparate Impact

Congress later clarified that its intent in prohibiting discrimination was to eliminate practices that contributed to economic inequality. What it found was that, although companies could adhere to the disparate treatment definition of discrimination, this did not eliminate all of the discriminatory practices that existed. For example, a company could use two neutral, color-blind criteria for selection—a high school diploma and a standardized ability test. Minority group members might be treated the same under the criteria, but the problem arose when it became apparent that the policy of equal treatment resulted in unequal *consequences* for minorities. Minority members might be less likely to have high school diplomas, and those who took the test might be less likely to pass it. Therefore, a second, more expanded idea of what constituted discrimination was needed.

The Supreme Court had to decide whether an action was discriminatory if it resulted in unequal consequences in the *Griggs v. Duke Power Company* case.[84] Duke Power had required that employees transferring to other departments have a high school diploma or pass a standardized intelligence test. This requirement excluded a disproportionate number of minority workers. The court noted that there were nonminorities who performed satisfactorily and achieved promotions though they did not have diplomas. The court then reached the groundbreaking conclusion that it was the *consequences* of an employer's actions, not only its intentions, which determined whether discrimination had taken place. If any employment practice or test had an adverse or differential effect on minorities, it was a discriminatory practice.

An unequal impact, or disparate impact, means that fewer minorities are included in the outcome of the test or the hiring or promotion practice than would be expected by their numerical proportion in society. The court also held that a policy or procedure with a disparate impact would be permissible if the employer could demonstrate that it was a business- or job-related necessity. In the *Duke Power* case, however, a high school diploma and good scores on a general intelligence test did not have a clearly demonstrable relationship to successful performance on the job under consideration.[85]

The concept of "unequal impact" is quite significant, because it runs counter to so many traditional employment practices. For example, the minimum height and weight requirements of some police departments have unequal impact and have been struck down by courts because they tend to screen out women, people of Asian heritage, and Latinos disproportionately.[86] Several Supreme Court rulings have addressed the issue of the kind of evidence needed to document or prove discrimination. Typically, if a member of a minority group does not have a success rate at least 80 percent that of the majority group, the practice may be considered to have an adverse impact unless business necessity can be proven.[87] When this **four-fifths rule** is triggered, the firm will not necessarily be found guilty of having a disparate impact. However, it will be incumbent upon the firm to show that the selection practice is job related and necessary for the business.[88]

Figure 19-4 summarizes the characteristics of disparate treatment and disparate impact.

FIGURE 19-4 Two Kinds of Employment Discrimination

Disparate Treatment	Disparate Impact
Primary discrimination	Secondary discrimination
Different treatment	Different results
Intentional discrimination	Unintentional discrimination
Biased actions	Neutral actions, biased impact
Different standards for different groups	Different consequences for different groups

Source: EEOC, "Employment Tests and Selection Procedures," http://www.eeoc.gov/policy/docs/factemployment_procedures.html. Accessed June 2, 2016.

19.5 Issues in Employment Discrimination

The essentials of the major federal laws on discrimination have been presented, and we have traced the evolution of the concept of discrimination. Now it is useful to discuss briefly some of the different issues that are related to the types of discrimination we have covered. It is also important to indicate some of the particular problems that have arisen with respect to each of the different issues.

19.5a Inequality Persists Despite Diversity Efforts

In spite of the efforts previously described, racial and other forms of inequality persist. The reasons are not necessarily a form of racism. The housing collapse that began the Great Recession in 2008 hit African American households particularly hard, and the social mobility that had allowed their earnings to grow until 2000, began to decline even more rapidly.[89] As a result, the black-white wealth gap is now higher than it was in 1989.[90] Other economic factors, like lower overall home ownership and higher unemployment rates reflect inequalities that may or may not have to do with racism.[91]

Often, psychological or sociological factors, removed from race, are at play. For example, **homosocial reproduction** is the tendency of people to be more comfortable with people who share our life experiences and preferences. The uncertainty in business leads us to seek homogeneity in our work groups. Rosabeth Kanter labeled this tendency to replicate ourselves when we hire and promote people as homosocial reproduction.[92] Homosocial reproduction explains, for example, why top management teams are typically not diverse.[93]

In her 2013 book, *The American Non-Dilemma: Racial Inequality without Racism*, Nancy DiTomaso explains how favoritism rather than racism can lead to racial inequality in the workplace.[94] She conducted 246 interviews with white men and women in three parts of the country and found that, throughout their lives, they got their jobs with the help and support of someone they knew (or someone their friends or family knew).[95] Almost every opportunity was attached to being someone's friend or acquaintance, but the advantage was forgotten by the people who used that connection. She had to probe them in the interview to find out about it.[96] The friends or family members who provide the connection are almost always the same race as the person receiving the leg up. DiTomaso explains, "The mechanism that reproduces inequality, in other words, may be inclusion more than exclusion."[97]

19.5b Race and Ethnicity

Although racial discrimination was one of the first forms of discrimination to attract the focus of the civil rights legislation, it remains a major problem in workplaces in the United States and throughout the world. Although racial discrimination is always hurtful, the nature of its form and impact has been different for people of different races. Race discrimination includes discrimination based on ancestry or physical or cultural characteristics associated with a certain race, such as skin color, hair texture or styles, or certain facial features.[98]

First, it is important to discuss the special situation of Hispanics. The word *Hispanic* fails to capture the diversity in this population and sometimes creates confusion. The term was created by the government and was first used in the 1980 census. Hispanics are the only major minority group to be classified by the language they speak. They can be Black (Cuba's population is 58 percent Black), Asian (Peru's former President Fujimori is 100 percent Japanese), or any of a variety of races. Accordingly, many people prefer to be described as Latino (which includes people from Portugal) or as hailing from their country of origin (e.g., of Puerto Rican descent).[99]

People who are Hispanic are faced with significant discrimination that can take the form of racial, national origin, and/or color discrimination. In a 2015 *Gallup Poll*, about 1 in 10 Hispanics say they have experienced discrimination because of their ethnicity in a prior month at each of several locations—their place of work, in dealings with police, while getting health care, and at an entertainment venue like a bar or restaurant.[100] Altogether, 25 percent of Hispanics have felt discriminated against in at least one of these settings, with foreign-born Hispanics reporting more mistreatment than U.S.-born.[101] To deal with this, and the complicating fact that people can be of mixed race or mixed heritage, the Equal Employment Opportunity Commission now uses seven categories to collect statistics about the U.S. workforce. They are:[102]

- Hispanic or Latino
- White (not Hispanic or Latino)
- Black or African American (not Hispanic or Latino)
- Native Hawaiian or Other Pacific Islander (not Hispanic or Latino)
- Asian (not Hispanic or Latino)
- American Indian or Alaska Native (not Hispanic or Latino)
- Two or More Races (not Hispanic or Latino)

In an increasingly diverse society, people are not easily characterized, but these categories help to give some sense of the aggregate makeup of the work force.

19.5c Color

Color bias is another issue that raises challenges for the workplace. As part of the Civil Rights Act of 1964, discrimination based on color has been illegal for a long period of time. As a practical matter, however, color bias has been largely misunderstood. The EEOC has clarified the definition of color discrimination. "Even though race and color clearly overlap, they are not synonymous. Thus, color discrimination can occur between persons of different races or ethnicities, or between persons of the same race or ethnicity. Although Title VII does not define 'color,' the courts and the EEOC read 'color' to have its commonly understood meaning—pigmentation, complexion, or skin shade or tone. Thus, color discrimination occurs when a person is discriminated against based on their lightness, darkness, or other color characteristic. Title VII prohibits race/color discrimination against all persons, including Caucasians."[103]

Most people do not realize that race and color are considered to be separate by law and both are covered by law, so many cases go unreported."[104] Nevertheless, some situations do surface. In June 2009, the EEOC sued a Puerto Rico–based furniture company for allegedly permitting a Puerto Rican store manager to harass a dark-complexioned Puerto Rican sales associate. The manager taunted him about his skin color (e.g., asking why he was "so black") and then fired him for complaining.[105]

19.5d Gender

Issues surrounding sex discrimination are different from those involving race, color, and national origin. Gender issues include discrimination against men, women, gay, lesbian, bisexual, and transgender (LGBT) employees alike. We focus on women first with managerial positions and pay, as this has received a lot of attention in both research and the media. We then expand our gender classifications in the areas of sexual harassment, sexual orientation, and gender identity discrimination. However, we note that the major issues for women today can also apply across all gender classifications.

The major issues for women today include (1) getting into professional and managerial positions and out of traditional female-dominated positions, (2) achieving pay commensurate with that of men, (3) eliminating sexual harassment, and (4) being able to take maternity leave without losing their jobs. Some progress is being made on each of these fronts but more work remains to be done.

Women in Professional/Managerial Positions. The fact that, in 2015, only 4 percent of Fortune 500 firms are headed by women, and this has been the same for several years, is an indication that progress in this area has been slow, given the percentage of women in the population.[106] In addition, *PwC* reported that of the 359 open CEO slots in 2015, women filled just 10.[107] Furthermore, the Catalyst Census found that while 19.2 percent of the board seats of the S&P 500 companies are held by women, the U.S. tied with Australia in tenth place among the 20 developed nations, and in general, European countries are doing much better.[108]

Some argue that it takes decades to become a CEO and so the pipeline for female CEOs is just starting to fill.[109] Others contend that women bear some responsibility. Sheryl Sandberg raised a media furor with her 2013 book, *Lean In*, which suggests women sabotage themselves by lacking self-confidence and not grabbing opportunities as they arise.[110] Of course, gender discrimination remains a key explanation for the disparity, and that explanation is supported by the scores of studies that show the significant pay discrepancy between men and women in the workplace.[111] One thing is clear, the explanation is not performance driven. Women-run hedge funds outperform those run by men, male retail investors outtrade but underperform women, and women-led companies in the S&P 1500 outperform those run by men.[112]

Equal Pay and Promotion. As we noted above, equal pay and specifically the gender pay gap is a hot-button issue for gender discrimination. While we noted that some critics have tried to explain the discrepancy by arguing that these statistics include women who lost both time and experience through extended maternity leave, the Bureau of Labor statistics shows that the gap exists at the start of women's careers, as well as for women who work full time.[113] The gap also exists for women in professional and technical occupations.[114] This issue affects families as well as the worker involved. A 2015 Pew Research Center survey found that women as a whole continue to work in lower-paying occupations than men do, and women are about twice as likely as men to say they had been discriminated against at work because of their gender.[115]

It might seem surprising that issues of gender pay inequality, like other forms of discrimination, still exist today, with more legislation and court cases trying to address the issues. However, in the case of gender pay inequality, a recent study conducted by women in the San Francisco Bay Area, called the "Elephant in the Valley," found that the workplace requires more than "equal pay for equal work" covered under the Equal Pay Act.[116] For example, they found that women were presented with fewer business opportunities, excluded from key social networking events, and had colleagues address questions to their male peers that should have been addressed to them.[117]

While these may be examples of more subtle versions of discrimination against women, current research shows that subtle forms are just as damaging as more overt forms, with a host of adverse work-related outcomes at the individual and organizational levels.[118] Additionally, both subtle and overt forms of discrimination against women have been said to contribute to a "toxic work world" where only the young, childless, and eldercare-less employees are valued (since it is mostly women who handle care giving in families).[119] In sum, employers must be prepared to address both overt and subtle forms of gender discrimination.

Sexual Harassment. Sexual harassment in the workplace is a worldwide problem with negative consequences that are pervasive and ongoing. A meta-analysis of sexual harassment studies found that victims of sexual harassment suffered a range of negative outcomes such as decreased job satisfaction, lower organizational commitment, withdrawal from work, poor physical and mental health, and even symptoms of posttraumatic stress disorder.[120]

The EEOC defines **sexual harassment** in the following way:

> *Unwelcome sexual advances, requests for sexual favors, and other verbal or physical conduct of a sexual nature constitute sexual harassment when submission to or rejection of this conduct explicitly or implicitly affects an individual's employment, unreasonably interferes with an individual's work performance, or creates an intimidating, hostile, or offensive work environment.*

Implicit in this definition are two broad types of sexual harassment. First is what has been called **quid pro quo** harassment. This is a situation where something is given or received for something else. For example, a boss may make it explicit or implicit that a sexual favor is expected if the employee wants a pay raise or a promotion. Second is what has been referred to as **hostile work environment** harassment. In this type, nothing is given or received, but the employee perceives a hostile or offensive work environment by virtue of uninvited sexually oriented behaviors or materials being present in the workplace. Examples of this might include sexual teasing or jokes or sexual materials, such as pictures or cartoons, being present in the workplace. A recent study of EEOC settlements over a ten-year period found that almost all of the cases (98.5 percent) included a hostile environment aspect and most of the cases (89.1 percent) only involved a hostile environment, that is, did not include a quid pro quo complaint.[121]

To clear up common misconceptions, the EEOC indicates that sexual harassment can occur in a variety of circumstances that include but are not limited to the following:[122]

- The victim as well as the harasser may be a woman or a man.
- The victim does not have to be of the opposite sex.
- The harasser can be the victim's supervisor, an agent of the employer, a supervisor in another area, a coworker, or a nonemployee.
- The victim does not have to be the person harassed but could be anyone affected by the offensive conduct.
- Unlawful sexual harassment may occur without economic injury to or discharge of the victim.
- The harasser's conduct must be unwelcome.

Figure 19-5 lists the kinds of experiences about which women are typically talking when they say they have been sexually harassed; however, men and LGBT employees sometimes make these complaints as well. The stereotypical view of sexual harassment is of a male supervisor harassing a female subordinate. However, this is not always the case. In 2015, the EEOC had 6,822 charges filed alleging sexual harassment,

FIGURE 19-5 Examples of Sexual Harassment Complaints

- Being subjected to sexually suggestive remarks and propositions
- Being sent on unnecessary errands through work areas where co-workers have an added opportunity to stare
- Being subjected to sexual innuendo and joking
- Being touched by a boss while working
- Co-workers' "remarks" about a person sexually cooperating with the boss
- Suggestive looks and gestures
- Deliberate touching and "cornering"
- Suggestive body movements
- Sexually oriented materials being circulated around the office
- Pornographic cartoons and pictures posted or present in work areas
- Pressure for dates and sexual favors
- Boss's cruelty after sexual advances are resisted
- A boss rubbing employee's back while he or she is typing

Note: It should be noted that these are "complaints." Whether each item turns out to be sexual harassment or not in the eyes of the law is determined in an official hearing or trial.

with 17.1 percent filed by males.[123] Of the 1,412 sex discrimination cases that we noted above filed by LGBT members in 2015, a majority of them appear to involve sexual harassment.[124]

Many people do not realize that Title IX offers protection against sexual harassment in a way that is essentially similar to Title VII. Title IX, the law that bans sex discrimination at schools receiving federal funds, is best known in its sports context for the formula that determines if schools are providing women with fair opportunities to play sports. Schools can be sued for monetary damages under Title IX for knowingly allowing sexual harassment to take place.

There are four parts to the burden of proof: (1) the school must be aware of the sexual harassment, (2) the school must fail to take steps to stop it, (3) the harassment must deny access to an educational opportunity, and (4) the harassment must take place in an educational setting.[125]

Supreme Court rulings underscore the importance of companies' being diligent in their efforts to discourage harassing behavior. For example, the Supreme Court ruled that employers might be held liable even if they did not know about the harassment or their supervisors never carried out any threatened job actions.[126] Clearly, employers must develop comprehensive programs to protect their employees from harassment. When businesses develop comprehensive and clear programs to prevent sexual harassment, they are legally rewarded. The Supreme Court ruled that good faith efforts to prevent and correct harassment are one prong of an "affirmative defense" that companies can employ when charged with harassment. The second prong is proving the employee failed to take advantage of opportunities the firm provided for correction or prevention.[127]

19.5e Other Forms of Employment Discrimination

Much of the attention surrounding employment discrimination has focused on racial and sexual discrimination. However, other important forms of discrimination represent critical issues for business today. It is important for managers to understand the many forms that discrimination can take in an increasingly diverse workforce and where courts currently stand on those issues.

ETHICS IN PRACTICE CASE

Gentleman's Club?

After only a few months of working with a new firm, my supervisor asked me to partake in a trip to Central America to tour our sister facility. The company had recently purchased a plant in Mexico and after several months of production, the main office needed to conduct a full inventory count. It sounded like a great opportunity and I gladly accepted the offer.

While abroad we spent several long days in the warehouse and when the work was finally complete, the Director of Operations took us out to celebrate at the company's expense. Following a nice dinner, a few of us were encouraged to continue the evening at a "Gentleman's Club." While there, the senior staff member began to urge us to take part in the extracurricular activities.

The peer pressure was rather intense, as the Director made it clear that either we would all participate or none of us would. Furthermore, he informed us that he would take care of the entire bill. To the disappointment of some and the relief of others, I explained that I was not feeling well and preferred to return to the hotel. After we returned home, the events of that evening were never openly discussed; however, a few co-workers always throw me a look of disappointment.

1. Was I wrong to avoid participating in the activities going on? Might I have put my job at risk? Should I have been put in that situation?
2. Does this practice discriminate against any protected groups? Which one(s)?
3. Does this practice discriminate against any nonprotected groups?
4. What should I do? Should I report my supervisor to the company? Will not participating in the "activities" affect my career trajectory? Should I care?

Contributed Anonymously

Religious Discrimination. Religious discrimination is one that is growing quickly; complaints more than doubled in the past 15 years.[128] According to the EEOC, violations of religious discrimination involve a variety of patterns, including:[129]

1. Refusing to hire or firing workers after learning their religion;
2. Discharging workers who take leave for religious-related events (such as observing the Sabbath);
3. Failing to accommodate religious-related garb choices; and
4. Retaliating against employees who requested religious accommodation or complained about religious discrimination.

Research has shown that religious discrimination is a continuing problem, as we noted above in the recent Abercrombie & Fitch case. In many cases, corporate policies are at issue. For example, in 2015, a Chicago-area woman accused Office Depot of religious discrimination when an employee declined to copy anti-Planned Parenthood fliers. Office Depot's corporate spokesperson said that corporate policy prohibits "the copying of any type of material that advocates any form of racial or religious discrimination or the persecution of certain groups of people." The flier, she said, advocated the persecution of those who support abortion rights.[130]

In another case, UPS's "no-beard" policy resulted in a religious discrimination suit from a Muslim who applied for a driver helper position.[131] Sometimes accommodation requires some ingenuity. IBM was faced with a challenge when a newly hired Muslim woman showed up for work the first day wearing the veil and was told she had to have her picture taken for the employee identification badge. For Muslim women, wearing the veil is a sign of modesty, and so the new employee objected on religious grounds to showing her face. IBM officials came up with an accommodation that met the needs of all involved. She had her picture taken in the veil and that was the picture on the employee identification badge she wore each day. In addition, a woman photographer took her picture without the veil for a second badge she carried in her bag. It was agreed that if she ever needed to show that badge she would only do so to a female security officer.[132]

ETHICS IN PRACTICE CASE

Bigotry in the Bakery?

Since my junior year in high school, I have been working in the same local supermarket. My main job was for me to get the bread set up ready before the following day. After working in the bakery for quite some time, I began to notice the difference between how I have been treated compared to other co-workers. At first, I didn't notice the differences but as time passed I saw how they were making me do work that others in my department have never done. For example, the manager of the store realized that the ceiling of the bakery department was dirty and had accumulated pesticides. He told me to go up and clean the ceiling; he gave me no mask to protect myself from the pesticides. He just told me to go up and use Windex and clean the ceiling. I was hesitant at first but I completed the task without asking why. At the time, I was still new so I didn't want to mention anything to my boss so I just did as I was told.

Now as this continued to happen I asked my co-workers, who were white, if they were ever told to complete this task. They all answered saying that none of them have ever been told to clean the ceiling and don't know of anyone in the store who has. They couldn't believe that I was cleaning the ceilings full of pesticides. For the past four years, they have been making me do this and it's not my job to do so. For this job, they should be hiring a cleaning crew to come in at night and clean the store. So I asked another Latino in the store who has been working there for more than ten years how he is treated. He answered saying that they have asked him do things around the store that aren't under his job description as well. Over the years, I've seen that the manager feels like it is okay for me to clean the ceilings even though that can potentially harm my health. It is not only happening to me but other Hispanic employees as well. However, I try to be a good employee and listen. The same is true for the other Latinos in the store who have not said anything to the manager and continue to perform these tasks.

1. Is discrimination taking place in this job assignment situation?
2. If it is, what should I do next? This job is important to me and I don't want to lose it.
3. Will the fact that I agreed to perform these dirty and dangerous tasks affect my case? I was always taught to work hard and earn the money I am paid. Was that the wrong thing to do?

Contributed anonymously

Retaliation. As noted earlier, the most cases filed with the EEOC are in response to retaliation. The same laws that protect individuals from discrimination protect them from being retaliated against for filing a discrimination claim. They also protect someone who is not the target of the discrimination but is retaliated against for supporting a person who files a claim. **Retaliation** can take many forms, including firing, demotion, or harassment. Retaliation also can be intimidation, threats, and untrue negative evaluations, denial of a promotion, negative references, increased surveillance, or any other kind of treatment that would make a person hesitate to file a claim. This prohibition against retaliation only applies to those who file claims on their own behalf and those who oppose discrimination by supporting victims, testifying at proceedings, or calling attention to unlawful practices. It does not apply to whistleblowers who call attention to illegal acts other than discrimination (although other whistleblower protections may apply in those instances). In addition to this being a legal issue, it also represents an ethical issue. Ethical principles discussed earlier in the text, for example, fair treatment, rights, and due process, would preclude responsible companies taking retaliatory actions against a worker for seeking to protect his or her job.

Sexual Orientation and Gender Identity Discrimination. Corporations have been faster than governments in instituting protections for lesbian, gay, bisexual, and transgender (LGBT) employees. As of 2015, 88 percent of the Fortune 500 companies include **sexual orientation** in their nondiscrimination policies and a majority (67 percent) provides domestic partner health insurance benefits to employees.[133] The greatest growth has been in prohibition of gender identity discrimination in the *Fortune* 500. In

2000, only three companies prohibited discrimination based on gender identity, but in 2016, two-thirds prohibit gender identity discrimination.[134]

A combination of new state legislation, private protections, and federal litigations have provided some momentum in ensuring employment protection for LGBT workers, but in the 28 states with no antidiscrimination laws based on sexual orientation and gender identity, the possibility of overt discrimination still exists, and this is especially true for transgender employees. A recent survey noted that 90 percent of transgender people reported harassment on the job and 47 percent experienced an "adverse job outcome."[135] Yet, changes have occurred on some issues. According to the 2016 Corporate Equality Index, two-fifths of the Fortune 500 and 60 percent of their 4,000+ corporate respondents offer transgender-inclusive health-care coverage, nearly six times as many businesses as five years ago.[136]

Business has been generally supportive of proposed federal and state legislation that would extend LGBT protections. The Business Coalition for Workplace Fairness is pushing for federal legislation to extend protections to both sexual orientation and gender identity.[137] Corporate advocacy has also extended to protests against state bills that businesses like Apple, Coca-Cola, and Delta perceive as targeting LGBT workers.[138] In 2016, several companies launched a boycott against the state of North Carolina in protest about a new state law that overturned local protections for gay and transgender people and bars transgender people from using public bathrooms that do not match the sexes stated on their birth certificates.[139]

Companies were also instrumental in pushing for the Supreme Court to overturn the section of the Defense of Marriage Act (DOMA) that disallowed recognition and federal benefits for same-sex couples. More than 200 companies, including Citigroup, Apple, Microsoft, and Marriott, signed a supporting brief that argued that the patchwork of state laws cost the companies' time and money because they had to maintain dual policies.[140] In June 2015, the Supreme Court ruled that gay marriage is legal in all 50 states.

Gender identity, among other issues, addresses the special challenges for business of the treatment of transgender and transsexual employees. "Transgender" is an umbrella term that refers to people who express a gender that does not match the one on their original birth certificate or physically change their sex through surgery. "Transsexual" refers specifically to a person who is undergoing or has undergone sex-change surgery.[141] This is not a new workplace issue. In 1993, the Washington State Supreme Court upheld Boeing Company's 1985 firing of a male software engineer who dressed in women's clothes and insisted on using the women's restroom while the sex-change operation was pending. The court ruled that discomfort with one's biological sex was not a handicap.[142]

What is new is the opinion of the courts and the stance that corporations have begun to take since that day. In June 2004, the Sixth U.S. Circuit Court of Appeals (which covers Michigan, Ohio, Kentucky, and Tennessee) heard the case of a transsexual Ohio firefighter who had been fired. In the first such action by a federal court, the court ruled that Title VII of the Civil Rights Act of 1964 protects transsexuals and that the sex-stereotyping doctrine covers people who change their sex.[143] In 2010, the Eighth Circuit Court decided in favor of a motel clerk whom the company had deemed too masculine for a daytime front desk clerk position.[144] According to InsideCounsel, "The ruling confirms a legal principle that recently has gained support in circuit courts across the country: Although Title VII does not deal with sexual orientation, courts have found that the statute protects individuals from discrimination for breaking gender stereotypes."[145] In 2015, the EEOC settled one of its first two lawsuits ever filed alleging sex discrimination against a transgender individual when a director in an eye clinic was fired when she made it known she was transgender and started dressing differently.[146]

The concept of gender identity and its legal protections continues to evolve, but the trend against gender stereotyping carries implications for future protections for various gender identity issues. InsideCounsel offers employers the following advice, "Employers across the nation should be scrutinizing their policies and practices with regard to discrimination against transgender and transsexual people as states pass laws prohibiting discrimination on the basis of gender identity and courts interpret existing civil rights laws to protect those individuals."[147]

19.6 Affirmative Action in the Workplace

Affirmative action is the process of taking positive steps to hire and promote people from groups previously discriminated against. The concept of affirmative action was formally introduced to the business world in 1965, when former President Lyndon B. Johnson signed Executive Order 11246, the purpose of which was to require all firms doing business with the federal government to engage in affirmative actions to accelerate the movement of minorities into the workforce. Few people realize, however, that the federal government did not make a real commitment to affirmative action until the administration of former President Richard M. Nixon, who revived the practice of racial hiring preferences.[148] Companies today have affirmative action programs because they do business with the government, have begun the plans voluntarily, or have entered into them through collective bargaining agreements with labor unions.

The increase in employee diversity in workplaces throughout the world has shifted the debate. Companies are realizing that a diverse workforce is key to business success and so many companies actively seek a workforce that not only matches their increasingly diverse world but also draws upon an underutilized talent pool.[149] Affirmative action becomes less of an issue when companies actively seek to increase diversity in their companies, as many of them are. Nevertheless, affirmative action remains an issue in access to education opportunities as well as opportunities for underrepresented groups to break new ground.

The meaning of affirmative action has changed since its introduction. It originally referred only to special efforts to ensure equal opportunity for members of groups that had been subject to discrimination. More recently, the term has come to refer to programs in which members of such groups are given some degree of definite preference in determining access to positions from which they were formerly excluded.[150] It is important to remember that affirmative action is not just one thing; it can be anything in a range of programs. Today, when people speak of affirmative action, they are typically referring to some degree of preferential selection. It has most recently been applied to admissions practices in higher education, where race and ethnicity have been used in admissions decisions. Figure 19-6 summarizes the key Supreme Court decisions to date on affirmative action.

The underlying rationale for affirmative action is the principle of **compensatory justice**, which holds that whenever injustice is done, just compensation or reparation is owed to the injured party or parties.[151] The principal objection to affirmative action and the reason it has become and remained controversial is that it leads to **reverse discrimination**. The public, in general, supports affirmative action when it is described as simply providing opportunities for previously disadvantaged groups. When the question is rephrased to include providing preferential treatment to minorities, the approval rate plummets by half.[152]

The possibility of reverse discrimination is at the core of the controversy surrounding affirmative action. The U.S. Supreme Court, for example, recently agreed to take another look at the 2013 case of *Fisher v. University of Texas*, where a young white female, Abigail Fisher, was rejected for admission to the university and said that her rights were violated by UT Austin's consideration of race and ethnicity in admissions decisions. The

FIGURE 19-6 Key Supreme Court Decisions on Affirmative Action

Year	Case	Issue	General Finding
2016	*Fisher v. University of Texas*	Admission to the university	U.S. Supreme Court upheld the affirmative action program at the University of Texas
2013	*Fisher v. University of Texas*	Admission to the university	Remanded the case to the lower court finding, it did not apply the standard of strict scrutiny
2009	*Ricci v. DeStefano*	Firefighter lieutenant and captain exams	Unconstitutional to discard exams due to concerns about disparate impact
2006	*Parents v. Seattle and Meredith v. Jefferson*	School integration	Unconstitutional to consider race when assigning students to schools
2003	*Grutter v. Bollinger*	Admission to law school	Race can be a factor (invalidates *Hopwood*)
1996	*Hopwood v. University of Texas Law School*	Admission to law school	Rejected legitimacy of diversity as a goal for AA
1995	*Adarand Constructors, Inc. v. Peña*	Federal affirmative action set asides	AA must pass "strict scrutiny" test of compelling interest and narrow tailoring
1989	*City of Richmond v. Croson*	Construction set asides for black-owned firms	AA unconstitutional unless racial discrimination proven widespread in industry
1987	*United States v. Paradise*	Hiring of state trooper in Alabama	Strict quotas accepted only because there was persistent and pervasive racism
1986	*Wygant v. Board of Education*	Layoff policy that protected minorities	Preferential layoffs unacceptable—greater injury than hiring policy
1980	*Fullilove v. Klutznick*	Set asides for minority contractors	Set asides acceptable due to narrow focus and limited intent
1979	*United Steelworkers v. Weber*	Admission to private employer training program (Kaiser)	Quotas acceptable if temporary and addressing a clear imbalance
1978	*Regents of the University of California v. Bakke*	Admission to medical school	Race deemed a legitimate factor but ruled against strict quotas

2013 and 2014 Court of Appeals rulings on the case allowed colleges to continue the practice, but raised the bar for colleges in how they must justify the consideration of race and ethnicity in admissions. In 2016, the Supreme Court reviewed the Fisher case again and upheld the constitutionality of affirmative action in admissions practices, thereby allowing the University of Texas to continue to use its "race-conscious" admissions program.[153]

Some have suggested that college admissions should focus on favoring preferences for low-income students as a way of achieving diversity; however, the University of Michigan, where affirmative action has not been allowed in admissions since 2009, has argued that it does not work. A recent study by The Century Foundation points to a different solution. It found that states that banned affirmative action in higher education have been successful in recruiting minorities by implementing new methods of promoting racial, ethnic, and socioeconomic diversity, including (1) guaranteeing admission to public colleges for top graduates from each high school in the state, (2) adding socioeconomic factors to admissions, (3) funding new financial aid programs, (4) improving recruitment and support, and (5) dropping legacy preferences.[154]

What is the future of affirmative action for higher education and businesses? Supporters of affirmative action point out that a strictly income-based version would produce much less racial diversity, given that fewer than one-third of households making $40,000 a year or less are black or Latino.[155] Many favor an approach that focuses on wealth, neighborhood, and family structure, as well as parents' income, education, and other factors. However, the spirit of affirmative action, and diversity, continues to be endorsed by businesses, with dozens of Fortune 500 companies in 2015 asking the Supreme Court to preserve universities' right to use it in their admissions.[156]

19.6a The Future of Diversity Management

We began this chapter by noting that diversity and inclusion is a top priority in businesses today as they actively pursue diversity management strategies in their companies. With the buying power of minority groups in the United States increasing dramatically, there is further incentive for business's achieving greater diversity. The University of Georgia's Selig Center charts the growth of consumer groups, and their findings are instructive. According to center director Jeff Humphries, "The $1.2 trillion Hispanic market is larger than the entire economies of all but 13 countries in the world."[157] The growth has also been dramatic in African American buying power, which, according to a 2015 Nielsen report, is the fastest growing segment in all income groups above $60,000.[158] Similarly, the Asian American buying power is also growing. According to the Selig Center for Economic Growth, their buying power is expected to increase to $1.1 trillion by 2020.[159]

Increasing minority buying power and influence are also incentivizing companies to want to undertake voluntary programs to increase the diversity in their workforce and their bottom lines. In one of life's ironies, the EEOC had to warn companies to not base employment decisions on race or any other protected category, even when the goal is greater diversity. According to former EEOC Chair Naomi Earp, customer preferences have never been an acceptable reason to discriminate in employment and reference to a global market is not sufficient justification either.[160] The legality of some diversity practices remains unsettled, and thus they may be risky. These include offering incentives for managers to achieve a diverse workforce or promoting affinity groups, formed by employees along race or gender lines.[161]

New analytical tools can provide opportunities to identify gender and race inequalities in the workforce and offer some new opportunities for diversity management. New software tools allow companies to detect potential gender and race gaps in outcomes like pay, recruitment, and promotion, given different inputs like training, mentoring, and company policies and practices.[162] These offer opportunities to provide "real fixes" for workplace bias that can be institutionalized in the design of the businesses themselves, and perhaps, even to put an end to discrimination.[163] While it is early to see if these tools can truly make the workplace fairer, more inclusive, and productive, they provide one more way to ensure that underrepresented groups receive a fair shot in the workforce.

Summary

This chapter addresses several subgroups of employee stakeholders whose job rights are protected by law, and whose issues are morally important, as well as important to effective stakeholder management. We noted that managing diversity in the workforce has evolved from a paradigm of recruitment and retention of protected class members to one that promotes active integration of diverse members into the workforce. As companies have sought to become better corporate citizens, the movement toward diversity has become a hallmark of these companies.

This movement toward a diverse workforce was initiated by and has been supported by numerous laws, beginning with the Civil Rights Act of 1964, which prohibited discrimination based on race, color, religion, sex, or national origin. Laws covering age and disabilities then followed. Other protections related to disability are prohibitions against pregnancy discrimination and genetic information discrimination. The EEOC was created to assume the major responsibility for enforcing the discrimination laws. Like other federal agencies, the EEOC has had problems. However, on balance, it has done a reasonable job of monitoring the two major forms of discrimination: disparate treatment and disparate impact. Discrimination issues discussed in this chapter include issues of racial discrimination, women moving into professional/managerial positions, pay equity, sexual harassment, pregnancy discrimination, fetal protection policies, age discrimination, and religious discrimination. In addition, new and evolving discrimination issues such as sexual orientation, gender identity, and color bias as separate from race were discussed.

Affirmative action, the taking of positive steps to hire and promote people from groups previously discriminated against, was one of the government's answers to the problem of discrimination. There is evidence that attitudes toward affirmative action are changing as the global economy brings a more diverse workforce and customer base. However, psychological and sociological aspects of people being people may mean that achieving diversity will be an elusive goal. Firms should follow best practices when designing diversity programs, and there is the potential of new analytical software tools to help them with this. Moral management and sound stakeholder management require companies to strive to be fair in their employment practices.

Key Terms

access-and-legitimacy, p. 581
affirmative action, p. 602
Age Discrimination in Employment Act (ADEA), p. 585
Americans with Disabilities Act (ADA), p. 586
bona fide occupational qualification (BFOQ), p. 585
Civil Rights Act of 1991, p. 591
color bias, p. 595
compensatory justice, p. 602
discrimination-and-fairness, p. 581
disparate impact, p. 592
disparate treatment, p. 592
diversity fatigue, p. 581
diversity management, p. 581
Equal Employment Opportunity Commission (EEOC), p. 591
Equal Pay Act of 1963, p. 585
essential functions, p. 587
ethical blindness, p. 585
fetal protection policies, p. 590
four-fifths rule, p. 593
gender identity, p. 601
Genetic Information Nondiscrimination Act, p. 590
homosocial reproduction, p. 594
hostile work environment, p. 597
integration-and-learning, p. 581
Lilly Ledbetter Fair Pay Act of 2009, p. 585
major life activities, p. 587
Pregnancy Discrimination Act of 1978, p. 589
protected groups, p. 580
quid pro quo, p. 597
reasonable accommodations, p. 587
retaliation, p. 600
reverse discrimination, p. 602
sexual harassment, p. 597
sexual orientation, p. 600
Title VII of the Civil Rights Act of 1964, p. 583
undue hardship, p. 587

Discussion Questions

1. Identify the major federal discrimination laws and indicate what they prohibit. Which agency is primarily responsible for enforcing these laws?
2. Give two different definitions of discrimination, and provide an example of each.
3. How has the Americans with Disabilities Act (ADA) evolved since its inception?
4. Do you think racial inequality is caused by racism, favoritism, or both? Explain your answer.
5. Do you agree with the Genetic Nondiscrimination Act? Do companies have a right to know and use genetic information about employees? Why or why not?
6. Has the concept of diversity supplanted the concept of affirmative action in leading companies today? Why or why not?

Endnotes

1. "Equal Employment Opportunity (EEO) Terminology," http://www.archives.gov/eeo/terminology.html#r. Accessed May 31, 2016.
2. "Statewide Employment Laws and Policies," http://www.hrc.org/state_maps. Accessed May 31, 2016.
3. Josh Bersin, "Why Diversity and Inclusion Will Be a Top Priority for 2016," *Forbes* (December 6, 2015), http://www.forbes.com/sites/joshbersin/2015/12/06/why-diversity-and-inclusion-will-be-a-top-priority-for-2016/#37dc803f4bd4. Accessed May 31, 2016.
4. Vivian Hunt, Dennis Layton, and Sara Prince, "Why Diversity Matters," McKinsey Study (January 2015), http://www.mckinsey.com/business-functions/organization/our-insights/why-diversity-matters. Accessed May 31, 2016.
5. David Thomas and Robin Ely, "Making Differences Matter: A New Paradigm for Managing Diversity," *Harvard Business Review* (September/October 1996), https://hbr.org/1996/09/making-differences-matter-a-new-paradigm-for-managing-diversity. Accessed May 31, 2016.
6. Ibid.
7. Ibid.
8. Ibid.
9. Karen C. Wise, "The Three Paradigms of Equality and Diversity," Review of session by Professor Robin Ely at the NHS Employers Conference (February 4, 2011), https://karenwise.wordpress.com/2011/02/04/the-three-paradigms-of-equality-diversity/. Accessed May 31, 2016.
10. Society for Human Resource Management, "Workplace Diversity Series Part I: Moving Forward with Diversity" (March 1, 2006), https://www.shrm.org/research/articles/articles/pages/workplacediversityseriespartimovingforwardwithdiversity.aspx. Accessed May 31, 2016.
11. Society for Human Resource Management Diversity and Inclusion Report (April 8, 2014), https://www.shrm.org/research/surveyfindings/articles/pages/diversity-inclusion.aspx. Accessed June 1, 2016.
12. "Diversity Fatigue," *The Economist* (February 13, 2016), http://www.economist.com/news/business/21692865-making-most-workplace-diversity-requires-hard-work-well-good-intentions-diversity. Accessed May 31, 2016.
13. Rachel Feintzeig, "More Companies Say Targets Are the Key to Diversity," *The Wall Street Journal* (September 30, 2016), http://www.wsj.com/articles/more-companies-say-targets-are-the-key-to-diversity-1443600464. Accessed May 31, 2016.
14. Ibid.
15. Ibid.
16. Tanzina Vega, "Working While Brown: What Discrimination Looks Like Now," CNN Money (November 25, 2016), http://money.cnn.com/2015/11/25/news/economy/racial-discrimination-work/. Accessed May 31, 2016.
17. Ibid.
18. *U.S. News and World Report*, "An Attorney for the ACLU Says Federal Officials Are Investigating Whether Gender Discrimination Exists in Hollywood" (May 11, 2016), http://www.usnews.com/news/entertainment/articles/2016-05-11/feds-eye-whether-gender-discrimination-exists-in-hollywood. Accessed June 2, 2016.
19. Seamus Kirst, "#OscarsSoWhite: Celebrities Denounce the Academy Awards and Criticize Hollywood's Business Model," http://www.forbes.com/sites/seamuskirst/2016/01/18/oscarssowhite-celebrities-denounce-the-academy-awards-and-criticize-hollywoods-business-model/#61786ba666e6. Accessed June 1, 2016.
20. William F. Glueck and James Ledvinka, "Equal Employment Opportunity Programs," in William F. Glueck, *Personnel: A Diagnostic Approach*, rev. ed. (Dallas, TX: Business Publications, 1978), 593–633.
21. Ibid., 597–599.
22. "Equal Opportunity: A Scorecard," *Dun's Review* (November 1979), 107.
23. Ibid., 108.
24. Department of Labor, Bureau of Labor Statistics (December 2015), http://www.bls.gov/opub/mlr/2015/article/labor-force-projections-to-2024.htm. Accessed June 1, 2016.
25. Ibid.
26. Ibid.
27. Catalyst, "Lesbian, Gay, Bisexual, Transgender Workplace Issues" (May 26, 2015), http://www.catalyst.org/knowledge/lesbian-gay-bisexual-transgender-workplace-issues. Accessed June 1, 2016.
28. EEOC, "Title VII: Enforces Job Rights" (Washington, DC: The U.S. Equal Employment Opportunity Commission, Office of Communications, October 1988), 1.
29. Gerald L. Maatman, Jr., "Supreme Court Rulings Score a Worker Trifecta," *Business Insurance* (October 16, 2006), 26.
30. Ibid.
31. "Supreme Court: Title VII Deadline Clock Resets with Each New Biased Decision," *The HR Specialist* (June 2010), http://www.thehrspecialist.com/article.aspx?articleid=32469. Accessed May 29, 2013.
32. U.S. Equal Employment Opportunity Commission, "What You Should Know about EEOC and Enforcement Protections for LGBT Workers," https://www.

eeoc.gov/eeoc/newsroom/wysk/enforcement_protections_lgbt_workers.cfm. Accessed June 1, 2016.

33. Ibid.
34. U.S. Equal Opportunity Commission, "Age Discrimination," http://www.eeoc.gov/youth/age.html. Accessed June 4, 2016.
35. *Legal Dictionary.net*, "Bona Fide Occupational Qualification," http://legaldictionary.net/bona-fide occupational-qualification/. Accessed June 4, 2016.
36. EEOC, "Age Discrimination Is against the Law" (Washington, DC: The U.S. Equal Employment Opportunity Commission, Office of Communications, April 1988), 1.
37. R. Scott Oswald and Tom Harrington, "What It Takes to Prove an Age Discrimination Case," *Forbes* (September 28, 2015), http://www.forbes.com/sites/nextavenue/2015/09/28/what-it-takes-to-prove-an-age-discrimination-case/#760a34a27dbe. Accessed June 1, 2016.
38. Guido Palazzo, Franciska Krings, and Ulrich Hoffrage, "Ethical Blindness," *The Journal of Business Ethics* (Vol. 109, 2012), 323–338.
39. EEOC, "Equal Work, Equal Pay" (Washington, DC: The U.S. Equal Employment Opportunity Commission, Office of Communications, October 1988), 1.
40. Harold M. Brody and Alexander Grodan, "The Effect of the Fair Pay Act on Disparate-Impact Cases," *Employment Relations Today* (Winter 2010), 73–78.
41. "A Backpay Bonanza," *The Wall Street Journal* (August 2, 2007), A10.
42. Sheryl Gay Stolberg, "Obama Signs Equal Pay Legislation," *The New York Times* (January 29, 2009), http://www.nytimes.com/2009/01/30/us/politics/30ledbetter-web.html. Accessed June 4, 2016.
43. AAUW, "2015 State Equal Pay Legislation by the Numbers" (August 20, 2015), http://www.aauw.org/2015/08/20/equal-pay-by-state/. Accessed May 31, 2016.
44. Sarah Ketterer, "The 'Wage Gap' Myth That Won't Die," *The Wall Street Journal* (October 1, 2015), A17.
45. Ibid.
46. EEOC, "Equal Employment Opportunity Is the Law" (Washington, DC: The U.S. Equal Employment Opportunity Commission, Office of Communications 1986), 1.
47. Henry H. Perritt, Jr., *Americans with Disabilities Act Handbook* (New York: John Wiley & Sons, 1990), vii.
48. U.S. Department of Justice, Office on the Americans with Disabilities Act, *The Americans with Disabilities Act: Questions and Answers* (Washington, DC: Government Printing Office, 1991), 1. Also see "Disabilities Act to Cover 500,000 More Firms," *The Atlanta Journal* (July 25, 1994), E1.
49. U.S. EEOC, "Questions and Answers on the Final Rule Implementing ADA Amendments Act of 2008," http://www.eeoc.gov/laws/regulations/ada_qa_final_rule.cfm. Accessed June 3, 2016.
50. Ibid.
51. Jen Wieczner, "Why the Disabled Are Suing Uber and Lyft," *Fortune* (May 22, 2015), http://fortune.com/2015/05/22/uber-lyft-disabled/. Accessed June 2, 2016.
52. Ibid.
53. Joe Palazzolo, "Disabled Sue over Web Shopping," *The Wall Street Journal* (March 21, 2013), B1.
54. Jacob Gershman, "Court Orders Company to Make Website Accessible to the Blind," *The Wall Street Journal* (March 25, 2016), http://blogs.wsj.com/law/2016/03/25/court-orders-company-to-make-website-accessible-to-the-blind/. Accessed June 2, 2016.
55. Palazzolo, 2013.
56. Beth Brophy, "Supreme Court Gives Motherhood Its Legal Due," *U.S. News & World Report* (January 26, 1987), 1212.
57. Gillian Flynn, "Watch Out for Pregnancy Discrimination," *Workforce* (November 2002), 84.
58. U.S. EEOC, "EEOC Enforcement Guidance on Pregnancy Discrimination," https://www.eeoc.gov/laws/guidance/pregnancy_qa.cfm. Accessed June 2, 2016.
59. VedderPrice, "EEOC Guidance on Pregnancy Discrimination Acts Stirs Controversy in Form and Content," http://www.vedderprice.com/eeoc-guidance-on-pregnancy-discrimination-act-stirs-controversy-in-form-and-content/. Accessed June 2, 2016
60. Ibid.
61. Ibid.
62. "Under a Civil Rights Cloud, Fetal Protection Looks Dismal," *Insight* (April 15, 1991), 40–41.
63. U.S. Department of Labor, "Safety and Health Topics," http://www.osha.gov/SLTC/reproductivehazards/. Accessed June 4, 2016.
64. Dan Markiewicz, "Avoid a Costly Court Challenge." *Industrial Safety & Hygiene News* 47.2 (2013): 18.
65. Jessica L. Roberts, "Preempting Discrimination: Lessons from the Genetic Information Nondiscrimination Act." *Vanderbilt Law Review* 63.2 (2010): 437–490.
66. Andrea Davis, "GINA Can't Prevent Employee Disclosure," *Employee Benefit News* 27.1 (2013), 9–10.
67. Thomas H. Christopher, Louis W. Doherty, and David C. Lindsay, "EEOC Issues Final Regulations on Genetic Discrimination in the Workplace," *Employee Relations Law Journal* 36.4 (2011), 45–49.
68. Ibid.

69. Kira Peikoff, "Fearing Punishment for Bad Genes," *The New York Times* (April 7, 2014), http://www.nytimes.com/2014/04/08/science/fearing-punishment-for-bad-genes.html?_r=0. Accessed June 1, 2016.

70. Ibid.

71. John D. Rapoport and Brian L. P. Zevnik, *The Employee Strikes Back* (New York: Collier Books, 1994), 233–234.

72. Ibid.

73. Jacqueline A. Berrien Statement, Chair U.S. Equal Employment Opportunity Commission, before the Committee on Health, Education, Labor and Pensions, United States Senate (May 6, 2010), http://www.eeoc.gov/eeoc/events/berrien_protecting_older_workers.cfm. Accessed June 2, 2016.

74. Berrien, 2010.

75. Elizabeth Olson, "Claims of Age Bias Rise, But Standards of Proof Are High," *The New York Times* (March 18, 2016), http://www.nytimes.com/2016/03/19/your-money/trying-to-make-a-case-for-age-discrimination.html?_r=0. Accessed June 1, 2016.

76. EEOC, "What You Should Know: The EEOC, Conciliation and Litigation," https://www.eeoc.gov/eeoc/newsroom/wysk/conciliation_litigation.cfm. Accessed June 4, 2016.

77. EEOC Charge Statistics, https://www.eeoc.gov/eeoc/statistics/enforcement/charges.cfm. Accessed June 1, 2016.

78. Ibid.

79. James Ledvinka, *Federal Regulation of Personnel and Human Resource Management* (Boston: Kent, 1982), 37. Also see W. N. Outten, R. J. Rabin, and L. R. Lipman, *The Rights of Employees and Union Members* (Carbondale, IL: Southern Illinois University Press, 1994), chapter VIII, 154–156.

80. Glueck and Ledvinka, 304.

81. Ledvinka, 37–38.

82. See Jess Bravin, "Employers Watch Court in Religious-Garb Case," *The Wall Street Journal* (February 23, 2015), B1; Richard Wolf, "Muslim Girl Wins in Job Dispute," *USA Today* (June 2, 2015), 8A.

83. Ibid.

84. *Griggs v. Duke Power Company*, 401 U.S. 424, 1971.

85. Theodore Purcell, "Minorities, Management of and Equal Employment Opportunity," in L. R. Bittel (ed.), *Encyclopedia of Professional Management* (New York: McGraw-Hill, 1978), 744–745.

86. Yiyang, Wu. "Scaling the Wall and Running the Mile: The Role of Physical-Selection Procedures in the Disparate Impact Narrative." *University Of Pennsylvania Law Review* 160.4 (2012): 1195–1238.

87. Mary-Kathryn Zachary, "Discrimination without Intent," *Supervision* (May 2003), 23–26.

88. Biddle Consulting Group, "Uniform Guidelines on Employee Selection Procedures," http://www.uniformguidelines.com/questionandanswers.html. Accessed June 4, 2016.

89. William A. Galston, "Not There Yet on Equal Opportunity," *The Wall Street Journal* (October 21, 2015), A11.

90. Ibid.

91. Tami Luhby, "The Black-White Economic Divide in 5 Charts," *CNN Money* (November 25, 2015), http://money.cnn.com/2015/11/24/news/economy/blacks-whites-inequality/. Accessed June 2, 2016.

92. Rosabeth Moss Kanter *Men and Women of the Corporation* (New York: Basic Books, 1977), 47–68.

93. Sabina Nielsen, "Why Do Top Management Teams Look The Way They Do? A Multilevel Exploration of the Antecedents of TMT Heterogeneity." *Strategic Organization* 7.3 (2009): 277–305.

94. Nancy DiTomaso, *The American Non-Dilemma: Racial Inequality Without Racism* New York: Russell Sage Foundation, 2013).

95. "Interview with Nancy DiTomaso," *Background Readings*, http://www.pbs.org/race/000_About/002_04-background-03-07.htm. Accessed June 2, 2016.

96. Ibid.

97. Nancy DiTomaso, "How Social Networks Drive Black Unemployment," *The New York Times* (May 5, 2013), http://opinionator.blogs.nytimes.com/2013/05/05/how-social-networks-drive-black-unemployment/. Accessed June 2, 2016.

98. EEOC, "Facts about Race/Color Discrimination," http://www.eeoc.gov/facts/fs-race.html. Accessed June 2, 2016.

99. Marie Arana, "The Elusive Hispanic/Latino Identity," *Nieman Reports* (Summer 2001), 8–9.

100. *Gallup*, "Immigrant Status Tied to Discrimination among Hispanics" (August 20, 2015), http://www.gallup.com/poll/184769/immigrant-status-tied-discrimination-among-hispanics.aspx. Accessed June 2, 2016.

101. Ibid.

102. EEOC Employer Information Report EEO-1 (Appendix), "Race and Ethnic Identification" (January 2006), https://www.eeoc.gov/employers/eeo1survey/2007instructions.cfm. Accessed June 2, 2016.

103. EEOC, "Facts about Race/Color Discrimination," http://www.eeoc.gov/facts/fs-race.html. Accessed June 2, 2016.

104. EEOC, "Significant EEOC Race/Color Cases," http://www.eeoc.gov/eeoc/initiatives/e-race/caselist.cfm#color. Accessed June 2, 2016.

105. Ibid.

106. *Catalyst*, "Women CEOs of the S&P 500" (February 3, 2016), http://www.catalyst.org/knowledge/women-ceos-sp-500. Accessed June 2, 2016.

107. Emily Peck, "It's Not Getting Any Easier for Women to Become CEOs," *The Huffington Post* (April 20, 2016), http://www.huffingtonpost.com/entry/female-ceos_us_57179bdde4b0018f9cbbc80c. Accessed June 2, 2016.

108. *Catalyst*, 2016.

109. Regina Herzlinger, "Has the Glass Ceiling Been Shattered for Women Leading Major Companies?" *The Huffpost Business* (June 2, 2013), http://www.huffingtonpost.com/regina-e-herzlinger/has-the-glass-ceiling-bee_b_3001344.html. Accessed June 2, 2016.

110. Jodi Kantor, "A Titan's How-To on Breaking the Glass Ceiling," *The New York Times* (February 21, 2013), http://www.nytimes.com/2013/02/22/us/sheryl-sandberg-lean-in-author-hopes-to-spur-movement.html?pagewanted=all. Accessed June 2, 2016.

111. Steven M. Davidoff, "Why So Few Women Reach the Executive Rank," *The New York Times* (April 2, 2013), http://dealbook.nytimes.com/2013/04/02/why-so-few-women-reach-the-executive-rank/. Accessed June 2, 2016.

112. Ibid.

113. Ibid.

114. Ibid.

115. Eileen Patten, "On Equal Pay Day, Key Facts about the Gender Pay Gap," *Pew Research Center* (April 14, 2015), http://www.pewresearch.org/fact-tank/2015/04/14/on-equal-pay-day-everything-you-need-to-know-about-the-gender-pay-gap/. Accessed June 2, 2016.

116. Sam Turner, "Gender Inequality in the Workplace Goes Beyond the 'Pay Gap'," *NewsOK* (January 20, 2016), http://newsok.com/article/5473647. Accessed May 31, 2016.

117. Trae Vassalo, Ellen Levy, Michele Madansky, Hillary Mickell, Bennett Porter, Monica Leas, and Julie Oberweis, *The Elephant in the Room Study*, http://www.elephantinthevalley.com/. Accessed June 2, 2016.

118. Kristen P. Jones, Chad I. Peddie, Veronica Gilrane, Eden King, and Alexis Gray, "Not So Subtle: A Meta-Analytic Investigation of the Correlates of Subtle and Overt Discrimination," *Journal of Management* (DOI: 10.1177/0149206313506466, 2013).

119. Anne-Marie Slaughter, "A Toxic Work World," *The New York Times* (September 201, 2015), SR1.

120. Chelsea R. Willness, Piers Steel, and Kibeom Lee, "A Meta-Analysis of the Antecedents and Consequences of Workplace Sexual Harassment," *Personnel Psychology* (Spring 2007), 127–162.

121. Jana Szostek, Charles J. Hobson, Andrea Griffin, Anna Rominger, Marilyn Vasquez, and Natalie Murillo. 2012. "EEOC Sexual Harassment Settlements: An Empirical Analysis." *Employee Relations Law Journal* 38, no. 1: 3–13.

122. Ibid.

123. EEOC, "Charges Alleging Sexual Harassment FYE 2010-2015," https://www.eeoc.gov/eeoc/statistics/enforcement/sexual_harassment_new.cfm. Accessed June 4, 2016.

124. Ibid.

125. Erik Brady, "Colorado Scandal Could Hit Home to Other Colleges," *USA Today* (May 26, 2004), http://usatoday30.usatoday.com/sports/college/football/big12/2004-05-26-colorado-cover_x.htm?csp=34. Accessed June 2, 2016.

126. Susan B. Garland, "Finally, a Corporate Tip Sheet on Sexual Harassment," *Businessweek* (July 13, 1998), 39.

127. Anita Cava, "Sexual Harassment Claims: New Framework for Employers," *Business and Economic Review* (July–September 2001), 13–16; Ted Meyer and Linda Schoonmaker, "Employers Must Think outside the Sexual Harassment Box," *Texas Lawyer* (February 12, 2001), 36.

128. EEOC, "Charge Statistics FY 1997 through FY 2015," http://www.eeoc.gov/eeoc/statistics/enforcement/charges.cfm. Accessed June 2, 2016.

129. EEOC, "Fact Sheet on Recent EEOC Religious Discrimination Litigation" (February 19, 2015) https://www.eeoc.gov/eeoc/litigation/selected/religious_discrimination_facts.cfm. Accessed June 2, 2016.

130. Claire Groden, "Office Depot Involved in Religious Discrimination Printing Tiff," *Fortune* (September 10, 2015), http://fortune.com/2015/09/10/office-depot-religious-discrimination/. Accessed June 2, 2016.

131. Claire Zillman, "UPS's No-Beard Policy Hit with Religious Discrimination Suit," *Fortune* (July 15, 2015), http://fortune.com/2015/07/15/ups-religious-discrimination-lawsuit/. Accessed June 2, 2016.

132. Kelley Holland, "When Religious Needs Test Company Policy," *The New York Times* (February 25, 2007), http://www.nytimes.com/2007/02/25/business/yourmoney/25mgmt.html. Accessed June 2, 2016.

133. *Catalyst* 2016, "Lesbian, Gay, Bisexual, Transgender Workplace Issues," http://www.catalyst.org/knowledge/lesbian-gay-bisexual-transgender-workplace-issues. Accessed June 2, 2016.

134. Lauren Godles, "What's Going on with LGBT Discrimination in the Workplace?" *onLabor* (April 6, 2016), https://onlabor.org/2016/04/06/whats-going-on-with-lgbt-discrimination-in-the-workplace/. Accessed June 2, 2016.

135. Jaime Grant, Lisa Mottet, and Justin Tanis, "Injustice at Every Turn," *A Report of the National Transgender Survey* (2011), http://www.thetaskforce.org/static_html/downloads/reports/reports/ntds_full.pdf. Accessed June 2, 2016.

136. Human Rights Campaign Foundation, "Corporate Equality Index 2016," http://hrc-assets.s3-website-us-east-1.amazonaws.com//files/assets/resources/CEI-2016-FullReport.pdf. Accessed June 2, 2016.

137. Human Rights Campaign, "Business Coalition for Workplace Fairness, Members," http://www.hrc.org/resources/entry/business-coalition-for-workplace-fairness-members. Accessed June 4, 2016.
138. Godles, 2016.
139. Richard Perez-Pena, "Suit Challenges North Carolina Law Overturning Anti-Discrimination Measures," *The New York Times* (March 28, 2016), http://www.nytimes.com/2016/03/29/us/north-carolina-anti-discrimination-lawsuit.html?_r=0. Accessed June 2, 2016.
140. Erik Eckholm, "Corporate Call for Change in Gay Marriage Case," *The New York Times* (February 27, 2013), http://www.nytimes.com/2013/02/28/business/companies-ask-justices-to-overturn-gay-marriage-ban.html?_r=0. Accessed June 4, 2016.
141. Human Rights Campaign, "Sexual Orientation and Gender Identity Definitions," http://www.hrc.org/resources/entry/sexual-orientation-and-gender-identity-terminology-and-definitions. Accessed June 4, 2016.
142. "HRC Lauds Federal Court Ruling Asserting Protection for Transsexual Employees under Existing Law," *Human Rights Campaign Press Release* (June 1, 2004), http://www.hrc.org/press-releases/entry/hrc-lauds-federal-court-ruling-asserting-protection-for-transsexual-employe. Accessed June 4, 2016.
143. Christopher Danzig, "Gender Stereotyping Leads to Title VII Claim," *Inside Counsel* (April 2010), 63–64.
144. Ibid.
145. Dave Wieczorek, "Transsexual Employee's Title VII Claim Goes Forward," *InsideCounsel* (May 2006), 77–79.
146. EEOC Press Release, "Lakeland Eye Clinic Will Pay $150,000 to Resolve Transgender/Sex Discrimination Lawsuit" (April 13, 2015), https://www.eeoc.gov/eeoc/newsroom/release/4-13-15.cfm. Accessed June 2, 2016.
147. David L. Chappell, "If Affirmative Action Fails … What Then?" *The New York Times* (May 8, 2004), B7; Terry H. Anderson, *The Pursuit of Fairness: A History of Affirmative Action* (New York: Oxford University Press, May 2004).
148. Thomas Nagel, "A Defense of Affirmative Action," *Report from the Center for Philosophy and Public Policy* (College Park, MD: University of Maryland, Fall 1981), 6–9.
149. Glenn Llopis, "America's Most Wanted: What Diversity Can Do for Business," *Forbes* (August 29, 2011), http://www.forbes.com/sites/glennllopis/2011/08/29/americas-most-wanted-what-diversity-can-do-for-business/. Accessed June 6, 2016.
150. Daniel Seligman, "How 'Equal Opportunity' Turned into Employment Quotas," *Fortune* (March 1973), 160–168.
151. Tom L. Beauchamp and Norman Bowie (eds.), Ethical Theory and Business, 2d ed. (Englewood Cliffs, NJ: Prentice Hall, 1983), 477–478.
152. Public Backs Affirmative Action, But Not Minority Preferences," *Pew Research Center* (June 2, 2009), http://pewresearch.org/pubs/1240/sotomayor-supreme court-affirmative-action-minority-preferences. Accessed June 2, 2016.
153. Adam Liptak, "Supreme Court Upholds Affirmative Action Program at University of Texas," *The New York Times* (June 23, 2016), http://www.nytimes.com/2016/06/24/us/politics/supreme-court-affirmative-action-university-of-texas.html?=&_r=0. Accessed July 29, 2016.
154. Halley Potter, "What Can We Learn from States That Ban Affirmative Action?" *The Century Foundation* (June 26, 2014), https://tcf.org/content/commentary/what-can-we-learn-from-states-that-ban-affirmative-action/?version=meter%20at%207&module=meter-Links&pgtype=article&contentId&mediaId&referrer=https%3A%2F%2Fwww.google.com&priority=true&action=click&contentCollection=meter-links-click. Accessed June 2, 2016.
155. David Leonhardt, "If Affirmative Action Is Doomed, What's Next?" *The New York Times* (June 17, 2014), http://www.nytimes.com/2014/06/17/upshot/if-affirmative-action-is-doomed-whats-next.html. Accessed June 2, 2016.
156. Roger Parloff, "Big Business Asks Supreme Court to Save Affirmative Action," *Fortune* (December 9, 2015), http://fortune.com/2015/12/09/supreme-court-affirmative-action/. Accessed June 2, 2016.
157. Matt Waldman, "Hispanic Consumer Market in the U.S.," Terry College of Business (May 1, 2012), http://www.terry.uga.edu/news/releases/hispanic-consumer-market-in-the-u.s.-is-larger-than-the-entire-economies-of. Accessed June 2, 2016.
158. *Nielsen*, "Increasingly Affluent, Educated and Diverse: African-American Consumers" (September 17, 2015), http://www.nielsen.com/us/en/insights/reports/2015/increasingly-affluent-educated-and-diverse-african-american-consumers.html. Accessed June 2, 2016.
159. *Nielsen*, "Asian-Americans Are Expanding Their Footprint in the U.S. and Making an Impact" (May 19, 2016), http://www.nielsen.com/us/en/insights/news/2016/asian-americans-are-expanding-their-footprint-and-making-an-impact.html. Accessed June 2, 2016.
160. "Voluntary Diversity Plans Can Lead to Risk," *HR Focus* (June 2007), 2.
161. Ibid., 2.
162. Iris Bohnet, "Real Fixes for Workplace Bias," *The Wall Street Journal* (March 12–13, 2016), C3.
163. Ibid.

Case

Case Analysis Guidelines

The guidelines presented below have been designed to help you analyze the cases that follow. The guidelines are presented in three stages, but they are not intended to be a rigid format. Each question is designed to elicit information that will help you in analyzing and resolving the case. Each case is different, and some parts of the guidelines may not apply to every case. The questions for discussion at the end of each case should be addressed in any complete case analysis. Use the Issue/Problem Identification and Analysis/Evaluation steps to focus on generating and defending the most effective set of recommendations possible because the objective of case analysis is making recommendations. In all stages of the case analysis, use the stakeholder, ethics, sustainability, and corporate social responsibility (CSR) concepts presented in the text.

Issue/Problem Identification

1. **Facts and Assumptions.** What are the *central facts* of the case and the assumptions you are making on the basis of these facts?
2. **Major Overriding Issues/Problems.** What are the *major overriding issues* in this case? (What major questions/issues does this case address that merit(s) their/its study in this course and in connection with the chapter/material you are now covering?)
3. **Subissues and Related Issues.** What *subissues* or *related issues* are present in the case that merit consideration, discussion, and action?

Analysis/Evaluation

4. **Stakeholder Analysis.** Who are the *stakeholders* in this case, and what are their stakes? (Create a stakeholder map to depict relationships.) What challenges, threats, or opportunities does each stakeholder face? What stakeholder characteristics are at work (legitimacy, power, urgency)?
5. **CSR Analysis.** What CSRs (*economic, legal, ethical, philanthropic*) does the company have, and what exactly are the nature and extent of these responsibilities to the various stakeholders?
6. **Evaluations.** If the case involves a company's or manager's actions, evaluate what the company or manager did or did not do correctly in handling the issue affecting it. How should actions have been handled?

Recommendations

7. **Recommendations and Implementation.** What *recommendations* would you make in this case? If a company's or a manager's strategies or actions are involved, should they have acted the way they did? What actions should they have taken? What actions should the company or manager take now, and why? Be specific and include a discussion of alternatives (*right now*, *short-term*, and *long-term*). Identify and discuss any important *implementation considerations.*

CASE 1

Walmart: The Main Street Merchant of Doom*

Sam Walton, founder, owner, and mastermind of Wal-Mart,[1] now spelled Walmart and often used that way in many advertisements, passed away on April 5, 1992, leaving behind his spirit to ride herd on the colossal Walmart organization. To the consumer in the small community, his store, Walmart, was seen as a friend when it came to town. On the flip side, many a small-town merchant had been the victim of Sam's blazing merchandising tactics. So what is Walmart to the communities it serves? Is Walmart the consumer's best friend, the purveyor of the free-enterprise system, the "Mother of All Discount Stores," or, conversely, is it really "The Main Street Merchant of Doom"?

THE MAN NAMED SAM

Samuel Moore Walton was born on March 29, 1918, near Kingfisher, Kansas. He attended the University of Missouri in the fall of 1936 and graduated with a degree in business administration. During his time there, he was a member of the Beta Theta Phi fraternity, was president of the senior class, played various sports, and taught what was believed to be the largest Sunday school class in the world, numbering over 1,200 Missouri students.[2]

At age 22, Sam joined JCPenney. One of his first tasks was to memorize and practice the "Penney Idea." Adopted in 1913, this credo exhorted the associate to serve the public; not to demand all the profit the traffic will bear; to pack the customer's dollar full of value, quality, and satisfaction; to continue to be trained; to reward men and women in the organization through participation in what the business produces; and to test every policy, method, and act against the question, "Does it square with what is right and just?"[3]

Sam's First Store

In 1962, at age 44, Sam Walton opened his first Walmart store in Rogers, Arkansas. He took all the money and expertise he could gather and applied the JCPenney idea to Middle America. Sam first targeted small, underserved rural towns with populations of no more than 10,000 people. The people responded and Walmart soon developed a core of loyal customers who loved the fast, friendly service coupled with consistently low prices. Later, Sam expanded his company into the large cities, often with numerous Walmart's spread throughout every part of the city.

THE STORE THAT SAM BUILT

By 1981, Walmart's rapid growth was evident to all and especially disturbing to Sears, JCPenney, Target, and Kmart, because Walmart had become America's largest retailer.

By 2001, Walmart Stores, Inc., had become the world's largest retailer with $191 billion in sales. The company employed one million associates worldwide through nearly 3,500 facilities in the United States and more than 1,000 stores throughout nine other countries. Walmart claimed that more than 100 million customers per week visited Walmart stores. The company had four major retail divisions—Walmart Supercenters, Discount Stores, Neighborhood Markets, and Sam's Club warehouses. As it entered the 2000s, Walmart had been named "Retailer of the Century" by *Discount Store News*, made *Fortune* magazine's lists of the "Most Admired Companies in America" and the "100 Best Companies to Work For," and was ranked on *Financial Times'* "Most Respected in the World" list.[4] By January 2016, Walmart's sales had grown to $486 billion.[5]

The Walmart Way

Sam's approach was to promote the associate—the hourly employee—to a new level of participation within the organization. Sam, as the head cheerleader, saw his job as the chief proponent of the "Walmart Way." The Walmart Way reflected Sam's idea of the essential Walmart culture that was needed for success. Sam felt that when a customer entered Walmart in any part of the country, he or she should feel at home. Examples of the culture included "exceeding customer expectations" and "helping people make a difference." He was a proponent of the *"Ten-Foot Rule,"* which meant that if a customer came within ten feet of an associate, the associate would look the customer in the eye, greet him or her, and ask if the customer needed help.[6]

Sam, the CEO, hired the best managers he could find. He let them talk him into buying an extensive computer network system. This network corporate

*This case, originally prepared by William T. Rupp, Austin Peay State University, was revised and updated by Archie B. Carroll, University of Georgia, in 2016.

satellite system enabled Sam to use round-the-clock inventory control and credit card sales control and provided him with information on total sales of which products, where, and when. This computer control center was about the size of a football field and used a satellite for uplinking and downlinking to each store.

SOCIAL AWARENESS: THE "BUY AMERICAN" PLAN

Sam, the innovator, was responsible for two early social responsibility innovations: Walmart's "Buy American" plan and its "Environmental Awareness" campaign.

Walmart's "Buy American" plan was in response to Sam's own realization that his company was adding to the loss of American jobs by buying cheaper foreign goods. This concern drove him to find a solution. In February 1986, about 12 months after the "Buy American" plan had begun, Sam held a press conference. He showed off all the merchandise Walmart was now buying domestically. He estimated that Walmart's "Buy American" plan had restored 4,538 jobs to the American economy and its people.[7] The "Buy American" plan was one of Walmart's early efforts at corporate social responsibility.

The "Buy American" plan morphed over the years into the well-publicized "Made in the USA" campaign in which Walmart called customers' attention to these domestic products with special labels. Ironically, Walmart eventually abandoned this program and became one of the largest purchasers of products made overseas. In fact, the company in time became the country's largest purchaser of Chinese goods in any industry. Some say that by taking its orders abroad, Walmart forced many U.S. manufacturers out of business.[8]

THE "ENVIRONMENTAL AWARENESS" CAMPAIGN

As awareness of the environment was on the rise, Sam looked for a way to involve Walmart in the environmental movement. In August 1989, an ad in *The Wall Street Journal* proclaimed Walmart's "commitment to our land, air and water." Sam envisioned Walmart as a leader among American companies in the struggle to clean up the environment.

Walmart wanted to use its tremendous buying power to aid in the implementation of the campaign. Walmart sent a booklet to manufacturers stating the following:

> *At Wal-Mart we're committed to help improve our environment. Our customers are concerned about the quality of our land, air and water, and want the opportunity to do something positive. We believe it is our responsibility to step up to their challenge.*[9]

In the stores, shelf tags made from 100 percent recycled paper informed customers as to the environmental friendliness of the highlighted product. As a result of these shelf tags and Walmart's advertising, customer awareness had increased, and some environmentally safe product manufacturers were reaping the rewards of increased Walmart orders.

SAM AND THE EARLY MERCHANTS OF MAIN STREET

Not everyone was excited to see Sam and his mechanized Walmart army arrive and succeed. Small merchants across America shuddered when the winds of the "Walmart Way" began to blow in their direction. Kennedy Smith of the National Main Street Center in Washington, DC, said, "The first thing towns usually do is panic." Once Walmart comes to town, Smith says, "Downtowns will never again be the providers of basic consumer goods and services they once were."[10]

Steamboat Springs

Some towns learned to "just say 'no'" to Walmart's overtures. Steamboat Springs, Colorado, was one such city. Colorado newspapers called it the "Shootout at Steamboat Springs." Walmart was denied permission to build on a nine-acre parcel along U.S. Route 40. Owners of upscale shops and condos were very concerned with the image of their resort and ski community, and Walmart, with its low-cost reputation, just did not fit. The shootout lasted for two years, and finally Walmart filed a damage suit against the city. Countersuits followed. A petition was circulated to hold a referendum on the matter. This was the shot that made Walmart blink and back down. Just before the vote, Don Shinkle, corporate affairs vice president, said, "A vote would not be good for Steamboat Springs, and it would not be good for Walmart. I truly believe Walmart is a kinder, gentler company, and, while we have the votes to win, an election would only split the town more."[11] Years later, Steamboat Springs finally got a Walmart. It won't be found on the tourist's lists of shopping places but it's there.

Iowa City

In Iowa City, Iowa (population more than 50,000), Walmart was planning an 87,000-square-foot store on the outskirts of the town. A group of citizens gathered enough signatures during a petition drive to put a referendum on the ballot to block Walmart and the city council from building the new store (the city council had approved the rezoning of the land Walmart wanted). Jim Clayton, a downtown merchant, said, "Walmart is a freight train going full steam in the opposite direction of this town's philosophy." If businesses wind up going down, Clayton says, "you lose their involvement in the community, involvement I promise you won't get with some assistant manager over at Walmart."[12] Efforts to stop Walmart and the Iowa City Council were not successful. Walmart opened its Iowa City store on November 5, 1991.

PAWHUSKA, OKLAHOMA

Meanwhile, in Pawhuska, Oklahoma, as a result of Walmart's entry in 1983 and other local factors, the local "five-and-dime," JCPenney, Western Auto, and a whole block of other stores closed their doors. Four years later, Dave Story, general manager of the local *Pawhuska Daily Journal Capital*, wrote that Walmart was a "billion-dollar parasite" and a "national retail ogre."[13]

Walmart managers have become very active in Pawhuska and surrounding communities since that time. A conversation with the editor of the Pawhuska paper, Judy Smith, and her advertising editor, Suzy Burns, revealed that Walmart sponsored the local rodeo, gave gloves to the local coat drive, and was involved with the local cerebral palsy and multiple sclerosis fund-raisers. On the other hand, Fred Wright, former owner of a TV and record store, said, "Walmart really craters a little town's downtown."[14]

OPPOSITION TO WALMART GETS ORGANIZED

By the 1990s, there were dozens of organized groups actively opposing Walmart's expansion.[15] Some of these groups were and still are run by social activists who are reliving the 1960s and 1970s. Instead of protesting the Vietnam War, nuclear proliferation, or the destruction of the environment, they turned their efforts to Walmart specifically and capitalism in general. One of these activists, Paul Glover, who was an antiwar organizer, defined Walmart as the epitome of capitalism, which he despises. For Glover and others, Walmart stands for "everything they dislike about American society—mindless consumerism, paved landscapes, and homogenization of community identity."[16]

Boulder, Colorado Opposition

In Boulder, Colorado, Walmart tried to counter these allegations by proposing a "green" store. Steven Lane, Walmart's real estate manager, said that a "green store" would be built that would be environmentally friendly, with a solar-powered sign out front and everything. His efforts were trumped by Spencer Havlick, an organizer of the first Earth Day in 1970, suggesting that the entire store be powered by solar energy. Mr. Lane did not respond.[17]

Protest organizers united against the spread of the "Walmart Way" differ from the downtown merchants in that these protesters have no financial stake though they still regard themselves as stakeholders. These activists attack Walmart on a higher, philosophical plane. The accusations ring with a tone of argument that was made by other activists protesting polluting industries (e.g., the coal, nuclear, and chemical industries). These activists accuse Walmart of "strip-mining" towns and communities of their culture and values.

One possible root of this culture clash may be attributed to the unique aspects of the internal corporate culture at Walmart's headquarters. This is a place where competition for the reputation as the "cheapest" was practiced. An example is the competition among employees in procuring the cheapest haircut, shoes, or necktie. Consequently, as a result of the internal culture of Walmart and the external environment, some analysts believe that a clash of priorities and values was inevitable as Walmart moved into larger, more urban settings.

New England Opposition

Some of the greatest opposition to Walmart's growth came from the New England area. This area holds great promise for Walmart because of the large, dense population and the many underserved towns. These towns are typically underserved in three ways: in variety of product choices, in value, and in convenience. The opposition to Walmart entering these New England markets includes some high-profile names, such as Jerry Greenfield, cofounder of Ben & Jerry's Homemade ice cream, and Arthur Frommer, a well-known travel writer.[18] In addition to New England, other areas, such as resort areas, opposed Walmarts because they have wanted to insulate their unique cultures from what they considered to be the offensive consumerism that is usually generated by Walmart's presence.

Sprawl-Busters

Al Norman, a lobbyist and media consultant, turned opposition to Walmart into a cottage industry. Norman developed a Web site (http://sprawl-busters.com/) that has vast information for citizens who are fighting to prevent Walmart or other "big box" stores from locating in their cities or neighborhoods. Norman achieved national attention in 1993, when he stopped Walmart from locating in his hometown of Greenfield, Massachusetts. Since then, he has appeared on *60 Minutes*, which called him "the guru of the anti-Walmart movement," and has gained widespread media attention. To this day, Norman remains active in his protestations against Walmart and other big box stores such as Home Depot, Target, Lowe's, Kohl's and others.[19] His latest book is *Occupy Walmart* in which he says that Walmart is the "Mother of all 1% corporations" as the Wall Street movement moves to main street.[20]

Sprawl-Busters is not alone in its on-line, focused criticism of Walmart's presence in communities.[21]

CONTINUING CHALLENGES AND ISSUES

For its part, Walmart has continued its aggressive diversification and growth pattern. In 2009, *The Wall Street Journal* said that Walmart's image had moved from demon to darling as a result of the strategies the company had employed. By 2013, however, questions such as "Is Walmart in Trouble?" continue to be asked.[22]

Figure 1 provides some interesting facts and statistics about Walmart.

FIGURE 1 Interesting Information About Walmart

Walmart's Locations

Walmart operates more than **11,500 stores in 28 countries** around the world.
Walmart operates stores under 72 different banners globally.

Walmart's Employees

Walmart employs 2.2 million associates around the world—1.4 million in the United States alone. About **75** percent **of its store management teams** started as hourly associates and they earn between $50,000 and $170,000 a year—similar to what firefighters, accountants, and some doctors make. Every year, **Walmart promotes about 170,000 people** to jobs with more responsibility and higher pay

Walmart's Customers

Walmart serves customers more than 200 million times per week. The average family of four spends over $4,000 per year at Walmart. One of every four dollars spent on groceries are spent at Walmart. Ninety percent of all Americans live within 15 miles of a Walmart.

Walmart's Financials

For the fiscal year ended January 2015, Walmart **increased net sales by 1.9** percent **to $482 billion** and returned $7.2 billion to shareholders through dividends and share repurchases.

Walmart's Size

If Walmart were a country, it would be the 26th **largest economy in the world.** If Walmart were an army, it would have the second largest military in the world, behind China. Walmart is bigger than Home Depot, Kroger, Target, Sears, Costco, and K-mart combined. Walmart's parking lots alone take up roughly the size of Tampa, Florida.

Community Giving

In 2014, Walmart and the Walmart Foundation gave **$1.4 billion** in cash and in-kind contributions around the world. In FY2015, Walmart's associates volunteered more than 1.5 million hours to organizations.

Environmental Sustainability

Walmart has three aspirational sustainability goals: to be supplied 100 percent by renewable energy, to create zero waste, and to sell products that sustain people and the environment. They also have a Responsible Sourcing program. As of September 2015, the Responsible Sourcing team numbered 200 associates in retail markets and sourcing offices around the world.

Hunger and Nutrition

Walmart has committed $2 billion to fight hunger and nutrition in the United States. The company is striving to make food healthier and more affordable. The company is using its size and scale to help support farmers and their communities to strengthen the global food supply chain.

Sources: Walmart, "Walmart's Facts," http://news.walmart.com/walmart-facts, Accessed May 18, 2016; Dina Spector, "18 Walmart Facts that will make your head explode," *Business Insider*, February 21, 2013, http://www.businessinsider.com/incredible-facts-about-walmart-2013-2?op=1, Accessed May 18, 2016; Walmart Foundation, "Our Volunteers," http://giving.walmart.com/our-volunteers/, Accessed May 18, 2016; "Wal-Mart: The Long Term Solution," 2015, http://www.economist.com/sites/default/files/unebraskalincoln_ws.pdf, Accessed May 18, 2016.

Clandestine Opposition to Grocery Sales

In the past decade, a new form of opposition to Walmart's growth has emerged. It was disclosed by *The Wall Street Journal* that rival grocery chains had secretly funded opposition to Walmart's entrance into communities because its grocery sales had reached such a large percentage of its total sales. By year end 2015, Walmart's grocery sales had grown to 56 percent of its U.S. sales.[23] What *The Wall Street Journal* learned through investigative research was that in Mundelein, Illinois, a town about 20 miles northwest of Chicago with a population of about 35,000, a grocery chain with about nine stores in the area had hired Saint Consulting Group to secretly operate an anti-Walmart campaign. It was revealed that Saint had developed a specialty in fighting proposed Walmarts in communities and were using techniques it described as "black arts."[24]

The techniques used by Saint Consulting were usually clandestine. In a typical anti-Walmart project, a Saint executive would drop into the town under an assumed name and take charge of the local opposition to the store. They would flood local politicians with calls, using multiple phone lines to make it look like they were coming from different people. They would hire lawyers and traffic experts to derail the project or stall it. They would flood neighborhoods with flyers outlining the purported evils of a Walmart entering their area and the subsequent traffic and increased police calls that would follow. Operating in secret, they would hope that the developer would back off, slow down, or drop the project altogether. They deployed their strategies under assumed names and never revealed their clients' names because clients didn't want their names publicly known for fear it would draw adverse publicity or lawsuits should they be known.[25]

Planet Walmart

In spite of its many achievements, article titles from newspapers and magazines have consistently raised questions about Walmart's power and impact in the United States and around the world. These article titles from the 2000s reveal some of the public's thinking about the giant corporation:

"The Wal-Martization of America"[26]

"Is Wal-Mart Too Powerful?"[27]

"Is Wal-Mart Good for America?"[28]

"One Nation under Wal-Mart"[29]

"Wal-Mart Gives Globalization a Bad Name"[30]

"Attack of the Wal-Martyrs"[31]

"Wal-Mart's Midlife Crisis"[32]

"Planet Wal-Mart"[33]

Sheer size has become a huge problem for Walmart because many citizens equate size with power. Being so highly visible makes the company a natural target of critics. *The New York Times* argued in 2004 that Walmart has become a nation unto itself. To document its point, the newspaper stated that if Walmart were an independent nation, it would be China's eighth-largest trading partner. In terms of its low prices and impact, however, some economists say that the company has single-handedly cut inflation by 1 percent in some years as it has saved customers billions of dollars annually.[34] It is little wonder the newspaper calls it "The Walmartization of America."[35] Because of its number one ranking in the *Fortune* 500 listing, based on size, the magazine referred to the company as "Planet Walmart."[36] In the 2015 Fortune 500 listing, Walmart has held on to its #1 position in terms of revenues.[37]

In addition to domestic growth, Walmart continues its growth internationally. By 2016, Walmart was operating 11,500 retail units under 72 banners in 28 countries. International units number 6,303 so it is apparent that global growth has been vital to the company.[38]

Millions of Supporters

In spite of its opponents and the challenges it faces every week, 100 million customers shop at Walmart. Ninety percent of Americans live within a 15-minute drive of a Walmart store. The total amount of money spent at Walmart every hour of every day is about $36.7 million.[39] By virtually any measure, the popularity of Walmart is staggering.

Many consider the company to be socially responsible in addition to being a provider of thousands of jobs, low prices, and high value and service. Walmart has numerous corporate citizenship initiatives at the local and national levels. Locally, Walmart stores underwrite college scholarships for high school seniors, raise funds for children's hospitals through the Children's Miracle Network Telethon, provide local fund-raisers money and workforce, and educate the public about recycling and other environmental topics with the help of "Green Coordinators."[40]

In 1998, the Walton Family Charitable Support Foundation, the charitable program created by Sam

Walton's family, announced what at the time was the largest ever single gift made to an American business school: $50 million to the College of Business Administration of the University of Arkansas. Helen R. Walton, the "first lady" of Walmart, said that she and her husband established the Foundation to support specific charities, including the University.[41] To no one's surprise, it is now called the Sam M. Walton College of Business.[42]

Global Responsibility and Sustainability Achievements

In its 2016 Global Responsibility Report, Walmart summarized some of its recent achievements:[43]

- Walmart and the Walmart Foundation committed $100 million over 5 years to increase economic mobility among U.S. retail and related sector workers.
- Walmart committed $20 million through 2019 to support the reintegration of U.S. veterans into civilian life.
- In terms of sustainability, the company diverted 75 percent of its global waste from landfills.
- 35.6 metric tons of greenhouse emissions were eliminated from its supply chain, based on supplier reports.
- $25 million was committed by the company over five years to improve community disaster response.
- Global giving totaled $1.2 billion.
- 800+ scholarships were awarded by Walmart Foundation to associates and dependents for higher education.

In 2015, Walmart announced a groundbreaking new animal welfare policy. The new policy includes the responsible use of antimicrobials, including antibiotics. Its new policy asks suppliers to be proactive in eliminating animal abuse, including reporting cases of animal abuses and taking corrective action; finding and implementing solutions to housing systems, painful procedures, and euthanasia or slaughter; and proving progress reports to Walmart and annually reporting on their corporate animal welfare position.[44] In 2016, Walmart announced its new cage-free promise, which could change the egg industry. Walmart is striving to join the "cage-free" eggs movement, which means that hens will have more space to move around and their eggs could become less expensive. Walmart's plan is to sell cage-free eggs only by 2015 and as they come to market, the usually pricier option is expected to become more affordable. Walmart's decision has been applauded by The Humane Society and the American Society for the Prevention of Cruelty to Animals.[45]

EPILOGUE TO SAM'S STORY

Sam learned his lessons well. The people who bought at his stores have been mostly satisfied. The downtown merchants who survived learned to coexist with the company's associates. But things would never be the same. The changes had come rapidly. The social fabric of the small town was changed forever. The larger cities continued to fight but had only limited success. The company continued its expansion, always searching for that next town that needed to be liberated from the downtown price-fixing bad guys. The search became more complicated as the opposition has risen but the spirit of Sam rides on.

A CONTINUING STREAM OF ISSUES

Walmart's size, power, and impact on local communities are where criticism of the company began. This included the threat of putting other merchants out of business, the creation of urban sprawl, the concern over impact on property values, and the traffic congestion created when the company decides to locate in a particular area. The public and various stakeholders seem to have a love or hate relationship with the company. There is a continuing stream of issues the company faces.

Labor Practices. In addition to antisprawl activists and merchants, Walmart continues to face new opposition from competitors, labor unions, other activist organizations, and lawsuits. Its labor practices have been increasingly questioned. The company has been accused of paying low wages such that workers cannot live off them, making employees work "off the clock" without overtime pay, paying few or low benefits, and taking advantage of undocumented immigrants.

In 2004, the company was hit with a class-action lawsuit on gender discrimination against women. This class action lawsuit covered 1.6 million current and former employees, making it the largest private civil rights case in the U.S. history. In late 2008, Walmart agreed to pay up to $640 million to settle 63 state class-action lawsuits regarding overtime.[46] In 2011, the U.S. Supreme Court ruled that the huge class-action lawsuit against the company could not move forward as a "class action" and that Walmart was entitled to individual determinations of its employees' eligibility for back pay. This was judged to be a huge victory for Walmart.[47]

Because the company's labor issues are so expansive and important, and why wouldn't they be with over a million employees, they are not addressed in this present case. Case 2, titled "Walmart's Labor Practices," focuses primarily on Walmart's labor practices and some of the issues mentioned above. Case 2 may be analyzed and discussed immediately following this case or it may be deferred until a more in-depth consideration of employee stakeholders is undertaken in connection with Chapters 17–19.

Bribery Scandal in Mexico. In 2012, the *New York Times* broke an investigative story into Walmart's activities as it has tried to expand in Mexico. The allegations stated that Walmart executives had learned of attempts by its Mexican subsidiary, Walmart de Mexico, to bribe Mexican officials to the tune of $24 million in exchange for getting building permits faster and other favors but chose to cover up these findings. It was alleged that the cover-up scheme went all the way to Walmart headquarters in Bentonville, Arkansas. If Walmart was to be found guilty of violations of the Foreign Corrupt Practices Act, fines into the millions of dollars and possible prison sentences could be given.[48] In the fall of 2015, the Justice Department concluded its investigation of the bribery charges and decided that it was a much smaller case than originally thought.[49] It was determined that Walmart executives were not likely to be charged.[50] But, with stores located all over the world, this has got to be a continuing challenge.

Fire in Bangladesh. Though Walmart claimed it was no longer permitting its subcontractors to make clothing at the apparel factories that burned down in 2012 in Bangladesh, the company has been implicated for its lax attention to labor policies and safety standards in sweatshops such as those in Bangladesh. Some of Walmart's brands were found in the fire ruins along with a dozen or more Western brands found in the charred remains. Walmart said it had revoked the factory's authorization to make its products there months before the fire but that one of its suppliers had given the business to Tazreen Fashions on its own. The major incident demonstrated how hard it is for companies to monitor and police its suppliers.[51] In early 2013, Walmart announced tougher supplier policies. It has warned suppliers that it is adopting a "zero tolerance policy" for violations of its global sourcing standards and will sever ties with anyone who subcontracts work to factories without the company knowing it.[52] By 2015, Walmart had become a founding member of an alliance to improve building, electrical and worker safety throughout Bangladesh.[53]

Buy American More Often. It may be because of consumers' more recent interest in "buying American" or it may be in response to the bad press it received in connection with the fire in Bangladesh, but the nation's largest retailer announced in early 2013 that it was embarking on a program to "buy American more often." Walmart officially announced that it would increase sourcing of American-made products by $50 billion over the next decade. The company also said it would help vendors in categories such as furniture and textiles to return production to America that had moved abroad. The challenge for Walmart, according to a spokesman for the American Apparel and Footwear Association, will be in finding vendors who can meet Walmart's price points.[54] Not everyone believes Walmart is serious about its new "Buy American" plan.[55]

Doug McMillon—New CEO

Doug McMillon, 49, a two-decade veteran at Walmart, was appointed CEO in 2014 succeeding Mike Duke who was CEO from 2009 to 2014.[56] McMillon immediately sensed the monumental task he faced as the new head of the world's largest employer. He sensed the scrutiny that Walmart was under because of its huge size. Walmart gets about 60,000 mentions a day on social media, so everything the company does and he does will be closely watched.[57]

In spite of Walmart's revenue growth over the previous five year period, the company's profits had been relatively flat. In addition to the poor economy beginning with the 2008 financial crisis, Walmart was being challenged by a number of the so-called dollar store chains, such as Dollar General and Family Dollar. In addition, it faced a significant threat in the rise of Amazon.com and other online retailers.[58] In fact, one retail analyst was quoted as saying that "Amazon and online retailing is probably the biggest disrupter of retail since Walmart itself."[59]

McMillon moved quickly during his first year-and-a-half on the job. He speeded up new investments in e-commerce, made news by raising the minimum wage for Walmart employees, and experimented with one of the company's newest retail models, Walmart Pickup Grocery, where the trial run for this business model was taking place right in the company's headquarters in Bentonville, Arkansas.[60]

As McMillon thought about the new challenges ahead, he set forth four steps to remaking the retail pioneer.[61]

1. Create a "Walmart sized" e-commerce business.
2. Think "Omnichannel" by making it easier for customers to buy anywhere, anytime and get their purchases anywhere and anyhow.
3. Rev up experimentation with innovations.
4. Bring back Mr. Sam's spirit.

Higher Minimum Wages but Store Closings. Walmart made important decisions in 2015 and 2016 to raise the minimum wage of its employees to \$9 an hour in 2015 increasing to \$10 an hour in 2016. The company made this decision after years of being hammered by protest groups and advocacy groups. But, the new CEO thought it was a good decision to raise productivity and get the employees more engaged.[62] This was the good news that its critics were pleased to see happen.

But, then came the bad news. Perhaps due to the sluggish economy, perhaps due to competition, possibly due to paying higher wages, Walmart announced in early 2016 its plans to close down 154 U.S. stores it said were underperforming.[63] As an example, one of those stores was located in Oriental, North Carolina. Residents there were upset when Walmart first entered the area because a local grocery store had to close its doors after 44 years because it was unable to compete with the retail giant. But, after only two years of being there, Walmart decided it had to close the store.[64] Walmart announced on January 15, 2016 that it would close all 102 of its Express stores, many of them in rural or isolated towns, and would focus on its supercenters and midsize Neighborhood Markets.[65]

Another important store closing occurred in Winnsboro, South Carolina, and residents there are very upset and began collecting petitions urging Walmart to reconsider the closing of the town's Supercenter that had opened in 1998. On a more optimistic note, some of the local residents expressed hope that Walmart's departure will leave room for smaller businesses to thrive once again.[66] Walmart also disappointed District of Columbia officials after it had announced plans to open three stores in the city's more affluent areas but also said it had changed its mind about opening two additional supercenters in some of the poorer neighborhoods. The company not only faced regulatory hurdles and lobbying fees but also faced a boost in the local minimum wage from \$11.50 to \$15.00 an hour. In addition, the city had proposed legislation that would mandate minimum hours for part-time workers and impose new family and medical-leave requirements.[67]

Walmart's woes, lackluster same-store sales, and store closings are a part of gloomy economic conditions and competition in the global economy. The challenges that Walmart has before it are faced by many other merchants and consumers and employees as well. Stagnant wages is a problem shared across the economy at large, and many consumers simply do not have money to spend.[68] But, at the same time, the company has a new CEO who Fortune magazine has dubbed the "chosen one," and has said that he may be the best-prepared executive to lead Walmart since Sam Walton himself.[69] The years ahead will be interesting to watch as Walmart plays out its "business in society" role.

QUESTIONS FOR DISCUSSION

1. What are the major issues in this case? What does Walmart's experience tell you about the business and society relationship?
2. Assess Walmart's corporate social responsibility using the four-part CSR model. Is Walmart socially responsible even though it has had a devastating impact on many small merchants?
3. What about Walmart's impact on communities in terms of sprawl, traffic congestion, and impact on the appearance of the environment? What responsibility, if any, does the company have to the communities it enters?
4. Sam Walton has been called a motivational genius. After reading this case, and with what you have observed at your local Walmart store, do you think his motivational genius is still felt by the associates. What is the "Walmart Way"? How would you characterize the store's culture now that Sam is no longer around to visit the stores?
5. Walmart was an early leader in the area of corporate social responsibility. Is the company's

detrimental impact on merchants offset by the benefits of its recent corporate citizenship and sustainability initiatives?

6. Walmart continues to find resistance to its expansion into New England and some parts of the United States. What are the true goals of the opponents of Walmart? Include a consideration of the following: (a) stopping Walmart's expansion, (b) preserving the status quo (e.g., downtown community and social fabric), (c) developing a cause that will pay their bills, (d) fighting for an ideology, or (e) something else. What should Walmart do when it encounters resistance?
7. With Walmart now having to close stores due to the economy and/or competition, does it have any social responsibilities to the communities it is leaving? If so, what would those responsibilities be?
8. When you are the largest company in the world, how do you protect yourself against the kind of criticism Walmart has received? Does it seem that no matter how hard you try, it's difficult to make things better?

ENDNOTES

1. Wal-Mart Stores, Inc. (NYSE: WMT) is the legal name of the corporation. The name "Walmart," expressed as one word and without punctuation, is a trademark of the company and is used analogously to describe the company and its stores.
2. Vance H. Trimble, *Sam Walton: The Inside Story of America's Richest Man* (New York: Penguin Books, 1990), 30. Also see Bob Ortega, *In Sam We Trust* (New York: Times Business, 1998).
3. Ibid., 34.
4. Walmart's Web Page, "News for List of Awards," http://corporate.walmart.com/search?ajaxMainObjectId=0000014f-b810-d55e-a3ff-fe1663dd0000&q=awards&media=all&years=all&sortby=new&view=grid&offset=0&count=20&scrollDown=true. Accessed May 18, 2016. Accessed May 20, 2013.
5. Wickinvest, Wal-Mart Revenue 2015, http://www.wikinvest.com/stock/Wal-Mart_(WMT)/Data/Revenue/2015. Accessed May 18, 2016.
6. For Up-to-Date Information on Walmart's Culture, see "Walmart's Enduring Values," http://news.walmart.com/executive-viewpoints/walmarts-enduring-values. Accessed May 18, 2016.
7. Ibid., 261.
8. "Store Wars: When Walmart Comes to Town," IMDb. Accessed May 18, 2016.
9. Ibid., 10.
10. Dan Koeppel, "Wal-Mart Finds New Rivals on Main Street," *Adweek's Marketing Week* (November 10, 1990), 5.
11. Trimble, 255.
12. "Just Saying No to Wal-Mart," *Newsweek* (November 13, 1989), 65.
13. Karen Blumenthal, "Arrival of Discounter Tears the Civic Fabric of Small-Town Life," *The Wall Street Journal* (April 14, 1987), 1, 23.
14. Ibid., 23.
15. Bob Ortega, "Aging Activists Turn, Turn, Turn Attention to Wal-Mart Protests," *The Wall Street Journal* (October 11, 1994), A1, A8.
16. Ibid., A1.
17. Ibid., A8.
18. Joseph Pereira and Bob Ortega, "Once Easily Turned Away by Local Foes, Wal-Mart Gets Tough in New England," *The Wall Street Journal* (September 7, 1994), B1.
19. Sprawl-Busters, http://sprawl-busters.com/. Accessed May 21, 2016.
20. "What Is Occupy Walmart?" http://sprawl-busters.com/occupywalmart.html. Accessed May 18, 2016.
21. Reclaim Democracy, "Anti-Walmart and Pro-Walmart Groups and Websites," http://reclaimdemocracy.org/walmart_links/. Accessed May 18, 2016.
22. Ann Zimmerman, "Wal-Mart's Image Moves from Demon to Darling," *The Wall Street Journal* (July 16, 2009), B1; also see Matthew Yglesias, "Is Walmart in Trouble?" *Slate*, http://www.slate.com/articles/business/moneybox/2013/05/wal_mart_sales_decline_america_s_largest_retailer_is_slipping_as_customers.html. Accessed May 18, 2016.
23. Market Realist, "Competitive Forces: Why Walmart Dominates the Grocery Industry," http://marketrealist.com/2015/02/competitive-forces-walmart-dominates-grocery-industry/. Accessed May 18, 2016.
24. Zimmerman, ibid.
25. Ibid.
26. *The New York Times* (November 15, 2003), A26.
27. *BusinessWeek* (October 6, 2003), 100–110.

28. *The New York Times* (December 7, 2003), 1WK.
29. *Fortune* (March 3, 2003), 66–78.
30. Jeffrey E. Garten, "Wal-Mart Gives Globalization a Bad Name," *BusinessWeek* (March 8, 2004), 24.
31. Barney Gimbel, "Attack of the Wal-Martyrs," *Fortune* (December 11, 2006), 125–130.
32. Anthony Bianco, "Wal-Mart's Midlife Crisis," *BusinessWeek* (April 30, 2007), 46–56.
33. "First," *Fortune* (May 3, 2010), 27.
34. Steven Greenhouse, "Wal-Mart, a Nation Unto Itself," *The New York Times* (April 17, 2004), A15.
35. "The Wal-Martization of America," *The New York Times* (November 15, 2003), A26.
36. "First," *Fortune* (May 3, 2010), 27.
37. Forbes, "The World's Biggest Public Companies," http://www.forbes.com/global2000/list/#header:revenue_sortreverse:true. Accessed May 18, 2016.
38. Walmart, "Where in the World is Walmart?" http://corporate.walmart.com/our-story/locations. Accessed May 18, 2016.
39. Statistic Brain, "Walmart Company Statistics," http://www.statisticbrain.com/wal-mart-company-statistics/. Accessed May 18, 2016.
40. Walmart Environmental Sustainability, http://corporate.walmart.com/global-responsibility/environment-sustainability. Accessed May 18, 2016.
41. University of Arkansas, Sam Walton College of Business, http://walton.uark.edu/about/walton-atrium.php. Accessed May 18, 2016.
42. Walton College, University of Arkansas, https://walton.uark.edu/. Accessed May 21, 2016.
43. Walmart, 2016 Global Responsibility Report, http://corporate.walmart.com/2016grr/performance-highlights. Accessed May 18, 2016.
44. Gina-Marie Cheeseman, "Walmart Adopts Groundbreaking Animal Welfare Policy," Triple Pundit, May 25, 2015, http://www.triplepundit.com/2015/05/walmart-adopts-groundbreaking-animal-welfare-policy/. Accessed May 18, 2016.
45. Hadley Malcolm, "Walmart's Cage-Free Vow Could Change Egg Industry," *USA Today* (April 11, 2016), 4B.
46. Ibid.
47. Jenna Goudreau, Forbes, June 20, 2011, "Walmart Wins Supreme Court Ruling in Historic Sex Discrimination Suit, http://www.forbes.com/sites/jennagoudreau/2011/06/20/wal-mart-wins-supreme-court-ruling-in-historic-sex-discrimination-suit/#7b8489193a7a. Accessed May 18, 2016.
48. David Barstow, "Wal-Mart Hushed up a Vast Mexican Bribery Case," *New York Times* (April 21, 2012); also see James B. Stewart, "Bribes without Jail Time," *New York Times*, April 27, 2012. "Walmart Faces Big Fines Amid Bribery Charges," *The Jakarta Globe*, April 24, 2012.
49. Phil Wahba, "Walmart Bribery Probe by Feds Finds No Major Misconduct in Mexico," *Fortune*, http://fortune.com/2015/10/18/walmart-bribery-mexico/. Accessed May 18, 2016.
50. NPR, Wal-Mart Executives unlikely to be Charged over Alleged Bribes in Mexico, Report Says," http://www.npr.org/sections/thetwo-way/2015/10/19/450031690/wal-mart-executives-unlikely-to-be-charged-over-alleged-bribes-in-mexico-report. Accessed May 18, 2016.
51. Miguel Bustillo, Tom Wright and Shelly Banjo, "Tough Questions in Fire's Ashes," *Wall Street Journal* (November 30, 2012), B1.
52. Shelly Banjo, "Wal-Mart Toughens Supplier Policies," *Wall Street Journal* (January 22, 2013), B1.
53. Walmart, "Responsible Sourcing in Bangladesh," http://corporate.walmart.com/our-commitment-to-the-workers-of-bangladesh. Accessed May 18, 2016.
54. Stephanie Clifford, "Walmart Plans to Buy American More Often," *New York Times* (January 15, 2013).
55. Robert Greenwald, "Wal-Mart's Newest Big Lie: Another Misleading Ad Campaign from the Job Killing Behemoth," Salon, http://www.salon.com/2014/03/07/walmarts_newest_big_lie_another_misleading_ad_campaign_from_a_job_killing_behemoth/. Accessed May 18, 2016.
56. Brian O'Keefe, "The Chosen One," *Fortune* (June 15, 2015), 134–144.
57. Ibid.
58. Ibid.
59. Quoted in ibid.
60. Ibid.
61. Ibid., 144.
62. Matt Krantz, "Walmart's Wages Get CEO's Attention," *USA Today* (March 2, 2015), 2B.
63. Holman W. Jenkins, Jr. "Bad Days for Wal-Mart Americans," *Wall Street Journal* (January 20, 2016), A11.

64. "No Cheers When Walmart Packs Up," *Bloomberg Businessweek* (February 1–7, 2016), 18–19.
65. Ibid., 19.
66. Sarah Nassauer, "Repercussions of a Wal-Mart Exit," *Wall Street Journal* (January 27, 2016), B1.
67. Jenkins, 2016, ibid.
68. Rana Foroohar, "Walmart's Woes Suggest a Bumpy Road for the American and Global Economies," *Time* (November 2, 2015), 28.
69. Krantz, 134.

CASE 2

Walmart's Labor Practices*

Historically, the primary criticism of Walmart, the world's largest company, has been its impact on communities and small merchants. Anti-sprawl activists and small-town merchants, in particular, have taken issue with the company moving into their communities.[1] In *Case 1—Walmart: The Main Street Merchant of Doom*, these issues were presented in some detail.

In the past decade or so, however, other issues concerning the company have become important as well and have begun dominating the news. In particular, Walmart's labor practices and treatment of its employees have raised many issues in public and business discussions. Paradoxically, Walmart refers to its employees as "associates," a term intended to bestow a more lofty status on its human resources than the term "employees."

Many consumers and citizens do view Walmart as an excellent provider of jobs in communities, and in spite of criticisms that have been raised, people continue to seek out employment with Walmart. Though it has high turnover, it is viewed by countless job seekers as a stable place to work, and some individuals have sought to establish careers at the company. In 2013, Walmart was ranked #27 in the top fifty of "World's Most Admired Companies" in the annual *Fortune* magazine rankings.[2] By 2016, it had fallen to position #42.[3] In spite of Walmart being ranked highly for years, *Fortune* writer Jerry Useem asked, "Should we admire Walmart?" He goes on to say, "Some say it's evil. Others insist it's a model of all that's right with America. Who are we to believe?"[4] For information about Walmart, review Figure 1 in Case 1.

Many different employee-related issues with respect to Walmart have been the focus of a great deal of news coverage in the past few years, and it is the purpose of Case 2 to explore those issues in more detail. The company has been accused of hiring too many part-time workers; offering jobs that are actually dead-end; paying low wages and poor benefits; forcing workers to work "off-the-clock," that is, to work overtime without overtime pay; and taking advantage of undocumented immigrants. Over the years, the company has also been accused of gender discrimination against women, who occupy most jobs at the company. Coupled with these allegations of employee treatment, the company, which currently is not unionized, has fought unions and unionization everywhere it locates. Figure 1 presents some basic information about Walmart and its associates.

Over the past several years, income inequality has become an important issue in the United States and worldwide and this has exacerbated the low-wage accusations against all merchants, especially the big box stores.[5] In addition, the minimum wage debate in the United States has been percolating to the top of news stories and a number of different cities and several states have been striving to move to a $15 minimum wage level. The "living wage" movement has continued to argue for minimum wage increases and this movement seems to be gaining some momentum even in the face of a sour economy and some companies having to lay off workers because they cannot afford higher minimum wages.[6] These national trends have created a backdrop against which Walmart and other stores that rely on many entry-level jobs have had to deal in recent years. However, most of Walmart's employee challenges began years ago.

*This case was prepared by Archie B. Carroll, University of Georgia. Revised and Updated in 2016.

FIGURE 1 Recent Facts (2016) About Walmart's Employees/Associates

- Walmart employs more than 1.3 million "associates" in the United States.
- Walmart promotes about 170,000 people every year to jobs with higher pay and more responsibility.
- Women make up more than 57 percent of the U.S. Walmart workforce. Walmart employs 784,000 female associates. Forty-two percent of the women are in management positions. Thirty-two percent of the women are corporate officers.
- Walmart USA employs more than 279,000 African-American associates, more than 185,000 Hispanic associates, and more than 48,000 Asian associates.
- Over the period 2012–2014, over 50 percent of the new hires at Walmart were women. Over the same three-year period, 45–51 percent of the new hires were people of color. (More recent data available.)
- In May 2015, Walmart announced it would guarantee a job offer to any eligible U.S. veteran honorably discharged from active duty since the original offer launch on Veteran's Day 2013.
- In February 2016, the minimum wage at Walmart was at least $10 per hour and the average wage of full-time employees was $13 per hour.
- In terms of health-care benefits, benefits for qualified associates at Walmart amount to $22 per pay period. In terms of 401K plan, associates at Walmart can begin contributing on their first day of employment and the company will match this amount up to 6 percent after one year on the job. The company also offers paid sick leave.
- Walmart gives eligible employees a 10 percent discount on general merchandise and select groceries purchased at a Walmart store.

Sources: Walmart, "Our people," http://careers.walmart.com/our-people/. Accessed May 18, 2016; "Diversity and Inclusion," http://cdn.corporate.walmart.com/01/8b/4e0af18a45f3a043fc85196c2cbe/2015-diversity-and-inclusion-report.pdf, Accessed May 18, 2016; "Walmart Facts," http://news.walmart.com/walmart-facts. Accessed May 18, 2016; "Working at Walmart," http://www.therealwalmart.com/people-associates.html. Accessed May 18, 2016.

LOW PAY, HARD WORK, QUESTIONABLE TREATMENT

Walmart is the nation's largest employer. It employs 2.2 million worldwide—1.3 million in the United States alone.[7] As such, it is not surprising that it has a large number of interactions with employees, and these interactions will be both positive and negative. Walmart claims to offer "good jobs, (and) good careers," but a number of employees have become vocal in recent years about their working conditions at the company. As with many retailers and service industries, Walmart is accused of offering low pay and few benefits. Many of these employees have been angered by the disparity between their low wages and the company's profits.[8] With the current economic malaise, however, the company's profits have not been high and the company has been struggling just as all retailers have.

One Person's Experience

Journalist Barbara Ehrenreich, author of the best-seller *Nickel and Dimed: On (Not) Getting by in America*," spent three weeks working at a Walmart to get insights into whether many of the claims she had heard about Walmart's treatment of employees was true.[9] Ehrenreich claimed she'd heard stories about Walmart workers being mistreated and being asked to work extra hours without overtime pay. During her three weeks there, she said she saw one facet of the mega-retailer that most people who shop there never get to see.[10]

Ehrenreich observed that many of the store's cheapest items were often unaffordable to the workers who sold them because of their low pay. She observed: "when you work for a company who you can't afford to buy their product, you're in trouble." She went on, "Here is this store that's oriented toward the lower end of the economic spectrum, but not low enough [for its own workers]." She said on one occasion she had to go to the local food bank and she was mistaken for another Walmart worker who had just been there.[11]

Of course, some people would say that there is nothing wrong with low pay and few benefits if a business can still find workers willing to work there. After all, in a free market, this is the way the economic system works. And, indeed, one reason Walmart has been so efficient and has contributed to nationwide productivity increases is precisely because of its tight controls on labor costs. The McKinsey consulting group has said that Walmart was responsible for roughly 25 percent of the nation's productivity gains in the 1990s. Their low prices have also contributed significantly to low inflation. Financial guru Warren Buffett expressed the opinion that Walmart has contributed more than any other company to the economic vigor that is found in America.[12]

Working Off-The-Clock and Without Breaks

One of the most troubling allegations of unfair treatment reported by some Walmart employees is that of being asked to work "off-the-clock." This means that employees are pressured to do overtime work for which they do not get paid. One employee reported that he was asked to work off-the-clock by both the store manager and the assistant manager. The allegation is that managers would wait until an employee had clocked out and then say something like, "Do me a favor. I don't have anyone coming in—could you stay here?" Before you knew it, four to five hours passed before you got away.[13] According to Walmart's *2015 Annual Report*, the company had, indeed, been the defendant in several cases pertaining to wage-and-hour class action since 2002. Settlement was reached on these charges but Walmart has continued to appeal them.[14]

The Pressure Is On

The company blamed individual store and department managers for any unpaid overtime. They claim it is against company policy to not pay for overtime. However, there is some evidence that managers have been under significant pressure from corporate headquarters to get more work done than can be done with the number of employees allowed. One attorney for an employee said that headquarters collect reams of data on every store and every employee and use sales figures to determine how many hours of labor it wants to allocate to each store. Then, the store managers were required to schedule fewer hours than allotted and their store performance is closely monitored on a daily basis. The store managers, in turn, put pressure on lower managers, and employees start feeling the pressure to work hours without pay. In another case, a former Walmart manager claimed that supervisors had been known to regularly delete hours from time records and even to reprimand employees who claimed overtime hours so the store could keep its labor costs under control.[15]

LABOR UNION RESISTANCE

Because of employee complaints and desires to have higher wages and more generous benefits, Walmart employees have been targeted by union organizers for decades. Walmart's huge size and number of employees allows the firm to increasingly "set the standard for wages and benefits throughout the U.S. economy."[16]

Across the country, workers in many states have tried to get unions organized, but so far they have not had much success. According to one report, employees at more than 100 stores in 25 states have been trying to get union representation. Walmart has tried in various ways to fight the union organizing efforts. The company has engaged in actions some of which have been judged to be in violation of federal labor laws. Walmart has been held to be in violation of the law in ten separate cases in which the National Labor Relations Board has ruled that it has engaged in illegal activities such as confiscating union literature, interrogating workers, and discharging union sympathizers.[17] According to one management consultant, Walmart will go to great lengths to keep unions out.

The United Food and Commercial Workers (UFCW) union has been most aggressively trying to unionize Walmart across the country. Several full-time union organizers have traveled the country trying to convince employees to agree to a union vote in their store. The UFCW, which represents 1.4 million workers in the grocery and retail industry, has representatives in many different cities attempting to convince workers to sign a card indicating they want a union vote held at their store. According to the National Labor Relations Board, a workplace needs 30 percent of its workers to sign cards calling for a union election to have one held. Unions often try to get 50 percent of the employees to sign a card, because they want to increase their chances of winning.[18]

Success in Union Resistance

There are several reasons why the unions have not been successful in unionizing Walmart. First, many employees feel intimidated by the company and fear signing on with a union. They fear retaliation of some kind, and many of the employees cannot afford to lose their jobs. Second, Walmart has mastered the art and science of fighting unionization. At one point, the company had a "union avoidance program." In this program, the company, with its vast resources, would wear people down and even destroy their spirit.

One consultant said that each Walmart manager is taught to take attempts at union organizing personally and to consider that supporting a union is like slapping the supervisor in the face.[19] Walmart is considered to be a very sophisticated adversary when it comes to fighting unionization. At one point managers had been asked to call a 24-hour hotline if they ever see a hint of unionization taking place, and a labor team can be dispatched to a store under threat at a moment's notice.[20] Third, many Walmarts are located in southern states that do not have a history and tradition of unionization.[21] Regardless, unions in cities in the north continue, most recently in Chicago, ferociously fighting the company's plans to locate in historically union territory, but they have not had great success. These cities are hungry for jobs and cheap products, and these factors seem to win out.[22]

In 2014, Anonymous, a network of hacker activists leaked two internal Walmart PowerPoint slideshows. One was a Labor Relations Training presentation for store managers on which it was suggested that labor unions were money grubbing outfits that cared little about the workers' welfare.[23] Walmart confirmed the slides' authenticity. One slide went on to say that the unions just want the associates' money and that they spend the dues money on other things than representing them.[24] After the slideshow episode, one of Walmart's orientation videos was leaked and it revealed more of Walmart's anti-union efforts. Walmart stated that it showed the videos to new hires between 2009 and 2014.[25]

With respect to its position, a Walmart spokesman says that the company is not anti-union, it is "pro-associate."[26] According to writer Karen Olsson, "Walmart has made it clear that keeping its stores union-free is as much a part of the culture as door greeters and blue aprons."[27]

USE OF UNDOCUMENTED IMMIGRANTS

Several years ago, a series of predawn raids by federal agents were conducted in which they rounded up 250 illegal immigrants working as cleaning crews in 61 Walmarts across 21 states. Although technically they were not employees of the company, the company was accused by federal officials of knowing that its contractors were using the illegal immigrants as employees. The Immigration and Customs Enforcement program claimed it has wiretaps revealing that Walmart knew contractors were using undocumented workers in their cleaning crews.[28]

Walmart claims that it did what it could to ensure that its contractors were hiring legal workers, both before and after the raid. Antidiscrimination provisions of the immigration code limit an employer's ability to investigate an employee's legal status, the company claimed. The company claimed that as far back as in 1996, the Immigration and Naturalization Service (INS) filed a complaint against Walmart for requiring prospective hires who were not U.S. citizens to show more verification than that required by law. The company paid $11 million to settle this case.[29] Walmart admitted that it unwittingly may have been doing business with some of the contractors that were in violation and that their own investigations revealed they were dealing with companies with different corporate identities and names that made it difficult to eliminate suspected violators.[30]

SEX DISCRIMINATION CHARGES

The most serious employee issues Walmart has faced in the past decade or so have been accusations of gender discrimination against women. In 2001, six women filed a gender bias lawsuit against Walmart, claiming they were discriminated against. The case, *Dukes v. Walmart*, started as an EEOC complaint by Betty Dukes, the lead plaintiff, who claimed she had been trying to get promoted from the cashier ranks for nine years.[31] In a landmark decision in June of 2004, a federal judge in San Francisco ruled that the sex discrimination lawsuit could proceed as a class-action lawsuit, affecting as many as 1.6 million current and former female employees who have worked for the company since December 26, 1998.[32] In February 2007, a federal appeals court upheld the 2004 decision that Walmart must face the class-action bias claim. Walmart appealed the decision but lost. It was said that the company could lose billions of dollars should it be found guilty of sex discrimination in a class action lawsuit.[33] The lawsuit, which has been called the "largest private civil rights case ever,"[34] had the potential to go on for years and doubtless will have significant repercussions for Walmart and other companies in the retail and other industries.

A summary of the major allegations against Walmart included three major areas. First, women claimed they had been denied equal promotions. Second, women claimed they had been paid less for the same jobs, even when they have more experience.

Third, women claimed they were subjected to sexist actions and gender stereotyping.[35]

Lawyers for the plaintiffs argued that top managers at Walmart knew about the sex bias that was taking place in the company. The lawyers argued that women complained to corporate executives, including then CEO Lee Scott, about pay disparities or sexism and received very little response. They also argued that information was shared with board members and that outsiders complained and got little or no response from corporate offices.[36]

The Company's Defense

Walmart has long argued that it treats its female employees fairly. The company has said that women do not apply for promotion as often as men, and this accounts for the underrepresentation of women.[37] The main argument by the company was its opposition to the lawsuit being categorized as a class-action lawsuit. The company argued that decisions about employees are made at the individual store level and that a class-action lawsuit is too unwieldy because it thinks it should be able to present evidence defending itself against each individual plaintiff's claims and that this would not be possible in a class-action trial. Walmart claimed that in a class-action lawsuit of this size, it means that store managers will not be given the opportunity to explain how they made individual compensation and promotion decisions.

The company argued in its appeal of the class-action judgment that the class was certified under laws intended to provide injunctive relief, that is, to stop a particular practice, but that the judge ruled that the class can also seek monetary damages that the company does not think applies to the case. Part of the monetary relief could be punitive damages, but for these to apply, it has to be proven that Walmart management "fostered or recklessly ignored discriminatory practices." The judge concluded that whereas the individual decisions were made at specific store locations, there was some evidence of a corporate culture of gender stereotyping that may have affected the decisions made at the store level.[38] Judge Martin Jenkins was not ruling on the merits of the case but was simply saying there was some evidence of a corporate culture permeating the organization that may be related to the discrimination, and thus he allowed the case to move forward as a class action.

In April 2010, a federal appeals court ruled that the gender discrimination lawsuit could move forward as a class action. It was estimated that if the company lost this lawsuit, it could cost Walmart upward of $1 billion. In addition, a loss would be a terrible blow to its reputation and much-improved corporate image.[39]

Walmart appealed this case and it went to the U.S. Supreme Court. In 2011, the court rendered its decision in a "5–4 decision" in favor of Walmart.[40] The court ruled that the class action suit could not move forward and that each woman would have to file her claim individually. The ruling did not decide whether Walmart was guilty of discrimination or not, but the Supreme Court decision will have far reaching effects on the future of class action lawsuits.[41]

Changes Made After Sex Discrimination Case

Partially as a result of criticism and bad publicity Walmart had been receiving, the company announced some changes that were planned to improve conditions for its workers. In 2004, then CEO Lee Scott outlined the changes that would be made but indicated it may take several years before the true impact of the changes take place and are felt throughout the company.[42]

One change would include the creation of a compliance group to oversee workers' pay, hours, and breaks. The company also began testing a new program that would alert cashiers when it is time for them to take a meal break. Another change was the implementation of a new system that would require employees to sign off on any changes that are made to their time cards. The company also planned to implement software that would force managers to adhere to state employment rules regarding areas such as how late teenagers can work. While announcing these new policies, Scott mentioned several times that he was tired of the adverse publicity that the company was getting.[43]

WALMART STRIVES TO IMPROVE ITS IMAGE AND POLICIES

Beginning in about 2005, the company ratcheted up its charm offensive by trying to enhance its public image. Then-CEO Lee Scott admitted that the company was trying to improve its image by being more open to its critics and trying to take specific steps to improve the way the world perceived the company. He admitted that when growth was easier, they could ignore their critics, but as the share price slowed its growth, the company had to start reaching out and being more responsive to the concerns raised.[44]

Walmart sought to improve its image with stakeholders on four fronts. First, in the area of outreach, the company opened offices in eight major cities in an attempt to improve community relations and be responsive to local critics. Second, the company met with several activist groups seeking to improve its environmental impact. Third, the company hired Business for Social Responsibility (BSR), a nonprofit organization, to help it establish better relations with anti-sweatshop advocates and to strengthen its global labor monitoring program. Fourth, the company set up quick-response teams in Washington and at its Arkansas headquarters, with the help of a public relations firm, so that it could be more responsive to public criticism.[45] It appeared that Walmart had finally realized the legitimacy of the "stakeholder effect": "As companies grow and develop, some stakeholders become more important than others, and new stakeholders sometimes emerge."[46] In 2009, one writer was exclaiming how Walmart's image had moved from demon to darling, but in the world of public relations, retaining a solid corporate image is a challenging task.[47]

Walmart's struggles with labor and labor unions, in particular, continued in 2011 and 2012 when the company heard rumors about the possibility of a strike on Black Friday, the day after Thanksgiving, 2012.[48] Sensing that billions in sales might be at stake on Black Friday, the company was duly concerned. Walmart learned about a new group, called OUR Walmart, which stood for **O**rganization **U**nited for **R**espect at Walmart.[49] OUR Walmart was a group of employees that had spun off from the United Food and Commercial Workers International (UFCW) union. OUR Walmart was asking for more full-time jobs with higher wages and more predictable schedules. Executives at Walmart thought the group to be a serious threat, however, and hired an intelligence-gathering service from Lockheed Martin, contacted the FBI, increased its staffing of its labor hotline, and started to monitor the prominent employees and activists in the group.[50]

In testimony that later came out, Walmart estimated that about 100 workers did go on strike on Black Friday, but OUR Walmart claimed it was closer to 400 employees spread over 1,200 stores. Walmart filed an unfair labor practice charge against the UFCW in November 2012 arguing that the one-day strikes were not legally protected. In January 2013, the UFCW and OUR Walmart agreed to refrain from picketing or other confrontational conduct for 60 days.[51] Later, OUR Walmart charged Walmart with unfair labor practices on behalf of 200 workers. The company denied any wrongdoing. The labor board dismissed some of the allegations but continued to investigate others, including a retaliation case. A resolution to these cases in expected late in 2016.[52] OUR Walmart said it planned to stage a 15-day fast leading up to Black Friday, 2016. Their hunger strike is in support of a $15 an hour minimum wage and to highlight problems the employees have with feeding their families.[53]

In 2015, led by new CEO Doug McMillon, Walmart decided to upgrade its investments in its employees over a two-year period, a criticism that had been hanging over the company for several years. The company committed $2.7 billion in wage increases, scheduling improvements, and employee training.[54] After years of complaints about low wages and poor employee treatment, Walmart increased its minimum wage to $9 an hour in 2015 and then to $10 per hour in 2016.[55]

In 2016, Walmart announced that it was closing more than 150 stores. This will require laying off thousands of workers. The company said it would try to place its laid off workers at other Walmart stores. Those who are not hired by nearby stores will get 60 days of pay and severance if eligible as well as resume and interview skills training.[56] CEO Doug McMillon said that "the decision to close stores is difficult and we care about the associates who will be impacted."[57] He went on to say "we invested considerable time assessing our stores and clubs and don't take this lightly."[58]

QUESTIONS FOR DISCUSSION

1. Identify and describe the major labor relations issues facing Walmart and the likely stakeholders to be affected.
2. Walmart has been said to have excessive power in its relationship with communities. How is its manifestation of power with employees similar to or different than with communities? Which is the most serious issue? Why?
3. Are many of the allegations by employees at Walmart just reflections of the changing social contract between companies and their workers? Are many of the so-called problems just the free-enterprise system at work? Discuss.
4. Is the practice of being required to work "off-the-clock" an unethical practice or just "to be expected" in the modern world of work? After all, many salaried employees are expected to work "until the job is done" no matter how many hours it takes.

5. Is it wrong for Walmart to fight unionization? Sam Walton always felt the company should function as one big happy family and that unions were to be resisted. What is your evaluation of the union opposition?
6. If Walmart can effectively argue that women are contributors to their plight by not applying for promotions or for seeking fewer responsibilities to accommodate family priorities, should the company be held to be in violation of sex discrimination laws because the statistics reveal differences between women and men?
7. Regarding the various labor practices discussed in this case, do they reflect questionable treatment of associates or just the business system at work?
8. Have increased competitiveness, globalization, higher wages, technology, and lack of a stronger e-commerce program affected Walmart's relations with its associates?
9. Conduct Internet research on Walmart and update allegations and lawsuits against the company.

ENDNOTES

1. Charles Fishman, "The Wal-Mart Effect and a Decent Society: Who Knew Shopping Was So Important," *Academy of Management Perspectives* (August 2006), 6–25.
2. Fortune's "The World's Most Admired Companies," *2013,* http://money.cnn.com/magazines/fortune/most-admired/2013/list/. Accessed May 18, 2016.
3. Fortune, "World's Most Admired Companies," 2016, http://fortune.com/worlds-most-admired-companies/. Accessed May 18, 2016.
4. Jerry Useem, "Should We Admire Wal-Mart?" *Fortune* (March 8, 2004), 118–120.
5. David Lauter, "Income Inequality Emerges as a Key Issue in 2016 Presidential Campaign," *Los Angeles Times*, February 5, 2015, http://www.latimes.com/nation/la-na-campaign-income-20150205-story.html. Accessed May 18, 2016.
6. "Living Wage NYC: A Growing Movement," http://livingwagenyc.org/pagedetail.php?id=5. Accessed May 18, 2016.
7. "Walmart Facts," http://news.walmart.com/walmart-facts. Accessed May 18, 2016.
8. Karen Olsson, "Up Against Wal-Mart," *Mother Jones* (March/April 2003), 54–59.
9. Barbara Ehrenreich, "*Nickled and Dimed: On (Not) Getting by in America*" (New York: Henry Holt and Company, 2001).
10. Tammy Joyner, "Author Had Eyes Opened at Work," *Atlanta Journal Constitution* (June 27, 2004), Q1.
11. Ibid.
12. George F. Will, "Waging War on Wal-Mart," *Newsweek* (July 5, 2004), 64.
13. Olsson, 58.
14. Wal-Mart's *2015 Annual Report*, p. 55, http://www.corporatereport.com/walmart/2015/ar/_downloads/walmart_2015_ar.pdf. Accessed May 18, 2015.
15. Olsson, 58.
16. Ibid., 55.
17. Ibid.
18. Cora Daniels, "Up Against the Wal-Mart," *Fortune* (May 17, 2004), 112–120.
19. Olsson, 56.
20. Daniels, 116.
21. Ibid.
22. "Unions vs. Wal-Mart: Belaboured," *The Economist* (May 29, 2010), 30–32.
23. Steven Greenhouse, "How Walmart Persuades Its Workers Not to Unionize," The Atlantic, June 8, 2015, http://www.theatlantic.com/business/archive/2015/06/how-walmart-convinces-its-employees-not-to-unionize/395051/. Accessed May 18, 2016.
24. Ibid.
25. Ibid.
26. Ibid.
27. Olsson, 58.
28. Ann Zimmerman, "After Huge Raid on Illegals, Wal-Mart Fires Back at U.S.," *The Wall Street Journal* (December 19, 2003).
29. CNN Money, "Wal-Mart Pays $11 Million over Illegal Labor," March 18, 2005, http://money.cnn.com/2005/03/18/news/fortune500/wal_mart_settlement/. Accessed May 18, 2016.
30. Ibid.
31. Cora Daniels, "Women vs. Wal-Mart," *Fortune* (July 21, 2003), 79–82.
32. Ann Zimmerman, "Judge Certifies Wal-Mart Suit as Class Action," *The Wall Street Journal* (June 23, 2004), A1.
33. David Kravets, "Wal-Mart Must Face Class-Action Bias Trial: Female Workers Say Men

Were Paid More," *USA Today* (February 7, 2007), 3B.

34. Stephanie Armour and Lorrie Grant, "Wal-Mart Suit Could Ripple through Industry," *USA Today* (June 23, 2004), 4B.
35. Stephanie Armour, "Rife with Discrimination: Plaintiffs Describe Their Lives at Wal-Mart," *USA Today* (June 24, 2004), 3B.
36. Stephanie Armour, "Women Say Wal-Mart Execs Knew of Sex Bias," *USA Today* (June 25, 2004), 1B.
37. "Wal-Mart: Trial by Checkout," *The Economist* (June 26, 2004), 64.
38. Zimmerman, 2004, B2.
39. Sean Gregory, "Walmart Faces a Gender Discrimination Suit," *Time* (April 29, 2010), http://www.time.com/time/business/article/0,8599,1985549,00.html. Accessed July 31, 2010.
40. Nina Martin, "The Impact and Echoes of the Walmart Discrimination Case," ProPublica, https://www.propublica.org/article/the-impact-and-echoes-of-the-wal-mart-discrimination-case. Accessed May 18, 2016.
41. AAUW, "Court Case: Walmart vs. Dukes," http://www.aauw.org/resource/wal-mart-stores-inc-v-dukes/. Accessed May 18, 2016.
42. Constance L. Hays, "Wal-Mart Plans Changes to some Labor Practices," *The New York Times* (June 5, 2004), B2.
43. Ibid.
44. Robert Berner, "Can Wal-Mart Fit into a White Hat?" *BusinessWeek* (October 3, 2005), 94–96.
45. Ibid., 96.
46. R. Edward Freeman, "The Wal-Mart Effect and Business, Ethics and Society," *Academy of Management Perspectives* (August 2006), 38–43.
47. Ann Zimmerman, "Wal-Mart's Image Moves from Demon to Darling," *The Wall Street Journal* (July 16, 2009), B1.
48. Susan Berfield, "How Walmart Watches Its Employees," *Bloomberg Businessweek* (November 24, 2015), 51–57
49. Ibid.
50. Ibid, 54.
51. Ibid., 56.
52. Ibid., 57.
53. Ibid.
54. Haley Peterson, Business Insider, "Walmart Spent $2.7 Billion Fixing a Major Weakness," http://finance.yahoo.com/news/walmart-spent-2-7-billion-143109126.html. Accessed May 20, 1016.
55. Matt Krantz, "Walmart's Wages Get CEO's Attention," *USA Today* (March 2, 2015), 2B.
56. Haley Peterson, Business Insider, "Walmart Is Closing Hundreds of Stores and Laying off Thousands of Employees," January 15, 2016, http://www.businessinsider.com/walmart-closes-hundreds-of-stores-2016-1. Accessed May 20, 2016.
57. Ibid.
58. Ibid.

CASE 3

The Body Shop: Poster Child of Early CSR Movement*

PART A: PURSUING SOCIAL AND ENVIRONMENTAL CHANGE

When North American consumers are asked to describe the cosmetics industry, they often respond with words such as "glamour" and "beauty." Beginning in 1976, The Body Shop International PLC (BSI) provided a contrast to this image by selling a range of 400 products designed to "cleanse and polish the skin and hair." The product line included such items as "Honeyed Beeswax, Almond, and Jojoba Oil Cleanser" and "Carrot Facial Oil." Women's cosmetics and men's toiletries were also available. They were all produced without the use of animal testing and were packaged in plain-looking, recyclable packages.[1]

The Body Shop's primary channel of distribution was a network of over 600 franchised retail outlets in

*This case was prepared initially by William A. Sodeman, Hawaii Pacific University, now of University of Alabama in Huntsville (UAH), using publicly available information. It was revised and updated in 2016 by Archie B. Carroll.

Europe, Australia, Asia, and North America.[2] The company had enjoyed annual growth rates of approximately 50 percent until 1990, when net income began to level off. The media raised few questions about this decline in performance, because the firm's social agenda and exotic product line captured most of the public's interest. Indeed, early on, The Body Shop was the poster-child company for the burgeoning corporate social responsibility (CSR) movement.

ANITA RODDICK: FOUNDER

The company's founder and managing director, Anita Roddick, was responsible for creating and maintaining much of the company's marketing strategy and product development.[3] Roddick believed that The Body Shop was fundamentally different from other firms in the cosmetics industry because, in her own words, "we don't claim that our products will make you look younger, we say they will only help you look your best."[4] She regularly assailed her competitors: "We loathe the cosmetics industry with a passion. It's run by men who create needs that don't exist."[5] During the 1980s, Anita Roddick became one of the richest women in the United Kingdom by challenging the well-established firms and rewriting the rules of the cosmetics industry.

Honors and Awards

Anita Roddick was greatly admired within the business community for the conviction of her beliefs and the success of her company. She received many honors and awards, including the U.K. Businesswoman of the Year in 1985, the British Retailer of the Year in 1989, and the Order of the British Empire.[6] The firm's customers included well-known celebrities, including Diana, Princess of Wales; Sting; and Bob Weir of the Grateful Dead. Ben Cohen, cofounder and chairman of Ben & Jerry's, described her as an incredibly dynamic, passionate, humorous, and intelligent individual who believes "it's the responsibility of a business to give back to the community … she understands that a business has the power to influence the world in a positive way."[7]

Roddick opened the first Body Shop store in Brighton, England, as a means of supporting her family while her husband, Gordon Roddick, was taking a year-long sabbatical in America. Gordon, a chartered accountant by trade, was using much of their savings to finance his trip. Anita Roddick had little money to open a store, much less to develop products or purchase packaging materials.[8]

Field Expeditions

Roddick called upon her previous experiences as a resource to get started. Having been a United Nations researcher for several years in the 1960s, she had had many opportunities during field expeditions to see how men and women in Africa, Asia, and Australia used locally grown plants and extracts, such as beeswax, rice grains, almonds, bananas, and jojoba, as grooming products. With some library research, she found several recipes, some of which were centuries old, that used these same ingredients to make cosmetics and skin cleansers. With the addition of inexpensive bottles and handwritten labels, Roddick quickly developed a line of products for sale in her first Body Shop store. She soon opened a second store in a nearby town. When Gordon Roddick returned to the United Kingdom in 1977, The Body Shop was recording sizable profits. At Anita's request, he joined the company as its chief executive officer.[9]

Early Strategy—The Power to do Good

The Body Shop's retail stores were somewhat different from the cosmetic salons and counters familiar to shoppers in highly commercialized nations. The typical retail sales counter relied on high-pressure tactics that included promotions, makeovers, and an unspoken contract with the customer that virtually required a purchase in order for the customer to receive any advice or consultation from a sales counter employee.[10] By contrast, The Body Shop employees were taught to wait for the customer to ask questions, be forthright and helpful, and not to press for sales.[11]

According to Roddick, "Businesses have the power to do good. That's why The Body Shop's Mission Statement opens with the overriding commitment, 'To dedicate our business to the pursuit of social and environmental change.' We use our stores and our products to help communicate human rights and environmental issues."[12]

Early on, The Body Shop had to rely on cost containment because it could not afford advertising, and Roddick didn't believe in it, so she resolved to succeed without it.[13]

Employees and Hiring Procedures

In addition to their regular wages, store employees were paid a half-day's wage every week to perform community service activities. There was nothing that resembled a marketing department at the company headquarters in Littlehampton, England. Husbands and wives frequently worked together and could visit their children during the workday at the on-site day-care center.[14] The company's hiring procedures included questions about the applicant's personal heroes and literary tastes, as well as their individual beliefs on certain social issues. On one occasion, Roddick was ready to hire a retail director but refused to do so when he professed his fondness for hunting, a sport that Roddick despised because of her support for animal rights.[15]

PROSPERITY AND SOCIAL ACTIVISM

As the company prospered, Anita Roddick used her enthusiasm and growing influence on her suppliers and customers. The Body Shop began to produce products in the country of origin when it was feasible and paid the workers wages that were comparable to those in the European Community.[16] Customers were asked to sign petitions and join activist groups that The Body Shop endorsed, mostly in the areas of animal rights and environmental causes. The company said it was contributing significant portions of its earnings to these groups, including Amnesty International and People for the Ethical Treatment of Animals (PETA). Roddick was careful to choose causes that were "easy to understand"[17] and could be communicated quickly to a customer during a visit to one of The Body Shop stores.

Opposition to Animal Testing

An example of The Body Shop's corporate activism was its opposition to a practice that had become common in the cosmetics industry—animal testing. Cosmetics firms were not *required* to perform animal testing of their products to comply with product safety and health regulations. However, many companies voluntarily adopted animal-based testing procedures to guard against product liability lawsuits.[18]

The Body Shop was not worried about such lawsuits, because Roddick claimed that the product ingredients it used had been used safely for centuries. In addition, the older recipes had been used for many decades without incident. These circumstances led to the company's rejection of animal-based product testing. Any supplier wishing to do business with The Body Shop had to sign a statement guaranteeing that it had done no animal testing for the previous five years and would never do such testing in the future. The Body Shop used human volunteers from its own staff and the University Hospital of Wales to test new and current products under normal use.[19]

Most other cosmetics firms used a variety of procedures to determine the safety of cosmetics products, with animal-based tests becoming the standard procedures.

Beginning in the 1970s, animal rights groups such as the Humane Society and PETA began protesting the use of animal testing by the cosmetics industry. The Body Shop lent its support to these groups' efforts, tagging all animal testing as "cruel and unnecessary." By 1991, alternative procedures that involved far less cruelty to animals had already been developed, but were yet to be approved for industry use.[20]

THE BODY SHOP IN THE UNITED STATES

When it moved to the United States, The Body Shop's market share was limited by two factors. First, its prices were significantly higher than those charged for mass-marketed products in drugstores, although they were generally comparable to the prices charged for cosmetics and cleansers at department store sales counters. Second, The Body Shop was constrained by the limited number of stores it had opened in the United States. By 1991, only 40 stores had been opened in a dozen metropolitan areas across the country. Roddick maintained that those consumers who sampled The Body Shop products became loyal customers: "Once they walk into one of our stores or buy from our catalogue, they're hooked."[21]

Going Public

The Body Shop was taken public in London in 1984, with the Roddicks owning a combined 30 percent of the outstanding stock. The firm's subsequent sales and net income figures grew during 1985–1990 from sales revenue of $15.3 and net income of $1.4 million to $137.7 and $14.7 million, respectively.[22] Without The Body Shop's monetary donations to various social causes, all of these net income figures would be higher than reported in the financial statements. Estimates of the company's annual contributions to outside organizations were claimed to be from several hundred thousand dollars to several million dollars.

Industry analysts considered The Body Shop to be a strong performer with the potential to prosper even in an economic downturn. The exotic nature of its products, such as hair conditioner made with 10 percent real bananas and a peppermint foot lotion, would attract consumers who desired affordable luxuries. Analysts regarded the public's desire for personal care products as "insatiable," especially in North America.[23] The addition of the strong emotional appeal of social issues formed the basis for one of the most successful marketing and promotional concepts in the cosmetics industry in decades.

Competition Becomes Active

Several new entrants and existing competitors challenged The Body Shop in the United States and Europe. Among the largest of these firms were Estée Lauder and Revlon. The Limited had opened 50 Bath & Body Works stores, patterned after The Body Shop's outlets and located in shopping malls across the United States. In addition, an English competitor, Crabtree & Evelyn, had held a significant presence in North America and Europe since the mid-1970s.

By 1991, The Body Shop was a successful and profitable firm that had attracted a variety of well-financed competitors. The company faced a genuine threat from these firms because they were all well financed and had a broad range of experience in marketing cosmetics. Each of these firms was well established in the United States, yet no one firm dominated the new product segment that The Body Shop had helped create.

There were indications that the environmental concerns that attracted customers to The Body Shop might not have permanent drawing power. Roddick had vowed never to sell anything but environmentally friendly cosmetics and grooming products in her stores, but the industry was growing and changing faster than anyone had anticipated. It seemed that The Body Shop needed to take some kind of action to ensure its long-term survival.

THE BODY SHOP'S ADVERTISING CAMPAIGN

The first appearance by Anita Roddick in a U.S. television commercial was in 1993 in an American Express ad. This came as something of a surprise to the long-time Body Shop customers and her competitors in the cosmetics industry. These people believed that Roddick abhorred advertising as a wasteful practice that "created" needs. The company did promote certain nonprofit groups in its stores and catalogs, including Greenpeace, PETA, and Amnesty International. However, The Body Shop had a policy of not advertising directly to consumers.[24]

Roddick appeared in three commercials and a series of print advertisements as part of this advertising campaign.

Selling Out?

Although the Roddick commercials received a positive response from advertising industry professionals, some long-time Body Shop customers accused Roddick of "selling out" and breaking her promise never to advertise The Body Shop products. Roddick responded that the commercials promoted American Express and did not specifically promote The Body Shop products. The advertisements gave The Body Shop valuable publicity in much the same way that Roddick's social activism and personal appearances had done in the past. In 1997, The Body Shop unveiled "Ruby," a voluptuous size 18 doll created to counter the media images of thin women.[25]

RODDICK'S ROLE AND BUSINESS PURPOSE

When asked about her role in the company, founder Anita Roddick stated:

> *The purpose of a business isn't just to generate profits to create an ever-larger empire. It's to have the power to effect social change, to make the world a better place. I have always been an activist. I have always been incredibly impassioned about human rights and environmental issues. The Body Shop is simply my stage.*[26]

PART B: THE COMPANY'S REPUTATION IS TARNISHED

Between 1991 and 1995, The Body Shop continued to expand its operations. The company had opened 1,200 stores by early 1995. Over 100 company-owned and franchised stores were operating in U.S. shopping malls and downtown shopping districts. During the period 1991–1994, sales and net income grew from $231 million and $41 million to $330 million and $47 million, respectively.

The Body Shop had moved its U.S. headquarters from Cedar Knolls, New Jersey, to a less expensive and more central location—Raleigh, North Carolina. Later, Anita Roddick realized that setting up her headquarters in a college town such as Boulder, Colorado, or a city such as San Francisco would have been a better choice than starting from scratch in New Jersey.[27]

PROBLEMS ARISE

The Body Shop had bigger problems to deal with than the location of its national headquarters. The Limited continued to open its chain of Bath & Body Works stores on a nationwide scale. Placement of a Bath & Body Works store in a mall usually precluded The Body Shop from entering the same mall. (There were some exceptions, most notably very large shopping malls such as the Mall of America in Bloomington, Minnesota.) All of The Limited's stores, from Express and Victoria's Secret to Structure and Lerner's, were company owned. The Limited's size and power as one of the major retailers in the United States made the company a strong threat to The Body Shop's continued presence in the U.S. retail market.

More Competition

Other companies had successfully introduced organic or natural beauty products in discount and drugstores, a market segment that The Body Shop had completely ignored in its global operations. Traditional retailers, including Woolworths and Kmart, had also entered what had come to be known as the minimalist segment of the personal care products industry. Woolworths's entry was an expanded selection of organic bath and body case products in its deep-discount Rx Place chain. Kmart's line of naturalistic cosmetics was sold in over 1,800 stores.[28] Other new companies included H_2O Plus, which sold its products in its own retail stores but did not make claims about animal testing as had The Body Shop and Bath & Body Works.

GOOD PRESS

The Body Shop continued to receive new accolades and to hit new heights of prosperity. Anita Roddick published her autobiography, *Body and Soul*, in late 1991. She donated her portion of the royalties to several groups, including the Unrepresented Nations and Peoples Organization, a self-governing group that spoke for Kurds, Tibetans, and Native Americans; the Medical Foundation, which treated victims of torture; and a variety of individual political prisoners. On the final page of the book, where one would expect to see the last page of the index, is the coda of the final chapter. The last line of text, printed in large boldface letters, reads "Make no mistake about it—I'm doing this for me."[29]

Media Attention

Partly as a result of the book's publication, The Body Shop received a great deal of flattering media attention. *Inc.*[30] and *Working Woman*[31] ran cover stories featuring Anita Roddick. *Fortune*[32] and *BusinessWeek*[33] published shorter articles that focused on Anita Roddick and the company's performance.[34]

BAD PRESS

In 1992, some members of the media began to criticize The Body Shop and the Roddicks. The *Financial Times* newspaper gave The Body Shop the dubious honor of headlining its 1992 list of top ten corporate losers after the price of The Body Shop stock dipped from $5.20 to $2.70 during September.[35] Stock analysts had reacted to a disappointing earnings report, and the news set some minds to wonder if the company could indeed grow quickly enough to capture a leadership position in the minimalist market, or if there was a minimalist market at all.

In 1993, a British television news magazine telecast a report on The Body Shop. The show alleged that the company knowingly sourced materials from suppliers that had recently performed animal testing. The Body Shop sued the TV station and the production company for libel and won a significant financial award after a six-week court battle. Anita Roddick sat in the courtroom every day and compared the experience to confinement in a "mahogany coffin." The Body Shop won the suit and a huge settlement by proving to the British court that the company had never intentionally misled consumers about the animal-testing policy, which encouraged manufacturers to give up animal testing but not claim that ingredients had never been tested on animals.[36]

JON ENTINE'S EXPOSÉ

In 1994, *Business Ethics* magazine, a well-respected U.S. publication, surprised the progressive community by publishing a cover story by Jon Entine on The Body Shop that built upon many of the allegations that others had presented over the years. The resulting controversy engulfed the journalist, the magazine, and The Body Shop in a new wave of controversy that threatened The Body Shop's already slow expansion into the U.S. market.

The story began in June 1993, when journalist Jon Entine had first been approached by disgruntled current and former Body Shop staffers about several of the company's practices. After overcoming his initial skepticism and doing some preliminary investigations in Littlehampton, The Body Shop's headquarters, Entine was convinced he had a sound basis on which to develop a story. Entine began his own investigation, which eventually resulted in the *Business Ethics* article.[37] Despite the magazine's admiration for Anita Roddick, it decided the greater good would best be served by publishing the article.

Entine's Allegations

In the lengthy article, Entine made several claims.[38] Among these claims were that Roddick had stolen the concept of the Body Shop, including the store name, recycling of bottles, store design, and products, from a store she had visited in Berkeley, CA in 1971, before she opened her first shop in Brighton in 1976. Entine further alleged that Roddick had not discovered exotic recipes for some of her products as she had previously claimed but that some were outdated, off-the-shelf formulas that had been used by other manufacturers.

Entine charged that many of The Body Shop products were full of petrochemicals, artificial colors and fragrances, and synthetic preservatives and contained only small amounts of naturally sourced ingredients. He said that quality control was a continuing problem with instances of mold, formaldehyde, and *E. coli* contamination reported around the world, thus requiring the use of large amounts of preservatives to give the products stable shelf lives. Entine further wrote that the U.S. FTC was investigating BSI's franchising practices, which included using deceptive financial data, unfair competition, and misleading representations. He also claimed that the Body Shop's "Trade Not Aid" program was a sham, providing only a small portion of The Body Shop's raw materials while failing to fulfill the company's promises to suppliers. Finally, Entine said that between 1986 and 1993, The Body Shop contributed far less than the average annual pretax charitable donations for U.S. companies, according to the Council on Economic Priorities.[39]

Entine published a similar article in a trade magazine, *Drug and Cosmetic Industry*, in February 1995.[40]

Reaction to Entine's Article

The reaction to Entine's *Business Ethics* magazine article was swift and furious. In June, well before the article's publication, Franklin Development and Consulting, a leading U.S.-based provider of social investment services, had sold 50,000 shares of The Body Shop because of "financial concerns."[41] With rumors spreading about the article in early August, the stock fell from $3.75 to $3.33 per share. Ben Cohen, cofounder of Ben & Jerry's and a *Business Ethics* advisory board member severed his ties with the magazine. The U.S. and British press ran numerous pieces on the article and its allegations. These articles appeared in newspapers and magazines such as *USA Today*,[42] *The Economist*,[43] *The New York Post*,[44] and *The San Francisco Chronicle*.[45] *The London Daily Mail* secured an exclusive interview with one of the founders of the California Body Shop, who described the company's early years and how they eventually came to legal terms with the Roddicks over the rights to The Body Shop trademark.[46]

Entine was interviewed by a small newsletter, the *Corporate Crime Reporter*, in which he defended and explained his research and the article.[47] One point of interest was Entine's claim that The Body Shop products were of "drugstore quality," which he based on the company's use of obsolete ingredients and formulas and a *Consumer Reports* ranking that placed The Body Shop Dewberry perfume last out of 66 tested.[48] *Corporate Crime Reporter* also noted that another reporter, David Moberg, had brought similar allegations against The Body Shop in a separate article published the same month as Entine's.[49]

Rift in Progressive Community

In January 1995, *Utne Reader* published a forum including commentaries by Anita Roddick, Entine, Moberg, and Franklin Research founder Joan Bavaria. Editor Eric Utne noted the rift that the article had caused in the progressive business community and described how the Roddicks, Marjorie Kelly (editor of *Business Ethics*), and other parties had begun holding face-to-face meetings to mend their relationships.[50] Entine described the same meetings as "a family gathering a few days after everyone's favorite uncle was found molesting a neighbor's child. The scandal was on everyone's mind, few would openly talk about it, and most hoped that ignoring it would make it fade away. It didn't."[51] Roddick maintained that the truth had been sacrificed in a rush to judgment but that she had managed to cope with and learn from the experience.[52]

GORDON RODDICK TO THE DEFENSE

Entine's *Business Ethics* article aroused Gordon Roddick to new heights of anger. He was now ready to play hard ball.[53] Early in Entine's investigation, The Body Shop had hired the public relations firm of Hill & Knowlton (H&K) to launch a counterattack on Entine's credibility and motives.[54] H&K used its contacts at NPR to place an interview with Entine and a follow-up story that included comments from The Body Shop supporters on NPR news programs such as "All Things Considered." Attempts by The Body Shop to intimidate *Business Ethics* magazine failed. The editor and publisher, Marjorie Kelly, knew from the beginning that publishing the article was a risk but she said she had checked and rechecked Entine's sources and was satisfied that his charges were sound.[55]

Gordon's Letter

Gordon Roddick responded to the *Business Ethics* article within a month of its publication by sending a ten-page letter on The Body Shop letterhead to all *Business Ethics* magazine subscribers. In this letter, he denied many of the charges made in the article. The letter offered statements by several people that appeared to contradict their own quotations in the article. Roddick seemed to have a reasonable defense for most of Entine's allegations.

Several staff members at *Business Ethics* magazine were not pleased with the letter, which they had received in the mail because they were included as decoys on the subscriber mailing list. This is a common practice in the mailing-list industry to help prevent the misuse of subscriber addresses. The publisher of *Business Ethics* magazine could not recall authorizing the magazine's mailing-list service to rent the list to The Body Shop. It did not take long for the mailing-list company to discover that The Body Shop had obtained the magazine's subscriber list through a third party. Said Ralph Stevens, president of the mailing-list firm, "The Body Shop duped a prominent and legitimate list-brokerage company, a respected magazine, and they duped us.... If this is any indication of the way [The Body Stop does] business, of their regard for honesty and integrity, I give them a failing mark on all counts."[56]

In late 1994, The Body Shop hired a business ethics expert to lead a social audit of the company.[57]

THE SITUATION AS OF 1995

By July 1995, Anita Roddick was already considering the possibility of opening The Body Shop stores in Cuba, hoping to beat her competitors to that market and at the same time convert the Cubans' social revolution into a profitable yet honorable business revolution.[58] The company was also considering opening retail stores in Eastern European countries. At the same time, the media attention on the company had raised serious concerns among customers, among The Body Shop supporters, and within the financial community. Since August 1994, the company's stock price plummeted by almost 50 percent to an all-time low.

Losses

The Roddicks took millions of dollars in paper losses on their holdings, despite having sold a portion of their stock in July 1994.[59] The company faced increased competition from several larger firms, including Procter & Gamble, Avon, Kmart, The Limited, L'Oreal, Crabtree & Evelyn, and Marks & Spencer. Other companies, such as H2O Plus, were making progress in their efforts to open retail stores that featured products similar to those of The Body Shop. The questions that had been raised as a result of media investigations and The Body Shop's responses left some observers wondering what principles the company espoused and if the company could regain its earlier level of success.

Anita's Fame Continues to be Rewarded

Anita Roddick continued to be recognized for her leadership on social and ethical causes. Because of her social activism, she won many awards in the mid-1990s. Among them were the following:[60]

1993—National Audubon Society Medal, USA

1994—Botwinick Prize in Business Ethics, USA

1994—University of Michigan's Annual Business Leadership Award, USA

1995—Women's Business Development Center's First Annual Woman Power Award, USA

PART C: UNIMPRESSIVE GROWTH

By 1998, The Body Shop International had grown into a multinational enterprise with almost 1,600 stores and 5,000 employees in 47 countries.[61] That year, after several years of lackluster financial performance, Anita Roddick gave the company's CEO post to a professional manager and became executive cochairman with her husband, Gordon.[62] Despite the change, the company's financial performance between 1995 and 1997 continued to be unimpressive:[63] Worldwide sales revenue and operating profits were $303 million and $21 million in 1995 and $377 million and $19 million, respectively, in 1997.

In 1995–1996, The Body Shop began to experiment with advertising in North American markets. According to one observer, the company originally thought that its brands and human rights agenda would create valuable word-of-mouth promotion among socially conscious consumers and that advertising would not be needed. The Body Shop's anti-advertising strategy largely paid off in the United Kingdom and other European nations, where human rights activism and commerce blended more seamlessly and consumers had fewer brands and retailers than in the United States. The strategy did not work effectively in the United States, where brand differentiation was crucial. In 1997, for example, The Body Shop's same-stores sales in the United States dropped by 6 percent, the company's worst performance since entering the U.S. market ten years earlier.[64]

BSI's U.S. advertising had always been piecemeal and quirky. For example, Anita Roddick taped a radio spot that slammed the cosmetics industry. In the radio spot, Roddick said, "If more men and more women understood what really makes people beautiful, most cosmetic companies would be out of business."[65]

TRYING TO GET ITS ACT TOGETHER

The Body Shop seemed to be trying hard to get its act together in the U.S. market. It hired a new CEO in the fall of 1998 and created the position of vice president for promotions. These were significant moves for the company, but it would take more than advertising to turn things around. The Body Shop typically plays down product efficacy in favor of hyping product ethicality. A case in point is its Mango Body Butter, whose ingredients the company promotes as from a "woman's cooperative in Ghana." Sean Mehegan, a writer for *Brandweek*, summarized the company's dilemma this way: "How much American consumers care about such claims lies at the heart of whether The Body Shop can turn itself around here."[66]

THE BODY SHOP'S SOCIAL AUDITS

In 1994, perhaps in response to the *Business Ethics* magazine article by Jon Entine calling its integrity into question and perhaps on its own initiative, The Body Shop began an elaborate program of annual social audits examining, in particular, its environmental, social, and animal protection initiatives. In its 218-page *Values Report 1997*, the company reported its progress.[67] This lengthy, landmark document is often held out to be one of the most significant social performance reports ever prepared.

As reported in its *Values Report*, The Body Shop established policies in three areas: human and civil rights, environmental sustainability, and animal protection. In each category, the company set forth a conceptual framework for the auditing process. The auditing process in each category depended heavily on stakeholder interviews. The stakeholders who were interviewed included employees, international franchisees, customers, suppliers, shareholders, and local community/campaigning groups. The company identified the media as a potential stakeholder group for inclusion in future social auditing cycles.[68]

FRANCHISEE ALLEGATIONS

In 1998, The Body Shop continued to face charges that could threaten its future. The company faced a flood of allegations and lawsuits by franchisees charging fraudulent presentations by the company when they bought their franchises. A number of U.S. franchisees had been angry at what they saw as unfair buyback terms if they wanted to get out of the business.[69] An example of the kind of lawsuit being filed was that of Jim White, who was asking for $32 million in damages. He was suing The Body Shop for fraud, fraudulent inducement, and inequitable treatment of franchisees. White claimed that the company offered rock-bottom buyback prices to franchisees caught in a five-year spiral of declining U.S. sales. White claimed he was offered only 20 cents on the dollar and that others were offered as low as 5 cents on the dollar.[70]

INTO THE NEW MILLENNIUM

The early 2000s continued to be tumultuous for The Body Shop. The company continued to grow, but sales and profits were not strong. In the United Kingdom, the company found itself operating in a much more competitive marketplace than in its beginnings 25 years before. Most high street retail chains now are fielding their own "natural" cosmetics and toiletries, and price and promotional battles left the company's products more expensive than those of its rivals.[71]

Conflicts with Franchisees Continue

In September 2001, a major *Fortune* magazine article featured some of the legal difficulties The Body Shop was facing because of conflicts with franchisees. It was reported that eight U.S. Body Shop franchisees, who owned 13 locations, were accusing the parent company of impeding their business. In December 2000, this group filed a lawsuit against the company, asking for damages in the neighborhood of $2 million. One major complaint was that the company-owned stores were getting much better treatment than the franchisee-owned stores. Franchisee owners complained of the company failing to deliver them products while the company-owned stores had no problem getting products. Some franchisee owners saw this chronic out of-stock problem as a ploy to force them to sell their franchises back for a fraction on the dollar.[72]

Roddicks Step Aside

In 2002, Anita and Gordon Roddick stepped down from their positions as cochairs of the board of directors. Along with their friend, and early investor, Ian McGlinn, they maintained control of more than 50 percent of the company's voting rights. Anita Roddick was to remain involved in a "defined consultant role." At about this same time, the company had been in discussions with potential buyers of the company, but these talks were abandoned when offers were below what the company expected.[73] Peter Saunders, former president and CEO of The Body Shop in North America, became the CEO of the company.

Also, during 2002, The Body Shop furthered its commitment to environmental sustainability through investments in renewable energy, funding of energy-efficient projects in the developing world, and incorporating postconsumer recycled materials into its packaging.[74] In 2003, the company started a global campaign to stop violence in the home. In 2003, Anita Roddick was appointed a Dame of the British Empire as part of the Queen's birthday honors.[75]

Sale to L'Oréal

In mid-2006, The Body Shop was sold to France's L'Oréal. Following the sale, Peter Saunders kept his CEO title and founder Dame Anita Roddick remained on the company's board. The plan was that the company would retain its unique identity and values and continue to be based in the United Kingdom. The company hoped to operate independently within the L'Oréal Group and would be led by its own management team, reporting directing to the CEO of L'Oréal.[76] By 2007, the company had 2,100 stores in 55 countries, and two-thirds of them are franchised.[77] In 2007, the company published its *Values Report 2007*, its first since it was acquired by L'Oréal. The company continued to emphasize its five core values: against animal testing, supporting community trade, activating self-esteem, defending human rights, and protecting the planet.[78] The company published another values report and it was called *Values Report 2011*.[79] The company published another *Values Report* in 2014 in which it reaffirmed its core values.[80]

The company continues to face stiff competition. Its top three competitors are Bath & Body Works, Estée Lauder, and Alliance Boots (the U.K.'s number 1 retail pharmacy). But the company has dozens of other competitors including familiar names such as Alberto-Culver, Avon, Coty, The Gap, Macy's, Mary Kay, Revlon, and Target.[81]

An article in *The Independent*, a newspaper in the United Kingdom, said in 2006 that The Body Shop's popularity plunged after the L'Oréal sale. The article argued that the sale had dented the company's reputation, and it was stated that Dame Anita Roddick had abandoned her principles by accepting the deal with L'Oréal. Roddick claimed that she would eventually give away the £130 million she made from the sale.[82]

Much of the targeted criticism of The Body Shop for the issues raised earlier, led in part by Jon Entine, has subsided. A review of Jon Entine's Web site, however, shows that he continued to critique The Body Shop and continues to write periodic articles and newspaper columns about the company. Entine's Web site may be accessed at http://www.jonentine.com/the-body-shop.html.

Roddick Turns to Publishing

Roddick published her second book, *Business as Unusual: The Triumph of Anita Roddick and the Body Shop*, in 2001. Also in 2001 she published *Take It Personally: How to Make Conscious Choices to Change the World*. She explained, "I'm at the point in my life where I want to be heard." She adds, "I have knowledge and I want to pass it on."[83] In an interview with *Across the Board* magazine, Anita commented on her experiences with professional consultants and executives who are not as concerned as she is about preserving The Body Shop's values. She stated: "The hardest thing for me are the marketing people, because they focus on us as a brand

and our customers as consumers. We've never called it a brand; we call it The Body Shop. In 25 years, we've never, ever, ever called a customer a consumer. Customers aren't there to consume. They're there to live, love, die, get married, have friendships—they're not put on this planet to bloody consume."[84]

In 2003 she published *A Revolution in Kindness*. Her last book, published in 2005, was *Business as Unusual: My Entrepreneurial Journey*. She continued to speak and write and raise money for social causes and even developed her own personal Web site, http://www.anitaroddick.com/ where you can track everything she did during the final years of her life.

ANITA'S UNTIMELY DEATH

Quite unexpectedly, and as a shock to all, Anita Roddick died on September 10, 2007. She was 64. She died of a brain hemorrhage, according to her family. As *The New York Times* summarized, she was "a woman of fierce passions, boundless energy, unconventional idealism, and sometimes diva-like temperament."[85]

The Future Under L'Oréal

Upon the sale of The Body Shop to L'Oréal in 2006, *The Independent* (newspaper) in the United Kingdom reported that BSI's popularity had plunged after the sale. An index that tracks public perception of consumer brands found that "satisfaction" with The Body Shop had slumped by almost half since the deal by its founder, Dame Anita Roddick, to sell the company to L'Oréal.[86]

Better progress was later made—in later years. The total number of The Body Shop company-owned stores grew from 1,088 in 2010 to 1,111 by year end 2012. Franchised stores increased from 1,517 stores in 2010 to 1,726 by year end 2012. Retail sales were up 3.7 percent from 2010 to 2012.[87]

In its *Values Report 2011-Striving to Be a Force for Good*, then-Executive Chairman Sophie Gasperment said that the theme of the report, "The Values Chain," reflects how the company works as a business with values integrated into everything that is done. She reiterated the company's key values as: defend human rights, support community fair trade, protect our planet, against animal testing, and activate self-esteem.[88]

When Anita Roddick sold her business to L'Oréal in 2006, she said that The Body Shop would be a "Trojan Horse." By that she meant that the ethical stance of the smaller group she founded would infiltrate the multinational.[89] Though it is not clear whether this infiltration has occurred, it does appear that the company is operating somewhat independently as one of L'Oréal divisions and is striving to uphold its socially oriented mission.

In 2013, after 20 years of campaigning, BSI celebrated a ban on the import and sale of animal-tested products and ingredients in the European Union. BSI was named International Responsible Business of 2013 by London based Business in the Community Organization, a business-led charity. Jeremy Schwarz became CEO.[90] In 2014, BSI became business of the year for the second-year running.[91]

The end of year 2015 data for The Body Shop reported the following:[92]

- 3,102 stores (1,134 company owned; 1,968 franchisee owned
- Total sales: €1559.6 million (up 2.8 percent in Europe; up 1.9 percent new markets; down 10.2 percent North America)

In 2016, The Body Shop was still a part of L'Oreal and it employed 22,000 people in over 60 countries.[93] Since The Body Shop's operating margin has been in decline over the past several years, CEO Jeremy Schwarz announced in 2016 the launch of a new campaign—*Enrich not Exploit*—in an effort to turn around the brand's fortunes. Schwarz hopes that the new campaign will invigorate consumer's commitment to ethical and sustainable ways of doing business and that the company will be the benefactor.[94] Whether a new or restated social mission can turn the company around remains to be seen.

QUESTIONS FOR DISCUSSION

Part A

1. As this case begins, how does The Body Shop address the four components of corporate social responsibility (CSR)? What tensions among these components are at work?
2. Does The Body Shop employ any questionable practices with respect to its hiring practices?
3. What is your assessment of Anita Roddick's philosophy regarding the "purpose of a business"?
4. Can a company such as The Body Shop succeed in trying to balance profitability with an obsession for social causes?

Part B

5. During Part B, how does The Body Shop continue to address the four components of CSR?
6. What is your assessment of Jon Entine's allegations? What is your assessment of The Body Shop's response? Was The Body Shop misrepresenting itself to its stakeholders?
7. Has The Body Shop's reputation been damaged by the incidents in Part B of the case? What are the most serious of the allegations?

Part C

8. In Part C, has the firm snapped back from any damage done to its reputation? Did The Body Shop's social auditing program help the firm?
9. Do the low buyback prices offered to U.S. franchisees reflect poorly on The Body Shop's ethics, or are these just the economic realities of risky investments such as franchises?
10. By the end of the case, what is your assessment of Anita Roddick? Was she a good business person and leader? Was the sale to L'Oreal an indication that Roddick's philosophy had finally failed?
11. Based on your own research, is The Body Shop still a vital part of L'Oreal's portfolios of businesses? Has The Body Shop been able to continue its values and priorities under L'Oreal's ownership?
12. Do you think the new CEO's social theme will invigorate shoppers and turn the company's sales around? What is the future of The Body Shop?

ENDNOTES

1. Catalog, The Body Shop (Fall 1990).
2. Laura Zinn, "Whales, Human Rights, Rain Forests—And the Heady Smell of Profits," *BusinessWeek* (July 15, 1991), 114.
3. Ibid., 114.
4. Samuel Greengard, "Face Values," *USAir Magazine* (November 1990), 89.
5. Zinn, 114.
6. Greengard, 93.
7. Ibid., 97.
8. Zinn, 115.
9. Greengard, 94.
10. Greengard, 90.
11. Maria Koklanaris, "Trio of Retailers Finds Soap and Social Concern an Easy Sell," *The Washington Post* (April 27, 1991).
12. AnitaRoddick.com, http://www.anitaroddick.com/aboutanita.php. Accessed May 20, 2016.
13. Zinn, 114.
14. Greengard, 90.
15. Zinn, 115.
16. The Body Shop promotional Literature, 1991.
17. Zinn, 115.
18. The Body Shop promotional Literature, 1991.
19. Ibid.
20. The Body Shop promotional Literature, 1991.
21. Greengard, 89.
22. Compact Disclosure database, 1991.
23. Koklanaris.
24. The Materials Used in This Section Are Based on Jennifer Conlin, "Survival of the Fittest," *Working Woman* (February 1994).
25. The Body Shop International PLC, "History," *Hoover's Online* (July 7, 2004).
26. Greengard, 97.
27. Anita Roddick, *Body and Soul: Profits with Principles, The Amazing Success Story of Anita Roddick & The Body Shop* (New York: Crown, 1991), 135–136.
28. Faye Brookman, "Prototypes Debut," *Stores* (April 1994), 20–22.
29. Roddick, 1991.
30. Bo Burlingame, "This Woman Has Changed Business Forever," *Inc.* (June 1990).
31. Conlin, 29.
32. Andrew Erdman, "Body Shop Gets into Ink," *Fortune* (October 7, 1991), 166.
33. Laura Zinn, "Whales, Human Rights, Rain Forests—And the Heady Smell of Profits," *BusinessWeek* (July 15, 1991), 114–115.
34. Philip Elmer-Dewitt, "Anita the Agitator," *Times* (January 25, 1993), 52–54.
35. Ibid., 54.
36. Conlin, 30–31.
37. Jon Entine, "Shattered Image," *Business Ethics* (October 1994), 23–28.
38. Ibid.
39. Ibid.
40. Jon Entine, "The Body Shop: Truth & Consequences," *Drug and Cosmetic Industry* (February 1995), 54–64.
41. Judith Valente, "Body Shop Shares Plunge on Reports of Sales by Funds and FTC Inquiry," *The Wall Street Journal* (August 24, 1994).
42. Ellen Neuborne, "Body Shop in a Lather over Ethics Criticism," *USA Today* (August 29, 1995), B1.
43. "Storm in a Bubble Bath," *The Economist* (September 3, 1994), 56.

44. Martin Peers, "Journalist's Probe Hits Body Shop," *New York Post* (August 25, 1994), 33.
45. Dirk Beveridge, "Uproar Threatens Body Shop Stock," *The San Francisco Chronicle* (August 25, 1994), D1.
46. Rebecca Hardy, "American Woman Recalls the Heady Days of Her Hippy Perfume Store … And a £2.3m Deal with the Roddicks," *London Daily Mail* (August 28, 1994).
47. "Interview with Jon Entine," *Corporate Crime Reporter* (September 19, 1994), 13–18.
48. Ibid., 17.
49. David Moberg, "The Beauty Myth," *In These Times* (September 19–October 2, 1994).
50. Eric Utne, "Beyond the Body Shop Brouhaha," *Utne Reader* (January–February 1995), 101–102.
51. Jon Entine, "Exploiting Idealism," *Utne Reader* (January–February 1995), 108–109.
52. Anita Roddick, "Who Judges the Judges?" *Utne Reader* (January–February 1995), 104.
53. Ruth G. Davis, "The Body Shop Plays Hardball," *New York Magazine* (September 19, 1994), 16.
54. Ibid.
55. Maureen Clark, "Socially Responsible Business Brawl," *The Progressive* (March 1995), 14.
56. Ibid.
57. "Ethics Study for Body Shop," *The New York Times* (October 31, 1994), C7.
58. Conlin, 73.
59. "Stake Reduced in Body Shop," *The New York Times* (July 11, 1994), C7.
60. About Dame Anita Roddick, http://www.anitaroddick.com/aboutanita.php. Accessed June 3, 2013.
61. "Capitalism and Cocoa Butter," *The Economist* (May 16, 1998), 66–67.
62. Ibid; also see Ernest Beck, "Body Shop Founder Roddick Steps Aside as CEO," *The Wall Street Journal* (May 13, 1998), B14.
63. *Values Report 1997*, The Body Shop (October 1997), 150.
64. Sean Mehegan, "Not Tested on Humans," *Brand-week* (May 19, 1997), 54.
65. Ibid.
66. Ibid.
67. *Values Report 1997*, 7–12.
68. Ibid., 10–12.
69. Jan Spooner, "Body Shop Faces U.S. Legal Fights," *Financial Mail* (London) (February 22, 1998).
70. Ibid.
71. Harriet Marsh, "Has the Body Shop Lost Its Direction for Good?" *Marketing* (London) (May 10, 2001), 19.
72. Carlye Adler, "The Disenfranchised," *Fortune* (September 2001), 66–72.
73. Sarah Ellison, "Body Shop's Two Founders to Step aside; Sale Talks End," *The Wall Street Journal* (February 13, 2002), A15.
74. Company Profile: The Body Shop, http://www.thebodyshop-usa.com/. Accessed May 20, 2016.
75. Ibid.
76. Ibid.
77. The Body Shop International PLC, "Overview," *Hoover's Online*. Accessed September 6, 2007.
78. The Body Shop Values Report, http://www.thebodyshop-usa.com/about-us/aboutus_history.aspx. Accessed May 20, 2016.
79. Values Report 2011, http://www.thebodyshop.com/content/pdf/global-values_report.pdf. Accessed May 20, 2016.
80. Prezi, "The Body Shop's Values Report, 2014, https://prezi.com/pezbmxtnzjxp/the-body-shops-value-report-2014/. Accessed May 23, 2016.
81. The Body Shop International PLC, "Overview," *Hoover's Online*. Accessed September 6, 2007.
82. Cahal Milmo, "UK: Body Shop's Popularity Plunges after L'Oréal Sale," *The Independent* (UK), April 10, 2006, http://www.corpwatch.org/article.php?id=13469. Accessed May 20, 2016.
83. Mike Hofman, "Anita Roddick: The Body Shop International, Established in 1976," *Inc.* (April 30, 2001), 61.
84. Matthew Budman, "Questioning Authority," *Across the Board* (January 2001), 15–16.
85. "Anita Roddick, Body Shop Founder, Dies at 64," *The New York Times* (September 12, 2007).
86. "Body Shop's Popularity Plunges after L'Oréal Deal," *The Independent*, http://www.corpwatch.org/article.php?id=13469. Accessed June 3, 2013.
87. The Body Shop Sales and Stores, http://www.loreal-finance.com/eng/brands/the-body-shop. Accessed May 20, 2016.
88. Values Report 2011, http://www.thebodyshop.com/content/pdf/global-values_report.pdf. Accessed May 20, 2016.
89. "Body Shop's Popularity Plunges after L'Oréal Deal," *The Independent*, http://www.corpwatch.org/article.php?id=13469. Accessed May 20, 2016.

90. The Body Shop, "The Body Shop History," http://www.thebodyshop-usa.com/about-us/aboutus_history.aspx. Accessed May 20, 2016.
91. Ibid.
92. L'Oreal, The Body Shop, http://www.loreal-finance.com/eng/brands/the-body-shop. Accessed May 20, 2016.
93. L'Oreal, "The Body Shop," http://www.loreal.com/brand/the-body-shop/the-body-shop. Accessed May 20, 2016.
94. Krysia McKechnie, "New Body Shop Chief Executive Is on a Mission," The National, April 27, 2016, http://www.thenational.ae/business/the-life/new-body-shop-chief-executive-is-on-a-mission. Accessed May 23, 2016.

CASE 4

Chipotle's Struggle with Food Safety*

When five customers entered the Chipotle restaurant, Seattle, Washington, in July of 2015, they placed their normal orders…burritos, bowls, tacos—you name it. These customers expected to indulge in what they had come to love over the years, what Chipotle has preached since opening its doors in 1993, "Food with Integrity." Real, fresh, responsibly raised ingredients that "just taste better."[1]

Unfortunately, for these five patrons, integrity was not served up on that summer day. Approximately three days after consumption, the symptoms of an *E. coli* bacterial infection began to set in—upset stomach, body aches, sporadic cramping, and worst of all, persistently bloody stools. The infected people were able to trace their ingestion of bacteria back to their beloved Chipotle meals.[2] However, the source ingredient of this particular outbreak was not immediately determined. Unfortunately, this incident was just a precursor of the crisis to come.

Months later, in December of 2015, Boston College students flocked to their local Brighton, Massachusetts Chipotle restaurant, looking for a quick and hearty meal. Members of the varsity men's basketball team, club hockey players, and many others were expecting to have their cravings satisfied as usual and placed their orders without hesitation. However, like the Chipotle patrons in Seattle, the students became ill shortly after they ate their food. Unbeknownst to the diners, the chicken that had been prepared in the restaurant was not kept at a warm enough temperature in the assembly line. The lack of heat combined with workers showing physical symptoms of illness provided the perfect breeding grounds for a Norovirus to spread. Like an *E. coli* infection, a Norovirus infection is not instantaneous, so these folks still enjoyed their meals, but they certainly paid for them later on. The students found themselves with persistent diarrhea, painful stomach cramps, fevers, and vomiting.[3]

The problems did not stop with this incident. Within weeks of the Boston incident, outbreaks of *E. coli* from Chipotle meals began to occur across the nation with no explanation as to their origins. The company's stock price began to slide, making the fall of 2015 a very difficult quarter for Chipotle. Overall, from July to December 2015, there were over 10 reported outbreaks nationwide, ranging from *E. coli* to Norovirus to Salmonella. At least 500 people across 13 states were affected by the outbreaks—luckily, no deaths were reported.[4]

TWELVE MONTHS EARLIER…

In January of 2014, Chipotle was ranked by *The Daily Meal* as the number one Tex-Mex chain restaurant in America, beating out Baja Fresh, Qdoba, and Moe's Southwest Grill. The ranking, published in *USA Today*, noted how the chain produced fresh and tasty food, with customers appreciating the fresh and local supply of food.[5] Everything seemed to be great for Chipotle, with revenues up almost 28 percent from 2013 to $4.11 billion. Stores were continuously opening nation and worldwide, with further

*This case was written by Thomas Hart, Bentley University, in 2016.

plans of expansion in the future. Additionally, stockholder earnings for 2014 had increased 35 percent from the prior year.[6] Customers (and investors) were extremely satisfied—in fact; even President Obama visited the chain, hosting a roundtable chat with working families in August of 2014 at a location in Washington, D.C. Chipotle appeared to be unstoppable, as if nothing could stand in its way.[7]

THE HISTORY OF CHIPOTLE

Steve Ells, the founder of Chipotle, is a man who has always enjoyed cooking. Ells began cooking at a very young age, as his mother would put him to work in the kitchen helping her bake and prepare meals. As he grew, it was not uncommon in high school and college for Ells to host elaborate dinner parties for his friends and family, where he would serve them with delicious meals. Upon completion of his undergraduate degree and unsure of where he was going to go next, the aspiring chef made a deal with his father. He had to work for a year in the restaurant industry to ensure that he truly wanted to be in the business, and then his father would pay for culinary school—but, it had to be "the best culinary college in America."[8]

Ells held up his end of the bargain and went on to the Culinary Institute, graduating in 1990. After graduating, Ells soon moved to San Francisco where he gained both experience as a sous-chef and an appreciation for Mission-style burritos. Ells was not just attracted to San Francisco's Mexican food itself, but the way it was prepared and packaged, the simplicity of a foil wrap with everything tucked away inside. After receiving a loan from his father and locking down a storefront, Ells opened the first Chipotle restaurant in Denver in July of 1993.

No recipes, no calculated formulas, just fresh ingredients for customers to look at and choose from—this is the way Ells designed his business so that it would be extremely simple to manage and operate, because, in his words, "I didn't want to spend much time there."[9] The first restaurant had no individual menus and no menu board as you see when you walk into a current-day Chipotle. Customers were supposed to order what they wanted based on what they saw in front of them. Although reportedly some customers walked back outside confused, the majority were happy that they had so many fresh food options. Ells was fast to respond to customer demands and quickly created the concept of the burrito bowl when he was trying to shed the tortilla. He wanted all of his customers to enjoy their meals, leaving them with a desire to come back again.

It was not long before the business started to take off. The first few Chipotle restaurants were established with the help of Ells' parents; however, Ells soon realized that larger investors would be necessary to continue to fuel the company's growth. Ells' parents were able to gather just over $1 million from close friends and then they began to hunt for larger contributors. In 1998, when Chipotle had just 13 stores opened, McDonald's invested approximately $50 million.

More significant than the cash received, Chipotle gained access to McDonald's supply chain, construction knowledge, and vast industry knowledge because of the buy-in. The two chains had an interesting relationship in that the only common menu items were the soft drinks. From 1998 to McDonald's divestiture in Chipotle in 2006, the chain grew to just over 500 restaurants, and its growth did not cease after parting ways with McDonald's.[10] Today, Chipotle boasts over 1,900 locations.[11]

PROMISING STOCK PRICE BEGINS TO FALL

The company's initial public offering (IPO) in January of 2006 was priced at $22, opened at $45, and closed at $44 per share.[12] From 2006 on, Chipotle's share price rose steadily until the economic crash of 2007–2008, which sent the stock plummeting, closing below the IPO price at just under $39 a share in November of 2008.

As the U.S. recovered, Chipotle did too. The stock price climbed to $442 per share in April of 2012, and then hit a stock price high of just under $758 in early August of 2015, right around the time of the first *E. coli* outbreak.[13] By mid-2016, following the additional food safety scandals, the stock price tumbled to $426 a share. While the Centers for Disease Control (CDC) had ceased its investigation into the *E. coli* outbreaks and deemed Chipotle to be safe once again, there was no specific determination about the source of the various outbreaks. As a result, many shareholders and consumers were leery about the restaurant.[14] Same-store sales (the metric of customers repeatedly dining at one location) dropped 14.6 percent in the fourth quarter of 2015, and many restaurants were permanently shut down—at least 43 stores in the Northwestern region of the United States.[15]

LAWSUITS

Several civil lawsuits have been brought against Chipotle following the outbreak epidemic. Most prominent is a suit accusing employees of the Simi Valley, California store of attempting to hide evidence of the August 2015 Norovirus outbreak. According to witnesses, the kitchen manager was sick and continued to work days after displaying signs of illness. The restaurant closed its doors shortly after symptoms worsened, and employees allegedly posted signs on the doors to the building stating a staffing shortage was the cause. The lawsuit claimed that after closing the store, employees threw out all of the food in stock, bleached every cooking and preparation surface, and once reopened, brought in alternate employees from other locations to cover for the sick (by then more staff had become ill). County health officials were not contacted until two days after the restaurant closed its doors, a period in which at least 234 customers reported some form of gastrointestinal illness.[16]

Chipotle continues to face multiple negligence suits by/on behalf of affected victims. The majority of these suits aim to obtain compensation to cover medical bills, loss of wages, and other damages. One woman in Boston is suing on behalf of her child who caught Norovirus after eating in the Chipotle restaurant, causing the mother to have to miss work and forgo other responsibilities. It is likely that the chain will settle many of these suits out of court.[17]

Managing the "Perfect (PR) Storm"

Some experts believe that Chipotle managed the crisis well. Chipotle was noted to be "aggressive and forthcoming" in its approach to closing affected stores for deep cleaning; going so far as to close all their stores on one day to hold a company-wide meeting to discuss the changes.[18] In addition, the company revealed it would provide fully paid sick days to ill employees who are now required to stay home an additional five days from the time their symptoms disappear. *Fortune* magazine referred to this as a "one–two approach" that not only addressed Norovirus concerns but also proved Chipotle's loyalty to its employees.[19] Many have said that the chain's ability to be upfront and honest with the public through the years has been the key to its success, as well as key to helping them stay afloat during times of crisis. Chipotle was founded and grown as an "anti-fast food" fast-food restaurant, sacrificing efficiencies and cost savings to prioritize quality and customer satisfaction—"people-before-profits"—and this message resonated even during the food safety issues.[20] The chain posted information to its Web site regarding the outbreaks and released information to media when appropriate.

In 2016, Chipotle implemented a new food safety program to assess the safety risks of every ingredient on its menu. This included DNA-based testing of its ingredients before being shipped to Chipotle locations and changes to food prep and handling, including new training for safety standards for workers. The goal continued to be to provide the freshest food possible at a low cost to customers, despite the challenges of using local supply chains. Nevertheless, one article about Chipotle, postcrisis, was titled, "Chipotle Struggling to Get Customers Back."[21] It cited the need for Chipotle to "tweak" its food safety changes and beef up its advertising. That month, Chipotle issued free burritos to any customer who texted a code to a designated phone number. This marketing campaign proved very successful, with 5.3 million people texting the number, and 67 percent of those people redeeming the coupon.[22] In March 2016, Chipotle announced it would double-down on its free-burrito strategy, announcing that it would mail 21 million coupons to households across the United States. By combining damage control tactics, positive press, and driving traffic to its locations, Chipotle attempted to gain back its lost customer loyalty and trust. So, will these tactics be enough to get Chipotle customers hooked again and ultimately regain their trust? Only time will tell.

QUESTIONS FOR DISCUSSION

1. What are the ethical issues of this case?
2. How would you describe Chipotle's handling of the food safety crisis?
3. In Chapter 6, we identified that Chipotle did not seem to have time to completely develop a plan to manage its crises. Looking back at Chapter 6's "*5 Steps in Managing Crises,*" what might the Chipotle management team have done differently?
4. What is the role of the Center for Disease Control (CDC) in food safety situations? How did they help or hurt Chipotle in managing the crisis?

ENDNOTES

1. Chipotle, "Food with Integrity," (Chipotle, 2016), https://www.chipotle.com/food-with-integrity. Accessed February 1, 2016.
2. Susan Berfield, "Inside Chipotle's Contamination Crisis," *Bloomberg* (December 22, 2015), http://www.bloomberg.com/features/2015-chipotle-food-safety-crisis/. Accessed December 27, 2015.
3. Maggie Fox, "Norovirus Caused Chipotle Outbreak in Boston, Officials Say," *NBC News* (December 8, 2015), http://www.nbcnews.com/health/health-news/chipotle-outbreak-grows-80-boston-college-students-n476316. Accessed February 10, 2016.
4. Coral Beach, "Nothing Ruled out Yet as Cause of Chipotle E. coli Outbreaks," Food Safety News (January 22, 2016), http://www.foodsafetynews.com/2016/01/122728/#.V1oVM-SUQmQ. Accessed January 27, 2016.
5. Samantha Neudorf, "America's 15 Best Tex-Mex Chain Restaurants," *The Daily Meal* (December 10, 2013) http://www.thedailymeal.com/america-s-15-best-tex-mex-chain-restaurants/121213. Accessed February 1, 2016.
6. Chipotle, Investor Relations (January 30, 2014), http://ir.chipotle.com/phoenix.zhtml?c=194775&p=irol-newsArticle&ID=1895464. Accessed February 10, 2016.
7. Jessica Sidman, "Obama Visits D.C.'s Best Chipotle," Washington City Paper (June 23, 2014), http://www.washingtoncitypaper.com/food/blog/20677586/obama-visits-d-c-s-best-chipotle. Accessed February 1, 2016.
8. Kyle Stock and Vanessa Wong, "Chipotle: The Definitive Oral History," (February 2, 2015), http://www.bloomberg.com/graphics/2015-chipotle-oral-history/. Accessed February 10, 2016.
9. Ibid.
10. Ibid.
11. Aaron Smith and Ahiza Garcia, "Chipotle to Close All Restaurants on Feb.8 for Food Safety Meeting," CNN Money (January 15, 2016), http://money.cnn.com/2016/01/15/news/companies/chipotle-food-safety-meeting/index.html. Accessed February 10, 2016.
12. Lynn Cowan, "Chipotle Mexican Grill's IPO Sizzles," *The Wall Street Journal* (January 27, 2006), http://www.wsj.com/articles/SB113829672351557263. Accessed February 10, 2016.
13. Craig Giammona, "Chipotle Outbreaks Send Wall Street Looking for Price Bottom," *Chicago Tribune* (January 11, 2016), http://www.chicagotribune.com/business/ct-chipotle-outbreaks-wall-street-20160111-story.html. Accessed January 27, 2016.
14. Monica Watrous, "CDC Concludes Chipotle Investigation," *Food Business News* (February 2, 2016), http://www.foodbusinessnews.net/articles/news_home/Food_Safety_News/2016/02/CDC_concludes_Chipotle_investi.aspx?ID={57F84B31-7C86-4961-A38D-95828451A884}&cck=1. Accessed February 10, 2016.
15. Kerry Close, "Chipotle Tried to Cover Up Food-Borne Illness Outbreak, Lawsuit Says," *Time* (January 21, 2016), http://time.com/money/4189356/chipotle-cover-up-food-borne-illness-outbreak-lawsuit/. Accessed January 27, 2016.
16. Ibid.
17. O'Ryan Johnson, "Brookline Woman Sues Chipotle, Says Bad Burrito Sickened Son," *Boston Herald* (December 17, 2015), http://www.bostonherald.com/news/local_coverage/herald_bulldog/2015/12/brookline_woman_sues_chipotle_says_bad_burrito_sickened. Accessed February 10, 2016.
18. Daniel B. Kline, "Here's Everything Chipotle Has Done to Handle Its E. Coli Crises; Is it Enough?" *The Motley Fool* (February 10, 2016).
19. Tyler Barnett, "Chipotle Knows What It's Doing by Closing Its Stores," *Fortune* (February 10, 2016), http://fortune.com/2016/02/10/chipotle-temporarily-closing-pr/. Accessed May 31, 2016.
20. Geoff Williams, "Chipotle's E. coli Crisis: P.R. Experts Say It's Handling It Right," *Forbes* (November 4, 2015), http://www.forbes.com/sites/geoffwilliams/2015/11/04/can-chipotle-survive-its-e-coli-crisis-pr-experts-seem-to-think-so-and-offer-advice/#6d8544ab1644. Accessed February 1, 2016.
21. Sam Oches, "Chipotle Struggling to Get Customers Back," *QSR* (March 17, 2016), https://www.qsrmagazine.com/news/chipotle-struggling-get-customers-back. Accessed March 31, 2016.
22. Ibid.

CASE 5

Direct-to-Consumer Advertising for Pills: Is It Ethical?*

What do Tamiflu® and Natazia® have in common? They are both gold medal winners for their direct-to-consumer advertising (DTCA).[1] Although their brand name recognition does not rival that of Coca-Cola, their names are familiar to consumers across the nation. As flag bearers of the DTCA efforts of the pharmaceutical industry, they are at the forefront of the DTCA debate. At this writing, the United States and New Zealand are the only developed countries that permit DTCA. However, the pharmaceutical lobby has been pressuring European regulators to open the European Union to DTCA and so the debate is certain to continue.[2]

Why debate DTCA? In his testimony before the Senate Commerce Subcommittee on Consumer Affairs, Dr. Sidney Wolfe, director of the Public Citizen's Health Research Group, expressed the following concern: "There is little doubt that false and misleading advertising to patients and physicians can result in prescriptions being written for drugs that are more dangerous and/or less effective than perceived by either the doctor or the patient."[3] Beyond safety concerns, there are also concerns over the additional costs that consumers bear with DTCA, as well as the emotional impact and tone of images used in the advertising. In November 2015, the American Medical Association called for a ban on DTCA practices for prescription drugs and medical devices with concerns that the growing proliferation of ads is driving demand for expensive treatments, despite the effectiveness of less costly alternatives.[4]

The findings of a CMI/Compas survey of 104 physicians across multiple specialties underscore these concerns: 89 percent of the physicians indicated that a patient requested a prescription because of seeing a DTCA and 43 percent of the physicians reported changing their prescribing as a result.[5] Only 20 percent agree (5 percent strongly and 15 percent somewhat) that DTCA improves the relationship between a clinician and the patient.[6] The FDA is currently in the process of surveying physician, nurse practitioners, and physician assistants again about their experience with DTC ads, including questions about the impact of social media advertising.[7]

On the positive side, DTCA can also help patients. In the CMI/Compas Survey, 48 percent of the same physicians agreed (5 percent strongly and 43 percent somewhat) that DTCA educates patients and 52 percent agreed (9 percent strongly and 43 percent somewhat) that DTCA lessened the stigma of some diseases.[8] Dr. Richard Dolinar, an endocrinologist, says that the ads empower consumers, "Direct-to-consumer advertising is getting patients with diabetes into my office sooner so they can be treated."[9] Professor Dhaval Dave of Bentley University conducted a study for the National Bureau of Economic Research (NBER) and found that "advertising directed at consumers can expand the total market for drug treatment by educating consumers with regard to treatment options for their symptoms, by facilitating contact between the patient and the physicians, and by reminding patients who already have prescribed medications to adhere to their drug therapy."[10]

With strong arguments for and against DTCA, many people find their opinions evolving. John LaMattina, the former president of Pfizer Global Research and Development, is an expert on the pharmaceutical industry. In a *Forbes* article entitled, "Maybe It's Time for Drug Companies to Drop TV Ads," he questions whether the negatives of DTCA are starting to outweigh the benefits.[11] He was an early supporter of DTCA based on its education value for the consumer and he still believes that some benefits remain; however, he now feels that the ads are having too many negative effects due to industry missteps. For example, some of the commercials are not age appropriate for children and so are subject to tighter industry standards.[12] Denis Arnold and James Oakley found that, over a four-year period, five major pharmaceutical companies violated industry standards in their marketing of erectile dysfunction drugs, leading to children being exposed to sexually themed advertising over one billion times.[13] Another issue Mattina raises is that the endless listing of negative side effects creates problems. He quotes Elizabeth Rosenthal's *New York Times* article:[14]

> *When the Food and Drug Administration in the 1990s first mandated that drug makers list medicines' side*

---

*This case was written by Ann K. Buchholtz, Rutgers University. Updated in 2016 by Jill A. Brown, Bentley University.

effects in order to advertise prescription drugs, there was a firestorm of protest from the industry. Now the litany of side effects that follows every promotion is so mind-numbing — drowsiness, insomnia, loss of appetite, weight gain — as to make the message meaningless.

QUESTIONS FOR DISCUSSION

1. What are the ethical issues in this case?
2. Should DTCA be judged by the same criteria as other advertising? If not, how should it be judged differently?
3. What public policy changes would you advocate regarding DTCA? Should the United States and New Zealand ban them? Should the EU allow them?
4. How will changes in technology and viewing habits change the DTCA issue?

ENDNOTES

1. "Long-Standing DTC National Advertising Awards Honor Diverse Group of DTC Marketing Campaigns," http://www.cvent.com/events/2013-dtc-national-conference/custom-36-16f0d91afe954c9ab932b619722d4642.aspx. Accessed June 11, 2016.
2. Denis G. Arnold and James L. Oakley, "The Politics and Strategy of Industry Self-Regulation: The Pharmaceutical Industry's Principles for Ethical Direct-to-Consumer Advertising as a Deceptive Blocking Strategy," *Journal of Health Politics, Policy and Law* (Advance Publication, February 15, 2013), http://jhppl.dukejournals.org/content/early/2013/02/11/03616878-2079496.full.pdf+html. Accessed June 11, 2016.
3. Sidney M. Wolfe, "Direct-to-Consumer (DTC) Ads: Illegal, Unethical, or Both," *Public Citizen's Health Research Group Health Letter* (September 2001), 3–4.
4. "AMA Calls for Ban on Direct to Consumer Advertising of Prescription Drugs and Medical Devices," *American Medical Association News Room* (November 17, 2015), http://www.ama-assn.org/ama/pub/news/news/2015/2015-11-17-ban-consumer-prescription-drug-advertising.page. Accessed June 11, 2016.
5. "CMI/Compas Survey Finds Doctors' True Opinions of DTC Advertising" (May 1, 2013), http://www.prweb.com/releases/2013/5/prweb10733538.htm. Accessed June 11, 2016.
6. Ibid.
7. "FDA to Survey Direct to Consumers Advertising and Prescribers," *Policy and Medicine* (June 4, 2013), http://www.policymed.com/2013/06/fda-to-survey-direct-to-consumer-advertising-and-prescribers.html. Accessed June 11, 2016.
8. Ibid.
9. Ira Teinowitz, "DTC Regulation by FDA Debated," *Advertising Age* (July 30, 2001), 6.
10. Coalition for HealthCare Communication, "Study Cites Benefits of Pharma's Promotional Efforts," (March 4, 2013), http://www.cohealthcom.org/2013/03/04/study-cites-benefits-of-pharma%E2%80%99s-promotional-efforts/. Accessed June 11, 2016.
11. John LaMattina, "Maybe It's Time for Drug Companies to Drop TV Ads," *Forbes* (February 15, 2012), http://www.forbes.com/sites/johnlamattina/2012/02/15/maybe-its-time-for-drug-companies-to-drop-tv-ads/. Accessed June 11, 2016.
12. Ibid.
13. Arnold and Oakley, 2013.
14. Elizabeth Rosenthal, "I Disclose … Nothing," *The New York Times* (January 21, 2012), SR1. Cited in Mattina, 2012.

CASE 6

Using Ex-Cons to Teach Business Ethics*

After the Enron scandal of 2001 and the WorldCom, Tyco, and Adelphia debacles that followed a couple of years later, the business ethics industry really started to take off. Business ethics consulting and training became a booming field of expertise and those business schools that had not yet started teaching business ethics quickly created new courses to take advantage of the newly energized topic. Business schools that had ethics courses already in their curricula ramped up the number of offerings per year and started looking for innovative and interesting ways to attract students to the courses.

The early wave of ethics scandals brought about two major events that became driving forces in corporate and educational change. First, the Sarbanes–Oxley Act was passed by Congress in 2002. SOX elevated the interest in and incentives for stronger financial controls and compliance, and this led to related initiatives in the realm of business ethics. Second, the Federal Sentencing Guidelines were revised in 2004. The U.S. Sentencing Commission revised its guidelines and created a new ruling that rewarded companies for developing ethics programs and offering ethics training. The Commission passed a ruling that among the different factors to be taken into consideration when a company was accused of wrongdoing was whether or not company management had provided ethics training for its employees. If the company had not offered ethics training as part of an ethics program, the company could be more severely disciplined than if it had offered its employees such training.

On both the business school and corporate fronts, as a result, the demand for ethics training and education quickly grew in importance. In partial response to this new demand, a new category of ethics education arrived on the scene—the use of ex-cons to teach business ethics via presentations in business schools and companies.

WALT PAVLO: AN EARLY CASE STUDY

Walter A. Pavlo, Jr., had achieved many things by the time he was 40 years old. He had graduated from business school with a master's degree, worked as a manager at MCI, devised a $6 million money laundering scheme, and served two years in federal prison. Along the way he became divorced and unemployed, and had to move back in with his parents. As *Business-Week* reported, it was "a story that should scare any MBA straight."[1]

Walt Pavlo, the convicted white collar criminal, has been called by ABC *News* the "Visiting Fellow of Fraud" for his appearances on many campuses. At an appearance for a business school lecture, Pavlo claimed he was once a God-fearing student who played hard and straight. He told ABC's *Nightline* that he was taught the catechism and Ten Commandments as a child and was taught not to steal, cheat, or curse. He was taught to be honest and truthful in all that he did. Upon completion of his MBA, he got a position at MCI, the communications giant, and started working in the collections department. He became very competitive and began fretting that the next guy might be outperforming him, so he ratcheted up his efforts.[2]

Pavlo eventually became a senior manager at MCI. He was responsible for the billing and collection of almost $1 billion in monthly revenue for MCI's carrier finance division. He had a meritorious employment history. In March 1996, Pavlo, a member of his staff, and an outside business associate began to carry out a fraud involving several of MCI's customers. When completed, the scheme had involved seven customers who were defrauded of $6 million over a six-month period. The money was stashed away in a Grand Cayman bank account.[3]

In explaining his going astray, Pavlo detailed how much pressure he had been under and how he was having a difficult time meeting the targets and goals that had been set for him. He told a colleague about his struggle, and the colleague said that "everybody was cheating" because "that's the way you make it." This became a pivotal moment in Pavlo's life, he reported, and that started him down the path to white collar crime.[4] After stealing the $6 million, he began to live according to his newfound means—an expensive new car, hand-tailored Italian suits, and frequent holidays often to the Cayman Islands.

Six months into the fraud, auditors at MCI realized what he was doing and he was forced to resign. He thought the company would just write off the loss as

---

*This case was prepared by Archie B. Carroll, University of Georgia, using public sources. Updated in 2016 by Jill A. Brown, Bentley University.

bad debt to avoid adverse publicity, but his prayers were not answered. MCI brought in the FBI. Knowing he could not withstand a trial, Pavlo made a full confession and was sentenced to three years and five months in prison. He was required to pay recompense from any subsequent earnings for the next 27 years. Pavlo served his time in prison, and after getting out, learned that his wife had filed for divorce. Penniless and homeless, he returned home to live with his parents but found no success in looking for work.[5]

PAVLO'S SECOND CAREER

At the end of one of his unsuccessful job interviews, Pavlo was told he did not get the job but was asked whether he could return to the company and speak to the employees about white collar crime. This was the beginning of his second career. Over the next couple of years, he spoke to the FBI, some of the nation's top accounting firms, professional societies, and numerous business schools. He is now a finance and ethics professor in the MBA program at Ithaca College and a contributor to *Forbes Magazine*. He is described as a "poster boy for white collar crime."[6] Pavlo was asked by ABC's *Nightline*: "You are a convicted felon and an accomplished liar. Why should anybody listen to you?"

Pavlo responded:[7]

> *Before I was a criminal or committed a criminal act, I was someone. I was someone who was on the fast track and did a lot of things right in my life. I've paid a significant price for what I've done, and I tell people that, and I educate people with a cautionary tale about what's going on out there. I'm trying to make a difference, and it's a chance for me to move on with my life and I feel good about my career, for once. For once in my life, I enjoy my work.*

THE PROS & THE CONS

The Pros & The Cons, a Web-based company offering up an array of speakers on the subjects of white collar crime, fraud, and business ethics, demonstrates how the use of ex-cons in teaching business ethics has become a profitable enterprise. In addition to Walt Pavlo, the company features several other speakers whose expertise grew out of their having spent time behind bars. Scott London was a big-4 regional audit partner who was arrested for insider trading. Chuck Gallagher embezzled his clients' trust funds, served time in prison, and is now on the lecture circuit. Mark Morze committed an infamous fraud when he bilked banks and investors of $100 million before getting caught and serving time. Nick Wallace served six years in federal prison for bankrupting 69 savings and loan associations. Now, each of these speakers is ready and willing, for a price, to come to your business school or place of employment and share with you the secrets they learned "from behind bars." These speakers earn thousands of dollars per talk to speak to groups.[8]

Some convicted business people have gone out on their own and written books about their experiences and also lecture to business schools, companies and government. Perhaps most famous is the story of Frank William Abagnale, who wrote over $2.5 million in fraudulent checks and successfully posed as an airline pilot, doctor, lawyer, and college professor. His story was made into a film, "Catch Me If You Can," directed by Steven Spielberg and starring Leonardo DiCaprio in his character.[9] He now runs a successful fraud consulting company. Aaron Beam, one of the cofounders and first Chief Financial Officers of HealthSouth, one of America's most successful health-care companies, is another prime example.[10] Beam tells the story of his role in helping to perpetrate one of the biggest frauds in history. After prison time, Beam gives talks on business ethics and how to prevent corporate fraud, but also has to operate a one-man lawn care business to make a living. Beam thinks there are still those who think he is still wealthy, but he denies it. He observes "Trust me—if you can—I would not be mowing lawns in the South Alabama summer heat if it was not necessary."[11]

OPPONENTS TO USING EX-CONS

Not everyone is satisfied with the idea of using ex-cons to speak to business students. Business ethicist, Professor John C. Knapp has said, "I'm disturbed that so many professors seem to be willing to invite Pavlo and other convicted felons into the classroom without verifying that their stories are true. Paying the ex-cons is rewarding them for committing a crime."[12] A reader of *BusinessWeek* chimed in: "Too bad they don't pay $2,500 to honest people who never embezzled a penny to tell students that they shouldn't be crooks."[13] Similar outrage has taken place when ex-Enron offender Andy Fastow is invited to speak at different venues. Fastow spent six years in prison for securities fraud. At a recent engagement where he was speaking on the topic of Jewish Ethics, the rabbi who introduced Fastow mentioned that she had received numerous complaints for including Fastow in the program. In defending the invitation, she noted, "The wisest person learns from somebody else."[14]

QUESTIONS FOR DISCUSSION

1. What are the ethical issues in this case?
2. What are the advantages and disadvantages of hiring ex-cons to speak to college students on the subject of business ethics? Is it appropriate for colleges and universities to pay felons to be guest speakers?
3. What do you think you could learn from an ex-con speaking on business ethics?
4. Successful business executives who speak to students on the subject of business ethics typically do not get paid. They do this as a service. Is it wrong to pay ex-cons to speak on their illicit motives and activities?

ENDNOTES

1. Jane Porter, "Using Ex-Cons to Scare MBAs Straight," *Bloomberg Businessweek* (April 24, 2008).
2. Martin Bashir, "Walt Pavlo: The Visiting Fellow of Fraud—Ex-Corporate Criminal Makes a Good Living Talking Up Ethics," *ABC News* (January 30, 2006).
3. "Walter Walt Pavlo," The Pros & The Cons: The Only Speakers Bureau for White-Collar Criminals in the U.S., http://www.theprosandthecons.com/. Accessed June 10, 2016.
4. Bashir.
5. Ibid.
6. "Former White-Collar Criminal Uses Experience as a Lesson in Business Ethics," *Tampa Bay Business Journal* (October 1, 2014), http://www.bizjournals.com/tampabay/blog/2014/10/former-white-collar-criminal-uses-experience-as-a.html. Accessed June 10, 2016.
7. Ibid.
8. Christopher S. Stewart, "After Serving Time, Executives Now Serve up Advice," *The New York Times* (June 1, 2004).
9. Samantha Cortex and Vivian Giang, "11 Ex-Criminals Who Completely Turned Their Lives Around," *Business Insider* (June 19, 2012), http://www.businessinsider.com/10-ex-criminals-who-completely-turned-their-careers-around-2012-6?op=1. Accessed June 11, 2016.
10. Aaron Beam with Chris Warner, "*HealthSouth: The Wagon to Disaster*" (Fairhope, AL: Wagon Publishing, 2011); also see "Aaron Beam," http://www.aaronbeam.net/. Accessed June 10, 2016.
11. Ibid., 199.
12. Quoted in Porter (2008).
13. Ibid.
14. Mimi Swartz, "Forgive Those Who Trespass Against Us?" *Texas Monthly* (April 20, 2016), http://www.texasmonthly.com/articles/andy-fastow-enron-cfo-apology-tour/. Accessed June 11, 2016.

CASE 7

Volkswagen's Diesel Deception*

Between 2009 and 2015, Volkswagen manufactured and marketed clean diesel automobiles that were designed to provide high performance without the polluting emissions commonly associated with diesel engines. These turbocharged direct injection (TDI) clean diesel vehicles were very popular in Western Europe, where environmentally conscious or "green" consumers found they could have fast, responsive cars that seemed to sip diesel. On September 18, 2015, the U.S. Environmental Protection Agency announced that it was suing the Volkswagen Group for selling over 482,000 diesel Volkswagens and Audis with software "defeat devices" that caused the vehicles to be far more polluting than expected during normal driving. The vehicles would be recalled for repairs.[1]

In the following weeks, the U.S. and German investigators swarmed into Volkswagen offices,

*This case was written by William A. Sodeman, University of Alabama in Huntsville (UAH)

including the company's international headquarters in Wolfsburg, Germany, and the corporate offices of the company's U.S. subsidiary, Volkswagen Group of America (VWoA).[2] The Volkswagen group manufactures and markets automobiles, vans, and trucks around the world in a variety of brands. The Volkswagen marque is the company's most popular brand. Prestige brands such as Audi, Porsche, and Bentley have significantly lower sales volumes, but much higher margins.[3] In May 2016, VW reported a quarterly profit on Volkswagen-branded cars of only €73 million for the first quarter of 2016, a significant decrease from the €514 million profit it posted in the first quarter of 2015. Much of the profits were erased by dealer incentives and consumer rebates that supported sales of gasoline-powered Volkswagen-branded vehicles. As a whole, Volkswagen Group posted a quarterly profit of €2.4 billion; Audi and Porsche accounted for two-thirds of that profit.[4]

FIGURE 1 Volkswagen Automotive Brands

Volkswagen*
Audi*
Bentley*
Bugatti*
Lamborghini*
Ducati
MAN
Porsche
Scania
SEAT
ŠKODA

*Indicates Volkswagen brands marketed in the United States by VWoA.

Sources: Volkswagen, "Brands and products," http://www.volkswagenag.com/content/vwcorp/content/en/brands_and_products.html. Accessed June 8, 2016.

VOLKSWAGEN'S HISTORY AND CULTURE

Founded in 1937, Volkswagen was intended to produce a "people's car," designed by Ferdinand Porsche, for the citizens of the Third Reich. The town of Wolfsburg was established in 1938 for VW employees.

U.S. distribution of the VW Beetle, a modified version of the original "people's car" design, began in 1949. The company founded Volkswagen Group of America (VWoA) in 1955, and created the Audi marque in 1969.[5] VW's international success helped spur the recovery of West Germany.[6] VW opened a U.S.$1 billion manufacturing facility in Chattanooga, Tennessee, in 2008. To secure Volkswagen's commitment, the state of Tennessee offered Volkswagen a package of tax incentives that grew to almost $U.S.1 billion by 2015.[7] Porsche took over VW in 2009[8] after decades of cooperation and conflict between the Porsche family and Volkswagen management.[9]

In 2015, Volkswagen was tightly controlled by the billionaire descendants of Ferdinand Porsche, who own 50 percent. Independent shareholders own about 12 percent of the stock. The north German state government of Lower Saxony, where Wolfsburg is located, and Qatar's sovereign wealth fund[10] own the rest. A network of powerful German labor unions participate in management decisions, as compensation for funds that were confiscated after World War II.[11] Volkswagen had a fleet of corporate jets, including an Airbus A319; VW owned over 100 factories in 31 countries[12] across 12 different brands (see Figure 1), and the Volkswagen air services subsidiary that flew company executives as needed.[13]

"Be aggressive at all times" was how one Volkswagen executive described the company's confident approach to global competition. Volkswagen chief executives including Ferdinand Piëch, a grandson of Ferdinand Porsche, and Piëch's successor, Martin Winterkorn, heavily promoted clean diesel technology as part of the company's environmental commitment. He had promised that Volkswagen would surpass Toyota to become the world's largest automobile manufacturer, and that clean diesel vehicles, not hybrids, were the key to global domination.[14]

Soon after the EPA recall announcement in September 2015, Winterkorn resigned. In December 2015, the new CEO, Mathias Müller, and the chairman of Volkswagen's supervisory board announced in a press conference that Volkswagen employees had created the emissions test scheme in 2005, after realizing the company's diesel technology could not pass U.S. environmental standards.[15] CEO Müller, announced that the company might have to sell the corporate Airbus A319 corporate jet, among other major changes. The company set aside €6.7 billion to cover the costs of repairing faulty diesel cars, including the option of repurchasing some diesel vehicles from consumers.[16] While Volkswagen planned to keep its 12 different brands, plans for a €100 million corporate design center intended for Wolfsburg were scrapped.[17]

In January 2016, members of the Porsche and Piëch families, who owned half of Volkswagen, made public statements endorsing Müller after his controversial visit to the United States.[18] In an NPR interview recorded during a visit to Detroit, Müller apologized for the scandal, and promised to "deliver appropriate solutions to [VWoA] customers."[19] Earlier in the interview, Müller claimed that Volkswagen did not lie to the American public:

> Frankly spoken, it was a technical problem. We made a default, we had a ... not the right interpretation of the American law. And we had some targets for our technical engineers, and they solved this problem and reached targets with some software solutions which haven't been compatible to the American law. That is the thing. And the other question you mentioned — it was an ethical problem? I cannot understand why you say that.[20]

NPR interviewed Müller the next day, and the CEO attempted to mitigate the damage of his previous statements:

> We have to accept that the problem was not created three months ago. It was created, let me say, 10 years ago. ... We had the wrong reaction when we got information year by year from the EPA and from the [California Air Resources Board].... We have to apologize for that, and we'll do our utmost to do things right for the future.[21]

In April 2016, Volkswagen agreed to repurchase almost all the affected 2 L diesel vehicles in the United States, and further agreed to provide owners with additional compensation. This buyback program was estimated to cost U.S.$7 billion, but it did not include 3-liter diesel vehicles from Audi and Porsche.[22] Later in April, Müller personally apologized to President Barack Obama for the emissions scandal.[23] The following month, Volkswagen challenged the U.S. Department of Justice's authority in the matter, claiming that the affected cars were sold not by the European parent companies, but by local businesses in the United States.[24] While Volkswagen's European operations designed the automobiles and their emissions systems, many of the affected diesel automobiles were manufactured in Volkswagen's Chattanooga facility.[25]

CHEATING THE SYSTEM

The emissions control systems used in the affected Volkswagen, Audi, and Porsche cars included software designed by Volkswagen engineers to deceive or cheat emissions tests. Automakers often use common body frames, engines, components, and software across multiple brands to reduce duplication and costs. Emissions tests usually involve running at several different speeds while the driving wheels of the vehicle rest on a treadmill. When testing a front wheel drive model, the back wheels remain stationary.[26] To test an all-wheel or four-wheel drive vehicle, treadmills are placed under both axles. The vehicle is connected to a dynamometer, a device that measures the torque or power of an engine.[27] Sensors attached to the vehicle's exhaust pipe measure the vehicle's emissions.

The test or "dyno" mode used in the engine control unit (ECU)[28] of VW diesel vehicles was activated only when the following conditions were met:

> the steering wheel was not being moved;
> the vehicle was operating at a constant speed; and
> the atmospheric barometric pressure was steady.[29]

In April 2016, German newspapers and television broadcasts revealed that an early version of this "dyno" mode plan was found in a 2006 PowerPoint presentation that had been prepared by a German Volkswagen executive.[30] Under normal driving conditions, the vehicle's braking and stability control systems might take over the vehicle because a lack of steering column movement; this is one indication of a loss of vehicular control, such as a skid. Therefore, the test or "dyno" mode performed a useful function by allowing the vehicle to be driven normally on a dynamometer.

The ECU, braking, and stability control modules for VW diesel vehicles were manufactured by Bosch, a major manufacturer of automotive components.[31] These components were programmed by VW engineers, using proprietary code developed within the company. The U.S. Environmental Protection Agency (EPA) performs emission testing on only about 10 to 15 percent of new cars each year, and relies on automobile manufacturers to certify the emissions performance of its vehicles. According to Columbia University law professor Eben Moglen, "[s]oftware is in everything ... proprietary software is an unsafe building material. You can't inspect it."[32] In the summer of 2015, the EPA announced that it opposed inspection of proprietary automobile software, supporting automobile manufacturers who claimed that people might try to reprogram their vehicles systems to increase performance in unsafe ways.[33]

Volkswagen engineers took advantage of "dyno" mode by programming the ECU to shift the vehicle's emissions control systems into a full power mode that significantly reduced emissions, but used significantly more fuel to operate.[34] Diesel engines produce emissions that include nitrogen oxides (NO_x) and ozone. These are chemical compounds that, according to the EPA, can cause "adverse respiratory effects including airway inflammation in healthy people and increased respiratory symptoms in people with asthma," especially inside vehicles and near roads.[35] Emissions control systems are installed in vehicles to reduce the production and/or emissions of compounds. Volkswagen started selling diesel cars in the United States in 1977, taking advantage of increased consumer interest in diesel fuel economy.[36]

One form of Volkswagen's diesel emissions control systems used a technology called selective catalytic reduction (SCR).[37] This method used a solution of 70 percent water and 30 percent urea to convert NO_x emissions to nitrogen, oxygen, water, and carbon dioxide (CO_2).[38] A computerized controller sprayed an optimal amount of liquid as the emissions passed through the exhaust system. The liquid is sold in the United States as AdBlue.[39] This system required drivers to have the urea tank refilled periodically at a service center.

A different system was installed in the Golf and other small cars, partly because the SCR system required more space than was available. This version did not require refills; it used a nitrogen oxide trap located before the exhaust valve and catalytic converter to capture and reduce emissions. The vehicle used about 4 percent more diesel fuel when the trap was operating at full power.[40] Some industry experts claimed that traps were less effective than urea-based systems.[41]

VW engineers changed the vehicle's software to turn off the nitrogen oxide trap or catalytic scrubbers[42] during the "on road" mode that was used for normal operation of the vehicle.[43] This boosted the vehicle's overall speed and acceleration but reduced fuel economy while increasing NO_x emissions by a factor of 40. VW's diesel emissions control systems also increased the price of each vehicle between U.S.$5,000 and U.S.$8,000.[44]

CATCHING THE CHEAT

Government reliance upon manufacturer testing can be problematic. According to Zeynep Tufekci, an assistant professor at the University of North Carolina, smart cars and other smart devices should be tested in realistic conditions, not in a controlled environment. Companies should not be able to use copyright and intellectual property laws to restrict inspection of proprietary software, especially when the code is used in important processes such as voting and public safety. Developers should also include logs and audit trails in their software, to help document its operation.[45]

Volkswagen's "dyno" or cheat mode was discovered in 2014 by researchers at West Virginia University (WVU) who measured the emissions of VW diesel vehicles during long-distance driving tests. One vehicle had a nitrogen oxide trap, while two other vehicles used urea-based SCR systems. WVU was contracted by an NGO, the International Council on Clean Transportation (ICCT), to perform these tests after European investigators noticed discrepancies in their emissions tests of VW and BMW diesel vehicles. U.S. emissions testing is more stringent than European testing, and California automobile emissions standards are more stringent that Federal standards.[46]

While the WVU report only mentioned Volkswagen once,[47] it was clear that the VW diesel vehicles produced much higher levels of NO_x emissions during the WVU road tests than were seen in dynamometer tests performed by the California Air Resources Board.[48] ICCT posted the findings to its Web site in May 2014 and notified the EPA. Investigations by CARB and the EPA led to the EPA's September 2015 announcement. The regulators refused to certify VW's 2016 diesel vehicles for sale, leaving VW and its North American dealers with billions of dollars in new car inventory that could not legally be sold.[49] On September 21, VW's stock price dropped 23 percent.[50]

Over 11 million diesel vehicles worldwide had engines that were affected by VW's unorthodox technology; 660,000 were sold in the United States. The EPA ordered a recall of over a dozen diesel-powered models.[51] (See Figure 2)

U.S. consumers were assured that they could continue to drive their affected vehicles while the recall was being organized. For 2015 and 2016 model year vehicles that used the nitrogen oxide trap, the repair was most likely a software patch, installed by a dealer.[52] More extensive modifications were needed for SCR models.

FIGURE 2 Diesel Automobiles Recalled by the EPA
Audi A3 (2010–2015)
Audi A6 Quattro (2014–2016)
Audi A7 Quattro (2014–2016)
Audi A8 (2014–2016)
Audi A8L (2014–2016)
Audi Q5 (2014–2016)
Audi Q7 (2009–2016)
Porsche Cayenne (2013–2016)
Volkswagen Beetle (2012–2015)
Volkswagen Beetle Convertible (2012–2015)
Volkswagen Golf (2010–2015)
Volkswagen Golf SportWagen (2015)
Volkswagen Jetta (2009–2015)
Volkswagen Passat (2012–2015)
Volkswagen Touareg (2009–2016)

MARKETING THE CLEAN DIESEL

Between 2009 and 2015, VWoA bought significant amounts of advertising for diesel vehicles in the United States, which was one of the Volkswagen's most profitable markets. Diesel vehicle sales accounted for about 5 percent of the North American market,[53] but about 25 percent of VW's sales were in the diesel category.[54] While VW is a market leader in China, diesel engines are unpopular there. There are stringent emissions control rules in European countries, especially in cities such as Paris, but diesel vehicles held a 50 percent market share in Western Europe.[55] Between January and September 2015, VW spent $77 million on U.S. television advertising for diesel vehicles, which was about 45 percent of the company's total in that market.

VW diesel ads used humor to emphasize the high performance and clean emissions of its diesel cars. In a 2015 campaign, three older women discussed the drawbacks of diesel cars while being driven in a VW diesel vehicle. The series, titled "Old Wives Tales," focused on consumer complaints regarding diesel cars, including sluggish performance, loud noise, and the scarcity of diesel fuel. The passengers in the commercials were always surprised when their VW vehicle overcame the problems they discussed.[56] Another 2015 VW advertisement showed precocious boys who cause chaos in a convenience store, to the sounds of Waylon Jennings' country music song "Mommas, don't let your babies grow up to be cowboys." Their mother notices the boys are missing while she refuels their vehicle outside. A VW diesel Jetta drives by, and the viewers see the mother who is driving that vehicle while her three boys sit quietly.[57]

Another benefit that VW and Audi emphasized in their marketing was decreased diesel fuel consumption. During the 2010 Super Bowl, Audi ran a television advertisement for its A3 TDI hatchback that showed the car as the only vehicle that could pass through a fictional "green police" checkpoint. For the 2015 diesel Jetta, VW aired a television advertisement that claimed "When you're driving, things aren't always what they appear to be." The advertisement only aired a few times before it was pulled in September 2015.[58] After the EPA's September 18 announcement, VWoA paused its national advertising through October 11, including the company's non-diesel vehicles.[59] Advertising for gasoline and electric vehicles resumed slowly, as VWoA managers and ad agencies scrambled to create new campaigns and content.

GOVERNMENT INVESTIGATIONS

Over 450 VW and third-party investigators conducted a probe during late 2015 and early 2016, coordinated by the accounting firm Deloitte and a U.S.-based law firm, Jones Day. There were many obstacles in VW's internal reports and documentation on the affected diesel systems. VW engineers used dozens of code words such as "acoustical software" when referring to the emission control countermeasures. The investigators turned their focus on about 20 VW employees. Many persons interviewed during the investigation were "reluctant to provide insight because they were afraid of the legal consequences."[60] The German employees under investigation were not executives. However, the idea that VW executives were unaware of the diesel defeat designs "just doesn't' pass the launch test," to quote John German, a former EPA official who became a senior fellow at ICCT and helped begin that group's investigation of VW in 2013.[61] French authorities launched their own investigation into intentional fraud by VW.[62]

German law exempts companies from being prosecuted for crimes; the German Penal Code or *Strafgesetzbuch (StGB)* stipulates that only individuals can be held liable for criminal acts. Six Volkswagen employees were under investigation for charges of corporate tax evasion. In the United States, Senators Ron Wyden (D-OR) and Orrin Hatch (R-UT) accused Volkswagen and VWAG of accepting as much as

U.S.$51 million in tax incentive credits for diesel vehicles.[63] Margo Oge, who was director of the EPA Office of Transportation and Air Quality in 2011, revealed that German Volkswagen executives had pressured the EPA for "special fuel economy credits for environmental friendliness" that were equivalent to those awarded to zero-emissions vehicles such as electric cars.[64] Oge perceived that the German Volkswagen executives believed their diesel technology was superior to electric motors: "I never had a problem dealing with the Americans. The U.S. Volkswagen people would always come and apologize to us after meeting with the Germans. My sense was that things were being dictated by Germany."[65]

Whistleblowers also came forward. David Donovan, who worked at VWoA in electronic discovery and information management, claims he was fired in December 2015 after he reported his concerns to the company's legal department.[66] Volkswagen acknowledged that there were at least 50 other whistleblowers.[67]

The legal responsibilities of Volkswagen and VWoA executives is also of concern. CIOs are responsible for finding and archiving data, messages, and other corporate information. In September 2015, U.S. Deputy Attorney General Sally Quillian Yates announced that the U.S. Department of Justice planned to increase its efforts to prosecute corporate executives for their involvement in corporate misconduct.[68] Investors criticized Volkswagen's executive compensation practices. Billionaire investor Christopher Hohn of TCI Fund Management wrote in a letter to Volkswagen's executive supervisory boards that top management compensation appeared to be "excessive," and was "unlinked to transparent metrics and paid in cash with no vesting or deferral, and has encouraged aggressive management behavior, contributing to the diesel scandal."[69]

Michael Schrage, a research fellow at MIT's Center for Digital Business, noted that Volkswagen had brought the crisis on itself by failing to acknowledge societal and technological change. The emergence of the Internet of Things (IoT), in which products are embedded with sensors and smart systems, coupled with societal acceptance of social media, made the revelation of corporate deception far more likely than ever before.[70]

VOLKSWAGEN DIESEL TIMELINE

2005: Volkswagen executives make diesel the focus of the company's U.S. marketing efforts. A small group of Volkswagen engineers and employees in Germany decide to find ways to cheat emissions testing.

2006: A Volkswagen executive prepares a PowerPoint presentation that describes how to cheat U.S. emissions testing.

2007: Martin Winterkorn becomes CEO of Volkswagen.

2008: Volkswagen opens a U.S.$1 billion production facility in Chattanooga, Tennessee, in return for U.S.$577 million in state tax incentives.

2009: Volkswagen and Porsche merge. Diesel vehicles with the altered software go on sale. VWAG launches diesel vehicle marketing campaign in the United States.

2011: Volkswagen opens a new manufacturing facility in Chattanooga, Tennessee.

2014: Volkswagen decides to expand the Chattanooga plant instead of moving production to Puebla, Mexico, based on an additional $U.S.230 million in state tax incentives.

September 18, 2015: The EPA orders Volkswagen to recall 486,000 because they used software designed to cheat emissions tests.

September 22, 2015: Volkswagen reveals that 11 million diesel cars worldwide used the affected software.

September 25, 2015: Winterkorn resigns as CEO. Matthias Müller, the head of the company's Porsche unit, is named as his replacement.

November 2, 2015: The EPA discovers cheating software on more cars than previously disclosed and, for the first time, also finds the illegal software in a Porsche model.

November 3, 2015: Volkswagen announces that it understated emissions of gasoline powered cars in Europe.

November 9, 2015: VWoA offers $1,000 gift cards to owners of affected diesel vehicles in the United States. Volkswagen later states that this offer does not apply to owners in the EU.

November 11, 2015: Volkswagen halts production of the 2016 diesel Passat at its Chattanooga manufacturing facility.

November 25, 2015: Volkswagen announces that a set of simple repairs could bring the affected diesel cars in to compliance with European standards.

December 10, 2015: The chairman and CEO of VW presented the results of an internal inquiry, revealing that the decision by employees to cheat on emissions tests was made in 2005.

January 10, 2016: CEO Müller claims in a radio interview that the emissions scandal was a technical issue, not an ethical concern. He changes his statement the next day.

March 2, 2016: Volkswagen reveals that former CEO Winterkorn received a memo on problems with diesel emissions in Volkswagen vehicles in May 2014, but did not indicate if Winterkorn had ever read the document.

April 22, 2016: Volkswagen agrees to fix or buyback almost all affected diesel cars in the United States.

April 24, 2016: CEO Müller personally apologizes to President Barack Obama for the emissions scandal, during a state dinner hosted by German Chancellor Angela Merkel.

May 24, 2016: Volkswagen claims that the U.S. Government has no jurisdiction over the emissions scandal. The company will continue its own internal investigation.

QUESTIONS FOR DISCUSSION

1. Consider the corporate culture of Volkswagen in Germany. How did it affect this situation?
2. Why did Volkswagen engineers decide to cheat the emissions tests? Should the engineers have consulted with executives?
3. What is your assessment of VW's sense of business ethics and fair play as manifested in the emissions cheating scandal?
4. VW has always been perceived to be a socially responsible corporation. In light of this, how could an emissions cheating scandal like this occur?
5. What roles should government regulators play in terms of emissions and fuel economy testing?
6. Assume that you are a consumer who purchased one of the affected diesel vehicles in 2014, before the EPA made its announcement. What might your reaction have been? What forms of restitution would you have sought from VWoA and Volkswagen?
7. Do research into what has taken place in the VW case since the end of this case. Are circumstances looking better or worse for the company?

ENDNOTES

1. Nathan Bomey, "EPA Accuses Volkswagen, Audi of Evading Emission Laws," *USA Today* (September 18, 2015). http://www.usatoday.com/story/money/cars/2015/09/18/epa-accuses-volkswagen-audi-evading-emission-laws/72400018/. Accessed May 31, 2016.
2. Danielle Ivory and Keith Bradsher, "Regulators Investigating 2nd VW Computer Program on Emissions," *New York Times* (October 8, 2015). http://nytimes.com/2015/10/09/business/international/vw-diesel-emissions-scandal-congressional-hearing.html. Accessed October 9, 2015.
3. Jack Ewing and Graham Bowley, "The Engineering of Volkswagen's Aggressive Ambition," *New York Times* (December 13, 2015). http://www.nytimes.com/2015/12/14/business/the-engineering-of-volkswagens-aggressive-ambition.html. Accessed December 14, 2015.
4. Jack Ewing, "Volkswagen Reports Profit Drop as It Grapples with Emissions Scandal," *New York Times* (May 31, 2016). http://www.nytimes.com/2016/06/01/business/international/volkswagen-q1-earnings.html. Accessed May 31, 2016.
5. Zachary Wilson, "The History of Volkswagen," *Fast Company* (February 1, 2010). http://www.fastcompany.com/1512941/history-volkswagen. Accessed June 6, 2016.
6. Bowler.
7. Sue Sturgis, "Reminder: Here's What One State Paid to Lure Lawbreaking VW," *Blue Nation Review* (September 25, 2015). http://bluenationreview.com/reminder-heres-what-one-state-paid-to-lure-lawbreaking-vw. Accessed October 6, 2015.
8. Wilson, ibid.
9. Luca Ciferri, "Winners and Losers in the VW Scandal," *Automotive News* (November 9, 2015).
10. Dietmar Hawranek, "The Porsche Story: The Downfall of a Corporate Upstart," *Der Speigel* (July 22, 2009). http://www.spiegel.de/international/business/the-porsche-story-the-downfall-of-a-corporate-upstart-a-637542-druck.html. Accessed June 9, 2016.
11. Ewing and Bowley.
12. Bowler.
13. Ibid.
14. Danny Hakim, Aaron M. Kessler, and Jack Ewing, "As Volkswagen Pushed to Be No. 1, Ambitions Fueled a Scandal," *New York Times* (September 26, 2015) http://www.nytimes.com/2015/09/27/business/as-vw-pushed-to-be-no-1-ambitions-fueled-a-scandal.html. Accessed September 26. 2015.

15. Ibid.
16. Ewing and Bowley.
17. Rauwald.
18. Jan Schwartz, "Porsch, Piech Families Support Embattled Volkswagen CEO: Sources," *Reuters* (January 17, 2016). http://www.reuters.com/article/us-volkswagen-emissions-porsche-idUSKCN0UV0JW. Accessed June 8, 2016.
19. Sonari Glinton, "'We Didn't Lie,' Volkswagen CEO Says of Emissions Scandal," *NPR* (January 11, 2016). http://www.npr.org/sections/thetwo-way/2016/01/11/462682378/we-didnt-lie-volkswagen-ceo-says-of-emissions-scandal. Accessed March 5, 2016.
20. Glinton, ibid.
21. Glinton, ibid.
22. Jack Ewing, "Volkswagen Reaches Deal in U.S. over Emissions Scandal," *New York Times* (April 21, 2016). http://www.nytimes.com/2016/04/22/business/international/volkswagen-emissions-settlement.html. Accessed April 21, 2016.
23. Jack Ewing, "VW Chief 'Personally' Apologized to Obama over Cheating," *New York Times* (April 28, 2016). http://www.nytimes.com/2016/04/29/business/international/volkswagen-legal-costs-emissions-cheating.html. Accessed June 10, 2016.
24. Hiroko Tabuchi, "Volkswagen Challenges U.S. Jurisdiction in Emissions Scandal," *New York Times* (May 25, 2016). http://www.nytimes.com/2016/05/26/business/volkswagen-challenges-us-jurisdiction-in-emissions-scandal.html. Accessed May 27, 2016.
25. Geoffrey Smith, "Scandal Halts VW's Diesel Passat Production in U.S." *Fortune* (November 11, 2015). http://fortune.com/2015/11/11/scandal-halts-vws-diesel-passat-production-in-u-s. Accessed June 10, 2016.
26. Jon Linkov, "Volkswagen Emissions Cheat Exploited 'Test Mode'," *Consumer Reports* (September 25, 2015). http://www.consumerreports.org/cro/cars/volkswagen-emissions-cheat-exploited-test-mode.htm. Accessed October 3, 2015.
27. Tom Lish, "What Is a Dynamometer and How Does It Work?" http://www.setra.com/blog/test-and-measurement-dynamometer. Accessed June 6, 2016.
28. Linkov.
29. Jim Dwyer, "Volkswagen's Diesel Fraud Makes Critic of Secret Code a Prophet," *New York Times* (September 22, 2015). http://www.nytimes.com/2015/09/23/nyregion/volkswagens-diesel-fraud-makes-critic-of-secret-code-a-prophet.html. Accessed September 24, 2015.
30. Jack Ewing, "VW Presentation in '06 Showed How to Foil Emissions Tests," *New York Times* (April 26, 2016). http://www.nytimes.com/2016/04/27/business/international/vw-presentation-in-06-showed-how-to-foil-emissions-tests.html. Accessed June 10, 2016.
31. Linkov.
32. Dwyer.
33. Dwyer.
34. Ian Mouawad and Sydney Ember, "VW's Pitch to Americans Relied on Fun and Fantasy," *New York Times* (September 27, 2015). Accessed May 31, 2016.
35. Health. https://www3.epa.gov/airquality/nitrogenoxides/health.html. Accessed April 26, 2016.
36. Mouawad and Ember.
37. Ewing (2015).
38. Eric Niiler, "VW Could Fool the EPA, But It Couldn't Trick Chemistry," *Wired* (September 22, 2015). http://www.wired.com/2015/09/vw-fool-epa-couldnt-trick-chemistry/. Accessed September 22, 2015.
39. Jack Ewing, "VW Says Emissions Cheating Was Not a One-Time Error," *New York Times* (December 10, 2015). http://www.nytimes.com/2015/12/11/business/international/vw-emissions-scandal.html. Accessed December 10, 2015.
40. Ewing (2015).
41. Ewing (2015).
42. Gilbert Gates, Jack Ewing, Karl Russell, and Derek Watkins, "Explaining Volkswagen's Emissions Scandal," *New York Times* (June 1, 2016). http://www.nytimes.com/interactive/2015/business/international/vw-diesel-emissions-scandal-explained.html. Accessed June 6, 2016.
43. Linkov.
44. Niiler.
45. Zeynep Tufekci, "Volkswagen and the Era of Cheating Software," *New York Times* (September 23, 2015). http://www.nytimes.com/2015/09/24/opinion/volkswagen-and-the-era-of-cheating-software.html. Accessed September 24, 2015.
46. Jeff Plungis and Dana Hull, "VW's Emissions Cheating Found by Curious Clean-Air Group," *Bloomberg* (September 20, 2015). http://www.bloomberg.com/news/articles/2015-09-19

/volkswagen-emissions-cheating-found-by-curious-clean-air-group. Accessed September 23, 2015.

47. Gregory G. Thompson, "In-Use Emissions Testing of Light-Duty Diesel Vehicles in the United States," *Center for Alternative Fuels, Engines & Emissions, West Virginia University* (May 15, 2014). http://www.theicct.org/sites/default/files/publications/WVU_LDDV_in-use_ICCT_Report_Final_may2014.pdf. Accessed January 5, 2016.
48. Gregory J. Thompson, Daniel K. Carder, Marc C. Besch, Arvind Thiruvengadam, and Hemanth K. Kappanna, "In-Use Emissions Testing of Light-Duty Diesel Vehicles in the U.S." http://www.theicct.org/use-emissions-testing-light-duty-diesel-vehicles-us. Accessed January 5, 2016.
49. Plungis and Hull.
50. Naomi Kresge and Richard Weiss, "Volkswagen Drops 23% after Admitting Diesel Emissions Cheat," *Bloomberg* (September 21, 2015). http://www.bloomberg.com/news/articles/2015-09-21/volkswagen-drops-15-after-admitting-u-s-diesel-emissions-cheat. Accessed September 23, 2015.
51. Gates *et al.*
52. Jeff S. Bartlett, "Guide to the Volkswagen Emissions Recall," *Consumer Reports* (April 28, 2016). http://www.consumerreports.org/cro/cars/guide-to-the-volkswagen-dieselgate-emissions-recall. Accessed May 14, 2016.
53. Ciferri.
54. Mouawad and Ember.
55. Ciferri.
56. Mouawad and Ember.
57. Volkswagen Passat TDI TV Spot, Mom song by Waylon Jennings. https://www.ispot.tv/ad/78QS/volkswagen-passat-tdi-mom-song-by-waylon-jennings. Accessed March 20, 2016.
58. Mouawad and Embry.
59. Bond.
60. "Volkswagen Code Words Trip up Diesel Investigators," *Automotive News* (April 25, 2016). Accessed May 28, 2016.
61. Ewing and Bowley.
62. Jack Ewing, "Volkswagen Inquiry Expands to 17 Suspects," *New York Times* (March 8, 2016). http://nytimes.com/2016/03/09/business/international/volkswagen-inquiry-germany.html. Accessed March 8, 2016.
63. Kelly Phillips Erb, "Germany Investigating Volkswagen Employees for Emissions Scandal Related Tax Evasion," *Forbes* (December 1, 2015). http://www.forbes.com/sites/kellyphillipserb/2015/12/01/germany-investigating-volkswagen-employees-for-emissions-scandal-related-tax-evasion. Accessed June 8, 2016.
64. Aaron M. Kessler, "Volkswagen Sought a Green Seal for Its Diesel Cars," *New York Times* (October 6, 2015). http://www.nytimes.com/2015/10/07/business/international/volkswagen-sought-a-green-seal-for-its-diesel-cars.html. Accessed October 7, 2015.
65. Kessler.
66. Kim S. Nash and Steven Norton, "Electronic Discovery Can Bring CIOs to Court," *The Wall Street Journal* (March 25, 2016). http://blogs.wsj.com/cio/2016/03/25/electronic-discovery-can-bring-cios-to-court/. Accessed June 6, 2016.
67. Ewing and Bowley.
68. Nash and Norton.
69. Antoine Gara, "Billionaire Christopher Hohn Says Lavish Bonuses Contributed to Volkswagen's Emissions Scandal," *Forbes* (May 6, 2016). http://www.forbes.com/sites/antoinegara/2016/05/06/billionaire-christopher-hohn-says-exec-bonuses-contributed-to-volkswagens-emissions-scandal. Accessed May 24, 2016.
70. Michael Schrage, "Is VW's Fraud the End of Large-Scale Corporate Deception?" *Harvard Business Review* (September 29, 2015). https://hbr.org/2015/09/is-vws-fraud-the-end-of-large-scale-corporate-deception. Accessed September 29, 2015.

CASE 8

Unlocking the Secrets of the Apple iPhone in the Name of Antiterrorism*

THE SAN BERNARDINO MASSACRE

On December 2, 2015, a married couple used automatic weapons to attack and kill 14 people during an employee training event and holiday party at the Inland Regional Center in San Bernardino, California. One of the shooters was an employee of San Bernardino County, the sponsor of the event. Nine of the 14 victims died in an 85 × 50 foot conference room during an ambush. Three victims died just outside the building, and the remaining 2 victims died in a triage station that emergency responders had set up nearby. Twenty-two additional people were injured.[1] Survivors identified the two shooters, who were killed by local police in a shootout later that day in the nearby town of Redlands. The male shooter had briefly attended the event, left, and returned with his wife to commit the attack.[2] During a televised address from the Oval Office of the White House on December 6, President Barack Obama declared the attack was a terrorist act.[3] The next day, the Federal Bureau of Investigation (FBI) began a counter-terrorism investigation.

On February 9, 2016, the FBI announced that they could not unlock the Apple iPhone 5c that belonged to the male suspect. The specific iPhone ran the iOS 9 operating system.[4] The county of San Bernardino had previously purchased the phone for the suspect's use in his role as a county employee. The suspect also owned and used an Android phone that government investigators were able to access. The FBI was concerned that the male suspect's iPhone 5c might have additional data that would be useful in identifying any links the couple had to terrorist groups. The FBI asked Apple to create a new version of iOS that could unlock the phone and allow the FBI access to the phone's content. Apple was given until February 26 to comply. On February 16, 2016, Apple CEO Tim Cook released a public letter explaining why the company was not cooperating with Federal requests to access the male San Bernardino suspect's iPhone 5c. Cook stated:

> *We are challenging the FBI's demands with the deepest respect for American democracy and a love of our country. We believe it would be in the best interest of everyone to step back and consider the implications.*
>
> *While we believe the FBI's intentions are good, it would be wrong for the government to force us to build a backdoor into our products. And ultimately, we fear that this demand would undermine the very freedoms and liberty our government is meant to protect.*[5]

APPLE IPHONE ENCRYPTION POLICIES

Apple Inc. designs and manufactures the iPhone, one of the most popular lines of smartphones in the United States. Consumers use their iPhones to send and read messages, post to social media, and access apps. Apple's iPhones, as well as the iPad tablet computer, run an operating system called iOS. Competing models from Samsung, Motorola, and dozens of other manufacturers use Google's Android operating system. By 2015, smartphones had become the dominant product category in the U.S. wireless phone industry, surpassing a more limited category called feature phones that could run only a few specialized apps.

Because smartphones also contained GPS technology, law enforcement officials can use the smartphone as a convenient means of determining where a suspect has been, with whom the suspect communicated, and more. However, mobile devices such as smartphones and tablets are also tempting targets for hackers and criminals because users often store valuable data such as passwords, financial data, and other records. Encryption is used to protect data within these devices through a mathematical process that scrambles or encrypts the data. Encryption is also used to protect data in transit; one example is HTTPS, a secure mode used in Web browsers. The data can be decrypted by providing appropriate credentials, such as passwords or cryptographic keys. The encrypted data is only as secure as the credentials themselves.

SECURING AND ENCRYPTING DATA

The iPhone 5c was a low-end model that Apple introduced in September 2013 for value-conscious customers and emerging markets. This model was also a

*This case was written by William A. Sodeman, University of Alabama in Huntsville (UAH), in 2016.

popular choice for companies and organizations that provided iPhones to their employees for business use. The iPhone 5c was easily identified by its colorful polycarbonate case, which was visually different from the aluminum case used in the iPhone 5 and 5s. In this phone, and earlier models, lockcodes and data encryption were handled exclusively by iOS, which created security issues. Third parties such as investigators, hackers, and criminals could exploit vulnerabilities in iOS to intercept, record, and access devices. The iPhone 5c did not include the Touch ID sensor, which, in later models, allowed users to unlock a specific iPhone with a fingerprint. The iPhone 5c was the last iPhone that carried the "squircle" symbol on the home button. The iPhone 5c faced steep competition from low-priced Android smartphones, as well as less powerful feature phones, and became a disappointment for Apple. The 5c model was discontinued in September 2015, when Apple introduced the iPhone 6 and iPhone 6 Plus.

The Touch ID sensor is installed in the home button, and is electronically linked to the specific iPhone, making it impossible to unlock an iPhone by replacing the home button. Touch ID sensors allow the individual user to enroll several fingerprints to unlock their iPhone or iPad. The device does not save a picture of the fingerprints. In the iPhone 5s and later models, Apple saved the fingerprint data as encrypted maps in the Secure Enclave, a separate CPU embedded within the device's CPU. Apple designed and manufactured its own CPUs for iPhones and iPads. The Secure Enclave was specifically designed to handle data encryption and Touch ID processes for the device, using a small and efficient operating system that was much more secure than iOS.[6] By removing encryption and lock features from the CPU and putting them into the Secure Enclave, Apple made it far more difficult for unauthorized third parties to unlock and decrypt its newer devices.[7] This change also prevented Apple from creating customized versions of iOS to unlock the iPhone 5s and later devices, because Apple had no access to the Secure Enclave and UID inside of these devices.

APPLE RESISTS DECRYPTION REQUESTS

Prior to this incident, Apple had resisted government requests to provide access to iPhone and iPad data in criminal proceedings. In October 2015, U.S. Magistrate Judge James Ornstein of the U.S. District Court for the Eastern District of New York asked federal prosecutors why they needed access to an iPhone 5c that belonged to a male suspect, Jun Feng, who had already pled guilty to methamphetamine distribution in New York City. Feng had previously configured his iPhone 5c to erase its data after 10 consecutive unsuccessful attempts to unlock the phone. The Erase Data feature was available in iOS 7, the operating system version that originally shipped with the iPhone 5c in 2013, as well as iOS 8 and iOS 9. The 10-attempt policy could completely erase data from the affected phone, in a manner that made data recovery from the device virtually impossible. When Apple was asked to help retrieve the data, Apple lawyer Marc Zwillinger responded, "Right now Apple is aware that customer data is under siege from a variety of different directions. Never has the privacy and security of customer data been as important as it is now." He continued, "A hypothetical consumer could think if Apple is not in the business of accessing my data and if Apple has built a system to prevent itself from accessing my data, why is it continuing to comply with orders that don't have a clear lawful basis in doing so?"[8] The Judge appeared to agree, strongly resisting the prosecutors' requests to unlock Feng's phone:

> In light of the fact that the defendant against whom evidence from the subject telephone was to be used has pleaded guilty, I respectfully direct the government to explain why the application is not moot. To the extent the response requires the disclosure of information occurring before a grand jury, the government may file its response under seal, along with a redacted version suitable for public access.[9]

Law enforcement officials in New York City had been vocal advocates for government regulation of encryption. In May 2016, Cyrus R. Vance Jr., the district attorney of Manhattan, stated that his office had over 230 iPhones that could not be used in criminal proceedings because they were locked. Apple had refused to assist his offices with these devices,[10] including Feng's iPhone 5c.[11] Apple had built several features into iOS to prevent unauthorized users from gaining access to a device. Four-digit passwords are one example; iOS 7 and iOS 8 users had the option of enabling six digit or alphanumeric passwords. iOS also restricted access to a device after consecutive unsuccessful login attempts, by using a one-minute timer to force the user to wait, or requiring the user to connect the iPhone to a computer that is running iTunes.[12] For these iPhones, even Apple could not bypass the user's lockcode as all data saved in the device's SSC was encrypted with a 256-bit key. iPhone and iPad users were forced to set up a lockcode when they started using iOS 8, and that lockcode was "entangled" with the unique identifier (UID) of the specific device in such a way that the device's data could not be accessed directly, even if the SSD chips are removed from the iPhone or iPad. The UID itself is a 256-bit number, stored in a permanent form in the CPU and available nowhere else on the device.

THE GOVERNMENT HACKS ITS WAY IN

On February 22, 2016, the Department of Justice indicated that it wanted access to locked iPhones involved in 12 separate criminal cases. These phones were in government custody as evidence, but could not be unlocked because the owners were unable or unwilling to provide their lockcodes. While there was no indication that any of these dozen cases were linked to the San Bernardino crimes or other terrorist acts, it seemed clear that the Department wanted to use the San Bernardino situation as advantage for additional powers over encryption.[13]

On March 28, 2016, the Department of Justice announced that it had found a way to unlock the San Bernardino male suspect's iPhone 5c without assistance from Apple.[14] After weeks of speculation, FBI Director Covey announced that the U.S. Government had paid an undisclosed third party at least $1.3 million to defeat the 10 login limit on the male suspect's iPhone. This allowed investigators to repeatedly try different passwords until the iPhone was finally unlocked. At that point, investigators could access the specific phone's encrypted contents.[15]

It is possible that the Federal government could not tell Apple how it gained access to iPhone, if the exploit was done as part of a Vulnerabilities Equities Process (VEP) performed by the Federal government against the specific iPhone.[16] The VEP framework was established by the White House in 2010 to allow various Federal government agencies to discuss how they each deal with information security flaws. The National Security Agency (NSA) tends to keep flaws and vulnerabilities secret so that they may be reused as needed; it also allows them to resist efforts by other Federal agencies to release or disclose this information.[17]

The FBI has a history of overcoming and sidestepping encryption. Details about specific operations are difficult to find, as the Bureau tends to classify many of its tools and techniques. In 2003, FBI investigators requested and received permission to install eavesdropping software in personal computers used by an animal rights group that was under secret investigation for industrial sabotage. Codenamed Operation Trail Mix, the investigation resulted in the convictions of six activists under the Animal Enterprise Protection Act. The activists used encryption software called PGP (Pretty Good Privacy) that encrypted their e-mail messages. Decrypting the messages required a password or digital encryption keys. It is possible that the FBI's software captured every keystroke on one or more specific computers, eventually yielding the password or keys. The *New York Times* sued for and received access to Operation Trail Mix records under the Freedom of Information Act; however, details regarding the eavesdropping software had already been classified secret by the FBI.[18]

Governmental agencies have used encryption since the 19th century. In 1994, the U.S. National Security Agency (NSA) and the White House asked AT&T to add an encryption mechanism called a Clipper chip into a new model of secure telephone. The Clipper chip included backdoors or secret points of access that government investigators could use to access and intercept telephone calls.[19] Public outcry stopped this effort, and the U.S. Government finally allowed strong cryptography to be implemented in consumer devices. In 2016, the U.S. Government's request that Apple provide access to unlock iPhones was regarded as a heavyhanded attempt to add backdoors to hundreds of millions of mobile devices.[20]

While the FBI and NSA fought vigorously for backdoors, other federal agencies helped fund the creation of encryption software, such as to aid activists in other countries.[21] Technology companies acted on their own to add encryption to their services. In March 2016, Whatsapp, a messaging service operated by Facebook, turned on end-to-end encryption. Viber, a competing messaging service, added a similar feature the following month.[22]

APPLE VOWS TO INCREASE SECURITY

For its part, following the San Bernandino incident and federal intervention, Apple executives vowed to improve iPhone and iPad security and privacy.

While Apple had refused government requests to unlock iPhones and iPads, Apple had generally cooperated with government requests to extract and transfer user data stored in the iCloud service. Companies such as Apple, Google, Microsoft, Twitter, and Facebook regularly publish transparency reports that list instances when user data have been turned over to governmental authorities in many countries. In Apple's report for the first half of 2015, the company revealed it had received almost 11,000 requests for iCloud user data tied to approximately 60,000 Apple iPhones and iPads. Apple provided some iCloud data for about 7,100 of the estimated 11,000 requests. A form of end-to-end encryption that allowed only the sender and receiver to encrypt and decrypt messages already protected one popular Apple service, iMessage.[23] iMessages are used as a substitute for text messaging on Apple devices, and can transmit text, emojis, photos, and videos.

Apple executives decided to add automatic encryption to the iCloud service, which meant that Apple itself would be unable to decrypt any user data stored in iCloud, including iPhone and iPad backups. The service is also used to store encrypted copies of user passwords entered into Safari and other iOS apps through a system called iCloud Keychain. The Keychain helps users who have more than one iOS device access stored passwords across the devices. However, the service already had a destruct switch that would purge the Keychain from the iCloud servers after ten incorrect login attempts. By encrypting the entire iCloud service, Apple could provide better security and privacy for its customers, while reducing the company's exposure to law enforcement investigations.[24] iCloud backups of iMessage data were already encrypted.[25]

Because of the difficulties involved in adding encryption to existing online services, Apple was also developing more secure chips and hardware for future iPhones and iPads. It is far easier to encrypt data on a device than on a separate storage device or service. It was also generally expected that Apple would enhance the Secure Enclave. As older iPhones fell out of use, the opportunities to use third-party attacks and customized operating systems to open these devices would dwindle.[26]

QUESTIONS FOR DISCUSSION

1. What was Apple's motive in not giving the FBI access to the San Bernadino suspect's iPhone? Is Apple genuinely interested in protecting consumers' privacy or in protecting its brand and products?
2. What responsibilities should device manufacturers like Apple have to assist in government investigations, especially when serious crimes such as terrorism are involved?
3. Should the use of encryption be more tightly regulated?
4. Should device manufacturers be compelled to unlock or decrypt devices under extraordinary circumstances such as the San Bernardino case?
5. Apple tried to balance user experience, user convenience, and security in its devices. Should Apple continue to do this, or attempt to emphasize one specific area?
6. One potential solution is to minimize the amount of data stored within a device by relying on the cloud as the main storage medium. How might this approach affect consumers? Apple? Law enforcement?
7. Overall, how do you evaluate Apple's handling of this case? Was the company being socially responsible or self-interested?

ENDNOTES

1. "Autopsies of San Bernardino Victims Reveal Details of Carnage," *New York Times* (May 29, 2016). http://www.nytimes.com/2016/05/29/us/autopsies-of-san-bernardino-victims-reveal-details-of-carnage.html. Accessed June 2, 2016.
2. "What Investigators Know about the San Bernardino Shooting," *New York Times* (December 10, 2015). http://www.nytimes.com/interactive/2015/12/02/us/california-mass-shooting-san-bernardino.html. Accessed June 2, 2016.
3. Carol E. Lee and Damian Paletta, "Terrorist Threat Has 'Evolved' into a New Phase, Obama Says," *The Wall Street Journal* (December 7, 2015). http://www.wsj.com/articles/terrorist-threat-has-evolved-into-a-new-phase-obama-says-1449451592. Accessed February 12, 2016.
4. Katie Benner and Eric Lichtblau, "U.S. Says It Has Unlocked iPhone without Apple," *New York Times* (March 28, 2016). http://nytimes.com/2016/03/29/technology/apple-iphone-fbi-justice-department-case.html. Accessed March 29, 2016.
5. Tim Cook, "A Message to Our Customers," http://www.apple.com/customer-letter/. Accessed February 17, 2016.

6. Mike Lash, "What Is the Secure Enclave?" https://www.mikeash.com/pyblog/friday-qa-2016-02-19-what-is-the-secure-enclave.html. Accessed June 1, 2016.
7. Lash.
8. Collier and Turton.
9. Cyrus Farivar, "After Guilty Plea, Judge Confused as to Why Prosecutors still Want iPhone Unlocked," *Ars Technica* (October 30, 2015). http://arstechnica.com/tech-policy/2015/10/feds-apple-must-still-unlock-iphone-5s-even-after-defendant-pled-guilty/. Accessed June 6, 2016.
10. Bryan R. Smith, "Police and Tech Giants Wrangle over Encryption on Capitol Hill," *New York Times* (May 9, 2016). http://www.nytimes.com/2016/05/09/technology/police-and-tech-giants-wrangle-over-encryption-on-capitol-hill.html. Accessed May 9, 2016.
11. Kevin Collier and William Turton, "Here's Why Apple Will No Longer Unlock Phones for Police," *Daily Dot* (January 25, 2016). http://www.dailydot.com/politics/apple-unlock-iphone-court/. Accessed January 25, 2016.
12. Ashley Poland, "What Happens If You Enter the Wrong Password into an iPhone too many Times?" http://smallbusiness.chron.com/happens-enter-wrong-password-iphone-many-times-69874.html. Accessed June 6, 2016.
13. Devlin Barrett, "Justice Department Seeks to Force Apple to Extract Data from about 12 other iPhones," *The Wall Street Journal* (February 22, 2016). http://www.wsj.com/articles/justice-department-seeks-to-force-apple-to-extract-data-from-about-12-other-iphones-1456202213. Accessed February 23, 2016.
14. Benner and Lichtblau.
15. Aspen Security Forum, "F.B.I. Director Suggests Bill for iPhone Hacking Topped $1.3 Million," *New York Times* (April 22, 2016). http://www.nytimes.com/2016/04/22/us/politics/fbi-director-suggests-bill-for-iphone-hacking-was-1-3-million.html. Accessed April 22, 2016.
16. Jamie Condliffe, "FBI Might Not Be Able to Tell Apple How It Unlocked the San Bernardino iPhone Even If It Wanted to," http://gizmodo.com/fbi-might-not-be-able-to-tell-apple-how-it-unlocked-the-1770914956. Accessed April 14, 2016.
17. Joseph Menn and Mark Hosenball, "Apple iPhone Unlocking Maneuver Likely to Remain Secret," *Reuters* (April 13, 2016). http://www.reuters.com/article/us-apple-encryption-white house-idUSKCN0XB05D. Accessed June 6, 2016.
18. Matt Apuzzo, "F.B.I. Used Hacking Software Decade Before iPhone Fight," *New York Times* (April 13, 2016). http://www.nytimes.com/2016/04/14/technology/fbi-tried-to-defeat-encryption-10-years-ago-files-show.html. Accessed May 9, 2016.
19. Steven Levy, "Battle of the Clipper Chip," *New York Times* (June 12, 1994). http://www.nytimes.com/1994/06/12/magazine/battle-of-the-clipper-chip.html. Accessed on September 5, 2013.
20. Steven Levy, "Why Are We Fighting the Crypto Wars Again?" *Medium* (March 11, 2016). https://backchannel.com/why-are-we-fighting-the-crypto-wars-again. Accessed March 13, 2016.
21. Damian Palatta, "How the U.S. Fights Encryption—And Also Helps Develop It," *The Wall Street Journal* (February 21, 2016). http://www.wsj.com/articles/how-the-u-s-fights-encryptionand-also-helps-develop-it-1456109096. Accessed February 22, 2016.
22. Brian Barrett, "700 Million People Just Got Encryption That Congress Can't Touch," *Wired* (April 20, 2016). https://www.wired.com/2016/04/viber-encrytpion. Accessed on April 30, 2016.
23. Mike Issac, "Apple Still Holds the Keys to Its Cloud Service, But Reluctantly," *New York Times* (February 21, 2016). http://www.nytimes.com/2016/02/22/technology/apple-still-holds-the-keys-to-its-cloud-service-but-reluctantly.html. Accessed February 26, 2016.
24. Daisuke Wakabayashi, "In Beefing Up iCloud Security, Apple Weighs Privacy Against Convenience," *The Wall Street Journal* (March 15, 2016). http://www.wsj.com/articles/in-beefing-up-icloud-security-apple-weighs-privacy-against-convenience-1458089515. Accessed March 15, 2016.
25. Isaac.
26. Lash.

CASE 9

To Hire or Not to Hire*

SELECTING A NEW COMPUTER ANALYST

As a manager in human resources, part of my job is to guide the process by which my company selects new employees. Recently, we selected an applicant to fill a computer analyst position. The supervising manager and a selection panel selected this applicant over a number of others based on her superior qualifications and interview.

BACKGROUND CHECK

However, a routine background check indicated that the applicant had been convicted 18 years earlier for false check writing. The application form has a section where the applicant is asked if he or she has ever been convicted of anything other than a traffic violation. In response to that question, this applicant wrote "no." When informed of this, the supervising manager stated that she would still like to hire the applicant, but asked me for my recommendation. The job does not involve money handling.

*This case was prepared by Tim Timmons.

QUESTIONS FOR DISCUSSION

1. If the applicant mistakenly thought that her record had been cleared over time and therefore did not lie intentionally, would that make any difference in the hiring decision?
2. Should the fact that the applicant did not tell the truth on one part of the application automatically disqualify her from further consideration?
3. Should the supervising manager be allowed to hire this applicant despite the fact that the applicant lied on her application, provided the manager is willing to take the risk and assume responsibility for the applicant?
4. If the applicant freely admitted the conviction, should she still be considered for the position? Should a minor offense committed 18 years ago, when the applicant was in her early 20s, disqualify her when she is overall the most qualified applicant? What types of convictions, and how recent, should disqualify potential new hires?

CASE 10

Payday Loans: A Needed Product or a Scam?*

Ethan Dorsett was a retired and disabled Marine living in Missouri.[1] He struggled for five years trying to pay back a $2,500 payday loan, which had escalated to $50,000 in interest due. Ethan's plight began when his wife, Emily, slipped on ice and broke her ankle. Needing surgery, she was unable to work in her retail job for several months. Her medical bills came to $26,000, and she was ineligible for insurance at her work. With two children in college, Ethan found himself unable to pay his wife's medical bills. Ethan tried borrowing the money from family, friends, banks, and credit unions. He had a "fair" credit rating, but it was not good enough to borrow such a large sum of money.[2]

Out of desperation, Ethan turned to store front lenders (another name for payday loan companies). He took out five $500 loans and paid interest every week. Every two weeks, each of the five loans carried $95 in interest for a total of $475 and he had to take out new loans to cover the old ones.[3] Eventually, through taking various jobs over the five years, Ethan somehow got the loans paid off. It was tough. Ethan said "We ended up losing our home. We lost our car."[4]

Ethan was one of the fortunate ones. Not everyone is able to get out from under the burden of high-interest loans. Quite often, these type of store front loans are given to people in more desperate

*This case was written by Archie B. Carroll, University of Georgia, in 2016.

circumstances who are not able to pay off their loans like Ethan did.

Many consumers who take out payday loans are not as good a credit risk as Ethan. More frequently, payday loan borrowers are living on the ragged edge financially and end up borrowing, paying interest, and borrowing some more. Many end up going to title loan companies, which are somewhat similar to payday loans, where they end up signing over the title to their cars. One 66-year-old woman and her jobless son in Las Vegas took out a $2,000 title loan and pledged his 2002 Ford F-150 truck as collateral. Both say no one verified whether she or her son would be able to repay the loan, which carried 121.5 percent interest. When they finally paid the loan off, she said the company did not give them the truck title back, rather, the company talked them into borrowing another $2,000.[5]

WHAT IS A PAYDAY LOAN?

A payday loan is a short-term loan, generally for $500 or less, that is usually due on your next payday.[6] Payday loans typically have the following characteristics. In addition to these loans typically being for a small amount and due on your next payday, they generally require that the lender is given access to the borrower's checking account or they must write a check for the full balance in advance so the lender has the option of depositing the check when the loan comes due (on the borrower's payday).[7]

Payday loans often have features other than those described. Though they are usually paid off in one lump sum, it is possible to set them up so that the borrower pays interest-only payments resulting in "renewals" or "rollovers" that may result in installment payments over a longer period of time.[8]

The borrower may receive his or her loan in a variety of ways. It could be given as cash or a check; it could be received through funds loaded onto a prepaid debit card; or, the borrower could have the funds electronically deposited into a checking account. The finance charge for the loan (the cost of borrowing) may range from $10 to $30 for each $100 borrowed, which equates to an Annual Percentage Rate (APR) of almost 400 percent. To appreciate this rate, compare it with the APR on a credit card where the range usually runs 12–30 percent, depending on the card holder's credit rating.[9]

Example: Let's say you need to borrow $300 until your next payday, which is two weeks away. To pay it back, you will owe $345 assuming a fee of $15 per each $100 borrowed. Let's assume you need to renew or roll over your loan. You get charged a $45 fee when the extension is over. That comes to a $90 charge for borrowing $300 for several weeks.[10]

In addition to the fixed fees for a payday loan, other fees may be added on. If you renew or roll over your loan, for example, you will be charged an added fee and you still owe the original amount. In addition, if you do not repay the loan on time, you might be charged a late fee or a returned check fee. If your loan is loaded onto a prepaid debit card, there are other possible fees. These could include fees to add the funds to your card, fees for checking your balance, fees each time you use your card and/or regular monthly fees.[11]

STATES PUSH BACK

Payday loans are governed by state laws. Some states do not permit payday lending storefronts because the loans are not permitted by state laws. Or, some payday lending businesses may opt not to do business in a state because of its regulations.[12] Twenty-two states have already regulated the industry, but in some states the industry has protected itself from regulations by making huge donations to the state lawmakers. Further, those donations are carefully targeted at key leaders in the legislature and to members of important committees when legislation has stalled or died in recent years.[13]

Some states, such as Colorado and Indiana, say they have found a balanced approach to payday lending which keeps the payday loans available but heavily regulates them.[14] In Colorado, many have praised the state for effectively reducing the interest rates on such loans by two-thirds and slowing down the rate that the lenders can roll over the loans. Some say Colorado is the most consumer-friendly payday loan market in the United States, but others say that there is still evidence of repeat reborrowing and high default rates.[15]

One credit counselor observed that before Colorado's new rules, families with numerous payday loans, all from different lenders, would spend Saturdays driving all over town rolling over their loans, but now that doesn't happen much anymore. According to Colorado state data, the number of payday loan stores has dropped from 486 before 2010 to 188. In addition, 15 states have effectively banned payday loans by imposing strict caps on interest rates.[16]

NEW FEDERAL CONTROLS

Beginning in 2015, the relatively new Consumer Financial Protection Bureau (CFPB) began studying ways that payday lenders would be required to make sure that borrowers can pay back their loans.[17] By spring 2016, it was becoming evident what the new CFPB regulations might look like. The draft of the new regulations issued by CFPB director Richard Corday was 1,300 pages long.[18] Under the new regulations, payday lenders would be required to run full credit checks on prospective borrowers to check out their sources of income, need for the loan, and ability to keep paying their living expenses while paying the loan back.[19] In short, potential borrowers would be subject to the same kinds of screens that banks and credit unions now use and for which the typical payday borrower cannot qualify.

The new regulations, of course, will make it difficult or impossible for the typical payday loan borrower to take advantage of the service because they likely will not meet the requirements for the loans. In addition, huge record keeping requirements being foisted on the industry will likely force the small, local lenders who have dominated the industry out of business, and favor the large firms and consolidators who can afford and manage the regulatory overhead.[20]

THE GOOGLE BAN

Just before the CFPB announced its proposed regulations on the payday lending industry, Google announced that it would no longer run ads for payday loans, a decision that would impact significantly the online-lending sector of the industry. Online loans account for about half of the payday lending market.[21] The payday loan industry did not respond well to Google's decision. They claimed the new policy was "discriminatory and a form of censorship."[22] The president and CEO of the Online Lenders Alliance said that Google's new policy "will prohibit legal loans for many Americans who otherwise do not have access to the financial system."[23] She added, "The policy discriminates against those among us who rely on online loans."[24] In its defense, Google said that it hopes that fewer people will be exposed to misleading or harmful products.[25]

According to a *Wall Street Journal* (WSJ) editorial, Google may be getting plaudits from some observers, but maybe Google's motivations are not entirely pure. Apparently, the venture capital arm of Google's parent company, Alphabet, has invested in LendUp, a company that offers short-term loans at high interest rates and competes with the payday lenders. Google responded that it planned to block LendUp's ads too. The *WSJ* editorial also pointed out that Google had invested about $125 million in the online Lending Club and posed the question of how much that firm would pick up in business due to the ban.[26]

DON'T RUSH IN

Supporters of the payday lending industry point out that the government should not rush into payday loan regulations. One writer pointed out that when the CFPB conducted a study of consumer complaints, less than 1 percent of the consumer complaints were related to payday lending. This was a small percentage compared to the complaints related to mortgages, debt collection, and credit cards, which made up about two-thirds of the complaints.[27]

A further issue is that proposed new regulations would further reduce alternatives for consumers who already lack access to the banking system. The CEO of the Community Financial Services Association of America, which represents the storefront payday lenders, said "payday loans represent an important source of credit for millions of Americans who live from paycheck to paycheck."[28] He went on to say that we need to find ways to increase not limit the ways that these persons can get access to the credit they need.[29] Pew Charitable Trusts research found that some consumers turn to pawning their belongings or borrowing further from families and that these were not good options for people in a financial pinch.[30]

QUESTIONS FOR DISCUSSION

1. Who are the stakeholders in this case and what are their stakes?
2. Have you ever taken out a payday loan or title loan? What was your experience?
3. What is your evaluation of the corporate social responsibility of the payday lending industry, using the four-part definition of CSR? Is payday lending an exploitive industry that snares borrowers in a never ending cycle of debt?
4. Is the industry socially responsible but some of its members are engaging in questionable practices? What questionable practices are most troublesome?
5. Given the strong need for payday loans on the part of some citizens, should the industry be further regulated such that borrowers no longer have

access? What are borrowers to do who do not meet the new federal regulations?

6. Is the title loan industry the same as the payday lending industry? How do they compare?
7. The states have regulated the payday lending industry. Should the federal government be getting involved with regulating this industry? What will be the effects of the proposed CFPB regulations?
8. What is your assessment of the Google ban? Does Google have a conflict of interests in imposing this ban?
9. Should the CFPB back off and let the marketplace and the states handle payday lending issues?

ENDNOTES

1. Susanna Kim, "Missouri Man Paid $50,000 in Interest After Taking $2,500 in Payday Loans," *ABC13Eyewitness News* (May 21, 2016). http://abc13.com/news/missouri-man-paid-$50000-in-interest-after-taking-$2500-in-payday-loans/1349121/. Accessed May 29, 2016. Note: the name given him in this case has been changed.
2. Ibid.
3. Ibid.
4. Ibid.
5. Fred Schulte, "Title Loan Companies Under Scrutiny Across the U. S.," *USA Today* (December 9, 2015), 5B.
6. Consumer Financial Protection Bureau, "What Is a Payday Loan?" http://www.consumerfinance.gov/askcfpb/1567/what-payday-loan.html. Accessed May 29, 2016.
7. Ibid.
8. Ibid.
9. Ibid.
10. Ibid.
11. Ibid.
12. Ibid.
13. Kyle Whitmire, "Which Lawmakers Go Payday Cash for Free?" *The Huntsville Times* (March 29, 2015), A10.
14. Yuka Hayashi, "States Push Back on Payday," *The Wall Street Journal* (March 17, 2016), C2.
15. Ibid.
16. Ibid.
17. Alan Zibel, "Payday Loans Face New Controls," *Wall Street Journal* (January 5, 2015), C1.
18. Holman W. Jenkins, Jr., "Payday Loans a Crony Capitalist Target," *The Wall Street Journal* (June 4–5, 2016), A11.
19. Ibid.
20. Ibid.
21. Yuka Hayashi, "Google to Pull Plug on Ads for Payday Lenders," *The Wall Street Journal* (May 12, 2016), C1.
22. Ibid.
23. Ibid.
24. Ibid.
25. "Google's Payday Lending Ban," *Wall Street Journal* (May 31, 2016), A12.
26. Ibid.
27. Dennis Shaul, "We Shouldn't Rush into Payday Lending Regulations," *The Huntsville Times* (March 29, 2015), A13.
28. Ibid.
29. Ibid.
30. Sarah Skidmore Sell, Associated Press, "Payday Loans 101," *Athens Banner-Herald* (June 12, 2016), B8.

CASE 11

You Punch Mine and I'll Punch Yours

When I was in college, I worked part-time one summer at a childcare center that was in a fitness center. Most mornings, I worked from 8 A.M. until noon, but some days I was scheduled to work from 7 A.M. until 11 A.M. My roommate also worked there, and our start times typically varied by that first hour. If I went in at 8 A.M., she had already gone in at 7 A.M. She would leave at 11 A.M. and I would work until noon.

One morning when I got in at 8 A.M., she told me that she had punched my timecard for me when she came in at 7 A.M., and if I would punch her out at noon when I left then we would each make a few extra bucks. She thought this would be a great plan. After all, who would know? The folks who actually processed paychecks were in another location; our total hours were just submitted to them every two weeks. There wasn't anyone who signed off on them, and most of the other folks who worked there paid very little attention to the childcare folks. She said we were only getting minimum wage, so what would it hurt to give ourselves a little raise because we were taking fantastic care of the children.

QUESTIONS FOR DISCUSSION

1. What are the ethical issues in this case?
2. What should I have done in this situation?
3. Should I have confronted my roommate? What should I have said?
4. Should I have gone to management and told them what happened? If I did nothing I would be paid for an hour that I did not work.

Contributed Anonymously

CASE 12

Phantom Expenses*

Jane Adams had just completed a sales training course with her new employer, a major small appliance manufacturer. She was assigned to work as a trainee under Ann Green, one of the firm's most productive sales reps on the East Coast. At the end of the first week, Jane and Ann were sitting in a motel room filling out their expense vouchers for the week.

INFLATING EXPENSES

Jane casually remarked to Ann that the training course had stressed the importance of filling out expense vouchers accurately. Ann immediately launched into a long explanation of how the company's expense reporting resulted in underpayment of actual costs. She claimed that all the sales reps on the East Coast made up the difference by padding their expenses under $25, which did not require receipts. A rule of thumb used was to inflate total expenses by 25 percent. When Jane questioned whether this was honest, Ann said that even if the reported expenses exceeded actual expenses, the company owed them the extra money, given the long hours and hard work they put in.

FOLLOW THE AGREED-UPON PRACTICE

Jane said that she did not believe that reporting fictitious expenses was the correct thing to do and that she would simply report her actual expenses. Ann responded in an angry tone, saying that to do so would expose all the sales reps. As long as everyone cooperated, the company would not question the expense vouchers. However, if one person reported only actual expenses, the company would be likely to investigate the discrepancy and all the sales reps could lose their jobs. She appealed to Jane to follow the agreed-upon practice, stating that they would all be better off, that no one would lose his or her job, and that the company did not really need the money because it was very profitable.

QUESTIONS FOR DISCUSSION

1. What are the ethical issues in this case?
2. Given all the factors, what should Jane have done?
3. What would have been the consequences for Jane and the company if she had accurately reported her expenses? What would the consequences have been if she had inflated her expense account as Ann had urged her to do?
4. What ethical principles would be useful here?

*This case was written by David J. Fritzsche, Penn State Great Valley. Permission to reprint granted by Arthur Andersen & Co., SC.

CASE 13

Family Business*

Jane had just been hired as the head of the payroll department at R&S Electronic Service Company, a firm comprising 75 employees. She had been hired by Eddie, the general manager, who had informed her of the need for maintaining strict confidentiality regarding employee salaries and pay scales. He also told her that he had fired the previous payroll department head for breaking that confidentiality by discussing employee salaries. She had also been formally introduced to Brad, the owner, who had told her to see him if she had any questions or problems. Both Brad and Eddie had made her feel welcome.

GREG'S HIGH COMMISSIONS

After three months of employment, Jane began to wonder why Greg, a service technician and Eddie's brother, made so much more in commissions than the other service technicians. She assumed that he must be highly qualified and must work rapidly because she had overheard Brad commending Greg on his performance on several occasions. She had also noticed Brad, Eddie, and Greg having lunch together frequently.

One day, Eddie gave Jane the stack of work tickets for the service technicians for the upcoming week. The technicians were to take whatever ticket was on top when they finished the job they were working on. After putting the tickets where they belonged, Jane remembered that she had a doctor's appointment the next morning and returned to Eddie's office to tell him she would be reporting late for work.

EDDIE SHOWS FAVORITISM

When she entered Eddie's office, she saw Eddie give Greg a separate stack of work tickets. As she stood there, Eddie told her that if she mentioned this to anyone, he would fire her. Jane was upset because she understood that Eddie was giving the easier, high commission work to his brother. Jane also realized that Eddie had the authority to hire and fire her. Because she had been at the company for only a short time, she was still a probationary employee. This was her first job since college. She wondered what she should do.

QUESTIONS FOR DISCUSSION

1. What are the ethical issues in this case?
2. Is a family business different from other types of businesses with respect to employee treatment?
3. What was Jane's ethical dilemma?
4. What should Jane have done? Why?

*This case was written by Marilyn M. Helms, University of Tennessee at Chattanooga. Permission to reprint granted by Arthur Andersen & Co., SC.

CASE 14

The Waiter Rule: What Makes for a Good CEO?*

As the topic of corporate governance has been in the news more and more during the past several decade, it is useful to reflect on what boards of directors have to do in terms of their roles and responsibilities. Acting on behalf of shareholders, one of the board's most important jobs is selection of the CEO, who will provide strategic direction for the firm, and in turn, hire the top management team. But how does a board go about hiring a CEO? Certainly, this has got to be one of the toughest jobs of selection in the business world.

In recent years, so many contentious issues have surrounded CEOs that the board's task is no small one. Many CEOs have been implicated in ethics scandals, and many of them have been criticized for what the public considers excessive compensation. Today especially, boards want to be sure they hire CEOs

*This case was prepared by Archie B. Carroll, University of Georgia. Revised in 2016.

with high integrity and impeccable character. It is a lofty goal and things don't always turn out the way boards wish. With a record number of CEO firings in the past five years, it is little wonder boards of directors are always seeking insights as to how to make these selection decisions.

Business people are always on the alert for guidance, for suggestions, for tips that would make their hiring more successful or run more smoothly. But if an elusive quality such as character is so important, how does one gauge a prospective CEO's or top executive's character? Or, for that matter, how can we gauge the character of anyone at any level of management?

SWANSON'S UNWRITTEN RULES

In an important *USA Today* article, it was revealed that Bill Swanson, CEO of Raytheon, the defense contractor based in Waltham, Massachusetts, that has 80,000 employees and more than $22 billion in annual sales, had published a booklet containing 33 brief leadership observations.[1] The booklet was titled *Swanson's Unwritten Rules of Management*.[2] It turns out that Raytheon has given away close to 300,000 copies of the booklet to members of its own organization and to virtually anyone who inquires about it. The book is filled with commonsense maxims, observations, rules, and guidelines considered to be something of a cult hit in corporate America.[3] Among the 33 guidelines or rules compiled in the booklet is one rule that Swanson has said never fails in terms of helping to assess someone's character.

THE WAITER RULE

Known as the "Waiter Rule," the observation says that "A person, who is nice to you but rude to the waiter, or to others, is not a nice person." A number of CEOs and other corporate executives have all agreed with the Waiter Rule. They basically concur that how a privileged corporate executive treats people in subordinate roles, whether they be waiters, clerks, maids, bellmen, golf caddies, or any other service-type worker, reveals insights into the executive's character that should be taken into consideration in hiring decisions.

Former Office Depot CEO Steve Odland recalls that when he was working in a restaurant in Denver many years ago, he spilled a glass of purple sorbet all over the expensive white gown of an apparently important and rich woman. Though it occurred over 30 years ago, he can't get the spill out of his mind. But what struck him most was her reaction to his careless spill. The woman responded in a very kind and understanding way. She kept her composure and in a calm voice said, "It's okay. It wasn't your fault." Years later, the former CEO of Office Depot recalls what he learned about this incident: "You can tell a lot about a person by the way he or she treats the waiter."[4]

CHARACTER REVEALED

As it turns out, just about every CEO has a waiter story to tell. The opinion they hold in common, moreover, is that the Waiter Rule is a valid way to gain insights into the character of a person, especially someone who may be in a position of authority over thousands of workers. The cofounder of Au Bon Pain, the leading urban bakery and sandwich café, Ron Shaich, became CEO of Panera Bread. He tells the story of interviewing a woman for general counsel, who was "sweet" to him but turned "amazingly rude" to the person cleaning tables. She didn't get the job.[5] She had failed the Waiter Rule.

Author Bill Swanson is quoted as having written, "Watch out for people who have a situational value system, who can turn the charm on and off depending on the status of the person they are interacting with."[6] Related to this observation, Steve Odland, formerly of Office Depot, has been quoted as saying, "People with situational values have situational ethics, and those are people to be avoided."[7]

QUESTIONS FOR DISCUSSION

1. Is character an essential ingredient in ethical leadership? Is it especially important in managers? In leadership, especially among CEOs, is character important? Why?
2. Do you agree with the Waiter Rule? Does it provide useful insights into who might be an ethical or unethical leader? Should corporate boards consider character when hiring someone for the top position?
3. Is using the Waiter Rule too simplistic a guideline for hiring people in important positions such as CEO? Is it too simplistic a guideline for judging one's ethics?
4. Do you have a "Waiter Rule" story or experience to tell?

ENDNOTES

1. Del Jones, "CEOs Vouch for Waiter Rule: Watch How People Treat Staff," *USA Today* (April 14,

2006), B1; see also http://usatoday30.usatoday.com/money/companies/management/2006-04-14-ceos-waiter-rule_x.htm. Accessed June 11, 2016.
2. William H. Swanson, *Swanson's Unwritten Rules of Management, Raytheon* (2005).
3. David Leonhardt, "Rule No. 35: Reread Rule on Integrity," *The New York Times* (May 3, 2006).
4. Jones, ibid.
5. Ibid.
6. Quoted in Jones (2006).
7. Quoted in Jones (2006).

CASE 15

Nike, Inc. and Sweatshops*

Jonah Peretti decided to customize his Nike shoes and visited the NikeiD Web site. The company allowed customers to personalize their Nikes with the colors of their choice and their own personal 16-character message. Peretti chose the word "sweatshop" for his Nikes.

After receiving his order, Nike informed Peretti via e-mail that the term "sweatshop" represents "inappropriate slang" and is not considered viable for printing on a Nike shoe. Thus, his order was summarily rejected. Peretti e-mailed Nike, arguing that the term "sweatshop" is found in *Webster's* dictionary and could not possibly be considered inappropriate slang. Nike responded by quoting the company's rules, which state that the company can refuse to print anything on its shoes that it does not deem appropriate. Peretti replied that he was changing his previous order and would instead like to order a pair of shoes with a "color snapshot of the ten-year-old Vietnamese girl who makes my shoes." He never received a response.[1]

THE PR NIGHTMARE BEGINS

Before Nike could blink an eye, the situation turned into a public relations nightmare. Peretti forwarded the e-mail exchange to a few friends, who forwarded it to a few friends, and so on. Within six weeks of his initial order, the story appeared in *The Wall Street Journal, USA Today*, and *The Village Voice*. Peretti himself appeared on *The Today Show*, and he estimates that 2 million people have seen the e-mail. At the height of the incident, Peretti was receiving 500 e-mails a day from people who had read the e-mail from as far away as Asia, Australia, Europe, and South America.[2,3]

Nike refused to admit any wrongdoing in the incident and stated that they reserved the right to refuse any order for whatever reason. Beth Gourney, a spokesperson for Nike, claimed that Peretti was just trying to create trouble. She said he is not an activist and he doesn't understand the company's labor policy. If he understood the policy he would know that 18 is the minimum age for hiring. She went on to say that Nike does not need to apologize for not using "sweatshop" because company policy clearly says the company can cancel any order within 24 hours of its submission.[4]

Nike, Inc. is no stranger to sweatshop allegations. Since the mid-1990s, the company has been imperiled by negative press, lawsuits, and demonstrations on college campuses alleging that the firm's overseas contractors subject employees to work in inhumane conditions for low wages. As Philip Knight, the CEO and cofounder of Nike, once lamented, "The Nike product has become synonymous with slave wages, forced overtime, and arbitrary abuse."[5]

NIKE, INC. IS FOUNDED

Philip Knight started his own athletic shoe distribution company in 1964. Using his Plymouth Reliant as a warehouse, he began importing and distributing track shoes from Onitsuka Company, Ltd., a Japanese manufacturer. First-year sales of $8,000 resulted in a profit of $254. After eight years, annual sales reached $2 million, and the firm employed 45 people.

*This case was written initially by Bryan S. Dennis, Idaho State University. Revised and updated by Archie B. Carroll, University of Georgia, in 2016.

However, Onitsuka saw the huge potential of the American shoe market and dropped Knight's relatively small company in favor of larger, more experienced distributors. Knight was forced to start anew. However, instead of importing and distributing another firm's track shoes, he decided to design his own shoes and create his own company. The name he chose for his new company was "Nike."[6]

Nike's Use of Contract Labor

When the company began operations, Knight contracted the manufacture of Nike's shoes to two firms in Japan. Shortly thereafter, Nike began to contract with firms in Taiwan and Korea. In 1977, Nike purchased two shoe-manufacturing facilities in the United States—one in Maine, the other in New Hampshire. Eventually, the two plants became so unprofitable that the firm was forced to close them. The loss due to the write-off of the plants was approximately $10 million in a year in which the firm's total profit was $15 million. The firm had a successful IPO in 1980, eight years after the company was founded. Nike became the largest athletic shoe company in the world.[7]

Nike does not own a single shoe or apparel factory. Instead, the firm contracts the production of its products to independently owned manufacturers. Today, practically all Nike subcontracted factories are in countries such as Indonesia, Vietnam, China, and Thailand, where the labor costs are significantly less than those in the United States. Worldwide, over 530,000 people are employed in factories that manufacture Nike products. In an earlier calculation of labor costs for a pair of shoes, the labor costs amounted to less than 4 percent of the consumer's price for the shoes.[8]

Even in today's hi-tech environment, the production of athletic shoes is still a labor-intensive process. Although most leaders in the industry are confident that practically the entire production process will someday be automated, it may still be years before the industry will not have to rely on inexpensive human labor.

After some bad press in the early 1990s, Nike sought to improve the working conditions of its plants by establishing a code of conduct for its suppliers.[9] This was not seen as enough by outside critics, however.

Other Firms in the Industry

Nike's use of overseas contractors is not unique in the athletic shoe and apparel industry. All other major athletic shoe manufacturers also contract with overseas manufacturers, albeit to various degrees. Athletic shoe firm New Balance Inc. is somewhat of an anomaly as it continues to operate five factories in the United States and is the only company to continue U.S. production. New Balance makes about 25 percent of its shoes in the United States.[10]

Nike spends heavily on endorsements and advertising and pays several top athletes well over a million dollars a year in endorsement contracts. In contrast, New Balance has developed a different strategy. They do not use professional athletes to market their products. According to their "Endorsed by No One" policy, New Balance instead has chosen to invest in product research and development and foregoes expensive endorsement contracts.[11]

THE ANTI-SWEATSHOP MOVEMENT

There is one pivotal event largely responsible for introducing the term "sweatshop" to the American public. In 1996, Kathie Lee Gifford, cohost of the formerly syndicated talk show "Live with Regis and Kathie Lee," endorsed her own line of clothing for Walmart. During that same year, labor rights activists disclosed that her "Kathie Lee Collection" was made in Honduras by seamstresses who earned 31 cents an hour and were sometimes required to work 20-hour days. Traditionally known for her pleasant, jovial demeanor and her love for children, Kathie Lee was outraged. She tearfully informed the public that she was unaware that her clothes were being made in so-called sweatshops and vowed to do whatever she could to promote the anti-sweatshop cause.[12]

Nike Is Accused

In a national press conference, Gifford named Michael Jordan as another celebrity who, like herself, endorsed products without knowing under what conditions the products were made. At the time, Michael Jordan was Nike's premier endorser and was reportedly under a $20 million per year contract with the firm.[13] Nike, the number-one athletic shoe brand in the world, soon found itself under attack by the rapidly growing anti-sweatshop movement.

Shortly after the Gifford story broke, Joel Joseph, chairperson of the Made in the USA Foundation,[14] accused Nike of paying underage Indonesian workers 14 cents an hour to make the company's line of Air Jordan shoes. He also claimed that the total payroll of Nike's six Indonesian subcontracted factories was less than the reported $20 million per year that Jordan was receiving from his endorsement contract with Nike. The Made in the USA Foundation is one of the organizations that ignited the Gifford controversy and is largely financed by labor unions and U.S. apparel manufacturers that are against free trade with low-wage countries.[15]

Nike quickly pointed out that Air Jordan shoes were made in Taiwan, not Indonesia. Additionally, the company maintained that employee wages were fair and higher than the government-mandated minimum wage in all of the countries where the firm has contracted factories. Nike avowed that the entry-level income of an Indonesian factory worker was five times that of a farmer. The firm also claimed that an assistant line supervisor in a Chinese subcontracted factory earned more than a surgeon with 20 years of experience.[16] In response to the allegations regarding Michael Jordan's endorsement contract, Nike stated that the total wages in Indonesia were $50 million a year, which is well over what the firm pays Jordan.[17]

Nike soon faced more negative publicity. Michael Moore, the movie director whose documentary *Roger and Me* shed light on the plight of laid-off autoworkers in Flint, Michigan, and damaged the reputation of General Motors chairperson Roger Smith, interviewed Nike CEO Philip Knight for his movie *The Big One*. On camera, Knight referred to some employees at subcontracted factories as "poor little Indonesian workers."[18]

Knight, the only CEO interviewed in the movie, received harsh criticism for his comments. Nike alleged that the comments were taken out of context and were deceitful because Moore failed to include Knight's pledge to make a transition from a 14- to a 16-year-old minimum age labor force. Nike prepared its own video that included the entire interview.[19]

Thomas Nguyen, founder of Vietnam Labor Watch, inspected several of Nike's plants in Vietnam in 1998 and reported cases of worker abuse. At one factory that manufactured Nike products, a supervisor punished 56 women for wearing inappropriate work shoes by forcing them to run around the factory in the hot sun. Twelve workers fainted and were taken to the hospital. Nguyen also reported that workers were allowed only one bathroom break and two drinks of water during each eight-hour shift. Nike responded that the supervisor who was involved in the fainting incident had been suspended and that the firm had hired an independent accounting firm to look into the matters further.[20]

Nike Responds

In 1997, Nike hired former Atlanta Mayor Andrew Young, a vocal opponent of sweatshops and child labor, to review the firm's overseas labor practices. Neither party disclosed the fee that Young received for his services. Young toured 12 factories in Vietnam, Indonesia, and China, and was reportedly given unlimited access. However, he was constantly accompanied by Nike representatives during all factory tours. Furthermore, Young relied on Nike translators when communicating with factory workers.[21]

In his 75-page report, Young concluded, "Nike is doing a good job, but it can do better." He provided Nike with six recommendations for improving the working conditions at subcontracted factories. Nike immediately responded to the report and agreed to implement all six recommendations. Young did not address the issue of wages and standards of living because he felt he lacks the "academic credentials" for such a judgment.[22]

Public reaction to Young's report was mixed. Some praised Nike. However, many of Nike's opponents disregarded Young's report as biased and incomplete. One went so far as to state the report could not have been better if Nike had written it themselves and questioned Young's independence.[23,24]

In 1998, Nike hired Maria Eitel to the newly created position of vice president for corporate and social responsibility. Eitel was formerly a public relations executive for Microsoft. Her responsibilities were to oversee Nike's labor practices, environmental affairs, and involvement in the global community. Although this move was applauded by some, others were skeptical and claimed that Nike's move was nothing more than a publicity stunt.[25]

Later that same year, Philip Knight gave a speech at the National Press Club in Washington, DC, and announced six initiatives that were intended to improve the working conditions in its overseas factories. The firm chose to raise the minimum hiring age from 16 to 18 years. Nike also decided to expand its worker education program so that all workers in Nike factories would have the option to take middle and high school equivalency tests.[26] The director of Global Exchange, one of Nike's staunchest opponents, called the initiatives "significant and very positive." He also added, "we feel that the measures—if implemented could be exciting."[27]

STUDENTS AND ORGANIZED LABOR GET INVOLVED

Colleges and universities have direct ties to the many athletic shoe and apparel companies (such as Nike, Champion, and Reebok) that contract with overseas manufacturers. Most universities receive money from athletic shoe and apparel corporations in return for outfitting the university's sports teams with the firm's products. In 1997, Nike gave $7.1 million to the University of North Carolina (UNC) for the right to outfit all of UNC's sports teams with products bearing the Nike Swoosh logo.[28] Additionally, academic institutions allow firms to manufacture apparel bearing the university's official name, colors, and insignias in return for a fee. In 1998, the University of Michigan received $5.7 million in licensing fees.[29] Most of these contract and licensing fees are allocated toward scholarships and other academic programs. Today, these practices continue and the amounts of money are much larger.

Organized Labor

In 1995, the Union of Needletrades, Industrial and Textile Employees (UNITE) was founded. The union, a member of the AFL-CIO, represented 250,000 workers in North America and Puerto Rico. Most of the union members work in the textile and apparel industry. In 1996, UNITE launched a "Stop Sweatshops" campaign after the Kathy Lee Gifford story broke to "link union, consumers, student, civil rights and women's groups in the fight against sweatshops at home and abroad."[30] The unions had a deep interest in this issue as they would prefer that the shoes be made by them in the United States.

In 1997, UNITE, along with the AFL-CIO, recruited dozens of college students for summer internships. Many of the students referred to that summer as "Union Summer and it had a similar impact as Freedom Summer did for students during the civil rights movement."[31] The United Students against Sweatshops (USAS) organization was formed the following year. It was founded and led by former UNITE summer interns and remains active today.[32]

University Organizations

The USAS established chapters at dozens of universities across the United States. Since its inception, the organization has staged a large number of campus demonstrations that are reminiscent of the 1960s. One notable demonstration occurred on the campus of UNC in 1997. Students of the Nike Awareness Campaign protested against the university's contract with Nike due to the firm's alleged sweatshop abuses. More than 100 students demanded that the university not renew its contract with Nike and rallied outside the office of the university's chancellor. More than 50 other universities, such as the University of Wisconsin and Duke, staged similar protests and sit-ins.[33]

In response to the protests at UNC, Nike invited the editor of the university's student newspaper to tour Nike's overseas contractors to examine the working conditions firsthand. Nike offered to fund the trip by pledging $15,000 toward the students' travel and accommodation costs. Ironically, Michael Jordan is an alumnus of UNC.[34]

Critics of the USAS contend that the student organization is merely a puppet of UNITE and organized labor. They cite the fact that the AFL-CIO has spent more than $3 million on internships and outreach programs with the alleged intent of interesting students in careers as union activists. The founders of the USAS are former UNITE interns. The USAS admits that UNITE has tipped off the student movement as to the whereabouts of alleged sweatshop factories. According to Allan Ryan, a Harvard University lawyer who has negotiated with the USAS, "[T]he students are vocal, but it's hard to get a viewpoint from them that does not reflect that of UNITE."[35]

Many students denied allegations that they are being manipulated by organized labor and claim that they discovered the sweatshop issues on their own. Others acknowledge the assistance of organized labor but claim it is "no different from [student] civil rights activists using the NAACP in the 1960s."[36] John Sweeney, president of the AFL-CIO, claimed the role of organized labor was not one of manipulation but of motivation. Others assert that the union merely provides moral support.[37]

Regardless of the AFL-CIO's intentions, the students have had a positive impact on the promotion of organized labor's anti-sweatshop agenda over the years. According to the director of one of the several human rights groups that are providing assistance to the students, the sweatshop protests were being carried on the backs of the university students. A major reason for this is that they get more press coverage than do the union people.[38]

In telling the world about itself, in 2016 USAS stated that it "is a national student labor organization fighting for workers' rights with chapters at over 150 campuses."[39] USAS's anti-sweatshop campaign continues under its "Garment Worker Solidarity" initiative.

THE FAIR LABOR ASSOCIATION (FLA)

In 1996, a presidential task force of industry and human rights representatives was given the job of addressing the sweatshop issue. The key purpose of this task force was to develop a workplace code of conduct and a system for monitoring factories to ensure compliance. In 1998, the task force created the Fair Labor Association (FLA) to accomplish these goals. This organization was made up of consumer and human rights groups as well as footwear and apparel manufacturers. Nike was one of the first companies to join the FLA. Many other major manufacturers (Levi Strauss & Co., Liz Claiborne, Patagonia, Polo Ralph Lauren, Reebok, Eddie Bauer, and Phillips-Van Heusen) along with hundreds of colleges and universities also joined the FLA.[40]

FLA Requirements

Members of the FLA must follow the principles set forth in the organization's Workplace Code of Conduct. The Code of Conduct is based on international labor and human rights standards—primarily Conventions of the International Labor Organization (ILO)—and prohibits discrimination, the use of child or forced labor, and harassment or abuse. It also establishes requirements related to health and safety; freedom of association and collective bargaining; wages and benefits; hours of work; and overtime compensation.[41]

THE WORKER RIGHTS CONSORTIUM

The USAS opposed several of the FLA's key components and created the Worker Rights Consortium (WRC) as an alternative to the FLA. The WRC asserts that the prevailing industry or legal minimum wage in some countries is too low and does not provide employees with the basic human needs they require. They proposed that factories should instead pay a higher "living wage" that takes into account the wage required to provide factory employees with enough income to afford housing, energy, nutrition, clothing, health care, education, potable water, child care, transportation, and savings. Additionally, the WRC supports public disclosure of all factory locations and the right to monitor any factory at any time. As of May, 2016, 183 colleges and universities had joined the WRC and agreed to adhere to its policies.[42]

Nike, a member and supporter of the FLA, did not support the WRC. The firm states that the concept of a living wage is impractical as "there is no common, agreed-upon definition of the living wage. Definitions range from complex mathematical formulas to vague philosophical notions." Additionally, Nike was once opposed to the WRC's proposal that the location of all factories be publicly disclosed. Nike also has claimed that the monitoring provisions set out by the WRC are unrealistic and biased toward organized labor.[43]

The University of Oregon, Philip Knight's alma mater, joined the WRC in the year 2000. Alumnus Knight had previously contributed over $50 million to the university—$30 million for academics and $20 million for athletics. Upon hearing that his alma mater had joined the WRC, Knight was shocked. He withdrew a proposed $30 million donation and stated that "the bonds of trust, which allowed me to give at a high level, have been shredded" and "there will be no further donations of any kind to the University of Oregon."[44,45]

NIKE COMES AROUND

In May 2001, Harsh Saini, Nike's corporate and social responsibility manager, acknowledged that the firm may not have handled the sweatshop issue as well as it could have and stated that Nike had not been adequately monitoring its subcontractors in overseas operations until the media and other organizations revealed the presence of sweatshops.

> *We were a bunch of shoe geeks who expanded so much without thinking of being socially responsible that we went from being a very big sexy brand name to suddenly becoming the poster boy for everything bad in manufacturing.*[46]

She added, "We realized that if we still wanted to be the brand of choice in 20 years, we had certain responsibilities to fulfill."[47]

Oregon Reverses its Decision

In early 2001, Oregon's state board of higher education cast doubt on the legality of the University of Oregon's WRC membership, and the university dissolved its ties with the labor organization.[48] In September of the same year, Phil Knight renewed his financial support.

Although the exact amount of Knight's donation was kept confidential, it was sufficient to ensure that the $85 million expansion of the university's football stadium would go through as originally planned. In 2000, the stadium expansion plans suffered a significant setback when Knight withdrew his funding. Many of the proposed additions, such as a 12,000 seat capacity increase and 32 brand new skyboxes, could happen, largely due to Knight's pledge of financial support.[49,50]

Nike released its first corporate social responsibility report in October 2001. According to Phil Knight, "[I] n this report, Nike for the first time has assembled a comprehensive public review of our corporate responsibility practices."[51] The report cited several areas in which the firm could have done better, such as worker conditions in Indonesia and Mexico. The report, compiled by both internal auditors and outside monitors, also noted that Nike was one of only four companies that had joined a World Wildlife Fund program to reduce greenhouse admissions. Jason Mark, a spokesperson for Global Exchange, one of Nike's chief critics, praised the report and stated that Nike is "obviously responding to consumer concerns."[52]

Kasky V. Nike, Inc.

Nike's problems with fair labor issues continued on a related front. Labor activist Mark Kasky had sued Nike in 1998, arguing that Nike had engaged in false advertising when it denied that there was mistreatment of workers in Southeastern Asian factories. At issue was the question of whether Nike's defense of its practices was commercial speech or not, for which free speech protections apply. The California Supreme Court ruled that Nike's statements about labor conditions could be construed as false advertising. Nike appealed this ruling to the U.S. Supreme Court, which sent it back to the California court, without making a judgment on the free speech issue. In September 2003, Kasky and Nike settled the case for a $1.5 million donation to the FLA.[53] The settlement, however, left many questions unanswered.[54] Many feared that the risk of lawsuit would have a chilling effect, causing firms to no longer release social responsibility reports, which, unlike the SEC financial reports, are all voluntary. Though Nike issued a corporate social responsibility report in 2001, the company announced that, due to the California decision, they would not release a corporate social responsibility report in 2002–2003. Nike released a "Community Investment" report detailing its philanthropic efforts instead.[55] The company later released a corporate responsibility report in 2005–2006 and again in 2008–2009. In 2016, Nike released its most recent Corporate Responsibility Report, now called a Sustainability Report.[56]

CRITICS QUIET DOWN BUT DON'T GO AWAY

Nike's critics never go away, but they have quieted down as the company has taken steps to address many of the criticisms made over the years. Typical of the ongoing opposition is the organization Educating for Justice (EFJ) that runs a continuing "Stop Nike Sweatshops" campaign.[57] In 2006, EFJ planned a film titled *Sweat*. The film, as described on EFJ's Web site, describes the journey of two young Americans uncovering the story behind the statistics about Nike factory workers. Through the lens of their experiences, they claim viewers will discover the injustices of Nike's labor practices in the developing world, specifically in Indonesia, and how Nike's cutthroat, bottom-line economic decisions have a profound effect on human lives.[58] EFJ announced that the film was going to production in 2009, but in 2016, it appeared that EFJ was still trying to raise money to complete the film and to release it for public viewing.[59]

One organization that remains somewhat active in taking Nike to task is "Team Sweat." Team Sweat identifies itself as an "international coalition of consumers, investors, and workers committed to ending the injustices in Nike's sweatshops around the world." It goes on to say "Team Sweat is striving to ensure that all workers who produce Nike products are paid a living wage."[60] As of Fall, 2015, James Keady, organizer of the group, was still appearing at various university campuses and calling for a boycott of Nike. Its initiative is called "Behind the swoosh: Sweatshops and social justice."[61] One other organization that conducts an ongoing campaign against Nike's and other companies' sweatshops is Oxfam Australia. Among other charges, Oxfam complained about Nike paying Tiger Woods $25 million a year, while the workers who make its products receive poverty wages and endure harsh working conditions.[62] In addition to Nike, Oxfam pursues its initiatives against Puma, Adidas, and Fila, and the companies that sell their products.[63]

NIKE TURNS IT AROUND BUT SWEAPSHOPS DON'T GO AWAY

In spite of its controversial record on the issue of sweatshops and monitoring labor practices abroad, in 1998, then-CEO Phil Knight announced that changes would be coming in how the company dealt with the sweatshop situation. By 2005, Nike was the first company in its industry to adopt a policy of transparency and to publish a complete list of its contract companies.[64] Once the company publically proclaimed it would change, it seemed to take this mandate seriously and eventually became a company that would be regarded as one of the leaders in CSR.[65] Also in 2005, Nike published a detailed report revealing conditions and pay in its factories and acknowledging widespread issues, especially in its south Asian factories. Since that time, the company has continued to post its commitments, standards, and audit data as part of its CSR reports.[66] In 2016, Nike was ranked 28th in Corporate Responsibility's "100 Best Corporate Citizens Awards."[67]

In spite of turnarounds such as that witnessed at Nike, sweatshops have not gone away and protest groups continue to monitor what companies are doing and raise issues about their questionable practices. Since the tragic Rana Plaza factories collapse in Bangladesh in 2013 that resulted in more than 1,100 deaths, the world's awareness of what has been going on in the shoe and apparel industries has been significantly energized.[68]

QUESTIONS FOR DISCUSSION

1. What are the ethical and social issues in this case?
2. Why should Nike and other companies be held responsible for what happens in factories that they do not own? Does Nike have a responsibility to ensure that factory workers receive a "living wage"? Do the wage guidelines of FLA or WRC seem most appropriate to you? Why?
3. Is it fair for Nike to pay endorsers millions, while its factory employees receive a few dollars a day?
4. Is Nike's responsibility to monitor its subcontracted factories a legal, economic, social, or philanthropic responsibility? What was it ten years ago? What will it be ten years from now?
5. What was behind the turnaround at Nike? Is it "good business" for Nike to acknowledge its past errors and become more socially responsible?
6. What are the motivations of student organizations when they get involved in the anti-sweatshop movement? Why is their activism present on some campuses but not on others?
7. Nike seems to be a much more respected company today than it was back when the anti-sweatshop movement began. What has changed in Nike and the world to explain this?

ENDNOTES

1. Copy of E-Mail Exchange Found at The Life of an Internet Meme, http://www.shey.net/niked.html. Accessed May 23, 2016.
2. Ibid.
3. ABC News, "When Nike Just Couldn't Do It," http://abcnews.go.com/Technology/story?id=98680&page=1#.Ua9C50Ckobw. Accessed May 23 2016.
4. Ibid.
5. Bien Hoa, "Job Opportunity or Exploitation," *Los Angeles Times* (April 18, 1999).
6. Philip Knight, "Global Manufacturing: The Nike Story Is just Good Business," *Vital Speeches of the Day* 64(20): 637–640.
7. Ibid.
8. These data were presented on an earlier Nike Web site that is no longer available. The site was http://nikeinc.com/.
9. "Working Conditions in Factories: When the Jobs Inspector Calls," *The Economist* (March 31, 2012), 73–74.
10. "New Balance," Wikipedia, https://en.wikipedia.org/wiki/New_Balance. Accessed May 23, 2016.
11. Ibid.
12. David Bauman, "After the Tears, Gifford Testifies on Sweatshops—She Turns Lights, Cameras on Issue," *Seattle Times* (July 16, 1996), A3.
13. Del Jones, "Critics Tie Sweatshop Sneakers to 'Air' Jordan," *USA Today* (June 6, 1996), 1B.
14. Made in USA Foundation, http://www.madeinusa.org/. Accessed June 21, 2010.
15. Ibid.
16. Nike Press Release (June 6, 1996).
17. Del Jones, 1B.
18. Garry Trudeau, "Sneakers in Tinseltown," *Time* (April 20, 1998), 84.
19. William J. Holstein, "Casting Nike as the Bad Guy," *U.S. News & World Report* (September 22, 1997), 49.
20. Verena Dobnik, "Nike Shoe Contractor Abuses Alleged," *The Atlanta Journal-Constitution* (March 18, 1997), A14.

21. Simon Beck, "Nike in Sweat over Heat Raised by Claims of Biases Assessment," *South China Morning Post* (July 6, 1997), 2.
22. Matthew C. Quinn, "Footwear Maker's Labor Pledge Unlikely to Stamp Out Criticism," *The Atlanta Journal-Constitution* (June 25, 1997), F8.
23. G. Pascal Zachary, "Nike Tries to Quell Exploitation Charges," *The Wall Street Journal* (June 15, 1997).
24. Beck, 2.
25. Bill Richards, "Nike Hires an Executive from Microsoft for New Post Focusing on Labor Policies," *The Wall Street Journal* (January 15, 1998), B14.
26. Knight, 640.
27. Patti Bond, "Nike Promises to Improve Factory Worker Conditions," *The Atlanta Journal-Constitution* (May 13, 1998), 3B.
28. Allan Wolper, "Nike's Newspaper Temptation," *Editor & Publisher* (January 10, 1998), 8–10.
29. Gregg Krupa, "Antisweatshop Activists Score in Campaign Targeting Athletic Retailers," *Boston Globe* (April 18, 1999), F1.
30. UNITE, http://www.unitehere.org/about/apparel.php. Accessed June 5, 2013.
31. Krupa, F1.
32. USAS, http://usas.org/. Accessed May 23, 2016.
33. Wolper, 8–10.
34. Ibid., 8.
35. Jodie Morse, "Campus Awakening," *Time* (April 12, 1999), 77–78.
36. Krupa, F1.
37. Morse, 77–78.
38. Ibid.
39. USAS About Us, http://usas.org/about/mission-vision-organizing/. Accessed May 23, 2016.
40. Fair Labor Association, http://www.fairlabor.org/. Accessed May 23, 2016.
41. Fair Labor Association Workplace Code of Conduct, http://www.fairlabor.org/blog/entry/fair-labor-association-enhances-its-workplace-code-conduct. Accessed May 23, 2016.
42. Worker's Rights Consortium, Affiliated Colleges and Universities, http://www.workersrights.org/about/as.asp. Accessed May 23, 2016.
43. Nike Web site, http://www.nikebiz.com/labor/index.shtml. Current Web site is: http://nikeinc.com/search?search_terms=labor. Accessed May 23, 2016.
44. Philip Knight Press Release (April 24, 2000). Found at http://www.nikebiz.com/media/n_uofo.shtml (Web site no longer active).
45. Louise Lee and Aaron Bernstein, "Who Says Student Protests Don't Matter?" *BusinessWeek* (June 12, 2000), 96.
46. Ravina Shamdasani, "Soul Searching by 'Shoe Geeks' Led to Social Responsibility," *South China Morning Post* (May 17, 2001), 2.
47. Ibid.
48. Greg Bolt, "University of Oregon Ends Relationship with Antisweatshop Group," *The Register Guard* (March 6, 2001).
49. Hank Hager, "Frohnmayer: It's a Very Happy Day for Us," *Oregon Daily Emerald* (September 27, 2001).
50. Ron Bellamy, "Nike CEO to Resume Donations to University of Oregon," *The Register Guard* (September 26, 2001).
51. William McCall, "Nike Releases First Corporate Responsibility Report," *Associated Press State & Local Wire* (October 9, 2001).
52. Ibid.
53. Adam Liptak, "Nike Move Ends Case over Firm's Free Speech," *New York Times* (September 13, 2003).
54. For a more thorough discussion of this controversy, see David Hess and Thomas Dunfee, "The KaskyNike Threat to Corporate Social Reporting," *Business Ethics Quarterly* (January 2007), 5–32, and Don Mayer, "Kasky v. Nike and the Quarrelsome Question of Corporate Free Speech," *Business Ethics Quarterly* (January 2007), 65–96.
55. For detailed coverage of this case and its implications, see http://reclaimdemocracy.org/nike/. Accessed June 5, 2013.
56. Nike, FY 14/15 Sustainable Business Report, http://news.nike.com/news/sustainable-innovation. Accessed May 27, 2016.http://nikeinc.com/pages/responsibility
57. Educating for Justice, http://educatingforjustice.org/about/history/. Accessed May 27, 2016.
58. Educating for Justice, SWEAT, http://www.sweatthefilm.org/story.htm. Accessed May 27, 2016.
59. Ibid.
60. Team Sweat, https://www.facebook.com/TeamSweat/timeline. Accessed May 27, 2016.

61. Corporate Crime Reporter, "James Keady and the Coming Boycott of Nike," http://www.corporatecrimereporter.com/news/200/james-keady-and-the-coming-boycott-of-nike/. Accessed May 27, 2016.
62. Oxfam Australia, https://www.oxfam.org.au/what-we-do/ethical-trading-and-business/workers-rights-2/nike/. Accessed May 27, 2016.
63. Oxfam Australia, https://www.oxfam.org.au/explore/workers-rights/which-brands-are-dodging-the-hard-questions/. Accessed May 27, 2016.
64. Andrea Newell, "How Nike Embraced CSR and Went from Villain to Hero," *TriplePundit,* June 19, 2015, http://www.triplepundit.com/special/roi-of-sustainability/how-nike-embraced-csr-and-went-from-villain-to-hero/. Accessed May 27, 2016.
65. Ibid.
66. Max Nisen, "How Nike Solved Its Sweatshop Problem," *Business Insider* (May 9, 2013), http://www.businessinsider.com/how-nike-solved-its-sweatshop-problem-2013-5. Accessed May 27, 2016.
67. CR's 100 Best Corporate Citizens Awards, http://www.thecro.com/wp-content/uploads/2016/04/100best_1.pdf. Accessed May 27, 2016.
68. Judy Gearhart, "Remembering Rena Plaza, Advancing Women Workers' Rights in Global Supply Chains," Huffpost Women, April 27, 2016, http://www.huffingtonpost.com/judy-gearhart/remembering-rana-plaza-ad_b_9781538.html. Accessed May 27, 2016.

CASE 16

Coke and Pepsi in India: Issues, Ethics, and Crisis Management*

There is nothing new about multinational corporations (MNCs) facing challenges as they do business around the world, especially in developing nations or emerging markets. Royal Dutch Shell had to greatly reduce its production of oil in Nigeria due to guerrilla attacks on its pipelines. Cargill was forced to shut down its soy-processing plant in Brazil because of the claim that it was contributing to the destruction of the Amazon rainforest. Tribesmen in Botswana accused De Beers of pushing them off their land to make way for diamond mines.[1] Google was kicked out of China only to be later restored. Global business today is not for the faint hearted.

It should not come as a surprise, therefore, that MNC giants such as Coca-Cola and PepsiCo—highly visible, multibillion dollar corporations with well-known, iconic brands around the world—would encounter challenges in the creation and distribution of their products in some countries. After all, soft drinks are viewed as discretionary and sometimes luxurious products when compared to the staples of life that are often scarce in developing countries. One of those scarce staples is water. Many observers think a shortage of water is the next burgeoning global resource crisis.[2]

Whether it is called an issue, an ethics challenge, or a scandal, the situation confronting both Coke and Pepsi in India, beginning in 2003, richly illustrates the many complex and varied social challenges companies face once they decide to embark on other country's shores. Their experiences in India may predict other issues they may eventually face elsewhere or trials other companies might face as well. With a billion-plus people and an expanding economy, and with markets stagnating in many Western countries, India, along with China and Russia, represent immense opportunities for growth for virtually all businesses. Hence, these companies cannot afford to ignore these burgeoning markets.

INITIAL ALLEGATIONS

Coke and Pepsi's serious problems in India began in 2003. In that year, India's Center for Science and Environment (CSE), an independent public interest group, made allegations that tests they had conducted revealed dangerously high levels of pesticide residue in the soft drinks being sold all over India. The director of CSE, Sunita Narain, stated that such residues could cause cancer and birth defects as well as harm nervous and immune systems if the products were

*This case was prepared by Archie B. Carroll, University of Georgia. Updated and revised most recently in 2016.

consumed over long periods of time.[3] Further, CSE stated that the pesticide levels in Coke's and Pepsi's drinks were much higher than that permitted by European Union standards. On one occasion, Narain accused Pepsi and Coke of pushing products that they wouldn't dare sell at home.[4]

In addition to the alleged pesticides in the soft drinks, another special interest group, India Resource Center (IRC), accused the companies of over consuming scarce water and polluting water sources due to its operations in India.[5] IRC intensely criticized the companies, especially Coca-Cola, by detailing a number of different "water woes" experienced by different cities and regions of the country. IRC's allegations even more broadly accused the companies of water exploitation and of controlling natural resources, and thus communities. Examples frequently cited were the impact of Coke's operations in the communities of Kerala and Mehdiganj.[6]

In 2004, IRC continued its "Campaign to Hold Coca-Cola Accountable" by arguing that communities across India were under assault by Coke's practices. Among the continuing allegations were communities' experiencing severe water shortages around Coke's bottling plants, significant depletion of the water table, strange water tastes and smells, and pollution of groundwater as well as soil. IRC said that in one community Coke was distributing its solid waste to farmers as fertilizer and that tests conducted found cadmium and lead in the waste, thus making it toxic waste. And the accusation of high levels of pesticides continued. According to IRC, the Parliament of India banned the sale of Coca-Cola in its cafeteria.[7] In December 2004, India's Supreme Court ordered Coke and Pepsi to put warning labels on their products. This caused a serious slide in sales for the next several years.[8]

Sunita Narain

One major reason that Indian consumers and politicians took seriously the allegations of both CSE and IRC was CSE's director, Sunita Narain—a well-known activist in New Delhi. Narain was born into a family of freedom fighters whose support of Mahatma Gandhi goes back to the days when Gandhi was pushing for independence in India over 60 years ago. She took up environmental causes in high school. One major cause she adopted was to stop developers from cutting down trees. Her quest was to save India from the ravages of industrialization. She became the director of CSE in 2002.[9]

According to a *BusinessWeek* writer, Narain strongly holds forth on the topic of MNCs exploiting the natural resources of developing countries, especially India. She manifests an alarmist tone that tends toward the end-is-near level of fervency. She is skilled at getting media attention. In 2005, she won the Stockholm Water Prize, one of a number of environmental accolades she has received.[10] In addition, she has been very successful in taking advantage of India's general suspicion of huge MNCs, dating back to its tragic Bhopal gas leak in 1984. Narain claims she does not intend to hurt companies but only to spur the country to pass stricter regulations.[11]

Sacred Water

Coke and Pepsi's problems in India have been complicated by the fact that water carries considerable significance in India. We are often told about cultural knowledge we should have before doing business in other countries. Water is one of those issues in India. Although the country has some of the worst water in the world, due to poor sewage, pollution, and pesticide use, according to UN sources, water carries an almost-spiritual meaning to Indians. Bathing is viewed by many of them to be a sacred act, and tradition for some residents holds that one's death is not properly noted until one's ashes are scattered in the Ganges River. In one major poll, Indians revealed that drinking water was one of their major life activities to improve their well-being.[12] Indians' sensitivity to the subject of water has undoubtedly played a role in the public's reactions to the allegations.

COKE'S AND PEPSI'S EARLY RESPONSES

Initially, Coke and Pepsi denied the allegations of CSE and IRC, primarily through the media. It was observed that their response was limited at best as they got caught up in the technical details of the tests. Coke conducted its own tests, the conclusion of which was that their drinks met demanding European standards.[13] Over the next several years, the debate continued as the companies questioned the studies and conducted studies of their own. The companies also pointed out that other beverages and foods in the Indian food supply, and indeed water, had trace pesticide levels in it and they sought to deflect the issue in this manner.

The IRC also attacked Coke and Pepsi for not taking the crisis seriously. They argued that the companies were "destroying lives, livelihoods, and communities" while viewing the problems in India as "public relations" problems that they could "spin" away. IRC pointed out that Coca Cola had hired a new public relations firm to help them build a new image in India, rather than addressing the real issues. According to IRC, the then-new CEO of Coke, Neville Isdell, immediately made a visit to India, but it was a "stealth" visit designed to avoid the heavy protests that would have met him had the trip been public. IRC also pointed out that Coke had just increased its marketing budget by a sizable amount in India. IRC then laid out the steps it felt Coke should take to effectively address its problems.[14]

PESTICIDE RESIDUE AND PARTIAL BANS

The controversy flared up again in August of 2006 when the CSE issued a new study. The new test results showed that 57 samples from 11 Coke and Pepsi brands contained pesticide residue levels 24 times higher than the maximum allowed by the Indian government. Public response was swift. Seven of India's 28 states imposed partial bans on the two companies, and the state of Kerala banned the drinks completely. Officials there ignored a later court ruling reversing the ban.[15] During 2006, the United Kingdom's Central Science Laboratory questioned the CSE findings Coca Cola sought a meeting with CSE that it denied. Also that year, India's Union Health Ministry rejected the CSE study as "inconclusive."

THE COMPANIES RATCHET UP THEIR RESPONSES

As a result of the second major flurry of studies and allegations in 2006, both Coke and Pepsi ratcheted up their responses, sometimes acting together, sometimes taking independent action. They responded almost like different companies than they were before. Perhaps they finally reckoned this issue was not going to go away and had to be addressed more forcefully.

Coke's Response

Coke started with a more aggressive marketing campaign. It ran three rounds of newspaper ads refuting the new study. The ads appeared in the form of a letter from more than 50 of India's company-owned and franchised Coke bottlers, claiming that their products were safe. Letters with a similar message went out to retailers and stickers were pressed onto drink coolers, declaring that Coke was "safety guaranteed." Coke also hired researchers to talk to consumers and opinion leaders to find out what exactly they believed about the allegations and what the company needed to do to convince them the allegations were false.[16]

Based on its research findings, Coke created a TV ad campaign that featured testimonials by well-respected celebrities. One of the ads featured Aamir Khan, a popular movie star, as he toured one of Coke's plants. He told the people that the product was safe and that if they wanted to see for themselves they could personally do so. In August and September 2006, over 4,000 people took him up on his offer and toured the plants. Opening up the plants sent the message that the company had nothing to hide, and this was very persuasive.[17]

The TV ads, which were targeted toward the mass audience, were followed by giant posters with movie star Khan's picture drinking a Coke. These posters appeared in public places such as bus stops. In addition, other ads were targeted toward adult women and housewives, who make the majority of the food-purchasing decisions. One teenager was especially impressed with Khan's ads because she knew he was very selective about which movies he appeared in and that he wouldn't take a position like this if it wasn't appropriate.[18]

In a later interview, Coke's CEO Isdell said he thought the company's response during the second wave of controversy was the key reason the company began turning things around. After the 2003 episode, the company changed management in India to address many of the problems, both real and imagined. The new management team was especially concerned about how it would handle its next public relations crisis. Weeks later, in December 2006, India's Health Ministry said that both Coke's and Pepsi's beverages tested in three different labs contained little or no pesticide residue.

Pepsi's Response

Pepsi's response was similar to Coke's. Pepsi decided to go straight to the Indian media and try to build relationships there. Company representatives met with editorial boards, presented its own data in press conferences, and also ran TV commercials. Pepsi's commercials featured the then president of

PepsiCo India, Rajeev Bakshi, shown walking through a polished Pepsi laboratory.[19]

In addition, Pepsi increased its efforts to cut down on water usage in its plants. Employees in the plants were organized into teams and used Japanese-inspired *kaizens* and suggested improvements to bring waste under control. The company also employed lobbying of the local government.

Indra Nooyi becomes CEO Pepsi had an advantage in rebuilding its relationships in India, because in October 2006, an Indian-born woman, Indra Nooyi, was selected to be CEO of the multinational corporation. It is not known whether Pepsi's problems in India were in any way related to her being chosen CEO, but it definitely helped. After graduating from the prestigious Indian Institute of Management, and later Yale University, Nooyi worked her way up the hierarchy at PepsiCo before being singled out for the top position.[20] She previously held positions at the Boston Consulting Group, Motorola, and ABB Group.

Prior to becoming CEO, Nooyi had a number of successes in Pepsi and became the company's chief strategist. She was said to have a perceptive business sense and an irreverent personal style. One of Nooyi's first decisions was to take a trip to India in December 2006. While there, she spoke broadly about Pepsi's programs to improve water and the environment. The Indian media loved her, beaming with pride, and covered her tour positively as she shared her own heartwarming memories of her life growing up in India. She received considerable praise. Not surprisingly, Pepsi's sales started moving upward.[21]

While all the criticism of Coke and Pepsi was going on, roughly from 2003 to 2006, both companies were pursuing corporate social responsibility (CSR) initiatives in India, many of them related to improving water resources for communities, while the conflict was center stage.

A COMMENTARY ON "WHAT'S GOING ON"

Because of all the conflicting studies and the stridency of CSE and IRC, one has to wonder what was going on in India to cause this developing country to so severely criticize giant MNCs such as Coke and Pepsi. Many developing countries would be doing all they could to appease these companies. It was speculated by a number of different observers that what was at work was a form of backlash against huge MNCs that come into countries and consume natural resources.[22] Why were these groups so hostile toward the companies? Was it really pesticides in the water and abuse of natural resources? Or was it environmental interest groups using every opportunity to bash large corporations on issues sensitive to the people? Were CSE and IRC strategically making an example of these two hugely successful companies and trying to put them in their place?

Late in 2006, an interesting commentary appeared in *BusinessWeek* exploring the topic of what has been going on in India with respect to Coke and Pepsi.[23] This commentary argued that the companies may have been singled out because they are foreign owned. It appears that no Indian soft drink companies were singled out for pesticide testing, though many people believe pesticide levels are even higher in Indian milk and bottled tea. It was pointed out that pesticide residues are present in most of India's groundwater, and the government has ignored or has been slow to move on the problem. The commentary went on to observe that Coke and Pepsi have together invested $2 billion in India over the years and have generated 12,500 jobs and support more than 200,000 indirectly through their purchases of Indian-made products including sugar, packing materials, and shipping services.[24]

CONTINUING PROTESTS, RENEWED PRIORITIES, AND STRATEGIES

Eventually, the open conflict settled down and sales took an upturn for both companies, but the issue lingered. In June 2007, the IRC continued its attacks on Coca-Cola. It accused the company of "greenwashing" its image in India.[25] The IRC staged a major protest at the new Coke Museum in Atlanta on June 30, 2007, questioning the company's human rights and environmental abuses. They erected a 20-foot banner that read "Coca-Cola Destroys Lives, Livelihoods, Communities" in front of the New World of Coke that opened in May 2007. Amit Srivastava of the IRC was quoted as saying, "This World of Coke museum is a fairy tale land and the real side of Coke is littered with abuses." A representative of the National Alliance of People's Movements, a large coalition of grassroots movements in India, said, "The museum is a shameful attempt by the Coca-Cola Company to hide its crimes."[26]

Piling On

The protestations by these groups apparently motivated other groups to take action against Coke. It was reported that United Students Against Sweatshops also staged a "die-in" around one of Coke's bottling facilities in India. And more than 20 colleges and universities in the United States, Canada, and the United Kingdom removed Coca-Cola from campuses because of student-led initiatives to put pressure on the company. In addition, the protests in Atlanta were endorsed by a host of groups that participated in the U.S. Social Forum.[27]

Coke's Renewed Priorities

Undaunted, Coca-Cola continued its initiatives to improve the situation in India and around the world. Coke faces water problems around the world because it is the key natural resource that goes into its products. The company had 70 clean-water projects in 40 countries aimed at boosting local economies. It was observed that these efforts were part of a broader strategy on the part of CEO Neville Isdell to build Coke's image as a local benefactor and a global diplomat.[28]

The criticism of Coke has been most severe in India. CEO Isdell admits that the company's experience in India has taught some humbling lessons. Isdell, who took over the company after the crisis had begun, told *The Wall Street Journal*, "It was very clear that we had not connected with the communities in the way we needed to." He indicated that the company has now made "water stewardship" a strategic priority, and in a recent 10-K securities filing, had listed a shortage of clean water as a strategic risk.[29] In August 2007, Coca-Cola India unveiled its "5-Pillar" growth strategy to strengthen its bonds with India. Coke's new strategy focuses on the pillars of People, Planet, Portfolio, Partners, and Performance. The company also announced a series of initiatives under each of the five pillars and its "Little Drops of Joy" proposal, which tries to reinforce the company's connection with stakeholders in India.[30]

Though most of the attention focused on Coca-Cola, it should also be noted that Pepsi has continued taking steps on a number of projects as well. One novel initiative is that the company now gathers rainwater in excavated lakes and ponds and on the rooftops of its bottling plants in India. The company sponsors other community water projects as well.[31]

Indian Beverage Association Formed

Though Coke and Pepsi are typically fighting each another in their longstanding "cola wars," due to their mutual problems in India they formed the Indian Beverage Association (IBA) in the summer of 2010. Other beverage companies were quick to join.[32] Because of continuous hostility from regulators and activist groups, the two companies decided that a joint effort to address issues might make sense.[33]

The IBA was formed to address the issues related to the government of Kerala's charge that Coke is polluting the groundwater in the state and other taxation issues that affect both companies. Their issues have been ongoing, but Kerala's government decided to form a tribunal against Coca-Cola, seeking $48 million in compensation claims for allegedly causing pollution and depleting the groundwater level there. Another important issue was the value-added tax (VAT) by the Delhi government. The IBA brought in other bottlers and packaging firms that had similar interests and issues in India.[34]

WATER ISSUES CONTINUE

Coke and Pepsi's issues in India, especially surrounding the issue of water, never seem to go away. Beginning in fall 2011, The India Resource Center (IRC) alleged that Pepsico's water claims have been "deception with a purpose.[35] According to the IRC, Pepsico's claims of achieving "positive water balance" are misleading and do not stand up to scrutiny. IRC accuses that Pepsico (1) severely underestimates the amount of water it uses in India, (2) has flawed water balance accounting techniques, (3) just doesn't get it that water issues are local issues in India, (4) has one in four of its plants operating in a water stressed area, and (5) lacks commitment to local water stewardship in India.[36]

In 2012–2013, the IRC's campaigns against Coca-Cola continued as well. According to IRC, fifteen village councils (panchayats) have called upon their government to reject Coca-Cola's application for expansion because it would further worsen the water conditions in the area. They have also called for an end to Coca-Cola's current groundwater extraction in Mehdiganj in Varanasi district in India. The 15 village councils are located within a 5-km radius of the Coca-Cola bottling plant and are affected by Coca-Cola's bottling operations.[37] For the past several years, and on a continuing basis, the IRC has been extremely activist toward Coca-Cola and continues its "Campaign to Hold Coca-Cola Accountable."[38]

In February 2016, Coke announced that it was closing a bottling plant in north India. Activists campaigning against the plant said that the facility was depleting groundwater and undermining agriculture in the area.[39] The opposition to Coke was led by the Indian Resource Center and several other activist groups that have been targeting the company for well over a decade. One activist claimed that "Coke has drained us of water." He went on to say that "water meant for poor farmers and their fields was time and again diverted to the factory."[40] A Coca-Cola spokesman in India said that the plant only uses a miniscule share of the water there and that it was using less than 1 percent of the area's water.[41] For Coke, the plant closure was the most recent challenge the company faced in India, the company's sixth largest market by sales volume. In spite of the challenges, Coca-Cola said it planned to inject $5 billion into the country by the year 2020.[42]

In May 2016, PepsiCo was put on notice that it is contributing to the water shortage in parts of India and the company is being asked to stop its operations for some months until the situation improves.[43]

QUESTIONS FOR DISCUSSION

1. Identify the ongoing issues in this case with respect to global business ethics, issue management, crisis management, and stakeholder management. Rank these in terms of their priorities for Coca-Cola and for PepsiCo.
2. Assess the corporate social responsibility (CSR) of Coke and Pepsi in India.
3. Are these companies ignoring their responsibilities in India, or is something else at work?
4. Why does it seem that Coke has become a larger and more frequent target than Pepsi in India? Does having an Indian-born CEO help Pepsi's case?
5. How do companies defend themselves against the nonstop allegations of activist groups that have made them a target? Is any form of stakeholder management workable?
6. IRC seems to have made it its life's work to defeat Coca-Cola. Is IRC an interest group that has just gone too far?
7. What lessons do Coke and Pepsi's experiences in India present for multinationals in their global business and society relationships? Enumerate three to five lessons and give examples from the case to document them.

ENDNOTES

1. "Beyond India, More Battles," *BusinessWeek* (June 11, 2007), 52.
2. Annie Chernish, "Is Water the Next Resource Crisis?" PRI, http://www.pri.org/stories/2016-02-18/water-next-resource-crisis. Accessed May 27, 2016.
3. Duane D. Stanford, "Coke's PR Offensive in India Pays Off," *Atlanta Journal Constitution* (December 3, 2006), D1, D9.
4. Diane Brady, "Pepsi: Repairing a Poisoned Reputation in India," *BusinessWeek* (June 11, 2007), 50.
5. Amit Srivastava, "Communities Reject Coca-Cola in India," *India Resource Center* (July 10, 2003), http://www.corpwatch.org/article.php?id=7508. Accessed May 27, 2016.
6. Ibid.
7. Ibid.
8. Stanford, D1.
9. Diane Brady, "Pepsi: Repairing a Poisoned Reputation in India," *BusinessWeek* (June 11, 2007), 46–54.
10. Ibid.
11. Sunita Narain, *Time*, http://www.time.com/time/specials/2007/article/0,28804,1652689_1652372_1652366,00.html. Accessed June 6, 2013.
12. Brady, 50.
13. Stanford, D9.
14. "Campaign to Hold Coca-Cola Accountable: Coca-Cola Crisis in India," *India Resource Center* (2004), http://www.indiaresource.org/campaigns/coke/. Accessed June 11, 2016.
15. Stanford, D9.
16. Stanford, D9.
17. Ibid.
18. Ibid.
19. Brady, 54.
20. Ibid., 46.
21. Ibid., 54.
22. Ibid., 48.
23. Brian Bremner, Nandini Lakshman, and Diane Brady, "Commentary India: Behind the Scare over Pesticides in Pepsi and Coke," *BusinessWeek* (September 4, 2006), 43.
24. Ibid.
25. New America Media, "Coke Accused of 'Greenwashing' Its Image in India" (June 8, 2007),

http://www.indybay.org/newsitems/2007/06/08/18426206.php. Accessed June 6, 2013.

26. India Resource Center, "Major Protest at Coke Museum in Atlanta" (June 30, 2007), http://www.indiaresource.org/news/2007/1049.html. Accessed May 27, 2016.
27. Ibid.
28. Betsy McKay, "Why Coke Aims to Slake Global Thirst for Safe Water," *The Wall Street Journal* (March 15), 2007.
29. Ibid.
30. Ibid.
31. McKay.
32. India Beverage Association, http://www.in-beverage.org/aboutiba.htm. Accessed May 27, 2016.
33. Anuradha Shukla, "Taxation Issues Bring Arch Rivals Coke and Pepsi on the Same Platform," *India Today* (July 6, 2010), http://indiatoday.intoday.in/story/taxation-issues-bring-archrivals-coke-&-pepsi-on-same-platform/1/104338.html. Accessed May 27, 2016.
34. Ibid.
35. India Resource Center, November 30, 2011, "Deception with Purpose: Pepsico's Water Claims in India," http://www.indiaresource.org/news/2011/pepsipositivewater.html. Accessed May 27, 2016.
36. Ibid.
37. India Resource Center, "Coca Cola," http://www.indiaresource.org/. Accessed May 27, 2016.
38. India Resource Center, "Campaign to Hold Coca-Cola Accountable," Campaign to Hold Coca-Cola Accountable: Coca-Cola Crisis in India. Accessed May 27, 2016.
39. Preetika Rana, "Coca-Cola Closes Plant in India," *Wall Street Journal* (February 10, 2016), http://www.wsj.com/articles/coca-cola-closes-plant-in-india-1455122537. Accessed May 27, 2016.
40. Ibid.
41. Ibid.
42. Ibid.
43. "After Coke, Palakaad now Wants PepsiCo to Shut Its Plant due to Water Crisis," *The Economic Times*, http://articles.economictimes.indiatimes.com/2016-05-11/news/72987643_1_pepsico-india-pepsi-co-india-water-exploitation. Accessed May 27, 2016.

CASE 17

Chiquita: An Excruciating Dilemma between Life and Law*

AN ETHICAL DILEMMA

Assume that you are the top executive for a firm doing business in Colombia, South America. If a known terrorist group threatens to kill your employees unless you pay extortion money, should the company pay it?

If you answer "no," how would you respond to the family of an employee who is later killed by the terrorist group?

If you answer "yes," how would you respond to the family of an innocent citizen who is killed by a bomb your money funded?[1]

*This case was written by Archie B. Carroll, University of Georgia. Updated in 2016.

BACKGROUND

In many parts of the world, doing business is a dangerous proposition. Such has been the case in the country of Colombia in South America. The danger has been described in the following way: "In Colombia's notoriously lawless countryside, narco-terrorists ran roughshod over the forces of law and order—or collaborated with them in a mutual game of shakedowns, kidnappings, and murders."[2] Foreign companies that choose to do business in many parts of the world are easy targets. These companies have resources, they care about their employees, and many of them have been willing to negotiate with terrorists and just consider it one of the costs of doing business. Security in many of these countries is available only at a price.[3]

Formerly known as United Fruit Company and then United Brands, Chiquita Brands International, based in Cincinnati, Ohio, has faced the kind of situation described above. Today, Chiquita is a global food company that employs more than 20,000 employees across 70 countries in six different continents. The company has strong brand name recognition and premium positioning in the United States and Europe and operates with solid logistics and an efficient supply chain.[4]

BUYING SECURITY: PROTECTING ITS' EMPLOYEES

According to then-CEO Fernando Aguirre, Chiquita started making payments to paramilitary groups in Colombia beginning in 1997 and extending into 2004. The payments came to a total of about $1.7 million. The company felt it was forced to make these payments because the lives of its employees were at stake.[5] During the period 2001–2004, the company was making payments to the terrorist group United Self-Defense Forces of Colombia (AUC). AUC was the group's Spanish acronym, by which the group was primarily known. A major complication during this period was that the U.S. government had declared AUC to be a specially designated terrorist organization, making it illegal to provide funds for them, and the Bush Administration had vowed to go after any company that funded terrorist groups.[6]

CHIQUITA TURNS ITSELF IN

Chiquita turned itself in and reported to the government that it had made the payments to AUC during the years indicated.

In 2007, CEO Fernando Aguirre released a public statement outlining what he called "an excruciating dilemma between life and law."[7] Following are some excerpts from his statement:

- In February 2003, senior management of Chiquita Brands International learned that protection payments the company had been making to paramilitary groups in Colombia to keep our workers safe from the violence committed by those groups were illegal under U.S. law.
- The company had operated in Colombia for nearly a century, generating 4,400 direct and an additional 8,000 indirect jobs. We contributed almost $70 million annually to the Colombian economy in the form of capital expenditures, payroll, taxes, social security, pensions, and local purchases of goods and services.
- However, during the 1990s, it became increasingly difficult to protect our workforce. Among the hundreds of documented attacks by left- and right-wing paramilitaries were the 1995 massacre of 28 innocent Chiquita employees who were ambushed on a bus on their way to work, and the 1998 assassination of two more of our workers on a farm while their colleagues were forced to watch.
- Despite the harsh realities on the ground, the discovery that our payments were violating U.S. law created a dilemma of more than theoretical proportions for us: the company could stop making the payments, complying with the law but putting the lives of our workers in immediate jeopardy; or we could keep our workers out of harm's way while violating American law.[8]
- Each alternative was unpalatable and unacceptable. So the company decided to do what we believe any responsible citizen should do under the circumstances: We went to the U.S. Department of Justice and voluntarily disclosed the facts and the predicament. The U.S. government had no knowledge of the payments and, had we not come forward ourselves, it is entirely possible that the payments would have remained unknown to American authorities to this day.[9]

In a plea deal, the company was fined $25 million, and in September 2007 it made its first installment payment of $5 million. Chiquita's general counsel said that "this was a difficult situation for the company and that the company had to do it to protect the wellbeing of our employees and their families." The Department of Justice prosecutor called the payments "morally repugnant" and said that the protection payments "fueled violence everywhere else."[10]

BOARD KNOWLEDGE REVEALED

During the investigation of this incident, it was discovered that the Board of Directors of the company came to know that the questionable payments were going on. A prosecution document, according to the *Miami Herald*, presented the following timeline of events:[11]

2000—Chiquita's audit committee, composed of board members, heard about the payments and took no action.

2002—Soon after AUC had been designated a terrorist organization; a Chiquita employee learned about this and alerted the company.

2003—Chiquita consulted with a Washington attorney who told the company, "Bottom line: Cannot make the payment."

2003—Two months later, Chiquita executives reported to the full board of directors that the company was still making payments. One board member objected and the directors agreed to make the payments known to the Department of Justice.

CHIQUITA'S SOCIAL RESPONSIBILITY INITIATIVES

An interesting description of the company's track record in the area of corporate social responsibility (CSR) makes this case particularly unusual. Jon Entine's account of Chiquita's turnaround as a company is enlightening. Apparently, Chiquita spent at least 15 years living down its longstanding reputation as a "ruthless puppeteer manipulating corrupt Latin American banana republics."[12] Once operating as United Fruit, the company began turning itself around in 1990 and remade itself into a model food distributor, complete with high environmental and ethical standards.

Better Banana Project

In the early 1990s, the company separated itself from its competitors by teaming up with the Rainforest Alliance on sustainability and labor standards. This became known as the Better Banana Project.[13] Rainforest Alliance had the following to say about Chiquita's adoption of the Better Banana Project, "The Rainforest Alliance monitors and verifies that Chiquita's farms abide by strong environmental and social standards, which have positive impacts on rural communities and tropical landscape."[14] The Better Banana Project's ability to be responsive to environmental concerns without threatening the livelihood of companies and employees earned it the 1995 Peter F. Drucker Award for Nonprofit Innovation. Chiquita also became well known through its publications of its corporate social responsibility reports. The company issued public reports on its CSR efforts each year starting in 2000.[15]

Regarding its CSR initiatives and payments to terrorist groups, CEO Fernando Aguirre pointed to the fact that the company came forward voluntarily to disclose the payments to the paramilitaries as an indication that Chiquita is "completely committed to corporate responsibility and compliance."[16] He noted too that the voluntary action involved considerable cost. In June 2004, Chiquita sold its Colombian farms at a loss of $9 million in order to bring closure to the issue and remove itself from a difficult situation.[17] The company settled its case with the U.S. Justice Department for $25 million.[18]

LAWSUITS AGAINST CHIQUITA

After this, Chiquita faced a host of lawsuits related to its time in Colombia. These included one from three U.S. citizens who survived a five-year hostage ordeal by Colombia's notorious FARC paramilitary group.[19] The employees' lawsuit suggested that Chiquita's connection with FARC may have been more proactive than just paying protection money. The suit also claimed that Chiquita used its network of local transportation contractors to transport weapons to the group.[20]

These same charges have propelled the largest lawsuit, based on the Alien Torts Claims Act (ATCA), filed by family members of thousands of Colombians who were tortured or killed by paramilitaries in Colombia. Cases from around the country were consolidated and put before a South Florida federal judge.[21] Chiquita asked the judge to dismiss the case arguing that, as a victim of extortion, Chiquita was not responsible for the crimes that the paramilitary groups committed.[22] U.S. District Judge Kenneth A Marra granted Chiquita's motion to dismiss terrorism-related claim; however, he allowed the plaintiffs to move forward with claims against Chiquita for torture, war crimes, and crimes against humanity.[23] If the plaintiffs succeed, the cost to Chiquita could be in the billions.[24] In 2014, Chiquita won dismissal of this lawsuit by 4,000 Colombians who sought to hold the company responsible for the deaths relatives. The court said it lacked the power to review the claims because all relevant conduct took place outside the United States and that Chiquita's mere presence in the United States did not confer jurisdiction.[25]

A TALE OF TWO COMPANIES

The Chiquita payment controversy has been called a "tale of two companies."[26] One face of Chiquita comes across as a defiant, secretive multinational, with lots of resources, determined to break the law to keep its employees safe and its businesses running. The other face of Chiquita builds partnerships with groups such as Rainforest Alliance to support the

Better Banana Project and issues frequent corporate social responsibility reports to keep its stakeholders pleased and informed. The company tried to extricate itself by turning itself in, paying a huge fine, suffering tremendous embarrassment and loss of reputational capital, and finally selling its farms to help reach closure. Which is the real Chiquita?

QUESTIONS FOR DISCUSSION

1. Go to the ethical dilemma at the beginning of the case. Which position did you take and why? Did your position change after you read the case?
2. Was Chiquita justified in making the extortion payments to protect its employees? Was the company really between a rock and a hard place? What should it have done differently?
3. Using your knowledge of business ethics and global practices, what concepts, principles, or ideas from your study have a bearing on this case? Explain how some of them might have guided Chiquita toward better decisions.
4. What is your assessment of then-CEO Aguirre's statements? Did he come across as sincere or just making excuses?
5. What is your analysis of the Chiquita board of directors' handling of this case? Do you think selling the farms at a loss in Colombia was the right thing to do? Why?
6. If you were the judge in the consolidated case, what would you decide?
7. In the "tale of two companies," which do you think is the real Chiquita and why?

ENDNOTES

1. Denis Collins, Edgewood College, Madison, Wisconsin, posed these questions in an e-mail to an International Association for Business and Society ListServ discussing the Chiquita Banana situation, on June 18, 2007. Used with permission.
2. Rushworth M. Kidder, "Ethical Bananas," *Ethics Newsline* (March 19, 2007), a publication of the Institute for Global Ethics, http://www.globalethics.org/newsline/2007/03/19/. Accessed May 27, 2016.
3. Ibid.
4. "Chiquita Brands International, Inc. SWOT Analysis." *Chiquita Brands International SWOT Analysis* (2012), 1–8, http://www.marketresearch.com/MarketLine-v3883/Chiquita-Brands-International-SWOT-6552405/. Accessed May 27, 2016.
5. Kidder.
6. Jane Bussey, "Chiquita Disregarded Warnings, Records Show," *The Miami Herald* (April 16, 2007).
7. Fernando Aguirre, "An Excruciating Dilemma between Life and Law: Corporate Responsibility in a Zone of Conflict," *The Corporate Citizen* (U.S. Chamber of Commerce, April 2007), 1–2.
8. Ibid.
9. Ibid.
10. Pablo Bachelet, "Chiquita Pays Fine for Supporting Colombian Terrorist Group," McClatchy Washington Bureau, McClatchy Newspapers, http://www.mcclatchydc.com/news/nation-world/world/article24469555.html#.Ua4Fe9LVB8E. Accessed May 27, 2016.
11. Jane Bussey, "Documents: Chiquita Paid up Despite Warnings," *Miami Herald* (April 17, 2007), http://www.miamiherald.com/news/nation-world/world/americas/article1927938.html. Accessed May 27, 2016.
12. Jon Entine, "Chiquita Counts the Cost of Honesty," *Ethical Corporation* (May 2007), 74.
13. Ibid.
14. Earth Times, "The Rainforest Alliance Helps Chiquita Produce a Better Banana and Transforms an Industry," http://www.sdearthtimes.com/et1200/et1200s10.html. Accessed May 27, 2016.
15. Chiquita, "Corporate Social Responsibility Reports," http://www.chiquita.com/The-Chiquita-Difference/Reports.aspx. Accessed May 27, 2016.
16. *The Corporate Citizen* (April 2007)
17. Ibid.
18. Associated Press, "Chiquita Settles Case on Payments to Rebel Groups," *The New York Times* (March 15, 2007), http://www.nytimes.com/2007/03/15/business/worldbusiness/15bananas.html?ref=chiquitabrandsinternationalinc. Accessed May 27, 2016.
19. Daniel Tencer, "Lawsuit: Chiquita Fruit Company Funded Death Squads in Colombia," *The Raw Story* (April 7, 2010), http://www.rawstory.com/rs/2010/04/07/chiquita-funded-death-squads-colombia/. Accessed May 27, 2016.

20. Ibid.
21. Associated Press, "Chiquita Sued over Colombian Paramilitary Payments," May 30, 2011, http://www.syracuse.com/news/index.ssf/2011/05/chiquita_sued_over_colombian_p.html. Accessed May 27, 2016.
22. CNN Wire Staff, "Florida Judge Allows Suits against Chiquita to Move Forward," *CNNWorld* (June 4, 2011), http://www.cnn.com/2011/WORLD/americas/06/03/florida.colombia.chiquita.lawsuits/index.html. Accessed May 27, 2016. 2013.
23. Ibid.
24. Anderson. http://www.reuters.com/article/chiquita-colombia-decision-idUSL2N0PZ28P20140724. Accessed May 27, 2016.
25. Jonathan Stempl, "Chiquita Wins Dismissal of U.S. Lawsuits over Colombian Abuses," *Reuters* (July 24, 2014).
26. Jon Entine, 74.

CASE 18

The Betaseron® Decision (A)[1]

The United States Food and Drug Administration's (FDA) approval of interferon beta-1b (brand name Betaseron®) made it the first multiple sclerosis (MS) treatment to get FDA approval in 25 years. Betaseron was developed by Berlex Laboratories, a U.S. unit of Schering AG, the German pharmaceutical company. Berlex handled the clinical development, trials, and marketing of the drug, while Chiron Corporation, a biotechnology firm based in California, manufactured it. The groundbreaking approval of Betaseron represented not only a great opportunity for Berlex but a dilemma. Supplies were insufficient to meet initial demand, and shortages were forecast for three years. With insufficient supplies and staggering development costs, how would Berlex allocate and price the drug?

THE CHALLENGE OF MULTIPLE SCLEROSIS

MS is a disease of the central nervous system that interferes with the brain's ability to control functions such as seeing, walking, and talking. The nerve fibers in the brain and spinal cord are surrounded by myelin, a fatty substance that protects the nerve fibers in the same way that insulation protects electrical wires. When the myelin insulation becomes damaged, the ability of the central nervous system to transmit nerve impulses to and from the brain becomes impaired. With MS, there are sclerosed (i.e., scarred or hardened) areas in multiple parts of the brain and spinal cord when the immune system mistakenly attacks the myelin sheath.

The Impact of MS

The symptoms of MS depend to some extent on the location and size of the sclerosis. Symptoms may include numbness, slurred speech, blurred vision, poor coordination, muscle weakness, bladder dysfunction, extreme fatigue, and paralysis. There is no way to know how the disease will progress for any individual, because the nature of the disease can change. Some people will have a relatively benign course of MS with only one or two mild attacks, nearly complete remission, and no permanent disability. Others will have a chronic progressive course resulting in severe disability. A third group displays the most typical pattern, which is periods of exacerbations, when the disease is active, and periods of remission, when the symptoms recede, yet generally leave some damage. People with MS live with an exceptionally high degree of uncertainty because their disease can change from one day to the next. Dramatic downturns as well as dramatic recoveries are not uncommon.

[1]This case was prepared by Ann K. Buchholtz, Rutgers University.

This case was written from public sources, solely for the purpose of stimulating class discussion. All events are real. The author thanks Dr. Stephen Reingold, Vice President Research and Medical Programs at the National Multiple Sclerosis Society, and Avery Rockwell, Chapter Services Associate of the Greater Connecticut Chapter of the Multiple Sclerosis Society, for their helpful comments.

THE PROMISE OF BETASERON

Interferon beta is a naturally occurring protein that regulates the body's immune system. Betaseron is composed of interferon beta-1b that has been genetically engineered and laboratory manufactured as a recombinant product. Although other interferons (i.e., alpha and gamma) had been tested, only beta interferon had been shown, through large-scale trials, to affect MS. Because it is an immunoregulatory agent, Betaseron was believed to combat the immune problems that make MS worse. However, the exact way in which it works was yet to be determined.

Research

In clinical studies, Betaseron was shown to reduce the frequency and severity of exacerbations in ambulatory MS patients with a relapsing-remitting form of the disease. It did not reverse damage nor did it completely prevent exacerbations. However, Betaseron could dramatically improve the quality of life for the person with MS. For example, people taking Betaseron were shown to have fewer and shorter hospitalizations. Betaseron represented the first and only drug to have an effect on the frequency of exacerbations.

Administration

Betaseron is administered subcutaneously (under the skin) every other day by self-injection. To derive the most benefits from the therapy, it was important that the MS patient maintain a regular schedule of the injections. Some flu-like side-effects, as well as swelling and irritation around the injection, had been noted. However, these side-effects tended to decrease with time on treatment. In addition, one person who received Betaseron committed suicide, while three others attempted it. Because MS often leads to depression, there was no way to know whether the administration of Betaseron was a factor. Last, Betaseron was not recommended for use during pregnancy.

THE BETASERON DILEMMA

FDA approval for Betaseron allowed physicians to prescribe the drug to MS patients who were ambulatory and had a relapsing-remitting course of MS. An estimated one-third of the 300,000 people with MS in the United States fell into that category, resulting in a potential client base of 100,000. The expedited FDA approval process for Betaseron took only 1 year instead of the customary 3. As a result, Berlex was unprepared to manufacture and distribute the treatment. Chiron Corporation had been making the drug in small quantities for experimental use and did not have the manufacturing facilities to handle the expected explosion in demand. Chiron estimated that it would have enough of the drug for about 12,000–20,000 people by the end of the year. By the end of the second year, Chiron expected to be able to provide the drug to 40,000 patients. Depending on demand, it might take about three years to provide the drug to all patients who requested it. Chiron's expanded manufacturing represented the only option for Berlex because the process required for another company to get FDA approval to manufacture the drug would take even longer.

Pricing

In addition to availability, price was a concern because successes must fund the failures that precede them. Betaseron represented years of expensive, risky research by highly trained scientists in modern research facilities. Furthermore, genetically engineered drugs were extremely expensive to manufacture. In the case of Betaseron, a human interferon gene is inserted into bacteria, resulting in a genetically engineered molecule. The stringent quality controls on the procedure take time and are expensive. As a result, the price of Betaseron was expected to be about $10,000 per year for each patient.

Betaseron brought great hope to people with MS and a great quandary to Berlex. How should Berlex handle the supply limitations, the distribution, and the pricing of this drug?

QUESTIONS FOR DISCUSSION

1. What are the ethical issues in this situation? Which issues must Berlex consider first when determining how to distribute Betaseron?
2. Given the shortage of the drug, how should Berlex decide who receives it and who waits? Give a specific plan.
3. How should Berlex handle the logistics of distribution?
4. How should Berlex determine the drug's relative pricing (assume the drug costs about $12,000 per year)?
5. Who, if anyone, should be involved in the decision making?

CASE 19

Should Directors Shine Light on Dark Money?*

Recent election cycles have brought new challenges for corporations and their boards of directors. For example, in the 2016 presidential election campaign, candidate Hillary Clinton unveiled a prescription drug plan to lower prescription prices following the Turing Pharmaceutical price gouging scandal. Yet ironically, the pharmaceutical industry was one of the most generous industry donators to her campaign, as well as those of the other candidates.[1] In fact, the health industry overall (including health professionals, hospitals, HMOs, and pharmaceutical companies) donated over $10 million to the presidential candidates by spring of 2016.[2] In essence, the pharmaceutical companies and health-care professionals spent money to promote policies that went against their own financial interests.

This happened in congressional elections as well. In 2010, the pharmaceutical industry's trade group, PhRMA, donated funds to nonprofit groups that used those funds to help elect 23 representatives who subsequently voted to limit access to contraceptives. Some of those funds came from firms like Pfizer, Bayer, and Merck—all manufacturers of contraceptives.[3]

Political spending is also an issue with individual companies. Target Corporation, a company that had positioned itself as an LGBT-friendly corporation, found itself the target of angry employees and customers when they learned about Target's political spending. Target, a sponsor of the annual Twin Cities Gay Pride Festival, donated money to a business group that supported an antigay rights candidate for Minnesota governor. Angry employees and consumers conducted protests outside Target stores and threatened a boycott.[4]

These examples show how political spending can have dramatic consequences for corporations. Politicians take positions on a range of policies and so the same politician may hold some positions that support and other positions that damage a corporation's best interests. This problem was exacerbated when the U.S. Supreme Court's *Citizen United* decision changed the political spending landscape for corporations. Before that decision, political spending was constrained to political action committees (PACs), and PAC political activity had to be disclosed to the FEC (Federal Election Commission). Now firms can make unlimited contributions directly to candidates or indirectly to 501c4 nonprofits and trade associations, who can then hide both the donors who provided the money and the way the money was spent. Firms are now freer to become politically involved but, as Target and the pharmaceutical companies found out, that freedom comes with risk. Shareholders and other stakeholders are asking firms to be transparent in their political spending. They want to judge those expenditures for themselves to avoid agency problems and other conflicts of interest.

Ira M. Millstein, founder of the Ira M. Millstein Center for Global Markets and Corporate Ownership at Columbia Law School, proposes a new policy for boards of directors to follow in this new landscape. He suggests that (1) companies should require trade associations of which they are members to report to them on their political spending, (2) companies should require trade associations of which they are members to disclose the donors who provide the money for their political spending, and (3) companies should then disclose the information they receive from their trade associations when they disclose their other spending to shareholders and other stakeholders.[5]

QUESTIONS FOR DISCUSSION

1. What is your reaction to the problem of political spending? What would you do if you were the CEO of a pharmaceutical company? Would you still belong to PhRMA? Would your membership have any conditions attached?
2. What is your reaction to the Target situation? How would you handle it if you were the CEO?
3. Do you agree with Ira Millstein? Should companies require trade associations to disclose this information before they join? Should companies then disclose the information they receive? If a trade association refuses to provide that information, should the company refuse to join?

*This case was written by Ann K. Buchholtz, Rutgers University. Updated in 2016 by Jill A. Brown, Bentley University.

ENDNOTES

1. Nadia Kounang, "Big Pharma's Big Donations to 2016 Presidential Candidates," *CNN* (February 11, 2016), http://www.cnn.com/2016/02/11/health/big-pharma-presidential-politics/
2. Ibid.
3. See Bruce F. Freed and Karl Sandstrom, "Political Spending: Directors Responsible for Protecting Companies," *Directors and Boards* (July 2013); Bruce F. Freed and Karl Sandstrom, "How Dark Money Is Distorting Politics and Undermining Democracy," *The Fiscal Times* (February 24, 2015), http://rebootamerica.thefiscaltimes.com/index.php/how-dark-money-is-distorting-politics-and-undermining-democracy/; Jonathan D. Salant, "Merck, Pfizer Back Lawmakers Who Oppose Company Products," *Bloomberg* (May 31, 2012), http://www.bloomberg.com/news/2012-05-31/merck-pfizer-back-lawmakers-who-oppose-company-products.html. Accessed June 7, 2016. Center for Political Accountability, "The 2015 CPA-Zicklin Index," http://www.politicalaccountability.net/index.php?ht=a/GetDocumentAction/i/1433. Accessed June 9, 2016.
4. Brian Bakst, "Target Apologizes for Political Donation in Minnesota," *USA Today* (August 5, 2010), http://usatoday30.usatoday.com/money/industries/retail/2010-08-05-target-campaign-donation_N.htm. Accessed June 7, 2016
5. Bruce F. Freed, "Report on the Proceedings of the Roundtable on Corporate Political Accountability: The Importance of Educating Future Business Leaders Post-Citizens United," (February 14–15, 2013), http://files.cfpa.gethifi.com/reports/cpa-reports/Roundtable_Report.pdf, Accessed June 11, 2016

CASE 20

Big Pharma's Marketing Tactics*

"Big Pharma" is the name the business press uses for the gigantic pharmaceutical industry. Most of us are familiar with Big Business and Big Government. Now Big Pharma continues to be in the news and has been for several years regarding its marketing, advertising, pricing, and sales tactics. The pharmaceutical industry has been under attack by consumers and patient groups for well over a decade now. But, in 2015 and 2016, two companies, Valeant Pharmaceuticals International and Turing Pharmaceuticals, became headliners in an issue that has touched many families and has energized a national debate about the drug industry and especially drug pricing.

Valeant would buy patents for unique, lifesaving drugs, raise their prices steeply and watch the profits roll in.[1] While raising prices is a common industry practice, it all boils down to the degree. Valeant was doubling and tripling its prices of new drugs, while other companies used smaller price hikes imposed over a number of years. Valeant got into trouble because it didn't follow the industry practice called the rule of three. If you are raising prices, do it quietly, modestly and over time.[2] The immediate response was outrage by the public and some members of Congress. In 2015, drug companies jacked up the prices on their brand-name products an average of 16.2 percent.[3]

In 2015, Turing Pharmaceuticals and its 32-year-old founder and CEO Martin Shkreli, bought a drug named Daraprim and quickly raised its price more than 5,000 percent.[4] Shkreli, a former hedge fund manager, quickly drew the wrath of consumers and has since been called the "bad boy" of Big Pharma.[5] Shkreli's tactics became a talking point during the 2016 presidential elections, and Bernie Sanders even refused to take his $2,700 campaign donation and turned it over to a health clinic.[6] Mr. Shkreli is now the subject of congressional hearings into skyrocketing drug prices.[7] The Valeant and Turing cases are just part of the recent backdrop in the continuing controversial pharmaceutical industry.

As *Time* magazine has stated, it's hard to empathize with the drug industry these days because of the

*This case was written and revised by Archie B. Carroll, University of Georgia. Updated in 2016.

high cost of our prescriptions. We either just emptied our wallets in paying for our latest prescription or some consumers just returned on a Greyhound bus from Canada, where we bought our prescriptions for less.[8] Consistently negative public perceptions of the pharmaceutical industry add to its problems. Big Pharma has ranked negatively in the eyes of the public for well over a decade, and the positive views of the industry dropped from 40 percent in 2014 to 35 percent in 2015.[9]

Big Pharma has been aware that it faces challenges to its marketing, pricing, and sales tactics. One gets the impression that the industry does not try to repair its negative image as much as it calls upon its huge army of lobbyists in Washington, DC to protect its interests. According to the Center for Responsive Politics, Big Pharma had just over 1,000 lobbyists at work in 2016 and has spent about $24 million annually in lobbying expenses over the past several years.[10] Though the public values the drugs the industry makes available for sale, increasingly, the multibillion dollar industry's social responsibilities and business ethics are being questioned.[11]

THE PHARMACEUTICAL INDUSTRY

The pharmaceutical industry is one of the healthiest and wealthiest in America. However, astronomical drug prices recently have continued to result in push back against the industry. For example, of 12 cancer drugs released in 2012, 11 of them cost more than $100,000. More and more drugs are being offered at this level of pricing, and the more they get away with it the more it becomes a standard that emboldens the companies to push the envelope on pricing. Anger is percolating about this level of pricing.[12]

The top pharmaceutical companies, according to Fortune's 2015 sales data, include the familiar names, with the most profitable at the top of the list:[13]

1. Johnson & Johnson
2. Pfizer
3. Merck
4. Gilead Sciences
5. Amgen
6. Abb Vie
7. Eli Lilly
8. Bristol-Meyers Squibb
9. Biogen
10. Celgene

Among this group, only Johnson & Johnson (J&J) was ranked among *Fortune*'s "most admired companies in the world in 2016."[14] And, in spite of its relatively high ranking (#15), J&J has increasingly been under the gun in recent years as allegations of questionable marketing of its products have come to light and resulted in huge settlements. For example, in 2013, J&J paid $2.2 billion to settle charges of illegally marketing Risperdal, which was once the company's top-selling drugs before generic versions hit the market.[15] One of the charges against J&J was that it was encouraging the use of Risperdal for elderly nursing home patients suffering from dementia though such a use had not been approved by health regulators and could prove to be life-threatening. J&J disputed the accusations and said that its settlement was not an admission of wrongdoing or liability.[16]

Depending on the study considered and how expenses are calculated, the pharmaceutical industry spends much more on advertising than on research and development.[17] In spite of its size and success, Big Pharma has been called into question for a number of years now for its questionable marketing, advertising, pricing, and sales techniques. The charges have included questionable direct-to-consumers (DTC) advertising (see Case 5) and dubious ethics, and a number of them have resulted in lawsuits. It seems quite amazing, actually, that the pharmaceutical industry has not been more in the spotlight than it has been.

By one estimate, Big Pharma has paid out more than $30 billion during the past decade to resolve government allegations and to settle criminal and civil lawsuits involving illegal marketing practices, Medicaid overcharges, and kickbacks.[18] Dr. Eric Campbell, a medical school professor, has stated that the settlements and fines these companies pay "far outstrip any penalties they pay."[19] Campbell argues that the pharmaceutical firms view these payments as a cost of doing business and this appears to be the business model the firms are using.[20]

SALESMANSHIP OVER SCIENCE

An overall criticism of Big Pharma is that the industry has abandoned science for salesmanship.[21] That is, the industry has become more concerned with pushing pills for whatever problem than for developing new and important drugs. An example of this was provided in the aggressive marketing by Novartis of its fourth biggest selling drug. Was this drug a life-saver? No, it's Lamisil, a pill for toenail fungus. Yes, toenail fungus can turn a nail yellow, but apparently no one has died of this illness. On the other hand, a few people may have died taking the drug as regulators linked the drug to at least 16 cases of liver failure, including 11 deaths. Novartis claimed most of these patients had preexisting illnesses or were on other drugs.[22]

Many patients taking Lamisil were enticed to the drug by a grotesque cartoon creature named Digger the Dermatophyte, who is a squat, yellowish character with a dumb-guy big city accent. In the TV ads, Digger lifts a toenail, creeps beneath it, and declares, "I'm not leavin'!"[23] One group calculated that Novartis spent $236 million on Lamisil ads over three years, but Novartis denies this figure. In the first run of the commercial, Digger is crushed by a giant Lamisil tablet. Regulators thought the ad so overstated the drug's benefits that the company had to pull that particular version of the ad. It has been reported that the drug cured the problem in only 38 percent of patients, but Lamisil's sales increased 19 percent after it.[24] In short, it was alleged that the industry spends a fortune on remedies to cure trivial maladies, while its drug research pipelines are running dry. This has been dubbed "salesmanship over science."[25] Others have said it represents marketing and profits being considered more important than consumer safety and wellness.[26]

Another way pharmaceutical firms emphasize sales over science was illustrated in when the *New York Times* revealed that drug giant SmithKline Beecham had secretly compared its own diabetes drug, Avandia, to a competing medicine, Actos, which was produced by Takeda. The company discovered that its own drug was riskier, but the company spent the next 11 years trying to cover up the results. According to the *New York Times,* sales of Avandia were crucial to the company and the company failed to disclose the research so that it could keep making money.[27] Once again, sales trumped science. After an investigation, the FDA review panel recommended that the drug should be kept on the market.[28]

PROMOTIONS TO MED STUDENTS

Big Pharma starts its promotional techniques while the doctors are still students in medical school. There the med students have in the past received free lunches, pens, notepads, and other gifts that are given by the companies. The companies start early trying to persuade the young doctors-to-be to prescribe their products by inundating them with logo-infested products and other gifts. Some medical students have become fed up with the practice and have resisted the free gifts and have started movements to stop the practice from occurring in the first place.

One med student, Jaya Agrawal, launched a national campaign calling on students to sign a pledge saying they would not accept drug-industry gifts. Medical students on other campuses have organized seminars and lectures on the issue. Agrawal was reminded of how difficult it would be to get everyone to think like her when she moved into an apartment she was planning to share with two other med students and noticed a Big Pharma logo on a clock in three rooms of the apartment.[29]

In recent years, some med schools have banned pharmaceutical reps from giving gifts to their students and some improvements in their graduates being more objective later in terms of prescribing medicines has been evident.[30]

CHARGES AND LAWSUITS SPAN MULTIPLE ISSUES

Pricing

Though Valeant and Turing have dominated the news recently about skyrocketing drug prices, it is an industry-wide problem. These two companies have given the entire industry a black eye and are inviting increased regulatory scrutiny.[31] *Bloomberg Businessweek* ran an article recently titled "Big Pharma's Favorite Prescription: Higher Prices."[32] Between 2006 and 2013, medication prices rose more than six times the rate of inflation and the increases do not appear to be slowing down.[33] Though many companies are raising prices more slowly, the trend has been toward higher prices at escalating rates.

What is driving prices up? Many companies raise prices just because they can. There are no simple answers. The United States has the highest drug prices in the world, and the high prices are a function of a complex set of circumstances including the complicated interplay between the insurance industry, the Affordable Care Act, Medicare, and Medicaid systems. Medicare is the single largest payer for health care in the United States and it is barred by law from negotiating directly with drug companies. As a result, the United States is a drugmakers' gold mine. According to recent statistics, the U.S. drug spending was more than twice that of France, Germany, Italy and Britain combined.[34]

Mergers and acquisitions in the drug industry have reduced the number of competitors and this has been an influential factor in drug pricing, especially among generic drugs. During the decade 2002–2013, for example, the number of drug companies making oral digoxin, a heart drug, decreased from eight to three companies. The cost soared 637 percent during this time.[35] The recent price increases of many medicines has climbed so steeply in the last couple years that some analysts see a crisis looming. More and more, insurers, health maintenance organizations, pharmacy association and patient groups are sounding the alarm that prices are becoming unsustainable.[36]

Off-Label Marketing and Prescribing

Another questionable and illegal practice that some companies are charged with involve promoting drugs for uses for which they were not approved of by the FDA or run counter to state consumer protection laws. The result of this is that doctors may be prescribing, and patients may be using, drugs for conditions for which those medicines are not needed, are not appropriate, or might hurt patients.[37]

In a huge settlement, the biotech giant Amgen agreed to pay $762 million for marketing its anemia drug Aranesp for off-label uses. According to the then acting U.S. attorney, Amgen was "pursuing profits at the expense of patient safety."[38] A federal prosecutor in this case said that in some cases Amgen sales people were so indoctrinated to sell the drug for off-label uses that many of them didn't even know that the drug was not approved for the use for which they were selling it.[39]

Another example was the promotion of Paxil. The New York attorney general filed a lawsuit alleging that drug company GlaxoSmithKline (GSK) had covered up results from clinical trials of its drug, Paxil, an antidepressant. It was alleged that the drug was at best ineffective in children and at worst could increase suicidal thoughts. GSK denied the charges. The company was charged with "repeated and persistent fraud" in promoting the drug.[40] In the largest health-care settlement in history, GSK pleaded guilty and paid $3 billion to settle criminal and civil charges of promoting Paxil and another drug, Wellbutrin, for uses not approved by the FDA. Wellbutrin was an approved drug for major depressive disorders but it was being promoted for unapproved uses such as weight loss and sexual dysfunction.[41]

In another case, Glaxo was also accused of using spa treatments, trips to Hawaii, and hunting excursions to charm doctors into writing prescriptions for unapproved uses of certain drugs.[42]

The FDA and state attorneys general have been up in arms about drug companies marketing their products for "off-label" uses and continue to pursue companies for these violations. The anomaly is this: doctors may prescribe drugs for off-label use when they believe they are appropriate, but it is illegal for the drug companies to market or promote the drugs for off-label use.[43] But, the future is uncertain for these types of charges. A U.S. Court of Appeals in 2012 threw out the conviction of a pharmaceutical salesman for marketing drugs for unapproved uses on the grounds that his actions involved free-speech rights. Big Pharma has argued that it should be legally permitted to make truthful statements about its drugs even if the statements are not related to an FDA-approved use of the drug.[44] The FDA plans to fight this ruling and it will be important to watch over the next several years of litigation.[45]

IMPROPER PAYMENTS AND BRIBES

Sometimes the questionable marketing of drugs entails improper payments or bribes. In a landmark case, the Securities and Exchange Commission (SEC) announced that the drug maker Schering-Plough Corporation would pay a $500,000 penalty to settle claims that one of its subsidiaries made improper payments to a Polish charity in a quest to get a Polish government health official to buy the company's products.[46]

The SEC claimed that Schering-Plough Poland donated about $76,000 to a Polish charity over a three-year period. Chudnow Castle Foundation, the charity, was headed up by a health official in the Polish government. Apparently, this information came to light while regulators were investigating several pharmaceutical companies for compliance with the U.S. Foreign Corrupt Practices Act. The SEC charged that the payments were not accurately shown on the company's books and that the company's internal controls failed to prevent or detect them. The SEC said that the charity was legitimate, but that the company made the contributions with the expectation of boosting drug sales. In addition to paying the fine, the company also agreed to hire an independent consultant to review the company's internal control system and to ensure the firm's compliance with the Foreign Corrupt Practices Act (FCPA).[47]

Johnson & Johnson is another company that has been pursued for improper payments. In its case, the improper payments were in connection with the sale of medical devices in two foreign countries. Johnson & Johnson turned itself in, and the worldwide chairperson of medical devices and diagnostics took responsibility and retired.[48] In a related case, the company was being investigated for possible bribery in its medical device unit in Shanghai, in which it is alleged that the company bribed the deputy chief of the Chinese state FDA.[49]

Even while it was trying to repair the injury to its image in relation to drug-marketing tactics, it was revealed in 2013 that Glaxo was being investigated for allegations that its sales staff in China was involved in general payments to doctors to prescribe their drugs, some for unauthorized uses. China is one of Glaxo's most important markets and the problem is complicated by the fact that the health-care system in China is owned and controlled by the state and that it has a tradition of government patronage and gift-giving.[50] Since the China allegations arose, Glaxo's name continues to pop up with allegations of bribery and corruption, most recently in Yemen in 2016. The company claims it that it is conducting an internal probe into the allegations.[51]

QUESTIONABLE PAYMENTS TO DOCTORS

Few cases more vividly illustrate the questionable marketing tactics of Big Pharma than that of the allegations made against Schering-Plough. According to an investigation by the *New York Times*, Schering-Plough used the marketing tactic of making payments to doctors in exchange for their commitment to exclusively prescribe the company's medications. One doctor reported receiving an unsolicited check for $10,000 in the mail. He said it had been made out to him personally in exchange for an enclosed "consulting" agreement in which all he had to do was prescribe the company's medicines.[52]

"Shadowy" Financial Lures

Interviews with 20 doctors, industry executives, and observers close to the investigation of Schering-Plough and other drug companies revealed a "shadowy system of financial lures" that the companies had been using to convince the physicians to favor their drugs. In the case of Schering-Plough, the tactics included paying doctors large sums of money to prescribe its drug for hepatitis C and to participate in the company's clinical trials that turned out to be thinly disguised marketing ploys that required very little on the part of the doctors. The company even barred doctors from participating in the program if they did not exhibit loyalty to the company's drugs.[53]

One doctor, a liver specialist, and eight others who were interviewed, said that the company paid them $1,000–$1,500 per patient for prescribing Intron A, the company's hepatitis C medicine. The doctors were supposed to gather data, in exchange for the fees, and pass it on to the company. Apparently, many doctors were not diligent in recordkeeping, but the company did little. Another liver disease specialist said that the trials were "merely marketing gimmicks."[54] According to some doctors, the company would even shut off the money if one of the doctors wrote prescriptions for competing drugs, or even spoke favorably about other competing drugs. Other doctors reported being signed up for consulting services and being paid $10,000, and the only purpose was to keep them loyal to the company's products.[55]

In response to the allegations against the company, former Schering-Plough CEO Fred Hassan reported that the violations took place before he took office. He went on to outline steps he was taking to get the company on track. This included instituting an "integrity hotline" for employees to report wrongdoing and the creation of a chief compliance officer to report directly to the CEO and the board. Hassan said that compliance has to become "part of the DNA" of a drug company.[56] Another company official said that the company has been "undergoing a company-wide transformation since the arrival of new leadership in mid-2003," which is a "commitment to quality compliance and business integrity."[57]

In 2013, Novartis AG was accused by federal prosecutors of paying kickbacks to doctors to get them to prescribe certain of their brand-name drugs. Novartis disputes the charges and defends its payments to doctors as "accepted and customary practice." Prosecutors claimed that the inducements included lavish dinners, fishing trips off the Florida coast, and outings to expensive restaurants (as well as meals at Hooters) around the country. Though Novartis claimed the speakers' fees were paid to the doctors for educational purposes, some of the dinners in which the "speaking" was taking place appeared dubious. For example, one dinner was attended only by three people, including the doctor/speaker, at a Smith & Wollensky steakhouse in Washington, DC and the bill came to $2,016, or $672 per person. The lawsuit alleges that Novartis simply wined and dined doctors at high-end restaurants with cosmic prices. In one instance, prosecutors said the company paid a Florida doctor $3,750 for speaking to the same four doctors about a Novartis drug five times in a nine-month period.[58]

As it turns out, most doctors take money from drug and device companies. According to research by NPR, about three quarters of all doctors take at least one payment and in some states such as Nevada that percentage was over 90 percent.[59] Further, a study by ProPublica has found that there is a high correlation between payments received from drug companies and prescribing patterns of doctors. The more doctors receive, the more they prescribe the brand-name medications from the giving company. In spite of the patterns, most doctors still claim they are not prescribing based upon payments received.[60]

Paying Questionable Doctors

Some Big Pharma companies have continued to pay doctors with questionable credentials to oversee their drug trials and contribute to marketing. One representative case was a doctor whose medical license was suspended in 1997 by the Minnesota Board of Medical Practice. *The New York Times* reported that from 1997 to 2005, this same doctor was hired by several drug firms to conduct multiple drug trials and he was paid for speaking and consulting fees as well.[61] *The New York Times'* investigation found that 103 doctors in Minnesota, who had been disciplined by the Minnesota Board of Medical Practice, received a total of $1.7 million in payments for research and marketing services rendered.[62] Though Minnesota was the only state willing to make its records available for inspection, experts say this is a national problem.

GIFTS TAKE MANY FORMS

Not only do pharmaceutical companies give cash payments to doctors under a variety of justifications, but many payments come in the form of meals, tickets to shows and sporting events, ski and beach vacations disguised as medical education seminars, consulting "jobs" for which the doctors do no work, and other gifts, as part of their marketing strategies. The companies expect something in return. They expect the doctors to prescribe their medicines. It is estimated that there is an army of 88,000 or more pharmaceutical reps, many of them young and beautiful, supplying the doctors and their staffs with gifts and freebies. It is argued that these gifts damage the doctors' integrity.[63]

An article published in the *New England Journal of Medicine* reported on a survey of doctors and found that 94 percent of them had some type of relationship with the drug industry. The most frequent drug-industry ties were food and drinks in the workplace (83 percent), drug samples (78 percent), payments for consulting (18 percent), payments for speaking (16 percent), reimbursement for meeting expenses (15 percent), and tickets to cultural or sporting events (7 percent).[64] Some argue that these financial relationships between doctors and companies reflect a conflict of interests making it appear that the drug companies are rewarding the doctors for prescribing their lucrative drugs to patients. Others in the industry say that doctors have a right to make this money because they are providing research and access for the drug companies.[65]

A new requirement, instituted by the Affordable Care Act, is that the Centers for Medicare and Medicaid Services (CMS) must collect information from applicable manufacturers and group purchasing organizations about their financial relationships with doctors and hospitals. The Open Payments Web site allows the public access to their data. Therefore, the public should be able to see what payments are being made by companies to doctors though the data reported occurs on a two-year lag basis as it takes time to collect this information.[66] Whether this effort to provide transparency will make a difference or not remains to be seen.

BIG BUCKS, BIG PHARMA

The Media Education Foundation, a nonprofit corporation that produces and distributes educational materials observing the impact and ethics of the media industry, released a hard-hitting film, *Big Bucks, Big Pharma: Marketing Disease and Pushing Drugs*, that continues to be available in 2016.[67]

According to the Media Education Foundation, the 46-minute film, *Big Bucks, Big Pharma* pulled back the curtain on the multibillion dollar pharmaceutical industry to expose the insidious ways that illness is used, manipulated, and in some instances created for capital gain. Focusing on the industry's marketing practices, media scholars and health professionals helped viewers understand the ways in which direct-to-consumer (DTC) pharmaceutical advertising glamorizes and normalizes the use of prescription medication and works in tandem with promotion to doctors. Combined, these industry practices have shaped how both patients and doctors understand and relate to disease and treatment.

Big Pharma = Big Lobbying

Big Pharma is able to ward off most government regulations and actions to control it through the power of its huge lobbying force. According to the Center on Public Integrity, Big Pharma has a stranglehold on Washington. The pharmaceutical industry spends more each year on lobbying than any other industry and that includes the nation's defense and aerospace industries, and Big Oil.[68] We might call this process Big Pharma doing Big Lobbying. The pharmaceutical lobby has defeated most attempts over the years to restrain drug marketing. In September 2007, Congress passed a sweeping drug safety bill, but before it was passed, it was stripped of provisions that were intended to limit the ability of the industry to market directly to consumers. In addition, in 11 states that considered legislation to expose pharmaceutical gift-giving, the bills were either defeated or stalled.[69]

In 2012, it was revealed both by *The New York Times* and *The Wall Street Journal* how successfully Big Pharma had lobbied for its own self-interest and won in the passage of the Affordable Care Act (Obamacare).[70] According to the *New York Times*, the administration's unlikely collaboration with the drug industry forced unappealing trade-offs. Of particular importance was the industry's writing into the proposed law the provision that the Medicare program could not negotiate prices with the drug industry. The result was there would be no lower prices for drugs in the new legislation.[71]

Congress has been fighting this provision for years but has not been successful in its dealings with Big Pharma because of the industry's lobbying power. At this writing, the Medication Prescription Drug Price Negotiation Act of 2015 was assigned to a committee in January of 2016. This bill has been stalled in Congress since its introduction in 2011.[72] With respect to the Affordable Care Act, *The Wall Street Journal* complained that "a Pfizer CEO and Big Pharma colluded with the White House at the public's expense."[73] What is clear is that Big Pharma's behind-the-scenes lobbying has paid big dividends for the industry.

QUESTIONS FOR DISCUSSION

1. What are the ethical issues in this case?
2. Who are the primary stakeholders in these incidents and what are their stakes?
3. Is there any justification for the marketing and pricing tactics described in the case? Which are acceptable and which are questionable?
4. What ethical principles may be violated by the marketing tactics described? Do any of these ethical principles *support* the companies' actions?
5. Big Pharma needs enormous sums of money to conduct R&D and to advance its innovations. Do the ends justify the means because our health is at stake?
6. What response do you think physicians should take when approached regarding some of the schemes presented in this case? Are doctors in a conflict of interest situation when taking Big Pharma's money?

ENDNOTES

1. Haley Sweetland Edwards, "Public Outrage: What's behind the Gouging?" *Time* (May 30, 2016), 38–43.
2. Ibid., 42.
3. Ibid., 40.
4. Ben Elgin and Robert Langreth, "Pharma's Play," *Bloomberg Businessweek* (May 23–29, 2016), 44–49.
5. Julie Creswell and Andrew Pollack, "The Bad Boy of Pharmaceuticals Hits Back," *New York Times* (December 6, 2015), 1BU.
6. Ibid.
7. Ibid.
8. Daren Fonda and Barbara Kiviat, "Curbing the Drug Marketers," *Time* (July 5, 2004), 40–42.
9. "American's Views of Pharmaceutical Industry Take a Tumble," *Gallup* (September 14, 2015), http://www.gallup.com/poll/185432/americans-views-pharmaceutical-industry-tumble.aspx. Accessed May 30, 2016.
10. Center for Responsive Politics, OpenSecrets.org, "Pharmaceuticals/Health Products," http://www.opensecrets.org/lobby/indusclient.php?id=h04&year=2016. Accessed May 30, 2016.

11. Michael A. Santoro and Thomas M. Gorrie, "*Ethics and the Pharmaceutical Industry*" (Cambridge: Cambridge University Press, 2005); see also Public Citizen, "The Other Drug War: Big Pharma's 625 Washington Lobbyists," http://www.citizen.org/congress/article_redirect.cfm?ID=6537. Accessed June 13, 2013.
12. Bernard Munos, "We the People vs the Pharmaceutical Industry," *Forbes* (April 29, 2013), http://www.forbes.com/sites/bernardmunos/2013/04/29/the-pharmaceutical-industry-vs-society/. Accessed May 30, 2016.
13. Sy Mukherjee, "Pharma's Fortune 500: The Top Ranked Companies of 2015," *BioPharma Dive*, http://www.biopharmadive.com/news/fortune-500-pharmaceutical-companies/400691/. Accessed May 30, 2016.
14. *Fortune*'s World's Most Admired Companies 2016, http://fortune.com/worlds-most-admired-companies/. Accessed May 30, 2016.
15. Jonathan D. Rockoff, "J & J Pays $2.2 Billion to Settle Probe," *The Wall Street Journal* (November 5, 2013), B3.
16. Ibid.
17. Randal S. Olsen, "Putting Big Pharma Spending in Perspective" (March 1, 2015), http://www.randalolson.com/2015/03/01/design-critique-putting-big-pharma-spending-in-perspective/. Accessed May 30, 2016.
18. Consuella Pachio, "Billions of Dollars Paid Out for Illegal Marketing Practices," *Legalreader* (May 8, 2016), http://www.legalreader.com/billions-of-dollars-paid-out-for-illegal-marketing-practices/. Accessed June 6, 2016.
19. Ibid.
20. Ibid.
21. Robert Langreth and Matthew Herper, "Pill Pushers: How the Drug Industry Abandoned Science for Salesmanship," *Forbes* (May 8, 2006), 94–102.
22. Ibid., 94.
23. Ibid.
24. Ibid.
25. Ibid., 96.
26. Dani Veracity, "Pharmaceutical Fraud: How Big Pharma's Marketing and Profits Come Before Consumer Safety and Wellness," http://www.naturalnews.com/z020345.html. Accessed June 13, 2013.
27. Gardiner Harris, "Diabetes Drug Maker Hid Test Data on Risks, Files Indicate," *The New York Times* (July 12, 2010), http://www.nytimes.com/2010/07/13/health/policy/13avandia.html?_r=0. Accessed June 13, 2013.
28. "Avandia on Trial," *The Wall Street Journal* (July 16, 2010), A16.
29. Chris Adams, "Student Doctors Protest Largess of Drug Makers," *The Wall Street Journal* (June 24, 2002), B1.
30. Kevin B. O'Reilly, "Pharma Gift Bans for Budding Doctors have Long Term Impact," amednews.com (February 18, 2013), http://www.amednews.com/article/20130218/profession/130219950/6/. Accessed June 25, 2013.
31. Knight Kiplinger, "Are Drug Prices Unethically High?" *Kiplinger's Personal Finance* (January 2016, 18).
32. "Big Pharma's Favorite Prescription: Higher Prices," *Bloomberg Businessweek* (May 12–18, 2014), 22–24.
33. Jeffrey Pfeffer, "To Fix High Drug Prices, Stop the Merger Madness," *Fortune* (May 17, 2016), http://fortune.com/2016/05/17/high-drug-prices-mergers-pharma-competition/. Accessed June 6, 2016.
34. Laura Lorenzetti, "The U.S. Has the Highest Drug Prices in the World. And Hating Martin Shkreli Won't Be Enough to Change It," *Fortune* (November 1, 2015), 17.
35. Peter Jaret, "Price Spike for Some Generics: Brand-Name Drug Costs Also Soaring," *AARP Bulletin* (July–August 2015), 8–10.
36. Ibid., 10.
37. Carolyn Susman, "False Marketing of Drugs Raises Red Flags," *Cox News Service* (May 25, 2004).
38. Andrew Pollack and Mosi Secret, "Amgen Agrees to Pay $762 Million for Marketing Anemia Drug for Off-Label Use," *New York Times* (December 18, 2012), http://www.nytimes.com/2012/12/19/business/amgen-agrees-to-pay-762-million-in-drug-case.html. Accessed June 6, 2016.
39. Ibid.
40. "Business: Trials and Tribulations; Pharmaceuticals," *The Economist* (June 19, 2004), 74.
41. Pachio, ibid.
42. "Mis-selling Drugs: The Settlers," *The Economist* (July 7, 2012), 61.

43. Joseph V. Gulfo, "Ending the Prescribe-Don't-Tell Charade for Off-Label Drugs," *The Wall Street Journal* (March 28, 2016), A15.
44. Ibid.
45. Thomas M. Burton, "Courts to Weigh Free Speech Rights in Pharmaceutical Marketing Cases," *The Wall Street Journal* (December 6, 2012), B6.
46. Judith Burns, "SEC Settles Bribery Case vs. Schering-Plough Corp.," *The Wall Street Journal* (June 9, 2004).
47. Ibid.
48. Peter Loftus, "Ex-Health Executives Go on Trial," *The Wall Street Journal* (May 23, 2106), B1.
49. Jim Edwards, "J&J's Other Headache: Foreign Bribery Probe Targets Shanghai Unit," *CBS Moneywatch* (June 25, 2010), http://www.cbsnews.com/8301-505123_162-42845025/j038js-other-headache-foreign-bribery-probe-targets-shanghai-unit/. Accessed June 6, 2016.
50. Christopher Matthews and Jessica Hodgson, "Glaxo Probes Claims It Paid Bribes in China," *The Wall Street Journal* (June 13, 2013), B1.
51. Carly Helfand, "Add It to the List: GSK Corruption Claims Crop Up in Yemen," *FiercePharma* (April 18, 2016), http://www.fiercepharma.com/pharma/add-it-to-list-gsk-corruption-claims-crop-up-yemen. Accessed June 6, 2016.
52. Gardiner Harris, "As Doctor Writes Prescription, Drug Company Writes a Check," *The New York Times* (June 27, 2004), 1YT.
53. Ibid.
54. Ibid.
55. Ibid.
56. Fonda and Kiviat, 41.
57. Reuters (June 28, 2004).
58. Chad Bray and Jeanne Whalen, "U.S. Accuses Novartis of Kickbacks," *The Wall Street Journal* (April 27/28, 2013), B1.
59. Charles Ornstein, Ryann Jones, and Mike Tigas, "Drug Company Payments Mirror Doctors' Brand Name Prescribing," *NPR* (March 17, 2016), http://www.npr.org/sections/health-shots/2016/03/17/470679452/drug-company-payments-mirror-doctors-brand-name-prescribing. Accessed June 6, 2016.
60. Ibid.
61. Gardiner Harris and Janet Roberts, "After Sanctions, Doctors Get Drug Company Pay," *New York Times* (June 3, 2007), A1.
62. Ibid., 20.
63. "Gifts from Drugmakers Damage Doctors' Integrity," *USA Today* (February 8, 2006), 10A.
64. Reported in Rita Rubin, "Most Doctors Get Money, Gifts from Industry," *USA Today* (April 26, 2007), 4D; see also "Doctors Still Chummy with Drug Sales Reps," *AARP Bulletin* (June 2007).
65. "Is Your Doctor Taking Money from Drug Companies? *1-1.5 WPDH* (February 9, 2015), http://wpdh.com/is-your-doctor-taking-money-from-drug-companies/. Accessed June 6, 2016.
66. CMS.gov, "Open Payments," https://www.cms.gov/openpayments/. Accessed June 6, 2016.
67. "Big Bucks, Big Pharma: Marketing Disease and Pushing Drugs," Media Education Foundation, http://store.nexternal.com/mef/big-bucks-big-pharma-p49.aspx. Accessed June 6, 2016.
68. Center for Public Integrity, "Opinion: Big Pharma's Stranglehold on Washington," https://www.publicintegrity.org/2013/02/11/12175/opinion-big-pharmas-stranglehold-washington. Accessed June 6, 2016.
69. Arlene Weintraub, "Drug Marketing: Will Pharma Finally Have to Fess Us?" *Business Week* (October 8, 2007), 36.
70. Peter Baker, "Obama Was Pushed by the Drug Industry, E-mails Suggest," *New York Times* (June 8, 2012). Accessed June 18, 2013; see also "ObamaCare's Secret History," *The Wall Street Journal* (June 12, 2012), A12.
71. Baker, ibid.
72. Govtrack.us, "S.31: Medicare Prescription Drug Price Negotiation Act of 2015," https://www.govtrack.us/congress/bills/114/s31. Accessed June 6, 2016.
73. "ObamaCare's Secret History," *The Wall Street Journal*, June 12, 2012, A12, http://www.wsj.com/articles/SB10001424052702303830204577446470015843822. Accessed June 6, 2016.

CASE 21

McDonald's—The Coffee Spill Heard 'Round the World*

The McDonald's coffee spill is the most famous consumer lawsuit in the world. Everyone knows about this case, and the details involved in it continue to be debated in many different venues—classrooms, Web sites, blogs, law schools, and business schools. Regardless, it serves as one of the best platforms in the world for discussing what companies owe their consumer stakeholders and what responsibilities consumers have for their own well-being. Consumers, lawyers, and analysts are still debating the world famous coffee spill case.

Keeping the topic hot was the 2011 documentary film, *Hot Coffee*, which analyzed the famous coffee spill, set the facts straight, and highlighted the ongoing debate about the impact of tort reform on the U.S. judicial system. The film premiered at the 2011 Sundance Film Festival and aired on HBO during June 2011.[1] The film won many awards.

STELLA LIEBECK

Stella Liebeck and her grandson, Chris Tiano, drove her son, Jim, to the airport 60 miles away in Albuquerque, New Mexico, on the morning of February 27, 1992. Because she had to leave home early, she and Chris missed having breakfast. Upon dropping Jim off at the airport, they proceeded to a McDonald's drive-through for breakfast. Stella, an active, 79-year-old, retired department-store clerk, ordered a McBreakfast, and Chris parked the car so she could add cream and sugar to her coffee.[2]

What occurred next was the coffee spill that has been heard 'round the world. A coffee spill, serious burns, a lawsuit, and an eventual settlement made Stella Liebeck (pronounced Lee-beck) the "poster lady" for the bitter tort reform discussions that have dominated the news for more than 20 years. To this day, the issue is still debated, with cases similar to Stella's continuing to be filed.

THIRD-DEGREE BURNS

According to Liebeck's testimony, she tried to get the coffee lid off. She could not find any flat surface in the car, so she put the cup between her knees and tried to get it off that way. As she tugged at the lid, scalding coffee spilled into her lap. Chris jumped from the car and tried to help her. She pulled at her sweatsuit, but the pants absorbed the coffee and held it close to her skin. She was squirming as the 170-degree coffee burned her groin, inner thigh, and buttocks. Third-degree burns were evident as she reached an emergency room. A vascular surgeon determined she had third-degree (full thickness) burns over 6 percent of her body.

Hospitalization

Following the spill, Liebeck spent eight days in the hospital and about three weeks at home recuperating under the care of her daughter, Nancy Tiano. She was then hospitalized again for skin grafts. Liebeck lost 20 pounds during the ordeal and at times was practically immobilized. Another daughter, Judy Allen, recalled that her mother was in tremendous pain both after the accident and during the skin grafts.[3]

According to a *Newsweek* magazine report, Liebeck wrote to McDonald's in August 1994, asking them to turn down the coffee temperature. Though she was not planning to sue, her family thought she was due about $2,000 for out-of-pocket expenses plus the lost wages of her daughter who stayed at home with her. The family reported that McDonald's offered her $800.[4]

STELLA FILES A LAWSUIT

After this, the family went looking for a lawyer and retained Reed Morgan, a Houston attorney, who had won a $30,000 settlement against McDonald's in 1988 for a woman whose spilled coffee had caused her third-degree burns. Morgan filed a lawsuit on behalf of Liebeck, charging McDonald's with "gross negligence" for selling coffee that was "unreasonably dangerous" and "defectively manufactured." Morgan asked for no less than $100,000 in compensatory damages, including pain and suffering, and triple that amount in punitive damages.

McDonald's Motion Rejected

McDonald's moved for summary dismissal of the case, defending the coffee's heat and blaming Liebeck for spilling it. According to the company, she was the "proximate cause" of the injury. With McDonald's motion rejected, a trial date was set for August 1994.

*This case was written by Archie B. Carroll, University of Georgia, and updated in 2016.

As the trial date approached, no out-of-court settlement occurred. Morgan, the attorney, said that at one point he offered to drop the case for $300,000 and was willing to settle for half that amount, but McDonald's would not budge. Days before the trial, the judge ordered the two parties to attend a mediation session. The mediator, a retired judge, recommended McDonald's settle for $225,000, using the argument that a jury would likely award that amount. Again, McDonald's resisted settlement.[5]

THE TRIAL

The trial lasted seven days, with expert witnesses dueling over technical issues, such as the temperature at which coffee causes burns. Initially, the jury was annoyed at having to hear what at first was thought to be a frivolous case about spilled coffee, but the evidence presented by the prosecution grabbed its attention. Photos of Liebeck's charred skin were introduced. (These dramatic photos are shown in the documentary, *Hot Coffee*.) A renowned burn expert testified that coffee at 170 degrees would cause second-degree burns within 3.5 seconds of hitting the skin.

The Defense Helped Liebeck

Defense witnesses inadvertently helped the prosecution. A quality-assurance supervisor at McDonald's testified that the company did not lower its coffee heat despite 700 burn complaints over ten years. A safety consultant argued that 700 complaints—about 1 in every 24 million cups sold—were basically trivial. This comment was apparently interpreted to imply that McDonald's cared more about statistics than about people. An executive for McDonald's testified that the company knew its coffee sometimes caused serious burns, but it was not planning to go beyond the tiny print warning on the cup that said, "Caution: Contents Hot!" The executive went on to say that McDonald's did not intend to change any of its coffee policies or procedures, saying, "There are more serious dangers in restaurants."

In the closing arguments, one of McDonald's defense attorneys acknowledged that the coffee was hot and that that is how customers wanted it. She went on to insist that Liebeck had only herself to blame as she was unwise to put the cup between her knees. She also noted that Liebeck failed to leap out of the bucket seat in the car after the spill, thus preventing the hot coffee from falling off her. The attorney concluded by saying that the real question in the case is how far society should go to restrict what most of us enjoy and accept.[6]

THE JURY DECIDES

The jury deliberated about four hours and reached a verdict for Liebeck. It decided on compensatory damages of $200,000, which it reduced to $160,000 after judging that 20 percent of the fault belonged to Liebeck for spilling the coffee. The jury concluded that McDonald's had engaged in willful, reckless, malicious, or wanton conduct, which is the basis for punitive damages. The jury decided upon a figure of $2.7 million in punitive damages.

Company Neglected Customers

One juror later said that the facts were overwhelmingly against the company and that the company just was not taking care of its customers. Another juror felt the huge punitive damages were intended to be a stern warning for McDonald's to wake up and realize its customers were getting burned. Another juror said he began to realize that the case was really about the callous disregard for the safety of customers.

Public opinion polls after the jury verdict were squarely on the side of McDonald's. Polls showed that a large majority of Americans—including many who usually support the little guy—were outraged at the verdict.[7] But, of course, the public did not hear all the details presented in the trial.

JUDGE REDUCES AWARD

The judge later slashed the jury award by more than 75 percent to $640,000. Liebeck appealed the reduction, and McDonald's continued fighting the award as excessive. In December 1994, it was announced that McDonald's had reached an out-of-court settlement with Liebeck, but the terms of the settlement were not disclosed due to a confidentiality provision. The settlement was reached to end appeals in the case. We will never know the final ending to this case because the parties entered into a secret settlement that has never been revealed to the public. Since this was a public case, litigated in public, and subjected to extensive media reporting, some lawyers think that such secret settlements, after public trials, should not be condoned.[8]

Debate over Coffee Temperature

Coffee suddenly became a hot topic in the industry. The Specialty Coffee Association of America put coffee safety on its agenda for discussion. A spokesperson for the National Coffee Association said that McDonald's coffee conforms to industry temperature standards. A spokesperson for Mr. Coffee, the coffee-machine maker, said that if customer complaints are any indication, industry settings may be too low. Some customers like it hotter. A coffee connoisseur who imported and wholesaled coffee said that 175 degrees is probably the optimum temperature for coffee because that's when aromatics are being released. Coffee served at home is generally 135–140 degrees. McDonald's continued to say that it is serving its coffee the way customers like it. As one writer noted, the temperature of McDonald's coffee helps to explain why it sells a billion cups a year.[9]

LATER INCIDENTS

In August 2000, a Vallejo, California, woman sued McDonald's, saying she suffered second-degree burns when a handicapped employee at a drive-through window dropped a large cup of coffee in her lap. The suit charged that the handicapped employee could not grip the cardboard tray and was instead trying to balance it on top of her hands and forearms when the accident occurred in August 1999. The victim, Karen Muth, said she wanted at least $10,000 for her medical bills, pain and suffering, and "humiliation." But her lawyer, Dan Ryan, told the local newspaper that she was entitled to between $400,000 and $500,000. Attorney Ryan went on to say, "We recognize that there's an Americans with Disabilities Act, but that doesn't give them (McDonald's) the right to sacrifice the safety of their customers." It is not known how this lawsuit was settled.

Suits Go Global

It was also announced in August 2000 that British solicitors had organized 26 spill complainants into a group suit against McDonald's over the piping hot nature of its beverages. One London lawyer said, "Hot coffee, hot tea, and hot water are at the center of this case. We are alleging they are too hot." Since that time other lawsuits have been filed around the world.

Burned by a Hot Pickle

In a related turn of events, a Knoxville, Tennessee, woman, Veronica Martin, filed a lawsuit in 2000 claiming that she was permanently scarred when a hot pickle from a McDonald's hamburger fell on her chin. She claimed the burn caused her physical and mental harm. Martin sued for $110,000. Martin's husband, Darrin, also sought $15,000 because he "has been deprived of the services and consortium of his wife." According to Veronica Martin's lawsuit, the hamburger "was in a defective condition or unreasonably dangerous to the general consumer and, in particular, to her." The lawsuit went on to say, "while attempting to eat the hamburger, the pickle dropped from the hamburger onto her chin. The pickle was extremely hot and burned the chin of Veronica Martin." Martin had second-degree burns and was permanently scarred, according to the lawsuit. One report was that the McDonald's owner settled this case out of court.[10]

ISSUE WON'T GO AWAY

The Stella Awards

For 25 years now, the coffee spill heard 'round the world continues to be a subject of heated debate. The coffee spill and subsequent trial, publicity, and resolution "prompted a tort reform storm that has barely abated."[11] One school of thought held that it represents the most frivolous lawsuit of all time. In fact, a program called the "Stella Awards" was begun to recognize each year's most outrageous lawsuit. The awards were the creation of humorist Randy Cassingham, and his summaries of award-winning cases may be found on the Stella Awards Web site.[12] In actuality, most of the lawsuits he chronicles are far more outrageous than the coffee spill in which Stella Liebeck did get seriously injured. On the other hand, consumer groups are still concerned about victims of what they see as dangerous products, and they continue to assail McDonald's callous unconcern for Stella Liebeck.

In the ensuing decades, lawsuits over spilt beverages have continued to come and go, but most of them have been resolved with less fanfare than Stella's case. As for S. Reed Morgan, the lawyer who successfully represented Stella Liebeck, he has handled only three cases involving beverages since Liebeck's suit. Morgan has turned down many plaintiffs, but said he is interested in such cases only if they involve third-degree burns.

A Lawsuit in Moscow

Coffee spill cases have even gone global. In fact, a long-running case against McDonald's in Moscow was closed in 2006 by a Moscow court after the claimant withdrew her $34,000 lawsuit. Olga Kuznetsova filed a lawsuit against the company after hot coffee was spilled on her in a Russian McDonald's. Kuznetsova claimed that a swinging door hit her while she was walking out onto the restaurant's terrace with a full tray. She demanded 900,000 rubles (then about $34,000) in damages. McDonald's lawyers said she had nobody to blame but herself because the paper cup carried a warning that the coffee was hot, which prompted her to go to court.[13]

Coffee Spill Suits Continue

There is likely no end in sight for coffee spill-type cases. In a 2013 lawsuit, a woman passenger on Continental Airlines sued the company for $170,550 after a cup of hot coffee was spilled on her during her flight. She claimed the hot coffee resulted in second-degree burns and permanent scarring on her inner thighs.[14]

Consumers can learn more about the Stella Liebeck case and many others by visiting Ralph Nader's newly opened American Museum of Tort Law in Winsted, Connecticut, his home town.[15] The new museum features groundbreaking civil cases on auto safety, tobacco, asbestos, and, yes, spilled coffee, along with many others.[16]

QUESTIONS FOR DISCUSSION

1. What are the major issues in the Liebeck case and in the following incidents? Was the lawsuit "frivolous" as some people thought, or serious business regarding safety and treatment of consumers?
2. What are McDonald's social (economic, legal, and ethical) responsibilities toward consumers in the Liebeck case and the other cases? What are consumers' responsibilities when they buy a product such as hot coffee or hot hamburgers? How does a company give consumers what they want and yet protect them at the same time?
3. What are the arguments supporting McDonald's position in the Liebeck case? What are the arguments supporting Liebeck's position? Should McDonald's have settled this case when it had a chance?
4. If you had been a juror in the Liebeck case, which position would you most likely have supported? Why? What if you had been a juror in the pickle burn case?
5. What are the similarities and differences between the coffee burn cases and the pickle burn case? Does one represent a more serious threat to consumer harm? What should McDonald's, and other fast food restaurants, do about hot food, such as hamburgers, when consumers are injured?
6. Why did Stella Liebeck win this case and what implications does it pose for businesses' responsibility toward consumers?
7. What is your assessment of the "Stella Awards"? Is this making light of a serious problem?
8. Do we now live in a society where businesses are responsible for customers' accidents or carelessness in using products? We live in a society that is growing older. Does this fact place a special responsibility on merchants who sell products to senior citizens?

ENDNOTES

1. Hot Coffee, http://www.hotcoffeethemovie.com/. Accessed June 8, 2016.
2. Andrea Gerlin, "A Matter of Degree: How a Jury Decided That a Coffee Spill Is Worth $2.9 Million," *The Wall Street Journal* (September 1, 1994), A1, A4.
3. Theresa Howard, "McDonald's Settles Coffee Suit in Out-of-Court Agreement," *Nation's Restaurant News* (December 12, 1994), 1.
4. Aric Press and Ginny Carroll, "Are Lawyers Burning America?" *Newsweek* (March 20, 1995), 30–35.
5. Howard, 1.
6. "Coffee-Spill Suits Meet ADA," Overlawyered.com, http://www.overlawyered.com/archives/00aug1.html. Accessed June 8, 2016.
7. Gerlin, A4.
8. "The Actual Facts about the McDonald's Coffee Case," The 'Lectric Law Library, http://www.lectlaw.com/files/cur78.htm. Accessed June 8, 2016.
9. Ibid.
10. Associated Press, "Couple Seeks $125,000 for Pickle Burn on Chin," *Athens Banner Herald* (October 8, 2000), 6A. Also see Associated Press, "Couple Sues over Hot Pickle Burn" (October 7, 2000), http://www.washingtonpost.com/wp-srv/aponline/20001007/aponline154419_000.htm. Accessed June 8, 2016.

11. Matt Fleisher-Black, "One Lump or Two?" *The American Lawyer* (June 4, 2004).
12. StellaAwards.com, http://www.stellaawards.com/. Accessed June 8, 2016.
13. "Moscow McDonald's Coffee-Spill Case Closed," *RIA Novosti* (January 11, 2006), http://en.rian.ru/russia/20061101/55304783.html. Accessed June 8, 2016.
14. Daily Mail, "Woman Sues United or $170,000 over Spilled Hot Coffee," http://www.dailymail.co.uk/news/article-2333908/Woman-sues-United-170-000-spilled-hot-coffee.html. Accessed June 8, 2016.
15. American Museum of Tort Law, https://www.tortmuseum.org/. Accessed June 8, 2016.
16. PBS News Hour, "Inside Ralph Nader's American Museum of Tort Law," http://www.pbs.org/newshour/bb/inside-ralph-naders-american-museum-of-tort-law/. Accessed June 8, 2016.

CASE 22

General Electric and the Hudson River Cleanup*

One of the major challenges businesses face with respect to government regulations is that often compliance with existing regulations during an earlier period does not protect them against expensive problems that occur or come to light later. The plight of General Electric (GE) with respect to its dumping of PCBs (polychlorinated biphenyls) over 30 years ago is a classic case in point.

For decades, GE had electrical-equipment-making plants along the Hudson River in New York. During the period prior to 1977, GE discharged more than 1.3 million pounds of PCBs into a 40-mile stretch of the Hudson before the chemicals were banned in 1977. In 2001, the PCB-contaminated upper Hudson River had become the largest EPA Superfund site in the nation and has become the most expensive to clean up.[1]

In August 2001, the Environmental Protection Agency (EPA) circulated a draft proposal informing GE that it would have to spend hundreds of millions of dollars to clean up the PCBs that were legally dumped over a 30-year period that ended in 1977.[2] According to *Businessweek*, the Bush Administration and the EPA, under fire for its environmental policies, ordered GE to clean up the Hudson in what has been called the biggest environmental dredging project in U.S. history. The decision reaffirmed a plan developed in the waning days of the Clinton Administration.

A GE representative stated that the company was "disappointed in the EPA's decision," which it said, "will cause more harm than good." Environmentalists, predictably, praised the decision, and the Sierra Club executive director called the decision a "monumental step toward protecting New Yorkers from cancer-causing PCBs."[3]

The cleanup plan became a heated and politically charged debate beginning in fall of 2001, as an investigative report detailed how environmentalists (the Greens) claimed that GE and the EPA used the terrorist attacks on the World Trade Center and Pentagon as a distraction from the priority of the planned cleanup. The Greens charged that GE and the EPA, under the leadership of EPA administrator Christine Todd Whitman, delayed the cleanup and were "negotiating in the shadow of September 11." The executive director of the Clearwater advocacy groups and spokesperson for the coalition said regarding the meetings between GE and EPA, "It smells really bad."[4]

USE OF PERFORMANCE STANDARDS

The Greens charged that a modification of the cleanup plan was in the works that would favor GE. This would be the establishment of "performance standards" to measure the effectiveness of dredging

*This case was prepared by Archie B. Carroll, University of Georgia. Revised and updated in 2016.

to remove the PCBs. In a change from the original Clinton Administration plan, the revised goal of the EPA would be to roll out the dredging project in stages with periodic testing for PCBs. EPA stated: "The performance indicators being considered will include measuring PCB levels in the soil and the water column, as well as measuring the percentage of dredged material that gets re-suspended." The agency added: "Based on these objective scientific indicators, EPA will determine at each stage of the project whether it is scientifically justified to continue the cleanup. PCB levels in fish will be monitored throughout the project as well."[5]

Would GE Be Favored?

Environmentalists believed that the performance standards would be weighted in ways that would favor GE's position and would put an early lid on the project. They communicated to the EPA that they did not want any standards built into the project that would offer GE an "out." Environmentalists who met with the EPA claimed they were talking to a brick wall—that their arguments were brushed off. One stated: "That office (EPA), with all due respect, seems to get its information from G.E. It's a political process being handled inside the [Washington] beltway; it's inappropriate and possibly illegal." The Greens stated they planned to start an advertising blitz hammering on its claim that terrorism was used as a cover while EPA and GE schemed a way to dilute the plan.[6]

THE HUDSON RIVER

Close to 40 miles of the half-mile-wide Hudson River is involved in the cleanup. It is a pastoral and wooded stretch of the river that winds in the shadows of the Adirondacks, which serve recreational activities of numerous towns and villages. At one time, these villages were thriving examples of American industrial power. Today, most of the factories, mills, and plants are closed. Like in many other industries, jobs headed south, west, across borders, or across oceans as companies tried to extricate themselves from what they saw as devastating taxes and regulations. Though not obvious to the observer, the hidden problem of hazardous waste pollution has been a significant barrier to redevelopment of the area.[7]

SUPERFUND SITE

In 1983, the upper Hudson was named a Superfund site by the EPA. This meant that GE would be held responsible by law for cleaning up the pollution resulting from years of disposal of pollutants, regardless of whether the disposal was legal at the time.

John Elvin, an investigative reporter, claimed that the Hudson River was just 1 of 77 alleged sites to be in need of cleanup under the EPA's Superfund program. Also, it is believed that there are numerous other sites in addition to the upper Hudson River where PCBs were dumped. In addition to the Hudson River area, the chemicals were used at plants throughout the New England area.[8]

PCBs

PCBs are a large family of fire-retardant chemicals that GE once used in the production of electrical products. There are over 200 variations of the chemical, which were, for the most part, dumped legally in the years before it was determined they posed a possible cancer risk. The PCBs were oily and tarry and were disposed of as fill for roadbeds, housing developments, and other such uses. It was reported that GE often dispensed the material free to residents surrounding its factories. In various forms, the company sold or gave away what is now considered a contaminated waste product to be used as a wood preservative, fertilizer, termite inhibitor, and component in house paints. As for directly dumped wastes, the PCBs are thought to be leaking into groundwater from landfills that GE had put caps on.[9]

The Dangers of PCBs

According to the EPA, PCBs have been found to cause cancer and can also harm the immune, nervous, and reproductive systems of humans, fish, and wildlife. They think the chemicals are especially risky for children.[10] David O. Carpenter, the director of the Institute for Health and the Environment at the State University of New York at Albany and professor of Environmental Health Sciences within the School of Public Health, has been a critic of GE. According to Carpenter, all experts except those allied with GE believe PCBs to be a "probable" cause of cancer in humans. Carpenter lashed out at GE for "deceitful and unscientific" claims that are "preposterous." Carpenter claims that PCBs are linked to reduced IQs in children, attention deficit disorder, suppressed immune systems, diabetes, and heart disease.[11]

Controversy over Safety

There is controversy over whether PCBs are dangerous or not. Like the EPA, environmental groups believe they are dangerous. A handout from the Friends of a Clean Hudson coalition states strongly: "PCBs are a class of synthetic toxic chemicals universally recognized as among the world's most potent and persistent threats to human health." On the other hand, a former GE employee who worked intimately with PCBs for 25–30 years offered a different perspective. To put it in layman's terms, he said, "You're talking about a big, fat, slippery, stable molecule that doesn't break down. That's why it was used in lubrication and cooling in the manufacturing process. It's just plain sludge, that's all."[12]

Another hazardous-waste-management expert was reported as saying that he had been in PCBs up to his armpits and so had many others working with GE and other firms. He also affirmed that he had drunk half a glass of PCBs accidentally 25 years earlier. (But, we don't know what happened to him after that period.) The expert went on to say that there are no reported cases of cancer traced to PCBs. He expressed the opinion that this controversy is 25 percent an environmental concern and 75 percent politics in a state and towns abandoned by GE that are left with no industry and a lot of trash. In spite of his views, the expert does think that GE should clean up the "hot spots" where dumping was most severe and the rest of the river should be left to heal on its own.[13]

GE'S POSITION ON CLEANUP PLAN

GE did not accept EPA's cleanup plan as a done deal. The huge, wealthy company, one of the largest in the world, cranked up a barrage of TV infomercials, radio and TV ads, and initiatives by top-tier Washington lobbyists to sway the public, media, and government. The company fielded an imposing cadre of Washington lobbyists. Among these lobbyists were former Senator George Mitchell, former House Speaker-Designate Bob Livingston, and several other prominent people.[14]

Former CEO Jack Welch Chimes In

Retired former chief executive officer (CEO) of GE, the legendary Jack Welch, was negotiating with regulators over this issue as far back as the 1970s. Welch summarized the company's position in a statement he made to GE stockholders while he was the CEO: "We simply do not believe that there are any adverse health effects from PCBs."[15] At the time, GE has already spent millions of dollars fighting the proposal to clean up the river. The company contended that the proposed dredging would actually be more destructive because it would stir up PCBs buried in the mud and recontaminate the river. Supporting GE's position, Rep. John Sweeney said that he would continue to fight the dredging plan because it would have an adverse impact on local residents.[16]

One journalist estimated that GE would end up spending as much fighting the EPA plan as it would if they just went ahead with the cleanup. This raises the obvious question as to why GE would fight the plan. According to John Elvin, investigative reporter, it was because the company thought it was a precedent-setting case that would leave the company open to a tobacco industry-sized settlement claim. As it turns out, this was only one of the many sites GE used legally to dispose of manufacturing by-products, and PCBs were just one of the many possibly hazardous wastes that the company had to deal with over the years. Apparently, GE used as many as 77 sites alleged to be in need of cleanup under the Superfund program.[17]

CITIZENS AND ENVIRONMENTAL GROUPS' CHIME IN

Many of the residents of the upstate area that would be most affected by a GE cleanup preferred to just leave the situation alone and let the river heal itself. A poll commissioned by GE and handled by Zogby International found that 59 percent of the residents in the region favored letting the river deal with the pollutants naturally. Another poll done by Siena College Research Institute found that 50 percent of all the residents along the entire length of the Hudson wanted the river to be left alone. On the other side of the issue, polls showed that a large majority of the citizens did want a cleanup.[18] The survey results seem to depend on which citizens are chosen to be polled, how the questions are framed, and who was doing the polling.

Grassroots Opposition

There was even some grassroots opposition to EPA's dredging plan. An example is found in Citizen Environmentalists Against Sludge Encapsulation (CEASE) and Farmers Against Irresponsible Remediation (FAIR). CEASE proposed acts of civil disobedience to prevent the government from coming onto private property. According to one CEASE activist, "the downstate enviros are only interested in punishing GE at the expense of agriculture, recreation, and other economic interests in our community."[19] FAIR, for its part, asked a federal district court in Albany, New York, for a preliminary injunction blocking EPA from issuing a final decision until it provided additional information on the impact of the dredging project. However, the U.S. District Court for the Northern District of New York ruled that it did not have jurisdiction over the case because the Superfund Amendments and Reauthorization Act of 1986 prohibited judicial review at that point in the case.[20]

Supporters of the Cleanup

For their part, most of the environmental groups continued to think that the cleanup was the right thing to do. Advocates of the cleanup said that the project would be a "gift from heaven" to the rustbelt towns along the Hudson River. Friends of a Clean Hudson, a coalition of 11 major environmental groups, commissioned a study in which they concluded that thousands of jobs and hundreds of millions of dollars would come into the area once the project was under way. The coalition claimed benefits that could include the creation of close to 9,000 new jobs with annual payrolls of up to $346 million. In a reaction to this report, Rep. Maurice Hinchey, whose district includes a downstate portion of the river, claimed that as a result of the dredging, "tourism will increase, the fishing industry will be revived, thousands of jobs will be created and property values will rise."[21]

According to reporter John Elvin, there are many festering grudges still held against GE. GE was once the centerpiece of the bustling and prosperous area. He contends that GE eventually left the region because of New York's antibusiness environment and that, in recent years, legislators have felt free to tax the company to their heart's content, but the company expressed its own right to pack up and leave. Elvin maintains that many state and local officials, and some citizens, just wanted a last piece of GE's hide—a last chance to make GE pay.[22]

WORKING TOWARD A SETTLEMENT

Companies may resist, but government agencies do not go away. Such is the case in the continuing saga of the Hudson River cleanup. In 2001, the Bush Administration ordered a full-scale dredging of a 40-mile stretch of the river. It was to be the largest environmental dredging project in history. GE was expected to pay the estimated $490 million charge for the cleanup and the project was expected to take about a decade, with plans for the dredging to begin in 2005.

In 2003, it was reported that the Hudson River cleanup was moving on schedule although at the time GE was withholding payments, according to environmental groups. A spokesman for Environmental Advocates, one of 13 concerned groups that formed the Friends of a Clean Hudson coalition said, "contrary to dire predictions of two or three years ago, the project is on track." Critics said that GE had not been cooperative, but the company denied this evaluation of its efforts. At that time, the environmental groups graded the key players in the cleanup. The EPA got a "B" and GE got a "D."[23]

Performance Standards Finalized

In May 2004, the EPA finally released its final quality of life performance standards for the Hudson River cleanup.[24] By March 2004, an environmental progress report was released in which it was stated that more than 290,000 pounds of PCBs had been removed from the Hudson Falls Plant Site. GE installed a comprehensive network of collection and monitoring wells to capture PCBs in the bedrock and prevent them from reaching the river. Also in 2004, the New York State Department of Environmental Conservation (DEC) approved GE's plan to build innovative under-the-river tunnels to capture the final few ounces a day of PCBs that are thought to trickle out of the river bottom near the Hudson Falls Plant.[25]

Dredging Delayed, Backroom Deals

According to environmental groups, GE dragged its feet in moving forward with the cleanup. Initially, dredging was to begin in 2005, but due to GE-requested delays, the start date got pushed back to 2009. Also, the Natural Resources Defense Council (NRDC), an environmental group, claimed that in 2005 the EPA rewarded GE's foot dragging by striking a backroom deal that required GE to commit only to completing the Phase 1 of the cleanup—just 10 percent of the total job.[26]

Settlement Reached

On November 2, 2006, the federal district court signed off on the EPA–GE settlement. This agreement allowed for the dredging of the PCB-contaminated river sediments to proceed. GE continued to challenge the EPA over important details, and it continued to press a federal lawsuit challenging the EPA's authority to require GE in the future to complete Phase 2 of the cleanup. If GE got out of the second phase, taxpayers would have to foot the bill to clean up the remaining mess, face protracted legal battles with GE to get it to complete the job, or else be forced to live with a polluted river indefinitely. Much of the upper Hudson River had already been closed to fishing. South of Troy, New York, women of childbearing age and children have been advised not to eat fish at all. In addition, according to the NRDC, the pollution was spreading, continuing to move downriver from Albany.[27]

PHASE 1 (2009) OF DREDGING PROJECT COMPLETED

After legal squabbling, Phase 1 of the GE dredging project began and was completed in 2009. The work spanned the period of May 15 to November 15, 2009. The task focused on removal of PCB-contaminated sediment from a six-mile stretch of the upper Hudson River. GE removed approximately 10 percent of the contamination scheduled to be dredged during the expected six-year project. During this time, the depth of contamination was found to be greater than expected due to dense logging debris.

In addition to the PCB removal, Phase 1 was intended to allow GE and EPA to evaluate project progress and to make program adjustments to improve compliance with EPA's performance standards. The standards were intended to ensure that dredging operations were done safely and with public health being protected at all times.[28]

At the same time that GE was pursuing Phase 1 of the dredging, it had an outstanding lawsuit filed in 2000 in which it challenged the EPA Superfund law's application to the Hudson River case as unconstitutional. In June 2010, GE lost this lawsuit and its appeal to the U.S. Court of Appeals. A spokesman for the company said, "GE is evaluating the decision and reviewing its options."[29]

PHASE 2 (2011–2015)

According to the Phase 2 Fact Sheet issued by the EPA, Phase 2 of the dredging by GE took place between 2011 and 2015.[30] In November, 2015, the EPA approved the PCB Facility Demobilization Restoration Plan that allowed GE to dismantle and decontaminate the 110 acre sediment processing facility that was built to support the dredging of the Hudson River by GE.[31] With the dredging now complete, the demobilization process will run into 2016. In general, the multistep demobilization process includes:

- Decontamination of equipment and infrastructure (e.g., unloading equipment, buildings, concrete surfaces)
- Sampling of equipment/materials
- Final placement of equipment/materials (e.g., sale, reuse, salvage/recycling, or off-site disposal)
- Environmental sampling (soil, groundwater, sediment, and surface water)
- Property restoration[32]

For GE, even winding down has been a complicated process and differences of opinion about what to do and when to do it generated considerable discussion. Some commenters did not want the EPA to allow the demobilization to occur in case there is an opportunity for more dredging. Other observers requested that the infrastructure remain in place to support future development of the site for the economic benefit of the local municipalities. The final determination as to what will be left in place is still ongoing.[33]

The Hudson River cleanup turned out to be the "largest environmental river-dredging project in the history of the nation," said the EPA's regional administrator, Judith Enck.[34] Even as the cleanup was ending, GE has received overtures from the state to move its corporate headquarters back after 40 years in Connecticut.[35] In 2016, GE announced they would move their headquarters to Massachusetts.

IS IT EVER OVER?

As GE is wrapping up the \$1.6 billion, seven-year dredging project, environmental groups, and some government agencies say that it still has not done enough. The Natural Resources Defense Council and other agencies that have a role in the next stage of river restoration say that GE is being allowed to exit the project despite solid evidence that the dredging has worked as planned. The National Oceanic & Atmospheric Administration (NOAA) and the Fish and Wildlife Service, the appointed trustees for the cleanup, have said that the PCB levels will not fall enough to levels allowing safe consumption of fish for decades longer than EPA's projection.[36] EPA issued a white paper in which it responded to

NOAA's predictions. EPA says that NOAA's conclusions about delayed fish recovery were based on an analysis of a limited number of fish species collected at only one location. Further, EPA claims that NOAA's study does not reflect fish and water data that have been collected over a long period of time.[37]

Both GE and the EPA reject the idea that more dredging may need to be done. The EPA says that 65 percent of the contaminants have been removed, and it thinks PCB levels will decline significantly in the coming years. A GE spokesman asserts that the company has met every obligation it had imposed on it. Next, GE and EPA will commence the next phase of the cleanup; a $20 million study trying to estimate how much GE will have to pay to clean up some related land projects that could take another decade.[38]

QUESTIONS FOR DISCUSSION

1. What are the social, ethical, and political issues in this case? Which are major and which are minor?
2. Who are the stakeholders and what are their stakes? Assess the different stakeholders' legitimacy, power, and urgency.
3. Do your own research on PCBs. Do your findings clarify their status as being so hazardous they must be removed? Or should they best have been left where they had been settled?
4. When GE contaminated the Hudson River, it was not breaking the law. Who is responsible for the contaminated Hudson River? GE? EPA? State of New York? Local citizens? What ethical principles help to answer this question?
5. Do research on the EPA Superfund. Does it appear to be fair environmental legislation? Should a company have to pay for something that was legal at the time they did it?
6. Do research on this case and update the case facts. Has anything changed since the facts were presented that affects its resolution?
7. What lessons about environment and sustainability do you take away from this complex, lengthy pollution and cleanup of the Hudson River? Will it ever be over?

ENDNOTES

1. James L. Nash, "Compliance Not Good Enough, GE Finds Out," *Occupational Hazards* (September 2001), 47ff.
2. "Hudson River Cleanup," *Business Insurance* (August 6, 2001), 2.
3. Monica Roman, "GE's Hudson River Blues," *Businessweek* (August 13, 2001), 40.
4. John Elvin, "Greens Exploit Terror against GE," *Insight* (November 19, 2001), 22–25.
5. Glenn Hess, "Hudson River Cleanup Could Cost GE about $460 Million," *Chemical Market Reporter* (August 6, 2001), 1, 29.
6. Ibid., 23.
7. Ibid.
8. Ibid., 24.
9. Ibid.
10. Ibid., 1, 29.
11. Elvin, 25.
12. Ibid., 24.
13. Ibid.
14. Ibid., 23.
15. Ibid., 25.
16. Hess, 29.
17. Ibid., 24.
18. Ibid.
19. Ibid.
20. "New York Attacks Push Back Decision on Hudson Dredging," *Chemical Market Reporter* (October 1, 2001), 18.
21. Elvin, 25.
22. Ibid., 22.
23. Yancey Roy, "Environmental Groups Check on Hudson River Cleanup," *Rochester Democrat and Chronicle* (February 7, 2003).
24. Hudson River PCBs Superfund Site, http://www.epa.gov/hudson/. Accessed June 15, 2016.
25. "New York State Approves GE Plan for Hudson River Tunnel Project" (press release) (March 16, 2004), http://www.ge.com/en/company/news/hudson_tunnel.htm.
26. National Resources Defense Council, https://www.nrdc.org/issues/healthy-rivers-and-ecosystems. Accessed June 15, 2016.
27. Ibid.
28. Environmental Protection Agency, "Hudson River PCBs Superfund Site—Phase 1 Dredging Fact Sheet" (November 2009), http://www.hudsondredgingdata.com/. Accessed June 15, 2016.
29. Mary Esch, "GE loses appeal of Superfund case," *Timesunion*, June 30, 2010, http://www.timesunion.com/news/article/GE-loses-appeal-of

-Superfund-case-562833.php. Accessed June 15, 2016.

30. U.S. EPA, Hudson River PCBs Superfund Site, "Phase 2 Overview Fact Sheet 2015," https://www3.epa.gov/hudson/pdf/Phase2_Overview-2015.pdf. Accessed June 15, 2016.
31. U.S. EPA, "EPA Statement on Approval of PCB Processing Facility Demobilization and Restoration Plan for Hudson River Clean Up," November 12, 2015, http://www.hudsondredgingdata.com/documents/pdf/DemobPlan_ApprovalStatement_Final.pdf. Accessed June 15, 2016.
32. Ibid.
33. Ibid.
34. Ted Mann, "GE Nears End of Hudson Cleanup," *The Wall Street Journal*, November 12, 2015, B3.
35. Ibid.
36. Ibid.
37. U.S. EPA, Hudson River PCBs Superfund Site, "EPA Response to NOAA Hudson River PCB Fish Analysis," March 29, 2016, http://www.hudsondredgingdata.com/documents/pdf/EPA%20Response%20to%20NOAA%20-%20Factsheet.pdf. Accessed June 15, 2016.
38. Ibid.

CASE 23

What Have You Done for Me Lately? The Case of Amazon in South Carolina*

Often, state and local governments use tax cuts (abatements) or other types of incentives to entice firms to locate within their area. While tax abatements remain useful incentives to help governments achieve job creation goals, those same cuts may create undue burdens for other stakeholders such as taxpayers, and local businesses who do not benefit from tax cuts. The case of Amazon in South Carolina (S.C.) may be one such example.

BRIEF HISTORY OF AMAZON.COM

Amazon.com began in 1995 as one of the earliest online bookstores. Jeff Bezos started the online bookstore in his garage in Seattle, Washington, and within 30 days, the company sold books online to customers in all 50 U.S. states as well as in 45 countries.[1] Amazon.com is a 24/7 e-commerce retailer with nearly 240,000 employees.[2] Since its inception, Amazon has leveraged its technology to offer customers personalized services such as "1-Click® Shopping," Wish Lists, personalized suggestions, and customer reviews of products. In addition to the United States, the company operates in several countries including the United Kingdom, Germany, Canada, and France.

Over the last two decades, Amazon has engaged in over 60 acquisitions to expand the firm with online retailers like ShopBop.com, Zappos.com, Soap.com, and Endless.com, as well as online payment companies like Emvantage, and advanced delivery options like Prime and Prime Now.[3] Amazon maintains a large inventory of downloadable films and TV shows, and they continue to expand their store concepts (e.g., Groceries, Motorcycles) each year. Their Kindle e-book reader is now its eighth generation.[4] In sum, Amazon's focus for growth since its beginnings has been upon exploiting technology efficiently for the benefit of their customers and shareholders.

"Fulfillment centers," where goods and services are held and then distributed, are instrumental to Amazon's success in their distribution strategy.[5] Amazon started with two fulfillment centers in Seattle and Delaware; currently they have approximately 78 centers in the United States, and another 87 sorting centers and hubs—amounting to almost 70 million active square feet of storage space.[6] They also have 84 international fulfillment and storage centers in countries like Japan, Ireland, China, Costa Rica, the United Kingdom, and India.[7]

---

*This case was prepared by Linda Rodriguez, University of South Carolina-Aiken, and Jill A. Brown, Bentley University, in 2016.

AMAZON IN SOUTH CAROLINA

In 2012, Amazon decided to build a fulfillment center in Lexington, South Carolina. It was an ideal location for its southeast distribution network. Along with plans to do the same in Tennessee, it began to negotiate with the S.C. state legislature. Specifically, Jeff Bezos said that he would not open a fulfillment center in South Carolina unless the state agreed that Amazon would not have to collect sales tax from S.C. residents.[8] He had negotiated this deal with other states under a 1992 U.S. Supreme Court ruling holding that the Constitution's commerce clause prevents state officials from requiring retailers who have no physical presence in their states to collect their sales taxes.[9]

South Carolina agreed with his request after initially voting it down.[10] They did this, in part, because Amazon immediately canceled $52 million in procurement contracts and removed all job postings from their Web site when they encountered opposition.[11] To incentivize the company to locate to Lexington, the state legislature of South Carolina, in conjunction with Lexington County, granted Amazon approximately 90 acres of land, a five-year exemption from charging S.C. residents state sales tax, capital property tax cuts, and state job tax credits. Further, the long-standing Sunday-morning sales restrictions were lifted so that Amazon could fill orders around the clock.[12]

At the time of the negotiations, South Carolina had been experiencing some of the highest unemployment in the country. The Bureau of Labor listed South Carolina's unemployment in August 2011 as 10.9 percent, causing the state to be ranked at 48 out of 50 in unemployment.[13] The lure of new job opportunities through Amazon was hard for the S.C. legislature to resist. Amazon agreed that in return for building and tax concessions, they would hire primarily from within S.C., adding 1,250 jobs in the first year, with an additional 750 jobs over the next five years. However, the deal was highly debated.

At first, Governor Nikki Haley staunchly opposed the S.C. sales tax exemption because many local businesses believed that the exemption would create an unfair tax advantage for Amazon relative to other S.C. firms. At least 20 S.C. lawmakers agreed, including S.C. State Representative Gary Simrill (R-York), who claimed that the sales tax break gave Amazon an unfair advantage over local brick and mortar businesses.[14]

However, the S.C. legislature let the deal pass, and Governor Haley capitulated by not vetoing the bill. In the end, the legislature supported the bill with the notion that building the distribution center would support job creation, and the staffing of the distribution center from local labor pools would help South Carolina's economic recovery. Further, South Carolina expected to net $11 million in payroll and property taxes per year regardless of losing the S.C. state sales tax revenues from Amazon.[15] In essence, the legislature, the Governor and Amazon stuck to "quid pro quo" negotiations, essentially ignoring many local stakeholder interests and the opposing voices from the community.

Table 1 presents the estimated costs of the deal between Amazon and the state of South Carolina.

TABLE 1 Estimated Costs for First Five Years of Operations

	Amazon	S.C.
Estimated (cost) of 90-acre land grant and other concessions		(4,000,000)
Estimated tax break impact in first five years of operation ($2.5 million per year)		(12,500,000)
Estimated income to S.C. from collecting Amazon payroll and property taxes in first five years		11,000,000
Gain of jobs in first five years		2,000
Estimated cost to Amazon for building	125,000,000	
Estimated total of major (costs) during the first five years	**125,000,000**	**(5,500,000)**
Estimated 20-year gain to S.C. after 20 years of operations		1,700,000,000
Estimated long-term gain to S.C. revenue after 20 years		**1,694,500,000**

NIKKI HALEY, GOVERNOR OF SOUTH CAROLINA

Nikki Haley, in 2011, was the nation's youngest governor at age 39.[16] Governor Haley ran as a fiscal conservative becoming South Carolina's first female and ethnic minority governor.[17] She was born in Bamberg, S.C., to Indian immigrants, where her first job was in her family's clothing store as a bookkeeper; she started the job when she was 13. She attended and graduated from Clemson University with a B.S. degree in accounting. Upon graduation, she worked as an accounting supervisor for FCR Recycling, Inc., and five of its subsidiaries. Eventually, she returned to the family business, growing it into a multimillion dollar operation.[18]

At the time of the Amazon deal, Governor Haley was in a tough position. Former Governor Mark Sanford, who finished his office under the scandal of an extramarital affair, had promised Amazon the tax breaks in late 2010.[19] When Governor Haley relented to the decision of the S.C. legislature, she said that although she opposed the tax breaks, she would honor the commitments made by the previous administration. However, she vowed that, "we will never have a change like this in tax policy under the Haley administration in order to get jobs. It is bad policy and it is not something we are going to have happen."[20]

AMAZON.COM'S OPPOSITION

Local groups and businesses most opposed to the bill becoming law spent nearly $166,000 for lobbyists to halt the sales tax break.[21] To fight back, Amazon spent nearly $200,000 for their own set of lobbyists, although various reports said the total amount was more because neither side was compelled to disclose total costs. Some claimed that the costs to battle the sales tax break approached $2 million.[22] Among those opposed to the Amazon.com deal was the S.C. Alliance for Main Street Fairness, which formed a coalition of local businesses.[23]

THE RESULT

In 2012, Amazon built the fulfillment center in Lexington, South Carolina, at a total cost of around $2 million.[24] Then, it announced plans to open a second fulfillment center in Spartanburg County, South Carolina, such that the total investment in South Carolina fulfillment centers would be close to $50 million.[25] Vice President of Amazon Global Customer Fulfillment David Clark announced, "We had a great first holiday season in Lexington County and we look forward to serving our customers from both Lexington and Spartanburg Counties by the fall."[26]

CORPORATE WELFARE

The subject of tax and other incentives to lure businesses to an area is an example of what has been called "corporate welfare." Corporate welfare are those actions that governments take that provide benefits to a corporation or industry and may include things like grants, tax breaks, and regulatory preference.[27] However, the example of Amazon in South Carolina shows how contentious corporate welfare might be. Some say that the uncollected sales tax from Amazon costs each state quite a bit of lost revenue. According to a 2014 report by the National Conference of State Legislatures, South Carolina lost out on an estimated $254 million in taxes from out-of-state sales, mostly online.[28] One expert estimated that in total, Amazon's Sales-Tax-Free Status has cost states almost $8.6 billion in tax revenues.[29]

On New Year's Day, 2016, the sales tax breaks the South Carolina Legislature gave Amazon in 2011 expired. The Department of Revenue and Fiscal Affairs in South Carolina estimates that now the state will start taking in $13.8 million in sales tax revenue through Amazon purchases annually.[30] Was it worth it? By 2015, Amazon had brought more than 1500 full-time jobs to the area, and around the time the tax incentives expired, Amazon announced they would hire another 500 additional workers.[31] Governor Haley responded to the announcement of its new hiring with the following message:

> *For a company like Amazon to make the decision to expand its operations in South Carolina, it is a special source of pride and a reason to celebrate because it proves what we already know—that we have a world class work force and competitive business environment. The 500 new jobs this expansion will create is terrific news for the Midlands community, and we look forward to watching Amazon continue to grow here for many years to come.*[32]

QUESTIONS FOR DISCUSSION

1. Who is helped and who gets hurt in the use of tax incentives? Draw a stakeholder map for Amazon and the governments involved, who was excluded, or who could have been included?

2. Did Amazon, the South Carolina State Legislature, and the county of Lexington, S.C., arrive at creating shared value for the greatest number of stakeholders?
3. What is the nature of the various stakeholder stakes? Are they owners or community members? Analyze their legitimacy, power, and urgency characteristics.
4. Was Amazon abusing its power when it canceled procurement contracts and job postings if it did not get its way?
5. Could the state of South Carolina, or Lexington County, have asked for more or were they fortunate to get what they got?
6. Do "corporate welfare" deals like this give Amazon an unfair advantage over other businesses that do not receive tax breaks? What are the ethical issues involved in this decision?
7. What updates can you find about this tax break issue in South Carolina or in other states?

ENDNOTES

1. Amazon.com, https://www.amazon.com/p/feature/rzekmvyjojcp6uc?ref_=aa_nav_footer. Accessed June 21, 2016.
2. Philip Elmer-DeWitt, "Amazon Now Has Twice as Many Employees as Apple," Fortune (February 8, 2016), http://fortune.com/2016/02/08/apple-amazon-hiring-spree/. Accessed June 23, 2016.
3. Kristin Pryor, "A History of Amazon's Acquisitions," *Tech.Co* (May 23, 2016), http://tech.co/history-amazon-acquisitions-2016-05. Accessed June 21, 2016.
4. Mike Brown, "Fans to Amazon: Either Leave 'Perfect' Kindle Alone or Make It an iPad," *Inverse.com* (April 7, 2016), https://www.inverse.com/article/13942-fans-to-amazon-either-leave-perfect-kindle-alone-or-make-it-an-ipad. Accessed June 21, 2016.
5. Dan Berthiaume, "Amazon's Expanding Footprint Includes New Fulfillment Centers, College Pickup Locations," *Retailing Today* (April 27, 2016), http://www.retailingtoday.com/article/amazons-expanding-footprint-includes-new-fulfillment-centers-college-pickup-locations. Accessed June 22, 2016.
6. MWPVL International, "Amazon Global Fulfillment Center Network," (June 2016), http://www.mwpvl.com/html/amazon_com.html. Accessed June 22, 2016.
7. Ibid.
8. Tim Flach, "Amazon Packing after South Carolina Tax Vote," *McClatchyDC*, http://www.mcclatchydc.com/news/nation-world/national/economy/article24626677.html. Accessed June 21, 2016.
9. Janet Novack, "Amazon's Special Deals with States Unconstitutional, Law Profs Say," Forbes (December 4, 2011), http://www.forbes.com/sites/janetnovack/2011/12/04/amazons-special-deals-with-states-unconstitutional-law-profs-say/#4ddfcf2c73c7. Accessed June 22, 2016.
10. Ibid.
11. Ibid.
12. Charles Reynolds, "Sunday Blue Laws Ended in Lexington County," *The Examiner* (December 23, 2010), http://www.examiner.com/article/sunday-blue-laws-ended-lexington-county. Accessed June 23, 2016.
13. Bureau of Labor Statistics, "State Unemployment Rates 2011," http://www.bls.gov/opub/ted/2012/ted_20120313.htm. Accessed June 23, 2016.
14. Cassie Cope, "Controversial Amazon SC Tax Break Set to Expire in 2016, The State (December 28, 2014), http://www.thestate.com/news/local/article13930880.html. Accessed June 23, 2016.
15. Ibid.
16. K Severson, "South Carolina's Young Governor Has a High Profile and Higher Hopes," *Spartanburg Herald Journal* (July 3, 2011), 1.
17. Leah Jessen, "29 Facts about Nikki Haley," *The Daily Signal* (January 12, 2016), http://dailysignal.com/2016/01/12/29-facts-about-nikki-haley-who-will-give-the-gop-response-to-the-state-of-the-union/. Accessed June 23, 2016.
18. Ibid.
19. Rosalie Thompson, "Nikki Haley Will Leave Amazon Tax Breaks up to Legislature," Examiner (April 6, 2011), http://www.examiner.com/article/nikki-haley-will-leave-amazon-tax-breaks-up-to-legislature. Accessed June 22, 2016.
20. Ibid.
21. Tim Flatch, "Reports Hint at High Cost of Amazon Tax-Break Battle," *The State 2011*(July 12, 2011), 1.
22. Ibid.
23. Ibid.

24. John Cook, "Amazon Fulfillment Centers Planned for India, South Carolina," *Geekwire* (January 23, 2012), http://www.geekwire.com/2012/amazoncom-plans-distribution-centers-india-south-carolina/. Accessed June 23, 2016.
25. Ibid.
26. "Amazon Announces New Facility in Spartanburg County, South Carolina," South Carolina Department of Commerce (January 23, 2012), http://sccommerce.com/news/press-releases/amazon-announces-new-facility-spartanburg county-south-carolina. Accessed June 22, 2016.
27. C.E. Dawkins, "Corporate Welfare, Corporate Citizenship and the Question of Accountability," *Business & Society* (Volume 41, Issue 3, 2002), 269–291.
28. "No More Tax Breaks for S.C. Amazon Shoppers," *WYFF4.com* (January 3, 2016), http://www.wyff4.com/news/No-more-tax-breaks-for-S-C-Amazon-shoppers/37242228. Accessed June 23, 2016.
29. Peter Cohan, "Amazon's Sales-Tax-Free Status Cost States $8.6 Billion," *Forbes* (October 17, 2012), http://www.forbes.com/sites/petercohan/2012/10/17/amazons-sales-tax-free-status-cost-states-8-6-billion/#1a0fcc452234. Accessed June 22, 2016.
30. Turnage, 2015.
31. Jeremy Turnage, "500 More Jobs Heading to Amazon Distribution Center," *WISTV.com* (March 20, 2015), http://www.wistv.com/story/28352665/500-more-jobs-heading-to-amazon-distribution-center. Accessed June 22, 2016.
32. "Amazon Expanding Lexington County Operations," South Carolina Department of Commerce (March 10, 2015), http://sccommerce.com/news/press-releases/amazon-expanding-lexington-county-operations. Accessed June 22, 2016.

CASE 24

Everlane: Ethical Chic and Radical Transparency in Global Supply Chains*

Global supply chains have been wrought with controversy for decades now. Images and stories of global manufacturing, and particularly textile manufacturing, have highlighted issues of unsafe working conditions, child labor, unfair wages, and corruption.

Enter a company called Everlane, an online clothing company founded in 2010 and committed to "radical transparency." Its founder, Michael Preysman, wanted to develop a clothing brand that was both ethical and trendy, commonly known as *ethical fashion*, or, as Preysman described it, a brand that followed the "look of Céline and the ethics of Patagonia."[1] He started with venture capital money to offer high-quality clothes at lower prices that would be sold online under the mission to provide radical transparency. This included providing customers information about how Everlane found "the best factories in the world" to ensure a factory's integrity.[2]

Preysman then began publicizing the costs of making Everlane shirts on Facebook, which broke tradition from the unspoken protocol of keeping this information as a trade secret.[3] He noted that in "traditional retail," a designer shirt is marked up eight times by the time it reaches the customer and he promised to be fairer to the consumer by passing on the cost savings of being an online-only store to the customer.[4] More transparency followed, focusing in on its global supply chain partners. For example, in response to the Rana Plaza collapse in Bangladesh in 2013, when more than 1,100 workers died in factories that supplied clothes to European and American retailers, Everlane posted videos and photos of the workers and factories that they use for their production.

To do business with Everlane, factories have to be willing to be photographed and have their costs and audit scores made public. They must supply information about their workers' dorms, including the

*This case was prepared by Jill A Brown, Bentley University, in 2016.

availability of hot water, heating, and air conditioning. All of this information reinforces Everlane's commitment to radical transparency, noted on their Web site byline as, "Know your factories. Know your costs. Always ask why."[5]

ETHICAL FASHION

Companies like Everlane are part of a bigger fashion trend that supports the concept of ethical fashion and sustainable practices. This trend is associated with a rise in conscious consumerism that has driven many companies to make serious changes to their global supply chains and increase their reputation as good corporate citizens.[6] Some companies have chosen to be Fair Trade certified through the nonprofit corporation, Fair Trade USA, which introduced more than 334 compliance criteria for textile factories in 2012, and whose certification now appears on 20 brands, including Patagonia and Bed Bath & Beyond.[7] Others have chosen to pursue a "slow fashion" trend that involves taking the time to source organic materials and articles made by artisans and craftspeople around the globe and viewing apparel as a more long-term investment.[8] This trend has sparked an annual "Fashion Revolution Day" to generate awareness of slow fashion and a call for accountability through all steps in the clothes-making process."[9]

Everlane has not pursued certification or slow fashion, but the company is very much aware of the steps in its supply chain; it is committed to ethical production. Everlane searches for factories certified by independent outside organizations—in fact, Preysman himself spends time with each factory's owner to get some idea about whether he or she is "a decent human being."[10] The focus of Everlane is on an ethical production process, rather than using organics or fair trade collections, or "artisan made" classifications, which are other alternatives for ethical fashion.[11]

During a recent review of one of their Chinese suppliers, Everlane was deciding whether to break ties with the factory after it twice failed an independent audit that tried to reconcile workers' hours with wages paid.[12] Everlane was trying to work with the supplier to raise it audit scores, rather than simply cut ties with the organization in part because of a sense of loyalty to the relationship, but also because Everlane has struggled over the years to find good suppliers in China that were willing to take on a smaller company. Everlane sales are said to be around $25 million, and they simultaneously compete against and rely upon large global buyers to recommend them to good suppliers.[13] If they do not get a recommendation, they are often at a loss to find anyone to work with them.[14]

SUPPLY CHAIN CHALLENGES

So, the question becomes, how can a smaller company like Everlane locate good, but cheap and efficient suppliers for their products, who are also willing to be transparent and accountable to the company? Sourcing goods and suppliers in China, which still offers the lowest relative costs of manufacturing, can be very difficult, in general, for smaller U.S. companies.[15] Some Business-to-Business sourcing platforms have endorsed service provider lists and supplier blacklists that can be helpful, but it is often a question of access for smaller companies like Everlane.[16]

Some suggest that companies like Everlane become more integrated with Chinese companies and offer Chinese suppliers the opportunity for them to move up the value chain by offering more design input, more make-on-demand, and venturing into higher-technology components.[17] However, Everlane likes the ability to control costs and quality in their current model. They share production costs with their customers, and when they see an increase in costs, they try to figure out how to lower them.[18] Therefore, while it is difficult to get in the door with suppliers who agree to be transparent, once they are in the door, they work hard to train their suppliers to be efficient as well.

TRANSPARENCY AT ALL COSTS

On the upside, because Everlane is relatively small, it has the opportunity to visit, vet, and negotiate with suppliers. For example, executives from Everlane, including Preysman, often visit Chinese suppliers after the Lunar New Year holiday in February, when they can get a sense of how many workers return to work after the holiday—an important indicator of how well the factory treats them.[19] So, while Everlane faces some significant challenges in holding to its mission of ethical production through transparency, they feel comfortable with a model that allows them some control over cost and quality. According to Preysman, "We look for partners with the same aesthetics."[20] While some worry that Everlane's ambitions to be ethical and transparent cannot keep up with its growth, Preysman argues that the bigger his company is, the more impact he can make.[21]

QUESTIONS FOR DISCUSSION

1. What are the ethical and social issues in this case?
2. How difficult is it for a company like Everlane to follow through on its mission? What are the challenges to its commitment to radical transparency in global supply chains?
3. What are the different ways that a fashion company can be ethical?
4. What interest groups might support an ethical fashion group like Everlane? How could they do this?
5. What are the other stakeholder groups that are involved with Everlane? How would each stakeholder view Everlane's quest for transparency and ethical production?
6. How does Everlane's approach to their supply chain differ from a large global buyer like Nike?
7. Is the Everlane business model sustainable? Or, is it just temporarily popular because it is unique? Are competitors likely to follow?

ENDNOTES

1. Susan Berfield, "Making Ethical Chic," *Bloomberg Businessweek* (December 7–13, 2015), 58.
2. Everlane, https://www.everlane.com/about. Accessed June 20, 2016.
3. Berfield, 2015.
4. Ibid.
5. Ibid.
6. Nayelli Gonzalez, "A Brief History of Sustainable Fashion," *TriplePundit* (February 19, 2015), http://www.triplepundit.com/special/sustainable-fashion-2014/brief-history-sustainable-fashion/#. Accessed June 22, 2016.
7. Andria Cheng, " 'Fair trade' Becomes a Fashion Trend," *The Wall Street Journal* (July 7, 2015), http://www.wsj.com/articles/fair-trade-becomes-a-fashion-trend-1436307440. Accessed June 21, 2016.
8. Colleen Kane, "Who Made Your Clothes? A 'Slow Fashion' Revolution Rises," *Fortune* (April 24, 2015), http://fortune.com/2015/04/24/clothes-slow-fashion-zady/. Accessed June 22, 2016.
9. Ibid.
10. Stephanie Clifford, "Some Retailers Say More about Their Clothing's Origins," *The New York Times* (May 8, 2013), http://www.nytimes.com/2013/05/09/business/global/fair-trade-movement-extends-to-clothing.html. Accessed June 21, 2016.
11. Fair Trade Winds and The Good Trade, "35 Fair Trade and Ethical Clothing Brands That Are Betting against Fast Fashion," *The Good Trade* (2015), http://www.thegoodtrade.com/features/fair-trade-clothing. Accessed June 21, 2016.
12. Berfield, 2015.
13. Ibid.
14. Ibid.
15. Rick Frasch, "Sourcing Goods and Suppliers in China: A How-to-Guide for Small Businesses," *Forbes* (January 6, 2014), http://www.forbes.com/sites/allbusiness/2014/01/06/sourcing-goods-and-suppliers-in-china-a-how-to-guide-for-small-businesses/#126f84fb5e5b. Accessed June 21, 2016.
16. Ibid.
17. Michael Zakkour, "Supply Chain Key to Success in China-Outlook 2014," *Forbes Asia* (February 6, 2014), http://www.forbes.com/sites/michaelzakkour/2014/02/06/supply-chain-key-to-success-in-china-outlook-2014/#70dedbc12e35. Accessed June 21, 2016.
18. Berfield, 2015.
19. Ibid.
20. Ibid.
21. Ibid.

CASE 25

New Belgium Brewing: Defining a Business on Sustainability*

When Jeff Lebesch and Kim Jordan expanded from home beer brewing to commercial production in 1991, they envisioned two goals for their new company: they believed they could produce world-class beers and they believed they could do this while kindling social, environmental, and cultural change. In 2012, their company, New Belgium Brewing Company (NBB), has become the third largest craft brewery in the United States and the eighth largest producer in the overall industry.[1] The brewery also stands as a corporate leader in environmental sustainability and provides an example of how a company can incorporate environmental concerns into everyday business decisions.[2] However, as NBB continues to expand, the company faces a number of challenges in reaching its environmental goals, many of which it cannot directly control.

HISTORY OF NEW BELGIUM BREWERY

Jeff was inspired to found New Belgium Brewing (NBB) while on a 1989 bike ride through the Belgian countryside.[3] During his trek, he perceived a lack of flavor in American beers compared to those he was drinking in Europe. When he returned home to Colorado, he set out on a quest to introduce American beer drinkers to the unique essence found in traditional Belgian brews, from the tart framboise, the light saison, and the truly one-of-a-kind trappist ales. Using his home brewing experience, Jeff was able to develop a distinctive recipe for traditional Belgian amber ale. The ale, dubbed Fat Tire in commemoration to the inspirational bike trip, became the brewery's flagship beer. By 1991, Jeff and Kim formally organized the brewery as New Belgium Brewing Company and began selling the first bottles of Fat Tire around their hometown of Fort Collins, Colorado.

Kim, serving as the businessperson of the two, engaged in the marketing and distribution operations, selling the beer to friends, neighbors, and local bars/stores. A neighbor provided the watercolors that adorn the beers' labels, a tradition that lives on today. The beers were brewed in the couple's basement, using an 8.5-barrel system (one barrel is 31 gallons) allowing for total production in 1992 of 993 barrels.[4] By 2012, NBB produced over 750,000 barrels and sold in 31 states.[5] In 1991, the company only produced two types of beer, the signature Fat Tire Amber Ale and the darker Abbey Dubbel. Today, NBB regularly produces 21 different styles, 11 being produced year-round. The main brewery is still located in Fort Collins, Colorado, and a new second brewery is opening in Ashville, North Carolina.

CORE VALUES

Unique in the founding story of New Belgium Brewing is a commitment to a set of values that were adopted from the beginning. Before initial production and during the planning stages of the business, Kim and Jeff developed a set of core values and beliefs by which they would guide their company. Listed below, it is clear from this set of values that profitability is secondary to a sense of social responsibility. This responsibility is centered on two core concepts: the production of quality beer and beer culture and a business that can produce this beer while paying attention to environmental and social concerns. All business decisions are made according to the core values and beliefs, and everything is done with the mission "to operate a profitable company which is socially, ethically, and environmentally responsible, and that produces high quality beer true to Belgian styles."[6] The values live on today, unchanged from their original conception, guiding the 300-plus person company into the new era of craft brewing.

Our Core Values and Beliefs[7]

- ***Remembering*** that we are incredibly lucky to create something fine that enhances people's lives while surpassing our consumers' expectations.
- ***Producing*** world-class beers.
- ***Promoting*** beer culture and the responsible enjoyment of beer.
- ***Kindling*** social, environmental, and cultural change as a role model of a sustainable business.
- ***Environmental stewardship***: Honoring nature at every turn of the business.
- ***Cultivating*** potential through learning, high-involvement culture, and the pursuit of opportunities.

*This case was prepared by Revised and updated in 2016 by Jill Brown, Bentley University.

- ***Balancing*** the myriad needs of the company, our co-workers, and families.
- ***Trusting*** each other and committing to authentic relationships and communications.
- ***Continuous***, innovative quality and efficiency improvements.
- ***Having fun.***

NEW BELGIUM'S SUSTAINABILITY EFFORTS

In the spirit of the core values, NBB has attempted to implement sustainable efforts in all aspects of the brewing process. Some of NBB's efforts include the following.[8]

Electricity

In 1998, NBB conducted a study to analyze its carbon emissions. It was found that the single largest factor was emissions generated from its electricity consumption—emissions released by coal-fired power plants. In response, NBB owners (which included the founders and approximately 90 employees) unanimously voted to source their electricity from 100 percent renewable, carbon-free wind sources. At a premium of 57 percent on its electricity bill, NBB became the first completely wind powered brewery. NBB also introduced a combination of solar PV, co-generation, metering, and control initiatives in an attempt to become a net-zero purchaser of electricity. A further example of its efficiency and conservation efforts includes the development of a "natural draft cooling" system, which utilizes outside air for refrigeration when the temperature is below 40 degrees. By 2015, 12.6 percent of NBB electricity was produced on-site.[9] Also in 2015, the company began using and Internal Energy Tax to charge themselves based on the amount of energy purchased.[10] The money funds future renewable energy projects like more solar panels and lighting upgrades.

Water

The average brewery uses five gallons of water to produce one gallon of beer. NBB's ratio is 4.2:1. The majority of its water use efficiencies come from its conservation efforts.[11] The company has analyzed all of its water consumption activities and has attempted to reduce use at every stage of production. NBB also has invested in an on-site water treatment facility Wastewater is treated in its "bio-digester" plant before being released into Fort Collins wastewater streams. NBB tries to use this processed water where it can throughout the brewery. In addition, the process creates methane that is captured and used to co-generate power for the brewery.

Waste and Recycling

NBB has made a number of conscious efforts to reduce input materials. NBB is also a believer in recycling; 99.8 percent of its waste escapes the landfill.[12] The majority of its waste consists of spent grain, which is sold as feedstock for cattle. The remainder of its recycled waste includes a combination of glass, cardboard, and general office and industrial waste.

Carbon Emissions (Six-Pack of Fat Tire Amber Ale)

New Belgium partnered with The Climate Conservancy to assess the greenhouse gases emitted across the lifecycle of its signature Fat Tire Amber Ale.[13] The assessment was born from a goal to reduce the carbon footprint per barrel by 50 percent. It was found that over half of the total emissions came from "downstream" activities: distribution and retail storage. The majority of the remaining contribution comes from production and transportation of the raw inputs (barley and hops), bottles, and cardboard. Only 8 percent is produced directly from brewing activities, with nearly half of this being the actual CO_2 found in the beer itself. Surprisingly, over a quarter of the total carbon equivalent emissions come from refrigeration at retail locations, something that is completely out of the control of NBB. By understanding where the emissions are generated, New Belgium is better able to target specific initiatives to reduce its impact.

MAKING A BIGGER SPLASH

While NBB is proud of its sustainability efforts, the company also recognizes that much remains to be done. Specifically, NBB wants to make a stronger impact on the upstream (materials sourcing) and downstream (recycling) factors—factors controlled by suppliers and consumers. Beer products, by nature, involve a great deal of packaging, most of which is still ending up in landfills. NBB, as well as the entire craft brewing industry, realizes that it must do what it can to encourage more consumer recycling. One possibility is the enactment of a national "bottle bill," which would require consumers to pay a refundable deposit on glass bottles. When the consumer returns the bottle for recycling, they receive their deposit back and thus have a material incentive to recycle. The brewing and packaging industries do not generally support these kinds of bills, and many within the two industries have actively attempted to stop their passage. Opponents see the deposit as a kind of tax or price increase on the product. NBB, however, has shown an inclination for support, saying that "perhaps it is time for the domestic and craft brewers to support Bottle Bills to reduce our industry CO_2 footprint."[14] In the meantime, NBB continues to use as much recycled glass as it can.

An additional effort to impact consumer decisions to recycle is centered on packaging. In an initiative begun in 2008, NBB started selling a small percentage of Fat Tire Amber Ale in lightweight aluminum 12-ounce cans.[15] Because cans weigh less than bottles, they are more efficient to transport around the country. Transporting a bottle emits 20 percent more greenhouse gases than transporting a can.[16] Consumers are also much more likely to recycle cans than bottles. Studies have shown that over half of all drinking cans are recycled and new cans generally contain more recycled content that new bottles (40 percent for cans versus 10 to 30 percent for bottles).

However, switching from bottles to cans is easier said than done. There are two central issues. The first is perception. As the Brewers Association noted, "Canned beer is commonly associated with mass marketed light American lager beer, budget beer and perceived inferior quality."[17] Additionally, NBB has crafted its image around uniquely styled bottles, complete with the company's embossed logo and watercolor labels. By switching to cans, NBB would have to be willing to sacrifice this unique characteristic of the company. The second issue is the total environmental impact of cans. Even though cans have recycling and transportation benefits, they still have a negative impact on the environment. For example, the mining of bauxite and smelting of aluminum cans are more damaging to the environment than the production of glass bottles.[18] Thus, the environmental benefits of cans over bottles remain unclear.

Despite the negative perceptions and unique environmental issues, canned beer sales are increasing, and today many craft breweries offer canned beer.[19] New Belgium Beer began selling canned beers in 2013 with some success; by 2015, they had a recycle content of 68 percent on canned beers, far outperforming their peers with their recycle content.

A FUTURE OF SUSTAINABILITY

Perhaps the biggest sustainability accomplishment of Belgium Beer is its achievement of Certified B Corporation status in 2013 and rising B Corp scores in 2015 due to a jump from 42 percent to 100 percent employee ownership.[20] With the opening of a second facility in Asheville, North Carolina, the company is poised to expand. In fact, New Belgium donated land to the City of Asheville to build a new greenway in a previously urban zone. However, it is their new policy of employee ownership that experts believe is NBB's latest win in sustainability. In fact, the competition for jobs at the new Asheville plant was so fierce that one new hire moved to Asheville more than a year before it opened to improve his chances of landing a job with the company.[21]

The only dark cloud on the horizon is a rumor that Belgium Beer may "sell out." In 2015, rumors began that the company was engaging in discussions with potential buyers.[22] While co-founder Kim Jordan denies any deal, it is possible that this craft beer company, which built its reputation on sustainability, will join the ranks of the mega-brewers.

QUESTIONS FOR DISCUSSION

1. What are the ethical issues in this case?
2. What keeps other companies from having the commitment to environmental sustainability that NBB has evidenced?
3. Are you more likely to purchase a product from a company with a strong commitment to sustainability?
4. The benefits of cans over bottles are unclear. Has NBB done the right thing by focusing more on canned beer? Should NBB continue to make a greater commitment to cans? What additional options can NBB explore in the future?
5. Are New Belgium Brewing's Core Values and Beliefs sustainable?
6. How do employee stock ownership plans (ESOPs) align with the sustainability goals of NBB?
7. Do you think that the sale of New Belgium Brewing Company will affect the company's sustainability focus if they lost their independence and were taken over by a large brewing company?

ENDNOTES

1. Press Release, "Brewers Association Releases Top 50 Breweries of 2012," *Brewers Association* (April 10, 2013).
2. "The Green 50: The Integrators," *Inc. Magazine* (November 1, 2006), 84.

3. Newbeligum.com, http://www.newbelgium.com/brewery/company. Accessed May 19, 2013.
4. Christopher Asher, Elina Bidner, and Christopher Greene, "New Belgium Brewing Company: Brewing with a Conscious," *University of Colorado, Graduate School of Public Affairs* (January, 2003), 7.
5. Newbelgium.com
6. Asher, Bidner, and Greene, 1.
7. New Belgium Brewing Company, "Company Core Values and Beliefs," http://www.newbelgium.com/brewery/company. Accessed May 19, 2013.
8. The data provided in this section comes from "2007 Sustainability Report," *New Belgium Brewing Company*; and from New Belgium's sustainability Web site, http://www.newbelgium.com/sustainability.aspx. Accessed May 19, 2013.
9. 2015 New Belgium Sustainability Report, https://www.newbelgium.com/files/sustainability/New_Belgium_Sustainability_Brochure.pdf?pdf=sustainabilityreport. Accessed June 21, 2016.
10. Ibid.
11. Asher, Bidner, and Green, 11.
12. 2015 New Belgium Sustainability Report.
13. "The Carbon Footprint of Fat Tire Amber Ale," *The Climate Conservancy,* 2007. See also Jeffery Ball, "Six Products, Six Carbon Footprints," *The Wall Street Journal* (October 6 2008), R1.
14. 2007 Sustainability Report, 10.
15. Steve Raabe, "New Belgium Brewing Turns to Cans," *The Denver Post* (May 15, 2008). Available online at: http://www.denverpost.com/commented/ci_9262005?source=commented-.
16. Brendan Koerner, "Wear Green, Drink Greenly: The Eco-Guide to Responsible Drinking," *The Slate* (March 16, 2009). http://www.slate.com/id/2186219. Accessed July 7, 2010.
17. Charlie Papazian, "52 Small Craft Brewers Put Beer in a Can," *Brewers Association.* http://www.brewersassociation.org/pages/community/charlies-blog/show?title=52-small-craft-brewers-put-beer-in-a-can. Accessed May 19, 2013.
18. New Belgium's sustainability Web site, http://www.newbelgium.com/sustainability.aspx. Accessed May 19, 2013.
19. Alissa Walker, "Ditch the Bottle? Microbreweries Say Can-Do," *Fast Company* (August 10, 2009). http://www.fastcompany.com/blog/alissa-walker/designerati/real-can-do-attitude-more-microbreweries-saying-no-bottles. Retrieved July 7, 2010. See also Papazian.
20. 2015 New Belgium Sustainability Report.
21. Darren Dahl, "What's So Special about Employee-Owned Companies like New Belgium Brewing?" *Forbes* (May 2, 2016), http://www.forbes.com/sites/darrendahl/2016/05/02/whats-so-special-about-employee-owned-companies-like-new-belgium-brewing/#67a3e7cd353f. Accessed June 21, 2016.
22. Aldo Svaldi, "New Belgium Brewing Is Said to Be Looking for Buyer," *The Denver Post* (December 18, 2015), http://www.denverpost.com/2015/12/18/new-belgium-brewing-said-to-be-looking-for-buyer/. Accessed June 22, 2016.

CASE 26

Altruism versus Profit: The Challenges of Clean Water in India*

Lack of safe drinking water is a global issue. One of the United Nations Millennium goals is to "halve, by 2015, the proportion of the population without sustainable access to safe drinking water and basic sanitation." Climate change has made this goal difficult to achieve, and the updated 2030 UN Sustainable Development Goals require investments in infrastructure, sanitation, and increased education. By 2050, water shortages are projected to impact 25 percent of the population.[1]

Water is needed every day, several times a day, by all people. This makes long-term sustainability critical to any water project. A recent study in rural India found that 82 percent of the villagers collect water

*This case was prepared by Brenda Eichelberger, Portland State University, 2016.

from a well or a pond, travelling up to one kilometer each time.[2] This is a low prestige task most often done by women and girls. Over 70 percent of the surface water in India is contaminated and in many cases have been rendered unsafe for human consumption.[3] This inaccessibility and increased pollution continues to be a serious health and economic issue in India and globally. UNICEF found that unsafe water worldwide causes four billion cases of diarrhea annually and "in India alone, the single largest cause of ill health and death among children is diarrhea, which kills nearly half a million children each year."[4]

The water crisis in India has been addressed in several ways, but with limited success. One of the solutions for water problems includes retail for-profit water sales and buying from mobile suppliers. Both Coke and Pepsi bottled waters are present in shops and restaurants in India through their Dasani and Aquafina brands, as are a variety of local providers, all part of the $300 billion global bottled water industry. However, the World Resources Institute report finds that bottled water comes at a significant price penalty compared to surface or piped water systems. Studies show mobile distributors charge up to ten times more than public utilities.[5] Unfortunately, India faces many "basic service" issues and a fully functioning water system is very costly.

In addition to large, for-profit companies distributing bottled water in India, several socially responsible companies are also exploring the water filtration market in India. One example is WaterHealth International. They were profiled in *Inc.* magazine as the "Do Good Capitalist of the Year" in 2007. WaterHealth installs a water filtration system and offers financing to local villages to purchase their water center packages. The villages then repay their loans with the profits of the water sales.[6] However, many critics express concern at the expense of the WaterHealth Systems. Initial cost and financing issues are challenges for rural India and many areas trying to expand access to clean water.

Another developing for-profit enterprise is Hyderabad's Waterlife. It is a franchise opportunity that offers a franchisee the ability to pay Rs. 30,000 (approximately Rs. 45 per US dollar) for the right to sell water at Rs. 5 per 20 liters; the franchisee keeps Rs. 2 per 20 liters for themselves and pays Rs. 3 to Waterlife. Gaurav Dwivedi, author of *Public-Private Partnerships in the Water Sector; Partnerships or Privatization*, writes that these for-profit enterprises "are being designed to enhance private profits without taking any serious responsibilities for extending coverage, or improving efficiency."[7] One concern in letting the market decide water access is that large areas of rural India will be left without coverage as they continue to face poor health and continued poverty. According to one KPMG study, only 32 percent of the rural population in India has access to safe water, in contrast to 73 percent of the population in large cities who has access.[8] The challenge of assuming the private market will respond is that it is not lucrative enough to help the poor and the rural areas. The challenge in waiting for governmental response is that even more urgent social and economic issues overwhelm the priorities of the Indian government.

Nonprofit organizations are also attempting to address the water crises. One such organization is the Byrraju SWEET (Safe Water for Everyone using Effective Technology) water project, which was started in 2004. To build a water treatment plant, a village contacts the Byrraju Foundation and submits an application; residents are then asked to raise or donate 75 percent of the total plant, building and equipment costs, approximately $15,000. Byrraju adds the remaining loaned funds and provides expertise, supervision, and quality control. The village hires at least two residents to run the facility and offers a delivery route to enterprising entrepreneurs who earn a commission with each delivery. The water treatment plant is a "shared investment" between the foundation and the village. The village pays a percentage of sales to Byrraju for the 25 percent initial cost and for continued maintenance and water quality testing. This allows the "loan" to be paid back and villagers to have continued access to technological resources. Currently, they have nearly 60 water plants serving 1.2 million people.[9]

However, the Foundation has been controversial. Ramalinga Raju, CEO and founder of Satyam Computer Services, founded the foundation in 2001, and over 90 percent of the Byrraju Foundation's funding has historically come from Raju and his family members. Satyam was one of the top companies in India, employing over 30,000 people. Nevertheless, in January 7, 2009, Raju confessed to accounting fraud at Satyam and falsely reporting over a billion dollars in profits. Even in light of his well-known philanthropic efforts, per an article in the Indian Express.[10] Raju was sentenced to, and is serving, seven years in jail. The Foundation continues to provide clean water to the villages with established water systems; however, it has been unable to expand due to its limited donations and fees.

QUESTIONS FOR DISCUSSION

1. Looking at the options for addressing India's water crisis, how do these reflect community partnerships and/or strategic philanthropy?
2. The Byrraju Foundation requires the village to donate funds. Is this a good strategy? Why/Why not?
3. Per the United Nation's report, India's water quality ranks 120th among the 122 rated countries in terms of quality water available to its citizens.[11] What are the challenges to addressing environmental issues in emerging countries, and how does that differ from developed countries?
4. What are the differences in nonprofit versus for profit organizational forms of business when addressing these types of social problems? Is market demand the best determinant for basic necessities?
5. Which of the five stakeholder groups might have the most power to address social problems in developing countries, especially when there is instability in the government due to transitions, crisis, or corruption?
6. Corporate philanthropy has become more globalized and international development has seen increased funding even through recessionary times. Why are MNC's interested in international giving?

ENDNOTES

1. United Nations, Sustainable Development Goal 6: Clean Water and Sanitation. (2015, September 25). Retrieved May 21, 2016, from http://www.undp.org/content/undp/en/home/sdgoverview/post-2015-development-agenda/goal-6.html.
2. Bhola Nath Ghosh and Utpal Kumar De, "Women in Natural Resource Collection: Experience from Rural Jharkhand in India," *AIP Conference Proceedings* 1643, no. 1 (February 3, 2015): 476–86. doi:10.1063/1.4907483.
3. Hemant Pathak, "Effect of Water Borne Diseases on Indian Economy: A Cost-Benefit Analysis," *Annals of the University of Oradea, Geography Series / Analele Universitatii Din Oradea, Seria Geografie* 25, no. 1 (June 2015): 74–78.
4. "World Water Day 2010, Water Quality Facts and Statistics," *Welcome to UN-Water*. United Nations, 2010, http://www.unwater.org/. Accessed July 26, 2011.
5. Mukami Kariuki and Jordan Schwartz, "Small-Scale Private Service Providers of Water Supply and Electricity," World Resources Institute, Policy Research Working Paper 3727 (Washington, DC: World Bank, 2005), http://www.wri.org.
6. Hadiya Faheem and Debapratim Purkayastha, "WaterHealth International—Oikos International," *Www.oikos-international.org - Oikos International*. Oikos International, 2010, http://www.oikos-international.org/academic/case-collection/inspection-copies/alphabetical-list/waterhealth-international.html. Accessed July 26, 2011.
7. Gaurav Dwivedi, "Public Private Partnerships in the Water Sector: Partnerships or Privatisation—A Report and Video by Manthan Adhyayan Kendra | India Water Portal," *India Water Portal | Safe, Sustainable Water for All*, Manthan Adhyayan Kendra, 2010, http://www.indiawaterportal.org/node/9614. Accessed July 26, 2011.
8. Gauri Kamath, "Special Report: Water, 'Off the Beaten Path'," *BusinessWorld* (10 May 2010), http://www.businessworld.in. Accessed July 22, 2011.
9. "Byrraju Foundation Web Page," *Rural Transformation, Rural Development Services Andhra Pradesh, India, Asia by Byrraju Foundation*, http://www.byrrajufoundation.org/. Accessed May 21, 2016.
10. Judge Cites SC Verdict to Reject Pleas for Lenience (2015, April 10). Retrieved May 21, 2016, from http://www.newindianexpress.com/cities/hyderabad/Judge-Cites-SC-Verdict-to-Reject-Pleas-for-Lenience/2015/04/10/article2757126.ece.
11. Pathak, ibid.

CASE 27

Safety? What Safety?*

KIRK'S FIRST YEAR

Kirk was a bright individual who was being groomed for the controller's position in a medium-sized manufacturing firm. After his first year as assistant controller, the officers of the firm started to include him in major company functions. One day, for instance, he was asked to attend the monthly financial statement summary at a prestigious consulting firm. During the meeting, Kirk was intrigued at how the financial data he had accumulated had been transformed by the consultant into revealing charts and graphs.

NEW MANUFACTURING PLANT

Kirk was generally optimistic about the session and the company's future until the consultant started talking about the new manufacturing plant the company was adding to the current location and the per-unit costs of the chemically plated products it would produce. At that time, Bob, the president, and John, the chemical engineer, started talking about waste treatment and disposal problems. John mentioned that the current waste treatment facilities could not handle the waste products of the "ultramodern" new plant in a manner that would meet the industry's fairly high standards, although the plant would still comply with federal standards.

COST INCREASES

Kirk's boss, Henry, noted that the estimated per-unit costs would increase if the waste treatment facilities were upgraded according to recent industry standards. Industry standards were presently more stringent than federal regulations, and environmentalists were pressuring strongly for stricter regulations at the federal level. Bob mentioned that since their closest competitor did not have the waste treatment facilities that already existed at their firm, he was not in favor of any more expenditures in that area. Most managers at the meeting resoundingly agreed with Bob, and the business of the meeting proceeded to other topics.

Kirk's Dilemma

Kirk did not hear a word during the rest of the meeting. He kept wondering how the company could possibly have such a casual attitude toward the environment. Yet he did not know if, how, when, or with whom he should share his opinion. Soon he started reflecting on whether this firm was the right one for him.

QUESTIONS FOR DISCUSSION

1. Who are the stakeholders in this case, and what are their stakes?
2. What social responsibility does the firm have for the environment? How would you assess the firm's CSR using the four-part CSR definition presented in Chapter 2?
3. Identify the different competing "standards" at issue in this case. Which standard seems most defensible for this company considering all factors?
4. How should Kirk reconcile his own thinking with the thinking being presented by the firm's management?
5. What should Kirk do? Why?

---

*This case was written by Donald E. Tidrick, Northern Illinois University. Permission to reprint granted by Arthur Andersen & Co., SC.

CASE 28

Targeting Consumers (and Using Their Secrets)*

Data mining of large data sets, frequently called Big Data, has become a big part of analyzing consumer-related data that companies collect. Basically, data mining is a computational process of extracting information patterns from data sets and transforming it into more organized uses for the future. Usually this information is used to increase sales, reduce costs, or otherwise improve operations or profits.[1] Obviously, if retailers could predict based on past purchasing patterns what consumers might buy in the future, this would be extremely valuable in target marketing.

The statistical team at Target, the giant national retailer, used data mining techniques to determine whether and when a woman was going to have a baby long before she ever purchased diapers from their stores. The marketing plan was then to target ads toward the woman for purchases she might be thinking about for the future. A conversation with one of Target's statisticians revealed how this worked.

Apparently, Target assigns every customer a Guest ID number and links this with your name, the credit cards you use, addresses, phone numbers, and e-mail addresses they are able to ascertain. They collect all the demographic data they can gather or perhaps buy from others. Their statisticians then decided to analyze the women's purchases who had signed up on Baby Registries in the past and then study their purchasing patterns before their babies were born. They discovered through data analysis that certain purchasing patterns did emerge. For example, the analysts noticed that women started buying huge quantities of lotion during the beginning of their second trimester of pregnancy. They also discovered that during their first 20 weeks of pregnancy, women stocked up on calcium, magnesium, and zinc supplements. The analysts also detected that as the woman was approaching her delivery date, she bought larger quantities of scent-free soap, cotton balls, hand sanitizer, and washcloths.[2]

After their analysis, the Target team concluded that there was a set of 25 products, which when analyzed together yielded what they termed a "pregnancy prediction score." They concluded they could closely predict that a woman was pregnant and when the baby was due to be born and could target their ads to the woman based on what they expected her needs at that time would be.[3] To their benefit, by getting the women to shop at Target during an expensive and habit-forming period of her life, she could be made a customer for life.[4]

THE FATHER FROM MINNEAPOLIS

As a result of one set of mailings going out, an angry father showed up at his Target store one day demanding to speak to the manager. In his hands were a fistful of coupons sent to his daughter who lived at home in Minneapolis. His complaint was that his daughter, who was still in high school, was receiving mailed ads for maternity clothes and cribs. He angrily asked the manager "Are you trying to encourage her to get pregnant?"[5]

Not sure what was going on, the manager apologized to the angry father and called him on the phone several days later to apologize again. At this point, the father started changing his tune. He uncomfortably told the manager that he'd had a talk with his daughter and discovered that there were some things going on around his house of which he was unaware. He confessed that he'd discovered that his daughter was due in August and he said that he owed the manager an apology himself.[6]

As a result of the *New York Times* reporter investigating Target's data mining approaches and wanting to know more, Target decision makers finally figured out that some of what they were doing may not be appropriate. They eventually concluded that not everyone wanted them to know this much about their personal lives. They discovered that as long as women didn't know they were being spied on they would use the coupons sent them. But, once they discovered how Target knew to send them these coupons—because of their reproductive status—some of them were quite upset. The company decided to slow down and think about this target marketing scheme a bit more.[7]

Realizing that the company had the ability to create custom advertising booklets, a process that they had used in the past with other products, the company decided to put its ads for baby items in booklets

*This case was prepared by Archie B. Carroll, University of Georgia, using publically available information. The case was revised and updated in 2016.

where the baby products were paired with other items such as wine glasses or lawn mowers so that the advertising appeared to be random and not profiled toward an expectant mother. This advertising program was then used. Target discovered that not too long after this revised advertising approach was begun, its sales in the Mom and Baby category increased impressively.[8]

OTHERS USE OF BIG DATA

Many companies today mine Big Data to gather insights into consumers' likely purchasing habits. For example, Facebook recently reported that it collects data on 1.6 billion consumers, including their "likes" and social connections, to identify behavioral patterns that they might use in their product design and marketing.[9] Increasingly, companies are mining social media data, Internet searches, purchasing behavior, and publically available data sets to improve their products, track trends, and place ads. Recently, Microsoft reported that it had conducted a study suggesting that a consumer's search queries might provide clues that a person has cancer even before such a diagnosis is made.[10]

Because of the concern for consumer users' privacy and the public furor it has caused in the past, Facebook announced that it was starting to use an internal review process to assess the ethical impact of each of its research efforts. It has established a five-person group of employees, including experts in law and ethics. Then, if a manager thinks that a research project deals with a sensitive topic, the proposal will get a review by the group to consider its risks and benefits and to consider consumers' expectations about how their personal information is being used.[11]

QUESTIONS FOR DISCUSSION

1. What are the social and ethical issues in this case? Who are the affected stakeholders and what are their stakes?
2. Target's practice of predicting a woman's pregnancy and then exploiting it commercially was legal. Was it ethical? If you were the woman in the case and you learned what Target had done, what terms would you use to describe their practice?
3. Would you feel deceived, tricked, or exploited if a company predicted a purchasing expectation of yours that you felt was private or intimate? What, if anything, would you do about it?
4. How do you evaluate Target's new approach to disguise the ads by mixing them in with other, unrelated ads?
5. What is your assessment of Facebook's efforts to protect consumers' privacy? Or, is it really to protect the company should questions be raised?
6. Have companies gone too far in their statistical analytics and use of Big Data and data mining such as that described in this case? Is it ethical for companies to use data mining to target market customers based on the patterns they detected?

ENDNOTES

1. "Data Mining: What is Data Mining?" http://www.anderson.ucla.edu/faculty/jason.frand/teacher/technologies/palace/datamining.htm. Accessed June 20, 2016.
2. Charles Duhigg, "How Companies Learn Your Secrets," *The New York Times* (February 16, 2012), http://www.nytimes.com/2012/02/19/magazine/shopping-habits.html?src=xps. Accessed June 15, 2016; see also Kashmir Hill, "How Target Figured Out a Teen Girl Was Pregnant before Her Father Did," *Forbes* (February 16, 2012), http://www.forbes.com/sites/kashmirhill/2012/02/16/how-target-figured-out-a-teen-girl-was-pregnant-before-her-father-did/#33bfbecf34c6. Accessed June 15, 2016.
3. Duhigg, ibid.
4. "The Incredible Story of How Target Exposed a Young Girl's Pregnancy," *Business Insider*, (February 16, 2012), http://www.businessinsider.com/the-incredible-story-of-how-target-exposed-a-teen-girls-pregnancy-2012-2. Accessed June 15, 2016.
5. Duhigg, 2012, ibid.
6. Ibid.
7. Ibid.
8. Ibid.
9. Daniela Hernandez and Deepa Seethraraman, "Facebook Reveals Research Methods," *The Wall Street Journal* (June 15, 2016), B1.
10. Ibid., B2.
11. Ibid.

CASE 29

The Perils of Student Loan Debt*

Following the lessons learned in the 2008/2009 mortgage crisis, one would think that issues of egregious lending practices would have gone away. Instead, they have taken a different twist in the context of student loans. Take the example of Scott Burnside.[1]

Scott Burnside was very excited when he opened the letter that said he had been accepted to an Ivy League university. He had worked very hard in high school, determined to be the first from his family to attend an Ivy League institution. He accepted his offer, sent in a deposit to hold his slot, and figured that he would apply for student loans and grants to facilitate his tuition payments. He filled out his FAFSA (Free Application for Federal Student Financial Aid) form and waited to hear about his options. Although both of Scott's parents had gone to college and had good full-time jobs, there was no way that they could pay for Scott's $65,000 annual estimated tuition and expenses. However, Scott was not too worried. He wanted to do it on his own, anyway. He felt confident that if he did well in college he would get a great job later and repay his loans over the next few years.

Five years and $207,000 of debt later, Scott graduated with an engineering degree. He began working at a large engineering company with a starting salary of $65,000 per year before taxes. His monthly payments toward his FAFSA student loans ran approximately $2,100 a month. The interest rates on his loans were 6 percent, but payments became due right after he graduated. Before he knew it, his interest began compounding and he was struggling to meet his payments while covering his rent for an apartment plus transportation to work in the metropolitan area where his firm was located.

Embarrassed and humiliated, Scott asked his parents if he could move back in with them. Even though he would have a long commute to work, he had no choice because he was risking his credit rating if he fell behind with his payments. As it stood, his parents had to guarantee his credit on his apartment because he was not deemed "credit worthy" with the extensive loans taken out under his name.

*This case was prepared by Jill A Brown, Bentley University in 2016.

Scott's story is actually a more fortunate one that many other students' debt stories. At least his university was accredited and provided him an excellent education and the opportunity to be recruited for a good job. Additionally, his loans were Federal Direct Subsidized student loans, at a reasonable interest rate. There are horror stories of students being recruited by colleges with deceptive marketing tactics to attend less-than-legitimate colleges that misrepresent graduates' job prospects.[2] Additionally, private lenders, including banks, colleges, private organizations and state government agencies, charge higher rates than those of federal loans, and these might rise over time. Finally, private collection agencies, some of whom were hired by the U.S. Education Department, have been accused of using illegal, high-pressure debt-collection tactics.[3] Worse yet, federal investigators caught private lenders including Sallie Mae, Citibank, and Bank of America allegedly paying financial aid officers to steer students to their loans, which had significant mark-ups over federal loans.[4]

THE NUMBERS

Student loans have surpassed credit cards to become the second largest source of outstanding debt in the U.S. after mortgages.[5] It is estimated that more than 40 percent of student borrowers from the government's direct loan program are not making their loan payments on more than $200 billion owed.[6] The economic recession in 2008/2009 drove many people back to school and the demand for student loans exploded. By 2016, the government held $1.2 trillion in student loans, nearly triple what they held in 2006. Federal student loans can be in the form of Direct loans for undergraduates, Direct loans for graduate students, and Plus loans for parents and graduates. The federal student loan rates are set by Congress in the spring for the upcoming academic year based on the auction of 10-year Treasury notes.[7]

Private debt collection agencies, employed by the Education Department, garnished $176 million in Americans' wages in the last three months of 2015.[8] The government lends to students and parents without any sort of credit check, but the risks are limited because it can garnish wages, Social Security benefits and tax refunds to collect the money.[9] Parents and graduate students can borrow up to the full cost of attendance as long as they have not defaulted recently on a loan, declared bankruptcy, or had any other black marks on a credit report in the past two years.[10] As a result, it is not just students who are at risk of perennial debt. In fact, there are 2.2 million borrowers age 60 years and up who have student debts that financed their own schooling and/or their children's, and the total outstanding education loans held by people 65 years or older is over $18 billion.[11]

PUSHBACK

Students and parents are beginning to push back. Many are seeking loans to be forgiven based on an obscure 1994 federal "forgiveness" law that allows debts to be forgiven if fraud has occurred.[12] Prior to 2015, the law had rarely been applied because it is vague, with little guidance about what proof is needed to demonstrate that a school committed fraud. However, in 2016, the U.S. Education Department agreed to cancel $28 million of debt under the law for 1,300 former students of Corinthian Colleges—a for-profit chain that went bankrupt in 2015.[13] Since then, students have been flooding the government with appeals to have their loans forgiven. By early 2016, 7,500 borrowers owing $164 million had applied to have their student debt expunged.[14] President Obama initiated a Student Aid Enforcement Unit within the Education Department to deal with such claims.

A WAY FORWARD

Federal regulators, and specifically the Consumer Financial Protection Bureau, are in the process of putting in place new rules to change a number of practices in the student loan industry. Under consideration are:[15]

- Putting requirements on student-loan servicers to help lower monthly payments and lessen the chances of default
- Addressing debt-collection tactics when borrowers fall behind
- Reviewing the oversight of federal student lending, which is handled by the Education Department
- Addressing poor customer service and routine transfers of student loan servicing rights from one company to another
- Making sure that service providers provide borrowers with adequate information about affordable repayment options, including income-driven repayment plans
- Reviewing private student loan providers to ensure they are providing information about how they could receive federal income tax benefits
- Reviewing procedures for cosigners who may be having difficulty when they try to get out of a loan years after student borrowers are making payments

ONGOING PROBLEMS

Nobody disputes the fact that the U.S. student loan system needs overhaul. However, debates continue over the source of the problems and the solutions. For example, some feel that the federal safety net of forgiving student loans will become outrageously costly down the road for taxpayers who had nothing to do with the student loan system; the Brookings Institution estimated that it could cost taxpayers $250 billion over the next 10 years.[16] Further, there are already safety programs in place that are both underutilized and costly, like the Income Driven Repayment Plan (IDRP), originally passed under President Bill Clinton and the Public Service Loan Forgiveness Plan (PSLF), started under President George W. Bush.

The IDRP allows debtors to cap their monthly payments at a maximum of 15 percent of their discretionary income. After a maximum of 25 years, any remaining balance is wiped off. The PSLF plan allows debtors with federal direct loans to have their remaining balance on student loans forgiven after 10 years of full-time government or nonprofit service. Critics of these plans point out that they act as a powerful, indirect subsidy for the $488 billion higher education industry, which then has no incentive to lower tuition costs.[17]

Other debates are more philosophical. Some debate whether everyone is qualified to go to college and whether the United States has encouraged millions of unprepared people to enroll in college, who end up dropping out and defaulting on student loans.[18] They point to the fact that most borrowers who have defaulted owe relatively little—a median of $8,900—but cumulatively they contribute to the growing problem.[19] Others point to the idea that a college education is the most effective intervention to help people obtain economic security.[20] Therefore, they argue, the student loan problem is a systems failure of for-profit institutions and community colleges that increase their rates in line with the total amount of federal loans their students receive.[21] Finally, some argue that fixing the system will probably involve significant costs to the taxpayers, including raising money for the new Student Aid Enforcement Unit to adjudicate claims of deceptive practices.[22]

What can be done to solve the student loan problem? It is obvious that the system needs an overhaul. Meanwhile, students are begging for debt relief, moving back home with their parents, delaying buying homes, and contemplating other career options. Additionally, some say there is less obvious damage to the economy that occurs as well. For example, with rising student debt, small business creation suffers because young entrepreneurs cannot afford to take on any more liabilities.[23] In any case, the student loan business continues to see increasing defaults with lenders like the U.S. government scrambling to collect.

QUESTIONS FOR DISCUSSION

1. What are the ethical issues involved with student loans? How do these parallel issues that were involved with the mortgage lending crisis of 2008/2009?
2. As a matter of public policy, should the federal government be getting involved in providing these funds for education?
3. Who are the stakeholders involved in student lending?
4. Should large sums of money (tens-of-thousands of dollars) be loaned to students and parents without any sort of credit check?
5. How can responsible lending take place in this sort of environment? Is it ethical and responsible for private lenders to make such loans just because they are backed by taxpayer's money?
6. Should the federal government be involved in guaranteeing loans provided by private lending groups? Why or why not?
7. Should student loan forgiveness be limited to situations where a college has engaged in deceptive practices? If so, why should taxpayers be responsible for bad judgments being made?
8. What do you think about the IDRP and PSLF programs for student loan relief?

ENDNOTES

1. Names have been changed to protect the identity of the student.
2. Josh Mitchell and Douglas Belkin, "New Office Will Probe Colleges," *The Wall Street Journal* (February 9, 2016), A2.
3. National Consumer Law Center, "Pounding Student Loan Borrowers," (September 3, 2014), http://www.nclc.org/issues/pounding-student-loan-borrowers.html, Accessed June 21, 2016.
4. Danielle Douglas-Gabriel, "How the Attempt to Fix Student Loans Got Bogged Down by the Middlemen," *The Washington Post* (August 23, 2016), https://www.washingtonpost.com/business/economy/how-the-education-department-turned-into-a-massive-bank/2015/08/23/7618f2fa-1442-11e5-9ddc-e3353542100c_story.html. Accessed June 21, 2016.
5. Natalie Kitroeff, "The Student Debt Collection Mess," *Bloomberg Businessweek* (June 8, 2016), 45.
6. Josh Mitchell, "More than 40% of Student Borrowers Aren't Making Payments," *The Wall Street Journal* (April 7, 2016), http://www.wsj.com/articles/more-than-40-of-student-borrowers-arent-making-payments-1459971348. Accessed June 21, 2016.
7. Tom Anderson, "The Fed and the Future of Student Loan Rates," *Forbes* (March 17, 2016), http://www.forbes.com/sites/tomanderson/2016/03/17/the-fed-and-the-future-of-student-loan-rates/#2ecb6caa30a0. Accessed June 21, 2016.
8. Ibid.
9. Douglas-Gabriel, 2016.
10. Ibid.
11. Natalie Kitroeff, "Hey, Pops, My Student Loans Are Due," *Bloomberg Businessweek* (December 21, 2015), 24.
12. Josh Mitchell, "Thousands Want Student Loans Canceled," *The Wall Street Journal* (January 21, 2016), A3.
13. Ibid.
14. Ibid.
15. AnnaMaria Andriotis, "Regulator to Revamp Student-Loan Rules," *The Wall Street Journal* (September 30, 2015), C4.
16. Haley Sweetland Edwards, "But Can America Afford This Approach to Solving Student Debt?" *Time* (November 30, 2015), 93.
17. Ibid.

18. Neal McCluskey, "We End up Hurting the Students We Are Trying to Help," *The Wall Street Journal* (February 29, 2016), R7.
19. Mitchell, 2016.
20. Sara Goldrick-Rab, "Lenders Shouldn't Pick Which Students Get an Education," *The Wall Street Journal* (February 29, 2016), R7.
21. Ibid.
22. Jorge Klor de Alva and Mark Schneider, "The Feds and Students vs. Taxpayers," *The Wall Street Journal* (March 4, 2016), A13.
23. "The Student-Loan Siphon," Op-Ed, *The Wall Street Journal* (August 29, 2015), A10.

CASE 30

"Dead Peasant" Life Insurance Policies*

Caroline Murray was mourning the death of her husband, Mike, when she received a call from the employee benefits division of his company requesting a copy of the death certificate.[1] After asking why they needed the certificate, Caroline was surprised to learn that her husband's company had purchased a life insurance policy on her husband. Especially surprising was the fact that Caroline had no record of the policy, and apparently, neither did her husband. This particular policy listed only the company as beneficiary and allowed the company to borrow against Mike's policy, write-off the loan's interest on its taxes, and receive a tax-free payout upon Mike's death. Mike's position at the company was not an executive one; he was the security guard at a local manufacturing company, and his company received $80,000, tax-free, upon his death. His family received nothing. How did this happen? Through the company's purchase of a life insurance policy nicknamed "dead peasant" life insurance.

CORPORATE-OWNED LIFE INSURANCE POLICIES

The Prevalence of COLIs. Corporate-owned life insurance policies (COLI) have been around for years. They are used as funding mechanisms for protecting businesses against the loss of its "human capital." Additionally, until the 1990s, these policies provided financial gains for companies as a form of "tax arbitrage" where they could deduct the interest on leveraged insurance transactions while simultaneously avoiding tax payments on the interest credited to the policies' cash values. In the mid-1990s, the federal government closed most of the tax loopholes and opportunity for arbitrage; however, the tax-free benefits and tax deferrals on the policies still exist as financial incentives for companies. It is estimated that about a quarter of the Fortune 500 either have or had "broad-based" COLI policies covering about 5 million employees.[2]

The pseudonym, "broad-based" refers to the policies' coverage of both executive and lower-level employees. Until the mid-1980s, most states required that an employer have an "insurable interest" in the lives of the employees that they insured, so these plans were limited to executives. Because of federal tax law changes that limited the amount that companies might deduct per insured employee, many states relaxed the "insurable interest" requirement, and businesses began taking life insurance policies out on rank-and-file workers to retain profitability on their policies. Hence, the term, "dead peasants," was used to reference the lower social status of some employees.

In 2009, a Michael Moore documentary, "*Capitalism: A Love Story*" highlighted this practice and drew attention to some of the problems. Lawsuits of families of deceased employees challenged the practice and began suing corporations and their insurers for allegedly misrepresenting what the policies offer. Many cases settled out of court, including a 2004 class action suit against Wal-Mart that settled for $10.3 million and another in 2006 that settled for $5 million.[3] However, the practice continues today. Despite the negative press and lawsuits, statistics show that employers are still utilizing Dead Peasants Life insurance policies. In

*This case was written by Jill A. Brown, Bentley University.

2004, the *Wall Street Journal* reported the estimated value of these policies was $65.8 billion. In 2008, it had doubled to $122.3 billion.[4]

Currently, top employers engaged in this practice include Wells Fargo ($17 billion), Bank of America ($17 billion), JP Morgan Chase ($11 billion), Winn-Dixie, Citi Bank, Walt Disney, Wal-Mart, American Electric Company, Dow Chemical, Procter & Gamble, and many others.[5] In a horrible twist of fate, in 2011, police in Ohio arrested the owner of an oil-change business and charged him with trying to hire a hit man to kill a former employee to collect on a $250,000 COLI policy.[6]

THE LAWS REGARDING COLIS

How is it that companies were able to take life insurance out on employees without their knowledge? Part of the confusion was with the different state laws back in the 1980's and 1990's when these policies became popular. Some state laws, like those in Texas, required that employees "consent" to having their lives insured while other states, like Georgia, did not require consent. Additionally, some employees "consented" without knowing it. In one Texas lawsuit, Wal-Mart employees alleged that they consented without knowing it when they were offered a special $5,000 death benefit when Wal-Mart launched the program. Wal-Mart disputed the claim by stating that the policies were signed in Georgia with an insurance management company located in Georgia, and therefore the more lenient Georgia law applied, regardless of the consent issue.[7] However, the term "consent" was, and is still, vague because some states consider consent granted if an employee *does not object* to a notice of the employer's intent to purchase a policy.[8]

In recent years, regulators have stepped in to address the practice. The IRS cracked down on deductions, Congress approved stricter consent laws, and state laws were modified.[9] Insurance law is regulated by states, and some have responded by passing "insurable interest" laws, which require that employers have the possibility of financial loss because of an employee's death before they can take out a life insurance policy on them.[10]

In 2006, The COLI Best Practices Provision, within The Pension Protection Act of 2006, was signed into federal law. Among other issues, it addressed COLI employee notice and consent requirements—noting that the employee must be notified in writing, as well as provide written consent. Of course, the law was designed to codify the industry and identify "best practices." In fact, many policies for which employers did not obtain consent are still in effect because those purchased before the law became effective in 2006 were grandfathered from its provisions.[11] Additionally, as noted above, what constitutes "consent" could simply be an employee not noticing that he or she had to "opt out."

THE COLI DEBATE

Critics of dead peasant insurance policies point to the disincentives for employee safety; after all, if a company is going to collect money on an employee's death, what incentives do they really have to protect that employee? Additionally, critics point to the comparison to slaveholders' policies, the loss of tax revenues, and the use of these policies to fund exorbitant executive compensation programs.

Supporters of these insurance policies cite the fact that it is no different than insuring a business asset and it is perfectly legal. For years, companies have protected their interests with life insurance policies on their CEOs, top management team members and executives whose deaths could seriously affect a company's bottom line. Finally, many supporters point out that these insurance policies provide a beneficial vehicle for funding the growing costs of retiree benefits, so there is financial soundness to these policies that offer benefit to all employees of the companies. However, there is room for more debate in that the proceeds are often directed toward funding executive benefits, not for general retirees.

THE CURRENT SITUATION

While different states continue to set the parameters for the legalities of these policies, some companies have decided to cancel these COLI policies to avoid the risk of lawsuits from family members of the deceased who say that they are the rightful owners of the policies. Wal-Mart canceled most of these policies after several lawsuits with similar companies resulted in stiff penalties and settlements. Wal-Mart continues to settle claims from the estates of deceased Wal-Mart employees.

In 2011, President Obama's proposed budget included further decreases in the amount of allowable interest deductions for borrowing against COLI policies. Although this did not outlaw the practice, it was designed to influence businesses to put a halt to these policies. By 2015, with the removal of many tax incentives, it was estimated that the dead peasant insurance policies might go away, although it has fostered larger debates about life insurance schemes and corporate tax loopholes.[12] Perhaps at some point, the widows and widowers of "dead peasants" like Caroline Murray will be able to mourn the death of their loved ones without surprise calls from benefits divisions.

QUESTIONS FOR DISCUSSION

1. What are the major ethical issues involved in this case? Is it ethical for an employer to benefit from the death of an employee if they took out and paid for the policy?
2. How does the idea that these policies help to fund executive compensation and/or retiree benefits affect your answer to #1?
3. Should Congress create more stringent guidelines, beyond "best practices," for the administration and use of these types of COLI policies? Should states be pressured to conform to stricter "consent" policies?
4. What are other ways that federal and state governments could encourage businesses to avoid these COLI policies?

ENDNOTES

1. Fictional characters based on a true story.
2. David Gelles, "An Employee Dies and the Company Collects the Insurance," *DealBook*, (June 22, 2014), http://dealbook.nytimes.com/2014/06/22/an-employee-dies-and-the-company-collects-the-insurance/?_r=1. Accessed June 15, 2016.
3. Michelle Fablo, "Can Your Employer Make Money on Your Death? Corporate-Owned Life Insurance Policies," *Legal Zoom* (August 2010), https://www.legalzoom.com/articles/can-your-employer-make-money-on-your-death-corporate-owned-life-insurance-policies. Accessed June 15, 2016
4. McClanahan Myers Espy, "Which Employers Bought Policies on the Lives of Their Employees," (October 10, 2014), http://www.deadpeasantinsurance.com/which-employers-bought-policies-on-the-lives-of-employees/. Accessed June 12, 2016.
5. Gelles, 2014.
6. Jay MacDonald, "Does a Sneaky Boss Have Life Insurance on You?" *Bankrate.com* (June 26, 2014), http://www.bankrate.com/finance/insurance/dead-peasant-life-insurance.aspx. Accessed June 12, 2016.
7. Sixel, L. "Profiting from Death? Lawsuit Filed in Wal-Mart Life Insurance Case," *The Houston Chronicle* (April 25, 2002), 1.
8. Ibid.
9. Fablo, 2010.
10. Ibid.
11. David McCann, "'Dead Peasant Insurance' Still Alive in Corporate America," *CFO.com* (January 31, 2014), http://ww2.cfo.com/tax/2014/01/dead-peasant-insurance-still-alive-corporate-america/. Accessed June 12, 2016.
12. Warren S. Hersch, "4 Threats to the Insurance Industry: Tax Reform (and 3 Others)," *LifeHealthPro* (May 20, 2016), http://www.lifehealthpro.com/2016/05/20/4-threats-to-the-insurance-industry-tax-reform-and. Accessed June 20, 2016.

CASE 31

The Case of the Fired Waitress*

Ruth Hatton, a waitress for a Red Lobster restaurant in Pleasant Hills, Pennsylvania, was fired from her job because she was accused of stealing a guest-comment card that had been deposited in the customer comment box by a disgruntled couple.[1] The couple, who happened to be black, had been served by Hatton and was unhappy with the treatment they felt they got from her. At the time of her firing, Hatton, age 53 years, had been a 19-year-old veteran employee. She said, "It felt like a knife going through me."

*This case was prepared by Archie B. Carroll, University of Georgia. Updated in 2016.

THE INCIDENT

The couple had gone to the Red Lobster restaurant for dinner. According to Hatton, the woman had requested a well-done piece of prime rib. After she was served, she complained that the meat was fatty and undercooked. Hatton then said she politely suggested to the woman that prime rib always has fat on it. Hatton later explained, based on her experience with customers in the working-class area in which the restaurant was located, that the customer might have gotten prime rib confused with spare rib.

Upset Customer Leaves

Upon receiving the complaint, Hatton explained that she returned the meat to the kitchen to be cooked further. When the customer continued to be displeased, Hatton offered the couple a free dessert. The customer continued to be unhappy, doused the prime rib with steak sauce, and then pushed it away from her plate. The customer then filled out a restaurant comment card, deposited it in the customer comment box, paid her bill, and left with her husband.

Inadvertently Thrown Out

Hatton explained that she was very curious as to what the woman had written on the comment card, so she went to the hostess and asked for the key to the comment box. She said she then read the card and put it in her pocket with the intention of showing it to her supervisor, Diane Canant, later. Hatton said that Canant, the restaurant's general manager, had commented earlier that the prime rib was overcooked, not undercooked. Apparently, the restaurant had had a problem that day with the cooking equipment and was serving meat that had been cooked the previous day and so it was being reheated before being served. Later, Hatton said that she had forgotten about the comment card and had inadvertently thrown it out. It also came out that it is against Red Lobster's policy to serve reheated meat, and the chain no longer serves prime rib.[2]

HATTON IS FIRED

Canant said that she fired Hatton after the angry customer complained to her and to her supervisor. Somehow, the customer had learned later that Hatton had removed the comment card from the box. Canant recalled, "The customer felt violated because her card was taken from the box and she felt that her complaint about the food had been ignored." Referring to the company's policy manual, Canant said Hatton was fired because she violated the restaurant's rule forbidding the removal of company property.

Not a Big Deal

Another person to comment on the incident was the hostess, Dawn Brown, then a 17-year-old student, who had been employed by the restaurant for the summer. Dawn stated, "I didn't think it was a big deal to give her the key (to the comment box). A lot of people would come and get the key from me."[3]

THE PEER REVIEW PROCESS

Hatton felt she had been unjustly fired for this incident. Rather than filing suit against the restaurant, however, she decided to take advantage of the store's peer review process.[4] The parent company of Red Lobster, Darden Restaurants, four years earlier had adopted a peer review program as an alternative dispute resolution (ADR) mechanism. Many companies across the country have adopted the peer review method as an alternative to lengthy lawsuits and as an avenue of easing workplace tensions.

Success of Peer Review

Executives at Red Lobster observed that the peer review program had been "tremendously successful." It helped to keep valuable employees from unfair dismissals, and it had reduced the company's legal bills for employee disputes by $1 million annually. Close to 100 cases had been heard through the peer review process, with only ten resulting in lawsuits. Executives at the company also said that the process had reduced racial tensions. In some cases, the peer review panels have reversed decisions made by managers who had overreacted to complaints from minority customers and employees.[5]

HATTON'S PEER REVIEW PANEL

The peer review panel chosen to handle Ruth Hatton's case was a small group of Red Lobster employees from the surrounding area. The panel included a general manager, an assistant manager, a hostess, a server, and a bartender, all of whom had volunteered to serve on the panel. The peer review panel members had undergone special peer review training and were being paid their regular wages and travel expenses. The peer review panel was convened about three weeks after Hatton's firing. According to Red Lobster policy, the panel was empowered to hear testimony and to even overturn management decisions and award damages.

Testimony and a Decision

The panel met in a conference room at a hotel near Pittsburgh and proceeded to hear testimony from Ruth Hatton, store manager Diane Canant, and hostess Dawn Brown. The three testified as to what they believed had happened in the incident.

Through careful deliberations, the panelists tried to balance the customer's hurt feelings with what Hatton had done and why, and with the fact that a company policy may have been violated. Initially, the panel was split along job category lines, with the hourly workers supporting Hatton and the managers supporting store management. After an hour and a half of deliberations, however, everyone was finally moving in the same direction and the panel finally came to a unanimous opinion as to what should be done.[6]

QUESTIONS FOR DISCUSSION

1. What are the ethical issues in this case from an employee's point of view? From management's point of view? From a customer's point of view?
2. Who are the stakeholders, and what are their stakes?
3. As a peer review panel member, how would you judge this case? Do you think Hatton "stole" company property or inadvertently threw it away? Do you think the discharge should be upheld?
4. Do you think the peer review method of resolving work complaints is a desirable substitute for lawsuits? What are its strengths and weaknesses?
5. If you had been Hatton, would you be willing to turn your case over to a peer review panel like this and then be willing to live with the results?

ENDNOTES

1. Margaret A. Jacobs, "Red Lobster Tale: Peers Decide Fired Waitress's Fate," *The Wall Street Journal* (January 20, 1998), B1, B4.
2. Ibid.
3. Ibid.
4. "Peer Review," U.S. Equal Employment Opportunity Commission, http://www.eeoc.gov/federal/adr/peerreview.cfm. Accessed June 15, 2016; see also ADR Synopsis, http://www.contilaw.com/adrsyn.html. Accessed June 15, 2016.
5. Jacobs, ibid.
6. Ibid.

CASE 32

After-Hours Activities: The Case of Peter Oiler*

Few people question an employer's right to control an employee's behavior on the job. However, when an employer takes action based on an employee's off-duty conduct, questions of ethics arise. More than half of all states prohibit firing based on various types of after-hours conduct.[1] Federal law prohibits firing that is discriminatory.[2] Some cases, however, fall through the cracks. If you were the judge in the Peter Oiler lawsuit, how would you rule?

WORK HISTORY

By all accounts, Peter Oiler was a good worker. Hired to drive a truck for Winn-Dixie, his responsibilities included driving a 50-foot truck, loading supplies from the company warehouse, driving them to Winn-Dixie stores throughout southeastern Louisiana, and unloading them. Oiler received above average performance ratings and was promoted three times during his tenure at Winn-Dixie. He adhered to company policies in all ways, including his attire and his presentation.[3] In his private time, Oiler liked to take on the persona of "Donna" at home, donning women's clothing, accessories, makeup, wigs, and fake breasts. Though he usually stayed home, Oiler would sometimes go out as Donna with his wife and friends to restaurants, the shopping mall, or church.[4]

A SITUATION ARISES

In 1999, Oiler had a meeting with his supervisor Greg Miles. A year earlier, Oiler had been bothered by a rumor that had been circulating that Oiler was gay and so he asked Miles to take action against it. At

*This case was prepared by Ann K. Buchholtz, Rutgers University, and updated by Jill A Brown, Bentley University in 2016.

the meeting, Miles asked if the rumors had subsided and Oiler said that they had. Miles asked Oiler why the rumors bothered him and Oiler said it was because he is transgender instead of gay. When Miles asked what transgender was, Oiler explained that it refers to people who have feelings about their gender that are sometimes inconsistent with their anatomical sex. Oiler added that he had no intention of ever changing his sex or living as a woman full-time.[5] He was a happily married, heterosexual man, about to celebrate his 25th wedding anniversary.

WINN-DIXIE RESPONDS

Miles said he would have to check the company policy about transgender employees. On November 1, 1999, Miles informed Oiler that a supervisor had seen Oiler dressed as a woman off-duty. Oiler said that he did sometimes dress as a woman but never on-duty. Miles responded that Oiler's activities could harm Winn-Dixie's image and so the company was asking him to resign. He recommended that Oiler look for another job. Oiler said he did not want another job because he was happy at Winn-Dixie. He continued to work in his position. From November 4, 1999 to January 5, 2000, Winn-Dixie managers had five meetings with Oiler. They told him to find another job because he was about to be terminated. They said they had no problem with his work performance but his off-duty dressing as a woman could hurt Winn-Dixie's public image. Oiler reiterated that he would not wear women's clothing at work. At the January 5, 2000 meeting, Oiler was terminated.[6]

THE AFTERMATH

Oiler sued Winn-Dixie for gender discrimination. He argued that the company fired him because he did not fit the company's gender stereotype of a man. Ken Choe, an American Civil Liberties Union attorney who represented Oiler, said, "Everyone agrees he was not terminated for anything related to his job performance. All of the cross dressing behavior occurred off the job." In September 2002, a federal judge in New Orleans ruled that transgendered people were not a protected class and so laws against sex discrimination did not apply to them.[7]

Although Oiler lost in court, he may have won the battle for public opinion. According to Oiler, "Quite a few people told me, 'You're not hurting anybody. You do your job extremely well. How can they do this?'" Oiler added that Winn-Dixie's reaction made other workers feel less secure. "The common theme (among former coworkers) was, 'If they can get away with this, what can they do to me?' It's got a lot of people saying, 'Where's the limit?'"[8]

ADDENDUM

In 2007, Representative Barney Frank (D-MA) sponsored HR 2015, the Employment Nondiscrimination Act (ENDA). The purpose of this legislation was to prohibit employment discrimination on the basis of actual or perceived sexual orientation or gender identity.[9] For almost two decades, similar laws had been debated in the legislature, without much progress. In 2013, the ENDA bill was passed by the U.S. Senate on a bipartisan basis, but it died in the House of Representatives.

In 2014, President Obama signed an executive order expanding the protections for federal workers and contractors from discrimination based on sexual orientation; however, broader legislation remains elusive at this writing.[10] A recent study noted that about half of Americans are protected against anti-LGBT employment discrimination—living in cities, states, or counties with regulations that explicitly prevent employers from firing workers for their sexual orientation or gender identity on or off the job.[11] These employment protections are concentrated in 30 percent of the country geographically, with the most nondiscrimination ordinances and laws clustered in the West, Midwest, and Northeast—and the most protections in urban areas.[12]

QUESTIONS FOR DISCUSSION

1. What are the ethical issues in this case?
2. Who are the stakeholders and how are they impacted by this situation?
3. Did Winn Dixie have a legitimate concern that Peter's off-the-job behavior might adversely affect the company's reputation?
4. In today's social media crazed environment, an employee's off-the-job behavior could be reported and go viral overnight and adversely impact the reputation of an employer. Should this be taken into consideration in designing policies to address after-hours conduct?
5. Do you agree with the federal judge's decision? If you were the judge what would you do?
6. An ordinance in New Orleans prohibited discrimination against off-the-job cross-dressing. However, the Winn-Dixie branch that fired Oiler

is located just outside that jurisdiction. Does this affect your answer to #2?

7. For what after-hours behavior do you think it is appropriate to discipline or terminate an employee? For what after-hours behavior is it not appropriate? Where do you draw the line and how would you describe that line if you were developing a policy to put into an employee manual?

ENDNOTES

1. Carolyn Hirschman, "Off Duty, Out of Work," *HR Magazine* (February 2003), 50–56.
2. Lisa Guerin, "Off-Duty Conduct and Employee Rights," Nolo, http://www.nolo.com/legal-encyclopedia/off-duty-conduct-employee-rights-33590.html. Accessed June 22, 2016.
3. ACLU, http://www.aclu.org. Accessed June 24, 2016.
4. Hirschman, 50–56.
5. http://www.aclu.org, ibid.
6. Ibid.
7. Hirschman, 52.
8. Ibid., 52.
9. Congress.gov, http://thomas.loc.gov. Accessed June 24, 2016.
10. Gregory Korte, "Obama Signs Executive Order Banning LGBT Discrimination," *USA Today* (July 21, 2014), http://www.usatoday.com/story/news/politics/2014/07/21/obama-executive-order-lgbt-discrimination/12944523/. Accessed June 24, 2016.
11. Mollie Reilly, "Report Finds Just Half of Americans Are Protected from Anti-LGBT Discrimination at Work," *The Huffington Post* (October 27, 2015), http://www.huffingtonpost.com/entry/lgbt-discrimination-study_us_562f9d9fe4b06317990f7971. Accessed June 22, 2016.
12. Ibid.

CASE 33

Location, Location, Location

Our department has two buildings about three miles apart. The extension office operates quite differently from headquarters. Folks seem to come and go as they please, and the atmosphere is casual. April works in the extension office and takes full advantage of this environment to maximize her second income; selling real estate. Her office—a cubicle in the back of the building—is a disaster area of sales paraphernalia, billing statements from investment properties that she owns, and a smattering of work-related papers. She uses her computer and e-mail account to close deals and is constantly chattering in full voice on her cell phone as she woos potential buyers and schedules appointments. The departmental fax machine and photocopier also come in handy as a part of April's burgeoning real estate endeavors.

Management is aware of April's situation. However, they struggle with the other side of her story. Her job is unique in that it requires her to work in very hot or very cold environments depending on weather. The storage building, out of which she must work daily, does not have heating or air conditioning, but must be fully ventilated. The bottles, jerricans, and drums that she handles are heavy, cumbersome, and dangerous. Sometimes the items April handles as a part of her duties are poisonous, extremely flammable, and even carcinogenic. At least once a month she has to don a respirator, a suffocating protective suit, and rubber boots as protection while she consolidates chemicals into larger drums. Temperatures in the protective suit easily exceed 100 degrees in the summer months. Finally, April is on the low end of the department's salary range taking home less than $35,000 per year.

April's coworkers understand what her job entails, but her unabashed real estate transactions during work hours are creating a toxic environment for the rest of the staff—many of whom are in the same salary range as April, but with jobs that are not as difficult.

Contributed Anonymously

QUESTIONS FOR DISCUSSION

1. What are the ethical issues in this case?
2. Should management do something about this situation? What? Why?
3. Do April's extremely difficult working conditions factor into your decision?
4. How should management respond to the coworkers?

CASE 34

Looks Discrimination at A&F*

When then-Abercrombie & Fitch (A&F) CEO Michael Jeffries said the following in a *Salon* interview, relatively few took notice:

> *Candidly, we go after the cool kids. We go after the attractive all-American kid with a great attitude and a lot of friends. A lot of people don't belong [in our clothes], and they can't belong. Are we exclusionary? Absolutely.*[1]

Years later, *Business Insider* unearthed the quote and included it in an article about A&F's unwillingness to make clothing for larger women.[2] In the words of Robin Lewis, that 2006 spark then became a 2013 conflagration.[3] The quote went viral through social networks, Twitter, YouTube, and blogs. As a result, A&F stores around the country found themselves to be targets of boycotts and protests.[4] This time the issue was A&F's unwillingness to carry larger sizes, but that is not the only "exclusion" for which A&F has been called to task. Over many years, A&F has been charged with bias and discrimination for its attempts to promote a consistent A&F look.

Looksism, also referred to as Lookism, refers to discrimination or prejudice based on a person's appearance.[5] It has long been regarded as an ethical issue, but when it begins to affect protected groups, it can be a legal issue as well.[6] Over a decade ago, a coalition of four organizations filed an employment discrimination lawsuit against A&F. The coalition filing the lawsuit included the Mexican American Legal Defense Fund, the Asian Pacific American Legal Center, the NAACP Legal Defense and Educational Fund, and the law firm of Lieff Cabraser Heimann & Bernstein, LLP. The nine plaintiffs to the lawsuit claimed that A&F discriminated against people of color, including Latinos, Asian Americans, and African Americans, in its hiring practices, job assignments once hired, compensation, termination, and conditions of employment—they settled the case for $50 million minus attorney fees and costs.[7]

In 2009, an Oklahoma teen, employed by A&F, filed suit against the company, claiming she was told her *hijab*, a headscarf she wore in keeping with her Muslim beliefs, was not consistent with the A&F "look."[8] More recently, a corporate jet pilot who claimed A&F fired him and then replaced him with a younger man charged A&F with age discrimination.[9]

Later, a Denver judge ruled that the entrances to A&F's surfing-themed Hollister stores violated the Americans with Disabilities Act (ADA)'s requirements for accessibility.[10] In 2011, the firm managed to insult the *Jersey Shore* cast by offering to pay them if they would stop wearing A&F clothing.[11]

Retail consumer expert Robin Lewis pondered why a 2006 quote, which was largely ignored after its utterance, would create such a firestorm seven years later.[12] Of course, the speed with which messages can go around the world is a factor, but he also wonders if a change in societal values could be a factor as well. Might the backlash be due to an increased sensitivity toward exclusion and a desire to be more inclusive in an increasingly diverse world?[13] Celebrities such as Miley Cyrus publicly joined the boycott and comedians like Ellen DeGeneres made the A&F issue part of their routines.[14] Greg Karber, an L.A. filmmaker, created a short video called "Fitch the Homeless" in which he drives to poor areas to give A&F clothing to poor people to "rebrand" the product.[15]

Some observers question whether A&F has now lost its cultural relevance. In a post-economic recession world, is elitism something that A&F's target

*This case was written by Archie B. Carroll, University of Georgia. Updated in 2016.

demographic no longer values? Abe Sauer of *Brandchannel* draws a comparison to the 2012 movie *21 Jump Street*, in which two young police officers go undercover in a high school, thinking that what was cool in 2000 is still cool today.[16] They are confused when the students they meet find the officers' year 2000 conception of "cool" to be offensive. Those students value compassion, environmentalism, and earnestness instead. Sauer asks if A&F might be about to learn the same lesson as the officers did.[17]

Returning back to the Oklahoma teen who did not conform to the A&F "look," this case, involving Samantha Elauf, resulted in a discrimination suit being filed on her behalf by the Equal Employment Opportunity Commission (EEOC). The EEOC thought A&F should have accommodated her religious beliefs and not held this against her. A&F said they could not have made such an accommodation at the time because Elauf did not request one.[18]

A court ruled in A&F's favor, but this decision was appealed to the U.S. Supreme Court. In June 2015, the Supreme Court ruled that A&F "may" have discriminated against Elauf, and they sent the case back to the lower court for further consideration. The Supreme Court held that management cannot make employment decisions based on an applicant's religious practice. A&F was quick to respond that the ruling did not conclude that it *had* discriminated against Elauf but that she may continue pursuing her claim in court.[19] A&F appealed the Supreme Court's decision and lost. Soon after, A&F announced a $25,000 settlement of the lawsuit with Samantha Elauf.[20]

In an announcement on its Web site regarding employment practices that may violate Title VII of the Civil Rights Act, the EEOC has stated that employers should be particularly sensitive to potential discrimination against individuals who are, or are perceived to be, Muslim Arab, Afghani, Middle Eastern, or South Asian.[21]

In December 2014, Michael Jeffries, A&F's CEO, was forced to step down. One reason was the controversial remarks he had made about the brand's exclusivity. Jeffries' departure signaled a new era in the company, and soon after his departure the company began a rebranding process, which is still underway. The company overhauled its strict look policy, decided it should no longer hire employees based on their physical attractiveness, and softened its dress code to permit employees to be more "individualistic."[22] Store employees would now be renamed to be "brand representatives" instead of "models," and the company planned to stop featuring sexualized marketing, sell black clothing, and add larger sizes.[23]

QUESTIONS FOR DISCUSSION

1. What are the legal and ethical issues in this case?
2. What is your evaluation of the concept of the "A&F look?" Have you personally observed this concept in practice? Have other retailers used this approach?
3. Are the employment practices of A&F intended to be discriminatory? Are they unfair? What ethical principles or precepts guide your analysis?
4. Did the EEOC go too far in naming specific groups about whom employers should be particularly sensitive? Could this have been a political decision?
5. What could A&F and other retailers be doing, that they are not doing, to make their hiring practices less controversial? Are the changes being made in A&F's "brand" enough to help it to grow again?
6. Will A&F be able to be "cool" again? Would you work at the company or invest in the company?
7. Are there other companies that promote a particular look? Are they being discriminatory? Where do you draw the line?

ENDNOTES

1. Benoit Denizet-Lewis, "The Man Behind Abercrombie & Fitch," *Salon* (January24, 2006), http://www.salon.com/2006/01/24/jeffries/. Accessed June 15, 2016.
2. Ashley Lutz, "Abercrombie & Fitch Refuses to Make Clothes for Large Women," *Business Insider* (May 3, 2013), http://www.businessinsider.com/abercrombie-wants-thin-customers-2013-5. Accessed June 15, 2016.
3. Robin Lewis, "A&F: Exclusive or Exclusionary?" *The Huffington Post* (May 31, 2013), http://www.huffingtonpost.com/robin-lewis/af-exclusive-or-exclusionary_b_3360354.html. Accessed June 15, 2016.
4. Ibid.
5. "Lookism," Dictionary.com, http://www.dictionary.com/browse/lookism. Accessed June 15, 2016.
6. M.S. "Looksism and the Law," *The Economist* (May 24, 2010), http://www.economist.com/blogs/democracyinamerica/2010/05/appearance_discrimination. Accessed June 17, 2013.

7. "$50 Million, Less Attorneys' Fees and Costs, Paid to Class Members in December 2005 in Abercrombie & Fitch Discrimination Lawsuit Settlement," AFjustice.com, http://afjustice.com/. Accessed June 15, 2016.
8. "Abercrombie & Fitch Sued over Head Scarf," *CBS News* (September 18, 2009), http://www.cbsnews.com/2100-201_162-5320868.html. Accessed June 15, 2016.
9. Sapna Maheshwari, "Models on Abercrombie Jet Had Rules on Proper Underwear," *Bloomberg* (October 18, 2012), http://www.bloomberg.com/news/2012-10-18/models-on-abercrombie-jet-had-rules-on-proper-underwear.html?cmpid=yhoo. Accessed June 15, 2016.
10. Terri Pous, "We, the Underdressed: A Brief History of Discrimination and Indifference in Fashion Retail," *Time* (May 22, 2013), http://style.time.com/2013/05/22/we-the-underdressed-a-history-of-discrimination-and-indifference-in-fashion/. Accessed June 15, 2016.
11. Abe Sauer, "Why A&F's 'Cool Kids' Stance Will Damage the Brand Now More Than Ever," *Brandchannel* (May 13, 2013), http://www.brandchannel.com/home/post/2013/05/13/Abercrombie-Brand-Damage-051313.aspx. Accessed June 15, 2016.
12. Lewis, 2013.
13. Ibid.
14. "Miley Cyrus and US Stars Boycott Abercrombie & Fitch After Discrimination of Overweight," *gulfnews.com* (June 16, 2013), http://gulfnews.com/arts-entertainment/celebrity/miley-cyrus-and-us-stars-boycott-abercrombie-fitch-after-discrimination-of-overweight-1.1197732. Accessed June 15, 2016.
15. Sami K. Martin, "Abercrombie & Fitch Homeless Campaign by Greg Karber Gives Store 'New Image'," *CP N.America* (May 15, 2013), http://www.christianpost.com/news/abercrombie-fitch-homeless-campaign-by-greg-karber-gives-store-new-image-95905/. Accessed June 15, 2016.
16. Sauer, 2013.
17. Ibid.
18. Dave Jamieson, "Supreme Court Rules against Abercrombie & Fitch in Discrimination Case," *The Huffington Post* (June 2, 2015), http://www.huffingtonpost.com/2015/06/01/supreme-court-abercrombie_n_7464534.html. Accessed June 20, 2016.
19. Ibid.
20. Michele Gorman, "Abercrombie & Fitch Pays More than $25,000 to Settle Headscarf Lawsuit," *Newsweek* (July 21, 2015), http://www.newsweek.com/abercrombie-fitch-pays-25000-settle-headscarf-lawsuit-356004. Accessed June 20, 2016.
21. U.S. Equal Employment Opportunity Commission, "Employment Discrimination Based on Religion, Ethnicity, or Country of Origin," https://www.eeoc.gov/laws/types/fs-relig_ethnic.cfm. Accessed June 20, 2016.
22. Karizza Sanchez, "Can Abercrombie & Fitch Be Cool Again?" *Complex.com* (March 24, 2016), http://www.complex.com/style/2016/03/can-abercrombie-fitch-be-cool-again. Accessed June 20, 2016.
23. Ibid.

CASE 35

Two Vets, Two Dogs, and a Deadlock*

When a roadside explosion in Afghanistan blew up his Humvee, Russ Murray sustained brain and back injuries as well as posttraumatic stress disorder that made it very difficult to leave his home in Watkinsville, Georgia. Getting Ellie, his service dog, made it possible for him to leave the house and the two became inseparable.[1] When he visited Clyde's Armory Gun Shop in a nearby town, however, he was told by the owner, Andrew Clyde, that Ellie could not come in the store because she was disturbing the owner's security dog, Kit. Kit is a Doberman pinscher who roams freely from the store to the warehouse and, according Clyde, "does not interact well with other dogs."[2]

*This case was prepared by Ann K. Buchholtz, Rutgers University. Updated by Archie B. Carroll in 2016.

Clyde, a veteran himself, served three combat missions in Iraq. Clyde maintained that he had a right not to allow Murray in with his dog because "The store was private property, therefore, the owner of the facility decides who is allowed to enter."[3] Clyde also said that he wanted his store to be a safe environment, "but when someone becomes confrontational and refuses to follow instructions, at that point the only recourse is to ask them to leave."[4] Clyde said that he is a disabled veteran too but that he is allowed to ask a customer with a service dog to leave if the dog is being disruptive.[5]

Murray received his service dog from the Dog Tag program of Puppies Behind Bars, an organization that trains prison inmates to raise service dogs for disabled Afghanistan and Iraq war veterans.[6] Ellie, a black lab, is able to respond to about 80 commands—she can pick up items, help with laundry, and call 911.[7] According to Gloria Stoga, president of Puppies Behind Bars, the organization has placed about 54 dogs with wounded veterans. She notes that the dogs they place are "fully trained service dogs."[8] Murray said he intended to file a complaint under the Americans with Disabilities Act of 1990 (ADA) adding, "I don't want this to happen to anyone else."[9]

Clyde asked Murray to leave the store, and when he refused, two employees escorted him out. Murray then called the police and an officer was dispatched to the scene. In the officer's presence, Clyde told Murray he was barred from the store for two years.[10] Murray later told reporters that he thought Clyde would be in trouble with the law for asking him to leave. Clyde said Murray's final warning to him was "Don't worry, I won't be back until I own the place." Clyde reported that he thought Murray had a vendetta against him because Murray had contacted several news outlets about the issue.[11]

QUESTIONS FOR DISCUSSION

1. Before doing any more research on service dogs and the ADA, think about what happened. Was this a violation of the ADA or does the store owner have rights too that confound matters in terms of providing a clear answer?
2. When Clyde said the service dog, Ellie, was disturbing his security dog, Kit, could this have been construed that he thought the service dog was out of control? If he did think the service dog was out of control, does this influence his decision about removing them from his store?
3. Should Clyde have accommodated Murray in any way? If so, how?
4. Now check out the ADA policy on service animals.[12] Taking this into consideration, who is in the right in the above scenario? Does your answer change from the one you gave in Question #1?

ENDNOTES

1. "Disabled Vet, Service Dog, Reportedly Kicked Out of Georgia Gun Shop," Fox News, April 10, 2013, http://www.foxnews.com/us/2013/04/10/disabled-veteran-service-dog-reportedly-kicked-out-georgia-gun-store.html. Accessed June 22, 2016.
2. Wayne Ford, "Two War Vets Disagree Over 'Service Dog' in Athens Gun Store," Online Athens (April 10, 2013), http://onlineathens.com/local-news/2013-04-10/two-war-vets-disagree-over-service-dog-athens-gun-store. Accessed June 22, 2016.
3. Ibid.
4. Ibid.
5. Fox News, ibid.
6. http://www.puppiesbehindbars.com/home. Accessed June 22, 2016.
7. Ford, 2013.
8. Ford, ibid.
9. Ford, ibid.
10. Ford, ibid.
11. Ford, ibid.
12. U.S. Department of Justice, Civil Rights Division, Disability Rights Section, ADA Requirements, "Service Animals," http://www.ada.gov/service_animals_2010.htm. Accessed June 22, 2016.

CASE 36

Are Criminal Background Checks Discriminatory?*

In April 2012, the Equal Employment Opportunity Commission (EEOC) issued revised guidance on the use of arrest and conviction records in employment decisions. In it, the EEOC warned that the use of criminal background as an exclusion must be "job related and consistent with business necessity."[1] The EEOC noted that arrest and incarceration rates are high for African American and Hispanic men and so a blanket exclusion of applicants with criminal backgrounds is likely to have disparate impact and thus be a violation of Title VII of the Civil Rights Act of 1964.[2]

A year later, June 2013, the EEOC filed its first lawsuits under the revised guidance against Dollar General and a BMW manufacturing plant in South Carolina. Both companies were accused of discriminating against African Americans. In the case of BMW, the issue arose when a new logistics service was hired. The previous service had a policy of only screening convictions that occurred in the past seven years. BMW did not have a screening time limit and ordered the new logistics service to do a new screening. Employees with convictions that violated the BMW policy of no time limit were terminated, even if they had worked for the company for years.[3] The Dollar General case involves two applicants. One had her conditional job offer revoked due to a six-year old conviction, even though she disclosed the conviction in the interview and worked for another retailer in a similar position for four years.[4]

Reaction to the filing of the lawsuit was swift. The *Wall Street Journal* opined, "We would have thought that criminal checks discriminate against criminals, regardless of race, creed, gender or anything else."[5] The editorial goes on to say that one can argue that criminals deserve a second chance but "business owners and managers ought to be able to decide if they want to take the risk of hiring felons."[6] An EEOC spokesperson told the Associated Press, "Overcoming barriers to employment is one of our strategic enforcement priorities. We hope that these lawsuits will further educate the public and the employer community on the appropriate use of conviction records."[7]

*This case was prepared by Ann K. Buchholtz, Rutgers University, and updated by Jill Brown, Bentley University in 2016.

QUESTIONS FOR DISCUSSION

1. Do you agree with the EEOC or the WSJ?
2. Are blanket exclusions of people with criminal backgrounds discriminatory or should businesses be given the discretion to make the employment decision when a potential or current employee is found to have a criminal background?
3. How would you determine whether a conviction record is "job related and consistent with business necessity?"
4. What factors would affect your decision? Would it vary by the nature of the conviction? If so, how would it vary? Would it vary by the nature of your business and industry? If so, how would it vary?

ENDNOTES

1. "Consideration of Arrest and Conviction Records in Employment Decisions under Title VII of the Civil Rights Act of 1964," http://www.eeoc.gov/laws/guidance/arrest_conviction.cfm. Accessed June 22, 2016.
2. Ibid.
3. Tess Stynes, "EEOC Files Suits Against BMW Manufacturing, Dollar General," *The Wall Street Journal* (June 11, 2013), http://www.advfn.com/nasdaq/StockNews.asp?stocknews=UTIW&article=57945371. Accessed June 22, 2016.
4. Scott Thurm, "Employment Checks Fuel Race Complaints," *The Wall Street Journal* (June 11, 2013), http://www.wsj.com/articles/SB1000142412788732349560457853928351885502O. Accessed June 22, 2016.
5. "Banning Background Checks: The EEOC Says That Screening for Felonies Is Discriminatory," *The Wall Street Journal* (June 15, 2013), A14.
6. Ibid.
7. Bruce Kennedy, "BMW, Dollar General Hit with Discrimination Suits," *MSN Money* (June 12, 2013), http://money.msn.com/now/blog--bmw-dollar-general-hit-with-discrimination-suits. Accessed June 22, 2016.

CASE 37

To Take or Not to Take*

As a State employee, I am restricted from receiving excessive gifts because of my opportunity to direct business toward certain vendors. Currently, the State forbids acceptance of gifts that exceed $100 in value. Regardless of the limit, I make it a personal policy not to receive gifts of any value in order to be equitable to all vendors.

Recently, however, a vendor to whom I frequently provide business (because of the great value in their products and services) offered me two tickets to a sold-out concert for a group that my wife greatly enjoys. With our anniversary approaching, I had tried unsuccessfully to purchase the tickets on my own. The face value of the two tickets does not exceed the $100 limit, but I still do not feel comfortable taking them. I am torn because of the joy it would bring to my wife to attend the concert.

QUESTIONS FOR DISCUSSION

1. What are the ethical issues in this case?
2. Am I being too hard on myself? Should I accept the tickets? On what are you basing that decision?
3. Should I change my practice of refusing all gifts?
4. Should the State's policies be modified regarding gifts? If so, how should they be modified?

*This case was prepared by Ken Crowe.

CASE 38

Tragedy in Bangladesh—the Rana Plaza Factory Collapse*

On April 24, 2013, an eight-story garment factory building collapsed in Rana Plaza, which is on the outskirts of Dhaka, Bangladesh. The Rana Plaza building is located in Savar, near Dhaka. The collapse occurred just after work had begun that morning in several companies that were all housed in the building. Roughly 5,000 workers, mostly women, worked in the complex. By that evening, 1,000 people had been rescued and it was reported the next day that at least 119 were killed. This building collapse occurred months after more than 100 workers had died in a fire at the Tazreen Fashions factory near Dhaka.[1]

As the weeks passed, the death toll continued to rise. By a month later, it was apparent that over 1,100 garment workers perished in the collapse of the substandard factory building. The gruesome calamity already has been called the worst industrial accident since the Bhopal disaster in 1984 and the worst ever in the garment industry.[2]

What makes the tragedy such a monumental story is that it is the worst event to occur in the decades-long debate over the use of sweat shops and related labor rights issues in these controversial links in supply chains typically used by well-to-do multinational industries to manufacture cheap products for the Western world. At issue are the safety, health, and security of the employees at these work sites.

Since the building collapse occurred and the total costs in lives, injuries, and property losses have been tallied, the logical questions about responsibility for the tragedy have been raised. In a complex disaster such as this, there is considerable finger pointing and the parties being identified as responsible continue to multiply.

Reports are that the owners of the building had been warned that it was unsafe and one response by the owners was to threaten to fire the people who didn't just keep working.[3] Within a month of the building collapse, the government created a panel to study the accident and the panel issued a 400-page report claiming that substandard building materials, failure to comply with building regulations, and the use of heavy equipment on upper floors were key factors in the disaster. The panel also recommended that the owner of Rana Plaza, Sohel Rana, and the owners

*This case was written by Archie B. Carroll, University of Georgia, and updated in 2016.

of the five garment factories located in the building should be charged with "culpable homicide" for allegedly forcing the employees to return to work on April 24 after cracks had been seen on the exterior of the building the previous day.[4]

The Bangladeshi government has been pressured by many diverse groups to take action to overhaul workplace safety in the aftermath of the building collapse. A more serious problem viewed by others has been the lack of acceptable regulations and their enforcement on the part of the government itself. Many blame the government for not setting and enforcing safety standards in much the same way these type regulations work in more developed countries. The government has taken some steps in the aftermath of the tragedy. It shut down 20 sites for safety improvements.[5] One reason the government started working quickly after this tragedy is because it feared losing millions of jobs to another poor country if companies exited en masse.[6]

The government also said it would broker talks for higher garment industry minimum wages, residing at $38 per month on average at the time of the accident. The country of Bangladesh is second only to China in terms of garment manufacturing for the developed world; however, its minimum wages are paltry in comparison to the $138 per month received on average by workers in China at the time.[7]

As so often is the case involving sweatshops and their consequences, however, the primary public discussion about the Rana Plaza disaster quickly turned to U.S. and other wealthy nations' corporations who have taken advantage of the low costs in Bangladesh and thought to be indifferent to the working conditions in the low-cost providing countries. Product remnants of two companies were found in the rubble of the building collapse: Primark, a cut-rate British brand and Canada's Loblaw, including its Joe Fresh brand.[8]

Other national brands, though they have not been significantly linked to the Rana Plaza fire, are also under the gun to take some substantial action on the worker safety front. Among these companies are such familiar names as Walmart, Gap, Dress Barn, H&M, Benetton, J. C. Penney, Mango, Target, Sears, Walt Disney Co., and Nike. These companies are not new to sweatshop allegations and challenges as they have been using them for decades. And, many of them have been striving for years to improve workplace conditions but the challenges posed in countries such as Bangladesh are formidable.

To ensure safe and good practices, does a company need to check the supplier of its supplier's supplier? Is seeing a certificate that a factory is safe an adequate assurance? Should the company send people in to check every safety feature of the building and to observe working conditions? If so, how often and for how long?[9]

According to *The Economist*, Western firms can decide to respond to the Bangladeshi tragedy in one of three ways: they can overlook attempts at CSR and just take advantage of cheap labor wherever it exists; they can exit countries like Bangladesh and operate only in countries where risks are less; or, they can stay and try to improve upon conditions there.[10] Interestingly, some companies had already been working to improve conditions there. Walmart had started a fire-safety training academy there even before the disaster. Gap had already announced a plan to help factory owners upgrade their plants. The clothing industry had already held meetings with NGOs and governments seeking to develop a strategy to improve safety in Bangladesh's 5,000 factories.[11] Another reason why companies might stay in Bangladesh is because the world is running out of low cost countries to turn to for their production.

Two major approaches surfaced for companies to respond to the serious workplace safety situation in Bangladesh—(1) form a group, or an accord, and act together or (2) each company act independently and go its own way.

EUROPEAN ACCORD ON FIRE AND BUILDING SAFETY IN BANGLADESH

In mid-May 2013, some of Europe's largest retailers took the first approach and decided to create and sign an accord to improve fire and building safety conditions in Bangladesh. The accord would be a legally binding five-year agreement not to hire manufacturers whose factories failed to meet safety standards. The group also agreed to pay for necessary factory repairs and renovations. This agreement was negotiated with global worker-safety advocates, overlapping with the Bangladeshi government in its efforts to raise the minimum wage and making it easier for workers to join unions.[12] Leaders of the accord said they need widespread participation to make the agreement work.

Two of the companies leading the proposed European accord were Sweden's Hennes & Mauritz AB (H&M), and Spain's Inditex. H&M is the leading buyer of clothing from Bangladesh's $20 billion garment industry. Observers have said that H&M had no choice but to take the lead since the volume it requires from there is so large.[13] Other signers of the accord include Italy's Benetton Group, Spain's Mango MNG Holdings SL, France's Carrefour SA and the U.K.'s Marks & Spencer.[14]

COMPANIES ACTING INDEPENDENTLY

When the European-led accord was being developed, two leading companies, Walmart and Gap, indicated they would not join the accord but would put together their own safety plans for improving conditions in Bangladesh. One major objection they had to the accord was that it was legally binding and it was unclear what all that might mean. Other companies have been reluctant to sign the accord for the same reason.

Walmart's initial plan, which it called a commitment, would involve hiring outside auditors to inspect 279 Bangladesh factories and publish the results on its Web site. When warranted, Walmart said it would require the factory owners to make needed renovations or risk being removed from its list of authorized factories. Walmart said that it believed its safety plan would meet or exceed the accord's plan and would get results faster. The company also reported that it had already met and revoked authorization for more than 250 factories in the country. Another part of Walmart's plan was to set up an independent call center for workers to call and report unsafe conditions. Walmart also planned to conduct safety training for every worker in plants making its products.[15]

Though Gap did not agree with the European-led accord, the company indicated that if certain revisions were made to the legally binding agreement, it may join the accord. Other companies initially indicating they would craft their own safety plans for Bangladesh included JCPenney, Sears, and Japan's Fast Retailing Co., operator of the Uniqlo casual clothing chain.[16]

Several companies decided to downplay their use of manufacturing in Bangladesh because of the risks involved. Nike, for example, said that Bangladesh is a high-risk country for them and they plan to keep their footprint very limited there. Nike said that only eight of the 896 factories it worked with were in Bangladesh. To ensure compliance with its safety requirements, Nike has its own system of grading or judging the suppliers.[17] Walt Disney Co. had told its licensees in March, before the building collapse, that they could no longer produce Disney branded products in Bangladesh because some boxes of Disney sweatshirts were found at the site of the major Tazreen factory fire that had occurred in Bangladesh the previous November. Disney and Walmart claimed that they did not know their goods were being produced at the plant that burned and that it was not an authorized manufacturer.[18] It is difficult for companies to always know or control where their products are sometimes made because subcontractors hire subcontractors, and so on, often without the company's knowledge.

UNITED STATES' RETAILERS ALLIANCE FORMED

Just over a month after saying they would act alone, it was announced in late June 2013 that Walmart, Gap, Inc., VF Corp., Macy's, Sears Holdings, and other large U.S. retailers would establish their own accord to improve safety conditions in Bangladesh garment factories. The agreement became known as the Alliance for Bangladesh Worker Safety. The agreement would be a $50 million, five-year fund for improving safety conditions. There were several key differences between the European-led and the U.S.-led proposals. Whereas the European plan does not require participation of the Bangladesh government, the U.S. plan does require the government's participation. Another major difference is in the realm of legal liability. The European plan requires signatories to accept broad legal liability whereas the U.S. plan calls for limited legal liability.[19]

The $50 million U.S.-led plan would be contingent upon the Bangladesh government meeting certain criteria ensuring accountability and compliance for safety improvements. This was included because many safety codes were often ignored by governmental officials responsible for enforcing them. As for legal liability, the U.S. proposal stipulated that signatories to their plan not have broad but rather limited legal liability. In the U.S. proposal, firms could be held legally liable if they agree to commit resources and then renege or if they continue to use the unsafe factories.[20] Another major difference between the two plans is the amount of resources required for improvements. Under the European plan, companies would be required to pay for all upgrades to factories at an estimated cost of $600,000 per factory. In the U.S. plan, companies would set up a $50 million fund to help cover the upgrade costs.

ARE CONSUMERS THE RESPONSIBLE PARTY?

By implication, the world's consumers of "fast fashion" and other cheaply produced products are identified by some as responsible parties in the tragedy in Bangladesh. Though surveys report that consumers will reward responsible business practices or punish violators, this doesn't happen very often. *USA Today* writer Jayne O'Donnell reported on a 23-year-old woman who said she would pay a little more for her clothes if she knew the companies were "socially responsible in the way that they gave their workers safe conditions and adequate pay." But, O'Donnell observes that this woman may be the exception; consumers will be troubled by these news accounts, but they quickly forget. Consumer psychologist Kit Yarrow is quoted as observing that "denial is a pretty powerful thing if something is beautiful and you really want it."[21]

THE EUROPEAN ACCORD CONTINUES ITS WORK

The European Accord continues it work and reports periodically on its progress on its Web site.[22] The Accord's initiatives include inspections, remediation, and workplace programs. The remediation process requires the factory owner and the companies to develop a Corrective Action Plan that specifies what remedial actions will be taken along with clear deadlines and a financial plan signed off by each party.[23] In its March 2016, quarterly report, the Accord showed that real and important progress was being made in the remediation of safety hazards identified.[24] In spite of progress being made, the report indicated that the majority of factories monitored by the Accord are behind schedule with remediation. The Accord reports that it has been accelerating the pace of remediation.[25]

THE U.S.-LED ALLIANCE FOR WORKER SAFETY MAKES PROGRESS

The Alliance for Bangladesh Worker Safety is a collaborative process involving apparel companies and stakeholders including the U.S. and Bangladeshi governments, policymakers, NGOs, labor organizations and members of civil society.[26] The Alliance's initiatives include standards and inspections, remediation, worker empowerment, worker helpline, training, and sustainability/capacity building. The Alliance claims it coordinates and collaborates with all groups that are committed to bringing about the sustainable transformation of the garment sector in Bangladesh.[27] In its June 2016 report, the Alliance provides a snapshot of the progress being made along with key statistics in its programmatic areas.[28]

The European Accord has over 200 signatories and the U.S.-led Alliance has 28 signatories. This may be why *Triple Pundit*, in its report that that worker safety has improved in the three years since the Rana Plaza tragedy, focuses exclusively on the efforts of the Accord.[29] Despite the progress being made, safety inspections in Bangladesh continue to report several dozen safety violations, on average, at the plants inspected. This may be why the Rana Plaza event occurred in the first place; unfortunately, something like it may occur again.[30] Bringing about a high level of safety in the sweatshop industry in underdeveloped countries will be an ongoing challenge for large global buyers and smaller suppliers alike.

QUESTIONS FOR DISCUSSION

1. Who are the stakeholders in this case and what are their stakes? What are the ethical issues?
2. Based on your study of the building collapse in Bangladesh, which party or parties do you think are responsible and why?
3. What role does the government of Bangladesh assume in this building collapse and other safety violations?
4. Do Western companies have an obligation to safeguard the safety of workers in foreign lands where the products they sell are made?
5. What are the pros and cons of companies working together in an accord to address safety violations versus taking independent action to address the issues in the plants they use? Do both approaches represent sound global corporate citizenship?
6. Which plan is best for addressing the factory safety problem in Bangladesh—the European-led Accord or the U.S.-led Alliance? What are the pros and cons of each?
7. Do research on this case to bring all the facts up to date. Has anything significant changed? If so, integrate these findings into your analysis.
8. What is your appraisal of companies that decide Bangladesh is too risky a country for them to do business in?
9. What is the responsibility of consumers to the employees in other countries where our products are made? Is the writer correct, "we quickly forget?" What can consumers do to address this mindset?

ENDNOTES

1. Syed Zain Al-Mahmood and Shelly Banjo, "Deadly Collapse," *Wall Street Journal* (April 25, 2013), A1.
2. "Disaster at Rana Plaza," *The Economist* (May 4, 2013), 12.
3. Ibid.
4. Syed Zain Al-Mahmood, "Shoddy Materials Are Blamed for Building Collapse," *Wall Street Journal* (May 24, 2012), B4.
5. Syed Zain Al-Mahmoud, "Bangladesh Factory Toll Passes 800," *Wall Street Journal* (May 9, 2013), A10.
6. Adam Davidson, "Clotheslined," *New York Times Magazine* (May 19, 2013), 16.
7. Syed Zain Al-Mahmood, "Bangladesh to Raise Workers' Pay," *Wall Street Journal* (May 13, 2013), B4.
8. *The Economist* (May 4, 2013), ibid.
9. Ibid.
10. Ibid.
11. Ibid.
12. Shelly Banjo and Christina Passariello, "Promises in Bangladesh," *Wall Street Journal* (May 14, 2013), B1.
13. Jens Hansegard, Tripti Lahiri, and Christina Passariello, "Retailers' Dilemma: Cut Off or Help Fix Unsafe Factories," *Wall Street Journal* (May 29, 2013), B1.
14. Shelly Banjo, Ann Zimmerman, and Suzanne Kapner, "Wal-Mart Crafts Own Bangladesh Safety Plan," *Wall Street Journal* (May 15, 2013), B1.
15. Ibid.
16. Mayumi Negishi, "Uniqlo Won't Join Accord on Bangladesh Labor Safety," *Wall Street Journal* (May 28, 2013), B1.
17. "Nike's Game Plan for Policing Its Suppliers: Try to Avoid Bangladesh," *Wall Street Journal* (November 30, 2012).
18. Hansegard et al., ibid.
19. Suzanne Kapner and Shelly Banjo, "Plan B for Bangladesh," *The Wall Street Journal* (June 27, 2013), B1.
20. Ibid.
21. Jayne O'Donnell, "Treat Workers Well, or Kiss Our Cash Goodbye," *USA Today* (May 23, 2013), 5B.
22. Accord on Fire and Building Safety in Bangladesh, http://bangladeshaccord.org/about/. Accessed June 20, 2016.
23. Ibid, Remediation Process, http://bangladeshaccord.org/remediation/. Accessed June 20, 2016.
24. Quarterly Aggregate Report, March 31, 2016, http://bangladeshaccord.org/wp-content/uploads/Quarterly-Aggregate-Report-11-May-2016.pdf. Accessed June 20, 2016.
25. Ibid.
26. Alliance for Bangladesh Worker Safety, "Who We Are," http://www.bangladeshworkersafety.org/who-we-are/about-the-alliance. Accessed June 20, 2016.
27. Ibid.
28. Ibid., Alliance Progress June 2016, http://www.bangladeshworkersafety.org/progress-impact/alliance-statistics. Accessed June 20, 2016.
29. Leon Kaye, "Three Years After Rana Plaza, Worker Safety Improves in Bangladesh," *TriplePundit* (June 10, 2016), http://www.triplepundit.com/special/cotton-sustainability-c-and-a-foundation/bangladesh-worker-accord-fire-and-building-safety/#. Accessed June 20, 2016.
30. Ibid.

CASE 39

Workplace Spying*

Investment banking company Goldman Sachs flags employee e-mails that contain inappropriate "swear" words.[1] Bank of America's call centers track employee movements.[2] Other companies check their employees' browser histories, log their keystrokes for productivity checks, and pinpoint their locations. In fact, Boston-based Sociometric Solutions provides companies with employee ID badges fitted with microphones, location sensors, and accelerometers (to track the motions of employees).[3] How is it that employers can track

*This case was prepared by Jill A Brown, Bentley University, in 2016.

employees in this way? Moreover, what are the consequences of employee monitoring?

In general, it is legal for a company to monitor the usage of its own property, including equipment, computers, laptops, and cellphones. Only two states, Connecticut and Delaware, require employers to notify employees that their e-mail is being monitored.[4] Professional lawyers suggest a clear and reasonable monitoring policy that is linked to a firm's mission and goals.[5] However, regardless of the legality, many feel that workplace monitoring has gone too far.

Some say that this is the case at United Parcel Service (UPS). The company claims to save millions of dollars each year by using a computer analysis program that guides drivers to avoid time-and-fuel wasting left turns and even steers them to drive past a stop and come back later if it is more efficient.[6] The "telematics" tracking system involves putting sensors on the trucks that report everything from an open door to a buckled (or unbuckled) seatbelt.[7] With over 200 sensors on each delivery truck, the data is fed in real time to a supervisor.[8] At the end of each day, the data are sent to a central data center where computers crunch the data.[9] However, reports abound of stressed UPS drivers being called to account for their every movement.[10]

UPS drivers allege "metrics-based harassment," including supervisors posting printouts of drivers' data every day to keep the pressure on for better efficiency.[11] The drivers also note potential safety hazards from such monitoring, such as when workers use tricks to keep up—like sitting on top of already-fastened seat belts to save time.[12] Inevitably, drivers end up over their allotted times by at least an hour or two due to traffic or other holdups. The real concern for UPS safety, however, may be the handful of trainees who come in as much as two hours under. As one UPS supervisor stated in an interview with *Harpers Magazine*, "...there's no way drivers could be beating their time quotes by that much without sprinting the entire day and recklessly cutting corners on safety."[13] She pointed to the telematics as the source of the pressure, "It's like when they ship animals. But this is a mental whip."[14]

QUESTIONS FOR DISCUSSION

1. What are the benefits of employee monitoring? What are the downside consequences?
2. Do you consider any of the company practices reported in this case to be ethically questionable? Which ones and why?
3. What is the correct balance of monitoring of, and discretion for, employees? When does workplace spying cross the line?
4. Should companies place this much stress on their employees?
5. Is this an example of dehumanizing employees?
6. Do you think workplace monitoring can be an effective part of an employee engagement program?

ENDNOTES

1. "The Rise of Workplace Spying," *The Week* (July 5, 2015), http://theweek.com/articles/564263/rise-workplace-spying. Accessed June 24, 2016.
2. Ibid.
3. Ibid.
4. "USA Employee Monitoring Laws: What Are Employers Allowed and Not Allowed Doing in the Workplace?" *WorkTime* (June 2016), http://www.worktime.com/usa-employee-monitoring-laws-what-can-and-cant-employers-do-in-the-workplace/. Accessed June 28, 2016.
5. Ibid.
6. Lee Michael Katz, "Monitoring Employee Productivity: Proceed with Caution," *Society for Human Resource Management (SHRM)* (June 1, 2015), https://www.shrm.org/publications/hrmagazine/editorialcontent/2015/0615/pages/0615-employee-monitoring.aspx. Accessed June 22, 2016.
7. Jessica Bruder, "These Workers Have a New Demand: Stop Watching Us," *The Nation* (May 27, 2015), https://www.thenation.com/article/these-workers-have-new-demand-stop-watching-us/. Accessed June 23, 2016.
8. Esther Kaplan, "The Spy Who Fired Me," *Harper's Magazine* (March 2015), http://harpers.org/archive/2015/03/the-spy-who-fired-me/2/. Accessed June 22, 2016.
9. Jacob Goldstein, "To Increase Productivity, UPS Monitors Drivers' Every Move," *South Carolina Public Radio* (April 17, 2014), http://www.npr.org/sections/money/2014/04/17/303770907/to-increase-productivity-ups-monitors-drivers-every-move. Accessed June 23, 2016.
10. Ibid.
11. Ibid.
12. Ibid.
13. Kaplan, 2015.
14. Ibid.

Subject Index

Page numbers in italics refer to figures

D

E

F

T

Name Index

Ethics in Practice and End-of-Text Case Matrix

#	End of Text Case	1–3	4–6	7–8	9–10	11–12	13–14	15–16	17–19
1	Walmart: The Main Street Merchant of Doom	X					X	X	
2	Walmart's Labor Practices			X					X
3	The Body Shop: Poster Child for Early CSR Movement	X	X						
4	Chipotle's Struggle with Food Safety	X	X				X		
5	Direct-to Consumer Advertising for Pills: Is it Ethical?		X			X	X		
6	Using Ex-Cons to Teach Ethics	X		X					
7	Volkswagen's Diesel Deception	X	X	X	X				
8	Unlocking the Secrets of the Apple iPhone in the Name of Terrorism	X	X		X	X	X		
9	To Hire or Not to Hire			X					X
10	PayDay Loans: A Needed Product or a Scam?	X	X	X			X		
11	You Punch Mine & I'll Punch Yours			X					
12	Phantom Expenses			X					
13	Family Business		X	X					
14	The Waiter Rule		X	X					X
15	Nike, Inc. and Sweatshops		X		X				X
16	Coke and Pepsi in India: Issues, Ethics and Crisis Mgt		X		X		X	X	
17	Chiquita: An Excruciating Dilemma Between Life & Law		X	X	X				X
18	The Betaseron Decision (A)	X	X	X			X		
19	Should Directors Shine Light on Dark Money?	X				X			
20	Big Pharma's Marketing Tactics		X		X	X	X		
21	McDonald's—Coffee Spill Heard 'Round the World	X	X	X			X		
22	General Electric and Hudson River Cleanup	X	X			X		X	
23	What Have You Done for Me Lately? The Case of Amazon in South Carolina	X	X			X			